MODERN
CRIMINAL LAW
CASES, COMMENTS AND QUESTIONS
Second Edition

By

Wayne R. LaFave
David C. Baum Professor of Law and Professor
in the Center for Advanced Study,
University of Illinois

AMERICAN CASEBOOK SERIES

WEST PUBLISHING CO.
ST. PAUL, MINN., 1988

COPYRIGHT © 1978 By WEST PUBLISHING CO.
COPYRIGHT © 1988 By WEST PUBLISHING CO.
                        610 Opperman Drive
                        P.O. Box 64526
                        St. Paul, Minnesota 55165–0526

Library of Congress Cataloging-in-Publication Data

LaFave, Wayne R.
    Modern criminal law: cases, comments, and questions / by Wayne R. LaFave. — 2nd ed.
    p.   cm. — (American casebook series)
    Includes index.
    ISBN 0-314–82177–5
    1. Criminal law—United States—Cases.   I. Title.   II. Series.

KF9218.L25   1988
345.73—dc19   [347.305]   88–4262
                                                                         CIP

 *TEXT IS PRINTED ON 10% POST
CONSUMER RECYCLED PAPER*

3rd Reprint–1997

        LaFave—Mod.Crim.Law, 2nd Ed. ACB

Preface

This casebook is intended for use in a basic course on the substantive criminal law, which at most law schools is a required part of the first year curriculum. In selecting, editing, and organizing these materials, I have sought to bring together a collection of cases and secondary sources which will serve what I perceive to be the primary functions of such a course. These are: (1) together with the other first-year courses, to provide training in the case method and techniques of legal analysis; (2) also with the other first year courses, to afford the student with new insights into the fundamental question of how and to what extent the law can be effectively utilized as an instrument of social control; (3) to compare and evaluate the actual and potential contributions of legislatures (through codification), courts (through the common law and by "interpretation" of statutes) and administrators (by certain enforcement policies) in defining and grading crimes; (4) to provide the fundamental information and impart those skills which are the necessary foundation for criminal law practice, either as a prosecutor or defense counsel; (5) to provide an awareness of the inherent difficulties in trying to control antisocial behavior through the criminal law without encroaching upon basic democratic values, an appropriate matter of concern to all members of the legal profession.

This Book does not attempt to cover both substantive criminal law and criminal procedure. This is not to suggest that criminal procedure is unimportant. Rather, the assumption here is that both subjects are important parts of the law school curriculum, and that neither substantive criminal law nor criminal procedure should be shortchanged by compaction into a single course. There has been a growing realization that there is no particular advantage in teaching the two subjects together (any more than, say, combining torts and civil procedure); in recent years more and more schools have chosen to offer them separately.

It is important, however, for the student studying criminal law to have a general understanding of how the criminal process works. Thus, I have included herein textual material on that subject (Chapter 1).[1] Also, there are some aspects of substantive criminal law which simply cannot be meaningfully understood unless they are considered together with certain matters which, literally speaking, fall within the realm of criminal procedure. When this is the case, I have included the relevant procedural material.[2] Thus, for example, Chapter 6, dealing with mental disease or defect, treats incompetency to stand trial (which often

1. This material, largely the work of Professor Jerold H. Israel of the University of Michigan, is abridged from *Modern Criminal Procedure*, a casebook which I have co-authored with Professor Israel and Professor Yale Kamisar.

2. On the other hand, I have not covered the subject of entrapment in this Book. Though strictly speaking it is a matter of substantive criminal law, it is more meaningfully studied in the context of that part of criminal procedure dealing with restrictions upon police investigative practices.

is a "substitute" for an insanity defense) and various procedural aspects of the insanity defense.

The reach of the substantive criminal law is constantly expanding, and thus today's law student is much more likely than his counterpart of some years ago to find himself engaged to some extent in the practice of criminal law after graduation. This practice may involve the prosecution of or defense against charges of such familiar crimes as robbery, battery, and rape; it may instead or in addition be concerned with the increasing body of regulatory crimes which have been enacted in response to such contemporary concerns as consumer protection and environmental control. An adequate preparation for such practice requires an *understanding* of the fundamental bases of our system of substantive criminal law, rather than *knowledge* of the precise definitions of the growing list of crimes. Consequently, the major emphasis in this casebook is upon what is usually referred to as the "general part" of the criminal law: mental state (Chapter 3) and act (Chapter 4); responsibility (Chapters 6 and 7); justification and excuse (Chapter 8); inchoate crimes (Chapters 9 and 10); and liability for the conduct of another (Chapter 11).

Although I believe that the imparting of detailed information about many different crimes is *not* the goal of a basic course in criminal law, I have included within the coverage of this Book the subject of criminal homicide (Chapter 5). It is important for students of the criminal law to consider not only the question of what conduct should be made criminal, but also the question of how various forms of criminal conduct should be classified into separate crimes so as to reflect their respective seriousness. Although this problem of classification arises in a great many areas of the criminal law, undoubtedly the courts and legislatures have experienced the greatest difficulty in articulating intelligent classifications in the area of homicide. Moreover, study of homicide provides a necessary background to consideration of certain doctrines which come into play almost exclusively in a homicide context (e.g., the insanity defense) or which raise the most difficult issues in that context (e.g., the defense of duress or of self-defense).

I have attempted to place special emphasis upon the actual and potential contributions of the legislative branch in resolving the difficult policy questions which exist in this field. (This matter is first confronted in Chapter 2, Section 2, but is a recurring theme in the balance of the Book.) This emphasis takes proper account of the contribution which legislatures have made to the criminal law in recent years; a total of thirty-six states have adopted new substantive criminal law codes, and such revisions are pending in several other jurisdictions. Moreover, this emphasis aids in presenting the first-year student, often preoccupied with the common law in his other courses, with a more balanced picture of our legal system. Thus, while it is my belief that this Book is readily adaptable to a wide range of teaching styles, it is especially suited to those professors who have found it useful to require their students to work intensively with the Model Penal Code (major portions of which appear in the Appendix) or with the code of a particular jurisdiction.[3]

---

3. I have for some years required my students to have the Illinois Criminal Code (one of the first of the modern recodifications, with a heavy Model Penal Code influence) with them in class and to make frequent reference to the Code in connection with the assigned cases and materials.

Although the subject of criminal law has not been "constitutionalized" to the same extent as criminal procedure, it is fair to say that there is a significant degree of overlap between the law school subjects of constitutional law and substantive criminal law. This gives rise to the very difficult question of how much constitutional law to include in a first-year criminal law course, which the authors of extant casebooks have resolved in quite different ways.[4] It is my judgment that the constitutional limits on the substantive criminal law cannot be ignored in a criminal law course, for without some appreciation of those limitations the student cannot evaluate in a meaningful way alternative legislative proposals for dealing with various issues. On the other hand, it is hardly appropriate to subsume most of constitutional law into the criminal law offering, if for no other reason than that the beginning law student would probably be overwhelmed as a consequence. I have attempted to strike a fair balance. As for the broad question of what constitutional limits exist with respect to penal legislation, this is treated rather briefly by focusing upon one particular type of legislation—that dealing with the so-called "crimes against nature" (Chapter 2, Section 3). Beyond this, I have included certain Supreme Court decisions (e.g., *Powell v. Texas*) which raise very basic issues about the permissible reach of the substantive criminal law.

One important constitutional limitation unique to criminal law is the requirement that the prosecution prove the defendant's guilt beyond a reasonable doubt. An appreciation of the significance of this requirement aids in understanding how crimes may or should be defined and classified. On a great variety of legislative issues—e.g., whether to limit a crime to intentional wrongdoing, whether to make possession a punishable act, whether to articulate certain defenses—the practical consequences in terms of how a particular choice will affect the prosecution's burden of proof cannot be overlooked. Consequently, I have given attention at several points in these materials to the constitutionality of putting some proof burdens on the defendant (i.e., the impact of *Mullaney v. Wilbur* and its progeny) or of "lightening" the prosecutor's burden by resort to inferences and presumptions (i.e., the impact of *Barnes v. United States* and related cases). However, a professor who feels that these matters should be reserved until later in the student's legal education will find it easy to omit the aforementioned cases and the few others of the same character without interrupting the flow of the remaining material.

Following the introductory chapter, this Book begins with an inquiry into the purposes of the criminal law and, in particular, the considerations which ought to bear upon the imposition of a criminal sentence (Chapter 2, Section 1). Although sentencing issues are also raised from time to time at other points in the Book,

My purpose is not primarily to ensure that all of them learn the criminal law of this state, but rather is to give them experience in working closely with a particular code, which I believe provides a beneficial background wherever the student ultimately practices. It has been my experience that intensive work with a particular set of legislative materials throughout the course better prepares the student to work with any criminal code than isolated examination of the statutes appearing in cases drawn from many jurisdictions.

4. Some virtually ignore the matter of constitutional limitations; others devote several hundred pages to the constitutional limits on the legislative power to define and create crimes.

the matter of sentencing—or, indeed, the broader subject of corrections—is not given major emphasis in this Book. This reflects the fact that the law of corrections has developed to the point where at a great many law schools it has become the basis of a separate course.[5] Where such an offering is not available, an expanded treatment of corrections within the context of these materials can be readily achieved by examination of relevant parts of the Model Penal Code or some state penal or corrections code.

The first edition of this Book was 705 pages long, excluding the Appendix and index. My intention then was to produce a volume which was sufficiently compact that it could be covered within the confines of the typical criminal law course, at a pace which is realistic for first-year students. Though I still believe that the objectives of the criminal law course listed earlier can be best achieved by intensive study of a limited number of cases, this second edition is (consistent with the suggestion of several of the users of the first edition) a bit longer. This greater length is attributable to the addition of a few new sections (e.g., in Chapter 10, a section on RICO) and by addition of more depth to some old sections (e.g., in the section on self-defense, addition of a case and several notes on the battered spouse syndrome). This longer edition should better serve those who like to proceed at a somewhat faster pace, while at the same time providing other users with more choices in terms of what subject matter to include in the criminal law course.

I have attempted to present the subject of criminal law in a modern setting. Over three-quarters of the main cases in the first edition were decided in the 1970's, and about 20% of the principal cases in this second edition were decided since publication of the first edition. This second edition has a total of over 250 new principal and note cases, and nearly 100 new excerpts from books, articles and secondary sources. This means that the cases and other materials present issues within the context of current events with which the students will be familiar.

In selecting the major cases which appear in this Book, I have included those which, in my judgment, are most likely to stimulate an interesting and profitable classroom dialogue. That is, inclusion of a particular case does not necessarily rest upon the conclusion that it was rightly decided or that the court's analysis was in all respects sound, but rather is grounded on the belief that the facts or the analysis or both provide a useful vehicle for classroom discussion. The book is intended as a teaching tool, not a research tool, and thus the primary objective throughout has been to provide the teacher and student with a common source of material upon which they may interact in the classroom. As for the notes and questions which often follow the cases, their purpose is not to upstage the teacher, but rather to direct the student's thoughts down certain avenues prior to class so that the class time may be utilized more effectively and efficiently.[6]

5. Teaching materials on the subject are available. See, e.g., Krantz, *The Law of Corrections and Prisoners' Rights* (3d ed. 1986).

6. Not infrequently, the notes will contain one or more fact situations accompanied by the question of what the result should be on such facts.

When, as is usually the case, the fact situation is taken from an actual case, I have provided the citation in a footnote. This is not intended to suggest, however, that it is either necessary or desirable that the student consult the cited case in preparing for class. An evaluation of the fact

Students desiring to do additional reading on the subject may wish to consult one or both of the available student texts: LaFave and Scott, *Criminal Law* (2d ed. 1986), which generally follows the organization of this casebook; and Perkins and Boyce, *Criminal Law* (3d ed. 1982). Also very useful are the many outstanding articles on a variety of substantive criminal law topics appearing in the four-volume *Encyclopedia of Crime and Justice* (1983). Particularly with respect to how the problems discussed herein may best be dealt with through recodification, there are two most useful sources: the updated *Model Penal Code and Commentaries* published by the American Law Institute commencing in 1980 and ending in 1985; and the two volumes of *Working Papers* published in 1970 by the National Commission on Reform of the Federal Criminal Laws.

Case citations in opinions and footnotes of the courts and commentators have been omitted without so specifying. Numbered footnotes are from the original materials; my footnotes are lettered.

* * *

I am especially grateful to The American Law Institute for permission to include as an Appendix the Model Penal Code, copyright 1985 by The American Law Institute, and to include portions of the updated Commentary, copyright 1980 and 1985, reprinted with permission of The American Law Institute. I am also grateful to the following for permission to reproduce extracts from the works indicated. American Bar Association Journal: Goldberg, *Misprision of Felony: An Old Concept in a New Context*, 52 A.B.A.J. 148 (1966); Wechsler, *The American Law Institute: Some Observations on Its Model Penal Code*, 42 A.B.A.J. 321 (1956). American Bar Foundation: S. Brakel, J. Parry & B. Weiner, *The Mentally Disabled and the Law* (3d ed. 1985); Enker, *Mens Rea and Criminal Attempt*, 1977 A.B.F.Res.J. 845; A. Matthews, *Mental Disability and the Criminal Law* (1970). American Criminal Law Review: Allen & DeGrazia, *The Constitutional Requirement of Proof Beyond a Reasonable Doubt in Criminal Cases*, 20 Am.Crim.L.Rev. 1 (1982); Saltzburg, *Burdens of Persuasion in Criminal Cases: Harmonizing the Views of the Justices*, 20 Am.Crim.L.Rev. 393 (1983). American Journal of Criminal Law: Alderstein, *Felony–Murder in the New Criminal Codes*, 4 Am.J.Crim.L. 249 (1976); Treiman, *Recklessness and the Model Penal Code*, 9 Am.J.Crim.L. 281 (1981). Arizona Law Review: Note, 18 Ariz.L.Rev. 207 (1976), copyright © 1977 by the Arizona Board of Regents. The Bobbs–Merrill Company: J. Hall, *General Principles of Criminal Law* (2d ed. 1960); R. Moreland, *Law of Homicide* (1952). Buffalo Law Review: Comment, 21 Buff.L.Rev. 188 (1971). Butterworths: Smith, *A Case of Reckless Murder*, 123 New L.J. 792 (1973); Sullivan, *Self Induced and Recurring Automatism*, 123 New L.J. 1093 (1973). California Law Review and Fred B. Rothman & Co.: Johnson, *The Unnecessary Crime of Conspiracy*, 61 Calif.L.Rev. 1137 (1973); Johnson, *Multiple Punishment and Consecutive Sentences*, 58 Calif.L.Rev. 357 (1970). Columbia Law Review: Sayre, *Public Welfare Offenses*, 33 Colum.L.Rev. 55 (1933); Notes, 86 Colum.L.Rev. 348 (1986); 75 Colum.L.Rev. 1517 (1975); 75 Colum.L.Rev. 1122 (1975); 47 Colum.L.Rev. 1332 (1947). Cornell Law Review: Roth & Sundby, *The*

situation provided should be possible on the basis of the immediately preceding material in this Book.

Felony–Murder Rule: A Doctrine at Constitutional Crossroads, 70 Cornell L.Rev. 446 (1985). DePaul Law Review: Burgman, *Unilateral Conspiracy: Three Critical Perspectives,* 29 DePaul L.Rev. 75 (1979). Duke University School of Law: Schroeder, *Two Methods for Evaluating Duty to Rescue Proposals,* 49 Law & Contemp.Probs. 181 (1986); Greenawalt, *Distinguishing Justifications from Excuses,* 49 Law & Contemp.Probs. 89 (1986). Food Drug Cosmetic Law Journal: Cohen, *Enforcement Under the Food, Drug and Cosmetic Act—The Park Case in Perspective,* 30 Food Drug Cosmetic L.J. 676 (1975); O'Keefe & Shapiro, *Personal Criminal Liability Under the Federal Food, Drug and Cosmetic Act,* 30 Food Drug Cosmetic L.J. 5 (1975). Fordham Law Review: Comment, 45 Fordham L.Rev. 553 (1976). Georgetown Law Journal: Note, 60 Geo.L.J. 667 (1972), copyright © 1972 by The Georgetown Law Journal. Harcourt Brace Jovanovich, Inc.: B. Cardozo, *Law and Literature* (1931). Harvard Journal on Legislation: Note, 9 Harv.J.Legis. 469 (1972). Harvard Law Review: Landis, *A Note on "Statutory Interpretation,"* 43 Harv.L.Rev. 886 (1930); *Developments in the Law—Criminal Conspiracy,* 72 Harv.L.Rev. 920 (1968); Note, 94 Harv.L.Rev. 1660 (1981), copyright 1930, 1968 and 1981, by the Harvard Law Review Association. Hill and Wang (now a division of Farrar, Straus & Giroux, Inc.): M. Frankel, *Criminal Sentences* (1972), copyright © 1972, 1973 by Marvin E. Frankel. Iowa Law Review: Comment, 56 Iowa L.Rev. 658 (1971). Journal of Criminal Law: Comment, 39 J.Crim.L. 264 (1975). Kansas Law Review: Note, Kansas L.Rev. 272 (1974). Kentucky Law Journal: Moreland, *A Reexamination of the Law of Homicide in 1971: The Model Penal Code,* 59 Ky.L.J. 788 (1971). Prof. Paul Marcus: Marcus, *Criminal Conspiracy: The State of Mind Crime,* 1976 U.Ill.L.F. 627. Minnesota Law Review: Enker, *Impossibility in Criminal Attempts—Legality and the Legal Process,* 53 Minn.L.Rev. 665 (1969). Modern Law Review: Samuels, *Excusable Loss of Self–Control in Homicide,* 34 Mod.L.Rev. 163 (1971). National Law Journal: Wehrwein, 'Samaritan' Law Poses Difficulties, Nat'l L.J., Aug. 22, 1983. Nebraska Law Review: Ludwig, *Responsibility for Young Offenders,* 29 Neb.L.Rev. 521 (1950). The New York Times: Editorial, June 18, 1976; Articles, June 17, June 19, July 3, Sept. 2, Sept. 15, Sept. 17, 1976, copyright © 1976 by The New York Times Company. New York University Review of Law and Social Change: Uviller, *Seizure by Gunshot: The Riddle of the Fleeing Felon,* 14 N.Y.U.Rev.L. & Soc.Chg. 705 (1986). Notre Dame Law Review: Recent Decision, 59 Notre Dame L.Rev. 253 (1983). Stanford Law Review: Kelman, *Interpretive Construction in the Substantive Criminal Law,* 33 Stan.L.Rev. 591 (1981); Misner, *The New Attempt Laws: Unsuspected Threat to the Fourth Amendment,* 33 Stan.L.Rev. 201 (1981); Note, 26 Stan.L.Rev. 923 (1974), copyright 1974 and 1981 by the Board of Trustees of the Leland Stanford Junior University. St. John's Law Review: Holtzman, *Premenstrual Symptoms: No Legal Defense,* 60 St. John's L.Rev. 712 (1986). Sweet & Maxwell, Ltd.: 1 *Russell on Crime* (12th ed. 1964); G. Williams, *Criminal Law—The General Part* (2d ed. 1961); Brett, *The Physiology of Provocation,* 1970 Crim.L.Rev. 634; Buxton, *Incitement and Attempt,* 1973 Crim.L.Rev. 656; Elliott, *Offences Against the Person—Murder,* 1977 Crim.L.Rev. 70; Stuart, *The Actus Reus in Attempts,* 1970 Crim.L.Rev. 505; Glazebrook, *Should We Have a Law of Attempted Crime?,* 85 L.Q.Rev. 28 (1969). Syracuse Law Review: Lewin, *Psychiatric Evidence in Criminal Cases for Purposes Other than the Defense of Insanity,* 26 Syracuse L.Rev. 1051 (1975). Tulane Law

Review: Comment, 47 Tulane L.Rev. 1017 (1973). The University of Chicago Press: Packer, *Mens Rea and the Supreme Court,* 1962 Sup.Ct.Rev. 107, copyright © 1962 by The University of Chicago. University of Chicago Law Review: Burt & Morris, *A Proposal for the Abolition of the Incompetency Plea,* 40 U.Chi.L.Rev. 66 (1972); Levi, *An Introduction to Legal Reasoning,* 15 U.Chi.L.Rev. 501 (1948). U.C.L.A. Law Review and Fred B. Rothman & Co.: Abrams, *Criminal Liability of Corporate Officers for Strict Liability Offenses—A Comment on Dotterweich and Park,* 28 U.C.L.A.L.Rev. 463 (1981); Comments, 33 U.C.L.A.L.Rev. 1679 (1986); 16 U.C.L.A.L.Rev. 155 (1968). University of Illinois Law Forum: Paulsen, *Intoxication as a Defense to Crime,* 1961 U.Ill.L.F. 1; Remington & Rosenblum, *The Criminal Law and the Legislative Process,* 1960 U.Ill.L.F. 481. University of Missouri–Kansas City Law Review: Comment, 44 U.M.K.C.L.Rev. 438 (1976). University of Pennsylvania Law Review and Fred B. Rothman & Co.: Filvaroff, *Conspiracy and the First Amendment,* 121 U.Pa.L.Rev. 189 (1972); Fletcher, *The Theory of Criminal Negligence: A Comparative Analysis,* 119 U.Pa.L.Rev. 401 (1971); Comments, 135 U.Pa.L.Rev. 427 (1987); 121 U.Pa.L.Rev. 120 (1972); Notes, 109 U.Pa.L.Rev. 67 (1960); 106 U.Pa.L.Rev. 1021 (1958). University of Pittsburgh Law Review: Skilton, *The Requisite Act in a Criminal Attempt,* 3 U.Pitt.L.Rev. 308 (1937). Virginia Law Review and Fred B. Rothman & Co.: Hoffman & Dunn, *Beyond Rouse and Wyatt: An Administrative Law Model for Expanding and Implementing the Mental Patient's Right to Treatment,* 61 Va.L.Rev. 297 (1975); Whitebread & Stevens, *Constructive Possession in Narcotics Cases: To Have and Have Not,* 58 Va.L.Rev. 751 (1972); Note, 72 Va.L.Rev. 619 (1986). Warren, Gorham & Lamont: Acker & Toch, *Battered Women, Straw Men, and Expert Testimony,* 21 Crim.L.Bull. 125 (1985); Lunde & Wilson, *Brainwashing as a Defense to Criminal Liability: Patty Hearst Revisited,* 13 Crim.L.Bull. 341 (1977). Washington Law Review Association: Notes, 52 Wash.L.Rev. 142 (1976); 50 Wash.L.Rev. 755 (1975). Wayne Law Review: Frankel, *Criminal Omissions: A Legal Microcosm,* 11 Wayne L.Rev. 367 (1965). William and Mary Law Review: Fox, *Responsibility in the Juvenile Court,* 11 Wm. & Mary L.Rev. 659 (1970). Wisconsin Law Review: Remington & Helstad, *The Mental Element in Crime—A Legislative Problem,* 1952 Wis.L.Rev. 644; Remington & Joseph, *Charging, Convicting, and Sentencing the Multiple Criminal Offender,* 1961 Wis.L.Rev. 528; Comment, 1956 Wis.L.Rev. 641; Note, 1976 Wis.L.Rev. 623, copyright by the University of Wisconsin. John Wright & Sons, Ltd.: O'Connor, *The Voluntary Act,* 15 Med.Sci. Law 31 (1975). Yale Law Journal and Fred B. Rothman & Co.: Estrich, *Rape,* 95 Yale L.J. 1087 (1986); Fingarette, *Addiction and Criminal Responsibility,* 84 Yale L.J. 413 (1975); Goldstein, *Conspiracy to Defraud the United States,* 68 Yale L.J. 405 (1959); Hughes, *Criminal Omissions,* 67 Yale L.J. 590 (1958); Notes, 70 Yale L.J. 160 (1960); 67 Yale L.J. 916 (1958). Yale University Press: A. Goldstein, *The Insanity Defense* (1967).

I would also like to thank Carol Haley for able secretarial assistance. Jim LaFave and Terri LaFave, who served as manuscript paginator and manuscript agglutinator, respectively, on the first edition, resisted conscription for similar operosity on the second edition. I attribute this to their intervening majority rather than any dubitation on their part concerning the indefectibility of the aggregate undertaking.

WAYNE R. LAFAVE

March, 1988

✳

Summary of Contents

	Page
PREFACE	iii
TABLE OF CASES	xxxv
TABLE OF OTHER AUTHORITIES	xliii

CHAPTER 1. THE CRIMINAL JUSTICE SYSTEM

Sec.
1. The Steps in the Process _____ 1
2. The Agencies of the Criminal Justice System _____ 14

CHAPTER 2. PURPOSES, SOURCES AND LIMITS OF THE CRIMINAL LAW

1. The Purposes of the Criminal Law _____ 23
2. Sources: The Role of Courts, Legislatures and Administrators in Creating and Defining Crimes _____ 42
3. Constitutional Limitations: "Crimes Against Nature" _____ 71

CHAPTER 3. MENTAL STATE

1. General Considerations _____ 96
2. Intent _____ 102
3. Knowledge _____ 122
4. Recklessness and Negligence _____ 137
5. Strict Liability _____ 150
6. Ignorance or Mistake of Fact or Law _____ 165

CHAPTER 4. THE ACT REQUIREMENT

1. Voluntary Act _____ 187
2. The "Act" of Possession _____ 203
3. Omissions _____ 217
4. One Act or Related Acts as a Basis for Multiple Charges, Prosecutions and Sentences _____ 225

CHAPTER 5. HOMICIDE: USING MENTAL STATE AND OTHER FACTORS TO CLASSIFY CRIMES

1. Intentional Killing: The "Heat of Passion" Test _____ 238
2. Intentional Killing: The "Deliberate"—"Premeditated" Test _____ 264
3. Reckless and Negligent Killing _____ 278
4. Killing by Unlawful Act _____ 296

Sec.   Page
5. Causation _____ 315
6. The Death Penalty _____ 334

CHAPTER 6. MENTAL DISEASE OR DEFECT

1. Competency to Stand Trial _____ 354
2. Tests for the Insanity "Defense" _____ 371
3. The Insanity Defense—Procedural Aspects _____ 393
4. Diminished Capacity _____ 408

CHAPTER 7. ALCOHOLISM AND ADDICTION; INTOXICATION; IMMATURITY

1. Chronic Alcoholism and Drug Addiction _____ 419
2. Voluntary and Involuntary Intoxication _____ 439
3. Immaturity _____ 455

CHAPTER 8. JUSTIFICATION AND EXCUSE

1. Introduction _____ 460
2. Defense of Self and Others _____ 462
3. Defense of Property _____ 484
4. Law Enforcement and Response Thereto _____ 491
5. Domestic Authority _____ 509
6. Duress, Necessity and Choice of Evils _____ 514
7. Consent and Condonation _____ 533

CHAPTER 9. ATTEMPTS

1. Mental State _____ 540
2. Acts _____ 549
3. Impossibility _____ 563
4. Abandonment _____ 575
5. Prosecution and Punishment _____ 581
6. Attempt–Like Crimes _____ 583

CHAPTER 10. CONSPIRACY AND SOLICITATION

1. Conspiracy: Introduction _____ 596
2. The Agreement _____ 598
3. Mental State _____ 610
4. The Objective _____ 632
5. Impossibility _____ 640
6. The Overt Act Requirement _____ 645
7. Scope: The Object Dimension _____ 646
8. Scope: The Party Dimension _____ 650
9. Duration of the Conspiracy _____ 661
10. Withdrawal _____ 668
11. The Plurality Requirement _____ 670
12. Conspiracy: A Final Look _____ 682

Sec.		Page
13.	Beyond Conspiracy: RICO	683
14.	Solicitation	696

CHAPTER 11. PARTIES; LIABILITY FOR CONDUCT OF ANOTHER

1.	The Common Law Classification	704
2.	Acts or Omissions	706
3.	Mental State	717
4.	The Conspiracy–Complicity Relationship	732
5.	Foreseeable or Related Crimes	737
6.	Must the Principal Be Guilty?	745
7.	Withdrawal	757
8.	Exceptions to Accomplice Liability	760
9.	Vicarious Liability	762
10.	Liability of Organizations, Their Officers and Agents	775
11.	Post–Crime Aid	793

APPENDIX: AMERICAN LAW INSTITUTE MODEL PENAL CODE	809
INDEX	895

*

Table of Contents

[This table contains main cases, abstracted cases, and extracts from secondary authorities.]

	Page
PREFACE	iii
TABLE OF CASES	xxxv
TABLE OF OTHER AUTHORITIES	xliii

CHAPTER 1. THE CRIMINAL JUSTICE SYSTEM

Section 1.   The Steps in the Process — 1
 Step 1: The Report of the Crime — 2
 Step 2: Pre–Arrest Investigation — 2
 Step 3: The Arrest — 3
 Step 4: Booking — 3
 Step 5: Post–Arrest Investigation — 4
 Step 6: The Decision to Charge — 4
 Step 7: Filing the Complaint — 6
 Step 8: The First Appearance — 6
 Step 9: Preliminary Hearing — 8
 Step 10: Grand Jury Review — 9
 Step 11: The Filing of the Indictment or Information — 9
 Step 12: Arraignment on the Information or Indictment — 10
 Step 13: Pretrial Motions — 10
 Step 14: The Trial — 10
 Step 15: Sentencing — 11
 Step 16: Appeals — 12
 Step 17: Postconviction Remedies — 12
 The Criminal Justice Funnel — 13

Section 2.   The Agencies of the Criminal Justice System — 14
 Police Agencies — 14
  Fragmentation — 14
  Federal agencies — 14
  State agencies — 15
  Local police agencies — 15
 Prosecutors — 15
  Federal prosecutors — 16
  Local prosecutors: the rural and small suburban office — 17
  Local prosecutors: the urban and large suburban office — 17
  Local prosecutors: prosecutor/police relations — 18
  State attorneys general — 18

Section 2. The Agencies of the Criminal Justice System—Continued Page

Defense Counsel _____ 19

Public defenders _____ 19

Private practitioners _____ 20

The Judiciary _____ 20

Magistrate courts _____ 20

Trial courts of general jurisdiction _____ 21

Appellate courts _____ 22

CHAPTER 2. PURPOSES, SOURCES AND LIMITS OF THE CRIMINAL LAW

Section 1. The Purposes of the Criminal Law _____ 23

Frankel, Criminal Sentences (1973) _____ 23

Bergman Urges Judge to "Show Mercy" and Not Jail Him for Aged–Home Fraud, N.Y. Times (1976) _____ 27

United States v. Bergman (Fed.1976) _____ 28

Bergman Sentence is Discussed, N.Y. Times (1976) _____ 36

Editorial—Equal Justice?, N.Y. Times (1976) _____ 36

Sentencing Commission, Sentencing Guidelines (1987) _____ 39

Section 2. Sources: The Role of Courts, Legislatures and Administrators in Creating and Defining Crimes _____ 42

State v. Palendrano (N.J.1972) _____ 42

State v. Egan (Fla.1973) _____ 45

Commonwealth v. Mochan (Pa.1955) _____ 45

Note, Colum.L.Rev. (1947) _____ 46

Wechsler, A.B.A.J. (1956) _____ 46

Keeler v. Superior Court (Cal.1970) _____ 47

Comment, Iowa L.Rev. (1971) _____ 57

Commonwealth v. Cass (Mass.1984) _____ 58

People v. Smith (Cal.1976) _____ 58

People v. Saldano (Cal.1975) _____ 59

People v. Sobiek (Cal.1973) _____ 60

People v. Rossi (Cal.1976) _____ 60

Comment, U.Pa.L.Rev. (1972) _____ 62

Notes on the Role of Courts in Construing Criminal Statutes _____ 62

Levi, U.Chi.L.Rev. (1948) _____ 63

Hall, General Principles of Criminal Law (1960) _____ 63

United States v. Hartwell (S.Ct.1868) _____ 64

Caminetti v. United States (S.Ct.1917) _____ 64

Landis, Harv.L.Rev. (1930) _____ 64

Leflar, Statutory Construction (1975) _____ 65

McBoyle v. United States (S.Ct.1931) _____ 65

People v. Nichols (Cal.1970) _____ 65

State v. Bradley (Kan.1974) _____ 66

Notes on the Respective Roles of the Federal, State and Local Legislative Bodies _____ 66

Federal Power _____ 66

State Power _____ 66

Municipal Power _____ 66

Section 2. Sources: The Role of Courts, Legislatures and Administrators in Creating and Defining Crimes—Continued   **Page**

Federal Pre-emption _____ 67

State Pre-emption and Other State–Local Conflicts _____ 67

Notes on the Role of Administrative Officers and Agencies _____ 68

State v. Boyajian (Me.1975) _____ 68

Sundberg v. State (Ga.1975) _____ 68

Poe v. Ullman (S.Ct.1961) _____ 68

Remington & Rosenblum, U.Ill.L.F. (1960) _____ 68

Section 3. Constitutional Limitations: "Crimes Against Nature" _____ **71**

Locke v. State (Tenn.1973) _____ 71

Locke v. Rose (Fed.1975) _____ 74

Rose v. Locke (S.Ct.1975) _____ 75

McBoyle v. United States (S.Ct.1931) _____ 80

Note, Harv.L.Rev. (1948) _____ 80

Nash v. United States (S.Ct.1913) _____ 80

Winters v. New York (S.Ct.1948) _____ 81

Kelman, Stan.L.Rev. (1981) _____ 81

Papachristou v. City of Jacksonville (1972) _____ 81

Note, U.Pa.L.Rev. (1960) _____ 81

Bowers v. Hardwick (S.Ct.1986) _____ 82

The Supreme Court, Harv.L.Rev. (1986) _____ 92

Lovisi v. Slayton (Fed.1976) _____ 93

Note, N.Y.U.L.Rev. & Soc.Chg. (1986) _____ 93

Comment, Ford L.Rev. (1976) _____ 93

Note, supra _____ 94

Comment, supra _____ 94

Comment, Harv.J.L. & Pub.Pol. (1987) _____ 94

Solem v. Helm (S.Ct.1983) _____ 94

CHAPTER 3. MENTAL STATE

Section 1. General Considerations _____ **96**

Regina v. Cunningham (Engl.1957) _____ 98

Pembliton (Engl.1874) _____ 100

Faulkner (Engl.1877) _____ 100

Martin (Engl.1881) _____ 100

Latimer (Engl.1886) _____ 101

State v. Hatley (N.M.1963) _____ 101

United States v. Zapata (Fed.1974) _____ 101

Section 2. Intent _____ **102**

State v. Rocker (Hawaii 1970) _____ 102

In re Smith (Cal.1972) _____ 105

Notes and Questions on Motive and on Criminal, Constructive, General, Specific, Conditional, Multiple and Transferred Intent _____ 105

People v. Connors (Ill.1912) _____ 106

People v. Hamil (Ill.1974) _____ 107

State v. Kinnemore (Ohio 1972) _____ 107

Section 2.   Intent—Continued   Page
  State v. Simonson (Minn.1974) _____ 108
  Gladden v. State (Md.1974) _____ 108
  United States v. Melton (Fed.1973) _____ 109
    Commonwealth v. Freeman (Pa.1973) _____ 112
    Lee v. State (Tenn.1972) _____ 112
    Patterson v. Commonwealth (Va.1975) _____ 113
  State v. Odom (Wash.1974) _____ 113
    People v. Serra (Mich.1974) _____ 117
    Stone v. State (Ark.1973) _____ 117
    Commonwealth v. Horton (Pa.1975) _____ 117
    O'Neal v. State (Wyo.1972) _____ 117
  Sandstrom v. Montana (S.Ct.1979) _____ 117
    Francis v. Franklin (S.Ct.1985) _____ 121
    Allen & DeGrazia, Am.Crim.L.Rev. (1982) _____ 122
    Devitt & Blackmar, Federal Jury Practice and Instructions (1977) _____ 122

Section 3.   Knowledge _____ 122
  State v. Beale (Me.1973) _____ 122
    People v. Prante (Colo.1972) _____ 125
    State v. Ware (Ariz.1976) _____ 125
    State v. Jantzi (Or.1982) _____ 125
  United States v. Jewell (Fed.1976) _____ 127
    State v. Nations (Mo.1984) _____ 131
    United States v. Bright (Fed.1975) _____ 131
    United States v. Slater (Fed.1975) _____ 132
    Commonwealth v. Thureson (Mass.1976) _____ 132
  Barnes v. United States (S.Ct.1973) _____ 132
    State v. Attardo (S.Car.1975) _____ 135
    People v. Kirkpatrick (N.Y.1973) _____ 135
    People v. Theel (Colo.1973) _____ 136

Section 4.   Recklessness and Negligence _____ 137
  State v. Jones (Me.1956) _____ 137
    State v. Williams (Wash.1971) _____ 140
    State v. Hodgdon (Or.1966) _____ 140
    Treiman, Am.J.Crim.L. (1981) _____ 141
    Boggess v. State (Utah 1982) _____ 143
    Regina v. Caldwell (Engl.1981) _____ 144
    Smith, Vill.L.Rev. (1982) _____ 144
    Duff, Crim.L.Rev. (1980) _____ 144
    Fletcher, U.Pa.L.Rev. (1971) _____ 144
    State v. Lucero (N.M.1975) _____ 146
    Speidel v. State (Alaska 1969) _____ 147
    State v. Smith (Conn.1981) _____ 147
  State v. Cushman (Vt.1974) _____ 147
    State v. Wong (N.H.1984) _____ 150

Section 5.   Strict Liability _____ 150
  State v. Stepniewski (Wis.1982) _____ 150
    Morissette v. United States (S.Ct. 1952) _____ 157
    Stepniewski v. Gagnon (Fed.1984) _____ 157
    Remington & Helstad, Wis.L.Rev. (1952) _____ 157
    People v. Arnold (Ill.1972) _____ 158
    Packer, Sup.Ct.Rev. (1962) _____ 158

Section 5. Strict Liability—Continued Page

Note, Colum.L.Rev. (1975) 158

Comment, Wis.L.Rev. (1956) 159

United States v. Balint (S.Ct.1922) 160

Packer, supra 160

Note, supra 161

State v. Campbell (Alaska 1975) 161

Section 6. Ignorance or Mistake of Fact or Law 165

Director of Public Prosecutions v. Morgan (Engl.1975) 165

People v. Mayberry (Cal.1975) 171

Estrich, Yale L.J. (1986) 172

Temkin, Crim.L.Rev. (1983) 172

Model Penal Code § 2.04, Comment (1985) 173

Braun v. State (Md.1962) 174

People v. Vogel (Cal.1956) 174

People v. Cash (Mich.1984) 174

State v. Elton (Utah 1984) 174

United States v. Hamilton (Fed.1972) 174

White v. State (Ohio 1933) 175

Liparota v. United States (S.Ct.1985) 175

United States v. Baker (Fed.1986) 180

Lambert v. California (S.Ct.1957) 181

Hughes, Yale L.J. (1958) 182

Hall, General Principles of Criminal Law (1960) 182

Holmes, The Common Law (1948) 183

Gordon v. State (Ala.1875) 183

State v. Boyett (N.Car.1849) 183

State v. Cude (Utah 1963) 183

Morgan v. District of Columbia (D.C.1984) 184

Notes and Questions on Mistake of Law and Reasonable Reliance 184

State v. O'Neal (Iowa 1910) 184

State v. Striggles (Iowa 1926) 184

United States v. Irwin (Fed.1976) 185

State v. Goodenow (Me.1876) 185

State v. DeMeo (N.J.1955) 185

State v. Davis (Wis.1974) 185

Hopkins v. State (Md.1950) 185

United States v. Insco (Fed.1974) 186

United States v. Barker (Fed.1975) 186

Regina v. Prairier Schooner News Ltd. and Powers (Can.1970) 186

Long v. State (Del.1949) 186

People v. Snyder (Cal.1982) 186

CHAPTER 4. THE ACT REQUIREMENT

Section 1. Voluntary Act 187

State v. Caddell (N.Car.1975) 187

People v. Newton (Cal.1970) 195

People v. Grant (Ill.1978) 196

Fulcher v. State (Wyo.1981) 196

State v. Pierson (Conn.1986) 196

People v. Decina (N.Y.1956) 197

George v. State (Tex.1984) 197

State v. Boleyn (La.1976) 198

Section 1. Voluntary Act—Continued   Page
    Sullivan, New L.J. (1973) _____ 198
    O'Connor, Med.Sci.Law (1975) _____ 198
    Lunde & Wilson, Crim.L.Bull. (1977) _____ 199
    Delgado, Minn.L.Rev. (1978) _____ 199
    Dressler, Minn.L.Rev. (1979) _____ 199
    Erlinder, B.C.L.Rev. (1984) _____ 200
    State v. Jerrett (N.Car.1983) _____ 200
    State v. Grimsley (Ohio 1982) _____ 200
    Recent Decision, Notre Dame L.Rev. (1983) _____ 201
    Holtzman, St. John's L.Rev. (1986) _____ 201
    Dalton, Once a Month (1983) _____ 201
    Williams, Criminal Law (1961) _____ 201
    Martin v. State (Ala.1944) _____ 201
    People v. Newton (N.Y.1973) _____ 202
    People v. Shaughnessy (N.Y.1971) _____ 202
    Williams v. City of Petersburg (Va.1975) _____ 202

Section 2. The "Act" of Possession _____ 203
    People v. Gory (Cal.1946) _____ 203
    Commonwealth v. Lee (Mass.1954) _____ 205
    Commonwealth v. Rambo (Pa.1980) _____ 206
    State v. Flaherty (Me.1979) _____ 206
    People v. Norris (Mich.1972) _____ 206
    Wheeler v. United States (D.C.1985) _____ 206
    Whitebread & Stevens, Va.L.Rev. (1972) _____ 209
    People v. Ireland (Ill.1976) _____ 209
    United States v. Martinez (Fed.1979) _____ 209
    United States v. Martorano (Fed.1983) _____ 209
    County Court of Ulster County v. Allen (S.Ct.1979) _____ 210
    Saltzburg, Am.Crim.L.Rev. (1983) _____ 216
    Allen & DeGrazia, Am.Crim.L.Rev. (1983) _____ 217

Section 3. Omissions _____ 217
    State v. Williquette (Wis.1986) _____ 217
    Commonwealth v. Konz (Pa.1982) _____ 221
    State v. Tennant (W.Va.1984) _____ 222
    United States v. Spingola (Fed.1972) _____ 223
    Davis v. Commonwealth (Va.1985) _____ 223
    Commonwealth v. Cali (Mass.1923) _____ 223
    State v. Harrison (N.J.1931) _____ 223
    Moreland, Law of Homicide (1952) _____ 224
    Moreland v. State (Ga.1927) _____ 224
    Wehrwein, Nat'l L.J. (1983) _____ 224
    Schroeder, Law & Contemp.Probs. (1986) _____ 224

Section 4. One Act or Related Acts as a Basis for Multiple Charges, Prosecutions and Sentences _____ 225
    Gore v. United States (S.Ct.1958) _____ 225
    Johnson, Calif.L.Rev. (1970) _____ 228
    Note, Yale L.J. (1958) _____ 228
    Irby v. United States (Fed.1967) _____ 229
    Neal v. State (Cal.1960) _____ 233
    Johnson, Calif.L.Rev. (1970) _____ 234

Section 4.   One Act or Related Acts as a Basis for Multiple Charges, Prosecutions and Sentences—Continued   **Page**

Remington & Joseph, Wis.L.Rev. (1961) _____ 234
State v. Dunlop (Alaska 1986) _____ 234
Commonwealth v. Donovan (Mass.1985) _____ 234
Notes on Prosecuting the Multiple Offender _____ 235
Remington & Joseph, supra _____ 235
Missouri v. Hunter (S.Ct.1983) _____ 236
Ashe v. Swenson (S.Ct.1970) _____ 237

CHAPTER 5. HOMICIDE: USING MENTAL STATE AND OTHER FACTORS TO CLASSIFY CRIMES

Section 1.   Intentional Killing: The "Heat of Passion" Test _____ **238**

Mullaney v. Wilbur (S.Ct.1975) _____ 238
Patterson v. New York (S.Ct.1977) _____ 245
People v. Washington (Cal.1976) _____ 250
Bedder v. Director of Public Prosecutions (Engl.1954) _____ 251
Rex v. Raney (Engl.1942) _____ 252
Samuels, Mod.L.Rev. (1971) _____ 253
State v. Hoyt (Wis.1964) _____ 253
State v. Little (N.H.1983) _____ 255
Dressler, J.Crim.L. & C. (1982) _____ 255
People v. Berry (Cal.1976) _____ 256
Note, U.Pa.L.Rev. (1958) _____ 259
Holmes v. Director of Public Prosecutions (Engl.1946) _____ 259
People v. Arnold (Ill.1974) _____ 260
State v. Harwood (Ariz.1974) _____ 260
State v. Madden (N.J.1972) _____ 260
United States v. Collins (Fed.1982) _____ 261
Ex parte Fraley (Okla.1910) _____ 261
Comment, U.C.L.A.L.Rev. (1986) _____ 261
State v. Tilson (Tenn.1974) _____ 262
Notes and Questions on Assisting Suicide _____ 262
Note, Colum.L.Rev. (1986) _____ 262
State v. Mays (W.Va.1983) _____ 263
In re Joseph (Cal.1983) _____ 264

Section 2.   Intentional Killing: The "Deliberate"—"Premeditated" Test _____ **264**

United States v. Brown (Fed.1975) _____ 264
People v. Gill (Mich.1972) _____ 267
Cardozo, Law and Literature (1931) _____ 268
State v. Schrader (W.Va.1982) _____ 269
Model Penal Code § 210.6, Comment (1980) _____ 269
State v. Jenkins (Ohio 1976) _____ 270
Fisher v. United States (Fed.1946) _____ 271
People v. Wolff (Cal.1964) _____ 272
State v. Johnson (N.Car.1986) _____ 273
People v. Anderson (Cal.1968) _____ 273
People v. Craig (Cal.1957) _____ 278

Section 2. Intentional Killing: The "Deliberate"—"Premeditated" Test—Continued

Page

Hemphill v. United States (Fed.1968) _____ 278
United States v. Blue Thunder (Fed.1979) _____ 278

Section 3. Reckless and Negligent Killing _____ 278
Hyam v. Director of Public Prosecutions (Engl.1974) _____ 278
Notes and Questions on Killing by Gross Recklessness (Depraved Heart) 285
Smith, New L.J. (1973) _____ 285
Elliott, Crim.L.Rev. (1977) _____ 286
Commonwealth v. Ashburn (Pa.1975) _____ 286
State v. Chalmers (Ariz.1966) _____ 287
Model Penal Code § 210.2, Comment (1980) _____ 288
Note, Colum.L.Rev. (1985) _____ 288
State v. Randolph (Tenn.1984) _____ 289
State v. Ibn Omar–Muhammad (N.M.1985) _____ 289
People v. Watson (Cal.1981) _____ 289
Notes and Questions on Killing With Intent to Do Serious Bodily Injury 289
Elliott, Crim.L.Rev. (1977) _____ 289
English, Crim.L.Rev. (1977) _____ 290
Model Penal Code § 210.2, Comment (1980) _____ 290
United States v. Escamilla (Fed.1972) _____ 290
Remington & Helstad, Wis.L.Rev. (1952) _____ 293
People v. Strong (N.Y.1975) _____ 294
People v. Arndt (Ill.1972) _____ 294
State v. Gooze (N.J.1951) _____ 295
Commonwealth v. Welansky (Mass.1944) _____ 296

Section 4. Killing by Unlawful Act _____ 296
State v. Goodseal (Kan.1976) _____ 296
State v. Underwood (Kan.1980) _____ 301
State v. Lashley (Kan.1983) _____ 301
Notes and Questions on the Rationale and Status of the Felony–Murder Rule _____ 302
Roth & Sundby, Cornell L.Rev. (1985) _____ 302
People v. Aaron (Mich.1980) _____ 303
People v. Dillon (Cal.1983) _____ 305
Roth & Sundby, supra _____ 305
Moreland, Ky.L.J. (1971) _____ 306
Notes and Questions on the Dimensions of the Felony–Murder Rule __ 306
State v. Thompson (Wash.1977) _____ 307
People v. Wilson (Cal.1969) _____ 307
People v. Miller (N.Y.1973) _____ 308
Note, Stan.L.Rev. (1970) _____ 308
People v. Gladman (N.Y.1976) _____ 308
Campbell v. State (Md.1982) _____ 311
Notes and Questions on the Misdemeanor–Manslaughter Rule _____ 313
Model Penal Code § 201.3, Comment (1959) _____ 314

Section 5. Causation _____ 315
Model Penal Code § 2.03, Comment (1985) _____ 316
Hassett, Syrac.L.Rev. (1987) _____ 316

Section 5. Causation—Continued Page
State v. Rose (R.I.1973) _____ 316
People v. Dlugash (N.Y.1977) _____ 318
State v. Southern (Minn.1981) _____ 318
Fine v. State (Tenn.1952) _____ 319
State v. Minster (Md.1985) _____ 319
Kibbe v. Henderson (Fed.1976) _____ 319
Henderson v. Kibbe (S.Ct.1977) _____ 322
Regina v. Blaue (Engl.1975) _____ 324
Williams, Cambr.L.J. (1976) _____ 327
State v. Chavers (La.1974) _____ 327
Notes and Questions on Intervening Acts by the Victim _____ 328
Commonwealth v. Atencio (Mass.1963) _____ 328
State v. Hallett (Utah 1980) _____ 329
United States v. Hamilton (Fed.1960) _____ 329
State v. Casper (Neb.1974) _____ 330
People v. Goodman (N.Y.1943) _____ 330
Commonwealth v. Bianco (Mass.1983) _____ 330
Commonwealth v. Feinberg (Pa.1969) _____ 330
United States v. Guillette (Fed.1976) _____ 331
People v. Lewis (Cal.1899) _____ 331
Notes and Questions on Intervening Acts by Third Parties and Outside
Forces _____ 331
People v. Stewart (N.Y.1976) _____ 331
Matter of J.N. (D.C.1979) _____ 332
Bush v. Commonwealth (Ky.1880) _____ 332
Regina v. Michaels (Engl.1840) _____ 332
Notes and Questions on Intervening Acts by the Defendant _____ 332
Thabo Meli v. Regina (Engl.1954) _____ 332
Russell, Crime (1964) _____ 333
Lingras Das v. King (India 1945) _____ 333
Regina v. Chiswibo (S.Afr.1961) _____ 333

Section 6. The Death Penalty _____ 334
Gregg v. Georgia (S.Ct.1976) _____ 335
Jurek v. Texas (S.Ct.1976) _____ 345
Proffitt v. Florida (S.Ct.1976) _____ 345
Lockett v. Ohio (S.Ct.1978) _____ 346
Spaziano v. Florida (S.Ct.1984) _____ 347
Woodson v. North Carolina (S.Ct.1976) _____ 347
Roberts v. Louisiana (S.Ct.1976) _____ 348
Roberts v. Louisiana (S.Ct. 1977) _____ 349
Sumner v. Shuman (S.Ct.1987) _____ 349
Coker v. Georgia (S.Ct.1977) _____ 350
Enmund v. Florida (S.Ct.1982) _____ 351
Tison v. Arizona (S.Ct.1987) _____ 352

CHAPTER 6. MENTAL DISEASE OR DEFECT

Section 1. Competency to Stand Trial _____ 354
Brakel et al., The Mentally Disabled and the Law (1985) _____ 354
Matthews, Mentally Disabled and the Criminal Law (1970) _____ 355

Section 1.   Competency to Stand Trial—Continued   **Page**
    Pate v. Robinson (S.Ct.1966) _____ 356
      Drope v. Missouri (S.Ct.1975) _____ 359
      Dusky v. United States (S.Ct.1960) _____ 360
      State v. Johnson (Wis.1986) _____ 360
      People v. Francabandera (N.Y.1974) _____ 361
    Jackson v. Indiana (S.Ct.1972) _____ 362
      State ex rel. Matalik v. Schubert (Wis.1973) _____ 369
      People v. Garlick (Ill.1977) _____ 369
      Spencer v. Zant (Fed.1983) _____ 369
      United States v. DeBellis (Fed.1981) _____ 369
      Burt & Morris, U.Chi.L.Rev. (1972) _____ 369
      Winick, U.C.L.A.L.Rev. (1985) _____ 370
      Ford v. Wainwright (S.Ct.1986) _____ 370

Section 2.   Tests for the Insanity "Defense" _____ 371
    Daniel M'Naghten's Case (Engl.1843) _____ 372
      State v. Coombs (Ohio 1985) _____ 374
      People v. Skinner (Cal.1985) _____ 374
      State v. Boan (Kan.1984) _____ 374
      Parsons v. State (Ala.1887) _____ 375
    United States v. Brawner (Fed.1972) _____ 376
      Insanity Defense Reform Act of 1984 _____ 387
      Brakel et al, The Mentally Disabled and the Law (1985) _____ 387
      State v. Korell (Mont.1984) _____ 388
      Morris & Hawkins, The Honest Politician's Guide to Crime Control (1970) 388
      Brakel et al., supra _____ 388
      Wexler, Ariz.L.Rev. (1984) _____ 389
    Notes on the Borderland of Responsibility _____ 389
      People v. Yukl (N.Y.1975) _____ 389
      United States v. Gould (Fed.1984) _____ 391
      Holtzman, St. John's L.Rev. (1986) _____ 392
      Brakel et al., supra _____ 393

Section 3.   The Insanity Defense—Procedural Aspects _____ 393
A. Raising the Defense—Why and by Whom? _____ 393
    Matthews, Mental Disability and the Criminal Law (1970) _____ 393
    State v. Jones (Wash.1983) _____ 394
B. Raising the Defense—When and How? _____ 397
    Williams v. Florida (S.Ct.1970) _____ 397
    Wardius v. Oregon (S.Ct.1973) _____ 397
    Note, Yale L.J. (1972) _____ 398
C. Examination and Diagnosis Before Trial _____ 398
    Riles v. McCotter (Fed.1986) _____ 398
    United States v. Byers (Fed.1984) _____ 399
    Ake v. Oklahoma (S.Ct.1985) _____ 399
    State v. Gambrell (N.Car.1986) _____ 400
    Matthews, Mental Disability and the Criminal Law (1970) _____ 400
D. Burden of Proof _____ 400
    Insanity Defense Reform Act of 1984 _____ 401
    Leland v. Oregon (S.Ct.1952) _____ 401
    Rivera v. Delaware (S.Ct.1976) _____ 401

Page

Section 3.   The Insanity Defense—Procedural Aspects—Continued

E.   Presentation of Evidence at Trial 401
    United States v. Milne (Fed.1973) 401
    Jones v. State (Fla.1974) 401
    Goldstein, The Insanity Defense (1967) 402
    In re Pray (Vt.1975) 402

F.   The Bifurcated Trial 402
    State v. Helms (N.Car.1974) 403
    United States v. Bennett (Fed.1972) 403

G.   Instructions and Verdict 403
    Lyles v. United States (Fed.1957) 403
    People v. Ramsey (Mich.1985) 404
    Keener v. State (Ga.1985) 404
    Mickenberg, U.Cin.L.Rev. (1987) 405

H.   Commitment and Release 405
    Brakel et al., The Mentally Disabled and the Law (1985) 405
    Jones v. United States (S.Ct.1983) 406

I.   The Right to Treatment 408
    Rouse v. Cameron (Fed.1967) 408
    Goldstein, The Insanity Defense (1967) 408
    Hoffman & Dunn, Va.L.Rev. (1975) 408

Section 4.   Diminished Capacity 408
    State v. McVey (Iowa 1985) 408
    Muench v. Israel (Fed.1983) 413
      State v. Flattum (Wis.1985) 417
      Robinson, Criminal Law Defenses (1987) 417
      People v. Wetmore (Cal.1978) 418

CHAPTER 7. ALCOHOLISM AND ADDICTION; INTOXICATION; IMMATURITY

Section 1.   Chronic Alcoholism and Drug Addiction 419
    Powell v. Texas (S.Ct.1968) 419
      People v. Davis (Ill.1963) 427
      State ex rel. Harper v. Zegeer (W.Va.1982) 428
      Note, Harv.L.Rev. (1981) 428
    United States v. Moore (Fed.1973) 429
      People v. Davis (N.Y.1973) 435
      Fingarette, Yale L.J. (1975) 436
      Note, Geo.L.J. (1972) 436
      Gorham v. United States (D.C.1975) 437
      Vorenberg & Lukoff, Fed.Prob. (1973) 438

Section 2.   Voluntary and Involuntary Intoxication 439
    Director of Public Prosecutions v. Majewski (Engl.1976) 439
      United States v. Nix (Fed.1974) 444
      State v. Vaughn (S.C.1977) 445
      Terry v. State (Ind.1984) 445
      State v. Schulz (Wis.1981) 446
      United States ex rel. Goddard v. Vaughn (Fed.1980) 446
      Hall, General Principles of Criminal Law (1960) 446

Section 2.   Voluntary and Involuntary Intoxication—Continued   **Page**

People v. Crittle (Mich.1973) _____ 447

Parker v. State (Mo.1969) _____ 447

Paulsen, U.Ill.L.F. (1961) _____ 448

State v. Hall (Iowa 1974) _____ 448

City of Minneapolis v. Altimus (Minn.1976) _____ 448

Paulsen, U.Ill.L.F. (1961) _____ 453

State v. Hall (Iowa 1974) _____ 454

People v. Walker (Ill.1975) _____ 454

Section 3.   Immaturity _____ **455**

State v. Q.D. (Wash.1984) _____ 455

In re Michael (R.I.1981) _____ 458

Ludwig, Neb.L.Rev. (1950) _____ 458

Walkover, U.C.L.A.L.Rev. (1984) _____ 458

Couch v. State (Ga.1985) _____ 458

CHAPTER 8. JUSTIFICATION AND EXCUSE

Section 1.   Introduction _____ **460**

Greenawalt, Law & Contemp.Probs. (1986) _____ 460

Model Penal Code Art. 3, Introduction (1985) _____ 461

Section 2.   Defense of Self and Others _____ **462**

United States v. Peterson (Fed.1973) _____ 462

Coleman v. State (Del.1974) _____ 467

State v. Faulkner (Md.1984) _____ 467

People v. Townes (Mich.1974) _____ 468

Townsend v. Commonwealth (Ky.1971) _____ 468

McMahon v. State (Alaska 1980) _____ 469

Ashworth, Cambr.L.J. (1975) _____ 469

Commonwealth v. Palmer (Pa.1976) _____ 469

Commonwealth v. Shaffer (Mass.1975) _____ 469

State v. Bonano (N.J.1971) _____ 469

Cooper v. United States (D.C.1986) _____ 470

State v. Harris (Iowa 1974) _____ 470

People v. Adams (Ill.1972) _____ 471

United States v. Black (Fed.1982) _____ 472

United States v. Panter (Fed.1982) _____ 472

Martin v. Ohio (S.Ct.1987) _____ 472

State v. Hodges (Kan.1986) _____ 474

Note, Va.L.Rev. (1986) _____ 478

Acker & Toch, Crim.L.Bull. (1985) _____ 479

Comment, U.Pa.L.Rev. (1987) _____ 479

Jahnke v. State (Wyo.1984) _____ 480

People v. Goetz (N.Y.1986) _____ 480

Werner v. State (Tex.1986) _____ 481

Commonwealth v. Martin (Mass.1976) _____ 481

Section 3.   Defense of Property _____ **484**

Law v. State (Md.1974) _____ 484

Bishop v. State (Ga.1987) _____ 488

Page

Section 4. Law Enforcement and Response Thereto 491
   Kohler v. Commonwealth (Ky.1973) 491
     Reigan v. People (Colo.1949) 493
     Lilly v. West Virginia (Fed.1928) 493
   Tennessee v. Garner (S.Ct.1985) 495
     Uviller, N.Y.U.L.Rev. & Soc.Chg. (1986) 501
     Commonwealth v. Klein (Mass.1977) 503
   People v. Curtis (Cal.1969) 504
     Wainwright v. New Orleans (S.Ct.1968) 507
     Chevigny, Yale L.J. (1969) 508
     People v. Alexander (Mich.1972) 508
     Johnson v. State (Ind.1972) 508

Section 5. Domestic Authority 509
   People v. Ball (Ill.1973) 509
     State v. Thorpe (R.I.1981) 513
     People v. DeCaro (Ill.1974) 513
     Ingraham v. Wright (S.Ct.1977) 514
     State v. Pittard (N.C.1980) 514

Section 6. Duress, Necessity and Choice of Evils 514
   Director of Public Prosecutions v. Lynch (Engl.1975) 514
     Dennis, L.Q.Rev. (1980) 523
     State v. Toscano (N.J.1977) 524
     State v. Knapp (Vt.1986) 525
     People v. Unger (Ill.1975) 525
     People v. Court (N.Y.1976) 525
     People v. Colgan (N.Y.1975) 526
     United States v. Stevison (Fed.1972) 526
   State v. Warshow (Vt.1979) 527
     United States v. Montgomery (Fed.1985) 530
     Sigma Reproductive Health Center v. State (Md.1983) 532
     United States v. Holmes (Fed.1842) 532
     Commonwealth v. Lindsey (Mass.1986) 532
     People v. Patrick (Colo.1975) 533
     State v. Diana (Wash.1979) 533
     United States v. Bailey (S.Ct.1980) 533

Section 7. Consent and Condonation 533
   Model Penal Code § 2.11 533
     People v. Evans (N.Y.1975) 534
     Regina v. Collins (Engl.1972) 534
     Halushka v. University of Saskatchewan (Can.1965) 535
     Flakne & Caplan, Trial (1977) 535
     Recent Case, Harv.L.Rev. (1968) 536
     Kennedy, Crim.L.Rev. (1976) 536
     Note, Colum.L.Rev. (1986) 536
     Note, Harv.L.Rev. (1986) 536
   State v. Garoutte (Ariz.1964) 537

CHAPTER 9. ATTEMPTS

Page

Section 1. Mental State 540
    People v. Harris (Ill.1978) 540
      People v. Castro (Colo.1983) 544
      Amlotte v. State (Fla.1984) 544
      People v. Weeks (Ill.1967) 544
      People v. Brown (N.Y.1964) 545
      State v. Grant (Me.1980) 545
      Enker, A.B.F.Res.J. (1977) 545
      Model Penal Code § 5.01, Comment (1985) 545
      Gardner v. Akeroyd (Engl.1952) 547
    In re Smith (Cal.1970) 547

Section 2. Acts 549
      Buxton, Crim.L.Rev. (1973) 549
    Regina v. Eagleton (Eng.1855) 550
      Rex v. White (Engl.1910) 551
    People v. Rizzo (N.Y.1927) 551
    People v. Orndorff (Cal.1968) 553
    Commonwealth v. Skipper (Pa.1972) 555
      Skilton, U.Pitt.L.Rev. (1937) 556
    People v. Bowen (Mich.1968) 556
      Campbell & Bradley v. Ward (N.Z.1955) 559
      Stuart, Crim.L.Rev. (1970) 559
      Williams, Criminal Law (1961) 559
    United States v. Mandujano (Fed.1974) 560
      Stuart, Crim.L.Rev. (1970) 562
      Misner, Stan.L.Rev. (1981) 562

Section 3. Impossibility 563
    United States v. Thomas (Fed.1962) 563
      United States v. Berrigan (Fed.1973) 571
      Model Penal Code § 5.01, Comment (1985) 571
      Enker, Minn.L.Rev. (1969) 572
      United States v. Oviedo (Fed.1976) 572
      Weigand, DePaul L.Rev. (1977) 573
      Note, Yale L.J. (1960) 574
      Commonwealth v. Johnson (Pa.1933) 574
      Wilson v. State (Miss.1905) 574
      Kelman, Stan.L.Rev. (1981) 575

Section 4. Abandonment 575
    People v. Staples (Cal.1970) 575
      People v. Von Hecht (Cal.1955) 578
      Commonwealth v. McCloskey (Pa.1975) 579
      United States v. McDowell (Fed.1983) 579
      People v. Crary (Cal.1968) 580
      LeBarron v. State (Wis.1966) 580
      Kelman, Stan.L.Rev. (1981) 580

Page

Section 5.   Prosecution and Punishment **581**
  Charge of completed crime, conviction of attempt 581
  Charge of attempt, proof of completed crime 582
  Punishment 582

Section 6.   Attempt–Like Crimes **583**
  Glazebrook, L.Q.Rev. (1969) 583
A.   Vagrancy 584
  Papachristou v. City of Jacksonville (S.Ct.1972) 584
  Kolender v. Lawson (S.Ct.1983) 588
    State v. Young (N.J.1970) 589
    People v. Johnson (N.Y.1959) 589
B.   Assault 590
  In re M. (Cal.1973) 590
    State v. Wilson (Or.1959) 592
    Robinson v. United States (D.C.1986) 593
C.   Burglary 593
  Model Penal Code § 221.1, Comment (1980) 593
    DeGidio v. State (Minn.1980) 595

CHAPTER 10.   CONSPIRACY AND SOLICITATION

Section 1.   Conspiracy: Introduction **596**
  Vagueness 596
  Venue 596
  Hearsay Exception 597
  Circumstantial Evidence 597
  Joint Trial 598
  Rationale 598

Section 2.   The Agreement **598**
  United States v. James (Fed.1976) 598
    United States v. Brown (Fed.1985) 602
    Ziatz v. People (Colo.1970) 602
    Commonwealth v. Cook (Mass.1980) 603
    United States v. Alvarez (Fed.1977) 603
  State v. St. Christopher (Minn.1975) 604
    Note, Colum.L.Rev. (1975) 608
    Burgman, DePaul L.Rev. (1979) 608
    Hutchinson v. State (Fla.1975) 609
    State v. Sexton (Kan.1983) 609
    United States v. Kasvin (Fed.1985) 609

Section 3.   Mental State **610**
  United States v. Chagra (Fed.1986) 610
    People v. Horn (Cal.1974) 614
    Model Penal Code § 5.03, Comment (1985) 615
    United States v. U.S. Gypsum Co. (S.Ct.1978) 615
    State v. Beccia (Conn.1986) 616
  People v. Lauria (Cal.1967) 616
    Marcus, U.Ill.L.F. (1976) 621

Section 3.   Mental State—Continued   **Page**
     United States v. Rush (Fed.1982) _____ 622
     United States v. Gallishaw (Fed.1970) _____ 622
   United States v. Feola (S.Ct.1975) _____ 623
     United States v. Prince (Fed.1976) _____ 630
     Model Penal Code § 5.03, Comment (1985) _____ 631
     Church v. Walton (Engl.1967) _____ 632

Section 4.   The Objective _____ **632**
   Shaw v. Director of Public Prosecutions (Engl.1961) _____ 632
     Commonwealth v. Bessette (Mass.1966) _____ 635
     State v. Bowling (Ariz.1967) _____ 636
     United States v. Burgin (Fed.1980) _____ 637
     Goldstein, Yale L.J. (1959) _____ 638
     United States v. Conover (Fed.1985) _____ 639
     Note, Colum.L.Rev. (1975) _____ 639

Section 5.   Impossibility _____ **640**
   Ventimiglia v. United States (Fed.1957) _____ 640
     United States v. Thomas (Fed.1962) _____ 643
     State v. Moretti (N.J.1968) _____ 644
     People v. Tinskey (Mich.1975) _____ 644

Section 6.   The Overt Act Requirement _____ **645**
   Developments, Harv.L.Rev. (1959) _____ 645
     Note, Colum.L.Rev. (1975) _____ 646

Section 7.   Scope: The Object Dimension _____ **646**
   Braverman v. United States (S.Ct.1942) _____ 646
     Lievers v. State (Md.1968) _____ 648
     People v. Burleson (Ill.1977) _____ 649
     Note, Colum.L.Rev. (1975) _____ 649
     Albernaz v. United States (S.Ct.1981) _____ 649
     Mason v. State (Md.1985) _____ 650

Section 8.   Scope: The Party Dimension _____ **650**
   Model Penal Code § 5.03, Comment (1985) _____ 650
   Johnson, Calif.L.Rev. (1973) _____ 650
   Kotteakos v. United States (S.Ct.1946) _____ 651
     Blumenthal v. United States (S.Ct.1947) _____ 653
     Anderson v. Superior Court (Cal.1947) _____ 654
     United States v. Cole (Fed.1983) _____ 655
     Rex v. Myrick & Ribuffi (Engl.1929) _____ 655
   United States v. Bruno (Fed.1939) _____ 655
   United States v. Michelena–Orovio (Fed.1983) _____ 656

Section 9.   Duration of the Conspiracy _____ **661**
   Grunewald v. United States (S.Ct.1957) _____ 661
     Comment, Ga.L.Rev. (1983) _____ 664
     United States v. Girard (Fed.1984) _____ 664
     United States v. Yow (Fed.1972) _____ 666
     State v. Yslas (Ariz.1984) _____ 666

Section 9.   Duration of the Conspiracy—Continued   **Page**
    United States v. Smith (Fed.1972) _____ 667
    Note, Colum.L.Rev. (1975) _____ 667

Section 10.   Withdrawal _____ **668**
    Note, Colum.L.Rev. (1975) _____ 668
    United States v. U.S. Gypsum Co. (S.Ct.1978) _____ 670

Section 11.   The Plurality Requirement _____ **670**
    Iannelli v. United States (S.Ct.1975) _____ 670
    Jeffers v. United States (S.Ct.1977) _____ 675
    United States v. Lupino (Fed.1973) _____ 676
    United States v. Helmich (Fed.1983) _____ 676
    People v. Carter (Mich.1982) _____ 676
    Note, Wash.L.Rev. (1976) _____ 676
    State v. Cornman (Mo.1985) _____ 677
    Note, Colum.L.Rev. (1975) _____ 677
    Gebardi v. United States (S.Ct.1932) _____ 678
    Eyman v. Deutsch (Ariz.1962) _____ 679
    United States v. Espinoza–Cerpa (Fed.1980) _____ 679
    Note, Colum.L.Rev. (1975) _____ 680
    United States v. Hartley (Fed.1982) _____ 680
    Welling, Hastings L.J. (1982) _____ 680
    Brickey, U.Cin.L.Rev. (1983) _____ 681
    United States v. Dege (S.Ct.1960) _____ 681

Section 12.   Conspiracy: A Final Look _____ **682**
    Johnson, Calif.L.Rev. (1973) _____ 682

Section 13.   Beyond Conspiracy: RICO _____ **683**
    United States v. Turkette (S.Ct.1981) _____ 683
    United States v. Elliott (Fed.1978) _____ 689
    Holderman, U.Cin.L.Rev. (1983) _____ 691
    United States v. Bledsoe (Fed.1982) _____ 691
    United States v. Lemm (Fed.1982) _____ 692
    United States v. Thompson (Fed.1982) _____ 692
    United States v. Ivic (Fed.1983) _____ 693
    United States v. Bagaric (Fed.1983) _____ 693
    Sedima v. Imrex Co. (S.Ct.1985) _____ 694
    United States v. Barton (Fed.1981) _____ 695
    Tarlow, Ford.L.Rev. (1980) _____ 695
    Dombrink & Meeker, Rutgers L.J. (1985) _____ 695

Section 14.   Solicitation _____ **696**
    People v. Lubow (N.Y.1971) _____ 696
    People v. Werblow (N.Y.1925) _____ 698
    Smith v. Commonwealth (Pa.1867) _____ 699
    Kelly v. United States (Fed.1952) _____ 699
    City of Columbus v. Scott (Ohio 1975) _____ 700
    United States v. Carson (D.C.1974) _____ 700
    State v. Boehm (Wis.1985) _____ 701
    Leffel v. Municipal Court (Cal.1976) _____ 701

Section 14.   Solicitation—Continued   **Page**
    State v. Bush (Mont.1981) _____ 701
    Shannon v. United States (D.C.1974) _____ 703

CHAPTER 11. PARTIES; LIABILITY FOR CONDUCT OF ANOTHER

Section 1.   The Common Law Classification _____ **704**
    Principal in the First Degree _____ 704
    Principal in the Second Degree _____ 705
    Accessory Before the Fact _____ 705
    Legislative Reform _____ 705

Section 2.   Acts or Omissions _____ **706**
    Hicks v. United States (S.Ct.1893) _____ 706
        Pace v. State (Ind.1967) _____ 707
        State v. Walden (N.Car.1982) _____ 708
        State v. Tazwell (La.1878) _____ 709
        State v. Ulvinen (Minn.1981) _____ 709
        State ex rel. Martin v. Tally (Ala.1894) _____ 709
        People v. Bohmer (Cal.1975) _____ 711
        Dressler, Hastings L.J. (1985) _____ 712
    Bailey v. United States (Fed.1969) _____ 712
        Settles v. United States (D.C.1987) _____ 716
        Commonwealth v. Drew (Mass.1976) _____ 716
        Hodges v. Commonwealth (Ky.1971) _____ 716
        United States v. McCall (Fed.1972) _____ 717

Section 3.   Mental State _____ **717**
    State v. Grebe (Mo.1970) _____ 717
        State v. Davis (Wash.1984) _____ 719
        United States v. Gregg (Fed.1979) _____ 720
        Wilson v. People (Colo.1939) _____ 720
    State v. Gladstone (Wash.1970) _____ 721
        United States v. Peoni (Fed.1938) _____ 724
        Backun v. United States (Fed.1940) _____ 724
        N.Y. Penal Law § 115.00 _____ 726
        Commonwealth v. Simione (Pa.1972) _____ 727
        State v. Hecht (Wis.1984) _____ 727
    People v. Marshall (Mich.1961) _____ 728
        State v. Foster (Conn.1987) _____ 729
        People v. Turner (Mich.1983) _____ 730
        Johnson v. Youden (Engl.1950) _____ 731

Section 4.   The Conspiracy–Complicity Relationship _____ **732**
    Pinkerton v. United States (S.Ct.1946) _____ 732
        Model Penal Code § 2.06, Comment (1985) _____ 734
        Note, Colum.L.Rev. (1975) _____ 735
        United States v. Alvarez (Fed.1985) _____ 735
        State v. Anderberg (S.D.1975) _____ 737

Page

Section 5.   Foreseeable or Related Crimes _____ **737**
United States v. Carter (Fed.1971) _____ 737
N.Y. Penal Law § 125.25 _____ 740
People v. Kessler (Ill.1974) _____ 740
United States v. Greer (Fed.1972) _____ 744
Model Penal Code § 2.06, Comment (1985) _____ 744

Section 6.   Must the Principal Be Guilty? _____ **745**
People v. Taylor (Cal.1974) _____ 745
Standefer v. United States (S.Ct.1980) _____ 749
United States v. Bryan (Fed.1973) _____ 750
United States v. Azadian (Fed.1971) _____ 754
State v. Hayes (Mo.1891) _____ 754
Bailey v. Commonwealth (Va.1985) _____ 755
Dusenbery v. Commonwealth (Va.1980) _____ 756

Section 7.   Withdrawal _____ **757**
State v. Thomas (N.J.1976) _____ 757
Commonwealth v. Huber (Pa.1958) _____ 759

Section 8.   Exceptions to Accomplice Liability _____ **760**
Queen v. Tyrrell (Engl.1893) _____ 760
State v. Bearcub (Or.1970) _____ 761
Model Penal Code § 2.06, Comment (1985) _____ 761

Section 9.   Vicarious Liability _____ **762**
State v. Beaudry (Wis.1985) _____ 762
Vachon v. New Hampshire (S.Ct.1974) _____ 768
Commonwealth v. Koczwara (Pa.1959) _____ 769
Davis v. City of Peachtree (Ga.1983) _____ 769
State v. Guminga (Minn.1986) _____ 770
State v. Akers (N.H.1979) _____ 770
City of Missoula v. Shea (Mont.1983) _____ 770

Section 10.   Liability of Organizations, Their Officers and Agents ___ **775**
Commonwealth v. Beneficial Finance Co. (Mass.1971) _____ 775
Developments, Harv.L.Rev. (1979) _____ 782
Miller, Fed.B.J. (1979) _____ 782
Coffee, Encyclopedia of Crime & Justice (1983) _____ 782
Granite Construction Co. v. Superior Court (Cal.1983) _____ 782
Gordon v. United States (Fed.1953) _____ 783
United States v. A & P Trucking Co. (S.Ct.1958) _____ 783
United States v. Park (S.Ct.1975) _____ 784
O'Keefe & Shapiro, Food, Drug & Cosm.J. (1975) _____ 790
Cohen, Food, Drug & Cosm.J. (1975) _____ 791
McVisk, J.Crim.L. & C. (1978) _____ 791
Abrams, U.C.L.A.L.Rev. (1981) _____ 791
Brickley, Vand.L.Rev. (1982) _____ 791
United States v. Y. Hata & Co. (Fed.1976) _____ 792
State v. Riley (W.Va.1975) _____ 792
Day v. State (Ind.1976) _____ 792
People v. Cheff (Mich.1971) _____ 793

	Page
Section 11. Post–Crime Aid	**793**
Stephens v. State (Wyo.1987)	793
Commonwealth v. Devlin (Mass.1974)	796
United States v. Hobson (Fed.1975)	797
United States v. Prescott (Fed.1978)	798
United States v. Balano (Fed.1979)	798
Model Penal Code § 242.3, Comment (1980)	799
State v. Cole (Mo.1973)	799
United States v. Magness (Fed.1972)	800
Holland v. State (Fla.1974)	802
Goldberg, A.B.A.J. (1966)	804
United States v. Kuh (Fed.1976)	805
United States v. Ciambrone (Fed.1984)	806
APPENDIX: AMERICAN LAW INSTITUTE MODEL PENAL CODE	809
INDEX	895

Table of Cases

The principal cases are in bold type. Cases cited or discussed in the text are roman type. References are to pages. Cases cited in principal cases and within other quoted materials are not included.

Aaron, People v., 303, 305
Abbott v. R., 523
Ake v. Oklahoma, 399, 400
Akers, State v., 770
Albernaz v. United States, 308, 649, 650
Alexander, People v., 508
Allsip, People v., 754
Alvarez, United States v., 603, 735
Amlotte v. State, 544, 545
Anderberg, State v., 737
Anderson, People v., 273, 679
Anderson v. Superior Court In and For Alameda County, 654
Anderson v. United States, 639
A & P Trucking Company, United States v., 783
Arnold, People v., 158, 260
Ashburn, Com. v., 286
Ashe v. Swenson, 237
Atencio, Com. v., 328, 329
Attardo, State v., 135
Aurora, City of v. Martin, 67
Azadian, United States v., 754

Babcock v. State, 754
Backun v. United States, 724, 726
Bagaric, United States v., 693
Bailey v. Com., 755
Bailey, United States v., 306, 533, **712,** 716
Baker, United States v., 180
Balano, United States v., 798
Balint, United States v., 160, 161
Ball, People v., 509, 513
Bantum v. State, 290
Barker, Rex v., 559
Barker, United States v., 186
Barnes v. United States, 132
Barney, State v., 412
Barton, United States v., 695
Batiste, State v., 315
Beale, State v., 122
Bearcub, State v., 761
Beaudry, State v., 762, 769, 770
Beccia, State v., 616
Bedder v. Director of Public Prosecutions, 251, 253
Beneficial Finance Co., Com. v., 775, 781, 783
Bennett, United States v., 403
Benson v. Superior Court of Los Angeles County, 700

Bergman, United States v., 28
Berrigan, United States v., 571
Berry, Com. v., 259, 260
Berry, People v., 256, 258, 261, 262
Bessette, Com. v., 635
Bianco, Com. v., 330
Bias, State v., 290
Bishop v. State, 453, 488
Black, United States v., 472
Blaue, Regina v., 324, 327, 328
Bledsoe, United States v., 692
Blockburger v. United States, 236, 237, 650
Blumenthal v. United States, 653
Boan, State v., 374
Boehm, State v., 701
Boggess v. State, 143
Bohmer, People v., 711
Boleyn, State v., 198
Bonano, State v., 469
Bouie v. City of Columbia, 60
Bowen, People v., 550, 556, 558, 559
Bowers v. Hardwick, 82, 92, 93
Bowling, State v., 636
Boyett, State v., 183
Bradley, State v., 66
Braun v. State, 174
Braverman v. United States, 646, 648, 650
Brawner, United States v., 372, 376
Bright, United States v., 131
Brody, People v., 60
Brown v. Ohio, 237, 308
Brown, People v., 545
Brown, State ex rel. v. Thompson, 799
Brown, United States v., 264, 271
Browning v. Michigan Dept. of Corrections, 508
Bryan, United States v., 750, 754
Bugger, State v., 203
Burge, State v., 412
Burgin, United States v., 637, 639
Burleson, People v., 649
Burroughs, People v., 306
Burton, People v., 308
Bush v. Commonwealth, 332
Bush, State v., 701
Butler, State v., 261
Byers, United States v., 399

Caddell, State v., 187, 200
Caldrain, State v., 444

Caldwell, Regina v., 144, 196
Cali, Com. v., 223
Calvaresi, People v., 140
Cameron, State v., 447
Caminetti v. United States, 64
Campbell and Bradley v. Ward, 559
Campbell v. State, 161, 311
Carbajal-Portillo v. United States, 754
Carson, United States v., 700
Carter, People v., 676
Carter, United States v., 737
Cash, People v., 174, 175
Casper, State v., 330
Cass, Com. v., 58
Castro, People v., 544, 545
Chadwick v. United States, 678
Chagra, United States v., 610, 616
Chalmers, State v., 287
Chambers, State v., 307
Champagne, State v., 360
Chavers, State v., 327, 328
Chavez, People v., 60
Cheff, People v., 793
Chermansky, Com. v., 504
Cherry v. State, 700
Chiswibo, Regina v., 333
Churchill v. Walton, 632
Ciambrone, United States v., 806
City of (see name of city)
Coates, State v., 445, 446
Coker v. Georgia, 350, 351
Cole, State v., 799
Coleman v. State, 467, 468
Collins, United States v., 261
Columbus, City of v. Scott, 700
Com. v. ___ (see opposing party)
Commonwealth v. ___ (see opposing party)
Commonwealth of Pennsylvania v. Nelson, 67
Connors, People v., 106, 107
Conover, United States v., 639
Cook, Com. v., 603
Coombs, State v., 374
Cooper v. State, 404
Cooper v. United States, 470
Cornman, State v., 677
Couch v. State, 458
**County Court of Ulster County, New York v.
   Allen, 116, 210**
Crackerneck Country Club, Inc. v. City of Inde-
   pendence, 67
Craig, State v., 311
Crawford, State v., 532
Crittle, People v., 447
Crocker, State v., 315
Cude, State v., 183
Cunningham, Regina v., 98, 100, 303
Curl v. State, 412
Curtis, People v., 504
Curtis, State v., 397
Cushman, State v., 147, 150

Damms, State v., 574
Davis v. City of Peachtree City, 769, 770
Davis v. Com., 223

Davis, People v., 427, 435
Davis, State v., 701, 719
Day v. State, 792
Debellis, United States v., 369
Decaro, People v., 513
Decina, People v., 197
Dege, United States v., 681
Degidio v. State, 595
De Meo, State v., 185
Dennis v. United States, 638
De Petro, Com. v., 105
Devlin, Com. v., 796, 799
Diana, State v., 533
Difrancesco, United States v., 695
Dillon, People v., 305
Director of Public Prosecutions v. Beard, 444
Director of Public Prosecutions v. Lynch, 514, 523
**Director of Public Prosecutions v. Majewski,
   439,** 444
Director of Public Prosecutions v. Morgan, 165,
   172, 173, 174, 175, 756
Dissicini, State v., 524
District Court of Thirteenth Judicial Dist. In and
   For Yellowstone and Stillwater Counties, State
   ex rel. Sikora v., 397
Dlugash, People v., 318
Dombroski, State v., 171
Donovan, Com. v., 234
Dorsey v. Commonwealth, 721
Dotterweich, United States v., 790
Drew, Com. v., 716
Drope v. Missouri, 359, 360, 370
Dunbar Contracting Co., People v., 680
Dunlop, State v., 234
Durham v. United States, 372
Dusenbery v. Com., 756
Dusky v. United States, 360

Eagleton, Regina v., 550
Egan, State v., 45
Ehrlichman, United States v., 186
Elliott, United States v., 689
Elmore v. Com., 262
Elton, State v., 174
Enmund v. Florida, 306, 351, 352, 353
Enriquez v. Procunier, 360
Escamilla, United States v., 290
Espinosa Cerpa, United States v., 679
Essex v. Com., 289
Etzweiler, State v., 730
Evans, People v., 534
Evans v. State, 453
Ex parte (see name of party)
Eyman v. Deutsch, 679

Falcone, United States v., 621
Farnsworth v. Zerbst, 680
Faulkner, 100
Faulkner, State v., 100, 467, 468
Feinberg, Com. v., 330
Feola, United States v., 623
Fine v. State, 319
Fisher v. United States, 271, 272
Fiswick v. United States, 667

Flaherty, State v., 206
Flattum, State v., 417
Flick Case, The, 531
Ford v. Wainwright, 370
Foster, State v., 729
Fraley, Ex parte, 261
Francabandera, People v., 361
Francis v. Franklin, 121, 122
Franzese, United States v., 667
Fraser, State v., 761
Frazier, State v., 314
Freeman, Com. v., 112
Fulcher v. State, 196
Furman v. Georgia, 345, 347, 348

Gaddis, United States v., 236
Gaetano v. United States, 184
Gallishaw, United States v., 622
Gambrell, State v., 400
Gardner v. Akeroyd, 547
Gardner, State v., 108
Garlick, People v., 369
Garoutte, State v., 537
Gebardi v. United States, 678, 761
Gelb, State v., 710
George v. State, 197
Gerak, State v., 314, 315
Gibson, People v., 270
Gilday v. Com., 397
Gill, People v., 267
Giordano v. United States, 667
Girard, United States v., 664
Gladden v. State, 108
Gladman, People v., 308
Gladstone, State v., 721, 724, 727
Goddard, United States ex rel. v. Vaughn, 446
Goetz, People v., 480
Goldstein v. California, 67
Goldstein, United States v., 667
Goodenow, State v., 185
Goodman, People v., 330
Goodseal, State v., 296, 301, 306
Goodwin v. State, 526
Gordon v. State, 183
Gordon v. United States, 783
Gore v. United States, 24, 225, 228
Gorham v. United States, 437
Gory, People v., 203
Gould, United States v., 391
Granite Const. Co. v. Superior Court of Fresno County, 782
Grant, People v., 196
Grant, State v., 545
Grebe, State v., 717, 719, 720
Greer, United States v., 744
Gregg v. Georgia, 335
Gregg, United States v., 720
Griffiths, Regina v., 655
Grimsley, State v., 200
Grunewald v. United States, 661
Guillette, United States v., 331
Guminga, State v., 770

Hairston v. State, 106, 107
Hall, State v., 448, 454
Hallett, State v., 329
Halushka v. University of Saskatchewan, 535
Hamaker, People v., 508
Hamil, People v., 107
Hamilton, United States v., 174, 175, 329
Hansen, People v., 304
Harper, State ex rel. v. Zegeer, 428
Harris v. Oklahoma, 237, 308
Harris, People v., 540, 544, 545
Harris, State v., 470
Harrison, State v., 223, 224
Hartley, United States v., 680
Hartwell, United States v., 64
Harwood, State v., 260
Hatley, State v., 101
Hawes v. Dinkler, 67
Hayes, State v., 360, 754
Hayes, United States v., 360
Hecht, State v., 727, 728
Helmich, United States v., 676
Helms, State v., 403
Hendershott v. People, 412
Henderson v. Kibbe, 322
Hicks v. United States, 706, 709
Hill v. Baxter, 189
Hobson, United States v., 797
Hodgdon, State v., 140
Hodges v. Com., 716
Hodges, State v., 474, 480
Holland v. State, 802
Holmes v. Director of Public Prosecutions, 259, 260
Holmes, United States v., 532
Holsemback v. State, 315
Holt, People v., 272
Holzer, People v., 679
Hopkins v. State, 185
Horn, People v., 614
Horton, State v., 314
Hoyt, State v., 253, 260
Huber, Commonwealth v., 759
Hudson, United States v., 47
Hughes v. Mathews, 413, 414
Hurwitz v. State, 679
Hutchinson v. State, 609
Hyam v. Director of Public Prosecutions, 278, 286, 287

Iannelli v. United States, 670, 675, 677
Ibn Omar-Muhammad, State v., 289
Ingraham v. Wright, 514
In re (see name of party)
Insco, United States v., 186
International Minerals & Chemical Corp., United States v., 182
Irby v. United States, 229
Ireland, People v., 209, 307
Irwin, United States v., 185
Ivic, United States v., 693

Jackson v. Indiana, 362, 369
Jacobs v. State, 329

Jaffe, People v., 571, 572, 573, 575
Jahnke v. State, 480
James, United States v., 598, 603
Jantzi, State v., 125
Jeffers v. United States, 237, 675
Jenkins, State v., 270
Jerrett, State v., 200
Jewell, United States v., 127
J. N., Matter of, 332
Johnson, Com. v., 574
Johnson, People v., 447, 589
Johnson, State v., 314, 360, 508
Johnson, State ex rel. v. Richardson, 399
Johnson, United States ex rel. Matthews v., 260
Johnson v. Youden, 731
Jones, People v., 754
Jones, State v., 137, 144, 394, 397, 401
Jones v. United States, 406
Jurek v. Texas, 345

Karstetter, State v., 399
Kasvin, United States v., 609
**Keeler v. Superior Court of Amador County,
47,** 57, 58, 59, 60, 62
Keener v. State, 404
Kelly v. United States, 699
Kessler, People v., 740
Kibbe v. Henderson, 319
Kilgus, State v., 701
Kinnemore, State v., 107
Kirkpatrick, People v., 135
Klein, Com. v., 503
Koczwara, Commonwealth v., 769
Kohler v. Com., 491
Kolender v. Lawson, 588
Konz, Com. v., 221
Korell, State v., 388
Kotteakos v. United States, 651, 653
Krulewitch v. United States, 596
Kuh, United States v., 805

Lambert v. People of the State of California, 181,
182
Lancaster v. Municipal Court for Beverly Hills
Judicial Dist. of Los Angeles County, 67
Lane v. State, 360
Langworthy, People v., 444
Lashley, State v., 301
Lauria, People v., 616, 726
Law v. State, 484
Lawrance, United States v., 403
Leary v. United States, 116
Leavine v. State, 721
Lee, Com. v., 205, 206
Lee v. State, 112, 113
Leffel v. Municipal Court of Fresno County, 701
Legg, Com. v., 311
Leland v. State of Oregon, 401
Lemm, United States v., 692
Levia, Com. v., 235
Lewis, People v., 331
Lievers v. State, 648
Light, State v., 314
Lilly v. State of W. Va., 493

Lindsey, Com. v., 532
Lingras Das v. King, 333
Linscott, State v., 745
Liparota v. United States, 175, 181, 182
Little, State v., 255
Locke v. Rose, 74
Locke v. State, 71
Lockett v. Ohio, 346
Long v. State, 186
Love, People v., 332
Lovisi v. Slayton, 93
Lowenfield, State v., 395
Lubow, People v., 696, 699, 700
Lucero, State v., 146
Lupino, United States v., 676
Lyles v. United States, 403, 404

M., In re, 590, 593
MacAndrews & Forbes Co., United States v., 680
Madden, State v., 260
Magness, United States v., 800
Mandujano, United States v., 550, 560
Marshall, People v., 728, 729, 730
Martin, Com. v., 481
Martin v. Ohio, 446, 472
Martin v. State, 201
Martin, State ex rel. Tally v., 709
Martinez, United States v., 209
Martorano, United States v., 209
Mason v. State, 650
Massey, State v., 799
Matalik, State ex rel. v. Schubert, 369
Matchett, Com. v., 306
Matter of (see name of party)
Matthews, United States ex rel. v. Johnson, 260
Mayberry, People v., 171
Mayes v. People, 287
McAllister, State v., 721
McBoyle v. United States, 65, 80
McCall, United States v., 717
McCarthy v. State, 413
McCusker, Com. v., 412
McDowell, United States v., 579
McKim, State v., 719
McLaughlin, State v., 447
McLeod, Com. v., 315
McMahan v. State, 469
McVey, State v., 408, 412
Meeker, United States v., 444
Melton, United States v., 109, 112
Meyrick and Ribuffi, Rex v., 655
Michael, In re, 458
Michael, Regina v., 332
Michelena-Orovio, United States v., 656
Miller, Commonwealth v., 45
Miller, People v., 308
Milne, United States v., 401
Minneapolis, City of v. Altimus, 448, 453
Minster, State v., 319
Missoula, City of v. Shea, 770
Missouri v. Hunter, 236
M'Naghten's Case, Daniel, 371, **372,** 374, 375
Mobbley, State v., 799
Mobley v. State, 708

Mochan, Com. v., 45
Montgomery, United States v., 530
Moore v. Lowe, 721
Moore, United States v., 429, 437
Moreland v. State, 224
Moretti, State v., 644
Morgan v. District of Columbia, 184
Morissette v. United States, 157
Motes v. State, 399
Muench v. Israel, 413, 446
Mulcahy, People v., 314
Mullaney v. Wilbur, 238, 305, 334, 401

Nash v. United States, 80
Nations, State v., 131
Neal v. State, 233
Newton, People v., 195, 202
Nichols, People v., 65
Norris, People v., 206
Nuckolls, State v., 404

Odom, State v., 113, 117
O'Neal v. United States, 108
O'Neil, State v., 184
Orndorff, People v., 550, 553
Ortiz, State v., 360
Osborne v. State, 800
Otto, State v., 701
Oviedo, United States v., 572

Pace v. State, 707
Palendrano, State v., 42
Palmer, Com. v., 469
Panter, United States v., 472
Papachristou v. City of Jacksonville, 81, 584,
587, 588
Park, United States v., 784, 790, 791, 793
Parker v. State, 447, 448
Parsons v. State, 371, 375
Pate v. Robinson, 356, 360, 370
Patterson v. Com., 113
Patterson v. New York, 122, **245,** 401, 446, 472,
473
Pembliton, Regina v., 100
Peoni, United States v., 724
People v. ____(see opposing party)
Peterson, United States v., 462, 468, 469
Phillips, People v., 287
Pierson, State v., 196
Pinkerton v. United States, 670, **732,** 735
Pittard, State v., 514
Poe v. Ullman, 68
Pomponio, United States v., 105
Powell, People v., 632
Powell v. Texas, 388, **419,** 427
Prairie Schooner News Ltd. and Powers, Regina
v., 186
Prante, People v., 125
Pray, In re, 402
Prescott, United States v., 798
Price, State v., 799
Prince, 175
Prince, United States v., 175, 630
Proffitt v. Florida, 345

Q.D., State v., 455, 458
Quentin, People v., 700

R. v. Rancy, 252, 253
Rambo, Com. v., 206
Ramsey, People v., 404
Randolph, State v., 289
Reed v. State, 467
Regina v. _____ (see opposing party)
Regle v. State, 680
Reigan v. People, 493
Rex v. _____ (see opposing party)
Richardson, State ex rel. Johnson v., 399
Riles v. McCotter, 398
Riley, State v., 792
Ripley v. Ewell, 45
Rivera v. Delaware, 401
Rizzo, People v., 550, 551
Roberts v. Louisiana, 348, 349
Roberts, Regina v., 551
Robinson v. Com., 412
Robinson, State v., 404
Robinson v. State of California, 388, 427, 436
Robinson v. United States, 593
Rocker, State v., 102, 104, 105
Roe v. Wade, 59
Root, Com. v., 329
Rose v. Locke, 75
Rose, State v., 316, 318
Rossi, People v., 60
Rossi, State v., 702
Rouse v. Cameron, 408
Rozell v. State, 754, 761
Rummel v. Estelle, 95
Rush, United States v., 622

Sak v. State, 670
Salas v. State, 427
Saldana, People v., 59, 60
Samuels, People v., 536
Sandstrom v. Montana, 117, 121, 122, 150, 305
Santa Rita Store Co., United States v., 680
Santiago, Com. v., 526
Savoie, People v., 447
Schleifer, State v., 699
Schmidt, People v., 374
Schrader, State v., 269
Schubert, State ex rel. Matalik v., 369
Schulz, State v., 446
Scott, United States v., 444
Sedima, S.P.R.L. v. Imrex Co., Inc., 694
Serebin, State v., 315
Settles v. United States, 716
Sexton, State v., 609
Seyfried, Ex parte, 113
Shaffer, Com. v., 469
Shannon v. United States, 703
Shaughnessy, People v., 202
Shaw v. Director of Public Prosecutions, 632
Shine, State v., 445
Sikora, State ex rel. v. District Court of Thir-
teenth Judicial Dist. In and For Yellowstone
and Stillwater Counties, 397
Simione, Com. v., 727, 728

Simonson, State v., 108
Simpson v. Florida, 237
Skinner, People v., 374
Skipper, Com. v., 550, 555
Smith, In re, 105, 547
Smith v. Commonwealth, 45, 46, 699
Smith, People v., 58
Smith, State v., 147, 259
Smith, United States v., 667
Snyder, People v., 186
Sobiek, People v., 60
Solem v. Helm, 94
Southern, State v., 318
Spaziano v. Florida, 347
Speidel v. State, 147
Spencer v. Zant, 369
Spingola, United States v., 223
Standefer v. United States, 749
Staples, People v., 575
State v. ____ (see opposing party)
State ex rel. v. ____ (see opposing party and relator)
St. Christopher, State v., 604, 608
St. Clair, State v., 524
Stephens v. State, 793
Stepniewski, State v., 150, 157, 158, 159
Sterling, State v., 444
Stewart, People v., 331
St. Paul, City of v. Olson, 67
Striggles, State v., 184
Stuart, People v., 315
Suire, State v., 67
Sumner v. Shuman, 349
Sundberg v. State, 68

Tally, State ex rel. v. Marting, 709
Tate, State v., 533
Taylor, Commonwealth v., 46
Taylor v. District Court In and For Tenth Judicial Dist., 398
Taylor, People v., 142, 745
Taylor, State v., 721
Tazwell, State v., 709
Tennessee v. Garner, 495, 501, 503
Terry v. Ohio, 563, 588
Terry v. State, 445
Thabo Meli v. Regina, 332
Thacker v. State, 329
Theel, People v., 136
Thomas v. State, 757, 799
Thomas, United States v., 563, 571, 574, 643
Thompson, State v., 307
Thompson, State ex rel. Brown v., 799
Thompson, United States v., 692
Thorpe, State v., 513
Tilson, State v., 262
Tinskey, People v., 644
Tison v. Arizona, 352
Toscano, State v., 524
Townes, People v., 468
Townsend v. Com., 468
Travers, People v., 769
Tronca, State v., 761
Tully v. State, 524

Turkette, United States v., 683
Turner v. La Belle, 699
Turner, People v., 730
Turner v. United States, 116
Tyrrell, Queen v., 760

Ulvinen, State v., 709
Underwood, State v., 301, 302
Union Pac Coal Co. v. United States, 680
United States v. ____ (see opposing party)
United States ex rel. v. ____ (see opposing party and relator)
United States v. Bruno, 655
U. S. Gypsum Co., United States v., 615, 670

Vachon v. New Hampshire, 768
Vanderbilt, People v., 582
Vardas v. Estelle, 403
Vaughn, State v., 445
Vaughn, United States ex rel. Goddard v., 446
Ventimiglia v. United States, 640
Viser, People v., 544, 545
Vogel, People v., 174
Von Hecht, People v., 578

Wainwright v. City of New Orleans, Louisiana, 507
Walden, State v., 708
Walker, People v., 454
Waller v. Florida, 68
Wardius v. Oregon, 397, 398
Ware, State v., 125
Warshow, State v., 527, 531
Washington, People v., 250
Watson, People v., 289
Waye v. Com., 412
Weeks, People v., 544, 545
Werblow, People v., 698
Werner v. State, 481
Wetmore, People v., 413, 418
Wheeler v. United States, 206
White, Rex v., 551
White v. State, 175, 445
Wilcox, People v., 769
Wilcox, State v., 412
Wilder, People v., 308
Williams v. City of Petersburg, 202
Williams, Com. v., 315
Williams v. Florida, 397, 398
Williams, State v., 140, 799
Williquette, State v., 217, 221
Wilson, People v., 307, 308, 720
Wilson v. State, 574, 575
Wilson, State v., 592
Wilson v. United States, 361
Winn, United States v., 398
Winship, In re, 473
Winters v. People of State of New York, 81
Wiyott v. State, 203
Wolff, People v., 272
Wong, State v., 150
Woodson v. North Carolina, 334, 347, 349
Wright, United States v., 397
Wyant v. State, 446

Y. Hata & Co., Ltd., United States v., 792
Young, State v., 589, 754
Yow, United States v., 666
Yslas, State v., 666
Yukl, People v., 389

Zapata, United States v., 101
Zegeer, State ex rel. Harper v., 428
Zimmerman, People v., 545

*

Table of Other Authorities

References are to Pages

Books and Reports

ABA Comm'n on Organized Crime, Organized Crime and Law Enforcement (1952), 69

ACLU, Secret Detention by the Chicago Police (1959), 587

Administrative Office of U.S. Courts, Federal Offenders in the United States District Courts (1969), 24

Arnold, The Symbols of Government (1935), 71

Austin, Lectures on Jurisprudence (1879), 443

Bishop, Criminal Law (1923), 375, 568

Black, Law Dictionary (1968), 751

Blackstone, Commentaries (1775), 43, 54, 55, 76, 240, 380, 721, 797

Brakel, Parry & Weiner, The Mentally Disabled and the Law (1985), 354, 387, 388, 393, 405

Bucknill & Tuke, Psychological Medicine (1879), 375

Burdick, The Law of Crime (1946), 536

California Statistical Abstract (1969), 56

Capote, In Cold Blood (1965), 267

Cardozo, Law and Literature and Other Essays and Addresses (1931), 268

Clark, Analysis of Criminal Liability (1880), 443

Coke, Institutes (1648), 48

Dalton, Once a Month (1983), 201

Devitt & Blackmar, Federal Jury Practice and Instructions (1977), 122

Egan, Life in London (1821), 444

FBI, Annual Crime Reports (1973), 587

Frankel, Criminal Sentences (1973), 23

Gellhorn, American Rights (1960), 729

Goldstein, The Insanity Defense (1967), 377, 382, 384, 402, 408

Gray, Attorneys' Textbook of Medicine (1949), 188

Hale, Pleas of the Crown (1880), 325

Hall, General Principles of Criminal Law (1960), 63, 182, 446, 566, 567

Hart, Punishment and Responsibility (1968), 30, 351

Hicks, Human Jettison (1927), 532

Holmes, The Common Law (1881), 31, 46, 183, 302

Illinois Crime Survey (1929), 304

Kamisar, LaFave & Israel, Modern Criminal Procedure (1986), 1

Kant, Philosophy of Law (1887), 30

Kenny, Outlines of Criminal Law (Turner ed. 1952), 99

Kinsey, Sexual Behavior in the Human Female (1942), 72

LaFave & Scott, Criminal Law (1972), 176, 188, 218, 321, 323, 543

Law Commission, Working Paper No. 50 (1973), 635

Manual for Courts-Martial (1969), 566

Matthews, Mental Disability and the Criminal Law (1970), 355, 393, 400

Miller, Prosecution: The Decision to Charge a Suspect with a Crime (1970), 235

Moreland, Law of Homicide (1952), 224

Morris, The Future of Imprisonment (1974), 29, 31

Morris & Hawkins, The Honest Politician's Guide to Crime Control (1970), 388

National Comm'n on Reform of Federal Criminal Laws, Final Report (1971), 607, 699

National Comm'n on Reform of Federal Criminal Laws, Study Draft (1970), 432

New Jersey State Police, Crime in the United States: Uniform Crime Reports (1975), 304

Perkins & Boyce, Criminal Law (1982), 107, 128, 636

President's Comm'n on Law Enforcement and Administration of Justice, Task Force Report: The Police (1967), 496

Prosser, Torts (1984), 490

Robinson, Criminal Law Defenses (1984), 417

Roche, The Criminal Mind (1958), 410

Royal Comm'n on Capital Punishment, Report (1953), 280, 281, 283, 381

Russell, Crime (Turner ed. 1964), 169, 333

Salmond, Jurisprudence (1937), 105

Sedgwick, Statutory and Constitutional Law, 62

Smith & Hogan, Criminal Law (1965), 547, 583

Steadman, Beating a Rap? Defendants Found Incompetent to Stand Trial (1979), 354

Stephen, Digest of the Criminal Law (1877), 279, 518

Stephen, History of the Criminal Law (1883), 270
Stroud, Mens Rea (1914), 443
Stumpf, Morality and the Law (1966), 93

United States Sentencing Comm'n, Federal Sentencing Guidelines (1987), 39

von Hirsch, Doing Justice (1976), 31

Walker, The Battered Woman (1979), 476
Webster, New Collegiate Dictionary (1974), 119
Webster, New International Dictionary (1954), 727

Wharton, Criminal Law (1932), 375, 671
Wigmore, Evidence (1940), 115
Williams, Criminal Law: The General Part (1961), 105, 128, 169, 201, 559, 575, 606, 781
(Wolfenden Report) Report of the Committee on Homosexual Offenses and Prostitution (1963), 93
Wolfgang, Criminal Homicide (1958), 303

Zimring and Hawkins, Deterrence (1973), 30

Articles

Abrams, Criminal Liability of Corporate Officers for Strict Liability Offenses—A Comment on Dotterweich and Park, 28 U.C.L.A.L.Rev. 463 (1981), 791
Acker & Toch, Battered Women, Straw Men, and Expert Testimony, 21 Crim.L.Bull. 125 (1985), 479
Allen & DeGrazia, The Constitutional Right of Proof Beyond a Reasonable Doubt in Criminal Cases: A Comment on Incipient Chaos in the Lower Courts, 20 Am.Crim.L.Rev. 1 (1983), 122, 217
Andenaes, The Morality of Deterrence, 37 U.Chi.L.Rev. 649 (1970), 30
Aron & Katz, Corporal Punishment in the Public Schools, 6 Harv.Civ.Rts.—Civ.Lib.L.Rev. 583 (1971), 512
Ashworth, Self-Defence and the Right to Life, 34 Camb.L.J. 282 (1975), 469

Blackburn, Solicitation to Crimes, 40 W.Va.L.Rev. 135 (1934), 699
Bohlen & Burns, The Privilege to Protect Property by Dangerous Barriers and Mechanical Devices, 35 Yale L.J. 525 (1926), 490
Bonnie, The Moral Basis of the Insanity Defense, 69 A.B.A.J. 194 (1983), 404
Brett, The Physiology of Provocation, 1970 Crim.L.Rev. 634, p. 253
Brickey, Conspiracy, Group Danger and the Corporate Defendant, 52 U.Cin.L.Rev. 431 (1983), 681
Brickey, Criminal Liability of Corporate Officers for Strict Liability Offenses—Another View, 35 Vand.L.Rev. 1337 (1982), 791
Burgman, Unilateral Conspiracy: Three Critical Perspectives, 29 DePaul L.Rev. 75 (1979), 608
Burkhart, Is There a Rational Justification for Punishing an Accomplished Crime More Severely Than an Attempted Crime?, 1986 Brigham Young U.L.Rev. 553, p. 583
Burt & Morris, A Proposal for the Abolition of the Incompetency Plea, 40 U.Chi.L.Rev. 66 (1972), 369
Buxton, Incitement and Attempt, 1973 Crim.L.Rev. 656, p. 549

Chambliss, Types of Deviance and the Effectiveness of Legal Sanctions, 1967 Wis.L.Rev. 703, p. 31
Chevigny, The Right to Resist an Unlawful Arrest, 78 Yale L.J. 1128 (1969), 508
Coffee, Corporate Criminal Responsibility, 1 Encyclopedia of Crime and Justice 253 (1983), 782
Cohen, Enforcement Under the Food, Drug and Cosmetic Act—The Park Case in Perspective, 30 Food Drug Cosm.L.J. 676 (1975), 791
Cook, Act, Intention, and Motive in the Criminal Law, 26 Yale L.J. 645 (1917), 105

Delgado, Ascription of Criminal States of Mind: Toward a Defense Theory for the Coercively Persuaded ("Brainwashed") Defendant, 63 Minn.L.Rev. 1 (1978), 199
Dennis, Duress, Murder and Criminal Responsibility, 96 L.Q.Rev. 1208 (1980), 523
DiNicola & Mendeloff, Controlling Violence in Professional Sports, 21 Duquesne L.Rev. 843 (1983), 535
Dix, Mental Illness, Criminal Intent, and the Bifurcated Trial, 1970 Law & Soc. Order 559, p. 403
Dombrink & Meeker, Racketeering Prosecutions: The Use and Abuse of RICO, 16 Rutgers L.J. 633 (1985), 695
Dressler, Professor Delgado's "Brainwashing" Defense: Courting a Deterministic Legal System, 63 Minn.L.Rev. 335 (1979), 199
Dressler, Reassessing the Theoretical Underpinnings of Accomplice Liability: New Solutions to an Old Problem, 37 Hastings L.J. 91 (1985), 712
Dressler, Rethinking Heat of Passion: A Defense in Search of a Rationale, 73 J.Crim.L. & C. 421 (1982), 255
Duff, Recklessness, 1980 Crim.L.Rev. 282, p. 144

Edwards, The Criminal Degrees of Knowledge, 17 Mod.L.Rev. 294 (1954), 128
Elliott, Offences Against the Person—Murder, 1977 Crim.L.Rev. 70, pp. 286, 289
English, Homicides Other Than Murder, 1977 Crim.L.Rev. 79, p. 290

English, What Did Section Three Do to the Law of Provocation?, 1970 Crim.L.Rev. 249, p. 253

Enker, Impossibility in Criminal Attempts—Legality and the Legal Process, 53 Minn.L.Rev. 665 (1969), 572, 573

Enker, Mens Rea and Criminal Attempt, 1977 A.B.F.Res.J. 845, p. 545

Erlinder, Paying the Price for Vietnam: Post-Traumatic Stress Disorder and Criminal Behavior, 25 B.C.L.Rev. 305 (1984), 200, 393

Estrich, Rape, 95 Yale L.J. 1087 (1986), 172, 173

Fentiman, "Guilty But Mentally Ill": The Real Verdict is Guilty, 26 B.C.L.Rev. 601 (1985), 404, 405

Filvaroff, Conspiracy and the First Amendment, 121 U.Pa.L.Rev. 189 (1972), 640

Fingarette, Addiction and Criminal Responsibility, 84 Yale L.J. 413 (1975), 436

Flakne & Caplan, Sports Violence and the Prosecution, Trial 33 (Jan. 1977), 535

Fletcher, Should Intolerable Prison Conditions Generate a Justification or an Excuse for Escape?, 26 U.C.L.A.L.Rev. 1355 (1979), 533

Fletcher, The Theory of Criminal Negligence: A Comparative Analysis, 119 U.Pa.L.Rev. 401 (1971), 144

Forsythe, Homicide of the Unborn Child: The Born Alive Rule and Other Legal Anachronisms, 21 Val.U.L.Rev. 563 (1987), 58

Fridman, Mens Rea in Conspiracy, 19 Mod.L.Rev. 276, pp. 605, 606

Glazebrook, Should We Have a Law of Attempted Crime?, 85 L.Q.Rev. 28 (1969), 583

Goldberg, Misprision of Felony: An Old Concept in a New Context, 52 A.B.A.J. 148 (1966), 804

Goldstein, Conspiracy to Defraud the United States, 68 Yale L.J. 405 (1959), 638

Goldstein & Katz, Abolish the "Insanity Defense"—Why Not?, 72 Yale L.J. 853 (1963), 371

Greenawalt, Distinguishing Justifications from Excuses, 49 Law & Contemp.Probs. 89 (Summer 1986), 460

Hallowell & Meshbesher, Sports Violence and the Criminal Law, Trial 27 (Jan. 1977), 535

Harno, Intent in Criminal Conspiracy, 89 U.Pa.L.Rev. 624 (1941), 596

Hassett, Absolutism in Causation, 38 Syrac.L.Rev. 683 (1987), 316

Hoffman & Dunn, Beyond Rouse and Wyatt: An Administrative-Law Model for Expanding and Implementing the Mental Patient's Right to Treatment, 61 Va.L.Rev. 297 (1975), 408

Holderman, Reconciling RICO's Conspiracy and "Group" Enterprise Concepts with Traditional Conspiracy Doctrine, 52 U.Cin.L.Rev. 385 (1983), 691

Holtzman, Premenstrual Symptoms: No Legal Defense, 60 St. John's L.Rev. 712 (1986), 201, 392

Hughes, Criminal Omissions, 67 Yale L.J. 590 (1958), 182

Johnson, Multiple Punishment and Consecutive Sentences: Reflections on the Neal Doctrine, 58 Calif.L.Rev. 357 (1970), 228, 234

Johnson, The Unnecessary Crime of Conspiracy, 61 Calif.L.Rev. 1137 (1973), 650, 682

Keedy, Criminal Attempts at Common Law, 102 U.Pa.L.Rev. 464 (1954), 572

Kelman, Interpretive Construction in the Substantive Criminal Law, 33 Stan.L.Rev. 591 (1981), 81, 575, 580

Kennedy, The Legal Effect of Requests by the Terminally Ill and Aged Not to Receive Further Treatment from Doctors, 1976 Crim.L.Rev. 217, p. 536

LaFave, Penal Code Revision: Considering the Problems and Practices of the Police, 45 Texas L.Rev. 434 (1967), 589

Landis, A Note on "Statutory Interpretation," 43 Harv.L.Rev. 886 (1930), 64

Leflar, Statutory Construction: The Sound Law Approach (remarks, 1975), 65

Leigh, Sado-Masochism, Consent, and the Reform of the Criminal Law, 9 Mod.L.Rev. 130 (1976), 536

Lerblance, Impeding Unlawful Arrest: A Question of Authority and Criminal Liability, 61 Denver L.J. 655 (1984), 508

Levi, An Introduction to Legal Reasoning, 15 U.Chi.L.Rev. 501 (1948), 63

Lewin, Psychiatric Evidence in Criminal Cases for Purposes Other Than the Defense of Insanity, 26 Syracuse L.Rev. 1051 (1975), 412

Livermore & Meehl, The Virtues of M'Naghten, 51 Minn.L.Rev. 789 (1967), 377

Louisell & Hazard, Insanity as a Defense: The Bifurcated Trial, 49 Calif.L.Rev. 805 (1961), 403

Ludwig, Responsibility for Young Offenders, 29 Neb.L.Rev. 521 (1950), 458

Lunde & Wilson, Brainwashing is a Defense to Criminal Liability: Patty Hearst Revisited, 13 Crim.L.Bull. 341 (1977), 199

McVisk, Toward a Rationale Theory of Criminal Liabilty for the Corporate Executive, 69 J.Crim.L. & C. 75 (1978), 791

Marcus, Criminal Conspiracy: The State of Mind Crime—Intent, Proving Intent, and Anti-Federal Intent, 1976 U.Ill.L.F. 627, p. 621

Mickenberg, A Pleasant Surprise: The Guilty But Mentally Ill Verdict Has Both Succeeded in Its Own Right and Successfully Preserved the Traditional Role of the Insanity Defense, 55 U.Cin.L.Rev. 943 (1987), 405

Mickenberg, Competency to Stand Trial and the Mentally Retarded Defendant, 17 Cal.W.L.Rev. 365 (1981), 360

Miller, Corporate Criminal Liability: A Principle Extended to Its Limits, 38 Fed.B.J. 49 (1979), 782

Miller, The Compromise of Criminal Cases, 1 So.Cal.L.Rev. 1 (1927), 538

Misner, The New Attempt Laws: Unsuspected Threat to the Fourth Amendment, 33 Stan.L.Rev. 201 (1981), 562

Moreland, A Re-examination of the Law of Homicide in 1971: The Model Penal Code, 59 Ky.L.J. 788 (1971), 306

O'Connor, The Voluntary Act, 15 Med.Sci.Law 31 (1975), 198

O'Keefe & Shapiro, Personal Criminal Liability Under the Federal Food, Drug, and Cosmetic Act, 30 Food Drug Cosm.L.J. 5 (1975), 790

Orchard, Drunkenness, Drugs and Manslaughter, 1970 Crim.L.Rev. 214, p. 442

Packer, Mens Rea and the Supreme Court, 1962 Sup.Ct.Rev. 107, pp. 157, 158, 160

Paulsen, Intoxication as a Defense to Crime, 1961 U.Ill.L.F. 1, pp. 448, 453

Remington & Helstad, The Mental Element in Crime—A Legislative Problem, 1952 Wis.L.Rev. 644, pp. 104, 157, 293

Remington & Joseph, Charging, Convicting, and Sentencing the Multiple Criminal Offender, 1961 Wis.L.Rev. 528, pp. 234, 235, 236.

Remington & Rosenblum, The Criminal Law and the Legislative Process, 1960 U.Ill.L.F. 481, p. 68

Robinson, Criminal Law Defense: A Systematic Analysis, 82 Colum.L.Rev. 199 (1982), 411

Roth & Sundby, the Felony-Murder Rule: A Doctrine at Constitutional Crossroads, 70 Cornell L.Rev. 446 (1985), 302, 305

Sachs, Is Attempt to Commit Voluntary Manslaughter a Possible Crime?, 71 Ill.B.J. 166 (1982), 545

Saltzburg, Burdens of Persuasion in Criminal Cases: Harmonizing the Views of the Justices, 20 Am.Crim.L.Rev. 393 (1983), 216

Samuels, Excusable Loss of Self-Control in Homicide, 34 Mod.L.Rev. 163 (1971), 253

Sartorius, The Enforcement of Morality, 81 Yale L.J. 891 (1972), 93

Sayre, Criminal Conspiracy, 35 Harv.L.Rev. 393 (1922), 596

Sayre, Criminal Responsibility for the Acts of Another, 43 Harv.L.Rev. 689 (1930), 777

Sayre, Public Welfare Offenses, 33 Colum.L.Rev. 55 (1933), 160

Schaefer, Unresolved Issues in the Law of Double Jeopardy: Waller and Ashe, 58 Calif.L.Rev. 391 (1970), 237

Schroeder, Two Methods for Evaluating Duty to Rescue Proposals, 49 Law & Contemp.Prob. 181 (1986), 224

Schulhofer, Harm and Punishment: A Critique of Emphasis on the Results of Conduct in the Criminal Law, 122 U.Pa.L.Rev. 1497 (1974), 583

Schwartz, Federal Criminal Jurisdiction and Prosecutors' Discretion, 13 Law & Contemp.Prob. 64 (1948), 66

Scutt, Fraudulent Impersonation and Consent in Rape, 9 U.Queens L.J. 59 (1975), 534

"Sexual Behavior in the 1970's," Playboy Magazine (Oct. 1973), 72

Skegg, 'Informal Consent' to Medical Procedures, 15 Med.Sci.Law 125 (1975), 535

Skilton, The Requisite Act in a Criminal Attempt, 3 U.Pitt.L.Rev. 308 (1937), 556

Smith, A Case of Reckless Murder, 123 New L.J. 792 (1973), 285

Smith, Subjective or Objective?—Ups and Downs of the Test of Criminal Liability in England, 27 Vill.L.Rev. 1179 (1982), 144

Steadman, Monahan, Hartstone, Davis & Robbins, Mentally Disordered Offenders: A National Survey of Patients and Facilities, 6 Law & Hum.Behav. 31 (1982), 354

Stone, The Insanity Defense on Trial, 33 Hosp. & Comm.Psych. 636 (1982), 389

Stuart, The Actus Reus in Attempts, 1970 Crim.L.Rev. 505, pp. 559, 562

Sullivan, Self Induced and Recurring Automatism, 123 New N.J. 1093 (1973), 198

Tarlow, RICO: The New Darling of the Prosecutor's Nursery, 49 Fordham L.Rev. 165 (1980), 695

Temkin, The Limits of Reckless Rape, 1983 Crim.L.Rev. 5, p. 172

Treiman, Recklessness and the Model Penal Code, 9 Am.J.Crim.L. 281 (1981), 140, 141

Turner, Attempts to Commit Crimes, 5 Camb.L.J. 230 (1934), 558

Turner, The Mental Element in Crimes at Common Law, 6 Camb.L.J. 31 (1938), 104

Uviller, Seizure by Gunshot: The Riddle of the Fleeing Felon, 14 N.Y.U.Rev.L. & Soc.Chg. 705 (1986), 501, 503

Vorenberg & Lukoff, Addiction, Crime, and the Criminal Justice System, 37 Fed.Prob. 3 (Dec. 1973), 438

Walkover, The Infancy Defense in the New Juvenile Court, 31 U.C.L.A.L.Rev. 503 (1984), 458

Wechsler, The American Law Institute: Some Observations on Its Model Penal Code, 42 A.B.A.J. 321 (1956), 46

Weigand, Why Lady Eldon Should be Acquitted: The Social Harm in Attempting the Impossible, 27 DePaul L.Rev. 231 (1977), 573

Welling, Intracorporate Plurality and Criminal Conspiracy Law, 33 Hastings L.J. 1155 (1982), 680

Wexler, An Offense-Victim Approach to Insanity Defense Reform, 26 Ariz.L.Rev. 18 (1984), 389

Whitebread & Stevens, Constructive Possession in Narcotics Cases: To Have and Have Not, 58 Va.L.Rev. 751 (1972), 209

Winick Restructuring Competency to Stand Trial, 32 U.C.L.A.L.Rev. 921 (1985), 370

Annotations, Comments and Notes

52 A.L.R.2d 1458 (1958), 470
41 A.L.R.3d 584 (1972), 470
13 Am.Crim.L.Rev. 235 (1975), 535
22 Ariz.L.Rev. 919 (1980), 535
71 Calif.L.Rev. 1298 (1983), 289
35 Camb.L.J. 15 (1976), 327
47 Colum.L.Rev. 1332 (1947), 46
55 Colum.L.Rev. 1210 (1955), 445
75 Colum.L.Rev. 914 (1975), 483
75 Colum.L.Rev. 1122 (1975), 608, 639, 646, 649, 667, 668, 677, 680, 735
75 Colum.L.Rev. 1517 (1975), 158, 161
78 Colum.L.Rev. 1249 (1978), 316
85 Colum.L.Rev. 786 (1985), 288
86 Colum.L.Rev. 348 (1986), 262, 263, 536
1975 Crim.L.Rev. 584, p. 756
85 Dick.L.Rev. 289 (1981), 405
1986 Duke L.J. 1030, p. 535
45 Fordham L.Rev. 553 (1976), 93, 94
17 Ga.L.Rev. 539 (1983), 664
60 Geo.L.J. 667 (1972), 436, 438
46 Geo.Wash.L.Rev. 273 (1978), 533
10 Harv.J.L. & Pub.Pol. 213 (1987), 94
62 Harv.L.Rev. 77 (1948), 80
72 Harv.L.Rev. 920 (1959), 605, 607, 645, 679
81 Harv.L.Rev. 1339 (1968), 536
92 Harv.L.Rev. 1227 (1979), 782
94 Harv.L.Rev. 1660 (1981), 428
99 Harv.L.Rev. 1293 (1986), 536
100 Harv.L.Rev. 100 (1986), 92
56 Iowa L.Rev. 658 (1971), 57
39 J.Crim.L. 264 (1975), 171

22 Kan.L.Rev. 272 (1974), 728
88 L.Q.Rev. 458 (1972), 534
80 Mich.L.Rev. 271 (1981), 533
84 Mich.L.Rev. 1326 (1986), 400
61 N.Y.U.L.Rev. 703 (1986), 400
14 N.Y.U.Rev.L. & Soc.Chg. 973 (1986), 93
14 N.Y.U.Rev.L. & Soc.Chg. 995 (1986), 94
59 Notre Dame L.Rev. 253 (1983), 201
22 Stan.L.Rev. 1059 (1970), 308
26 Stan.L.Rev. 923 (1974), 438
32 Stan.L.Rev. 765 (1983), 370
47 Tulane L.Rev. 1017 (1973), 607, 640
24 U.Chi.L.Rev. 561 (1957), 236
43 U.Chi.L.Rev. 613 (1976), 534
48 U.Cin.L.Rev. 501 (1979), 532
29 U.C.L.A.L.Rev. 409 (1981), 531
33 U.C.L.A.L.Rev. 1679 (1986), 261
1970 U.Ill.L.F. 391, p. 595
106 U.Pa.L.Rev. 1021 (1958), 259
109 U.Pa.L.Rev. 67 (1960), 81
121 U.Pa.L.Rev. 120 (1972), 62
135 U.Pa.L.Rev. 427 (1987), 479
72 Va.L.Rev. 619 (1986), 477, 478
11 Wake Forest L.Rev. 253 (1975), 60
52 Wash.L.Rev. 142 (1976), 676
1956 Wis.L.Rev. 641, p. 159
1975 Wis.L.Rev. 771, p. 535
67 Yale L.J. 916 (1958), 228
70 Yale L.J. 160 (1960), 574
71 Yale L.J. 280 (1961), 780, 781
81 Yale L.J. 1342 (1972), 398

Newspapers

Nat'l L.J., July 20, 1987, at 3, col. 1, p. 289
N.Y. Times, June 17, 1976, at 39, col. 1, p. 27
N.Y. Times, June 18, 1976, at A22, col. 2, p. 36
N.Y. Times, June 19, 1976, at 46, col. 2, p. 36
N.Y. Times, July 3, 1976, at 18, col. 1, p. 37
N.Y. Times, July 10, 1976, at 21, col. 4, p. 37
N.Y. Times, Sept. 2, 1976, at 35, col. 1, p. 37
N.Y. Times, Sept. 15, 1976, at 1, col. 4, p. 38
N.Y. Times, Sept. 16, 1976, at 31, col. 3, p. 38
N.Y. Times, Sept. 17, 1976, at 12, col. 3, p. 38
N.Y. Times, Dec. 7, 1976, at 45, col. 6, p. 38

N.Y. Times, July 13, 1977, at 59, col. 4, p. 38
N.Y. Times, Jan. 6, 1977, at 27, col. 5, p. 38
N.Y. Times, Feb. 7, 1978, at 24, col. 5, p. 39
N.Y. Times, Oct. 20, 1979, at 26, col. 1, p. 39
N.Y. Times, May 17, 1981, at 48, col. 1, p. 39
N.Y. Times, June 22, 1984, at § 4, 6, col. 1, p. 39
N.Y. Times, Oct. 5, 1986, at L37, col. 1, p. 490
N.Y. Times, March 4, 1987, at 16, col. 1, p. 261
N.Y. Times, March 24, 1987, at 15, col. 2, p. 261
Wehrwein, 'Samaritan' Law Poses Difficulties, Nat'l L.J., Aug. 22, 1983, at 5, col. 1, p. 224

Federal: Constitution; Statutes; Regulations; Rules

U.S.Const., art. I, § 8, p. 66
U.S.Const., art. I, § 9, p. 52
U.S.Const., art. I, § 10, p. 52
U.S.Const., art. III, § 3, p. 66
U.S.Const., 1st Am., 85, 89, 711, 712
U.S.Const., 4th Am., 89, 496, 497, 499, 500, 501, 503, 505
U.S.Const., 5th Am., 84, 237
U.S.Const., 6th Am., 368, 398

U.S.Const., 8th Am., 85, 86, 87, 88, 94, 335, 336, 337, 342, 344, 346, 347, 348, 350, 351, 353, 425, 426, 427, 430, 433, 514
U.S.Const., 9th Am., 83, 85, 87
U.S.Const., 14th Am., 43, 45, 83, 87, 88, 336, 342, 344, 346, 347, 348, 351, 366, 368
1 U.S.C. § 1, p. 784
7 U.S.C. § 2024, pp. 175, 176, 177, 178, 179, 180
10 U.S.C. § 881, p. 644
10 U.S.C. § 920, p. 644

18 U.S.C. § 2, pp. 609, 751, 752, 798, 799
18 U.S.C. § 3, pp. 797, 798
18 U.S.C. § 4, pp. 802, 805, 806, 807
18 U.S.C. § 20, pp. 387, 401
18 U.S.C. § 88, p. 733
18 U.S.C. § 111, pp. 484, 623, 624, 625, 627, 628, 629
18 U.S.C. § 254, pp. 628, 629
18 U.S.C. § 371, pp. 623, 625, 626, 637, 638, 661, 665, 674, 690
18 U.S.C. § 641, p. 179
18 U.S.C. § 660, p. 720
18 U.S.C. § 751, p. 444
18 U.S.C. § 794, p. 676
18 U.S.C. § 834, p. 180
18 U.S.C. § 835, pp. 783, 784
18 U.S.C. § 1001, pp. 177, 665
18 U.S.C. § 1071, pp. 800, 801
18 U.S.C. § 1111, pp. 264, 265, 610, 611
18 U.S.C. § 1112, p. 290
18 U.S.C. § 1114, pp. 484, 610, 611, 623, 624
18 U.S.C. § 1117, pp. 610, 611
18 U.S.C. § 1201, p. 472
18 U.S.C. § 1202, pp. 472, 675
18 U.S.C. § 1511, p. 674
18 U.S.C. § 1708, p. 134
18 U.S.C. § 1792, p. 751
18 U.S.C. § 1952, p. 630
18 U.S.C. § 1955, pp. 670, 671, 672, 673, 674, 675, 676, 677
18 U.S.C. § 1961, pp. 683, 684, 685, 686, 687, 688, 694
18 U.S.C. § 1962, pp. 683, 684, 685, 696, 695
18 U.S.C. § 1964, p. 686
18 U.S.C. § 2113, pp. 623, 805, 806
18 U.S.C. § 2312, p. 666

18 U.S.C. § 2313, pp. 179, 666
18 U.S.C. § 2314, p. 744
18 U.S.C. § 2320, p. 180
18 U.S.C. § 2421, pp. 175, 227
18 U.S.C. § 2422, p. 175
18 U.S.C. § 2423, pp. 174, 175
18 U.S.C. § 3575, p. 695
21 U.S.C. § 174, p. 229
21 U.S.C. § 331, p. 784
21 U.S.C. § 333, p. 790
21 U.S.C. § 342, p. 784
21 U.S.C. § 841, pp. 128, 179
21 U.S.C. § 846, pp. 560, 561, 650, 660, 675
21 U.S.C. § 848, p. 675
21 U.S.C. § 952, p. 128
21 U.S.C. § 963, pp. 649, 660
26 U.S.C. § 2803, p. 647
26 U.S.C. § 2810, p. 647
26 U.S.C. § 2833, p. 647
26 U.S.C. § 2834, p. 647
26 U.S.C. § 3253, p. 647
26 U.S.C. § 3321, p. 647
26 U.S.C. § 4704, p. 225
26 U.S.C. § 4705, p. 225
26 U.S.C. § 5601, p. 215
26 U.S.C. § 5861, p. 626
28 U.S.C. § 2255, p. 229
29 U.S.C. § 186, p. 640
42 U.S.C. § 1983, p. 495
49 U.S.C. § 322, pp. 782, 784
49 U.S.C. § 1472, p. 344
49 U.S.C. § 1473, p. 344
U.C.M.J. art. 80, pp. 563, 571
U.C.M.J. art. 81, p. 563
U.C.M.J. art. 120, pp. 563, 664
U.C.M.J. art. 134, pp. 563, 571

Congressional Documents

H.R.Rep. No. 734, 76th Cong., 1st Sess. (1939), 134
S.Rep. No. 864, 76th Cong., 1st Sess. (1939), 134

State: Constitutions; Statutes

Alaska Const. art. I, § 7, p. 161
Alaska Stat. § 11.20.140, pp. 162, 165
Alaska Stat. § 11.20.260, pp. 161, 162, 163, 164, 165
Ariz.Rev.Stat. § 13–103, p. 538
Ariz.Rev.Stat. § 13–456, p. 537
Ariz.Rev.Stat. § 13–1591, pp. 537, 538
Ariz.Rev.Stat. § 28–691, p. 538
Cal.Const., art. I, § 16, p. 52
Cal.Gov't Code § 9608, p. 61
Cal.Health & Saf.Code § 11160, p. 203
Cal.Pen.Code § 4, pp. 51, 55
Cal.Pen.Code § 5, p. 48
Cal.Pen.Code § 6, pp. 51, 591
Cal.Pen.Code § 182, pp. 614, 615
Cal.Pen.Code § 187, pp. 48, 50, 51, 53, 54, 55, 59, 250

Cal.Pen.Code § 192, pp. 55, 258
Cal.Pen.Code § 240, p. 590
Cal.Pen.Code § 241, p. 590
Cal.Pen.Code § 245, pp. 590, 591
Cal.Pen.Code § 316, p. 621
Cal.Pen.Code § 485, p. 163
Cal.Pen.Code § 647, p. 588
Cal.Pen.Code § 653f, p. 698
Cal.Pen.Code § 654, p. 233
Cal.Pen.Code § 664, pp. 577, 591
Cal.Pen.Code § 834, p. 505
Cal.Pen.Code § 834a, pp. 504, 505, 506
Cal.Pen.Code § 835, p. 506
Cal.Pen.Code § 835a, p. 506
Cal.Welf. & Inst'ns Code § 602, p. 590
D.C.Code § 22–1801, pp. 110, 232
D.C.Code § 22–2401, p. 739

D.C.Code § 24–301, p. 407
Fla.Stat.Ann. § 775.01, p. 802
Fla.Stat.Ann. § 776.03, p. 802
Fla.Stat.Ann. § 843.14, p. 802
Fla.Stat.Ann. § 856.02, p. 584
Ga.Code Ann. § 16–3–1, p. 458
Ga.Code Ann. § 16–3–23, pp. 488, 489, 490
Ga.Code Ann. § 16–6–2, pp. 82, 86, 87, 88, 89, 90 91
Ga.Code Ann. § 26–1101, p. 340
Ga.Code Ann. § 27–2302, p. 341
Ga.Code Ann. § 27–2534.1, p. 341
Ga.Code Ann. § 27–2537, pp. 341, 343
Hawaii Rev.Stat. § 530, p. 669
Hawaii Rev.Stat. § 727–1, pp. 102, 103
Ill.Rev.Stat. ch. 38, § 2–4, p. 741
Ill.Rev.Stat. ch. 38, § 4–4, p. 743
Ill.Rev.Stat. ch. 38, § 4–5, p. 126
Ill.Rev.Stat. ch. 38, § 5–1, p. 741
Ill.Rev.Stat. ch. 38, § 5–2, pp. 741, 743
Ill.Rev.Stat. ch. 38, § 8–4, pp. 541, 743
Ill.Rev.Stat. ch. 38, § 9–1, pp. 541, 542, 543, 743
Ill.Rev.Stat. ch. 122, § 24–24, pp. 510, 512
Ind.Ann.Stat. § 9–1706a, pp. 363, 364, 365
Ind.Ann.Stat. § 22–1201, pp. 363, 364
Ind.Ann.Stat. § 22–1209, pp. 365, 366
Ind.Ann.Stat. § 22–1907, pp. 363, 365, 366
Iowa Code § 321.279, p. 408
Iowa Code § 701.4, p. 410
Iowa Code § 714.1, pp. 408, 409
Iowa Code § 714.2, p. 408
Kan.Stat.Ann. § 21–401, p. 298
Kan.Stat.Ann. § 21–3110, p. 301
Kan.Stat.Ann. § 21–3401, pp. 297, 301
Kan.Stat.Ann. § 21–3411, p. 66
Kan.Stat.Ann. § 21–3416, p. 66
Kan.Stat.Ann. § 21–3701, pp. 301, 302
Kan.Stat.Ann. § 21–3703, p. 301
Kan.Stat.Ann. § 21–3704, p. 301
Kan.Stat.Ann. § 21–3705, p. 301
Kan.Stat.Ann. § 60–456, p. 475
Me.Rev.Stat.Ann. tit. 17, § 2551, p. 239
Me.Rev.Stat.Ann. tit. 17, § 2651, p. 239
Me.Rev.Stat.Ann. tit. 17, § 3551, p. 122
Me.Rev.Stat.Ann. tit. 37, § 146, pp. 137, 139
Mass.Gen.Laws Ann. ch. 274, § 4, p. 797
Minn.Stat.Ann. § 340.96, p. 428
Minn.Stat.Ann. § 609.075, pp. 450, 451
Minn.Stat.Ann. § 609.17, p. 607
Minn.Stat.Ann. § 609.175, p. 607

Minn.Stat.Ann. § 611.026, pp. 451, 452, 453
Minn.Stat.Ann. § 613.70, p. 607
Mont.Code Ann. § 45–2–104, p. 775
Mont.Code Ann. § 45–2–301, p. 774
Mont.Code Ann. § 45–2–302, p. 774
N.H.Rev.Stat.Ann. § 269–C:24, p. 770
N.H.Rev.Stat.Ann. § 630:3, p. 150
N.J.Stat.Ann. 2A:85–1, pp. 42, 43, 44, 45
N.J.Stat.Ann. 2A:170–26, pp. 43, 44
N.Y.Pen.Law § 2, p. 552
N.Y.Pen.Law § 10.00, p. 214
N.Y.Pen.Law § 15.00, pp. 126, 323
N.Y.Pen.Law § 15.05, p. 126
N.Y.Pen.Law § 30.05, p. 390
N.Y.Pen.Law § 35.45, p. 760
N.Y.Pen.Law § 100.05, p. 696
N.Y.Pen.Law § 115.00, p. 726
N.Y.Pen.Law § 115.05, p. 726
N.Y.Pen.Law § 115.10, p. 727
N.Y.Pen.Law § 125.25, pp. 320, 321, 740
N.Y.Pen.Law § 265.15, p. 210
N.Y.Pen.Law § 265.20, p. 210
N.Y.Pen.Law § 2120, p. 552
N.Y.Pen.Law § 2124, p. 552
Or.Rev.Stat. § 161.085, p. 126
Or.Rev.Stat. § 164.065, p. 164
Or.Rev.Stat. § 418.140, p. 761
R.I.Gen.Laws § 14–1–2, p. 458
Tenn.Code Ann. § 39–707, pp. 71, 72, 74, 75, 77, 78
Texas Pen.Code art. 477, p. 419
Utah Code Ann. § 76–2–103, p. 143
Utah Code Ann. § 76–5–205, p. 143
Utah Code Ann. § 76–5–206, p. 143
Va.Code § 18.1–54, p. 203
Vt.Stat.Ann. ch. 13, § 1023, p. 148
Vt.Stat.Ann. ch. 13, § 1025, pp. 148, 149
Wash.Rev.Code § 9.41.030, p. 114
Wash.Rev.Code § 9A.04.050, pp. 455, 456, 457
Wis.Stat.Ann. § 100.20, pp. 150, 151, 153, 156
Wis.Stat.Ann. § 100.26, pp. 150, 151, 152, 153, 154, 155, 156
Wis.Stat.Ann. § 125.02, p. 765
Wis.Stat.Ann. § 125.04, pp. 762, 765
Wis.Stat.Ann. § 125.11, pp. 763, 765
Wis.Stat.Ann. § 125.68, pp. 763, 765, 768
Wis.Stat.Ann. § 939.30, p. 699
Wis.Stat.Ann. § 940.34, p. 220
Wis.Stat.Ann. § 940.201, pp. 217, 218, 220
Wyo.Stat. § 6–5–201, p. 791

English Statutes

Criminal Law Amendment Act of 1885, p. 760
Homicide Act of 1957, pp. 282, 306, 522
Malicious Damage Act, 100
Obscene Publications Act of 1959, p. 633
Offences Against the Person Act of 1861, pp. 98, 169, 170, 441, 442

Sexual Offences Act of 1956, pp. 166, 168
Street Offences Act of 1959, p. 633
7 & 8 Geo. 4, c. 18, p. 490
43 Geo. 3, c. 58, p. 282
24 Henry VIII, ch. 5, p. 463
25 Henry VIII, ch. 6, p. 73

Model Penal Code

Code Provisions:
  Section 1.05, p. 47
  Section 1.07, pp. 236, 237, 676
  Section 2.02, pp. 97, 104, 107, 126, 129, 130,
    131, 140, 418
  Section 2.03, p. 316
  Section 2.04, p. 184
  Section 2.05, p. 161
  Section 2.06, pp. 705, 710, 726, 754, 760
  Section 2.07, pp. 250, 775, 777, 782
  Section 2.08, pp. 440, 451, 452, 453, 454
  Section 2.09, pp. 454, 524
  Section 2.11, p. 533
  Section 3.02, p. 531
  Section 3.04, p. 483
  Section 3.05, p. 483
  Section 3.06, p. 488
  Section 3.07, pp. 471, 484, 498, 504
  Section 3.08, p. 484
  Section 3.09, pp. 483, 488
  Section 4.01, pp. 376, 381, 384
  Section 4.06, p. 368
  Section 5.01, pp. 550, 562, 566, 578, 711, 755
  Section 5.02, pp. 698, 701
  Section 5.03, pp. 606, 607, 639, 648, 649, 667,
    668, 735
  Section 5.04, pp. 679, 701, 702
  Section 5.05, pp. 677, 701
  Section 7.01, p. 30
  Section 210.2, pp. 288, 290, 306
  Section 210.3, pp. 255, 260, 290
  Section 210.6, p. 339
  Section 221.1, pp. 230, 595
  Section 223.5, p. 164

  Section 242.3, p. 799
  Section 250.6, p. 588
Revised Commentary (1980, 1985):
  Section 1.07, p. 236
  Section 2.02, p. 104
  Section 2.03, p. 316
  Section 2.04, p. 173
  Section 2.06, pp. 711, 734, 744, 761
  Article 3, p. 461
  Section 4.01, p. 371
  Section 5.01, pp. 545, 562, 571, 711
  Section 5.03, pp. 615, 631, 650
  Section 210.2, pp. 288, 290
  Section 210.3, p. 303
  Section 210.6, p. 269
  Section 221.1, p. 593
  Section 242.3, p. 799
Tent. Draft No. 1, Comments (1953):
  Section 2.04, p. 726
Tent. Draft No. 4, Comments (1955):
  Section 1.13, p. 246
  Section 2.02, pp. 106, 129, 147, 179
  Section 4.01, p. 384
Tent. Draft No. 5, Comments (1956):
  Section 1.08, p. 676
Tent. Draft No. 8, Comments (1958):
  Section 3.04, p. 506
  Section 3.06, p. 489
Tent. Draft No. 9, Comments (1959):
  Section 201.3, pp. 255, 314
  Section 201.6, p. 339
Tent. Draft No. 10, Comments (1960):
  Section 5.03, p. 606

Miscellaneous

ABA Standards Relating to Joinder and Severance § 1.1, p. 235
Restatement (First) of Torts § 216, p. 205

Uniform Alcoholism and Intoxication Treatment
Act, 428
Uniform Arrest Act, 505

MODERN
CRIMINAL LAW
CASES, COMMENTS AND QUESTIONS
Second Edition

*

Chapter 1

THE CRIMINAL JUSTICE SYSTEM *

This course has to do with the *substantive* criminal law. Substantive criminal law consists of that body of law which, for the purpose of preventing harm to society, declares what conduct is criminal and prescribes the punishment to be imposed for such conduct.

This field of law includes not only the definition of specific offenses (e.g., murder, robbery, rape), but also a good many general principles of liability. Those general principles, which receive primary emphasis in this Book, are of two types. One, represented by the principles that an insane person cannot be guilty of a crime, or that one coerced into committing what would otherwise be criminal conduct cannot be guilty of most crimes, has to do with *defenses to liability.* The second concerns principles of the *affirmative liability* sort—for example, those having to do with accomplice liability (who, other than the person who pulled the trigger, may be convicted of a murder?) or with the "inchoate crimes" of attempt, conspiracy and solicitation.

The criminal justice process consists of that series of procedures through which the substantive criminal law is enforced. In the typical law school curriculum, that

process is the subject of intense study in one or more courses often labelled *criminal procedure.* It is important, however, that students commencing their study of substantive criminal law have at least a general appreciation of how the criminal justice process is structured and who the persons responsible for administering the process are. The purpose of this Chapter is to provide a general overview of both the steps in the criminal justice process and the agencies which collectively make up the criminal justice system.

There is, of course, no single criminal justice system in this country. The United States consists of 51 jurisdictions (federal, plus the individual states), and thus it is fair to say that there are many systems which are quite similar but yet have individual uniqueness. Because that is so and because the description which follows is necessarily brief, some degree of overgeneralization is inevitable. The reader is forewarned.

SECTION 1. THE STEPS IN THE PROCESS

This section describes the major steps taken in the processing of a criminal case. The focus is on the processing of a "typical

* The material in this Chapter is abridged from Ch. 1 in Y. Kamisar, W. LaFave & J. Israel, *Modern Criminal Procedure* (6th ed. 1986).

1

case" in a "typical jurisdiction" (i.e., those procedures employed by most states in processing most of their criminal cases). The processing of both felony and misdemeanor cases is covered, but primary concentration is upon felony cases.[a]

Step 1: The Report of the Crime. The criminal justice process usually starts when the police receive information concerning the possible commission of a crime. The police may obtain that information either through their own observations or from the reports of interested citizens. In either case, if it appears likely that a crime was committed, the offense will be recorded in the police files as a "reported" crime (and will be listed statistically as an offense "known to the police").

Surprisingly, we have only limited data on the exact distribution of reported crimes in this country. That data is adequate, however, to provide a rough estimate of the likely distribution of reported offenses in a typical industrial state. Approximately 60% of all reported crimes will relate to the taking or destruction of property. The major offenses in this group will include the various forms of theft (perhaps 50% of all property offenses), burglary (15%), and vandalism (15%). Assaults of all varieties, ranging from assaults with weapons to simple assaults, may provide an additional 10% of the reported crimes. Offenses relating to the use of alcohol and drugs (e.g., public drunkenness, possession of drugs, and driving under the influence) are likely to constitute another 10% of the reported offenses. The remaining 20% of the reported crimes will be spread over a variety of offenses. Included in this group are the most serious violent felonies, such as rob-

bery (likely to constitute 2–4% of all reported offenses), and murder and forcible rape (each likely to fall below $1/2$ of 1%).

Step 2: Pre–Arrest Investigation. Once the police become aware of the possible commission of a crime, they must determine (1) whether the crime actually was committed and (2) if it was, whether there is sufficient information pointing to the guilt of a particular person to justify arresting and charging that person. Pre-arrest investigative procedures are designed to answer these questions and to collect evidence that may be helpful in establishing guilt at trial. The particular procedures used will vary with the circumstances of the crime. In some instances, a police officer will observe a crime being committed in his presence and will make an arrest "on the spot." In such cases, the pre-arrest investigation consists of no more than the officer's initial observation. In other cases, the officer will observe activity that is suspicious, though not necessarily criminal, and will seek further information to determine whether to make an arrest. Where an alleged offense has been called to the officer's attention by an interested citizen (usually a victim), the officer also is likely to seek information beyond that provided by the complainant.

Where additional information is sought, the officer may utilize a variety of investigatory techniques to gather that information. Perhaps the most common is to question the suspect. Pre-arrest questioning may be accompanied by the temporary detention of the suspect on the street or at home, but does not involve taking him into custody, as occurs with an arrest. The scope of the officer's questioning may range from merely asking the suspect to

---

a. American jurisdictions commonly use one of two different standards in distinguishing between felonies and misdemeanors. Some classify as felonies all offenses punishable by a maximum term of imprisonment of more than one year; offenses punishable by imprisonment for one year

or less are then misdemeanors. Others look to the location of the possible imprisonment: if the offense is punishable by incarceration in a penitentiary, it is a felony; if punishable only by a jail term, it is a misdemeanor.

identify himself to asking him to respond to an accusation made by others. Where the crime investigated involved violence, or there is some other reason to believe the suspect could be armed, the officer may undertake some sort of search of the temporarily detained suspect (usually a pat-down or "frisk" of the suspect's outer clothing). In a small percentage of these police-suspect encounters, the officer also may search the car of a suspect who was stopped while driving.

Along with the police-suspect encounter, the other common pre-arrest investigatory techniques are the interviewing of potential witnesses and the examination of the scene of the crime. In certain types of cases (e.g., homicides), that examination may include the collection of physical evidence (e.g., fingerprints) that will be subjected to scientific analysis. For other offenses, commonly those committed by specialized professional criminals, police informants may be contacted for information concerning possible offenders. Thorough searches of homes and offices, and electronic eavesdropping through wiretaps and similar devices, are also used in certain types of investigations. However, those procedures, which commonly require prior judicial authorization through the issuance of a search warrant, are used in only a very small portion of all investigations. Most prearrest investigations will be completed in a relatively short period of time, whether successful or not. The vast majority of burglary and robbery cases, for example, are investigated in no more than 4 hours, although that investigation may be spread over several days.

Step 3: The Arrest. Once the officer has acquired sufficient information to justify arresting a suspect, the arrest ordinarily is the next step in the criminal justice pro-

cess. An arrest generally occurs when the officer takes the suspect into custody for the purpose of transporting him to the station and then charging him with a crime.[b] Although an arrest may be authorized in advance by a judicially issued warrant, the vast majority of all arrests are made on the officer's own initiative, without a warrant.

As with reported crimes, arrests will be distributed over a variety of offenses. The distribution of arrests will differ substantially from the distribution of reported crimes, however, because some reported crimes are more likely to lead to arrests than others. While the exact distribution of arrests will vary with the individual jurisdiction, a general pattern emerges that roughly fits most jurisdictions. Typically, only 20–30% of the arrests will be for felonies, with the remainder being for misdemeanors. Though the theft group of offenses constitutes the number one category of reported crimes, it will rank slightly behind the alcohol/drug offenses as a basis for arrests. A substantial percentage of the arrests, perhaps as high as 20%, will be for public disorder misdemeanors, such as simple assaults, vandalism, and disorderly conduct. Less than 10% will be for serious felony offenses against the person, with aggravated assault and robbery likely to account for 2% each and forcible rape and murder for less than one-half of one percent each. The remaining arrests, approximately 10%, will be spread over a wide variety of offenses, including arson, nonviolent sex offenses, and possession of weapons.

Step 4: Booking. Immediately after making an arrest, the arresting officer usually will search the arrestee's person and remove any weapons, contraband, or evidence relating to a crime. He then will

---

b. As an alternative to the traditional "custodial arrest," many jurisdictions grant the officer discretion to briefly detain a person subject to arrest and to then release him upon issuance of a

citation (sometimes called an "appearance ticket"). This alternative is most commonly authorized for misdemeanor offenses, and sometimes is limited to particular types of misdemeanors.

arrange for the transportation of the arrestee to the police station, a centrally located jail, or some similar "holding" facility. It is at this facility that the arrestee will be taken through a process known as "booking." Initially, the arrestee's name, the time of his arrival, and the offense for which he was arrested are noted in the police "blotter" or "log." The arrestee then will be photographed and fingerprinted. Typically, he also will be informed of the charge on which he has been booked and will be allowed to make at least one telephone call. When booked on a minor offense, he may be able to obtain his release on "stationhouse bail," i.e., by posting cash as a security payment and promising to appear before a magistrate at a specified date. Persons arrested on serious offenses, and those arrested on minor offenses but unable to gain their release, will remain at the holding facility until ready to be presented before a magistrate (see step 8). Ordinarily, they will be placed in a "lockup," which usually is some kind of cell. Before entering the lockup, they will be subjected to another search, more thorough than that conducted at the point of arrest. This search is designed primarily to inventory the arrestee's personal belongings and to prevent the introduction of contraband into the lockup.

Step 5: Post–Arrest Investigation. The extent of the post-arrest investigation will vary with the fact situation. In some situations, such as where the arrestee was caught "red-handed," there will be little left to be done. In other situations, police will utilize many of the same kinds of investigative procedures as are used before arrest (e.g., interviewing witnesses, searching the suspect's home, and viewing the scene of the crime). Post-arrest investigation does offer one important investigative source, however, that ordinarily is not available prior to the arrest—the person of the arrestee. Thus, the arrestee may be placed in a lineup or simply taken to a place where a witness can view him individually (a "showup"). He may be required to provide handwriting or hair samples that can be compared with evidence the police have found at the scene of the crime. He also may be questioned at length about the crime for which he was arrested and any other crime thought to be related. Although we do not have precise data on these post-arrest procedures involving the arrestee, the best available estimates indicate they are not applied to the vast majority of arrestees. In most communities, they are used almost exclusively in the investigation of felony cases and even then not in most of those investigations.

Step 6: The Decision to Charge. Sometime between the booking of the arrestee and his presentation before a magistrate, there will be a review of the decision to file charges. Initially, the police officer making the arrest fills out an arrest report, which is reviewed by a higher ranking police officer. That officer may conclude either that charges should not be brought or that they should be based on a lower level offense than that for which the arrestee was booked. The decision not to charge may be based upon the officer's conclusion that there is insufficient evidence or that the particular offense can more appropriately be handled by a "stationhouse adjustment" (e.g., in the case of a fight among acquaintances, a warning and lecture may be deemed sufficient). If the officer decides against prosecution, the arrestee may be released from the lockup on the officer's direction (although some departments follow the practice of seeking prosecutor approval before releasing felony arrestees). In some jurisdictions, the police will drop as many as 10–15% of their arrests (predominantly misdemeanor arrests) at this point.

The second review of the decision to charge is usually the review by the prosecuting attorney. Prosecutors' offices vary, however, both as to the timing and extent of their review. In some jurisdictions, prosecutors regularly screen all felony and misdemeanor cases before charges are filed with the court. In other jurisdictions, pre-charge prosecutorial review is limited to exceptional cases, primarily those in which the police seek the prosecutor's advice. Here, the primary prosecutorial screening occurs sometime after charges have been filed. In the case of felonies, the prosecutor may not review the case until he is required to present it at a preliminary hearing or a grand jury screening. In misdemeanor cases, the prosecutor may not review the case until it goes to trial (and thus he may never screen misdemeanor charges to which the defendant pleads guilty). Still other jurisdictions prefer a midway position, with prosecutors undertaking a pre-charge screening of all felony cases, but utilizing a post-charge review for all but the most serious misdemeanors.

The timing of the screening is likely to have an impact upon the scope of the screening, as prosecutors tend to have less information available to them the earlier their review is undertaken. However, even among prosecutors utilizing the most prompt post-arrest screening, there is considerable variation in the sources considered in deciding whether to charge. The practice ranges from prosecutors who read only the police reports to those who regularly interview the police officer and often the victim of the crime as well.

Prosecutor offices also vary in the weight that will be given to a particular factor in determining whether to prosecute. The most significant factor, of course, is the strength of the evidence. If the evidence clearly is insufficient to gain a conviction, the case will be dropped. Similarly, if the evidence will support only a lesser offense than that suggested by the police, the charge will be reduced. Where the evidence arguably is sufficient to support the requested charge, the prosecutor will then turn to other factors that might suggest the case is inappropriate for prosecution in light of the equities of the situation and the overall caseload of the prosecutor's office. Such factors include the harm caused by the offense, the victim's attitude toward pressing the case, the arrestee's criminal record, and the adequacy of alternative remedies.[e] It is in the consideration of these factors that differences between prosecutors are most likely to be significant.

Though we can hardly characterize any particular pre-charge screening program as typical of most jurisdictions, a fairly common pattern is found in the eventual results of the overall prosecutorial screening through the entire criminal justice process. In the end, at least as to felonies, the cases against 30–60% of all arrestees will be dropped as a result of such screening. If only a small percentage of the felony cases are rejected at pre-charge screening, then there will be a much higher percentage rejected at subsequent stages when the prosecutor engages in more thorough screening.

The prosecutor's post-charge screening is more likely to focus primarily upon the sufficiency of the evidence, but the prosecutor remains free to consider also all of the factors that are considered in pre-charge screening. If the prosecutor decides in his post-charge screening that the case does not merit prosecution, he will file a motion to terminate the prosecution

c. Many prosecutor offices have developed pre-charge "diversion programs" that provide a formal structure for the prosecutor's refusal to charge notwithstanding sufficient evidence. Under these programs, certain types of charges (usu-

ally misdemeanors) will not be prosecuted if the arrestee agrees to comply with specified "rehabilitative conditions" (e.g., making restitution to the victim, maintaining regular employment, etc.).

(a *nolle prosequi* motion), which will be granted almost automatically by the court. In jurisdictions in which pre-charge screening is not extensive, post-charge screening may account for the disposition of more charges than any other step in the criminal justice process.

Statistics on charge reductions reflect a less consistent pattern than that characterizing dismissals. The percentage of reductions attributable to the screening process varies considerably, but prosecutors have been known to reduce the offense from that designated in the police booking in as many as 30% of the felony cases subjected to pre-charge screening. In many jurisdictions, certain types of felony arrests, most notably those involving non-professional thefts, are almost automatically reduced to misdemeanors (e.g., first-offense shoplifting reduced to petty theft). While most reductions occur before the initial charge is filed, a substantial number of reductions often occur later in the proceedings on the prosecutor's motion. Where plea bargaining takes the form of a charge bargain rather than a sentence bargain (see step 12), most of the later reductions are likely to be attributable to plea bargaining rather than post-charge prosecutorial screening.

Step 7: Filing the Complaint. Assuming that the pre-charge screening results in a decision to prosecute, the next step in the criminal justice process is the filing of charges with the lowest level court, the magistrate court. Typically, the initial charging instrument will be called a "complaint." In misdemeanor cases, which may be tried before the magistrate court, the complaint will serve as the charging instrument throughout the proceedings. In felony cases, on the other hand, the complaint serves to set forth the charges only before the magistrate court; felony cases may be adjudicated only in a trial court of general jurisdiction, and an information or indictment will replace the complaint as the charging instrument when the

case reaches that court. The complaint ordinarily includes a brief description of the offense and is sworn to by a complainant. The complainant usually will be either the victim or the investigating officer. When an officer-complainant did not observe the offense being committed, but relied on information received from the victim or other witnesses, he will note that the facts alleged in the complaint are based on "information or belief."

In most jurisdictions, at some point between the filing of the complaint and the first appearance (see step 8), the magistrate will conduct an *ex parte* review of the case. The purpose of this review is to ensure that the arrest and complaint are supported by sufficient incriminating information to establish probable cause to believe the defendant committed the crime charged. The magistrate's review may be based on the complaint itself where the complaint alleges the facts establishing probable cause (e.g., that the complainant observed the offense). In other cases, it may be based on a police officer's affidavit setting forth available information establishing probable cause. In some jurisdictions, the magistrate also may base his determination upon a brief oral statement presented by the complainant. If the magistrate finds that probable cause has not been established, he will direct the prosecution to promptly produce more information or release the arrested person. Such instances tend to be quite rare, however.

Step 8: The First Appearance. After the complaint has been filed and reviewed, the arrestee (who is now formally a defendant) is presented before the magistrate. This proceeding before the magistrate usually is described as the "first appearance," although some jurisdictions call it the "initial presentment" or the "arraignment on the warrant." Where the arrested person was released by police on a citation or stationhouse bail, the first appearance will not be scheduled until several days after the arrest. In most instances, however, the arrestee will still be in custody, and state law will require that he be brought before the magistrate without unnecessary delay. Ordinarily, the time consumed in booking, transportation, reviewing the decision to charge, and limited post-arrest investigation makes it unlikely that the arrestee will be presented before the magistrate until at least several hours after his arrest. Thus, if the magistrate court does not have an evening session, a person arrested in the afternoon or evening will not be presented before the magistrate until the next day. If arrested on a Friday or a weekend, he will not be presented until the next Monday, unless the magistrate court has a special weekend session.

The first appearance often is a quite brief proceeding. Initially, the magistrate will make certain that the person before him is the person named in the complaint. The magistrate then will inform the defendant of the charge in the complaint and will note various rights that the defendant may have in further proceedings. The range of rights mentioned will vary from one jurisdiction to another. Commonly, the magistrate will inform the defendant of his right to remain silent and warn him that anything he says in court or to the police may be used against him at trial. The magistrate also will inform the defendant of his right to be represented by counsel and his right to appointed counsel if he is indigent. Although the timing varies, most jurisdictions at least initiate the process of providing counsel for the indigent at the first appearance. The magistrate first will determine that the defendant is indigent and desires the assistance of appointed counsel. The magistrate then will either himself arrange for representation by the public defender or appointed private counsel or notify the judge in charge of appointments.

Other aspects of the first appearance are likely to depend upon whether the defen-

dant is charged with a felony or misdemeanor. In the felony case, the magistrate will advise the defendant of the next step in the process, the preliminary hearing, and will set a date for that hearing unless the defendant desires to waive it. If the defendant is charged with a misdemeanor, he will not be entitled to a preliminary hearing (or a subsequent grand jury review). The misdemeanor charge is triable to the magistrate, and the magistrate therefore can proceed with a misdemeanor case in the same fashion as a general trial court receiving a felony case. For the misdemeanor, the first appearance becomes an arraignment on the complaint, equivalent to the arraignment on the information or indictment in a felony case (see step 12).

The final function of the magistrate at the first appearance is to set bail (i.e., set the conditions under which the defendant can obtain his release from custody pending the final disposition of his case). If the defendant obtained his release previously by posting stationhouse bail, the magistrate will merely review that bail. In felony cases, the defendant ordinarily will still be in custody and the magistrate will be making the initial decision on bail. At one time, bail was limited almost entirely to the posting of cash or a secured bond, purchased from a professional bondsman. Today, the defendant may also be able to obtain his release by depositing with the court cash equal to 10% of the amount of the bond set by the magistrate. Indeed, several states make such extensive use of the 10% alternative that they have effectively eliminated the role of the professional bondsman. In addition, courts today frequently authorize release upon the defendant's unsecured promise to appear (commonly called "release on personal recognizance" or "personal bond"). In some jurisdictions, as many as 50% of all defendants are released under this procedure. Other non-financial bail conditions that may be imposed include curfews, regular reporting to a designated pretrial services agency, and avoiding contact with the victim.

While most felony arrestees will be released prior to trial, a substantial percentage will not gain their release. In some jurisdictions, preventive detention statutes allow the magistrate to deny bail upon a finding (made after a hearing) that the accused is so likely to flee, obstruct justice, or pose a threat to the community that no condition of release will be satisfactory. Most of those who fail to gain release, however, have had bail set, but have been unable to meet the financial conditions of that bail. In a jurisdiction in which liberal use is made of non-financial alternatives, the percentage of those felony defendants who fail to gain their release is likely to be in the neighborhood of 15–20%, but in other jurisdictions that figure may be twice as high. In misdemeanor cases, the percentage remaining in custody will be much lower, very often less than 10%.

Step 9: Preliminary Hearing. Following the first appearance, the next scheduled step in a felony case ordinarily is the preliminary hearing. In many jurisdictions, however, a substantial portion of the felony caseload will be disposed of during the period (usually one or two weeks) between the first appearance and the scheduled preliminary examination. As mentioned previously, where the primary screening by the prosecutor occurs after charges are filed, a substantial number of felony charges are likely to be dismissed or reduced to a misdemeanor during this period. Even for those felony charges that remain, a preliminary hearing will not necessarily be held. The defendant ordinarily may waive his right to a preliminary hearing, and it is not unusual for a substantial percentage (e.g., 20–30%) to waive, usually because they intend to plead guilty. Also, even if the defendant desires a preliminary hearing, state law commonly allows the prosecutor to bypass the hearing

by taking the case directly to the grand jury (a practice infrequently followed in some jurisdictions and very often followed in others). In those jurisdictions in which plea negotiations (see step 12) begin at this stage of the proceedings, a substantial percentage of the felony cases (e.g., 30%) may be resolved prior to a preliminary hearing upon agreement of the defendant to enter a plea of guilty before the magistrate to a charge reduced to the misdemeanor level.

Where the preliminary hearing is held, it will provide, like grand jury review, a screening of the decision to charge by a neutral body. In the preliminary hearing, that neutral body is the magistrate, who must determine whether, on the evidence presented, there is probable cause to believe that defendant committed the crime charged. Ordinarily, the magistrate will already have determined that probable cause exists as part of the *ex parte* screening of the complaint (see step 7). The preliminary hearing, however, provides screening in an adversary proceeding in which both sides are represented by counsel. Jurisdictions vary in the evidentiary rules applicable to the preliminary hearing, but most require that the parties rely primarily on live witnesses rather than affidavits. Typically, the prosecution will present its key witnesses and the defense will limit its response to the cross-examination of those witnesses. The defendant has the right to present his own evidence at the hearing, but traditional defense strategy advises against subjecting defense witnesses to prosecution cross-examination in any pretrial proceeding.

If the magistrate concludes that the evidence presented establishes probable cause, he will "bind the case over" to the next stage in the proceedings. In an indictment jurisdiction (see step 10), the case is bound over to the grand jury, and in a jurisdiction that permits the direct filing of an information (see step 11), the case is bound over directly to the general trial court. If the magistrate finds that the probable cause supports only a misdemeanor charge, he will reject the felony charge and allow the prosecutor to substitute the lower charge, which will then be set for trial in the magistrate court. If the magistrate finds that the prosecution's evidence does not support any charge, he will order that the defendant be released. The rate of dismissals at the preliminary hearing quite naturally varies with the degree of previous screening exercised by the prosecutor. In a jurisdiction with fairly extensive screening, the percentage of dismissals is likely to fall in the range of 5–15% of the cases heard.

Step 10: Grand Jury Review. Although all American jurisdictions still have provisions authorizing grand jury screening of felony charges, such screening is mandated only in those states requiring felony prosecutions to be instituted by an indictment, a charging instrument issued by the grand jury. About one-third of the states and the federal system currently require grand jury indictments for all felony prosecutions (unless waived by the defendant). If there has been a preliminary hearing, the magistrate's decision at that hearing is not binding on the grand jury. It can reject prosecution notwithstanding a preliminary hearing bindover, or reinstitute prosecution even though the magistrate concluded that the prosecution's evidence was inadequate.

The grand jury is composed of a group of private citizens who are selected to review cases presented over a term that may range from one to several months. Traditionally the grand jury consisted of 23 persons with the favorable vote of a majority needed to indict. Today, many states use a somewhat smaller grand jury (e.g., 12) and some require more than a simple majority to indict. As in the case of the magistrate at the preliminary hearing, the primary function of the grand jury

is to determine whether there is sufficient evidence to justify a trial on the charge sought by the prosecution. The grand jury, however, participates in a screening process quite different from the preliminary hearing. It meets in a closed session and hears only the evidence presented by the prosecution. The defendant has no right to offer his own evidence or to be present during grand jury proceedings. If a majority of the grand jurors conclude that the prosecution's evidence is sufficient, the grand jury will issue the indictment requested by the prosecutor. The indictment will set forth a brief description of the offense charged, and the grand jury's approval of that charge will be indicated by its designation of the indictment as a "true bill." If the grand jury majority refuses to approve a proposed indictment, the charges against the defendant will be dismissed. In most indictment jurisdictions, grand juries refuse to indict in only a small percentage (e.g., 3–8%) of the cases presented before them.

Step 11: The Filing of the Indictment or Information. If an indictment is issued, it will be filed with the general trial court and will replace the complaint as the accusatory instrument in the case. Where grand jury review either is not required or has been waived in the particular case, an information will be filed with the general trial court. Like the indictment, the information is a charging instrument which replaces the complaint, but it is issued by the prosecutor rather than the grand jury. Approximately two-thirds of the states do not require prosecution by indictment, and prosecutors in these jurisdictions generally proceed by information in all but a very small portion of their prosecutions. In these "information states," the charge in the information ordinarily must be supported by a preliminary hearing bindover (unless the preliminary hearing was waived).

Step 12: Arraignment on the Information or Indictment. After the indictment or information has been filed, the defendant is arraigned—i.e., he is brought before the trial court, informed of the charges against him, and asked to enter a plea of guilty, not guilty, or, as is permitted under some circumstances, *nolo contendere.* The vast majority of the cases that reach the arraignment stage will not go to trial. Depending upon the quality of pre-arraignment screening, anywhere from 10–30% of the felony cases will be dismissed as a result of a *nolle prosequi.* Of the remaining felony cases, 70–90% will be resolved by a guilty plea in most jurisdictions. Whether the guilty plea rate in a particular jurisdiction is closer to 70% or 90% depends upon several factors. One very significant variable may be the extent to which the prosecutor is willing to plea bargain—i.e., grant concessions in return for a guilty plea. While the vast majority of prosecutors make substantial use of plea bargaining, they vary markedly both as to the type of cases in which they will grant major concessions and as to the nature of those concessions. One of the most common concessions is the reduction of the offense charged in return for a guilty plea to a lesser offense. Thus, in a jurisdiction with extensive plea bargaining, it is not unusual to find that only a small percentage of the defendants plead guilty to the original charge. In other jurisdictions, prosecutors will offer concessions that deal directly with the sentence as opposed to the level of the charge. Such sentencing concessions often take the form of a prosecutorial recommendation of a lenient sentence (which will be given great weight by the sentencing judge) or the promise of a specific sentence agreed to by the judge.

Step 13: Pretrial Motions. In most jurisdictions, a broad range of objections must be raised by a pretrial motion. Those motions commonly present challenges to the institution of the prosecution (e.g., claims regarding the grand jury or the preliminary hearing), attacks upon the sufficiency of the charging instrument, requests for discovery of the prosecution's evidence, and requests for the suppression of evidence allegedly obtained through a constitutional violation. While some pretrial motions are made only by defendants who intend to go to trial, other motions are advanced almost as frequently by defendants expecting to plead guilty even if the motion succeeds. Nevertheless, pretrial motions are likely to be made in no more than 10% of all felony cases that reach the trial court. In misdemeanor cases, pretrial motions may be made in less than one percent of the cases before the magistrate court. The use of pretrial motions varies, of course, with the nature of the case. In narcotics cases, for example, motions to suppress are quite common. In the typical forgery case, on the other hand, pretrial motions of any type are quite rare.

As a group, pretrial motions are likely to result in the dismissal of not substantially more than 5% of all of the felony cases before the trial judge (and they are likely to have even less impact on the misdemeanor docket). The pretrial motion most likely to produce a dismissal is the motion to suppress. Quite frequently, if the defendant gains suppression of unconstitutionally obtained evidence, there will be insufficient remaining evidence to continue with the prosecution.

Step 14: The Trial. As noted previously, most felony and misdemeanor cases are likely to be disposed of either by a guilty plea or by a dismissal. Quite commonly, only 10–15% of the felony cases that reach the trial court actually will go to trial. Misdemeanor cases tend to have an even lower trial rate. Magistrate courts often have trials in less than 5% of the cases presented before them. Most trials will not be lengthy affairs. Misdemeanor trials typically last less than one day. Felony trials may occupy somewhat more time, particularly when tried to a jury, but most will be completed within a few days.

In all jurisdictions, the defendant will have a right to a jury trial for all felony offenses and for misdemeanors punishable by more than 6 months imprisonment (although the jury trial right in the misdemeanor cases may exist only through a trial *de novo*). Most states also provide a jury trial for lesser misdemeanors as well. Juries traditionally were composed of 12 persons, but many states now utilize 6 person juries in misdemeanor cases and several use the smaller juries in non-capital felony cases as well. Of course, the right to a jury trial can be waived, and in most jurisdictions, a significant number of defendants will waive the jury in favor of a bench trial. Over the country as a whole, however, a clear majority (perhaps 60–65%) of all felony trials are tried to a jury. In several jurisdictions, the percentage of jury trials comes close to 80%, although in one state, it often is as low as 15%. In misdemeanor cases, bench trials often are in the majority even in jurisdictions that extend the defendant's jury trial right to all misdemeanors. In all but a few jurisdictions, the jury verdict in misdemeanor and felony cases, whether for acquittal or conviction, must be unanimous. Where the jurors cannot agree, no verdict is entered and the case may be retried. Such "hung juries" occur in only a small percentage of tried cases (e.g., 3–6%).

The criminal trial resembles the civil trial in many respects. There are, however, several distinguishing features that are either unique to criminal trials or of special importance in such trials. These include (1) the presumption of defendant's innocence, (2) the requirement of proof beyond a reasonable doubt, (3) the right of the defendant not to take the stand, (4) the exclusion of evidence obtained through unconstitutional police procedures, and (5) the more frequent use of incriminating statements of defendants. In most jurisdictions, the misdemeanor trial will be almost indistinguishable from a felony trial. In some jurisdictions, however, misdemeanor trials tend to be less formal, with rules of evidence applied in a rather loose fashion.

Whether a criminal case is tried to the bench or to a jury, the odds favor conviction over acquittal. The acquittal rate for felonies generally does not exceed one-third. At the misdemeanor level, the rate of acquittals often is somewhat lower. A substantial variation exists, however, among the different types of crimes. Acquittal rates for rape and robbery tend to be considerably higher, for example, than acquittal rates for forgery or assault. Where the offense is one that is not likely to produce either an offender caught "red-handed," more than one eyewitness, or contraband discovered in the defendant's possession, the acquittal rate for the offense is likely to be higher than the average for offenses generally.

Step 15: Sentencing. If the defendant pleads guilty or is found guilty at trial, the judge will enter a judgment of conviction and set the case for sentencing. The structure of the sentence and the discretion of the judge in choosing among sentencing alternatives will be controlled by statute. For misdemeanors a judge ordinarily has discretion to impose a fine, probation, suspended sentence, or fixed jail term not to exceed a statutorily prescribed maximum. For felony offenses, the choice ordinarily is between imprisonment and probation, although the legislature is likely to have prohibited probation for some offenses. When imprisonment is imposed, most states continue to use the indeterminate sentences, i.e., the court sets a minimum and maximum term, with the parole board determining the actual release date between the minimum and maximum. State law will set the highest maximum sentence permissible for the particular crime and will also require that the minimum be no greater than a certain percentage (e.g., one-half) of the maximum. Some jurisdictions also impose other restrictions upon the trial court (e.g., compliance with sentencing guidelines) in its setting of the maximum and minimum terms. In recent years, many states have moved from indeterminate to determinate prison sentences for most felonies. Under determinate sentencing, the judge sets a single fixed term of imprisonment, which must fall within a fairly narrow range set by the legislature for the particular crime. This sentencing structure eliminates earlier parole release except for limited good-behavior credits.

In the case of misdemeanor sentences, there often is a substantial difference in the pattern of dispositions for those persons originally charged with misdemeanors and those originally charged with felonies that were reduced to misdemeanors as part of a plea bargain. The vast majority of the defendants in the former category will be fined, placed on probation, or receive a suspended sentence. Where the initial charge was a felony, the defendant is much more likely to receive a jail sentence (often combined with probation). Defendants convicted on felony charges are even more likely to be incarcerated for at least a short period. Prison sentences usually are imposed in anywhere from one-third to one-half of the felony convictions. Many jurisdictions also make extensive use of short jail sentences, combined with probation, in felony cases.

Step 16: Appeals.[d] In felony cases, initial appeals will be taken to the intermediate appellate court or to the state supreme court if there is no intermediate appellate court. Initial appeals in misdemeanor cases will be taken to the general trial court, and in some jurisdictions will consist

of a trial *de novo.* Although all convicted defendants are entitled to appeal their conviction, appeals are taken predominantly by those defendants who were sentenced to imprisonment. In several states, a fairly substantial portion of felony appeals (perhaps as many as 20%) come from imprisoned defendants who pled guilty and are challenging their pleas. Most felony appeals, however, are taken by imprisoned defendants who are seeking review of a trial conviction. In some jurisdictions, as many as 90% of the defendants who were both convicted after a trial and sentenced to imprisonment will appeal their convictions. Even with almost automatic appeals by this group of defendants, however, the total number of felony appeals is still not likely to exceed 15% of all felony convictions. In misdemeanor cases, the appeal rate is much lower.

The rate of reversals on appeal varies with the particular appellate court, but tends to fall within the range of 10–20%. In many jurisdictions, the most common objection raised on appeal is the trial court's admission of evidence obtained through an allegedly unconstitutional search. That objection also provides the most common basis for reversal. Other grounds raised quite frequently (but with much less success) are the insufficiency of the evidence, the incompetency of counsel, constitutional violations in identification procedures, and challenges to the admission of defendant's incriminating statements made to the police.

Step 17: Postconviction Remedies. After the appellate process is exhausted, imprisoned defendants may be able to use postconviction remedies to challenge their convictions on limited grounds. In particular, federal postconviction remedies allow state

---

d. This discussion of defense appeals is limited to challenges to the conviction rather than requests for appellate review of sentences. Prosecution appeals also are possible, but there are far fewer prosecution appeals than defense appeals. Most prosecution appeals must be taken prior to trial from an adverse pretrial order, although some jurisdictions permit an appeal from a dismissal at trial. Prosecution appeals may not be taken from an acquittal.

as well as federal prisoners to challenge their convictions in the federal courts on certain constitutional grounds. The federal district courts receive roughly 9,000 such postconviction applications each year. Relief is granted on less than 4% of these petitions, however, and the relief often is limited to requiring a further hearing. In the state systems, postconviction remedies are used far less frequently.

THE CRIMINAL JUSTICE FUNNEL

If one were to draw a diagram of the criminal justice process, charting the numbers of persons processed at each stage, the shape of the diagram would be roughly that of a funnel. A great number of persons are subjected to the process at its initial stage (pre-arrest investigation), and at each subsequent stage, fewer and fewer persons are involved. There are more persons investigated as suspects than arrested, more persons arrested than charged, more persons charged than finally brought to adjudication, more persons adjudicated than found guilty, and more persons found guilty than subjected to incarceration. As the caseload moves through it, the criminal justice process sifts out cases in much the same manner as a sieve. A rough picture of the actual contours of this "funnel analogy" or "sieve effect" is provided by the following "model" of the distribution of a cross-section of felony cases in a typical jurisdiction. While our model probably is not duplicated in any particular jurisdiction, available figures suggest it approximates the distribution found in various communities.

Assume that 5,000 possible felonies have come to the attention of the police either through citizen complaint or officer observations. Although the investigation of some of these possible felonies will not point to any suspects, the investigation of others will require police encounters with more than one suspect. As a result, the police investigation process for 5,000 felonies can readily produce more than 5,000 police-suspect encounters. Assuming a typical mix of reported felonies (i.e., with a heavy emphasis on property crimes), the investigation of the 5,000 felonies is likely to lead to the arrest of no more than 1,500 persons. Out of this group of arrestees, approximately 400 will be juveniles. They will be transferred to the juvenile process, leaving 1,100 adult arrestees for possible criminal prosecution. After the police and prosecutor have reviewed the cases against these arrestees, about 350 will be released without any charges being pressed. In an additional 150 cases, the charges will immediately be reduced to misdemeanors. Thus, of 1,500 felony arrestees, only 600 will have felony charges filed against them.

The 600 felony charges will then be screened at preliminary hearings or grand jury proceedings, and will be subject to challenge by defense motions of various sorts. These procedures are likely to result in the dismissal of roughly 50 cases. Still another 50 cases may be dismissed by the prosecutor as a result of his review of the case once it reaches the trial court. Of the 500 felony cases that are left, approximately 400 will be resolved by guilty pleas. Perhaps half of those pleas will be to misdemeanor charges, and the others will be to the felony charged or to a lesser felony. There remain roughly 100 felony cases that will go to trial. Approximately 70 of the trials will result in convictions, although not necessarily for felonies.

In the end, of the 1,100 adult arrestees, approximately 250 will be convicted on a felony charge (including felonies lesser than that originally charged) and 300 will be convicted of misdemeanor charges. Of the 550 arrestees eventually convicted, as many as 250 may receive a sentence that includes some incarceration, but for most of the 250, incarceration will be limited to a short jail term, typically combined with probation. Approximately 100 will be sentenced to prison terms.

SECTION 2. THE AGENCIES OF THE CRIMINAL JUSTICE SYSTEM

Throughout this book, you will find both commentators and appellate judges referring to "police," "prosecutors," "defense counsel" and "judges." This section describes the variety of officials that fit under these generic terms.

POLICE AGENCIES

Fragmentation. Police agencies constitute the largest and most complex group of participants in the administration of the criminal justice system. They have the greatest volume of work, the most diverse range of functions, and the greatest number of employees. They also clearly operate in the most decentralized fashion. Over 20,000 different governmental agencies in the United States can be classified as "police" agencies. Most of them are units of local government (counties, cities, townships), but close to a thousand are part of a state government and about fifty are part of the federal government. Many of the agencies at the state and federal level are "specialized" police agencies; they have authority to enforce only a limited group of criminal laws (as in the case of state conservation officers) or to deal with offenses committed within a special geographic enclave (as in the case of campus police). However, the vast majority of all police agencies, including almost all of those that are part of local governments, are "general" police agencies. Such agencies have authority to enforce all of the state's criminal laws throughout the geographical limits of their particular unit of government.

One consequence of this fragmentation of police authority is that over 100 different police agencies may be operating within a single metropolitan area. In the tri-county area of metropolitan Detroit, for example, over 125 police agencies are separately engaged in the investigation of crime. Initially, over a dozen federal agencies have agents assigned to the area. The state adds several agencies, including the state police. Each of the three counties contributes its sheriff's department. Finally, over 100 cities and townships provide their own police departments.

Federal agencies. Leaving aside the special case of the District of Columbia police department (which is more appropriately viewed as a local government agency), all but one of the major federal police agencies are clearly specialized agencies. Most, like the Drug Enforcement Agency, are assigned to enforcement of a limited group of crimes. Others, like the United States Park Police, have enforcement responsibility only within a specified enclave. The Federal Bureau of Investigation is the one federal police agency that might be classified as a "general" agency. Its enforcement responsibility extends to violations of all federal laws other than those laws assigned to specialized agencies such as the D.E.A.

Though considered a general police agency, the F.B.I. is quite unlike any local or state general police agency. With over 8,500 agents, it is larger than any other police agency except for the police departments of New York and Chicago. It insists upon educational prerequisites for its agents (generally a law degree or a bachelor's degree with expertise in accounting or other specialized field) that go beyond those found in any local or state agency. The mix and volume of the crimes it investigates are substantially different from those found in any other jurisdiction. Finally, and most significantly, the F.B.I. does not bear the general peacekeeping, traffic control, and social service functions that occupy so much of the effort of local and state agencies.

State agencies. At the state level, like the federal level, most police agencies are specialized agencies assigned to the enforcement of specific laws. These agencies typically enforce regulatory laws that have criminal sanctions (e.g., liquor laws or fish and gaming provisions). The state agency commonly known as the "state police," "state patrol" or "state troopers" is a specialized agency in some states and a general police agency in others. Where a specialized agency, its basic responsibility is to enforce state traffic laws and the authority of its officers to arrest for violations of the state's general criminal laws is tied to the state highway systems (i.e., officers can make arrests only if the offense took place on the highway, in the immediate vicinity of the highway, or in their presence). In other states, the state police have a general law enforcement responsibility that extends throughout the state in addition to their highway responsibilities. Such state police departments usually include a criminal investigative unit, a uniformed patrol force, a criminal intelligence network of some type, and a forensic science laboratory. Ordinarily, the department will limit its patrol efforts to the state highways and to rural areas that are not serviced by a local police department. Where local departments are quite small (as is often the case), the investigative unit of the state police will assist the local department in the investigation of serious crime. Even larger police departments will make use of the state police department's criminal intelligence network and forensic laboratory.

Local police agencies. The local police agencies perform the bulk of the police work in this country and contain approximately 85% of our law enforcement officers. At the county level, the primary police agency is the sheriff's department. While the sheriff's departments in some states are limited to the administration of the county jail and the service of process, most states grant those department full law enforcement responsibilities. To avoid overlap, sheriff's deputies commonly concentrate their efforts in those communities that lack their own police departments (usually villages and some townships) and are not patrolled by the state police.

The great majority of the local police agencies are found at the city and township level. They include over 11,000 municipal police departments. Over 90% of all municipalities with a population of 2,500 or more have their own police force. As might be expected, most municipal police agencies have small staffs. Close to two-thirds have less than 20 sworn officers, and over one-third employ less than 5 officers. In such departments, all officers except the chief are likely to be assigned to patrol. Standing in sharp contrast to the typical small municipal department are the roughly 100 local departments employing more than 300 sworn officers, with the largest, the New York City police department, having over 20,000 officers.

PROSECUTORS

Although the British common law tradition was one of private prosecution (i.e., the complainant hired private counsel to press the prosecution), Americans had established an office of public prosecutor even before the Revolution. In most of the colonies, public prosecution was originally superimposed upon a system of private prosecution, but private prosecution was eventually seen as impracticable, too often subject to abuse, and inconsistent with the view that crimes were "acts against the state" and not simply wrongs inflicted upon an individual victim. As the office of public prosecutor grew in status and prosecutors became elected officials (a product of the Jacksonian reform movement), the public prosecutor was gradually given a virtual monopoly over criminal prosecutions with extensive discretion over both the filing and selection of criminal charges.

As in the case of police power, the authority of the public prosecutor has not been centralized, but divided among a group of officials. Initially, there is the division between state officials responsible for prosecutions under state laws (the vast majority of all prosecutions), and federal officials responsible for prosecutions under federal laws. The Attorney General of the United States is the chief federal prosecutor, but federal prosecutorial authority has long been divided among a series of lesser officials (most noteably, the United States Attorneys) who are responsible to the Attorney General. At the state level, the primary recipient of prosecutorial authority is the local prosecutor, commonly known as the "prosecuting attorney," "county prosecutor," "state attorney" or "district attorney." These prosecutors represent districts consisting of a single county or a group of counties that coincide with a judicial district. While the local prosecutors tend to have virtually autonomous authority in prosecuting for crimes committed in their districts, that authority may not be exclusive. In many states, the state attorney general also may bring prosecutions for at least some crimes and the city attorney may prosecute for violations of local ordinances.

Federal prosecutors. The primary responsibility for federal prosecutions rests with the United States Attorney, an office created in 1789. There are 94 United States Attorneys, one for each of the federal judicial districts. Those offices range in size from one or two assistants in the sparsely populated districts to over 50 assistants in the large urban districts. By and large, political considerations play a substantial role in the selection of the U.S. Attorney, but not in the selection of their assistants. The U.S. Attorney is a presidential appointee, confirmed by the Senate. In practice, the appointee is almost invariably a member of the President's political party and is appointed on the recommendation of the Senators or Representatives from the particular state who are members of that party. When a president of a different political party takes office, the U.S. Attorney usually is replaced (tradition dictates that the U.S. Attorney, though appointed to a four year term, resign upon presidential request). The assistants are hired by the U.S. Attorney, usually without reference to their political affiliation. When a new U.S. Attorney is appointed, even after a shift in political party, the assistants no longer are replaced en masse. Nevertheless, assistants do not view their jobs as career positions, and the vast majority stay no more than several years, (usually leaving to return to private practice).

Like many state prosecutors, U.S. Attorneys have various civil enforcement responsibilities (e.g., debt collection) as well as their criminal enforcement responsibilities. However, unlike most local prosecutors, the U.S. Attorney can obtain substantial support services from beyond his local district. The U.S. Attorney's office can utilize the investigative assistance of offices of the F.B.I. located throughout the United States, the legal expertise provided by the Justice Department's Criminal Division, and the data collection and case management systems provided by other divisions within the Justice Department.

Although U.S. Attorneys are subject to the supervisory authority of the Attorney General, they are given considerable autonomy in their exercise of prosecutorial discretion. The Attorney General has set forth a series of departmental guidelines, contained in the United States Attorney's Manual, but those guidelines allow for considerable flexibility both as to prosecution priorities and practices. However, the use of certain types of litigation and investigative practices (e.g., the use of electronic surveillance or the granting of immunity to witnesses) requires the approval of the Attorney General's designated representative in Washington. Such approval is also required in several substantive areas where a national enforcement policy is deemed essential (e.g., internal security violations).

The U.S. Attorneys offices present the vast majority of the approximately 35,000 federal criminal prosecutions brought in a typical year, but various divisions within the Justice Department also exercise prosecutorial authority as to particular types of offenses. Criminal antitrust prosecutions are developed and presented by the Antitrust Division, and the Civil Rights Division often brings prosecutions within its area of expertise. The Criminal Division itself initiates prosecutions in several fields (e.g., organized crime, public corruption, and narcotics distribution), acting through its special Strike Forces and regional offices located in 25 major cities.

Local prosecutors: the rural and small suburban office. There are over 2,500 local prosecutor's offices in the United States, and a substantial majority represent districts with populations under 60,000. In contrast to large urban or suburban offices, many prosecutors in these districts operate without even one full time assistant. Indeed, less than 20% of all local prosecutor's offices have four or more assistants. In districts with an especially small population, the prosecutor is likely to be a part-time official, maintaining a private practice in addition to his public office.

The criminal caseload in small districts often is fairly light, particularly as to felonies. Solo prosecutors may process no more than two felonies per month. Indeed, one national survey of the total range of local prosecutor's offices reported that 45% process fewer than 200 felony cases per year. Of course, in most of these districts, the prosecutor's responsibility is not limited to criminal prosecution. The prosecutor also handles juvenile cases and often has extensive civil responsibilities; these include advising the county board of supervisors, representing the county in civil actions, and representing the state in mental commitments and in the enforcement of health and safety regulations.

Small prosecutor's offices have no need for a bureaucratic structure. The assistants, if any, work closely with the prosecutor and should fully understand his prosecutorial policies. Dealings with defense counsel, who are likely to be known socially as well as professionally, require no formal guidelines. There is neither the resources nor the need for highly structured programs dealing with matters such as diversion or the investigation and prosecution of complex fraud or narcotics offenses. The former can be handled through relatively informal arrangements, and the latter is often best handled by turning the matter over to the state attorney general or federal authorities.

Local prosecutors: the urban and large suburban office. Prosecuting attorneys in metropolitan districts not uncommonly have a larger legal staff than even the largest of the private law firms in the community. Los Angeles County, for example, has over 600 assistant prosecutors. Notwithstanding their size, these offices commonly have extraordinarily heavy caseloads per prosecutor, often four or five times that found in smaller offices. To assist the local prosecutor in handling that caseload, some counties have relieved the prosecutor's office of most of its civil responsibilities, or provided a separate staff for civil cases. Prosecutors in metropolitan areas are also provided with various support services, including special investigators, librarians, record control clerks, and where the office is large enough to support an automated case tracking system, computer programers and systems analysts. Large offices may also support a substantial diversion program staffed by a director and several counselors.

In a large office, the assignment of prosecutors may have a substantial bearing on the operation of the office. The two most common assignment systems are the vertical or integrated system and the horizontal or process system. The vertical system is most commonly found in districts in which a complaint once filed will be assigned to a specified caseflow resulting in its eventual presentation in a particular courtroom or before a particular judge. A single assistant prosecutor or a team of assistants will then be assigned to all cases docketed for that courtroom or judge, with the assistant handling those cases from the point of filing through their final disposition. Where special units are established to handle particular types of cases (e.g., narcotics) or particular types of offenders (e.g., career criminals), the assignment will start at an even earlier point, with the prosecutor assuming responsibility for the case prior to the decision to charge and carrying it through to disposition. The horizontal assignment system, in contrast, revolves around each process step rather than the individual case. Thus, separate assistants may be assigned to intake, preliminary hearings, grand jury review, arraignments, trials, and appeals. As the case moves from one step to another, a new prosecutor will take over. Under this system, the newest assistants are commonly assigned to the preliminary steps or to misdemeanor trials, with the more seasoned prosecutors handling felony trials or supervising at one of the other stages.

Large offices also vary in the degree to which they seek to control the assistants in their exercise of discretion. Some assign experienced assistants to major areas of discretionary decisionmaking (e.g., charging and plea negotiation) and allow basically autonomous exercise of that authority by each assistant. Others utilize detailed guidelines, require assistants to justify their decision in writing by reference to those guidelines, and require all variations to be approved by one of a selected group of senior assistants. Spot checks and statistical analysis are run to ensure that all prosecutors are adhering basically to the same policies. Even here, however, individual prosecutors retain considerable flexibility, particularly in evaluating the factual elements of the case.

Local prosecutors: prosecutor/police relations. The local prosecutor is commonly described as the "chief law-enforcement officer" of the local district, but this does not mean that the prosecutor has the authority to simply order the police to engage or not engage in certain investigative practices as he so directs. Police departments commonly do follow the legal advice of the prosecutor but they do so because the interaction of police and prosecutor make cooperation necessary, not because they are legally required to do so. The local prosecutor and the local police are separate agencies, often receiving their funding from separate sources. Unlike the federal system, where the U.S. Attorney and F.B.I. are both subject to the supervisory power of the Attorney General, the local police and local prosecutor are not subject to the higher authority of a single executive. Short of threatening to withdraw his power to prosecute, the prosecutor must rely on his power of persuasion to gain any changes in police practices thought to be desirable.

State attorneys general. In all but a few states, the state attorney general also has prosecutorial authority with respect to at least some state law violations. In approximately a dozen states, that authority is limited to cases in which the governor, legislature, or some other body (e.g., a grand jury) has requested that the attorney general replace the prosecutor. In such cases, the attorney general may intervene in prosecutions already initiated by the local prosecuting attorney or initiate his own prosecutions. In approximately half of the states, the attorney general has a general authority to intervene in pending prosecutions at his discretion. In many of those states, he also is given authority to institute prosecutions at his discretion, although this authority sometimes is limited to specific groups of offenses, such as tax fraud and criminal antitrust violations. In practice, the state attorneys general rarely exercise their authority to intervene in pending prosecutions. The authority to initiate prosecutions also is used very sparingly in most of the jurisdictions in which it exists. However, there has been a growing trend to make use of that authority with respect to certain types of criminal activity, most noteably organized crime and public corruption. In those areas, several state attorneys general have developed extensive investigative units and are frequently initiating prosecutions. Finally, notice should be taken of three states (Alaska, Delaware, and Rhode Island) in which there are no independent local prosecutors; all prosecuting authority is granted to the attorney general, who may assign particular assistants to exercise that authority in each of the judicial districts.

DEFENSE COUNSEL

Public defenders. In most jurisdictions, 60–70% of all felony defendants are "indigent" in the sense that they lack the funds to hire defense counsel. The percentage of misdemeanor defendants who are indigent usually is somewhat lower, but it can easily fall in the range of 30–50%. Indigent felony defendants are constitutionally entitled to defense representation paid for by the state. Indigent misdemeanor defendants have a similar right only when sentenced to incarceration, but many jurisdictions provide free representation for all indigent misdemeanor defendants charged with a misdemeanor or ordinance violation

that carries a potential sentence of imprisonment. A majority of local judicial districts provide counsel for the indigent defendant through an assigned counsel system; the court makes individual appointments of private practitioners who receive compensation from the state for the work done in the particular case, usually at a rate somewhat lower than that which would be earned in private practice. In the more heavily populated districts, however, a public defender agency is likely to be the primary provider of counsel for the indigent. Only one-third of all counties have defender agencies, but those counties contain over 60% of the nation's population. In most of these districts, defender agencies are the almost exclusive provider of representation for the indigent, with private counsel being assigned only to avoid potential conflicts in cases of jointly charged codefendants. In other districts, a "mixed system" is used, with the defender agency and appointed counsel each representing a substantial portion of the indigents (although the defender agency usually has the larger group).

Public defender programs may be either statewide or local programs. Under a statewide system, a chief defender is appointed either by the governor or the judiciary and is charged with providing a system of representation for each of the counties in the state. The chief defender commonly establishes branch offices staffed by his assistants, although a contractual arrangement with a local law firm may be used for some counties. The local branches are subject to the supervisory authority of the chief defender and receive support services from the central office. Local defender agencies are organized by county or judicial district. They usually are government agencies, but some are private non-profit organizations receiving funding from the local courts (based on the number of indigents represented) or the community's charitable giving program. Where the defender agency is a governmental agency, the chief defender may be elected, but most chief defenders of such agencies are selected by the local legislative body or a governing board appointed by that body.

In many respects, local defender agencies or local branches of statewide agencies present a mirror image of a local prosecutor's office. Individual offices range in size from a single part-time defender to a staff of more than 200 lawyers. A majority of all local public defender offices employ 3 or fewer lawyers. Larger offices are likely to include such support personnel as investigators and paralegals. However, lawyers in those offices are also likely to have very heavy caseloads (e.g., close to 200 cases per year for a deputy handling felonies, and nearly 500 for the misdemeanor deputy). While most offices assign each client to a single lawyer, some use a horizontal assignment system similar to that found in prosecutor's offices. Separate deputies may handle the first appearance, preliminary hearing, pretrial motions, and the trial.

Private practitioners. The representation of criminal defendants is shared by a surprisingly small segment of the roughly 400,000 members of the private bar. A good many general practitioners, particularly in smaller communities, will handle a few criminal cases each year, but studies of defense representation in medium and large cities indicate that the private bar is represented primarily by a small group of attorneys who specialize in criminal cases.

THE JUDICIARY

Magistrate courts. The courts of first instance in the administration of the criminal justice process ordinarily are the courts of limited jurisdiction. These courts are known in different jurisdictions as magistrate courts, justice of the peace courts, municipal courts, district courts, police courts, and recorder's courts. They will be referred to here simply as magistrate courts. The magistrate courts traditionally have trial jurisdiction over lower-level criminal offenses. In some states, this trial jurisdiction extends to all misdemeanors; in other states, it is limited either to misdemeanors punishable by no more than 90 days imprisonment or to misdemeanors punishable by no more than 6 months imprisonment. In addition to their trial jurisdiction, magistrate courts have a limited jurisdiction in the processing of felonies and any misdemeanors that are beyond their trial authority. Cases involving those offenses are brought before the magistrate court for preliminary processing before they are sent to the courts of general jurisdiction where they can be tried. The preliminary matters that may be handled by the magistrate include: the issuance of search and arrest warrants; the first appearance of the arrested person before a court; the setting of bail; the appointment of counsel for indigent defendants; and a preliminary hearing review of the sufficiency of the evidence to proceed on the charge. As we shall see in later chapters, these are most important functions that can have considerable bearing on the disposition of the case. Of course, magistrate courts also handle those preliminary procedures that are applicable to the misdemeanors within their trial jurisdiction.

The structure and staffing of magistrate courts differ considerably from state to state. Perhaps the greatest variation is found in the drawing of the judicial districts served by the magistrate courts. Some states have divided the state into uniform districts with the same type of magistrate court for each district. Others have districts that coincide with different political subdivisions (city, township, village, etc.). In these states, there may be several different types of magistrate courts, each with different limits on their trial jurisdiction, different qualifications required for their judges, and even different procedures for review of their decisions. In New York state, for example, there are seven different courts that perform the traditional functions of magistrate courts. These include a special criminal court for New York City, a county court for two of the more populous counties, city courts in most cities, and justice of the peace courts in various towns and villages.

In over half of the states, at least one of the magistrate courts is a court "not of record." Historically, courts not of record lacked the capacity to prepare a fairly complete transcript of their trials. Without that record, their decisions in misdemeanor cases could not be subjected to the traditional form of appellate review. Accordingly, on appeal, the higher court simply gave the case *de novo* consideration through a new trial. Today, the magistrate courts not of record often have the facilities to provide a verbatim transcript of their proceedings, but convictions in their court remain subject to review by a trial *de novo* before a trial court of general jurisdiction. The trial *de novo* procedure has been retained, in large part, due to concern that a person convicted of a misdemeanor should be entitled to a more formal and thorough trial than is provided in courts not of record. Magistrates in such courts often are not lawyers, and they may follow the traditional rules governing trials only in a rather loose fashion.

Almost all states permit judges in at least some magistrate courts to serve as part-time jurists. Where the judges are lawyers, state law commonly restricts their private practice to avoid a conflict of interest with their judicial duties. In approximately 40 states, judges in at least some magistrate courts need not be lawyers. Typically, a state will require that judges of magistrate courts in metropolitan areas be lawyers and serve full-time, while judges in rural magistrate courts may be non-lawyers and may serve part-time. Ordina-

rily, lay judges sit only in courts not of record so that defendants convicted in their courts may obtain a trial *de novo* review before general trial court (which will have an attorney-judge). In most jurisdictions, judges of the magistrate court, whether lawyers or laymen, are elected to office. The remaining states fill magistrate judgeships through the appointment process, with appointment made either by the governor or by local government officials.

Trial courts of general jurisdiction. The courts that try felony cases (and any misdemeanors beyond the magistrate court's trial jurisdiction) are the basic trial courts that you will also encounter in your civil law courses. In the federal system, that court is the United States District Court. In the state system, the felony trial court is the court of general jurisdiction (commonly called the superior court, circuit court, or district court). In addition to its felony trial jurisdiction, this court will also provide the first level of appellate review for misdemeanors tried in the magistrate court (although, as noted previously, that review may be by trial *de novo* in many states).

Judges of courts of general jurisdiction are selected in a variety of different ways. A few states use an appointive process similar to that found in the federal system, but the majority use a contested election (either partisan or non-partisan). Even with an election system, however, a majority of the judges will have been initially appointed to fill an interim vacancy and then elected as an incumbent.

The criminal caseload of the general trial court typically constitutes anywhere from 15 to 40 percent of the court's docket, with the lower figure applicable primarily where that docket includes juvenile and probate cases in addition to the traditional civil cases. Moreover, when caseloads are weighted according to the time spent on the particular type of case, the significance of the criminal docket increases at least twofold. Weighted caseload formulas commonly attach a substantially higher weight to criminal cases than to almost all types of civil cases. Although only a small percentage of felony cases actually go to trial, that rate is still much higher than the trial rate in civil cases. Thus, in a jurisdiction in which criminal cases constitute no more than 25% of the total docket, they can readily provide over 50% of all jury trials.

Appellate courts. Except for a few state appellate courts that hear only criminal appeals, the appellate courts reviewing decisions in criminal cases are the same courts that deal with civil appeals. In approximately two-thirds of the states, those courts are, first, an intermediate court of appeals, and then the highest state court. In the remainder of the states, there is simply the state supreme court. In the federal system, appeals are taken initially to the United States Court of Appeals and then to the Supreme Court. Most of the cases reviewed by the various appellate courts involve convictions at the trial level that are being appealed by the defendant. The convicted defendant ordinarily will have an automatic right to appeal to the next highest court. Any further appellate review generally lies in the discretion of the higher appellate court. In those appellate courts as to which there is an automatic right to review, criminal cases are likely to constitute at least one-third, and often more than half, of the total docket. Among appellate courts having discretion as to the cases they review, the proportion of criminal cases may be somewhat lower, but the percentage still is not likely to dip below 25%.

Chapter 2

PURPOSES, SOURCES AND LIMITS OF THE CRIMINAL LAW

SECTION 1. THE PURPOSES OF THE CRIMINAL LAW

JUDGE MARVIN E. FRANKEL— CRIMINAL SENTENCES

7–8, 23–24, 105–111 (1973).

Why do we impose punishment? Or is it properly to be named "punishment"? Is our purpose retributive? Is it to deter the defendant himself or others in the community from committing crimes? Is it for reform? rehabilitation? incapacitation of dangerous people? Questions like these have engaged philosophers and students of the criminal law for centuries. There are no easy—probably no single, simple—answers. But perhaps differing from concerns about angels and pins, these problems as to the purposes of criminal sanctions are, or should be, at the bedrock of any rational structure of criminal law. It makes all the difference in the world, for instance, whether we think, as it is fashionable nowadays to say, that only rehabilitation of the offender can justify confinement. It is impossible on that premise to order a week in jail for the elderly official finally caught after years of graft, now turned out of office and disgraced, and neither in need of nor susceptible to any extant kinds of rehabilitation. Leaving this subject for the time being

* * *, I make the point that our legislators have not done the most rudimentary job of enacting meaningful sentencing "laws" when they have neglected even to sketch democratically determined statements of basic purpose. Left at large, wandering in deserts of uncharted discretion, the judges suit their own value systems insofar as they think about the problem at all. * * *

Beyond the random spreads of judicial attitudes, there is broad latitude in our sentencing laws for kinds of class bias that are commonly known, never explicitly acknowledged, and at war with the superficial neutrality of the statute as literally written. Judges are on the whole more likely to have known personally tax evaders, or people just like tax evaders, than car thieves or dope pushers. Dichotomies of a similar kind are obvious beyond the need to multiply examples. Can such items of personal experience fail to have effects upon sentencing? I do not stop at simpleminded observations about the substantial numbers of judges who simply do not impose prison sentences for tax evasion though the federal law, for example, provides a maximum of five years per count (and tax-evasion prosecutions frequently involve several tax years, with each a separate count). There are more things at stake than judicial "bias" when tax evaders average relatively rare and brief prison terms, while more frequent and much longer average terms (under a statute carrying the same five-year maximum) are imposed for interstate transport of stolen motor vehicles.* Whatever other factors may be operating, however, it is not possible to avoid the impression that the judges' private senses of good and evil are playing significant parts no matter what the law on the books may define as the relative gravity of the several crimes. And, although it anticipates a later subject, this is certainly the focus of the familiar jailhouse complaint that "the more you steal, the less of a sentence you get." I believe the complaint has a basis in the fundamental realities and in the way justice is seen to be dispensed. The latter aspect is important in itself; among our sounder aphorisms is the one teaching that justice must not only be done, but must appear to be done. Both objectives are missed by a system leaving to individual preferences and value judgments the kind of discretion our judges have over sentencing.

* * *

A Supreme Court opinion in 1958 made the obvious point that the "apportionment of punishment," its "severity," "its efficacy or its futility," all "are peculiarly questions of legislative policy." ** Fully agreeing that this *ought to be* so, I have been saying at some length that the legislature has for too long abdicated this basic function. To begin at the elementary beginning, we have an almost entire absence in the United States of legislative determinations—of "law"—governing the basic questions as to the purposes and justifications of criminal

sanctions. Without binding guides on such questions, it is inevitable that individual sentencers will strike out on a multiplicity of courses chosen by each decision-maker for himself. The result is chaos.

The writings of philosophers and lawyers about sentencing have identified a familiar small list of purposes to be sought through the imposition of criminal sanctions. There is not universal agreement on the list. There are bookshelves of disputation concerning the feasibility or moral propriety of one asserted objective or another. Skirting that interesting subject, let me just note for present uses the main ends of criminal sentences that have been posited at one time or another:

Retribution, the exaction of payment—"an eye for an eye."

Deterrence, which may be "general" (i.e., discouraging others than the defendant from committing the wrong), "special" (discouraging the specific defendant from doing it again), or both.

Denunciation, or condemnation—as a symbol of distinctively criminal "guilt," as an affirmation and re-enforcement of moral standards, and as reassurance to the law-abiding.

Incapacitation, during the time of confinement.

Rehabilitation or *reformation* of the offender.

Different scholars would shorten or lengthen the list, or prefer other terminology. While the academic debate continues, it is ignored by those empowered (and expected) to make uniform rules of law. We have in our country virtually no legislative declarations of the principles

---

* It may serve only to confirm a priori hunches, but consider these illustrative figures for federal sentences in the fiscal year 1969. Of 502 defendants convicted for income tax fraud, 95, or 19 percent, received prison terms, the average term being three months. Of 3,791 defendants sentenced for auto theft, 2,373, or 63 percent, went to prison, the average term being 7.6 months.

From the Administrative Office of the U.S. Courts' publication, *Federal Offenders in the United States District Courts,* 1969, pp. 146–7 (1971).

** *Gore v. United States,* 357 U.S. 386, 393 (1958).

justifying criminal sanctions. It will take only a minute or two to show that this is much more than an aesthetically regrettable lack. It is the omission of foundation stones, without which no stable or reliable structure is possible.

To begin at the first item on the debatable list, there is in contemporary jurisprudential literature a large majority for, but a vocal minority against, the view that retribution is not an acceptable aim of sentencing. There are judges, naturally, on both sides of the issue. While that is to be expected, the power of the judges to go their variable and conflicting ways in sentencing is not tolerable. And it is perfectly clear that divergent opinions on the purposes of punishment will lead to divergent decisions as to the appropriate sentence. We expect judges, like others, to hold varying opinions on many things—on the scope and limits of permissible wiretapping, on the desirability of outlawing gambling, on bank loans for securities purchases, on prostitution, whatever. But we neither expect nor permit that each judge should follow his private judgment in deciding the legal consequences of these—or any—forms of conduct. The consequences are matters of law, prescribed legislatively and equally for all.

It seems clear to me that judgments affecting consequences so grave as the length and character of sentences should similarly be matters of law. Whatever our individual preferences may be, it is for the legislature in our system to decide and prescribe the legitimate bases for criminal sanctions. Accordingly, while it may remain a matter for debate and amendment in the future, there ought to be one uniform rule now on such questions as whether retribution is a legitimate concept to be entertained by a judge in determining a sentence. There should be at a minimum a basic provision of the criminal code listing and defining the legislatively decreed purposes or objectives the community has

chosen to pursue, for the time being, by means of criminal sanctions. * * *

To illustrate these points, let us hypothesize a sentencing code with an initial section declaring the permissible objects of sentencing. Suppose the list is the one I tendered awhile ago: retribution, deterrence ("general" and "special"), denunciation, incapacitation, and rehabilitation. Assume that the sentencer must decide and state which of these purposes underlie the judgment in each individual case. Assume, finally, that the system is to include both definite and indeterminate sentences—i.e., some to be fixed in length at the time of sentencing, others to be fixed finally by later decisions of a parole board.

One clear benefit of such provisions would be a long step toward sense and rationality in choosing for the particular case between the two kinds of sentences. If the sentencer determines that the particular case implicates the goals of general deterrence and, perhaps, retribution—and determines at the same time that the defendant is neither dangerous nor a suitable candidate for rehabilitation—there should be no occasion for an indeterminate sentence. Whatever complexities and imponderables there are—and there are plenty, some to be touched upon below—there is none that is not knowable on the day of sentencing. Or, to note the other side of the coin, there is none that is justifiably postponed for, or assigned to, parole-board consideration. There are no factors or questions peculiarly suited—or, indeed, suited at all—to handling by the supposed expertise of parole officials. The impact of the sentence in such a case is presumably achieved in the very fact, and at the very time, of its pronouncement. Assuming, of course, that sentences are known to be carried out, the effect of the example on other people is achieved and the desire for vengeance is satisfied without regard to the kinds of treatment and observation to which the prisoner is thereafter subjected. It is arguable, in fact, that indeterminacy in such a case is unsound, quite apart from its oppressive impact upon the defendant. Since the effects for general deterrence and retribution are really aimed at people other than the defendant himself, uncertainty in the sentence tends to diminish or dissipate its impact.

To elaborate this simple analysis a little more, take the case where the sentencer has studied the defendant and found concrete needs for incapacitation and rehabilitation. This, of course, presents the arguable occasion for an indeterminate sentence. In this sort of case, the intended effect is upon the defendant and is to be achieved, in considerable measure at least, over some period of time, not at the instant of sentencing. The questions presented at the time of the sentence entail predictions: when, if ever, will the defendant's dangerous propensities subside? How soon may we hope to cure or alleviate the defects disposing him to violate the criminal law? Being in their nature risky predictions, the answers to such questions must be tentative, subject to later verification or correction.

It should be obvious that the purpose or purposes of a sentence are first steps toward deciding whether a definite or indeterminate term is appropriate. However obvious, the point is systematically ignored both in existing statutes prescribing penalties and in the current judgments of the courts. Existing codes, buttressed by still prevalent professional opinion, rarely make distinctions along the lines of purpose. They tend simply to provide for indeterminacy across the board. They do not call upon the sentencer even to consider, let alone to state, whether any rehabilitative or incapacitating goal is involved. There is no suggestion of what a parole board is to be looking at or looking for as it hears the prisoner's application for release. Small wonder that our parole boards characteristically never tell the prisoner—or anyone—the grounds of their decisions. Who knows if they know?

Without pretending to follow the whole course of implications and issues, we can readily see further stages of judgment after the choice between a definite and an indefinite sentence has been made. Where we seek only general deterrence, say, of tax evaders or bribetakers, we may come to see that relatively short but substantially inexorable sentences to prison are the prescription. More complex questions present themselves when we think the case involves a need or a desire for rehabilitation. It does not follow as a matter of good sense—though it appears currently to be a matter of practice—that such a sentence must or should be indeterminate. First off, it is not definitive that a judge (perhaps echoing, without deep insight, the debatable views of others) is led to say there is a need for rehabilitation. He may be wrong. If he is right, there is still the question whether and where appropriate rehabilitative resources may be found. It is a familiar kind of well-intended mockery for our judges to imagine vaguely, or to say, that psychotherapy or some other form of treatment is the proper course for a defendant, to impose a supposedly rehabilitative sentence, and to ignore that there is no pertinent treatment available where the defendant is sent or anywhere else in the state's penal facilities.

Compelled to focus on what he thinks he means by rehabilitation, the sentencer should be better able to know whether he really means it at all. He should be able to see with some clarity whether and why the sentence should be indeterminate. He should be moved to ask insistently where the defendant will be taken from the courtroom, what will be done to or for him, and why that course is thought to present realistic prospects of rehabilitation.

BERGMAN URGES JUDGE TO 'SHOW MERCY' AND NOT JAIL HIM FOR AGED–HOME FRAUD

New York Times, June 17, 1976, at 39, col. 1.

Bernard Bergman, the nursing home promoter, appealed to a Federal judge yesterday not to send him to prison for his confessed role in a $1.2 million Medicaid and tax fraud.

Mr. Bergman, with his voice breaking, asked Judge Marvin Frankel to "spare me more suffering" and "show me mercy." The judge, who expressed impatience with defense arguments minimizing the crime, said he would pass sentence this morning. Mr. Bergman faces a maximum term in prison of eight years.

"I pleaded guilty to those charges because I permitted my business to be conducted in a manner that violated the law," he said. "I intended no evil and I am not the monster I was portrayed as being."

Nathan Lewin, one of three lawyers appearing for Mr. Bergman at the presentence hearing in United States District Court at Foley Square, argued that the major fraud had been committed by an accountant and that the offenses admitted by Mr. Bergman were "technical."

Judge Frankel retorted that the defendant had pleaded guilty to "a serious Federal offense" that indeed had cost the Government money in the form of a "no-show" job by Mr. Bergman's wife and a contract with a company secretly controlled by Mr. Bergman for services paid by Medicaid.

"At this point," the judge said, "I begin to wonder whether there has been a failure to plead guilty. Now you tell me that although he admitted these facts, there were no untoward effects."

Mr. Bergman's lawyers disclosed that they had suggested to the court alternatives to imprisonment, such as assigning him to teach high school students about the lessons of the Holocaust, or visiting the sick and incapacitated.

Sentencing had originally been set for last Monday, but had been postponed during negotiations between Mr. Bergman and Federal and state prosecutors over the amount of restitution. Monroe Friedman, another of Mr. Bergman's lawyers, revealed that he had offered to pay back about one-third of a million dollars.

The New York State Health Department has claimed overpayments of more than $2 million for capital costs alone at Mr. Bergman's Park Crescent Nursing Home at 87th Street and Riverside Drive in Manhattan. Other large claims are pending for allegedly padded operating costs at the Park Crescent and the now closed Towers Nursing Home, at 106th Street and Central Park West.

Following plea bargaining, Mr. Bergman pleaded guilty three months ago to the Federal conspiracy indictment and to a state indictment alleging that he had bribed Albert H. Blumenthal, the Assembly majority leader, to obtain his influence in getting a license for the Park Crescent. In return, he and his family were granted immunity from further prosecution.

* * *

Mr. Friedman told the court yesterday that Mr. Bergman had cooperated with the prosecution in testifying about his relations with politicians, adding that the plea-bargain had excused the operator from testifying about other nursing homes. Jeremy Epstein, an Assistant United States Attorney, said the defendant's information had been of little value aside from the Blumenthal case.

[Mr. Friedman] argued also that other nursing-home operators who had pleaded guilty had not been sent to prison. Mr. Lewin, the lawyer, cited the cases of Eugene Hollander and Frank Trippi. Mr. Hollander was sentenced to spend five nights a week for six months in a Federal treatment center. Mr. Trippi, of Buffalo, drew 10 years, but is free on bail pending appeal.

Mr. Hollander agreed to withdraw from the nursing home business and to make restitution, but officials said yesterday that he had not yet begun to pay back the more than $1 million he was committed to pay nor the nearly $6 million in other overpayments claimed by the state. * * *

UNITED STATES v. BERGMAN

United States District Court, Southern District of
New York, 1976.
416 F.Supp. 496.

SENTENCING MEMORANDUM

FRANKEL, DISTRICT JUDGE.

Defendant is being sentenced upon his plea of guilty to two counts of an 11–count indictment. The sentencing proceeding is unusual in some respects. It has been the subject of more extensive submissions, written and oral, than this court has ever received upon such an occasion. The court has studied some hundreds of pages of memoranda and exhibits, plus scores of volunteered letters. A broad array of issues has been addressed. Imaginative suggestions of law and penology have been tendered. A preliminary conversation with counsel, on the record, preceded the usual sentencing hearing. Having heard counsel again and the defendant speaking for himself, the court postponed the pronouncement of sentence for further reconsideration of thoughts generated during the days of studying the briefs and oral pleas. It seems fitting now to report in writing the reasons upon which the court concludes that defendant must be sentenced to a term of four months in prison.[1]

I. Defendant and His Crimes

Defendant appeared until the last couple of years to be a man of unimpeachably high character, attainments, and distinction. A doctor of divinity and an ordained rabbi, he has been acclaimed by people around the world for his works of public philanthropy, private charity, and leadership in educational enterprises. Scores of letters have come to the court from across this and other countries reporting debts of personal gratitude to him for numerous acts of extraordinary generosity. (The court has also received a kind of petition, with fifty-odd signatures, in which the signers, based upon learning acquired as newspaper readers, denounce the defendant and urge a severe sentence. Unlike the pleas for mercy, which appear to reflect unquestioned facts inviting compassion, this document should and will be disregarded.) In addition to his good works, defendant has managed to amass considerable wealth in the ownership and operation of nursing homes, in real estate ventures, and in a course of substantial investments.

Beginning about two years ago, investigations of nursing homes in this area, including questions of fraudulent claims for Medicaid funds, drew to a focus upon this defendant among several others. The results that concern us were the present indictment and two state indictments. After extensive pretrial proceedings, defendant embarked upon elaborate plea negotiations with both state and federal prosecutors. A state guilty plea and the instant plea were entered in March of this year. (Another state indictment is expected to be dismissed after defendant is sentenced on those to which he has pled guilty.) As part of the detailed plea arrangements, it is

---

1. The court considered, and finally rejected, imposing a fine in addition to the prison term. Defendant seems destined to pay hundreds of thousands of dollars in restitution. The amount is being worked out in connection with a state

criminal indictment. Apart from defendant's further liabilities for federal taxes, any additional money exaction is appropriately left for the state court.

expected that the prison sentence imposed by this court will comprise the total covering the state as well as the federal convictions.[2]

For purposes of the sentence now imposed, the precise details of the charges, and of defendant's carefully phrased admissions of guilt, are not matters of prime importance. Suffice it to say that the plea on Count One (carrying a maximum of five years in prison and a $10,000 fine) confesses defendant's knowing and wilful participation in a scheme to defraud the United States in various ways, including the presentation of wrongfully padded claims for payments under the Medicaid program to defendant's nursing homes. Count Three, for which the guilty plea carries a theoretical maximum of three more years in prison and another $5,000 fine, is a somewhat more "technical" charge. Here, defendant admits to having participated in the filing of a partnership return which was false and fraudulent in failing to list people who had bought partnership interests from him in one of his nursing homes, had paid for such interests, and had made certain capital withdrawals.

The conspiracy to defraud, as defendant has admitted it, is by no means the worst of its kind; it is by no means as flagrant or extensive as has been protrayed in the press; it is evidently less grave than other nursing-home wrongs for which others have been convicted or publicized. At the same time, the sentence, as defendant has acknowledged, is imposed for two federal felonies including, as the more important, a knowing and purposeful conspiracy to mislead and defraud the Federal Government.

II. The Guiding Principles of Sentencing

Proceeding through the short list of the supposed justifications for criminal sanctions, defense counsel urge that no licit purpose could be served by defendant's incarceration. Some of these arguments are plainly sound; others are not.

The court agrees that this defendant should not be sent to prison for "rehabilitation." Apart from the patent inappositeness of the concept to this individual, this court shares the growing understanding that no one should ever be sent to prison *for rehabilitation.* That is to say, nobody who would not otherwise be locked up should suffer that fate on the incongruous premise that it will be good for him or her. Imprisonment is punishment. Facing the simple reality should help us to be civilized. It is less agreeable to confine someone when we deem it an affliction rather than a benefaction. If someone must be imprisoned—for other, valid reasons—we should seek to make rehabilitative resources available to him or her. But the goal of rehabilitation cannot fairly serve in itself as grounds for the sentence to confinement.[3]

Equally clearly, this defendant should not be confined to incapacitate him. He is not dangerous. It is most improbable that he will commit similar, or any, offenses in the future. There is no need for "specific deterrence."

Contrary to counsel's submissions, however, two sentencing considerations demand a prison sentence in this case:

First, the aim of *general deterrence,* the effort to discourage similar wrongdoing by others through a reminder that the law's warnings are real and that the grim

---

2. This is not absolutely certain. Defendant has been told, however, that the imposition of any additional prison sentence by the state court will be an occasion for reconsidering today's judgment.

3. This important point, correcting misconceptions still widely prevalent, is developed more fully by Dean Norval Morris in *The Future of Imprisonment* (1974).

consequence of imprisonment is likely to follow from crimes of deception for gain like those defendant has admitted.

Second, the related, but not identical, concern that any lesser penalty would, in the words of the *Model Penal Code,* § 7.01(1)(c), "depreciate the seriousness of the defendant's crime."

Resisting the first of these propositions, defense counsel invoke Immanuel Kant's axiom that "one man ought never to be dealt with merely as a means subservient to the purposes of another." [4] In a more novel, but equally futile, effort, counsel urge that a sentence for general deterrence "would violate the Eighth Amendment proscription against cruel and unusual punishment." Treating the latter point first, because it is a short subject, it may be observed simply that if general deterrence as a sentencing purpose were now to be outlawed, as against a near unanimity of views among state and federal jurists, the bolt would have to come from a place higher than this.[5]

As for Dr. Kant, it may well be that defense counsel mistake his meaning in the present context.[6] Whether or not that is so, and without pretending to authority on that score, we take the widely accepted stance that a criminal punished in the interest of general deterrence is not being employed *"merely* as a means ＊ ＊ ＊." Reading Kant to mean that every man must be deemed *more* than the instrument of others, and must "always be treated as an end in himself," [7] the humane principle is not offended here. Each of us is served by the enforcement of the law—not least a person like the defendant in this case, whose wealth and privileges, so long enjoyed, are so much founded upon law. More broadly, we are driven regularly in our ultimate interests as members of the community to use ourselves and each other, in war and in peace, for social ends. One who has transgressed against the criminal laws is certainly among the more fitting candidates for a role of this nature. This is no arbitrary selection. Warned in advance of the prospect, the transgressor has chosen, in the law's premises, "between keeping the law required for society's protection or paying the penalty." [8]

But the whole business, defendant argues further, is guesswork; we are by no means certain that deterrence "works." The position is somewhat overstated; there is, in fact, some reasonably "scientific" evidence for the efficacy of criminal sanctions as deterrents, at least as against some kinds of crimes.[9] Moreover, the time is not yet here when all we can "know" must be quantifiable and digestible by computers. The shared wisdom of generations teaches meaningfully, if somewhat amorphously, that the utilitarians have a point; we do, indeed, lapse often into rationality and act to seek pleasure and avoid pain.[10] It would be better, to be sure, if we had more certainty and precision. Lacking these comforts, we continue to include among our working hypotheses a belief (with some concrete evidence in its support) that crimes like those in this case—deliberate, purposeful, continuing, non-impulsive, and committed for profit—are among those most likely to

---

4. Quoting from I. Kant, *Philosophy of Law* 1986 (Hastie Trans.1887).

5. To a large extent the defendant's eighth amendment argument is that imprisoning him because he has been "newsworthy" would be cruelly wrong. This thought is accepted by the court without approaching the Constitution. (See below.) The reference at this point is meant to acknowledge, if only to reject, a seemingly broader submission.

6. See H.L.A. Hart, *Punishment and Responsibility* 243–44 (1968).

7. Andenaes, *The Morality of Deterrence,* 37 U.Chi.L.Rev. 649 (1970). See also O. Holmes, *Common Law* 43–44, 46–47 (1881).

8. H.L.A. Hart, supra note 6, at 23.

9. See, e.g., F. Zimring and G. Hawkins, *Deterrence* 168–71, 282 (1973).

10. See Andenaes, supra note 7, at 663–64.

be generally deterrable by sanctions most shunned by those exposed to temptation.[11]

The idea of avoiding depreciation of the seriousness of the offense implicates two or three thoughts, not always perfectly clear or universally agreed upon, beyond the idea of deterrence. It should be proclaimed by the court's judgment that the offenses are grave, not minor or purely technical. Some attention must be paid to the demand for equal justice; it will not do to leave the penalty of imprisonment a dead letter as against "privileged" violators while it is employed regularly, and with vigor, against others. There probably is in these conceptions an element of retributiveness, as counsel urge. And retribution, so denominated, is in some disfavor as a reason for punishment. It remains a factor, however, as Holmes perceived,[12] and as is known to anyone who talks to judges, lawyers, defendants, or people generally. It may become more palatable, and probably more humanely understood, under the rubric of "deserts" or "just deserts."[13] However the concept is formulated, we have not yet reached a state, supposing we ever should, in which the infliction of punishments for crime may be divorced generally from ideas of blameworthiness, recompense, and proportionality.

III. An Alternative, "Behavioral Sanction"

Resisting prison above all else, defense counsel included in their thorough memorandum on sentencing two proposals for what they call a "constructive," and therefore a "preferable" form of "behavioral sanction." One is a plan for Dr. Bergman to create and run a program of Jewish vocational and religious high school training. The other is for him to take charge of a "Committee on Holocaust Studies," again concerned with education at the secondary school level.

A third suggestion was made orally at yesterday's sentencing hearing. It was proposed that Dr. Bergman might be ordered to work as a volunteer in some established agency as a visitor and aide to the sick and the otherwise incapacitated. The proposal was that he could read, provide various forms of physical assistance, and otherwise give comfort to afflicted people.

No one can doubt either the worthiness of these proposals or Dr. Bergman's ability to make successes of them. But both of the carefully formulated "sanctions" in the memorandum involve work of an honorific nature, not unlike that done in other projects to which the defendant had devoted himself in the past. It is difficult to conceive of them as "punishments" at all. The more recent proposal is somewhat more suitable in character, but it is still an insufficient penalty. The seriousness of the crimes to which Dr. Bergman has pled guilty demands something more than "requiring" him to lend his talents and efforts to further philanthropic enterprises. It remains open to him, of course, to pursue the interesting suggestions later on as a matter of unforced personal choice.

IV. "Measuring" the Sentence

In cases like this one, the decision of greatest moment is whether to imprison or not. As reflected in the eloquent submissions for defendant, the prospect of the closing prison doors is the most appalling concern; the feeling is that the length of the sojourn is a lesser question once that threshold is passed. Nevertheless, the set-

11. For some supporting evidence that "white-collar" offenses are somewhat specially deterrable, see Chambliss, *Types of Deviance and the Effectiveness of Legal Sanctions*, 1967 Wis.L.Rev. 703, 708–10.

12. See O. Holmes, *Common Law* 41–42, 45 (1881).

13. See A. von Hirsch, *Doing Justice* 45–55 (1976); see also N. Morris, *The Future of Imprisonment* 73–77 (1974).

ting of a term remains to be accomplished. And in some respects it is a subject even more perplexing, unregulated, and unprincipled.

Days and months and years are countable with a sound of exactitude. But there can be no exactitude in the deliberations from which a number emerges. Without pretending to a nonexistent precision, the court notes at least the major factors.

The criminal behavior, as has been noted, is blatant in character and unmitigated by any suggestion of necessitous circumstance or other pressures difficult to resist. However, metaphysicians may conjure with issues about free will, it is a fundamental premise of our efforts to do criminal justice that competent people, possessed of their faculties, make choices and are accountable for them. In this sometimes harsh light, the case of the present defendant is among the clearest and least relieved. Viewed against the maxima Congress ordained, and against the run of sentences in other federal criminal cases, it calls for more than a token sentence.[14]

On the other side are factors that take longer to enumerate. Defendant's illustrious public life and works are in his favor, though diminished, of course, by what this case discloses. This is a first, probably a last, conviction. Defendant is 64 years old and in imperfect health, though by no means so ill, from what the court is told, that he could be expected to suffer inordinately more than many others of advanced years who go to prison.

Defendant invokes an understandable, but somewhat unworkable, notion of "disparity." He says others involved in recent nursing home fraud cases have received relatively light sentences for behavior more culpable than his. He lays special

emphasis upon one defendant whose frauds appear indeed to have involved larger amounts and who was sentenced to a maximum of six months' incarceration, to be confined for that time only on week nights, not on week days or weekends. This court has examined the minutes of that sentencing proceeding and finds the case distinguishable in material respects. But even if there were a threat of such disparity as defendant warns against, it could not be a major weight on the scales.

Our sentencing system, deeply flawed, is characterized by disparity. We are to seek to "individualize" sentences, but no clear or clearly agreed standards govern the individualization. The lack of meaningful criteria does indeed leave sentencing judges far too much at large. But the result, with its nagging burdens on conscience, cannot be meaningfully alleviated by allowing any handful of sentences in a short series to fetter later judgments. The point is easy, of course, where Sentence No. 1 or Sentences 1–5 are notably harsh. It cannot be that a later judge, disposed to more leniency, should feel in any degree "bound." The converse is not identical, but it is not totally different. The net of this is that this court has considered and has given some weight to the trend of the other cited sentences (though strict logic might call for none), but without treating them as forceful "precedents" in any familiar sense.

How, then, the particular sentence adjudged in this case? As has been mentioned, the case calls for a sentence that is more than nominal. Given the other circumstances, however—including that this is a first offense, by a man no longer young and not perfectly well, where danger of recidivism is not a concern—it verges on cruelty to think of confinement

---

14. Despite Biblical teachings concerning what is expected from those to whom much is given, the court has not, as his counsel feared might happen, held Dr. Bergman to a higher standard of responsibility because of his position in the community. But he has not been judged under a lower standard either.

for a term of years. We sit, to be sure, in a nation where prison sentences of extravagant length are more common than they are almost anywhere else. By that light, the term imposed today is not notably long. For this sentencing court, however, for a nonviolent first offense involving no direct assaults or invasions of others' security (as in bank robbery, narcotics, etc.), it is a stern sentence. For people like Dr. Bergman, who might be disposed to engage in similar wrongdoing, it should be sufficiently frightening to serve the major end of general deterrence. For all but the profoundly vengeful, it should not depreciate the seriousness of his offenses.

V. Punishment in or for the Media

Much of defendant's sentencing memorandum is devoted to the extensive barrage of hostile publicity to which he has been subjected during the years before and since his indictment. He argues, and it appears to be undisputed, that the media (and people desiring to be featured in the media) have vilified him for many kinds of evildoing of which he has in fact been innocent. Two main points are made on this score with respect to the problem of sentencing.

First, as has been mentioned, counsel express the concern that the court may be pressured toward severity by the force of the seeming public outcry. That the court should not allow itself to be affected in this way is clear beyond discussion. Nevertheless, it is not merely permissible, but entirely wholesome and responsible, for counsel to bring the expressed concern out in the open. Whatever our ideals and mixed images about judges, it would be naive to doubt that judges have sometimes been swept by a sense of popular demand toward draconian sentencing decisions. It cannot hurt for the sentencing judge to be reminded of this and cautioned about it. There can be no guarantees. The sentencer must confront and regulate himself.

But it bears reaffirmance that the court must seek to discount utterly the fact of notoriety in passing its judgment upon the defendant. Defense counsel cite reported opinions of this court reflecting what happens in a large number of unreported cases, by the present sentencer and many others, in which "unknown" defendants have received prison sentences, longer or shorter than today's, for white-collar or comparably nonviolent crimes. The overall run of cases, with all their individual variations, will reflect, it is hoped, earnest efforts to hew to the principle of equal treatment, with or without publicity.

Defendant's second point about his public humiliation is the frequently heard contention that he should not be incarcerated because he "has been punished enough." The thought is not without some initial appeal. If punishment were wholly or mainly retributive, it might be a weighty factor. In the end, however, it must be a matter of little or no force. Defendant's notoriety should not in the last analysis serve to lighten, any more than it may be permitted to aggravate, his sentence. The fact that he has been pilloried by journalists is essentially a consequence of the prestige and privileges he enjoyed before he was exposed as a wrongdoer. The long fall from grace was possible only because of the height he had reached. The suffering from loss of public esteem reflects a body of opinion that the esteem had been, in at least some measure, wrongly bestowed and enjoyed. It is not possible to justify the notion that this mode of nonjudicial punishment should be an occasion for leniency not given to a defendant who never basked in such an admiring light at all. The quest for both the appearance and the substance of equal justice prompts the court to discount the thought that the public humiliation serves the function of imprisonment.

Writing, as judges rarely do, about a particular sentence concentrates the mind with possibly special force upon the experience of the sentencer as well as the person sentenced. Consigning someone to prison, this defendant or any other, "is a sad necessity." There are impulses of avoidance from time to time—toward a personally gratifying leniency or toward an opposite extreme. But there is, obviously, no place for private impulse in the judgment of the court. The course of justice must be sought with such objective rationality as we can muster, tempered with mercy, but obedient to the law, which, we do well to remember, is all that empowers a judge to make other people suffer.

SUPPLEMENTAL SENTENCING MEMORANDUM ON ADJOURNMENT OF SURRENDER

The defendant moves to adjourn his surrender on the ground that interrelated plea bargains by state and federal prosecutors contemplate coordinated sentencing decisions in this and the state court. Apparently recognizing the soundness of defendant's basic position, the United States Attorney agreed last week that this court should not even impose sentence until the state court was ready to sentence on the same day. Now, however, citing the court's refusal to postpone sentencing, the United States Attorney takes a fundamentally changed position on surrender. But it was or should have been plain that this court's decision to impose sentence, and the simultaneous delay of surrender, was meant to leave time for an intervening state sentence, since it was understood that an additional state sentence might warrant some further application here. In any case, as events have developed, the propriety of postponing surrender is obvious. The reasons why this is so, given the history of these proceedings, merit some explication.

This is a case in which two prosecutors, state and federal, brought indictments charging monstrous frauds and larcenies, but then chose to deal away most of the

charges in two narrowly drawn plea bargains. It is highly probable that if either prosecutor had proved even a substantial part of his charges in open court, Dr. Bergman would have faced a heavy sentence indeed. Instead of taking these charges to trial, however, the prosecutors entered into interrelated plea bargains with the defendant's counsel. Both agreements were reduced to writing, signed by the parties, and made a part of the public record.

The federal and state plea bargains provided that the Special State Prosecutor was to drop his fraud and larceny indictment altogether and only require the defendant to plead to a much narrower one charging bribery of a state legislator. (That indictment was dismissed as against the legislator. The dismissal is being appealed.) Both plea agreements provided that Dr. Bergman was to plead guilty to only Counts One and Three of the 11–count federal indictment. Although these are serious crimes, they are moderate in comparison to the full panoply of the offenses originally charged. Under the federal agreement, the defendant was permitted to plead guilty by reading a prepared statement of narrowly drawn, tightly limited admissions of fact, which were to be all the defendant would confess (and all he could justly be sentenced for). This statement contained nothing, for example, about $1.2 million or $2.5 million or any other astronomical sums of allegedly fraudulent Medicaid claims. There was certainly nothing about whether the Bergman nursing homes had given good or bad nursing care.

This court's duty was, of course, to sentence defendant for what he had admitted, not upon accusations that were not only unproved, but that the prosecutors had agreed to drop as criminal charges. The general public could easily have misunderstood this. But the plea bargainers certainly had no reason to misunderstand. It appears, however, that there have been, putting the best face upon things, some possible misunderstandings.

As part of the plea bargain, though his case has been scheduled as the first and primary one, the Special State Prosecutor agreed to have the problem of sentencing handled by the federal court.[1] He further agreed to "recommend to the Judge of the New York State Supreme Court who will sentence Bernard Bergman on his plea of guilty to making unlawful payments to [a state legislator] that, in light of Bernard Bergman having voluntarily disclosed the facts of the crime to the Special Prosecutor and since the Federal Judge will know of these facts when he imposes sentence on the Federal charges, no sentence additional to that imposed by the United States District Court Judge on the federal indictment be imposed here."

The occasion for the application to postpone surrender is an unresolved dispute, evidently in progress for some time, over the restitution aspect of the state plea bargain. It has been agreed that the defendant "will pay to the State of New York, voluntarily, without any civil action or litigation of any kind, whatever sums of money are owing to the State of New York * * *," the amount to be determined after accountants representing the United States, the State of New York, and the defendant have consulted and examined the relevant financial records. The Special Prosecutor has argued in the state court that the main fault for failing to reach an

agreement as to the amount to be paid lies on Dr. Bergman's side. He has said that the plea agreement might well become "a nullity" if the defendant's resistance continues, and might amount after all only to "froth."

If the state plea bargain, for any reason, becomes "a nullity," serious questions will arise as to the closely connected federal bargain. If the Special Prosecutor is forced, after all, to go first, as had been planned, and prove his charges in open court, as he has thus far chosen not to do, there may be an issue as to whether the secondary federal case is barred by double jeopardy or other defenses. More significantly, the federal plea bargain and the state plea bargain are tied inseparably together. The court may not overlook the evident possibility that nullification of the state plea bargain may lead to nullification of the one here and a substantial motion to withdraw the guilty plea and vacate the sentence.

Nobody should be made to begin serving a sentence in such circumstances. Courts serve the public, to be sure. That cannot mean bowing to passing waves of popular frenzy goaded by misunderstanding.

The motion to postpone surrender is granted. Defendant will surrender to begin service of his sentence at 10:30 a.m. on July 7, 1976.

It is so ordered.[2]

---

1. Implementing the understanding that the state case would go to trial first, and might well obviate a trial of the federal case altogether, this court on September 29, 1975, deferred the federal prosecution, noting "that the central concerns of the two prosecutions relate primarily to matters of state interest." The adjournment was granted on papers that included an affidavit by the Special State Prosecutor, who pointed out that his office had conducted "a thorough investigation into alleged abuses and fraudulent practices in the nursing home industry." There was every reason to expect that the results of that investigation would be made the subjects of lawful proof, under familiar safeguards, in the state prosecu-

tion. On that anticipation, a month later this court disposed very briefly of a substantial motion in which the defendant urged that the federal indictment alleged essentially state claims and was not a valid indictment at all. In thus deciding that the motion should not be granted, this court observed that the case might well have a different aspect after the completion of the state prosecution, and that it might well prove unnecessary to consider whether there was any sufficient federal interest to pursue.

2. Defendant has also applied to have the court recommend that his sentence be served in a halfway house. The Government opposes on

BERGMAN SENTENCE IS DISCUSSED

New York Times, June 19, 1976, at 46, col. 2.

When former Vice President Spiro T. Agnew pleaded "no contest" to an income tax evasion charge in 1973 and received no prison sentence, large segments of the public reacted with shock, disbelief and outrage. Similarly, many felt that sentences meted out to several Watergate figures were too lenient. Those same reactions were evident yesterday—from taxi drivers, dozens of irate individuals who telephoned newspapers, politicans, lawyers and judges—following the four-month prison term given Bernard Bergman, the central figure in the New York nursing home scandal. * * *

While expressing admiration for Judge Frankel, Morris B. Abram, the lawyer who headed the state's Moreland Act Commission that investigated nursing homes, said: "The sentence failed to meet society's justified expectations."

"The 'Bergman' has become a new unit of sentencing," said Justice James J. Leff of State Supreme Court. "This becomes the standard. Every lawyer will ask that his client be treated no more harshly than Mr. Bergman." * * *

Coming to Judge Frankel's defense, Adrian W. DeWind, president of the Association of the Bar of the City of New York said:

"Judge Frankel had better access to all matters relevant to the Bergman sentencing than anyone else. He obviously was not motivated by whether or not his sentence would be popular. In this situation, his reputation as a fair-minded, conscientious jurist of unquestioned integrity should not be overlooked."

seemingly sound grounds. Halfway houses serve special purposes, none of which appears pertinent to this case. The recommendation defendant seeks will not be made. Ultimately, of course,

But Mr. Abram said: "If the public perceives a wide disparity between sentences inflicted upon the rich and the poor, the cement that holds the society together is impaired."

EDITORIAL—EQUAL JUSTICE?

New York Times, June 18, 1976, at A. 22, col. 2.

Bernard Bergman was brought to justice yesterday. He got four months.

In imposing sentence, United States District Judge Marvin Frankel said, "I've undertaken to impose sentence on what you did and admitted, and not what was reported and rumored." It therefore is hardly useful, in discussing the sentence, to rehearse the history of Mr. Bergman's involvement in the nursing-home business. It is worth noting, however, that after his arrest, Mr. Bergman entered into negotiations with the prosecutor which resulted in his plea of guilty to a charge of conspiring to commit fraud against the United States, a felony carrying a top sentence of five years, and of filing a false income-tax return, another felony, carrying a top sentence of three years.

Judge Frankel said that Mr. Bergman's "imperfect health," the fact that he was a first offender and had been "pilloried in the press," along with considerations of his earlier "unimpeachable high character, attainments and distinction," had an impact on the sentencing process. As a result, on charges of defrauding the Government of $1.2 million and filing a false return, Mr. Bergman was sentenced to four months in prison.

One of the most prominent current theories is that sentences should serve to deter others from committing similar crimes. Though this view is most regularly applied to street crime, it would seem to be sub-

the place of confinement is for the Attorney General, through his Bureau of Prisons, not for the court.

stantially more applicable to white-collar criminals to whom prison is much more jarring than to criminals who live at society's economic and social margins. Yet, Mr. Bergman now joins a parade of formerly respectable white-collar criminals who have received sentences which make the odds on white-collar crime look rather good.

A second popular notion about sentencing is that it should show the criminal justice system to be even-handed. At a time when the Legislature is moving toward mandatory sentences of three years for juveniles convicted of serious crimes, a four-month sentence for a rich felon, guilty of a million-dollar fraud, can only reinforce cynicism about the realities of equal justice under law.

———

At a hearing in state court on July 2, the defendant and the special prosecutor both requested a deferral of sentencing on the plea of guilty to bribery pending an audit which would determine the amount of restitution Bergman was to make. As reported in *N.Y. Times,* July 3, 1976, at 18, col. 1:

"At the close of the hearing, Justice Melia, reading from notes, commented sharply on the pressures that he said had been brought upon him in this case. He said he had received 400 letters in favor of Mr. Bergman, many of them apparently 'solicited.' In the last 24 hours, he continued, he received 19 telegrams, 250 letters and many telephone calls, mostly demanding a harsh sentence.

"Most of these, the judge said, were 'in response to a call by a public official.' The reference was to Assemblyman Andrew Stein, Democrat of Manhattan, who visited Justice Melia on Wednesday and, in a news conference, called for measures by the public to urge a maximum sentence of four years.

" 'This is an indecent assault on the court,' Justice Melia said. 'I hope we will not have a repetition of that kind of thing.'

"Mr. Stein, who attended the court session, said in a statement later:

" 'The courts belong to the people and they have a right to air their views. * * *' "

On July 9, the federal sentence was again stayed pending sentencing in the state court. *N.Y. Times,* July 10, 1976, at 21, col. 4.

———

When the fall term commenced at Hofstra University law school, Dean Monroe Freedman appeared before the student body to explain why he had defended Mr. Bergman. As reported in *N.Y. Times,* Sept. 2, 1976, at 35, col. 1:

"He was not a 'hired gun' who represented anyone who could afford his services, the dean said. Nor did he represent 'only those he loved.'

"Rather, he agreed to help with the Bergman defense because it was 'a cause I believe in.'

" 'Should a 64–year–old man, broken in spirit, broken in health serve time in prison?' he asked.

"The question was rhetorical and not meant to be answered, but many of the students muttered, 'Yes.'

"The dean asked angrily if any students had been inside prisons, which he described as 'cages.'

"A student shot back, 'Have you ever been inside a nursing home?'

"Mr. Freedman replied that his client was the 'victim of some of the most irresponsible and malicious character assassination I have ever seen.'

"But the chief reason for his helping in the case, the dean said, was that it provided an opportunity for him to argue that the theory of general deterrence—punishing an individual so that others would be deterred from committing similar crimes— was an improper rationale for sentencing.

" 'Judge Frankel did not write the opinion I had hoped for,' the dean said. * * *

" 'I think Bernard Bergman should have spent no time at all,' he said."

On Sept. 14th, Bergman was sentenced in state court to one year in a city prison for bribery. The sentencing judge "said Mr. Bergman's long 'shilly-shallying' about the debt [i.e., the amount owed the state because of his Medicaid fraud, which he acknowledged on the date of sentencing was $2.5 million] confirmed a probation report that he appeared to be 'an unscrupulous and corrupt individual,' warped by greed, and with 'no compunction' and 'little or no remorse.' * * *

"Taking in consideration, on the one hand, the prosecutor's recommendation for no additional time and, on the other, 'concern for the proper effect of a sentence on society,' Justice Melia said he was imposing a sentence of one year, rather than the maximum of four years. In reply to a question from the defense, he added, 'consecutive.' " N.Y. Times, Sept. 15, 1976, at 1, col. 4.

The following day, Judge Frankel ordered Bergman to begin his federal sentence. He rejected a defense motion to suppress the sentence on the ground that the state plea bargain had been breached, saying that the place to settle that issue was in state court. N.Y. Times, Sept. 16, 1976, at 31, col. 3. Bergman was sent to the minimum-security federal prison in Allenwood, Pa. "The 400-acre Allenwood prison was described by its Superintendent, L. Eldon Jensen, as 'a very-minimum-security prison.'

" 'There are fences,' he said, 'but they are not designed to keep people in or out, they're just designed to let us know where our property ends.'

"He added that the prisoners—about 500 of them—live in open, dormitorylike accommodations and have access to a game room, television and a library. They work either in the prison's furniture factory or on its farm.

" 'It doesn't have the feel of a prison in a James Cagney sense,' Mr. Jensen said. 'It's the opposite end of the scale from Lewisburg and Terre Haute and the others.' " N.Y. Times, Sept. 17, 1976, at 12, col. 3.

Bergman was released from the federal prison after serving three and a half months of his federal sentence. N.Y. Times, Jan. 6, 1977, at 27, col. 5. He sought unsuccessfully to recover his assets from a receivership which was set up as part of his plea bargain with the state, People v. Bergman, 54 A.D.2d 83, 389 N.Y.S.2d 589 (1976), and to withdraw his state guilty plea, N.Y. Times, Sept. 17, 1976, at 12, col. 3. The state sentence, which he was scheduled to commence serving in mid-January, was stayed pending his appeal, N.Y. Times, Dec. 7, 1976, at 45, col. 6, which was unsuccessful, 395 N.Y.S.2d 872 (1977). On the day he was scheduled to commence serving the state sentence, he obtained a stay from federal judge Robert Ward pending a hearing in federal court on the state conviction. "Alan Dershowitz, a lawyer for Mr. Bergman, contended that Mr. Bergman's agreement to plead guilty in both cases had been violated by Charles J. Hynes, the special state prosecutor on nursing homes. Mr. Dershowitz said that Mr. Hynes had broken the agreement by criticizing the four-month Federal sentence imposed on Mr. Bergman by Judge Marvin E. Frankel." N.Y. Times, July 13, 1977, at 59, col. 4. That contention was rejected by the federal district court and court of appeals. See Bergman v. Lefkowitz, 569 F.2d 705 (2d Cir.1977).

Bergman then surrendered to serve his state sentence, *N.Y. Times,* Feb. 7, 1978, at 24, col. 5, but even thereafter some two dozen lawyers and numerous state and federal officials struggled to untangle Bergman's business affairs. *N.Y. Times,* Oct. 20, 1979, at 26, col. 1. A few years later, the nursing home reopened despite the efforts of community groups contending that Bergman and his family owned the holding company that sold the home to Beth Rifka, a Hasidic organization which assumed operation of the home. *N.Y. Times,* May 17, 1981, at 48, col. 1. At the age of 73, Bernard Bergman died of a heart attack. *N.Y. Times,* June 22, 1984, § 4, p. 6, col. 1.

Notes and Questions

1. Do you agree with Judge Frankel's sentence? Does it square with the points made by author Frankel?

2. Largely because of concerns of the kind raised in the Frankel book, Congress adopted the Comprehensive Crime Control Act of 1984, creating a Sentencing Commission and assigning to that body the responsibility to develop sentencing guidelines. The Commission has approved an initial set of guidelines, which took effect on November 1, 1987. See 41 *Criminal Law Reporter* 3087 (1987), setting out the guidelines in full.

3. Assess, to the extent you can, what Bergman's fate would have been regarding the conspiracy to defraud the government charge had these guidelines been applicable to his case.

The first step under the guidelines is to determine the "base offense level and apply any appropriate specific offense characteristics." [a] For conspiracy, the base offense level is determined from the object offense [b] or most analogous offense,[c] ex-

cept that it is necessary to "decrease by 3 levels, unless the defendant or a co-conspirator completed all the acts the conspirators believed necessary on their part for the successful completion of the offense or the circumstances demonstrate that the conspirators were about to complete all such acts but for apprehension or interruption by some similar event beyond their control." [d]

Because the object of the conspiracy was fraud, applicable here is the guideline regarding such conduct, which reads in relevant part:

"(a) Base Offense Level: 6

"(b) Specific Offense Characteristics

"(1) If the estimated, probable or intended loss exceeded $2,000, increase the offense level as follows:

Loss	Increase in Level
(A) $2,000 or less	no increase
(B) $2,001–$5,000	add 1
(C) $5,001–$10,000	add 2
(D) $10,001–$20,000	add 3
(E) $20,001–$50,000	add 4
(F) $50,001–$100,000	add 5
(G) $100,001–$200,000	add 6
(H) $200,001–$500,000	add 7
(I) $500,001–$1,000,000	add 8
(J) $1,000,001–$2,000,000	add 9
(K) $2,000,001–$5,000,000	add 10
(L) over $5,000,000	add 11

"(2) If the offense involved (A) more than minimal planning; (B) a scheme to defraud more than one victim; (C) a misrepresentation that the defendant was acting on behalf of a charitable, educational, religious or political organization, or a government agency; or (D) violation of any judicial or administrative order, injunction, decree or process; increase by 2 levels, but if the result is

a. Guideline 1B1.1(b).

b. 2X1.1(a).

c. 2X5.1.

d. 2X1.1(b)(2).

less than level 10, increase to level 10." [e]

The next step is to "apply the adjustments as appropriate related to victim, role, and obstruction of justice." [f] The only adjustments arguably possible here have to do with the defendant's role in the offense, as follows:

"Based on the defendant's role in the offense, increase the offense level as follows:

"(a) If the defendant was an organizer or leader of a criminal activity that involved five or more participants or was otherwise extensive, increase by 4 levels.

"(b) If the defendant was a manager or supervisor (but not an organizer or leader) and the criminal activity involved five or more participants or was otherwise extensive, increase by 3 levels.

"(c) If the defendant was an organizer, leader, manager, or supervisor in any criminal activity other than described in (a) or (b), increase by 2 levels.

"If the defendant abused a position of public or private trust, or used a special skill, in a manner that significantly facilitated the commission or concealment of the offense, increase by 2 levels. This adjustment may not be employed in addition to that provided for in § 3B1.1, nor may it be employed if an abuse of trust or skill is included in the base offense level or specific offense characteristic." [g]

The third step is to "apply the adjustment as appropriate for the defendant's acceptance of responsibility," [h] as follows:

"(a) If the defendant clearly demonstrates a recognition and affirmative acceptance of personal responsibility for the offense of conviction, reduce the offense level by 2 levels.

"(b) A defendant may be given consideration under this section without regard to whether his conviction is based upon a guilty plea or a finding of guilt by the court or jury or the practical certainty of conviction at trial.

"(c) A defendant who enters a guilty plea is not entitled to a sentencing reduction under this section as a matter of right." [i]

The fourth step is to "compute the defendant's criminal history category," [j] and where (as here) there are no prior convictions the category is 0.[k]

The fifth step is to "determine the guideline range * * * that corresponds to the total offense level and criminal history category." [l] For criminal history category 0, this table applies:

Offense Level	Guideline Range
1	0–1
2	0–2
3	0–3
4	0–4
5	0–5
6	0–6
7	1–7
8	2–8
9	4–10
10	6–12
11	8–14
12	10–16
13	12–18
14	15–21
15	18–24
16	21–27
17	24–30
18	27–33

e. 2F1.1.

f. 1B1.1(c).

g. 3B1.1, 3B1.3.

h. 1B1.1(e).

i. 3E1.1.

j. 1B1.1(f).

k. 4A1.1.

l. 1B1.1(g).

Offense Level	Guideline Range
19	30–37
20	33–41
21	37–46
22	41–51
23	46–57
24	51–63
25	57–71
26	63–78
27	70–87
28	78–97
29	87–108
30	97–121
31	108–135
32	121–151
33	135–168
34	151–188
35	168–210
36	188–235
37	210–262
38	235–293
39	262–327
40	292–365
41	324–405
42	360–life
43	life [m]

The last step is to apply the sentencing requirements "for the particular guideline range." [n] Probation is permissible if the minimum in the applicable range is 6 or less, except if that minimum is 1 or more a condition requiring intermittent confinement or community confinement is necessary.[o] "A sentence [of imprisonment] conforms with the guidelines for imprisonment if it is within the minimum and maximum terms of the guideline range," [p] expressed in the above table in terms of months. (For example, if you were to conclude the offense level was 10, then a sentence anywhere from 6 to 12 months of imprisonment would be within the guidelines.) But, the sentence imposed may not exceed any maximum or minimum set for that crime by statute.[q] Also, a fine not exceeding $250,000 (but subject to the statutory maximum) is called for, unless the defendant is unable to pay or its imposition would unduly burden the defendant's dependents,[r] as follows:

"(1) The minimum fine range is the greater of:

"(A) the amount shown in column A of the table below; or

"(B) any monetary gain to the defendant, less any restitution made or ordered.

"(2) Except as specified in (4) below, the maximum fine is the greater of:

"(A) the amount shown in column B of the table below;

"(B) twice the estimated loss caused by the offense; or

"(C) three times the estimated gain to the defendant.

"(3)

Fine Table

Offense Level	A Minimum	B Maximum
1	$25	$250
2–3	$100	$1,000
4–5	$250	$2,500
6–7	$500	$5,000
8–9	$1,000	$10,000
10–11	$2,000	$20,000
12–13	$3,000	$30,000
14–15	$4,000	$40,000
16–17	$5,000	$50,000
18–19	$6,000	$60,000
20–22	$7,500	$75,000
23–25	$10,000	$100,000
26–28	$12,500	$125,000
29–31	$15,000	$150,000

m. Ch. 5, Part A.

n. 1B1.1(h).

o. 5B1.1(a).

p. 5C2.1.

q. 5G1.1.

r. 5E4.2(f).

Offense	A	B
Level	Minimum	Maximum
32–34	$17,500	$175,000
35–37	$20,000	$200,000
38 and above	$25,000	$250,000" s

In the event of a plea agreement, it is still necessary that the recommended or agreed to sentence fall within the applicable guideline range.[t] A court may depart from a guideline-specified sentence only when it finds "an aggravating or mitigating circumstance * * * that was not adequately taken into consideration by the Sentencing Commission." [u]

4. Would these guidelines have produced a "wiser" sentence in the Bergman case? Will they in other cases?

SECTION 2. SOURCES: THE ROLE OF COURTS, LEGISLATURES AND ADMINISTRATORS IN CREATING AND DEFINING CRIMES

STATE v. PALENDRANO

Superior Court of New Jersey, 1972.
120 N.J.Super. 336, 293 A.2d 747.

McGANN, J.C.C. (temporarily assigned).

Marion Palendrano was indicted on three counts: the first charged an atrocious assault and battery by her on Margaret P. Maguire on July 21, 1970; the second with threatening to take the life of Margaret P. Maguire on the same date. The third count is the subject matter of this decision and is set forth at length:

THIRD COUNT

And the Grand Jurors of the State of New Jersey, for the County of Monmouth upon their oaths do further present that MARION PALENDRANO on

s. 5E4.2(c).

t. 6B1.2.

u. 18 U.S.C.A. § 3553(b).

the Twenty-First day of July, 1970, and divers other days and times as well as before and afterwards in the Township of Middletown, in the County of Monmouth aforesaid and within the jurisdiction of this Court, was and yet is a common scold and disturber of the peace of the neighborhood and of all good and quiet people of this State to the common nuisance of the people of this State, contrary to the provisions of N.J.S. 2A:85–1 and against the peace of this State, the Government and dignity of the same.

When the matter came on for trial the Court severed the third count on its own motion and requested memoranda and the benefit of oral argument from counsel.[1]

In contemporary society the average citizen, as well as the professional lawyer or jurist, may reasonably ask two questions: (1) What is a Common Scold? (2) Is that status still criminal?

What is a Common Scold? * * * The incidents of the offense may be summarized as follows:

A Common Scold is a troublesome and angry woman, who, by brawling and wrangling among her neighbors, breaks the public peace, increases discord, and becomes a nuisance to the neighborhood. At common law, common brawler or common scold meant a person of an habitually quarrelsome, noisy, and wrangling nature, although brawler denoted something harsher than scold, namely anger, loud outcries and tumult.

A peculiar feature of the offense of being a common scold has been said to be that it reduces woman to a mere thing, to a nuisance, and does not consider her as a person. The offense does not consist of a single act, but in an habitual

1. After a jury trial, the defendant was adjudged not guilty of the first two counts.

course of conduct; therefore, the element of continuity is essential, and there must be a habit or practice of scolding. It is not necessary, however, that the scolding be done in anger or turbulence. While a common scold may be indictable as a common nuisance, the offense of being a common scold or a common brawler was indictable at common law.

Being a Common Scold was a crime under the Common Law of England. * * * It is defined as follows:

COMMON SCOLDS—Lastly, a common scold, *communis rixatrix* (for our laws—Latin confines it to the feminine gender), is a public nuisance to her neighborhood, for which offense she may be indicted, and, if convicted, shall be sentenced to be placed in a certain engine of correction called a trebucket, castigatory, or cucking-stool, which in the Saxon language signifies the scolding stool, though now it is frequently corrupted into ducking-stool, because the residue of the judgment is, that when she is so placed therein, she shall be plunged in the water for her punishment.

IV Blackstone, *Commentaries on the Laws of England,* 168 (Seventh Ed. Oxford, Clarendon Press, 1775).

With a certain syllogistic nicety the State argues that the indictment is valid. The argument is thusly stated: "(N)uisances * * * and all other offenses of an indictable nature at common law and not otherwise expressly provided for by statute, are misdemeanors." N.J.S.A. 2A:85–1. Being a common scold was an offense of an indictable nature at common law (and not otherwise expressly provided for by statute). Therefore, being a common

scold is a misdemeanor under the laws of New Jersey.

The defendant concedes that the offense was indictable at common law but urges, alternatively (1) that the legislature has expressly provided by statute that such conduct now be deemed a disorderly persons offense or (2) that the charge is unconstitutionally vague and therefore unenforceable under "due process" concepts of the 14th Amendment of the United States Constitution, or (3) that an attempt to criminally prosecute such conduct is violative of the equal protection of the laws guarantee of the 14th Amendment.

There is merit to each argument. The motion to dismiss the Third Count of the Indictment is granted for the reasons hereinafter set forth.

Being a Common Scold is no longer a crime.

It is undeniable that as late as 1890, the Courts of this State did not question the fact that being a Common Scold was criminal conduct. *Baker v. State,* 53 N.J.L. 45, 20 A. 858 (Sup.Ct.1890).[3] This is understandable since the antecedents of N.J.S.A. 2A:85–1 had been in effect since 1796. Oddly enough, note was not then taken that being a Common Scold had not been viewed as a crime in England for many years.

Chief Justice Vanderbilt in *State v. Maier,* 13 N.J. 235, 99 A.2d 21, (1953) made a most comprehensive review of the common law precedents to determine that conduct known as "simple assault and battery" was triable at common law in a summary manner and that a statute (N.J.S.A. 2A:170–26) making it a Disorderly Persons offense did not violate constitutional guarantees of right to indictment and trial by jury. * * *

---

3. *State v. Fuller,* 42 N.J.L.J. 149 (Oyer and Terminer 1919) indicates an indictment charging the defendant with being a Common Scold was returned as late as 1919. A motion to quash was

denied, relying on *State v. Baker,* supra. That reliance seems misplaced since no mention was made of the broad Disorderly Persons Act passed in 1898.

As pointed out in *Maier,* in enacting the Disorderly Persons law from its beginning in 1799 to the present, the Legislature has encompassed in it many offenses which formerly had been considered crimes. Most, if not all of the elements of being a common scold are found in our present Disorderly Persons Act, N.J.S.A. 2A:170–26 through N.J.S.A. 2A:170–30, and have been so categorized at least since the general enactment in L.1898 c. 239. To the extent not found, such conduct is no longer an offense and has been ignored by the law. If, in this case, the State wished to prosecute the defendant she should have been charged with specific violation of the appropriate sections of the Disorderly Persons Act.

In almost two centuries of statehood, our Legislature has never once addressed itself to the offense. In all of the official and unofficial reports of judicial proceedings in this State, it is mentioned just twice. Being a Common Scold is no longer a crime in this State.

One of the great virtues of the common law is its dynamic nature that makes it adaptable to the requirements of society at the time of its application in court. There is not a rule of the common law in force today that has not evolved from some earlier rule of common law, gradually in some instances, more suddenly in others, leaving the common law of today when compared with the common law of centuries ago as different as day is from night.

It is a basic principle of due process that an enactment is void for vagueness if its prohibitions are not clearly defined. Vague laws offend several important values. First, because we assume that man is free to steer between lawful and unlawful conduct, we insist that laws give the person of ordinary intelligence a reasonable opportunity to know what is prohibited, so that he may act accordingly. Vague laws may trap the innocent by not providing fair warning. Second, if arbitrary and discriminatory enforcement is to be prevented, laws must provide explicit standards for those who apply them. A vague law impermissibly delegates basic policy matters to policemen, judges, and juries for resolution on an ad hoc and subjective basis, with the attendant dangers of arbitrary and discriminatory application. Third, but related, where a vague statute " 'abut(s) upon sensitive areas of basic First Amendment freedoms,' it 'operates to inhibit the exercise of [those] freedoms.' Uncertain meanings inevitably lead citizens to 'steer far wider of the unlawful zone' * * * than if the boundaries of the forbidden areas were clearly marked." *Grayned v. City of Rockford,* 408 U.S. 104, 92 S.Ct. 2294, 33 L.Ed.2d 222 (1972). * * *

Against the background of these constitutional guidelines, can it be said that there is easily understood, recognizable conduct for which one may be prosecuted as a Common Scold. There is not and never has been a legislative definition of the offense. "Common Scold" does not appear in any law ever enacted by the duly elected representatives of the people. All that the average person has to guide his conduct is N.J.S.A. 2A:85–1. That is a catch-all statute which tells him that if [in addition to the expressly enacted statutory crimes together with assaults, batteries, false imprisonments, affrays, riots, routs, unlawful assemblies (whatever they may be), nuisances, cheats and deceits] his conduct would have been indictable at common law (i.e. pre–1776), he is a criminal. One can scarcely conceive of anything more vague or indefinite. To know the criminal risks he might run, the average citizen would be obliged to carry a pocket edition of Blackstone with him.

To a die-hard male chauvinist the public utterances of a dedicated woman's liberationist may be those of a "communis rixatrix" yet his judgment would immediately run afoul of basic 1st Amendment concepts. A neighborhood gossip could, with but little imagination, be indicted as a Common Scold. To state the proposition reveals its absurdity. If N.J.S.A. 2A:85–1 purports to make criminal the common law offense of being a Common Scold it is void because of its vagueness and is constitutionally unenforceable.

By definition only a woman can be a "Common Scold." A man might be "troublesome and angry" and by his "brawling and wrangling among" his "neighbors break the peace, increase discord and become a nuisance to the neighborhood" yet he could not be a common scold. The discrimination between the sexes is obvious. It is senseless. It is unconstitutional under the Equal Protection Clause of the 14th Amendment.

* * *

Notes and Questions

1. Compare *State v. Egan*, 287 So.2d 1 (Fla.1973), upholding a charge of "the common-law offense of nonfeasance" in light of a state statute providing: "The common law of England in relation to crimes * * * shall be of full force in this state where there is no existing provision by statute on the subject." As to the vagueness objection, the court responded that the statute was not vague because (i) "the legislative intent * * * is plain and unambiguous," and (ii) it is not objectionable that "the statute imposes the duty upon the reader thereof to ascertain for himself what the common law is." As for the claim that there was no longer any need for common law crimes, the court replied: "Whenever a principle of the common law has been once clearly established, the courts of this country must enforce it until repealed by the legislature, as long as there is a subject matter for the principle to operate on, and although the reason, in the opinion of the court, which

induced its original establishment may have ceased to exist. Of course, when the rules of the common law are in doubt, or when a factual situation is presented which is not within the established precedents, courts are called upon to determine what general principles are to be applied, and, in so doing, of necessity, must exercise a broad judicial discretion. The courts of this jurisdiction do, and properly so, take into account the changes in our social and economic customs and present day conceptions of right and justice. But the fact remains, as this Court said in *Ripley v. Ewell*, [61 So.2d 420 (Fla.1952)] 'When the common law is clear we have no power to change it.'"

2. In *Commonwealth v. Mochan*, 177 Pa. Super. 454, 110 A.2d 788 (1955), the defendant was indicted and convicted for a common law misdemeanor on evidence that on numerous occasions he telephoned a married woman to suggest sexual intercourse and sodomy. The court affirmed, reasoning:

"It is of little importance that there is no precedent in our reports which decides the precise question here involved. The test is not whether precedents can be found in the books but whether the alleged crimes could have been prosecuted and the offenders punished under the common law. In *Commonwealth v. Miller*, 94 Pa.Super. 499, 507, the controlling principles are thus stated: 'The common law is sufficiently broad to punish as a misdemeanor, although there may be no exact precedent, any act which directly injures or tends to injure the public to such an extent as to require the state to interfere and punish the wrongdoer, as in the case of acts which injuriously affect public morality, or obstruct, or pervert public justice, or the administration of government.' * * *

"To endeavor merely to persuade a married woman to commit adultery is not indictable. *Smith v. Commonwealth*, [p. 699

of this Book]. The present defendant's criminal intent was evidenced by a number of overt acts beyond the mere oral solicitation of adultery. The vile and disgusting suggestions of sodomy alone and the otherwise persistent lewd, immoral and filthy language used by the defendant, take these cases out of the principle of the *Smith* case. Moreover potentially at least, defendant's acts injuriously affected public morality. The operator or any one on defendant's four-party telephone line could have listened in on the conversations, and at least two other persons in Mrs. Zivkovich's household heard some of defendant's immoral and obscene language over the telephone."

A dissenting judge objected: "There is no doubt that the common law is a part of the law of this Commonwealth, and we punish many acts under the common law. But after nearly two hundred years of constitutional government in which the legislature and not the courts have been charged by the people with the responsibility of deciding which acts do and which do not injure the public to the extent which requires punishment, it seems to me we are making an unwarranted invasion of the legislative field when we arrogate that responsibility to ourselves by declaring now, for the first time, that certain acts are a crime."

3. Note, 47 Colum.L.Rev. 1332, 1336 (1947): "The most obvious argument favoring the retention of common law is that, in its breadth, it effectively precludes the possibility of those lacunae which must appear to some extent in even the best code. The existence of such lacunae is said to constitute a threat to the public security,[35] and, moreover, to do violence to that retributive instinct of society which

Holmes once called ' * * * a felt necessity that punishment should follow wrongdoing.' [36] Supporting arguments are that today the operation of the common law is so restricted to the field of petty offenses as not to be sufficiently important to merit legislative treatment; and that within this field history has shown the common law technique to be adequate."

4. In 1962 the American Law Institute adopted the Model Penal Code, portions of which appear as an Appendix to this Book. As the Chief Reporter explained in Wechsler, *The American Law Institute: Some Observations on Its Model Penal Code,* 42 A.B. A.J. 321 (1956): "Our belief that such a model can contribute to the sound development of the criminal law does not, of course, imply that we are seeking uniformity in penal law throughout the country or that we wish to standardize the law of crimes. Uniformity is not as such a value of importance in this field, as it is, for example, in the case of the commercial code. It is to be expected that substantial differences of social situation or of point of view among the states should be reflected in substantial variation in their penal laws. But what is generally needed, we believe, is systematic re-examination of the subject—to the end that the law may represent the mature sentiment of our respective jurisdictions—sentiment formed after a fresh appraisal of the situation, with attention to the goals to be achieved, the legislative possibilities for their attainment and the knowledge or experience that bears upon the choices to be made."

The Code has had a very significant impact. In recent years 36 states have enacted comprehensive new criminal codes, 5 others have completed work on but have not yet enacted new codes, and

---

35. "It is impossible to find precedents for all offenses. The malicious ingenuity of mankind is constantly producing new inventions in the art of disturbing their neighbors. To this invention must be opposed general principles. * * *";

Commonwealth v. Taylor, 5 Binn. 276, 281 (Pa. 1812).

36. Holmes, *The Common Law* 42 (1881).

another 2 have revisions under way. These codes draw heavily upon the Model Penal Code, and most of them have followed its lead (see § 1.05) in abolishing common law crimes.

5. It has long been settled that there are no federal common law crimes. *United States v. Hudson and Goodwin,* 11 U.S. (7 Cranch) 32, 3 L.Ed. 259 (1812). The need for recodification of the federal statutory criminal law was recognized by the Congress when, in 1966, it established a National Commission on Reform of Federal Criminal Laws. The Commission issued its final report, a proposed revision of Title 18 of the U.S.Code, in 1971, but Congress never adopted the Commission's recommendations or alternative proposals recommended by the Administration or by certain members of Congress.

KEELER v. SUPERIOR COURT OF AMADOR COUNTY

Supreme Court of California, 1970.
2 Cal.3d 619, 87 Cal.Rptr. 481, 470 P.2d 617.

MOSK, JUSTICE. * * *

The evidence received at the preliminary examination may be summarized as follows: Petitioner and Teresa Keeler obtained an interlocutory decree of divorce on September 27, 1968. They had been married for 16 years. Unknown to petitioner, Mrs. Keeler was then pregnant by one Ernest Vogt, whom she had met earlier that summer. She subsequently began living with Vogt in Stockton, but concealed the fact from petitioner. Petitioner was given custody of their two daughters, aged 12 and 13 years, and under the decree Mrs. Keeler had the right to take the girls on alternate weekends.

On February 23, 1969, Mrs. Keeler was driving on a narrow mountain road in Amador County after delivering the girls to their home. She met petitioner driving in the opposite direction; he blocked the road with his car, and she pulled over to the side. He walked to her vehicle and began speaking to her. He seemed calm, and she rolled down her window to hear him. He said, "I hear you're pregnant. If you are you had better stay away from the girls and from here." She did not reply, and he opened the car door; as she later testified, "He assisted me out of the car. * * * [I]t wasn't roughly at this time." Petitioner then looked at her abdomen and became "extremely upset." He said, "You sure are. I'm going to stomp it out of you." He pushed her against the car, shoved his knee into her abdomen, and struck her in the face with several blows. She fainted, and when she regained consciousness petitioner had departed.

Mrs. Keeler drove back to Stockton, and the police and medical assistance were summoned. She had suffered substantial facial injuries, as well as extensive bruising of the abdominal wall. A Caesarian section was performed and the fetus was examined *in utero.* Its head was found to be severely fractured, and it was delivered stillborn. The pathologist gave as his opinion that the cause of death was skull fracture with consequent cerebral hemorrhaging, that death would have been immediate, and that the injury could have been the result of force applied to the mother's abdomen. There was no air in the fetus' lungs, and the umbilical cord was intact.

Upon delivery the fetus weighed five pounds and was 18 inches in length. Both Mrs. Keeler and her obstetrician testified that fetal movements had been observed prior to February 23, 1969. The evidence was in conflict as to the estimated age of the fetus; the expert testimony on the point, however, concluded "with reasonable medical certainty" that the fetus had developed to the stage of viability, i.e., that in the event of premature birth on the date in question it would have had a 75 percent to 96 percent chance of survival.

An information was filed charging petitioner, in Count I, with committing the crime of murder in that he did "unlawfully kill a human being, to wit Baby Girl VOGT, with malice aforethought." In Count II petitioner was charged with wilful infliction of traumatic injury upon his wife and in Count III, with assault on Mrs. Keeler by means of force likely to produce great bodily injury. His motion to set aside the information for lack of probable cause was denied, and he now seeks a writ of prohibition * * *.

Penal Code section 187 provides: "Murder is the unlawful killing of a human being, with malice aforethought." The dispositive question is whether the fetus which petitioner is accused of killing was, on February 23, 1969, a "human being" within the meaning of this statute. If it was not, petitioner cannot be charged with its "murder" and prohibition will lie.

Section 187 was enacted as part of the Penal Code of 1872. Inasmuch as the provision has not been amended since that date, we must determine the intent of the Legislature at the time of its enactment. But section 187 was, in turn, taken verbatim from the first California statute defining murder, part of the Crimes and Punishments Act of 1850. (Stats.1850, ch. 99, § 19, p. 231.) Penal Code section 5 (also enacted in 1872) declares: "The provisions of this Code, so far as they are substantially the same as existing statutes, must be construed as continuations thereof, and not as new enactments." We begin accordingly, by inquiring into the intent of the Legislature in 1850 when it first defined murder as the unlawful and malicious killing of a "human being."

It will be presumed, of course, that in enacting a statute the Legislature was familiar with the relevant rules of the common law, and, when it couches its enactment in common law language, that its intent was to continue those rules in statutory form. This is particularly appropriate in considering the work of the first session of our Legislature: its precedents were necessarily drawn from the common law, as modified in certain respects by the Constitution and by legislation of our sister states.

We therefore undertake a brief review of the origins and development of the common law of abortional homicide. From that inquiry it appears that by the year 1850—the date with which we are concerned—an infant could not be the subject of homicide at common law *unless it had been born alive.* Perhaps the most influential statement of the "born alive" rule is that of Coke, in mid–17th century: "If a woman be quick with childe,[5] and by a potion or otherwise killeth it in her wombe, or if a man beat her, whereby the childe dyeth in her body, and she is delivered of a dead childe, this is a great misprision [*i.e.* misdemeanor], and no murder; but if the childe be born alive and dyeth of the potion, battery, or other cause, this is murder; for in law it is accounted a reasonable creature, *in rerum natura,* when it is born alive." (3 Coke, *Institutes* *58 (1648).) In short, "By Coke's time, the common law regarded abortion as murder only if the foetus is (1) quickened, (2) born alive, (3) lives for a brief interval, and (4) then dies." Whatever intrinsic defects there may have been in Coke's work, the common law accepted his views as authoritative. In the 18th century, for example, Coke's requirement that an infant be born alive in order to be the subject of homicide was reiterated and expanded by both Blackstone and Hale.

---

5. "Quickening" is said to occur when movements of the fetus are first sensed or observed, and ordinarily takes place between the 16th and 18th week of pregnancy. Although much of the history of the law of abortion and abortional homicide revolves around this concept, it is of no medical significance and was never adopted into the law of California.

Against this background, a series of infanticide prosecutions were brought in the English courts in mid-19th century. In each, a woman or her accomplice was charged with murdering a newborn child, and it was uniformly declared to be the law that a verdict of murder could not be returned unless it was proved the infant had been born alive. Thus in *Rex v. Brain* (1834) 6 Carr. & P. 349, 350, 172 Eng.Rep. 1272, the court instructed the jury that "A child must be actually wholly in the world in a living state to be the subject of a charge of murder; but if it has been wholly born, and is alive, it is not essential that it should have breathed at the time it was killed; as many children are born alive, and yet do not breathe for some time after their birth. But you must be satisfied that the child was wholly born into the world at the time it was killed, or you ought not to find the prisoner guilty of murder."

Of these decisions, some pointed out that evidence of breathing is not conclusive because that function may begin before the infant is fully born, while others observed that the infant can possess an "independent circulation"—one of the tests used to determine live birth—even though the umbilical cord may not yet be severed. But all were in agreement that however live birth was to be proved, unless that event had occurred before the alleged criminal act there could be no conviction of homicide.

By the year 1850 this rule of the common law had long been accepted in the United States. As early as 1797 it was held that proof the child was born alive is necessary to support an indictment for murder (*State v. McKee* (Pa.) 1 Add. 1), and the same rule was reiterated on the eve of the first session of our Legislature (*State v. Cooper* (N.J.1849) 22 N.J.L. 52).

* * *

While it was thus "well settled" in American case law that the killing of an unborn child was not homicide, a number of state legislatures in the first half of the 19th century undertook to modify the common law in this respect. The movement began when New York abandoned the common law of abortion in 1830. The revisers' notes on that legislation recognized the existing rule, but nevertheless proposed a special feticide statute which, as enacted, provided that "The wilful killing of an unborn quick child, by any injury to the mother of such child, which would be murder if it resulted in the death of such mother, shall be deemed manslaughter in the first degree." At the same time the New York Legislature enacted a companion section (§ 9) which, although punishing a violation thereof as second degree manslaughter, was in essence an "abortion law" similar to those in force in most states today.

In the years between 1830 and 1850 at least five other states followed New York and enacted, as companion provisions, (1) a statute declaring feticide to be a crime, punishable as manslaughter, and (2) a statute prohibiting abortion. In California, however, the pattern was not repeated. Much of the Crimes and Punishments Act of 1850 was based on existing New York statute law; but although a section proscribing abortion was included in the new Act (§ 45), the Legislature declined to adopt any provision defining and punishing a special crime of feticide.

We conclude that in declaring murder to be the unlawful and malicious killing of a "human being" the Legislature of 1850 intended that term to have the settled common law meaning of a person who had been born alive, and did not intend the act of feticide—as distinguished from abortion—to be an offense under the laws of California.

Nothing occurred between the years 1850 and 1872 to suggest that in adopting the new Penal Code on the latter date the Legislature entertained any different intent. The case law of our sister states, for example, remained consonant with the common law. * * *

Any lingering doubt on this subject must be laid to rest by a consideration of the legislative history of the Penal Code of 1872. The Act establishing the California Code Commission required the commissioners to revise all statutes then in force, correct errors and omissions, and "recommend all such enactments as shall, in the judgment of the Commission, be necessary to supply the defects of and give completeness to the existing legislation of the State * * *." In discharging this duty the statutory schemes of our sister states were carefully examined, and we must assume the commissioners had knowledge of the feticide laws noted hereinabove. Yet the commissioners proposed no such law for California, and none has been adopted to this day.

That such an omission was not an oversight clearly appears, moreover, from the commissioners' explanatory notes to Penal Code section 187. After quoting the definitions of murder given by Coke, Blackstone, and Hawkins, the commissioners conclude: "A child within its mother's womb is not a 'human being' within the meaning of that term as used in defining murder. The rule is that it must be born.—*Rex vs. Brain*, 6 Car. & P., p. 349. That every part of it must have come from the mother before the killing of it will constitute a felonious homicide. * * *"

When there is persuasive evidence of a legislative intent contrary to the views expressed in code commissioners' notes, those views will not be followed in construing the statute. Here, however, the views of the commissioners are in full accord with the history of section 187; and as we have seen, the Legislature made no significant change in that statute when it was codified into the Penal Code. The

rule is therefore applicable that "Reports of commissions which have proposed statutes that are subsequently adopted are entitled to substantial weight in construing the statutes. This is particularly true where the statute proposed by the commission is adopted by the Legislature without any change whatsoever and where the commission's comment is brief, because in such a situation there is ordinarily strong reason to believe that the legislators' votes were based in large measure upon the explanation of the commission proposing the bill."

It is the policy of this state to construe a penal statute as favorably to the defendant as its language and the circumstances of its application may reasonably permit; just as in the case of a question of fact, the defendant is entitled to the benefit of every reasonable doubt as to the true interpretation of words or the construction of language used in a statute. We hold that in adopting the definition of murder in Penal Code section 187 the Legislature intended to exclude from its reach the act of killing an unborn fetus.

The People urge, however, that the sciences of obstetrics and pediatrics have greatly progressed since 1872, to the point where with proper medical care a normally developed fetus prematurely born at 28 weeks or more has an excellent chance of survival, i.e., is "viable"; that the common law requirement of live birth to prove the fetus had become a "human being" who may be the victim of murder is no longer in accord with scientific fact, since an unborn but viable fetus is now fully capable of independent life; and that one who unlawfully and maliciously terminates such a life should therefore be liable to prosecution for murder under section 187. We may grant the premises of this argument; indeed, we neither deny nor denigrate the vast progress of medicine in the century since the enactment of the Penal Code. But we cannot join in the conclusion sought to be deduced: we cannot hold this petitioner to answer for murder by reason of his alleged act of killing an unborn— even though viable—fetus. To such a charge there are two insuperable obstacles, one "jurisdictional" and the other constitutional.

Penal Code section 6 declares in relevant part that "No act or omission" accomplished after the code has taken effect "is criminal or punishable, except as prescribed or authorized by this Code, or by some of the statutes which it specifies as continuing in force and as not affected by its provisions, or by some ordinance, municipal, county, or township regulation * * *." This section embodies a fundamental principle of our tripartite form of government, i.e., that subject to the constitutional prohibition against cruel and unusual punishment, the power to define crimes and fix penalties is vested exclusively in the legislative branch. Stated differently, there are no common law crimes in California. * * *

Settled rules of construction implement this principle. Although the Penal Code commands us to construe its provisions "according to the fair import of their terms, with a view to effect its objects and to promote justice" (Pen.Code, § 4), it is clear the courts cannot go so far as to create an offense by enlarging a statute, by inserting or deleting words, or by giving the terms used false or unusual meanings. Penal statutes will not be made to reach beyond their plain intent; they include only those offenses coming clearly within the import of their language. Indeed, "Constructive crimes—crimes built up by courts with the aid of inference, implication, and strained interpretation—are repugnant to the spirit and letter of English and American criminal law."

Applying these rules to the case at bar, we would undoubtedly act in excess of the judicial power if we were to adopt the People's proposed construction of section 187. As we have shown, the Legislature has defined the crime of murder in California to apply only to the unlawful and malicious killing of one who has been born alive. We recognize that the killing of an unborn but viable fetus may be deemed by some to be an offense of similar nature and gravity; but as Chief Justice Marshall warned long ago, "It would be dangerous, indeed, to carry the principle, that a case which is within the reason or mischief of a statute, is within its provisions, so far as to punish a crime not enumerated in the statute, because it is of equal atrocity, or of kindred character, with those which are enumerated." (*United States v. Wiltberger* (1820) 18 U.S. (5 Wheat.) 76, 96, 5 L.Ed. 37.) Whether to thus extend liability for murder in California is a determination solely within the province of the Legislature. For a court to simply declare, by judicial fiat, that the time has now come to prosecute under section 187 one who kills an unborn but viable fetus would indeed be to rewrite the statute under the guise of construing it. Nor does a need to fill an asserted "gap" in the law between abortion and homicide—as will appear, no such gap in fact exists—justify judicial legislation of this nature: to make it "a judicial function 'to explore such new fields of crime as they may appear from time to time' is wholly foreign to the American concept of criminal justice" and "raises very serious questions concerning the principle of separation of powers."

The second obstacle to the proposed judicial enlargement of section 187 is the guarantee of due process of law. Assuming *arguendo* that we have the power to adopt the new construction of this statute as the law of California, such a ruling, by constitutional command, could operate only prospectively, and thus could not in any event reach the conduct of petitioner on February 23, 1969.

The first essential of due process is fair warning of the act which is made punishable as a crime. "That the terms of a penal statute creating a new offense must be sufficiently explicit to inform those who are subject to it what conduct on their part will render them liable to its penalties, is a well-recognized requirement, consonant alike with ordinary notions of fair play and the settled rules of law." (*Connally v. General Constr. Co.* (1926) 269 U.S. 385, 391, 46 S.Ct. 126, 127, 70 L.Ed. 322.)

* * *

This requirement of fair warning is reflected in the constitutional prohibition against the enactment of ex post facto laws (U.S. Const., art. I, §§ 9, 10; Cal.Const., art. I, § 16). When a new penal statute is applied retrospectively to make punishable an act which was not criminal at the time it was performed, the defendant has been given no advance notice consistent with due process. And precisely the same effect occurs when such an act is made punishable under a preexisting statute but by means of an unforeseeable *judicial* enlargement thereof. (*Bouie v. City of Columbia* (1964) 378 U.S. 347, 84 S.Ct. 1697, 12 L.Ed.2d 894.)

In *Bouie* two Negroes took seats in the restaurant section of a South Carolina drugstore; no notices were posted restricting the area to whites only. When the defendants refused to leave upon demand, they were arrested and convicted of violating a criminal trespass statute which prohibited entry on the property of another "after notice" forbidding such conduct. Prior South Carolina decisions had emphasized the necessity of proving such notice to support a conviction under the statute. The South Carolina Supreme Court nevertheless affirmed the convictions, construing the statute to prohibit not only the act of entering after notice not to do so but also the wholly different act of remaining on the property after receiving notice to leave.

The United States Supreme Court reversed the convictions, holding that the South Carolina court's ruling was "unforeseeable" and when an "unforeseeable state-court construction of a criminal statute is applied retroactively to subject a person to criminal liability for past conduct, the effect is to deprive him of due process of law in the sense of fair warning that his contemplated conduct constitutes a crime." Analogizing to the prohibition against retrospective penal legislation, the high court reasoned "Indeed, an unforeseeable judicial enlargement of a criminal statute, applied retroactively, operates precisely like an *ex post facto* law, such as Art. I, § 10, of the Constitution forbids. An *ex post facto* law has been defined by this Court as one 'that makes an action done before the passing of the law, and which was *innocent* when done, criminal; and punishes such action,' or 'that *aggravates a crime,* or makes it *greater* than it was, when committed.' *Calder v. Bull,* 3 Dall. 386, 390, 1 L.Ed. 648. If a state legislature is barred by the *Ex Post Facto* Clause from passing such a law, it must follow that a State Supreme Court is barred by the Due Process Clause from achieving precisely the same result by judicial construction. The fundamental principle that 'the required criminal law must have existed when the conduct in issue occurred,' must apply to bar retroactive criminal prohibitions emanating from courts as well as from legislatures. If a judicial construction of a criminal statute is 'unexpected and indefensible by reference to the law which had been expressed prior to the conduct in issue,' it must not be given retroactive effect."

The court remarked in conclusion that "Application of this rule is particularly compelling where, as here, the petitioners' conduct cannot be deemed improper or immoral." In the case at bar the conduct with which petitioner is charged is certainly "improper" and "immoral," and it is not contended he was exercising a constitutionally favored right. But the matter is simply one of degree, and it cannot be denied that the guarantee of due process extends to violent as well as peaceful men. The issue remains, would the judicial enlargement of section 187 now proposed have been foreseeable to this petitioner?

* * *

Turning to the case law, we find no reported decision of the California courts which should have given petitioner notice that the killing of an unborn but viable fetus was prohibited by section 187. Indeed, the contrary clearly appears from *People v. Eldridge* (1906) 3 Cal.App. 648, 649, 86 P. 832, in which the defendant challenged as uncertain an information which charged him with the murder of "a human being," to wit, the infant child "born to the said Glover H. Eldridge and said Mabel Eldridge on or about said twentieth day of February, 1905." It was urged that "such charge might include the killing before birth, and therefore it cannot be determined from the information whether murder or abortion was intended to be charged." The Court of Appeal rejected the contention, observing that "The only reasonable construction which can be given to the language employed in the information is to say that it charges that a child born to the defendant was by him unlawfully killed and murdered. That it was born is clearly stated; that it could be killed after birth of necessity implies that *it was born alive,* and we think the charge of murder was set forth with the degree of certainty required."

Properly understood, the often cited case of *People v. Chavez* (1947) 77 Cal.App. 2d 621, 176 P.2d 92, does not derogate from this rule. There the defendant was charged with the murder of her newborn child, and convicted of manslaughter. She testified that the baby dropped from her womb into the toilet bowl; that she picked it up two or three minutes later, and cut

but did not tie the umbilical cord; that the baby was limp and made no cry; and that after 15 minutes she wrapped it in a newspaper and concealed it, where it was found dead the next day. The autopsy surgeon testified that the baby was a full-term, nine-month child, weighing six and one-half pounds and appearing normal in every respect; that the body had very little blood in it, indicating the child had bled to death through the untied umbilical cord; that such a process would have taken about an hour; and that in his opinion "the child was born alive, based on conditions he found and the fact that the lungs contained air and the blood was extravasated or pushed back into the tissues, indicating heart action."

On appeal, the defendant emphasized that a doctor called by the defense had suggested other tests which the autopsy surgeon could have performed to determine the matter of live birth; on this basis, it was contended that the question of whether the infant was born alive "rests entirely on pure speculation." The Court of Appeal found only an insignificant conflict in that regard, and focused its attention instead on testimony of the autopsy surgeon admitting the possibility that the evidence of heart and lung action could have resulted from the child's breathing "after presentation of the head but before the birth was completed".

The court cited the mid–19th century English infanticide cases mentioned hereinabove, and noted that the decisions had not reached uniformity on whether breathing, heart action, severance of the umbilical cord, or some combination of these or other factors established the status of "human being" for purposes of the law of homicide. The court then adverted to the state of modern medical knowledge, discussed the phenomenon of viability, and held that "a viable child *in the process of being born* is a human being within the meaning of the homicide statutes, whether or not the process has been fully completed. It should at least be considered a human being where it is a living baby and where in the natural course of events *a birth which is already started* would naturally be successfully completed." Since the testimony of the autopsy surgeon left no doubt in that case that a live birth had at least begun, the court found "the evidence is sufficient here to support the implied finding of the jury that this child *was born alive and became a human being within the meaning of the homicide statutes.*"

Chavez thus stands for the proposition—to which we adhere—that a viable fetus "in the process of being born" is a human being within the meaning of the homicide statutes. But it stands for no more; in particular it does not hold that a fetus, however viable, which is *not* "in the process of being born" is nevertheless a "human being" in the law of homicide. On the contrary, the opinion is replete with references to the common law requirement that the child be "born alive," however that term is defined, and must accordingly be deemed to reaffirm that requirement as part of the law of California.

The *Chavez* court relied in part on *Scott v. McPheeters* (1939) 33 Cal.App.2d 629, 92 P.2d 678, 93 P.2d 562, a decision holding that an unborn child is an "existing person," within the meaning of Civil Code section 29, for the purpose of bringing a postnatal action for prenatal injuries. In *People v. Belous* (1969) 71 A.C. 996, 80 Cal.Rptr. 354, 362, 458 P.2d 194, 202, however, a majority of this court distinguished such civil law rules on the ground they either "require a live birth or reflect the interest of the parents." We need not repeat that analysis here; but two further bases of distinction deserve mention. First, *Scott* emphasized that the child's right of action for prenatal injuries was unknown to the common law and would not exist in California but for statutory authorization. By the same token, as we have seen, the fetus' status as a "human being" within the definition of murder was unknown to the common law and exists only where special feticide statutes have been enacted. Secondly, the law's protection of the *property* interests of an unborn child dates not from *Scott* but from a far earlier time: for example, in Blackstone's day it was already well settled that "An infant *in ventre sa mere,* or in the mother's womb, is supposed in law to be born for many purposes. It is capable of having a legacy, or a surrender of a copyhold estate, made to it. It may have a guardian assigned to it; and it is enabled to have an estate limited to its use, and to take afterwards by such limitation, as if it were then actually born." (1 Blackstone, *Commentaries* * 130 (1765).) Inasmuch as such rules coexisted for centuries with the common law requirement of live birth to support a conviction of homicide, they cannot reasonably be deemed to have given petitioner notice that the killing of an unborn but viable fetus would now be murder.

Finally, although a defendant is not bound to know the decisional law of other states, the United States Supreme Court in *Bouie* referred to reported cases of jurisdictions other than South Carolina in concluding that the South Carolina Supreme Court's construction of the statute "is no less inconsistent with the law of other States than it is with the prior case law of South Carolina and, of course, with the language of the statute itself." Here, too, the cases decided in our sister states from *Chavez* to the present are unanimous in requiring proof that the child was born alive before a charge of homicide can be sustained. And the text writers of the same period are no less unanimous on the point.

We conclude that the judicial enlargement of section 187 now urged upon us by the People would not have been foreseeable to this petitioner, and hence that its adoption at this time would deny him due process of law. * * *

BURKE, ACTING CHIEF JUSTICE (dissenting). * * *

The majority cast a passing glance at the common law concept of quickening, but fail to explain the significance of that concept: At common law, the quickened fetus *was* considered to be a human being, a second life separate and apart from its mother. As stated by Blackstone, in the passage immediately preceding that portion quoted in the majority opinion, "Life is the immediate gift of God, a right inherent by nature in every individual; *and it begins in contemplation of law as soon as an infant is able to stir in the mother's womb.*" (1 Blackstone, *Commentaries,* p. 129.) * * *

This reasoning explains why the killing of a quickened child was considered "a great misprision," although the killing of an unquickened child was no crime at all at common law. Moreover, although the common law did not apply the labels of "murder" or "manslaughter" to the killing of a quickened fetus, it appears that at common law this "great misprision" was severely punished. As late as 1837, the wilful aborting of a woman quick with child was punishable by *death* in England.

Thus, at common law, the killing of a quickened child was severely punished, since that child was considered to be a human being. The majority would have us assume that the Legislature in 1850 and 1872 simply overlooked this "great misprision" in codifying and classifying criminal offenses in California, or reduced that offense to the lesser offense of illegal abortion with its relatively lenient penalties.

In my view, we cannot assume that the Legislature intended a person such as defendant charged with the malicious slaying of a fully viable child, to suffer only the mild penalties imposed upon common abortionists who, ordinarily, procure only

the miscarriage of a nonviable fetus or embryo. To do so would completely ignore the important common law distinction between the quickened and unquickened child.

Of course, I do not suggest that we should interpret the term "human being" in our homicide statutes in terms of the common law concept of quickening. At one time, that concept had a value in differentiating, as accurately as was then scientifically possible, between life and nonlife. The analogous concept of viability is clearly more satisfactory, for it has a well defined and medically determinable meaning denoting the ability of the fetus to live or survive apart from its mother.

The majority opinion suggests that we are confined to common law concepts, and to the common law definition of murder or manslaughter. However, the Legislature, in Penal Code sections 187 and 192, has defined those offenses for us: homicide is the unlawful killing of a "human being." Those words need not be frozen in place as of any particular time, but must be fairly and reasonably interpreted by this court to promote justice and to carry out the evident purposes of the Legislature in adopting a homicide statute. Thus, Penal Code section 4, which was enacted in 1872 along with sections 187 and 192, provides: "The rule of the common law, that penal statutes are to be strictly construed, has no application to this Code. All its provisions are to be construed according to the fair import of their terms, with a view to effect its objects and to promote justice." * * *

Penal Code section 4, which abolishes the common law principle of the strict construction of penal statutes, permits this court fairly to construe the terms of those statutes to serve the ends of justice. Consequently, nothing should prevent this court from holding that Baby Girl Vogt was a human ("belonging or relating to man; characteristic of man") being ("existence, as opp. to nonexistence; specif. life") under California's homicide statutes.

We commonly conceive of human existence as a spectrum stretching from birth to death. However, if this court properly might expand the definition of "human being" at one end of that spectrum, we may do so at the other end. Consider the following example: All would agree that "Shooting or otherwise damaging a corpse is not homicide. * * *" In other words, a corpse is not considered to be a "human being" and thus cannot be the subject of a "killing" as those terms are used in homicide statutes. However, it is readily apparent that our concepts of what constitutes a "corpse" have been and are being continually modified by advances in the field of medicine, including new techniques for life revival, restoration and resuscitation such as artificial respiration, open heart massage, transfusions, transplants and a variety of life-restoring stimulants, drugs and new surgical methods. Would this court ignore these developments and exonerate the killer of an apparently "drowned" child merely because that child would have been pronounced dead in 1648 or 1850? Obviously not. Whether a homicide occurred in that case would be determined by medical testimony regarding the capability of the child to have survived prior to the defendant's act. And that is precisely the test which this court should adopt in the instant case.

The common law reluctance to characterize the killing of a quickened fetus as a homicide was based solely upon a presumption that the fetus would have been born dead. This presumption seems to have persisted in this country at least as late as 1876. Based upon the state of the medical art in the 17th, 18th and 19th centuries, that presumption may have been well-founded. However, as we approach the 21st century, it has become apparent that "This presumption is not only contra-

ry to common experience and the ordinary course of nature, but it is contrary to the usual rule with respect to presumptions followed in this state." (*People v. Chavez, supra.*)

There are no accurate statistics disclosing fetal death rates in "common law England," although the foregoing presumption of death indicates a significantly high death experience. On the other hand, in California the fetal death rate in 1968 is estimated to be 12 deaths in 1,000, a ratio which would have given Baby Girl Vogt a 98.8 percent chance of survival. (*California Statistical Abstract* (1969) Table E–3, p. 65.) If, as I have contended, the term "human being" in our homicide statutes is a fluid concept to be defined in accordance with present conditions, then there can be no question that the term should include the fully viable fetus.

The majority suggest that to do so would improperly create some new offense. However, the offense of murder is no new offense. Contrary to the majority opinion, the Legislature has not "defined the crime of murder in California to apply only to the unlawful and malicious killing one who has been born alive." Instead, the Legislature simply used the broad term "human being" and directed the courts to construe that term according to its "fair import" with a view to effect the objects of the homicide statutes and promote justice. What justice will be promoted, what objects effectuated, by construing "human being" as excluding Baby Girl Vogt and her unfortunate successors? Was defendant's brutal act of stomping her to death any less an act of homicide than the murder of a newly born baby? No one doubts that the term "human being" would include the elderly or dying persons whose potential for life has nearly lapsed; their proximity to death is deemed immaterial. There is no sound reason for denying the viable fetus, with its unbounded potential for life, the same status.

The majority also suggest that such an interpretation of our homicide statutes would deny defendant "fair warning" that his act was punishable as a crime. Aside from the absurdity of the underlying premise that defendant consulted Coke, Blackstone, or Hale before kicking Baby Girl Vogt to death, it is clear that defendant had adequate notice that his act could constitute homicide. Due process only precludes prosecution under a new statute insufficiently explicit regarding the specific conduct proscribed, or under a pre-existing statute "by means of an unforeseeable *judicial* enlargement thereof."

Our homicide statutes have been in effect in this state since 1850. The fact that the California courts have not been called upon to determine the precise question before us does not render "unforeseeable" a decision which determines that a viable fetus is a "human being" under those statutes. Can defendant really claim surprise that a 5-pound, 18-inch, 34-week-old, living, viable child is considered to be a human being?

The fact is that the foregoing construction of our homicide statutes easily could have been anticipated from strong dicta in *People v. Chavez,* supra, wherein the court reviewed common law precedents but disapproved their requirement that the child be born alive and completely separated from its mother. The court in *Chavez* held that a viable child killed during, but prior to completion of, the birth process, was a human being under the homicide statutes. However, the court did not hold that partial birth was a prerequisite, for the court expressly set forth its holding "Without drawing a line of distinction applicable to all cases * * *." In dicta, the court discussed the question when an unborn infant becomes a human being under the homicide statutes, as follows: "There is not much change in the child itself between a moment before and a moment after its expulsion from the body of its mother, and normally, while still dependent upon its mother, the child for some time before it is born, has not only the possibility but a strong probability of an ability to live an independent life. * * * While before birth or removal it is in a sense dependent upon its mother for life, there is another sense in which it has started an independent existence after it has reached a state of development where it is capable of living and where it will, in the normal course of nature and with ordinary care, continue to live and grow as a separate being. While it may not be possible to draw an exact line applicable to all cases, the rules of law should recognize and make some attempt to follow the natural and scientific facts to which they relate. * * * [I]t would be a mere fiction to hold that a child is not a human being because the process of birth has not been fully completed, when it has reached that state of viability when the destruction of the life of its mother would not end its existence and when, if separated from the mother naturally or by artificial means, it will live and grow in the normal manner."

Thus the *Chavez* case explodes the majority's premise that a viability test for defining "human being" under our homicide statutes was unforeseeable; *Chavez* approved and advocated this interpretation 23 years ago. (See also *Scott v. McPheeters,* ["Who may say that such a viable child is not in fact a human being in actual existence?"].) I would conclude that defendant had sufficient notice that the words "human being" could include a viable fetus. * * *

Notes and Questions

1. Consider Comment, 56 Iowa L.Rev. 658, 671–72 (1971): "In adopting this position, however, the *Keeler* court failed to consider certain realities. It apparently did not attach significance to the fact that

the born alive rule is a rule of judicial interpretation, not of legislative enactment. No California statute specifically limited the word homicide to human beings born alive. * * * Consequently, the judicial abrogation of the born alive rule cannot realistically be considered tantamount to the judicial creation of a new crime. Rather, the judicial definition of the scope of homicide appears to be an act which manifests legislative intent, and not one which usurps legislative power.

"The most significant failure on the part of the *Keeler* court, however, was its unwillingness to make a judgment consistent with the pattern of priorities in our criminal law system because of a feeling that to do so would constitute judicial legislation. * * * By refusing to extend the sanctions of the homicide statute for the protection of a medically ascertainable human life, the court made a decision that some human lives deserve protection while others do not. Such a decision, being inconsistent with the pattern of priorities of our criminal law system, can only be made by a legislature. Consequently, by not abrogating the born alive rule in California, the court usurped the power of the legislature."

2. By a recent tabulation, courts in 22 states have held to the "born alive" rule, while those in just three states have decided otherwise. (Several other states have abandoned the rule by statute.) Forsythe, *Homicide of the Unborn Child: The Born Alive Rule and Other Legal Anachronisms,* 21 Val.U.L.Rev. 563, 595–96 (1987). One of the three is *Commonwealth v. Cass,* 392 Mass. 799, 467 N.E.2d 1324 (1984), a 4–3 prospective ruling that a viable fetus is a 'person' within the meaning of the vehicular homicide statute. The majority in *Cass* rejected "the suggestion that, in using the term 'person' in defining a statutory crime, the Legislature intended to crystallize the *preexisting* common law with regard to who may be the victim of a homicide. Preex-

isting common law meaning may be a useful indication of legislative intent. However, to conclude that mere use of the term was intended to freeze its meaning is to make a shibboleth of a rule of construction."

The dissenters objected: "If the court truly believed that the Legislature intended to include a viable fetus within the meaning of 'person' in the motor vehicle homicide statute, it should have made its interpretation applicable to this defendant. How can it justify ignoring such a legislative determination? As it is, the court has prospectively amended the statute. I think that this is an inappropriate 'exercise of raw judicial power.'"

3. Following *Keeler,* the California legislature amended the murder statute to read:

"(a) Murder is the unlawful killing of a human being, or a fetus, with malice aforethought.

"(b) This section shall not apply to any person who commits an act which results in the death of a fetus if any of the following apply:

"(1) The act complied with the Therapeutic Abortion Act * * *.

"(2) The act was committed by a holder of a physician's and surgeon's certification * * * in a case where, to a medical certainty, the result of childbirth would be death of the mother of the fetus or where her death from childbirth, although not medically certain, would be substantially certain or more likely than not.

"(3) The act was solicited, aided, abetted, or consented to by the mother of the fetus.

"(c) Subdivision (b) shall not be construed to prohibit the prosecution of any person under any other provision of law."

4. In *People v. Smith,* 59 Cal.App.3d 751, 129 Cal.Rptr. 498 (1976), the defen-

dant was charged under the amended statute with the murder of a fetus. At the preliminary hearing, the evidence was that defendant kicked his wife in the stomach at a time when she was 12 to 15 weeks pregnant, resulting in a miscarriage of a nonviable fetus. The court affirmed the dismissal of the murder charge, reasoning:

"Legally and factually, a non-viable fetus does not possess the capability for independent existence and has not attained the status of independent human life. Logically, one cannot destroy independent human life prior to the time it has come into existence. Until the capability for independent human life is attained, there is only the expectancy and potentiality for human life. This was the prevailing view at common law, which required birth to recognize human life, and in the then state of the medical art the legal requirement for birth before recognition of human life harmonized with practical realities. With the advance in the medical art in recent years the capability for independent human life prior to birth has increased, and the period of successful gestation has shortened. This increased capability for independent human life justifies increased legal protection for human beings, but it does not separate us from the underlying realities and limitations of gestation. We, therefore, construe section 187 as making its protection coextensive with the capability for independent human life, a concept embraced within the term *viability.* If future medical art succeeds in further lowering the age of viability, then the protection of the statute will follow, for it protects human life at the stage it has achieved the capability for independent existence.

"From the constitutional view, this construction leaves section 187 consistent with due process of law. If destruction of a non-viable fetus were susceptible to classification as the taking of human life and therefore murder, then the mother no more than the father would have the right to take human life. Yet we know from *Roe v. Wade* (1973) 410 U.S. 113, 93 S.Ct. 705, 35 L.Ed.2d 147, that the mother has an absolute right to destroy the fetus during the first trimester of gestation, and, under some of the language of that opinion, a right that is almost absolute to destroy the fetus during the second trimester, the latter right being restricted only by the state's interest in regulating abortion to promote 'the health of the mother.' We do not believe the court intended to suggest that the mother has a constitutional right to destroy a fetus after it has become viable, but rather that the court assumed the commencement of viability at the end of the second trimester. The compelling point, said the court, is viability, and until viability has been reached the state has no interest in the fetus that it is entitled to protect against the wishes of the mother. The underlying rationale of *Wade,* therefore, is that until viability is reached, human life in the legal sense has not come into existence. Implicit in *Wade* is the conclusion that as a matter of constitutional law the destruction of a non-viable fetus is not a taking of human life. It follows that such destruction cannot constitute murder or other form of homicide, whether committed by a mother, a father (as here), or a third person."

5. With respect to when one ceases to be a "human being," raised by Justice Burke in his *Keeler* dissent, consider *People v. Saldana,* 47 Cal.App.3d 954, 121 Cal. Rptr. 243 (1975). Defendant shot Fenoff in the neck on Dec. 10; Fenoff was taken to the hospital where, by resort to drugs and a respirator, his heart and lungs were kept functioning. On Dec. 17 it was determined that there was no electrical activity in the brain, and thereafter Fenoff was removed from the respirator. His heart and lungs then ceased to function. Defendant, convicted of murder, claimed on appeal that the cause of death was the removal of the artificial life-support systems.

The court affirmed, stating: "The evidence presented clearly points to the cessation of Joe Fenoff's brain functions, and thereby his death, prior to the removal of such systems." It was also noted that *after* the murder the California legislature had defined death for the purpose of organ transplantations in terms of when a person "has suffered a total and unreversible cessation of brain function." The *Saldana* court did not refer to prior appellate decisions in California and elsewhere which had held in noncriminal contexts that "[a]s long as the heart remains beating and there is breathing, death has not occurred." Comment, 11 Wake Forest L.Rev. 253 (1975).

6. Consider again the *Chavez* case discussed in *Keeler.* Can the conviction of Ms. Chavez be squared with the fair warning requirement as later defined in *Bouie?*

7. In *People v. Sobiek,* 30 Cal.App.3d 458, 106 Cal.Rptr. 519 (1973), the state appealed the quashing of an indictment for theft which alleged that the defendant had embezzled or stolen partnership property. The applicable statute reads: "Every person who shall feloniously steal, take, carry, lead, or drive away the personal property of another, or who shall fraudulently appropriate property which has been entrusted to him, or who shall knowingly and designedly, by any false or fraudulent representation or pretense, defraud any other person of money, labor or real or personal property, * * * is guilty of theft." The court acknowledged that in *People v. Brody,* 29 Cal.App.2d 6, 83 P.2d 952 (1938), it had been held, relying upon dictum in two California Supreme Court cases, that it was "settled law" that it was not theft for a partner to take partnership property. But, the *Sobiek* court, noting that this view had been rejected in the Model Penal Code and in the recent recodifications in other jurisdictions, concluded it was "both illogical and unreasonable to hold that a partner cannot steal from his partners merely be-

cause he has an undivided interest in the partnership property" and that there was nothing in the statute quoted above "which requires an interpretation different from that in [the] Model Penal Code."

The defendant objected that such a construction of the statute, if applied to him, would violate the principles of the *Bouie* and *Keeler* cases. The court responded that this was not so because "in the case at bar, 'common social duty' would have forewarned respondent that 'circumspect conduct' prohibited robbing his partners and also would have told him that he was stealing 'property of another.'" Is the distinction persuasive?

8. The *Bouie* doctrine and the ex post facto clause, both discussed in *Keeler,* afford a defendant protection against the adverse consequences of an expansion of the criminal law by the courts or the legislature, respectively, occurring after his conduct. What, then, of the somewhat reverse situation, i.e., when a change in the substantive criminal law which would be beneficial to the defendant occurs after his conduct?

In *People v. Rossi,* 18 Cal.3d 295, 134 Cal.Rptr. 64, 555 P.2d 1313 (1976), defendant was convicted under a statute proscribing all oral copulation. Before the time for appeal had expired, the legislature amended the statute so that it only proscribed such conduct when done by force, while confined in prison, or with a minor. Because the defendant's acts would not be criminal under the statute as amended, the defendant on appeal sought a reversal of her conviction. The court held:

"At common law, a statute mitigating punishment applied to acts committed before its effective date as long as no final judgment had been rendered. Similarly, when a statute proscribing certain designated acts was repealed without a saving clause, all prosecutions for such act that had not been reduced to final judgment were barred.[a] Until a decade ago, however, a line of California cases—primarily Court of Appeal decisions—had interpreted the general saving clause embodied in Government Code section 9608 [4] and its predecessors as completely abrogating these common law rules.

"In *In re Estrada* (1965) 63 Cal.2d 740, 48 Cal.Rptr. 172, 408 P.2d 948, this court undertook an extensive review of this entire line of authority and concluded that the earlier cases had improperly extended the application of Government Code section 9608 far beyond its intended scope. In *Estrada* we observed that at common law when a statute was passed that *increased* the punishment for a crime, a defendant who committed the proscribed acts prior to the effective date of the new law could not be punished under the old law because it no longer existed, and he could not be punished under the new law because its attempted application would render it an ex post facto law.

"Section 9608, we explained in *Estrada*, was enacted simply to authorize prosecutions under the former statute in order to avoid this technically absurd result by which a defendant could be prosecuted under no law, simply because the Legislature had decided to *increase* the punishment for his crime. We concluded, however, that the provision was not intended to abrogate the well-established common law rule which, in the absence of clear legislative intent to the contrary, accorded a criminal defendant the benefit of a mitigation of punishment adopted before his

criminal conviction became final. Thus, we held that '[w]here the amendatory statute mitigates punishment and there is no saving clause, the rule is that the amendment will operate retroactively so that the lighter punishment is imposed.' * * *

"The People contend, however, that the case at bar is distinguishable from *Estrada,* pointing out that in the instant case the intervening amendment has entirely eliminated any criminal sanction for defendant's acts while in *Estrada* the intervening amendment merely reduced the punishment for the conduct. Although it is true that *Estrada* and recent California cases applying *Estrada* have involved intervening enactments which merely reduced, rather than entirely eliminated, penal sanctions, numerous precedents demonstrate that the common law principles reiterated in *Estrada* apply a fortiori when criminal sanctions have been completely repealed before a criminal conviction becomes final.

"In *Spears v. County of Modoc* (1894) 101 Cal. 303, 35 P. 869, for example, defendant was convicted in justice court of violating a local penal ordinance prohibiting 'the keeping of a saloon where spiritous liquors were sold' and was fined $500. Pending his appeal to the superior court, the local ordinance was repealed but the superior court nonetheless affirmed the conviction. In subsequent proceedings, this court determined that the superior court had been in error and explicitly held that the repeal of the ordinance before the judgment became final invalidated the conviction.

---

a. This is to be distinguished from the situation in which the statute is repealed because the prohibition is reenacted in another statute, as commonly occurs when all or a part of a criminal code is recodified. In such a case, even absent a saving clause, a court might well conclude the legislature did not intend any such bar. See, e.g., *State v. Armstrong*, 239 Kan. 559, 712 P.2d 1258 (1986).

4. Section 9608 provides in full: "The termination or suspension (by whatsoever means ef-

fected) of any law creating a criminal offense does not constitute a bar to the indictment or information and punishment of an act already committed in violation of the law so terminated or suspended, unless the intention to bar such indictment or information and punishment is expressly declared by an applicable provision of law."

"Citing numerous respected authorities, the *Spears* court explained its conclusion at some length: '[T]he effect of repealing a statute is "to obliterate it as completely from the records of the parliament as if it had never passed; and it must be considered as a law that never existed, except for the purpose of those actions which were commenced, prosecuted, and concluded while it was an existing law." This principle has been applied more frequently to penal statutes, and it may be regarded as an established rule that the repeal of a penal statute without any saving clause has the effect to deprive the court in which any prosecution under the statute is pending of all power to proceed further in the matter. "The repeal of a statute puts an end to all prosecutions under the statute repealed, and to all proceedings growing out of it pending at the time of the repeal." (Sedgwick's *Statutory and Constitutional Law,* 130.) * * * "If a penal statute is repealed pending an appeal, and before the final action of the appellate court, it will prevent an affirmance of a conviction, and the prosecution must be dismissed, or judgment reversed." ' "

A dissenting judge objected: "When a statute is repealed there is no new law to enter into consideration. [T]herefore, the Legislature's intent that the offender be punished, expressed in section 9608, can only be given effect under the old law."

9. As a matter of policy, when should a criminal defendant be allowed to take advantage of decriminalization occurring after his conduct? Consider Comment, 121 U.Pa.L.Rev. 120, 148–49 (1972): "A criminal statute might be repealed due to a present legislative determination that the conduct proscribed should never have been criminal,[176] that a change in societal mores demands that the conduct be decriminalized,[177] or that a sudden change in circumstances or conditions renders the proscription unnecessary.[178] In each of the cases, the prudence of retroactivity or nonretroactivity must be measured in terms of serving the possible goals of punishment: prevention, restraint, rehabilitation, deterrence, education, and retribution. For example, if upon repeal of a law a determination that the proscribed conduct should never have been criminal can be attributed to the legislature, the 'no benefit' rule clearly does not advance the goals of punishment. Prevention or particular deterrence is not served since the defendant cannot commit the same crime again once the conduct has been decriminalized. Further restraint is unnecessary to protect society from the now legalized conduct, and to the extent that rehabilitation is aimed at eliminating any predisposition to repeat the same criminal act, decriminalization completes rehabilitation. General deterrence is not fostered since decriminalization ends the need to dissuade others from committing the previously proscribed act.[180] Public education about the criminality of the act becomes anachronistic. The only remaining goal, retribution, *is* served by continued punishment, but is a generally discredited goal."

NOTES ON THE ROLE OF COURTS IN CONSTRUING CRIMINAL STATUTES

In the great majority of the cases which follow in this Book, as in *Keeler,* the appellate court is confronted with the necessity

---

176. Repeal of prohibition by the 21st amendment is illustrative of such a change.

177. The absolute decriminalization of abortions performed in New York by licensed physicians on women less than 24 weeks pregnant is such an example.

178. This type of change is illustrated by the repeal of a variety of price controls at the end of World War II.

180. Of course, one possible objective of punishment may be the deterrence of law-breaking in general. Under this rationale, it is a disregard for law, and not a substantive offense, that is punished.

of construing a criminal statute. The question of how courts ought to perform that task, therefore, is one which frequently arises in these materials. The following notes are intended merely to introduce the student to this complex subject.

1. *Construing statutes vs. construing cases.* Levi, *An Introduction to Legal Reasoning,* 15 U.Chi.L.Rev. 501, 521 (1948): "[It is necessary] to reexamine whether there is any difference between case-law and statutory interpretation. It is not enough to show that the words used by the legislature have some meaning. Concepts created by case law also have some meaning, but the meaning is ambiguous. It is not clear how wide or narrow the scope is to be. Can it be said that the words used by the legislature have any more meaning than that, or is there the same ambiguity? One important difference can be noted immediately. Where case law is considered, there is a conscious realignment of cases; the problem is not the intention of the prior judge. But with a statute the reference is to the kind of things intended by the legislature. All concepts suggest, but case-law concepts can be re-worked. A statutory concept, however, is supposed to suggest what the legislature had in mind; the items to be included under it should be of the same order. We mean to accomplish what the legislature intended. * * * The difficulty is that what the legislature intended is ambiguous. In a significant sense there is only a general intent which preserves as much ambiguity in the concept used as though it had been created by case law."

2. *Why ambiguity?* Levi, supra, at 521–22: "This is not the result of inadequate draftsmanship, as is so frequently urged. Matters are not decided until they have to be. For a legislature perhaps the pressures are such that a bill has to be passed dealing with a certain subject. But the precise effect of the bill is not something upon which the members have to reach agreement. If the legislature were a court, it would not decide the precise effect until a specific fact situation arose demanding an answer. Its first pronouncement would not be expected to fill in the gaps. But since it is not a court, this is even more true. It will not be required to make the determination in any event, but can wait for the court to do so. * * *

"Controversy does not help. Agreement is then possible only through escape to a higher level of discourse with greater ambiguity. This is one element which makes compromise possible. Moreover, from the standpoint of the individual member of the legislature there is reason to be deceptive. He must escape from pressures at home. Newspapers may have created an atmosphere in which some legislation must be passed. Perhaps the only chance to get legislation through is to have it mean something not understood by some colleagues. * * * And if all this were not sufficient, it cannot be forgotten that to speak of legislative intent is to talk of group action, where much of the group may be ignorant or misinformed."

3. *Strict construction.* J. Hall, *General Principles of Criminal Law* 46–47 (2d ed. 1960): "[W]e know that the strict construction of penal statutes played an extraordinary role in the eighteenth century when a humanitarian ideology propagated by Beccaria, Romilly, Howard, Buxton and others rose against severe, indiscriminate penalization. Statutes which were quite clear in their meaning were completely distorted. 'Strict construction' then was any interpretation, however fantastic, which saved minor offenders from the capital penalty. * * * What seems to have been rather definitely established is that statutory interpretation is a relative process in the sense that it changes and must be appraised in relation to time, facts, sanctions, and ideals."

In *United States v. Hartwell,* 73 U.S. (6 Wall.) 385, 18 L.Ed. 830 (1868), in holding that the defendant (a clerk appointed by the assistant treasurer, with approval of the Secretary of the Treasury) came within the phrase "an officer or person charged with the safekeeping of the public money," the Court observed:

"We are not unmindful that penal laws are to be construed strictly. It is said that this rule is almost as old as construction itself. But whenever invoked it comes attended with qualifications and other rules no less important. It is by the light which each contributes that the judgment of the court is to be made up. The object in construing penal, as well as other statutes, is to ascertain the legislative intent. That constitutes the law. If the language be clear it is conclusive. There can be no construction where there is nothing to construe. The words must not be narrowed to the exclusion of what the legislature intended to embrace; but that intention must be gathered from the words, and they must be such as to leave no room for a reasonable doubt upon the subject. It must not be defeated by a forced and overstrict construction. The rule does not exclude the application of common sense to the terms made use of in the act in order to avoid an absurdity, which the legislature ought not to be presumed to have intended. * * * The rule of strict construction is not violated by permitting the words of the statute to have their full meaning, or the more extended of two meanings, as the wider popular instead of the more narrow technical one; but the words should be taken in such a sense, bent neither one way nor the other, as will best manifest the legislative intent."

4. *Plain meaning.* Defendant, who transported his mistress across state lines, was convicted of violating the Mann Act. The Supreme Court, in *Caminetti v. United States,* 242 U.S. 470, 37 S.Ct. 192, 61 L.Ed. 442 (1917), rejected the defendant's

contention that the Act was intended to reach only commercialized vice:

"Where the language is plain and admits of no more than one meaning, the duty of interpretation does not arise, and the rules which are to aid doubtful meanings need no discussion. There is no ambiguity in the terms of this act. It is specifically made an offense to knowingly transport or cause to be transported, etc., in interstate commerce, any woman or girl for the purpose of prostitution or debauchery, or for 'any other immoral purpose,' or with the intent and purpose to induce any such woman or girl to become a prostitute or to give herself up to debauchery, or to engage in any other immoral practice.
* * *

"[W]hen words are free from doubt they must be taken as the final expression of the legislative intent, and are not to be added to or subtracted from by considerations drawn from titles or designating names or reports accompanying their introduction, or from any extraneous source. In other words, the language being plain, and not leading to absurd or wholly impracticable consequences, it is the sole evidence of the ultimate legislative intent."

5. *Legislative intent.* Landis, *A Note on "Statutory Interpretation,"* 43 Harv.L.Rev. 886, 888–89, (1930): "The assumption that the meaning a representative assembly attached to the words used in a particular statute is rarely discoverable, has little foundation in fact. The records of legislative assemblies once opened and read with a knowledge of legislative procedure often reveal the richest kind of evidence. To insist that each individual legislator besides his aye vote must also have expressed the meaning he attaches to the bill as a condition precedent to predicating an intent on the part of the legislator, is to disregard the realities of legislative procedure. Through the committee report, the explanation of the committee chairman, and

otherwise, a mere expression of assent becomes in reality a concurrence in the expressed views of another. A particular determinate thus becomes the common possession of the majority of the legislature, and as such a real discoverable intent."

Compare Leflar, *Statutory Construction: The Sound Law Approach* (remarks delivered to Federal Appellate Judges Conference, Federal Judicial Center, Washington, D.C., May 13, 1975): "We say frequently that in interpreting a statute we want to discover the intent of the legislature. I think that it was Chief Justice Hingham, I'm not sure, who said that the devil himself 'knoweth not the mind of man.' It is difficult to discover intent; and when you cannot discover with any authority the state of mind of one man, the process of discovering the states of mind, the intent of 535 men, who make up the Federal Congress, becomes an extremely difficult matter. The United States Supreme Court, as I said a few moments ago, has time and again referred back to legislative debates, to discussions in committee and to all other background sources. We could cite dozens of U.S. cases in which that has occurred. But if you have to work with state law few legislatures have transcripts of proceedings comparable to those that are available at the federal level. The problem of legislative intent as such seems to me to involve as much in the way of possibility of being misled as almost anything one can get into. There are bits of legislative record that are devised peculiarly by congressmen or senators for the purpose of misleading judges. And sometimes it is difficult to know which of those you are looking at."

6. *Ejusdem generis.* Defendant was convicted of the interstate transportation of a "motor vehicle" known to be stolen, in that he transported an airplane from Illinois to Oklahoma. The statute read: "The term 'motor vehicle' shall include an automobile, automobile truck, automobile wagon, motor cycle, or any other self-propelled vehicle not designed for running on rails." In *McBoyle v. United States,* 283 U.S. 25, 51 S.Ct. 340, 75 L.Ed. 816 (1931), the Court reversed: "No doubt etymologically it is possible to use the word ['vehicle'] to signify a conveyance working on land, water or air, and sometimes legislation extends the use in that direction * * *. But in everyday speech 'vehicle' calls up the picture of a thing moving on land. * * * So here, the phrase under discussion calls up the popular picture. For after including automobile truck, automobile wagon and motor cycle, the words 'any other self-propelled vehicle not designed for running on rails' still indicate that a vehicle in the popular sense, that is a vehicle running on land is the theme. It is a vehicle that runs, not something, not commonly called a vehicle, that flies. Airplanes were well known in 1919 when this statute was passed, but it is admitted that they were not mentioned in the reports or in the debates in Congress. It is impossible to read words that so carefully enumerate the different forms of motor vehicles and have no reference of any kind to aircraft, as including airplanes under a term that usage more and more precisely confines to a different class."

7. *Expressio unius est exclusio alterius.* The defendant was convicted of murder under the California felony-murder statute, which (in the part here relevant) permitted such a conviction where a death occurred in the perpetration of an "arson" by the defendant. The jury had been instructed it would suffice that the death occurred as a result of defendant's malicious burning of a car. In *People v. Nichols,* 3 Cal.3d 150, 89 Cal.Rptr. 721, 474 P.2d 673 (1970), the court reversed. Noting that the arson statute did not specifically refer to motor vehicles and that in 1959 one type of conveyance, "trailer coaches," had been

added to the arson statute, the court stated: "This enactment, expressly making the burning of trailer coaches arson, implies that the burning of motor vehicles is not arson."

8. *In pari materia.* The defendant was convicted of aggravated assault under a statute (§ 21–3411) defining the crime as an assault "committed against a uniformed or properly identified state, county or city law enforcement officer while such officer is engaged in the performance of his duty." On appeal, defendant claimed the evidence was insufficient under his interpretation of the statute, namely, that it required proof that the defendant knew the person assaulted was a police officer. In *State v. Bradley,* 215 Kan. 642, 527 P.2d 988 (1974), the court disagreed with that construction. Noting that § 21–3411 was enacted at the same session of the legislature as § 21–3416 and that both statutes had to do with public employees performing dangerous and vital duties, the court concluded that "the statutes are *in pari materia* and they must be read together when interpreting section 21–3411." Because § 21–3416 made it a crime for one "knowingly and intentionally" to assault a fireman, the court reasoned:

"In section 21–3416 the legislature expressly included *scienter* as an element of the offense. Therefore, it may be concluded the term 'knowingly' would have been used in section 21–3411, if the legislature had intended that *scienter* also be an element of aggravated assault on a law enforcement officer. Its absence is compelling evidence that the legislature did not intend to require *scienter.*"

NOTES ON THE RESPECTIVE ROLES OF FEDERAL, STATE AND LOCAL LEGISLATIVE BODIES

1. *Federal power.* The federal government has the power to create statutory crimes where the Constitution expressly grants Congress the power (e.g., art. I, § 8, power to punish counterfeiting; art. III, § 3, power to punish treason). In addition, art. I, § 8 of the Constitution provides that the Congress has the power "to make all Laws which shall be necessary and proper for carrying into Execution the foregoing [express] Powers, and all other Powers vested by this Constitution in the Government of the United States." Thus, many federal criminal statutes have been enacted on the theory that they are "necessary and proper" to such powers as the power to regulate interstate commerce, to establish post offices, and to tax. It has been noted that in fact the federal criminal law is utilized to punish antisocial conduct primarily injurious to the federal government (e.g., bribery of federal officers) and also to punish antisocial conduct of primarily local concern with which local officials are unable or unwilling to cope (e.g., use of the mails to defraud, kidnapping across state lines). See Schwartz, *Federal Criminal Jurisdiction and Prosecutors' Discretion,* 13 Law & Contemp. Prob. 64 (1948).

2. *State power.* A state, unlike the federal government, may declare activities to be criminal without the necessity of finding some express or implied authority therefor in its constitution. It is commonly said that a state has regulatory power (usually termed its "police power") to regulate its internal affairs for the protection or promotion of public health, safety and morals, or—somewhat more vaguely—for the protection or promotion of the public welfare. There are, however, constitutional limits on this power; they will be considered in the following section.

3. *Municipal power.* Pursuant to authorization from the legislature, local governmental units have the police power to regulate for the protection of the lives, health and property of their inhabitants and the preservation of good order and morals. In most states the typical munici-

pality has numerous ordinances on local traffic matters, on local nontraffic matters (e.g., regulating garbage disposal), and on matters also covered by state criminal laws (e.g., assault and battery). These ordinances frequently provide for fines or imprisonment or both for their violation, although sometimes the power to imprison is limited to imprisonment for failure to pay a fine. While the prevailing view is that violation of a municipal ordinance is a civil wrong rather than a crime, the modern trend is in the direction of calling such violations criminal, at least where imprisonment is authorized or where the ordinance prohibits the same conduct as does the state criminal law.

4. *Federal pre-emption.* A state criminal statute and a federal criminal statute may proscribe identical or substantially identical conduct. In such a case, the state law may be upheld on the theory that the two statutes do not conflict and that Congress did not intend to make its law exclusive, or the state legislation may be held unconstitutional under the supremacy clause, art. VI of the Constitution, on the theory that the federal legislation has occupied the field. While "[n]o simple formula can capture the complexities of this determination," *Goldstein v. California,* 412 U.S. 546, 93 S.Ct. 2303, 37 L.Ed.2d 163 (1973), the Supreme Court in *Pennsylvania v. Nelson,* 350 U.S. 497, 76 S.Ct. 477, 100 L.Ed. 640 (1956), set forth three tests for determining the pre-emption issue: (1) Is the federal legislative scheme as to the subject matter in question so pervasive as to indicate that Congress must have meant the states were not to supplement the federal legislation? (2) Is the federal interest in the subject matter so dominant that Congress must have meant to preclude the states from dealing with the matter? (3) Would state enforcement in the matter present a serious danger to effective federal enforcement?

5. *State pre-emption and other state-local conflicts.* A municipal ordinance may not permit what state law proscribes. For example, where a state law prohibits the sale of liquor at certain times, such sales may not be permitted by local law. *Hawes v. Dinkler,* 224 Ga. 785, 164 S.E.2d 799 (1968). And if a state law expressly permits certain conduct, such as the sale of liquor by the drink in establishments having a state license, this conduct may not be proscribed by local ordinance. *Crackerneck Country Club v. Independence,* 522 S.W.2d 50 (Mo.App.1974). Municipal regulations proscribing what the state has impliedly permitted are often upheld, e.g., *St. Paul v. Olson,* 300 Minn. 455, 220 N.W.2d 484 (1974). Though the rule is otherwise if the regulations conflict with some general state policy, the prevailing view is that there is no conflict merely because a local ordinance duplicates a state statute, *Aurora v. Martin,* 181 Colo. 72, 507 P.2d 868 (1973). See also *State v. Suire,* 319 So.2d 347 (La.1975), holding that an ordinance which punishes aggravated battery as a misdemeanor is not unconstitutional as inconsistent with a state law punishing such conduct as a felony. A local ordinance may be voided on the ground that the state has occupied or pre-empted the field. See *Lancaster v. Municipal Court,* 6 Cal.3d 805, 100 Cal.Rptr. 609, 494 P.2d 681 (1972), striking down a county ordinance making it a misdemeanor for a person to massage a member of the opposite sex as a commercial business, on the ground that "the state had adopted a general scheme for the regulation of the criminal aspects of sexual activity and that the state had occupied the field to the exclusion of all local regulation."

Assume that in a state where the criminal code makes possession of marijuana a misdemeanor punishable by up to a year in jail and/or a fine of $500, and sale of marijuana a felony punishable by up to 5 years in the penitentiary, the students at the state university manage to elect a majority of the city council in the city where the university is located, after which the council adopts an ordinance making possession or sale of marijuana an offense punishable by not more than a fine of $5. Is the ordinance valid? Of what relevance, if any, is *Waller v. Florida,* 397 U.S. 387, 90 S.Ct. 1184, 25 L.Ed.2d 435 (1970), holding that the constitutional protection against double jeopardy bars a state prosecution of a defendant for the "same acts" for which he was previously tried under a city ordinance.

NOTES ON THE ROLE OF ADMINISTRATIVE OFFICIALS AND AGENCIES

1. *Delegation.* A legislature may delegate to an administrative agency the power to make rules, the violation of which is punishable as a crime by virtue of penalties set by statute. However, it has often been held that such delegation is proper only if the legislature, in its delegation statute, sets forth sufficient standards to guide the administrative agency. There is considerable difference of opinion in the cases as to what standards will suffice. In *State v. Boyajian,* 344 A.2d 410 (Me.1975), the court upheld a statute making it unlawful to sell "any drug designated by the Board [of Commissioners of the Profession of Pharmacy] as a 'potent medicinal substance.'" The court noted that a companion statute said such designation could be made as to any "central nervous system stimulants or depressants, psychic energizers or any other drugs having a tendency to depress or stimulate which are likely to be injurious to health if improperly used," and concluded that this statute "contains limitations, readily understandable by experienced pharmacists, on the type of materials to be designated."

But in *Sundberg v. State,* 234 Ga. 482, 216 S.E.2d 332 (1975), a statute prohibit-ing the possession of a "depressant or stimulant drug" as designated by the State Board of Pharmacy was struck down. Though the statute went on to say that such a drug is "[a]ny substance which the State Board shall determine to be habit-forming because of its stimulant effect on the central nervous system or any drug which the State Board shall determine to contain any quantity of a substance having a potential for abuse because of its depressant or stimulant effect on the central nervous system or its hallucinogenic effect," the court concluded that "this paragraph says a depressant or stimulant drug is anything the State Board of Pharmacy says it is."

2. *Discretionary enforcement.* In *Poe v. Ullman,* 367 U.S. 497, 81 S.Ct. 1752, 6 L.Ed.2d 989 (1961), Justice Frankfurter, after noting that the criminal statute there challenged apparently had never been enforced, commented: "What was said in another context is relevant here. 'Deeply embedded traditional ways of carrying out state policy * * *'—or not carrying it out—'are often tougher and truer law than the dead words of the written text.'" In that sense, it may be said that those responsible for enforcing the criminal law determine, within the statutory limits, what the actual content of the criminal law will be. This subject is helpfully discussed in Remington & Rosenblum, *The Criminal Law and the Legislative Process,* 1960 U.Ill. L.F. 481. They note that "[w]here the substantive law is ambiguous there is an opportunity, indeed a necessity, for the exercise of discretion by enforcement agencies and courts as to what conduct ought to be subjected to the criminal process," and observe that such ambiguity may be: (i) "by default" [i.e., resulting from "inadequacies of legislative draftsmanship in the criminal law"]; (ii) "unavoidable" [i.e., resulting from "theoretical and practical limitations upon the capacity for precise legislative formulation"]; or

(iii) "by design." As to the latter, they comment at 490–94:

"One who sets out to eliminate ambiguity in the substantive law very soon is confronted with the argument that he thus creates loopholes through which the guilty can escape.

"The effort to be explicit as to the precise mental state required is often resisted by law enforcement agencies, not on the grounds that persons ought to be convicted who lack the prescribed mental state, but rather on the ground that the explicit requirement will create a loophole through which some of the guilty can escape.

"If the legislative contribution is to be a major one, clarity as an objective ought to prevail even at the cost of creating opportunity of escape for some who ought to be convicted. There are, however, some situations in which the line is not easily drawn in a way that will exempt conduct which it is not desired to proscribe without seriously hindering enforcement against conduct which it is desirable to proscribe. In this case the temptation is strong to overgeneralize, leaving it to enforcement agencies not to invoke the process against conduct which is not serious. The consequence is, of course, the delegation of broad discretion. For example, this problem confronted the draftsmen of the Model Anti-Gambling Act:

'The Commission has also had great difficulty with this problem of finding a formula which would exclude the social or casual gambler from prosecution and punishment, yet which would not result in opening a large breach in the statute for the benefit of professional gamblers and their patrons. The Commission recognizes that it is unrealistic to promulgate a law literally aimed at making a criminal offense of the friendly election

bet, the private, social card game among friends, etc. Nevertheless, it is imperative to confront the professional gambler with a statutory facade that is wholly devoid of loopholes.' [27]

"The combination of the attitude that loopholes might result and that overgeneralization has not been abused in practice tends to support a continuation of the ambiguity created by criminal statutes which are intended to proscribe a much narrower range of conduct than that defined by the terms of the statute.

"In the field of regulation of economic activity it is assumed that the legislature is incapable of dealing with the details of regulation and that these are best left to administrative agencies staffed by persons expert in the particular aspect of the economy involved. The legislature contents itself with a broad policy directive, leaving to the administrative agency the task of taking steps to implement that policy. The actions of the administrative agency are subject to judicial review to determine whether the action was arbitrary.

"In the field of criminal law, the regulation of social behavior, there has been little explicit recognition given to the role of administrative expertness in determining, within a legislative policy framework, what conduct ought to be treated as criminal. The tradition of the criminal law, in recent years, has been to assume that the legislature is responsible for the definition of criminal conduct and the administrative agencies are responsible for discovering such conduct and subjecting persons who engage in it to arrest, prosecution, and conviction. Expertise relates to efficiency of investigation, apprehension, and conviction rather than to issues relating to whether it is desirable, under particular circumstances, to subject conduct to part or all of the criminal process. * * *

27. 2 ABA Comm'n on Organized Crime, *Organized Crime and Law Enforcement* 57 (1952).

"Perhaps there is a difference in principle between the exercise of discretion by an agency primarily responsible for economic regulation which uses the criminal sanction as an incident to regulation and the exercise of discretion by the police, but the difference, if one, is not easy to see or to formulate. It is not clear, for example, why the Supreme Court's per curiam support of the discretionary power of the Federal Trade Commission to select the businessmen against whom the Robinson-Patman Act is to be enforced should not apply equally to similar problems of enforcement of criminal law by the police. In *Moog Industries v. FTC,*[29a] the Supreme Court upheld the power of the FTC to put into operation a cease and desist order against a single firm, despite the firm's offer to show that its competitors engaged in the same proscribed practices and that it would suffer serious financial loss if prohibited from engaging in these practices that remained open to their competitors. Stressing the 'specialized experienced judgment,' the 'expert understanding,' and the 'special competence' of the Commission, the Court concluded that 'the Commission alone is empowered to develop that enforcement policy best calculated to achieve the ends contemplated by Congress and to allocate its available funds and personnel in such a way as to execute its policy efficiently and economically.'

"When a Pennsylvania court was faced recently with a similar assertion of discretionary power by Philadelphia's Police Commissioner in enforcing the city's Sunday Blue Law, the court held his action a violation of the fourteenth amendment's equal protection clause. Apparently, the Commissioner's mistake was to assert that, for lack of funds and personnel, he would limit initial enforcement of the Sunday closing law to large retail establishments.[29b]

"A careful study of legislative attitude in relation to certain kinds of criminal conduct might well disclose a legislative willingness to delegate a measure of discretion to an enforcement agency thought to be expert in the matter involved. One explanation, and perhaps justification, of current, broadly formulated gambling statutes is that they are a delegation of discretion to police, who have expert knowledge, to apply the statute with the objective of eliminating organized commercial gambling. The continuation of broadly phrased gambling statutes may well be on the assumption that the wide discretion thus conferred has not been abused.

"It is well known that some criminal statutes reflect the hope rather than the expectation that the community will conform to the standard set forth in the statute. Vigorous enforcement is not resorted to because, although there is general support for proscribing the conduct, there is no such support for a program of systematic enforcement. Thus statutes prohibiting fornication and adultery, for example, stand relatively immune from repeal although it can be demonstrated that they are seldom invoked in practice. In part their continued existence undoubtedly reflects a desire to reassert the validity of certain standards of morality by keeping them in the criminal code. In part this also undoubtedly reflects the fact that it is difficult to repeal such statutes because of practical legislator's judgment that his vote for repeal is likely to be interpreted as a vote in favor of the conduct of which most of his constituents disapprove. Perhaps the most important reason is the lack of an adequate demonstration that harm results from the continued existence of such legislation. The assertion that such statutes give enforcement agencies the power to invoke the statute only against those whom they desire to convict rests upon an as-

---

29a. 355 U.S. 411, 78 S.Ct. 377, 2 L.Ed.2d 370 (1958).

29b. *Bargain City v. Dilworth,* 29 U.S.L.Week 2002 (Pa.Ct.Com.Pls. June 10, 1960).

sumption that the existence of such power, within the prescribed limits, is necessarily undesirable.[30] For example, a recent Wisconsin case involved a situation where a woman was charged and convicted of fornication. It appears quite clearly that the prosecution resulted primarily because she had agreed, and then refused, to testify against her hoodlum boyfriend. Is this different from the situation where an Al Capone is prosecuted for income tax violation primarily because of his gangster activities which are more difficult to prove? There is no consensus that the income tax penalty ought to be repealed. Is there a difference in regard to the offense of fornication? If so, it is one so subtle in nature it is not surprising that it is not reflected in typical state legislative action. It is obvious that the issue may be one of degree and that the power to invoke the income tax penalty selectively against persons suspected of other criminal conduct does not necessitate the conclusion that the fornication statute must be retained. But, it does mean that opposition to a fornication-type statute on the ground that it creates a discretionary power in law enforcement agencies is not a completely persuasive one when the total system is, realistically viewed, characterized by broad discretionary power."

SECTION 3. CONSTITUTIONAL LIMITATIONS: "CRIMES AGAINST NATURE"

LOCKE v. STATE

Court of Criminal Appeals of Tennessee, 1973.
501 S.W.2d 826.

RUSSELL, JUDGE.

Harold Locke was charged and convicted of committing a "crime against nature"

as proscribed by T.C.A. § 39–707 against Minnie R. Rogers, and his punishment set at not less than five (5) nor more than seven (7) years in the penitentiary. The State's theory of the case was that Locke entered the apartment of a neighbor, Mrs. Rogers, late at night on the pretext of using the telephone, presented a butcher knife, and forced Mrs. Rogers to submit to two episodes of cunnilingus. This theory is adequately supported by the evidence * * *.

We next confront the question of whether or not cunnilingus is an act made unlawful as a "crime against nature" by T.C.A. § 39–707. We hold that it is. Our Supreme Court has heretofore held that fellatio is such a crime. *Fisher v. State,* 197 Tenn. 594, 277 S.W.2d 340. And, in *Sherrill v. State,* 204 Tenn. 427, 321 S.W.2d 811, our Supreme Court has specifically adopted the liberal Maine doctrine defining crimes against nature as bringing "all unnatural copulation with mankind or a beast, including sodomy, within its scope", as first pronounced in the Maine case of *State v. Cyr,* 135 Me. 513, 198 S. 743. Maine has since broadened its case law to specifically hold cunnilingus included. *State v. Townsend,* 145 Me. 384, 71 A.2d 517. It would be a paradox of legal construction to say that fellatio, "which in common language means sexual perversion committed with the male sexual organ and the mouth", *Sherrill v. State,* supra, is proscribed as a crime against nature, but cunnilingus is not. We recognize that many states limit crimes against nature strictly to sodomy; but the weight of authority supports the view which we follow, said to be the better reasoned in 48 Am. Jur. 549, *Sodomy* § 2. This court used the

---

30. The position that criminal statutes are the arsenal available to enforcement officials is advanced in Arnold, *The Symbols of Government* (1935). In omitting some sex offenses, the Model Penal Code advances the argument that such offenses are used for purposes of discriminatory

enforcement. See *Model Penal Code* 204–10 (Tent.Draft No. 4, 1955). Yet, there is no adequate empirical basis for concluding that these offenses are more susceptible to selective enforcement than certain other kinds of offenses, like worthless checks, which are retained as crimes.

following language in *Stephens v. State,* Tenn.Cr.App., 489 S.W.2d 542 (1972):

" * * * In its narrower sense sodomy is the carnal copulation between two human beings per anus, or by a human being in any manner with a beast. In its broader sense it is the carnal copulation by human beings with each other against nature or with a beast in which sense it includes all acts of unnatural copulation. Our Courts probably accept the broader meaning since they have held that the proscribed acts may be per os as well as per anus. * * * "

Finally, T.C.A. § 39–707 is said to be unconstitutionally vague and indefinite. We disagree.

We express no opinion as to the constitutionality of the application of this statute to the private acts of married couples, a question inapplicable to the facts of this case, and not briefed herein. Nor does the case sub judice involve the application of the statute to consenting adults.

Affirmed.

WALKER, P.J., concurs.

GALBREATH, JUDGE (dissenting).

I must with all due respect for my colleagues in the majority point out that cursory research does not appear to substantiate the holding that "the weight of authority supports the view" that oral caressing of the vagina, or cunnilingus, is included in the acts proscribed by Section 39–707 of our criminal code which sets out:

"Crimes against nature, either with mankind or any beast, are punishable by imprisonment in the penitentiary not less than five (5) years nor more than fifteen (15) years."

Less than one half of the jurisdictions in the nation have a statute such as ours which is a reiteration of the common law

2. "Sexual Behavior in the 1970's" *Playboy Magazine,* October, 1973, p. 85. See also Kinsey's

definition of sodomy. In at least two states the statute has been declared unconstitutional. See *Harris v. State* (Alaska), 457 P.2d 638, and *Franklin v. State* (Fla.), 257 So.2d 21. From a review of the many cases cited in West's Fifth through Seventh Decennial Digests under Key Number 1 for Sodomy, nature and elements of offenses, the courts of six states have ruled that cunnilingus is not a form of sodomy while four states seem to have adopted the view expressed by the majority.

To hold that cunnilingus (an act approved by almost 90% of adults between 18 and 34 according to an exhaustive study) [2] is a crime would seem to me to be judicial legislation of the plainest kind. The writer of this opinion is a strict constructionist. I firmly believe courts must take the law as it is made up for us by legislative bodies and higher judicial authority. One of the most basic canons of judicial behavior is incorporated in the doctrine of stare decisis. Although the issue involved in this case has never been passed on by either our Supreme Court or made the subject of legislation, we are firmly bound by many decisions which hold that when a statute is based on the common law, courts must look to the common law to determine the elements of the offense. Our own Court has emphasized this in pointing out that acts of sexual deviation other than sodomy could never be the subject of prosecution under the statute:

"Since crime against nature means the common law offense of sodomy and the crime is well defined and described at common law, T.C.A. 39–707 is not unconstitutionally vague. There is no danger that some kind of sexual perversion apart from unnatural carnal copulation, unnatural sexual intercourse, could be

Sexual Behavior in the Human Female, p. 257 (1942).

embraced in the definition and description as plaintiff in error contends." *Stephens v. State,* Tenn.Cr.App., 489 S.W.2d 542.

Affirmation of the conviction here for a perversion that did not involve copulation or sexual intercourse, natural or unnatural, is a direct refutation of what this Court said in *Stephens,* supra, and points up the danger inherent in judicial legislation. Where do we stop if we decree that any form of sexual activity is the equivalent of copulation or sexual intercourse so as to be unlawful if not confined to penis-vaginal connection? Even if we had the authority to legislate on the subject, where would we draw the line? * * *

From what has been pointed out above, it is clear that the laws in this State dealing with sexual perversions are in need of clarification. What is, or is not, illegal sexual activity could be, and in my view should be, set out in clear and precise terms so as to remove the present confusion and uncertainty. Surely we have progressed some from the dim past when Lord Coke spoke of sodomy as being "a detestable and abominable sin among Christians not to be named," although affirmation here would seem to be a regression since not even Lord Coke and his fellow English jurists through the centuries have felt it legally permissible to include cunnilingus, or even fellatio, within the definition of sodomy. See *Rex v. Jacobs,* 168 Eng.Rep. 830 (1817), construing 25 Henry VIII, C 6, 1533, the first statutory enactment of the common law offense Crime Against Nature.

The reticence expressed by Lord Coke and the framers of our statute to deal explicitly with the offense involved is a singular departure from one of the most basic rules of criminal procedure, i.e., that an accused is entitled to be notified of just what he has allegedly done to violate the law, usually by an indictment. To hold as

has the puritanical court in Illinois would not seem to even slightly conform to this long established rule of law:

"It was never the practice to describe the particular manner or the details of the commission of the act, but the offense was treated in the indictment as the abominable crime not fit to be named among Christians. * * * The existence of such an offense is a disgrace to human nature. The legislature has not seen fit to define it further than by the general term, and the records of the courts need not be defiled with the details of different acts which may go to constitute it. A statement of the offense in the language of the statute, or so plainly that its nature may be easily understood by the jury, is all that is required." *Honselman v. People,* 168 Ill. 172, 48 N.E. 304 (1897).

This reasoning seems to suggest two fallacies to me. Firstly, that sodomy is the most abhorrent of all crimes, so much so that it may not even be defined in writing. Any person who believes that sodomy is more abhorrent than murder, which is sharply defined by statute, in my opinion has a misplaced sense of priority. Secondly, the attitude of the Maine Court, now adopted by the majority, seems to be "everyone knows what a crime against nature is, so why spell it out?" In the first place, there have been so many disagreements as to what constitutes the offense that such reasoning falls under its own weight. (The legal paradox mentioned by the majority has not prevented some few states, at least two, from holding that while fellatio is proscribed as a crime against nature, cunnilingus is not. *State v. Tarrant,* 83 Ohio App. 199, 80 N.E.2d 509, and *Riley v. Garrett,* 219 Ga. 345, 133 S.E.2d 637.) Secondly, if there is no need to define this offense, why should it be necessary to define every other offense in our statutes exacting penal sanctions? Are arson, rape, robbery, burglary, forgery, etc. so little understood that they must be carefully defined while the never before in this State judicially encountered activity involved here is so familiar to all that one accused of committing a "crime against nature" must of necessity know what he is supposed to have done so as to be able to prepare a defense? The defendant here has the dubious distinction of being the only person in the history of this State, so far as reference to our case law is concerned, who has ever been sentenced to prison for committing this act which, as aforesaid, has been statistically attributed to some 46% of the adult population.

Cunnilingus, unlike fellatio, does not involve the virile male organ of reproduction. It would seem that it is the penis that must penetrate in order to accomplish the offense. Regardless of how loathsome one might view such conduct, surely, inserting any other part of the body against, or even in, the vagina would not be an offense under the common law or our statute. For instance, if the defendant had forced his victim onto the bed as the proof shows and had her remove her clothing and then placed his hand or one of his fingers against her vagina, this would not be punishable under the statute. Even if penetration should be made with the finger, or nose, toe, lips, tongue, or some foreign object, it is doubtful if this would meet the test under the common law or statute.

Proof of penetration is lacking.

"Penetration has been held an essential element of the crime of sodomy both at common law and under a number of the statutes defining and punishing the offense, but any penetration, however slight, is sufficient, and on penetration the crime becomes complete. The view that cunnilingus is not within the crime against nature, as discussed supra subdivision b(1) of this section, has been based on the lack of penetra-

tion of the body." 81 C.J.S. *Sodomy* § 1(4). * * *

Under the evidence the defendant is certainly guilty of an aggravated assault and battery since the proof is that he employed a deadly weapon to force his will on the prosecutrix, but under the present posture of the law in this State, in my considered opinion, he did not commit sodomy. I would reverse with a suggestion that a more appropriate prosecution be considered.

LOCKE v. ROSE

United States Court of Appeals, Sixth Circuit, 1975.
514 F.2d 570.

PER CURIAM.

Plaintiff-appellant ("appellant") was convicted in state court of committing a "crime against nature," by forcibly performing cunnilingus on a neighbor. The Tennessee court of criminal appeals (2:1) affirmed the conviction, rejecting appellant's claim that section 39–707 was unconstitutionally vague, *Locke v. State,* and the Tennessee Supreme Court denied certiorari (November 28, 1973).

Thereafter, appellant filed, *pro se,* the instant petition for writ of habeas corpus in the district court. That court, by order, rejected appellant's claim of unconstitutional vagueness in light of *Wainwright v. Stone,* 414 U.S. 21, 94 S.Ct. 190, 38 L.Ed. 2d 179 (1973), and denied relief. We reverse.

We do not understand defendant-appellee ("appellee") as arguing that the statutory term, "crimes against nature," could in and of itself withstand a charge of unconstitutional vagueness. Neither could appellee so argue, *Harris v. State,* 457 P.2d 638 (Alaska 1969), see *Perkins v. State,* 234 F.Supp. 333, 336 (W.D.N.C.1964), *Hogan v. State,* 84 Nev. 372, 441 P.2d 620, 621 (1968), particularly since courts have differed widely in construing the reach of "crimes against nature" to cunnilingus.

Although *Stone* upheld the constitutionality of Florida's "crime[s] against nature statute," as applied to copulation per os and per anum, the Court noted that the Florida statute had long been construed as proscribing "[t]hese very acts." Conversely, no reported Tennessee opinion had previously applied the Tennessee statute to cunnilingus. Section 39–707 had been applied exclusively as proscribing copulation per anum.

Appellee, however, argues that language in prior state court opinions, particularly in *Sherrill,* supra, has cured the unconstitutional vagueness of section 39–707 as applied to cunnilingus. Though *Sherrill* explicitly adopted the "liberal" statutory construction of *State v. Cyr,* 135 Me. 513, 198 A. 743 (1938), *Cyr* involved fellatio rather than cunnilingus. Moreover, *Sherrill* failed to cite *State v. Townsend,* 145 Me. 384, 71 A.2d 517, 518 (1950), which applied the Maine statute to cunnilingus. Even had *Sherrill* cited *Townsend,* however, such citation most likely would still have failed in putting "[m]en of common intelligence," *Winters v. New York,* 333 U.S. 507, 515, 68 S.Ct. 665, 92 L.Ed. 840 (1948), on notice of the court's cunnilingus-reaching interpretation. Likewise, *Stephens,* supra, even assuming that it preceded appellant's challenged act [3] cannot preclude "men of common intelligence [from] necessarily guess[ing] at its meaning and differ[ing] [at] its application" as applied to cunnilingus. *Bouie v. Columbia,* 378 U.S. 347, 351, 84 S.Ct. 1697, 1701, 12 L.Ed.2d 894 (1964).

Stephens, the Tennessee courts' most candid attempt at outlining the scope of section 39–707, defined the statutory "crime against nature" as

"a euphemism for the particular acts that constitute the offense of sodomy at common law. * * * In its narrower sense sodomy is the carnal copulation between two human beings per anus, or by a human being in any manner with a beast. In its broader sense it is the carnal copulation by human beings with each other against nature or with a beast in which sense it includes all acts of unnatural copulation. Our courts *probably* accept the broader meaning * * *." (Emphasis added.)

First, sodomy at common law included only copulation per anum. Second, *Stephens* only hinted that Tennessee "probably" accepts the broader view of crimes against nature. Moreover, even had the court expressly adopted the broader view, such view, as described, proscribing "carnal copulation by human beings with each other against nature * * * includ[ing] all acts of unnatural copulation," would still fail to give "fair warning," *Bouie,* supra, of the proscription of cunnilingus.

In accordance with the foregoing, the judgment of the district court is reversed and the case is remanded to the district court for remand to the Criminal Court of Knox County for such further proceedings as may be deemed appropriate and permissible under the applicable law, such as a prosecution for aggravated assault and battery; and provided further that if no such proceedings are instituted within sixty days of such remand, the writ shall issue and appellant shall stand discharged.

ROSE v. LOCKE

Supreme Court of the United States, 1975.
423 U.S. 48, 96 S.Ct. 243, 46 L.Ed.2d 185.

PER CURIAM. * * *

It is settled that the fair-warning requirement embodied in the Due Process Clause

---

3. *Stephens* was filed on September 28, 1972. Appellant's petition for writ of habeas corpus indicates that he was convicted on October 3,

1972, the forced cunnilingus thereby virtually certainly occurring prior to September 28, 1972.

prohibits the States from holding an individual "criminally responsible for conduct which he could not reasonably understand to be proscribed." *United States v. Harriss,* 347 U.S. 612, 617, 74 S.Ct. 808, 812, 98 L.Ed. 989 (1954); see *Wainwright v. Stone,* 414 U.S. 21, 94 S.Ct. 190, 38 L.Ed.2d 179 (1973). But this prohibition against excessive vagueness does not invalidate every statute which a reviewing court believes could have been drafted with greater precision. Many statutes will have some inherent vagueness, for "[i]n most English words and phrases there lurk uncertainties." *Robinson v. United States,* 324 U.S. 282, 286, 65 S.Ct. 666, 668, 89 L.Ed. 944 (1945). Even trained lawyers may find it necessary to consult legal dictionaries, treatises, and judicial opinions before they may say with any certainty what some statutes may compel or forbid. Cf. *Nash v. United States,* 229 U.S. 373, 33 S.Ct. 780, 57 L.Ed. 1232 (1913); *United States v. National Dairy Corp.,* 372 U.S. 29, 83 S.Ct. 594, 9 L.Ed.2d 561 (1963). All the Due Process Clause requires is that the law give sufficient warning that men may conform their conduct so as to avoid that which is forbidden.[3]

Viewed against this standard, the phrase "crime against nature" is no more vague than many other terms used to describe criminal offenses at common law and now codified in state and federal penal codes. The phrase has been in use among English-speaking people for many centuries, see 4 W. Blackstone, *Commentaries* * 216, and a substantial number of jurisdictions in this country continue to utilize it. Anyone who cared to do so could certainly determine what particular acts have been considered crimes against nature, and there can be no contention that the respondent's acts were ones never before considered as such.

Respondent argued that the vice in the Tennessee statute derives from the fact that jurisdictions differ as to whether "crime against nature" is to be narrowly applied to only those acts constituting the common-law offense of sodomy, or is to be broadly interpreted to encompass additional forms of sexual aberration. We do not understand him to contend that the broad interpretation is itself impermissibly vague; nor do we think he could successfully do so. We have twice before upheld statutes against similar challenges. In *State v. Crawford,* 478 S.W.2d 314 (Mo.1972), the Supreme Court of Missouri rejected a claim that its crime against nature statute was so devoid of definition as to be unconstitutional, pointing out its provision was derived from early English law and broadly embraced sodomy, bestiality, buggery, fellatio, and cunnilingus within its terms. We dismissed the appeal from this judgment as failing to present a substantial federal question. *Crawford v. Missouri,* 409 U.S. 811, 93 S.Ct. 176, 34 L.Ed.2d 66 (1972); see *Hicks v. Miranda,* 422 U.S. 332, 343–345, 95 S.Ct. 2281, 2289, 45 L.Ed.2d 223 (1975). And in *Wainwright v. Stone,* supra, we held that a Florida statute proscribing "the abominable and detestable crime against nature" was not unconstitutionally vague, despite the fact that the State Supreme Court had recently changed its mind about the statute's permissible scope.

The Court of Appeals, relying on language in *Stone,* apparently believed these cases turned upon the fact that the state courts had previously construed their statutes to cover the same acts with which the defendants therein were charged. But although *Stone* demonstrated that the existence of previous applications of a particular statute to one set of facts forecloses lack-of-fair-warning challenges to subse-

3. This is not a case in which the statute threatens a fundamental right such as freedom of speech so as to call for any special judicial scruti-

ny, see *Smith v. Goguen,* 415 U.S. 566, 572–573, 94 S.Ct. 1242, 1246, 39 L.Ed.2d 605 (1974).

quent prosecutions of factually identical conduct, it did not hold that such applications were a prerequisite to a statute's withstanding constitutional attack. If that were the case it would be extremely difficult ever to mount an effective prosecution based upon the broader of two reasonable constructions of newly enacted or previously unapplied statutes, even though a neighboring jurisdiction had been applying the broader construction of its identically worded provision for years.

Respondent seems to argue instead that because some jurisdictions have taken a narrow view of "crime against nature" and some a more broad interpretation, it could not be determined which approach Tennessee would take, making it therefore impossible for him to know if § 39-707 covered forced cunnilingus. But even assuming the correctness of such an argument if there were no indication of which interpretation Tennessee might adopt, it is not available here. Respondent is simply mistaken in his view of Tennessee law. As early as 1955 Tennessee had expressly rejected a claim that "crime against nature" did not cover fellatio, repudiating those jurisdictions which had taken a "narrow restrictive definition of the offense." *Fisher v. State,* 197 Tenn. 594, 277 S.W.2d 340. And four years later the Tennessee Supreme Court reiterated its view of the coverage intended by § 39-707. Emphasizing that the Tennessee statute's proscription encompasses the broad meaning, the court quoted from a Maine decision it had earlier cited with approval to the effect that " 'the prohibition brings all unnatural copulation with mankind or a beast, including sodomy, within its scope.' " *Sherrill v. State,* 204 Tenn. 427, 429, 321 S.W.2d 811, 812 (1959), quoting from *State v. Cyr,* 135 Me. 513, 198 A. 743 (1938). And the Maine statute, which the Tennessee court had at that point twice equated with its own, had been applied to cunnilingus before either Tennessee deci-

sion. *State v. Townsend,* 145 Me. 384, 71 A.2d 517 (1950). Thus, we think the Tennessee Supreme Court had given sufficiently clear notice that § 39-707 would receive the broader of two plausible interpretations, and would be applied to acts such as those committed here when such a case arose.

This also serves to distinguish this case from *Bouie v. City of Columbia,* 378 U.S. 347, 84 S.Ct. 1697, 12 L.Ed.2d 894 (1964), a decision the Court of Appeals thought controlling. In *Bouie,* the Court held that an unforeseeable judicial enlargement of a criminal statute narrow and precise on its face violated the Due Process Clause. It pointed out that such a process may lull "the potential defendant into a false sense of security, giving him no reason even to suspect that conduct clearly outside the scope of the statute as written will be retroactively brought within it by an act of judicial construction." But as we have noted, respondent can make no claim that § 39-707 afforded no notice that his conduct might be within its scope. Other jurisdictions had already reasonably construed identical statutory language to apply to such acts. And given the Tennessee court's clear pronouncements that its statute was intended to effect broad coverage, there was nothing to indicate, clearly or otherwise, that respondent's acts were outside the scope of § 39-707. There is no possibility of retroactive lawmaking here. Accordingly, the petition for certiorari and respondent's motion to proceed *in forma pauperis* are granted, and the judgment of the Court of Appeals is reversed.

Judgment of Court of Appeals reversed.

So ordered.

MR. JUSTICE BRENNAN, with whom MR. JUSTICE MARSHALL concurs, dissenting.

I dissent from the Court's summary reversal. The offense of "crimes against nature" at common law was narrowly limited to copulation *per anum.* American jurisdictions, however, expanded the term—some broadly and some narrowly—to include other sexual "aberrations." Of particular significance for this case, as the Court of Appeals accurately stated, "courts have differed widely in construing the reach of 'crimes against nature' to cunnilingus."

The Court holds, however, that because "other jurisdictions had already reasonably construed identical statutory language to apply to [cunnilingus] * * * given the Tennessee court's clear pronouncements that its statute was intended to effect broad coverage, there was nothing to indicate, clearly or otherwise, that respondent's acts were outside the scope of § 39–707." In other words the traditional test of vagueness—whether the statute gives fair warning that one's conduct is criminal—is supplanted by a test whether there is anything in the statute "to indicate, clearly or otherwise, that respondent's acts were outside the scope of" the statute. This stands the test of unconstitutional vagueness on its head. And this startling change in vagueness law is accompanied by the equally startling holding that, although the Tennessee courts had not previously construed "crimes against nature" to include cunnilingus, respondent can not be heard to claim that § 39–707, therefore afforded no notice that his conduct fell within its scope, because he was on notice that Tennessee courts favored a broad reach of "crimes against nature" and other state courts favoring a broad reach had construed their state statutes to include cunnilingus.

Yet these extraordinary distortions of the principle that the Due Process Clause prohibits the States from holding an individual criminally responsible for conduct when the statute did not give fair warning that the conduct was criminal, are perpetrated without plenary review affording the parties an opportunity to brief and argue the issues orally. It is difficult to recall a more patent instance of judicial irresponsibility. For without plenary review the Court announces today, contrary to our prior decisions, that even when the statute he is charged with violating fails of itself to give fair warning, one acts at his peril if the state court has indicated a tendency to construe the pertinent statute broadly, and some other state court of like persuasion has construed its state statute to embrace the conduct made the subject of the charge. I simply cannot comprehend how the fact that one state court has judicially construed its otherwise vague criminal statute to include particular conduct can, without explicit adoption of that state court's construction by the courts of the charging State, render an uninterpreted statute of the latter State also sufficiently concrete to withstand a charge of unconstitutional vagueness. But apart from the merits of the proposition, surely the citizens of this country are entitled to plenary review of its soundness before being required to attempt to conform their conduct to this drastically new standard. Today's holding surely flies in the face of the line of our recent decisions that have struck down statutes as vague and overbroad, although other state courts had previously construed their like statutes to withstand challenges of vagueness and overbreadth.

Nor will the Court's assertions that the Tennessee courts had in any event in effect construed the Tennessee statute to include cunnilingus withstand analysis. The Court relies on a 1955 Tennessee decision that had held that "crimes against nature" include fellatio, the Tennessee court rejecting the contention that the statute was limited to the common-law copulation *per anum* scope of the phrase. The Tennessee court in that opinion cited a Maine case, decided in 1938, *State v. Cyr,* where the Maine court had applied a "crimes against nature" statute to fellatio. But the Tennessee court did not also cite a 1950

Maine decision, *State v. Townsend,* 145 Me. 384, 71 A.2d 517 (1950), that applied Maine's "crimes against nature" statute to cunnilingus. *Fisher v. State,* 197 Tenn. 594, 277 S.W.2d 340 (1955). Four years later, in 1959, in another fellatio case, the Tennessee court again made no mention of *Townsend,* although quoting from *Cyr's* holding that the Maine statute applies to "all unnatural copulation with mankind or a beast, including sodomy." *Sherrill v. State,* 204 Tenn. 427, 321 S.W.2d 811, 812 (1959). Despite this significant failure of the Tennessee court to cite *Townsend,* and solely on the strength of the Tennessee court's general "equating" of the Maine statute with the Tennessee statute, this Court holds today that respondent had sufficient notice that the Tennessee statute would receive a "broad" interpretation that would embrace cunnilingus.

This 1974 attempt to bootstrap 1950 Maine law for the first time into the Tennessee statute must obviously fail if the principle of fair warning is to have any meaning. When the Maine court in 1938 applied its statute broadly to all "unnatural copulation," nothing said by the Maine court suggested that that phrase reached cunnilingus. The common-law "crimes against nature," limited to copulation *per anum,* required penetration as an essential element. In holding that a "broad" reading of that phrase should encompass all unnatural copulation including fellatio— copulation *per os*—Maine could not reasonably be understood as including cunnilingus in that category. Other jurisdictions, though on their States' particular statutory language, have drawn that distinction. Thus, when the Tennessee court in 1955 adopted the language of Maine's 1938 *Cyr* case, a Tennessee citizen had at most notice of developments in Maine law through 1938. That Maine subsequently in 1950 applied its statute to cunnilingus is irrelevant, for such subsequent developments were not "adopted" by the Tennessee

court until the case before us. Indeed, the Tennessee court's failure in its 1955 *Fisher* opinion to cite *Townsend,* Maine's 1950 cunnilingus decision, although citing *Cyr,* Maine's 1938 fellatio decision, more arguably was notice that the Tennessee courts considered fellatio but not cunnilingus as within the nebulous reach of the Tennessee statute.

Moreover, I seriously question the Court's assumption that the "broad interpretation" of the phrase "crimes against nature" is not unconstitutionally vague. The Court's assumption rests upon two supposed precedents, (1) this Court's dismissal for want of a substantial federal question of the appeal in *Crawford v. Missouri,* 409 U.S. 811, 93 S.Ct. 176, 34 L.Ed.2d 66 (1972), and (2) the Court's *per curiam* opinion in *Wainwright v. Stone,* 414 U.S. 21, 94 S.Ct. 190, 38 L.Ed.2d 179 (1973). That reliance is plainly misplaced.

In *Crawford,* the appellant had been convicted of coercing a mentally retarded individual to perform fellatio on appellant. The Supreme Court of Missouri did not, as the Court implies, for the first time in that case adopt a "broad" construction of its statute and apply that construction in appellant's case. Rather, the Supreme Court of Missouri first noted that the original statute, probably reaching only common-law "crimes against nature," had been legislatively amended in express terms to expand the offense to conduct committed "with the sexual organs or with the mouth," thereby "enlarg[ing] the common law definition of the crime * * *." *State v. Crawford,* 478 S.W.2d 314, 317 (Mo.1972). Moreover, the court, observing that a "court's construction of statutory language becomes a part of the statute ' "as if it had been so amended by the legislature," ' ", stated that in the 60 years since that amendment, the Missouri courts had "adjudicated" that the statute embraced "bestiality, buggery, fellatio

* * * and cunnilingus," and that "[a]t least five [Missouri] cases have specifically held that the act charged [against appellant] is within the statute." In light of that prior judicial and legislative construction of the statutory phrase, and its specific prior application to acts identical to the appellant's, the dismissal in *Crawford* simply cannot be treated as holding that the phrase "crimes against nature" is not in itself vague.

Wainwright v. Stone, as MR. JUSTICE STEWART correctly observes, also involved a statute already construed to cover the conduct there in question. Indeed, it was for that very reason that we held that the "judgment of federal courts as to the vagueness or not of a state statute must be made in the light of prior state constructions of the statute." The reversal of the Court of Appeals' holding finding the statute unconstitutional was explicitly based on the fact that the state statute had previously been applied to identical conduct, which decisions "require[d] reversal" in *Wainwright* since they put the particular conduct expressly within the statute.

No spectre of increasing caseload can possibly justify today's summary disposition of this case. The principle that due process requires that criminal statutes give sufficient warning to enable men to conform their conduct to avoid that which is forbidden is one of the great bulwarks of our scheme of constitutional liberty. The Court's erosion today of that great principle without even plenary review reaches a dangerous level of judicial irresponsibility. I would have denied the petition for certiorari, but now that the writ has been granted would affirm the judgment of the Court of Appeals or at least set the case for oral argument.

MR. JUSTICE STEWART, with whom MR. JUSTICE MARSHALL concurs, dissenting.

I would have denied the petition for certiorari in this case, but, now that the writ has been granted, I would affirm the judgment of the Court of Appeals. * * *

As the Court of Appeals pointed out, the defendant in this case could, and probably should, be prosecuted for aggravated assault and battery. But I think the Court of Appeals was correct in holding that the Tennessee statute under which the defendant was in fact prosecuted was unconstitutionally vague as here applied.

Notes and Questions

1. Did Locke *really* receive the warning to which he was entitled? Would the case have come out the same way if the sodomy had been consensual? Consider the following.

2. Justice Holmes, in *McBoyle v. United States,* 283 U.S. 25, 51 S.Ct. 340, 75 L.Ed. 816 (1931): "Although it is not likely that a criminal will carefully consider the text of the law before he murders or steals, it is reasonable that a fair warning should be given to the world in language that the common world will understand, of what the law intends to do if a certain line is passed. To make the warning fair, so far as possible the line should be clear."

3. Note, 62 Harv.L.Rev. 77, 80 (1948): "In general, it would seem fair to charge the individual with such knowledge of a statute's meaning and application as he could obtain through competent legal advice, provided that the statute gives him enough warning that he ought reasonably to see the need of obtaining such advice."

4. Justice Holmes, in *Nash v. United States,* 229 U.S. 373, 33 S.Ct. 780, 57 L.Ed. 1232 (1913): "[T]he law is full of instances where a man's fate depends on his estimating rightly, that is, as the jury subsequently estimates it, some matter of degree. If his judgment is wrong, not only may he incur a fine or a short imprisonment, as here; he may incur the penalty of death. 'An act causing death may be

murder, manslaughter, or misadventure, according to the degree of danger attending it' by common experience in the circumstances known to the actor. 'The very meaning of the fiction of implied malice in such cases at common law was, that a man might have to answer with his life for consequences which he neither intended nor foresaw.' 'The criterion in such cases is to examine whether common social duty would, under the circumstances, have suggested a more circumspect conduct.' "

5. Justice Frankfurter, dissenting in *Winters v. New York,* 333 U.S. 507, 68 S.Ct. 665, 92 L.Ed. 840 (1948): "There is no such thing as 'indefiniteness' in the abstract, by which the sufficiency of the requirement expressed by the term may be ascertained. The requirement is fair notice that conduct may entail punishment. But whether notice is or is not 'fair' depends upon the subject matter to which it relates. Unlike the abstract stuff of mathematics, or the quantitatively ascertainable elements of much of natural science, legislation is greatly concerned with the multiform psychological complexities of individual and social conduct. Accordingly, the demands upon legislation, and its responses, are variable and multiform. [It is thus necessary to ask, in the particular case, such questions as:] How easy is it to be explicitly particular?"

6. Kelman, *Interpretive Construction in the Substantive Criminal Law,* 33 Stan.L. Rev. 591, 662 (1981): "Vagueness doctrine is *predominantly* used when the conduct that is *ambiguously* covered by the statute, conduct that the court fears will be deterred because citizens are unsure whether or not it falls within the ambit of the statute, is either affirmatively constitutionally protected or at least desirable. When this 'nearby' conduct is unprotected or affirmatively undesirable in the judge's

eyes, courts are less likely to overturn. Naturally, the court's interpretation of the breadth of conduct that may be deterred is quite flexible. For instance, does a facially vague statute outlawing vexatious phone-calling chill protected 'speech' or less protected 'telephoning to strangers'?"

7. Justice Douglas, in *Papachristou v. City of Jacksonville,* 405 U.S. 156, 92 S.Ct. 839, 31 L.Ed.2d 110 (1972): "Another aspect of the ordinance's vagueness appears when we focus, not on the lack of notice given a potential offender, but on the effect of the unfettered discretion it places in the hands of the Jacksonville police. * * *

"Those generally implicated by the imprecise terms of the ordinance—poor people, nonconformists, dissenters, idlers—may be required to comport themselves according to the life style deemed appropriate by the Jacksonville police and the courts. Where, as here, there are no standards governing the exercise of the discretion granted by the ordinance, the scheme permits and encourages an arbitrary and discriminatory enforcement of the law. It furnishes a convenient tool for 'harsh and discriminatory enforcement by local prosecuting officials, against particular groups deemed to merit their displeasure.' "

8. Note, 109 U.Pa.L.Rev. 67, 73–75 (1960): "[W]here the opinions do attempt to expound some policy bases for the doctrine, the holdings often fail to bear these bases out: it is common ground, for example, to explain the antivagueness prescription as a constitutional mandate that 'no one may be required at peril of life, liberty or property to speculate as to the meaning of penal statutes. All are entitled to be informed as to what the State commands or forbids.' [33] Yet the Supreme Court, in passing on these penal statutes, has invariably allowed them the benefit of

33. *Lanzetta v. New Jersey,* 306 U.S. 451, 453 (1939).

whatever clarifying gloss state courts may have added in the course of litigation of the very case at bar. This would indicate, inconsistently with the 'warning' rationale, that 'the defendant, at the time he acted, was chargeable with knowledge of the scope of subsequent interpretation.' [35] Nor is this practice of the Court—'for the purpose of deciding the constitutional questions * * * [taking] the statute as though it read precisely as the highest court of the State has interpreted it' [36]— quite compatible with another claimed foundation for the vagueness doctrine: that 'it would certainly be dangerous if the legislature could set a net large enough to catch all possible offenders and leave it to the courts to step inside and say who could be rightfully detained and who should be set at large.' [37] These several circumstances indicate that vagueness alone, although helpful and important, does not provide a full and rational explanation of the case development in which it appears so prominently. Together with certain further indications which may be derived from the history of the doctrine and from the settings in which it is invoked successfully, they rather compel the conclusion that in the great majority of instances the

35. *Winters v. New York,* 333 U.S. 507, 514–15 (1948) (dictum). As *Winters* and *Kunz v. New York,* 340 U.S. 290 (1951), demonstrate, *post hoc* state construction may be heavily relied on by the Court in striking down, as well as in sustaining, a challenged statute. Such reliance for purposes of voiding is of course not, as is saving reliance, inconsistent with the fair warning rationale.

36. *Minnesota ex rel. Pearson v. Probate Court,* 309 U.S. 270, 273 (1940).

37. *United States v. Reese,* 92 U.S. 214, 221 (1875).

1. Ga.Code Ann. § 16–6–2 (1984) provides, in pertinent part, as follows:

"(a) A person commits the offense of sodomy when he performs or submits to any sexual act involving the sex organs of one person and the mouth or anus of another. * * *

"(b) A person convicted of the offense of sodomy shall be punished by imprisonment for not less than one nor more than 20 years. . . . ."

concept of vagueness is an available instrument in the service of other more determinative judicially felt needs and pressures."

BOWERS v. HARDWICK

Supreme Court of the United States, 1986.
__ U.S. __, 106 S.Ct. 2841, 92 L.Ed.2d 140.

JUSTICE WHITE delivered the opinion of the Court.

In August 1982, respondent was charged with violating the Georgia statute criminalizing sodomy [1] by committing that act with another adult male in the bedroom of respondent's home. After a preliminary hearing, the District Attorney decided not to present the matter to the grand jury unless further evidence developed.

Respondent then brought suit in the Federal District Court, challenging the constitutionality of the statute insofar as it criminalized consensual sodomy.[2] He asserted that he was a practicing homosexual, that the Georgia sodomy statute, as administered by the defendants, placed him in imminent danger of arrest, and that the statute for several reasons violates the Federal Constitution. The District Court

2. John and Mary Doe were also plaintiffs in the action. They alleged that they wished to engage in sexual activity proscribed by § 16–6–2 in the privacy of their home, and that they had been "chilled and deterred" from engaging in such activity by both the existence of the statute and Hardwick's arrest. The District Court held, however, that because they had neither sustained, nor were in immediate danger of sustaining, any direct injury from the enforcement of the statute, they did not have proper standing to maintain the action. The Court of Appeals affirmed the District Court's judgment dismissing the Does' claim for lack of standing, and the Does do not challenge that holding in this Court.

The only claim properly before the Court, therefore, is Hardwick's challenge to the Georgia statute as applied to consensual homosexual sodomy. We express no opinion on the constitutionality of the Georgia statute as applied to other acts of sodomy.

granted the defendants' motion to dismiss for failure to state a claim.

A divided panel of the Court of Appeals for the Eleventh Circuit reversed. * * * Relying on our decisions in *Griswold v. Connecticut*, 381 U.S. 479, 85 S.Ct. 1678, 14 L.Ed.2d 510 (1965), *Eisenstadt v. Baird*, 405 U.S. 438, 92 S.Ct. 1029, 31 L.Ed.2d 349 (1972), *Stanley v. Georgia*, 394 U.S. 557, 89 S.Ct. 1243, 22 L.Ed.2d 542 (1969), and *Roe v. Wade*, 410 U.S. 113, 93 S.Ct. 705, 35 L.Ed.2d 147 (1973), the court went on to hold that the Georgia statute violated respondent's fundamental rights because his homosexual activity is a private and intimate association that is beyond the reach of state regulation by reason of the Ninth Amendment and the Due Process Clause of the Fourteenth Amendment. The case was remanded for trial, at which, to prevail, the State would have to prove that the statute is supported by a compelling interest and is the most narrowly drawn means of achieving that end.

Because other Courts of Appeals have arrived at judgments contrary to that of the Eleventh Circuit in this case, we granted the State's petition for certiorari questioning the holding that its sodomy statute violates the fundamental rights of homosexuals. We agree with the State that the Court of Appeals erred, and hence reverse its judgment.

This case does not require a judgment on whether laws against sodomy between consenting adults in general, or between homosexuals in particular, are wise or desirable. It raises no question about the right or propriety of state legislative decisions to repeal their laws that criminalize homosexual sodomy, or of state court decisions invalidating those laws on state constitutional grounds. The issue presented is whether the Federal Constitution confers a fundamental right upon homosexuals to engage in sodomy and hence invalidates

the laws of the many States that still make such conduct illegal and have done so for a very long time. The case also calls for some judgment about the limits of the Court's role in carrying out its constitutional mandate.

We first register our disagreement with the Court of Appeals and with respondent that the Court's prior cases have construed the Constitution to confer a right of privacy that extends to homosexual sodomy and for all intents and purposes have decided this case. The reach of this line of cases was sketched in *Carey v. Population Services International*, 431 U.S. 678, 97 S.Ct. 2010, 52 L.Ed.2d 675 (1977). *Pierce v. Society of Sisters*, 268 U.S. 510, 45 S.Ct. 571, 69 L.Ed. 1070 (1925), and *Meyer v. Nebraska*, 262 U.S. 390, 43 S.Ct. 625, 67 L.Ed. 1042 (1923), were described as dealing with child rearing and education; *Prince v. Massachusetts*, 321 U.S. 158, 64 S.Ct. 438, 88 L.Ed. 645 (1944), with family relationships; *Skinner v. Oklahoma ex rel. Williamson*, 316 U.S. 535, 62 S.Ct. 1110, 86 L.Ed. 1655 (1942), with procreation; *Loving v. Virginia*, 388 U.S. 1, 87 S.Ct. 1817, 18 L.Ed.2d 1010 (1967), with marriage; *Griswold v. Connecticut, supra*, and *Eisenstadt v. Baird, supra*, with contraception; and *Roe v. Wade, supra*, with abortion. The latter three cases were interpreted as construing the Due Process Clause of the Fourteenth Amendment to confer a fundamental individual right to decide whether or not to beget or bear a child. *Carey v. Population Services International, supra*.

Accepting the decisions in these cases and the above description of them, we think it evident that none of the rights announced in those cases bears any resemblance to the claimed constitutional right of homosexuals to engage in acts of sodomy that is asserted in this case. No connection between family, marriage, or procreation on the one hand and homosexual activity on the other has been demonstrated, either by the Court of Appeals or by respondent. Moreover, any claim that these cases nevertheless stand for the proposition that any kind of private sexual conduct between consenting adults is constitutionally insulated from state proscription is unsupportable. Indeed, the Court's opinion in *Carey* twice asserted that the privacy right, which the *Griswold* line of cases found to be one of the protections provided by the Due Process Clause, did not reach so far.

Precedent aside, however, respondent would have us announce, as the Court of Appeals did, a fundamental right to engage in homosexual sodomy. This we are quite unwilling to do. It is true that despite the language of the Due Process Clauses of the Fifth and Fourteenth Amendments, which appears to focus only on the processes by which life, liberty, or property is taken, the cases are legion in which those Clauses have been interpreted to have substantive content, subsuming rights that to a great extent are immune from federal or state regulation or proscription. Among such cases are those recognizing rights that have little or no textual support in the constitutional language. *Meyer, Prince,* and *Pierce* fall in this category, as do the privacy cases from *Griswold* to *Carey.*

Striving to assure itself and the public that announcing rights not readily identifiable in the Constitution's text involves much more than the imposition of the Justices' own choice of values on the States and the Federal Government, the Court has sought to identify the nature of the rights qualifying for heightened judicial protection. In *Palko v. Connecticut,* 302 U.S. 319, 326, 58 S.Ct. 149, 152, 82 L.Ed. 288 (1937), it was said that this category includes those fundamental liberties that are "implicit in the concept of ordered liberty," such that "neither liberty nor justice would exist if [they] were sacrificed." A different description of fundamental liberties appeared in *Moore v. East*

Cleveland, 431 U.S. 494, 97 S.Ct. 1932, 52 L.Ed.2d 531 (1977) (opinion of POWELL, J.), where they are characterized as those liberties that are "deeply rooted in this Nation's history and tradition."

It is obvious to us that neither of these formulations would extend a fundamental right to homosexuals to engage in acts of consensual sodomy. Proscriptions against that conduct have ancient roots. Sodomy was a criminal offense at common law and was forbidden by the laws of the original thirteen States when they ratified the Bill of Rights. In 1868, when the Fourteenth Amendment was ratified, all but 5 of the 37 States in the Union had criminal sodomy laws. In fact, until 1961, all 50 States outlawed sodomy, and today, 24 States and the District of Columbia continue to provide criminal penalties for sodomy performed in private and between consenting adults. Against this background, to claim that a right to engage in such conduct is "deeply rooted in this Nation's history and tradition" or "implicit in the concept of ordered liberty" is, at best, facetious.

Nor are we inclined to take a more expansive view of our authority to discover new fundamental rights imbedded in the Due Process Clause. The Court is most vulnerable and comes nearest to illegitimacy when it deals with judge-made constitutional law having little or no cognizable roots in the language or design of the Constitution. That this is so was painfully demonstrated by the face-off between the Executive and the Court in the 1930's, which resulted in the repudiation of much of the substantive gloss that the Court had placed on the Due Process Clause of the Fifth and Fourteenth Amendments. There should be, therefore, great resistance to expand the substantive reach of those Clauses, particularly if it requires redefining the category of rights deemed to be fundamental. Otherwise, the Judiciary necessarily takes to itself further authority to govern the country without express constitutional authority. The claimed right pressed on us today falls far short of overcoming this resistance.

Respondent, however, asserts that the result should be different where the homosexual conduct occurs in the privacy of the home. He relies on *Stanley v. Georgia,* where the Court held that the First Amendment prevents conviction for possessing and reading obscene material in the privacy of his home: "If the First Amendment means anything, it means that a State has no business telling a man, sitting alone in his house, what books he may read or what films he may watch."

Stanley did protect conduct that would not have been protected outside the home, and it partially prevented the enforcement of state obscenity laws; but the decision was firmly grounded in the First Amendment. The right pressed upon us here has no similar support in the text of the Constitution, and it does not qualify for recognition under the prevailing principles for construing the Fourteenth Amendment. Its limits are also difficult to discern. Plainly enough, otherwise illegal conduct is not always immunized whenever it occurs in the home. Victimless crimes, such as the possession and use of illegal drugs do not escape the law where they are committed at home. *Stanley* itself recognized that its holding offered no protection for the possession in the home of drugs, firearms, or stolen goods. And if respondent's submission is limited to the voluntary sexual conduct between consenting adults, it would be difficult, except by fiat, to limit the claimed right to homosexual conduct while leaving exposed to prosecution adultery, incest, and other sexual crimes even though they are committed in the home. We are unwilling to start down that road.

8. Respondent does not defend the judgment below based on the Ninth Amendment, the Equal Protection Clause or the Eighth Amendment.

Even if the conduct at issue here is not a fundamental right, respondent asserts that there must be a rational basis for the law and that there is none in this case other than the presumed belief of a majority of the electorate in Georgia that homosexual sodomy is immoral and unacceptable. This is said to be an inadequate rationale to support the law. The law, however, is constantly based on notions of morality, and if all laws representing essentially moral choices are to be invalidated under the Due Process Clause, the courts will be very busy indeed. Even respondent makes no such claim, but insists that majority sentiments about the morality of homosexuality should be declared inadequate. We do not agree, and are unpersuaded that the sodomy laws of some 25 States should be invalidated on this basis.[8]

Accordingly, the judgment of the Court of Appeals is

Reversed.

CHIEF JUSTICE BURGER, concurring.

I join the Court's opinion, but I write separately to underscore my view that in constitutional terms there is no such thing as a fundamental right to commit homosexual sodomy.

To hold that the act of homosexual sodomy is somehow protected as a fundamental right would be to cast aside millennia of moral teaching.

This is essentially not a question of personal "preferences" but rather of the legislative authority of the State. I find nothing in the Constitution depriving a State of the power to enact the statute challenged here.

JUSTICE POWELL, concurring.

I join the opinion of the Court. I agree with the Court that there is no fundamental right—*i.e.,* no substantive right under the Due Process Clause—such as that claimed by respondent, and found to exist by the Court of Appeals. This is not to suggest, however, that respondent may not be protected by the Eighth Amendment of the Constitution. The Georgia statute at issue in this case authorizes a court to imprison a person for up to 20 years for a single private, consensual act of sodomy. In my view, a prison sentence for such conduct—certainly a sentence of long duration—would create a serious Eighth Amendment issue. Under the Georgia statute a single act of sodomy, even in the private setting of a home, is a felony comparable in terms of the possible sentence imposed to serious felonies such as aggravated battery, first degree arson, and robbery.

In this case, however, respondent has not been tried, much less convicted and sentenced.[2] Moreover, respondent has not raised the Eighth Amendment issue below. For these reasons this constitutional argument is not before us.

JUSTICE BLACKMUN, with whom JUSTICE BRENNAN, JUSTICE MARSHALL, and JUSTICE STEVENS join, dissenting.

This case is no more about "a fundamental right to engage in homosexual sodomy," as the Court purports to declare, than *Stanley v. Georgia* was about a fundamental right to watch obscene movies, or *Katz v. United States,* 389 U.S. 347, 88 S.Ct. 507, 19 L.Ed.2d 576 (1967), was about a fundamental right to place interstate bets from a telephone booth. Rather, this case is about "the most comprehensive of rights and the right most valued by civilized men," namely, "the right to be

let alone." *Olmstead v. United States,* 277 U.S. 438, 478, 48 S.Ct. 564, 572, 72 L.Ed. 944 (1928) (Brandeis, J., dissenting).

The statute at issue denies individuals the right to decide for themselves whether to engage in particular forms of private, consensual sexual activity. The Court concludes that § 16–6–2 is valid essentially because "the laws of * * * many States * * * still make such conduct illegal and have done so for a very long time." But the fact that the moral judgments expressed by statutes like § 16–6–2 may be "natural and familiar * * * ought not to conclude our judgment upon the question whether statutes embodying them conflict with the Constitution of the United States." *Roe v. Wade.* Like Justice Holmes, I believe that "[i]t is revolting to have no better reason for a rule of law than that so it was laid down in the time of Henry IV. It is still more revolting if the grounds upon which it was laid down have vanished long since, and the rule simply persists from blind imitation of the past." I believe we must analyze respondent's claim in the light of the values that underlie the constitutional right to privacy. If that right means anything, it means that, before Georgia can prosecute its citizens for making choices about the most intimate aspects of their lives, it must do more than assert that the choice they have made is an "'abominable crime not fit to be named among Christians.'"

First, the Court's almost obsessive focus on homosexual activity is particularly hard to justify in light of the broad language Georgia has used. Unlike the Court, the

---

2. It was conceded at oral argument that, prior to the complaint against respondent Hardwick, there had been no reported decision involving prosecution for private homosexual sodomy under this statute for several decades. Moreover, the State has declined to present the criminal charge against Hardwick to a grand jury, and this is a suit for declaratory judgment brought by respondents challenging the validity of the stat-

ute. The history of nonenforcement suggests the moribund character today of laws criminalizing this type of private, consensual conduct. Some 26 states have repealed similar statutes. But the constitutional validity of the Georgia statute was put in issue by respondents, and for the reasons stated by the Court, I cannot say that conduct condemned for hundreds of years has now become a fundamental right.

Georgia Legislature has not proceeded on the assumption that homosexuals are so different from other citizens that their lives may be controlled in a way that would not be tolerated if it limited the choices of those other citizens. Rather, Georgia has provided that "[a] person commits the offense of sodomy when he performs or submits to any sexual act involving the sex organs of one person and the mouth or anus of another." Ga.Code Ann. § 16–6–2(a). The sex or status of the persons who engage in the act is irrelevant as a matter of state law. In fact, to the extent I can discern a legislative purpose for Georgia's 1968 enactment of § 16–6–2, that purpose seems to have been to broaden the coverage of the law to reach heterosexual as well as homosexual activity. I therefore see no basis for the Court's decision to treat this case as an "as applied" challenge to § 16–6–2, or for Georgia's attempt, both in its brief and at oral argument, to defend § 16–6–2 solely on the grounds that it prohibits homosexual activity. Michael Hardwick's standing may rest in significant part on Georgia's apparent willingness to enforce against homosexuals a law it seems not to have any desire to enforce against heterosexuals. But his claim that § 16–6–2 involves an unconstitutional intrusion into his privacy and his right of intimate association does not depend in any way on his sexual orientation.

Second, I disagree with the Court's refusal to consider whether § 16–6–2 runs afoul of the Eighth or Ninth Amendments or the Equal Protection Clause of the Fourteenth Amendment. Respondent's complaint expressly invoked the Ninth Amendment, and he relied heavily before this Court on *Griswold v. Connecticut,* which identifies that Amendment as one of the specific constitutional provisions giving "life and substance" to our understanding of privacy. More importantly, the procedural posture of the case requires that we affirm the Court of Appeals' judgment if there is *any* ground on which respondent may be entitled to relief. This case is before us on petitioner's motion to dismiss for failure to state a claim. It is a well settled principle of law that "a complaint should not be dismissed merely because a plaintiff's allegations do not support the particular legal theory he advances, for the court is under a duty to examine the complaint to determine if the allegations provide for relief on any possible theory." Thus, even if respondent did not advance claims based on the Eighth or Ninth Amendments, or on the Equal Protection Clause, his complaint should not be dismissed if any of those provisions could entitle him to relief. I need not reach either the Eighth Amendment or the Equal Protection Clause issues because I believe that Hardwick has stated a cognizable claim that § 16–6–2 interferes with constitutionally protected interests in privacy and freedom of intimate association. But neither the Eighth Amendment nor the Equal Protection Clause is so clearly irrelevant that a claim resting on either provision should be peremptorily dismissed.[2]

2. In *Robinson v. California,* the Court held that the Eighth Amendment barred convicting a defendant due to his "status" as a narcotics addict, since that condition was "apparently an illness which may be contracted innocently or involuntarily." In *Powell v. Texas,* where the Court refused to extend *Robinson* to punishment of public drunkenness by a chronic alcoholic, one of the factors relied on by JUSTICE MARSHALL, in writing the plurality opinion, was that Texas had not "attempted to regulate appellant's behavior in the privacy of his own home." JUSTICE WHITE wrote separately:

"Analysis of this difficult case is not advanced by preoccupation with the label 'condition.' In *Robinson* the Court dealt with 'a statute which makes the "status" of narcotic addiction a criminal offense. * * *' By precluding criminal conviction for such a 'status' the Court was dealing with a condition brought about by acts remote in time from the application of the criminal sanctions contemplated, a condition which was relatively permanent in duration, and a condition of great magnitude and significance in terms of human behavior and values * * *. If it were necessary to distinguish between 'acts' and 'con-

The Court's cramped reading of the issue before it makes for a short opinion, but it does little to make for a persuasive one.

"Our cases long have recognized that the Constitution embodies a promise that a certain private sphere of individual liberty will be kept largely beyond the reach of government." In construing the right to privacy, the Court has proceeded along two somewhat distinct, albeit complementary, lines. First, it has recognized a privacy interest with reference to certain *decisions* that are properly for the individual to make. Second, it has recognized a privacy interest with reference to certain *places* without regard for the particular activities in which the individuals who occupy them are engaged. The case before us implicates both the decisional and the spatial aspects of the right to privacy.

The Court concludes today that none of our prior cases dealing with various decisions that individuals are entitled to make free of governmental interference "bears any resemblance to the claimed constitutional right of homosexuals to engage in acts of sodomy that is asserted in this case." While it is true that these cases may be characterized by their connection to protection of the family, the Court's conclusion that they extend no further

than this boundary ignores the warning in *Moore v. East Cleveland,* 431 U.S. 494, 501, 97 S.Ct. 1932, 1936, 52 L.Ed.2d 531 (1977) (plurality opinion), against "clos[ing] our eyes to the basic reasons why certain rights associated with the family have been accorded shelter under the Fourteenth Amendment's Due Process Clause." We protect those rights not because they contribute, in some direct and material way, to the general public welfare, but because they form so central a part of an individual's life. * * *

Only the most willful blindness could obscure the fact that sexual intimacy is "a sensitive, key relationship of human existence, central to family life, community welfare, and the development of human personality." The fact that individuals define themselves in a significant way through their intimate sexual relationships with others suggests, in a Nation as diverse as ours, that there may be many "right" ways of conducting those relationships, and that much of the richness of a relationship will come from the freedom an individual has to *choose* the form and nature of these intensely personal bonds.

* * *

The behavior for which Hardwick faces prosecution occurred in his own home, a

---

ditions' for purposes of the Eighth Amendment, I would adhere to the concept of 'condition' implicit in the opinion in *Robinson* * * *. The proper subject of inquiry is whether volitional acts brought about the 'condition' and whether those acts are sufficiently proximate to the 'condition' for it to be permissible to impose penal sanctions on the 'condition.' "

Despite historical views of homosexuality, it is no longer viewed by mental health professionals as a "disease" or disorder. But, obviously, neither is it simply a matter of deliberate personal election. Homosexual orientation may well form part of the very fiber of an individual's personality. Consequently, under JUSTICE WHITE's analysis in *Powell*, the Eighth Amendment may pose a constitutional barrier to sending an individual to prison for acting on that attraction regardless of the circumstances. An individual's ability to make constitutionally protected "decisions concerning sexual relations," is

rendered empty indeed if he or she is given no real choice but a life without any physical intimacy.

With respect to the Equal Protection Clause's applicability to § 16–6–2, I note that Georgia's exclusive stress before this Court on its interest in prosecuting homosexual activity despite the gender-neutral terms of the statute may raise serious questions of discriminatory enforcement, questions that cannot be disposed of before this Court on a motion to dismiss. The legislature having decided that the sex of the participants is irrelevant to the legality of the acts, I do not see why the State can defend § 16–6–2 on the ground that individuals singled out for prosecution are of the same sex as their partners. Thus, under the circumstances of this case, a claim under the Equal Protection Clause may well be available without having to reach the more controversial question whether homosexuals are a suspect class.

place to which the Fourth Amendment attaches special significance. The Court's treatment of this aspect of the case is symptomatic of its overall refusal to consider the broad principles that have informed our treatment of privacy in specific cases.

* * *

The Court's interpretation of the pivotal case of *Stanley v. Georgia* is entirely unconvincing. *Stanley* held that Georgia's undoubted power to punish the public distribution of constitutionally unprotected, obscene material did not permit the State to punish the private possession of such material. According to the majority here, *Stanley* relied entirely on the First Amendment, and thus, it is claimed, sheds no light on cases not involving printed materials. But that is not what *Stanley* said. Rather, the *Stanley* Court anchored its holding in the Fourth Amendment's special protection for the individual in his home. * * *

The central place that *Stanley* gives Justice Brandeis' dissent in *Olmstead,* a case raising *no* First Amendment claim, shows that *Stanley* rested as much on the Court's understanding of the Fourth Amendment as it did on the First. Indeed, in *Paris Adult Theatre I v. Slaton,* 413 U.S. 49, 93 S.Ct. 2628, 37 L.Ed.2d 446 (1973), the Court suggested that reliance on the Fourth Amendment not only supported the Court's outcome in *Stanley* but actually was *necessary* to it: "If obscene material unprotected by the First Amendment in itself carried with it a 'penumbra' of constitutionally protected privacy, this Court would not have found it necessary to decide *Stanley* on the narrow basis of the 'privacy of the home,' which was hardly more than a reaffirmation that 'a man's home is his castle.'" "The right of the people to be secure in their * * * houses," expressly guaranteed by the Fourth Amendment, is perhaps the most "textual"

of the various constitutional provisions that inform our understanding of the right to privacy, and thus I cannot agree with the Court's statement that "[t]he right pressed upon us here has no * * * support in the text of the Constitution." Indeed, the right of an individual to conduct intimate relationships in the intimacy of his or her own home seems to me to be the heart of the Constitution's protection of privacy.

The Court's failure to comprehend the magnitude of the liberty interests at stake in this case leads it to slight the question whether petitioner, on behalf of the State, has justified Georgia's infringement on these interests. I believe that neither of the two general justifications for § 16–6–2 that petitioner has advanced warrants dismissing respondent's challenge for failure to state a claim.

First, petitioner asserts that the acts made criminal by the statute may have serious adverse consequences for "the general public health and welfare," such as spreading communicable diseases or fostering other criminal activity. Inasmuch as this case was dismissed by the District Court on the pleadings, it is not surprising that the record before us is barren of any evidence to support petitioner's claim. In light of the state of the record, I see no justification for the Court's attempt to equate the private, consensual sexual activity at issue here with the "possession in the home of drugs, firearms, or stolen goods," to which *Stanley* refused to extend its protection. None of the behavior so mentioned in *Stanley* can properly be viewed as "[v]ictimless": drugs and weapons are inherently dangerous, and for property to be "stolen," someone must have been wrongfully deprived of it. Nothing in the record before the Court provides any justification for finding the activity forbidden by § 16–6–2 to be physically dangerous, either to the persons engaged in it or to others.[4]

The core of petitioner's defense of § 16–6–2, however, is that respondent and others who engage in the conduct prohibited by § 16–6–2 interfere with Georgia's exercise of the " 'right of the Nation and of the States to maintain a decent society,' " Essentially, petitioner argues, and the Court agrees, that the fact that the acts described in § 16–6–2 "for hundreds of years, if not thousands, have been uniformly condemned as immoral" is a sufficient reason to permit a State to ban them today.

I cannot agree that either the length of time a majority has held its convictions or the passions with which it defends them can withdraw legislation from this Court's scrutiny. As Justice Jackson wrote so eloquently for the Court in *West Virginia Board of Education v. Barnette,* 319 U.S. 624, 63 S.Ct. 1178, 87 L.Ed. 1628 (1943), "we apply the limitations of the Constitution with no fear that freedom to be intellectually and spiritually diverse or even contrary will disintegrate the social organization. . . . [F]reedom to differ is not limited to things that do not matter much. That would be a mere shadow of freedom. The test of its substance is the right to differ as to things that touch the heart of the existing order." It is precisely because the issue raised by this case touches the heart of what makes individuals what they are that we should be espe-

cially sensitive to the rights of those whose choices upset the majority.

The assertion that "traditional Judeo–Christian values proscribe" the conduct involved cannot provide an adequate justification for § 16–6–2. That certain, but by no means all, religious groups condemn the behavior at issue gives the State no license to impose their judgments on the entire citizenry. The legitimacy of secular legislation depends instead on whether the State can advance some justification for its law beyond its conformity to religious doctrine. Thus, far from buttressing his case, petitioner's invocation of Leviticus, Romans, St. Thomas Aquinas, and sodomy's heretical status during the Middle Ages undermines his suggestion that § 16–6–2 represents a legitimate use of secular coercive power. A State can no more punish private behavior because of religious intolerance than it can punish such behavior because of racial animus. * * *

Nor can § 16–6–2 be justified as a "morally neutral" exercise of Georgia's power to "protect the public environment." Certainly, some private behavior can affect the fabric of society as a whole. Reasonable people may differ about whether particular sexual acts are moral or immoral, but "we have ample evidence for believing that people will not abandon morality, will not think any better of murder, cruelty and dishonesty, merely because some private sexual practice which they abominate is not punished by the

---

4. Although I do not think it necessary to decide today issues that are not even remotely before us, it does seem to me that a court could find simple, analytically sound distinctions between certain private, consensual sexual conduct, on the one hand, and adultery and incest (the only two vaguely specific "sexual crimes" to which the majority points), on the other. For example, marriage, in addition to its spiritual aspects, is a civil contract that entitles the contracting parties to a variety of governmentally provided benefits. A State might define the contractual commitment necessary to become eligible for these benefits to include a commitment of fidelity and then punish individuals for breaching

that contract. Moreover, a State might conclude that adultery is likely to injure third persons, in particular, spouses and children of persons who engage in extramarital affairs. With respect to incest, a court might well agree with respondent that the nature of familial relationships renders true consent to incestuous activity sufficiently problematical that a blanket prohibition of such activity is warranted. Notably, the Court makes no effort to explain why it has chosen to group private, consensual homosexual activity with adultery and incest rather than with private, consensual heterosexual activity by unmarried persons or, indeed, with oral or anal sex within marriage.

law." Petitioner and the Court fail to see the difference between laws that protect public sensibilities and those that enforce private morality. Statutes banning public sexual activity are entirely consistent with protecting the individual's liberty interest in decisions concerning sexual relations: the same recognition that those decisions are intensely private which justifies protecting them from governmental interference can justify protecting individuals from unwilling exposure to the sexual activities of others. But the mere fact that intimate behavior may be punished when it takes place in public cannot dictate how States can regulate intimate behavior that occurs in intimate places.

This case involves no real interference with the rights of others, for the mere knowledge that other individuals do not adhere to one's value system cannot be a legally cognizable interest, let alone an interest that can justify invading the houses, hearts, and minds of citizens who choose to live their lives differently.

* * *

JUSTICE STEVENS, with whom JUSTICE BRENNAN and JUSTICE MARSHALL join, dissenting.

Like the statute that is challenged in this case, the rationale of the Court's opinion applies equally to the prohibited conduct regardless of whether the parties who engage in it are married or unmarried, or are of the same or different sexes. * * *

Because the Georgia statute expresses the traditional view that sodomy is an immoral kind of conduct regardless of the identity of the persons who engage in it, I believe that a proper analysis of its constitutionality requires consideration of two questions: First, may a State totally prohibit the described conduct by means of a

neutral law applying without exception to all persons subject to its jurisdiction? If not, may the State save the statute by announcing that it will only enforce the law against homosexuals? The two questions merit separate discussion. * * *

Society has every right to encourage its individual members to follow particular traditions in expressing affection for one another and in gratifying their personal desires. It, of course, may prohibit an individual from imposing his will on another to satisfy his own selfish interests. It also may prevent an individual from interfering with, or violating, a legally sanctioned and protected relationship, such as marriage. And it may explain the relative advantages and disadvantages of different forms of intimate expression. But when individual married couples are isolated from observation by others, the way in which they voluntarily choose to conduct their intimate relations is a matter for them—not the State—to decide.[10] The essential "liberty" that animated the development of the law in cases like *Griswold, Eisenstadt,* and *Carey* surely embraces the right to engage in nonreproductive, sexual conduct that others may consider offensive or immoral.

Paradoxical as it may seem, our prior cases thus establish that a State may not prohibit sodomy within "the sacred precincts of marital bedrooms," *Griswold,* or, indeed, between unmarried heterosexual adults. *Eisenstadt.* In all events, it is perfectly clear that the State of Georgia may not totally prohibit the conduct proscribed by § 16–6–2 of the Georgia Criminal Code.

If the Georgia statute cannot be enforced as it is written—if the conduct it seeks to prohibit is a protected form of

---

10. Indeed, the Georgia Attorney General concedes that Georgia's statute would be unconstitutional if applied to a married couple. See Tr. of Oral Arg. 8 (stating that application of the statute to a married couple "would be unconstitution-

al" because of the "right of marital privacy as identified by the Court in Griswold"). Significantly, Georgia passed the current statute three years after the Court's decision in *Griswold.*

liberty for the vast majority of Georgia's citizens—the State must assume the burden of justifying a selective application of its law. Either the persons to whom Georgia seeks to apply its statute do not have the same interest in "liberty" that others have, or there must be a reason why the State may be permitted to apply a generally applicable law to certain persons that it does not apply to others.

The first possibility is plainly unacceptable. Although the meaning of the principle that "all men are created equal" is not always clear, it surely must mean that every free citizen has the same interest in "liberty" that the members of the majority share. From the standpoint of the individual, the homosexual and the heterosexual have the same interest in deciding how he will live his own life, and, more narrowly, how he will conduct himself in his personal and voluntary associations with his companions. State intrusion into the private conduct of either is equally burdensome.

The second possibility is similarly unacceptable. A policy of selective application must be supported by a neutral and legitimate interest—something more substantial than a habitual dislike for, or ignorance about, the disfavored group. Neither the State nor the Court has identified any such interest in this case. The Court has posited as a justification for the Georgia statute "the presumed belief of a majority of the electorate in Georgia that homosexual sodomy is immoral and unacceptable."

* * *

Nor, indeed, does the Georgia prosecutor even believe that all homosexuals who violate this statute should be punished. This conclusion is evident from the fact that the respondent in this very case has formally acknowledged in his complaint and in court that he has engaged, and intends to continue to engage, in the prohibited conduct, yet the State has elected not to process criminal charges against him. As JUSTICE POWELL points out, moreover, Georgia's prohibition on private, consensual sodomy has not been enforced for decades. The record of nonenforcement, in this case and in the last several decades, belies the Attorney General's representations about the importance of the State's selective application of its generally applicable law. * * *

The Court orders the dismissal of respondent's complaint even though the State's statute prohibits all sodomy; even though that prohibition is concededly unconstitutional with respect to heterosexuals; and even though the State's *post hoc* explanations for selective application are belied by the State's own actions. At the very least, I think it clear at this early stage of the litigation that respondent has alleged a constitutional claim sufficient to withstand a motion to dismiss.[13]

I respectfully dissent.

Notes and Questions

1. *Right to privacy.* (a) Consider *The Supreme Court—Leading Cases,* 100 Harv.L. Rev. 100, 217–18 (1986): "In declining to view the right to privacy as protecting the right to make personal decisions in intimate relationships, the *Hardwick* Court also refused to declare a new fundamental right, because the claimed right lacked a historical or traditional basis. The Court's use of history and tradition, rather than

---

13. Indeed, at this stage, it appears that the statute indiscriminately authorizes a policy of selective prosecution that is neither limited to the class of homosexual persons nor embraces all persons in that class, but rather applies to those who may be arbitrarily selected by the prosecutor for reasons that are not revealed either in the record of this case or in the text of the statute. If

that is true, although the text of the statute is clear enough, its true meaning may be "so intolerably vague that evenhanded enforcement of the law is a virtual impossibility." *Marks v. United States,* 430 U.S. 188, 198, 97 S.Ct. 990, 996, 51 L.Ed.2d 260 (1977) (STEVENS, J., concurring in part and dissenting in part).

the underlying values protected by the right of privacy, to analyze Hardwick's claim is nothing less than an abdication of judicial responsibility. The Court apparently assumed that because intrusive and oppressive legislation is long-standing, it is no longer oppressive and is in fact justified. However, the long history of restrictions on homosexuals, like the long history of state-sanctioned racial discrimination before it, illustrates the need for judicial intervention, not the legitimacy of the oppression. To cite a shameful history of prejudice, and to adopt it as support for the constitutionality of Georgia's law, is to relegate constitutional analysis to preserving the status quo without regard for those who cannot vindicate their rights through the political process. As numerous observers have noted, the case for active judicial review is especially compelling when the Court is evaluating a statute penalizing a minority group with a long history of political powerlessness and social stigmatization."

(b) How would the Court have come out as to John and Mary Doe (fn. 2 in *Hardwick*) had they not lacked standing? How would the Court come out on the facts of *Lovisi v. Slayton,* 539 F.2d 349 (4th Cir.1976), where Margaret Lovisi performed fellatio upon her husband and Earl Dunn (who had answered the Lovisis' ad

in "Swinger's Life") in the Lovisis' bedroom?

(c) Note, 14 N.Y.U.Rev.L. & Soc.Chg. 973, 994 (1986): "Many state constitutions provide either explicit or court-inferred privacy guarantees, and state courts present a forum in which to pursue sodomy law reform. * * * State constitutional privacy guarantees offer an exciting and largely untapped opportunity to meet the important goal of sodomy law reform."

2. *Substantive due process.* Comment, 45 Fordham L.Rev. 553, 580–81 (1976), though noting that the Supreme Court "has found no difficulty in upholding federal and state laws legislating morality," made this pre-AIDS observation:

"Since it can be demonstrated that deviate sexual practices carried out in private by willing adults result in no mental or physical danger to the health or safety of the participants or of others, the only possible interest capable of being safeguarded by the prohibition of such conduct is the moral interest. Adult consensual sodomy, if it does any harm at all, harms the soul of the actor, as Plato would say. But while the welfare of its citizens' souls may have been the most important concern of Plato's ideal state, it is questionable whether such a concern is proper to a secular, pluralistic society.[147] Critics of sodomy laws argue

---

147. After all, whose morals are to be enforced? In 1957 England's Wolfenden Committee recommended that private homosexual acts between consenting adults be decriminalized, reasoning that, unless crime is to be made synonymous with sin, "there remains a realm of private morality and immorality which is, in brief and crude terms, not the law's business." *Report of the Committee on Homosexual Offenses and Prostitution* ¶ 62 (Stein & Day eds. 1963) (Wolfenden Report).

On the other hand, many of our legal writers and judges have expressed the view that morality is the source and inspiration of lawmaking. "Dean Pound has said that 'the attempt to make law and morals identical by covering the whole field of morals with legal precepts, and by conforming existing precepts to the requirements of

a reasoned system of morals, made the modern law.' In a similar generalization, Justice Cardozo held that 'The scope of legal duty has expanded in obedience to the urge of morals.'" S. Stumpf, *Morality and the Law* 9 (1966) (footnotes omitted); see U.C.L.A. Comment, supra note 144, at 582.

Lord Devlin, one of the most vigorous advocates of society's right to use the law to prevent moral harm, has relied on two principal arguments. The first is that a set of shared moral values is essential to society and, therefore, private conduct that threatens a moral principle, though it may not be a menace to particular individuals, is a threat to the existence of society. The second argument holds that a sincere moral conviction that certain activity is wrong justifies the individual or community in seeking to outlaw it. Sarto-

that majority opinion as to what is moral and rational should not carry the sanction of the criminal law. Indeed, they point out that such moral condemnation cannot satisfy the rational basis test required by substantive due process."

3. *Equal protection of the laws.* (a) Note, 14 N.Y.U.Rev.L. & Soc.Chg. 995, 1014 (1986): "Ironically, had Hardwick decided to press an equal protection claim, a showing of a history of discrimination would have been required for a finding that lesbian and gay litigants deserve special protection. But even an equal protection claim would have left Hardwick pleading for rights this Court would not grant. An equal protection argument would have required Hardwick to jump through legal hoops, meeting the required 'indicia of suspectness': a history of discrimination against lesbians and gay men, their discreteness and insularity today, and a biological basis of same-sex attraction. Again Hardwick would have been forced to analogize the lesbian and gay experience to that of the few other groups to whom the Court has begrudgingly granted special protection status."

(b) Comment, 45 Fordham L.Rev. 553, 585–87 (1976): "Justice Holmes once characterized the equal protection challenge as 'the usual last resort of Constitutional arguments.' It is an attack, not upon what a law directs, but upon the classification of citizens to whom it is or is not to be applied. Thus, as concerns a statute making consensual sodomy illicit, the issue is whether the distinction between married people and single people or between heterosexuals and homosexuals is the type of 'invidious discrimination' that offends the Constitution. * * *

"If single people or homosexuals can be deemed to form a suspect class, they will qualify for the added protection of the

rius, *The Enforcement of Morality,* 81 Yale L.J. 891, 892–93 (1972). * * *

compelling state interest test. Suspect classes are those composed of 'discrete and insular minorities,' groups therefore meriting judicial protection. These groups must be readily definable. Thus the category 'poor people' has been held not to qualify inasmuch as it was 'a large, diverse, and amorphous class.' To date, only race, alienage, and national origin have been specifically denominated as suspect classes. It may be noted that these are congenital attributes, over which the individual has no control and to which opprobrium has frequently attached."

4. *Cruel and unusual punishment.* (a) Taking note of Justice Powell's concurring opinion, Comment, 10 Harv.J.L. & Pub. Pol. 213, 227 (1987), opines "that if a State chooses to express its morality by criminalizing sodomy, then, in the case of a private act of sodomy between consenting adults, any punishment involving imprisonment would be violative of the Eighth Amendment."

(b) Is this so? Consider *Solem v. Helm,* 463 U.S. 277, 103 S.Ct. 3001, 77 L.Ed.2d 637 (1983), where Helm was convicted of uttering a "no account" check for $100, ordinarily punishable by a 5–year maximum, but received a sentence of life imprisonment without parole under a recidivist statute because of his prior convictions for six felonies, all of which were minor and nonviolent. Applying the Eighth Amendment "principle that a criminal sentence must be proportionate to the crime for which the defendant has been convicted," the Court first cautioned that proportionality analysis "should be guided by objective criteria, including (i) the gravity of the offense and the harshness of the penalty; (ii) the sentences imposed on other criminals in the same jurisdiction; and (iii) the sentences imposed for commission of the same crime in other jurisdictions.

* * * Applying objective criteria, we find that Helm has received the penultimate sentence for relatively minor criminal conduct. He has been treated more harshly than other criminals in the State who have committed more serious crimes. He has been treated more harshly than he would have been in any other jurisdiction, with the possible exception of a single State. We conclude that his sentence is significantly disproportionate to his crime, and is therefore prohibited by the Eighth Amendment." But the Court repeated its admonition in *Rummel v. Estelle,* 445 U.S. 263, 100 S.Ct. 1133, 63 L.Ed.2d 382 (1980), that "outside the context of capital punishment, *successful* challenges to the proportionality of particular sentences [will be] exceedingly rare."

Chapter 3

MENTAL STATE

SECTION 1. GENERAL CONSIDERATIONS

Introductory Notes

1. It is commonly stated that a crime consists of both a physical part and a mental part; that is, both an act or omission (and sometimes also a prescribed result of action or omission, or prescribed attendant circumstances, or both) and a state of mind. This Chapter is concerned with what is required of crimes in the way of the mental part, variously called *mens rea* ("guilty mind") or *scienter* or criminal intent.

Actually, the terms "mental part" and "*mens rea*" and "state of mind" are somewhat too narrow to be strictly accurate, for they include matters that are not really mental at all. Thus we shall see that, though many crimes do require some sort of mental fault (*i.e.,* a bad mind), other crimes (which are commonly said to require *mens rea*) require only some sort of fault which is not mental.[a] The unadorned word "fault" is thus a more accurate word to describe what crimes

generally require in addition to their physical elements.

2. During the early days of the development of common law crimes, the judges often declared conduct to be criminal which did not include any bad state of mind. But in more recent times (*i.e.,* since about 1600), the judges have generally defined common law crimes in terms which require, in addition to prescribed action or omission, some prescribed bad state of mind, although that state of mind has differed from one common law crime to another. The basic premise that for criminal liability some *mens rea* is required is expressed by the Latin maxim *actus not facit reum nisi mens sit rea* (an act does not make one guilty unless his mind is guilty). The words and phrases used by the judges to express the bad mind necessary for common law crimes include "maliciously" (as in murder, arson, malicious mischief), "fraudulently" (forgery), "feloniously" (larceny), "wilfully and corruptly" (perjury), and "with intent to * * *" (*e.g.,* "with intent to steal," another phrase used in defining larceny; "with intent to commit a felony therein," in burglary).[b]

---

a. In addition, some crimes require no fault at all, mental or otherwise; these impose liability without fault. But such crimes are said not to require *mens rea*.

b. The common law did occasionally depart from the requirement of a literally bad mind.

Thus manslaughter could be committed by a type of negligent conduct which, in England, did not require a subjective bad mind, though it did require objective fault. In two crimes, libel and nuisance, vicarious liability was imposed upon a faultless employer for the conduct of his employee.

3. Most crimes today, of course, are statutory crimes. In some jurisdictions common law crimes have been abolished; in others common law crimes are sparingly used. In all jurisdictions most of the common law crimes have been stated in the form of statutory law. And of course, in modern times, new statutory crimes, unknown to the common law, far outnumber the relatively few common law crimes originally created by the judges. The "mental" aspects of statutory crimes may be roughly classified as follows as to type:

(1) Many statutes defining conduct which is criminal employ words (usually adverbs) or phrases indicating some type of bad-mind requirement: "intentionally" or "with intent to * * *"; "knowingly" or "with knowledge that * * *"; "purposely" or "for the purpose of * * *"; "fraudulently" or "with intent to defraud"; "wilfully"; "maliciously"; "corruptly"; "designedly"; "recklessly"; "wantonly"; "unlawfully"; "feloniously" and so on. (2) Some of the statutes use words or phrases indicating a requirement of fault, but not necessarily mental fault— *e.g.,* "negligently", "carelessly", or "having reason to know * * *" (3) Some statutes define criminal conduct without any words or phrases indicating any express requirement of fault; thus "whoever does so-and-so (or: whoever omits to do so-and-so) is guilty of a crime and subject to the following punishment * * *" c However, although the statute may contain no adverbs or phrases indicating a requirement of fault, some fault may be inherent in a verb which the statute employs (*e.g.,* whoever "refuses" to do something or "permits" another to do something).

It may be said of statutory crimes that, so far as the mental element is concerned,

(1) some crimes (like most of the common law crimes) require "subjective fault"— actually a bad mind of some sort; (2) others require only "objective fault"— fault which is not a matter of the mind; and (3) others require no fault at all, either subjective (mental) or objective (nonmental), such statutes providing instead for "liability without fault."

4. The difficulties inherent in such a variety of expressions as to *mens rea* as is used by the common law and by statutes in defining crimes have led modern thinkers to classify the mental aspects of crime into a few general types; and to urge that, in drafting penal codes, a single expression be used to express a single type of *mens rea* culpability. The Model Penal Code has thus reduced the matter to four basic types of crimes which require fault: (1) crimes requiring *intention* (or *purpose*) to do the forbidden act (omission) or cause the forbidden result; (2) crimes requiring *knowledge* of the nature of the act (omission) or of the result which will follow therefrom or of the attendant circumstances; (3) those requiring *recklessness* in doing the act (omission) or causing the result (subjective fault in that the actor must in his own mind realize the risk which his conduct involves); and (4) those requiring only *negligence* in so doing or causing (objective fault in creating an unreasonable risk; but, since the actor need not realize the risk in order to be negligent, no subjective fault is required).[d] Most of the modern criminal codes expressly provide for these four basic types of culpability. Of course, there remains the possibility that, for some crimes or for some elements of a crime, a statute may impose strict liability.

---

c. Legislatures seldom if ever expressly provide that lack of fault shall be irrelevant, by any such phrase as "without regard to fault."

d. *Model Penal Code* § 2.02(2).

REGINA v. CUNNINGHAM

Court of Appeal, Criminal Division, England, 1957.
[1957] 2 Q.B. 396, [1957] 3 W.L.R. 56, [1957] 2 All E.R. 412.

BYRNE, J.: * * *

The appellant was convicted at Leeds Assizes upon an indictment framed under section 23 of the Offences against the Person Act, 1861, which charged that he unlawfully and maliciously caused to be taken by Sarah Wade a certain noxious thing, namely, coal gas, so as thereby to endanger the life of the said Sarah Wade.

The facts were that the appellant was engaged to be married and his prospective mother-in-law was the tenant of a house, No. 7a, Bakes Street, Bradford, which was unoccupied but which was to be occupied by the appellant after his marriage. Mrs. Wade and her husband, an elderly couple, lived in the house next door. At one time the two houses had been one, but when the building was converted into two houses a wall had been erected to divide the cellars of the two houses, and that wall was composed of rubble loosely cemented. On the evening of January 17 last the appellant went to the cellar of No. 7a, Bakes Street, wrenched the gas meter from the gas pipes and stole it, together with its contents, and in a second indictment he was charged with the larceny of the gas meter and its contents. To that indictment he pleaded Guilty and was sentenced to six months' imprisonment. In respect of that matter he does not appeal. The facts were not really in dispute, and in a statement to a police officer the appellant said: "All right I will tell you. I was short of money, I had been off work for three days, I got eight shillings from the gas meter. I tore it off the wall and threw it away." Although there was a stop tap within two feet of the meter, the appellant did not turn off the gas, with the result that a very considerable volume of gas escaped, some

of which seeped through the wall of the cellar and partially asphyxiated Mrs. Wade, who was asleep in her bedroom next door, with the result that her life was endangered.

At the close of the case for the prosecution Mr. Brodie, who appeared for the appellant at the trial and who has appeared for him again in this court, submitted that there was no case to go to the jury, but the learned judge, quite rightly in our opinion, rejected this submission. The appellant did not give evidence.

The act of the appellant was clearly unlawful and therefore the real question for the jury was whether it was also malicious within the meaning of section 23 of the Offences against the Person Act, 1861. Before this court Mr. Brodie has taken three points, all dependent upon the construction of that section. Section 23 provides as follows: "Whosoever shall unlawfully and maliciously administer to or cause to be administered to or taken by any other person any poison or other destructive or noxious thing, so as thereby to endanger the life of such person, or so as thereby to inflict upon such person any grievous bodily harm, shall be guilty of felony." Mr. Brodie argued, first, that *mens rea* of some kind is necessary. Secondly, that the nature of the *mens rea* required is that the appellant must have an intention to do the particular kind of harm that was done, or alternatively he must foresee that that harm may occur, yet nevertheless continue recklessly to do the act. Thirdly, that the learned judge misdirected the jury as to the meaning of the word "maliciously." He cited the following cases: *Pembliton* (1874) L.R. 2 C.C.R. 119; *Latimer* (1886) 17 Q.B.D. 359; and *Faulkner* (1877) 13 Cox 550. In reply Mr. Snowden, on behalf of the Crown, cited *Martin* (1881) 8 Q.B.D. 54.

We have considered those cases, and we have also considered, in the light of those cases, the following principle which was propounded by the late Professor C. S. Kenny in the first edition of his *Outlines of Criminal Law*, published in 1902, and repeated in the sixteenth edition edited by Mr. J. W. Cecil Turner and published in 1952: "In any statutory definition of a crime, malice must be taken not in the old vague sense of wickedness in general but as requiring either (1) An actual intention to do the particular kind of harm that in fact was done; or (2) Recklessness as to whether such harm should occur or not (i.e., the accused has foreseen that the particular kind of harm might be done and yet has gone on to take the risk of it). It is neither limited to nor does it indeed require any ill will towards the person injured." * * * We think that this is an accurate statement of the law. It derives some support from the judgments of Lord Coleridge, C.J. and Blackburn, J. in *Pembliton's* case. In our opinion, the word "maliciously" in a statutory crime postulates foresight of consequence.

In his summing-up the learned judge directed the jury as follows: "You will observe that there is nothing there about 'with intention that that person should take it.' He has not got to intend that it should be taken; it is sufficient that by his unlawful and malicious act he causes it to be taken. What you have to decide here, then, is whether, when he loosed that frightful cloud of coal gas into the house which he shared with this old lady, he caused her to take it by his unlawful and malicious action. 'Unlawful' does not need any definition. It is something forbidden by law. What about 'malicious'? 'Malicious' for this purpose means wicked—something which he has no business to do and perfectly well knows it. 'Wicked' is as good a definition as any other which you would get. The facts which face you (and they are uncontradicted and undisputed; the prisoner has not gone into the box to seek to give any particular

explanation) are these. Living in the house, which was now two houses but which had once been one and had been rather roughly divided, the prisoner quite deliberately, intending to steal the money that was in the meter * * * broke the gas meter away from the supply pipes and thus released the mains supply of gas at large into that house. When he did that he knew that this old lady and her husband were living next door to him. The gas meter was in a cellar. The wall which divided his cellar from the cellar next door was a kind of honeycomb wall through which gas could very well go, so that when he loosed that cloud of gas into that place he must have known perfectly well that gas would percolate all over the house. If it were part of this offence—which it is not—that he intended to poison the old lady, I should have left it to you to decide, and I should have told you that there was evidence on which you could find that he intended that, since he did an action which he must have known would result in that. As I have already told you, it is not necessary to prove that he intended to do it; it is quite enough that what he did was done unlawfully and maliciously."

With the utmost respect to the learned judge, we think it is incorrect to say that the word "malicious" in a statutory offence merely means wicked. We think the learned judge was in effect telling the jury that if they were satisfied that the appellant acted wickedly—and he had clearly acted wickedly in stealing the gas meter and its contents—they ought to find that he had acted maliciously in causing the gas to be taken by Mrs. Wade so as thereby to endanger her life.

In our view, it should have been left to the jury to decide whether, even if the appellant did not intend the injury to Mrs. Wade, he foresaw that the removal of the gas meter might cause injury to someone but nevertheless removed it. We are unable to say that a reasonable jury, properly directed as to the meaning of the word "maliciously" in the context of section 23, would without doubt have convicted.

In these circumstances this court has no alternative but to allow the appeal and quash the conviction.

Notes and Questions

1. Reassess *Cunningham* in light of the four cases the court notes were cited by counsel:

(a) *Pembliton* (1874): The defendant threw a stone at some persons with whom he had been fighting; the stone passed over their heads and broke a large plate glass window. The jury found that the defendant threw the stone intending to strike one or more of those persons and not intending to break the window. This finding, the court held per Lord Coleridge, C.J., was not sufficient to convict under a statute making it a misdemeanor for one to "unlawfully and maliciously" commit any damage upon real or personal property: "[W]hat was intended to be provided against by the Act is the wilfully doing an unlawful Act, and that the Act must be wilfully and intentionally done on the part of the person doing it, to render him liable to be convicted. Without saying that, upon these facts, if the jury had found that the prisoner had been guilty of throwing the stone recklessly, knowing that there was a window near which it might probably hit, I should have been disposed to interfere with the conviction, yet as they have found that he threw the stone at the people he had been fighting with intending to strike them and not intending to break the window, I think the conviction must be quashed."

(b) *Faulkner* (1877): The defendant, a sailor, went into the hold of a ship to steal some rum; he lit a match to see better, but this ignited the rum and the resulting fire destroyed the ship. The defendant was convicted by a jury of violating the Mali-cious Damage Act by maliciously setting fire to the ship. The court, per Barry, J., reversed: "The jury were, in fact, directed to give a verdict of guilty upon the simple ground that the firing of the ship, though accidental, was caused by an act done in the course of, or immediately consequent upon, a felonious operation, and no question of the prisoner's malice, constructive or otherwise, was left to the jury. I am of opinion that, according to *Reg. v. Pembliton*, that direction was erroneous, and that the conviction should be quashed."

(c) *Martin* (1881): Shortly before the conclusion of a performance at a theatre, the defendant, with the intention and with the result of causing terror in the minds of persons leaving the theatre, put out the gaslights on a staircase which a large number of them had to descend in order to leave. He also, with the intention and with the result of obstructing the exit, placed an iron bar across the doorway. Upon the lights being extinguished a panic seized a large portion of the audience, and they rushed in fright down the staircase, forcing those in front against the iron bar and causing those persons to be injured. The defendant was indicted under a statute providing that "whosoever shall unlawfully and maliciously wound, or inflict any grievous bodily harm upon any other person, either with or without a weapon or instrument, shall be guilty of a misdemeanor." The jury was charged that if they concluded the conduct of the defendant in extinguishing the lights and putting the bar across the doorway amounted to nothing more than a mere piece of foolish mischief they might acquit, but that if they believed the acts were done with a deliberate and malicious intention they ought to convict. The defendant was convicted. The court, per Lord Coleridge, C.J., affirmed: "The prisoner must be taken to have intended the natural consequences of that which he did. He acted 'unlawfully and maliciously,' not that he had any personal malice against the particular individuals injured, but in the sense of doing an unlawful act calculated to injure, and by which others were in fact injured. Just as in the case of a man who unlawfully fires a gun among a crowd, it is murder if one of the crowd is thereby killed." Stephen, J., concurring, commented: "I wish to add that the Recorder seems to have put the case too favourably for the prisoner, for he put it to the jury to consider whether the prisoner did the act 'as a mere piece of foolish mischief.' Now, it seems to me, that if the prisoner did that which he did as a mere piece of foolish mischief unlawfully and without excuse, he did it 'wilfully,' that is 'maliciously,' within the meaning of the statute."

(d) *Latimer* (1886): The defendant, a soldier, quarreled with Chapple in a public-house, and Chapple knocked him down. The defendant left but returned about five minutes later and walked over to Chapple and swung a leather belt at him. The belt struck Chapple slightly, bounded off and struck Ellen Rolston, cutting her face open. The defendant was convicted under a statute making it a misdemeanor to "unlawfully and maliciously wound or inflict any grievous bodily harm upon any other person." The court, per Lord Coleridge, C.J., affirmed: "It is common knowledge that a man who has an unlawful and malicious intent against another, and, in attempting to carry it out, injures a third person, is guilty of what the law deems malice against the person injured, because the offender is doing an unlawful act, and has that which the judges call general malice, and that is enough. * * * He intended to do an unlawful act, and in course of doing it the consequence was that somebody was injured." Esher, M. R., elaborated: "The only case which could be cited against the well-known principle of law applicable to this case was *Reg. v. Pembliton,* but, on examination, it is found to have been decided on this ground, viz., that there was no intention to injure any property at all. It was not a case of attempting to injure one man's property and injuring another's, which would have been wholly different."

2. Compare *State v. Hatley,* 72 N.M. 377, 384 P.2d 252 (1963), where the defendant was convicted of mayhem. Though the defendant struck the blow which put out the victim's eye, he claimed there was no proof he intended to maim the victim and that the harm resulted from the victim turning his head at the moment of the blow. The court affirmed: "We think the conduct of appellant falls well within the rule so as to make him liable for the consequences of an unlawful act, even though such consequences may not have been intended. One who, in the commission of a wrongful act, commits another wrong not meant by him, is nevertheless liable for the latter wrong. Here, the appellant deliberately committed the crime of assault and battery, and, in so doing, committed mayhem."

3. Consider *United States v. Zapata,* 497 F.2d 95 (5th Cir.1974), where defendant, upon her entry into the United States, was found to have 2,000 grams of pure cocaine in her undergarments. Questioned concerning the possession, she indicated an awareness of wrongdoing but did not specify whether she meant she was aware (i) she was illegally importing cocaine, (ii) she had failed to declare the packages on her person, or (iii) she had tried to enter on a false passport. She was charged with "knowingly and intentionally" importing the cocaine. At trial, she testified a stranger had given her money to transport unspecified "raw material" into the country for him and that he had assured her this was perfectly legal. Query, which of the following jury instructions, if any, would be proper: (a) that requested by the government, namely, that the "test is whether there was a conscious purpose to avoid enlightenment"; (b) that requested by the

defendant, namely, that there must be "proof that the defendant knew the substance she was carrying was cocaine"; or (c) that given by the court, namely, that it must be shown the defendant "was aware of the fact that he was committing some kind of wrong, or some sort of crime—not necessarily the crime of bringing in cocaine itself."

SECTION 2. INTENT

STATE v. ROCKER

Supreme Court of Hawaii, 1970.
52 Hawaii 336, 475 P.2d 684.

RICHARDSON, CHIEF JUSTICE.

Defendants-appellants, having waived a jury trial, were tried in the circuit court of the second circuit and found guilty as charged for violation of HRS § 727–1 for creating a common nuisance. The complaint read: "That Richard Barry Rocker and Joseph Cava [defendants] at Puu Olai, Makena, District of Makawao, County of Maui, State of Hawaii, on the 26th day of February, 1969, did openly sun bathe in the nude, which was offensive and against common decency or common morality, thereby committing the offense of common nuisance, contrary to the provisions of Section 727–1 of the Hawaii Revised Statutes."

It is undisputed that on February 26, 1969, police officers of the Maui Police Department received a phone call from an

anonymous person and, thereafter, on the day of the call, proceeded to the Puu Olai beach at Makena to look for nude sunbathers. On reaching their destination, the police surveyed the beach from a ridge using both their naked eyes and binoculars and saw the defendants lying on the beach completely nude, one on his stomach and the other on his back. The officers then approached the defendants and arrested them for indecent exposure. It was admitted by the police officers that defendants were not at any time engaged in any activity other than sunbathing. At the time of the arrest there were several other people on the beach where the defendants were nude. Defendant Rocker was nude at the Puu Olai beach on other days before and after he was arrested on February 26, 1969. Defendant Cava likewise frequently sunbathed in the nude at the same beach prior to his arrest on February 26, 1969.

* * *

HRS § 727–1, unlike statutes of most states, incorporates indecent exposure as an example of what the legislature has defined to constitute common nuisances.[a] The statute does not specifically delineate the elements of the crime of indecent exposure, and although reference to the common law or to cases decided in other jurisdictions based upon statutes different from ours may be helpful, neither is controlling.[1] The question of whether sunbathing in the nude on a public beach is

---

a. The statute reads as follows:

"The offense of common nuisance is the endangering of the public personal safety or health, or doing, causing or promoting, maintaining or continuing what is offensive, or annoying and vexatious, or plainly hurtful to the public; or is a public outrage against common decency or common morality; or tends plainly and directly to the corruption of the morals, honesty, and good habits of the people; the same being without authority or justification by law:

"As for example: * * *

"Open lewdness or lascivious behavior, or indecent exposure; * * * "

1. It should be noted that the Hawaii Penal Code (Proposed Draft) 1970 adopts the American Law Institute Model Penal Code classification and definition of indecent exposure. It is classified as a sexual offense and is defined as follows:

(1) A person commits the offense of indecent exposure if, with intent to arouse or gratify sexual desire of himself or of any person, he exposes his genitals to a person to whom he is not married under circumstances in which he knows his conduct is likely to cause affront or alarm.

(2) Indecent exposure is a petty misdemeanor.

punishable as a common nuisance is one of construction of our statute. * * *

Sunbathing in the nude is not per se illegal. It must be coupled with the intent to indecently expose oneself. Intent is an element of the crime of common nuisance defined by HRS § 727–1. The intent necessary is a general intent, not a specific intent; *i.e.,* it is not necessary that the exposure be made with the intent that some particular person see it, but only that the exposure was made where it was likely to be observed by others. Thus, the intent may be inferred from the conduct of the accused and the circumstances and environment of the occurrence. The criminal intent necessary for a conviction of indecent exposure is usually established by some action by which the defendant either (1) draws attention to his exposed condition or (2) by a display in a place so public that it must be presumed it was intended to be seen by others.

The defendants argue that there is no circumstantial evidence in the record from which a trier of fact could conclude that the element of intent had been proved beyond a reasonable doubt. The issue, therefore, is whether defendants' nude sunbathing at Puu Olai beach at Makena, Maui, was at a place so *public* that a trier of fact could infer it was intended to be seen by others. The prosecution offered testimony of one of the arresting police officers that the beach was a popular location for fishermen and was in fact one of his favorite fishing spots. Defendants testified that the public in general used the beach, that it was used by fishermen and local residents, and that they observed between 20 and 25 people on the beach over a two-month period. Although the Puu Olai beach is isolated by a hill and a ledge, away from the view of the public road and

adjoining beaches, it is accessible by a well-worn path and known to be a favorite location of fishermen to cast and throw fish nets. In view of this and other evidence in the record, we cannot agree with defendants' argument that the trier of fact could not find the beach so public as to justify an inference of intent on the part of defendants to be seen by others. * * *

The third issue raised on this appeal is whether the trial court erred in denying the defendants' motion for judgment of acquittal at the end of the prosecution's case. * * *

At the close of the prosecution's case it had been established that the defendants were seen by two police officers sunbathing in the nude at Puu Olai beach, a beach isolated by a hill and a ledge but accessible by a well worn path. One of the officers testified that the beach was a popular location for fishermen and was in fact one of his favorite fishing spots. From these facts the trial judge ruled that a prima facie case had been established and denied the defendants' motion for acquittal. We affirm this ruling. There was sufficient evidence at the close of the prosecution's case to justify an inference beyond a reasonable doubt that the Puu Olai beach was so public that the defendants could be attributed with the necessary knowledge to know that their acts under the circumstances were likely to offend members of the general public. * * *

Affirmed.

LEVINSON, JUSTICE (dissenting).

I dissent because I think that the evidence adduced by the government at the close of the prosecution's case was insufficient to sustain a conviction of either defendant. The trial judge erroneously denied the defendants' motion for acquittal

---

See Hawaii Penal Code (Proposed Draft) 1970, Chapter 7, Part V, Section 738.

This classification and definition of the crime of indecent exposure takes it out of the realm of

common nuisances and makes it a specific sexual offense.

made at that time. My view of the role that the motion for acquittal plays in the criminal process leads me to conclude that in reviewing a denial of such a motion, the appellate court should consider only the record as it existed when the motion was made. The majority opinion appears to concur in this view. * * *

My reading of the majority opinion leads me to conclude that in order to prove a prima facie case against the defendants it was necessary for the prosecution to demonstrate that the defendants possessed a general intent to expose themselves in a place where it would be likely that they would be observed by others. To prove this, it would be enough for the prosecution to establish the defendants' awareness of sufficient facts and circumstances from which a trier of fact could infer such intent beyond a reasonable doubt. From the evidence in the record at the close of the prosecution's case I do not think that a trier of fact could be justified in inferring beyond a reasonable doubt that the defendants possessed the necessary general intent to be seen by others.

Although there was testimony that the beach was visited by fishermen there was no link established between the visits by the fishermen and visits to the beach by the defendants. Officer Matsunaga, one of the fishermen who used the beach, did not testify to ever having observed the defendants on this beach prior to arresting them. Thus, this evidence could not be used to support an inference that the defendants were aware that this beach was used by fishermen and therefore public.

Nor could a trier of fact infer beyond a reasonable doubt that the defendants were aware of the "well-worn" path leading

over the hill to the beach and therefore knew that they were sunbathing in an area readily accessible to the public. One of the police officers testified that the beach was accessible by another trail which was *not* "well-used." There was no other evidence that would eliminate as a reasonable doubt the possibility that the defendants had used this other path and therefore inferred from its unused nature that the public would not be likely to see them. The majority opinion does not mention this possibility in assessing the adequacy of the prosecution's case. In failing to prove that the defendants were aware of the visits of the fishermen or the well-worn path I believe the State failed to prove beyond a reasonable doubt defendants' awareness of facts sufficient to establish a general intent to be seen by others.

* * *

Notes and Questions

1. There is some disagreement as to what ought to be encompassed within the term "intent." Compare Turner, *The Mental Element in Crimes at Common Law,* 6 Camb.L.J. 31, 39 (1938) (" 'Intention' describes the state of mind of the man who not only foresaw, but also desired the possible consequences of his conduct"); with Remington & Helstad, *The Mental Element in Crime—A Legislative Problem,* 1952 Wis. L.Rev. 644, 675 ("As to the meaning of intent, the word usually is identified with desire, but in the final analysis it means no more than that the person who intends something knows or believes that it is certain to result from his conduct"). How is the word being used in *Rocker*? Which definition is preferable? [a]

a. See *Model Penal Code* § 2.02(2)(a). The Comment thereto (1985) states: "In defining the kinds of culpability, the Code draws a narrow distinction between acting purposely and knowingly, one of the elements of ambiguity in legal usage of 'intent.' Knowledge that the requisite

external circumstances exist is a common element in both conceptions. But action is not purposive with respect to the nature or the result of the actor's conduct unless it was his conscious object to perform an action of that nature or to cause such a result. * * *

2. How would the defendants have fared under the proposed statute set out in footnote 1 of *Rocker*? Cf. *In re Smith*, 7 Cal.3d 362, 102 Cal.Rptr. 335, 497 P.2d 807 (1972), reversing the defendant's conviction for "willfully and lewdly" exposing the private parts of his body. The defendant had fallen asleep while sunbathing in the nude on a public but then vacant beach, but when he awakened several other persons were present. The court concluded there was "no doubt" that the defendant had " 'willfully'—i.e., intentionally—expose[d] himself," but that it was not shown he had done so lewdly, which the court concluded "requires proof beyond a reasonable doubt that the actor not only meant to expose himself, but intended by his conduct to direct public attention to his genitals for purposes of sexual arousal, gratification, or affront."

NOTES AND QUESTIONS ON MOTIVE AND ON CRIMINAL, CONSTRUCTIVE, GENERAL, SPECIFIC, CONDITIONAL, MULTIPLE, AND TRANSFERRED INTENT

1. *Motive.* What is the difference between "intent" and "motive"? It has been said that when A kills B in order to obtain B's money, A's intent was to kill and his motive was to get the money.[a] This suggests intent is limited to one's purpose to commit the proscribed act, and that all inquiries into why one did the proscribed act are concerned with motive.[b] If this is so, then if A breaks into B's house to get B's money, it must be said that the intent was to break and enter and the motive was to get the money. But the better view is that this is not so; rather, the question of why A broke into B's home is a matter of intent (the so-called "special intent" required for the crime of burglary) rather than motive. This suggests that intent relates to the means and motive to the ends, but that where the end is the means to yet another end, then the medial end may also be considered in terms of intent.[c] Thus, when A breaks into B's house in order to get money to pay his debts, it is appropriate to characterize his purpose to take the money as his intent and the desire to pay his debts as the motive. Under this definition, it may be said that motive is not relevant in substantive criminal law[d] except as circumstantial evidence bearing on intent.[e]

2. *"Criminal" and "constructive" intent.* The phrase "criminal intent" is often taken to be synonymous with *mens rea,* the general notion that except for strict liability offenses some form of mental state is a prerequisite to guilt. As a result, that phrase is sometimes used to refer to criminal negligence or recklessness. Similarly, the notion of "constructive intent" has been used by some courts; it is first asserted that intent is required for all crimes, and then it is added that such intent may be inferred from recklessness or negli-

---

"It is true, of course, that this distinction is inconsequential for most purposes of liability; acting knowingly is ordinarily sufficient. But there are areas where the discrimination is required and is made under traditional law, which uses the awkward concept of 'specific intent.' "

a. Cook, *Act, Intention, and Motive in the Criminal Law,* 26 Yale L.J. 645, 660 (1917).

b. This view has sometimes been taken; see Salmond, *Jurisprudence* § 134 (9th ed. 1937).

c. See G. Williams, *Criminal Law: The General Part* 48 (2d ed. 1961).

d. See, e.g., *United States v. Pomponio,* 429 U.S. 10, 97 S.Ct. 22, 50 L.Ed.2d 12 (1976), holding

that the term "willful" in the statute prohibiting the wilful filing of a false income tax return requires only an intent to violate a known legal duty and that consequently the trial judge did not err in instructing that "[g]ood motive alone is never a defense where the act done or omitted is a crime" and that motive was thus irrelevant except as it bore on intent.

e. See, e.g., *Commonwealth v. DePetro,* 350 Pa. 567, 39 A.2d 838 (1944), holding evidence defendant was in financial difficulties admissible on charge of arson with intent to defraud insurance company.

gence. It would make for clearer analysis if courts would merely acknowledge that for some crimes intent is not needed and that recklessness or negligence will suffice.

3. *"General" and "specific" intent.* The cases often distinguish "general" from "specific" intent, although the distinction being drawn by the use of these two terms often varies. Sometimes "general intent" is used in the same way as "criminal intent." Or, "general intent" may be used to encompass all forms of the mental state requirement, while "specific intent" is limited to the one mental state of intent. Another possibility is that "general intent" will be used to characterize an intent to do something on an undetermined occasion, and "specific intent" to denote an intent to do that thing at a particular time and place.

But the most common usage of "specific intent" is to designate a special mental element which is required above and beyond any mental state required with respect to the *actus reus* of the crime. Common law larceny, for example, requires the taking and carrying away of the property of another, and the defendant's mental state as to this act must be established, but in addition it must be shown that there was an "intent to steal" the property. Similarly, common law burglary requires a breaking and entry into the dwelling of another, but in addition to the mental state connected with these acts it must also be established that the defendant acted "with intent to commit a felony therein." The same situation prevails with many statutory crimes, such as assault "with intent to kill" or kidnapping "for the purpose of ransom or reward." Although this distinction between "general" and "specific" intent has

not been without importance in the criminal law,[f] greater clarity may be accomplished by abandoning this terminology, and this has been done in the Model Penal Code [g] and in many of the modern recodifications.

4. *"Conditional" and "multiple" intent.* In *People v. Connors,* 253 Ill. 266, 97 N.E. 643 (1912), the defendants appealed their convictions of assault with intent to kill. The evidence was that they approached Bell, a member of a certain union, with drawn guns and told him that unless he took off his overalls and went down and joined a competing union he would "get killed" because they "would bore a hole through him" and "shoot [him] like a dog." Bell took off his overalls and went with the defendants, who fled when the police approached. In affirming the convictions, the court reasoned: "In support of the view that an assault with a loaded revolver and a threat to shoot unless the party assaulted complies with a demand is not an assault with an intent to murder, plaintiffs in error rely with great confidence upon the case of *Hairston v. State,* 54 Miss. 689, 28 Am.Rep. 392. In that case Hairston, in company with others, attempted to remove the personal effects of a laborer from the plantation of his employer, Richards, to whom said laborer was indebted on account of advances of money or provisions made to said laborer. Hairston was in the act of hauling away the household furniture when Richards attempted to stop the wagon, and took hold of Hairston's mules, saying that he could not move the household goods until his debt was settled. Thereupon Hairston drew a pistol and pointed it at Richards

---

f. As we shall see, the traditional view was that the rules on when mistake of fact or mistake of law are a defense differ depending upon what kind of intent is involved. Also, some courts have taken the view that intent may be presumed (i.e., a person is "presumed to intend the natural and probable consequences of his acts") only as to a general intent.

g. *Model Penal Code* § 2.02, Comments (Tent. Draft No. 4, 1955): "[W]e can see no virtue in preserving the concept of 'general intent,' which has been an abiding source of ambiguity and of confusion in the penal law."

and said, 'I came here to move Charles Johnson, and by God I am going to do it, and I will shoot any God damned man who attempts to stop my mules,' at the same time urging his mules forward as he spoke. His manner was threatening and angry, and his voice loud and boisterous. Other persons who were accompanying Hairston, some of whom were armed with guns, pressed around Richards, as if they intended to aid Hairston if necessary. Richards was deterred by the apparent danger, and released the mules and the wagon moved on. Under the above facts Hairston was convicted of an assault with an intent to murder Richards. The conviction was reversed by the Supreme Court of Mississippi. The reasoning of the court in that case is as follows: Richards was in the act of committing a trespass upon Hairston's property by laying his hands upon the mules, and forcibly stopping Hairston upon the public highway. Hairston had a right to protect his property from such unlawful trespass, using no more force than was necessary. His threat to shoot was conditioned upon a demand which he had a right to make. In disposing of the case the Supreme Court of Mississippi uses the following language: 'Here there was only a conditional offer to shoot, based upon a demand which the party had a right to make. While the law will not excuse the assault actually committed in leveling the pistol within shooting distance, it cannot, from this fact alone, infer an intent to murder. The intent must be actual—not conditional—and especially not conditioned upon noncompliance with a proper demand.' A careful analysis of that case will show that the court laid special stress on the circumstance that the threat to shoot was coupled with a demand

which the prisoner had a lawful right to make."

Are *Connors* and *Hairston* really distinguishable? May they be explained on the ground that in *Hairston* the evidence "is insufficient to support an inference of an actual intent to kill," while in *Connors* "there was enough to support the inference that the defendants actually had homicide in mind"[h]? Does the approach taken in *Model Penal Code* § 2.02(6) help?

What should the result be in the following situations? (a) Hamil has been charged with attempted rape, which requires proof that he intended to have carnal knowledge of a female against her will by means of force. He grabbed a young woman into his car and then parked the car against a building to prevent her from opening the door. He pulled off some of her clothes and said that if she was a virgin he would let her go, but if she was not he was going to have intercourse with her. She said she was a virgin and the defendant thereafter said she was "nothing but a virgin and no good." He then started the car and pulled away, at which the girl jumped out of the car.[i]

(b) Kinnemore has been charged with assault with intent to kill. He was apprehended by department store security personnel for shoplifting. After he was taken to an office, he grabbed a female store employee around the neck and placed a scissors to her neck and stated that he would kill her if the others did not allow him to leave. At that point other store personnel intervened and disarmed him without any injury to his hostage.[j]

(c) Simonson has been charged with receiving stolen property, which requires proof that he knew the property was stolen

---

h. R. Perkins & R. Boyce, *Criminal Law* 647 (3d ed. 1982).

i. See *People v. Hamil*, 20 Ill.App.3d 901, 314 N.E.2d 251 (1974), affirming the conviction on the ground that "the defendant's actions, both before and after his equivocal statement about the vic-

tim's virginity, bespeak his intent much louder than his words alone."

j. *State v. Kinnemore*, 34 Ohio App.2d 39, 295 N.E.2d 680 (1972), reversing the conviction, and noting that "the exclamation tends to show that its objective was escape—not murder. The threat

and that he intended to deprive the owner of his property. Simonson bought tools worth $800 for $60 shortly after they had been stolen, and he then contacted the company from which they had been stolen and negotiated a reward of $125 for return of the tools. He was arrested before the exchange occurred.[k]

Sometimes a person may act with two or more intentions, in which case, so long as he had the intention required by the definition of the crime, it is immaterial that he also had some other intention as well. Illustrative is *O'Neal v. United States,* 240 F.2d 700 (10th Cir.1957), affirming defendant's conviction of a Mann Act violation where he transported a female interstate with the intent to have her work as a waitress in the day and as a prostitute at night; the court held the purpose of prostitution need not be the sole purpose of the trip.

5. *"Transferred" intent.* In *Gladden v. State,* 273 Md. 383, 330 A.2d 176 (1974), the defendant was convicted of the murder of Nixon. The evidence was that the defendant shot at Siegel in the street and that one of the bullets entered a home and struck Nixon. The trial judge charged the jury: "The fact that the person actually killed was killed instead of the intended victim is immaterial and the only question is what would have been the degree of guilt if the result intended had actually been accomplished. The intent is transferred to the person whose death has been caused." Citing a host of decisions from other jurisdictions in support, the court affirmed:

"Where, as here, there was evidence that the conduct of the petitioner, Gladden, in a reprobated state of mind, was willful, deliberate and premeditated toward Siegel, the *mens rea* for murder in the first degree was established, notwithstanding that the decedent was an unintended victim. All the elements of an intentional first degree killing were present. His responsibility for the commission of conduct proscribed by the law cannot extenuate the offense because he did not kill his supposed enemy. The purpose and malice with which the shots were fired are not changed in any degree by circumstances showing that they did not take effect— because of bad aim—upon Siegel. Gladden's culpability under the law and the resultant harm to society is the same as if he had accomplished the result he intended when he caused the death of the innocent youngster. The punishment is imposed in accordance with the culpability of the accused under the law and justice is served by punishing him for a crime of the same seriousness as the one he undertook to commit."

Is this reasoning persuasive? Consider *State v. Gardner,* 57 Del. 588, 203 A.2d 77 (1964), which, though in accord with *Gladden,* asserts that "the purely logical view is that *A,* the killer, should be charged with an attempt [requiring intent to kill] to murder *B,* his intended victim, and manslaughter [requiring recklessness] of *C,* his real victim."

---

was conditional, whereas an assault coupled with a present intent to kill necessarily involves continuous, sequential, and uninterrupted conduct. The state was required to prove that Kinnemore intended to kill Miss Frazier at the time of the assault, but the evidence upon this issue, which consists entirely of the exclamation of the defendant at the time of the assault, is not sufficient to sustain an essential element of the crime beyond a reasonable doubt."

k. *State v. Simonson,* 298 Minn. 235, 214 N.W.2d 679 (1974), affirming the conviction, as "with reference to the matter of intent, we believe that the rule should be that one who receives or conceals what he knows to be stolen property with the intent to restore it to the owner only if the owner pays a reward does have the requisite wrongful intent."

UNITED STATES v. MELTON

United States Court of Appeals, District of Columbia Circuit, 1973.
491 F.2d 45.

BAZELON, CHIEF JUDGE:

Appellant was tried before a jury and convicted of first degree burglary. At trial, the following story emerged. At about 10 p.m. on January 29, 1971, Mrs. Vessels was asleep on the second floor of her home, when she was awakened by a loud noise from downstairs. She went to the foot of the stairs where she could clearly see that the noise had been caused by someone knocking over several pieces of plywood, which had been stacked against a door opening inward from an unheated sunroom. When she went outside, she discovered that a screen door to the kitchen had been cut but the door itself had not been opened and that a window leading into the sunroom had been opened and left ajar.

After surveying the outside of the house, Mrs. Vessels went to her next door neighbor's home and called the police. A patrol car responded in about five minutes. After Mrs. Vessels told the policemen what had happened, they went to her house to investigate. Coming to the partially opened sunroom door, they immediately saw appellant lying on the floor. They arrested and searched him without incident; no weapons, burglary tools or stolen goods were found. Nothing of value in the house had been moved so as to indicate an attempt to steal.

Appellant was charged with first degree burglary—the unlawful breaking and entering into the dwelling of another while a person was present therein with the intent to commit a criminal offense—in this case, larceny. At the close of the government's case, defense counsel moved for a directed verdict of acquittal for a failure of proof on the question of ultimate criminal intent. * * * [T]he trial judge concluded that mere unlawful entry into another's house supports an inference that the interloper was there to steal. Accordingly, he denied the defense motion for acquittal and submitted the charge of burglary to the jury. * * *

The trial judge erred in submitting a burglary charge to the jury where he found a complete absence of any evidence of an intent to commit a crime after the unlawful entry. By doing so, the trial judge invited the jury "to conjecture merely, or to conclude upon pure speculation or from passion, prejudice or sympathy," rather than any factual predicate, why appellant entered the dwelling.

In addition, the trial court's ruling conflicts with the statutory scheme of property offenses. Unlawful entry carries a maximum penalty of six months' imprisonment. First degree burglary carries a penalty of not less than five or more than thirty years. The element that distinguishes burglary from unlawful entry is the intent to commit a crime once unlawful entry has been accomplished. To allow proof of unlawful entry, *ipso facto,* to support a burglary charge is, in effect, to increase sixty-fold the statutory penalty for unlawful entry. * * *

In each of the cases on which the trial judge relied in making his ruling, some circumstantial evidence of the requisite intent to commit a crime on the premises was either shown or noted—flight upon discovery, carrying or trying to conceal stolen goods, an assault upon a resident. Here, as the trial judge noted, there does not appear to be any circumstantial evidence of an ulterior criminal purpose other than the unlawful entry itself. Appellant did not attack Mrs. Vessels after she had discovered his presence. Despite a readily accessible means of escape provided by the nearby opened window, appellant did not escape during the several minutes between his discovery and his apprehension. Appellant had no stolen goods, weapons, or burglary tools with him when apprehended. He could not have been concealed, since the arresting officers saw him immediately upon peering through the door into the sunroom, nor did he resist arrest.

Nor should the fact that the unlawful entry occurred in the nighttime support the inference of intent to steal. An element of common law burglary was that it occurred at night; nighttime entry was seen as more likely to pose a threat to occupants. Congress abolished the "nighttime" requirement and focused instead on the specific consideration—the danger to occupants of a home. First degree burglary requires entrance into a dwelling while someone is present; second degree burglary, to which lesser penalties attach, requires neither that the building be a dwelling nor that it be occupied.[7] The "common law" nighttime element, clearly abandoned by Congress, should not be resurrected by judicial fiat to make an act proscribed by Congress as a breaking and entering into a first degree burglary. It is true that some courts would infer an intent to steal from an unexplained nighttime intrusion. Some states provide by statute for a presumption of burglarious intent to arise from such unexplained conduct. Congress has not done so. Rather, it enacted a comprehensive scheme of property offenses which should not be confounded by us.   *   *   *

Reversed.

MacKINNON, CIRCUIT JUDGE, dissenting: *   *   *

The majority opinion states, *inter alia,* "*Nothing of value in the house had been moved so as to indicate an attempt to steal.*" (Emphasis added.) This statement is erroneous as the transcript discloses:

Q. Now when you [Mrs. Vessels] came down and after you went back in the house, when the police came, did you find anything else [other than the plywood] disturbed in the house?

A. *Yes, there were things disturbed in the sunroom.*

Q. What?

A. Well, there were things which were broken in there because there were things stored there. There was a *clock which was broken, a lamp, some paintings in frames,* which were there, and there were some pieces of gill [*sic*] which had been bent because they were on the floor. (Emphasis added.)

The clock, the lamp and the pictures were clearly "items of value," and there is no evidentiary support in the record for the gratuitous conclusion of the majority opinion that these items of value had *not* "been moved so as to indicate an attempt to steal."   *   *   *

The majority opinion also asserts that appellant did not "resist arrest" but the transcript is silent or equivocal on this point. Appellant's trial counsel attempted to suggest in his cross examination of Mrs. Vessels that the "items of value" in the sun room were "destroyed in the arrest of the Defendant," which suggests that he resisted arrest. The suggestion was not denied by Mrs. Vessels, but neither was it

---

7. 22 D.C.Code § 1801(b) (Supp. V. 1972). Allowing *nighttime* entry to *ipso facto* support a burglary conviction would produce anomalous results that could not have been intended by Congress. Defendant A enters an occupied dwelling half an hour after sunset. Defendant B did so an hour earlier. Defendant C unlawfully enters an empty warehouse late at night. Defendant A could be found guilty of first degree burglary, and sentenced to 30 years. Defendant B who poses as great a threat to the security of the occupants, could be found guilty only of breaking and entering and subject to a maximum sentence of 6 months. Defendant C, who poses no threat to anyone may be found guilty of second degree burglary and sentenced to 15 years in prison. Congress wisely concluded that the issue should be why—not at what time—the defendant unlawfully entered.

admitted. His counsel in his opening statement also stated that when appellant was arrested, "he started to struggle." * * * The record thus would permit the jury to have inferred that appellant had disturbed these items while searching for something to steal before his arrest or that he did resist arrest. Either finding would support a conclusion under applicable burglary law that appellant had an intent to steal.

* * * As to the additional facts which support a finding that appellant entered the house with intent to steal, there are a number of facts here from which the jury could infer that appellant entered the house with an intent to steal, and thus place the jury verdict beyond one based on conjecture or speculation.

First, and most important, is the fact that the entry was made in the nighttime. The law is clear in this circuit that a jury may infer an intent to steal from a breaking and entering of an occupied dwelling place in the nighttime, where the defendant can offer no other explanation for his presence. This is *not* a required inference which the jury must make when there is a breaking and entering in the nighttime, but it is almost universally held that the jury may draw this inference based *solely* upon such an entry in the nighttime, in the absence of evidence suggesting another explanation for the unlawful entry. And where there is additional evidence tending to show intent to steal, as there is here, it is universally recognized that forcible entry in the *nighttime* is strong circumstantial evidence indicating the entrant had such an intent.

The majority opinion asserts that the "'common law' nighttime element [was] abandoned by Congress." * * * In attempting to make its point in this respect the majority opinion gets mixed up over what is involved and completely misses the mark, i.e., that we are not relying upon the provisions of a statute but upon an evidentiary inference that, while it may have been recognized at common law, really rests on common sense and is just as valid today as heretofore. * * * The cases cited above are based on the common sense rationale that a person who breaks into and enters a dwelling or building in the nighttime, if no other motive is apparent, generally has the purpose of stealing something. Were the law otherwise, every unsuccessful nighttime burglar, caught before he could steal anything, would be guilty only of unlawful entry * * *. Certainly there are situations where a person may break into a dwelling or building in the nighttime with an innocent intent. However, the cases cited above recognize such an innocent intent might occur, and they hold only that where a defendant completely fails to explain his presence or there is a lack of another explanation, then the jury *may* infer an intent to steal. * * *

The majority further attempts to support its interpretation of the innocent nature of appellant's forcible midnight entry by noting that he failed to attack Mrs. Vessels when she discovered his presence. The record, however, indicates that Mrs. Vessels never directly saw appellant, but only suspected he was still in the sun room and the plywood which had been knocked over when appellant attempted to open the French doors presented some obstacle to easy entry from the sun room to the dining room. Further, it finds significantly exculpatory the fact that appellant did not escape during the several minutes between discovery of his presence and his apprehension, even though there was an open window nearby. There is no evidence that appellant could have escaped had he attempted to do so. The policemen were undoubtedly armed and with armed policemen in close proximity, an open window is no guarantee of escape—so a refusal to attempt to so escape is not any indication of the absence of criminal intent. The point the majority opinion attempts to make in this respect is merely another example of where it is straining at gnats and thus indicating the weakness of its entire conclusion. * * *

In this general discussion it should also be noted that the facts were such that the jury could have concluded that he was attempting to "conceal" himself by the open window through which he had gained entry into the house by breaking the lock. To argue, as the majority opinion does that "He could not have been concealed, since the arresting officers saw him immediately upon peering through the door into the sunroom * * *" attempts to embellish the cold facts. The reason he was discovered so quickly was because Mrs. Vessels told the police officers where she thought he was and he was trapped between the French doors which were difficult to negotiate because of the fallen plywood, and the open window only led outside where Mrs. Vessels might see him. By being on the floor next to the wall under the window, the jury would be justified in inferring that he was attempting concealment—so the fact is that he tried to conceal himself, but the physical layout of the sun room prohibited him from effectively concealing himself. To my knowledge it has never before been suggested that an inability to conceal oneself or to escape is a defense to the crime of housebreaking. * * *

Notes and Questions

1. The applicable statute in *Melton* required an "intent * * * to commit any criminal offense," but the indictment charged the defendant with the "intent to steal the property of another." Does it make some difference which it is that must be proved? Are you satisfied beyond a reasonable doubt that Melton intended to commit *some* crime? That he intended to commit a theft instead of, say, rape? Is it unfair to the prosecutor to require him, as many jurisdictions do, to charge and prove what particular crime was intended? Is it unfair to the defendant to permit, as some jurisdictions do, pleading and proof merely that some crime was intended?

2. Consider, in this regard, *Commonwealth v. Freeman,* 225 Pa.Super. 396, 313 A.2d 770 (1973). The police saw defendant enter an apartment by force and then exit emptyhanded a few minutes later. He was apprehended thereafter while attempting to hide in some bushes. He was charged and convicted of burglary, an offense requiring proof of "an intent to commit any felony therein." The court reversed, but then remanded with directions to enter a verdict of guilty of the lesser offense of unlawful entry, which requires proof of an "intent to commit a crime therein." "While the evidence is insufficient to support the inference that he intended to commit [the felony of] larceny, it does show that * * * he intended to commit some crime."

3. Consider also *Lee v. State,* 489 S.W.2d 61 (Tenn.App.1972), where the court quotes a leading treatise as follows: "There is a lack of unanimity of opinion among the courts on the question whether the intent to commit larceny in connection with a burglary charge must be affirmatively shown to exist as distinct from some other offense which might have been intended. Numerous cases, however, hold that an unexplained breaking and entering into a dwelling house in the nighttime is in itself sufficient to sustain a verdict that the breaking and entry was done with the intent to commit larceny rather than some other felony. The fundamental theory, in the absence of evidence of other intent or explanation for breaking and entering, is that the usual object or purpose of burglarizing a dwelling house at night is theft."

Does this suggest that where the prosecutor is required to particularize the intent in his pleading and proof, this burden is being eased by what was characterized in *Ex parte Seyfried,* 74 Idaho 467, 264 P.2d 685 (1953), as "a strong presumption and inference" that a nocturnal breaking and entry of a dwelling at night is "made with the purpose of committing larceny, no other purpose appearing"?

4. In *Patterson v. Commonwealth,* 215 Va. 698, 213 S.E.2d 752 (1975), a woman found a man hiding behind the shower door in her bathroom. He had entered at night through the bathroom window while she was wearing only a gown. When she screamed, he fled. She recognized the man as the same person who had trailed her home several weeks earlier. The defendant's conviction on a charge of burglary "with intent to rape" was reversed: "Here, a trier of fact could find an intent to rape only by resorting to surmise and speculation. Neither a spoken word of the defendant nor any other action on his part justifies the inference that he harbored the intent to ravish Mrs. Horton. So far as the evidence shows, the defendant's intent might just as well have been to commit larceny or any of a number of offenses other than rape." In light of what was said in *Lee,* did the prosecutor err in charging intent to rape instead of intent to steal?

STATE v. ODOM

Supreme Court of Washington, 1974.
83 Wash.2d 541, 520 P.2d 152.

UTTER, ASSOCIATE JUSTICE.

The state appeals from a judgment of the Court of Appeals reversing the defendant's conviction on one count of first-degree assault. That opinion affirmed the defendant's conviction on three other counts of first-degree assault. * * *

The necessary facts from which the jury could have determined the guilt of the defendant, as set forth in the Court of Appeals opinion, are:

[O]n November 24, 1970, the defendant went to the Tacoma offices of the Department of Employment Security to make his weekly report in support of his application for unemployment compensation benefits. While there, he objected to filling out a particular form and to reporting to the adjudication section. After having been told by the supervisor of benefits to complete the form and return with it the next week, and after having expressed his dissatisfaction with that procedure in an angry fashion, he left the office only to return within a half hour. Upon his return, he approached the supervisor's desk, declared that he was tired of being pushed around, and announced an intention to settle this matter once and for all. At that time he was carrying a holstered .44 caliber magnum pistol in his left hand. He grasped the pistol in his right hand, pointed it at the supervisor and fired twice. On one occasion the projectile pierced through the supervisor's left lower chest, exiting to the right of the lumbar area of the spine. As a result of this gunshot wound, the supervisor suffered permanent paralysis of both lower extremities together with other permanent and incapacitating internal injuries.

After firing the pistol, he reloaded it, left the office by a rear exit and returned to his automobile in a nearby alley. In the meantime, police had been summoned. Two patrolmen approached in a "paddy wagon" and noticed the defendant sitting in his vehicle. The patrolman driver emerged from the police vehicle and the defendant fired at him. The patrolman returned the fire, and the defendant then fired at and into the windshield of the "paddy wagon" while the other patrolman was still sitting in the front seat. After a brief exchange of gunfire during which no one appears to have been hit by a projectile, the defendant ran down the alley and into another street, reloading his pistol as he ran.

At this point, a police lieutenant, driving a police prowl car, approached the defendant. The defendant pointed his pistol toward the windshield of the prowl car, but apparently did not fire the weapon. When the prowl car was approximately 25 feet from the defendant, the police lieutenant saw the gun pointed in his direction, and he believed Odom "was trying to kill me." He accelerated the vehicle and ran into the defendant, knocking him over and leaving him momentarily in a dazed condition. The lieutenant jumped out of the police car, approached the defendant from behind, and took the pistol from him. At that time the pistol was in a cocked position and was still loaded with two live rounds of ammunition. Before the gun was taken from the defendant, he said, "I've had enough," and after having been relieved of the gun, he addressed the lieutenant, "You son of a bitch, I wish I had shot you."

Mr. Odom purchased the gun in 1969. He applied for a permit to carry the weapon while he was working alone late at night in a drive-in restaurant. His application was denied.

The defendant was arrested and subsequently was charged with having committed four counts of first degree assault—each count alleging a separate victim which he had assaulted "with intent to kill." The victims were—the supervisor of benefits, the two patrolmen who had been in the "paddy wagon", and the lieutenant who had been in the prowl car.

The defendant assigned error to the giving of instruction No. 25, which reads:

You are instructed that under the laws of the State of Washington no person shall carry a pistol concealed on or about his person, except in his place of abode or place of business, without a license therefor.

You are further instructed that in the trial of a person who has been charged with a crime of violence, the fact that the defendant was armed with a pistol and had no license to carry the same shall be prima facie evidence of his intention to commit such crime of violence.

"Prima facie evidence" means evidence which may be accepted for proof of a particular fact. Such evidence even if not refuted by the defendant, should be given just such weight as it seems to you to merit.

He contends that the statute upon which this instruction is based deprives him of his presumption of innocence and allows the jury to convict him on proof of guilt less than beyond a reasonable doubt. RCW 9.41.030 provides: "In the trial of a person for committing or attempting to commit a crime of violence, the fact that he was armed with a pistol and had no license to carry the same shall be prima facie evidence of his intention to commit said crime of violence."

It is further urged that even if the statutory presumption is valid, the instruction improperly extends the use the jury may make of it.

The constitutionality of the statute in question has been affirmed in *State v. Person,* 56 Wash.2d 283, 352 P.2d 189 (1960), and in *State v. Thomas,* 58 Wash. 2d 746, 364 P.2d 930 (1961) as applied to first-degree assault. Statutory criminal presumptions in Washington have established a prima facie case for the prosecution by allowing, but not requiring, the jury to infer the presumed fact from proof of the operative facts. * * *

The evidentiary effect of this presumption is that once the operative facts are proved and that presumption attaches, the case must go to the jury and there can be no directed verdict of acquittal. * * *

Substantial changes in the law have occurred since these opinions, which force a reexamination of our position taken in them and the other cases based upon them.

Two theories, closely related, apply to the administration of the criminal laws of this state. The defendant is presumed innocent until proven guilty and his guilt must be proved by competent evidence beyond a reasonable doubt. *In re Winship,* 397 U.S. 358, 90 S.Ct. 1068, 25 L.Ed.2d 368 (1970). The presumption of innocence stresses that the jury is to consider in the material for their belief *"nothing but the evidence,* i.e., no surmises based on the present situation of the accused." 9 J. Wigmore, *Evidence,* § 2511 at 407 (3d ed. 1940). The requirement of proof beyond a reasonable doubt has not only common law and statutory origins but also has been recently given constitutional stature in *Winship,* where the court stated: "we explicitly hold that the Due Process Clause protects the accused against conviction except upon proof beyond a reasonable doubt of every fact necessary to constitute the crime with which he is charged." The court described the reasonable doubt standard as a "prime instrument for reducing the risk of convictions resting on factual error." Its role in criminal prosecution was recognized as vital to an accused because "he may lose his liberty upon conviction and because of the certainty that he would be stigmatized by the conviction." The fact that in litigation there is always a margin of error was conceded by the court, and in recognition of this they held the reasonable doubt standard indispensible because it " 'impresses on the trier of fact the necessity of reaching a subjective state of certitude of the facts in issue.' "

The apparent inconsistency between the newly emphasized standard of proof beyond a reasonable doubt and criminal presumptions has troubled many writers. The United States Supreme Court recently has, as well, reevaluated its earlier approach to the validity of criminal presumptions in *Leary v. United States,* 395 U.S. 6, 89 S.Ct. 1532, 23 L.Ed.2d 57 (1969) and *Turner v. United States,* 396 U.S. 398, 90 S.Ct. 642, 24 L.Ed.2d 610 (1970).

In *Leary,* a presumption that one knew marijuana had been illegally imported from proof of its possession was struck down as failing the rational connection test. The court held that "it was incumbent upon the prosecution to demonstrate that the inference was permissible before the burden of coming forward could be placed upon the defendant." The court required that it should "at least be said with substantial assurance that the presumed fact is more likely than not to flow from the proved fact on which it is made to depend."

The court also indicated an even stricter standard might be applied, [for] it stated that inasmuch as the presumption was unconstitutional under the more-likely-than-not standard "we need not reach the question whether a criminal presumption which passes muster when so judged must also satisfy the criminal 'reasonable doubt' standard if proof of the crime charged or an essential element thereof depends upon its use."

In a later case, the court in *Turner* sustained a presumption which inferred knowledge of the unlawful importation of heroin from its unexplained possession by stating that it met both the more-likely-than-not standard and the reasonable-doubt test. The court likewise invalidated the same presumption as applied to cocaine, stating that it could not be sustained even under the "more-likely-than-not standard." Subsequent to *Leary* and *Turner,* many courts which have recognized the problem, have concluded that the beyond a reasonable doubt test must be applied to find the rational relation to the presumed fact from the proved fact. * * *

The answer to whether it has been shown beyond a reasonable doubt in this case that the fact the defendant was armed with an unlicensed pistol proves his intent to commit a crime of violence can only be no. The facts in this case amply illustrate the failure of proof on this issue. The defendant purchased the gun two years before the crime was committed. He applied for a license, which was denied. He believed at that time that he needed the gun for self-protection while working as a night-time janitor. The failure to license a gun, standing alone, hardly can be said to create an inference beyond a reasonable doubt of an intent to commit a crime of violence with that gun two years after the gun's purchase.

The prosecutor has presented, in his brief, statistics showing that of seven homicides by gun in 1971, six were with unlicensed guns; in 1972, that six homicides were by gun, all of them unlicensed and that to date in 1973, six homicides have been committed by gun with three of the guns unlicensed. These figures, while of interest, fail to show the necessary correlation between the proved fact and the presumed fact beyond a reasonable doubt and only serve to demonstrate the unsatisfactory methods which we use in dealing with the use of presumptions and problems of proof relative to them in criminal law. * * *

The jury was entitled to find an intent to kill from the fact that the defendant fired at the victims in the first three counts. Although the instruction on the presumption was erroneous, we agree with the Court of Appeals that as to those three counts the mind of the average juror would not have found the prosecutor's

case significantly less persuasive had the jury not utilized the statutory presumption as a basis to find in the defendant a specific intent to kill the alleged victims. The error was harmless.

The same cannot be said for count 4. There was no shot fired at the intended victim and although this, in itself, is not determinative, the use of the presumption creates a doubt as to its effect on the jury to the extent we cannot say its use was harmless.

The judgment of the trial court is affirmed as to counts 1, 2 and 3 and reversed and remanded for a new trial as to count 4. * * *

HALE, CHIEF JUSTICE (concurring in part; dissenting in part). * * *

The legislature, quite logically, I think, recognizes that there exists a direct rational connection between the carrying of a concealed—*i.e.,* unlicensed—firearm and its use in crimes of violence. But in doing so, this lays down no more than a rebuttable presumption, and the defendant is at liberty to present whatever explanations he may have for carrying a concealed unlicensed pistol immediately prior to using it in the commission of an act of violence. If one does not wish to be saddled with the presumption, he has a ready remedy: not to carry a concealed pistol. By declaring a rebuttable presumption, the statute simply adds to already existing sanctions one more legitimate sanction against the illegal carrying of a deadly weapon.

I would, therefore, affirm on all counts.

Notes and Questions

1. The question not reached in *Leary* and *Turner* was finally resolved in *County Court of Ulster County v. Allen*, p. 210 of this Book, where the Supreme Court held that a "rational connection" between the proved and presumed facts exists whenever the latter is more likely than not to flow

from the former. Had the *Odom* court correctly anticipated this development, would the case have come out differently?

2. Which, if any, of the following provisions are constitutional?

(a) Possession of marijuana is a misdemeanor, but possession of marijuana "with intent to deliver" is a felony. The statute goes on to provide: "Possession of more than 2 ounces of marijuana is prima facie evidence of possession with intent to deliver." [a]

(b) Possession of heroin with intent to deliver is a more serious offense than mere possession. The statute provides: "Possession by any person of a quantity of Heroin in excess of 100 milligrams shall create a rebuttable presumption that such person possesses such Heroin with intent to deliver, provided however, the presumption provided for herein may be overcome by the submission of evidence sufficient to create a reasonable doubt that the person charged possessed Heroin with intent to deliver in violation of the law." [b]

(c) A statute makes it a crime for one, with intent to defraud, to make, draw, utter, or deliver any check upon any bank, knowing at the time of such making, drawing, uttering, or delivery, that the maker

or drawer has not sufficient funds in such bank for the payment of the check. The statute continues: "In any prosecution under this section, the making, drawing, uttering or delivering of a check, payment of which is refused by the drawee because of lack of funds or credit, shall be prima facie evidence of intent to defraud and of knowledge of insufficient funds in, or credit with, such bank unless such maker or drawer shall have paid the drawee thereof the amount due thereon within 10 days after receiving notice." [c]

(d) A somewhat similar statute regarding the delivery of fraudulent checks instead provides: "It shall be prima facie evidence upon proof of the fact that the drawer or maker did not have an account with the drawee, at the time of issuance, that the drawer or maker intended to defraud." [d]

SANDSTROM v. MONTANA

Supreme Court of the United States, 1979.
442 U.S. 510, 99 S.Ct. 2450, 61 L.Ed.2d 39.

MR. JUSTICE BRENNAN delivered the opinion of the Court.

The question presented is whether, in a case in which intent is an element of the crime charged, the jury instruction, "the

***

a. See *People v. Serra,* 55 Mich.App. 514, 223 N.W.2d 28 (1974), concluding that the statute does not meet the requirements of either *Leary* or *Turner* and that in addition it violates the privilege against self-incrimination. "The quite unobjectionable compulsion to testify arising from natural facts and inferences becomes objectionable when created by a presumption because in creating the presumption the state interferes, in a potentially misleading and unfair manner, with the jury's role as trier of fact. The state compels defendants to testify by telling them, in effect, that if they don't the jury will be told to convict them, even if conviction would be totally unwarranted without the presumption."

b. See *Stone v. State,* 254 Ark. 1011, 498 S.W.2d 634 (1973), where the court held (i) that the burden was on the defendant to show the lack of a "rational connection" and that he had not done so; and (ii) that the privilege against self-incrimination was not violated because "the appropriate evidentiary rebuttal might come

through the testimony of others than the accused himself."

c. In *Commonwealth v. Horton,* 465 Pa. 213, 348 A.2d 728 (1975), the court construed the statute as being not applicable where the defendant, who cashed the check, was not the maker or drawer of the check. "Without considering whether either or both of these inferences could pass constitutional muster, it is obvious that in the instance of a drawer or maker, the nexus to the inference to be inferred is infinitely stronger than when it is applied to a payee negotiator."

d. See *O'Neal v. State,* 498 P.2d 1232 (Wyo. 1972), deciding only that it was reversible error to instruct in the words of the statute, as "the giving of the instruction in the words of the statute without explanation or definition, particularly as to its rebuttable character, might well lead a jury to believe the State was relieved of its burden of proof beyond a reasonable doubt."

law presumes that a person intends the ordinary consequences of his voluntary acts," violates the Fourteenth Amendment's requirement that the State prove every element of a criminal offense beyond a reasonable doubt.

On November 22, 1976, 18–year–old David Sandstrom confessed to the slaying of Annie Jessen. Based upon the confession and corroborating evidence, petitioner was charged on December 2 with "deliberate homicide," in that he "purposely or knowingly caused the death of Annie Jessen." * * *

The prosecution requested the trial judge to instruct the jury that "[t]he law presumes that a person intends the ordinary consequences of his voluntary acts." Petitioner's counsel objected, arguing that "the instruction has the effect of shifting the burden of proof on the issue of" purpose or knowledge to the defense, and that "that is impermissible under the Federal Constitution, due process of law." He offered to provide a number of federal decisions in support of the objection, including this Court's holding in *Mullaney v. Wilbur,* [p. 238 of this Book], but was told by the judge: "You can give those to the Supreme Court. The objection is overruled." The instruction was delivered, the jury found petitioner guilty of deliberate homicide, and petitioner was sentenced to 100 years in prison.

Sandstrom appealed to the Supreme Court of Montana, again contending that the instruction shifted to the defendant the burden of disproving an element of the crime charged, in violation of *Mullaney v. Wilbur, supra, In re Winship,* 397 U.S. 358, 90 S.Ct. 1068, 25 L.Ed.2d 368 (1970), and *Patterson v. New York,* [p. 245 of this Book]. The Montana court conceded that these cases did prohibit shifting the burden of proof to the defendant by means of a presumption, but held that the cases "do not prohibit allocation of *some* burden of

proof to a defendant under certain circumstances." Since in the court's view, "[d]efendant's sole burden under instruction No. 5 was to produce *some* evidence that he did not intend the ordinary consequences of his voluntary acts, not to disprove that he acted 'purposely' or 'knowingly,' * * * the instruction does not violate due process standards as defined by the United States or Montana Constitution * * *." (emphasis added). * * *

Respondent argues, first, that the instruction merely described a permissive inference—that is, it allowed but did not require the jury to draw conclusions about defendant's intent from his actions—and that such inferences are constitutional. These arguments need not detain us long, for even respondent admits that "it's possible" that the jury believed they were required to apply the presumption. Sandstrom's jurors were told that "[t]he law presumes that a person intends the ordinary consequences of his voluntary acts." They were not told that they had a choice, or that they might infer that conclusion; they were told only that the law presumed it. It is clear that a reasonable juror could easily have viewed such an instruction as mandatory.

In the alternative, respondent urges that, even if viewed as a mandatory presumption rather than as a permissive inference, the presumption did not conclusively establish intent but rather could be rebutted. On this view, the instruction required the jury, if satisfied as to the facts which trigger the presumption, to find intent *unless* the defendant offered evidence to the contrary. Moreover, according to the State, all the defendant had to do to rebut the presumption was produce "some" contrary evidence; he did not have to "prove" that he lacked the required mental state. Thus, "[a]t most, it placed a *burden of production* on the petitioner," but "did not shift to petitioner the *burden of persuasion* with respect to any element of the offense

* * *" Again, respondent contends that presumptions with this limited effect pass constitutional muster. * * *

The Supreme Court of Montana is, of course, the final authority on the legal weight to be given a presumption under Montana law, but it is not the final authority on the interpretation which a jury could have given the instruction. If Montana intended its presumption to have only the effect described by its Supreme Court, then we are convinced that a reasonable juror could well have been misled by the instruction given, and could have believed that the presumption was not limited to requiring the defendant to satisfy only a burden of production. Petitioner's jury was told that *"[t]he law presumes* that a person intends the ordinary consequences of his voluntary acts." They were not told that the presumption could be rebutted, as the Montana Supreme Court held, by the defendant's simple presentation of "some" evidence; nor even that it could be rebutted at all. Given the common definition of "presume" as "to suppose to be true without proof," Webster's New Collegiate Dictionary 911 (1974), and given the lack of qualifying instructions as to the legal effect of the presumption, we cannot discount the possibility that the jury may have interpreted the instruction in either of two more stringent ways.

First, a reasonable jury could well have interpreted the presumption as "conclusive," that is, not technically as a presumption at all, but rather as an irrebuttable direction by the court to find intent once convinced of the facts triggering the presumption. Alternatively, the jury may have interpreted the instruction as a direction to find intent upon proof of the defendant's voluntary actions (and their "ordinary" consequences), unless *the defendant* proved the contrary by some quantum of proof which may well have been considerably greater than "some" evidence—thus

effectively shifting the burden of persuasion on the element of intent. * * *

In *Winship,* this Court stated:

"Lest there remain any doubt about the constitutional stature of the reasonable-doubt standard, we explicitly hold that the Due Process Clause protects the accused against conviction except upon proof beyond a reasonable doubt *of every fact* necessary to constitute the crime with which he is charged." (emphasis added).

The petitioner here was charged with and convicted of deliberate homicide, committed purposely or knowingly. It is clear that under Montana law, whether the crime was committed purposely or knowingly is a fact necessary to constitute the crime of deliberate homicide. Indeed, it was the lone element of the offense at issue in Sandstrom's trial, as he confessed to causing the death of the victim, told the jury that knowledge and purpose were the only questions he was controverting, and introduced evidence solely on those points. Moreover, it is conceded that proof of defendant's "intent" would be sufficient to establish this element. Thus, the question before this Court is whether the challenged jury instruction had the effect of relieving the State of the burden of proof enunciated in *Winship* on the critical question of petitioner's state of mind. We conclude that under either of the two possible interpretations of the instruction set out above, precisely that effect would result, and that the instruction therefore represents constitutional error.

We consider first the validity of a conclusive presumption. This Court has considered such a presumption on at least two prior occasions. In *Morissette v. United States,* 342 U.S. 246, 72 S.Ct. 240, 96 L.Ed. 288 (1952), the defendant was charged with willful and knowing theft of Government property. Although his attorney argued that for his client to be found guilty, " 'the taking must have been with felonious intent'," the trial judge ruled that " '[t]hat is presumed by his own act.' " After first concluding that intent was in fact an element of the crime charged, and after declaring that "[w]here intent of the accused is an ingredient of the crime charged, its existence is * * * a jury issue," *Morissette* held:

"It follows that the trial court may not withdraw or prejudge the issue by instruction that the law raises a presumption of intent from an act. It often is tempting to cast in terms of a 'presumption' a conclusion which a court thinks probable from given facts. * * * [But] [w]e think presumptive intent has no place in this case. *A conclusive presumption which testimony could not overthrow would effectively eliminate intent as an ingredient of the offense.* A presumption which would permit but not require the jury to assume intent from an isolated fact would prejudge a conclusion which the jury should reach of its own volition. A presumption which would permit the jury to make an assumption which all the evidence considered together does not logically establish would give to a proven fact an artificial and fictional effect. In either case, *this presumption would conflict with the overriding presumption of innocence with which the law endows the accused and which extends to every element of the crime."* (Emphasis added; footnote omitted.)

Just last Term, in *United States v. United States Gypsum Co.,* 438 U.S. 422, 98 S.Ct. 2864, 57 L.Ed.2d 854 (1978), we reaffirmed the holding of *Morissette.* In that case defendants, who were charged with criminal violations of the Sherman Act, challenged the following jury instruction:

"The law presumes that a person intends the necessary and natural consequences of his acts. Therefore, if the effect of the exchanges of pricing information was to raise, fix, maintain and stabilize prices, then the parties to them are presumed, as a matter of law, to have intended that result."

After again determining that the offense included the element of intent, we held:

"[A] defendant's state of mind or *intent is an element of a criminal antitrust offense which * * * cannot be taken from the trier of fact through reliance on a legal presumption* of wrongful intent from proof of an effect on prices. Cf. *Morissette v. United States * * *.*

* * *

"Although an effect on prices may well support an inference that the defendant had knowledge of the probability of such a consequence at the time he acted, the jury must remain free to consider additional evidence before accepting or rejecting the inference. * * * [U]ltimately the decision on the issue of intent must be left to the trier of fact alone. The instruction given invaded this factfinding function." (emphasis added).

As in *Morissette* and *United States Gypsum Co.,* a conclusive presumption in this case would "conflict with the overriding presumption of innocence with which the law endows the accused and which extends to every element of the crime," and would "invade [the] factfinding function" which in a criminal case the law assigns solely to the jury. The instruction announced to David Sandstrom's jury may well have had exactly these consequences. Upon finding proof of one element of the crime (causing death), and of facts insufficient to establish the second (the voluntariness and "ordinary consequences" of defendant's action), Sandstrom's jurors could reasonably have concluded that they were directed to find against defendant on the element of intent. The State was thus not forced to prove "beyond a reasonable doubt * * * every fact necessary to constitute the crime * * * charged," and defendant was deprived of his constitutional rights as explicated in *Winship.*

A presumption which, although not conclusive, had the effect of shifting the burden of persuasion to the defendant, would have suffered from similar infirmities. If Sandstrom's jury interpreted the presumption in that manner, it could have concluded that upon proof by the State of the slaying, and of additional facts not themselves establishing the element of intent, the burden was shifted to the defendant to prove that he lacked the requisite mental state. Such a presumption was found constitutionally deficient in *Mullaney v. Wilbur.* In *Mullaney,* the charge was murder, which under Maine law required proof not only of intent but of malice. The trial court charged the jury that " 'malice aforethought is an essential and indispensable element of the crime of murder.' " However, it also instructed that if the prosecution established that the homicide was both intentional and unlawful, malice aforethought was to be implied unless the defendant proved by a fair preponderance of the evidence that he acted in the heat of passion on sudden provocation. As we recounted just two Terms ago in *Patterson v. New York,* "[t]his Court * * * unanimously agreed with the Court of Appeals that Wilbur's due process rights had been invaded by the presumption casting upon him the burden of proving by a preponderance of the evidence that he had acted in the heat of passion upon sudden provocation." And *Patterson* reaffirmed that "a State must prove every ingredient of an offense beyond a reasonable doubt, and * * * may not shift the burden of proof to the defendant" by means of such a presumption.

Because David Sandstrom's jury may have interpreted the judge's instruction as constituting either a burden-shifting presumption like that in *Mullaney,* or a conclusive presumption like those in *Morissette* and *United States Gypsum Co.,* and because

either interpretation would have deprived defendant of his right to the due process of law, we hold the instruction given in this case unconstitutional.

Notes and Questions

1. In *Francis v. Franklin,* 471 U.S. 307, 105 S.Ct. 1965, 85 L.Ed.2d 344 (1985), the respondent, a state prisoner, while attempting to escape after receiving treatment at a dentist's office, shot and killed the resident of a nearby house with a stolen pistol when, at the moment the resident slammed the door as respondent demanded the key to the resident's car, the pistol fired and a bullet pierced the door, hitting the resident in the chest. At his Georgia trial for malice murder, he claimed the killing was an accident. The trial judge instructed: "The acts of a person of sound mind and discretion are presumed to be the product of a person's will, but the presumption may be rebutted. A person of sound mind and discretion is presumed to intend the natural and probable consequences of his acts, but the presumption may be rebutted. A person will not be presumed to act with criminal intention but the trier of facts * * * may find criminal intention upon a consideration of the words, conduct, demeanor, motive and all of the circumstances connected with the act for which the accused is prosecuted." Though the state supreme court had characterized this as merely a permissive inference and had upheld respondent's murder conviction, the Supreme Court held, 5–4, that this instruction was unconstitutional under *Sandstrom.* Because the "challenged sentences are cast in the language of command," they would be viewed by jurors either as a conclusive presumption or as a burden-shifting rebuttable presumption. The majority also concluded the general instructions on the prosecution's burden of proof and respondent's presumption of innocence did not dissipate the error. Nor, they concluded,

did the more specific "criminal intention" instruction, but the four dissenters felt otherwise.

2. Is the Court's conclusion in *Sandstrom* and *Francis* regarding the so-called conclusive presumption correct? Consider Allen & DeGrazia, *The Constitutional Requirement of Proof Beyond a Reasonable Doubt in Criminal Cases: A Comment Upon Incipient Chaos in the Lower Courts,* 20 Am.Crim.L. Rev. 1, 13 (1982): "If the instruction is given in every case of murder, a traditional element of the definition of the crime has been removed. If the instruction accurately describes state law, intent is not included as an element of murder; rather, the state must show only a voluntary act and its ordinary consequences. Alternatively, the instruction may be read to define the crime to require either proof of intent or proof that the defendant's act was voluntary and that the ordinary consequences of that act would be death. In either case, the instruction merely provides an untraditional definition of homicide that foregoes the usual requirement of intent. This involves no burden shifting at all; the issue has simply been removed as an absolute requirement. Consequently, neither alternative should have been objectionable to the Court on the grounds that the reasonable doubt requirement was violated. Montana may very well have defined homicide in an unusual fashion, but under the Court's theory *all* it did was define the crime. Without a constitutional limitation on a state's definition of crime, Montana's statute should have been perfectly acceptable."

3. As we will see in *Patterson v. New York,* p. 245 of this Book, at least when a crime may constitutionally be defined without a particular factual matter being stated as an element, then that matter may be expressed as an affirmative defense and the burden of proof as to it placed on the defendant. Allen & DeGrazia, supra at 13–14, therefore assert that *Sandstrom,*

which does not disapprove of *Patterson,* thus "appears to approve of traditionally constructed affirmative defenses, but to regard as constitutionally impermissible the unorthodox method of creating affirmative defenses through presumptions. This distinction, however, is difficult to support because placing a burden of persuasion on a defendant by a presumption is the functional equivalent of creating an affirmative defense in the conventional manner. * * * To be constitutional, the state need only use the correct words in its statute. If the state makes the mistake of effectively creating an affirmative defense through the use of mandatory presumption language rather than in the manner approved in *Patterson,* then the statute is unacceptable even though there is no functional difference between the two methods."

4. After *Sandstrom,* what is the status of 1 E. Devitt & C. Blackmar, *Federal Jury Practice and Instructions* § 14.13 (3d ed. 1977): "You may consider it reasonable to draw the inference and find that a person intends the natural and probable consequences of acts knowingly done or knowingly omitted. As I have said, it is entirely up to you to decide what facts to find from the evidence."

SECTION 3. KNOWLEDGE

STATE v. BEALE
Supreme Court of Maine, 1973.
299 A.2d 921.

WEATHERBEE, JUSTICE.

The Defendant, who operates an antique shop in Hallowell, was convicted under 17 M.R.S.A. § 3551 of the offense of knowingly concealing stolen property. His appeal presents us for the first time with the opportunity to construe the phrase "knowing it to be stolen" found in this statute.

One Saturday during the summer of 1971, when the Defendant was absent and his store was in Mrs. Beale's care, a prospective customer, a Mrs. Johnson, noticed that some of the displayed merchandise looked familiar. On examining it further she became convinced that several items were in fact pieces of silverware and glass which had been stolen from her several months earlier.

She left and returned after a short interval with a Hallowell police officer. She then pointed out to Mrs. Beale the items which she believed to have been stolen from her. The officer told Mrs. Beale that these items were "possibly stolen" and that they should be placed aside and not displayed or sold. She then gathered these items and put them on a shelf. The officer testified that he told Mrs. Beale to tell her husband to "contact me as soon as he got back". He later testified that he said that she "would be contacted, probably, later on that day".

There was no further contact between the Beales and the police during the weekend. The following Monday morning the investigation was apparently taken over by a deputy sheriff from the county where the theft had occurred. When he called at Defendant's store Defendant informed him that he had put the articles back in the counter for sale Sunday morning and that he had sold many of these items that day in spite of knowing that the police officer had requested that they be withdrawn from sale. Among those which the Defendant said he had sold were all the articles which bore the distinctive initials by which the owner had identified them as hers.

The Defendant testified that he had purchased these items at different times from people whom he considered to be reliable, that he had receipts for many of them and that he was entitled to sell them regardless

of the officer's warning. The only testimony as to the details of the complaint by Mrs. Johnson and the officer's admonitions to Mrs. Beale which were in fact related to Mr. Beale was given by Mrs. Beale (called by the State) and the Defendant himself. The Defendant and Mrs. Beale testified that Mrs. Beale told the Defendant that Mrs. Johnson claimed that these items had been stolen from her home, and that the officer had asked Mrs. Beale to put the items aside saying that he would be back later.

[Over defense counsel's objection, the trial court instructed the jury that "knowing" includes the situation in which a reasonable prudent man would be led to believe the items were stolen.]

* * * The issue is one of statutory interpretation of the words "knowing it to be stolen". Did the Legislature intend that the jury be satisfied as to the knowledge of the Defendant by testing it subjectively or objectively? To put it another way, must the State satisfy the jury that the Defendant himself actually had knowledge that the goods were stolen or is it enough that a reasonable person, with the information that was available to the Defendant, would have known that the goods were stolen?

We find a split of authority among the jurisdictions which have had the occasion to examine this issue, with the majority requiring that the State's proof should meet the subjective test. * * *

A minority of jurisdictions apply the so-called objective test as to knowledge, being impressed perhaps, by the difficulties of proof as to the actual state of a defendant's mind. * * * [1]

We consider that the distinction between the bases of the two points of view was clarified by an opinion from the Cir-

---

1. In some states the statutes define the offense as being committed by one who knows or

who has reasonable cause to believe that the property received had been stolen.

cuit Court of Appeals, 2nd Circuit, written by Judge Learned Hand. He wrote:

"The defendants ask us to distinguish between 'knowing' that goods are stolen and merely being put upon an inquiry which would have led to discovery; but they have misconceived the distinction which the decisions have made. The receivers of stolen goods almost never 'know' that they have been stolen, in the sense that they could testify to it in a court room. The business could not be so conducted, for those who sell the goods—the 'fences'—must keep up a more respectable front than is generally possible for the thieves. Nor are we to suppose that the thieves will ordinarily admit their theft to the receivers: that would much impair their bargaining power. For this reason, some decisions even go so far as to hold that it is enough, if a reasonable man in the receiver's position would have supposed that the goods were stolen. That we think is wrong; and the better law is otherwise, although of course the fact that a reasonable man would have thought that they had been stolen, is some basis for finding that the accused actually did think so. But that the jury must find that the receiver did more than infer the theft from the circumstances has never been demanded, so far as we know; and to demand more would emasculate the statute, for the evil against which it is directed is exactly that: i.e., making a market for stolen goods which the purchaser believes to have probably been stolen." *United States v. Werner,* 160 F.2d 438, 441–442 (2nd Cir.1947). * * *

It appears to us that the minority jurisdictions which follow the "ordinary reasonable man" test are failing to stress sufficiently the distinction between civil and criminal responsibility. In civil cases the failure of the defendant to act with the degree of care which a person of ordinary prudence would have used may be the test of his responsibility without any determination that the defendant, himself, was a person of ordinary prudence or that he had any wrongful intent. On the other hand, the very essence of this criminal offense is the intentional wrongdoing of the defendant.

Such was the case at common law and if the Legislature had intended something less than actual knowledge, more appropriate language could easily have been chosen.

The distinction is more than one of semantics. It is made necessary by the fact that while a defendant may have received information which would have convinced a person of ordinary intelligence and average capacity to comprehend and evaluate facts, a defendant may be a person of less than average intelligence, comprehension and reasoning powers. The true test is, did the *defendant* know the goods were stolen.

This is not to say that the defendant must have direct knowledge or positive proof that the goods were stolen, such as he would have gained by actually witnessing the theft or hearing the admission of the thief. It is enough if he was made aware of circumstances which caused him to believe that they were stolen.

The fact that the jury must be satisfied as to the state of the defendant's personal belief does not present the State with an insurmountable task when direct proof of his belief is absent. Juries have been instructed from time immemorial as to other offenses that they may draw rational inferences as to intent from a defendant's speech and conduct in relation to the subject matter and from evidence showing the information of which a defendant was aware. The state of a defendant's belief may be resolved by inference in the same manner.

While the objective test of what an ordinary intelligent man would have believed cannot serve as the absolute standard which determines the defendant's guilt or innocence, the jury, in making its determination as to the state of a defendant's belief, may properly take into consideration, among other things, the belief which the jury concludes a person of ordinary intellectual capacity would have formed from such facts and circumstances. The jury may consider this in the light of its evaluation of a defendant as an intelligent person, based upon what the jury has learned about the defendant from testimony and observation. * * * Appeal sustained. Remanded for new trial.

Notes and Questions

1. In *People v. Prante,* 177 Colo. 243, 493 P.2d 1083 (1972), the defendant was convicted of the crime of assaulting a police officer, defined by statute as requiring that a defendant "knew or reasonably should have known that the person assaulted was a peace officer engaged in the performance of his duties." On appeal, the defendant claimed that this language was (i) void for vagueness, and (ii) not a sufficient standard for criminal guilt. The court responded:

"The statute under consideration here states clearly the behavior sought to be proscribed. In a statute so framed as to clearly put before the public notice of what is prohibited, those who risk violation and seek escape through an exceptional fact situation are not protected by the Fourteenth Amendment * * *.

"In situations where it is difficult to determine what an actor knows or knew, there can be no better appraisal of it than for a jury to educe what a temperate and measured man would know in the same circumstances. Indeed, this is the function of the jury at any rate whether statutorily delegated or not. And framing a statute

in such a way as to give this function to the jury is not arbitrary or unreasonable."

2. Compare *State v. Ware,* 27 Ariz. App. 645, 557 P.2d 1077 (1976), where defendant was convicted of the sale of stolen property. The statute provided the defendant must have dealt with the property while "knowing or having reason to believe the property was stolen." In response to defendant's assertion that this language rendered the statute unconstitutional, the court stated:

"We hold that [the statute] requires a finding and proof that the defendant *himself* possessed actual knowledge or belief that the goods he retained were stolen. We reject the 'reasonable man' approach which attempts to integrate the civil negligence standard into the criminal law, primarily for the reason that implementation of this test would allow juries to return guilty verdicts against those who may be less circumspect and intelligent than the average man. * * *

"No legislative history has been presented by counsel as to the specific reason why the phrase 'having reason to believe' was added to the statute when it was amended in 1969 to raise the monetary amount from $50 to $100, differentiating a felony from a misdemeanor. In light of our holding regarding the impropriety of a 'reasonable man standard', it is our view that the language added in 1969 * * * merely codified the law in Arizona as set down by the Arizona Supreme Court in *Reser v. State* [27 Ariz. 43, 229 P. 936 (1924), adopting the subjective test]. Change in statutory language is presumed to be a change in form only, unless it is clearly shown that the Legislature intended to change the meaning of the law."

3. *State v. Jantzi,* 56 Or.App. 57, 641 P.2d 62 (1982): "The trial court stated for the record at the close of the evidence that it believed defendant's version of what occurred in the incident from which

this charge arose. Defendant testified that he was asked to accompany Diane Anderson, who shared a house with defendant and several other people, to the home of her estranged husband, Rex. While Diane was in the house talking with Rex, defendant was using the blade of his knife to let the air out of the tires on Rex's van. Another person put sugar in the gas tank of the van.

"While the Andersons were arguing, Diane apparently threatened damage to Rex's van and indicated that someone might be tampering with the van at that moment. Rex's roommate ran out of the house and saw two men beside the van. He shouted and began to run toward the men. Rex ran from the house and began to chase defendant, who ran down a bicycle path. Defendant, still holding his open knife, jumped into the bushes beside the path and landed in the weeds. He crouched there, hoping that Rex would not see him and would pass by. Rex, however, jumped on top of defendant and grabbed his shirt. They rolled over and Rex was stabbed in the abdomen by defendant's knife. Defendant could not remember making a thrusting or swinging motion with the knife; he did not intend to stab Rex.

"The indictment charged that defendant 'did unlawfully and knowingly cause physical injury to Rex Anderson by means of a deadly weapon, to-wit: knife, by stabbing the said Rex Anderson with said knife.' ORS 163.175 provides that:

1. The commentary to the Oregon Criminal Code of 1971 (1975 ed.) indicates that the definitions of the culpable mental states set out in ORS 161.085 are derived from the New York Revised Penal Law §§ 15.00–15.05, and that

"[t]he definition of 'knowingly' or 'with knowledge' in subsection (8) was changed by the New York reporters to eliminate any reference to result of conduct and to restrict the term to awareness of the nature of one's conduct or of the existence of specified circumstances (*e.g.*, that property is stolen, that one has no right to enter a building, etc.).

The New York commentary has this to say:

'(1) A person commits the crime of assault in the second degree if he:

' * * *

'(b) Intentionally or knowingly causes physical injury to another by means of a deadly or dangerous weapon;

' * * *

'Knowingly' is defined in ORS 161.085(8):

' "Knowingly" or "with knowledge" when used with respect to conduct or to a circumstance described by a statute defining an offense, means that a person acts with an awareness that his conduct is of a nature so described or that a circumstance so described exists.'[1]

The trial court stated:

'Basically, the facts of this case are: that Defendant was letting air out of the tires and he has an open knife. He was aware of what his knife is like. He is aware that it is a dangerous weapon. He runs up the bicycle path. He has a very firm grip on the knife, by his own admission, and he knows the knife is dangerous. It is not necessary for the state to prove that he thrust it or anything else. Quite frankly, this could have all been avoided if he had gotten rid of the knife, so he "knowingly caused physical injury to Rex Anderson." And, therefore, I find him guilty of that particular charge.'

" 'Under the formulations of the Model Penal Code (§ 2.02[2bii]) and the Illinois Criminal Code (§ 4–5[b]), "knowingly" is, in one phase, almost synonymous with "intentionally" in that a person achieves a given result "knowingly" when he "is practically certain" that his conduct will cause that result. This distinction between "knowingly" and "intentionally" in that context appears highly technical or semantic, and the Revised Penal Law does not employ the word "knowingly" in defining *result* offenses. Murder of the common law variety, for example, is committed *intentionally* or not at all.' (Commentary § 15.05, New York Revised Penal Law)."

"Although the trial judge found defendant guilty of 'knowingly' causing physical injury to Anderson, what he described in his findings is recklessness. The court found that defendant knew he had a dangerous weapon and that a confrontation was going to occur. The court believed that defendant did not intend to stab Anderson. The court's conclusion seems to be based on the reasoning that because defendant knew it was possible that an injury would occur, he acted 'knowingly.' However, a person who 'is aware of and consciously disregards a substantial and unjustifiable risk' that an injury will occur acts 'recklessly,' not 'knowingly.' Recklessly causing physical injury to another is assault in the third degree."

UNITED STATES v. JEWELL

United States Court of Appeals, Ninth Circuit, 1976.
532 F.2d 697

BROWNING, CIRCUIT JUDGE.[a] * * *

It is undisputed that appellant entered the United States driving an automobile in which 110 pounds of marihuana worth

a. Joined by 8 other members of the court, which heard the case en banc.

1. Appellant testified that a week before the incident in question he sold his car for $100 to obtain funds "to have a good time." He then rented a car for about $100, and he and a friend drove the rented car to Mexico. Appellant and his friend were unable to adequately explain their whereabouts during the period of about 11 hours between the time they left Los Angeles and the time they admitted arriving in Mexico.

Their testimony regarding acquisition of the load car follows a pattern common in these cases: they were approached in a Tijuana bar by a stranger who identified himself only by his first name—"Ray." He asked them if they wanted to buy marihuana, and offered to pay them $100 for driving a car north across the border. Appellant accepted the offer and drove the load car back, alone. Appellant's friend drove appellant's rented car back to Los Angeles.

Appellant testified that the stranger instructed him to leave the load car at the address on the car registration slip with the keys in the ashtray. The person living at that address testified that he had sold the car a year earlier and had not seen

$6,250 had been concealed in a secret compartment between the trunk and rear seat. Appellant testified that he did not know the marijuana was present. There was circumstantial evidence from which the jury could infer that appellant had positive knowledge of the presence of the marihuana, and that his contrary testimony was false.[1] On the other hand there was evidence from which the jury could conclude that appellant spoke the truth—that although appellant knew of the presence of the secret compartment and had knowledge of facts indicating that it contained marijuana, he deliberately avoided positive knowledge of the presence of the contraband to avoid responsibility in the event of discovery.[2] If the jury concluded the latter was indeed the situation, and if positive knowledge is required to convict, the jury would have no choice consistent with its oath but to find appellant not guilty even though he deliberately contrived his lack of positive knowledge. Appellant urges this view. The trial court rejected the premise that only positive knowledge would suffice, and properly so.

it since. When the Customs agent asked appellant about the secret compartment in the car, appellant did not deny knowledge of its existence, but stated that it was in the car when he got it.

There were many discrepancies and inconsistencies in the evidence reflecting upon appellant's credibility. Taking the record as a whole, the jury could have concluded that the evidence established an abortive scheme, concocted and carried out by appellant from the beginning, to acquire a load of marihuana in Mexico and return it to Los Angeles for distribution for profit.

2. Both appellant and his companion testified that the stranger identified as "Ray" offered to sell them marihuana and, when they declined, asked if they wanted to drive a car back to Los Angeles for $100. Appellant's companion "wanted no part of driving the vehicle." He testified, "It didn't sound right to me." Appellant accepted the offer. The Drug Enforcement Administration agent testified that appellant stated "he thought there was probably something wrong and something illegal in the vehicle, but that he checked it over. He looked in the glove box and under the front seat and in the trunk, prior to driving it. *He didn't find anything, and, there-*

Appellant tendered an instruction that to return a guilty verdict the jury must find that the defendant knew he was in possession of marihuana. The trial judge rejected the instruction because it suggested that "absolutely, positively, he has to know that it's there." * * *

* * * The court told the jury that the government must prove beyond a reasonable doubt that the defendant "knowingly" brought the marihuana into the United States (count 1: 21 U.S.C. § 952(a)), and that he "knowingly" possessed the marihuana (count 2: 21 U.S.C. § 841(a)(1)). The court continued:

> The Government can complete their burden of proof by proving, beyond a reasonable doubt, that if the defendant was not actually aware that there was marijuana in the vehicle he was driving when he entered the United States his ignorance in that regard was solely and entirely a result of his having made a conscious purpose to disregard the nature of that which was in the vehicle, with a conscious purpose to avoid learning the truth.

The legal premise of these instructions is firmly supported by leading commentators

here and in England. Professor Rollin M. Perkins writes, "One with a deliberate antisocial purpose in mind * * * may deliberately 'shut his eyes' to avoid knowing what would otherwise be obvious to view. In such cases, so far as criminal law is concerned, the person acts at his peril in this regard, and is treated as having 'knowledge' of the facts as they are ultimately discovered to be." [4] J. Ll. J. Edwards, writing in 1954, introduced a survey of English cases with the statement, "For well-nigh a hundred years, it has been clear from the authorities that a person who deliberately shuts his eyes to an obvious means of knowledge has sufficient *mens rea* for an offence based on such words as * * * 'knowingly.' " [5] Professor Glanville Williams states, on the basis [of] both English and American authorities, "To the requirement of actual knowledge there is one strictly limited exception. * * * [T]he rule is that if a party has his suspicion aroused but then deliberately omits to make further enquiries, because he wishes to remain in ignorance, he is deemed to have knowledge." [6] Professor Williams concludes, "The rule that wilful blindness is equivalent to knowledge is essential, and is found throughout the criminal law." [7]

---

fore, he assumed that the people at the border wouldn't find anything either". (Emphasis added.) Appellant was asked at trial whether he had seen the special compartment when he opened the trunk. He responded, "Well, you know, I saw a void there, but I didn't know what it was." He testified that he did not investigate further. The Customs agent testified that when he opened the trunk and saw the partition he asked appellant "when he had that put in." Appellant told the agent "that it was in the car when he got it."

The jury would have been justified in accepting all of the testimony as true and concluding that although appellant was aware of facts making it virtually certain that the secret compartment concealed marihuana, he deliberately refrained from acquiring positive knowledge of the fact.

4. R. Perkins, *Criminal Law* 776 (2d ed. 1969).

5. Edwards, *The Criminal Degrees of Knowledge,* 17 Modern L.Rev. 294, 298 (1954). * * *

6. G. Williams, *Criminal Law: The General Part,* § 57 at 157 (2d ed.1961).

7. Id. at 159. Mr. Williams' concluding paragraph reads in its entirety:

The rule that wilful blindness is equivalent to knowledge is essential, and is found throughout the criminal law. It is, at the same time, an unstable rule, because judges are apt to forget its very limited scope. A court can properly find wilful blindness only where it can almost be said that the defendant actually knew. He suspected the fact; he realised its probability; but he refrained from obtaining the final confirmation because he wanted in the event to be able to deny knowledge. This, and this alone, is wilful blindness. It requires in effect a finding that the defendant intended to cheat the administration of justice. Any wider definition would make the doctrine of wilful blindness indistinguishable

The substantive justification for the rule is that deliberate ignorance and positive knowledge are equally culpable. The textual justification is that in common understanding one "knows" facts of which he is less than absolutely certain. To act "knowingly," therefore, is not necessarily to act only with positive knowledge, but also to act with an awareness of the high probability of the existence of the fact in question. When such awareness is present, "positive" knowledge is not required.

This is the analysis adopted in [§ 2.02(7) of] the Model Penal Code. * * * As the Comment to this provision explains, "Paragraph (7) deals with the situation British commentators have denominated 'wilful blindness' or 'connivance,' the case of the actor who is aware of the probable existence of a material fact but does not satisfy himself that it does not in fact exist." [9] * * *

Appellant's narrow interpretation of "knowingly" is inconsistent with the Drug Control Act's general purpose to deal more effectively "with the growing menace of drug abuse in the United States." Holding that this term introduces a requirement of positive knowledge would make deliberate ignorance a defense. It cannot be doubted that those who traffic in drugs would make the most of it. This is evident from the number of appellate deci-

sions reflecting conscious avoidance of positive knowledge of the presence of contraband—in the car driven by the defendant or in which he is a passenger, in the suitcase or package he carries, in the parcel concealed in his clothing.

It is no answer to say that in such cases the fact finder may infer positive knowledge. It is probable that many who performed the transportation function, essential to the drug traffic, can truthfully testify that they have no *positive* knowledge of the load they carry. Under appellant's interpretation of the statute, such persons will be convicted only if the fact finder errs in evaluating the credibility of the witness or deliberately disregards the law. * * *

It is worth emphasizing that the required state of mind differs from positive knowledge only so far as necessary to encompass a calculated effort to avoid the sanctions of the statute while violating its substance. "A court can properly find wilful blindness only where it can almost be said that the defendant actually knew." In the language of the instruction in this case, the government must prove, "beyond a reasonable doubt, that if the defendant was not actually aware * * * his ignorance in that regard was *solely* and *entirely* a result of * * * a conscious purpose to avoid learning the truth." [21]

---

from the civil doctrine of negligence in not obtaining knowledge.

9. *Model Penal Code* 129–30 (Tent.Draft No. 4, 1955). Comment 9 reads in full as follows:

Paragraph (7) deals with the situation British commentators have denominated "wilful blindness" or "connivance," the case of the actor who is aware of the probable existence of a material fact but does not satisfy himself that it does not in fact exist. Whether such cases should be viewed as instances of acting recklessly or knowingly presents a subtle but important question.

The draft proposes that the case be viewed as one of acting knowingly when what is involved is a matter of existing fact, but not when what is involved is the result of the defendant's conduct, necessarily a matter of the future at

the time of acting. The position reflects what we believe to be the normal policy of criminal enactments which rest liability on acting "knowingly," as is so commonly done. The inference of "knowledge" of an existing fact is usually drawn from proof of notice of substantial probability of its existence, unless the defendant establishes an honest, contrary belief. The draft solidifies this usual result and clarifies the terms in which the issue is submitted to the jury.

21. We do not suggest that the instruction given in this case was a model in all respects. The jury should have been instructed more directly (1) that the required knowledge is established if the accused is aware of a high probability of the existence of the fact in question, (2) unless he actually believes it does not exist.

No legitimate interest of an accused is prejudiced by such a standard, and society's interest in a system of criminal law that is enforceable and that imposes sanctions upon all who are equally culpable requires it.

The conviction is affirmed.

ANTHONY M. KENNEDY, CIRCUIT JUDGE, with whom ELY, HUFSTEDLER and WALLACE, CIRCUIT JUDGES, join (dissenting). * * *

One problem with the wilful blindness doctrine is its bias towards visual means of acquiring knowledge. We may know facts from direct impressions of the other senses or by deduction from circumstantial evidence, and such knowledge is nonetheless "actual." Moreover, visual sense impressions do not consistently provide complete certainty.

Another problem is that the English authorities seem to consider wilful blindness a state of mind distinct from, but equally culpable as, "actual" knowledge. When a statute specifically requires knowledge as an element of a crime, however, the substitution of some other state of mind cannot be justified even if the court deems that both are equally blameworthy.

Finally, the wilful blindness doctrine is uncertain in scope. There is disagreement as to whether reckless disregard for the existence of a fact constitutes wilful blindness or some lesser degree of culpability. Some cases have held that a statute's scienter requirement is satisfied by the constructive knowledge imputed to one who simply fails to discharge a duty to inform himself. There is also the question of whether to use an "objective" test based on the reasonable man, or to consider the defendant's subjective belief as dispositive.

The deficiency in the instruction does not require reversal, however. Appellant did not object to the instruction on this ground either below or in this court. Since both of the elements referred

The approach adopted in section 2.02(7) of the Model Penal Code clarifies, and, in important ways restricts, the English doctrine. * * *

In light of the Model Penal Code's definition, the "conscious purpose" jury instruction is defective in three respects. First, it fails to mention the requirement that Jewell have been aware of a high probability that a controlled substance was in the car. It is not culpable to form "a conscious purpose to avoid learning the truth" unless one is aware of facts indicating a high probability of that truth. To illustrate, a child given a gift-wrapped package by his mother while on vacation in Mexico may form a conscious purpose to take it home without learning what is inside; yet his state of mind is totally innocent unless he is aware of a high probability that the package contains a controlled substance. Thus, a conscious purpose instruction is only proper when coupled with a requirement that one be aware of a high probability of the truth.

The second defect in the instruction as given is that it did not alert the jury that Jewell could not be convicted if he "actually believed" there was no controlled substance in the car. The failure to emphasize, as does the Model Penal Code, that subjective belief is the determinative factor, may allow a jury to convict on an objective theory of knowledge—that a reasonable man should have inspected the car and would have discovered what was hidden inside. * * *

Third, the jury instruction clearly states that Jewell could have been convicted even if found ignorant or "not actually aware" that the car contained a controlled substance. This is unacceptable because true ignorance, no matter how unreasona

to are implied in the instruction, the deficiency in the instructions is not so substantial as to justify reversal for plain error. * * *

ble, cannot provide a basis for criminal liability when the statute requires knowledge. A proper jury instruction based on the Model Penal Code would be presented as a way of defining knowledge, and not as an alternative to it. * * *

We do not agree with the majority that we can only reverse if the conscious purpose instruction constituted "plain error." Before the instruction was given, the defense counsel objected "strenuously" on the basis that the jury could convict Jewell for failure to make an adequate attempt to check out the car. When the trial judge rejected this argument, the defense counsel further requested that he "add an addendum" to the charge so the jury would understand it properly. * * *

* * * We believe these objections were sufficient to require reversal on appeal unless the deficiencies in the instruction were harmless error. * * *

Notes and Questions

1. Compare *State v. Nations,* 676 S.W.2d 282 (Mo.App.1984), where defendant was convicted under a statute making punishable one who "knowingly encourages, aids or causes a child less than seventeen years old to engage in any conduct" tending to injure the child's welfare. The evidence was that police found a scantily clad 16-year-old girl dancing for tips in the Main Street Disco, operated by the defendant. The defendant claimed on appeal that the state had failed to prove she knew the girl was under 17. After taking note of Model Penal Code § 2.02(7), the court stated:

"Our legislature, however, did not enact this proposed definition of 'knowingly'. Although the definitions of 'knowingly' and 'recklessly' in our Criminal Code are almost identical to the primary definitions of these terms as proposed in the Model Penal Code, *see* Model Penal Code § 2.02(2)(b)–(c) (Proposed Official Draft

1962), the Model Penal Code's proposed expanded definition of 'knowingly', encompassing wilful blindness of a fact, is absent from our Criminal Code. The sensible, if not compelling, inference is that our legislature rejected the expansion of the definition of 'knowingly' to include wilful blindness of a fact and chose to limit the definition of 'knowingly' to actual knowledge of the fact. Thus, in the instant case, the state's burden was to show defendant actually was aware the child was under seventeen, a heavier burden than showing there was a 'high probability' that defendant was aware the child was under seventeen. In short, the state's burden was to prove defendant acted 'knowingly', not just 'recklessly'. The state proved, however, that defendant acted 'recklessly', not 'knowingly'."

2. Compare also *United States v. Bright,* 517 F.2d 584 (2d Cir.1975), where the defendant was convicted of knowing possession of stolen mail. The trial judge instructed: "You may also find that the defendant had the requisite knowledge if you find that she acted with reckless disregard as to whether the checks were stolen, but with a conscious effort to avoid learning the truth, even though you may find that she was not specifically aware of the fact which would establish the stolen character of the checks." Accepting the definition in *Model Penal Code* 2.02(7) as applicable, the court reversed because the above instruction "was in no way balanced by an instruction that if the jury nevertheless found that 'the defendant actually believed that the bills were not stolen' they should acquit."

3. Slater has been charged with the knowing failure to report for induction into the armed forces. At trial, the government established that induction orders were mailed to his last known address and to the address of his grandmother in Georgia. Both were returned unopened and were marked "unclaimed" by postal au-

thorities. The government concedes that it thus is not established that Slater had actual knowledge of the orders, but, noting that the law imposes a duty upon registrants to keep Selective Service authorities informed of their current address, asserts that because the defendant did not comply with this duty he "should not now be permitted to take the position that he never received the notice of induction." [a] Is the government's position sound?

4. Thureson has been charged with the dissemination of obscene matter, knowing it to be obscene. "In September, 1974, a Cambridge police officer entered a bookstore advertising peep shows, observed six machine booths in the back of the store, approached the defendant at the front of the store for change with which to operate the machines, and deposited a quarter in one machine which then showed a brief film depicting explicit sexual conduct. Returning the next day with a search warrant, the officer questioned the defendant. She told him she had 'a pretty good idea' what was in the machines but had never viewed them. When the defendant claimed she did not know for whom she worked, the officer arrested her. At trial, she testified that she had been hired two or three days before her arrest to act as cashier. In her few days of employment, she worked alone in the store and performed no tasks related to the peep show machines beyond making change. She had accepted this employment over the telephone from an acquaintance, because its flexible hours suited her needs as a mother. Although the defendant gave testimony on her understanding of 'adult movies,' no evidence introduced indicated that she had ever viewed the contents of the peep show machines." [b] Ms. Thureson has moved for a directed verdict of acquittal. Should the motion be granted?

a. Based on *United States v. Slater*, 524 F.2d 987 (5th Cir.1975).

BARNES v. UNITED STATES

Supreme Court of the United States, 1973.
412 U.S. 837, 93 S.Ct. 2357, 37 L.Ed.2d 380.

MR. JUSTICE POWELL delivered the opinion of the Court.

Petitioner Barnes was convicted in United States District Court on two counts of possessing United States Treasury checks stolen from the mails, knowing them to be stolen, two counts of forging the checks, and two counts of uttering the checks, knowing the endorsements to be forged.

* * *

The evidence at petitioner's trial established that on June 2, 1971, he opened a checking account using the pseudonym "Clarence Smith." On July 1, and July 3, 1971, the United States Disbursing Office at San Francisco mailed four Government checks in the amounts of $269.02, $154.70, $184, and $268.80 to Nettie Lewis, Albert Young, Arthur Salazar, and Mary Hernandez, respectively. On July 8, 1971, petitioner deposited these four checks into the "Smith" account. Each check bore the apparent endorsement of the payee and a second endorsement by "Clarence Smith."

At petitioner's trial the four payees testified that they had never received, endorsed, or authorized endorsement of the checks. A Government handwriting expert testified that petitioner had made the "Clarence Smith" endorsement on all four checks and that he had signed the payees' names on the Lewis and Hernandez checks. Although petitioner did not take the stand, a postal inspector testified to certain statements made by petitioner at a post-arrest interview. Petitioner explained to the inspector that he received the checks in question from people who sold furniture for him door to door and that the checks had been signed in the payees' names when he received them. Petitioner

b. Based on *Commonwealth v. Thureson*, 371 Mass. 387, 357 N.E.2d 750 (1976).

further stated that he could not name or identify any of the salespeople. Nor could he substantiate the existence of any furniture orders because the salespeople allegedly wrote their orders on scratch paper that had not been retained. Petitioner admitted that he executed the Clarence Smith endorsements and deposited the checks but denied making the payees' endorsements.

The District Court instructed the jury that "[p]ossession of recently stolen property, if not satisfactorily explained, is ordinarily a circumstance from which you may reasonably draw the inference and find, in the light of the surrounding circumstances shown by the evidence in the case, that the person in possession knew the property had been stolen." [3] * * *

The teaching of [our prior] cases is not altogether clear.[a] To the extent that the "rational connection," "more likely than not," and "reasonable doubt" standards bear ambiguous relationships to one another, the ambiguity is traceable in large part to variations in language and focus rather than to differences of substance. What has

been established by the cases, however, is at least this: that if a statutory inference submitted to the jury as sufficient to support conviction satisfies the reasonable-doubt standard (that is, the evidence necessary to invoke the inference is sufficient for a rational juror to find the inferred fact beyond a reasonable doubt) as well as the more-likely-than-not standard, then it clearly accords with due process.

In the present case we deal with a traditional common-law inference deeply rooted in our law. * * * This longstanding and consistent judicial approval of the instruction, reflecting accumulated common experience, provides strong indication that the instruction comports with due process.

This impressive historical basis, however, is not in itself sufficient to establish the instruction's constitutionality. Common-law inferences, like their statutory counterparts, must satisfy due process standards in light of present-day experience. In the present case the challenged instruction only permitted the inference of guilt from *unexplained* possession of recently stolen

---

3. The full instruction on the inference arising from possession of stolen property stated:

"Possession of recently stolen property, if not satisfactorily explained is ordinarily a circumstance from which you may reasonably draw the inference and find, in the light of the surrounding circumstances shown by the evidence in the case, that the person in possession knew the property had been stolen.

"However, you are never required to make this inference. It is the exclusive province of the jury to determine whether the facts and circumstances shown by the evidence in this case warrant any inference which the law permits the jury to draw from the possession of recently stolen property.

"The term 'recently' is a relative term, and has no fixed meaning. Whether property may be considered as recently stolen depends upon the nature of the property, and all the facts and circumstances shown by the evidence in the case. The longer the period of time since the theft the more doubtful becomes the inference which may reasonably be drawn from unexplained possession.

"If you should find beyond a reasonable doubt from the evidence in the case that the mail described in the indictment was stolen, and that while recently stolen the contents of said mail here, the four United States Treasury checks, were in the possession of the defendant you would ordinarily be justified in drawing from those facts the inference that the contents were possessed by the accused with knowledge that it was stolen property, unless such possession is explained by facts and circumstances in this case which are in some way consistent with the defendant's innocence.

"In considering whether possession of recently stolen property has been satisfactorily explained, you are reminded that in the exercise of constitutional rights the accused need not take the witness stand and testify.

"Possession may be satisfactorily explained through other circumstances, other evidence, independent of any testimony of the accused."

a. The reference is to the *Leary* and *Turner* cases, discussed in *State v. Odom*, p. 113 of this Book, and to their predecessors.

property.[9] The evidence established that petitioner possessed recently stolen Treasury checks payable to persons he did not know, and it provided no plausible explanation for such possession consistent with innocence. On the basis of this evidence alone common sense and experience tell us that petitioner must have known or been aware of the high probability that the checks were stolen. Such evidence was clearly sufficient to enable the jury to find beyond a reasonable doubt that petitioner knew the checks were stolen. Since the inference thus satisfies the reasonable doubt standard, the most stringent standard the Court has applied in judging permissive criminal law inferences, we conclude that it satisfies the requirements of due process.[11]

Petitioner also argues that the permissive inference in question infringes his privilege against self-incrimination. The Court has twice rejected this argument, and we find no reason to re-examine the issue at length. The trial court specifically instructed the jury that petitioner had a constitutional right not to take the witness stand and that possession could be satisfactorily explained by evidence independent of petitioner's testimony. Introduction of any evidence, direct or circumstantial, tending to implicate the defendant in the alleged crime increases the pressure on him to testify. The mere massing of evidence against a defendant cannot be regarded as a violation of his privilege against self-incrimination.

Petitioner further challenges his conviction on the ground that there was insufficient evidence that he knew the checks were stolen *from the mails.* He contends that 18 U.S.C. § 1708 requires knowledge not only that the checks were stolen, but specifically that they were stolen from the mails. The legislative history of the statute conclusively refutes this argument [14] and the courts of appeals that have addressed the issue have uniformly interpreted the statute to require only knowl-

9. Of course, the mere fact that there is some evidence tending to explain a defendant's possession consistent with innocence does not bar instructing the jury on the inference. The jury must weigh the explanation to determine whether it is "satisfactory." The jury is not bound to accept or believe any particular explanation any more than it is bound to accept the correctness of the inference. But the burden of proving beyond a reasonable doubt that the defendant did have knowledge that the property was stolen, an essential element of the crime, remains on the Government.

11. It is true that the practical effect of instructing the jury on the inference arising from unexplained possession of recently stolen property is to shift the burden of going forward with evidence to the defendant. If the Government proves possession and nothing more, this evidence remains unexplained unless the defendant introduces evidence, since ordinarily the Government's evidence will not provide an explanation of his possession consistent with innocence. In *Tot v. United States,* 319 U.S. 463, 63 S.Ct. 1241, 87 L.Ed. 1519 (1943), the Court stated that the burden of going forward may not be freely shifted to the defendant. *Tot* held, however, that where there is a "rational connection" between the facts proved and the fact presumed or inferred, it is permissible to shift the burden of going forward to the defendant. Where an inference satisfies the reasonable-doubt standard, as in the present case, there will certainly be a rational connection between the fact presumed or inferred (in this case, knowledge) and the facts the Government must prove in order to shift the burden of going forward (possession of recently stolen property).

We do not decide today whether a judge-formulated inference of less antiquity or authority may properly be emphasized by a jury instruction.

14. Prior to 1939 the statute required proof of possession of articles stolen from the mail "knowing the same to have been *so* stolen." In 1939 Congress eliminated the word "so" preceding the word "stolen." H.R.Rep. No. 734, 76th Cong., 1st Sess., 1 (1939), explains the change:

"The reported bill amends the existing law so that it will sustain a conviction for the Government to prove that the property was in fact stolen from the mails and that the defendant knew the property he received had been stolen. The committee feel that this should be sufficient without requiring the Government to prove also that the defendant knew the property received had been stolen from the mails." See also S.Rep. No. 864, 76th Cong., 1st Sess. (1939).

edge that the property was stolen. * * *

Affirmed.

MR. JUSTICE DOUGLAS, dissenting.

* * *

[W]ithout a nexus with the "mails" there is no federal offense. How can we rationally say that "possession" of a stolen check allows a judge or jury to conclude that the accused knew the check was *stolen from the mails?* * * *

[W]e have no evidence whatsoever showing what amount of stolen property, let alone stolen checks, *implicates the mails.* Without some evidence or statistics of that nature we have no way of assessing the likelihood that this petitioner knew that these checks were *stolen from the mails.* We can take judicial notice that checks are stolen from the mails. But it would take a large degree of assumed omniscience to say with "substantial assurance" that this petitioner more likely than not knew from the realities of the underworld that this stolen property came *from the mails.* But without evidence of that knowledge there would be no federal offense of the kind charged. * * *

MR. JUSTICE BRENNAN, with whom MR. JUSTICE MARSHALL joins, dissenting.

* * *

We held in *In re Winship,* 397 U.S. 358, 364, 90 S.Ct. 1068, 1073, 25 L.Ed.2d 368 (1970), that the Due Process Clause requires "proof beyond a reasonable doubt of every fact necessary to constitute the crime * * *." Thus, in *Turner v. United States,* 396 U.S. 398, 417, 90 S.Ct. 642, 653, 24 L.Ed.2d 610 (1970), we approved the inference of "knowledge" from the fact of possessing smuggled heroin because " '[c]ommon sense' * * * tells us that those who traffic in heroin will *inevitably* become aware that the product they deal in is smuggled * * *." (Emphasis added.) The basis of that "common sense" judgment was, of course, the indisputable

fact that all or virtually all heroin in this country is necessarily smuggled. Here, however, it cannot be said that all or virtually all endorsed United States Treasury checks have been stolen. Indeed, it is neither unlawful nor unusual for people to use such checks as direct payment for goods and services. Thus, unlike *Turner,* "common sense" simply will not permit the inference that the possessor of stolen Treasury checks *"inevitably"* knew that the checks were stolen.

* * * The instruction thereby violated the principle of *Winship* that every essential element of the crime must be proved beyond a reasonable doubt.

Notes and Questions

1. Compare *State v. Attardo,* 263 S.C. 546, 211 S.E.2d 868 (1975), where defendant was convicted under a statute making it a crime to "knowingly" possess a controlled substance. The trial judge instructed the jury that "normally where a person is in possession of contraband, there is a factual presumption that he knows what it is, and the burden is then on him to prove that he did not have actual knowledge." Reversed: "In this case, knowledge, the element in question, *must* be established by the State before the accused has to put forth *any* defenses. Even where the State establishes a prima facie case, the burden of proof in a criminal case does *not* shift but the accused is only required to overcome inferences the State has established. A shifting of the burden of proof would impose a significantly greater onus on the defendant and, even more significantly, it would obliterate the presumption of innocence."

2. In *People v. Kirkpatrick,* 32 N.Y.2d 17, 343 N.Y.S.2d 70, 295 N.E.2d 753 (1973), the court, in a 4–3 decision, upheld a statute providing: "A person who promotes obscene material, or possesses the same with intent to promote it, in the

course of his business is presumed to do so with knowledge of its content and character." The majority concluded "it is hardly arguable that by a purely logical test the presumption of knowledge in an obscenity statute is amply supported by the probabilities. Even the largeness of the bookshop does not lessen the probabilities; if anything, with respect to egregiously packaged or conspicuously bizarre material it will stand out, as the trial court said, 'like a sore thumb', in a staid collection of books. Nor should the test be easier for the large bookseller as contrasted with the small one. Indeed, the small one may well be victimized by tie-in sales or lack of knowledge of his wares because his books and magazines are only a small part of his stock. In any event, no merchant, regardless of the size and scope of his inventory, can survive economically unless he knows his stock. This is a truism and an ancient one.

"Although no courts have made the distinctions it would seem too that in sustaining legislatively enacted presumptions one must look to counterbalancing factors. It is one thing to have presumptions in crimes punishable by long imprisonment, or even capital punishment. It is another to utilize presumptions in minor crimes and offenses where the policing problem is aggravated and the escape of responsibility by studied ignorance or denial too easy. Moreover, one must look to the ease with which a presumption may be rebutted. If it is easy for the defendant to rebut then the presumption is a tolerable burden."

The dissenters objected: "It is most unlikely that a bookseller—especially in a store such as those in which the defendants were employed—would have knowledge of the content of the publications being offered for sale. To say that booksellers in the circumstances of this case are 'more likely than not' to know the character and content of all the material they sell is to ignore not only the record evidence re-

garding the manner in which books and magazines are ordered but the very 'circumstances of life' itself. The New Yorker Bookstore—in which Kirkpatrick was employed—carried over 10,000 titles, while the East Side shop—where Dargis worked—carried about 16,000 titles. Reason and experience tell us that it would be impossible for a bookseller in either store to acquaint himself with the content and character of so large a number of titles. In any event, it may not be said with 'substantial assurance'—as required by the cases—that such booksellers may be 'presumed' to know the content and character of a publication merely upon proof that they sold it.

"However, even if the statutory presumption were able to withstand an attack based on due process grounds, I would be impelled to stamp it unconstitutional as an infringement on the freedom of expression guaranteed by the First Amendment. The presumption violates that amendment because it creates and occasions a system of 'self-censorship' on the part of booksellers which affects the sale and distribution of all books—those that are constitutionally protected as well as those that are obscene."

3. In *People v. Theel*, 180 Colo. 348, 505 P.2d 964 (1973), defendant was convicted of knowing possession of marijuana. The evidence was that "a trace amount" of less than one gram was found in a plastic bag carried by defendant, who had been arrested for hitchhiking. The court reversed:

"There are some narcotic drug possession cases where the direct evidence of possession also is a basis for a reasonable inference that the accused knew that the substance found in his possession was a narcotic drug. In such cases, once the possession of at least a usable quantity is established, the knowledge of the presence and nature of the substance may be inferred. However, evidence that the accused possessed only a minute quantity of a substance shown to be marijuana, and nothing more, does not formulate any basis for an inference that the defendant knew he possessed marijuana. Where the quantity involved is so minute that it amounts to only a trace, there is no basis, from that fact alone, for any logical or reasonable inference that the defendant had knowledgeable possession." [a]

SECTION 4. RECKLESSNESS AND NEGLIGENCE

STATE v. JONES

Supreme Court of Maine, 1956.
152 Me. 188, 126 A.2d 273.

TAPLEY, JUSTICE.

On exceptions. The respondent was tried on an indictment charging that he, while being then and there on a hunting trip, did feloniously, negligently and carelessly shoot and wound a human being. The case was tried at the December Term, 1955 of the Superior Court within and for the County of Hancock. Upon conviction by the jury the respondent was sentenced. The case is before us on the following exceptions:

1. To a portion of the presiding Justice's charge to the jury which, in substance, charged civil negligence and carelessness. * * *

2. The respondent requested the following instruction which was denied:

"Criminality is not predicated upon mere negligence necessary to impose civil liability, but upon that degree of negligence or carelessness which is denominated gross or culpable." * * *

a. In *People v. Harrington*, 396 Mich. 33, 238 N.W.2d 20 (1976), the court construed the state possession-of-narcotics statute in accordance with the view taken in the majority of jurisdictions, which is that possession of any quantity is sufficient. In rejecting the minority "usable amount"

The basis of the prosecution is found in the provisions of Sec. 146, Chap. 37, R.S.1954, the pertinent portion of which reads as follows:

"Whoever, while on a hunting trip or in the pursuit of wild game or game birds, negligently or carelessly shoots and wounds, or kills any human being, shall be punished by a fine of not more than $1,000, or by imprisonment for not more than 10 years."

The first two exceptions concerning the charge as to negligence and carelessness and the refusal to instruct as to "criminal negligence" so-called, brings in sharp focus the interpretation of the words "negligently or carelessly" as used in the statute upon which the respondent was prosecuted and convicted. * * *

There would be no problem if the prosecution under Sec. 146, Chap. 37, R.S.1954, was for the killing of a human being by the respondent while he was "then and there on a hunting trip." The instructions of the presiding Justice would, no doubt, have followed the well accepted and recognized rule of gross or culpable negligence which it is necessary to establish in a conviction of involuntary manslaughter.

The statute is not only penal but, by the punishment it prescribes, puts itself in the category of a felony statute. In order to approve the instruction of the presiding Justice of civil negligence, we must say that this penal statute is divisible by interpretation to the extent that the homicidal portion requires instructions on gross and culpable negligence, while the crime of a lesser degree is committed by a person who is guilty of civil negligence and carelessness.

rule and the "remnant of a usable amount" test used by the court of appeals, the court said these limitations were unnecessary in light of the fact that a conviction could be obtained only upon proof of knowing possession.

We start with the premise that we are considering a statute which defines a crime and provides punishment for its violation; in other words, it is a "criminal statute." The attorney for the respondent cites with confidence the case of *State v. Wright,* 128 Me. 404, 148 A. 141. The *Wright* case treats of the crime of manslaughter and holds that the degree of negligence or carelessness in such a case must be gross or culpable. The prosecution in the *Wright* case was based on Sec. 3, Chap. 129, R.S.1930, the pertinent provisions of which are identical with the statute involved in the instant case. Sec. 146, Chap. 37, R.S.1954. The late Chief Justice Sturgis wrote:

> "At the trial, the prosecution relied upon involuntary manslaughter and offered evidence to prove that the respondent, while on a hunting trip, negligently shot the deceased as he rode by on horseback."

and following this statement he said:

> "Criminality is not predicated upon mere negligence necessary to impose civil liability, but upon that degree of negligence or carelessness which is denominated gross or culpable. * * * In his charge to the jury, the presiding justice inadvertently failed to observe this distinction between civil and criminal negligence, instructing the jury to measure the respondent's guilt by the rules of negligence applicable only to civil cases."

The interesting portion of this quote, insofar as the instant case is concerned, is not the degree of negligence or carelessness determined to be necessary in the manslaughter case in which these elements were involved but rather the reference to *"criminality* is not predicated upon mere negligence necessary to impose civil liability" and "the presiding Justice inadvertently failed to observe this distinction between *civil* and *criminal* negligence".

(Emphasis ours.) *Turner v. State,* 65 Ga. App. 292, 16 S.E.2d 160, 161. This case involved a statute prohibiting any person from unlawfully, carelessly or negligently setting fire to woods, land or marshes thereby causing injury to others and further providing that such acts shall be termed misdemeanors. The Court determined that the words " 'carelessly or negligently' " as used in the statute meant criminal negligence. In defining criminal negligence the Court said:

> " 'Criminal negligence is something more than ordinary negligence which would authorize a recovery in a civil action. Criminal negligence as used in our Criminal Code is the reckless disregard of consequences, or a heedless indifference to the rights and safety of others and a reasonable foresight that injury would probably result.' "

* * *

We are considering a penal statute and, what is more, a felony statute. The rule of strict construction is applicable.

This respondent is entitled to an interpretation of the words "negligently or carelessly" which would be most favorable to him.

The respondent was indicted under the provisions of a felony statute and, according to the statute, he upon conviction could be subject to a sentence of great severity. Conformably to the rules of criminal procedure, the State had the burden of proving beyond a reasonable doubt every essential element necessary to establish the offense. The subject matter of the crime as defined by the statute is the *negligent* or *careless* shooting and wounding of a human being. We have determined that negligence as used in this criminal statute is criminal negligence. There is a definite line of demarcation between civil and criminal negligence and the two classes are not consistent one with the other. Good reasoning dictates that a criminal statute that could in effect deprive a person of his liberty should not be subjected to both civil and criminal procedures. It must fall within one category or the other. A conviction could more easily be obtained on instructions of that degree of negligence which would support civil liability than the degree necessary to establish criminal responsibility.

The Court below was in error in instructing the jury on civil negligence, and refusing to give the requested instruction.

* * *

WEBBER, JUSTICE (dissenting).

* * *

I do not understand that the Court intends by its opinion to question the power of the Legislature to define crimes so long as it keeps within the bounds of the constitution. * * * The power of a legislature to define a crime based upon ordinary negligence has been recognized in other jurisdictions. I conclude that our Legislature could then, if it saw fit, impose criminal penalties for ordinary negligence on the part of a hunter resulting in the shooting and wounding or killing of a human being. The issue is rather whether it has done so by the definition of the crime set forth in R.S.1954, Chap. 37, Sec. 146.

The Court holds that the negligence and carelessness referred to in that statute must be of the degree usually referred to as gross and culpable such as has always been required for a conviction for involuntary manslaughter at common law. The statute itself does not specify the degree of negligence. The question can be resolved only by ascertaining what the Legislature intended by its use of the words "negligently or carelessly" in this particular enactment. The shooting and killing of another as the result of gross and culpable negligence spells involuntary manslaughter and is punishable under the provisions of R.S. 1954, Chap. 130, Sec. 8 by "a fine of not more than $1000 or by imprisonment for

not more than *20 years*." (Emphasis supplied.) The maximum sentence to imprisonment imposable under R.S.1954, Chap. 37, Sec. 146, is, however, but *ten years*. If the negligence referred to in Chap. 37, Sec. 146, means what the Court now holds that it means, we have an interesting paradox, for the Legislature is providing two different punishments for the same crime, i.e., involuntary manslaughter. If the respondent killer is a hunter and prosecuted as such, the maximum term of years to which he can be sentenced is ten, but if he is a non-hunter, he faces a maximum sentence of twenty years. I cannot believe the Legislature so intended. In my view, the Legislature had in mind the alarming increase in so-called hunting accidents in our Maine forests. The recreation industry is one of the most valuable assets of the state. It will most certainly be impaired if hunters fear to enter the woods. An even greater consideration is the protection of our Maine citizens and our guests from death or bodily harm. I think it can safely be asserted that most of these tragic accidents result, not from any wanton or reckless indifference to the safety of others such as would base a charge of manslaughter, but rather from a simple failure to exercise ordinary care in the use of a deadly firearm. All too often, the respondent and his victim are related by ties of blood or marriage or have for many years been close friends or hunting companions. Rare indeed would be the case in which the State could show that one was recklessly indifferent to the safety of another to whom he was bound by such relationship. Rather are we dealing for the most part with the respondent who was morally certain that he saw game and who merely failed to take that long and careful second look which reasonable prudence demands before pulling the fatal trigger. In my view, the Legislature in its wisdom has concluded that only by imposing rigorous penalties for the failure to exercise ordinary care and prudence can the hunters who roam our woods be compelled to be careful. It seems clear to me that the Legislature has defined a new crime made purposely severe as to the degree of negligence to be proven and limited in its application only to hunters. The holding of the Court, requiring as it does proof by the State of gross and culpable negligence and a wanton disregard of consequences, seems to me to depart from the practical realities of the situation and virtually to emasculate the statute.   *   *   *

Notes and Questions

1. In *State v. Williams,* 4 Wash.App. 908, 484 P.2d 1167 (1971), the defendants, husband and wife (respectively, a 24–year–old laborer with a sixth grade education and a 20–year–old with an eleventh grade education) were convicted of manslaughter for negligently failing to supply their 17–month–old child with necessary medical attention, as a result of which he died. The trial court expressly found:

"That both defendants were aware that William Joseph Tabafunda was ill during the period September 1, 1968 to September 12, 1968. The defendants were ignorant. They did not realize how sick the baby was. They thought that the baby had a toothache and no layman regards a toothache as dangerous to life. They loved the baby and gave it aspirin in hopes of improving its condition. They did not take the baby to a doctor because of fear that the Welfare Department would take the baby away from them. They knew that medical help was available because of previous experience. They had no excuse that the law will recognize for not taking the baby to a doctor."

The applicable statute provided that "homicide, not being excusable or justifia-

a. In *People v. Calvaresi,* 188 Colo. 277, 534 P.2d 316 (1975), the variation adopted in that state,

ble, is manslaughter." In affirming the convictions, the court noted:

"The concept of simple or ordinary negligence describes a failure to exercise the 'ordinary caution' necessary to make out the defense of excusable homicide. Ordinary caution is the kind of caution that a man of reasonable prudence would exercise under the same or similar conditions. If, therefore, the conduct of a defendant, regardless of his ignorance, good intentions and good faith, fails to measure up to the conduct required of a man of reasonable prudence, he is guilty of ordinary negligence because of his failure to use 'ordinary caution'"

2. In *State v. Hodgdon,* 244 Or. 219, 416 P.2d 647 (1966), the defendant was convicted under a statute making it a crime to cause death by the "driving of any motor vehicle * * * in a grossly negligent manner," that is, in "reckless disregard of the rights of others." In affirming the conviction, the court concluded that the definition of recklessness in the law of torts governed, namely:

"The actor's conduct is in reckless disregard of the safety of another if he intentionally does an act or fails to do an act which it is his duty to the other to do, knowing or having reason to know of facts which would lead a reasonable man to realize that the actor's conduct not only creates an unreasonable risk of bodily harm to the other but also involves a high degree of probability that substantial harm will result to him."

3. Most of the modern recodifications contain their own definitions of such words as "recklessness" and "negligence," indicating what degree of risk is required and whether an objective or subjective test is intended. The definitions in *Model Penal Code* § 2.02(2)(c) and (d) are often but not always [a] used. See Treiman, *Reck-*

whereby inadvertence would suffice for either recklessness or negligence, was found wanting:

lessness and the Model Penal Code, 9 Am.J. Crim.L. 281, 375–86 (1981).

4. To what extent are the Model Penal Code definitions of recklessness and negligence really different? In what ways should they be different? Consider Treiman, supra, at 351–69:

"The requirement that the actor *consciously disregard* the risk is probably the most significant part of the definition of recklessness. * * * It is the concept of conscious disregard that distinguishes recklessness from negligence. * * *

"Since the *Model Penal Code* defines both knowledge and recklessness in terms of awareness, this suggests that conscious and knowledge might mean the same thing. However, some writers have suggested that knowledge is broader in meaning than conscious or aware. Being aware or conscious of something suggests that the something is in the person's thoughts at the moment. Knowledge, on the other hand, may be in a person's conscious thoughts, or may be something tucked away in the person's memory. Obviously we all have considerably more knowledge than we have in our conscious thoughts at any moment. We may know something without being currently aware or conscious of that fact or idea. * * *

"Since the *Model Penal Code* concept of recklessness utilizes awareness rather than knowledge of the risk, this would appear to exclude the situation in which the actor had knowledge of a risk, but was not aware of it at the moment. Having

knowledge of a risk involved in specific conduct, but not being aware of the risk at the moment, that is, not stopping to think of the consequences, may be negligent but it is not reckless. * * *

"With respect to recklessness, there is also a problem of lack of certainty. Can one claim he was not reckless because he was not certain that he was aware of the risk? Awareness of a risk involves a different mental process than awareness of an object being before one's eyes. Simple perception is sufficient to inform one of the object before his eyes. When one does not actually see the object, but is aware of a risk that the object is present, a mental process more complex than perception is required. One must reason from perceptions and previous knowledge and experience to make a judgment that something might be present. Can one be certain that there is a risk of the object being present? It is unlikely that a judgment or calculation of risks will be as fixed or clear in one's mind as perceptions. Just as requiring absolute certainty for knowledge would negate the usefulness of the concept of knowledge, requiring certain awareness or consciousness of a risk would make recklessness an almost useless concept. * * *

'In addition to the confusion resulting from proof of subjective mental states, there is also the danger that in defining consciousness of the risk the standard might be converted into an objective one.

"Under the manslaughter statute in question, a jury must determine if an accused acted 'recklessly,' i.e., whether he failed to perceive a risk, of which he should have been aware, and whether he acted in wanton and willful disregard of the standard of conduct that a reasonable person would observe in a given situation. Under the criminal negligence statute, the jury must determine whether the failure to perceive an unjustifiable risk constitutes a gross deviation from the standard of care that a reasonable person would observe in the situation. The distinction between

a gross deviation from, and a wanton and willful disregard of, a standard of care is not sufficiently apparent to be intelligently and uniformly applied. The legislative attempt to distinguish between recklessness, and its purportedly less culpable counterpart, criminal negligence, constitutes a distinction without a sufficiently pragmatic difference. To base a conviction of a felony, rather than a misdemeanor, upon the shifting sands of these semantics does not constitute substantial justice."

An illustration of this is found in *People v. Taylor*.[301] In finding that recklessness had not been established, the court stated the standard for recklessness as 'when the actor *has knowledge* of the highly dangerous nature of his actions or *knowledge of such facts* as under the circumstances would disclose to a reasonable man the dangerous character of his action, and despite this knowledge he so acts.' Since the prosecution's evidence was unable to meet this test, the misstatement of the standard was not harmful to Mr. Taylor, but it was a misstatement nevertheless.

"Though the standard in *Taylor* is more demanding than the definition of recklessness found in the *Restatement of Torts,* which does not even require knowledge of the circumstances, it fails to require any subjective awareness of the risk of harm. This is clearly insufficient for recklessness. The second sentence of both recklessness and negligence judge the nature and the degree of the risk based on the circumstances known to the actor. What distinguishes recklessness from negligence is awareness of the risk itself, not just the circumstances. * * *

" * * * There is strong support for the view that the actor must be aware of a substantial risk, not just any risk. * * *

"When the actor underestimates the risk so much that he believes the risk is not substantial at all, can he be found to have consciously disregarded a substantial risk? A very cautious person might be aware of a remote risk because he carefully considers his actions, but because of mistaken judgment or evaluation of facts he *did* perceive, think that the risk is much less than it is. Unless the actor is at least aware of a substantial risk, it is difficult to separate this actor from the negligent actor. Even if this mistake were unreasonable, in terms of culpability it is difficult to see why such a cautious actor should be

301. 31 A.D.2d 852, 297 N.Y.S.2d 192 (1969).

any more culpable than the person who unreasonably failed to see any risk whatsoever. * * *

"For the actor to be reckless with respect to a result or a circumstance, must the actor be aware that the risk he is disregarding is unjustifiable? * * *

"The *Model Penal Code* Commentary suggests that the weighing of interests to determine recklessness is an objective standard. After pointing to the factors to be weighed, the Commentary states, 'Some principle must be articulated, however, to indicate what final judgment is demanded after everything is weighed. There is no way to state this value-judgment that does not beg the question in the last analysis; the point is that the *jury must evaluate* the conduct and determine whether it should be condemned.'

"Several writers are also fairly explicit that the actor need not be conscious that his conduct is unjustifiable. This is a social judgment, determined by the trier of fact looking back at the actor's conduct and judging it by objective standards, and not by the actor's belief that the conduct is justifiable. * * *

"However, the conclusion that the unjustifiability of the risk is to be determined for purposes of recklessness by a purely objective standard is misleadingly oversimplified. * * *

"[T]he requirement for recklessness of conscious disregard should require the trier of fact to look at the purpose the actor had for engaging in the conduct, at the likelihood the actor thought existed of achieving the goal by his conduct, and at the harm he thought was risked by the conduct. However, the trier of fact should assign a value to the harm threatened and to the goal the actor sought. Finally, the trier of fact should weigh the factors, without regard to how the actor might have weighed those factors."

5.   What then of *Boggess v. State,* 655 P.2d 654 (Utah 1982), where the defendant, convicted of recklessness-manslaughter, objected on appeal that the trial judge should have instructed upon the lesser offense of negligent homicide. The majority reasoned: "Section 76–5–206, U.C.A. 1953 provides:

(1) Criminal homicide constitutes negligent homicide if the actor, acting with criminal negligence, causes the death of another.

"Section 76–2–103(4) provides that a person is criminally negligent when

he ought to be aware of a substantial and unjustifiable risk that circumstances exist or the result will occur. The risk must be of such a nature and degree that the failure to perceive it constitutes a gross deviation from the standard of care that an ordinary person would exercise in all the circumstances as viewed from the actor's standpoint.

"The defendant did not claim that he was unaware of the danger associated with the use of guns. He admitted that he should have looked to have seen if the gun was unloaded before he fired it, but he did not. He noted that his action was a 'hell of a way to show it's unloaded.' Even though he thought the gun was unloaded, defendant knew it was dangerous to have pointed it at his wife and pulled the trigger. In view of this evidence as to the defendant's knowledge concerning the inherent danger of firearms and the recklessness of his conduct towards his wife, the evidence would not admit of a finding that he was unaware but should have been aware of a substantial and unjustifiable risk, or that he failed to perceive the nature and degree of the risk—all of which is necessary to constitute criminal negligence. To the contrary, the defendant's own testimony establishes a state of mind

found in manslaughter. He repeatedly characterized his action as 'reckless' which under § 76–5–205 constitutes manslaughter. There being no evidence to support a verdict of negligent homicide under the peculiar facts of this case, it clearly was not error for the court to have failed to have given an instruction on that crime."

Stewart, J., concurring only because the defendant failed to ask for a negligent homicide instruction, responded: "In *People v. Stanfield,* 36 N.Y.2d 467, 330 N.E.2d 75, 369 N.Y.S.2d 118 (1975), a case not unlike the instant, defendant was convicted of reckless manslaughter for shooting his common law wife. The defendant had cocked the hammer of his pistol, pointed the barrel upward at about a 45 degree angle but in the direction of his wife who stood very close to him, and told her he was going to shoot her. His wife responded, ' "[D]on't mess with the gun like that," and then slapped his hand or arm.' The weapon discharged and inflicted the mortal wound. In holding that the trial court erred in not instructing on criminal negligence, the court stated:

[C]riminal recklessness and criminal negligence with respect to a particular result—there homicide—may in a particular case, if not hypothetically or definitionally, be but shades apart on the scale of criminal culpability. And the distinction between the two mental states is less clear practically than theoretically * * *.

[I]t seems manifest that in a practical, if not a literal definitional sense, if one acts with criminal recklessness he is at least criminally negligent. Moreover, negligence may, in a particular case, quickly, even imperceptibly, aggravate on the scale of culpability to recklessness.

"On the particular facts of this case, I think the conclusion is inescapable that there is a reasonable view of the evidence which would support an acquittal of reckless manslaughter and a conviction for criminal negligent homicide. The defendant testified, *and the State concedes, that the defendant did not think that the gun was loaded.* Thus, the State in effect concedes that defendant did not consciously disregard the risk because, if as believed, the gun was unloaded, there was no risk."

6. In *Regina v. Caldwell,* [1982] A.C. 341, [1981] 2 W.L.R. 509, [1981] 1 All E.R. 961, the House of Lords concluded that recklessness "includes not only deciding to ignore a risk of harmful consequences resulting from one's acts that one has recognised as existing, but also failing to give any thought to whether or not there is any such risk in circumstances where, if any thought were given to the matter, it would be obvious that there was." Is this to be preferred over the Model Penal Code approach? Consider:

(a) Smith, *Subjective or Objective? Ups and Downs of the Test of Criminal Liability in England,* 27 Vill.L.Rev. 1179, 1201–02 (1982): "Why did the House of Lords in *Caldwell* take this step? In the first place Lord Diplock thought that there was no difference in culpability between the defendant in *Caldwell* and one who was reckless in the previously accepted sense.

*   *   *

"Is it proper to equate the blameworthiness of a person who fails to realize that there is a risk of some harmful consequence with that of one who does realize that there is such a risk and decides to take it? It is submitted that there is a real distinction in degree of blameworthiness between the two cases."

(b) Duff, *Recklessness,* 1980 Crim.L.Rev. 282, 291: "Some failures of attention or realisation may manifest, not mere stupidity or 'thoughtlessness,' but the same indifference or disregard which characterises the conscious risk-taker as reckless. If I intend to injure someone seriously, I may

not realise that this might kill them: not because I am *mistaken* about the likely effects of my assault, but because it 'just doesn't occur to me'—I am blind to that aspect of my action. But such blindness to such an essential and integral aspect of a serious assault, though possible, itself manifests a 'reckless disregard' for my victim's life no different from that of an assailant who knows he is endangering life."

7. In *Jones,* Justice Webber concludes that the legislature "in its wisdom" decided to make inadvertent negligence a basis for criminal conviction. If he is correct in this, did the legislature act wisely? Consider Fletcher, *The Theory of Criminal Negligence: A Comparative Analysis,* 119 U.Pa.L. Rev. 401, 415–18 (1971):

"At first blush it seems odd that anyone would argue that negligence is not an appropriate ground for censuring the conduct of another. From the late Roman Empire to the present, in Continental and common law jurisdictions, the courts have punished acts negligently causing harm. In daily conduct, we all confidently blame others who fail to advert to significant risks. If we confront a motorist driving without his lights on and thereby endangering the lives of many others, we would hardly condition our condemnation of his conduct on whether he knew his lights were off. His failure to find out whether his lights were on or off would itself be a basis for condemning him. Yet theorists have repeatedly argued that this judicial practice is primitive and that, as a matter of principle, an actor must *choose* to do harm in order to be culpable and fairly subject to penal sanctions. Jerome Hall has vigorously advanced this view. And in Germany, Arthur Kaufmann is the latest in a line of commentators who have maintained that guilt is always attributable to an act of the will. From the fourteenth century legal renaissance in Italy to H.L.A. Hart's analysis, the proponents of punishing negligence have relied upon the same reply: the culpability of negligence is not the culpability of choice, but rather of failing to bring to bear one's faculties to perceive the risks that one is taking. Though joined for centuries, the issue is hardly resolved. It might be helpful to develop some perspective on the conflict between these two theories of culpability in an effort to understand why some theorists tenaciously reject predicating culpability on an actor's failure to bring to bear his capacity to perceive and avoid a substantial and unjustified risk.

"There are at least two sophisticated strategies that one might pursue in upholding a sharp differentiation between the culpability of choice and the culpability of inadvertence. The battleground of one segment of the literature is the role of culpability in justifying criminal sanctions. Jerome Hall argues, for example, that 'in the long history of ethics * * * *voluntary* harm-doing is the essence of [culpability].' From this premise he reasons that negligence is involuntary, and that therefore it is unjust to punish negligent risk-taking. The question Hall raises is the right one. We do wish to know whether it is just to punish the negligent actor. It is not enough to show that punishing negligence has a deterrent impact on other potential risk-creators, for the goal of deterrence, however sound, does not speak to the fairness of forcing the specific defendant to be the object of exemplary sanctioning. Yet the issue of fairness to the defendant is not resolved by positing that negligence is not voluntary and therefore not culpable. Surely, the negligent actor, like the intentional actor, has the capacity of doing otherwise; he could have brought to bear his faculties to perceive and to avoid the risk he created. That is all we typically require to label conduct as voluntary. But Hall has a more limited concept of voluntariness in mind. He equates voluntariness with

choice and thus has little difficulty with the question whether negligence is voluntary. Yet unsupported definitions of voluntariness will not still the debate. We still wish to know whether the proper interpretation of voluntariness and culpability would confine these concepts to instances of choice or would expand them to encompass cases of culpable inadvertence.

"It might be helpful to start with a clearer account of why criminal sanctions should be limited to culpable, voluntary conduct. The usual account is negative in form: one should not punish involuntary conduct because it is unjust to the individual to expose him to sanctions for blameless conduct. Yet that negative perspective provides little assistance in clarifying the concepts of culpability and voluntariness. When we turn to positive accounts, however, we find a divergence of views that does correspond to the dispute between conflicting schools on the contours of culpability and voluntariness. If one focuses on the just desert of the offender, as do strict retributivists, one is likely to reason along the following lines. Justice requires that punishment be inflicted to the extent that the offender deserves punishment. To assess a man's just desert, we must fathom the kind of a man he is; to do that within the criminal law, we must rely exclusively on the offender's illegal act as the index of his moral character. The choice to do harm manifests character flaws, such as moral arrogance and greed; and these flaws reveal the offender to be a man deserving of punishment. Negligent acts, on the other hand, at best ambiguously manifest an actor's character; it tells us little about a man to know that on one occasion of nighttime driving he forgot to turn on his headlights. As Holmes said, negligence does not reveal the 'condition of a man's heart or conscience.' And if it does not, then it is not a fitting ground for blame and punishment.

"This approach to the punishability of negligence invites replies at several levels. One can dispute the alleged link between choosing to do harm and moral character. After all, insensitivity and egocentricity are moral flaws and both of these manifest themselves in incidents of negligent risk-taking. Also, it is far from clear that every intentional violation of the law (even of a just law) demonstrates a defect in the violator's character. In specific instances, such as draft evasion and euthanasia, one might regard the illegal conduct as morally sound, yet favor a conviction to inhibit others from asserting their private moral views at the expense of the community. These lines of criticism are worth pursuing, but alas, they meander on the surface of the issue.

"At the core of this case against punishing negligence is the premise that culpability functions as a standard for assessing the moral desert of the offender. Yet the requirement of culpability shields the individual from unjust punishment even if the standard is viewed not as one of moral desert, but as one of moral forfeiture. With the idea of forfeiture in the foreground, culpability functions as the touchstone of the question whether by virtue of his illegal conduct, the violator has lost his moral standing to complain of being subjected to sanctions. If his illegal conduct is unexcused, if he had a fair chance of avoiding the violation and did not, we are inclined to regard the state's imposing a sanction as justified. The defendant's failure to exercise a responsibility shared by all, be it a responsibility to avoid intentional violations or to avoid creating substantial and unjustified risks, provides a warrant for the state's intrusion upon his autonomy as an individual. From the viewpoint of culpability as a standard of moral forfeiture, it seems fair and consistent to regard negligence as culpable and to subject the negligent offender to criminal sanctions.

"The dispute about the contours of culpability is reduced, then, into a conflict about the role of culpability in justifying criminal sanctions. Is culpability a standard of moral desert or of moral forfeiture? Negligence is arguably an unreliable index of the actor's moral desert, but it does qualify as a plausible rationale for the partial forfeiture of the actor's autonomy. The conflict between these two views is not readily resolved. According to the former view, the criminal act is significant because it reveals the moral character of the offender; according to the latter view, the act is abstracted from the actor's character and treated as the sole test of liability to punishment. It is fair to say that most common law commentators regard culpability as a standard of moral forfeiture and thus pay little heed to the connections between culpability and character traits of the offender. Yet a significant tradition supports the view that punishment is justified solely by the desert of the offender, and this view inclines us toward insisting that criminal acts manifest character traits relevant to assessing the offender's just desert. Though we cannot now resolve this conflict, we may at least note the depth of the differences between those who would reject and those who would acknowledge the culpability of inadvertence. If a theorist wishes to exclude negligence from the criminal law, he should provide a convincing account of why culpability ought never to function as a standard of moral forfeiture. Yet neither that convincing account nor its definitive refutation has emerged in the literature of criminal theory."

8. If, as Fletcher suggests, the negligent defendant is culpable, may it be said that he is not nearly as culpable as the defendant who acts with intent? If so, is it desirable or essential that the criminal law recognize this difference? In *State v. Lucero,* 87 N.M. 242, 531 P.2d 1215 (1975), the defendant challenged a statute which

made it a felony to "knowingly, intentionally or negligently" abuse a child. The trial court granted the defendant's motion to dismiss on the ground that "the statute makes no distinction among intentional, knowing or negligent acts and makes no provision for lesser included offenses or degrees of offense according to the degree of culpability of the defendant, as do other criminal statutes of a similar nature which cover similar kinds of prohibited behavior, and that the statute thus denies defendants equal protection of the laws." On appeal this order was vacated, with the explanation that the legislature "has the authority to make a negligent act a crime as well as an intentional one."

9. At least one court has not accepted this last statement in absolute terms. In *Speidel v. State,* 460 P.2d 77 (Alaska 1969), the challenged statute made it a felony if one who had rented a car "refuses or wilfully neglects to return it" at the time and place specified in the rental agreement. The statute defined "wilfully neglects" as meaning "omits, fails, or forbears, with a conscious purpose to injure, or without regard for the rights of the owner, or with indifference whether a wrong is done the owner or not." The court concluded that a part of this statute was unconstitutional:

"Although an act may have been objectively wrongful, the mind and will of the doer of the act may have been innocent. In such a case the person cannot be punished for a crime, unless it is one such as the 'public welfare' type of offense * * * where the penalties are relatively small and conviction does no great damage to an offender's reputation. Under the terms of [this statute] there is no escape from a felony conviction and a possible five-year prison term for simple neglectful or negligent failure to return a rented automobile at the time specified in the rental agreement. To make such an act, without consciousness of wrongdoing or

intention to inflict injury, a serious crime, and criminals of those who fall within its interdiction, is inconsistent with the general law. To convict a person of a felony for such an act, without proving criminal intent, is to deprive such person of due process of law."

Does this mean that the statute in the *Williams* case, Note 1 supra, is unconstitutional?

10. In *State v. Smith,* 185 Conn. 63, 441 A.2d 84 (1981), the court rejected defendant's claim that his reckless homicide conviction could not stand because the evidence showed the defendant acted with intent to kill: "*State v. Rodriguez,* 180 Conn. 382, 429 A.2d 919 (1980), established that in prosecutions for homicides despite the differences between acting intentionally, acting recklessly, and acting with criminal negligence, we will deem the more culpable of those mental states to include the less culpable when both apply to actions with respect to an identical result or circumstance. Therefore the defendant could not prevent his conviction by preserving a reasonable doubt that he intentionally rather than recklessly killed Curmon and seriously injured Nichols. See Model Penal Code, § 2.02(5), comment, p. 129 (tentative draft No. 4, 1955) (applying the analysis which we adopted in *Rodriguez* to all offenses)."

STATE v. CUSHMAN
Supreme Court of Vermont, 1974.
133 Vt. 121, 329 A.2d 648.

SMITH, JUSTICE. The defendant was charged by information and warrant with the offense of recklessly engaging in conduct which placed another person in danger of death or serious bodily injury. On June 1, 1973, the defendant was tried in the District Court of Vermont, Unit No. 4, Caledonia Circuit, by a jury and was found guilty. Defendant's appeal from this conviction has been timely taken to this Court.

The appeal of the defendant is mainly premised on what he claims to be a wrongful interpretation by the trial court of the statute under which he was charged. This challenged interpretation was the source of allegedly erroneous jury instructions. Because of the points raised by the defendant, we believe it essential to quote the statute in its entirety for a proper understanding of the questions presented, as well as the resolution thereof.

§ 1025. Recklessly endangering another person

A person who recklessly engages in conduct which places or may place another person in danger of death or serious bodily injury shall be imprisoned for not more than one year or fined not more than $1,000.00 or both. Recklessness and danger shall be presumed where a person knowingly points a firearm at or in the direction of another, whether or not the actor believed the firearm to be loaded.

Taken in the light most favorable to the State, the prevailing party below, the factual situation is not complicated. Trooper McDonald came to the home of the defendant in the evening of January 1, 1973. The visit was in response to a call made to the State Police by a Mrs. Aldrich, who lived with the defendant at his home on Bible Hill. Mrs. Aldrich was disturbed, because of her young daughter, by the presence of an individual brought to the house by the defendant, and for whom defendant had furnished bail. An argument ensued between the defendant and the trooper, the details of which are not relevant to this decision. The evidence of the State was that the defendant, during this argument, took a firearm from a rack in the kitchen and pointed it in the direction of the police officer. It was the contention of the defendant, who took the stand in his own behalf, that the weapon was of antique vintage and not loaded.

The first point briefed by the defendant is that the trial court committed error by instructing the jury that it need not find that the weapon used by the defendant was loaded in order to convict him. What defendant argues, as we understand it, is that he has not been charged with assault, but with placing another in danger of death or bodily injury. The claim of the defendant is that in order to convict him under 13 V.S.A. § 1025 it is essential that actual power to commit bodily injury must rest in the actor's hand, and the apparent power which is adequate for the finding of an assault is inadequate under the above statute.

We agree with the defendant that 13 V.S.A. § 1025 does not charge a simple assault, the definitions of which are set forth in 13 V.S.A. § 1023. The Legislature, in its general revision of the laws relative to breach of the peace in the 1971 Adjourned Session of the General Assembly, set forth a separate offense directly concerned with the use of firearms under § 1025. There is a clearly expressed legislative intent in the second sentence of this provision that even if the actor has knowledge, or is presumed to have knowledge, that the gun he is pointing in the direction of another is unloaded, the recklessness of his conduct is presumed from such action, as is the fact that he is placing the other person in danger of death or bodily injury.

We are aware of the principle cited by the defendant that, in interpreting a penal statute, the interpretation most favorable to the accused must be the one adopted. But the fundamental rule is to ascertain and give effect to the intention of the Legislature, and "construction of a statute leading to an absurd consequence must be avoided, if possible."

It can hardly be doubted that a person threatened by another with a firearm has no way of ascertaining whether or not such weapon is loaded, but the state of mind of the victim is irrelevant under this statute. The danger of death or of bodily injury is equally acute, no matter what knowledge the actor may possess on the loaded or unloaded condition of the firearm which he points in the direction of the victim. To accept the defendant's contention that the Legislature, in enacting this statute, only intended to prevent the pointing of a loaded weapon at another but not to proscribe the pointing of an unloaded weapon would require us to construe the statute to lead to an absurd result. The most dangerous weapon is the "unloaded gun", and the Legislature's intent was to proscribe the pointing of all firearms at others.

* * *

The defendant next briefs a contention that the denial of his request to charge that "To find the Respondent Guilty, you must find beyond a reasonable doubt: (c) That J. Bruce McDonald was actually placed in danger" was error. He argues that the court's charge on this issue was that, "The testimony is not whether, in fact, the weapon was loaded, but whether it reasonably appeared to the person that he was placed in such danger." Taken out of context, as this quotation is, it would appear to be an instruction more favorable to the defendant than he would be entitled to under 13 V.S.A. § 1025. It would require proof on the part of the State that a person toward whom an actor pointed a firearm could reasonably believe that he was in danger of death or bodily injury from the firearm.

However, reading the charge as a whole, as we must, we find that the court correctly charged the jury. The charge was directly based on the words of the statute, and the jury was instructed several times during the charge that the crucial issue was whether or not the defendant pointed a firearm at the officer. As we have already pointed out, under the second sentence of 13 V.S.A. § 1025 the danger to the victim is presumed once the jury decides that the defendant pointed a firearm in the direction of the victim. While the loaded or unloaded condition of the firearm is irrelevant, an accused can, of course, introduce potentially exculpatory evidence for the jury's consideration that the firearm was actually a toy and incapable, under any conditions, of inflicting injury. As no such evidence was adduced below, defendant takes nothing by his exception to the charge on this issue.

* * *

Judgment affirmed.

DALEY, JUSTICE (dissenting).

While I fully concur with the view of the majority that under the statute the knowledge of the actor as to the loaded or unloaded nature of the firearm is an irrelevancy, I cannot subscribe to my associates' further conclusion that the question of whether the gun is *actually* loaded or unloaded is similarly nongermane.

In my opinion, one cannot be placed in an objective state of danger when an unloaded gun is pointed at him. He may well be "in fear", but he is not, as I see it, "in danger". In cases of this nature I would recognize the presumption of danger (loaded gun) from the act of pointing, but permit the defendant to present evidence that the gun was not, in fact, loaded. The ultimate determination as to whether the gun was loaded, and thus whether the victim was placed in danger, would then properly rest with the jury.

Defendant in the case before us testified at trial that the gun was not loaded, and I feel that the trial court committed reversible error in instructing the jury that "the fact that a firearm is or is not loaded is of no importance." The jury was thereby prevented from considering an important factor bearing on the essential element of danger.

I would reverse.

Notes and Questions

1. Is the majority correct in saying that defendant's construction of the statute would "lead to an absurd result"?

2. In *State v. Wong,* 125 N.H. 610, 486 A.2d 262 (1984), the court ruled that defendant, who was driving while intoxicated at the time of his death-causing conduct, was properly convicted of negligent homicide despite the absence of a specific allegation or proof of criminal negligence. (The negligent homicide statute says that a "person is guilty of a class B felony when he causes the death of another: I. Negligently; or II. In consequence of his being under the influence of intoxicating liquor or controlled drug while operating a propelled vehicle.")

"The plain meaning of RSA 630:3 comports with the comments of the drafters of the statute. The statute is based, in part, on the 'determination' by the drafters that 'using an instrumentality as dangerous to human life as a vehicle . . . while in a state of intoxication is *per se* negligence.' Report of Commission to Recommend Codification of Criminal Laws, Comments, at 36 (1969). ✳ ✳ ✳

1. Sec. 100.26(3), Stats.1977, provides:

"Any person who violates s. 100.15, 100.19, 100.20 or 100.22, or who intentionally refuses, neglects or fails to obey any regulation made under s. 100.19 or 100.20, shall, for each offense, be fined not less than $25 nor more than $5,000, or imprisoned in the county jail for not more than one year or both."

3. Ch. AG 110 Wis.Adm.Code, in pertinent part, states:

"AG 110.02 **Prohibited trade practices.** No seller shall engage in the following unfair methods of competition or unfair trade practices:

" ✳ ✳ ✳

"(7) PERFORMANCE ✳ ✳ ✳.

"(b) Fail to begin or complete work on the dates or within the time period specified in the home improvement contract, or as otherwise rep-

"Accordingly, it is clear that the legislature, in adopting the drafter's formulation of the negligent homicide statute, intended that the culpability requirement of negligent homicide can be satisfied *either* by showing that a person caused the death of another '[n]egligently,' *or* by establishing that the person caused the death in consequence of driving a propelled vehicle while under the influence of intoxicating liquor or a controlled drug."

3. Do not *Cushman* and *Wong* involve conclusive presumptions which are invalid under *Sandstrom,* p. 117 of this Book?

SECTION 5. STRICT LIABILITY

STATE v. STEPNIEWSKI

Supreme Court of Wisconsin, 1982.
105 Wis.2d 261, 314 N.W.2d 98.

STEINMETZ, JUSTICE.

The principal issue in this case is whether the state must prove intentional conduct by a defendant in all charged circumstances of a violation of sec. 100.26(3), Stats.1977,[1] for a conviction. ✳ ✳ ✳

The defendants, Malec and Stepniewski, were each convicted of trade practice violations, Malec of six violations and Stepniewski of 12 counts. The evidence showed that the two defendants violated ch. AG 110 Wis.Adm.Code.[3] In particu-

resented, unless the delay is for reason of labor stoppage, unavailability of supplies or materials, unavoidable casualties, or any other cause beyond the seller's control. Any changes in the dates or time periods stated in a written contract shall be agreed to in writing."

"AG 110.05 **Home improvement contract requirements.** ✳ ✳ ✳

" ✳ ✳ ✳

"(2) Home improvement contracts and all changes in the terms and conditions thereof, required under this section to be in writing, shall be signed by all parties thereto, and shall clearly and accurately set forth in legible form all terms and conditions of the contract, and particularly the following:

" ✳ ✳ ✳

lar, the defendants on several occasions failed to state in writing projects' starting and completion dates. On other occasions, while the defendants did enter such dates in writing, they then failed to complete the projects. In two cases where work was left undone, severe damage occurred to the homes when winter arrived. Many of the homeowners victimized by the defendants were elderly and retired citizens. * * *

The defendants interpret the focused language of sec. 100.26(3), Stats.1977, "or who intentionally refuses, neglects or fails to obey any regulation made under s. 100.19 or 100.20, shall, * * *" as meaning that "intentionally" modifies all the words following it. * * *

The words following "intentionally" are *"refuses," "neglects"* or *"fails."* (Emphasis added.) The Random House Dictionary of the English Language, Unabridged Edition, relevant definitions of those words as verbs are:

"refuse— * * * to express a determination not to (do something) * * * to decline to submit to * * * to decline acceptance, consent, or compliance * * *"

"neglect—to pay no attention * * * to omit, through indifference or carelessness * * * to fail to carry out or perform (order, duties, etc.) * * *"

"fail—to fall short of success or achievement in something expected, attempted, desired, or approved * * * to be or become deficient or lacking * * *"

Since "refuses" has usages ranging from an expression of determination to not do something to a more passive declination of compliance, it is apparent the legislature

"(d) The dates or time period on or within which the work is to begin and be completed by the seller."

preceded the word "refuses" with "intentionally" to make it understood that the refusal intended was the determination to not do something. This was done so mere declination to comply would be understood to be the same as a failure to carry out or perform an order or duties, which is the meaning of *neglect*. Neglect was, therefore, not modified by "intentionally," since the conduct described was something less than determination to not act.

The word "fails" was intended to mean a failure to obey a regulation by a lack of success or achievement, where the performance in compliance was deficient or lacking.

The legislature intended to provide for as wide a range of conduct to be included as an offense of sec. 100.26(3), Stats.1977, as penalties provided: "shall for each offense, be fined not less than $25 nor more than $5,000, or imprisoned in the county jail for not more than one year or both."

The legislature has shown its awareness of the use of intentional in respect to neglect and other words in other statutes, *i.e.*:

"52.05 **Abandonment; uniform act.** (1) PENALTY. Any person who, without just cause, deserts or wilfully [intentionally] neglects *or* refuses to provide for the support and maintenance of his or her spouse or child under 18 years * * *." (Emphasis added.)

"947.15 **Contributing to the delinquency of children; neglect; neglect contributing to death.** (1) The following persons * * *

"(a) Any person * * * who intentionally encourages *or* contributes to the delinquency * * * *or* the neglect of any child * * *." (Emphasis added.)

When the legislature intended in those statutes that the modifying word "intentionally" apply to other words and also "neglect," it used the conjunctive word "*or*." It did not do so in sec. 100.26(3), Stats.1977, until after the word neglect and before the word "fails." Intentionally cannot modify "fails," since one who has intentionally failed to obey is one who has a mental purpose of refusal to obey and such use would be duplicitous.

The defendant argues that sec. 100.26(3), Stats.1977, was meant to include only intentional conduct or, alternatively, that it violates due process to convict a person of a crime with no *mens rea.* This idea was rejected by the U.S. Supreme Court and this court in several instances over the years. The first rejection in Wisconsin was in *State v. Hartfiel,* 24 Wis. 60 (1869), which involved the prosecution of a saloon keeper for serving a minor an intoxicating liquor when the statute did not include the words "knowingly" or "wilfully." The jurors were instructed that ignorance or mistake on the part of the accused as to the fact that the six-foot-one-inch person who was served was a minor was no defense. The court held:

> "The act in question is a police regulation, and we have no doubt that the legislature intended to inflict the penalty, irrespective of the knowledge or motives of the person who has violated its provisions. Indeed, if this were not so, it is plain that the statute might be violated times without number, with no possibility of convicting offenders, and so it would become a dead letter on the statute book, and the evil aimed at by the legislature remain almost wholly untouched. To guard against such results, the legislature has, in effect, provided that the saloon keeper, or other vendor of intoxicating liquors or drinks, must know the facts—must know that the person to whom he sells is a *qualified drink-*

er, within the meaning of the statute; and, if not, he acts at his peril in disobeying the requirements of the law."

The U.S. Supreme Court stated the history of crime without intent in *Morissette v. United States,* 342 U.S. 246, 72 S.Ct. 240, 96 L.Ed. 288 (1952) and declared:

* * *

> "The industrial revolution multiplied the number of workmen exposed to injury from increasingly powerful and complex mechanisms, driven by freshly discovered sources of energy, requiring higher precautions by employers. Traffic of velocities, volumes and varieties unheard of came to subject the wayfarer to intolerable casualty risks if owners and drivers were not to observe new cares and uniformities of conduct. Congestion of cities and crowding of quarters called for health and welfare regulations undreamed of in simpler times. Wide distribution of goods became an instrument of wide distribution of harm when those who dispersed food, drink, drugs, and even securities, did not comply with reasonable standards of quality, integrity, disclosure and care. Such dangers have engendered increasingly numerous and detailed regulations which heighten the duties of those in control of particular industries, trades, properties or activities that affect public health, safety or welfare.

> "While many of these duties are sanctioned by a more strict civil liability, lawmakers, whether wisely or not, have sought to make such regulations more effective by invoking criminal sanctions to be applied by the familiar technique of criminal prosecutions and convictions. This has confronted the courts with a multitude of prosecutions, based on statutes or administrative regulations, for what have been aptly called 'public welfare offenses.' These cases do not fit neatly into any of such accepted classifi-

cations of common-law offenses, such as those against the state, the person, property, or public morals. Many of these offenses are not in the nature of positive aggressions or invasions, with which the common law so often dealt, but are in the nature of neglect where the law requires care, or inaction where it imposes a duty. Many violations of such regulations result in no direct or immediate injury to person or property but merely create the danger or probability of it which the law seeks to minimize. While such offenses do not threaten the security of the state in the manner of treason, they may be regarded as offenses against its authority, for their occurrence impairs the efficiency of controls deemed essential to the social order as presently constituted. In this respect, whatever the intent of the violator, the injury is the same, and the consequences are injurious or not according to fortuity. Hence, legislation applicable to such offenses, as a matter of policy, does not specify intent as a necessary element. The accused, if he does not will the violation, usually is in a position to prevent it with no more care than society might reasonably expect and no more exertion than it might reasonably exact from one who assumed his responsibilities. Also, penalties commonly are relatively small, and conviction does no grave damage to an offender's reputation. Under such considerations, courts have turned to construing statutes and regulations which make no mention of intent as dispensing with it and holding that the guilty act alone makes out the crime. This has not, however, been without expressions of misgiving. * * * "

The statement of purpose for creating sec. 100.26(3), Stats.1977, is reflected in sec. 100.20(1) and (2):

"100.20 **Methods of competition and trade practices.** (1) Methods of competition in business and trade practices in business shall be fair. Unfair methods of competition in business and unfair trade practices in business are hereby prohibited.

"(2) The department, after public hearing, may issue general orders forbidding methods of competition in business or trade practices in business which are determined by the department to be unfair. The department, after public hearing, may issue general orders prescribing methods of competition in business or trade practices in business which are determined by the department to be fair."

The statement of purpose as appears in subsecs. (1) and (2) reflect a concern of the legislature with protection of the public, and it has chosen a proper means of exercising its police power to protect the public welfare. The literal reading of the statute urged by the defendants would interfere with the substantive purpose of the legislature. * * *

The defendants held themselves out to the public as persons having an expertise in home improvement. They sought out, by advertising and referrals, those persons in society who were in need of help and for the most part uninformed as to the law and construction practices. It is reasonable and necessary for the legislative body to protect the innocent who need services by placing a burden of regularity, evenhandedness and legal guidelines on the purveyors of the services. It is as much a part of competition to be honest, forthright and fulfilling as it is to work for a lower bid. The public does not always recognize this. Good, honest entrepreneurs recognize it and are not hurt by the law holding them strictly liable in a punitive statute which requires minimum standards of behavior. It is not offensive to require starting dates and completion dates to be stated in a contract. It would appear offensive only to persons not wishing to be held to any semblance of accountability.

* * *

ABRAHAMSON, JUSTICE (dissenting).

* * *

The instant case differs from the usual case raising the issue of whether the legislature intended scienter to be an element of a crime, in that in the usual case, the statutory definition of the crime is silent as to the element of scienter. In the case at bar, as the state and the majority acknowledge, the legislature specifically includes scienter in the definition of the offense; scienter is required for at least one type of violation of sec. 100.26(3), namely the state must prove that a defendant intentionally refuses to obey the regulation. While in the usual case the state urges this court not to read the element of scienter into a statute which is silent as to mens rea, in this case the state urges us to read the statute to create three ways of committing a crime, only one of which requires proof of scienter. The state is in effect asking the court to read scienter out of a portion of the statute.

The cases and commentators suggest that courts consider the following factors in deciding whether a statute should be interpreted as requiring scienter as an element of the crime or as imposing liability without fault:

1. The language of the statute.

2. The legislative history of the statute.

3. The seriousness of the penalty.

4. The purpose of the statute.

5. The practical requirements of effective law enforcement. * * *

In determining legislative intent and in analyzing the five factors outlined above, a key principle is that "the element of scienter is the rule rather than the exception in our criminal jurisprudence." This court has frequently recognized that a primary ethical foundation of the criminal justice system is that criminal liability is premised on individual blameworthiness. Reviewing these factors in the context of the case at bar, I conclude that they weigh heavily in favor of holding that the legislature intended scienter to be a necessary element of sec. 100.26(3).

Language of the Statute. As the majority concedes, the statute can reasonably be read so that intentionally modifies all three verbs. The majority then labors mightily to limit "intentionally" to modifying the verb "refuses" and to define "refuses," "neglects" and "fails" as three totally separate and distinct ways of committing a single offense. There are several flaws in the majority's analysis. First, the majority defines "refuses" as meaning intentional conduct, and the majority's conclusion that the word "intentionally" modifies only the verb "refuses" renders the word "intentionally" redundant. Second, the majority's dictionary definitions of the three verbs—and especially the definitions of neglect and fail—demonstrate that the meanings of the three verbs are not totally different and in fact overlap. * * *

Legislative History. Although the legislative history does not provide a definitive answer to the proper construction of the statute, it does point toward the legislature intending scienter to be an element of the crime. As the majority points out, the original 1921 version of sec. 100.26(3) does not include any words indicating that scienter is an element of the crime. In 1923 the legislature revised sec. 100.26(3), specifically adding the element of scienter. The 1923 statute reads "wilfully violates or refuses, neglects or fails to obey any order or regulation."

* * *

Severity of the Penalty. One of the principal indices courts consider to determine whether the legislature intended to require scienter is the severity of the penalty involved. Penalties imposed on the basis of strict liability "commonly are relatively small and conviction does no grave damage to an offender's reputation." *Morissette v. United States.*

In the instant case the potential maximum penalty is relatively severe in the context of criminal sanctions. The penalty under sec. 100.26(3)—up to one-year imprisonment in the county jail or a fine from $25 to $5,000, or both—is more severe—at least as to the term of imprisonment—than the penalty for the highest classification of misdemeanors in the criminal code. * * *

The state and the majority would have us look not at the maximum penalty possible but at the minimum penalty allowable, and the majority apparently reasons that the range of penalties illustrates that the legislature meant the statute to include various degrees of scienter. One way the majority opinion can be read is that it concludes that any problem caused by the severity of the sentence is cured by the prosecutors exercising discretion in selecting persons for prosecution and in charging the appropriate degree of scienter, and by the trial courts exercising discretion in imposing the severest penalties only on those who acted most culpably. This solution is not satisfactory; the solution merely dispenses with the safeguards of a trial on the critical issue of blameworthiness. The defendants in this case were charged with and convicted of "failing" to obey the regulations, the least culpable behavior under the reasoning of the majority. Yet the defendants were sentenced to one-year terms of imprisonment on each charge, several to be served consecutively. I recognize that the defendants had been previously charged with crimes involving property improvements and that execution of the present sentences was stayed pending probation. Nevertheless, if either defendant violates one of the numerous terms of probation, he will be subject to a lengthy period of imprisonment on conviction of "strict liability" offenses.

In my view, a determinative factor in the case at bar is the severity of the penalty. I do not believe the legislature intended a person who is blameless to be subjected to the harsh consequences sec. 100.26(3) imposes. It is one thing to accept the idea that a blameless person might occasionally be required to pay a fine and quite another to speak of a blameless person spending a year in county jail.

* * * Under the [Model Penal] Code a conviction resting on strict liability may result only in a civil penalty of monetary forfeiture. The rationale for the position taken in the Model Penal Code is explained as follows:

"* * * The liabilities involved are indefensible in principle, unless reduced to terms that insulate conviction from the type of moral condemnation that is and ought to be implicit when a sentence of imprisonment may be imposed. In the absence of minimal culpability, the law has neither a deterrent nor corrective nor an incapacitative function to perform. * * *"

Purpose of the Statute. * * *

Although one purpose of sec. 100.20, pursuant to which the regulations in the case at bar were issued, is to implement a high standard of care in the public's interest of protecting competition, I conclude that an additional purpose of sec. 100.20, and the primary purpose of the regulations in the case at bar and of sec. 100.26(3), is to punish wrongdoers. If the primary purpose of sec. 100.26(3) is to punish wrongdoers, the legislature must have intended that scienter be an element of the criminal offense set forth in sec. 100.26(3). I reach these conclusions for several reasons.

First, strict liability has generally been imposed on people who engage in acts which in and of themselves are not innocent or on people who engage in unusual or highly regulated activities and who may reasonably be held to know of and conform to government regulations. Such is not the case here.

Unlike the usual strict liability statutes which affect special, highly regulated businesses or activities such as drugs, intoxicating liquors, or firearms, sec. 100.20 and the regulations adopted under sec. 100.20, the violation of which are penalized under sec. 100.26(3), Stats., affect potentially all business people in the state. * * *

Thus when the majority decides that the legislature did not intend that scienter be proved for violations of home improvement regulations, it ignores the fact that its decision governs violations not only of the regulations of home improvement contracts but also of regulations which potentially govern every person engaged in almost any trade or business in this state. I find it hard to believe that the legislature intended criminal sanctions ranging up to a $5,000 fine and one year imprisonment to be imposed on each business person in the state who without fault fails to comply with one of the multitude of administrative regulations adopted under sec. 100.20, Stats.

Second, most of the home improvement regulations deal with false statements and misrepresentations and thus prescribe offenses which are supplementary to and extensions of the common law crimes of larceny, false pretenses and cheat. The purpose of these regulations is to prevent unscrupulous, fraudulent business practices which harm individual consumers. Many other regulations adopted pursuant to sec. 100.20 have a similar purpose. It is apparent that the Department of Agriculture, Trade and Consumer Protection has interpreted sec. 100.20 to authorize regulations to protect the pocket book of the individual consumer. These regulations primarily expand common-law and statutory property offenses; they do not primarily protect the public safety or the physical welfare or economic order of the community. Because the regulations of Ag ch. 110 (as well as other regulations) proscribe in large part variants of the classic larceny offense, a traditional property offense protecting individual private property, and because ordinarily scienter is an element of such an offense at common law, I conclude that the legislature intended scienter to be an element of sec. 100.26(3).

Third, as is explained more fully below, the legislature provided a multitude of civil remedies for violation of a regulation issued under sec. 100.20 in lieu of or in addition to criminal prosecution under sec. 100.26(3). The multitude of civil remedies indicates that the legislature intended criminal prosecution to be used to punish only "intentional" offenses.

Effective enforcement of the law. The larger the number of prosecutions expected or required to enforce the law, the more likely the legislature meant to impose liability without fault; the fewer the expected or required prosecutions, the more likely the legislature meant the prosecutor to prove scienter.

The legislature did not envisage a large number of criminal prosecutions under sec. 100.26(3) which had to be quickly processed. Quick criminal trials unhindered by proof of scienter are not needed for effective enforcement of sec. 100.20 or the regulations. The Wisconsin legislature has enacted a multitude of civil administrative and judicial remedies to enable the department of agriculture, trade and consumer protection, the department of justice, the district attorneys and the injured parties to stop the prohibited practices and to afford relief to the injured parties.

With this arsenal of weapons available to the state and the injured party against the violator, the argument that requiring proof of scienter in criminal prosecutions imposes severe difficulties in enforcement of the statute and regulations is not persuasive in the instant case.

The defendant argues that if the statute does not require scienter the statute violates due process. The majority apparently rejects this argument quoting at length various cases that have upheld strict liability statutes. I recognize that this court has, as have many federal and state courts, upheld the constitutionality of legislative acts creating crimes without a requirement of intent. Nevertheless the majority errs in intentionally neglecting to acknowledge that many courts and commentators have expressed misgivings about the constitutionality of strict liability statutes and that courts have recognized that due process may be violated when imprisonment and the stigma of a conviction are imposed on acts done innocently.

Professor Packer concludes that one of the major flaws in the jurisprudence concerning mens rea is that courts have consistently avoided trying to define the constitutional limits of the problem by employing the conclusory label, "public welfare offense." Packer, *Mens Rea and The Supreme Court,* 1962 The Supreme Court Review 149–52. The majority by not tackling the constitutional issue raised by its holding that scienter is not an element of the offense does nothing to provide future guidance for the legislature, litigants or the courts. For even if it is difficult to analyze the interrelation of scienter and due process, this court should try to begin to define the limits, if any, on the legislature's power to define a crime.

Notes and Questions

1. In *Morissette,* quoted in *Stepniewski,* the defendant had been convicted of converting government bomb casings which he had found on a government target range while deer hunting. The district

court had refused to instruct on the issue of intent, holding no intent was required by the statute, and the court of appeals affirmed. In reversing, the Supreme Court distinguished the instant case from those dealing with regulatory or "public welfare offenses" not requiring proof of intent. In concluding that Congress must not have intended merely by omission of fault words from the statute to make this crime a strict liability offense, the Court stressed (i) that the crime is a felony when the value of the property taken exceeds $100; (ii) that conviction of such a crime would gravely besmirch the defendant as a thief; and (iii) that the offense was taken over from the common law, which required proof of intent.

2. Stepniewski challenged his conviction in federal court via habeas corpus. The district court granted relief, relying upon *Morissette,* but the court of appeals reversed: "Although the *Morissette* court enunciated various factors, including those used by the district court, for federal courts to consider when reviewing statutes that arguably impose strict liability, the Court did not establish those factors as principles of constitutional law." *Stepniewski v. Gagnon,* 732 F.2d 567 (7th Cir. 1984).

3. Remington & Helstad, *The Mental Element in Crime—A Legislative Problem,* 1952 Wis.L.Rev. 644, 670: "How can these strict liability crimes be distinguished from those requiring proof of a mental element? Several tests have been suggested. Perhaps the one most frequently suggested is the determination of whether the crime is 'malum in se' or 'malum prohibitum.' Others seem to think it depends on whether the crime is a common-law crime or a statutory one. The size of the possible penalty also has been suggested as a test. Since most of these offenses are of relatively recent origin, having resulted from the need for social regulation brought about by the industrial revolution,

they usually can be recognized by their regulatory character. It has been pointed out that most of them fall into one or the other of the following categories: 1. illegal sales of intoxicating liquor; 2. sales of impure or adulterated food or drugs; 3. sales of misbranded articles; 4. violations of antinarcotic acts; 5. criminal nuisances; 6. violations of traffic regulations; 7. violations of motor-vehicle laws; and 8. violations of general police regulations, passed for the safety, health, or well-being of the community. If these categories could be depended on as being the exclusive ones where strict liability is imposed, the problem would be simplified considerably, but they cannot. The tendency is to every now and then extend strict liability to much more serious crimes. Thus, strict liability is quite frequently imposed for sex crimes committed against persons below a certain age, for adultery, and for bigamy."

4. State court decisions on the question of whether a criminal statute empty of words denoting fault was intended by the legislature to be a strict liability statute are typically based upon some or all of the factors discussed in *Stepniewski.* However, in the modern codes there is a greater likelihood that the court will find more guidance as to when absence of fault words in a statute means strict liability. Thus, in *People v. Arnold,* 3 Ill.App.3d 678, 279 N.E.2d 436 (1972), the court relied upon a criminal code provision which stated that an offense is not of the strict liability type unless it "is a misdemeanor which is not punishable by incarceration or by a fine exceeding $500, or the statute defining the offense clearly indicates a legislative purpose to impose absolute liability for the conduct described," in holding that the statute under which the defendant was charged required proof of a mental state.

5. Packer, *Mens Rea and the Supreme Court,* 1962 Sup.Ct.Rev. 107, 109: "The role of *mens rea* in the criminal law has been the subject of much discussion. The

consensus can be summarily stated: to punish conduct without reference to the actor's state of mind is both inefficacious and unjust. It is inefficacious because conduct unaccompanied by an awareness of the factors making it criminal does not mark the actor as one who needs to be subjected to punishment in order to deter him or others from behaving similarly in the future, nor does it single him out as a socially dangerous individual who needs to be incapacitated or reformed. It is unjust because the actor is subjected to the stigma of a criminal conviction without being morally blameworthy. Consequently, on either a preventive or a retributive theory of criminal punishment, the criminal sanction is inappropriate in the absence of *mens rea.*"

6. Compare Note, 75 Colum.L.Rev. 1517, 1537, 1564 (1975): "Punishing those in excusing conditions can have utile consequences. While the *threat* of punishment may indeed be inefficacious in deterring crimes by those in excusing conditions, the actual infliction of such punishment on *blameless* offenders may well serve to increase adherence to the law by members of the general public not in excusing conditions. Primarily, it would deter those potential offenders who *believe* (correctly or incorrectly) that their fault in committing a crime is probably unprovable in a court of law. * * *

"The retributivist reminds us that a state of affairs in which undeserved punishment is imposed is worse than one in which it is not imposed, and that since the institution of a system of strict liability leads with virtual certainty to such undeserved punishment, it is unacceptable.

"The retributivist, however, fails to consider the total context in which strict liability has been defended. It is not only undeserved punishment that is an evil, but also any undeserved *suffering.* Strict liability may well prevent undeserved suffering by victims of crime. Where some few individuals suffer undeserved punishment under a system which thereby deters many harmful offenses against individuals equally undeserving of harm, the total degree of desert requital may be greater than under a system which does not impose liability without fault."

7. The dissent in *Stepniewski* points out that strict liability statutes are selectively enforced. In assessing whether such crimes have a legitimate place in a rational system of criminal law, is this a plus or a minus? Consider the description of the enforcement of the food and drug laws by the Wisconsin Department of Agriculture in Comment, 1956 Wis.L.Rev. 641, 653–55:

"The general policy of the department has been to refrain from prosecuting inadvertent violations of the food and drug sections until a specific warning has been given and the violator has had ample opportunity to cease the offending action or correct the offensive condition. The considerations underlying this policy are many. Some of the more clearly defined factors include: (1) The department believes that the most effective control and the best public relations can be achieved by co-operation with the regulated group and correction of the average offender, coupled with selective prosecution of only the uncooperative recalcitrant minority. (2) The state would incur substantial cost from large numbers of food and drug prosecutions. (3) Administrative officers and field inspectors alike share a natural reluctance to be responsible for the imposition of punishment for a wholly unintended violation by a defendant free from any subjective fault. (4) The department faces the necessity of convincing the appropriate district attorney to institute prosecution, even after the inspector has decided that prosecution is desirable and has prepared a case. Evidence that a warning has been issued to the prospective defendant and has been ignored will often encourage a district attorney, who might otherwise be hesitant to do so, to prosecute. (5) Courts and juries may be reluctant to find an offender guilty even in the face of conclusive evidence of an actual violation, unless this evidence is accompanied by some showing of moral culpability, or subjective fault, such as might be provided by proof of failure to heed an express warning issued by the department. * * *

"To a certain extent the practical effect of these enforcement policies is to nullify the significance of the liability without fault character of the food and drug sections, since prosecution under them takes place only when the defendant has demonstrated subjective fault by showing a conscious intent to violate or, at least, a wilful heedlessness in failing to respond to repeated warnings. However, the liability without fault character of these provisions is still of prime importance to successful regulation of foods and drugs because the necessity of proving guilty knowledge or intent to the satisfaction of a court or jury would in many instances present an insurmountable burden to the department and greatly hinder efforts at control and regulation. This would be true even in many cases of conscious and advertent violation."

8. Taking into account the reasons for and objections to strict liability in criminal law, may it be said that there are preferable alternatives? Consider:

(a) *Increased penalties.* Note, supra, at 1548, observes that Bentham's oft-quoted principle (that when "the value of the punishment falls short, either in point of certainty, or of proximity, of that of the profit of the offense, it must receive a proportionable addition in point of magnitude") "suggests that it is possible to gain conformity to law by those who would be deterred by strict liability by increasing the penalties associated with crimes. Since the deterrent effect of a punishment is a function of the severity of the threatened punishment and the probability of incurring it, in those cases in which the latter is low, we may increase the former to achieve substantial deterrence."

(b) *Shifting the burden of proof.* Sayre, *Public Welfare Offenses,* 33 Colum.L.Rev. 55, 82 (1933): "It is fundamentally unsound to convict a defendant for a crime involving a substantial term of imprisonment without giving him the opportunity to prove that his action was due to an honest and reasonable mistake of fact or that he acted without guilty intent. If the public danger is widespread and serious, the practical situation can be met by shifting to the shoulders of the defendant the burden of proving a lack of guilty intent."

(c) *Using objective negligence standard.* Packer, supra, at 109–10: "If there is no concept between *mens rea* in the conventional sense and strict liability, then the agencies of enforcement will choose strict liability when the pressure to do so exists, as it notably does in the case of offenses that are handled on an assembly-line basis. But there is a 'half-way house': criminal liability predicated upon negligence. * * * [T]he idea of criminal responsibility based upon the actor's failure to act as carefully as he should affords an important and largely unutilized means for avoiding the tyranny of strict liability in the criminal law."

9. In *United States v. Balint,* 258 U.S. 250, 42 S.Ct. 301, 66 L.Ed. 604 (1922), the defendants were charged with the sale of narcotics not in pursuance of a written order. The defendants demurred to the indictment on the ground it failed to charge they had sold the drugs knowing them to be such. The district court sustained the demurrer, but the Supreme Court reversed, holding that consistent with Fourteenth Amendment due process "the state may in the maintenance of a

public policy provide 'that he who shall do them shall do them at his peril and will not be heard to plead in defense good faith or ignorance.' "

As noted in Packer, *Mens Rea and the Supreme Court,* 1962 Sup.Ct.Rev. 107, 113–16: "The Government's brief relied upon the numerous State cases in which criminal convictions had been upheld (usually without discussion of constitutionality) even though the statutes were construed to dispense with *mens rea.* There was no appearance for the defendants in the Supreme Court. So it came about that this all-important case was presented on an abstract issue and decided on the basis of an *ex parte* presentation.

"Unfortunately, the unanimous opinion of the Court, written by Mr. Chief Justice Taft, did not remedy the deficiency in the presentation. The constitutional point, only fleetingly referred to in the Government's brief, was quickly dismissed by the Court. * * *

"By a similarly obscure process of divination, the Chief Justice concluded that the omission of any reference to knowledge in the statute indicated an intention on the part of Congress to force persons dealing in narcotic drugs to do so at their peril. 'Doubtless considerations as to the opportunity of the seller to find out the facts and the difficulty of proof of knowledge contributed to this conclusion.' * * * But the Court showed no concern about the imposition of severe criminal sanctions without proof of blameworthiness. There was not a whisper in the opinion about the maximum penalty under the Act: five years' imprisonment, as it then stood. Nor was anything said about the trivial nature of the offenses dealt with in the State cases cited by the Court, although the distinction had not escaped the attention of State court judges.

"Upon this flimsy basis, dictum became holding, and the doctrine passed into our constitutional law that severe criminal punishment may be inflicted at the legislature's will, regardless of whether the defendant had any opportunity to conform his conduct to the requirements of law. And the more far-reaching doctrine that legislative silence is to be construed as a direction to dispense with *mens rea* took a firm hold. One wonders whether the result would have been the same * * * if Balint had come before the Supreme Court after conviction and sentence of five years' imprisonment, rather than in the posture of one protesting the omission of a word from an indictment."

10. Whether as a matter of constitutional law or simply sound criminal law policy, may it be concluded that serious penalties should not be imposed whenever guilt has been established on a strict liability basis? Consider Note, 75 Colum.L. Rev. 1517, 1556 (1975):

"[I]t has been suggested that strict liability may be imposed only where the possible penalty is a (nominal) fine. This basic approach is adopted by the Model Penal Code in section 2.05 and most vigorously defended in the framers' Comments. Yet, the deterrent effect of a threatened punishment depends upon its severity when compared to the anticipated gain by the potential offender from his crime. In the case of selling adulterated foods, drugs, etc., the possible financial gains are often quite high. For that reason, a commensurably high punishment may be necessary to outweigh the lure of the envisaged profits. Nor must such punishment be restricted to severe fines, as the Code suggests, particularly where the potential harm of the offense is severe and widespread. In fact, to some individuals the harm inflicted by a fine of $10,000 would be more severe than a six-month prison sentence."

3. 460 P.2d 77 (Alaska 1969) [p. 147 of this Book].

11. If (at least so long as *Balint* survives) the penalty does not alone provide a basis for setting due process limits on strict liability, then how might such limits be drawn? Consider:

STATE v. CAMPBELL

Supreme Court of Alaska, 1975.
536 P.2d 105.

BOOCHEVER, JUSTICE.

Thomas H. Campbell was accused of having violated AS 11.20.260 which provides that one who finds lost property and appropriates it to his own use without either advertising his discovery in a paper of general circulation or notifying the police officer nearest to the place of the finding is guilty of larceny. An indictment was returned on June 11, 1974 charging the defendant with "wilfully, unlawfully and feloniously" finding and retaining certain specified items of personal property—silver painted aluminum cans containing .22 caliber target ammunition, an ASAHI Pentax 300 mm. telephoto lens and Bushnell 7 × 35 power "sportcaster" binoculars—valued at more than $100.00 without taking either of the steps prescribed by AS 11.20.260 to find the lawful owner.

* * *

The sole issue raised on this appeal is whether the superior court erred in granting the defendant's motion to dismiss the indictment based upon the court's conclusion that AS 11.20.260 does not require criminal intent for conviction and, therefore, constitutes a violation of due process of law guaranteed by the fourteenth amendment of the United States Constitution and art. I, § 7 of the Alaska Constitution.

The lower court's invalidation of AS 11.20.260 rested solely on our holding in *Speidel v. State.*[3] That decision, in turn, was influenced by and to a great extent followed the United States Supreme Court's opinion in *Morissette v. United States,*[4] [where] the court held that, except in a narrow class of public welfare offenses in which strict liability would be tolerated,[6] proof of criminal intent would ordinarily be a necessary prerequisite to any criminal conviction.

Morissette also indicates an important corollary to this fundamental principle of law; that is, wrongful intent when *omitted* from a statutory codification of a common law crime will be read into the statute as an implied requisite element. * * *

The problem confronted in *Speidel v. State* was similar to the situation presented in *Morissette v. United States.* * * *

Following the decision in *Morissette v. United States,* we held that as a general rule, subject to the public welfare offenses exception, "conduct cannot be criminal unless it is shown that one charged with criminal conduct had an awareness or consciousness of some wrongdoing". We further stated that, where statutes codifying common law felonies such as larceny-type offenses are silent as to criminal intent, it was proper for a court to find an implication of that intent. * * *

With this background in the substantive holdings of the leading precedents, we shall evaluate the arguments presented by the parties concerning the constitutionality of the statute being challenged in the instant case. AS 11.20.260 provides:

A person who finds lost property and appropriates it to his own use or to the use of another person not entitled to it, without (1) immediately or within a reasonable time advertising that fact in a paper of general circulation published nearest the place where found, and setting out a full and true description of the property, with marks of identification, if any, or (2) notifying the peace officer nearest to the place where found and giving a full and true description of the property, together with the time, place and circumstances under which found, is guilty of larceny and is punishable as provided in § 140 of this chapter. The finder of the property may retain it until reimbursed for the cost of advertising and preserving or protecting the property.

On its face then, the statute lists only three elements which together would constitute the offense of retention of lost property: (1) a person must find *lost* property, (2) appropriate it to his own use and (3) fail to take either of the prescribed steps to locate the owner. There is, obviously, no express requirement of larcenous intent. The offense is *punishable* as a misdemeanor or felony, dependent on the value of the property, pursuant to the provisions of AS 11.20.140, which otherwise codifies the common law crime of larceny.[14] Campbell argues that, since the statute contains no requirement of criminal intent and since

4. 342 U.S. 246, 72 S.Ct. 240, 96 L.Ed. 288 (1952).

6. The court justified exempting these regulatory offenses on the basis of the public policy which sought to prevent certain types of injury, the extent of which would be the same regardless of the intent of the violator. The court observed:

The accused, if he does not will the violation, usually is in a position to prevent it with no more care than society might reasonably expect and no more exertion than it might reasonably exact from one who assumed his responsibilities. Also, penalties commonly are relatively small, and conviction does no grave damage to an offender's reputation. Under

such considerations, courts have turned to construing statutes and regulations which make no mention of intent as dispensing with it and holding that the guilty act alone makes out the crime. This has not, however, been without expressions of misgiving. * * *

14. AS 11.20.140 provides in pertinent part: A person who steals money, goods, or chattels, * * * which is the property of another, is guilty of larceny. Upon conviction, if the property stolen exceeds $100 in value, a person guilty of larceny is punishable by imprisonment in the penitentiary for not less than one nor more than 10 years. If the property stolen does not exceed $100 in value, the person, upon conviction, is

the remaining elements of the felony described could consist of mere negligent failure to notify the police or to advertise the finding of truly lost items, the holding in *Speidel* directly controls and directs a ruling invalidating the statute. The facts of the instant case, however, are distinguishable from the facts of *Speidel.* There the statute specifically defined the state of mind necessary for conviction substituting a lesser and *unconstitutional* degree of culpability for the traditional wrongful intent. AS 11.20.260, on the contrary, is *silent* as to its intent requirement and, therefore, is closer to the statute construed by the United States Supreme Court in *Morissette* where the Court found the implication of intent inherent in the common law offense.

But, according to the principles of interpretation announced in *Morissette* and *Speidel,* intent can be found by implication only in statutes which represent codifications of a common law crime. The crucial question thus becomes whether the crime described in AS 11.20.260 is sufficiently related to the common law crime of misappropriation of lost property to justify the implication of intent.

For a person to be guilty of the common law offense of misappropriation of lost property, two elements must coexist at the time the finder discovers the lost property. The finder must intend to convert the property absolutely to his own use. Secondly, the circumstances surrounding the finding must afford some reasonable clues for determining the identity of the rightful owner. In the absence of the coincidental existence of these two elements at the time of the finding, there is no larceny.

From the above analysis, it is clear that, in at least two respects, other than the absence of an express requirement of crim-

inal intent, the present form of AS 11.20.260 departs from the common law. First, since it does not require that there be any "means of inquiry" or "clues" as to ownership of the lost items, the statute does away with what was considered an essential ingredient of the felony. Secondly, the statute purports to impose a duty upon the finder to seek out the true owner by means of either of two specifically described methods.   *   *   *

This court is admittedly under a duty to reconcile, whenever possible, challenged legislation with the constitution by rendering a construction that would harmonize the statutory language with specific constitutional provisions. However, in fulfilling that duty, the extent to which the express language of the provision can be altered and departed from and the extent to which the infirmities can be rectified by the use of implied terms is limited by the constitutionally decreed separation of powers which prohibits this court from enacting legislation or redrafting defective statutes. We cannot "bootstrap" the wrongful intent requirement into the statute by the wholesale implication of other necessary elements. At some point, it must be assumed that the legislature means what it says and that, in fact, in this instance, it was trying to delineate a new statutory offense. There is nothing, of course, inherently unconstitutional about purposeful omission of the "clues" requirement. However, once that is done, this court loses its common law reference point necessary for implication of wrongful intent. *   *   *

The state contends that both of these arguments (that the challenged statute is a mere modification of the common law rule) are strengthened by reference to the analogous California statute. The California Penal Code § 485 reads:

---

punishable by imprisonment in a jail for not less than one month nor more than one year, or by a fine of not less than $25 nor more than $100.

One who finds lost property under circumstances which give him knowledge of or means of inquiry as to the true owner, and who appropriates such property to his own use, or to the use of another person not entitled thereto, without first making reasonable and just efforts to find the owner and to restore the property to him, is guilty of theft.

It should be immediately apparent that the California statute expressly requires that there be some "means of inquiry" as to the owner. Since that section is silent as to the requisite *mens rea* but otherwise consistent with the common law, larcenous intent can readily be implied.[22]

The Oregon statute, while similar to California's, is more instructive for purposes of the instant case. Oregon Revised Statutes 164.065 provides:

A person who comes into control of property of another that he knows or has good reason to know to have been lost, mislaid or delivered under a mistake as to the nature or amount of the property or the identity of the recipient, commits theft if, *with intent to deprive the owner thereof,* he fails to take reasonable measures to restore the property to the owner. (Emphasis added.)

This statute is similar to AS 11.20.260 in that the clues as to ownership requirement has been deleted. However, in conjunction with that departure from the common law, the Oregon legislature apparently found it necessary to define specifically the element of wrongful intent required for conviction under the statute.

This concurrence of the elimination of the need for clues and the express inclusion of the larcenous intent can also be found in the present New York statute covering larceny of lost property. Furthermore, § 223.5 of the Model Penal Code also reflects this pattern of variation from the common law combined with the express requirement of wrongful intent.

Thus, the statutes of Oregon and New York as well as the Model Penal Code demonstrate a uniform sensitivity on the part of legislatures and criminal law scholars to the critical importance of incorporating the requisite criminal intent into newly created statutory offenses. The comparison of the Alaska statute to these others, however, is not dispositive of the issue before the court concerning the propriety of implicating wrongful intent into the provision. While research has not revealed any other statute similar to Alaska's, its uniqueness alone cannot be a basis for condemning it. However, the juxtaposition of the relevant statutes certainly provides evidence that our statute demands either invalidation or radical reconstruction. Such reconstruction could either be along the lines of the Oregon statute (specify the element of wrongful intent) or in the direction of the California statute (set forth the clues requirement and imply intent). It is the existence of this very option which demonstrates the *legislative* nature of the decision.[26]

---

22. A survey, although not exhaustive, of like statutes from other jurisdictions which have enacted separate statutes specifically dealing with the felonious misappropriation of lost property indicates that the California-type statute has been widely used.

26. Moreover, we are inclined to require a high degree of exactitude in and strict construction of any statute (even the classic common law variety) which purports to make it a felony wrongfully to retain lost objects. That is because there is a lesser degree of culpability which logically attaches to one who merely submits to the temptation presented by his discovery of lost goods and commits a crime of omission (failing to return the items found) than there would be to one who affirmatively acts to deprive another of his property. There is the added consideration that the owner is usually partially responsible for circumstances giving rise to that temptation either by negligently losing the property or, by his indifference, creating the impression that the items have been abandoned. While a victim's negligence is admittedly not a defense to commission of a crime, it does reflect on the nature of the fault or wrong committed by the defendant. * * *

We conclude that AS 11.20.260 fails to set forth the requirements of the common law crime of larceny by appropriation of lost property.[27] Instead, a new, distinct offense has been created, and the statute is constitutionally defective and invalid because of its omission of the requirement of criminal intent. We affirm the trial court's dismissal of the action.

Affirmed.

SECTION 6. IGNORANCE OR MISTAKE OF FACT OR LAW

DIRECTOR OF PUBLIC PROSECUTIONS v. MORGAN

House of Lords, 1975.

[1976] A.C. 182, [1975] 2 W.L.R. 913, [1975] 2 All E.R. 347.

Appeal by the defendants from an order of the Court of Appeal (Criminal Division) dismissing their appeals against conviction.

The appellants were convicted at Stafford Crown Court on January 24, 1974; Morgan of aiding and abetting rape, Parker of aiding and abetting rape and of rape; McLarty of aiding and abetting rape and of rape; McDonald of rape and of aiding and abetting rape. They were sentenced by Kenneth Jones J.: Parker, McLarty and McDonald to concurrent terms of four years' imprisonment and Morgan to concurrent terms of 10 years' imprisonment. * * *

Morgan was a senior N.C.O. in the Royal Air Force. He was 37 years old, his wife 34, and they had been married for about 13 years and had boys of 11 and 12. For some time husband and wife had been on poor terms, and she had engaged in two love affairs, at least one of them being (as Mrs. Morgan alleged) at her husband's

instigation. Of the other three accused, one was nearly 20, the other two were in their twenties, all three of them serving in the Royal Air Force and having arrived at the R.A.F. Depot at Cosford on August 15, 1973. It was common ground that Morgan invited the other three accused, all complete strangers to him, that night to go back to his house and have intercourse with his wife and that as he drove them from Wolverhampton to his home at Cosford he supplied each of them with a contraceptive. The only issue between the various accused relating to this part of the case was that Morgan denied the assertion of the others that during the car journey he told them that his wife might put up a show of struggling, but that this would only be a charade stimulating her sexual excitement, as in reality she would welcome intercourse with them. They claimed that, although they were at first incredulous, Morgan finally persuaded them that he was serious and that their behaviour thereafter was throughout based on their belief that Mrs. Morgan was indeed only play-acting. Certainly she could have done nothing more than she did to resist the attacks made upon her, and before the House of Lords counsel for the appellants accepted that in fact she never did consent to what transpired from the moment the four men reached Morgan's home. She was awakened from sleep in a bedroom which she shared with her 11-year-old son and her evidence was that all four accused in part dragged and in part carried her into another room which contained a double bed. She claimed that she struggled violently and shouted "Police!" several times until a hand was placed over her mouth, that both children were awakened and that thereafter each of the four

---

27. The common law crime of larceny is codified in AS 11.20.140 set forth in Footnote 14 of this opinion. Many states have only such general larceny or theft statutes in their penal codes, and these states have sometimes prosecuted finders who have committed common law larceny pursuant thereto. * * *

accused had sexual intercourse with her. It was established that, as soon as the three strangers had departed and Morgan had gone to bed, Mrs. Morgan drove off to Cosford Hospital and complained of having been raped, her case being that she did all she could to resist but that she was throughout held down on the bed by three men while the fourth had intercourse with her. * * *

LORD CROSS OF CHELSEA: * * * The question of law which is raised by the appeal is whether the judge was right in telling the jury that, if they came to the conclusion that Mrs. Morgan had not consented to the intercourse in question but that the defendants believed or may have believed that she was consenting to it, they must nevertheless find the defendants guilty of rape if they were satisfied that they had no reasonable grounds for so believing. * * * The Sexual Offences Act 1956, which provides by section 1(1) that it is an offence "for a man to rape a woman," contains no definition of the word "rape." No one suggests that rape is an "absolute" offence to the commission of which the state of mind of the defendant with regard to the woman's consent is wholly irrelevant. The point in dispute is as to the quality of belief which entitles the defendant to be acquitted and as to the "evidential" burden of proof with regard to it.

* * * Rape is not a word in the use of which lawyers have a monopoly and the question to be answered in this case, as I see it, is whether according to the ordinary use of the English language a man can be said to have committed rape if he believed that the woman was consenting to the intercourse and would not have attempted to have it but for his belief, whatever his grounds for so believing. I do not think that he can. * * *

LORD HAILSHAM OF ST. MARYLE-BONE: * * * Bridge J., in giving the judgment of the Court of Appeal, attempted to do so by three propositions which, again, I quote in extenso. He said: "The relevant principles can perhaps be restated in the following propositions:

1. In all crimes the Crown has both the evidential and the probative burden of showing that the accused did the prohibited act * * *.

2. Wherever the definition of a crime includes as one of its express ingredients a specific mental element both the evidential and the probative burden lie upon the Crown with respect to that element. * * * In seeking to rebut the Crown's case against him in reference to his state of mind the accused may and frequently does assert his mistaken belief in non-existent facts. Of course it is right that in this context the question whether there were reasonable grounds for the belief is only a factor for the jury's consideration in deciding whether the Crown has established the necessary mental element of the crime. This is because the issue is already before the jury and no evidential burden rests upon the accused. * * *

3. But where the definition of the crime includes no specific mental element beyond the intention to do the prohibited act, the accused may show that though he did the prohibited act intentionally he lacked *mens rea* because he mistakenly but honestly and reasonably, believed facts which, if true, would have made his act innocent. Here the evidential burden lies upon the accused but once evidence sufficient to raise the issue is before the jury the probative burden lies upon the Crown to negative the mistaken belief. The rationale of requiring reasonable grounds for the mistaken belief must lie in the law's consideration that a bald assertion of belief for which the accused can indicate no reasonable ground is evidence of insufficient substance to raise any issue requiring the jury's consideration. Thus, for example, a

person charged with assault upon a victim shown to have been entirely passive throughout who said he had believed himself to be under imminent threat of attack by the victim but could indicate no circumstance giving cause for such a belief would not discharge the evidential burden of showing a mistaken belief that he was acting lawfully in self-defence.''

In the event Bridge J. then went on to subsume rape under the third and not the second heading and so to reach the conclusion: "The correct view, we think, is that, on proof of the fact of absence of consent from circumstances which in the nature of the case must have come to the notice of the defendant, he may be presumed to have appreciated their significance, and it is this presumption which casts upon the defendant the evidential burden of showing an honest and reasonable belief in consent before any issue as to his state of mind can arise for the jury's consideration." He goes on to say that, once the "evidential" burden is discharged the "probative burden" is cast once more on the Crown.

With due respect * * * I do not believe the conclusion follows. * * * I can see no reason why the class of case to which his second proposition applies should be limited to cases where the mental ingredient is limited to a "specific mental element" * * * .

I believe the law on this point to have been correctly stated by Lord Goddard C.J. in *Steane* (1947) 32 Cr.App.R. 61, 66; [1947] K.B. 997, 1004, when he said: "if on the totality of the evidence there is room for more than one view as to the intent of the prisoner, the jury should be directed that it is for the prosecution to prove the intent to the jury's satisfaction, and if, on review of the whole evidence,

they either think the intent did not exist or they are left in doubt as to the intent, the prisoner is entitled to be acquitted."

* * *

Once one has accepted, what seems to me abundantly clear, that the prohibited act in rape is non-consensual sexual intercourse, and that the guilty state of mind is an intention to commit it, it seems to me to follow as a matter of inexorable logic that there is no room either for a "defence" of honest belief or mistake, or of a defence of honest and reasonable belief and mistake. Either the prosecution proves that the accused had the requisite intent, or it does not. In the former case it succeeds, and in the latter it fails. Since honest belief clearly negatives intent, the reasonableness or otherwise of that belief can only be evidence for or against the view that the belief and therefore the intent was actually held, and it matters not whether, to quote Bridge J. in the passage cited above: "the definition of a crime includes no specific element beyond the prohibited act." If the mental element be primarily an intention and not a state of belief it comes within his second proposition and not his third. Any other view, as for insertion of the word "reasonable" can only have the effect of saying that a man intends something which he does not.

* * *

LORD SIMON OF GLAISDALE. * * * [A]greeing as I do with the judgment of Bridge J. in the Court of Appeal, I feel no reluctance in coming to this conclusion, which seems to me to accord with legal principle and with good sense. * * *

The common law seems to be the same in the U.S.A.; see specifically as regards rape *U.S. v. Short* (1954) 4 U.S.C.M.A. 437; 16 C.M.R. 11.[a] * * *

a. In *Short,* the defendant was court-martialed for assault with intent to commit rape. At trial, he claimed he thought the girl was a consenting prostitute. His request for an instruction

that "the accused must think victim is not consenting" was refused. In affirming the conviction, Quinn, C. J., held the instruction was properly refused because it "fails to qualify the

It remains to consider why the law requires, in such circumstances, that the belief in a state of affairs whereby the *actus* would not be *reus* should be held on reasonable grounds. One reason was given by Bridge J. in the Court of Appeal: "The rationale of requiring reasonable grounds for the mistaken belief must lie in the law's consideration that a bald assertion of belief for which the accused can indicate no reasonable ground is evidence of insufficient substance to raise any issue requiring the jury's consideration." I agree; but I think there is also another reason. The policy of the law in this regard could well derive from its concern to hold a fair balance between victim and accused. It would hardly seem just to fob off a victim of a savage assault with such comfort as he could derive from knowing that his injury was caused by a belief, however absurd, that he was about to attack the accused. A respectable woman who has been ravished would hardly feel that she was vindicated by being told that her assailant must go unpunished because he believed, quite unreasonably, that she was consenting to sexual intercourse with him. * * *

LORD EDMUND DAVIES: * * * The parties to these appeals are at one in regarding the offence of rape as falling within the third of Bridge J.'s propositions, but they differ widely in relation to what is involved in "the intention to do the prohibited act." Before this House, learned prosecuting counsel submitted that rape consists simply in having sexual intercourse with a woman who does not in fact consent, and that more than this the Crown need not establish in order to secure a conviction. This simplistic approach is reminiscent of the minority judgments in

Tolson (1889) 23 Q.B.D. 168, of which more hereafter, that a man commits bigamy if he goes through a marriage ceremony while his wife is alive, even though he honestly and reasonably believes she is dead. Indeed, it would mean that rape involved no mental element save the intention to have intercourse * * *.

It was rightly submitted for the appellants that such an approach involves a fundamentally wrong conception of what constitutes rape. The offence lacks statutory definition, the Sexual Offences Act 1956, s. 1(1) merely declaring it an offence for a man to rape a woman. [But all the definitions in the treatises] indicate that knowledge by the accused of the woman's unwillingness to have intercourse is essential to the crime of rape. * * *

In the absence of contrary evidence, the accused may be presumed to have appreciated the significance of circumstances which must have come to his notice. But it does not follow inexorably that he in fact did so * * *. The presumption is not conclusive and, unless it emerges that there is a weight of authority compelling a different conclusion, I should have considered that the honest belief of an accused charged with rape that the woman was willing, being wholly inconsistent with the criminal intention necessary to constitute the crime, would call for his acquittal. * * *

In this country a long line of authorities and numerous dicta indicate that, when an accused challenges that he had the necessary *mens rea* involved in the offence charged by asserting that he committed the *actus reus* under a mistake of fact, his belief must have been based on reasonable

---

accused's belief by requiring that it be reasonable and honest." Brosman, J., dissenting argued that rape "has ordinarily been treated as requiring only a general criminal intent," while assault with intent to rape requires "a specific intent," so that an unreasonable belief would negative the prerequisites for finding guilt of the latter offense

but not the former. He added: "It may be regarded as anomolous to conclude that an accused may be exonerated for guilt of assault with intent to commit rape because of an unreasonable mistake, whereas he could have been convicted lawfully of rape had penetration been effected under the same misapprehension."

grounds. Of these cases, the best known are those arising from charges of bigamy.

*   *   *

Such an approach has been criticised. In America, for example, Professor Jerome Hall observed ((1957) 33 *Indiana Law Journal*), "Anglo-American law restricts the scope of *ignorantia facti* in ways which constitute serious limitations. * * * An honest mistake is not sufficient. [It] must be bona fide and reasonable * * * The plain consequences of this application of objective liability to *ignorantia facti* is that persons who commit harms solely because they are mistaken regarding the material facts are nonetheless criminally liable, i.e. despite the complete lack of criminal intent. * * * The elimination of 'reasonableness' as a substantive restriction of the doctrine of *ignorantia facti* would clarify the public mind regarding the nature of criminal conduct. It would facilitate analysis of the criminal law and stimulate a sounder administration of it." In this country, *Russell on Crime* (12th ed. Vol. 1, p. 76), in the course of a discussion of *mens rea*, refers to "the ancient doctrine that the mistake must be reasonable" and adds: "It is hardly necessary to point out that such a doctrine, based purely on an objective test, is out of keeping with the modern principle that the *mens rea* required by the common law is a subjective

element." And Professor Glanville Williams has commented (*Criminal Law,* 2nd ed. (1961) p. 177): "* * * it is not true to say that the general run of crimes can be committed by inattention. * * * It is submitted that this is not the law. In the absence of words in the statute dispensing with proof of *mens rea,* it should be held that the crime can be committed only intentionally or recklessly. If a person charged with bigamy believed that he was legally free to marry again, it cannot be said that the crime was committed either intentionally or recklessly, and the question whether the belief was unreasonable is irrelevant." And, after a discussion of reported cases, he concluded: "Even if, as a result of decisions like this, it must now be conceded that unreasonable mistake is no defence in bigamy, this only means that bigamy can be committed negligently. It does not prove that other crimes can be committed negligently."

For myself, I am greatly impressed by these forceful passages * * *. But regard must be had to the uniformity of approach over a wide area and for a long time—*Tolson* [b], it should be remembered, was decided nearly 90 years ago. Paying such regard, the conclusion I have come to is that the necessary course is to uphold, as being in accordance with established law, the direction given in this case by the

---

b. 23 Q.B.D. 168 (1889), described by Lord Cross in *Morgan* as follows: "The statute [Offences against the Person Act 1861, s. 57] there provided that 'whoever being married shall marry any other person during the life of the former husband or wife shall be guilty of felony' with a proviso that: 'nothing in this section contained shall extend * * * to any person marrying a second time whose husband or wife shall have been continually absent from such person for the space of seven years then last past, and shall not have been known by such person to be living within that time. * * *' The defendant who was found by the jury to have had reasonable grounds for believing that her husband was then dead—though in fact he was not—went through a ceremony of marriage with another man within seven years of the time when she last knew of his being alive. She therefore fell within the very

words of the statute. Nevertheless, the majority of the Court of Crown Cases Reserved held that she was entitled to be acquitted because on general principles of criminal liability, having no particular relation to the crime of bigamy, a mistaken belief based on reasonable grounds in the existence of facts, which, if true, would have made the act charged against her innocent, afforded her a defence since it was not to be supposed that Parliament intended bigamy to be an 'absolute' offence to the commission of which the state of mind of the defendant was wholly irrelevant. The minority of the judges, on the other hand, thought that the existence of the proviso which gave an express exemption from liability in certain circumstances made it impossible to imply an exemption from liability in other circumstances not covered by it."

learned trial judge as to the necessity for the mistake of fact urged to be based on reasonable grounds. The approach which I should have preferred must, I think, wait until the legislature reforms this part of the law * * *.

LORD FRASER OF TULLYBELTON: * * * All the definitions of rape quoted to us which made any reference to the state of mind required of the rapist included a statement to the effect that: "One of the elements of the crime of rape is an intention on the part of an accused person to have intercourse without consent." * * * If that is so, then the logical difficulty of requiring a belief in the woman's consent to be based on reasonable grounds arises sharply. If the effect of the evidence as a whole is that the defendant believed, or may have believed, that the woman was consenting, then the Crown has not discharged the onus of proving commission of the offence as fully defined and, as it seems to me, no question can arise as to whether the belief was reasonable or not. Of course, the reasonableness or otherwise of the belief will be important as evidence tending to show whether it was truly held by the defendant, but that is all.

The argument for the Crown in support of an affirmative answer to the question in this case was not supported by any English decision on rape. It was supported by reference to English decisions in relation to other offences which are more or less analogous to rape, and to Australian decisions on rape, some of which I have already referred to. The English case upon which most reliance was placed was *Tolson,* supra, which was concerned with bigamy, and which decided that a bona fide belief *on reasonable grounds* in the death of the husband at the time of the second marriage afforded a good defence to the indictment for bigamy. The main argument in the case concerned with the question whether a mistaken belief could be a de-

fence to a charge of bigamy at all, and comparatively little attention was given to the subsidiary point of whether the belief had to be based upon reasonable grounds. The case seems to me therefore of only limited assistance for the present purpose. We were invited to overrule *Tolson* but, as it has stood for over 80 years, and has been followed in many later cases, I would not favour that course. But in my opinion the case is distinguishable from the present. Bigamy was a statutory offence under the Offences against the Person Act 1861, s. 57. So far as appears from the words of the section, bigamy was an absolute offence, except for one defence set out in a proviso, and it is clear that the mental element in bigamy is quite different from that in rape. In particular, bigamy does not involve any intention except the intention to go through a marriage ceremony, unlike rape in which I have already considered the mental element. So, if a defendant charged with bigamy believes that his spouse is dead, his belief does not involve the absence of any intent which forms an essential ingredient in the offence, and it is thus not comparable to the belief of a defendant charged with rape that the woman consents. The difficulty of arguing by analogy from one offence to another is strikingly illustrated by reference to the case of *Prince* (1875) 13 Cox C.C. 138. That case dealt with abduction of a girl under the age of 16, an offence created by section 55 of the Act of 1861. Lord Bramwell, with whom five other judges concurred, held that a mistaken and reasonable belief by the defendant that the abducted girl was aged 16 or more was no excuse, because abduction of a young girl was immoral as well as illegal, although a mistaken and reasonable belief by the defendant that he had the consent of the girl's father would have been an excuse. If such differences can exist about mistaken beliefs of different facts in one offence, it is surely dangerous to argue from one offence to another. No doubt a rapist, who mistakenly believes that the woman is consenting to intercourse, must be behaving immorally, by committing fornication or adultery. But those forms of immoral conduct are not intended to be struck at by the law against rape; indeed, they are not now considered appropriate to be visited with penalties of the criminal law at all. There seems therefore to be no reason why they should affect the consequences of the mistaken belief. * * * c

Notes and Questions

1. In *People v. Mayberry*, 15 Cal.3d 143, 125 Cal.Rptr. 745, 542 P.2d 1337 (1975), the defendant, on trial for rape (defined by statute as "an act of sexual intercourse, accomplished with a female not the wife of the perpetrator, under either of the following circumstances: * * * 2. Where she resists, but her resistance is overcome by force or violence; 3. Where she is prevented from resisting by threats of great and immediate bodily harm, accompanied by apparent power of execution"), was refused his requested instruction that he should be acquitted if the jury had a reasonable doubt as to whether he "reasonably and genuinely believed" that the woman consented. Reversed: "If a defendant entertains a reasonable and bona fide belief that a prosecutrix voluntarily consented to accompany him and to engage in sexual intercourse, it is apparent he does not possess the wrongful intent that is a prerequisite

* * * to a conviction of * * * rape by means of force or threat. * * *

"The Attorney General further argues that a defense based on mistake of fact as to the prosecutrix' consent in prosecutions for * * * rape should not be permitted because it will promote greater resistance by the victim to assure there is no misunderstanding as to consent and that such resistance could result in harm to the victim. The Attorney General notes that utmost resistance by the female to establish lack of consent to intercourse is not required. Such an argument, in our view, invokes a policy consideration for the Legislature * * *."

Should the defendant have asked for more? Or, should the court have given less? Compare *State v. Dombroski*, 145 Minn. 278, 176 N.W. 985 (1920), where defendant was convicted of rape in that he had intercourse without force or threat with a woman of unsound mind. The trial judge instructed the jury that it was not necessary for the prosecution to prove the defendant knew the woman was of unsound mind. On appeal, affirmed:

"Subdivision 1 of section 8655, upon which the prosecution rests, declares in plain and unambiguous language, that whoever has carnal intercourse with a female so devoid of mental powers, as to be incapable of rational consent thereto shall be guilty of rape; it is positive in its terms and unqualifiedly prohibits an act of the kind. It does not make knowledge by the accused of the defective mental condition

c. Although a majority of the House of Lords concluded the instruction was incorrect, the appeal was dismissed on the ground, as stated by Lord Davies, that "no reasonable jury could have failed to convict all four accused even had they been directed as counsel for the appellants urges they should."

Consider Comment, 39 J.Crim.L. 264, 267 (1975): "At first sight, this may seem rather remarkable, in that there is nothing inherently unlikely in a group of very young soldiers being convinced by an older and senior N.C.O. that his wife was 'kinky' and enjoyed sexual intercourse

only when she was stimulated by feigning resistance. If a jury had been properly directed that such a belief honestly held was a defence, is it inevitable that they would have convicted? The view taken by the House of Lords appears to have depended on the fact that, at their trial, the defendants changed their story and asserted that the woman had actively participated in an orgy. If this were really the ground upon which the proviso was applied, four years' imprisonment seems to be a severe penalty for lying, however grossly."

of the female an element of the crime, and, construed in the light of subdivisions 4 and 5 of the same section, it is clear that the legislature did not intend to make that a necessary ingredient thereof. Subdivision 4 treats of such an act with a female while under stupor from liquor or narcotics administered to her by or with the privity of the accused; subdivision 5 expressly makes knowledge by the accused of the unconsciousness of the female an essential to a conviction. By thus making knowledge and intent necessary elements as to those subdivisions, and omitting it from subdivision 1, the legislature must be deemed to have deliberately made the distinction, and for reasons deemed by it satisfactory. We need not go into that field in inquiry."

2. Estrich, *Rape,* 95 Yale L.J. 1087, 1097–99 (1986): "In defining the crime of rape, most American courts have omitted *mens rea* altogether. In Maine, for example, the Supreme Judicial Court has held that there is no *mens rea* requirement at all for rape. In Pennsylvania, the Superior Court held in 1982 that even a reasonable belief as to the victim's consent would not exculpate a defendant charged with rape. In 1982 the Supreme Judicial Court of Massachusetts left open the question whether it would recognize a defense of reasonable mistake of fact as to consent, but it rejected the defendant's suggestion that any mistake, reasonable or unreasonable, would be sufficient to negate the required intent to rape; such a claim was treated by the court as bordering on the ridiculous. The following year the court went on to hold that a specific intent that intercourse be without consent was not an element of the crime of rape; that decision has since been construed to mean that there is no intent requirement at all as to consent in rape cases.

"To treat what the defendant intended or knew or even should have known about the victim's consent as irrelevant to his

liability sounds like a result favorable to both prosecution and women as victims. But experience makes all too clear that it is not. To refuse to inquire into *mens rea* leaves two possibilities: turning rape into a strict liability offense where, in the absence of consent, the man is guilty of rape regardless of whether he (or anyone) would have recognized nonconsent in the circumstances; or defining the crime of rape in a fashion that is so limited that it would be virtually impossible for any man to be convicted where he was truly unaware or mistaken as to nonconsent. In fact, it is the latter approach which has characterized all of the older, and many of the newer, American cases. In practice, abandoning *mens rea* produces the worst of all possible worlds: The trial emerges not as an inquiry into the guilt of the defendant (is he a rapist?) but of the victim (was she really raped? did she consent?). The perspective that governs is therefore not that of the woman, nor even of the particular man, but of a judicial system intent upon protecting against unjust conviction, regardless of the dangers of injustice to the woman in the particular case. * * *

" * * * Rather than inquire whether the man believed (reasonably or unreasonably) that his victim was consenting, the courts have demanded that the victim demonstrate her nonconsent by engaging in resistance that will leave no doubt as to nonconsent. The definition of nonconsent as resistance—in the older cases, as utmost resistance, while in some more recent ones, as 'reasonable' physical resistance—functions as a substitute for *mens rea* to ensure that the man has notice of the woman's nonconsent."

3. Does this mean that, as a matter of policy, *Morgan* represents the better view? Consider Temkin, *The Limits of Reckless Rape,* 1983 Crim.L.Rev. 5, 14–15: "Whether or not a man who honestly but wrongly and unreasonably believes in a woman's consent should be criminally lia-

ble raises a moral problem which is obscured by arguments which focus on the definition of the crime or the infrequency with which such a defence is likely to be raised. Professor Williams asserts that the matter is likely to crop up in two circumstances only, namely, where the defendant has been told a tale by a third party or where he is drunk. He omits to mention cases where the defendant argues quite genuinely as follows:

"(1) 'I know that the complainant is a "slut." I know for a fact that she regularly sleeps with my friends Tom, Dick and Harry to say nothing of numerous others. Of course, I did not believe her when she said "no." '

"(2) 'I met the complainant at a dance. She was wearing a mini-skirt and a transparent blouse with a plunging neckline. She drank a lot throughout the evening. She accepted a lift home from me. I took it for granted that she was out to have a good time. I did not believe her when she said "no." '

"Alternatively, the defendant might be a man who believes that most women really want to have sexual intercourse and their 'no' is but a sham or who has had sexual intercourse with the same woman in the past and therefore places no credence on her refusal.

"The question is whether arguments of this nature ought to constitute a sufficient answer to a charge of rape. The view taken here is that they should not. It has been suggested elsewhere and it is suggested here that the guiding principle in the law of rape should be the protection of sexual choice for women. There can be no accommodation between that principle and any of the defences raised above. Furthermore, no law can claim to protect

sexual choice for women if it permits as a defence a belief in consent based on what another person (usually the complainant's husband) has told the accused."

Compare Estrich, supra, at 1101–03, who follows her critique of American rape law with the observation that "the British courts may have gone too far in the other direction. * * *

"My view is that such a 'negligent rapist' should be punished, albeit—as in murder—less severely than the man who acts with purpose or knowledge, or even knowledge of the risk. First, he is sufficiently blameworthy for it to be just to punish him. Second, the injury he inflicts is sufficiently grave to deserve the law's prohibition."

4. *Morgan* differs from the typical mistake-of-fact case, where generalizations regarding the "defense" of mistake of fact are often made without any indication that the underlying question is what mental state the crime requires. As noted in *Model Penal Code* § 2.04, Comment (1985), to have a provision to the effect that a mistake of fact is a defense if it negatives the existence of a required mental state "is not to say anything that would not otherwise be true, even if no provision on the subject were made. As Glanville Williams summarized the matter, the rule relating to mistake 'is not a new rule; and the law could be stated equally well without reference to mistake * * * It is impossible to assert that a crime requiring intention or recklessness can be committed although the accused laboured under a mistake that negatived the requisite intention or recklessness. Such an assertion carries its own refutation.' [a] This obvious point has, however, sometimes been overlooked in general formulations

---

a. Consider, in this connection, that there is disagreement as to whether a defendant's claim of mistake of fact entitles him to a special jury instruction focusing on the mistake issue or instead necessitates nothing more than the usual

mental state jury instruction. Compare *State v. Freeman*, 267 N.W.2d 69 (Iowa 1978) (must give mistake instruction); with *State v. Molin*, 288 N.W.2d 232 (Minn.1979) (contra).

purporting to require that mistake be reasonable if it is to exculpate, without regard to the mode of culpability required to commit the crime. * * *

"It is true, of course, that whether recklessness or negligence suffices as a mode of culpability with respect to a given element of an offense is often raised for the first time in dealing with a question of mistake. That this may happen emphasizes the importance of perceiving that the question relates to the underlying rule as to the kind of culpability required with respect to the particular element of the offense involved."

Under recent recodifications generally following the Model Penal Code in this respect, it is much more likely that the required mental state will be clear and that consequently it will be apparent what character of mistake will show the absence of that mental state.

5. Most of the American cases have taken a strict view concerning mistake of fact in bigamy cases. Illustrative is *Braun v. State,* 230 Md. 82, 185 A.2d 905 (1962), noting that "the majority rule in this country [is] opposed to *Tolson*," discussed in fn. b of *Morgan,* and holding: "In the light of the majority American rule and of the prior expressions of this Court * * * and in view of the fact that honest belief is not one of the exceptions from liability enumerated in the statute itself, we think that even if the appellant had entertained a bona fide belief that his first wife had divorced him before his second marriage, and even if this erroneous belief were to be regarded as a mistake of fact and not of law (which we do not decide), this would not constitute a defense to the charge of bigamy under our statute."

Compare *People v. Vogel,* 46 Cal.2d 798, 299 P.2d 850 (1956): "The severe penalty imposed for bigamy, the serious loss of reputation conviction entails, the infrequency of the offense, and the fact that it

has been regarded for centuries as a crime involving moral turpitude, make it extremely unlikely that the Legislature meant to include the morally innocent to make sure the guilty did not escape."

6. Similarly, the prevailing view with respect to statutory rape (which does not require a threat or force, but rather that the girl be under a certain age, such as 16) is that mistake of fact as to age is no defense. See, e.g., *People v. Cash,* 419 Mich. 230, 351 N.W.2d 822 (1984), noting "that our decision is in line with the preponderant majority of jurisdictions, both state and federal, which do not recognize the reasonable-mistake-of-age defense for statutory rape offenses and have likewise upheld against due process challenges their respective statutes' imposition of criminal liability without the necessity of proving the defendant's knowledge that the victim was below the designated age."

Compare *State v. Elton,* 680 P.2d 727 (Utah 1984): "It is not consonant with our principles of criminal liability when dealing with *malum in se* crimes to hold a person responsible for a crime he did not intend to commit * * *.

"In addition, it is fundamentally unfair to allow the victim in such a crime—who necessarily has also violated the law—to mislead the defendant as to an element of the crime and then place the blame for the mistake on the defendant rather than the person who created the deceit and entrapped the defendant into committing a crime he or she attempted to avoid."

7. In *United States v. Hamilton,* 456 F.2d 171 (3d Cir.1972), the defendant was convicted of violating 18 U.S.C.A. § 2423, which reads: "Whoever knowingly persuades, induces, entices, or coerces any woman or girl who has not attained her eighteenth birthday, to go from one place to another by common carrier, in interstate commerce or within the District of Columbia or any Territory

or Possession of the United States, with intent that she be induced or coerced to engage in prostitution, debauchery or other immoral practice, shall be fined not more than $10,000 or imprisoned not more than ten years, or both." On appeal the defendant contended the government failed to prove he knew the victim was under 18. The court replied:

"While an examination of the statutes found within the White Slave Traffic Act, 18 U.S.C.A. §§ 2421, 2422 and 2423, shows that there must be proof that one knowingly transports or persuades, induces, entices or coerces a person to be transported in interstate commerce in order to engage in immoral practices including prostitution, § 2423 provides a more severe penalty when the girl is under eighteen years of age and, accordingly, knowledge that the girl is under eighteen years of age is not part of the proof requisite by the Government in order to sustain a conviction."

Are you convinced? Of what relevance is it that 18 U.S.C.A. § 2422 is essentially the same crime, except there is no age requirement for the victim, and that it is punishable by a fine of not more than $5,000 or imprisonment for not more than 5 years or both?

8. May the *Morgan* case be rightly criticized on the ground that the Lords failed to see the analogy to the *Prince* case, discussed by Lord Fraser? That is, may it not be concluded, as stated in *White v. State,* 44 Ohio App. 331, 185 N.E. 64 (1933), that the "sound doctrine underlying the rule that guilty knowledge is not required to accomplish the crime of rape with consent is that the act of the accused is at best an immoral one, and that he cannot enter upon the accomplishment of an admittedly immoral act except at his peril, and if in law his act is in fact felony he must suffer the consequences thereof although so far as his actual knowledge was concerned he

may not have known the enormity of the offense of which he is guilty"? Are not *Cash* and *Hamilton* likewise explainable on this basis?

LIPAROTA v. UNITED STATES

Supreme Court of the United States, 1985.
471 U.S. 419, 105 S.Ct. 2084, 85 L.Ed.2d 434.

JUSTICE BRENNAN delivered the opinion of the Court.

The federal statute governing food stamp fraud provides that "whoever knowingly uses, transfers, acquires, alters, or possesses coupons or authorization cards in any manner not authorized by [the statute] or the regulations" is subject to a fine and imprisonment. 7 U.S.C. § 2024(b). The question presented is whether in a prosecution under this provision the Government must prove that the defendant knew that he was acting in a manner not authorized by statute or regulations.

Petitioner Frank Liparota was the co-owner with his brother of Moon's Sandwich Shop in Chicago, Illinois. He was indicted for acquiring and possessing food stamps in violation of § 2024(b). The Department of Agriculture had not authorized petitioner's restaurant to accept food stamps. At trial, the Government proved that petitioner on three occasions purchased food stamps from an undercover Department of Agriculture agent for substantially less than their face value. On the first occasion, the agent informed petitioner that she had $195 worth of food stamps to sell. The agent then accepted petitioner's offer of $150 and consummated the transaction in a back room of the restaurant with petitioner's brother. A similar transaction occurred one week later, in which the agent sold $500 worth of coupons for $350. Approximately one month later, petitioner bought $500 worth of food stamps from the agent for $300.

In submitting the case to the jury, the District Court rejected petitioner's proposed "specific intent" instruction, which would have instructed the jury that the Government must prove that "the defendant knowingly did an act which the law forbids, purposely intending to violate the law." Concluding that "[t]his is not a specific intent crime" but rather a "knowledge case," the District Court instead instructed the jury as follows:

> "When the word 'knowingly' is used in these instructions, it means that the Defendant realized what he was doing, and was aware of the nature of his conduct, and did not act through ignorance, mistake, or accident. Knowledge may be proved by defendant's conduct and by all of the facts and circumstances surrounding the case."

The District Court also instructed that the Government had to prove that "the Defendant acquired and possessed food stamp coupons for cash in a manner not authorized by federal statute or regulations" and that "the Defendant knowingly and wilfully acquired the food stamps." Petitioner objected that this instruction required the jury to find merely that he knew that he was acquiring or possessing food stamps; he argued that the statute should be construed instead to reach only "people who

knew that they were acting unlawfully." The judge did not alter or supplement his instructions, and the jury returned a verdict of guilty. * * *

The definition of the elements of a criminal offense is entrusted to the legislature, particularly in the case of federal crimes, which are solely creatures of statute. With respect to the element at issue in this case, however, Congress has not explicitly spelled out the mental state required. Although Congress certainly intended by use of the word "knowingly" to require *some* mental state with respect to *some* element of the crime defined in § 2024(b), the interpretations proffered by both parties accord with congressional intent to this extent. Beyond this, the words themselves provide little guidance. Either interpretation would accord with ordinary usage.[7] The legislative history of the statute contains nothing that would clarify the congressional purpose on this point.

Absent indication of contrary purpose in the language or legislative history of the statute, we believe that § 2024(b) requires a showing that the defendant knew his conduct to be unauthorized by statute or regulations.[9] "The contention that an injury can amount to a crime only when

---

7. One treatise has aptly summed up the ambiguity in an analogous situation:

"Still further difficulty arises from the ambiguity which frequently exists concerning what the words or phrases in question modify. What, for instance, does 'knowingly' modify in a sentence from a 'blue sky' law criminal statute punishing one who 'knowingly sells a security without a permit' from the securities commissioner? To be guilty must the seller of a security without a permit know only that what he is doing constitutes a sale, or must he also know that the thing he sells is a security, or must he also know that he has no permit to sell the security he sells? As a matter of grammar the statute is ambiguous; it is not at all clear how far down the sentence the word 'knowingly' is intended to travel—whether it modifies 'sells,' or 'sells a security,' or 'sells a security without a permit.'" W. LaFave & A. Scott, Criminal Law § 27 (1972).

9. The Dissent repeatedly claims that our holding today creates a defense of "mistake of

law." Our holding today no more creates a "mistake of law" defense than does a statute making knowing receipt of stolen goods unlawful. In both cases, there is a legal element in the definition of the offense. In the case of a receipt of stolen goods statute, the legal element is that the goods were stolen; in this case, the legal element is that the "use, transfer, acquisition," etc. were in a manner not authorized by statute or regulations. It is not a defense to a charge of receipt of stolen goods that one did not know that such receipt was illegal, and it is not a defense to a charge of a § 2024(b) violation that one did not know that possessing food stamps in a manner unauthorized by statute or regulations was illegal. It *is*, however, a defense to a charge of knowing receipt of stolen goods that one did not know that the goods were stolen, just as it is a defense to a charge of a § 2024(b) violation that one did not know that one's possession was unauthorized. * * *

inflicted by intention is no provincial or transient notion. It is as universal and persistent in mature systems of law as belief in freedom of the human will and a consequent ability and duty of the normal individual to choose between good and evil." *Morissette v. United States,* 342 U.S. 246, 72 S.Ct. 240, 96 L.Ed. 288 (1952). Thus, in *United States v. United States Gypsum Co.,* 438 U.S. 422, 438, 98 S.Ct. 2864, 2874, 57 L.Ed.2d 854 (1978), we noted that "[c]ertainly far more than the simple omission of the appropriate phrase from the statutory definition is necessary to justify dispensing with an intent requirement" and that criminal offenses requiring no *mens rea* have a "generally disfavored status." Similarly, in this case, the failure of Congress explicitly and unambiguously to indicate whether *mens rea* is required does not signal a departure from this background assumption of our criminal law.

This construction is particularly appropriate where, as here, to interpret the statute otherwise would be to criminalize a broad range of apparently innocent conduct. For instance, § 2024(b) declares it criminal to use, transfer, acquire, alter, or possess food stamps in any manner not authorized by statute or regulations. The statute provides further that "[c]oupons issued to eligible households shall be used by them only to purchase food in retail food stores which have been approved for participation in the food stamp program *at prices prevailing in such stores.*" This seems to be the *only* authorized use. A strict reading of the statute with no knowledge of illegality requirement would thus render criminal a food stamp recipient who, for example, used stamps to purchase food from a store that, unknown to him,

charged higher than normal prices to food stamp program participants. Such a reading would also render criminal a nonrecipient of food stamps who "possessed" stamps because he was mistakenly sent them through the mail due to administrative error, "altered" them by tearing them up, and "transferred" them by throwing them away. Of course, Congress *could* have intended that this broad range of conduct be made illegal, perhaps with the understanding that prosecutors would exercise their discretion to avoid such harsh results. However, given the paucity of material suggesting that Congress did so intend, we are reluctant to adopt such a sweeping interpretation.

In addition, requiring *mens rea* is in keeping with our longstanding recognition of the principle that "ambiguity concerning the ambit of criminal statutes should be resolved in favor of lenity." * * *

The Government advances two additional arguments in support of its reading of the statute. First, the Government contends that this Court's decision last Term in *United States v. Yermian,* 468 U.S. 63, 104 S.Ct. 2936, 82 L.Ed.2d 53 (1984), supports its interpretation. *Yermian* involved a prosecution for violation of the federal false statement statute, 18 U.S.C. § 1001.[14] All parties agreed that the statute required proof at least that the defendant "knowingly and willfully" made a false statement. Thus, unlike the instant case, all parties in *Yermian* agreed that the Government had to prove the defendant's *mens rea.* The controversy in *Yermian* centered on whether the Government also had to prove that the defendant knew that the false statement was made in a matter within the jurisdiction of a federal agency.

---

14. The statute provides:

"Whoever, in any matter within the jurisdiction of any department or agency of the United States knowingly and willfully falsifies, conceals, or covers up by any trick, scheme, or device a material fact, or makes any false, fictitious or

fraudulent statements or representations, or makes or uses any false writing or document knowing the same to contain any false, fictitious or fraudulent statement or entry, shall be fined not more than $10,000 or imprisoned not more than five years, or both."

With respect to this element, although the Court held that the Government did not have to prove actual knowledge of federal agency jurisdiction, the Court explicitly reserved the question whether *some* culpability was necessary with respect even to the jurisdictional element. In contrast, the Government in the instant case argues that *no mens rea* is required with respect to any element of the crime. Finally, *Yermian* found that the statutory language was unambiguous and that the legislative history supported its interpretation. The statute at issue in this case differs in both respects.

Second, the Government contends that the § 2024(b) offense is a "public welfare" offense, which the Court defined in *United States v. Morissette* to "depend on no mental element but consist only of forbidden acts or omissions." Yet the offense at issue here differs substantially from those "public welfare offenses" we have previously recognized. In most previous instances, Congress has rendered criminal a type of conduct that a reasonable person should know is subject to stringent public regulation and may seriously threaten the community's health or safety. Thus, in *United States v. Freed,* 401 U.S. 601, 91 S.Ct. 1112, 28 L.Ed.2d 356 (1971), we examined the federal statute making it illegal to receive or possess an unregistered firearm. In holding that the Government did not have to prove that the recipient of unregistered hand grenades knew that they were unregistered, we noted that "one would hardly be surprised to learn that possession of hand grenades is not an innocent act." Similarly, in *United States v. Dotterweich,* 320 U.S. 277, 284, 64 S.Ct. 134, 138, 88 L.Ed. 48 (1943), the Court held that a corporate officer could violate the Food and Drug Act when his firm shipped adulterated and misbranded drugs, even "though consciousness of wrongdoing be totally wanting." The distinctions between these cases and the instant case are clear. A food stamp can

hardly be compared to a hand grenade, see *Freed,* nor can the unauthorized acquisition or possession of food stamps be compared to the selling of adulterated drugs, as in *Dotterweich.*

We hold that in a prosecution for violation of § 2024(b), the Government must prove that the defendant knew that his acquisition or possession of food stamps was in a manner unauthorized by statute or regulations. * * *

JUSTICE POWELL took no part in the consideration or decision of this case.

JUSTICE WHITE, with whom THE CHIEF JUSTICE joins, dissenting.

* * * Even accepting that "knowingly" does extend through the sentence, or at least that we should read § 2024(b) as if it does, the statute does not mean what the Court says it does. Rather, it requires only that the defendant be aware of the relevant aspects of his conduct. A requirement that the defendant know that he is acting in a particular manner, coupled with the fact that that manner is forbidden, does not establish a defense of ignorance of the law. It creates only a defense of ignorance or mistake of fact. Knowingly to do something that is unauthorized by law is not the same as doing something knowing that it is unauthorized by law.

This point is demonstrated by the hypothetical statute referred to by the majority, which punishes one who "knowingly sells a security without a permit." See *ante,* at n. 7. Even if "knowingly" does reach "without a permit," I would think that a defendant who knew that he did not have a permit, though not that a permit was required, could be convicted.

Section 2024(b) is an identical statute, except that instead of detailing the various legal requirements, it incorporates them by proscribing use of coupons "in any manner not authorized" by law. This shorthand approach to drafting does not transform knowledge of illegality into an element of the crime. As written, § 2024(b) is substantively no different than if it had been broken down into a collection of specific provisions making crimes of particular improper uses. For example, food stamps cannot be used to purchase tobacco. The statute might have said, *inter alia,* that anyone "who knowingly uses coupons to purchase cigarettes" commits a crime. Under no plausible reading could a defendant then be acquitted because he did not know cigarettes are not "eligible food." But in fact, that is exactly what § 2024(b) does say, it just does not write it out longhand.

The Court's opinion provides another illustration of the general point: someone who used food stamps to purchase groceries at inflated prices without realizing he was overcharged. I agree that such a person may not be convicted, but not for the reason given by the majority. The purchaser did not "knowingly" use the stamps in the proscribed manner, for he was unaware of the circumstances of the transaction that made it illegal.

The majority and I would part company in result as well as rationale if the purchaser knew he was charged higher than normal prices but not that overcharging is prohibited. In such a case, he would have been aware of the nature of his actions, and therefore the purchase would have been "knowing." I would hold that such a mental state satisfies the statute. Under the Court's holding, as I understand it, that person could not be convicted because he did not know that his conduct was illegal.

* * * The provision is much like statutes that forbid the receipt or sale of stolen goods. See, *e.g.,* 18 U.S.C. §§ 641, 2313.

Just as those statutes generally require knowledge that the goods were stolen, so § 2024(c) requires knowledge of the past impropriety. But receipt of stolen goods statutes do not require that the defendant know that receipt itself is illegal, and similarly § 2024(c) plainly does not require that the defendant know that it is illegal to present coupons that have been improperly used in the past. It is not inconceivable that someone presenting such coupons— again, like someone buying stolen goods— would think that his conduct was above board despite the preceding illegality. But that belief, however sincere, would not be a defense. In short, because § 2024(c) does not require that the defendant know that the conduct for which he is being prosecuted was illegal, it does not create an ignorance of the law defense.[5]

* * *

The broad principles of the Court's opinion are easy to live with in a case such as this. But the application of its reasoning might not always be so benign. For example, § 2024(b) is little different from the basic federal prohibition on the manufacture and distribution of controlled substances. 21 U.S.C. § 841(a) provides:

"Except as authorized by this subchapter, it shall be unlawful for any person knowingly or intentionally—

"(1) to manufacture, distribute, or dispense, or possess with intent to manufacture, distribute or dispense, a controlled substance. . . ."

I am sure that the members of the majority would agree that a defendant charged under this provision could not defend on the ground that he did not realize his manufacture was unauthorized

---

5. Similarly, it is a valid defense to a charge of theft that the defendant thought the property legally belonged to him, even if that belief is incorrect. But this is not because ignorance of the law is an excuse. Rather, "the legal element involved is simply an aspect of the attendant circumstances, with respect to which knowledge

* * * is required for culpability * * *. The law involved is not the law defining the offense; it is some other legal rule that characterizes the attendant circumstances that are material to the offense." American Law Institute, Model Penal Code § 2.02, Comment 11, p. 131 (Tent. Draft No. 4, 1955).

or that the particular substance was controlled. * * *

In relying on the "background assumption of our criminal law" that *mens rea* is required, the Court ignores the equally well-founded assumption that ignorance of the law is no excuse. It is "the conventional position that knowledge of the existence, meaning or application of the law determining the elements of an offense is not an element of that offense. . . ." Model Penal Code, at 130.

This Court's prior cases indicate that a statutory requirement of a "knowing violation" does not supersede this principle. For example, under the statute at issue in *United States v. International Minerals & Chemical Corp.,* 402 U.S. 558, 91 S.Ct. 1697, 29 L.Ed.2d 178 (1971), the Interstate Commerce Commission was authorized to promulgate regulations regarding the transportation of corrosive liquids, and it was a crime to "knowingly violat[e] any such regulation." 18 U.S.C. § 834(f) (1970 ed.). Viewing the word "regulations" as "a shorthand designation for specific acts or omissions which violate the Act," we adhered to the traditional rule that ignorance of the law is not a defense. The violation had to be "knowing" in that the defendant had to know that he was transporting corrosive liquids and not, for example, merely water. But there was no requirement that he be aware that he was violating a particular regulation. Similarly, in this case the phrase "in any manner not authorized by" the statute or regulations is a shorthand incorporation of a variety of legal requirements. To be con-

victed, a defendant must have been aware of what he was doing, but not that it was illegal.

In *Boyce Motor Lines, Inc. v. United States,* 342 U.S. 337, 72 S.Ct. 329, 96 L.Ed. 367 (1952), the Court considered a statute that punished anyone who "knowingly violates" a regulation requiring trucks transporting dangerous items to avoid congested areas where possible. In rejecting a vagueness challenge, the Court read "knowingly" to mean not that the driver had to be aware of the regulation, but that he had to know a safer alternative route was available. * * *

In each of these cases, the statutory language lent itself to the approach adopted today if anything more readily than does § 2024(b).[6] I would read § 2024(b) like those statutes, to require awareness of only the relevant aspects of one's conduct rendering it illegal, not the fact of illegality. This reading does not abandon the "background assumption" of *mens rea* by creating a strict liability offense, and is consistent with the equally important background assumption that ignorance of the law is not a defense. * * *

Notes and Questions

1. In *United States v. Baker,* 807 F.2d 427 (5th Cir.1986), the charge was violating 18 U.S.C.A. § 2320, which subjects to criminal penalties anyone who "intentionally traffics or attempts to traffic in goods or services and knowingly uses a counterfeit mark on or in connection with such goods and services." "Paul Baker was convicted under this new statute for deal-

---

6. The Court distinguishes these as "public welfare offense" cases involving inherently dangerous articles of commerce whose users should have assumed were subject to regulation. But see *United States v. Freed,* (BRENNAN, J., concurring in judgment). Apart from the fact that a reasonable person would also assume food stamps are heavily regulated and not subject to sale and exchange, this distinction is not related to the actual holdings in those cases. The Court's opin-

ion in *Boyce* and the concurrence in *Freed* do not discuss this consideration. And the Court's references to the dangerousness of the goods in *International Minerals* were directed to possible due process challenges to convictions without notice of criminality. As today's majority acknowledges, there is no constitutional defect with the holding of the court below. The only issue here is one of congressional intent.

ing in counterfeit watches. He does not dispute that he intentionally dealt in the watches. He also admits that he knew the 'Rolex' watches he sold were counterfeit. His contention is that the statute requires that he act with knowledge that his conduct is criminal. He asserts that he did not know trafficking in counterfeit goods is criminal and that he would not have done so had he known he was committing a crime. The district court denied a motion to dismiss on this ground and refused to instruct the jury that Baker could not be convicted if he did not have the purpose to 'disobey or disregard the law.'" What result on Baker's appeal, grounded in *Liparota*?

2. *Lambert v. California,* 355 U.S. 225, 78 S.Ct. 240, 2 L.Ed.2d 228 (1957), involved a Los Angeles ordinance which made it unlawful for any person with a prior felony conviction to be or remain in the city more than 5 days without registering. Ms. Lambert, arrested on suspicion of another offense, was charged with violating this ordinance; she was convicted, fined $250 and placed on 3 years probation. The Court, per Douglas, J., reversed:

"We must assume that appellant had no actual knowledge of the requirement that she register under this ordinance, as she offered proof of this defense which was refused. The question is whether a registration act of this character violates due process where it is applied to a person who has no actual knowledge of his duty to register, and where no showing is made of the probability of such knowledge.

"We do not go with Blackstone in saying that 'a vicious will' is necessary to constitute a crime, for conduct alone without regard to the intent of the doer is often sufficient. There is wide latitude in the lawmakers to declare an offense and to exclude elements of knowledge and diligence from its definition. But we deal

here with conduct that is wholly passive—mere failure to register. It is unlike the commission of acts, or the failure to act under circumstances that should alert the doer to the consequences of his deed. The rule that 'ignorance of the law will not excuse' is deep in our law, as is the principle that of all the powers of local government, the police power is 'one of the least limitable.' On the other hand, due process places some limits on its exercise. Engrained in our concept of due process is the requirement of notice. Notice is sometimes essential so that the citizen has the chance to defend charges. Notice is required before property interests are disturbed, before assessments are made, before penalties are assessed. Notice is required in a myriad of situations where a penalty or forfeiture might be suffered for mere failure to act. * * *

"Many [registration] laws are akin to licensing statutes in that they pertain to the regulation of business activities. But the present ordinance is entirely different. Violation of its provisions is unaccompanied by any activity whatever, mere presence in the city being the test. Moreover, circumstances which might move one to inquire as to the necessity of registration are completely lacking. At most the ordinance is but a law enforcement technique designed for the convenience of law enforcement agencies through which a list of the names and addresses of felons then residing in a given community is compiled. The disclosure is merely a compilation of former convictions already publicly recorded in the jurisdiction where obtained. Nevertheless, this appellant on first becoming aware of her duty to register was given no opportunity to comply with the law and avoid its penalty, even though her default was entirely innocent. She could but suffer the consequences of the ordinance, namely, conviction with the imposition of heavy criminal penalties thereunder. We believe that actual knowledge of the duty to register or proof of the probability of such knowledge and subsequent failure to comply are necessary before a conviction under the ordinance can stand. As Holmes wrote in *The Common Law,* 'A law which punished conduct which would not be blameworthy in the average member of the community would be too severe for that community to bear.' Its severity lies in the absence of an opportunity either to avoid the consequences of the law or to defend any prosecution brought under it. Where a person did not know of the duty to register and where there was no proof of the probability of such knowledge, he may not be convicted consistently with due process. Were it otherwise, the evil would be as great as it is when the law is written in print too fine to read or in a language foreign to the community."

Frankfurter, J., joined by Harlan and Whittaker, JJ., dissenting, objected that "what the Court here does is to draw a constitutional line between a State's requirement of doing and not doing. What is this but a return to Year Book distinctions between feasance and nonfeasance— a distinction that may have significance in the evolution of common-law notions of liability, but is inadmissible as a line between constitutionality and unconstitutionality." [a]

3. What, exactly, are the dimensions of the *Lambert* holding? Considering the fact that in *International Minerals,* discussed by the *Liparota* dissenters, the defendant was charged with the *failure* to set out certain matters on the shipping papers, why doesn't *Lambert* apply to that case? Indeed, may it not be concluded that the principle that ignorance of the law is no excuse simply is inapplicable to criminal omissions? Consider Hughes, *Criminal*

Omissions, 67 Yale L.J. 590, 600–01 (1958): "In an offense of commission, the mind of the actor is almost always to some extent addressed to the prohibited conduct, even though he may be unaware of the legal prohibition. In these offenses, *mens rea* can quite usefully be generalized as an intention to bring about the prohibited consequences or, at the least, recklessness with regard to such consequences. With omissions, the great difficulty is that the mind of the offender may not be addressed at all to the enjoined conduct, if he is unaware of the duty to act. One may not know that it is prohibited to place garbage cans on the sidewalk between 9:00 A.M. and 7:00 P.M., but one can hardly place such a can on the sidewalk without knowing that he is doing it. * * * This approach is clearly of no use with omissions, where the accused does not have to perform any act to incur liability. What of the offender who violates a regulation requiring garbage to be put out in suitable receptacles at certain times? If he was quite unaware of the existence of the rule, in what sense can he be said to have been addressing his mind at all to the conduct required of him by law? This is the difficulty which plagues the analysis of omissions in terms of the conventional concepts of *mens rea.*"

4. In *Lambert,* it is noted that the "rule that 'ignorance of the law will not excuse' is deep in our law." What is the basis for this? Consider:

(a) J. Hall, *General Principles of Criminal Law* 383 (2d ed. 1960): "To permit an individual to plead successfully that he had a different opinion or interpretation of the law would contradict the * * * postulates of a legal order. For there is a basic incompatibility between asserting that the law is what certain officials declare it to be

a. In *Texaco, Inc. v. Short,* 454 U.S. 516, 102 S.Ct. 781, 70 L.Ed.2d 738 (1982), the Court observed that *Lambert's* "application has been limited, lending some credence to Justice Frankfurt-

er's colorful prediction in dissent that the case would stand as 'an isolated deviation from the strong current of precedents—a derelict on the waters of the law.'"

after a prescribed analysis, and asserting, also, that those officials *must* declare it to be, i.e. that the law is, what defendants or their lawyers believed it to be. A legal order implies the rejection of such contradiction. It opposes objectivity to subjectivity, judicial process to individual opinion, official to lay, and authoritative to nonauthoritative declarations of what the law is."

(b) O. Holmes, *The Common Law* 47–48 (1948 ed.): "The true explanation of the rule is the same as that which accounts for the law's indifference to a man's particular temperament, faculties, and so forth. Public policy sacrifices the individual to the general good. It is desirable that the burden of all should be equal, but it is still more desirable to put an end to robbery and murder. It is no doubt true that there are many cases in which the criminal could not have known that he was breaking the law, but to admit the excuse at all would be to encourage ignorance where the lawmaker has determined to make men know and obey, and justice to the individual is rightly outweighed by the larger interests on the other side of the scales."

(c) *Gordon v. State,* 52 Ala. 308, 23 Am. Rep. 575 (1875): "On the presumption that every one capable of acting for himself knows the law, courts are compelled to proceed. If it should be abandoned, the administration of justice would be impossible, as every cause would be embarrassed with the collateral inquiry of the extent of legal knowledge of the parties seeking to enforce or avoid liability and responsibility."

(d) *State v. Boyett,* 32 N.C. 336 (1849): "[I]n criminal matters, the presumption [that everyone knows the law] most usually accords with the truth. As to such as are *mala in se,* every one has an innate sense of right and wrong, which enables him to know when he violates the law, and it is of no consequence, if he be not able to give the name, by which the offense is known in the law books, or to point out the nice distinctions between the different grades of offense. As to such as are *'mala prohibita,'* they depend upon statutes printed and published and put within the reach of every one; so that no one has a right to complain, if a presumption, necessary to the administration of the law, is applied to him. To allow ignorance as an excuse would be to offer a reward to the ignorant."

5. In *State v. Cude,* 14 Utah 2d 287, 383 P.2d 399 (1963), defendant left his car at a garage for repairs. The garage owner estimated the repairs would cost about $180, but he claimed the defendant told him to go ahead with the repairs irrespective of the cost. When he came for his car, he was presented with a bill for $345. Unable to pay, defendant was refused possession of the car. Later, after the garage had closed for the night, defendant returned and drove the car away. He was thereafter charged with grand larceny. (Under Utah law, an owner of personalty in the possession of another by virtue of some special right or title, such as a mechanic's lien, is guilty of larceny if he takes the property from the person in possession with the intention of depriving such person of his rights.) On appeal of defendant's conviction, the court held the trial judge erred in refusing defendant's requested instruction that he could not be found guilty if, at the time of the taking, he honestly believed he had a legal right to the possession of the automobile. "It is fundamental that an essential element of larceny is the intent to steal the property of another. Consequently, if there is any reasonable basis in the evidence upon which the jury could believe that the accused thought he had a right to take possession of his automobile, or if the evidence in that regard is such that it might raise a reasonable doubt that he had the

intent to steal, then that issue should be presented to the jury."

Did the court err in failing to take account of the rule that ignorance of the law is no excuse?

6. In *Morgan v. District of Columbia,* 476 A.2d 1128 (D.C.App.1984), the defendants, who had engaged in an unlawful assembly outside the hotel where the Air Force Association was holding a convention, asked the trial judge to permit them to introduce evidence showing that they believed the convention activities contravened the Charter of the International Military Tribunal, 59 Stat. 1544, which provides that "planning, preparation, initiation or waging a war of aggression" is unlawful, and that accordingly they were privileged or required under international and local law to violate the unlawful assembly statute to prevent the greater wrong. They rely upon *Gaestano v. United States,* 406 A.2d 1291 (D.C.App.1979), holding that in an unlawful assembly prosecution the defendant may not be convicted if he acted on "a reasonable belief in an individual's right to remain on property not owned or possessed by that individual," including a mistake of law by which one "could reasonably believe that he had title or a possessory interest in the land" entered. What should the judge rule?

NOTES AND QUESTIONS ON MISTAKE OF LAW AND REASONABLE RELIANCE

Even assuming the validity of the general rule that ignorance of the law is no excuse, should an exception be recognized where the defendant shows that he relied upon what, as it turns out, was an erroneous statement or interpretation of the law? A number of the modern codes speak to this issue, often with a provision similar to *Model Penal Code* § 2.04(3). Consider in

which of the following situations the law ought to recognize the mistake of law as a defense.

1. A state statute prohibiting the sale of intoxicants was held unconstitutional by the state supreme court on the ground it was in violation of the interstate commerce clause of the federal Constitution. O'Neil, relying upon that decision, proceeded to make sales in that state for a certain brewery. Thereafter, the state supreme court overruled its prior decision, relying upon a United States Supreme Court case decided before O'Neil's conduct and upholding a similar statute of another state.[a]

2. The municipal court held that a certain type of gum vending machine was not a gambling device. Armed with certified copies of that decree, the distributors of these machines presented themselves to Striggles, the operator of a restaurant, and induced him to allow them to install one of the machines in his place of business. Thereafter, Striggles was charged with having a gambling device in his restaurant. It now appears that the municipal court decision was in error.[b]

3. Irwin received a letter from his draft board ordering him to report for induction on a certain date. Thereafter, he was arrested for disorderly conduct and was arraigned in municipal court. The magistrate explained that Irwin would be released on bail and that a notice would be mailed informing him of the date of his court appearance. Irwin told the magistrate that he had received his draft notice, and the magistrate responded, "You have to take care of this first." Irwin inquired, "Well, suppose this doesn't come up before I am scheduled for induction, that is December 8." The magistrate again responded that Irwin would have to take care of the charge first. Irwin, who had

a. *State v. O'Neil,* 147 Iowa 513, 126 N.W. 454 (1910), reversing defendant's conviction.

b. *State v. Striggles,* 202 Iowa 1318, 210 N.W. 137 (1926), affirming defendant's conviction.

not yet received notice to appear in court, did not report for induction on December 8th. He was charged with knowingly failing to report for induction.[c]

4. Goodenow married a woman before a justice of the peace who erroneously advised the couple that they were entitled to marry in light of the fact that the woman's prior spouse, whom she had not divorced, had remarried. He was thereafter charged with adultery.[d]

5. DeMeo, who was married to Ann in New Jersey, obtain a Mexican mail order divorce from her. Thereafter, he married Josephine in New Jersey. In his application for a license to marry Josephine, DeMeo set out in full that he had been divorced by a Mexican divorce decree and gave the date it was granted and the court which granted it. The license was granted without question. In fact, the Mexican divorce has no validity in New Jersey, and this has resulted in DeMeo being charged with bigamy.[e]

6. Davis, a member of the county board, was a member of the board's airport committee and thereby became involved in problems encountered in the development of the airport. One of these was the forced resignation of the airport manager for inadequate performance. Davis, on behalf of the committee, acted as temporary manager while a replacement was sought. Being unable to find a qualified replacement, the airport committee, with the advice and approval of the county corporation counsel, asked Davis to accept the position of permanent airport manager. He accepted. Thereafter, a longtime political adversary swore out a complaint charging Davis with violating a statute prohibiting a public official from having a personal interest in a public contract. By law, the duties of the county corporation counsel "shall be limited to civil matters and may include giving legal opinions to the board and its committees and interpreting the powers and duties of the board and county officers." [f]

7. Rev. Hopkins wished to erect some advertising signs. He consulted the state's attorney, who told him that the proposed signs would not violate the law. Hopkins then put up a sign at the entrance to his home and another along side the highway. About 3 years later, he was charged with violating a statute making it unlawful to erect or maintain any sign intended to aid in the solicitation or performance of marriages.[g]

8. Insco, unsuccessful Republican candidate for Congress in 1972 against Democratic candidate Gunter, had printed and distributed 2,500 bumper stickers containing only the words "McGovern–Gunter." Insco was charged with violating a federal statute making it a crime to distribute "any card, pamphlet, circular, poster, dodger, advertisement, writing, or other statement" concerning a candidate in a federal election without indicating thereon the name of the person or organization responsible therefor. He understandably did not think his conduct was criminal, as the universal practice of federal candidates has been *not* to affix attribution clauses to bumper stickers, and there has never been a prosecution with respect to this universal practice. The legislative history of the statute indicates that this practice is consistent with the Congressional intent, which was not to cover the usual sticker which conveys only candidate identification. But the stickers distributed by Insco, by linking

c. *United States v. Irwin,* 546 F.2d 1048 (3d Cir.1976), affirming defendant's conviction.

d. *State v. Goodenow,* 65 Me. 30 (1876), affirming defendant's conviction.

e. *State v. DeMeo,* 20 N.J. 1, 118 A.2d 1 (1955), affirming defendant's conviction.

f. *State v. Davis,* 63 Wis.2d 75, 216 N.W.2d 31 (1974), reversing defendant's conviction.

g. *Hopkins v. State,* 193 Md. 489, 69 A.2d 456 (1950), affirming defendant's conviction.

Gunter and McGovern, are "political statements" and thus fall within the statute.[h]

9. Barker and others have been charged with burglary for breaking into the headquarters of the Democratic Party's National Committee in the Watergate office complex. The defendants, all Cuban refugees, were led to believe by Howard Hunt (their senior officer in the abortive CIA-sponsored invasion of the Bay of Pigs), who then had his office in the White House, that they were to work for a secretly sponsored government intelligence agency seeking to photograph documents containing financial information indicating Cuban communist money was going into the Democratic campaign.[i]

10. Powers, president of a magazine distributing company, has been charged with possession of obscene literature with intent to distribute same. The publications in question were imported into the country. Though the customs authorities are authorized by statute to bar entry into the country of obscene materials, these particular publications were allowed to enter. Powers, knowing of this, claims he thus concluded these publications did not meet the legal definition of obscenity.[j]

11. Long moved from Delaware to Arkansas and obtained a divorce from his wife; thereafter he moved back to Delaware and later remarried. Prior to the second marriage, Long consulted a Delaware attorney with respect to whether he was free to remarry. The attorney erroneously advised him that the Arkansas divorce was valid and that he was free to remarry. Long has now been charged with bigamy.[k]

12. Snyder was charged with violating a state statute subjecting to criminal penalties "any person who has been convicted of a felony * * * who owns * * * any pistol, revolver, or other firearm." Snyder, who in fact had a prior felony conviction for sale of marijuana, had entered a guilty plea in that earlier case as a result of a plea bargain which ensured she would receive no jail or prison time. Her attorney told her she was pleading guilty to a misdemeanor, and Snyder thereafter conducted herself accordingly (e.g., believing she was not a felon, she registered to vote and voted).[l]

h. *United States v. Insco,* 496 F.2d 204 (5th Cir.1974), reversing defendant's conviction.

i. *United States v. Barker,* 514 F.2d 208 (D.C. Cir.1975). A majority of the court, en banc, held that the district judge properly refused to allow the defendants to withdraw their pleas of guilty, and thus did not have to reach the merits of the claimed mistake of law defense. Bazelon, J., concurring, and MacKinnon and Wilkey, JJ., dissenting, all indicated they would recognize the defense on these facts.

See also *United States v. Barker,* 546 F.2d 940 (D.C.Cir.1976), reversing defendants' convictions of conspiracy to violate the civil rights of Dr. Fielding, whose office they burglarized in an effort to find records on his patient, Daniel Ellsberg. The court concluded that the district court erred in rejecting the possibility of a limited mistake of law defense where the defendants claimed they reasonably believed that Hunt, their White House superior, had authority to order such an operation. Compare *United States v. Ehrlichman,* 546 F.2d 910 (D.C.Cir.1976), holding it was no defense that a former presidential assistant mistakenly believed the break-in into Fielding's office was legal.

j. *Regina v. Prairie Schooner News Ltd. and Powers,* 75 W.W.R. 585 (Manitoba C.A.1970), dismissing defendant's appeal.

k. *Long v. State,* 44 Del. 262, 65 A.2d 489 (1949), reversing defendant's conviction.

l. *People v. Snyder,* 32 Cal.3d 590, 186 Cal. Rptr. 485, 652 P.2d 42 (1982), affirming exclusion of evidence of such mistaken belief.

Chapter 4

THE ACT REQUIREMENT

SECTION 1. VOLUNTARY ACT

STATE v. CADDELL

Supreme Court of North Carolina, 1975.
287 N.C. 266, 215 S.E.2d 348.

LAKE, JUSTICE. [Defendant, charged with kidnapping, pleaded not guilty and not guilty by reason of insanity. At trial, the victim, a 14–year–old girl, testified that he forced her into his car, drove to a wooded area, beat her and attempted to have sexual intercourse with her, and then ran away. The defendant testified that he remembered nothing about the events of that day and that his lack of recall began as of the time he drove his car over an embankment the day before the alleged kidnapping. A psychiatrist testified he had diagnosed the defendant's condition as "sociopathic personality and anti-social reaction" and that characteristics of that condition are "meanness toward other human beings," "an inability to get along with people," "an inability to abide by the rules of society," and, in defendant's case, "extreme aggressiveness toward other human beings." The defendant was convicted and sentenced to life imprisonment.]

We come now to the defendant's contention that the trial court erred in its instruction with reference to the burden of proof in connection with the defense of unconsciousness. That instruction was:

"Now, members of the jury, a person cannot be held criminally responsible for acts committed while he is unconscious. Unconsciousness is never an affirmative defense. Where a person commits an act without being conscious thereof, such act is not criminal even though if committed by a person who was conscious it would be a crime. The defendant has no burden to prove that he was unconscious. If you find that the defendant was completely unconscious of what transpired when Catherine Sutton was taken violently from her driveway at her residence * * * then he would not be guilty, and it would be your duty to so find."

The defendant contends that the instruction that the defendant does not have the burden of proof on this issue and the instruction that the jury would find him not guilty, if it found he was "completely unconscious of what transpired" at the time of the alleged offense, are inconsistent and the court should have charged the jury to find the defendant not guilty unless they found beyond a reasonable doubt that he was conscious of what allegedly transpired.

This assignment of error has merit if, but only if, under the law of this State, a criminal defendant relying upon the defense of unconsciousness, also called automatism, does not have the burden of proof thereof. If the burden of proof is upon the defendant on this issue, the error in the charge was favorable to the defendant and does not entitle him to a new trial.

The defense of unconsciousness, or automatism, while not an entirely new development in the criminal law, has been discussed in relatively few decisions by American appellate courts, most of these being in California where the defense is expressly provided by statute. In *Bratty v. Attorney General for Northern Ireland,* All E.R. 3 (1961) 523, Lord Denning observed: "Until recently there was hardly any reference in the English books to this so-called defense of automatism. There was a passing reference to it in 1951 in *R. v. Harrison–Owen* [1951] 2 All E.R. 726." The only express reference to it which we have found in our Reports is in *State v. Mercer,* 275 N.C. 108, 165 S.E.2d 328, which we discuss below.

Unconsciousness, as a defense to a criminal charge, is discussed briefly in most of the textbooks and treatises on criminal law, the most extensive treatment of it, which has come to our attention, being in LaFave and Scott, *Criminal Law,* § 44 (1972), where it is said, "[a] defense related to but different from the defense of insanity is that of unconsciousness, often referred to as automatism: one who engages in what would otherwise be criminal conduct is not guilty of a crime if he does so in a state of unconsciousness or semi-consciousness." In *State v. Mercer,* this Court said: "Upon the present record, defendant was entitled to an instruction to the effect the jury should return verdicts of not guilty if in fact defendant was *completely* unconscious of what transpired when [the victims] were shot."

The defenses of insanity and unconsciousness are not the same in nature, for unconsciousness at the time of the alleged criminal act need not be the result of a disease or defect of the mind. As a consequence, the two defenses are not the same in effect, for a defendant found not guilty by reason of unconsciousness, as distinct from insanity, is not subject to commitment to a hospital for the mentally ill.

* * *

Sources of unconsciousness, recognized as a defense by courts and textwriters, include somnambulism, somnolenture, hypnotism, cerebral concussion, delirium from fever or drugs, diabetic shock, epileptic black-outs, and drunkenness. Unconsciousness due to voluntary drunkenness was held no defense in *Lewis v. State,* 196 Ga. 755, 27 S.E.2d 659.

It is generally said that amnesia, in and of itself, is not a defense to a criminal charge. *Thomas v. State,* 201 Tenn. 645, 301 S.W.2d 358. In *Thomas* the Supreme Court of Tennessee quoted Gray, *Attorneys' Textbook of Medicine,* § 96.01 (3rd ed. 1949), as follows:

"Amnesia, loss of memory, may lead to crimes entirely unknown to the culprit at a later date. That is rare. More frequently, the accused, remembering full well what he has done, alleges amnesia in false defense. He is a malingerer. To prove his innocence or guilt may be most difficult. * * * Failure to remember later, when accused, is in itself no proof of the mental condition when crime was performed."

The principal point of difference among the few reported decisions on the defense of unconsciousness is with reference to the burden of proof. In *People v. Hardy,* supra, the California Supreme Court said:

"In *People v. Nihell,* 144 Cal. 200, 77 P. 916, where defendant claimed he was unconscious by reason of epilepsy, it was held that the burden was on him to establish the peculiar mental condition upon which he relied, and the Court stated * * * 'Men are presumed to be conscious when they act as if they were conscious, and if they would have the jury know that things are not what they seem, they must impart that knowledge by affirmative proof.' This is merely another way of saying that defendant has the duty of going forward with the evidence, and it is entirely consistent with the rule that defendant has only the burden of producing evidence which would raise a reasonable doubt in the minds of the jury."

In *Bratty v. Attorney General for Northern Ireland,* supra, the accused killed a girl, a passenger in his car, by strangling her with her own stocking. He testified that a "blackness" came over him and that "I didn't know what I was doing; I didn't realize anything," and that he had previously had "feelings of blackness and headaches." There was medical testimony that he *might have been* suffering from an attack of psychomotor epilepsy, a disease of the mind which could cause ignorance of the nature and quality of acts done. There was no medical evidence of any other pathological cause for a state of automatism. The trial judge refused to submit the defense of automatism to the jury but did submit the defense of insanity, which the jury rejected. The House of Lords held: "The trial judge was justified in not putting the defense of automatism to the jury since the evidence attributed any involuntariness in the appellant's act solely to a disease of the mind and there was no sufficient evidence of automatism, apart from insanity, to be left to the jury." The Lord Chancellor (Viscount Kilmuir) said:

"It is necessary that a proper foundation be laid before a judge can leave 'automatism' to the jury. That foundation, in my view, is not forthcoming merely from unaccepted evidence of a defect of reason from disease of the mind.

* * *

"[In *Hill v. Baxter* [1958] 1 All E.R. 193 [1958] 1 Q.B. 277] Lord Goddard expressed the view that the onus of proving the defendant was in a state of automatism was on him because automatism is akin to insanity and further is a fact exclusively within his own knowledge. The other members of the court reserved this point.

* * *

"If one subtracts the medical evidence directed to the establishment of psychomotor epilepsy, I am of the opinion that there was not any evidence on which a jury could properly have considered the existence of automatism. Counsel for the appellant directed our attention to the appellant's statement, to his evidence and to his previous conduct. In my view they do not provide evidence fit to be left to a jury on that question. They could not form the basis of reasonable doubt.

* * *

"[N]ormally the presumption of mental capacity is sufficient to prove that he acted consciously and voluntarily and the prosecution need go no further. But, if, after considering evidence properly left to them by the judge, the jury are left in real doubt whether or not the accused acted in a state of automatism, it seems to me that on principle they should acquit because the necessary mens rea—if indeed the actus reus—has not been proved beyond a reasonable doubt."

Lord Denning was of the opinion that while the ultimate burden rests on the prosecution to prove every element essential in the crime, it was entitled to rely on the presumption that every man has sufficient mental capacity to be responsible for his crimes. He said:

"[I]f the defence wish to displace that presumption they must give some evidence from which the contrary may reasonably be inferred. * * * The necessity of laying this proper foundation is on the defence: and if it is not so laid, the defence of automatism need not be left to the jury * * *. The evidence of the man himself will rarely be sufficient unless it is supported by medical evidence which points to the cause of the mental incapacity. It is not sufficient for a man to say 'I had a black-out:' for 'black-out' as Stable, J., said in *Cooper v. McKenna* [1960] Qd.R. at p. 419, 'is one of the first refuges of a guilty conscience and a popular excuse.' The words of Devlin, J., in *Hill v. Baxter* [1958], 1 All E.R. at p. 197 [1958], 1 Q.B. at p. 285, should be remembered:

> " 'I do not doubt that there are genuine cases of automatism and the like, but I do not see how the layman can safely attempt without the help of some medical or scientific evidence to distinguish the genuine from the fraudulent.' "

Although unconsciousness, or automatism, is a defense separate and apart from insanity, in that it may not be the result of a disease or defect of the mind, it does not necessarily follow that the two defenses are different in law with respect to the burden of proof. Somnambulism and epilepsy, two sources of the defense of unconsciousness, have been said to be like unto insanity.

In *State v. Davis,* 214 N.C. 787, 1 S.E.2d 104, Justice Barnhill, later Chief Justice, speaking for this Court, said:

> "[It has long been settled in this State that although the burden of establishing the *corpus delicti* is upon the state, when defendant relies upon some, independent, distinct, substantive matter of exemption, immunity or defense, beyond the essentials of the legal definition of the offense itself, the *onus* of proof as to such matter is upon the defendant."

> * * *

An affirmative defense is one in which the defendant says, "I did the act charged in the indictment, but I should not be found guilty of the crime charged because * * *." In *Bratty v. Attorney General for Northern Ireland,* supra, the House of Lords, and in *People v. Hardy,* supra, the California Court, were of the opinion that, once the defendant has introduced substantial evidence of unconsciousness, or automatism, the ultimate burden of proving consciousness, beyond a reasonable doubt, rests upon the prosecution, because an element of crime is the presence of *mens rea* at the time the act was done. The defense of insanity is said to be distinguishable because the law presumes sanity. We are unable to perceive a reasonable basis for distinction, in this respect, between *insanity* and *intoxication* on the one hand and *unconsciousness* from a different cause, on the other. In all three defenses the contention is the same—the defendant did the act, but should not be convicted because the requisite mental element was not present. The same presumption, which casts upon the defendant, claiming insanity, the burden of proving it to the satisfaction of the jury, and thus to negative the presence of *mens rea,* applies also to the defendant who asserts a temporary mental lapse due to concussion, somnolentia, epilepsy or the like.

In *State v. Mercer,* supra, the defendant, according to the State's evidence, went to the home of his estranged wife, armed with a pistol. When she refused to admit him, upon his knocking at the locked door, he kicked the door open, entered and immediately shot and killed his wife, her woman companion and the infant son of the other woman. His testimony was that he became "blank in his mind" when his wife ordered him off the porch and "when he became conscious, he was standing on the porch and the pistol, which was beside his head clicked." There was no medical, or other, evidence establishing any pathological explanation of the alleged "black-out." This Court, saying there was no evidence of insanity, held, as one of several grounds for a new trial, that the trial court's charge to the jury was deficient in that it limited the jury's consideration of the alleged unconsciousness to its bearing upon the matter of premeditation and deliberation. We said, "Unconsciousness is never an affirmative defense."

Upon further reflection, we are convinced that we erred in *State v. Mercer,* supra, in saying, "Unconsciousness is never an affirmative defense." In that respect, *State v. Mercer,* supra, is hereby overruled.

Our research has disclosed no decision, other than *State v. Mercer,* supra, in which any court has held that the defendant's uncorroborated and unexplained testimony that, at the moment of his otherwise criminal act, he "blacked-out," and so does not remember what, if anything, he did, is sufficient to carry to the jury the question of unconsciousness as a defense. * * *

We now hold that, under the law of this State, unconsciousness, or automatism, is a complete defense to a criminal charge, separate and apart from the defense of insanity; that it is an affirmative defense; and that the burden rests upon the defendant to establish this defense, unless it arises out of the State's own evidence, to the satisfaction of the jury.

In the present case, the learned trial judge fell into error, in his instruction as to the burden of proof on the question of unconsciousness, by reason of our own error in *State v. Mercer,* supra, but his error therein was in the defendant's favor and could not have prejudiced him in any way. It does not, therefore, afford a basis for granting him a new trial. * * *

SHARP, CHIEF JUSTICE (concurring in result and dissenting in part). * * *

[I]t seems to me utterly impossible that any juror could have construed this charge to place the burden of proof on defendant to establish his plea of unconsciousness.

As heretofore noted, at the beginning of the charge the jury were told the defendant had *no* burden to prove his innocence; that the burden was on the State to prove his guilt beyond a reasonable doubt. Later, in words too plain to be misunderstood, the judge charged that a person cannot be held criminally responsible for acts committed while he is unconscious even though such acts would be criminal if committed by a conscious person, and that *unconsciousness is never an affirmative defense.* He then said, *"The defendant has no burden to prove that he was unconscious.* If you find that the defendant was completely unconscious of what transpired when Catherine Sutton was taken violently from her driveway * * * put in an automobile [etc.] * * * he would not be guilty and it would be your duty to so find." (Emphasis added.) * * *

I can perceive no conflict between the judge's charge in this case and our decision in *Mercer.* On the contrary, the judge meticulously followed the law as laid down in that case. Hence, upon the present record, there is no need to consider whether the *Mercer* holding that unconsciousness is never an affirmative defense should be reaffirmed or overruled. Notwithstanding, the majority purport to overrule it upon the grounds stated in that opinion. Since I consider those grounds unsound, I am constrained to express my contrary view.

In writing the well documented opinion in *Mercer,* Chief Justice Bobbitt pointed out that if a person is actually unconscious when he does an act which would otherwise be criminal, the absence of consciousness not only excludes the existence of any specific mental state, but also excludes the *possibility of a voluntary act* without which there can be no criminal liability. Unconsciousness, therefore, can never be an affirmative defense, which imposes the burden of proof upon the defendant, because the State has the burden of proving the essential elements of the offense charged, and "a voluntary act is an absolute requirement for criminal liability." Although the defense of unconsciousness "is sometimes explained on the ground that such a person could not have the requisite mental state for commission of the crime, the better rationale is that the individual has not engaged in a voluntary act." * * *

Whether the offense charged be a specific-intent or a general-intent crime, in order to convict the accused the State must prove that he voluntarily did the forbidden act. Here I note that in *In Re Winship,* 397 U.S. 358, 90 S.Ct. 1069, 25 L.Ed.2d 368 (1970), in an opinion expressing the views of five members of the Court, Mr. Justice Brennan said: "Lest, there remain any doubt about the constitutional stature of the reasonable-doubt standard, we explicitly hold that the Due Process Clause protects the accused against conviction except upon proof beyond a reasonable doubt of every fact necessary to constitute the crime with which he is charged."

The plea of unconsciousness is analogous to a plea of accident or of alibi, neither of which is an affirmative defense. Each plea merely negates an essential element of the crime charged. The plea of accidental homicide imposes no burden upon the defendant because the State cannot convict unless it first proves that the killing was culpable. "The claim that the killing was accidental goes to the very gist of the charge, and denies all criminal intent, and throws on the prosecution the burden of proving such intent beyond a reasonable doubt." When proof of defendant's presence at the scene of the crime charged is essential to his guilt, his plea that he was elsewhere and therefore could not have committed the crime is merely a denial of guilt, not an affirmative defense. To convict, the State must prove beyond a

reasonable doubt that he was present at the scene and participating. "Such proof, of course, would demolish an alibi." Similarly, proof of a voluntary act negates unconsciousness; voluntary action and unconsciousness cannot coexist.

When the State's evidence tends to show that, at the time in question, a defendant was "up and about," acting as if he had full possession of his faculties and knew what he was doing, it makes out a prima facie case of consciousness, and nothing else appearing, the law will assume he was conscious. Thus no issue of unconsciousness or automatism arises until some evidence of it is adduced. If the defendant offers such evidence, or if it is elicited from the State's own witnesses, the jurors must determine whether they are satisfied beyond a reasonable doubt that defendant voluntarily committed the act. From the beginning of the case and throughout the trial the burden remains upon the State to establish defendant's guilt beyond a reasonable doubt. This rule is supported by both reason and authority.

In *Government of the Virgin Islands v. Smith,* 278 F.2d 169 (3rd Cir.1960), defendant, who was charged with involuntary manslaughter by automobile, defended on the ground that he was suddenly stricken by an epileptic seizure and was unconscious at the time of the accident which resulted in a death. In its findings, the trial court said that the question was whether defendant's evidence convinces the court that he had a seizure which rendered him unconscious. In awarding a new trial, the Court of Appeals said: "This was an erroneous statement of the law for the defendant did not have the burden of convincing the court he had an epileptic seizure. On the contrary, his burden was merely to go forward with the evidence to the extent necessary to raise a doubt * * * as to the defendant's consciousness * * *." In arriving at this conclusion the Third Circuit Court of Appeals relied heavily upon the reasoning of the Supreme Court of California in *People v. Hardy,* 33 Cal.2d 52, 198 P.2d 865 (1948), which is briefed below.

In *Hardy,* the defendant, whose defense was unconsciousness, was convicted of first degree murder. On appeal she assigned as error the trial court's charge that when the evidence shows a defendant acted as if he was conscious the law presumes he was then conscious, and that presumption remains until overcome by a preponderance of evidence to the contrary. In ordering a new trial the court said that this instruction deprived the defendant of the benefit of the "cardinal rule in criminal cases that the burden rests on the prosecution to prove the offense beyond a reasonable doubt."

"The mere fact that there is a presumption which tends to support the prosecution's case does not change the amount or quantum of proof which the defendant must produce. * * * The prosecution is required to prove the offense beyond a reasonable doubt and, in so doing, may rely on any applicable presumptions. The defendant, on the other hand, is not required to prove his innocence by a preponderance of the evidence, but only to produce sufficient evidence to raise a reasonable doubt in the minds of the jury. * * * 'Men are presumed to be conscious when they act as if they were conscious, and if they would have the jury know that things are not what they seem, they must impart that knowledge by affirmative proof.' This is merely another way of saying that defendant has the duty of going forward with the evidence, and it is entirely consistent with the rule that defendant has only the burden of producing evidence which would raise a reasonable doubt in the minds of the jury."

In *Bratty v. A.–G. for N. Ireland,* 3 All E.R. 523 (1961), a case from which the majority opinion quotes extensively but

which does not support its conclusion, the Lord Chancellor and each of the four Lords who considered the case with him, expressed views in accord with those of *Hardy.*

The Lord Chancellor (Viscount Kilmuir), while noting that "a defence of automatism is very near a defence of insanity," said, "Nevertheless, one must not lose sight of the overriding principle, laid down by this House in *Woolmington's* case, that it is for the prosecution to prove every element of the offence charged. One of these elements is the accused's state of mind; normally the presumption of mental capacity is sufficient to prove that he acted consciously and voluntarily and the prosecution need go no further. But, if, after considering evidence properly left to them by the judge, the jury are left in real doubt whether or not the accused acted in a state of automatism, it seems to me that on principle they should acquit because the necessary mens rea—if indeed the actus reus—has not been proved beyond reasonable doubt. * * * "

"My conclusion is, therefore, that once the defence have surmounted the initial hurdle to which I have referred and have satisfied the judge that there is evidence fit for the jury's consideration, the proper direction is that, if that evidence leaves them in a real state of doubt, the jury should acquit."

Lord Morris agreed that if, during the trial, defendant advanced the defense of unconsciousness in explanation of the act, "and if such explanation was so supported that it had sufficient substance to merit consideration by the jury, then the onus which is on the prosecution would not be discharged unless the jury, having considered the explanation, were sure that guilt in regard to the particular crime charged was established so that they were left in no reasonable doubt."

Lords Tucker and Hodson each agreed with the views of both the Lord Chancellor and Lord Morris.

Lord Denning began his remarks by saying, " 'When dealing with a murder case the Crown must prove (a) death as the result of a voluntary act of the accused and (b) malice of the accused.' The requirement that it should be a voluntary act is essential, not only in a murder case, but also in every criminal case. No act is punishable if it is done involuntarily. * * * " He then noted that (1) an act is not involuntary "simply because the doer does not remember it * * * (or) could not control his impulse to do it" or "because it is unintentional or its consequences are unforeseen"; (2) automatism which results from drunkenness cannot lead "to a complete acquittal"; (3) "if the involuntary act proceeds from a disease of the mind, it gives rise to a defence of insanity, but not to a defence of automatism." These exceptions noted, Lord Denning perceived that "the category of involuntary acts is very limited."

While Lord Denning did not doubt that there were "genuine cases of automatism and the like" he observed that "black-out" was a popular excuse and "one of the first refuges of a guilty conscience," and he doubted that without the help of scientific evidence the layman-juror could distinguish the genuine from the fraudulent. In his opinion the evidence of the defendant himself would *rarely* be a sufficient foundation for the defense unless supported by medical evidence which pointed to the cause of the unconsciousness. He was convinced, however, that "[o]nce a proper foundation is thus laid for automatism, the matter becomes at large and must be left to the jury. As the case proceeds, the evidence may weigh first to one side and then to the other; and so the burden may appear to shift to and fro. *But at the end of the day the legal burden* comes into play and requires that the jury should be satisfied beyond reasonable doubt that the act was a voluntary act." (Emphasis added.)

The *decision* in *Bratty* was that the trial judge had not erred when he refused to submit to the jury defendant's defense of unconsciousness. In my view this was clearly correct, for the evidence was that the defendant remembered and gave the police a detailed account of the manner in which he had murdered his victim, and his only explanation for his conduct was that "something terrible" came over him and that he "didn't mean to do what really happened." Obviously such testimony constituted neither a "proper foundation" nor "evidence fit to be left to the jury on the question."

In discussing the relationship between the defenses of automatism and insanity, the "Law Lords" noted that the defendant acquitted by reason of insanity could be detained in a hospital where he was not a continuing danger to the public, whereas one acquitted on the ground of unconsciousness was unconditionally released. LaFave and Scott have noted the judicial tendency to characterize instances in which the condition of unconsciousness is likely to recur as insanity rather than automatism so that the defendant may be committed.

It is quite obvious that judges everywhere distrust the plea of unconsciousness and apprehend that jurors may repose hasty confidence in it. I think, however, there is no need for such concern, since jurors are sensible people too. For example, the jurors who tried this case were no more impressed with defendant's plea of automatism than is this Court. In my view we can safely assume that ordinarily a defendant's unsupported plea of blackout will aid the prosecution rather than the defense. But however that may be, were we to deny a defendant the defense of unconsciousness unless his testimony tending to establish unconsciousness be corroborated by medical testimony, we would violate fundamental and long-established principles of our criminal jurisprudence—that defendant has no burden to prove his innocence and that he is entitled to testify in his own behalf. * * *

It is quite possible that to require corroboration of a defendant's testimony that he was unconscious at the time the act with which he is charged was committed would, in effect, deprive an accused, who was actually unconscious at the time in question, of that plea. Presumably such a person would have no recollection of the acts with which he is charged. In such a case if his automatism resulted from a concussion of the brain caused by an injury or attack which he does not remember, he might well be in no position to provide the testimony upon which to base a hypothetical question an expert medical witness might answer in his favor. Unconsciousness resulting from unknown causes, or as the first manifestation or symptom of a previously undiagnosed condition or disease, might create similar problems.

In support of its thesis that the defense of automatism should be equated with the affirmative defense of insanity, the majority opinion says, "An affirmative defense is one in which the defendant says, 'I did the act charged in the indictment, but I should not be found guilty of the crime charged because * * *.'" A plea of unconsciousness, however, is not routinely one of confession and avoidance. Assuming a genuine case of unconsciousness—and the majority opinion concedes the possibility—the defendant who had been unconscious could not always know for certain whether he committed the act charged, and it therefore seems most unlikely he would admit having done so. Of course, until the jury is satisfied beyond a reasonable doubt that the defendant indeed committed the act charged, his mental condition at the time is irrelevant. In this case the defendant did not admit he kidnapped Catherine. On

the contrary he denied having done so. * * *

The opinions in both *Mercer* and *Bratty* point out the fundamental difference in the pleas of insanity and automatism. A plea of insanity raises this question: Was the defendant, at the time he committed the offense charged, so incapacitated from *a disease of the mind* that he was incapable of knowing the nature and quality of his act, or if he did know, was he incapable of distinguishing between right and wrong with relation thereto? No such question arises upon a plea of unconsciousness. One who is completely unconscious *cannot* know the nature and quality of his act or judge whether it is right or wrong. He is incapable of any voluntary action. Automatism "means unconscious involuntary action, and it is a defence because the mind does not go with what is being done." Automatism is action by one who has no knowledge of action, "no consciousness of doing what was being done." *Bratty.*

For the reasons stated herein I concur in the decision of the Court that there is no reversible error in the trial below, but I dissent from the statement in the majority opinion that unconsciousness is an affirmative defense. In my view unconsciousness, as held in *Mercer,* is never an affirmative defense.

Notes and Questions

1. Compare *People v. Newton,* 8 Cal. App.3d 359, 87 Cal.Rptr. 394 (1970), where defendant was convicted of the murder of police officer Frey. Prosecution witnesses testified that an altercation ensued after Frey stopped the defendant's car; that defendant had drawn a gun and that it had fired, wounding another officer; that this officer then fired at defendant's midsection; and that the defendant then wrested the gun away and fired point blank at Frey. The defendant testified that he carried no gun, that he felt a

sensation like "boiling hot soup had been spilled on my stomach" and heard an "explosion," and that he remembered nothing else until he found himself at the entrance to a hospital some time later. A doctor testified on behalf of the defendant that "it is not at all uncommon for a person shot in the abdomen to lose consciousness and go into this reflex shock condition for short periods of time up to half an hour or so." Held, "that the trial court should have given appropriate unconsciousness instructions upon its own motion in the present case, and that its omission to do so was prejudicial error."

2. In *People v. Grant,* 46 Ill.App.3d 125, 4 Ill.Dec. 696, 360 N.E.2d 809 (1977), reversed 71 Ill.2d 551, 17 Ill.Dec. 814, 377 N.E.2d 4 (1978), defendant was charged with battery of a policeman. When the officer made an arrest at a tavern altercation, the defendant leaped out of the crowd and struck the officer in the face. He appeared to be very agitated and upset at the time, and great force was required to restrain him. An hour later, defendant was found on his jail cot gasping for breath. His eyes were fixed and his back formed a rigid reversed arch, typical symptoms of a grand mal convulsive seizure. He was hospitalized for 10 days. It was established that he suffers from psychomotor epilepsy and has a history of violent attacks on other persons. At trial, he interposed an insanity defense, but the jury returned a guilty verdict. The appellate court—in the course of holding that "the interests of justice require reversal of the defendant's conviction because the jury instructions are substantially defective in that they do not contain an instruction on the defense of involuntary conduct"—noted that defendant's "past history is replete with emotional outbursts and he has been convicted on separate occasions of involuntary manslaughter and aggravated assault."

Green, J., dissenting, concluded that such an instruction should have been given

if tendered, but that since it was not tendered justice did not require the "extraordinary step of granting a new trial so that another jury can make a new determination upon the proof rejected by the first jury" when it failed to find the defendant not guilty by reason of insanity. He added: "I share with Lord Denning and the majority of commentators on the subject a belief in the need for protective custody for persons who repeatedly attack others while in a state of automatism. The situation merits an attempt by the legislature to devise a procedure balancing the rights of the public to be protected against the rights of the person subject to automatism to be at liberty and basing any deprivation of that liberty upon the degree of danger presented by that individual."

3. Is the solution to draw the line between the insanity and unconsciousness defenses in terms of whether there is a need for post-acquittal commitment of the defendant? Consider *Fulcher v. State,* 633 P.2d 142 (Wyo.1981), holding that unconsciousness due to a concussion, when it involves "simple brain trauma with no permanent after effects," properly falls within the automatism defense, because commitment for treatment "is not suited to unconscious behavior resulting from a bump on the head," but that "brain damage" which amounts to "some serious and irreversible condition having an impact upon the ability of the person to function" is properly viewed as falling within the insanity defense.

4. On the burden of proof issue, compare *Caldwell* with *State v. Pierson,* 201 Conn. 211, 514 A.2d 724 (1986): "There are some basic aspects of criminal liability [e.g., absence of unconsciousness, insanity, duress, and entrapment] that may be presumed and thus need not be discussed in a charge to the jury, at least in the absence of a request or some evidence casting doubt upon the presumption. * * * Though the state bears the burden of dis-

proving these defenses, once they are raised by the presentation of some evidence supporting them, there is no requirement that evidence negating them be produced as part of the state's prima facie case. A fortiori there is no requirement that a court suo motu instruct a jury upon these defenses in cases where the evidence produced by both parties contains not the remotest hint of their applicability."

5. In *People v. Decina*, 2 N.Y.2d 133, 157 N.Y.S.2d 558, 138 N.E.2d 799 (1956), defendant was convicted of negligent homicide after his automobile struck and killed four children. On appeal, he claimed his demurrer should have been sustained because the indictment (stating defendant knowing "that he was subject to epileptic attacks or other disorder rendering him likely to lose consciousness for a considerable period of time" was culpably negligent "in that he consciously undertook to and did operate his Buick sedan on a public highway" and "while so doing" suffered such an attack which caused said auto "to travel at a fast and reckless rate of speed, jumping the curb and driving over the sidewalk" causing the death of four persons) failed to charge a crime. The court of appeals disagreed:

"Assuming the truth of the indictment, as we must on a demurrer, this defendant knew he was subject to epileptic attacks and seizures that might strike *at any time.* He also knew that a moving motor vehicle uncontrolled on a public highway is a highly dangerous instrumentality capable of unrestrained destruction. With this *knowledge,* and without anyone accompanying him, he deliberately took a chance by making a conscious choice of a course of action, in disregard of the consequences which he knew might follow from his conscious act, and which in this case did ensue. How can we say as a matter of law that this did not amount to culpable negligence within the meaning of section 1053–a?

" * * * His awareness of a condition which he knows may produce such consequences as here, and his disregard of the consequences, renders him liable for culpable negligence, as the courts below have properly held. To have a sudden sleeping spell, an unexpected heart or other disabling attack, without any prior knowledge or warning thereof, is an altogether different situation, and there is simply no basis for comparing such cases with the flagrant disregard manifested here."

Desmond, J., dissenting, objected: "Just what is the court holding here? No less than this: that a driver whose brief blackout lets his car run amuck and kill another has killed that other by reckless driving. But any such 'recklessness' consists necessarily not of the erratic behavior of the automobile while its driver is unconscious, but of his driving at all when he knew he was subject to such attacks. Thus, it must be that such a blackout-prone driver is guilty of reckless driving, whenever and as soon as he steps into the driver's seat of a vehicle. Every time he drives, accident or no accident, he is subject to criminal prosecution for reckless driving or to revocation of his operator's license. And how many of this State's 5,000,000 licensed operators are subject to such penalties for merely driving the cars they are licensed to drive?"

How would Judge Desmond deal with *George v. State,* 681 S.W.2d 43 (Tex.Crim. App.1984), where defendant was convicted of aggravated assault, defined by statute as intentionally, knowingly or recklessly shooting another? "In his confession and testimony at trial appellant described in greater detail that after he asked Martin a second time for a dollar he cocked the hammer back short of its locked position; that he 'struck [the gun] up in [Martin's] face;' that Martin 'turned his face away;' and then 'the hammer slipped off my thumb' and the gun 'went off.' Appellant further told the jury that he did not know the gun would nor did he mean for it to go off 'when he cocked the hammer back;' he denied ever pulling the trigger and stated that he did not intend to shoot Martin or harm him in any way—it was an accident." Was the Texas court correct in asserting, on the issue of whether a voluntary act had been proved, that "factually whether appellant's precise bodily movement that released the hammer of his handgun was voluntary or involuntary is of little moment"?

6. In *State v. Boleyn*, 328 So.2d 95 (La. 1976), defendant was convicted of escape, defined by statute as "the intentional departure of a person, while imprisoned, * * * from any place where he is lawfully detained." He and Manuel were discovered missing at 2:30 p.m. but were apprehended less than 12 hours later when police stopped a car defendant was driving. The trial judge excluded (i) evidence relating to defendant's state of consciousness at the time of the purported escape (i.e., that he fell asleep in the parked truck by which Manuel made his escape) and (ii) evidence of his consumption of alcohol and drugs immediately prior thereto. On appeal, the court first held that the latter exclusion was proper under the rule that "voluntary intoxication can be considered as a defense only in cases where specific intent is a necessary element of the crime," and then concluded that it was error to exclude the other evidence because it "would indicate to the jury that defendant did not *voluntarily* escape."

Marcus, J., dissenting, asserted: "Under the circumstances of the instant case, defendant's criminal intent is found in the accused's intention to become intoxicated or drugged, i.e., the accused is held to have intended, in law, all the consequences of his intoxicated or drugged condition. Therefore, the criminal act of escape is a consequence of defendant's voluntary intoxicated or drugged condition."

Is the dissent sound? Is it supported by *Decina*? Consider Sullivan, *Self Induced and Recurring Automatism,* 123 New L.J. 1093, 1094 (1973), commenting on *Regina v. Quick,* [1973] 3 W.L.R. 26, holding it was error not to instruct on the defense of automatism where defendant, a diabetic, assaulted another while in a hypoglycaemic episode after taking insulin but very little food:

"The law is unsatisfactory in that it would probably provide for an acquittal, despite the fact that Q., with a history of violent blackouts, negligently induced his automatous state. [T]he court was reluctant to concede that the defence would have succeeded if the condition had been caused by insulin. It was felt that much would have depended on the answers to the following questions: 'to what extent had he brought about his condition by not following his doctor's instructions about taking regular meals? Did he know he was getting into a hypoglycaemic episode? If yes, why did he not use the antidote of eating a lump of sugar as he had been advised to?' The court felt that Q. might have had difficulty in answering these questions in a manner which would have relieved him of responsibility for his acts.

"Yet, even though Q. may have been clearly responsible for his condition the defence of automatism may still have succeeded at trial. The charge was assault, [which requires] 'any act which intentionally—or possibly recklessly—causes another person to apprehend immediate and unlawful physical violence.' So, *at the very least,* the prosecution would have had to prove that Q. foresaw he would attack someone."

Compare O'Connor, *The Voluntary Act,* 15 Med.Sci.Law 31, 35 (1975), arguing that any "distinction between self-induced and other-induced malfunction is not useful in the criminal law. If it is a necessary part of the [prosecution's] case to show a voluntary act, and the [prosecution] is unable to prove it beyond a reasonable doubt because there is evidence of involuntary conduct, the question whether the involuntarism resulted from the accused's own conduct or was induced by some external cause does not seem to be relevant."

7. Lunde & Wilson, *Brainwashing as a Defense to Criminal Liability: Patty Hearst Revisited,* 13 Crim.L.Bull. 341, 341–42, 370 (1977): "The recent trial and conviction of Patricia Hearst for bank robbery has raised anew within American society, and the legal and psychiatric communities more specifically, the question of 'brainwashing' as a defense of exculpation or mitigation to criminal liability. The facts of the *Hearst* case are well known: On April 15, 1974 Hearst participated in a San Francisco bank robbery together with members of the Symbionese Liberation Army who had kidnapped Hearst some ten weeks before, on February 4, 1974. The central issue at trial was whether Hearst had joined her abductors subsequent to her kidnapping and participated in the robbery voluntarily, or whether she was forced to participate—either by threats of death if she refused or as a result of beliefs inculcated in her through an indoctrination process of the SLA.

"The jury in the *Hearst* case was faced with the question of where coerced behavior ends and truly voluntary action begins for persons who appear to have changed their loyalties and values while held in captivity. The answer to that question was thought to reside in a misunderstood, potentially powerful, yet quite simple, process developed by the Chinese Communists and called 'brainwashing.' Because of the term's popularization during the Korean War years, and its reappearance in everyday parlance, a widely held belief was that it was a recognized legal doctrine. In fact, the term 'brainwashing' was not used or defended to any extent during the trial itself and the jury rejected the implied

brainwashing defense while convicting Hearst. Most important, brainwashing is not a presently recognized defense to criminal liability. * * *

"Bringing coercive persuasion under this legal rubric [of automatism] has the advantage of not faltering on the disease or defect hurdle that the insanity defense does because the unconsciousness defense applies to persons of sound mind. However, coercive persuasion simply does not rise to the factual sufficiency necessary. In none of the prisoner of war cases, nor in the *Hearst* case would it be possible to argue that the defendants were not aware of what they were doing. All remembered their crimes and did not contend otherwise, when an allegation of lack of memory is usually the necessary, but not sufficient, condition for raising an unconsciousness defense."

8. Without regard to whether brainwashing fits within the traditional definition of automatism, should it be recognized as a defense? Compare: (a) Delgado, *Ascription of Criminal States of Mind: Toward a Defense Theory for the Coercively Persuaded ("Brainwashed") Defendant,* 63 Minn.L.Rev. 1, 11 (1978): "The victim of thought reform typically commits criminal acts fully aware of their wrongfulness. He acts consciously, even enthusiastically, and without overt coercion. Yet, in an important sense, the guilty mind with which he acts is not his own. Rather, his mental state is more appropriately ascribed to the captors who instilled it in him for their own purposes. Explication of the concept of transferred or superimposed mens rea—criminal intent that is not the actor's own—is thus the principal task of this Article."

(b) Dressler, *Professor Delgado's "Brainwashing" Defense: Courting A Deterministic Legal System,* 63 Minn.L.Rev. 335, 343 (1979): "Such a proposal is doctrinally untenable. All ideas and intents originate outside the individual, in the sense that they are shaped by experiences and environment. As we have seen, however, the law nevertheless considers intent to be personal—to be a product of each individual's free will. This is true whether the intent to commit the crime is initiated by an inanimate object ('I saw the painting and it made me think of killing'), an innocent third party ('X told me the victim had a lot of money so I killed the victim'), or a guilty third party. If this were not the case, one could plausibly argue that all mental states—for example, criminal intentions, or political or religious views—are inauthentic, thus unacceptably blurring concepts of moral and legal responsibility."

9. Erlinder, *Paying the Price for Vietnam: Post–Traumatic Stress Disorder and Criminal Behavior,* 25 B.C.L.Rev. 305, 310–11, 329 (1984): "Following the traumatic event, a person who suffers from PTSD may have a number of symptoms that include: self medication through substance or alcohol abuse, memory loss, loss of sleep, nightmares reliving the original traumatic event, intrusive thoughts, exaggerated startle response, reduction in emotional response, a feeling of alienation, and, 'disassociative states' during which the original event is relived and *'the individual behaves as though experiencing the event of the moment.'* * * * The more difficult aspect of PTSD for many to accept is that the *symptoms of PTSD can occur long after the original traumatic event has ended.* Thus, long after the traumatic event, persons affected by PTSD may react as though they were back in the original traumatic situation.

"This tendency to 'reexperience' or 'relive' the original event is common to those who experience PTSD symptoms after a traumatic event, regardless of its source. For those trained to survive in combat, a 'reexperiencing' of the original event may include combat-like reactions. * * *

"Perhaps the most likely alternative theory for the introduction of PTSD at trial lies in the well accepted, but little used defense of automatism."

In *State v. Jerrett,* 309 N.C. 239, 307 S.E.2d 339 (1983), defendant burglarized a farmhouse, shot and killed the owner, and then kidnapped the owner's wife. At trial, defendant testified he had been blacked out during those events and that he had been experiencing blackouts since his Vietnam service. His parents testified about his many blackouts. A state psychiatrist testified defendant was not suffering from PTSD, while a defense psychiatrist testified the state had not adequately tested the defendant. Relying on *Caddell,* the court ruled defendant should have had an automatism instruction "because here there was corroborating evidence tending to support the defense of unconsciousness. In addition to the testimonial corroborating evidence, defendant's very peculiar actions in permitting the kidnapped victim to repeatedly ignore his commands and finally lead him docilely into the presence and custody of a police officer lends credence to his defense of unconsciousness."

10. In *State v. Grimsley,* 3 Ohio App.3d 265, 444 N.E.2d 1071 (1982), an appeal of defendant's conviction for driving while intoxicated, the defendant, who had a multiple personality disorder, contended she should not have been convicted because at the time of her conduct she was disassociated from her primary personality (Robin) and in the state of consciousness of a secondary personality (Jennifer, who is impulsive, angry, fearful and anxious). The court responded:

"We disagree. Assuming *arguendo* that the evidence was sufficient to establish such a complete break between appellant's consciousness as Robin and her consciousness as Jennifer that Jennifer alone was in control (despite years of therapy), nevertheless the evidence fails to establish the fact that Jennifer was either unconscious or acting involuntarily. There was only one person driving the car and only one person accused of drunken driving. It is immaterial whether she was in one state of consciousness or another, so long as in the personality then controlling her behavior, she was conscious and her actions were a product of her own volition. The evidence failed to demonstrate that Jennifer was unconscious or otherwise acting involuntarily."

11. Consider the following comments on the premenstral syndrome: (a) Recent Decision, 59 Notre Dame L.Rev. 253, 257–58, 264–65 (1983): "Although medical experts disagree on the diagnosis, cause, and treatment of PMS, they do agree that the syndrome causes marked psychological anomalies. These psychological anomalies have significantly affected the behavioral patterns of thousands of women. These women demonstrate the greatest potential for PMS-induced criminal behavior. Medical studies have linked PMS to an increased number of suicide attempts, automobile accidents, and miscellaneous criminal acts. Nonetheless, the legal community has not yet paid sufficient attention to the correlation between PMS and crime. * * *

"Because PMS is not a disease or defect of the mind, it might fit more appropriately within the automatism defense. * * *

"American courts might find it equally appropriate to exclude PMS-induced conduct from the reach of the criminal law. Although a PMS sufferer may be conscious of her actions and devoid of any mental disease or defect, she is no more able to control her actions than the automaton or the legally insane. Physiological anomalies render the PMS sufferer unable to control her actions during the short time PMS symptoms surface. These symptoms surface, however, at regular, predictable

intervals which doctors can effectively control under appropriate medical supervision."

(b) Holtzman, *Premenstral Symptoms: No Legal Defense,* 60 St. John's L.Rev. 712, 713 (1986), concludes "that there is no scientific evidence for the proposition that the onset of the menstrual cycle provokes aggressive or violent behavior in women. The scientific evidence is confirmed by common sense experience—if women became violent each month our jails would be filled with women. But, as it is, the overwhelming number of jail inmates are men; no menstrual cycle caused their aggression."

(c) K. Dalton, *Once a Month* 207 (1983): "Those few women who lose control of themselves for a day or two, month after month, need help and help is available. However, they must not be confused with the other 99.9 percent of women who are well able to control their actions. PMS is not a universal defense, nor should it be allowed to become one. Medical evidence is required by the court and the doctor must become fully conversant with the recognition, diagnosis and treatment of the syndrome."

12. G. Williams, *Criminal Law: The General Part* § 9 (2d ed. 1961): "At the present day the exception from responsibility, such as it is, given by the 'act' doctrine could, in respect of the requirement of will, just as well be put on the ground of absence of mens rea." Why?

13. Compare the following three cases and consider whether they all involve applications of the same principle:

(a) *Martin v. State,* 31 Ala.App. 334, 17 So.2d 427 (1944): Police arrested defendant at his home and took him onto the highway, where he was boisterous. Defendant was convicted under a statute covering any "person who, while intoxicated or drunk, appears in any public place where one or more persons are present,

* * * and manifests a drunken condition by boisterous or indecent conduct." Reversed, as "an accusation of drunkenness in a designated public place cannot be established by proof that the accused, while in an intoxicated condition, was involuntarily and forcibly carried to that place by the arresting officer."

(b) *People v. Newton,* 72 Misc.2d 646, 340 N.Y.S.2d 77 (1973): The defendant was a passenger on a commercial flight originating in the Bahamas and destined for Luxembourg. The defendant was unruly on the plane, and the captain feared he might be armed, so he diverted the plane from over international waters and made an unscheduled landing in New York. Police came aboard and found defendant had a loaded gun on his person. Defendant was charged with the felony of carrying a loaded weapon. The court found that the defendant "did not subject himself to criminal liability by virtue of a voluntary act. Flight # 101 was not scheduled to terminate in or pass through the territorial jurisdiction of the United States. The landing at John F. Kennedy International Airport on December 8, 1972 was merely an interruption of flight not attributable to a voluntary action by the petitioner."

(c) *People v. Shaughnessy,* 66 Misc.2d 19, 319 N.Y.S.2d 626 (1971): The defendant was a passenger in a car she understood was headed for a certain public park. The driver instead pulled into private premises across the street from the park, where the car was stopped by a watchman. The occupants waited 20 minutes for a police officer to arrive, during which time the defendant never left the vehicle. The defendant was prosecuted for violating an ordinance forbidding entry on private property without permission of the owner or occupant. In granting the defendant's motion to dismiss, the court stated:

"In the case at bar, the People have failed to establish any act on the part of the Defendant. She merely was a passenger in a vehicle. Any action taken by the vehicle was caused and guided by the driver thereof and not by the Defendant. If the Defendant were to be held guilty under these circumstances, it would dictate that she would be guilty if she had been unconscious or asleep at the time or even if she had been a prisoner in the automobile. There are many situations which can be envisioned and in which the trespass statute in question would be improperly applied to an involuntary act. One might conceive of a driver losing control of a vehicle through mechanical failure and the vehicle proceeding onto private property which is the subject of a trespass.

"Although the Court need not pass on the question, it might very well be proper to hold the driver responsible for his act even though he was under the mistaken belief that he was on his way to Christopher Morley Park. The legislature has provided statutes which make mistakes of fact or lack of knowledge no excuse in a criminal action. However, if the driver had been a Defendant, the People could have established an act on the part of the Defendant driver, to wit, turning his vehicle into the private property."

14. In *Williams v. City of Petersburg,* 216 Va. 297, 217 S.E.2d 893 (1975), defendant was convicted of violating an ordinance providing that "[n]o person shall drive or operate any automobile * * * in the city while under the influence of alcohol." At 4 a.m. a police officer was attracted to a car with the engine running in a parking lot. The defendant, intoxicated, was slumped over the wheel. All the doors were locked, but the officer managed to get defendant's attention, and the defendant then turned off the car. On appeal, the court held that "the trial court could properly find beyond a reasonable doubt that the defendant was

in actual physical control of the vehicle and that he had engaged the machinery of the vehicle which alone, or in sequence, would have activated its motive power. Therefore, the defendant was 'operating' the vehicle within the meaning of the ordinance.

"The trial court was not required to accept the defendant's account of the incident, which was that he had started the engine merely for the purpose of using the car heater to keep warm and not for the purpose of driving the vehicle."

The dissenters objected: "Defendant did exactly what others should do upon finding that they have consumed too much alcohol to operate a vehicle—stop drinking and go to sleep. For security purposes he locked his car doors. To keep from getting too cold he started the heater. He did nothing with his car that was a menace to himself or to the public. For us to hold that what the defendant did in this case amounts to operating a car within the purview of Code § 18.1–54, or the Petersburg ordinance, is unrealistic and unreasonable."

Compare *State v. Bugger,* 25 Utah 2d 404, 483 P.2d 442 (1971) (where intoxicated person was asleep in a car on the shoulder of the road and the car was not running, he is not guilty of violating a statute making it unlawful "for any person who is under the influence of intoxicating liquor to drive or be in actual physical control of any vehicle within the state"); with *Wiyott v. State,* 284 Ark. 399, 683 S.W.2d 220 (1985) (defendant guilty under such a statute where he intoxicated and asleep in the car, parked in grocery store parking lot but, when a policeman banged on the window and hollered at him, defendant reached for key in ignition switch).

———

SECTION 2. THE "ACT" OF POSSESSION

PEOPLE v. GORY

Supreme Court of California, 1946.
28 Cal.2d 450, 170 P.2d 433.

SPENCE, JUSTICE.

In an information filed by the District Attorney of Los Angeles County, defendant was accused of * * * violating section 11160 of the Health and Safety Code in that he did, on or about June 2, 1944, "willfully, unlawfully and feloniously have in his possession flowering tops and leaves of Indian Hemp (cannabis sativa)," commonly called marijuana. * * * From the judgment of conviction entered upon this verdict and from an order denying his motion for a new trial, defendant prosecutes this appeal. * * *

There is practically no conflict in the testimony. At the time of the alleged possession of marijuana, defendant was a prisoner at the Los Angeles County Honor Farm near Castaic. He shared living quarters with some thirty odd prisoners in one of the camp's bunkhouses, to which he had been assigned in April, 1944. As part of the equipment issued to each prisoner, defendant received a metal box—18 inches long, 12 inches wide, 8 inches deep—in which he kept his toilet articles and small personal effects. There was no way of locking these boxes, each of which bore a number corresponding to the bed number of the space occupied by the particular prisoner. Each prisoner's box was placed on the floor near the head of his bed. During the day when the prisoners were engaged in their duties on the farm, one man was left in charge of the bunkhouse to "keep the inmates from monkeying with other people's property."

About 9:30 p.m. on June 2, 1944, Officer Gunderson and several accompanying officers entered the bunkhouse. While his associates searched the boxes of other prisoners in the bunkhouse, Officer Gunderson went to defendant's bed—on which defendant was lying—picked up the metal box bearing the number of defendant's bed, opened the box and found marijuana "scattered from the top down to the bottom * * * just loose in the box." Said officer took off defendant's clothes and examined them, turning the pockets "wrong side out," but found no marijuana either on his person or in his clothes. Deputy Sheriff Huber, who was present at the time, testified at the trial that he asked defendant what he knew about this marijuana, stating: "This is your marijuana; where did you get it?" and that defendant did not answer. In his own testimony at the trial, defendant admitted that the material which the officers identified as marijuana was taken from his box, but stated that he had never seen it before the officers removed it from the box.

With the evidence so presented at the trial, defendant challenges the propriety of the trial Court's action in reading, rereading, and then expressly withdrawing from the jury's consideration the following instructions, hereinafter designated "instruction 12" and "instruction 13."

Instruction 12: "In order for defendant to have in his possession the objects charged in the information, you must be convinced by the evidence and beyond a reasonable doubt that he *knowingly* had such objects in his possession. The meaning of the word 'possession' includes the exercise of dominion and control over the thing possessed."

Instruction 13: "Even if you find from the evidence beyond a reasonable doubt that the defendant had in his possession, flowering tops of Indian Hemp or locoweed, before you can find the defendant guilty of possessing the same, you must also be convinced beyond a reasonable doubt that the defendant had a *guilty knowledge* of the character of said flowering

tops of Indian Hemp and possessed a *guilty intent*. If you find that the defendant was innocent of the *knowledge of the character* of the flowering tops of Indian Hemp or did not have a *guilty knowledge* of possessing said flowering tops of Indian Hemp, then you will find the defendant not guilty and must acquit him." * * *

So far as pertinent to defendant's argument, section 20 of the Penal Code provides that "In every crime or public offense there must exist a union, or joint operation of act and intent * * *." But this does not mean that a positive, wilful intent to violate the law is an essential ingredient of every offense. Sometimes an act is expressly prohibited by statute, in which case the *intentional doing of the act,* regardless of good motive or ignorance of its criminal character, constitutes the offense denounced by law. * * * Speaking to this point, the court in *People v. Sweeney,* 66 Cal.App.2d 855, 153 P.2d 371, a case concerning violation of the same code section here involved, said: "Neither intent nor knowledge is an element of the offense herein charged. The mere possession, except as authorized by the provisions of the Health and Safety Code, is a violation of the act. * * *"

While it thus appears that "mere possession, except as authorized" is sufficient to constitute the statutory offense in question, without regard for *scienter* or specific intent to violate the law as would follow from evidence establishing defendant's *knowledge of the contraband character* of the property, the law makes the matter of knowledge in relation to *defendant's awareness of the presence* of the object a basic element of the offense of possession. It has been repeatedly held that the term "possession" as used in the State Poison Act (now embraced in the Health and Safety Code) means an "immediate and exclusive possession and one under the dominion and control of defendant." Thus it was said in *People v. Noland,* 61 Cal.App.2d 364, 366,

143 P.2d 86, 87: "A person has 'possession' of a chattel who has physical control with the intent to exercise such control, or, having had such physical control, has not abandoned it and no other person has obtained possession. (Restatement Torts, section 216.)" But knowledge of the *existence* of the object is essential to "physical control thereof with the intent to exercise such control" and such knowledge must necessarily precede the intent to exercise, or the exercise of, such control. * * *

The distinction which must be drawn, from a reading of the foregoing authorities, is the distinction between (1) *knowledge of the character of the object and the unlawfulness of possession thereof* as embraced within the concept of a specific intent to violate the law, and (2) *knowledge of the presence of the object* as embraced within the concept of "physical control with the intent to exercise such control," which constitutes the "possession" denounced by the statute. It is "knowledge" in the first sense which is mentioned in the authorities as being immaterial but "knowledge" in the second sense is the essence of the offense.

In line with these authorities, it plainly appears in this case that instruction 13, as above quoted, in requiring the finding of a "guilty knowledge" and a "guilty intent" on the part of defendant to sustain his conviction, was properly withdrawn from the jury as an improper matter for consideration.

But instruction 12, as above quoted, in its predication of a finding of guilt upon defendant's *"knowingly"* having "in his possession the objects charged in the information," should have been given to the jury. "The word 'knowingly' imports only a knowledge that the facts exist which bring the act or omission within the provisions of this code. It does not require any knowledge of the unlawfulness of such act or omission." Thus instruction 12 in-

voked the element of knowledge in the sense of defendant's *awareness of the presence* of the marijuana in the box given him for the storage of his personal effects at the prison farm and so presented to the jury an issue of fact determinative of defendant's guilt or innocence of the possession prohibited by statute. * * *

The judgment and the order denying defendant's motion for a new trial are reversed.

SCHAUER, JUSTICE.

I concur in the judgment and agree that it was prejudicial error to fail to give (to withdraw) instruction number 12. I do not agree to the implication, if there be such, that mere conscious possession of an object, not knowing its true character (as, for example, possession of marijuana believed in good faith to be ordinary tobacco), any more than conscious possession of an object lawful in itself but within which, unknown to the possessor, contraband is concealed, constitutes a criminal act.

Notes and Questions

1. Assume that defendant is arrested moments after he has received a package from postal authorities and that the police then open the package and find narcotics. In one such case, *Commonwealth v. Lee,* 331 Mass. 166, 117 N.E.2d 830 (1954), the court affirmed defendant's conviction for possession of narcotics, stating: "Before the package was opened the defendant had received it from the mail carrier and had claimed it as hers. She indicated no intent not to exercise control of it on her own behalf.

"We need not consider whether there was sufficient evidence that the defendant knew or had reason to believe that the package contained marijuana, until she opened it. And we need not consider cases in other jurisdictions, where a statute made criminal the possession of a drug or other harmful thing, in which it has been held that a defendant cannot be convicted unless he knowingly had possession of the forbidden thing, illustrated by *People v. Gory.*"

Compare *Commonwealth v. Rambo,* 488 Pa. 334, 412 A.2d 535 (1980), noting that a statute in the criminal code defined possession as "an act, within the meaning of this section, if the possessor knowingly procured or received the thing possessed or was aware of his control thereof for a sufficient period to have been able to terminate his possession," and concluding from this that defendant's conviction must be reversed because there was no "evidence which would establish, beyond a reasonable doubt, that appellant knew the packages contained hashish."

Are *Lee* and *Rambo* in conflict as to what constitutes the "act" of possession, or as to whether the particular possession crime also has a mental state element?

2. In *State v. Flaherty,* 400 A.2d 363 (Me.1979), defendant was convicted of unlawful possession of a firearm because a rifle owned by another person was found in defendant's car. Defendant claimed the owner of the rifle had mistakenly put it there and that he had just discovered it there shortly before. On appeal, the court ruled defendant should have received an instruction in the language of the statute (essentially like that in *Rambo*) because with such an instruction "the jury might reasonably have concluded that the Defendant had not been aware of his control of the rifle for a sufficient period to have been able to terminate his possession." The court explained such a provision provides a " 'grace' period * * * designed to separate illegal possession from temporary control incidental to the lawful purpose of terminating possession. Thus a 'sufficient period' is not always the absolute minimum time required to get rid of the contraband. So long as the Defendant's control of the contraband remains

incidental to the lawful purpose of terminating his possession and, viewed under the circumstances, remains 'temporary,' it falls within the 'sufficient period' permitted him by" the statute.

3. In *People v. Norris,* 40 Mich.App. 45, 198 N.W.2d 430 (1972), police raided defendant's home, where gambling was allegedly occurring, and arrested him for possession of a blackjack, for which he was thereafter convicted. Defendant, who testified he had taken the blackjack from a customer to ensure it would not be used and then had thrown it on the couch after a few minutes, was refused an instruction on "the difference between temporary custody and possession." The court affirmed, concluding "that the defendant's reason for having the blackjack was immaterial, and that his proffered defense was in reality no defense at all."

WHEELER v. UNITED STATES

District of Columbia Court of Appeals, 1985.
494 A.2d 170.

MACK, ASSOCIATE JUDGE: * * *

Viewing the evidence in the light most favorable to the government, the facts of this case are as follows. On January 17, 1982, a search warrant was executed for Room 201 of the Logan Inn at 1338 R Street, N.W. In an affidavit in support of the warrant, Detective Alan Penberg stated that a source had informed him that female occupants of Room 201 were selling heroin from that room. The police knocked on the door to Room 201, identifying themselves, but received no response. Instead, they heard what they described as "scurrying" noises behind the door. After at least a minute, they succeeded in breaking down the door. They found appellant and two other women coming out of the bathroom; the toilet had just been flushed. A fourth woman was sitting in a chair next to the bathroom. Two of the women were dressed in street clothes, but appellant and another woman, Mary Sales, were wearing sleeping attire. Luggage and clothes belonging to appellant were found in the room along with other personal effects. Appellant and Sales both gave aliases to the police. Both admitted, however, that they lived in Room 201. There were two beds in the hotel room, at opposite ends of the room. Sales retrieved some slippers from underneath a bed at one end. Under the second bed's pillow, the police found 3550 milligrams of 2.7% heroin. Sales and appellant were arrested. While the charges against Sales were subsequently dismissed, appellant was found guilty of possession of heroin after a bench trial. This appeal followed. * * *

This case was submitted to the trial court on a theory of constructive possession. An individual has constructive possession of an illegal substance when he is knowingly in a position or has the right to exercise dominion and control over it, and has some appreciable ability to guide its destiny. The right to exercise dominion and control may be jointly shared. In evaluating the sufficiency of the evidence submitted by the government, no distinction is made between direct and circumstantial evidence, and the trier may infer knowledge from circumstantial evidence.

Appellant contends that the heroin could have been placed under the pillow by any one of the three other women present in the room at the time the police arrived, and that to hold her responsible for the drug is mere speculation. The case law on the question of who may be held

responsible when the police find an illegal item in a location together with more than one individual demonstrates some inconsistency. Several general principles may be extracted from the cases, however. Mere proximity to an illegal substance will be insufficient to uphold a conviction on a theory of constructive possession when an individual is one of several people found by the authorities on the premises together with the substance. *Cook v. United States,* 272 A.2d 444, 447 (D.C.1971) (conviction for possession of narcotics paraphernalia reversed where the government did not show appellant to be a resident of the premises and the actual tenant and other occupants were also present on the scene at the time of the raid); *United States v. Holland,* 144 U.S.App.D.C. 225, 227, 445 F.2d 701, 703 (1971) (conviction for possession of heroin reversed where drugs were found in codefendant's apartment, and although appellant was present when drugs were found the government did not show that he was residing there); *see United States v. Pardo,* 204 U.S.App.D.C. 263, 277, 636 F.2d 535, 549 (1980) (conviction for possession with intent to distribute narcotics reversed where appellant was merely present while a drug transaction was consummated between other individuals); *United States v. Watkins,* 171 U.S. App.D.C. 158, 162, 519 F.2d 294, 298 (1975) (conviction for possession of narcotics reversed even though police found appellant and narcotics in the same room, where two other individuals were found on the premises and insufficient evidence of appellant's residency at that location was adduced).[1] A common theme running

1. *See also Easley v. United States,* 482 A.2d 779, 781 (D.C.1984) (conviction for possession of an unregistered gun and ammunition reversed where the gun was hidden under the front seat of the car and appellants were sitting in the back seat); *Hack v. United States, supra,* 445 A.2d at 639–40 (conviction for possession of narcotics reversed where appellant and a co-defendant had been transported by the police in a squad car and the police subsequently found the drugs under

the seat where the co-defendant had been sitting); *United States v. Bethea,* 143 U.S.App.D.C. 68, 71, 442 F.2d 790, 793 (1971) (conviction for distribution of heroin reversed where drugs were found together with a gun hidden behind the back seat of a car, appellant had been sitting in the front seat, and the police had observed another passenger place the gun in the rear hiding place); *United States v. Whitfield,* 203 U.S.App.D.C. 102, 109, 629 F.2d 136, 143 (1980) (conviction for possession

through many of these cases is the courts' reluctance to hold an individual responsible for controlled substances or drug paraphernalia found in a home absent some proof that he is something other than a visitor. In this case, however, the government's evidence showed that appellant admitted that she was living in Room 201.

Even where the government proves that the defendant is a resident of the place where illegal items are seized, the courts are wary of imputing possession to the defendant absent proof of his involvement in some criminal enterprise. *Thompson v. United States,* 293 A.2d 275, 276 (D.C.1972) (conviction for possession of marijuana reversed where drug was found, along with four individuals, in living room and appellant was found in bedroom); *United States v. Bonham,* 477 F.2d 1137, 1138–40 (3d Cir.1973) (en banc) (conviction for acquisition of heroin reversed where drugs were found hidden behind a false wall panel in a room appellant shared with his half-brother; informant's tip did not mention appellant; and half-brother was an addict).

On the other hand, where there are circumstances giving rise to an inference of a concert of illegal action involving drugs by the occupants of the premises where the drugs are found, those circumstances tend to dispel any fear that the "constructive possession" doctrine has cast too wide a net. We have held that proximity may establish a supportable case of constructive possession of narcotics when colored by evidence linking the accused to an ongoing criminal operation of which that possession is a part. Other circumstances that will buttress the "constructive possession" inference include attempts to hide or destroy evidence. *See Logan v. United States,* 489 A.2d 485, 491–92 (D.C.1985) (joint

constructive possession of weapon affirmed where appellants were observed jointly throwing something out of car and gun was thereafter recovered from roadbed); *United States v. Smith,* 171 U.S.App.D.C. 342, 344, 520 F.2d 74, 76 (1975) (constructive possession of phencyclidine found in closet affirmed despite fact that appellant was not sole occupant of apartment, where police had found appellant in bathroom and had discovered bag of marijuana directly below open bathroom window).

While this is a close case, we think that the government's evidence, albeit circumstantial, gives rise to sufficient inferences to support the judgment of conviction. As mentioned previously, appellant admitted to the police that she lived in the room, and the government's proof permitted the inference that appellant occupied the bed from which the heroin was recovered. Appellant failed to open the door or to respond in any way to the knock by the police. The observation by the officers that the toilet was flushed while three of the room's occupants, including appellant, were standing in the bathroom simultaneously, permitted the trier to infer that appellant used the period of time that the police required to break down the door to eliminate evidence. In addition, the fact that appellant identified herself to the police using an alias carries some weight on the question of whether she was involved in a criminal enterprise.

In sum, this is not a case in which the defendant's conduct, other than a shared proximity to the illegal item, is entirely innocent. It is unnecessary for the government either to adduce evidence that would compel a finding of guilt, or to negate every possible inference of innocence. The inference that appellant knew of the presence of the drug is not wholly

of an unregistered pistol reversed where appellant had taken a 5–10 minute car ride with his co-defendant, sitting in the front seat, and although the pistol was found under that front seat

it was hidden and there was no evidence that appellant knew of its presence), *cert. denied,* 449 U.S. 1086, 101 S.Ct. 875, 66 L.Ed.2d 812 (1981).

speculative, and that inference, combined with the other circumstances outlined above, suffice to attribute to appellant a measure of control over the heroin and thus to support a finding of constructive possession.

Affirmed.

Notes and Questions

1. In Whitebread & Stevens, *Constructive Possession in Narcotics Cases: To Have and Have Not,* 58 Va.L.Rev. 751, 766 (1972), the authors are critical of how courts typically establish constructive possession. They propose that "the prosecution should have to show either: (a) defendant's exclusive control over the area in which the drug is found, or (b) substantial evidence of the defendant's past possession of the drug on his person. Failure to meet one of these two standards should justify a directed verdict of acquittal at the close of the prosecution's evidence."

2. Steven married Kathy in May, and they moved into a house trailer. Kathy came from a wealthy family, and when in November the couple's financial picture darkened she told Steven she was considering selling marijuana. Steven told her he was against the idea, but a few weeks later he came home from work to find 200 pounds of marijuana in the trailer. When he questioned Kathy, she became very upset and threatened to go to England alone, as she had planned to do before they met. Steven then relented and did nothing further. In December police raided the trailer and found over 100 pounds of marijuana.[a] Is *Steven* guilty of possession of marijuana?

3. Harmon stopped at a border checkpoint near Sarita, Texas, at 4 a.m. A border patrol agent detected the smell of marijuana and asked Harmon to open his trunk; Harmon answered that he did not have the trunk key. Martinez arrived at the checkpoint in another car. The agent asked Harmon if he knew Martinez and Harmon answered in the affirmative. The agent asked Martinez if he had the key to Harmon's trunk; Martinez said yes and handed over a key ring. The agent opened the trunk of Harmon's car and found locked chests, which he opened with keys on Martinez's key ring. Marijuana was found within. Is *Martinez* guilty of possession of marijuana?[b]

4. Martorano, not knowing Raiton was an undercover informant for federal agents, arranged to buy controlled substance P–2–P from him. Raiton rented a van and turned it over to the FBI; FBI agents loaded it with P–2–P, placed a special padlock on the rear doors, and then parked it near Rittenhouse Square in Philadelphia. Raiton met Martorano at the Square as planned and received $100,000 from him upon revealing the location of the van. Martorano remained there with Raiton while accomplices Vadino and DeTullio were dispatched to "check out" the van's location. After they left, Raiton gave Martorano the van and padlock keys. Martorano later gave them to DeTullio, who returned to the van, unlocked it and entered the van. He sat there for less than two minutes before he was arrested by FBI agents, who were maintaining continued surveillance of the van to prevent its removal. Is *Martorano* guilty of possessing P–2–P?[c]

---

a. *People v. Ireland,* 38 Ill.App.3d 616, 348 N.E.2d 277 (1976), reversing the conviction because of insufficient jury instructions.

b. *United States v. Martinez,* 588 F.2d 495 (5th Cir.1979), affirming the conviction.

c. *United States v. Martorano,* 709 F.2d 863 (3d Cir.1983), a 2–1 affirmance of the conviction.

COUNTY COURT OF ULSTER COUNTY v. ALLEN

Supreme Court of the United States, 1979.
442 U.S. 140, 99 S.Ct. 2213, 60 L.Ed.2d 777.

MR. JUSTICE STEVENS delivered the opinion of the Court.

A New York statute provides that, with certain exceptions, the presence of a firearm in an automobile is presumptive evidence of its illegal possession by all persons then occupying the vehicle.[1] The United States Court of Appeals for the Second Circuit held that respondents may challenge the constitutionality of this statute in a federal habeas corpus proceeding and that the statute is "unconstitutional on its face." We granted certiorari to review these holdings and also to consider whether the statute is constitutional in its application to respondents.

Four persons, three adult males (respondents) and a 16–year–old girl (Jane Doe, who is not a respondent here), were jointly tried on charges that they possessed two loaded handguns, a loaded machinegun, and over a pound of heroin found in a Chevrolet in which they were riding when it was stopped for speeding on the New York Thruway shortly after noon on March 28, 1973. The two large-caliber handguns, which together with their ammunition weighed approximately six pounds, were seen through the window of the car by the investigating police officer.

1. New York Penal Law § 265.15(3) (McKinney 1967):

"The presence in an automobile, other than a stolen one or a public omnibus, of any firearm, defaced firearm, firearm silencer, bomb, bombshell, gravity knife, switchblade knife, dagger, dirk, stiletto, billy, blackjack, metal knuckles, sandbag, sandclub or slungshot is presumptive evidence of its possession by all persons occupying such automobile at the time such weapon, instrument or appliance is found, except under the following circumstances:

"(a) if such weapon, instrument or appliance is found upon the person of one of the occupants therein; (b) if such weapon, instrument or appliance is found in an automobile which is being

They were positioned crosswise in an open handbag on either the front floor or the front seat of the car on the passenger side where Jane Doe was sitting. Jane Doe admitted that the handbag was hers. The machinegun and the heroin were discovered in the trunk after the police pried it open. The car had been borrowed from the driver's brother earlier that day; the key to the trunk could not be found in the car or on the person of any of its occupants, although there was testimony that two of the occupants had placed something in the trunk before embarking in the borrowed car. The jury convicted all four of possession of the handguns and acquitted them of possession of the contents of the trunk.

Counsel for all four defendants objected to the introduction into evidence of the two handguns, the machinegun, and the drugs, arguing that the State had not adequately demonstrated a connection between their clients and the contraband. The trial court overruled the objection, relying on the presumption of possession created by the New York statute. Because that presumption does not apply if a weapon is found "upon the person" of one of the occupants of the car, see n. 1, *supra,* the three male defendants also moved to dismiss the charges relating to the handguns on the ground that the guns were found on the person of Jane Doe. Respondents made this motion both at the

operated for hire by a duly licensed driver in the due, lawful and proper pursuit of his trade, then such presumption shall not apply to the driver; or (c) if the weapon so found is a pistol or revolver and one of the occupants, not present under duress, has in his possession a valid license to have and carry concealed the same."

In addition to the three exceptions delineated in §§ 265.15(3)(a)–(c) above as well as the stolen-vehicle and public-omnibus exception in § 265.15(3) itself, § 265.20 contains various exceptions that apply when weapons are present in an automobile pursuant to certain military, law enforcement, recreational, and commercial endeavors.

close of the prosecution's case and at the close of all evidence. The trial judge twice denied it, concluding that the applicability of the "upon the person" exception was a question of fact for the jury.

At the close of the trial, the judge instructed the jurors that they were entitled to infer possession from the defendants' presence in the car. He did not make any reference to the "upon the person" exception in his explanation of the statutory presumption, nor did any of the defendants object to this omission or request alternative or additional instructions on the subject.

Defendants filed a post-trial motion in which they challenged the constitutionality of the New York statute as applied in this case. The challenge was made in support of their argument that the evidence, apart from the presumption, was insufficient to sustain the convictions. The motion was denied, and the convictions were affirmed by the Appellate Division without opinion.

The New York Court of Appeals also affirmed. It rejected the argument that as a matter of law the guns were on Jane Doe's person because they were in her pocketbook. Although the court recognized that in some circumstances the evidence could only lead to the conclusion that the weapons were in one person's sole possession, it held that this record presented a jury question on that issue. Since the defendants had not asked the trial judge to submit the question to the jury, the Court of Appeals treated the case as though the jury had resolved this fact question in the prosecution's favor. It therefore conclud-

ed that the presumption did apply and that there was sufficient evidence to support the convictions. It also summarily rejected the argument that the presumption was unconstitutional as applied in this case.

Respondents filed a petition for a writ of habeas corpus in the United States District Court for the Southern District of New York contending that they were denied due process of law by the application of the statutory presumption of possession. The District Court issued the writ, holding * * * that the mere presence of two guns in a woman's handbag in a car could not reasonably give rise to the inference that they were in the possession of three other persons in the car.

The Court of Appeals for the Second Circuit affirmed, but for different reasons. [T]he majority of the court, without deciding whether the presumption was constitutional as applied in this case, concluded that the statute is unconstitutional on its face because the "presumption obviously sweeps within its compass (1) many occupants who may not know they are riding with a gun (which may be out of their sight), and (2) many who may be aware of the presence of the gun but not permitted access to it." * * *

Without determining whether the presumption in this case was mandatory, the Court of Appeals analyzed it on its face as if it were. In fact, it was not, as the New York Court of Appeals had earlier pointed out.

The trial judge's instructions make it clear that the presumption was merely a part of the prosecution's case,[19] that it gave

---

19. "It is your duty to consider all the testimony in this case, to weigh it carefully and to test the credit to be given to a witness by his apparent intention to speak the truth and by the accuracy of his memory to reconcile, if possible, conflicting statements as to material facts and in such ways to try and get at the truth and to reach a verdict upon the evidence."

"To establish the unlawful possession of the weapons, again the People relied upon the pre-

sumption and, in addition thereto, the testimony of Anderson and Lemmons who testified in their case in chief."

"Accordingly, you would be warranted in returning a verdict of guilt against the defendants or defendant if you find the defendants or defendant was in possession of a machine gun and the other weapons and that the fact of possession was proven to you by the People beyond a reasonable doubt, and an element of such proof is the reason-

rise to a permissive inference available only in certain circumstances, rather than a mandatory conclusion of possession, and that it could be ignored by the jury even if there was no affirmative proof offered by defendants in rebuttal.[20] The judge explained that possession could be actual or constructive, but that constructive possession could not exist without the intent and ability to exercise control or dominion over the weapons. He also carefully instructed the jury that there is a mandatory presumption of innocence in favor of the defendants that controls unless it, as the exclusive trier of fact, is satisfied beyond a reasonable doubt that the defendants possessed the handguns in the manner described by the judge. In short, the instructions plainly directed the jury to consider all the circumstances tending to support or contradict the inference that all four occupants of the car had possession of the two loaded handguns and to decide the matter for itself without regard to how much evidence the defendants introduced.

Our cases considering the validity of permissive statutory presumptions such as the one involved here have rested on an evaluation of the presumption as applied to the record before the Court. None suggests that a court should pass on the constitutionality of this kind of statute "on its face." It was error for the Court of Appeals to make such a determination in this case.

able presumption of illegal possession of a machine gun or the presumption of illegal possession of firearms, as I have just before explained to you."

20. "Our Penal Law also provides that the presence in an automobile of any machine gun or of any handgun or firearm which is loaded is presumptive evidence of their unlawful possession.

"In other words, these presumptions or this latter presumption upon proof of the presence of the machine gun and the hand weapons, you may infer and draw a conclusion that such prohibited weapon was possessed by each of the defendants

As applied to the facts of this case, the presumption of possession is entirely rational. Notwithstanding the Court of Appeals' analysis, respondents were not "hitchhikers or other casual passengers," and the guns were neither "a few inches in length" nor "out of [respondents'] sight." The argument against possession by any of the respondents was predicated solely on the fact that the guns were in Jane Doe's pocketbook. But several circumstances—which, not surprisingly, her counsel repeatedly emphasized in his questions and his argument—made it highly improbable that she was the sole custodian of those weapons.

Even if it was reasonable to conclude that she had placed the guns in her purse before the car was stopped by police, the facts strongly suggest that Jane Doe was not the only person able to exercise dominion over them. The two guns were too large to be concealed in her handbag. The bag was consequently open, and part of one of the guns was in plain view, within easy access of the driver of the car and even, perhaps, of the other two respondents who were riding in the rear seat.

Moreover, it is highly improbable that the loaded guns belonged to Jane Doe or that she was solely responsible for their being in her purse. As a 16–year–old girl in the company of three adult men she was the least likely of the four to be carrying one, let alone two, heavy handguns. It is

who occupied the automobile at the time when such instruments were found. The presumption or presumptions is effective only so long as there is no substantial evidence contradicting the conclusion flowing from the presumption, and the presumption is said to disappear when such contradictory evidence is adduced."

"The presumption or presumptions which I discussed with the jury relative to the drugs or weapons in this case need not be rebutted by affirmative proof or affirmative evidence but may be rebutted by any evidence or lack of evidence in the case."

far more probable that she relied on the pocketknife found in her brassiere for any necessary self-protection. Under these circumstances, it was not unreasonable for her counsel to argue and for the jury to infer that when the car was halted for speeding, the other passengers in the car anticipated the risk of a search and attempted to conceal their weapons in a pocketbook in the front seat. The inference is surely more likely than the notion that these weapons were the sole property of the 16-year-old girl.

Under these circumstances, the jury would have been entirely reasonable in rejecting the suggestion—which, incidentally, defense counsel did not even advance in their closing arguments to the jury—that the handguns were in the sole possession of Jane Doe. Assuming that the jury did reject it, the case is tantamount to one in which the guns were lying on the floor or the seat of the car in the plain view of the three other occupants of the automobile. In such a case, it is surely rational to infer that each of the respondents was fully aware of the presence of the guns and had both the ability and the intent to exercise dominion and control over the weapons. The application of the statutory presumption in this case therefore comports with the standard laid down in *Tot v. United States,* 319 U.S. 463, 63 S.Ct. 1241, 87 L.Ed.2d 1519, and restated in *Leary v. United States,* 395 U.S. 6, 89 S.Ct. 1532, 23 L.Ed.2d 57. For there is a "rational connection" between the basic facts that the prosecution proved and the ultimate fact presumed, and the latter is "more likely than not to flow from" the former.

Respondents argue, however, that the validity of the New York presumption must be judged by a "reasonable doubt" test rather than the "more likely than not" standard employed in *Leary.* Under the more stringent test, it is argued that a statutory presumption must be rejected un-

less the evidence necessary to invoke the inference is sufficient for a rational jury to find the inferred fact beyond a reasonable doubt. Respondents' argument again overlooks the distinction between a permissive presumption on which the prosecution is entitled to rely as one not necessarily sufficient part of its proof and a mandatory presumption which the jury must accept even if it is the sole evidence of an element of the offense.

In the latter situation, since the prosecution bears the burden of establishing guilt, it may not rest its case entirely on a presumption unless the fact proved is sufficient to support the inference of guilt beyond a reasonable doubt. But in the former situation, the prosecution may rely on all of the evidence in the record to meet the reasonable-doubt standard. There is no more reason to require a permissive statutory presumption to meet a reasonable-doubt standard before it may be permitted to play any part in a trial than there is to require that degree of probative force for other relevant evidence before it may be admitted. As long as it is clear that the presumption is not the sole and sufficient basis for a finding of guilt, it need only satisfy the test described in *Leary.*

The permissive presumption, as used in this case, satisfied the *Leary* test. And, as already noted, the New York Court of Appeals has concluded that the record as a whole was sufficient to establish guilt beyond a reasonable doubt.

The judgment is reversed.

Mr. Chief Justice Burger, concurring.

I join fully in the Court's opinion reversing the judgment under review. In the necessarily detailed step-by-step analysis of the legal issues, the central and controlling facts of a case often can become lost. The "underbrush" of finely tuned legal analysis of complex issues tends to bury the facts.

On this record, the jury could readily have reached the same result without benefit of the challenged statutory presumption; here it reached what was rather obviously a compromise verdict. Even without relying on evidence that two people had been seen placing something in the car trunk shortly before respondents occupied it, and that a machinegun and a package of heroin were soon after found in that trunk, the jury apparently decided that it was enough to hold the passengers to knowledge of the two handguns which were in such plain view that the officer could see them from outside the car. Reasonable jurors could reasonably find that what the officer could see from outside, the passengers within the car could hardly miss seeing. Courts have long held that in the practical business of deciding cases the factfinders, not unlike negotiators, are permitted the luxury of verdicts reached by compromise.

MR. JUSTICE POWELL, with whom MR. JUSTICE BRENNAN, MR. JUSTICE STEWART and MR. JUSTICE MARSHALL join, dissenting. * * *

In sum, our decisions uniformly have recognized that due process requires more than merely that the prosecution be put to its proof. In addition, the Constitution restricts the court in its charge to the jury by requiring that, when particular factual inferences are recommended to the jury, those factual inferences be accurate reflections of what history, common sense, and experience tell us about the relations between events in our society. Generally, this due process rule has been articulated as requiring that the truth of the inferred fact be more likely than not whenever the premise for the inference is true. Thus, to be constitutional a presumption must be at least more likely than not true. * * *

Undeniably, the presumption charged in this case encouraged the jury to draw a particular factual inference regardless of any other evidence presented: to infer that respondents possessed the weapons found in the automobile "upon proof of the presence of the machine gun and the hand weapon" and proof that respondents "occupied the automobile at the time such instruments were found." I believe that the presumption thus charged was unconstitutional because it did not fairly reflect what common sense and experience tell us about passengers in automobiles and the possession of handguns. People present in automobiles where there are weapons simply are not "more likely than not" the possessors of those weapons.

Under New York law, "to possess" is "to have physical possession or otherwise to exercise dominion or control over tangible property." N.Y.Penal Law § 10.00(8). Plainly, the mere presence of an individual in an automobile—without more—does not indicate that he exercises "dominion or control over" everything within it. As the Court of Appeals noted, there are countless situations in which individuals are invited as guests into vehicles the contents of which they know nothing about, much less have control over. Similarly, those who invite others into their automobile do not generally search them to determine what they may have on their person; nor do they insist that any handguns be identified and placed within reach of the occupants of the automobile. Indeed, handguns are particularly susceptible to concealment and therefore are less likely than are other objects to be observed by those in an automobile.

In another context, this Court has been particularly hesitant to infer possession from mere presence in a location, noting that "[p]resence is relevant and admissible evidence in a trial on a possession charge; but absent some showing of the defendant's function at the [illegal] still, its connection with possession is too tenuous to permit a reasonable inference of guilt— 'the inference of the one from proof of the other is arbitrary * * *.' *Tot v. United States,* 319 U.S. 463, 467, 63 S.Ct. 1241, 1245, 87 L.Ed.2d 1519." *United States v. Romano.*ᵃ We should be even more hesitant to uphold the inference of possession of a handgun from mere presence in an automobile, in light of common experience concerning automobiles and handguns. Because the specific factual inference recommended to the jury in this case is not one that is supported by the general experience of our society, I cannot say that the presumption charged is "more likely than not" to be true. Accordingly, respondents' due process rights were violated by the presumption's use.

As I understand it, the Court today does not contend that in general those who are present in automobiles are more likely than not to possess any gun contained within their vehicles. It argues, however, that the nature of the presumption here involved requires that we look, not only to the immediate facts upon which the jury was encouraged to base its inference, but to the other facts "proved" by the prosecution as well. The Court suggests that

a. 382 U.S. 136, 86 S.Ct. 279, 15 L.Ed.2d 210 (1965), where the defendant, found within a few feet of a still, was convicted of being in "possession, custody and control" of an illegal still. 26 U.S.C. § 5601(b)(1) provides that presence at the site of an illegal still "shall be deemed sufficient evidence to authorize conviction, unless the defendant explains such presence to the satisfaction of the jury." The Court, distinguishing *United States v. Gainey,* 380 U.S. 63, 85 S.Ct. 754, 13 L.Ed.2d 658 (1965) (upholding a provision that such presence suffices to prove the offense of carrying on a distilling business), reversed:

"Presence at an operating still is sufficient evidence to prove the charge of 'carrying on' because anyone present at the site is very probably connected with the illegal enterprise. Whatever his job may be, he is at the very least aiding and abetting the substantive crime of carrying on the illegal distilling business. Section 5601(a)(1), however, proscribes possession, custody or control. This is only one of the various aspects of the total undertaking, many of which have nothing at all to do with possession * * *. Presence tells us only that the defendant was there and very likely played a part in the illicit scheme.

this is the proper approach when reviewing what it calls "permissive" presumptions because the jury was urged "to consider all the circumstances tending to support or contradict the inference."

It seems to me that the Court mischaracterizes the function of the presumption charged in this case. As it acknowledges was the case in *Romano, supra,* the "instruction authorized conviction even if the jury disbelieved all of the testimony except the proof of presence" in the automobile.[7] The Court nevertheless relies on all of the evidence introduced by the prosecution and argues that the "permissive" presumption could not have prejudiced defendants. The possibility that the jury disbelieved all of this evidence, and relied on the presumption, is simply ignored.

I agree that the circumstances relied upon by the Court in determining the plausibility of the presumption charged in this case would have made it reasonable for the jury to "infer that each of the respondents was fully aware of the presence of the guns and had both the ability and the intent to exercise dominion and control over the

But presence tells us nothing about what the defendant's specific function was and carries no legitimate, rational or reasonable inference that he was engaged in one of the specialized functions connected with possession, rather than in one of the supply, delivery or operational activities having nothing to do with possession."

7. In commending the presumption to the jury, the court gave no instruction that would have required a finding of possession to be based on anything more than mere presence in the automobile. Thus, the jury was not instructed that it should infer that respondents possessed the handguns only if it found that the guns were too large to be concealed in Jane Doe's handbag; that the guns accordingly were in the plain view of respondents, *ibid.*; that the weapons were within "easy access of the driver of the car and even, perhaps, of the other two respondents who were riding in the rear seat"; that it was unlikely that Jane Doe was solely responsible for the placement of the weapons in her purse; or that the case was "tantamount to one in which the guns were lying on the floor or the seat of the car in the plain view of the three other occupants of the automobile."

weapons." But the jury was told that it could conclude that respondents possessed the weapons found therein from proof of the mere fact of respondents' presence in the automobile. For all we know, the jury rejected all of the prosecution's evidence concerning the location and origin of the guns, and based its conclusion that respondents possessed the weapons solely upon its belief that respondents had been present in the automobile.[8] For purposes of reviewing the constitutionality of the presumption at issue here, we must assume that this was the case. * * *

In sum, it seems to me that the Court today ignores the teaching of our prior decisions. By speculating about what the jury may have done with the factual inference thrust upon it, the Court in effect assumes away the inference altogether, constructing a rule that permits the use of any inference—no matter how irrational in itself—provided that otherwise there is sufficient evidence in the record to support a finding of guilt. Applying this novel analysis to the present case, the Court upholds the use of a presumption that it makes no effort to defend in isolation. In substance, the Court—applying an unarticulated harmless-error standard—simply finds that the respondents were guilty as charged. They may well have been but rather than acknowledging this rationale, the Court seems to have made new law with respect to presumptions that could seriously jeopardize a defendant's right to a fair trial. Accordingly, I dissent.

8. The Court is therefore mistaken in its conclusion that, because "respondents were not 'hitchhikers or other casual passengers,' and the guns were neither 'a few inches in length' nor 'out of [respondents'] sight,'" reference to these possibilities is inappropriate in considering the constitutionality of the presumption as charged in this case. To be sure, respondents' challenge is to the presumption as charged to the jury in this case. But in assessing its application here,

Notes and Questions

1. Saltzburg, *Burdens of Persuasion in Criminal Cases: Harmonizing the Views of the Justices,* 20 Am.Crim.L.Rev. 393, 418–19 (1983): "The majority and the dissent differ more in their reading of what the trial judge did than in their approach to presumptions and inferences. Both appear to have examined exactly what the trial judge said and to have asked whether it was a fair statement of what the evidence actually offered could be said to have proved.

"Had the trial judge said to the jury, 'If you believe that the defendants were in the car and weapons were in open view, you could reason from this that the defendants were jointly in possession of the weapons; but this is not the only way to view the evidence, and the important thing is that you must believe beyond a reasonable doubt that a defendant possessed the weapons before voting to convict the defendant,' the entire Court might have viewed this as a fair statement of a possible way of looking at the evidence. Alternatively, had the trial judge said to the jury, 'If you believe that the defendants were in the car where weapons were found, this is sufficient for you to convict them of possession, unless there is some adequate explanation for the defendants' presence,' all members of the Court might have agreed that this statement overstated the significance of evidence of presence in the car, and that the instruction may have produced a conviction for the wrong reason because the jury may have believed the judge was saying that as a matter of law

we are not free, as the Court apparently believes, to disregard the possibility that the jury may have disbelieved all other evidence supporting an inference of possession. The jury may have concluded that respondents—like hitchhikers—had only an incidental relationship to the auto in which they were traveling, or that, contrary to some of the testimony at trial, the weapons were indeed out of respondents' sight.

the evidence proved guilt unless some explanation for presence was present.

"Both opinions in *Allen* support the first principle identified above, which complements *Mullaney* and *Patterson*. The government may not evade its responsibility to prove guilt of the offense it charges by relying on a judicial comment that goes beyond a fair assessment of the proof actually presented. In other words, the government may not prove guilt by having a judge tell a jury that something has been proved when it has not. The proof must be evident in the record, and any instruction may not go beyond the proof offered."

2. Allen & DeGrazia, *The Constitutional Requirement of Proof Beyond a Reasonable Doubt in Criminal Cases: A Comment Upon Incipient Chaos in the Lower Courts,* 20 Am. Crim.L.Rev. 1, 11 (1983): "One result of the *Ulster* Court's heavy emphasis on the evidence adduced at trial appears to be to transform the analysis of the instructions into a harmless error analysis. * * * A harmless error standard that looks heavily to the facts in the record can permit an instruction to be upheld, and a conviction affirmed, primarily on the basis of facts that a jury did not believe beyond reasonable doubt. The effect is to undercut both the right to a jury trial and the reasonable doubt standard."

SECTION 3. OMISSIONS

STATE v. WILLIQUETTE

Supreme Court of Wisconsin, 1986.
129 Wis.2d 239, 385 N.W.2d 145.

STEINMETZ, JUSTICE.

The issue in the case is whether a parent who allegedly knew her husband had re-

1. Sec. 940.201, Stats., provides as follows:

"**940.201 Abuse of children.** Whoever tortures a child or subjects a child to cruel maltreatment, including, but not limited, to severe bruising, lacerations, fractured bones, burns, internal

peatedly abused her two children both physically and sexually, but who took no action to stop the abuse and instead left the children in the father's sole physical custody for hours at a time, can be tried for the direct commission of the crime of child abuse under sec. 940.201, Stats.[1]

* * *

In a criminal complaint issued on November 15, 1983, Terri Williquette, the defendant, was charged with two counts of child abuse, contrary to sec. 940.201, Stats. Count one was based on the defendant's alleged failure to take any action to prevent her husband, Bert Williquette, from repeatedly "sexually abusing, beating, and otherwise mistreating" her seven year old son, B.W. Count two was based on the defendant's alleged failure to take any action to prevent her husband from committing similar acts against the defendant's eight year old daughter, C.P.

* * *

On June 6, 1984, the defendant filed a motion to dismiss the information. She claimed that she could not be charged with child abuse because she did not directly commit the abusive conduct. The circuit court granted the motion to dismiss. The court concluded that sec. 940.201, Stats., applies only to the intentional acts of a defendant who directly abuses a child. Accordingly, the mother's alleged failure to take any action to prevent her husband from abusing the children was not covered by the statute. * * *

The parties disagree as to whether sec. 940.201, Stats., requires a person to directly inflict child abuse in order to violate the statute. The defendant contends that the legislature intended the statute to apply only to persons who directly abuse children. She maintains that the statute

injuries or any injury constituting great bodily harm under s. 939.22(14) is guilty of a Class E felony. In this section, 'child' means a person under 16 years of age."

does not impose a duty on her to protect her own children from abuse. The state, however, argues that the statute is susceptible to an interpretation which includes persons having a special relationship to children who expose them to abuse. The state relies on the statutory language "subjects a child to cruel maltreatment." The state urges the court to construe this language to cover situations in which a parent knowingly exposes a child to abuse by placing the child in a situation where abuse has occurred and is likely to recur. * * *

There is no statutory definition of "subjects" in sec. 940.201, Stats. We therefore turn to standard dictionary definitions for guidance. Webster's Third New International Dictionary (1967) defines "subject" when used as a verb to mean: "a: to bring under control or dominion * * * b. to reduce to subservience or submission * * * 2a: to make liable * * * 4: to cause to undergo or submit to: make submit to a particular action or effect: expose." * * *

We conclude that the ordinary and accepted meaning of "subjects" does not limit the application of sec. 940.201, Stats., only to persons who actively participate in abusing children. The common meaning of "subjects" is broader than directly inflicting abuse on children. It covers situations in which a person with a duty toward a child exposes the child to a foreseeable risk of abuse. * * *

A person exposes a child to abuse when he or she causes the child to come within the influence of a foreseeable risk of cruel maltreatment. * * * In this case, Bert Williquette's conduct obviously was a direct cause of the abuse his children suffered. However, the defendant's alleged conduct, as the mother of the children, also was a contributing cause of risk to the children. She allegedly knew that the father abused the children in her absence,

but she continued to leave the children and to entrust them to his exclusive care, and she allegedly did nothing else to prevent the abuse, such as notifying proper authorities or providing alternative child care in her absence. We conclude that the defendant's conduct, as alleged, constituted a substantial factor which increased the risk of further abuse. * * *

The court also expressly rejects the defendant's claim that an act of commission, rather than omission, is a necessary element of a crime. The essence of criminal conduct is the requirement of a wrongful "act." This element, however, is satisfied by overt acts, as well as omissions to act where there is a legal duty to act. LaFave and Scott, *Criminal Law* sec. 26 at 182, states the general rule applicable to omissions:

"Some statutory crimes are specifically defined in terms of omission to act. With other common law and statutory crimes which are defined in terms of conduct producing a specified result, a person may be criminally liable when his omission to act produces that result, but only if (1) he has, under the circumstances, a legal duty to act, and (2) he can physically perform the act. The trend of the law has been toward enlarging the scope of duty to act."

The comments to this section then state the traditional rule that a person generally has no duty to rescue or protect an endangered person unless a special relationship exists between the persons which imposes a legal duty to protect:

"For criminal liability to be based upon a failure to act it must first be found that there is a duty to act—a legal duty and not simply a moral duty. As we have seen, some criminal statutes themselves impose the legal duty to act, as with the tax statute and the hit-and-run statute. With other crimes the duty must be found outside the definition of the crime itself—perhaps in another statute, or in the common law, or in a contract.

"Generally one has no legal duty to aid another person in peril, even when that aid can be rendered without danger or inconvenience to himself. He need not shout a warning to a blind man headed for a precipice or to an absentminded one walking into a gunpowder room with a lighted candle in hand. He need not pull a neighbor's baby out of a pool of water or rescue an unconscious person stretched across the railroad tracks, though the baby is drowning or the whistle of an approaching train is heard in the distance. A doctor is not legally bound to answer a desperate call from the frantic parents of a sick child, at least if it is not one of his regular patients. A moral duty to take affirmative action is not enough to impose a legal duty to do so. But there are situations which do give rise to a duty to act:

"(1) *Duty based upon relationship.* The common law imposes affirmative duties upon persons standing in certain personal relationships to other persons—upon parents to aid their small children, upon husbands to aid their wives, upon ship captains to aid their crews, upon masters to aid their servants. Thus a parent may be guilty of criminal homicide for failure to call a doctor for his sick child, a mother for failure to prevent the fatal beating of her baby by her lover, a husband for failure to aid his imperiled wife, a ship captain for failure to pick up a seaman or passenger fallen overboard, and an employer for failure to aid his endangered employee. Action may be required to thwart the threatened perils of nature (*e.g.,* to combat sickness, to ward off starvation or the elements); or it may be required to protect against threatened acts by third persons."

The requirement of a legal duty to act is a policy limitation which prevents most omissions from being considered the proximate cause of a prohibited consequence. In a technical sense, a person's omission, *i.e.,* whether the person fails to protect, warn or rescue, may be a substantial factor in exposing another person to harm. The concept of causation, however, is not solely a question of mechanical connection between events, but also a question of policy. A particular legal cause must be one of which the law will take cognizance. The rule that persons do not have a general duty to protect represents a public policy choice to limit criminal liability.

The requirement of an overt act, therefore, is not inherently necessary for criminal liability. Criminal liability depends on conduct which is a substantial factor in producing consequences. Omissions are as capable of producing consequences as overt acts. Thus, the common law rule that there is no general duty to protect limits criminal liability where it would otherwise exist. The special relationship exception to the "no duty to act" rule represents a choice to retain liability for some omissions, which are considered morally unacceptable. * * *

We next address the scope of the "legal duty" exception to the rule regarding criminal liability for omissions. Like most jurisdictions, Wisconsin generally does not require a person to protect others from hazardous situations. When a special relationship exists between persons, however, social policy may impose a duty to protect. The relationship between a parent and a child exemplifies a special relationship where the duty to protect is imposed. We stated the rule applicable to the parent and child relationship in *Cole v. Sears, Roebuck & Co.,* 47 Wis.2d 629, 634, 177 N.W.2d 866 (1970):

" 'It is the right and duty of parents under the law of nature as well as the common law and the statutes of many states to protect their children, to care for them in sickness and in health, and to do whatever may be necessary for their care, maintenance, and preservation, including medical attendance, if necessary. An omission to do this is a public wrong which the state, under its police powers, may prevent. The child has the right to call upon the parent for the discharge of this duty, and public policy for the good of society will not permit or allow the parent to divest himself irrevocably of his obligations in this regard or to abandon them at his mere will or pleasure. . . . '"

From the above discussion, we conclude that a parent who fails to take any action to stop instances of child abuse can be prosecuted as a principal for exposing the child to the abuse, contrary to sec. 940.201, Stats. Consistent with the common law rule, however, we do not hold that all persons, regardless of their relationship or lack of relationship to an abused child, violate the child abuse statute by failing to take remedial action to protect the child. Finally, when liability under sec. 940.201, depends on a breach of the parent's duty to protect, the parent must knowingly act in disregard of the facts giving rise to a duty to act. The "knowingly" requirement is necessary for a breach of the parent's duty to protect; it is not imposed as an element of sec. 940.201. * * *

The enactment of sec. 940.34, Stats.,[6] subsequent to the commencement of this

prosecution also does not indicate that the defendant was previously immune from criminal liability for her conduct. Section 940.34 is a "Good Samaritan" law which imposes criminal liability on "[a]ny person who knows that a crime is being committed and that a victim is exposed to bodily harm" but fails to summon help or provide assistance to the victim. The new statute does not deny the prior existence of a parent's duty to protect. We acknowledge that a parent now could be charged under either statute. Section 939.65, however, provides that if an act forms the basis for a crime punishable under more than one statutory provision, then the state can prosecute under any or all such provisions.

* * *

HEFFERNAN, CHIEF JUSTICE (dissenting). * * *

The majority correctly asserts the criminal conduct can be predicated upon the failure to act when action is required by law. The problem is that nothing in the statutes remotely suggests that a parent has the legislatively prescribed legal duty to act in the instant circumstances or that the omission of the alleged duty will result in criminal sanctions. Certainly, I agree with the majority who, after reciting the catalog of horrors perpetrated upon these children, asserts, citing *Cole v. Sears, Roebuck & Co.*:

> "An omission to do this [care for and protect children] is a public wrong which the state, under its police powers, may prevent."

"(b) Compliance would interfere with duties the person owes to others.

"(c) Assistance is being summoned or provided by others.

"(3) If a person renders emergency care for a victim, s. 895.48 applies. Any person who provides other reasonable assistance under this section is immune from civil liability for his or her acts or omissions in providing the assistance. This immunity does not apply if the person receives or expects to receive compensation for providing the assistance."

---

6. Sec. 940.34, Stats., provides as follows:

"940.34 Duty to aid endangered crime victim. (1) Whoever violates sub. (2) is guilty of a Class C misdemeanor.

"(2) Any person who knows that a crime is being committed and that a victim is exposed to bodily harm shall summon law enforcement officers or other assistance or shall provide assistance to the victim. A person need not comply with this subsection if any of the following apply:

"(a) Compliance would place him or her in danger.

The problem with this position is that it begs the question. Of course, the state has the police powers which may be exercised for that very purpose. The omission can be categorized as a public wrong which the legislature *may* prevent. But the police power is a power of the legislature. It is not an independent power conferred upon courts. Courts may validate a legislature's conduct by recognizing the legislature's police power, but courts cannot supply that exercise of power where there is no evidence that the legislature so intended to act.

We return to the fundamental defect in the position of the state. There is no evidence that the legislature intended to exercise its police power in the manner urged here. I reiterate, if it desired to do so, the appropriate statutory language was not beyond the capabilities of the legislature. * * *

One real problem revealed here is that the court does not have the investigative facilities to decide what ought to be done in a broad spectrum of cases involving child abuse. We do not have the legislature's fact-finding process to justify our determination of what the criminal law should be. We are assuming, without being sure, that the legislature, had it confronted the problem posed here, would have concluded, as the majority guesses it would have concluded, that the conduct of Terri Williquette was just as culpable as that of her husband, who was overtly and cruelly sodomizing and torturing the children. While that assumption could be correct, it is not an assumption that a court should make. We do not know how the legislature would have treated the present facts. Nor do we have the authority as a court to reach that conclusion. We are not the branch of the government that has been designated by the constitution to determine what conduct is criminal. Yet, in this case, we come forward with our own definition of criminality. While to do so

may give the proponents of this court-made legislation a self-satisfied glow of rectitude, in reality we are by this opinion usurping the legislative prerogative to make the criminal law. While we have responsibilities in the formulation of the common law, the wise sages of our jurisprudence have long recognized that, unless conduct is clearly and unequivocally declared to be criminal by the legislature, a court should restrain itself—even from the impulse to do what it believes to be morally justified. * * *

Notes and Questions

1. Considering the principles discussed in *Williquette,* did the court err in *Commonwealth v. Konz,* 498 Pa. 639, 450 A.2d 638 (1982), in reversing the conviction of Mrs. Konz and Erikson for involuntary manslaughter (causing death by reckless conduct) on the following facts?

"Reverend Konz was a thirty-four year old diabetic and had, for seventeen years, administered to himself daily doses of insulin. On March 4, 1974, however, following an encounter on campus with a visiting evangelist speaker, Reverend Konz publicly proclaimed his desire to discontinue insulin treatment in reliance on the belief that God would heal the diabetic condition. He assured the president of the College and members of the student body that he would carefully monitor his condition and would, if necessary, take insulin. On only one or two occasions did the Reverend thereafter administer insulin. On March 18, 1974, however, Erikson and Reverend Konz formed a pact to pray together to enable the latter to resist the temptation to administer insulin.

"Mrs. Konz was informed of the prayer pact, and, on the morning of Saturday, March 23, 1974, when her husband evidenced symptoms of insulin debt, she removed his insulin from the refrigerator and concealed it.[2]   Later that day, the Reverend attempted to obtain insulin from the refrigerator, and, upon discovering that the medicine had been removed, strongly indicated that it should be returned.   He then attempted to proceed from room to room but his passage was blocked by Erikson.   Harsh words were exchanged, and Erikson, after kneeling in prayer, forced the Reverend into a bedroom where, accompanied by Mrs. Konz, Erikson and the Reverend conversed for approximately one half hour.   During that time, the Reverend tried to telephone police to obtain assistance but was prevented from doing so by Erikson and Mrs. Konz, who, during a struggle with the Reverend, rendered at least that telephone permanently inoperable.[3]   Immediately after this confrontation, the Reverend, his wife, and Erikson returned amicably to the kitchen for coffee, and no further request for insulin was ever made.   In addition, the Reverend approached his aunt who resided in the same household and stated, in an apparent reference to the preceding confrontation with Erikson, that 'It's all settled now,' and told her that there was no cause for concern.   He also told his eleven year old daughter that 'Everything is fine,' and indicated to her that he did not intend to take insulin.   The Reverend then departed from the house, accompanied by Erikson, and returned an hour later.   As the day progressed, Reverend Konz cancelled his speaking commitment for the following day and drove his wife to an institution having hospital facilities to pick up a close friend who was a practical nurse.   Late on Saturday night, while waiting inside the institution for the nurse to complete her duties, the Reverend appeared very fatigued and complained that he was developing an upset stomach.   Both of these conditions were symptomatic of lack of insulin, but neither the Reverend nor his wife requested that insulin, which was available at the institution, be administered.   With regard to the Reverend's condition at that time, the nurse observed that he travelled with unimpaired mobility, and that he was conversant, rational, and cognizant of his environs.   Nevertheless, he made no mention of a need for insulin, and the nurse made no inquiry as to such a need because the Reverend had on a previous day become very upset at her inquiry as to his diabetic condition.

"Upon returning home from this errand, Reverend Konz experienced increasing illness, vomiting intermittently Saturday night and Sunday morning, and remained in bed all day Sunday except for trips into the bathroom.   On Sunday afternoon visitors arrived at the Konz residence.   The Reverend, recognizing their voices, called to them from his room to inquire whether they wished to see him; having been informed of the Reverend's nausea, however, the visitors declined to stay.   As the Reverend's condition worsened and he became restless, his wife and Erikson administered cracked ice but did not summon medical aid.   The Konz's eleven year old daughter then inquired as to why a doctor had not been summoned but Mrs. Konz responded that her husband was 'going to be getting better.'   Late Sunday night or early Monday morning everyone in the household fell asleep.   On Monday morning at approximately 6 AM, while the others were still asleep, Reverend Konz died of diabetic ketoacidosis."

2.   In *State v. Tennant,* ___ W.Va. ___, 319 S.E.2d 395 (1984), the defendant, convicted under a hit-and-run statute requiring that the "driver of any vehicle involved in an accident resulting in injury shall immediately stop such vehicle" and identify himself and give aid, successfully argued on appeal that the jury should have

---

2.   The insulin was returned to the refrigerator sometime prior to Sunday night.

3.   There was testimony as to the existence of two telephones in the residence.

been instructed that the defendant must have known of the accident. "A commonly given reason for this interpretation is summarized in [a case] where the Alaska Supreme Court concluded: '[W]e cannot believe that the legislature could have intended that persons who unknowingly fail to stop and render assistance could be subject to serious criminal penalties.' Similarly, the Virginia Supreme Court stated:

'The duty imposed upon the driver of a vehicle involved in an accident is not passive. It requires positive, affirmative action; that is, to stop and give the aid and information specified.

'How can a person perform these affirmative acts unless he knows that his vehicle has struck a person or an object? Knowledge necessarily is an essential element of the crime.' "

3. In *United States v. Spingola,* 464 F.2d 909 (7th Cir.1972), the defendant, secretary-treasurer of a trade union, was convicted on three counts of failing to file timely annual financial reports for the fiscal years 1966, 1967 and 1968 on behalf of the union. The trial court excluded evidence by which the defendant sought to show that the late filings were due to the inability of the union's office staff to bring its accounting records up to date, as was necessary in order to prepare the reports, that the needed records were in the possession of the government for extended periods, and that he was unable to complete the reports by himself. In reversing, the court of appeals noted that defendant's defense "is perhaps best characterized as the defense of physical impossibility—that, while the law imposed upon him a duty to file the annual financial report of his union, he possessed neither the sophistication necessary to prepare it himself nor the ability to compel its timely preparation by others. Genuine impossibility is a proper defense to a crime of omission."

4. In *Davis v. Commonwealth,* 230 Va. 201, 335 S.E.2d 375 (1985), the defendant was convicted of involuntary manslaughter on a finding that the death of her senile and disabled mother, Emily Carter, resulted from defendant's failure to provide heat, food, liquids and other necessities. In response to defendant's claim on appeal that she violated "at most a moral duty," the court stated: "The evidence makes clear that Davis accepted sole responsibility for the total care of Carter. This became her full-time occupation. In return, Carter allowed Davis to live in her home expense free and shared with Davis her income from social security. Additionally, Carter authorized Davis to act as her food stamp representative, and for this Davis received food stamp benefits in her own right. From this uncontroverted evidence, the trial court reasonably could find the existence of an implied contract. Clearly, Davis was more than a mere volunteer; she had a legal duty, not merely a moral one, to care for her mother."

5. In *Commonwealth v. Cali,* 247 Mass. 20, 141 N.E. 510 (1923), the defendant was convicted of having burned a building with intent to injure the insurer. The defendant's testimony was that he started the fire accidentally. The trial judge instructed the jury that if that was so but the defendant thereafter, with the requisite intent, failed to extinguish the fire though it was within his power to do so, he could be convicted. On appeal, the court held the instruction was proper.

6. In *State v. Harrison,* 107 N.J.L. 213, 152 A. 867 (1931), defendant was employed by a railroad as a crossing gateman. The defendant failed to lower the crossing gate when he was warned of the approach of a train, as a result of which Goble drove onto the tracks with his car and was struck and killed by the train. On appeal, the defendant's conviction of manslaughter was affirmed. "Certainly such failure of

duty justified a finding of gross negligence."

R. Moreland, *Law of Homicide* 177 (1952), observes: "The decision in the *Harrison* Case has been vigorously criticized in a note. It is argued that in many of the cases where an omission to act has been punished there has been a helplessness created as a result of the contract that would not have resulted but for the agreement. Thus, passengers on an excursion steamer are lulled into a sense of security by their belief that the master of the boat and regularly appointed inspectors have carried out their contractual duties to inspect life-preservers and life-boats. In fact, most of them would not dare take such a trip except for the known fact that such equipment is supposed to be checked and inspected. They are helpless if the contracts are not carried out."

7. In *Moreland v. State,* 164 Ga. 467, 139 S.E. 77 (1927), the defendant was convicted of manslaughter upon evidence showing that the defendant was a passenger in his car while his chauffeur drove at an excessive speed, causing an accident in which a person was killed. In affirming the conviction, the court stated: "It would be the owner's duty, when he saw that the law was being violated and that his machine was being operated in such a way as to be dangerous to the life and property of others on the highway, to curb and restrain one in his employment and under his control, and prevent him from violating the law with his own property."

8. Wehrwein, *'Samaritan' Law Poses Difficulties,* Nat'l L.J., Aug. 22, 1983, p. 5, col. 1: "Minnesota's new law that imposes a fine on bystanders who don't aid people in peril could pose some problems for prosecutors and insurance companies—if it is ever put to use. * * *

"The law, which took effect Aug. 1, requires a bystander to render 'reasonable assistance' during an emergency to anyone who is 'exposed to or has suffered grave physical harm.' The statute includes in its definition of reasonable assistance such acts as calling the police and getting medical help, but it does not require a bystander to do anything that involves 'danger or peril to himself or others.' * * *

"The bill's sponsor, Democratic state Rep. Randy Staten, said he was moved to introduce the bill by reports of the gang rape earlier this year of a woman in a New Bedford, Mass., barroom who was hoisted onto a pool table and repeatedly assaulted while spectators stood by and some reportedly shouted 'go for it!' More recently, a 14–year–old St. Louis girl was raped last month while bystanders did nothing for 40 minutes until an 11–year–old boy called police. Last week, Mr. Staten also cited this incident as an example of the kind of conduct his bill would prevent.

"The traditional common-law rule that a bystander has no duty to aid an endangered person would permit 'totally unacceptable conduct for civilized society,' Mr. Staten said. One example of such conduct, he said, would be an expert swimmer ignoring the plight of a drowning child. * * *

"France, the Netherlands, West Germany and other European countries impose the duty to assist in their criminal statutes and hold those who fail to render help civilly liable."

9. Schroeder, *Two Methods for Evaluating Duty to Rescue Proposals,* 49 Law & Contemp.Probs. 181, 192, 194 (1986): "The relative lack of causal cut-offs between failures to act and harms, as compared with those available in our normal understanding of actions, places tremendous pressure on the concept of 'reasonable expectations' within the definition of failures to act, because that limiting concept may be about all that will stand between us and legal responsibility for many, many harms that we could have prevented.

The usual hypotheticals enter in here to press our intuitions about whether that line can be held. As Richard Epstein questions, if a strong swimmer is legally liable for failure to make an easy rescue of a drowning infant in a swimming pool, will you be similarly liable for failure to donate $10 to African relief if you are substantially certain that that $10 will prevent a death through starvation? Similarly, as a note pinned recently to a bulletin board at Duke University Law School queried, if you make $45,000 per year as an entry level associate at a corporate law firm and can live securely on $20,000, are you legally answerable for the deaths of one hundred Africans, on the assumption that $250 per year would sustain a life indefinitely? Or, as someone asked in a penned response to the original note, if you go to work for legal services at $20,000 a year, but could have taken a job with a corporate law firm and then donated your surplus $25,000 to relief organizations, are you still culpable? * * *

"[W]hile it may be true that a firm, albeit somewhat arbitrary, line delimiting rescues to which a legal duty attaches would be superior to a legal regime wholly without such a duty * * *, it is nevertheless important to isolate those criteria that influence where that line ought to be drawn. These criteria serve at the least as counsel to a conscientious legislator, and also clarify what we actually believe separates the case involving the drowning child and the strong swimmer from the ten dollar charitable contribution. What functions, in other words, to make certain expectations about rescue reasonable to a degree that warrants legal sanction for a failure to rescue? * * *

"Some of those principles appear in the Vermont statute requiring easy rescue, which is often cited as a model. It reads:

A person who knows that another is exposed to grave physical harm shall, to the extent that the same can be rendered without danger or peril to himself or without interference with important duties owed to others, give reasonable assistance to the exposed person unless that assistance or care is being provided by others."

SECTION 4. ONE ACT OR RELATED ACTS AS A BASIS FOR MULTIPLE CHARGES, PROSECUTIONS AND SENTENCES

GORE v. UNITED STATES

Supreme Court of the United States, 1958.
357 U.S. 386, 78 S.Ct. 1280, 2 L.Ed.2d 1405.

MR. JUSTICE FRANKFURTER delivered the opinion of the Court.

This is a prosecution under an indictment containing six counts for narcotics offenses. Four counts were based on provisions of the Internal Revenue Code of 1954 and two counts on the Narcotic Drugs Import and Export Act, as amended. The first three counts derive from a sale on February 26, 1955, of twenty capsules of heroin and three capsules of cocaine; the last three counts derive from a sale of thirty-five capsules of heroin on February 28, 1955. Counts One and Four charged the sale of the drugs, on the respective dates, not "in pursuance of a written order" of the person to whom the drugs were sold on the requisite Treasury form, in violation of § 4705(a) of the Internal Revenue Code of 1954, 26 U.S.C.A. § 4705(a). Counts Two and Five charged the sale and distribution of the drugs on the respective dates not "in the original stamped package or from the original stamped package," in violation of § 4704(a) of the Internal Revenue Code of 1954, 26 U.S.C.A. § 4704(a). Counts Three and Six charged facilitating concealment and sale of the drugs on the respective dates, with knowledge that the drugs had been unlawfully imported, in violation of § 2(c) of the Narcotic Drugs Import and Export Act, as amended by the Act of November 2, 1951, 65 Stat. 767. In short, Congress had made three distinct offenses in connection with the vending of illicit drugs, and the petitioner, having violated these three independent provisions, was prosecuted for all three as separate wrongdoings, despite the fact that these violations of what Congress had proscribed were compendiously committed in single transactions of vending. Duly tried before a jury, petitioner was convicted, and no question touching the conviction is before us. In controversy is the legality of the sentences imposed by the trial court. These were imprisonment for a term of one to five years, imposed on each count, the sentences on the first three counts to run consecutively, the sentences on the remaining three counts to run concurrently with those on the first three counts. Thus the total sentence was three to fifteen years. Petitioner moved to vacate the sentence, claiming that for all three counts a sentence as for only one count could be imposed. The motion was denied and the Court of Appeals affirmed, with expressions of doubt by two of the judges, who felt themselves bound by *Blockburger v. United States,* 284 U.S. 299, 52 S.Ct. 180, 76 L.Ed. 306. We brought the case here, in order to consider whether some of our more recent decisions, while not questioning *Blockburger* but moving in related areas may not have impaired its authority.

We adhere to the decision in *Blockburger v. United States,* supra.[a] The considerations advanced in support of the vigorous attack against it have left its justification undisturbed, nor have our later decisions generated counter currents. * * *

We are strongly urged to reconsider *Blockburger* by reading the various specific enactments of Congress as reflecting a unitary congressional purpose to outlaw nonmedicinal sales of narcotics. From this the conclusion is sought to be drawn that since Congress had only a single purpose, no matter how numerous the violations by an offender, of the specific means for dealing with this unitary purpose, the desire should be attributed to Congress to punish only as for a single offense when these multiple infractions are committed through a single sale. We agree with the starting point, but it leads us to the opposite conclusion. Of course the various enactments by Congress extending over nearly half a century constitute a network of provisions, steadily tightened and enlarged, for grappling with a powerful, subtle and elusive enemy. If the legislation reveals anything, it reveals the determination of Congress to turn the screw of the criminal machinery— detection, prosecution and punishment— tighter and tighter. The three penal laws for which petitioner was convicted have different origins both in time and in design. * * * It seems more daring than convincing to suggest that three different enactments, each relating to a separate way of closing in on illicit distribution of narcotics, passed at three different periods, for each of which a separate punishment was declared by Congress, somehow or other ought to have carried with them an

a. In *Blockburger,* the Court adopted this rule: "A single act may be an offense against two statutes and if each statute requires proof of an additional fact which the other does not, an acquittal or conviction under either statute does not exempt the defendant from prosecution and punishment under the other."

Illustrative of *Blockburger* operating to the defendant's advantage is *Ball v. United States,* 470 U.S. 856, 105 S.Ct. 1668, 84 L.Ed.2d 740 (1985), where defendant was convicted of receipt of a firearm by a convicted felon and possession of the same firearm by a convicted felon. The Court held that while the prosecutor could prosecute simultaneously for those two offenses, the defendant could be convicted and sentenced on only one, as "it is clear that Congress did not intend to subject felons to two convictions; proof of illegal receipt of a firearm *necessarily* includes proof of illegal possession of that weapon."

implied indication by Congress that if all these three different restrictions were disregarded but, forsooth, in the course of one transaction, the defendant should be treated as though he committed only one of these offenses.

This situation is *toto coelo* different from the one that led to our decision in *Bell v. United States,* 349 U.S. 81, 75 S.Ct. 620, 99 L.Ed. 905. That case involved application of the Mann Act, 18 U.S.C.A. § 2421,—a single provision making it a crime to transport a woman in interstate commerce for purposes of prostitution. We held that the transportation of more than one woman as a single transaction is to be dealt with as a single offense, for the reason that when Congress has not explicitly stated what the unit of offense is, the doubt will be judicially resolved in favor of lenity. It is one thing for a single transaction to include several units relating to proscribed conduct under a single provision of a statute. It is a wholly different thing to evolve a rule of lenity for three violations of three separate offenses created by Congress at three different times, all to the end of dealing more and more strictly with, and seeking to throttle more and more by different legal devices, the traffic in narcotics. Both in the unfolding of the substantive provisions of law and in the scale of punishments, Congress has manifested an attitude not of lenity but of severity toward violation of the narcotics laws. * * *

Finally, we have had pressed upon us that the *Blockburger* doctrine offends the constitutional prohibition against double jeopardy. If there is anything to this claim it surely has long been disregarded in decisions of this Court, participated in by judges especially sensitive to the application of the historic safeguard of double jeopardy. In applying a provision like that of double jeopardy, which is rooted in history and is not an evolving concept like that of due process, a long course of adju-

dication in this Court carries impressive authority. Certainly if punishment for each of separate offenses as those for which the petitioner here has been sentenced, and not merely different descriptions of the same offense, is constitutionally beyond the power of Congress to impose, not only *Blockburger* but [many other] cases would also have to be overruled.

Suppose Congress, instead of enacting the three provisions before us, had passed an enactment substantially in this form: "Anyone who sells drugs except from the original stamped package and who sells such drugs not in pursuance of a written order of the person to whom the drug is sold, and who does so by way of facilitating the concealment and sale of drugs knowing the same to have been unlawfully imported, shall be sentenced to not less than fifteen years' imprisonment: *Provided, however,* That if he makes such sale in pursuance of a written order of the person to whom the drug is sold he shall be sentenced to only ten years' imprisonment: *Provided, further,* That if he sells such drugs in the original stamped package he shall also be sentenced to only ten years' imprisonment: *And provided further,* That if he sells such drugs in pursuance of a written order and from a stamped package, he shall be sentenced to only five years' imprisonment." Is it conceivable that such a statute would not be within the power of Congress? And is it rational to find such a statute constitutional but to strike down the *Blockburger* doctrine as violative of the double jeopardy clause?

In effect, we are asked to enter the domain of penology, and more particularly that tantalizing aspect of it, the proper apportionment of punishment. Whatever views may be entertained regarding severity of punishment, whether one believes in its efficacy or its futility, these are peculiarly questions of legislative policy. * * *

Affirmed.

MR. CHIEF JUSTICE WARREN, dissenting.

The problem of multiple punishment is a vexing and recurring one. It arises in one of two broad contexts: (a) a statute or a portion thereof proscribes designated conduct, and the question is whether the defendant's conduct constitutes more than one violation of this proscription. Thus, murdering two people simultaneously might well warrant two punishments but stealing two one-dollar bills might not. (b) Two statutes or two portions of a single statute proscribe certain conduct, and the question is whether the defendant can be punished twice because his conduct violates both proscriptions. Thus, selling liquor on a Sunday might warrant two punishments for violating a prohibition law and a blue law, but feloniously entering a bank and robbing a bank, though violative of two statutes, might warrant but a single punishment.

In every instance the problem is to ascertain what the legislature intended. Often the inquiry produces few if any enlightening results. Normally these are not problems that receive explicit legislative consideration. But this fact should not lead the judiciary, charged with the obligation of construing these statutes, to settle such questions by the easy application of stereotyped formulae. It is at the same time too easy and too arbitrary to apply a presumption for or against multiple punishment in all cases or even to do so one way in one class of cases and the other way in another. Placing a case in the category of unit-of-offense problems or the category of overlapping-statute problems may point up the issue, but it does not resolve it.

Where the legislature has failed to make its intention manifest, courts should proceed cautiously, remaining sensitive to the interests of defendant and society alike. All relevant criteria must be considered and the most useful aid will often be common sense. In this case I am persuaded, on the basis of the origins of the three statutes involved, the text and background of recent amendments to these statutes, the scale of punishments prescribed for second and third offenders, and the evident legislative purpose to achieve uniformity in sentences, that the present purpose of these statutes is to make sure that a prosecutor has three avenues by which to prosecute one who traffics in narcotics, and not to authorize three cumulative punishments for the defendant who consummates a single sale.

MR. JUSTICE DOUGLAS, with whom MR. JUSTICE BLACK concurs, dissenting.

* * *

MR. JUSTICE BRENNAN, dissenting.

* * *

Notes and Questions

1. Johnson, *Multiple Punishment and Consecutive Sentences: Reflections on the Neal Doctrine,* 58 Calif.L.Rev. 357, 359 (1970): "The *Gore* opinion is a classic example of arid technical reasoning devoid of any serious effort to justify the result in terms of a sensible sentencing policy. A court less eager to wring the last drop of harshness out of the statutory scheme could have concluded that Congress meant to punish all nonmedical sales of narcotics only once, and provided three statutes out of an excess of caution to ensure that an accused could not escape conviction altogether due to some technical failure in the proof. Yet if it is easy to criticize decisions like *Gore,* it is somewhat more difficult to formulate a doctrine that will properly measure a defendant's liability in the many and varied situations in which an issue of multiple punishment may be posed."

2. Note, 67 Yale L.J. 916, 928–31 (1958), after concluding that *Gore* "undermines the legislative objection to promote uniform sentencing procedure for narcot-

ics violators," continues: "In other contexts, a legislative intent to proscribe a course of conduct rather than its elements may not be readily discernible. Particularly will this be true of overlapping statutes obviously enacted without reference to one another. Indeed, investigation under these circumstances will most likely reveal no specific evidence of legislative intent. When confronted with a prosecution involving such unrelated offenses, the courts may have greatest success in divining legislative purpose if they consider the social norms vindicated by the relevant statutory provisions. Vindication of a single social norm should, consistent with the concept of lesser included offenses and the current adaptation of merger and consummation, be suggestive of an intent not to allow cumulative punishment. For example, assault with a deadly weapon and illegal possession of a firearm each assert society's interest in protection of the person; consequently, punishment geared to the graver rather than the sum of offenses should fulfill the community's penological objectives. In contrast, a single act which violates laws prohibiting Sunday sales and liquor sales to minors would be cumulatively punishable since one statute vindicates religious values and the other is directed toward protecting minors. The various objectives of criminal law—reformation, rehabilitation, retribution, isolation and deterrence—are also relevant in determining probable, but unexpressed, legislative design. For instance, if fragmentation would increase a forty-year maximum sentence to three hundred and sixty years, the more severe penalty is unlikely to serve any purpose not already fulfilled.[55] Acting in a context which limits punishment by the will of the body that defines crime, courts in multiple conviction cases should abandon automatic and inappropriate application of the same evidence test and focus on legislative intent instead."

IRBY v. UNITED STATES

United States Court of Appeals, District of Columbia Circuit, 1967.
390 F.2d 432.

McGOWAN, CIRCUIT JUDGE, with whom CIRCUIT JUDGES DANAHER, BURGER, and TAMM join:

In 1958 appellant, represented by counsel, pleaded guilty to the housebreaking and robbery counts of a 9–count indictment, and received consecutive sentences of two to eight years on the one, and four to twelve years on the other. The other counts were then dismissed. In 1965 he moved under 28 U.S.C. § 2255 to regain his liberty on the ground that the two sentences could not validly have been made to run consecutively. The District Court denied the motion in a long opinion which explored with care the single legal issue raised by the motion. Upon appeal, a panel of this court reversed, one judge dissenting. The Government's petition for rehearing en banc was granted; and, after rehearing, the District Court's judgment is herewith affirmed.

Because of the existence of District Judge (now Circuit Judge) Robinson's opinion referred to above, there is no occasion for us to cover the same ground in reaching the same result. He recognized, as this court has recently had occasion to do, that there are circumstances where it cannot safely be assumed that simply because the legislature has defined two separate crimes with differing elements and prescribed separate punishments for them, it contemplated that such punishments can be consecutively inflicted.

---

55. Under present narcotics laws, for example, a third offense may be punished by a no-parole sentence of forty years and a fine of $20,000. 70 Stat. 570 (1956), 21 U.S.C. § 174 (Supp. IV, 1957). Int.Rev.Code of 1954, § 7237. Thus, consecutive sentences could yield up to 360 years and fines totalling $180,000.

The nature of the two criminal specifications, and of the course of conduct in which both crimes may be thought to have been committed, may be such as to raise a doubt as to a legislative purpose to encompass both punishments. In such a case, an aid to the divination of such purpose in the form of a so-called "rule of lenity" has been devised to the end of barring double punishment where there is substantial doubt as to whether Congress would have intended it to be imposed. * * *

It is not novel that Congress has differentiated between housebreaking and robbery in terms of the one as an invasion of the security of the dwelling, and the other as an intrusion upon the security of the person. This was a distinction familiar to the common law, and it was perpetuated in the statutes found to have been violated here. Stealing something worth $1000 may be only an aggravation of the misdeed involved in stealing something worth $10. But taking something, whatever its worth, from another's person by force and putting in fear brings in a new and different interest which it has been thought important to protect, namely the person threatened as distinct from the property taken.

One who wrongfully goes into a house to pilfer what he can find may or may not start out with a purpose to rob, if necessary. If he consciously entertains both purposes from the beginning, it can be said that he sets out with an intent to commit both larceny and robbery, or

crimes against both property and person, if the opportunity presents itself. In such circumstances, he will be guilty of housebreaking in either event once he crosses the threshold, but, if he retires upon finding the house occupied and without robbing the occupant, he has made the decision which saves him from punishment for robbery. The point is, of course, that his invasion of the premises to steal does not irrevocably commit him to rob from the person of anyone he finds there. The choice is still his up to the moment of confrontation.[2] If he decided to rob, consecutive punishments are not made available solely as a means of exacting greater retribution. Congress could well have conceived of them as a deterrent to compromising the safety of the person as well as the security of the premises. They illuminate the differing dangers to society inherent in stealing what one finds in a vacant house, and robbing the occupant as well when he proves to be at home. We cannot, at any rate, say with confidence that Congress did not contemplate some additional disincentive for the latter.[3]

* * *

The judgment of the District Court is affirmed.

LEVENTHAL, CIRCUIT JUDGE (concurring):

I concur in the judgment, since I agree that it is possible that a combination at one scene of a housebreaking, with intent to

---

2. We do not think that the indictment can be characterized as asserting that appellant's course of conduct was motivated by a single criminal intent. In the housebreaking count, he was charged with entering a dwelling "with intent to steal property of another." In the robbery count, he was charged with taking two rings from the person and from the immediate possession of a named complainant "by force and violence and against resistance and by sudden and stealthy seizure and snatching and by putting in fear." The two are not the same, and they are fully consistent with either concurrent or consecutive criminal purposes of a different order. The Supreme Court has, of course, been alert to prohibit

double punishment for the commission of a federally-created crime and for the attempt to do so. See *Prince v. United States*, 352 U.S. 322, 77 S.Ct. 403, 1 L.Ed.2d 370 (1957).

3. The drafters of the American Law Institute's Model Penal Code were explicitly conscious of the unfairness involved in the imposition of "cumulative penalties * * * for entering with intent to steal and for stealing, although ordinarily attempt merges in the completed offense." Although proposing a burglary offense not essentially unlike our housebreaking statute, they added a ban on duplicate penalties in [§ 221.1].

commit larceny, and a robbery, may reflect sufficiently separate criminal purposes to permit consecutive punishment. While they may also, I think, be so integrated as to preclude consecutive punishment, that objection is one that should ordinarily be put forward when sentence is imposed, or timely in a motion to reduce the sentence. In any event, as will be indicated, I do not believe that appellant's pleading asserted the factual predicate necessary to sustain the conclusion that the "sentence was in excess of the maximum authorized by law." * * *

In the absence of other, specific legislative intention on the side of either lenity or harshness, we can only invoke a generalized legislative intent. This is more likely presumed than real, and embodies a large standard of reasonableness and fairness to offenders and society alike. The standard that best conforms to my estimate of a generalized legislative intention is this: A defendant guilty of a serious crime is subject to judgment of imprisonment. The sentencing judge is given latitude so that a heavier punishment will be appropriate for a crime that is aggravated in its particular facts. When the same act can be classified as different crimes, he may be punished with the most onerous penalty provided for the most extreme crime for which he was charged. But he is not to be given two or more consecutive punishments for what is essentially a single criminal episode—say a robbery, committed of course with intent to rob—merely because the law would also have punished him if he had stopped or been apprehended before completing the robbery, on the ground that his acts and intent constitute either an attempt to commit robbery or a substantive crime which is made punisha-

ble because it is a preliminary step taken with that ultimate intent.[4] * * *

[I]f a defendant breaks into a house at night for the purpose of relieving the bejeweled guests at a dinner party of material encumbrances, the robbery is indeed a heinous offense that should be severely punished. There is not merely a robbery, but a robbery aggravated by housebreaking. But in my view the defendant is not subject to consecutive punishment on the theory that there are consecutive crimes even though it is the same intention—intention to commit the felony of robbery—which makes a felony of his preliminary housebreaking as well as of the robbery that completes the sequence of the criminal episode.

If at the scene of the crime the defendant can be said to have realized that he has come to a fork in the road, and nevertheless decides to invade a different interest, then his successive intentions make him subject to cumulative punishment, and he must be treated as accepting that risk, whether he in fact knows of it or not. * * *

I think a rule that focuses on changes in the extent and direction of the defendant's criminal intention provides a basis for permitting cumulative punishment that is related to mens rea, and that this is sounder than a generalized approach that two or more consecutive punishments are proper for a single episode because criminality of the activity is established by more than one section of the code.

BAZELON, CHIEF JUDGE, with whom J. SKELLY WRIGHT, CIRCUIT JUDGE, concurs (dissenting):

There are two questions before us. The first is whether, in some cases, the D.C.

---

4. Of course if his housebreaking had a double objective and he, say, both raped and robbed the resident he could plainly be subject to consecutive punishment. If he completed the rape, and then fled before consummating the robbery, could he be sentenced consecutively for rape and for housebreaking with intent to commit robbery? My tentative view is yes, but it is unnecessary to ponder all possible permutations and refinements which will remain for resolution no matter what basic approach is used.

housebreaking and robbery statutes prohibit cumulative punishment. The second is whether Irby's is one of those cases.

The answer to the first question depends entirely upon statutory construction.

* * *

On the issue of separate punishment, the common law and legislative history are even more ambiguous. Around the time of codification there was a lively debate about the legality of cumulative punishment for crimes similar to housebreaking and robbery. Congress does not seem to have taken any position when it codified the D.C. laws, for there is no provision in the original D.C.Code (or the present one) about cumulative punishment. And there is no mention of this problem in the Congressional reports and debates which preceded passage of the Code.

We must turn, then, to the statutes themselves. The housebreaking statute reads as follows: "Whosoever shall, either in the night or in the daytime, break and enter, or enter without breaking, any dwelling * * * whether at the time occupied or not * * * with intent * * * to commit any criminal offense, shall be imprisoned for not more than fifteen years." 22 D.C.Code § 1801 (1961). Housebreaking, by the terms of the statute, is committed in preparation for some other criminal offense which is intended at the time of entry. It seems most likely that Congress, instead of desiring to punish for both the preparation and the completion, created two separate crimes in order to punish those housebreakers who are thwarted and who do not complete the intended crime.

The Supreme Court faced a similar situation in *Prince v. United States* [352 U.S. 322, 77 S.Ct. 403, 1 L.Ed.2d 370 (1957).] There the defendant was convicted of robbing a federally insured bank and entering the bank with intent to commit a felony. The Supreme Court reasoned that:

It is a fair inference from the wording in the Act, uncontradicted by anything in the meager legislative history, that the unlawful entry provision was inserted to cover the situation where a person enters a bank for the purpose of committing a crime, but is frustrated for some reason before completing the crime. The gravamen of the offense is not in the act of entering, which satisfies the terms of the statute even if it is simply walking through an open, public door during normal business hours. Rather the heart of the crime is the intent to steal. This mental element merges into the completed crime if the robbery is consummated.

Therefore, the Supreme Court held that Congress did not intend to punish cumulatively for the preparation and the completed crime.

A similar inference is warranted here, since, as in *Prince,* our statute defines housebreaking as entry with intent to commit another crime. And, as in *Prince,* the gravamen of the offense is not simply the act of entering, which need not be forcible to satisfy the terms of the statute. Indeed, it is possible that a person may be guilty of housebreaking although he has not committed a criminal trespass as long as he enters the premises with the required criminal intent.

Even if a criminal trespass is a necessary prerequisite to a finding of housebreaking, it is evident that the illegal act of entry is not the gravamen of housebreaking. If nothing more than entering without permission were involved, a penalty in the order of six months would probably be thought enough by Congress. However, Congress provided a much stiffer penalty for housebreaking. And the likely reason is that Congress believed that entry with an intent to commit another crime would often, in fact, lead to that other crime. As in *Prince,* the intent to commit another crime is at the heart of the offense. By deterring housebreaking Congress meant also to deter the intended crime which might follow. If so, then the housebreaking statute punishes for the possibility or probability of the intended crime. We do not think Congress would have wanted to impose punishment of fifteen years for the probability of the intended crime and an additional fifteen years for the crime itself.

Under this analysis, however, cumulative punishment is prohibited only if the crime defendant in fact committed was the same as the crime he intended to commit when he entered the dwelling. This seems to be the question which divides the court. The majority does not think "the indictment can be characterized as asserting that appellant's course of conduct was motivated by a single criminal intent." Judge Leventhal thinks the record is unclear and would require more specific allegations of a single intent. We think the record is clear enough to show that Irby had only one criminal purpose when he committed the two crimes.

According to the indictment, Irby entered the complainant's dwelling with an "intent to steal [his] property." While in the house, Irby carried out his intention and stole two rings worth $2,200.

The fact that in order to steal he did things which made his crime robbery, as opposed, for example, to grand larceny or petit larceny, does not negate the fact that what he did within the house was motivated by the same criminal purpose ("to steal property of another") as his illegal entry.

Furthermore, it is significant that Irby was originally charged with carrying a dangerous weapon and assault with a dangerous weapon. If these charges are correct, they suggest that when Irby entered the dwelling he was already prepared to use "force and violence" (i.e., to commit robbery) if necessary. * * *

We think the record sufficiently shows that defendant entered the dwelling with the objective of stealing property, by force if necessary, and that he carried out this objective. Since there is substantial doubt that Congress intended cumulative punishment in this situation, the rule of lenity must be applied. Irby should have been punished for either housebreaking or robbery but not both consecutively.

Notes and Questions

1. Compare *Neal v. State*, 55 Cal.2d 11, 9 Cal.Rptr. 607, 357 P.2d 839 (1960), where the defendant threw gasoline into a couple's bedroom and ignited it, resulting in their being severely burned. He was convicted of arson and two counts of attempted murder, and the trial judge ordered that the sentences for the attempted murders run consecutively. Cal. Penal Code § 654 provides that "an act or omission which is made punishable in different ways by different provisions of this code may be punishable under either of such provisions, but in no case can it be punished under more than one." On appeal, the court held:

"In the instant case the arson was the means of perpetrating the crime of attempted murder * * *. The conviction for both arson and attempted murder violated Penal Code section 654, since the arson was merely incidental to the primary objective of killing Mr. and Mrs. Raymond. Petitioner, therefore can only be punished for the more serious offense, which is attempted murder.

"The two attempted murder convictions, however, present a different problem. The purpose of the protection against multiple punishment is to insure that the defendant's punishment will be commensurate with his criminal liability. A defendant who commits an act of violence with the intent to harm more than one person or by a means likely to cause harm to several persons is more culpable than a defendant who harms only one person. For example, a defendant who chooses a means of murder that places a planeload of passengers in danger, or results in injury to many persons, is properly subject to greater punishment than a defendant who chooses a means that harms only a single person. This distinction between an act of violence against the person that violates more than one statute and such an act that harms more than one person is well settled. Section 654 is not '* * * applicable where * * * one act has two results each of which is an act of violence against the person of a separate individual.' "

2. Consider Johnson, *Multiple Punishment and Consecutive Sentences: Reflections on the Neal Doctrine,* 58 Calif.L.Rev. 357, 365–66 (1970): "Because it is more blameworthy to murder two people than one, the court upheld the two sentences for attempted murder. The reasoning is intelligible as far as it goes, but if pursued to its logical conclusion, it would require that the arson conviction and sentence also be upheld. Neal's single act had a third victim, represented somewhat inadequately by the Raymond's home. By setting fire to that home, Neal caused a financial loss to its owner or insurer and endangered the lives of the neighbors to whose houses the fire might have spread and of the firemen called to extinguish it. In choosing a means of accomplishing his objective that was in itself a serious and dangerous felony, he demonstrated greater culpability than if he had chosen a method that endangered only his intended victims."

3. Assume that Neal had recklessly or negligently started the fire and that the couple had been burned to death. Would this constitute one criminal homicide or two? Consider Remington & Joseph, *Charging, Convicting, and Sentencing the Multiple Criminal Offender,* 1961 Wis.L.Rev. 528, 549–50: "In principle, a distinction

might well be drawn based on defendant's knowledge that his act would likely produce harm to more than one person. For example, the person who blows up a plane with 44 persons in it knows of the probable existence of many passengers, and this might properly increase the extent of his criminal liability. On the other hand, a person who drives his car in a manner amounting to a high degree of negligence and who collides with and kills three occupants of another car, is no more culpable than he would have been had the other car contained only one occupant. The conclusion that there may be a number of convictions in the first situation, and only one in the second, would not seem to do violence to the legislative objective."

4. In *State v. Dunlop,* 721 P.2d 604 (Alaska 1986), involving the second Remington & Joseph hypothetical, the court overruled its prior holding that only one manslaughter offense was present in favor of the result adopted by "virtually every other state which has considered this issue," namely, that "where an act of violence injures multiple victims, there are as many punishable *offenses* as there are victims." As for the defendant's claim this meant his punishment would not be based on his culpability, the court responded this was not so because there was no "lack of foreseeable harm to multiple victims."

5. Compare *Commonwealth v. Donovan,* 395 Mass. 20, 478 N.E.2d 727 (1985), where the defendants were convicted of seven counts of larceny. They attached a phony night deposit box to the outside of a bank and, after seven depositors dropped in a total of $37,000, made off with the money. The court remanded for dismissal of six of the counts. "Consistent with the overwhelming weight of authority in other jurisdictions," the court concluded: "The stealing of property from different owners at the same time and at the same place constitutes but one larceny." But the court then cautioned: "We emphasize that

nothing in this opinion signals a retreat from our holding in *Commonwealth v. Levia,* 385 Mass. 345, 431 N.E.2d 928 (1982), where we affirmed the two armed robbery convictions of a defendant who had robbed two individuals in the course of a single criminal episode. Whenever a single criminal transaction gives rise to crimes of violence which are committed against several victims, then multiple indictments (and punishments) are appropriate." Is the distinction convincing?

NOTES ON PROSECUTING THE MULTIPLE OFFENDER

1. Remington & Joseph, supra, at 529: "Often a person's conduct violates more than one provision of the criminal law. A married person who has sexual intercourse with a person not his spouse violates both the fornication statute and the adultery statute. A person who steals a pistol and uses it in robbing a bank violates the theft statute and the robbery statute. A person who "borrows" a vehicle early in the evening and "borrows" another at a later time violates the "joyriding" statute twice.

"When such situations occur, the system for administering criminal justice is confronted with five basic issues:

"(1) For how many offenses should a suspect be prosecuted?

"(2) Of these offenses charged, which should be submitted to the jury for its consideration?

"(3) Where more than one offense is submitted to the jury, for how many offenses may the jury properly convict the defendant?

"(4) Where there is conviction for more than one offense, for how many

offenses is it proper to sentence the defendant?

"(5) Under what circumstances may an accused be subjected to separate, successive prosecutions instead of adjudicating his liability in a single proceeding?

"These are difficult and important issues which are reflected in an increasing amount of litigation both in federal and state courts. Too often, many of these issues are dealt with under the heading of double jeopardy without sufficient attention to the fact that each raises essentially different considerations."

These issues are dealt with only briefly in the following notes.

2. When a person's conduct violates more than one criminal statute, the prosecutor must decide how many offenses to charge.[a] Sometimes, as where the defendant is intending to plead guilty and it is believed the penalty for one offense is adequate, only a single violation will be charged. On other occasions the prosecutor will charge several offenses because a greater penalty is thought appropriate, because of possible strategic advantages at trial, or because this gives the prosecutor added leverage in plea bargaining. It is commonly provided that several offenses may be joined in a single prosecution if they "are of the same or similar character" or "are based on the same conduct or on a series of acts connected together or constituting parts of a single scheme or plan."[b]

3. At the conclusion of the evidence, the judge must determine what offenses to submit to the jury. Generally, it may be said that he must submit all of the charged offenses which are reasonably supported by the proof. The question is whether

---

a. This is one aspect of the prosecutor's discretion, which is not ordinarily subject to judicial review. See F. Miller, *Prosecution: The Decision to Charge a Suspect with a Crime* (1970).

b. *ABA Standards Relating to Joinder and Severance* § 1.1 (Approved Draft, 1968). A defen-

dant may seek a severance of the joined offenses, but such motions are not frequently granted, and "appellate reversal of a trial court's decision not to grant a severance is extremely rare." Id. at 30.

reasonable men could "conclude on the evidence taken in the light most favorable to the prosecution that guilt has been proved beyond a reasonable doubt." [c] The judge must also submit any lesser included offense,[d] even if not specifically charged,[e] provided there is some reasonable ground in the evidence for conviction of the lesser offense and an acquittal of the greater offense. "For example, if a defendant is charged with robbery and his sole defense is an alibi, he would have no right to require the submission of attempted robbery. This is because no view of the evidence would justify both an acquittal of robbery and a conviction of attempted robbery." [f]

4. Generally, it may be said that when several offenses have been submitted to the jury, the jury may convict for more than one so long as each offense requires proof of a fact not required by the other. A defendant may not be convicted (a) of both an offense and another lesser included offense [g]; (b) of two offenses which require inconsistent findings of fact [h]; (c) of offenses which "differ only in that one is defined to prohibit a designated kind of conduct generally and the other to prohibit a specific instance of such conduct" [i]; or (d) of several violations of the same offense if "the offense is defined as a continuing course of conduct and the defendant's course of conduct was uninterrupted, unless the law provides that specific periods of such conduct constitute separate offenses." [j]

5. Cumulative sentencing is permissible whenever authorized by the legislature. As stated in *Missouri v. Hunter,* 459 U.S. 359, 103 S.Ct. 673, 74 L.Ed.2d 535 (1983), upholding defendant's conviction and sentencing in a single trial for both armed criminal action and the lesser included offense of first degree robbery: "Where, as here, a legislature specifically authorizes cumulative punishment under two statutes, regardless of whether those two statutes proscribe the 'same' conduct under *Blockburger,* a court's task of statutory construction is at an end and the prosecutor may seek and the trial court or jury may impose cumulative punishment under such statutes in a single trial."

6. With respect to successive prosecutions, the double jeopardy clause of the

---

c. Comment, 24 U.Chi.L.Rev. 561, 562 (1957).

d. Usually defined as in *Model Penal Code* § 1.07(4).

e. The charge of the greater offense is deemed sufficient notice to the defendant that he must also be prepared to defend as to any lesser included offense.

f. Remington & Joseph, supra, at 542.

g. E.g., if the alternatives of robbery and armed robbery were submitted to the jury because it was disputed whether a weapon had been used, the jury would be instructed it could not convict of both.

Though not done frequently, a state *may* constitutionally authorize conviction on both a greater and lesser offense at the same trial. See Note 5, infra, noting there may even be cumulative sentencing in such circumstances. And this is so even though the two crimes could not be *separately* prosecuted; see Note 6, infra.

h. E.g., in *United States v. Gaddis,* 424 U.S. 544, 96 S.Ct. 1023, 47 L.Ed.2d 222 (1976), the Court stated: "Situations will no doubt often exist where there is evidence before a grand jury or prosecutor that a certain person participated in a bank robbery and also evidence that that person, though not himself the robber, at least knowingly received the proceeds of the robbery. * * * If, upon the trial of the case the District Judge is satisfied that there is sufficient evidence to go to the jury on both counts, he must * * * instruct the members of the jury that they may not convict the defendant both for robbing a bank and for receiving the proceeds of the robbery."

i. *Model Penal Code* § 1.07(1)(d). "For example, the same conduct cannot be the basis of conviction under a general statute prohibiting lewd conduct and under a specific statute prohibiting indecent exposure." *Model Penal Code* § 1.07, Comment (1985).

j. *Model Penal Code* § 1.07(1)(e). "For example, a person violates an unlawful cohabitation statute only once, no matter how long his unlawful cohabiting continues, where the conduct was not interrupted by issuance of process or otherwise." *Model Penal Code* § 1.07, Comment (1985).

Fifth Amendment, applicable to the states through the Fourteenth Amendment, provides that no person shall "be subject for the same offence to be twice put in jeopardy of life or limb." The *Blockburger* test is used to determine what is the same offense. Thus, for example, if a defendant is convicted or acquitted of the greater offense he may not thereafter be prosecuted for the lesser included offense.[k] And if the defendant is first convicted or acquitted of the lesser offense, he may not thereafter be prosecuted for the greater offense.[l]

7. In *Ashe v. Swenson*, 397 U.S. 436, 90 S.Ct. 1189, 25 L.Ed.2d 469 (1970), Brennan, Douglas, and Marshall, JJ., arguing that under "our tradition of virtually unreviewable prosecutorial discretion concerning the initiation and scope of a crime prosecution, the potentialities for abuse inherent in the 'same evidence' test are simply intolerable," concluded that "the Double Jeopardy Clause requires the prosecution, except in most limited circumstances, to join at one trial all the charges against a defendant which grow out of a single criminal act, occurrence, episode, or transaction." Though a major-

ity of the Court declined to accept this view, a number of states have adopted the "same transaction" test, either by court decision or through enactment of a statute along the lines of *Model Penal Code* § 1.07(2).

However, the Court in *Ashe* did adopt another position which sometimes protects defendants from successive prosecutions of offenses which are not the same under *Blockburger:* the Fifth Amendment double jeopardy protection includes the principle of "collateral estoppel," which "means simply that when an issue of ultimate fact has once been determined by a valid and final judgment, that issue cannot again be litigated between the same parties in any future lawsuit." Thus because the defendant had been acquitted of armed robbery of *X* at a trial where defendant's sole defense was mistaken identity, he could not constitutionally be tried thereafter for armed robbery of *Y,* which occurred at the same time and place and by the same persons.[m] But the collateral estoppel doctrine is "of limited value because it is not often possible to determine with precision how the judge or jury [in the first trial] has decided any particular issue."[n]

k. *Harris v. Oklahoma*, 433 U.S. 682, 97 S.Ct. 2912, 53 L.Ed.2d 1054 (1977): "When, as here, conviction for a greater crime, [felony-] murder, cannot be had without conviction for the lesser crime, robbery with firearms, the Double Jeopardy Clause bars prosecution for the lesser crime after conviction for the greater one."

l. In *Brown v. Ohio*, 432 U.S. 161, 97 S.Ct. 2221, 53 L.Ed.2d 187 (1977), holding defendant was improperly tried for theft of an automobile following his conviction of the lesser included offense of joyriding (taking or operating the car without the owner's consent), the Court said: "Whatever the sequence may be, the Fifth Amendment forbids successive prosecution and cumulative punishment for a greater and lesser included offense." But in a footnote the Court cautioned: "An exception may exist where the State is unable to proceed on the more serious charge at the outset because the additional facts necessary to sustain that charge have not oc-

curred or have not been discovered despite the exercise of due diligence." See also *Jeffers v. United States*, 432 U.S. 137, 97 S.Ct. 2207, 53 L.Ed.2d 168 (1977), holding that defendant's demand for separate trials on two indictments deprived him of any right he may have had under the double jeopardy clause to be protected from successive prosecutions for a lesser included offense and the greater offense.

m. In criminal cases, the doctrine works only to the benefit of the accused, *Simpson v. Florida*, 403 U.S. 384, 91 S.Ct. 1801, 29 L.Ed.2d 549 (1971). Thus, if the defendant had been convicted of robbing *X*, this would not foreclose his defense on grounds of mistaken identity at his trial for robbery of *Y.*

n. Schaefer, *Unresolved Issues in the Law of Double Jeopardy: Waller and Ashe*, 58 Calif.L. Rev. 391, 394 (1970).

Chapter 5

HOMICIDE: USING MENTAL STATE AND OTHER FACTORS TO CLASSIFY CRIMES

SECTION 1. INTENTIONAL KILL-ING: THE "HEAT OF PASSION" TEST

MULLANEY v. WILBUR

Supreme Court of the United States, 1975.
421 U.S. 684, 95 S.Ct. 1881, 44 L.Ed.2d 508.

MR. JUSTICE POWELL delivered the opinion of the Court.

The State of Maine requires a defendant charged with murder to prove that he acted "in the heat of passion on sudden provocation" in order to reduce the homicide to manslaughter. We must decide whether this rule comports with the due process requirement, as defined in *In re Winship,* 397 U.S. 358, 364, 90 S.Ct. 1068, 1072, 25 L.Ed.2d 368 (1970), that the prosecution prove beyond a reasonable doubt every fact necessary to constitute the crime charged.

In June 1966 a jury found respondent Stillman E. Wilbur, Jr., guilty of murder. The case against him rested on his own pretrial statement and on circumstantial evidence showing that he fatally assaulted Claude Hebert in the latter's hotel room. Respondent's statement, introduced by the prosecution, claimed that he had attacked Hebert in a frenzy provoked by Hebert's homosexual advance. The defense offered no evidence, but argued that the homicide was not unlawful since respondent lacked criminal intent. Alternatively, Wilbur's counsel asserted that at most the homicide was manslaughter rather than murder, since it occurred in the heat of passion provoked by the homosexual assault.

The trial court instructed the jury that Maine law recognizes only two kinds of homicide, murder and manslaughter, and that these offenses are not subdivided into different degrees. The common elements of both are that the homicide be unlawful—i.e., neither justifiable nor excusable [1]—and that it be intentional.[2] The prosecution is required to prove these elements by proof beyond a reasonable

1. As examples of justifiable or excusable homicides, the court mentioned a soldier in battle, a policeman in certain circumstances, and an individual acting in self-defense.

2. The court elaborated that an intentional homicide required the jury to find "either that the defendant intended death, or that he intended an act which was calculated and should have been understood by [a] person of reason to be one likely to do great bodily harm and that death resulted."

238

doubt, and only if they are so proved is the jury to consider the distinction between murder and manslaughter.

In view of the evidence the trial court drew particular attention to the difference between murder and manslaughter. After reading the statutory definitions of both offenses,[3] the court charged that "malice aforethought is an essential and indispensable element of the crime of murder," without which the homicide would be manslaughter. The jury was further instructed, however, that if the prosecution established that the homicide was both intentional and unlawful, malice aforethought was to be conclusively implied unless the defendant proved by a fair preponderance of the evidence that he acted in the heat of passion on sudden provocation.[4] The court emphasized that "malice aforethought and heat of passion on sudden provocation are inconsistent things," thus, by proving the latter the defendant would negate the former and reduce the homicide from murder to manslaughter.

3. The Maine murder statute, Me.Rev.Stat., Tit. 17, § 2651, provides:

"Whoever unlawfully kills a human being with malice aforethought, either express or implied, is guilty of murder and shall be punished by imprisonment for life."

The manslaughter statute, Tit. 17, § 2551, in relevant part provides:

"Whoever unlawfully kills a human being in the heat of passion, on sudden provocation, without express or implied malice aforethought * * * shall be punished by a fine of not more than $1,000 or by imprisonment for not more than 20 years * * *."

4. The trial court also explained the concept of express malice aforethought, which required a "premeditated design to kill" thereby manifesting "a general malignancy and disregard of human life which proceeds from a heart void of social duty and fatally bent on mischief." Despite this instruction, the court repeatedly made clear that express malice need not be established since malice would be implied unless the defendant proved that he acted in the heat of passion. Hence, the instruction on express malice appears to have been wholly unnecessary, as the Maine Supreme Judicial Court subsequently held. *State v. Lafferty*, 309 A.2d 647 (1973).

The court then concluded its charge with elaborate definitions of "heat of passion"[5] and "sudden provocation."[6] * * *

Respondent appealed to the Maine Supreme Judicial Court, arguing that he had been denied due process because he was required to negate the element of malice aforethought by proving that he had acted in the heat of passion on sudden provocation. * * *

The Maine Supreme Judicial Court rejected this contention, holding that in Maine murder and manslaughter are not distinct crimes but rather different degrees of the single generic offense of felonious homicide. * * * With respect to *Winship*, which was decided after respondent's trial,[8] the court noted that it did not anticipate the application of the *Winship* principle to a "reductive factor" such as the heat of passion on sudden provocation.

Respondent next successfully petitioned for a writ of habeas corpus in federal district court. The District Court ruled that * * * *Winship* requires the prose-

5. "Heat of passion * * * means that at the time of the act the reason is disturbed or obscured by passion to an extent which might [make] ordinary men of fair, average disposition liable to act irrationally without due deliberation or reflection, and from passion rather than judgment."

6. "[H]eat of passion will not avail unless upon sudden provocation. Sudden means happening without previous notice or with very brief notice; coming unexpectedly, precipitated, or unlooked for * * *. It is not every provocation, it is not every rage of passion that will reduce a killing from murder to manslaughter. The provocation must be of such a character and so close upon the act of killing, that for a moment a person could be—that for a moment the defendant could be considered as not being the master of his own understanding."

8. The Maine court concluded that *Winship* should not be applied retroactively. We subsequently decided, however, that *Winship* should be given complete retroactive effect. *Ivan v. City of New York*, 407 U.S. 203, 92 S.Ct. 1951, 32 L.Ed.2d 659 (1972).

cution to prove malice aforethought beyond a reasonable doubt; it cannot rely on a presumption of implied malice which requires the defendant to prove that he acted in the heat of passion on sudden provocation.

The Court of Appeals for the First Circuit affirmed, subscribing in general to the District Court's analysis and construction of Maine law. * * *

The Maine law of homicide, as it bears on this case, can be stated succinctly: Absent justification or excuse, all intentional or criminally reckless killings are felonious homicides. Felonious homicide is punished as murder—i.e., by life imprisonment—unless the defendant proves by a fair preponderance of the evidence that it was committed in the heat of passion on sudden provocation, in which case it is punished as manslaughter—i.e., by a fine not to exceed $1,000 or by imprisonment not to exceed 20 years. The issue is whether the Maine rule requiring the defendant to prove that he acted in the heat of passion on sudden provocation accords with due process.

Our analysis may be illuminated if this issue is placed in historical context.

At early common law only those homicides committed in the enforcement of justice were considered justifiable; all others were deemed unlawful and were punished by death. Gradually, however, the severity of the common-law punishment for homicide abated. Between the 13th and 16th centuries the class of justifiable homicides expanded to include, for example, accidental homicides and those committed in self-defense. Concurrently, the widespread use of capital punishment was ameliorated further by extension of the ecclesiastic jurisdiction. Almost any

person able to read was eligible for "benefit of clergy," a procedural device that effected a transfer from the secular to the ecclesiastic jurisdiction. And under ecclesiastic law a person who committed an unlawful homicide was not executed; instead he received a one-year sentence, had his thumb branded and was required to forfeit his goods. At the turn of the 16th century, English rulers, concerned with the accretion of ecclesiastic jurisdiction at the expense of the secular, enacted a series of statutes eliminating the benefit of clergy in all cases of "murder of malice prepensed." Unlawful homicides that were committed without such malice were designated "manslaughter" and their perpetrators remained eligible for the benefit of clergy.

Even after ecclesiastic jurisdiction was eliminated for all secular offenses the distinction between murder and manslaughter persisted. It was said that "manslaughter (when voluntary) [14] arises from the sudden heat of passions, murder from the wickedness of the heart." 4 Blackstone's *Commentaries* 190. Malice aforethought was designated as the element that distinguished the two crimes, but it was recognized that such malice could be implied by law as well as proved by evidence. Absent proof that an unlawful homicide resulted from "sudden and sufficiently violent provocation," the homicide was "presumed to be malicious." Id., at 201. In view of this presumption, the early English authorities, relying on the case of *The King v. Onerby,* 92 Eng.Rep. 465 (KB 1727), held that once the prosecution proved that the accused had committed the homicide, it was "incumbent on the prisoner to make out * * * all * * * circumstances of justification, excuse or alleviation * * * to the satisfaction of the court and jury." 4 Blackstone's *Commenta-*

---

14. Blackstone also referred to a class of homicides called involuntary manslaughter. Such homicides were committed by accident in the course of perpetrating another unlawful, al-

though not felonious, act. 4 Blackstone's *Commentaries* 192–193. This offense, with some modification and elaboration, generally has been recognized in this country.

ries 201. Thus, at common law the burden of proving heat of passion on sudden provocation appears to have rested on the defendant.

In this country the concept of malice aforethought took on two distinct meanings: in some jurisdictions it came to signify a substantive element of intent, requiring the prosecution to prove that the defendant intended to kill or to inflict great bodily harm; in other jurisdictions it remained a policy presumption, indicating only that absent proof to the contrary a homicide was presumed not to have occurred in the heat of passion.[17] In a landmark case, *Commonwealth v. York*, 9 Met. (50 Mass.) 93 (1845), Chief Justice Shaw of the Massachusetts Supreme Judicial Court held that the defendant was required to negate malice aforethought by proving by a preponderance of the evidence that he acted in the heat of passion. Initially, *York* was adopted in Maine as well as several other jurisdictions. In 1895, however, in the context of deciding a question of federal criminal procedure, this Court explicitly considered and unanimously rejected the general approach articulated in *York*. *Davis v. United States*, 160 U.S. 469, 16 S.Ct. 353, 40 L.Ed. 499.[21] And, in the past half century, the large majority of States have abandoned *York* and now require the prosecution to prove the absence of the heat of passion on sudden provocation beyond a reasonable doubt.

This historical review establishes two important points. First, the fact at issue here—the presence or absence of the heat of passion on sudden provocation—has been, almost from the inception of the common law of homicide, the single most important factor in determining the degree of culpability attaching to an unlawful homicide. And, second, the clear trend has been toward requiring the prosecution to bear the ultimate burden of proving this fact.

Petitioners, the warden of the Maine Prison and the State of Maine, argue that despite these considerations *Winship* should not be extended to the present case. They note that as a formal matter the absence of the heat of passion on sudden provocation is not a "fact necessary to constitute the *crime*" of felonious homicide in Maine. *In re Winship* (emphasis supplied). This distinction is relevant, according to petitioners, because in *Winship* the facts at issue were essential to establish criminality in the first instance whereas the fact in question here does not come into play until the jury already has determined that the defendant is guilty and may be punished at least for manslaughter. In this situation, petitioners maintain, the defendant's critical interests in liberty and reputation are no longer of paramount concern since, irrespective of the presence or absence of the heat of passion on sudden provocation, he is likely to lose his liberty and certain to be stigmatized.[23] In short,

---

17. Several jurisdictions also divided murder into different degrees, typically limiting capital punishment to first-degree murder and requiring the prosecution to prove premeditation and deliberation in order to establish that offense.

21. In *Leland v. Oregon*, 343 U.S. 790, 72 S.Ct. 1002, 96 L.Ed. 1302 (1952), the Court declined to apply the specific holding of *Davis*—that the prosecution must prove sanity beyond a reasonable doubt—to the States.

23. Relying on *Williams v. New York*, 337 U.S. 241, 69 S.Ct. 1079, 93 L.Ed. 1337 (1949), and *McGautha v. California*, 402 U.S. 183, 196, 91 S.Ct. 1454, 1461, 28 L.Ed.2d 711 (1971), petition-

ers seek to buttress this contention by arguing that since the presence or absence of the heat of passion on sudden provocation affects only the extent of punishment it should be considered a matter within the traditional discretion of the sentencing body and therefore not subject to rigorous due process demands. But cf. *United States v. Tucker*, 404 U.S. 443, 92 S.Ct. 589, 30 L.Ed.2d 592 (1972). There is no incompatibility between our decision today and the traditional discretion afforded sentencing bodies. Under Maine law the jury is given no discretion as to the sentence to be imposed on one found guilty of felonious homicide. If the defendant is found to

petitioners would limit *Winship* to those facts which, if not proved, would wholly exonerate the defendant.

This analysis fails to recognize that the criminal law of Maine, like that of other jurisdictions, is concerned not only with guilt or innocence in the abstract but also with the degree of criminal culpability. Maine has chosen to distinguish those who kill in the heat of passion from those who kill in the absence of this factor. Because the former are less "blameworth[y]," *State v. Lafferty,* 309 A.2d, at 671, 673 (concurring opinion), they are subject to substantially less severe penalties. By drawing this distinction, while refusing to require the prosecution to establish beyond a reasonable doubt the fact upon which it turns, Maine denigrates the interests found critical in *Winship.*

The safeguards of due process are not rendered unavailing simply because a determination may already have been reached that would stigmatize the defendant and that might lead to a significant impairment of personal liberty. The fact remains that the consequences resulting from a verdict of murder, as compared with a verdict of manslaughter, differ significantly. Indeed, when viewed in terms of the potential difference in restrictions of personal liberty attendant to each conviction, the distinction established by Maine between murder and manslaughter may be of greater importance than the difference between guilt or innocence for many lesser crimes.

Moreover, if *Winship* were limited to those facts that constitute a crime as defined by state law, a State could undermine many of the interests that decision sought to protect without effecting any substantive change in its law. It would only be necessary to redefine the elements that comprise different crimes, characterizing them as factors that bear solely on the extent of punishment. An extreme example of this approach can be fashioned from the law challenged in this case. Maine divides the single generic offense of felonious homicide into three distinct punishment categories—murder, voluntary manslaughter, and involuntary manslaughter. Only the first two of these categories require that the homicidal act either be intentional or the result of criminally reckless conduct. But under Maine law these facts of intent are not general elements of the crime of felonious homicide. Instead, they bear only on the appropriate punishment category. Thus, if petitioners' argument were accepted, Maine could impose a life sentence for any felonious homicide—even those that traditionally might be considered involuntary manslaughter—unless the *defendant* was able to prove that his act was neither intentional nor criminally reckless.[24]

Winship is concerned with substance rather than this kind of formalism.

* * *

In *Winship* the Court emphasized the societal interests in the reliability of jury verdicts:

"The requirement of proof beyond a reasonable doubt has [a] vital role in our criminal procedure for cogent reasons. The accused during a criminal prosecution has at stake interests of immense importance, both because of the

---

be a murderer, a mandatory life sentence results. On the other hand, if the jury finds him guilty only of manslaughter it remains for the trial court in the exercise of *its* discretion to impose a sentence within the *statutorily defined* limits.

24. Many States impose different statutory sentences on different degrees of assault. If *Winship* were limited to a State's definition of the

elements of a crime, these States could define all assaults as a single offense and then require the defendant to disprove the elements of aggravation—*e.g.,* intent to kill or intent to rob. But see *State v. Ferris,* 249 A.2d 523 (Me.1969) (prosecution must prove elements of aggravation in criminal assault case by proof beyond a reasonable doubt).

possibility that he may lose his liberty upon conviction and because of the certainty that he would be stigmatized by the conviction.

*   *   *

"Moreover, use of the reasonable-doubt standard is indispensable to command the respect and confidence of the community in applications of the criminal law. It is critical that the moral force of the criminal law not be diluted by a standard of proof that leaves people in doubt whether innocent men are being condemned."

These interests are implicated to a greater degree in this case than they were in *Winship* itself. Petitioner there faced an 18-month sentence, with a maximum possible extension of an additional four and one-half years, whereas respondent here faces a differential in sentencing ranging from a nominal fine to a mandatory life sentence. Both the stigma to the defendant and the community's confidence in the administration of the criminal law are also of greater consequence in this case, since the adjudication of delinquency involved in *Winship* was "benevolent" in intention, seeking to provide "a generously conceived program of compassionate treatment."

Not only are the interests underlying *Winship* implicated to a greater degree in this case, but in one respect the protection afforded those interests is less here. In *Winship* the ultimate burden of persuasion remained with the prosecution, although the standard had been reduced to proof by a fair preponderance of the evidence. In this case, by contrast, the State has affirmatively shifted the burden of proof to the defendant. The result, in a case such as this one where the defendant is required to prove the critical fact in dispute, is to increase further the likelihood of an erro-

neous murder conviction. Such a result directly contravenes the principle articulated in *Speiser v. Randall,* 357 U.S. 513, 525–526, 78 S.Ct. 1332, 1342, 2 L.Ed.2d 1460 (1958):

"[W]here one party has at stake an interest of transcending value—as a criminal defendant his liberty—th[e] margin of error is reduced as to him by the process of placing on the [prosecution] the burden *   *   * of persuading the factfinder at the conclusion of the trial *   *   *."

It has been suggested that because of the difficulties in negating an argument that the homicide was committed in the heat of passion the burden of proving this fact should rest on the defendant. No doubt this is often a heavy burden for the prosecution to satisfy. The same may be said of the requirement of proof beyond a reasonable doubt of many controverted facts in a criminal trial. But this is the traditional burden which our system of criminal justice deems essential.

Indeed, the Maine Supreme Judicial Court itself acknowledged that most States require the prosecution to prove the absence of passion beyond a reasonable doubt.[28] Moreover, the difficulty of meeting such an exacting burden is mitigated in Maine where the fact at issue is largely an "objective, rather than a subjective, behavioral criterion." In this respect, proving that the defendant did not act in the heat of passion on sudden provocation is similar to proving any other element of intent; it may be established by adducing evidence of the factual circumstances surrounding the commission of the homicide. And although intent is typically considered a fact peculiarly within the knowledge of the defendant, this does not, as the Court has

---

28. Many States do require the defendant to show that there is "some evidence" indicating that he acted in the heat of passion before requiring the prosecution to negate this element by

proving the absence of passion beyond a reasonable doubt. Nothing in this opinion is intended to affect that requirement.

long recognized, justify shifting the burden to him.

Nor is the requirement of proving a negative unique in our system of criminal jurisprudence. Maine itself requires the prosecution to prove the absence of self-defense beyond a reasonable doubt. See *State v. Millett,* 273 A.2d 504 (1971).[30] Satisfying this burden imposes an obligation that, in all practical effect, is identical to the burden involved in negating the heat of passion on sudden provocation. Thus, we discern no unique hardship on the prosecution that would justify requiring the defendant to carry the burden of proving a fact so critical to criminal culpability.[31]

Maine law requires a defendant to establish by a preponderance of the evidence that he acted in the heat of passion on sudden provocation in order to reduce murder to manslaughter. Under this burden of proof a defendant can be given a life sentence when the evidence indicates that it is *as likely as not* that he deserves a significantly lesser sentence. This is an intolerable result in a society where, to paraphrase Mr. Justice Harlan, it is far worse to sentence one guilty only of man-

slaughter as a murderer than to sentence a murderer for the lesser crime of manslaughter. We therefore hold that the Due Process Clause requires the prosecution to prove beyond a reasonable doubt the absence of the heat of passion on sudden provocation when the issue is properly presented in a homicide case. Accordingly, the judgment below is affirmed.

Affirmed.

MR. JUSTICE REHNQUIST, with whom THE CHIEF JUSTICE joins, concurring.

* * *

I agree with the Court that *In re Winship* does require that the prosecution prove beyond a reasonable doubt every element which constitutes the crime charged against a defendant. I see no inconsistency between that holding and the holding of *Leland v. Oregon,* 343 U.S. 790, 72 S.Ct. 1002, 96 L.Ed. 1302 (1952). In the latter case this Court held that there was no constitutional requirement that the State shoulder the burden of proving the sanity of the defendant.

The Court noted in *Leland* that the issue of insanity as a defense to a criminal charge was considered by the jury only

---

30. In *Millett* the Maine Supreme Judicial Court adopted the "majority rule" regarding proof of self-defense. The burden of producing "some evidence" on this issue rests with the defendant, but the ultimate burden of persuasion by proof beyond a reasonable doubt remains on the prosecution.

31. This conclusion is supported by consideration of a related line of cases. Generally in a criminal case the prosecution bears both the production burden and the persuasion burden. In some instances, however, it is aided by a presumption, see *Davis v. United States,* 160 U.S. 469, 16 S.Ct. 353, 40 L.Ed. 499 (1895) (presumption of sanity), or a permissible inference, see *United States v. Gainey,* 380 U.S. 63, 85 S.Ct. 754, 13 L.Ed.2d 658 (1965) (inference of knowledge from presence at an illegal still). These procedural devices require (in the case of a presumption) or permit (in the case of an inference) the trier of fact to conclude that the prosecution has met its burden of proof with respect to the presumed or inferred fact by having satisfactorily established

other facts. Thus, in effect they require the defendant to present some evidence contesting the otherwise presumed or inferred fact. See *Barnes v. United States,* 412 U.S. 837, 846 n. 11, 93 S.Ct. 2357, 2363, 37 L.Ed.2d 380 (1973). Since they shift the production burden to the defendant, these devices must satisfy certain due process requirements. See e.g., *Barnes v. United States,* supra; *Turner v. United States,* 396 U.S. 398, 90 S.Ct. 642, 24 L.Ed.2d 610 (1970).

In each of these cases, however, the ultimate burden of persuasion by proof beyond a reasonable doubt remained on the prosecution. See, e.g., *Barnes v. United States, Davis v. United States.* Shifting the burden of persuasion to the defendant obviously places an even greater strain upon him since he no longer need only present some evidence with respect to the fact at issue; he must affirmatively establish that fact. Accordingly, the Due Process Clause demands more exacting standards before the State may require a defendant to bear this ultimate burden of persuasion.

after it had found that all elements of the offense, including the *mens rea* if any required by state law, had been proven beyond a reasonable doubt. Although as the state court's instructions in *Leland* recognized, evidence relevant to insanity as defined by state law may also be relevant to whether the required *mens rea* was present, the existence or nonexistence of legal insanity bears no necessary relationship to the existence or nonexistence of the required mental elements of the crime. For this reason, Oregon's placement of the burden of proof on insanity on Leland, unlike Maine's redefinition of homicide in the instant case, did not effect an unconstitutional shift in the State's traditional burden of proof beyond a reasonable doubt of all necessary elements of the offense. Both the Court's opinion and the concurring opinion of Mr. Justice Harlan in *In re Winship,* supra, stress the importance of proof beyond a reasonable doubt in a criminal case as "bottomed on a fundamental value determination of our society that it is far worse to convict an innocent man than to let a guilty man go free." Having once met that rigorous burden of proof that, for example, in a case such as this, the defendant not only killed a fellow human being, but did it with malice aforethought, the State could quite consistently with such a constitutional principle conclude that a defendant who sought to establish the defense of insanity, and thereby escape any punishment whatever for a heinous crime, should bear the laboring oar on such an issue.

PATTERSON v. NEW YORK

Supreme Court of the United States, 1977.
432 U.S. 197, 97 S.Ct. 2319, 53 L.Ed.2d 281.

MR. JUSTICE WHITE delivered the opinion of the Court. * * *

Patterson was charged with second-degree murder. In New York there are two

a. *Rivera* is discussed at p. 401 of this Book.

elements of this crime: (1) "intent to cause the death of another person"; and (2) "caus[ing] the death of such person or of a third person." Malice aforethought is not an element of the crime. In addition, the State permits a person accused of murder to raise an affirmative defense that he "acted under the influence of extreme emotional disturbance for which there was a reasonable explanation or excuse."

New York also recognizes the crime of manslaughter. A person is guilty of manslaughter if he intentionally kills another person "under circumstances which do not constitute murder because he acts under the influence of extreme emotional disturbance." Appellant confessed before trial to killing Northrup, but at trial he raised the defense of extreme emotional disturbance.

The jury was instructed as to the elements of the crime of murder. * * * The jury was further instructed, consistently with New York law, that the defendant had the burden of proving his affirmative defense by a preponderance of the evidence. The jury was told that if it found beyond a reasonable doubt that appellant had intentionally killed Northrup but that appellant had demonstrated by a preponderance of the evidence that he had acted under the influence of extreme emotional disturbance, it must find appellant guilty of manslaughter instead of murder.

The jury found appellant guilty of murder. * * *

In convicting Patterson under its murder statute, New York did no more than *Leland* and *Rivera* [a] permitted it to do without violating the Due Process Clause. Under those cases, once the facts constituting a crime are established beyond reasonable doubt, based on all the evidence including the evidence of the defendant's mental state, the State may refuse to sustain the affirmative defense of insanity unless demonstrated by a preponderance of the evidence.

The New York law on extreme emotional disturbance follows this pattern. This affirmative defense, which the Court of Appeals described as permitting "the defendant to show that his actions were caused by a mental infirmity not rising to the level of insanity, and that he is less culpable for having committed them," does not serve to negative any facts of the crime which the State is to prove in order to convict for murder. It constitutes a separate issue on which the defendant is required to carry the burden of persuasion; and unless we are to overturn *Leland* and *Rivera,* New York has not violated the Due Process Clause, and Patterson's conviction must be sustained.

We are unwilling to reconsider *Leland* and *Rivera.* But even if we were to hold that a State must prove sanity to convict once that fact is put in issue, it would not necessarily follow that a State must prove beyond a reasonable doubt every fact, the existence or nonexistence of which it is willing to recognize as an exculpatory or mitigating circumstance affecting the degree of culpability or the severity of the punishment. Here, in revising its criminal code, New York provided the affirmative defense of extreme emotional disturbance, a substantially expanded version of the older heat of passion concept; but it was willing to do so only if the facts making out the defense were established by the defendant with sufficient certainty. The State was itself unwilling to undertake to establish the absence of those facts beyond reasonable doubt, perhaps fearing that proof would be too difficult and that too many persons deserving treatment as murderers would escape that punishment if the evidence need merely raise a reasonable doubt about the defendant's emotional state. It has been said that the new criminal code of New York contains some 25 affirmative defenses which exculpate or mitigate but which must be established by the defendant to be operative. The Due Process Clause, as we see it, does not put New York to the choice of abandoning those defenses or undertaking to disprove their existence in order to convict for a crime which otherwise is within its constitutional powers to sanction by substantial punishment. * * *

[I]n each instance of a murder conviction under the present law, New York will have proved beyond reasonable doubt that the defendant has intentionally killed another person, an act which it is not disputed the State may constitutionally criminalize and punish. If the State nevertheless chooses to recognize a factor that mitigates the degree of criminality or punishment, we think the State may assure itself that the fact has been established with reasonable certainty. To recognize at all a mitigating circumstance does not require the State to prove its nonexistence in each case in which the fact is put in issue, if in its judgment this would be too cumbersome, too expensive, and too inaccurate.[11]

We thus decline to adopt as a constitutional imperative, operative country-wide,

---

11. The drafters of the Model Penal Code would, as a matter of policy, place the burden of proving the nonexistence of most affirmative defenses, including the defense involved in this case, on the prosecution once the defendant has come forward with some evidence that the defense is present. The drafters recognize the need for flexibility, however, and would, in "some exceptional situations," place the burden of persuasion on the accused.

"Characteristically these are situations where the defense does not obtain at all under existing law and the Code seeks to introduce a mitigation. Resistance to the mitigation, based upon the prosecution's difficulty in obtaining evidence, ought to be lowered if the burden of persuasion is imposed on the defendant. Where that difficulty appears genuine and there is something to be said against allowing the defense at all, we consider it defensible to shift the burden in this way." ALI, Model Penal Code § 1.13, Comment, p. 113 (Tentative Draft No. 4, 1955). * * *

that a State must disprove beyond reasonable doubt every fact constituting any and all affirmative defenses related to the culpability of an accused. Traditionally, due process has required that only the most basic procedural safeguards be observed; more subtle balancing of society's interests against those of the accused have been left to the legislative branch. We therefore will not disturb the balance struck in previous cases holding that the Due Process Clause requires the prosecution to prove beyond reasonable doubt all of the elements included in the definition of the offense of which the defendant is charged. Proof of the nonexistence of all affirmative defenses has never been constitutionally required; and we perceive no reason to fashion such a rule in this case and apply it to the statutory defense at issue here.

This view may seem to permit state legislatures to reallocate burdens of proof by labeling as affirmative defenses at least some elements of the crimes now defined in their statutes. But there are obviously constitutional limits beyond which the States may not go in this regard. "[I]t is not within the province of a legislature to declare an individual guilty or presumptively guilty of a crime." The legislature cannot "validly command that the finding of an indictment, or mere proof of the identity of the accused, should create a presumption of the existence of all the facts essential to guilt." * * *

It is urged that *Mullaney v. Wilbur* necessarily invalidates Patterson's conviction. * * *

Mullaney's holding, it is argued, is that the State may not permit the blameworthiness of an act or the severity of punishment authorized for its commission to depend on the presence or absence of an identified fact without assuming the burden of proving the presence or absence of that fact, as the case may be, beyond reasonable doubt. In our view, the *Mullaney*

holding should not be so broadly read. The concurrence of two Justices in *Mullaney* was necessarily contrary to such a reading; and a majority of the Court refused to so understand and apply *Mullaney* when *Rivera* was dismissed for want of a substantial federal question.

Mullaney surely held that a State must prove every ingredient of an offense beyond a reasonable doubt, and that it may not shift the burden of proof to the defendant by presuming that ingredient upon proof of the other elements of the offense. This is true even though the State's practice, as in Maine, had been traditionally to the contrary. Such shifting of the burden of persuasion with respect to a fact which the State deems so important that it must be either proved or presumed is impermissible under the Due Process Clause.

It was unnecessary to go further in *Mullaney*. The Maine Supreme Court made it clear that malice aforethought, which was mentioned in the statutory definition of the crime, was not equivalent to premeditation and that the presumption of malice traditionally arising in intentional homicide cases carried no factual meaning insofar as premeditation was concerned. Even so, a killing became murder in Maine when it resulted from a deliberate, cruel act committed by one person against another, "suddenly, and without any, or without considerable, provocation." Premeditation was not within the definition of murder; but malice, in the sense of the absence of provocation, was part of the definition of that crime. Yet malice, i.e., lack of provocation, was presumed and could be rebutted by the defendant only by proving by a preponderance of the evidence that he acted with heat of passion upon sudden provocation. In *Mullaney* we held that however traditional this mode of proceeding might have been, it is contrary to the Due Process Clause as construed in *Winship*.

As we have explained, nothing was presumed or implied against Patterson; and his conviction is not invalid under any of our prior cases. The judgment of the New York Court of Appeals is

Affirmed.

MR. JUSTICE POWELL, with whom MR. JUSTICE BRENNAN and MR. JUSTICE MARSHALL join, dissenting. * * *

[The majority's] explanation of the *Mullaney* holding bears little resemblance to the basic rationale of that decision. But this is not the cause of greatest concern. The test the Court today establishes allows a legislature to shift, virtually at will, the burden of persuasion with respect to any factor in a criminal case, so long as it is careful not to mention the nonexistence of that factor in the statutory language that defines the crime. The sole requirement is that any references to the factor be confined to those sections that provide for an affirmative defense. * * *

With all respect, this type of constitutional adjudication is indefensibly formalistic. A limited but significant check on possible abuses in the criminal law now becomes an exercise in arid formalities. What [*In re Winship,* 397 U.S. 358, 90 S.Ct. 1068, 25 L.Ed.2d 368 (1970),] and *Mullaney* had sought to teach about the limits a free society places on its procedures to safeguard the liberty of its citizens becomes a rather simplistic lesson in statutory draftsmanship. Nothing in the Court's opinion prevents a legislature from applying this new learning to many of the

classical elements of the crimes it punishes.[8] It would be preferable, if the Court has found reason to reject the rationale of *Winship* and *Mullaney,* simply and straightforwardly to overrule those precedents.

The Court understandably manifests some uneasiness that its formalistic approach will give legislatures too much latitude in shifting the burden of persuasion. And so it issues a warning that "there are obviously constitutional limits beyond which the States may not go in this regard." The Court thereby concedes that legislative abuses may occur and that they must be curbed by the judicial branch. But if the State is careful to conform to the drafting formulas articulated today, the constitutional limits are anything but "obvious." This decision simply leaves us without a conceptual framework for distinguishing abuses from legitimate legislative adjustments of the burden of persuasion in criminal cases.

It is unnecessary for the Court to retreat to a formalistic test for applying *Winship.* Careful attention to the *Mullaney* decision reveals the principles that should control in this and like cases. *Winship* held that the prosecution must bear the burden of proving beyond a reasonable doubt "the existence of every fact necessary to constitute the crime charged." In *Mullaney* we concluded that heat of passion was one of the "facts" described in *Winship*—that is, a factor as to which the prosecution must bear the burden of persuasion beyond a reasonable doubt. We reached that result

8. For example, a state statute could pass muster under the only solid standard that appears in the Court's opinion if it defined murder as mere physical contact between the defendant and the victim leading to the victim's death, but then set up an affirmative defense leaving it to the defendant to prove that he acted without culpable *mens rea.* The State, in other words, could be relieved altogether of responsibility for proving *anything* regarding the defendant's state of mind, provided only that the face of the statute meets the Court's drafting formulas.

To be sure, it is unlikely that legislatures will rewrite their criminal laws in this extreme form. The Court seems to think this likelihood of restraint is an added reason for limiting review largely to formalistic examination. But it is completely foreign to this Court's responsibility for constitutional adjudication to limit the scope of judicial review because of the expectation—however reasonable—that legislative bodies will exercise appropriate restraint.

only after making two careful inquiries. First, we noted that the presence or absence of heat of passion made a substantial difference in punishment of the offender and in the stigma associated with the conviction. Second, we reviewed the history, in England and this country, of the factor at issue. Central to the holding in *Mullaney* was our conclusion that heat of passion "has been, almost from the inception of the common law of homicide, the single most important factor in determining the degree of culpability attaching to an unlawful homicide."

Implicit in these two inquiries are the principles that should govern this case. The Due Process Clause requires that the prosecutor bear the burden of persuasion beyond a reasonable doubt only if the factor at issue makes a substantial difference in punishment and stigma. The requirement of course applies *a fortiori* if the factor makes the difference between guilt and innocence. But a substantial difference in punishment alone is not enough. It also must be shown that in the Anglo–American legal tradition the factor in question historically has held that level of importance. If either branch of the test is not met, then the legislature retains its traditional authority over matters of proof. But to permit a shift in the burden of persuasion when both branches of this test are satisfied would invite the undermining of the presumption of innocence, "that bedrock 'axiomatic and elementary' principle whose 'enforcement lies at the foundation of the administration of our criminal law.' "

I hardly need add that New York's provisions allocating the burden of persuasion as to "extreme emotional disturbance" are unconstitutional when judged by these standards. "Extreme emotional disturbance" is, as the Court of Appeals recognized, the direct descendant of the "heat of passion" factor considered at length in *Mullaney.* I recognize, of course, that the differences between Maine and New York law are not unimportant to the defendant; there is a somewhat broader opportunity for mitigation. But none of those distinctions is relevant here. The presence or absence of extreme emotional disturbance makes a critical difference in punishment and stigma, and throughout our history the resolution of this issue of fact, although expressed in somewhat different terms, has distinguished manslaughter from murder.

* * *

The *Winship/Mullaney* test identifies those factors of such importance, historically, in determining punishment and stigma that the Constitution forbids shifting to the defendant the burden of persuasion when such a factor is at issue. *Winship* and *Mullaney* specify only the procedure that is required when a State elects to use such a factor as part of its substantive criminal law. They do not say that the State must elect to use it. For example, where a State has chosen to retain the traditional distinction between murder and manslaughter, as have New York and Maine, the burden of persuasion must remain on the prosecution with respect to the distinguishing factor, in view of its decisive historical importance. But nothing in *Mullaney* or *Winship* precludes a State from abolishing the distinction between murder and manslaughter and treating all unjustifiable homicide as murder. In this significant respect, neither *Winship* nor *Mullaney* eliminates the substantive flexibility that should remain in legislative hands.

Moreover, it is unlikely that more than a few factors—although important ones—for which a shift in the burden of persuasion seriously would be considered will come within the *Mullaney* holding. With some exceptions, then, the State has the authority "to recognize a factor that mitigates the degree of criminality or punishment" without having "to prove its nonexistence in each case in which the fact is put in issue".

New ameliorative affirmative defenses,[14] about which the Court expresses concern, generally remain undisturbed by the holdings in *Winship* and *Mullaney*—and need not be disturbed by a sound holding reversing Patterson's conviction.

Furthermore, as we indicated in *Mullaney,* even as to those factors upon which the prosecution must bear the burden of persuasion, the State retains an important procedural device to avoid jury confusion and prevent the prosecution from being unduly hampered. The State normally may shift to the defendant the burden of production, that is, the burden of going forward with sufficient evidence "to justify [a reasonable] doubt upon the issue." If the defendant's evidence does not cross this threshold, the issue—be it malice, extreme emotional disturbance, self-defense, or whatever—will not be submitted to the jury. * * *

PEOPLE v. WASHINGTON

Court of Appeals, Second District, 1976.
58 Cal.App.3d 620, 130 Cal.Rptr. 96.

ALLPORT, ASSOCIATE JUSTICE.

Following trial by jury defendant was convicted of murder in violation of Penal Code section 187, which was found to be in the second degree. The allegation of use of a firearm was found to be true. He was sentenced to state prison and now appeals from the judgment.

In view of the contentions made on appeal a plenary statement of the facts surrounding this sordid affair is not necessary. Suffice to say that the victim Owen Wilson Brady met his death when shot by his homosexual partner Merle Francis Washington on August 10, 1974, while the two were riding in the victim's car. The killing resulted from a lover's quarrel, claimed to have been provoked by unfaithfulness on the part of the victim and his expressed desire to terminate the relationship.

It is contended on appeal that because of instructional error and inadequacy of defense trial counsel, the conviction should either be reversed or reduced to voluntary manslaughter by this court. * * *

It is next suggested that, in defining "heat of passion" necessary to reduce murder to manslaughter in a case involving a homosexual, it is error to use the standard of "an ordinarily reasonable person of average disposition" but rather should be tested by a standard applicable to a female or to the average servient homosexual.

In this respect the jury was instructed that to reduce the homicide from murder to manslaughter upon the ground of sudden quarrel or heat of passion, the conduct must be tested by the ordinarily reasonable man test. Defendant argues without precedent that to so instruct was error because, "Homosexuals are not at present a curiosity or a rare commodity. They are a distinct third sexual class between that of male and female, are present in almost every field of endeavor, and are fast achieving a guarded recognition not formerly accorded them. The heat of their passions in dealing with one another should not be tested by standards applicable to the average man or the average

14. Numerous examples of such defenses are available: New York subjects an armed robber to lesser punishment than he would otherwise receive if he proves by a preponderance of the evidence that the gun he used was unloaded or inoperative. A number of States have ameliorated the usual operation of statutes punishing statutory rape, recognizing a defense if the defendant shows that he reasonably believed his partner was of age. Formerly the age of the minor was a strict liability element of the crime. The Model Penal Code also employs such a shift in the burden of persuasion for a limited number of defenses. For example, a corporation can escape conviction of an offense if it proves by a preponderance of the evidence that the responsible supervising officer exercised due diligence to prevent the commission of the offense. § 2.07(5) (Proposed Official Draft 1962).

woman, since they are aberrant hybrids, with an obvious diminished capacity.

"Defendant submits that since the evidence disclosed that he was acting as a servient homosexual during the period of his relationship with the victim, that his heat of passion should have been tested, either by a standard applicable to a female, or a standard applicable to the average homosexual, and that it was prejudicial error to instruct the jury to determine his heat of passion defense by standards applicable to the average male." We do not agree. In *People v. Bridgehouse*, 47 Cal.2d 406, 413, 303 P.2d 1018, 1022, it was said:

> "To be sufficient to reduce a homicide to manslaughter, the heat of passion must be such as would naturally be aroused in the mind of an ordinary, reasonable person, under the given facts and circumstances, or in the mind of a person of ordinary self-control."

In *People v. Morse*, 70 Cal.2d 711, 734–735, 76 Cal.Rptr. 391, 405, 452 P.2d 607, 613, the test announced in *Bridgehouse*, supra, was applied, the court saying in addition that "the evidence of defendant's extraordinary character and environmental deficiencies was manifestly irrelevant to the inquiry." In *People v. Logan*, 175 Cal. 45, 48–49, 164 P. 1121, 1122, the applicable test is clearly stated where the court said:

> "In the present condition of our law it is left to the jurors to say whether or not the facts and circumstances in evidence are sufficient to lead them to believe that the defendant did, or to create a reasonable doubt in their minds as to whether or not he did, commit his offense under a heat of passion. The jury is further to be admonished and advised by the court that this heat of passion must be such a passion as would naturally be aroused in the mind of an ordinarily reasonable person under the given

facts and circumstances, and that, consequently, no defendant may set up his own standard of conduct and justify or excuse himself because in fact his passions were aroused, unless further the jury believe that the facts and circumstances were sufficient to arouse the passions of the ordinarily reasonable man. Thus no man of extremely violent passion could so justify or excuse himself if the exciting cause be not adequate, nor could an excessively cowardly man justify himself unless the circumstances were such as to arouse the fears of the ordinarily courageous man. Still further, while the conduct of the defendant is to be measured by that of the ordinarily reasonable man placed in identical circumstances, the jury is properly to be told that the exciting cause must be such as would naturally tend to arouse the passion of the ordinarily reasonable man."

In the instant case the jury was properly instructed to use the ordinarily reasonable man test. * * *

The judgment is affirmed.

Notes and Questions

1. In *Bedder v. Director of Public Prosecutions*, [1954] 1 W.L.R. 1119, [1954] 2 All E.R. 801, the House of Lords dismissed the appeal of an 18–year–old youth who was convicted of murdering a prostitute. The facts, as set out by Lord Simonds, are: "The appellant has the misfortune to be sexually impotent, a fact which he naturally well knew and, according to his own evidence, had allowed to prey upon his mind. On the night of the crime he saw the prostitute with another man and when they had parted went and spoke to her and was led by her to a quiet court off a street in Leicester. There he attempted in vain to have intercourse with her, whereupon— and I summarise the evidence in the way most favourable to him—she jeered at him

and attempted to get away. He tried still to hold her, and then she slapped him in the face and punched him in the stomach: he grabbed her shoulders and pushed her back from him whereas (I use his words), 'She kicked me in the privates. Whether it was her knee or foot, I do not know. After that I do not know what happened till she fell.' She fell, because he had taken a knife from his pocket and stabbed her with it twice, the second blow inflicting a mortal injury."

The House concluded the Court of Criminal Appeal was correct in ruling that the trial judge had properly instructed that the provocation must be sufficient to cause a "reasonable person * * * to lose his self-control" and that "an unusually excitable or pugnacious individual, or a drunken one or a man who is sexually impotent is not entitled to rely on provocation which would not have led an ordinary person to have acted in the way which was in fact carried out." Stated Lord Simonds:

"I am at a loss to know what other direction than that which he gave could properly have been given by the learned judge to the jury in the present case. The argument, as I understood it, for the appellant was that the jury, in considering the reaction of the hypothetical reasonable man to the acts of provocation, must not only place him in the circumstances in which the accused was placed but must also invest him with the personal physical peculiarities of the accused. Learned counsel, who argued the case for the appellant with great ability, did not, I think, venture to say that he should be invested with mental or temperamental qualities which distinguished him from the reasonable man * * *. But he urged that the reasonable man should be invested with the peculiar physical qualities of the accused, as in the present case with the characteristic of impotence, and the question should be asked what would be the reaction of the impotent reasonable man in

the circumstances? For that proposition I know of no authority nor can I see any reason in it. It would be plainly illogical not to recognize an unusually excitable or pugnacious temperament in the accused as a matter to be taken into account but yet to recognize for that purpose some unusual physical characteristic, be it impotence or another. Moreover, the proposed distinction appears to me to ignore the fundamental fact that the temper of a man which leads him to react in such and such a way to provocation, is or may be itself conditioned by some physical defect. It is too subtle a refinement for my mind or, I think, for that of a jury to grasp that the temper may be ignored but the physical defect taken into account.

"It was urged upon your Lordships that the hypothetical reasonable man must be confronted with all the same circumstances as the accused and that this could not be fairly done unless he was also invested with the peculiar characteristics of the accused. But this makes nonsense of the test. Its purpose is to invite the jury to consider the act of the accused by reference to a certain standard or norm of conduct and with this object the 'reasonable' or the 'average' or the 'normal' man is invoked. If the reasonable man is then deprived in whole or in part of his reason or the normal man endowed with abnormal characteristics, the test ceases to have any value."

2. In *R. v. Raney*, 29 Crim.App. 14 (1942), the court reduced defendant's murder conviction to manslaughter, saying: "To a one-legged man like the appellant, who is dependent on his crutches, it is obvious that a blow to a crutch, whether it is a blow that knocks the crutch away or not, is something very different from mere words. It seems to us that, if the Judge had repeated that part of the appellant's evidence, it would have been very proper to do so, because a blow to a one-legged man's crutch might well be regarded by a

jury as an act of provocation." English, *What Did Section Three do to the Law of Provocation?,* [1970] Crim.L.Rev. 249, 254, concludes that *Raney* cannot be squared with *Bedder.* Is this so?

3. Samuels, *Excusable Loss of Self-Control in Homicide,* 34 Mod.L.Rev. 163, 166, 170–71 (1971): "Each man has a different level of tolerance, or threshold of uncontrollable anger, in respect of each and every given situation.[a] An assault, a sexual overture, a family or personal insult, a racial discrimination, a moral aspersion, cruelty to a child, or anything imaginable, will at a certain level of intensity break self-control. Each 'provocative' item will break that self-control at a different point on the graph of provocation set against loss of control. But [the reasonable man test] suggests that the direction of the line on the graph is the same for all persons, that although the threshold of uncontrollable anger differs according to the provocation it does not differ in respect of each different person. The fallacy is to deny that one average man may be impervious to moral aspersions but instantly enraged by a sexual overture and another average man may be impervious to a sexual overture but instantly enraged by a moral aspersion. Who is the average man here? The first man would be open to condemnation if in fact he unexpectedly lost control in the face of a moral aspersion, the second in the face of a sexual overture. Neither should be open to condemnation in the converse case.

a. Consider Brett, *The Physiology of Provocation,* [1970] Crim.L.Rev. 634, 637–38: "The degree of response to a stress situation varies considerably from one individual to another. Some men are highly vulnerable to stress, others are strikingly resistant to it. This fact has been demonstrated both by clinical observation and by experiment though it is as yet unknown why these differences should occur. It seems likely, however, that a number of factors, some genetic, others environmental, combine to produce the differences of susceptibility and response.

" * * * There is a lot to be said for the judge not attempting to describe the reasonable man but simply leaving the issue to the jury, provided that there is some evidence of loss of self-control. The jury might then take account of the virility or size or colour or psychological make-up of the accused and ask themselves what would be the effect of this provocation upon a person having these physical or mental characteristics but having that degree of self-control that can properly be expected from that person. The inscrutability of the jury verdict would then remove the matter from the ambit of the law. * * *

"Provocation as a head of manslaughter could be abolished and replaced with the offence of criminal loss of self-control causing the death of another person, sentence being for culpable failure to exercise self-control. Proposed new statutory offence:

'If the jury are satisfied that the accused lost his self-control so as to form the intent to kill [or to cause grievous bodily harm] and so caused the death of the deceased they shall return a verdict of criminal [culpable] killing [manslaughter] if, having regard to all the circumstances, including in particular the standard of self-control properly to be expected of the accused, they are satisfied that the act was to some degree excusable.' "

4. Consider the comments of Wilkie, J., concurring in *State v. Hoyt,* 21 Wis.2d 284, 128 N.W.2d 645 (1964):

"It would be perverse for the law to ignore these teachings of science, and absurd for it to doubt their validity. But if we pay attention to them, it at once becomes clear that the reasonable man of provocation law is a figment of the imagination.

"Plainly we cannot sensibly talk of the ordinary man in any meaningful way. There is a whole range of types of men, and it would be pointless and cruel to penalise a particular man merely because his type occurs nearer to one or other end of the range than to the centre of it."

"The majority would retain the 'ordinarily-constituted man' or the 'reasonable man' test of provocation. Yet critical issues in the administration of even this test remain unanswered. The 'reasonable man' concept in the law generally has two distinct meanings. There is the statistical concept under which the reasonable man does what most people do in fact under the circumstances. Yet if this is the meaning of the test, it is clear that as a matter of fact a great majority of people will never commit murder no matter how violently provoked by another. A consistent application of this test, viewing the reasonable man as the statistical *factual* norm would, in effect, read [the manslaughter statute] out of existence.

"However, in other contexts, there is the ethical concept under which the reasonable man functions as the person the law *expects* everyone to be, regardless of whether a majority, in fact, fall short of the *moral* norm in actual conduct. To take this view of the reasonable man for the purposes of the provocation test would propel courts and juries into the strange task of deciding when a person, taken as the ethical ideal, would commit murder. This may well result in reading [the manslaughter statute] out of existence. The person we *expect* people to be like would not likely solve his problems by murder. If we conclude that an ethical ideal—that person whom all others aspire to emulate—would be driven to kill under the circumstances of a given case, logically the verdict should be not guilty, nor morally blameworthy to any degree. Again, manslaughter, as conduct less blameworthy than non-provoked intentional killing but not guiltless, is practically eliminated from the code.

"This analysis brings me to the heart of my disagreement with the majority. The objective, the 'ordinarily-constituted man' or the 'reasonable man' test leads juries and courts into inquiries which are not relevant to the issue at hand. In assessing the manslaughter defense to a charge of a more serious homicide, we are not concerned with how most people would act under the circumstances of the case, nor are we concerned with what the defendant 'ought' to have done comparing him with the morally ideal response under the circumstances. * * * The manslaughter defense assumes that the defendant is morally blameworthy to some degree. The basic question is whether he is as culpable as a person who kills solely for self-aggrandizement or out of sheer malevolence. To answer this question, we must place ourselves empathetically in the actual situation in which the defendant was placed, a situation which may be relatively unique. Therefore, an inquiry into what *most* people would do in such circumstances cannot be completely determinative of the issue. The test cannot be wholly objective or wholly subjective. A person may become filled with murderous hate for another which can be discharged only by acting out the feeling and killing that person. The victim's conduct, in relation to the defendant, from the point of view of most people, may have been neutral if not benign. The sheer intensity of the defendant's hostile feeling cannot alone justify the manslaughter verdict. The victim's conduct must be such that we conclude that the feeling and conduct of the defendant can be understood sympathetically, albeit not condoned. The trier-of-fact must be able to say, 'although I would have acted differently, and I believe most persons would have acted differently, I can understand why this person gave way to the impulse to kill. He is different from the person who kills for personal gain alone.'

"To come to this judgment, the trier-of-fact must focus upon the defendant's total life experience in relation to the victim, and attempt to understand, in emotional as well as cognitive terms, the defendant's feelings toward the victim. Under the wholly objective test, the defendant's state of mind immediately before the act of homicide, and the victim's conduct at this precise moment, are the crucial objects of inquiry. Although the majority notes that the prior experience of the defendant and victim in relation to one another is relevant to the state of mind of the defendant at the moment of the homicide, the objective test shifts the focus of inquiry in a manner which is misleading. The total life experience of the defendant in relation to the victim determines the justification of the lesser verdict. As the majority notes, the act of homicide may be the culmination of a pattern of pressures of long duration. That the defendant may have been less angry with the victim at the moment of murder than at some time in the past (when he checked the impulse to kill) is irrelevant, if the trier-of-fact can conclude that, given the total experience of the defendant with the victim, the act of violence can be understood in terms which lessen the defendant's blameworthiness.

"The instances in which the issue of manslaughter or a more serious offense is sharply posed, are relatively predictable. Outside of murder for personal gain or murder by organized criminals, most homicides involve one family member killing another, against a background of personal insult, humiliation, and bullying, such as is present in the instant case. It is important that the legal standards defining the dimensions of the crime and defenses and thereby determining the relevancy and probative worth of lines of evidence and modes of argument, focus the attention of the trier-of-fact upon the basic issues. By providing gradations of intentional homicide, the legislature has announced that not all persons who consciously and purposively kill another are equally blameworthy. Some person's act of homicide

can be understood as a very human response to a desperate condition.

"The wholly objective ordinarily-constituted-man test, by failing to take account of the emotional dimensions of a concrete individual's specific situation, fails, in my view, to define sharply the issue posed by the legislatively-provided manslaughter defense.

"The provocation test formulated in the *Model Penal Code* [§ 210.3(1)(b)] of the American Law Institute, I believe, gives proper weight to all relevant factors. It is neither wholly objective or wholly subjective. * * *

"This test would enable the trier-of-fact to evaluate the defendant's conduct in a specific situation. The trier-of-fact is called upon to determine a degree of blameworthiness. This task cannot be accomplished by means of either a wholly objective or wholly subjective test. The Model Penal Code formulation permits the trier-of-fact to decide 'whether the actor's loss of self-control can be understood in terms that arouse sympathy enough to call for mitigation in the sentence.'[6] This is the critical issue surrounding the manslaughter defense."

5. Under any test which is not "either wholly objective or wholly subjective," is there any principled way to tell the jury just how subjective the test is? What of the instruction requested but rejected in *State v. Little,* 123 N.H. 433, 462 A.2d 117 (1983), that "ordinary human nature, or the nature of a man of fair, average mind and disposition, should be taken as a standard, unless you find that the defendant is shown to have some peculiar weakness of mind or emotion not arising from wickedness of heart."

6. In light of Judge Wilkie's observation that the reasonable man does not kill, consider Dressler, *Rethinking Heat of Pas-*

6. *Model Penal Code,* Comment p. 48, Tentative Draft No. 9 (1959).

sion: A Defense in Search of a Rationale, 73 J.Crim.L. & C. 421, 466–67 (1982): "The point of the partial defense should be that if the ordinarily law-abiding person would be expected to be in sufficient control of his emotions so as to respond in an inner directed fashion, or to respond externally, but non-violently, then homicidal conduct by the actor may be fairly perceived as an unreasonable response to reasonable anger. This homicidal conduct would not be entitled to any mitigation. If, however, the provocation is so great that the ordinarily law-abiding person would be expected to lose self-control to the extent that he could not help but act violently, yet he would still have sufficient self-control so that he could avoid using force likely to cause death or great bodily harm in response to the provocation, then we are saying that the actor's moral blameworthiness is found not in his violent response, but in his *homicidal* violent response. He did not control himself as much as he *should* have, or as much as common experience tells us he *could* have, nor as much as the ordinarily law-abiding person *would* have. Thus, his choice-capabilities were partially undermined by severe and understandable, non-blameworthy anger, but he was not sufficiently in control of his actions so as to merit total acquittal. It is in this case that the traditional defense should apply."

PEOPLE v. BERRY

Supreme Court of California, 1976.
18 Cal.3d 509, 134 Cal.Rptr. 415, 556 P.2d 777.

SULLIVAN, JUSTICE.

Defendant Albert Joseph Berry was charged by indictment with one count of murder and one count of assault by means of force likely to produce great bodily injury. * * * In each count, the alleged victim was defendant's wife, Rachel Pessah Berry. A jury found defendant guilty as charged and determined that the murder was of the first degree. Defendant was sentenced to state prison for the term prescribed by law. He appeals from the judgment of conviction. * * *

Defendant, a cook, 46 years old, and Rachel Pessah, a 20–year–old girl from Israel, were married on May 27, 1974. Three days later Rachel went to Israel by herself, returning on July 13, 1974. On July 23, 1974, defendant choked Rachel into unconsciousness. She was treated at a hospital where she reported her strangulation by defendant to an officer of the San Francisco Police Department. On July 25, Inspector Sammon, who had been assigned to the case, met with Rachel and as a result of the interview a warrant was issued for defendant's arrest.

While Rachel was at the hospital, defendant removed his clothes from their apartment and stored them in a Greyhound Bus Depot locker. He stayed overnight at the home of a friend, Mrs. Jean Berk, admitting to her that he had choked his wife. On July 26, he telephoned Mrs. Berk and informed her that he had killed Rachel with a telephone cord on that morning at their apartment. The next day Mrs. Berk and two others telephoned the police to report a possible homicide and met Officer Kelleher at defendant's apartment. They gained entry and found Rachel on the bathroom floor. A pathologist from the coroner's office concluded that the cause of Rachel's death was strangulation. Defendant was arrested on August 1, 1974, and confessed to the killing.

At trial defendant did not deny strangling his wife, but claimed through his own testimony and the testimony of a psychiatrist, Dr. Martin Blinder, that he was provoked into killing her because of a sudden and uncontrollable rage so as to reduce the offense to one of voluntary manslaughter. He testified that upon her return from Israel, Rachel announced to him that while there she had fallen in love with another man, one Yako, and had enjoyed his sexual favors, that he was coming to this country to claim her and that she wished a divorce. Thus commenced a tormenting two weeks in which Rachel alternately taunted defendant with her involvement with Yako and at the same time sexually excited defendant indicating her desire to remain with him. Defendant's detailed testimony, summarized below, chronicles this strange course of events.

After their marriage, Rachel lived with defendant for only three days and then left for Israel. Immediately upon her return to San Francisco she told defendant about her relationship with and love for Yako. This brought about further argument and a brawl that evening in which defendant choked Rachel and she responded by scratching him deeply many times. Nonetheless they continued to live together. Rachel kept taunting defendant with Yako and demanding a divorce. She claimed she thought she might be pregnant by Yako. She showed defendant pictures of herself with Yako. Nevertheless, during a return trip from Santa Rosa, Rachel demanded immediate sexual intercourse with defendant in the car, which was achieved; however upon reaching their apartment, she again stated that she loved Yako and that she would not have intercourse with defendant in the future.

On the evening of July 22d defendant and Rachel went to a movie where they engaged in heavy petting. When they returned home and got into bed, Rachel announced that she had intended to make love with defendant, "But I am saving myself for this man Yako, so I don't think I will." Defendant got out of bed and prepared to leave the apartment whereupon Rachel screamed and yelled at him. Defendant choked her into unconsciousness.

Two hours later defendant called a taxi for his wife to take her to the hospital.

He put his clothes in the Greyhound bus station and went to the home of his friend Mrs. Berk for the night. The next day he went to Reno and returned the day after. Rachel informed him by telephone that there was a warrant for his arrest as a result of her report to the police about the choking incident. On July 25th defendant returned to the apartment to talk to Rachel, but she was out. He slept there overnight. Rachel returned around 11 a.m. the next day. Upon seeing defendant there, she said, "I suppose you have come here to kill me." Defendant responded, "yes," changed his response to "no," and then again to "yes," and finally stated "I have really come to talk to you." Rachel began screaming. Defendant grabbed her by the shoulder and tried to stop her screaming. She continued. They struggled and finally defendant strangled her with a telephone cord.

Dr. Martin Blinder, a physician and psychiatrist, called by the defense, testified that Rachel was a depressed, suicidally inclined girl and that this suicidal impulse led her to involve herself ever more deeply in a dangerous situation with defendant. She did this by sexually arousing him and taunting him into jealous rages in an unconscious desire to provoke him into killing her and thus consummating her desire for suicide. Throughout the period commencing with her return from Israel until her death, that is from July 13 to July 26, Rachel continually provoked defendant with sexual taunts and incitements, alternating acceptance and rejection of him. This conduct was accompanied by repeated references to her involvement with another man; it led defendant to choke her on two occasions, until finally she achieved her unconscious desire and was strangled. Dr. Blinder testified that as a result of this cumulative series of provocations, defendant at the time he fatally strangled Rachel, was in a state of uncontrollable rage, completely under the sway of passion.

We first take up defendant's claim that on the basis of the foregoing evidence he was entitled to an instruction on voluntary manslaughter as defined by statute which is "the unlawful killing of a human being, without malice * * * upon a sudden quarrel or heat of passion." In *People v. Valentine* (1946) 28 Cal.2d 121, 169 P.2d 1, this court, in an extensive review of the law of manslaughter, specifically approved the following quotation from *People v. Logan* (1917) 175 Cal. 45, 48–49, 164 P. 1121 as a correct statement of the law: "In the present condition of our law *it is left to the jurors* to say whether or not the facts and circumstances in evidence are sufficient to lead them to believe that the defendant did, or to create a reasonable doubt in their minds as to whether or not he did, commit his offense under a heat of passion. The jury is further to be admonished and advised by the court that this heat of passion must be such a passion as would naturally be aroused in the mind of an ordinarily reasonable person under the given facts and circumstances, and that, consequently, no defendant may set up his own standard of conduct and justify or excuse himself because in fact his passions were aroused, unless further the jury believe that the facts and circumstances were sufficient to arouse the passions of the ordinarily reasonable man. * * * "

We further held in *Valentine* that there is no specific type of provocation required by section 192 and that verbal provocation may be sufficient. In *People v. Borchers* (1958) 50 Cal.2d 321, 329, 325 P.2d 97 in the course of explaining the phrase "heat of passion" used in the statute defining manslaughter we pointed out that " 'passion' need not mean 'rage' or 'anger' " but may be any "[v]iolent, intense, high-wrought or enthusiastic emotion" and concluded there "that defendant was aroused to a heat of 'passion' by a series of

events over a considerable period of time * * *." Accordingly we there declared that evidence of admissions of infidelity by the defendant's paramour, taunts directed to him and other conduct, "supports a finding that defendant killed in wild desperation induced by [the woman's] long continued provocatory conduct." We find this reasoning persuasive in the case now before us. Defendant's testimony chronicles a two-week period of provocatory conduct by his wife Rachel that could arouse a passion of jealousy, pain and sexual rage in an ordinary man of average disposition such as to cause him to act rashly from this passion. It is significant that both defendant and Dr. Blinder testified that the former was in the heat of passion under an uncontrollable rage when he killed Rachel.

The Attorney General contends that the killing could not have been done in the heat of passion because there was a cooling period, defendant having waited in the apartment for 20 hours. However, the long course of provocatory conduct, which had resulted in intermittent outbreaks of rage under specific provocation in the past, reached its final culmination in the apartment when Rachel began screaming. Both defendant and Dr. Blinder testified that defendant killed in a state of uncontrollable rage, of passion, and there is ample evidence in the record to support the conclusion that this passion was the result of the long course of provocatory conduct by Rachel, just as the killing emerged from such conduct in *Borchers.* * * *

Notes and Questions

1. More and more jurisdictions, especially under modern code substitutes for the "heat of passion" test, are taking the view, as stated in *Berry,* "that there is no specific type of provocation required." But it is still true in many states that the

"application by the courts of an objective doctrine has led to the establishment of certain concrete standards of conduct which a reasonable man is said to adhere to. Unfortunately many of these incidents have ossified into ironclad rules originally evolved in the nineteenth century. Under modern law, the categories of things which provoked the nineteenth century reasonable man continue to provoke the reasonable man of the twentieth century with the addition of a few new but rigid categories.

"In general, he is said to be provoked into taking human life when he is violently assaulted; when an unlawful attempt is made to arrest him; when he kills in mutual combat; [a] or when he sees his wife in an act of adultery and kills her or her paramour. On the other hand, he is said not to be provoked by insulting words [b] or gestures, nor, according to some authorities, is he provoked by a trespass against his land or goods. The outcome of the case which *clearly* falls within one of these rules may be predicted with a high degree of accuracy. However, the situations which develop are seldom clear cut. Some courts carefully scrutinize the evidence to determine if the facts can be forced into any of the established categories; if they cannot, the case is not one for manslaughter regardless of evidence of actual provocation or passion. The result has been an unrealistic interpretation of the facts to fit an appealing case neatly within an established category, thus lead-

ing to confusion as to the breadth of the categories and lack of uniformity in the application of the law. Other jurisdictions have refused to saddle themselves with the 'nineteenth century four' and have created some few new categories of adequate provocation as the cases arise." Note, 106 U.Pa.L.Rev. 1021, 1023–24 (1958).

2. Should the number and breadth of the categories be increasing or decreasing? In *Holmes v. Director of Public Prosecutions,* [1946] A.C. 588, 62 T.L.R. 466, [1946] 2 All E.R. 124, Viscount Simon reasoned that "the application of common law principles in matters such as this must to some extent be controlled by the evolution of society. For example, the instance given by Blackstone that if a man's nose was pulled and he thereupon struck his aggressor so as to kill him, this was only manslaughter, may very well represent the natural feelings of a past time, but I should doubt very much whether such a view should necessarily be taken nowadays. The injury done to a man's sense of honour by minor physical assaults may well be differently estimated in differing ages. And, in the same way, one can imagine in these days at any rate, words of a vile character which might be calculated to deprive a reasonable man of his customary self-control even more than would an act of physical violence. But, on the other hand, as society advances, it ought to call for a higher measure of self-control in all cases."

---

a. This does not necessarily cover all cases in which a fight ensues. At least one court has held that if one person uses lawful force on another to prevent a trespass and the individuals then begin to fight, culminating in a killing by the latter person, this is not manslaughter. *State v. Smith,* 123 N.H. 46, 455 A.2d 1041 (1983).

b. But, "while words of an insulting and scandalous nature are not sufficient cause of provocation, words conveying information of a fact which constitutes adequate provocation when that fact is observed would constitute sufficient provocation." *Commonwealth v. Berry*, 461 Pa. 233, 336 A.2d 262 (1975). The court thus held it was error

to instruct that there would be sufficient provocation only if defendant actually witnessed the assault of his mother instead of being told of it by her immediately after the culmination of the attack. *Berry* thus recognizes one common expansion of the categories; as the court explained: "The threatened or immediate infliction of serious injury upon a parent, spouse or child because of the relationship of the parties and the expected concern of one for the well being of the other, has occasioned courts to hold this conduct may be sufficient provocation to reduce the killing to voluntary manslaughter."

3. As noted in *Holmes,* the significance of the common law categories was that they served as a means of controlling the jury, as only if there was evidence fitting the case within an established category would the jury be given the alternative of finding the defendant guilty of manslaughter. Under the *Berry* approach and that of *Model Penal Code* § 210.3(1)(b), which has been adopted in several jurisdictions, how much of this control remains? Should every defendant charged with murder be entitled to a manslaughter instruction? [c] If, as Justice Wilkie said in *Hoyt,* the "basic question is whether he is as culpable as a person who kills solely for self-aggrandizement or out of sheer malevolence," should the jury be given the manslaughter alternative whenever there is some evidence of some other motive? Specifically, should the jury be given the opportunity to return a manslaughter verdict where:

(a) the defendant shot his wife, who had recently commenced divorce proceedings against him, because he had long believed she had committed adultery and because, just before the killing, she did not respond when the defendant asked her to give him custody of their three children? [d]

(b) the defendant shot a woman, with whom he had been out earlier that evening, who "was jealous of [him] and did not want him to stop at another bar to drink before going home," and who "threatened to follow him and raise a commotion at his home if he did stop, and she did, in fact, follow him everywhere he went" until he stopped and approached her car, when she "laughed and appeared to be taunting him"? [e]

(c) the defendant was part of a mob which beat a police officer to death after the officer, assigned to an area which had just experienced serious racial rioting, sought to arrest defendant's friend Williams and wounded Williams in the process? [f]

(d) the defendant, a probationary postal worker, shot and killed his supervisor after she lowered his rating because of an unex-

c. In *United States ex rel. Matthews v. Johnson,* 503 F.2d 339 (3d Cir.1974), the court held that where, under Pennsylvania law, the jury had the power and prerogative to return a verdict of voluntary manslaughter in any murder prosecution, even in the absence of any evidence of provocation or passion which would require an instruction on voluntary manslaughter, and where there were no legal standards to guide the judge in determining whether to submit a voluntary manslaughter instruction in the absence of such evidence, due process was denied in refusing a request for a voluntary manslaughter instruction.

d. See *People v. Arnold,* 17 Ill.App.3d 1043, 309 N.E.2d 89 (1974), holding defendant was not entitled to a manslaughter instruction on such facts.

e. See *State v. Harwood,* 110 Ariz. 375, 519 P.2d 177 (1974), holding it was error not to instruct on manslaughter on these facts.

f. See *State v. Madden,* 61 N.J. 377, 294 A.2d 609 (1972), where the defendant was convicted of murder notwithstanding the fact the jury was also instructed on manslaughter.

"Defendants now urge that the jury should have been told (1) that racial or like antagonism or grievances may constitute provocation, and may so serve whether or not the officer was acting in the execution of his duty; and (2) that the illegal arrest or the shooting of Williams could constitute a provocation of bystanders.

"The first proposition is frivolous. It is no more than this: that racial, ethnic, religious, economic, political, or like grievances within our social order should be deemed sufficient to provoke a member of one group to kill a member of a group he deems opposed to him, or to kill every police officer as a symbol of the social order within which such grievances exist. The proposition is foreign to the subject of voluntary manslaughter. * * *

"And as to the wounding of Williams, which for the purpose of the present discussion is assumed to have involved excessive force, we * * * think provocation should not be recognized in those circumstances, for two reasons. The first is that we believe a man of ordinary firmness would not be provoked to a deadly attack. The second reason, which buttresses the first, is that the protection a police officer should have in the public interest might be diluted if his mistaken use of force were accepted as an affront to a bystander."

cused absence, which he feared would result in him losing his job.[g]

(e) the defendant testified that he invited a young lady to go for a ride, that they drove to a secluded area where she seduced him, redressed herself and then calmly informed him she was going to "cry rape" because she needed an excuse for arriving home late, at which he "panicked" and shot her.[h]

(f) the defendant stabbed and killed another man with whom he had just had sex because the other man then told the defendant that he had AIDS.[i]

4. Under the traditional "heat of passion" doctrine, a provoked defendant cannot have his homicide reduced to voluntary manslaughter where the time elapsing between the provocation and the death blow is such that a reasonable man thus provoked would have cooled; and this is so even though the defendant, being slower to cool off than the ordinary person, has not in fact cooled off by the time he delivers the lethal blow.[j] What constitutes a reasonable cooling time in a particular case depends upon the nature of the provocation and the circumstances surrounding its occurrence—a matter to be determined by the jury as a question of fact, unless the time is so short or so long that the court may hold, as a matter of law, that it was reasonable or unreasonable.

Berry follows the prevailing but not unanimous view that some act immediately preceding the killing may rekindle a passion originally aroused by some earlier provocation.

How useful is the "cooling time" concept? Consider whether the jury should be allowed to consider the alternative of manslaughter on these facts: Parker was standing in front of a drug store conversing with friends when Fraley walked up, immediately fired six shots into Parker, and said: "You damned son of a bitch! I told you I'd kill you. You killed my boy." Parker had shot and killed Fraley's son some 10 months ago and had been tried and acquitted.[k]

5. Is the case for relaxing somewhat the sudden provocation requirement, as in *Berry*, more compelling in some circumstances than others? Is *Berry* such a case? Consider Comment, 33 U.C.L.A.L.Rev. 1679, 1719–20 (1986): "When women kill men, cumulative provocation (terror) involves physical abuse and threats from the men with whom the women live, yet these women struggle to admit evidence of continual physical abuse and expert testimony to explain their reactions. For men

---

g. See *United States v. Collins*, 690 F.2d 431 (5th Cir.1982), holding defendant was not entitled to a manslaughter instruction on such facts.

h. See *State v. Butler*, 277 S.C. 452, 290 S.E.2d 1 (1982), holding defendant was not entitled to a manslaughter instruction on such facts.

i. *N.Y. Times*, March 4, 1987, p. 16, col. 1, reporting such an incident, stating "the case was the first in the country in which a man accused of murder was using AIDS in connection with this line of defense, described as the classic 'heat of passion' reasoning. * * *

" 'It is an outrageous defense,' the executive director of the Lamba Legal Defense and Education Fund, Thomas B. Stoddard, said. 'And if it were ever accepted by a court, it would set very dangerous legal and social precedents.' * * *

"According to [defense counsel] Lewis, the reaction of his client was not unwarranted.

" 'He had been handed a death sentence,' Mr. Lewis said. 'This kid won't know for the next seven years whether he is going to die. * * *' "

The defendant was permitted to plead guilty to manslaughter. *N.Y. Times*, March 24, 1987, p. 15, col. 2.

j. A minority view eliminates the reasonable-time test, so that if there is a reasonable and actual provocation, the defendant's crime is manslaughter if in fact, because of his particular temperament, he has not cooled off, though a reasonable man's passion would have subsided.

k. *Ex parte Fraley*, 3 Okl.Cr. 719, 109 P. 295 (1910), upholding denial of bail on the ground this was murder and not manslaughter.

who kill women, cumulative provocation (rage) often occurs in a similar domestic setting, but this provocation is verbal, usually involving taunts of sexual infidelity, and courts find sufficient provocation in a long course of mere verbal abuse.

"Cumulative terror should serve as an emotion adequate for heat-of-passion manslaughter and cumulative rage should not. Affronts to dignity and sexual pride should be coped with over time. The law should not mitigate culpability—thus considering a passionate reaction 'reasonable'—when the defendant 'brood[s]' over his hurt' until a relatively trivial event—usually words, which traditionally do not serve as adequate provocation—triggers his rage. On the other hand, when affronts to physical safety occur repeatedly, the law should recognize that they need not be forgotten over time. The common pattern of violence against women by their male intimates demonstrates that earlier 'trivial' episodes of physical abuse are reliable predictors of future violence and that the violence is likely to escalate until it becomes life-threatening. When a woman kills a man in response to such physical abuse, whether she claims heat of passion or self-defense, she is acting reasonably, and the accumulated abuse is relevant to her degree of guilt."

6. Tilson became involved in a fight in the Cue Lounge with Solomon, Jennings and Ellison. Tilson hurried to his car, obtained a pistol, returned to the club minutes later and shot and killed King, a friend of Tilson's assailants. Though Tilson was convicted of murder, the court of appeals reduced the crime to voluntary manslaughter. In *State v. Tilson,* 503 S.W.2d 921 (Tenn.1974), the court reversed the appellate ruling:

"To sustain the Court of Criminal Appeals would add a new dimension to the definition of voluntary manslaughter. That is, if the Court of Criminal Appeals

holding was sustained, it would now constitute voluntary manslaughter for a defendant, under reasonable and legal provocation, such as sudden combat, to kill a noncombatant by-stander, provided either by association or friendship, or both, with the other combatant, the by-stander could be characterized as 'on the side' of the one actually provoking the fight."

Do you agree? Does it follow that the manslaughter alternative should *never* be available except when the defendant kills the provoking party? What if: (a) Tilson killed King in the mistaken belief that King had been one of his assailants? (b) Tilson killed King accidently while shooting at Solomon, one of his assailants? (c) Tilson killed King while shooting at Solomon, but under circumstances such that his firing at Solomon created a known and substantial risk that King might be hit instead?

7. In *Berry,* the defendant's objection on appeal was that the court failed to instruct the jury on manslaughter. Sometimes, where the instruction is given without having been requested by the defendant and defendant is convicted of manslaughter, the appeal will be based upon the claim that it was error to give the instruction and that without the manslaughter alternative the jury might have acquitted him. See, e.g., *Elmore v. Commonwealth,* 520 S.W.2d 328 (Ky.App. 1975) (manslaughter conviction reversed because instruction on that crime, given over defendant's objection, was improper, there being no evidence "which would in any way indicate that Taylor met his death * * * in a sudden affray or a sudden heat of passion").

NOTES AND QUESTIONS ON ASSISTING SUICIDE

1. Note, 86 Colum.L.Rev. 348, 350–52 (1986): "A survey of the criminal codes of the fifty states and three United

States territories reveals that no jurisdiction defines suicide, by statute, as a criminal act. Nor does any state, by statute, criminalize attempts to commit suicide. While there is some logical difficulty in punishing one who aids an act that is not itself a crime, many states nonetheless punish suicide assistance. States that do make suicide assistance an offense generally follow one of two approaches.

"A minority of states have statutes that punish aiding a suicide, causing a suicide or both as manslaughter or murder. * * * It appears to be generally accepted, however, that actual participation in suicide, as opposed to facilitating or aiding the act, is murder. The simple form of this doctrine is: ' "Murder is no less murder because the homicide is committed at the desire of the victim." ' No jurisdiction in the United States recognizes consent to homicide.

"The majority of states that have statutes imposing criminal liability for assisting a suicide, however, make the act a unique offense, as contrasted with making it a type of murder or manslaughter."

2. Is it sensible to treat as murder every case in which the assistance reached the level of active participation, or—perhaps by analogy to the heat-of-passion doctrine—should at least some instances be characterized as some lesser offense, either manslaughter or aiding suicide? Note, supra, at 355, 361, 363, notes that "psychological studies of suicide suggest that many persons who assist suicide may do so in response to active and relentless pressure created by a victim's dependent or aggressive behavior" and that defendants have "sought to plead assistance to suicide as an affirmative defense akin to the defense of provocation," and concludes that "if a defendant has acted, not from malice, but

from compassion or fear, insisting on a charge of first-degree murder is unnecessarily harsh." Consider, in this regard, what result should be reached in the following two fact situations.

3. "In September of 1980, John Wamsley approached his friend, Dexter Mays, and asked him if he knew of anyone who could do him a favor. When Mays asked the nature of the favor he was told that Wamsley wanted someone 'to shoot somebody.' Mays agreed to do Wamsley this 'favor' for the sum of $300.00.

"On the evening of 14 October 1980, Wamsley, Mays and a third individual, a blonde-haired man, drove from Huntington to Gallipolis. On the way back, they stopped in Mason County and Mays learned that the man whom Wamsley had targeted for death was Wamsley himself. Mays claims that he was unwilling to shoot his friend and acquiesced only because he feared for his own life. With Wamsley kneeling on the ground, Mays pulled the trigger and fired three bullets into his willing victim.

"Wamsley was a homosexual and a drug dealer. His religious beliefs created within him a strong feeling of self-disdain. He was also deeply in debt and had taken out a life insurance policy which would not pay the death benefit if Wamsley committed suicide. Therefore, he had arranged his own death and had sought Mays' assistance in carrying out his ghoulish plan." [a]

4. "The minor and his friend, Jeff W., both 16 years old, drove to the Fillmore library one evening and joined a number of their friends who had congregated there. During the course of the two hours they spent at the library talking, mention was made of a car turnout on a curve overlooking a 300 to 350–foot precipice on a country road known as 'the cliff.' Both

a. *State v. Mays,* ___ W.Va. ___, 307 S.E.2d 655 (1983), rejecting defendant's argument "that there was no evidence of malice" because "his

actions were motivated either by a fear for his own life or simple heat of passion."

the minor and Jeff declared that they intended to 'fly off the cliff' and that they meant to kill themselves. * * * Jeff repeatedly encouraged the minor by urging, 'let's go, let's go' whenever the minor spoke. * * *

* * * The minor then drove off in the direction of the cliff with Jeff in the passenger seat * * *.

"Two other vehicles were parked in the turnout, from which vantage point their occupants watched the minor's car plummeting down the hill at an estimated 50 mph. The car veered off the road without swerving or changing course; the witnesses heard the car accelerate and then drive straight off the cliff. No one saw brakelights flash. The impact of the crash killed Jeff and caused severe injuries to the minor, resulting in the amputation of a foot." [b]

SECTION 2. INTENTIONAL KILLING: THE "DELIBERATE"—"PREMEDITATED" TEST

UNITED STATES v. BROWN

United States Court of Appeals, Seventh Circuit, 1975.
518 F.2d 821.

PERRY, SENIOR DISTRICT JUDGE.

Defendant Robert Lee Brown, an inmate at the United States Penitentiary at Terre Haute, Indiana, was convicted by a

jury for the murder of Elijah Atkinson, another inmate. * * *

In the indictment the Government charged that on or about May 9, 1974 at the penitentiary, Brown "with premeditation and malice aforethought, and by means of stabbing, did murder Eijah [sic] Atkinson," in violation of Title 18, United States Code, Section 1111.[1] * * *

Defendant states that the "sole issue" that he is raising in this appeal "is whether there was sufficient evidence of premeditation to support the jury's verdict of guilty of first degree murder under 18 United States Code Section 1111". In determining the sufficiency of evidence, a Court of Appeals must view the evidence and all the reasonable inferences which may be drawn therefrom in the light most favorable to the Government. * * *

It is uncontroverted that on the evening of May 9, 1974 Brown stabbed Atkinson several times in D–Unit, a living quarters unit at the penitentiary, where both were residents. D–Unit is a long corridor with two tiers of cells on each side. On the west side of the cell house is a mop room and a supply room, approximately 20 to 25 feet apart. Anywhere between five and forty-five minutes, but within an hour before the stabbing occurred, Brown and his cell had been searched. No weapon

---

b. *In re Joseph,* 34 Cal.3d 429, 194 Cal.Rptr. 163, 667 P.2d 1176 (1983), reversing the minor's juvenile court adjudication of murder, where the court stressed that "the minor and Jeff, because of the instrumentality chosen, necessarily were to commit their suicidal acts simultaneously and were subject to identical risks of death. The potential for fraud is thus absent in a genuine suicide pact executed simultaneously by both parties by means of the same instrumentality. The traditional rationale for holding the survivor of the pact guilty of murder is thus not appropriate in this limited factual situation.

"* * * To make the distinction between criminal liability for first degree murder and merely aiding and abetting suicide turn on the fortuitous circumstance of which of the pair was actually driving serves no rational purpose. The illogic of such a distinction has been similarly recognized in the classic example of the parties to the pact agreeing to commit suicide by gassing themselves

in a closed room. If the party who turns on the gas survives, he is guilty of murder; if on the other hand, the other person survives, that person's criminal liability is only that of an aider and abettor."

1. Title 18, section 1111, of the United States Code provides in pertinent part:

(a) Murder is the unlawful killing of a human being with malice aforethought. Every murder perpetrated by poison, lying in wait, or any other kind of willful, deliberate, malicious, and premeditated killing; or committed in the perpetration of, or attempt to perpetrate, any arson, rape, burglary, or robbery; or perpetrated from a premeditated design unlawfully and maliciously to effect the death of any human being other than him who is killed, is murder in the first degree.

Any other murder is murder in the second degree.

was found in Brown's cell or on his person, although an item variously described as a radio speaker or piece of electronic equipment was found in the cell. As the search ended, James D. Smith, one of the three correctional officers making the search, said Brown asked him who was the "snitch". The officer testified Brown then said, "If I find that (expletive deleted), I send him to you in a pine box". Smith explained that a "snitch" is "someone that tell on another inmate; they are doing something wrong or have something in his possession". Another correctional officer, Robert Zink, said he heard Brown say to Smith that "the next time a (expletive deleted) leaves his name [Brown's] name down there, he [Brown] will send him back to him in a box". A third officer did not hear Brown make any statement.

Later, about 8 P.M., inmate Atkinson was cleaning his cell and spilled some water in the corridor area in front of his cell. Correctional Officer Zink, who was on duty in D–Unit at the time, told Atkinson to get a mop and remove the water before someone slipped in it. About the same time, Zink was asked by another inmate to get some supplies from the supply room. Atkinson headed toward the mop room just ahead of Zink as Zink went to the supply room. Zink said Brown passed him as he went to the supply room. While getting something from the supply room, Zink heard screaming and the sound of buckets being kicked over in the mop room area. Zink testified he went to the mop room looked in, saw Atkinson on his knees and Brown stabbing Atkinson with a long, pointed weapon. Zink further testified that he yelled to Brown to stop the stabbing but that Brown continued to stab Atkinson for about a minute and a half after he yelled to Brown to stop.

Atkinson managed to crawl from the mop room to the doorway of the mop room with the upper portion of his body being through the doorway into the corridor. Zink testified Brown followed Atkinson to the doorway and there Brown stood over Atkinson and stabbed him four to six times. Some of the inmates in D–Unit saw Brown stab Atkinson in the day room corridor. One saw Atkinson fall partway out of the doorway of the mop room and he testified Brown stepped over Atkinson, then stopped and stabbed him four or five times. Another inmate saw Brown stab Atkinson two times near the mop room. Another testified he saw Atkinson bleeding and on his knees in the mop room door and Brown standing in the hall.

* * *

Atkinson was pronounced dead shortly after 8 P.M. in the prison hospital. He had suffered 21 stab wounds on his face, neck, sides, chest and back. Brown was questioned in the captain's office and later taken to another cell. On the way another inmate asked Brown what had happened and a guard testified that Brown said, "I just got rid of a punk who's been bothering me". Another guard heard a similar statement. * * *

It is well settled that the question of whether or not reflection and consideration amounting to deliberation required for first degree murder actually occurred must be determined by the jury, properly instructed by the court, from the facts and circumstances of the case. The jury received from the court ample instructions as to malice, malice aforethought, premeditation, specific intent, self-defense and the essential disputed elements of first degree murder, second degree murder and voluntary manslaughter.[2] * * *

2. The court gave the following instruction on premeditation:

Section 1111 of Title 18 of the United States Code further provides that:

"Every murder perpetrated by * * * lying in wait, or any other kind of willful, deliberate,

malicious, and premeditated killing * * * is murder in the first degree. Any other murder is murder in the second degree."

By "willful, deliberate and premeditated" is meant that the killing is done after a period of time for prior consideration. The duration of

Although it is clear that deliberation and premeditation involve a prior design to commit murder, the authorities are in accord that no particular period of time is necessary for such deliberation and premeditation. Although there is some conflict among the courts as to whether there need be any appreciable time for reflection and consideration between the formation and execution of the design, the courts which have held that some appreciable time must elapse have not attempted to measure the time period. For example, in *Bostic v. United States,* 68 App.D.C. 167, 94 F.2d 636 (1937), the court held that some appreciable time must elapse but that the period of time "does not require the lapse of days or hours, or even minutes".[a]

Appellant argues that there is no affirmative proof of premeditation on his part. Despite the difficulties in adducing proof as to a state of mind, premeditation and deliberation are susceptible of proof. Of course the mental processes of Brown are wholly subjective and cannot be proved directly, but premeditation may be established by adducing evidence from the facts and circumstances surrounding the killing. * * * This was a vicious and prolonged attack. Brown stabbed Atkinson not once but 21 times. The stabbings in the corridor were deliberate and not committed on impulse. Atkinson was by then in a helpless position and offering no resistance, and certainly at this point Brown was not acting in fear of injury or in self-defense. The jury was entitled to make reasonable deductions and inferences from the proven facts. It could have concluded from the evidence that there was ample opportunity for premeditation, before and during the repeated stabbings in the mop room, and certainly during the time which elapsed between the stabbings in the mop room and the time it took for Atkinson to crawl out of the mop room into the corridor, where the stabbings were resumed. The jury was not compelled to draw such a conclusion, but it properly could so do. We believe the facts and circumstances surrounding the resumption of the stabbings in the corridor are the strongest in establishing premeditation and, standing alone, justified the jury's finding that the killing was willful, deliberate, malicious and premeditated, with malice afore-thought. * * *

Counsel for the defendant * * * claims that no inference of premeditation is to be drawn from the violence or brutality of the crime alone and that proof of a brutal crime standing alone is not sufficient evidence to support a finding of premeditation. To support this claim he cites * * * *Austin v. United States,* 127 U.S. App.D.C. 180, 382 F.2d 129 (1967)[b]

---

that period cannot be arbitrarily fixed. The time in which to form a deliberate design varies as the minds and temperaments of men differ, and according to the circumstances in which they may be placed. Any interval of time between the forming of the intent to kill and the execution of that intent, which is of sufficient duration for the accused to be fully conscious of what he intended, is sufficient to support a conviction for murder. Thus, a murder which is perpetrated by any kind of willful, deliberate and premeditated killing, with malice aforethought, is murder in the first degree.

But if done with malice aforethought, but without deliberation and premeditation, that is, without the willful, deliberate and premeditated intent to take life which is an essential element of first degree murder, then the offense is murder in the second degree. * * *

a. Compare *Government of Virgin Islands v. Lake,* 362 F.2d 770 (3d Cir.1966) ("a brief moment of thought may be sufficient to form a fixed, deliberate design to kill"); with *Bullock v. United States,* 122 F.2d 213 (D.C.Cir.1941) ("To speak of premeditation and deliberation which are instantaneous, or which takes no appreciable time, is a contradiction in terms.").

b. In *Austin* the court said:

"In homespun terminology, intentional murder is in the first degree if committed in cold blood, and is murder in the second degree if committed on impulse or in the sudden heat of passion. These are the archtypes, that clarify by contrast. The real facts may be hard to classify and may lie between the poles. A sudden passion, like lust, rage, or jealousy, may spawn an impulsive intent yet persist long enough and in such a way as to

where the evidence showed the defendant stabbed and cut the victim a total of 50 times. There the defendant and victim had been drinking in a bar prior to the killing. *Austin* is clearly distinguishable from the case at bar in that the court held that the evidence was as consistent with an impulsive and senseless frenzy, possibly heightened by drink, as with premeditation, and consequently did not permit a reasonable juror to find beyond a reasonable doubt that there was premeditation. We believe the evidence of such a violent killing strongly tends to prove the killing was done maliciously and with premeditation and that it also reflects the state of mind of Brown before and during the successive stabbings. The fact that cruelty or brutality is manifested in a killing will raise an inference of malice and the length of time of premeditation is not material.

The defense refers to the time between the stopping of the stabbings in the mop room and their resumption in the corridor as only a "pause," and contends it was not proved that the intervening time constituted a legitimate opportunity for premeditation. We have found the evidence showed an interval for reflection and that this killing was not a mere persistence of an initial impulse or passion. There was time for second thought. *Fisher v. United States,* 328 U.S. 463, 470, 66 S.Ct. 1318, 90 L.Ed. 1382 (1946). * * *

* * * Appellant argues that neither his statement made before the stabbing, about a "snitch," nor his statement, after

the killing, about getting rid of a "punk" bothering him, supports a finding of premeditation. We believe both statements were properly accorded probative value * * *. Reasonable jurors could have inferred from the first statement that Brown thought Atkinson was the "snitch" and had given information which led to the search of Brown's cell. * * * After the killing, Brown made the statement about getting rid of a "punk" bothering him, and from this the jury could have inferred that Brown harbored animosity toward Atkinson. As to intent, every sane man is presumed to intend the natural and probable consequences of his own act. *Allen v. United States,* 164 U.S. 492, 496, 17 S.Ct. 154, 41 L.Ed. 528 (1896). The jury could have fairly inferred that when Brown repeatedly stabbed Atkinson, was told to desist, stopped and then resumed the stabbings, the destruction of Atkinson's life was intended. * * *

We see no reason to disturb the judgment of conviction of the District Court and it is affirmed.

Notes and Questions

1. Compare *People v. Gill,* 43 Mich. App. 598, 204 N.W.2d 699 (1972): Gill was convicted of murdering Jones, a fellow prisoner at Jackson State Prison. Another prisoner, Knopek, testified that Jones had been his "protector," that on the day of the murder Gill was pressing him for homosexual purposes and became engaged in an argument with Jones. Gill told Jones,

permit that intent to become the subject of a further reflection and weighing of consequences and hence to take on the character of a murder executed without compunction and 'in cold blood.' The term 'in cold blood' does not necessarily mean the assassin lying in wait, or the kind of murder brilliantly depicted by Truman Capote in *In Cold Blood* (1965). Thus the common understanding might find both passion and cold blood in the husband who surprises his wife in adultery, leaves the house to buy a gun at a sporting goods store, and returns for a deadly sequel. The analysis of the jury would be illuminated, howev-

er, if it is first advised that a typical case of first degree is the murder in cold blood; that murder committed on impulse or in sudden passion is murder in the second degree; and then instructed that a homicide conceived in passion constitutes murder in the first degree only if the jury is convinced beyond a reasonable doubt that there was an appreciable time after the design was conceived and that in this interval there was a further thought, and a turning over in the mind—and not a mere persistence of the initial impulse of passion."

"If you don't leave here, let me talk to the boy * * * I will cut you off the gallery." Gill told Knopek that if he didn't do what Gill wanted, Gill would see that there was great bodily harm done to him and to Jones. Cottee, another prisoner, testified he heard a noise from a tier (or gallery) of cells above him and that when he moved to a position where he was able to see Gill and Jones fighting, he saw a dull-colored instrument in Gill's hand and saw Gill strike Jones with it twice, at which Jones fell to the floor. Jones suffered four stab wounds, including one which pierced the heart and caused his death. The murder weapon was never found. The court reversed Gill's conviction of second degree murder on the ground that he had been prejudiced by the fact that the trial judge had also submitted an instruction on first degree murder to the jury.

"In order to convict Gill of the more aggravated offense of first-degree murder, the people were obliged to establish the additional statutory elements of premeditation and deliberation. Recently, in *People v. Morrin,* 31 Mich.App. 301, 187 N.W.2d 434, we discussed at some length the history and underlying rationale of the premeditation and deliberation requirement.[a]

* * *

"Focusing on the facts of this case the sequence of events establishes a threat, a fight, and a killing. What is missing is the time factor [11] between the threat and the fight and any showing that there was an opportunity for cool-headed reflection on Gill's part. Without such evidence, the sequence of events is as consistent with an unpremeditated killing—following hard on the outset of the argument—as it is with a premeditated killing after an interval during which there was an opportunity for cool-headed reflection."

2. B. Cardozo, *Law and Literature and Other Essays and Addresses* 99–101 (1931): "I think the distinction is much too vague to be continued in our law. There can be no intent unless there is a choice, yet by the hypothesis, the choice without more is enough to justify the inference that the intent was deliberate and premeditated. The presence of a sudden impulse is said to mark the dividing line, but how can an impulse be anything but sudden when the time for its formation is measured by the lapse of seconds? Yet the decisions are to the effect that seconds may be enough. What is meant, as I understand it, is that the impulse must be the product of an emotion or passion so swift and overmastering as to sweep the mind from its moorings. A metaphor, however, is, to say the least, a shifting test whereby to measure degrees of guilt that mean the difference between life and death. I think the students of the mind should make it clear to the lawmakers that the statute is framed

---

a. In *Morrin,* the court stated: "[I]t underscores the difference between the statutory degrees of murder to emphasize that premeditation and deliberation must be given independent meaning in a prosecution for first-degree murder. The ordinary meaning of the terms will suffice. To premeditate is to think about beforehand; to deliberate is to measure and evaluate the major facets of a choice or problem. As a number of courts have pointed out, premeditation and deliberation characterize a thought process undisturbed by hot blood. While the minimum time necessary to exercise this process is incapable of exact determination, the interval between initial thought and ultimate action should be long enough to afford a reasonable man time to subject the nature of his response to a 'second look'."

11. The time element in this case was poorly established at trial, with relatively few questions directed toward the witnesses. It appears that the threat was followed in relatively short order by the killing.

Knopek indicated that the argument took place between 3:40 p.m. and 4 p.m. The testimony of inmates Maxwell and Bussel seemed to establish that Jones died from his wounds between 4:30 p.m. and 4:45 p.m. Dr. Bartholic pronounced Jones dead in the prison hospital at 4:50 p.m. Cottee, the only witness who observed the fight, was not questioned about the time element. There is no way of knowing when the struggle between Gill and Jones began, and, most importantly, how soon after the threat the struggle began.

along the lines of a defective and unreal psychology. If intent is deliberate and premeditated whenever there is choice, then in truth it is always deliberate and premeditated, since choice is involved in the hypothesis of the intent. What we have is merely a privilege offered to the jury to find the lesser degree when the suddenness of the intent, the vehemence of the passion, seems to call irresistibly for the exercise of mercy. I have no objection to giving them this dispensing power, but it should be given to them directly and not in a mystifying cloud of words. The present distinction is so obscure that no jury hearing it for the first time can fairly be expected to assimilate and understand it.[b] I am not at all sure that I understand it myself after trying to apply it for many years and after diligent study of what has been written in the books. Upon the basis of this fine distinction with its obscure and mystifying psychology, scores of men have gone to their death."

3. In *State v. Schrader*, ___ W.Va. ___, 302 S.E.2d 70 (1982), the court affirmed defendant's first degree murder conviction and approved a jury instruction that to prove premeditation and deliberation the state need only show that the intention came "into existence for the first time at the time of such killing." Such an instruction, the court emphasized, squared with

the longtime interpretation of the state's murder statute that the "distinctive element in wilful, deliberate, and premeditated murder, not in murder of the second degree, is the specific intention to take life." The court added:

"Unfortunately, all of the considerations to which Justice Cardozo alluded that can be subsumed under the category of 'culpability' cannot be reduced to neat, prepackaged, jury instructions. The traditional instructions on the subject of murder are continually repeated not because they succeed in converting subjective considerations to objective considerations, but rather because they have always been given and they do about as well in this regard as any other attempt. The instruction objected to in this case has been given for years and has withstood our scrutiny before."

4. *Model Penal Code* § 210.6, Comment (1980): "It seems clear that the deliberation standard ought to exclude from the capital category cases where the homicide is committed under the influence of an extreme mental or emotional disturbance produced by causes that give rise to proper sympathy for the defendant. * * * Given this recognition of the role of mental or emotional disturbance, the case for a mitigated sentence on conviction of murder does not depend on a distinction between impulse and deliberation. Prior

b. Consider, in this regard, *People v. Sneed*, 183 Colo. 96, 514 P.2d 776 (1973). The trial court dismissed a charge of first degree murder on the ground that the murder statute was unconstitutionally vague. The statute defined first degree murder as causing death "with premeditated intent to cause the death," second degree murder as causing death "intentionally, but without premeditation," and premeditation as "a design formed to do something at any time before it is done." The trial court emphasized that under *Van Houton v. People*, 22 Colo. 53, 43 P. 137 (1895), the length of time needed for premeditation is the time sufficient for "one thought to follow another." In reversing the trial court, the court asserted:

"It is true that if we apply the rule in *Van Houton* that premeditation occurs as fast as one

thought follows another, then there does not seem to be much difference between 'premeditated intent' and 'intentionally.' But as we have said, the legislature certainly intended that there be a meaningful distinction between first degree and second degree murder. Accordingly, it is clear that it, as it had the power to do, rejected the definition of premeditation as announced in *Van Houton*. In effect, by emphasizing that 'premeditated intent' and 'intentionally, but without premeditation' were different, and that premeditation required design before the act, it indicated deliberation and reflection were necessary to create the premeditated intent.

"This means that between the forming of the intent to do the act and the act itself, an appreciable length of time must have elapsed to allow deliberation, reflection and judgment."

reflection may reveal the uncertainties of a tortured conscience rather than exceptional depravity. The very fact of a long internal struggle may be evidence that the homicidal impulse was deeply aberrational and far more the product of extraordinary circumstances than a true reflection of the actor's normal character. Thus, for example, one suspects that most mercy killings are the consequence of long and careful deliberation, but they are not especially appropriate cases for imposition of capital punishment. The same is likely to be true with respect to suicide pacts, many infanticides and cases where a provocation gains in its explosive power as the actor broods about his injury.[c]

"It also seems clear, moreover, that some purely impulsive murders will present no extenuating circumstance. The suddenness of the killing may simply reveal callousness so complete and depravity so extreme that no hesitation is required. As Stephen put the point long ago:

As much cruelty, as much indifference to the life of others, a disposition at least as dangerous to society, probably even more dangerous, is shown by sudden as

by premeditated murders. The following cases appear to me to set this in a clear light. A, passing along the road, sees a boy sitting on a bridge over a deep river and, out of mere wanton barbarity, pushes him into it and so drowns him. A man makes advances to a girl who repels him. He deliberately but instantly cuts her throat. A man civilly asked to pay a just debt pretends to get the money, loads a rifle and blows out his creditor's brains. In none of these cases is there premeditation unless the word is used in a sense as unnatural as 'aforethought' in 'malice aforethought', but each represents even more diabolical cruelty and ferocity than that which is involved in murders premeditated in the natural sense of the word.[62]"

5. What is the best solution to the problems set out in the preceding notes? Should the premeditation-deliberation test and, indeed, any division of murder into degrees be abandoned, as a number of jurisdictions have done? Or, should a new test be devised? Consider *State v. Jenkins,* 48 Ohio App.2d 99, 355 N.E.2d 825 (1976), commenting upon the new

---

c. Consider, for example, *People v. Gibson,* 23 Cal.App.3d 917, 101 Cal.Rptr. 620 (1972), affirming a first degree murder conviction on these facts: "On January 4, 1971, the defendant fired a single shot into the head of his twelve-year-old son causing his almost immediate death. He called the police, informed them of the killing and was taken into custody at the scene. At the initial meeting with the arresting officers the defendant appeared to be calm and rational and in possession of his faculties. His constitutional rights were read to him from a '*Miranda*' advisement card, and he again stated that he had killed his son. He did not appear, at this time, to be confused, irrational, or in any type of trance or pain.

"The deceased son was described by his mother as an autistic child who was unable to speak, had no empathy, failed to relate to sadness, was self-destructive and hyperactive, with a sexual orientation which was causing his parents concern because of fear that he might harm someone.

"A psychiatrist described infantile autism as one of the most severe, if not the most severe

form of childhood mental disorder. It is characterized by failure to talk, severe motor disturbances, compulsive repetitious behavior, inability to learn, and problems with interpersonal relationships. The autistic child frequently becomes the focal point of his family because of the needs and demands he generates. Many times the family structure is severely disturbed by the intense and constant preoccupation with the problems of the autistic child.

"Defendant had suffered from a severe heart condition since approximately 1958 and had suffered an attack as recently as the day before the killing of the son. The years of hopeless search for assistance for the autistic son, coupled with physical deterioration of the defendant as a consequence of his heart disease, was proffered by defense to prove that defendant's mental state at the time of the offense was such that he could not by reason of diminished mental capacity form the degree of intent requisite for first degree murder."

62. 3 J. Stephen, *History of the Criminal Law* 94 (1883).

provision that the defendant must have purposely caused the death of another with "prior calculation and design":

"Prior calculation and design sets up a more demanding standard than the old first degree murder standard of 'deliberate and premeditated malice.' Prior calculation and design requires the accused to have killed purposefully after devising a plan or scheme to kill. There must be some kind of studied analysis with its object being the means by which to kill. The kind of momentary deliberation or instantaneous premeditation that was the accepted standard under the old statute is no longer sufficient or acceptable.

"The trier of fact must look to the context in which the killing occurred to determine whether there was prior calculation and design. Some of the important factors to be examined and considered in deciding whether a homicide was committed with prior calculation and design include: whether the accused knew the victim prior to the crime, as opposed to a random meeting, and if the victim was known to him whether the relationship had been strained; whether thought and preparation were given by the accused to the weapon he used to kill and/or the site on which the homicide was to be committed as compared to no such thought or preparation; and whether the act was drawn out over a period of time as against an almost instantaneous eruption of events. These factors must be considered and weighed together and viewed under the totality of all circumstances of the homicide."

6. In *Fisher,* relied upon in *Brown,* the Supreme Court affirmed a first degree murder conviction on the following facts, as stated by the Court:

"The homicide took place in the library building on the grounds of the Cathedral of Saint Peter and Saint Paul, Washington, D.C., between eight and nine o'clock, a.m., on March 1, 1944. The victim was the librarian. She had complained to the verger a few days before about petitioner's care of the premises. The petitioner was the janitor. The verger had told him of the complaint. Miss Reardon and Fisher were alone in the library at the time of the homicide. The petitioner testified that Miss Reardon was killed by him immediately following insulting words from her over his care of the premises. After slapping her impulsively, petitioner ran up a flight of steps to reach an exit on a higher level but turned back down, after seizing a convenient stick of firewood, to stop her screaming. He struck her with the stick and when it broke choked her to silence. He then dragged her to a lavatory and left the body to clean up some spots of blood on the floor outside. While Fisher was doing this cleaning up, the victim 'started hollering again.' Fisher then took out his knife and stuck her in the throat. She was silent. After that he dragged her body down into an adjoining pump pit, where it was found the next morning. The above facts made up petitioner's story to the jury of the killing.

"It may or may not have been accepted as a whole by the jury. Other evidence furnishes facts which may have led the jury to disbelieve some of the details of accused's version of the tragedy. In his original confession, the accused made no reference to Miss Reardon's use of insulting words. In his written confession, they were mentioned. In his testimony their effect upon him was amplified. There are minor variations between Fisher's written confession and his testimony. In the written confession Fisher admitted that his main reason for assaulting Miss Reardon was because she reported him for not cleaning the library floor. The Deputy Coroner said the knife wound was not deep, 'just went through the skin.' "

The trial court had refused to instruct the jury to consider the evidence of the defendant's psychopathic aggressive ten-

dencies, low emotional response and borderline mental deficiency in determining
whether he was guilty of murder in the
first or in the second degree. The Supreme Court, noting it would not interfere
with "local rules of law" in the District
"save in exceptional situations where egre-
gious error has been committed," concluded this was not such a case. Indeed, the
Court asserted that it had "long been the
law of the District" that such subjective
factors are not to be considered by the
jury, and cited in support a case decided
before murder was divided into degrees in
the District and which involved the question of whether such an instruction should
be given concerning the difference between murder and voluntary manslaughter. "Such a radical departure from common law concepts," the Court concluded
in *Fisher*, "is more properly a subject for
the exercise of legislative power." [d]

7. Compare *People v. Wolff,* 61 Cal.2d
795, 40 Cal.Rptr. 271, 394 P.2d 959
(1964), where the court reduced defen-

d. The *Fisher* rule was ultimately abandoned
in *United States v. Brawner,* p. 376 of this Book.

The question of whether a defendant's "diminished capacity" should be taken into account in
determining whether he has the requisite mental
state for the crime charged is considered further
in Chapter 6, Section 4 of this Book.

e. The court in *Wolff* described the facts in
this way:

"In the case at bench there was evidence that
in the year preceding the commission of the
crime defendant "spent a lot of time thinking
about sex." He made a list of the names and
addresses of seven girls in his community whom
he did not know personally but whom he planned
to anesthetize by ether and then either rape or
photograph nude. One night about three weeks
before the murder he took a container of ether
and attempted to enter the home of one of these
girls through the chimney, but he became wedged
in and had to be rescued. In the ensuing weeks
defendant apparently deliberated on ways and
means of accomplishing his objective and decided
that he would have to bring the girls to his house
to achieve his sexual purposes, and that it would
therefore be necessary to get his mother (and
possibly his brother) out of the way first.

dant's first degree murder conviction
down to murder in the second degree:

"Certainly in the case now at bench the
defendant had ample *time* for any normal
person to maturely and appreciatively reflect upon his contemplated act and to
arrive at a cold, deliberated and premeditated conclusion.[e] He did this in a
sense—and apparently to the full extent of
which he was capable. But, indisputably
on the record, this defendant was not and
is not a fully normal or mature, mentally
well person. He knew the difference between right and wrong; he knew that the
intended act was wrong and nevertheless
carried it out. But the extent of his understanding, reflection upon it and its consequences, with realization of the enormity
of the evil, appears to have been materially—as relevant to appraising the quantum
of his moral turpitude and depravity—
vague and detached. We think that our
analysis in [*People v. Holt,* 25 Cal.2d 59,
153 P.2d 21 (1944)] of the minimum
essential elements of first degree murder,
especially in respect to the quantum of

"The attack on defendant's mother took place
on Monday, May 15, 1961. On the preceding
Friday or Saturday defendant obtained an axe
handle from the family garage and hid it under
the mattress of his bed. At about 10 p.m. on
Sunday he took the axe handle from its hiding
place and approached his mother from behind,
raising the weapon to strike her. She sensed his
presence and asked him what he was doing; he
answered that it was 'nothing,' and returned to
his room and hid the handle under his mattress
again. The following morning defendant arose
and put the customary signal (a magazine) in the
front window to inform his father that he had not
overslept. Defendant ate the breakfast that his
mother prepared, then went to his room and
obtained the axe handle from under the mattress.
He returned to the kitchen, approached his mother from behind and struck her on the back of the
head. She turned around screaming and he
struck her several more blows. They fell to the
floor, fighting. She called out her neighbor's
name and defendant began choking her. She bit
him on the hand and crawled away. He got up to
turn off the water running in the sink, and she
fled through the dining room. He gave chase,
caught her in the front room, and choked her to
death with his hands."

reflection, comprehension, *and turpitude of the offender,* fits precisely this case: that the use by the Legislature of 'wilful, deliberate, and premeditated' in conjunction indicates its intent to require as an essential element of first degree murder (of that category) substantially more reflection; i.e., more understanding and comprehension of the character of the act than the mere amount of thought necessary to form the intention to kill. It bears repeating that 'Dividing intentional homicides into murder and voluntary manslaughter was a recognition of the infirmity of human nature. Again dividing the offense of murder into two degrees is a further recognition of that infirmity and of difference in the quantum of personal turpitude of the offenders. The difference is basically in the offenders.' " f

PEOPLE v. ANDERSON

Supreme Court of California, 1968.
70 Cal.2d 15, 73 Cal.Rptr. 550, 447 P.2d 942.

TOBRINER, JUSTICE.

Defendant was indicted for the murder of Victoria Hammond, a 10–year–old girl, in 1962. The jury found defendant guilty of first degree murder, found that he was sane, and fixed the penalty at death.

*   *   *

Defendant, a San Jose cab driver, had been living for about eight months with a Mrs. Hammond and her three children, Cynthia, aged 17, Kenneth, aged 13, and the victim, Victoria, aged 10. On the morning of the day of the murder, December 7, 1962, Mrs. Hammond left for work

at 7:30 a.m., leaving only Victoria at home with the defendant. Defendant was still in bed. He had been home from work for the previous two days, during which time he had been drinking heavily, and apparently he did not go to work on the day of the murder.

The owner of a nearby liquor store testified that defendant purchased a quart of whisky from him sometime between 1 and 2 p.m. on December 7, 1962. The only other witness who testified as to defendant's whereabouts that day prior to the discovery of the murder was the victim's 13–year–old brother Kenneth.

Kenneth testified that he arrived home from school at 3:30 p.m. on December 7. He found the front door locked, which was not unusual, so he went around to the back of the house and down to the basement. Kenneth stayed there awhile working with his microscope. In a short time he heard noise coming from upstairs in the house which sounded like boxes and other things being moved around, like someone was cleaning up. He then heard the shower water running. A police officer later verified that a person in the basement could hear water running in the shower and movement in Victoria's bedroom.

Kenneth testified further that he then came up from the basement and went to the back porch screen door. The screen door was locked, which also was not unusual, so Kenneth jerked on it so the hook would pop out. Kenneth then went from the back porch directly into his bedroom to change his clothes. He then returned

f. As for the state's claim that the crime was first degree murder because the killing was committed by "lying in wait" (also stated by statute to be first degree murder), the court responded: "It must be remembered that 'lying in wait' is simply evidence which, if unexplained and unqualified by other evidence, would ordinarily establish that the perpetrator was guilty of a 'wilful, deliberate, and premeditated killing.' "

Compare *State v. Johnson*, 317 N.C. 193, 344 S.E.2d 775 (1986), holding "that premeditation

and deliberation is not an element of the crime of first-degree murder perpetrated by means of poison, lying in wait, imprisonment, starving, or torture. Likewise, a specific intent to kill is equally irrelevant when the homicide is perpetrated by means of poison, lying in wait, imprisonment, starving, or torture; and we hold that an intent to kill is not an element of first-degree murder where the homicide is carried out by one of these methods. Cases from other jurisdictions support this view."

through the back porch to the kitchen door which was also locked. Kenneth knocked on the door and the defendant opened it. Kenneth testified that the defendant was wearing slacks only. Kenneth went into the kitchen and asked defendant for $1.00 for a teen club dance he intended to attend that evening. Defendant obtained a dollar for him out of the pocket of another pair of slacks hanging on the knob of a bedroom door. When Kenneth noticed the blood on the kitchen floor and asked defendant about it, the defendant told Kenneth that he had cut himself. This explanation apparently satisfied Kenneth, as he finished dressing and left the house sometime before 4 p.m.

Kenneth testified that no one else was at his house when he was there between 3:30 and 4 p.m. He further testified that about 6:30 he realized that he had forgotten his wallet and returned home. As he approached the front door, his mother came out and asked to see the cut on his arm, and Kenneth explained that he had no cut. His mother then asked defendant about the blood she had noticed and defendant told her that Victoria had cut herself, but that the mother should not worry, as the cut was not serious. After defendant told her that Victoria was at a friend's for dinner, the mother wanted to take Kenneth with her to get Victoria. Kenneth went back to his room to get a jacket. Because he had a "weird" feeling, he looked into Victoria's room. He found her nude, bloody body under some boxes and blankets on the floor near her bed. Kenneth ran out of the room screaming that defendant had killed her. Mrs. Hammond, after seeing Victoria's body, went next door to phone the police.

Mrs. Hammond testified that she returned home from work at 4:45 p.m. The front door was locked, she rang the doorbell, and defendant answered. Mrs. Hammond noticed blood on the couch in the living room, and when she asked defen-

dant about it, he told her that Kenneth had cut himself playing with a knife and that he was at a teenage dance. Mrs. Hammond then went to the grocery store and returned about 5:30 p.m. She testified that at both times she arrived home defendant was drinking a highball. She also testified as to examining Kenneth's arm for a cut when he returned home for his wallet and as to defendant's subsequent explanation that Victoria had been cut, but not seriously. Mrs. Hammond discovered Victoria's body after Kenneth came out of Victoria's room.

A classmate of Victoria, who was the last person to see Victoria alive, testified that she left Victoria in front of the Hammond house about 3:45 p.m. after the two of them had walked home from school.

When the police arrived at 7 p.m. the shades were down on all the windows and the doors were locked. Defendant finally opened the front door for one of the officers who arrested and handcuffed defendant. The arresting officer testified that defendant was wearing slacks, no shirt or shoes, and that there was no blood on him.

The arresting officer found Victoria's body on the floor near her bed. He found defendant's blood-spotted shorts on a chair in the living room, and a knife and defendant's socks, with blood encrusted on the soles, in the master bedroom. The evidence established that the victim's torn and blood-stained dress had been ripped from her, that her clothes, including her panties out of which the crotch had been ripped, were found in various rooms of the house, that there were bloody footprints matching the size of the victim's leading from the master bedroom to Victoria's room, and that there was blood in almost every room including the kitchen, the floor of which appeared to have been mopped.

The TV cameraman who covered the murder story for channel 11, the officer who drove defendant to the police station, and the officer who "observed" defendant for four hours at the station the night of December 7, 1962, all testified that defendant did not appear intoxicated. The officers who talked to defendant testified, however, that they smelled alcohol on his breath; a blood test taken at 7:45 p.m. indicated that the alcohol content in defendant's blood was .34 percent, which was more than necessary for an automobile driver to be classified as "under the influence."

Over 60 wounds, both severe and superficial, were found on Victoria's body. The cuts extended over her entire body, including one extending from the rectum through the vagina, and the partial cutting off of her tongue. Several of the wounds, including the vaginal lacerations, were post mortem. No evidence of spermatozoa was found in the victim, on her panties, or on the bed next to which she was found. * * *

We must, in the absence of substantial evidence to support the verdict of first degree murder, reduce the conviction to second degree murder. * * *

As we noted in *People v. Bender,* 27 Cal. 2d 164, 183, 163 P.2d 8, we find no indication that the Legislature intended to give the words "deliberate" and "premeditated" other than their ordinary dictionary meanings. Moreover, we have repeatedly pointed out that the legislative classification of murder into two degrees would be meaningless if "deliberation" and "premeditation" were construed as requiring no more reflection than may be involved in the mere formation of a specific intent to kill.

Thus we have held that in order for a killing with malice aforethought to be first rather than second degree murder, " '[t]he intent to kill must be * * * formed upon a *pre-existing* reflection' * * * [and have] been the subject of actual deliberation or *forethought.* * * * ''

The type of evidence which this court has found sufficient to sustain a finding of premeditation and deliberation falls into three basic categories: (1) facts about how and what defendant did *prior* to the actual killing which show that the defendant was engaged in activity directed toward, and explicable as intended to result in, the killing—what may be characterized as "planning" activity; (2) facts about the defendant's *prior* relationship and/or conduct with the victim from which the jury could reasonably infer a "motive" to kill the victim, which inference of motive, together with facts of type (1) or (3), would in turn support an inference that the killing was the result of "a pre-existing reflection" and "careful thought and weighing of considerations" rather than "mere unconsidered or rash impulse hastily executed"; (3) facts about the nature of the killing from which the jury could infer that the *manner* of killing was so particular and exacting that the defendant must have intentionally killed according to a "preconceived design" to take his victim's life in a particular way for a "reason" which the jury can reasonably infer from facts of type (1) or (2).

Analysis of the cases will show that this court sustains verdicts of first degree murder typically when there is evidence of all three types and otherwise requires at least extremely strong evidence of (1) or evidence of (2) in conjunction with either (1) or (3). As will become clear from the following analysis of representative cases, the present case lacks evidence of any of the three types.

In *People v. Hillery,* 62 Cal.2d 692, 44 Cal.Rptr. 30, 401 P.2d 382, the jury could reasonably infer that the defendant engaged in the following "extended course of conduct": defendant parked his car near the victim's (a 15–year–old girl's) house, entered the house surreptitiously, seized the victim while she was sewing and covered her head with a towel and slip to prevent outcry or identification, cut a length of cord in another room to secure her hands behind her, took the victim's scissors, dragged her to a nearby irrigation ditch where her body was subsequently found, engaged in a struggle with the victim, and then plunged the scissors directly into her chest.

Hillery represents a case of very strong type (1) evidence: the defendant's surreptitious conduct, subjection of his victim to his complete control, and carrying off of his victim to a place where others were unlikely to intrude, can be described as "planning" activity directly related to the killing. Moreover, there is also strong evidence of type (3): directly plunging a lethal weapon into the chest evidences a deliberate intention to kill as opposed to the type of "indiscriminate" multiple attack of both severe and superficial wounds which defendant engaged in in the instant case. * * *

People v. Cole (1956) 47 Cal.2d 99, 301 P.2d 854, 56 A.L.R.2d 1435, involved a defendant living with an impecunious woman (his victim) and desirous of marrying a well-to-do woman. The evidence established that the defendant secretly took the latter's gun from her dresser the week before the killing, that he was carrying it on the evening of the killing, and that he used it to kill his victim. Moreover, the evidence also tended to show that defendant planned to implicate the wealthier woman so as to secure her assistance in concealing his guilt and that he killed the victim to remove her as an obstacle to his marital plans. As the court pointed out, "a showing of motive indicating that the killing was planned" tends to support an inference of premeditation and deliberation. *Cole* thus represents a case of prima-

rily type (2) evidence supported by type (1) evidence. * * *

The present case is strikingly similar to *People v. Granados,* 49 Cal.2d 490, 319 P.2d 346, in which this court reduced a verdict of first degree murder to second degree murder * * *.

In *Granados,* defendant lived in a common law relationship with the mother of his victim, a 13–year–old girl. After taking the deceased and her brother to a real estate office, defendant gave the brother a note requesting money to take to his mother who worked nearby. When the brother returned home with the requested money he saw defendant at the rear of the house. As he started to enter the house, defendant came running to him and asked him to get some alcohol for his sister (decedent) who had fainted. The brother noticed blood on one of defendant's hands and that defendant had the other hand behind his back.

The brother unsuccessfully looked for some alcohol. Defendant then suggested they get a doctor and an ambulance. The brother then noticed that defendant's hand had been washed. Defendant then drove the brother to a drugstore, gave him 50 cents for some alcohol, and told him he would wait for him. The defendant drove away and did not return for the brother.

Defendant then called the mother and told her the victim had poisoned herself. The mother returned to the house with a friend who found the victim's body in the bedroom lying on the floor. Her skirt was pulled up exposing her private parts, there were bloodstains on the wall, floor, and decedent's head, and a machete covered with blood was lying in a corner of the living room behind a small heater.

Defendant testified that on the day of the killing the girl was helping him clean the house and that he asked her if she was a virgin, to which she replied that it was none of his business. Defendant said that she had never answered him in that way and that he therefore struck her with his hand, but did not remember striking her with the machete.

Decedent's mother testified that she had warned defendant that the next time he bothered her daughter, she would tell the police, and that defendant in reply threatened to kill her and both her children if she did.

The prosecution argued that the murder was sexually motivated. This court, per Justice McComb, held that the evidence was insufficient as a matter of law to support a verdict of first degree murder.

Applying the standards developed above to *Granados,* we find that the only evidence of (1) defendant's behavior prior to the killing which could be described as "planning" activity related to a killing purpose was defendant's sending the victim's brother on an errand and apparently returning home alone with the decedent. Such evidence is highly ambiguous in terms of the various inferences it could support as to defendant's purpose in so behaving. The evidence of (2) defendant's prior behavior with the victim (alleged sexual molestation and his question as to her virginity) is insufficient to support a reasonable inference that defendant had a "motive" to kill the girl, which could in turn support an inference that the striking with the machete was the result of a "preconceived design" and "forethought." Finally, the evidence of (3) the manner of killing (brutal hacking) does not support a reasonable inference of deliberately placed blows, which could in turn support an inference that the act of killing was premeditated rather than "hasty and impetuous." * * *

Finally, the defendant in *Granados,* as here, attempted to "cover up" the crime by lying to the brother and the mother of the victim. Although this type of evidence may possibly bear on defendant's

state of mind *after* the killing, it is irrelevant to ascertaining defendant's state of mind immediately prior to, or during, the killing. Evasive conduct shows fear: it cannot support the double inference that defendant planned to hide his crime at the time he committed it and that therefore defendant committed the crime with premeditation and deliberation. * * *

We conclude that a finding of premeditation and deliberation cannot be sustained in the absence of any evidence of (1) defendant's actions prior to the killing, (2) a "motive" or "reason" from which the jury could reasonably infer that defendant intended to kill Victoria, or (3) a manner of killing from which the jury could reasonably infer that the wounds were deliberately calculated to result in death. As in *People v. Granados,* the evidence suffices only to support a verdict of second degree murder. * * *

Notes and Questions

Consider in which of the following situations a conviction for first degree murder should be affirmed.

1. The defendant told someone the morning of the murder that he would "like to have a little loving." On the evening of the murder he went to a bar where he threatened a woman who refused to dance with him. Later that evening he left another bar with a man who saw the victim approaching the intersection where he parted company with the defendant. The victim was found the next morning under a car at a service station near that intersection. She apparently had been dragged there. She was wearing a raincoat with only a slip and panties on underneath. All three garments were ripped open so that the front part of her body was exposed. She was lying on her back with her legs spread apart. She had suffered multiple contusions, caused by an estimated 20 to 80 blows. Four heel

marks were found on her body, and a key to the defendant's hotel room was found in her clothing. The morning after the murder defendant told someone that "I beat up a woman" and that when he hit them "they stayed hit." [a]

2. Defendant was an acquaintance of Mrs. Southerland and had been an occasional visitor at her home. He stopped by unexpectedly one evening while Mrs. Southerland and her 10–year–old grandson were watching television. They talked for more than an hour, laughing and chatting amicably with no heated discussions, arguments, or threats. Defendant walked back and forth to the window on several occasions, and repeatedly asked when Mr. Southerland would be home. Some time after the grandson had retired, Mrs. Southerland gently suggested to defendant that she wished to go to sleep, but defendant did not take the hint. At about 10:40 p.m., as she began to doze off, she was struck on the head by a succession of blows. She heard quick footsteps which she thought were headed toward the front door, and she then managed to drag herself out the back door. She then heard her grandson scream from his upstairs bedroom. When the police arrived, they found the grandson on the bed in his bedroom. The lad, his bed, the walls, and the floor all were covered with blood. He had been hit repeatedly with a blunt instrument and the blows to his head killed him. The defendant was later arrested at his home. The police found in his closet a hammer with the victim's blood on it.[b]

3. Four eyewitnesses testified that defendant forced his way into the victim's automobile, parked on the pow-wow ground of the Rosebud Indian Reservation, put a butcher knife to her throat, and then stabbed her in the back as she attempted to escape his grasp. Defendant then threw the knife into the woods as he fled; it was recovered and was determined to be the knife which had disappeared from the residence of defendant's aunt several days earlier. Two witnesses placed defendant in the vicinity of the victim's parked car 30 minutes prior to the stabbing. The vehicle had been in good working order prior to its arrival, but some time during the celebration it had been disabled through disconnection of a coil wire. The victim, who had been defendant's wife during a brief and unstable marriage, died from the stab wound.[c]

SECTION 3. RECKLESS AND NEGLIGENT KILLING

HYAM v. DIRECTOR OF PUBLIC PROSECUTIONS

House of Lords, 1974.
[1975] A.C. 55, [1974] 2 W.L.R. 607, [1974] 2 All E.R. 41.

LORD HAILSHAM OF ST. MARYLEBONE. My Lords, * * * for the reasons I have given in my opinion the appeal fails and should be dismissed.

VISCOUNT DILHORNE. My Lords, for some considerable time the appellant had had regular sexual relations with a Mr. Jones. In consequence of her having some gynaecological trouble those relations ceased and were not resumed after she had had an operation in 1968. She became suspicious of Mr. Jones's relations with a Mrs. Booth and very jealous of her. She tried to break up that association by the writing of anonymous letters. In May

---

a. *People v. Craig,* 49 Cal.2d 313, 316 P.2d 947 (1957), holding the evidence only established second degree murder.

b. *Hemphill v. United States,* 402 F.2d 187 (D.C.Cir.1968), holding the evidence only established second degree murder.

c. *United States v. Blue Thunder,* 604 F.2d 550 (8th Cir.1979), affirming defendant's conviction of first degree murder.

1972 Mrs. Booth obtained a decree nisi of divorce from her husband. That decree was due to be made absolute towards the end of July 1972, and then Mrs. Booth would have been free to marry Mr. Jones.

On July 15, 1972, at about 2 a.m. the appellant drove a van to the house where Mrs. Booth lived with her son and two daughters aged, we were told, 17 and 11. On her way there she went past Mr. Jones's house to see if he was there. The lights were on so she decided that he was in. She did that, she said, because she did not want to do any harm to Mr. Jones. She parked the van round the corner from Mrs. Booth's house. She took a gallon can of petrol from the van and poured petrol through the letter box in Mrs. Booth's front door. She then put newspaper in the letter box and lit it. The petrol ignited and the appellant said that she realised that what she had done was tremendously dangerous to anyone living in the house. She, however, did nothing to alert the occupants of the house to the danger she had put them in or the fire brigade. She just drove to her home some five miles away.

Mrs. Booth and her son succeeded in escaping from the house. Her two daughters did not and were killed. The appellant was charged with and convicted of their murder.

At the beginning of his summing up Ackner J. told the jury that a person who unlawfully and deliberately causes the death of another intending either to kill or to do serious bodily harm is guilty of murder. He said that there was no dispute that the appellant had killed the two children and that it was not suggested that the setting fire to the house was other than a deliberate act. He told the jury that the only question on which they had to focus their attention was the appellant's intent.

He had written down, and he had handed to the jury, his direction with regard to intent. It was in the following terms:

"The prosecution must prove, beyond all reasonable doubt, that the accused intended to (kill or) do serious bodily harm to Mrs. Booth, the mother of the deceased girls. If you are satisfied that when the accused set fire to the house she knew that it was highly probable that this would cause (death or) serious bodily harm then the prosecution will have established the necessary intent. It matters not if her motive was, as she says, to frighten Mrs. Booth." * * *

In this House Mr. McCullough for the appellant * * * submitted that knowledge that a certain consequence was a highly probable consequence does not establish an intent to produce that result. "All consequences that are foreseen are not," he said, "necessarily intended."

He also contended that the direction given by Ackner J. was erroneous in another respect, namely, that * * * intent to do grievous bodily harm did not, nor did knowledge that such harm was the probable result, suffice to make a killing murder. For it to be murder, he contended that the intent must be to kill or to endanger life or, if knowledge was enough, knowledge that the act would kill or endanger life.

With regard to his first contention, [i]n his *Digest of the Criminal Law,* published in 1877, in art. 223, Sir James Stephen defined "malice aforethought" as involving the following states of mind:

"(*a*) An intention to cause the death of, or grievous bodily harm to, any person, whether such person is the person actually killed or not;

(*b*) Knowledge that the act which causes death will probably cause the death of, or grievous bodily harm to, some person, whether such person is the person actually killed or not, although such knowledge is accompanied by indifference whether death or grievous bodily harm is caused or not, or by a wish that it may not be caused; * * *."

The Royal Commission on Capital Punishment (1949–1953) in their report (Cmd. 8932) said, at p. 27, that this was the statement of the modern law most commonly cited as authoritative. * * *

Stephen in his *Digest* treated such knowledge as a separate head of malice aforethought and distinct from those in which intent is necessary. The Royal Commission treated it as justifying a conviction of murder even if the accused did not intend to kill or to do grievous bodily harm. If this view is right, then Ackner J. was wrong in telling the jury that proof of such knowledge established the necessary intent.

On the other hand, Lord Devlin in a lecture he gave in 1954 (reported at [1954] Crim.L.R. 661) said, at pp. 666–667, that where a man has decided that certain consequences would probably happen, then

"for the purposes of the law he intended them to happen, and it does not matter whether he wanted them to happen or not * * * it is criminal intent in the strict sense." * * *

Whether or not it be that the doing of the act with the knowledge that certain consequences are highly probable is to be treated as establishing the intent to bring about those consequences, I think it is clear that for at least 100 years such knowledge has been recognised as amounting to malice aforethought. * * *

I now turn to the second contention advanced on behalf of the appellant. This has two facets: first, that the reference to the intent to cause grievous bodily harm has been based on the law that killing in the course or furtherance of a felony is murder, and that when the Homicide Act 1957 was enacted abolishing constructive malice it meant that it no longer sufficed to establish intent to do grievous bodily harm; and, secondly, that, if intent to do grievous bodily harm still made a killing murder, it must be intent to do grievous bodily harm of such a character that life was likely to be endangered.

Committing grievous bodily harm was for many, many years, and until all felonies were abolished, a felony. Consequently so long as the doctrine of constructive malice was part of the law of England, to secure a conviction for murder it was only necessary to prove that the death resulted from an act committed in the course of or in furtherance of the commission of grievous bodily harm. But when one looks at the cases and the old textbooks, one does not find any indication that proof of intent to do grievous bodily harm was an ingredient of murder only on account of the doctrine of constructive malice. Indeed, one finds the contrary. * * *

Killing with intent to do grievous bodily harm has thus for many years been regarded as murder, quite apart from the doctrine of constructive malice. This was recognised in the report of the Royal Commission on Capital Punishment (1953) (Cmd. 8932). Their five propositions stated in paragraph 76 which were, so the report said, generally accepted to be properly included in the category of murder, were

" * * * all cases where the accused either *intended* to cause death or grievous bodily harm or *knew* that his act was likely to cause death or grievous bodily harm" (paragraph 77).

The Royal Commission went on to recommend the abolition of constructive malice, and in paragraph 123 suggested a clause for inclusion in a Bill to bring that about. * * *

I now turn to the second facet of the appellant's contention, namely, that the words "grievous bodily harm" are to be interpreted as meaning harm of such a character as is likely to endanger life.

* * *

If the words bore the meaning now contended for, there must have been many murder cases in which that was not explained to the jury and in which there was consequently a substantial misdirection. The Royal Commission on Capital Punishment in their review of the law did not suggest that the words had this limited meaning. Indeed, in paragraph 472 of the report [(1953) (Cmd. 8932)] the following appears:

"We should therefore prefer to limit murder to cases where the act by which death is caused is intended to kill or to 'endanger life' or is known to be likely to kill or endanger life. But we do not believe that, if this change were made, it would lead to any great difference in the day-to-day administration of the law."

In the same paragraph it is stated that Stephen expressed the opinion that to substitute "bodily injury known to the offender to be likely to cause death" would to some extent narrow the definition.

* * *

Our task is to say what, in our opinion, the law is, not what it should be. In the light of what I have said, in my opinion, the words "grievous bodily harm" must, as Viscount Kilmuir said, be given their ordinary and natural meaning and not have the gloss put on them for which the appellant contends. * * *

To change the law to substitute "bodily injury known to the offender to be likely to cause death" for "grievous bodily harm" is a task that should, in my opinion, be left to Parliament if it thinks such a change expedient. If it is made, an accused will be able to say: "True it is that I intended grievous bodily harm or that I knew such harm was likely to result but I never intended to kill the dead man or to put his life in danger and I did not know that by doing him serious bodily harm I would put his life in danger." But I share the view of the majority of the Royal Commission that such a change would not lead to any great difference in the day-to-day administration of the law.

For these reasons in my opinion this appeal should be dismissed.

LORD DIPLOCK. * * *

Upon the first question I do not desire to say more than that I agree with those of your Lordships who take the uncomplicated view that in crimes of this class no distinction is to be drawn in English law between the state of mind of one who does an act because he desires it to produce a particular evil consequence, and the state of mind of one who does the act knowing full well that it is likely to produce that consequence although it may not be the object he was seeking to achieve by doing the act. What is common to both these states of mind is willingness to produce the particular evil consequence: and this, in my view, is the mens rea needed to satisfy a requirement, whether imposed by statute or existing at common law, that in order to constitute the offence with which the accused is charged he must have acted with "intent" to produce a particular evil consequence or, in the ancient phrase which still survives in crimes of homicide, with "malice aforethought."

I turn then to the second question. I believe that all your Lordships are agreed that if the English law of homicide were based on concepts that are satisfactory, both intellectually and morally, the crime of murder ought to be distinguished from less heinous forms of homicide by restricting it to cases where the consequence of his act, which the accused desired or foresaw as likely, was the death of a human being. * * *

My Lords, the now familiar expression "grievous bodily harm" appears to owe its place in the development of the English law of homicide to its use in 1803 in Lord Ellenborough's Act (43 Geo. 3, c. 58), which made it a felony to shoot at, stab or cut any other person "with intent * * * to murder, * * * maim, disfigure, or disable, * * * or * * * do some other grievous bodily harm * * *" * * *

The felony created by Lord Ellenborough's Act was one in which the intent with which the physical act was done was a necessary ingredient of the offence; but the intent here, unlike that needed to constitute actual malice in the offence of murder, was defined in the statute itself. Consequently after the passing of Lord Ellenborough's Act, wherever the act that caused the death was shooting, stabbing or cutting, it became constructive malice and so made the killing murder if the intent with which the act was done was to do any "grievous bodily harm" within the meaning of the statute. * * *

In the result, so long as the doctrine of constructive malice continued to be part of the English law of murder, it ceased to matter whether the actual intent with which the act that caused the death was done was an intent to do "grievous bodily harm" within the meaning of the successive statutes or some more heinous intent that might have had to be proved in order to show actual malice sufficient to constitute the crime of murder at common law. So where, as in the generality of murder charges, the prosecution did not rely upon the intent of the accused to commit some other felony such as robbery, rape or abortion, but relied solely on his intent to do physical harm to any person, the distinction between constructive malice and actual malice had no practical consequences and in course of time came to be overlooked.

In 1957 all this was altered. The doctrine of constructive malice was abolished by section 1 of the Homicide Act 1957. * * *

So with the passing of the Homicide Act 1957 the courts were faced with a dual task: first, to discover as a matter of historical research what state of mind of the accused was regarded by the 18th century judges as constituting actual malice for the purposes of the crime of murder; and, secondly, to decide in what respects the views on this matter of subsequent generations of judges, if all of them were wise, would have been modified to take account of the way in which material circumstances and social concepts had been developed throughout the 19th and 20th centuries—a task which presents a challenge without precedent to the wisdom of those upon whom this decision rests.

The material for the task of historical research is scanty. There was no systematic contemporaneous reporting of criminal trials before the 19th century. There was no check upon how individual judges directed juries on the criminal law, unless the judge himself chose to reserve a point of law for the informal consideration of his brother judges at Serjeants' Inn—and even such reports as there are of the opinions expressed by all the judges on points of law which were reserved are sparse and haphazard. * * *

If what was written before the 19th century about the degree of violence that must have been intended by the accused in order to support a charge of murder is to be properly understood, there are several matters to be borne in mind.

(1) It must be remembered that, judged by present day standards, we are dealing with a violent age. Men were used to carrying deadly weapons and not slow to resort to them. So, at the beginning of the period Coke did not classify as murder a killing on "a sudden falling out." Later

when this defence became merged in the general doctrine of provocation most of the cases with which the writers were preoccupied involved the use of deadly weapons and it is not without significance that Lord Ellenborough's Act itself was concerned only with shooting, stabbing and cutting.

(2) Medical and surgical science were in a very primitive state. Any bodily injury, particularly if it involved risk of sepsis through an open wound, might well prove mortal although today the likelihood of its resulting in death would be insignificant. It was not until the last quarter of the 19th century that antiseptics came into general use.

(3) Until the 19th century the common law did not recognise unconsummated attempts to commit a crime as being criminal offences in themselves. So in relation to the crime of murder judges were dealing with bodily injuries which had in fact been fatal, and so demonstrated to have been of a kind which could endanger life.

(4) As stated by Foster J. it was accepted law in the 18th century that once the fact of killing was proved the onus lay upon the prisoner to prove facts negativing malice aforethought unless such facts arose out of the evidence produced against him.

(5) Until as late as 1898 persons accused of murder were incompetent to give evidence in their own defence. So the actual intent with which they had done the act which had in fact caused death could only be a matter of inference from the evidence of other witnesses as to what the accused had done or said. In drawing this inference from what he had done it was necessary to assume that the accused was gifted with the foresight and reasoning capacity of a "reasonable man" and, as such, must have foreseen as a possible consequence of his act, and thus within his intention, anything which, in the ordinary course of events, might result from it.

Bearing these considerations in mind, I for my part find it impossible to say with confidence whether or not by the close of this period judges, when in connection with malice aforethought they used various expressions connoting physical injuries, did so with the unexpressed major premise in mind: "All physical injuries, at any rate if they are serious, are likely to endanger life" and so equated intent to cause serious physical injuries with intent to endanger life. * * *

My Lords, even if the first step towards the solution of the problem with which the courts were confronted by the statutory abolition of the doctrine of constructive malice does not lead to a confident conclusion that judges at the close of the 18th century would only have regarded as sufficient to constitute the actual malice needed for the crime of murder an intention to inflict bodily injury if the intended injury was such as in the existing state of medical skill and science was likely to endanger life, any difficulty created by this is, I think, resolved when one proceeds to the second step, viz., a consideration of how the law in this matter would have developed in the 19th and 20th centuries if there had been no doctrine of constructive malice.

Since the first Commissioners on the Criminal Law issued their Fourth Report in 1839, it has been the uniform view of those who have assumed or been charged with the task of codifying the law of homicide that the relevant intention on a charge of murder should be an intention to kill or to cause any bodily injury which is known to the offender to be likely to endanger life. Such was the view expressed by the Criminal Code Commissioners in 1879, by Stephen in 1877 and 1833, by the Royal Commission on Capital Punishment in 1953 and by the Law Commission in 1966. [Report No. 10, Imputed Criminal Intention (*Director of Public Prosecutions v. Smith*)]. The significance of the citations that I have already made from all but the last of these is that they show that it was the opinion of these eminent lawyers at the various dates when they were writing that this would involve a rationalisation of the existing common law rather than any change in it. I have no doubt that the judges in the course of the 19th and 20th centuries would have held this to be the law as to express malice had they not been diverted from doing so by the doctrine of constructive malice.   *   *   *

For my part I would allow the appeal and substitute a verdict of guilty of manslaughter for the verdict of guilty of murder.

LORD CROSS OF CHELSEA.   *   *   * I agree with my noble and learned friend, Lord Kilbrandon, that now that murder no longer attracts the death penalty it would be logical to replace the two crimes of murder and manslaughter by a single offence of unlawful homicide; but there are considerations, in which logic plays little part, which tell against the making of such a change—and as long as one has the two separate crimes one has to decide on which side of the line any given state of mind falls. Stephen's definition covers four states of mind. A(1) an intent to kill, (2) knowledge that the act in question will probably cause death. B(1) an intent to cause grievous bodily harm, (2) knowledge that the act in question will probably cause grievous bodily harm. Counsel for the appellant argued strenuously that there was a great gulf fixed between A(1) and B(1) on the one hand, and A(2) and B(2) on the other, and that unless the accused believed that the consequences in question were certain to ensue, one ought not to equate mere foresight of consequences with an intention to produce them. Even if one views the matter simply from the point of view of linguistics I am not sure that the ordinary man would agree. If, for example, someone parks a car in a city street with a time bomb in it which ex-

plodes and injures a number of people I think that the ordinary man might well argue as follows: "The man responsible for this outrage did not injure these people unintentionally; he injured them intentionally. So he can fairly be said to have intentionally injured them—that is to say, to have intended to injure them. The fact that he was not certain that anyone would be injured is quite irrelevant (after all, how could he possibly be certain that anyone would be injured?); and the fact that, although he foresaw that it was likely that some people would be injured, it was a matter of indifference to him whether they were injured or not (his object being simply to call attention to Irish grievances and to demonstrate the power of the I.R.A.) is equally irrelevant." But I can see that a logician might object that the ordinary man was using the word "intentionally" with two different shades of meaning, and I am prepared to assume that as a matter of the correct use of language the man in question did not intend to injure those who were in fact injured by his act. But we are not debating a problem of linguistics; we are asking ourselves whether Stephen was right in saying that the states of mind labelled A(2) and B(2) constitute "malice aforethought." The first question to be answered is whether if an intention to kill—using intention in the strict sense of the word—is murder—as it plainly is— doing an unlawful act with knowledge that it may well cause death ought also to be murder. I have no doubt whatever that it ought to be.   *   *   * Turning now to the states of mind labelled B(1) and (2)—*if* it is the law that an intention to cause grievous bodily harm—using intention in the strict sense of the word—is "malice aforethought," whether or not one realises that one's act may endanger life, then I think that it is right that the doing of an act which one realises may well cause grievous bodily harm should also constitute malice aforethought whether or not one realises that one's act may endanger life.   *   *   *

LORD KILBRANDON.   *   *   *

My Lords, it is not so easy to feel satisfaction at the doubts and difficulties which seem to surround the crime of murder and the distinguishing from it of the crime of manslaughter. There is something wrong when crimes of such gravity, and I will say of such familiarity, call for the display of so formidable a degree of forensic and judicial learning as the present case has given rise to. I believe this to show that a more radical look at the problem is called for, and was called for immediately upon the passing of the Act of 1967. Until that time the content of murder—and I am not talking about the definition of murder—was that form of homicide which is punishable with death. (It is not necessary to notice the experimental period during which capital murder and non-capital murder existed side by side.) Since no homicides are now punishable with death, these many hours and days have been occupied in trying to adjust a definition of that which has no content. There does not appear to be any good reason why the crimes of murder and manslaughter should not both be abolished, and the single crime of unlawful homicide substituted; one case will differ from another in gravity, and that can be taken care of by variation of sentences downwards from life imprisonment. It is no longer true, if it was ever true, to say that murder as we now define it is necessarily the most heinous example of unlawful homicide. The present case could form an excellent example exhibiting as it does, assuming it to be capable of classification as manslaughter, a degree of cold-blooded cruelty exceeding that to be found in many an impulsive crime which could never, on our present law, be so classified.

My Lords, since the passage in the summing up of the learned judge which was

particularly noticed is not consistent with the common law as it has now, as I agree, been shown to be, and the proviso was not relied on, it follows that this appeal should be allowed.

Appeal dismissed.

NOTES AND QUESTIONS ON KILLING BY GROSS RECKLESSNESS (DEPRAVED HEART)

1. Smith, *A Case of Reckless Murder,* 123 New L.J. 792, 793 (1973), written before *Hyam* was decided by the House of Lords, expressed the fear that if the instructions were upheld juries "would then need to be very carefully directed that they must ascertain exactly what the accused foresaw, at the time he carried out his fateful act, as regards harm and the likelihood of such harm occurring. A great difficulty would be trying to communicate to the jury the meaning of 'highly probable', and how the jury could deduce the extent of danger apparent to the accused. It does not require much imagination to see that anything resembling a uniform standard of approach and result would be hard to achieve. The consequential danger of this could be a considerable blurring of the distinction between murder and manslaughter with the probable further effect of diluting the odium which is usually attached to murder.

"Having hinted at some of the dangers involved in embracing recklessness in the context of murder, one must put the question: should recklessness form the basis of a murder charge in any circumstances? A familiar example is that of the person who plants in an aircraft a bomb primed to explode at 25,000 feet in order to collect the insurance money on his fake Old Master being carried as freight. In such a case the chances of life not being lost are of course infinitesimal, but if such a person had no intention of seriously harming anyone he would not (without the aid of some form of liability based on recklessness) be liable for murder even though he had foreseen the virtual certainty of death. Such an extreme example of recklessness is only a hair's breadth away from intent to kill and certainly it manifests such a similar degree of "wickedness" (to borrow Lord Denning's terminology) as to warrant the stigma reserved for murder.

"The problem then is not one of possible fundamental ethical objections to accepting something other than direct intent to kill or cause grievous bodily harm as a basis of liability for murder, but rather where and how one is to draw the line between a reckless murder and manslaughter by recklessness, so as to be able to differentiate between cases equivalent to the bomb in the aircraft example from less extreme forms of recklessness."

2. Elliott, *Offences Against the Person—Murder,* [1977] Crim.L.Rev. 70, 74–75, 77, comments critically on the proposals of the Criminal Law Revision Committee which would limit the *Hyam* rule:

"A definition of murder which includes risk-taking they regard as too wide, partly because it would include cases which are in practice dealt with as manslaughter (or were until the decision in *Hyam v. D.P.P.*) and partly because it would include a person who takes the risk of serious injury with no foresight of death. It 'would have the effect that the motorist who drives recklessly and kills someone, and the architect who designs a building involving the use of material which he knows to be highly inflammable and who thus causes a death in a fire, will be classed as murderers together with the bomber who places a bomb in a supermarket, killing a shopper, and the bank robber who fires over the heads of people in the bank but kills someone when a bullet ricochets'.

"One notes that it is not the fact that some of these four cases will be classified as murder which bothers the committee; it is the fact that *all* of them will be. It is bracketing the motorist and the architect with the supermarket bomber and the bank robber which the committee assume is objectionable, although how that can be *assumed* when *ex hypothesi* they all exhibit the same mental attitude is not at all made plain. The committee recognise that what distinguishes these people from true murderers is their lack of knowledge of the likelihood of death. They agree that they could exclude all of them by a requirement of foresight of death, but rule that out because foresight of death would then mean foresight that death would *probably* or *very probably* ensue and that would be an uncertain test for a jury to apply.
* * *

"To catch such cases they propose that it should be murder to cause death by an unlawful act intended to cause fear and known to the defendant to involve a risk of causing death.

" * * * Murder is about contempt for life or safety, not about causing fear. The line they draw is tortuous, and unattractive in leaving many imaginable cases on what will seem to many to be the wrong side. Challenged to do better and propose a more appropriate factor than intent to cause fear, a critic might decline, rejecting the whole approach as a futile attempt to distinguish cases by rule in a field where experience and intuition unite in affirming that the only tool is, not rule, but discretion."

3. In *Hyam,* the instruction was in part stated in terms of whether the defendant "knew that it was highly probable" that her conduct would cause death. Can the line between murder and manslaughter be meaningfully drawn in terms of probabilities? If so, what degree of probability does it take to make death-causing conduct murder? Consider *Commonwealth v. Ashburn,* 459 Pa. 625, 331 A.2d 167

(1975), where the appellant contended "that the court's discussion of *Commonwealth v. Malone,* 354 Pa. 180, 47 A.2d 445 (1946), in its charge to the jury was tantamount to a direction to return a verdict of guilty of murder in the second degree. There is no merit to this contention.

"The *Malone* case bears certain striking factual similarities to the case at bar. Malone and Long, two adolescents on friendly terms with each other, procured a five chamber pistol and one cartridge, and decided to play 'Russian poker'. Malone then placed the muzzle of the pistol against Long's body and pulled the trigger three times, fatally discharging the pistol on the third pull. Malone was convicted of murder in the second degree. On appeal, this Court affirmed his conviction, remarking:

'The killing of William H. Long by this defendant resulted from an act intentionally done by the latter, in reckless and wanton disregard of the consequences which were at least sixty per cent certain from his thrice attempted discharge of a gun known to contain one bullet and aimed at a vital part of Long's body. This killing was, therefore, murder, for malice in the sense of a wicked disposition is evidenced by the intentional doing of an uncalled-for act in callous disregard of its likely harmful effects on others.'

"It was Ashburn's counsel who first broached the subject of the *Malone* case to the jury. Seizing on the passage quoted above, he argued that the odds that Ashburn's second pull of the trigger would result in Santagada's death were significantly less than three in five. In making this argument, counsel suggested that this Court in *Malone* had defined murder in the second degree as any act at least sixty per cent certain to result in the death of another.

"This was a misstatement of the law which the court was duty-bound to correct. This the court did in a fair and judicious manner. After defining the elements of murder in the second degree, the court delivered the standard charge, based on *Malone,* relative to acts of gross recklessness resulting in death. The court then briefly described the *Malone* case, and pointed out that the application of the general principles of law announced therein does not depend on any precise mathematical calculation of the probable consequences of the defendant's acts. This was an accurate statement of the law. Taken as a whole, the court's instructions clearly indicated that the task of applying the law to the facts of Ashburn's case was the jury's and the jury's alone. We find no error in it."

4. Some statutes and cases describe this variety of murder in more flowery language, such as that it is murder if "all the circumstances of the killing show an abandoned and malignant heart." E.g., *Mayes v. People,* 106 Ill. 306 (1883), affirming a murder conviction where the defendant threw a beer glass at his wife and the glass struck an oil lamp she was carrying, causing a fire which brought about her death. Is this language less or more helpful than the probability formula in *Hyam?* See *People v. Phillips,* 64 Cal.2d 574, 51 Cal.Rptr. 225, 414 P.2d 353 (1966), holding that the jury should not be instructed in such language, though it appears in the statutory definition of murder, because "it could lead the jury to equate the malignant heart with an evil disposition or a despicable character."

5. Would it be more meaningful to draw the murder-manslaughter distinction in terms of the means by which the killing was done? In *State v. Chalmers,* 100 Ariz. 70, 411 P.2d 448 (1966), reversing defendant's murder conviction for a death resulting from his driving between 80 and 100 m.p.h., the court took note of the

statutory provision "that in the crime of murder malice may be implied 'when the circumstances attending the killing show an abandoned and malignant heart.' This term also occurs in many other jurisdictions in defining the offense of murder. However, we have found no case which would indicate that gross negligence alone would constitute such conduct as appears to be contemplated when referring to 'an abandoned and malignant heart.' The latter phrase seems to mean conduct by the use of a weapon or other applicance likely to produce death, and by the brutal and blood-thirsty use of such instrumentality."

6. Consider *Model Penal Code* § 210.2. In support, the draftsmen state in *Model Penal Code* § 210.2, Comment (1980): "Since risk * * * is a matter of degree and the motives for risk creation may be infinite in variation, some formula is needed to identify the case where recklessness may be found and where it should be assimilated to purpose or knowledge for purposes of grading. * * * In a prosecution for murder, * * * the Code calls for the further judgment whether the actor's conscious disregard of the risk, under the circumstances, manifests extreme indifference to the value of human life. The significance of purpose or knowledge as a standard of culpability is that, cases of provocation or other mitigation apart, purposeful or knowing homicide demonstrates precisely such indifference to the value of human life. Whether recklessness is so extreme that it demonstrates similar indifference is not a question, it is submitted, that can be further clarified. It must be left directly to the trier of fact under instructions."

7. Note, 85 Colum.L.Rev. 786, 789–90 (1985), observes that "four distinct approaches dominate the modern treatment of unintended murder": (1) the *objective circumstances* approach, which focuses upon the circumstances surrounding the crime rather than the defendant's attitude toward the victim's life, such as with the New York requirement that the jury determine whether the defendant's acts were themselves "brutal, callous, dangerous and inhuman"; (2) the *degree of risk* approach, which limits murder to cases in which the defendant's acts created a particularly significant chance of causing a death; (3) the *multiple victim* approach, whereunder a defendant is guilty only if his reckless act endangers more than one individual; and (4) the *mens rea* approach, which requires some state of mind more culpable than recklessness. This Note concludes at 807 that the latter approach is best; that in jurisdictions where this approach obtains we "have failed to put the question of indifference to courts and juries in a sufficiently concrete and definite manner"; and that extreme indifference can best be discovered "by asking the finder of fact whether the actor would have committed the act *had he known* it would cause a death." Do you agree?

8. "Test" the approach you favor by applying it to these situations: (a) Randolph and Smith supplied heroin to seller Barnhill, who sold one gram to Jones on August 14th. Barnhill knew this was "pure" or "uncut" heroin, and claims to have warned Jones not to take quantities or injections as great as on previous occasions in that the heroin was uncut because she had not had an opportunity to dilute it. Jones died from a self-injected overdose on August 15th. On August 17th, an undercover agent recorded a conversation in which Smith said to Barnhill, "You can't say that I didn't tell you that that definitely needed to be cut before it went out on the street," and Randolph observed that the same thing had happened to one of his customers two weeks earlier. Ran-

dolph, Smith and Barnhill have been charged with murder.[a]

(b) Ibn was pursued by police while he was driving a stolen Mercedes, but they were unable to catch up to him despite speeds of 100 m.p.h. Ibn drove through one roadblock, and an officer had to jump off the road to avoid being hit. Ibn then drove through a second roadblock when an officer moved his car onto the shoulder to avoid a collision. Ibn then drove through a third roadblock and at that moment had a blowout. The car continued down the road until it hit a hay truck and then swerved about 50 feet into a field, where it struck and killed Cross, who was visible from the road. Ibn has been charged with murder.[b]

(c) Watson drove to a bar, where he consumed a large quantity of beer. At one a.m. he drove through a red light and barely missed a vehicle and then continued on into another intersection (apparently through a green light) at 70 m.p.h. He skidded and swerved into the only other car on the otherwise deserted streets. Two occupants of that car were killed. Watson's blood alcohol content was .23, more than twice the amount necessary to support a finding that he was legally intoxicated. Watson has been charged with murder.[c]

(d) Markowski, knowing that he had tested positive for the AIDS virus, sold some of his blood to a commercial blood bank. As a result, one recipient of Markowski's blood contracted AIDS and died.[d]

(c) Moore, a prison inmate who knew he had tested positive for the AIDS virus, got into a dispute with a prison guard and, in the course of an altercation, bit the guard. Though there had not theretofore been any documented cases in which the virus had been transmitted by bites, the guard contracted AIDS and died.[e]

NOTES AND QUESTIONS ON KILLING WITH INTENT TO DO SERIOUS BODILY INJURY

1. Elliott, *Offences Against the Person— Murder,* [1977] Crim.L.Rev. 70, 73–74, discusses the proposals of the Criminal Law Revision Committee on this subject:

"A minority of the Committee, who were in favour of an intent to cause serious injury, *simpliciter,* remaining a sufficient intent in murder, argued, first, that a person who inflicts serious injury on another intentionally must know that there is a real chance that the victim will die, so if he does die, it is right that the killer should be convicted of murder, and, secondly, that a person who is minded to use violence in achieving an unlawful purpose may take more care to refrain from inflicting serious injury if he knows that a murder conviction awaits him if the victim dies. The majority notice these arguments only to reject them, saying 'The majority of us, however, think that if an intent to cause serious injury is to remain part of the

a. *State v. Randolph,* 676 S.W.2d 943 (Tenn. 1984), reversing dismissal of the murder charge.

b. *State v. Ibn Omar–Muhammad,* 102 N.M.2d 274, 694 P.2d 922 (1985), reversing the murder conviction for an erroneous jury instruction stating an objective standard of knowledge of risk.

c. *People v. Watson,* 30 Cal.3d 290, 179 Cal. Rptr. 43, 637 P.2d 279 (1981), reversing dismissal of the murder charge. *Watson* is criticized in Note, 71 Calif.L.Rev. 1298 (1983). Compare *Essex v. Commonwealth,* 228 Va. 273, 322 S.E.2d 216

(1984), reversing a murder conviction on somewhat similar facts because the "jury could only speculate, upon this evidence, whether the defendant embarked upon his ill-fated course of conduct wilfully and with a malicious purpose."

d. *Nat'l L.J.,* July 20, 1987, p. 3, col. 1, reporting such a sale of blood without fatal consequences, resulting in the defendant being charged with attempted murder.

e. Id., reporting such a case without fatal consequences. The defendant was convicted of assault with a deadly weapon.

mens rea of murder, it should be limited in some way so that it is related more closely to the fact of death.' This is apparently because for a person to be convicted of murder if he caused death with the intention of inflicting serious harm but without knowing or foreseeing that death was likely would be unacceptable to them. They do not say why it would be unacceptable.

"Having decided that some limiting factor is needed, the majority disagree on whether objective likelihood of death or subjective knowledge in the accused of likelihood of death should be chosen."

2. English, *Homicides Other than Murder*, [1977] Crim.L.Rev. 79, asks: "Is someone who causes death intending only serious injury more culpable than someone who causes death recklessly?"

3. Although the intent-to-do-serious-bodily-injury type of murder is generally to be found in American jurisdictions, some of the modern codes have abandoned the doctrine, as does the Model Penal Code. As explained in *Model Penal Code* § 210.2, Comment (1980), "it is preferable to handle such cases under the standards of extreme recklessness and recklessness contained in Sections 210.2(1)(b) and 210.3(1)(a). That the actor intended to cause injury of a particular nature or gravity is, of course, a relevant consideration in determining whether he acted with 'extreme indifference to the value of human life' under Section 210.2(1)(b) or 'recklessly' with respect to death of another under Section 210.3(1)."

4. It has often been held that an "intent to kill or to do great bodily harm [is] inferable from the intentional use of a deadly weapon upon the body of the deceased." *Bantum v. State*, 46 Del. 487; 85 A.2d 741 (1952). Moreover, while "[o]rdinarily blows inflicted by one person on another with bare fists do not demonstrate the malice requisite to sustain a conviction of second degree murder[,]

* * * a protracted and continued beating with bare hands by a stronger person upon a weaker person can evince the malice necessary for a conviction of murder." *State v. Bias*, 156 W.Va. 569, 195 S.E.2d 626 (W.Va.1973).

UNITED STATES v. ESCAMILLA

United States Court of Appeals, Fourth Circuit, 1972.
467 F.2d 341.

WINTER, CIRCUIT JUDGE:

Defendant, Mario Jaime Escamilla, was convicted of involuntary manslaughter, in violation of 18 U.S.C.A. § 1112, perpetrated on Fletcher's Ice Island T–3, an unclaimed island of ice in the Arctic Ocean, and sentenced to imprisonment for three years. * * *

T–3 is an island of glacial ice, composed of approximately 99% ice and less than 1% land matter, which meanders slowly about the general area of the Arctic Ocean. First sighted by an American in 1947, T–3 has been occupied since 1952 under the auspices of the United States Government, particularly the Departments of the Air Force and Navy, except for part of the years 1961–1962 when the island was grounded on the coastline of Alaska near Point Barrow. T–3 is used as a research station—a platform for scientific study * * *.

Discipline and order on the island depend upon the cooperation of all of the men and the effectiveness of the group leader, particularly in the summer months when it is virtually impossible to remove any wrongdoer from the ice. There are no medical facilities on the island, no doctor and, indeed, during the summer of 1970, no person trained in any aspect of medical science.

In May of 1970, a group of men arrived on T–3 expecting to remain there until late September or early October. Included were (a) the deceased, Bennie Lightsey, an employee of the United States Weather Bureau, who had been designated as station manager by the Arctic Research Laboratory, (b) the defendant, an employee of General Motors Defense Research Laboratory, (c) Donald Leavitt, who was an employee of the Arctic Research Laboratory, and whose nickname was "Porky," and (d) sixteen others. During the summer an acute problem arose from Porky's excessive drinking and resultant uncontrolled behavior. Prior to July 16, 1970, the date on which Lightsey was killed, Porky, at least three times, attacked various personnel at the station, including defendant, with butcher cleavers, mainly in an effort to obtain access to alcoholic beverages.

On July 16, while defendant was working at the General Motors camp, approximately one mile from the main camp where he lived in a trailer, he received a telephone call from his roommate, Charles Parodi, who told him that Porky was drunk and had taken some wine from their trailer. It should be noted that locked doors on T–3 were unknown because of potential fire hazard. Parodi pleaded with defendant to return to the trailer and defendant undertook to do so. He took with him a rifle selected from the common store to protect himself from the drunken Porky when he arrived back at the camp and later he loaded it. When defendant returned to the trailer he left his rifle and went to the next trailer to warn Porky to stay away from the raisin wine which was stored in defendant's trailer. Defendant found Porky and the station manager, Lightsey, consuming 190 proof Ethyl alcohol cut with grape juice and home made raisin wine. Defendant then returned to his trailer and soon thereafter heard footsteps approaching. Believing that it was Porky, he raised the rifle, put the safety off, opened the bolt, and assuring himself that the rifle was loaded, returned the bolt to the firing position and pointed the gun

at the door. It was not Porky, but Lightsey, who entered the trailer.

A discussion of increasing intensity then ensued between the two over whether or not Porky should be allowed some of defendant's raisin wine. Parodi was present for part of the discussion, but after he left defendant ordered Lightsey out of the trailer, waving the gun back and forth at him. The gun discharged and Lightsey was hit. Lightsey died a short time after the wound, despite the efforts of members of the camp, including defendant, to save him. There was no witness to the actual shooting, except the two participants, but there was evidence, on which the defense heavily relied, that the rifle was defective in an unforeseeable but most deadly way, i.e., it could be discharged without pulling the trigger by banging it, dropping it, by putting the safety on and off, by ramming the bolt handle down, and by applying slight pressure to the bolt handle when holding it.

[D]efendant contends that these reversible errors were committed: * * * (b) the district court failed to charge the jury correctly on the necessary elements of the crime of involuntary manslaughter * * *.

We agree with defendant that nowhere in either [the original or supplementary] charge did the district judge tell the jury that they must find, as a necessary element of involuntary manslaughter by the commission of a lawful act without due caution and circumspection, that defendant must be shown to have actual knowledge that his conduct was a threat to the lives of others. In *United States v. Pardee,* 368 F.2d 368 (4 Cir.1966), we had occasion to discuss the crime of involuntary manslaughter. After concluding that it requires proof of *gross* negligence, and not simple negligence, we added:

"Gross negligence" is to be defined as exacting proof of a wanton or reckless disregard for human life. *Furthermore, to convict, the slayer must be shown to have had actual knowledge that his conduct was a threat to the lives of others, or to have knowledge of such circumstances as could reasonably be said to have made foreseeable to him the peril to which his acts might subject others.* The reason of the latter comment is that awareness of the tendency to danger, or the foreseeability of injury, from the act or omission is an indispensable element of negligence. This requirement of proof gains stature when it is recalled that death as a result of an accident, that is an occurrence unpurposed and unattributable to negligence, does not give rise to civil or criminal liability. (Emphasis added.)

There can be no doubt that the omission of a charge in accordance with *Pardee* was reversible error in this case. The evidence showed that defendant brandished a gun at the decedent and that the gun fired and killed him. But there was additional uncontroverted evidence from the government's experts that the gun was defective and could be discharged other than by pulling the trigger. Without the instruction, the jury may have convicted on the theory that pointing a gun capable of accidental discharge was an act of gross negligence even though it found that defendant did not discharge it, without consideration of whether defendant knew the gun was defective and thus capable of accidental discharge. If these were its findings, the conclusion of involuntary manslaughter could not follow unless the jury considered and concluded that defendant was aware that the gun was defective. On this ground alone, a new trial is required.

In a second aspect, we conclude that the charge was also defective in that it unduly restricted the jury in its consideration of the special circumstances obtaining on T–3 in its consideration of whether defendant committed an act which constituted gross negligence from which involuntary man-

slaughter could be found. Defendant requested that the jury be instructed:

> In determining whether or not the defendant is guilty of involuntary manslaughter, the jury must measure his conduct against all of the existing circumstances and determine therefrom whether what he did was in its nature dangerous to life or grossly negligent. Some of the special circumstances you may consider in this case are the location of the alleged act, and its lack of law enforcement and medical facilities and the good character of Mario Escamilla.

This instruction was not given * * *.

This we think was error. Gross negligence or even simple negligence is to be determined by all of the facts and circumstances surrounding an act which is asserted to be either. It would seem plain that what is negligent or grossly negligent conduct in the Eastern District of Virginia may not be negligent or grossly negligent on T–3 when it is remembered that T–3 has no governing authority, no police force, is relatively inaccessible from the rest of the world, lacks medical facilities and the dwellings thereon lack locks—in short, that absent self-restraint on the part of those stationed on T–3 and effectiveness of the group leader, T–3 is a place where no recognized means of law enforcement exist and each man must look to himself for the immediate enforcement of his rights. Certainly, all of these factors are ones which should be considered by a jury given the problem of determining whether defendant was grossly negligent. This is not to say that the standards of civilized conduct and the law of the United States do not prevail even on T–3, but those standards and that law admit of consideration of the circumstances surrounding alleged involuntary manslaughter both in the continental United States and on T–3. While defendant's request for instruction, particularly the aspect invoking defendant's good character, need not have been granted exactly as requested, the district court should have instructed in accordance with the principle of the request.

* * *

Reversed and remanded.

Notes and Questions

1. Courts and legislatures have experienced considerable difficulty in identifying precisely what standard should govern in determining what unintentional homicides are criminal. Considerable variation is to be found from jurisdiction to jurisdiction. As noted in Remington & Helstad, *The Mental Element in Crime—A Legislative Problem,* 1952 Wis.L.Rev. 644, 663–64, "there are several distinct bases upon which liability may rest. 1. It may be sufficient that the actor should have realized that his act created an unreasonable risk of some harm to another. This is ordinary negligence, which is completely objective, and has generally been held to be insufficient for purposes of criminal liability. 2. It may be sufficient that the actor should have realized that his act creates, not only unreasonable risk, but also a substantial probability that serious harm will result. This is an objective standard which differs from ordinary negligence to the extent that the risk created is more serious. 3. The state may be required to show that the actor was aware of the circumstances, and being aware of the circumstances should have realized that his act created a serious risk. 4. Finally, the state may be required to show that the actor was aware, not only of the circumstances, but also of the fact that his act created a serious risk of harm to another.

"Seldom is there any clear indication on the face of a statute as to which of these bases is intended. The lack of clarity at the present time is amply demonstrated by the fact that 'gross negligence' in Wisconsin is equivalent to 'wanton or reckless' conduct in Massachusetts; 'wanton or reckless' conduct in Massachusetts apparently means something quite different than 'wilful and wanton' conduct in New Jersey; 'culpable negligence,' 'high degree of negligence,' and 'gross negligence' may all mean the same thing, or may mean three distinct things depending upon the jurisdiction chosen as the basis for comparison."

2. In many of the modern codes an effort has been made to be more specific, and this has necessitated more careful attention to the question of what the "bottom line" should be with respect to criminal liability for unintentional homicides. Which of the aforementioned four standards is to be preferred? As an aid to making that judgment, consider (i) in which of the following fact situations (Notes 3–6) there should be criminal liability; and (ii) what standard would have to be applicable to produce the desired result.

3. "[T]he defendant, 57 years old at the time of trial, had left his native Arabia at the age of 19, emigrating first to China and then coming to the United States three years later. He had lived in Rochester only a short time before committing the acts which formed the basis for this homicide charge. He testified that he had been of the Sudan Muslim religious faith since birth, and had become one of the sect's leaders, claiming a sizable following. Defendant articulated the three central beliefs of this religion as 'cosmetic consciousness, mind over matter and psysiomatic psychomatic consciousness.' He stated that the second of these beliefs, 'mind over matter', empowered a 'master', or leader, to lie on a bed of nails without bleeding, to walk through fire or on hot coals, to perform surgical operations without anesthesia, to raise people up off the ground, and to suspend a person's heartbeat, pulse, and breathing while that person remained

conscious. In one particular type of ceremony, defendant, purportedly exercising his powers of 'mind over matter', claimed he could stop a follower's heartbeat and breathing and plunge knives into his chest without any injury to the person. There was testimony from at least one of defendant's followers that he had successfully performed this ceremony on previous occasions. Defendant himself claimed to have performed this ceremony countless times over the previous 40 years without once causing an injury. Unfortunately, on January 28, 1972, when defendant performed this ceremony on Kenneth Goings, a recent recruit, the wounds from the hatchet and three knives which defendant had inserted into him proved fatal." [a]

4. "The defendant shot and killed Richard Levine while target practicing at a theater which he managed. The incident occurred at about 4:00 A.M. The defendant and Orberry Jackson, Dennis Martin and Richard Levine (the victim), three sailors, then stationed at the Great Lakes Naval Station, whom he employed as part-time helpers, were present in the theater at that time.

"The defendant was in the spotlight room, approximately 100 feet from the stage, and was shooting at a wicker basket placed about 2 or 3 feet from an open curtain on the right-hand side of the stage. Levine was on the stage. He, along with the rest of the parties present, had been drinking. He crossed in front of the target area several times to change a tape recorder which was located behind the curtain, and then played the drums which were near the stage. Levine then started dancing on the stage and Jackson played the drums for a while; and then Jackson

went upstairs to the spotlight room. Several times when Levine walked near the target area, Jackson would guide him away—to the left of the stage—by means of the spotlight. The stage floodlights and footlights were turned off, apparently by Levine. Whenever Levine would change the tape on the tape recorder, he would walk near the target area and Jackson would use the spotlight to guide him away and then return the spotlight to the target.

"Ultimately, Levine changed a tape but did not cross back through the spotlight which was focused on the target. The defendant waited a while and then resumed firing. Jackson noted a heavy movement behind the curtain and ran to the stage. Some shots were fired while he was running to the stage. He found Levine lying on his back, partially in front of the curtain, with blood covering his face and legs." [b]

5. "On July 1, 1950, the defendant was driving a Cadillac car at a speed of approximately 40 miles per hour in a southerly direction on Route 9–W. One Carl W. Larsen, who was driving his automobile in the opposite direction, testified that when he was about two miles north of Tenafly he saw the approaching car of the defendant with apparently no driver at the wheel; that the defendant's car crossed the white line separating the lanes approximately 240 to 300 feet to the north of Larsen's car, whereupon Larsen swung sharply to his right, but the defendant's car struck Larsen's car in the left rear portion thereof; that the defendant's car continued in the same direction and crashed head-on into a Studebaker automobile approximately 40 feet in the rear of the Larsen car; that the latter collision caused the death of

---

a. *People v. Strong,* 37 N.Y.2d 568, 376 N.Y.S.2d 87, 338 N.E.2d 602 (1975), reversing defendant's conviction for second degree manslaughter (subjective standard) because the jury was not given an instruction on the lesser offense of negligent homicide (objective standard).

b. *People v. Arndt,* 50 Ill.2d 390, 280 N.E.2d 230 (1972), affirming defendant's conviction for involuntary manslaughter under a subjective awareness-high risk type of statute; Schaefer, J., dissented.

Glory Morrow Flobeck. When Mr. Larsen reached the defendant's car, he found that he had collapsed at the wheel and was in a semiconscious condition, so that it was necessary to assist him from the car; the defendant stated he had 'blacked out,' whereupon he collapsed and was taken to a hospital in an ambulance. It is conceded that defendant was not under the influence of intoxicating liquor nor was there any evidence thereof upon his person. In late February, 1949, the defendant, while at home, suffered a sudden attack of dizziness or unconsciousness; subsequent thereto he was treated by his family physician and shortly thereafter by one Dr. Moses Madonick, Assistant Professor of Clinical Neurology in the College of Physicians and Surgeons, Columbia University, who diagnosed the defendant's condition as Meniere's Syndrome. After treating him on two or three occasions, Dr. Madonick discharged him on July 26, 1949, advising him that he might suffer a recurrence of the disease and that if he should drive an automobile he should not drive alone, but someone should accompany him. The defendant testified that he remembers nothing about the accident; that immediately prior thereto he was proceeding at 35 to 40 miles per hour when all of a sudden he just 'blacked out' and remembered nothing until he came out of the 'black out' in the hospital. Dr. Madonick testified further that he examined the defendant after the accident on August 2, 1950, at which time he concluded there was a recurrence of the ailment and that in his opinion it was the cause of the defendant's 'black out' or loss of consciousness without warning on the date of the accident. [Prior to that date, the defendant] had been pursuing his ordinary occupations one year and three months without any recurrence of the attack." [c]

c. *State v. Gooze,* 14 N.J.Super. 277, 81 A.2d 811 (1951), affirming defendant's conviction for causing "the death of another by driving any

6. "The defendant was accustomed to spend his evenings at [his] night club, inspecting the premises and superintending the business. On November 16, 1942, he became suddenly ill, and was carried to a hospital, where he was in bed for three weeks and remained until discharged on December 11, 1942.

* * *

"A little after ten o'clock on the evening of Saturday, November 28, 1942, the night club was well filled with a crowd of patrons. It was during the busiest season of the year. An important football game in the afternoon had attracted many visitors to Boston. Witnesses were rightly permitted to testify that the dance floor had from eighty to one hundred persons on it, and that it was 'very crowded.'

* * *

"A bartender in the Melody Lounge noticed that an electric light bulb which was in or near the coconut husks of an artificial palm tree in the corner had been turned off and that the corner was dark. He directed a sixteen year old bar boy who was waiting on customers at the tables to cause the bulb to be lighted. A soldier sitting with other persons near the light told the bar boy to leave it unlighted. But the bar boy got a stool, lighted a match in order to see the bulb, turned the bulb in its socket, and thus lighted it. The bar boy blew the match out, and started to walk away. Apparently the flame of the match had ignited the palm tree and that had speedily ignited the low cloth ceiling near it, for both flamed up almost instantly. The fire spread with great rapidity across the upper part of the room, causing much heat. The crowd in the Melody Lounge rushed up the stairs, but the fire preceded them. People got on fire while on the stairway. The fire spread with great speed across the foyer and into the

vehicle carelessly and heedlessly in willful or wanton disregard of the rights or safety of others."

Caricature Bar and the main dining room, and thence into the Cocktail Lounge. Soon after the fire started the lights in the night club went out. The smoke had a peculiar odor. The crowd were panic stricken, and rushed and pushed in every direction through the night club, screaming, and overturning tables and chairs in their attempts to escape.

"The door at the head of the Melody Lounge stairway was not opened until firemen broke it down from outside with an axe and found it locked by a key lock, so that the panic bar could not operate. Two dead bodies were found close to it, and a pile of bodies about seven feet from it. The door in the vestibule of the office did not become open, and was barred by the clothing rack. The revolving door soon jammed, but was burst out by the pressure of the crowd. The head waiter and another waiter tried to get open the panic doors from the main dining room to Shawmut Street, and succeeded after some difficulty. The other two doors to Shawmut Street were locked, and were opened by force from outside by firemen and others. Some patrons escaped through them, but many dead bodies were piled up inside them. A considerable number of patrons escaped through the Broadway door, but many died just inside that door. Some employees, and a great number of patrons, died in the fire. Others were taken out of the building with fatal burns and injuries from smoke, and died within a few days." [d]

SECTION 4. KILLING BY UNLAWFUL ACT

STATE v. GOODSEAL
Supreme Court of Kansas, 1976.
220 Kan. 487, 553 P.2d 279.

HARMAN, COMMISSIONER.

This is an appeal from a conviction of first degree murder.

d. *Commonwealth v. Welansky*, 316 Mass. 383, 55 N.E.2d 902 (1944), affirming defendant's con-

Appellant Charles Goodseal, also known as Charles Jones, was initially charged and tried upon three separate counts arising from the same incident: Unlawful possession of a firearm, aggravated robbery, and felony murder. The murder count charged that the homicide occurred during the perpetration of the crimes of unlawful possession of a firearm and aggravated robbery. At this first trial appellant was convicted of unlawful possession of a firearm (from which no appeal has been taken), he was acquitted upon the aggravated robbery count and the jury was unable to agree as to the murder charge. Upon a second trial appellant was convicted of murder in the first degree, done in the commission of a felony, unlawful possession of a firearm after a felony conviction. Appellant brings the murder conviction here for review.

The evidence revealed the following. In August, 1969, appellant Goodseal was released from the Kansas state industrial reformatory where he had been serving sentences imposed upon two counts of forcible rape. In December, 1973, he left his home in Wichita to seek employment in Denver, Colorado. While there he stayed with a friend, Carl Davis. Davis testified appellant handled a .38 caliber revolver during his Colorado stay and that appellant stated during their return trip to Wichita in appellant's automobile he, appellant, had a gun in the car trunk. The two arrived in Wichita December 19, 1973. The next day they met a girl called "Silky" whose real name was either Diana Warren or Dianna Coleman. The three spent much of the day together drinking gin. Silky was to commence working that night as a topless dancer in a club in Wichita called the Golddigger's Lounge. She displayed a .22 caliber pistol which she was carrying in her purse and said she had another gun hidden at the club and that both guns were for her protection.

viction under a manslaughter statute requiring proof of "wanton and reckless conduct."

There were generally from seven to ten girls at the club who worked as dancers, some of whom doubled as well as prostitutes.

At the club that evening appellant told his friend Davis that he had a gun but Davis did not see him with one at any time during the afternoon or early evening. Late in the evening appellant intervened in an argument between the club bartender and the girl who was the manager of the dancers, offering to help the latter. At one point he commented, "If you're having some trouble I got a heater in my back pocket that will straighten it out".

The victim of the homicide, James Warren Hunter, arrived at the lounge about 10:30 p.m. During the evening he was seen talking to Silky and at one point fondled her breasts. At a time when Hunter paid five dollars to get some of the girls to pose for pictures the bartender noticed other currency in his billfold. Hunter, Davis and appellant remained in the lounge until closing time, which was 12:30 a.m. Outside the lounge appellant told Davis he was waiting to give Silky a ride home and that she was in a car in the parking lot. Davis assumed Silky was "turning a trick". Appellant and Silky had previously agreed appellant would pretend to be her husband and pull her from the car so that she would not actually have to have sexual relations with the man she was with. Appellant testified that after this agreement Silky handed him a .38 caliber revolver which she said was not loaded.

Appellant got out of his car and went to the other automobile in the parking lot. There were no lights on inside but the motor was running. Appellant tapped the back glass with the gun butt, Silky unlocked the door and appellant opened the passenger side door. Hunter and Silky were in the back seat. Silky got out of the car immediately, pulling on her pants and asking appellant to get her shoes. Appellant asked Hunter what he was doing with his "wife" and Hunter replied he had paid her. Hunter then pulled on his pants, turned the pockets partially inside out and said, "Hey, she got my money". Appellant testified he remembered saying, "No wonder she wanted me to play this little trick so she could steal somebody's money". Appellant further testified he then bent over to pick up Silky's shoes, he slipped in the snow, bumped into the door and the gun discharged. The bullet struck Hunter in the armpit beneath his right shoulder and penetrated the lung area, causing his death. Appellant's version was that the shooting was accidental and the only reason he took the gun was to scare Hunter with it.

After appellant returned to his car he told his friend Davis he had shot the victim in the chest. Davis had witnessed the shooting. As appellant left the area he took a cartridge out of the gun and threw it away. The next day appellant left for Denver and en route he threw the gun away. Silky vanished immediately after the shooting. In January, 1974, appellant was apprehended in Olathe, Kansas.

* * *

Appellant's principal point upon appeal is that the trial court erroneously denied his motions for acquittal and new trial because the offense of felonious possession of a firearm is not inherently dangerous to human life and therefore cannot be the basis for felony murder. K.S.A. 21–3401, under which appellant was convicted, provides:

> "*Murder in the first degree is the killing of a human being* committed maliciously, willfully, deliberately and with premeditation or *committed in the perpetration or attempt to perpetrate any felony.* * * *" (Emphasis supplied.)

Possession of a firearm with a barrel less than twelve inches long by a person who within five years has been released from imprisonment for a felony, is one form of unlawful possession of a firearm and is a class D felony.

Here there is no question that appellant within five years after his release from confinement for a felony had in his hand a firearm with a barrel less than twelve inches long at a time when a bullet from that weapon caused Hunter's death. Appellant's argument is this. He says that to sustain a conviction for felony murder the collateral felony must be one inherently dangerous to human life; that this court recognized and applied this rule in *State v. Moffitt*, 199 Kan. 514, 431 P.2d 879, and held that unlawful possession of a firearm by an ex-felon is inherently dangerous to human life as a matter of law; further that in reaching this conclusion in *Moffitt* we cited a line of California decisions holding that unlawful possession of a firearm constitutes a felony inherently dangerous to human life and, where causal connection is shown, a resulting homicide constitutes felony murder in the second degree under California law; that in 1971 the California supreme court receded from this position and in *People v. Satchell*, 6 Cal.3d 28, 98 Cal.Rptr. 33, 489 P.2d 1361, 50 A.L.R.3d 383, ruled that the unlawful possession of a firearm by a convicted felon, viewed in the abstract, is not a felony inherently dangerous to human life for purposes of the felony murder rule, and this court should similarly reverse its decision in *Moffitt* and so hold.

Appellee first responds that our present statute does not require that a felony be one inherently dangerous to human life in order to support a felony murder conviction. We cannot agree. At the time *Moffitt* was decided and prior to 1970, our felony murder statute (K.S.A. 21–401 [Corrick 1964]) provided:

"*Every murder* which shall be committed by means of poison or by lying in wait, or by any kind of willful, deliberate and premeditated killing, or *which shall be committed in the perpetration or an attempt to perpetrate any arson, rape, robbery, burglary, or other felony, shall be*

deemed murder in the first degree." (Emphasis supplied.) * * *

In *Moffitt* we were dealing with the "other felony" clause of the then felony murder statute and we concluded that to come within the clause such a felony must be one inherently dangerous to human life. Our present statute, and the one under which appellant is being prosecuted, uses the term "any felony". We see no significant distinction between the two expressions for purposes of determining the applicability of the felony murder rule and no reason to depart from the traditional requirement that the felony must be one inherently or foreseeably dangerous to human life. This limitation has always been imposed even in the absence of specific statutory mention and we adhere to that requirement. To go further could lead to manifestly unjust and even absurd results. In reaching the same conclusion the Delaware supreme court in *Jenkins v. State*, 230 A.2d 262, commented:

"* * * The only rational function of the felony-murder rule is to furnish an added deterrent to the perpetration of felonies which, by their nature or by the attendant circumstances, create a foreseeable risk of death. This function is not served by application of the rule to felonies not foreseeably dangerous. The rule should not be extended beyond its rational function. Moreover, application of the rule to felonies not foreseeably dangerous would be unsound analytically because there is no logical basis for imputing malice from the intent to commit a felony not dangerous to human life."

The next question is whether unlawful possession of a firearm by an ex-felon is an offense inherently dangerous to human life. In *Moffitt* we said that it was. In reaching this conclusion we did not specifically state whether we were viewing the felony in the abstract or, as several courts have done, were considering both the nature of the felony and the circumstances of its commission. In *Moffitt* the facts were that the defendant, a convicted felon, fired a pistol while assaulting two pedestrians and inadvertently killed a woman sitting on a motorcycle some distance down the street. We did comment in *Moffitt* upon legislative recognition that persons who had once committed a felony were dangerous to society and should not have in their possession concealable weapons. Beyond this, where doubt may exist, we see nothing wrong in considering both the nature of the offense in the abstract and the circumstances of its commission in determining whether a particular felony was inherently dangerous to human life. Some felonies, such as aggravated robbery, viewed in the abstract alone, are of such nature as to be inherently dangerous to human life, while another which seems of itself not to involve any element of human risk may be committed in such a dangerous manner as to be of the same character.

Hence we hold that the nature of the felony and, where necessary for determination, the circumstances of its commission are relevant factors in considering whether the particular felony was inherently and foreseeably dangerous to human life so as to support a conviction of felony murder. These are questions for the trial court and jury to decide in appropriate cases. In the case at bar appellant's own testimony was that he used the pistol to scare the victim. However, there was no evidence he made any presentment of the pistol in an offer to do corporal hurt to the victim so as to amount to an assault constituting an integral part of a murder charge as prohibited by *State v. Clark,* 204 Kan. 38, 460 P.2d 586. Under appellant's undisputed admissions the trial court in effect correctly held as a matter of law that the collateral felony, unlawful possession of a firearm, was a sufficient basis for application of the felony murder rule. * * *

PRAGER, JUSTICE (dissenting):

The issue before us in this case was determined by the Supreme Court of California in 1971 in *People v. Satchell.* In that case the California court pointed out that the felony-murder rule is a highly artificial concept and warned that "it should not be extended beyond any rational function that it is designed to serve." The court further held that the determination as to whether a felony is inherently dangerous for purposes of the felony-murder rule must be based upon an assessment of that felony in the abstract and not on the particular facts of a case. * * * It is important that we examine closely the rationale of the California court in *Satchell* where the court stated:

"It is manifest that the range of antisocial activities which are criminally punishable as felonies in this state is very wide indeed. Some of these felonies, such as certain well-known crimes against the person of another, distinctly manifest a propensity for acts dangerous to human life on the part of the perpetrator. Others * * * just as distinctly fail to manifest such a propensity. Surely it cannot be said that a person who has committed a crime in this latter category, when he arms himself with a concealable weapon, presents a danger to human life so significantly more extreme than that presented by a non-felon similarly armed as to justify the imputation of malice to him if a homicide should result. Accordingly, because we can conceive of such a vast number of situations wherein it would be grossly illogical to impute malice, we must conclude that the violation of section 12021 by one previously convicted of a felony is not itself a felony *inherently* dangerous to human life which will support a second degree felony-murder instruction."

The California court recognized that possession of a firearm is a passive act which in and of itself, is not inherently dangerous. The weapon becomes inherently dangerous when it is *used* in such a manner as to endanger a human life. The California court in its opinion stated as follows in this regard:

> "Viewing the matter from the standpoint of inherent danger, we find it difficult to understand how any offense of mere passive possession can be considered to supply the element of malice in a murder prosecution. To be sure, if such possession is of an extremely reckless nature manifesting a conscious disregard for human life, malice may be imputed by means of basic murder principles. * * * Moreover, if passive possession ripens into a felonious *act* in which danger to human life is inherent, the purpose of the felony-murder rule is served by its application—for it is the deterrence of such acts by felons which the rule is designed to accomplish. However, mere possession *in itself*—ignoring the propensities and conduct of the possessor—is essentially neutral in its intentional aspect and should not serve as the basis for the imputation of malice."

The rule adopted by the majority in the case before us is not sound for several reasons. In the first place, in my judgment, it is a rule which would be impossible for the trial courts of this state to apply. * * * The majority opinion has furnished no guidelines to assist the trial court in instructing the jury. This in my judgment places a difficult burden upon the district courts of this state in applying the rule adopted by the majority.

The rule of the majority opinion also may result in a serious conflict with the established principle of law that in a first-degree murder prosecution the felony-murder rule may not properly be invoked when it is based upon a felony which is an integral part of the homicide. * * * In the case now before us the majority relies upon the fact that the defendant had a gun in his hand in order to scare the deceased and thereby to coerce him into involuntary action. In order to avoid a conflict with the rule of *State v. Clark,* supra, the majority opinion emphasizes that there was no evidence the defendant made any presentment of the pistol in an offer to do corporal hurt to the victim so as to amount to an assault constituting an integral part of the murder charge as prohibited by *Clark.* The clear implication is that if the defendant had actually assaulted the deceased with a gun, then the felony-murder rule would not have been applicable since in that situation the assault would have been an integral part of the homicide. It would seem to follow that if a defendant unlawfully possessing a firearm does not commit an assault upon his victim but accidently kills him, then he may be found guilty of felony-murder. If, however, he assaults his victim then the felony-murder rule cannot be applied and in order to convict the defendant of murder the state must prove that the defendant intentionally and with malice committed the homicide. The irrationality of this distinction is obvious on its face.

Furthermore, I wish to point out that the practical application of the rule approved by the majority can produce other absurd results. For example, let us assume that a defendant, having been previously convicted of felony for writing an insufficient fund check, purchases a firearm to protect himself and his family against criminal invaders of his home. He accidently drops the gun, causing it to strike the floor and be discharged, killing a guest in his home. Since the killing occurred during commission of a felony, possession of the gun unlawfully, defendant would be precluded from interposing the defense of accident. Under the rule adopted by the majority defendant would be guilty of murder in the first degree and possibly subjected to a term of life imprisonment in the state penitentiary. * * *

Assuming that the rule of the majority should be adopted, it would still be necessary to reverse this case and grant the defendant a new trial. * * * The majority rule would, of necessity, require an instruction to the jury that before the felony-murder rule should be applied it must find that the factual circumstances of the case made felony possession an inherently dangerous crime. * * * In this case the jury was * * * not instructed to take into consideration the factual circumstances present in the case. Even the majority would appear opposed to this result. * * *

Notes and Questions

1. In *State v. Underwood,* 228 Kan. 294, 615 P.2d 153 (1980), also involving a felony-murder conviction where the underlying felony was possession of a firearm by an ex-felon, the court in a 4–3 decision concluded: "A majority of this court now are convinced that the logic, reasoning and rule urged by Mr. Justice Prager in the dissent in *State v. Goodseal,* should be adopted for Kansas. Accordingly, we hold that in determining whether a particular collateral felony is inherently dangerous to human life so as to justify a charge of felony murder under K.S.A. 21–3401, the elements of the collateral felony should be viewed in the abstract, and the circumstances of the commission of the felony should not be considered in making the determination."

2. In *State v. Lashley,* 233 Kan. 620, 664 P.2d 1358 (1983), the defendant was convicted of felony murder on a jury instruction that the alleged felony, theft, "must be proved" by a showing that the homicide victim owned the property in question, that defendant obtained unauthorized control over it, that defendant intended to personally deprive the deceased

of it, and that the property was worth over $100. On appeal, the defendant invoked *Underwood.* The court responded: "There are three statutes that deal with the offense of theft: (1) theft—K.S.A. 21–3701; (2) theft of lost or mislaid property—K.S.A. 21–3703; and (3) theft of services— K.S.A. 21–3704. If the value of the stolen item or service is $100.00 or more, then the offense is a felony under each statute.

"Theft, K.S.A. 21–3701, became effective July 1, 1969. The legislature consolidated the offenses of larceny, embezzlement, false pretense, extortion, and receiving stolen property into the single crime of theft. The prior law was unduly complex, and created unnecessary problems in pleading and proof. All involved the common element of obtaining property by dishonest means. Though consolidated into a single statute of theft, the former offenses retained a portion of their former identity in the subdivisions contained within K.S.A. 21–3701.

"Theft is not one of the specified forcible felonies included in K.S.A. 21–3110(8). Does theft therefore fall into the categories of '*any other felony which involves the use or threat of physical force or violence against any person?*' Emphasis supplied. Viewing the separate statutes and the subdivisions of theft in the abstract, we can determine that the following crimes are not inherently dangerous to human life: (1) theft of lost or mislaid property— K.S.A. 21–3703; (2) unlawful deprivation of property—K.S.A. 21–3705; (3) theft, obtaining by deception control over property—K.S.A. 21–3701(*b*); and (4) theft by control over stolen property knowing the property to have been stolen by another—K.S.A. 21–3701(*d*).

"K.S.A. 21–3701 incorporates two sections that are, when viewed in the abstract, offenses that are inherently dangerous to human life: (1) theft by obtaining or ex-

erting unauthorized control over property—K.S.A. 21–3701(*a*); and (2) theft by
obtaining control over property by
threat—K.S.A. 21–3701(*c*).

"Theft by obtaining or exerting unauthorized control over property (K.S.A.
21–3701[*a*]) is generally committed by
stealth, but secrecy, or the owner's ignorance, is not a necessary element of the
crime. The thief's intent is to deprive the
owner of his property and to appropriate
the property to his own use. The act of
taking may be open, with a reckless disregard of the consequences, and even with
knowledge of the owner.

"Theft—obtaining by threat control
over property (K.S.A. 21–3701[*c*]), is taking property by putting the owner in fear
of personal injury or injury to his property
through fear induced by threats. The taking is without the voluntary consent of the
owner and the owner allows the property
to be taken as a result of actual fear induced by threats calculated to excite a
reasonable apprehension of harm.

"The offense of theft set forth in the
court's instruction is a felony when viewed
in the abstract inherently dangerous to
human life and is a proper felony to sustain a conviction for murder in the first
degree under the felony murder rule.
However, we wish to emphasize that theft
may be the underlying felony in a charge
of felony murder only in cases where the
discovery of the thief during the course of
the theft results in the death of a person."

Did the court reach a sound result?
Was the court faithful to *Underwood* ?

---

26. Still the law is intelligible as it stands.
. . .

Now, if experience shows, or is deemed by the
law-maker to show, that somehow or other
deaths which the evidence makes accidental
happen disproportionately often in connection
with other felonies, or with resistance to officers, or if on any other ground of policy it is
deemed desirable to make special efforts for the
prevention of such deaths, the law-maker may
consistently treat acts which, under the known

NOTES AND QUESTIONS ON THE RATIONALE AND STATUS OF THE FELONY–MURDER RULE

1. Consider Roth & Sundby, *The Felony–Murder Rule: A Doctrine at Constitutional
Crossroads,* 70 Cornell L.Rev. 446, 450–58
(1985):

"The deterrence rationale consists of
two different strains. The first approach
views the felony-murder rule as a doctrine
intended to deter negligent and accidental
killings during commission of felonies.
Proponents argue that co-felons will dissuade each other from the use of violence
if they may be liable for murder. Justice
Holmes attempted to justify the rule on
this basis by arguing that the rule would
be justified if experience showed that
death resulted disproportionately from the
commission of felonies.[26] * * *

"The second view focuses not on the
killing, but on the felony itself, and en-
dorses the felony-murder rule as a deterrent to dangerous felonies. From this perspective, punishing both accidental and
deliberate killings that result from the
commission of a felony is 'the strongest
possible deterrent' to 'undertaking inherently dangerous felonies.' * * *

"The felony-murder rule may be conceptualized as a theory of 'transferred or
constructive intent.' This theory posits
that the intent to commit the felony is
'transferred' to the act of killing in order
to find culpability for the homicide. The
rule thus serves 'the purpose of . . .
reliev[ing] the state of the burden of proving premeditation or malice.' * * *

---

circumstances, are felonious, or constitute resistance to officers, as having a sufficiently
dangerous tendency to be put under a special
ban. The law may, therefore, throw on the
actor the peril, not only of the consequences
forseen by him, but also of consequences which,
although not predicted by common experience,
the legislator apprehends.

See O.W. Holmes, The Common Law 58–59
(1881).

" 'Constructive malice' is closely related to the concept of transferred intent and is also frequently used to describe the operation of the felony-murder rule. * * *

"Constructive malice, however, appears to be more akin to the legal concept of a presumption. Whereas transferred intent would allow the mental state required for Act A to substitute for the mental state required for Act B, constructive malice would 'impute' or presume the mental state required for Act B from the commission of Act A. The felony-murder rule thus acts as a 'mens rea-imposing mechanism.'

"As a form of constructive malice, the felony-murder rule is viewed as conclusively presuming homicidal mens rea from the commission of the felony. This approach allows the courts to avoid characterizing felony murder as a strict liability crime, because, at least in theory, the mens rea for the homicide is formally retained separate and apart from the mens rea for the felony." * * *

"Courts and commentators viewing the felony-murder rule as a conclusive presumption retain a separate mens rea element for the homicide, which is irrebuttably attributed to the defendant from the commission of the felony. An alternative approach is to view the rule as not requiring a separate mens rea element for the homicide, but as justifying conviction for murder simply on the basis that the defendant committed a felony and a killing occurred.

"Courts adopting this view see felony murder as a distinct form of homicide: '[T]he elements of felony-murder are simply the intentional commission of a felony and the killing of a human being in the course thereof.' The justifications advanced for this conceptualization are deterrence of the underlying felony, and the notion that the felon has exhibited an 'evil mind' justifying severe punishment.

"The 'evil mind' theory of felony murder finds its roots in seventeenth and eighteenth century English notions of criminology. Mens rea was a less developed concept and judges focused on the harm resulting from a defendant's illegal act, rather than the maliciousness of his intent. The felony-murder rule thus partly operated on an unarticulated rationale that one who does bad acts cannot complain about being punished for their consequences, no matter how unexpected. Moreover, the felony-murder rule conceived from an 'evil mind' perspective comported with the retribution theory of punishment prevailing at the time of the rule's development, which focused on the resulting harm, not on the actor's mental state, in deciding the appropriate punishment. A convict, therefore, bore responsibility for his felony and for any harmful result arising from the crime regardless of his specific intentions."

2. Which (if any) of the foregoing rationalizations provides a justification for the felony-murder rule? Can the rule be squared with *Regina v. Cunningham,* p. 98 of this Book? With the fact, as noted in *Model Penal Code* § 210.3, Comment (1980), that "there is no basis in experience for thinking that homicides *which the evidence makes accidental* occur with disproportionate frequency in connection with specified felonies [96]"?

3. Only one state has judicially abandoned the felony-murder rule. In *People v. Aaron,* 409 Mich. 672, 299 N.W.2d 304 (1980), the court concluded: "We believe that it is no longer acceptable to equate

96. In fact, the number of all homicides which occur in the commission of such crimes as robbery, burglary, or rape is lower than might be expected. For example, comparison of the figures for solved and unsolved homicides from M. Wolfgang, Criminal Homicide (1958), with statistics on basic felonies taken from the FBI Uniform Crime Reports reveals the following for Philadelphia from 1948–1952:

the intent to commit a felony with the intent to kill, intent to do great bodily harm, or wanton and willful disregard of the likelihood that the natural tendency of a person's behavior is to cause death or great bodily harm. In *People v. Hansen,* 368 Mich. 344, 350, 118 N.W.2d 422 (1962), this Court said that '[m]alice requires an intent to cause the very harm that results or some harm of the same general nature, or an act done in wanton or wilful disregard of the plaintiff and strong likelihood that such harm will result.' In a charge of felony murder, it is the murder which is the harm which is being punished. A defendant who only intends to commit the felony does not intend to commit the harm that results and may or may not be guilty of perpetrating an act done in wanton or willful disregard of the plain and strong likelihood that such harm will result. Although the circumstances surrounding the commission of the felony may evidence a greater intent beyond the intent to commit the felony, or a wanton and willful act in disregard of the possible consequence of death or serious injury, the intent to commit the felony, of itself, does not connote a 'man-endangering-state-of-mind'. Hence, we do not believe that it constitutes a sufficient *mens rea* to establish the crime of murder.

RELATION OF TOTAL FELONIES TO HOMICIDES OCCURRING DURING THE FELONY
PHILADELPHIA 1948–1952

Offense	No. of Crimes Reported	No. Accompanied by Homicide	%	No. per 1000
Robbery	6,432	38	0.59	5.9
Rape	1,133	4	0.35	3.5
Burglary	27,669	1	0.0036	.36
Auto Theft	10,315	2	0.019	1.9

Similar figures are found in Cook County, Illinois, robbery statistics from 1926–1930. There were 71 murders committed during robberies in Cook County during 1926 and 1927. Illinois Crime Survey 610 (1929). Although robbery statistics for those years are not available, 7,196 robberies were committed in the county in 1930.

"Accordingly, we hold today that malice is the intention to kill, the intention to do great bodily harm, or the wanton and willful disregard of the likelihood that the natural tendency of defendant's behavior is to cause death or great bodily harm. We further hold that malice is an essential element of any murder, as that term is judicially defined, whether the murder occurs in the course of a felony or otherwise. The facts and circumstances involved in the perpetration of a felony may evidence an intent to kill, an intent to cause great bodily harm, or a wanton and willful disregard of the likelihood that the natural tendency of defendant's behavior is to cause death or great bodily harm; however, the conclusion must be left to the jury to infer from all the evidence. Otherwise, 'juries might be required to find the fact of malice where they were satisfied from the whole evidence it did not exist'.

"From a practical standpoint, the abolition of the category of malice arising from the intent to commit the underlying felony should have little effect on the result of the majority of cases. In many cases where felony murder has been applied, the use of the doctrine was unnecessary because the other types of malice could have been inferred from the evidence."

Assuming this number of robberies in 1926 and 1927, it appears that only .49 per cent of the robberies in those two years resulted in homicide. More recent statistics derived from N.J. State Police, Crime in New Jersey: Uniform Crime Reports 42–45 (1975) reveal strikingly similar percentages. In 1975, 16,273 robberies were committed in New Jersey, and 66 homicides resulted from these robberies, only .41 per cent, a figure even lower than the earlier statistics from Cook County and Philadelphia. When other violent felonies are taken into account, this percentage drops even lower. In 1975, there were 1,382 forcible rapes and 111,264 forcible breaking-and-enterings in New Jersey in addition to the 16,273 robberies. These crimes resulted in 136 deaths. Thus only .10 per cent of these serious felonies resulted in homicide.

4. Compare *People v. Dillon,* 34 Cal.3d 441, 194 Cal.Rptr. 390, 668 P.2d 697 (1983): "[A] thorough review of legislative history convinces us that in California—in distinction to Michigan—the first degree felony-murder rule is a creature of statute. However much we may agree with the reasoning of *Aaron,* therefore, we cannot duplicate its solution to the problem: this court does not sit as a super-legislature with the power to judicially abrogate a statute merely because it is unwise or outdated."

5. What then of a *constitutional* attack upon the felony-murder rule? In *Dillon,* in response to the defendant's reliance upon *Mullaney v. Wilbur,* p. 238 of this Book, and *Sandstrom v. Montana,* p. 117 of this Book, the court stated: "Addressing the issue for the first time, we start with the indisputable fact that if the effect of the felony-murder rule on malice is indeed a 'presumption,' it is a 'conclusive' one. It does not simply shift to the defendant the burden of proving that he acted without malice, as in *Mullaney;* rather, in a felony-murder prosecution the defendant is not permitted to offer any such proof at all. Yet it does not necessarily follow that he is denied the presumption of innocence with regard to an element of the crime, as in *Sandstrom.* We are led astray if we treat the 'conclusive presumption of malice' as a true presumption; to do so begs the question whether malice is an element of felony murder. And to answer that question, we must look beyond labels to the underlying reality of this so-called 'presumption.'

"* * * In every case of murder other than felony murder the prosecution undoubtedly has the burden of proving malice as an element of the crime. Yet to say that (1) the prosecution must also prove malice in felony-murder cases, but that (2) the existence of such malice is 'conclusively presumed' upon proof of the defendant's intent to commit the underlying felony, is merely a circuitous way of saying

that in such cases the prosecution need prove only the latter intent. In Wigmore's words, the issue of malice is therefore 'wholly immaterial for the purpose of the proponent's case' when the charge is felony murder. In that event the 'conclusive presumption' is no more than a procedural fiction that masks a substantive reality, to wit, that as a matter of law malice is not an element of felony murder. * * *

"Because the felony-murder rule thus does not in fact raise a 'presumption' of the existence of an element of the crime, it does not violate the due process clause as construed in *Mullaney* or *Sandstrom.* This is also the holding of each of our sister jurisdictions that has addressed the issue.

"For the same reason we need not be detained by defendant's second due process claim, i.e., that the felony-murder doctrine violates the rule that a statutory presumption affecting the People's burden of proof in criminal cases is invalid unless there is a 'rational connection' between the fact proved (here, felonious intent) and the fact presumed (malice). (See *County Court of Ulster v. Allen* [p. 210 of this Book]). If, as we here conclude, the felony-murder doctrine actually raises no 'presumption' of malice at all, there is no occasion to judge it by the standard that governs the validity of true presumptions."

6. Roth & Sundby, supra, at 470–71, conclude that a challenge "based upon *Sandstrom* * * * would require a court either to eliminate a mens rea element for the homicide aspect of felony murder or to find the rule an unconstitutional presumption of the ultimate fact of culpability for the killing." The former course, they suggest at 478, cannot be squared with Supreme Court holdings which "indicate that imposition of severe punishments for nonregulatory crimes without a finding of culpability violates constitutional guarantees of the eighth amendment and the due

process clause." They rely firstly upon *Enmunds v. Florida,* p. 351 of this Book, asserting at 484 that "the Court's concern with severe punishment of unintended crime applies with equal force whether the defendant's actions or a co-defendant's actions directly lead to the victim's death"; and secondly upon *United States v. Bailey,* 444 U.S. 394, 100 S.Ct. 624, 62 L.Ed.2d 575 (1980), which they assert at 489 arguably "stands for the proposition that certain crimes must contain a mens rea element."

7. What is your assessment of the "solution" provided by *Model Penal Code* § 210.2(1)(b)? Consider Moreland, *A Re-examination of the Law of Homicide in 1971: The Model Penal Code,* 59 Ky.L.J. 788, 803–04 (1971): "The 1957 English Homicide Act expressly abolished the felony murder rule in England.[a] This is the logical and proper way to handle the felony murder * * *. To one who is no friend of 'presumptions of law,' the device in the Model Code appears as an attempt to preserve a portion of the historic survivor, the felony murder rule. Taken as a compromise, as a transition statute, it may well serve a temporary purpose. It would be better to abolish the felony murder rule and prosecute such killings as negligent murders. Then if the fact was that the killing was committed in the commission of a felony, the determining factors would be the amount of danger in the act and the indifference to human life and safety shown in its perpetration."

8. The felony-murder doctrine is well entrenched in American law. Though two-thirds of the states have enacted modern codes, only two of them (Kentucky and Hawaii) have totally abolished the rule, though two others (Arkansas and Delaware) have added a requirement of some mental state such as recklessness. Only one (New Hampshire) has adopted the Model Penal Code approach.

NOTES AND QUESTIONS ON THE DIMENSIONS OF THE FELONY–MURDER RULE

The dimensions of the felony-murder rule vary considerably from jurisdiction to jurisdiction. To some extent, especially in jurisdictions with modern codes, this may be attributable to the precise way in which the rule is set out by statute. In large measure, however, the differences may be explained by the fact that the courts in some jurisdictions are more determined than those in others to limit the reach of the felony-murder rule.

1. *What felonies will suffice?* As indicated by *Goodseal,* one important issue is that of what type of felony must have been committed in order for the felony-murder rule to be applicable. Query, which of the following alternatives is preferable:

(a) only such felonies which, when viewed in the abstract rather than upon the facts of the particular case, are inherently dangerous to human life (so that, as held in *People v. Burroughs,* 35 Cal.3d 824, 201 Cal.Rptr. 319, 678 P.2d 894 (1984), the felony-murder rule does not apply where defendant's felony of practicing medicine without a license hastened a leukemia victims' death).

(b) also such felonies which, upon the facts of the particular case, are dangerous to human life (so that, as held in *Commonwealth v. Matchett,* 386 Mass. 492, 436 N.E.2d 400 (1982), the felony-murder rule will apply to a death incidental to an

a. English Homicide Act of 1957, 5 & 6 Eliz. 2, c. 11, § 1:

"Where a person kills another in the course or furtherance of another offense, the killing shall not amount to murder unless done with the same

malice aforethought (express or implied) as is required for a killing to amount to murder when not done in the course or furtherance of another offense."

extortion scheme if the extortion was committed in such a fashion).

(c) any felony (so that, as held in *State v. Chambers,* 524 S.W.2d 826 [Mo.1975], the felony of theft of a vehicle will suffice even if it was not "inherently or foreseeably dangerous to human life").

2. *Merger.* In *State v. Thompson,* 88 Wash.2d 13, 558 P.2d 202 (1977), defendant was convicted of the felony-murder of her husband on the theory that his death had resulted from her felonious assault upon him. On appeal, the court recognized that virtually all "states which have considered the question have adopted the merger rule, resulting in a holding that only felonies independent of the homicide can support a felony murder conviction," but declined to reject earlier Washington authority to the contrary. Utter, J., dissenting, objected:

"The only act of the appellant relied upon to establish the felony necessary for conviction of murder in the second degree was the shooting itself, which, standing alone, constitutes the crime of second-degree assault. The application of the felony-murder rule thus eliminated the necessity for proof by the state of the element of specific intent, which is the distinguishing aspect, in our statutory scheme, of murder in the second degree. Absent the proof of acts constituting an assault, the appellant could not have been found guilty of murder. In this situation it is apparent that the single act of shooting the victim can constitute one crime and one crime only. There exists no general malicious intent based upon proof of the commission of a separate felony which may be 'transferred' from that crime to an independent homicide committed in the course thereof. The existence of such a separate intent is an analytical necessity to an inference of intent to kill. For this reason the felony-murder rule should not apply where the underlying felony sought to be used as a

basis for the operation of the rule is an offense included in fact in the homicide itself. To hold otherwise constitutes, as Chief Justice Cardozo observed, 'a futile attempt to split into unrelated parts an indivisible transaction.'

"[T]he use of the rule approved by the majority would effectively convert into second-degree murder any crime properly viewed as manslaughter, because manslaughter itself is a felony * * *."

Is the merger rule sound? If so, how far should the rule be extended? Consider, for example, *People v. Wilson,* 1 Cal.3d 431, 82 Cal.Rptr. 494, 462 P.2d 22 (1969), reversing the defendant's felony-murder conviction, obtained on the theory that the killing occurred in the commission of a burglary (i.e., the breaking and entry of a dwelling at night with intent to commit a felony therein) which had been undertaken with the intent to engage in an assault with a deadly weapon within the premises entered:

"In [*People v. Ireland,* 70 Cal.2d 522, 75 Cal.Rptr. 188, 450 P.2d 580 (1969)], we reasoned that a man assaulting another with a deadly weapon could not be deterred by the second degree felony-murder rule, since the assault was an integral part of the homicide. Here, the only distinction is that the assault and homicide occurred inside a dwelling so that the underlying felony is burglary based on an intention to assault with a deadly weapon, rather than simply assault with a deadly weapon. * * *

"In *Ireland,* we rejected the bootstrap reasoning involved in taking an element of a homicide and using it as the underlying felony in a second degree felony-murder instruction. We conclude that the same bootstrapping is involved in instructing a jury that the intent to assault makes the entry burglary and that the burglary raises the homicide resulting from the assault to first degree murder without proof of malice aforethought and premeditation."

Compare *People v. Miller,* 32 N.Y.2d 157, 344 N.Y.S.2d 342, 297 N.E.2d 85 (1973), rejecting the *Wilson* position: "It should be apparent that the Legislature, in including burglary as one of the enumerated felonies as a basis for felony murder, recognized that persons within domiciles are in greater peril from those entering the domicile with criminal intent, than persons on the street who are being subjected to the same criminal intent. Thus, the burglary statutes prescribe greater punishment for a criminal act committed within the domicile than for the same act committed on the street. Where, as here, the criminal act underlying the burglary is an assault with a dangerous weapon, the likelihood that the assault will culminate in a homicide is significantly increased by the situs of the assault. When the assault takes place within the domicile, the victim may be more likely to resist the assault; the victim is also less likely to be able to avoid the consequences of the assault, since his paths of retreat and escape may be barred or severely restricted by furniture, walls and other obstructions incidental to buildings. Further, it is also more likely that when the assault occurs in the victim's domicile, there will be present family or close friends who will come to the victim's aid and be killed. Since the purpose of the felony-murder statute is to reduce the disproportionate number of accidental homicides which occur during the commission of the enumerated predicate felonies by punishing the party responsible for the homicide not merely for manslaughter, but for murder, the Legislature, in enacting the burglary and felony-murder statutes, did not exclude from the definition of burglary, a burglary based upon the intent to assault, but intended that the definition be 'satisfied if the intruder's intent, existing at the time of the unlawful entry or remaining, is to commit *any* crime'."

Note, 22 Stan.L.Rev. 1059, 1067 (1970), concluded that under the analysis of *Wilson* "neither forcible rape nor armed robbery—two other felonies enumerated in the first degree felony-murder statute—will support the application of the felony-murder rule" because each of those offenses consists of two distinct elements, one of which is the assault element. But, as it turned out, the California Supreme Court did not go this far; see *People v. Burton,* 6 Cal.3d 375, 99 Cal.Rptr. 1, 491 P.2d 793 (1971) (armed robbery resulting in death is felony murder). Is there any rationale by which the results in *Wilson* and *Burton* may be reconciled?

3. *Double jeopardy.* The merger rule should not be confused with the double jeopardy question of whether a defendant may be prosecuted and punished for both felony murder and the underlying felony. Under *Brown v. Ohio,* 432 U.S. 161, 97 S.Ct. 2221, 53 L.Ed.2d 187 (1977), separate prosecutions are ordinarily barred unless "each provision requires proof of an additional fact which the other does not." This covers the felony-murder—felony situation. *Harris v. Oklahoma,* 433 U.S. 682, 97 S.Ct. 2912, 53 L.Ed.2d 1054 (1977). As for separate punishment for the two offenses, the constitutional question is simply that "of what punishment the Legislative Branch intended to be imposed." *Albernaz v. United States,* 450 U.S. 333, 101 S.Ct. 1137, 67 L.Ed.2d 275 (1981). In some states the courts have concluded the legislature had authorized cumulative punishment for the felony murder and underlying felony, but the prevailing view is to the contrary. See *People v. Wilder,* 411 Mich. 328, 308 N.W.2d 112 (1981), and cases cited therein.

4. *Duration of the felony.* In *People v. Gladman,* 41 N.Y.2d 123, 390 N.Y.S.2d 912, 359 N.E.2d 420 (1976), defendant was convicted of felony murder on evidence that he robbed a delicatessen of $145 at 8:10 p.m., left the shopping center

and walked through the surrounding neighborhood, and thereafter hid under a car at a bowling alley parking lot when he saw a police car enter the lot. When the defendant crawled out upon orders of a police officer, he shot and mortally wounded the officer. This occurred 15 minutes after and less than one-half mile from the robbery. In affirming the conviction, the court commented:

"Under older statutes which did not specifically address the issue, it was early held that a killing committed during an escape could, under some circumstances, constitute a felony murder. * * * [The analysis in the earlier cases] led to the development of some rather arbitrary rules. If the defendant left the premises without the loot, the criminal action was deemed either terminated or abandoned and a subsequent homicide would not be a felony murder. * * * On the other hand, both presence on the premises and retention of loot were not regarded as conclusive proof of felony continuation, but were merely evidence that the felony was continuing.[a] The term premises was rather strictly confined to 'within the four walls of the building' and a killing on an immediately adjoining public street would not be a killing on the 'premises'.

"The later New York cases indicate some dissatisfaction with the strict legal rules that had developed and tended to leave the question of escape killings to the jury as a question of fact, under appropriate instructions. The change was to point out 'generally that the killing to be felony murder must occur while the actor or one or more of his confederates is engaged in securing the plunder or in doing some-

thing immediately connected with the underlying crime; that escape may, under certain unities of time, manner and place, be a matter so immediately connected with the crime as to be part of its commission; but that, where there is no reasonable doubt of a complete intervening desistance from the crime, as by the abandonment of the loot and running away, the subsequent homicide is not murder in the first degree without proof of deliberation and intent.' The question of termination of the underlying felony was then left to the jury as a fact question.

"The New York approach was more rigid than that developed in other jurisdictions. The majority of the States tended to follow the 'res gestae' theory—i.e., whether the killing was committed in, about and as a part of the underlying transaction. California had adopted the *res gestae* theory, at least insofar as robbery is concerned, holding that a robbery is not complete if the 'conspirators have not won their way even momentarily to a place of temporary safety and the possession of the plunder is nothing more than a scrambling possession. In such a case the continuation of the use of arms which was necessary to aid the felon in reducing the property to possession is necessary to protect him in its possession and in making good his escape * * * The escape of the robbers with the loot, by means of arms, necessarily is as important to the execution of the plan as gaining possession of the property. Without revolvers to terrify, or, if occasion requires, to kill any person who attempts to apprehend them at the time of or immediately upon gaining possession of said property, their plan would be child-

---

a. Sometimes the argument is that the offense is by its nature a continuing one. For example, in *Doane v. Commonwealth,* 218 Va. 500, 237 S.E.2d 797 (1977), where defendant stole a car at noon on July 7th and ran over and killed someone with it at 6:15 p.m. on July 8th, the prosecutor relied upon established state law that larceny is a continuing offense which "is being committed

every moment of the time during which the thief deprives the owner of the stolen property or its possession." The court responded that while this fiction was accepted for purposes of establishing venue for prosecution wherever the property was taken, it would not be embraced as a means for broadening felony-murder liability.

like.' (*People v. Boss,* 210 Cal. 245, 250–251, 290 P. 881 [1930].) Subsequent case law indicates that, in California, the robbery is ongoing simply if the culprit had failed to reach a place of temporary safety. (*People v. Salas,* 7 Cal.3d 812, 103 Cal.Rptr. 431, 500 P.2d 7.) The comparative rigidity of the New York approach has been explained as stemming from the fact that, at the time, New York, with a minority of other States, provided that all felonies would support a conviction for felony murder. Of course, felony murder was also a capital offense and the cases attempted to narrow the scope of liability, particularly where it was an accomplice that did the actual killing.

"The 1967 Penal Law limited the application of the felony murder concept to nine serious and violent predicate felonies. At the same time, it was provided that the doctrine would apply to a killing committed in 'immediate flight'. This change was intended to do away with many of the old technical distinctions relating to 'abandonment' or 'completion'.

"Under the new formulation, the issue of whether the homicide occurred in 'immediate flight' from a felony is only rarely to be considered as a question of law for resolution by the court. Only where the record compels the inference that the actor was not in 'immediate flight' may a felony murder conviction be set aside on the law. Rather, the question is to be submitted to the jury, under an appropriate charge. The jury should be instructed to give consideration to whether the homicide and the felony occurred at the same location or, if not, to the distance separating the two locations. Weight may also be placed on whether there is an interval of time between the commission of the felony and the commission of the homicide. The jury may properly consider such additional factors as whether the culprits had possession of the fruits of criminal activity, whether the police, watchmen or concerned citizens

were in close pursuit, and whether the criminals had reached a place of temporary safety. These factors are not exclusive; others may be appropriate in differing factual settings. If anything, past history demonstrates the fruitlessness of attempting to apply rigid rules to virtually limitless factual variations. No single factor is necessarily controlling; it is the combination of several factors that leads to a justifiable inference.

"In this case, the jury could properly find, as a question of fact, that the killing of Officer Rose occurred in immediate flight from the delicatessen robbery. The shooting occurred less than 15 minutes after the robbery and less than a half mile away. The defendant had made off with cash proceeds and was attempting to secure his possession of the loot. The police had reason to believe that the robber was still in the immediate vicinity and had taken steps to seal off avenues of escape. In this regard, the absence of proof as to why Officer Rose turned into the bowling alley parking lot is no deficiency. The standard is not whether the police officer subjectively believed that the defendant was the robber. Indeed, the defendant's own apprehension may be more valuable. The defendant's response to the observation of the police car was to seek an immediate hiding place. This indicates that the defendant perceived that the police were on his trail. The record does not indicate that the officer knew or supposed, that defendant committed a crime; it does indicate that the defendant feared that the officer possessed such knowledge. Additionally, the defendant had not reached any place of temporary safety. In short, there is evidence from which the jury could conclude, as it did, that the defendant was in immediate flight from the robbery and that he shot the officer in order to make good his escape with the loot."

What if, on the other hand, the defendant contends that the killing occurred too early to come within the felony-murder rule? One view is that taken in *Commonwealth v. Legg,* 491 Pa. 78, 417 A.2d 1152 (1980), holding that "where an actor kills prior to formulating the intent to commit the underlying felony, we cannot say the actor knew or should have known death might occur from involvement in a dangerous felony because no involvement in a dangerous felony exists since the intent to commit the felony is not yet formulated. Also, the greater deterrent is not necessary, and the rule has no application." Compare *State v. Craig,* 82 Wash.2d 777, 514 P.2d 151 (1973): "Since the statute does not require the state to prove the intent with which a murder is committed, when it is done in connection with the perpetration of a robbery, mere lack of an intent to rob at the moment of the killing is not a defense. The court's refusal of instructions embodying this theory was not error."

5. *Liability of co-felon.* If *A* and *B* commit an armed robbery of *C,* in the course of which *C* is killed by a bullet fired from a gun held by *B,* under the felony-murder rule both *A* and *B* are guilty of murder. Although *A* did not fire the shot, he was a party to the felony and thus is deemed equally guilty of murder. Because this is essentially a matter of accomplice liability, further discussion of this aspect of the felony-murder rule will be deferred until Chapter 11.

·6. *Felon or non-felon status of the deceased or the person directly causing the death.* The typical felony-murder case is as stated in the preceding Note. It is not uncommon, however, for deaths to occur during dangerous felonies in other ways. Illustrative is *Campbell v. State,* 293 Md. 438, 444 A.2d 1034 (1982), where the defendant's partner in an armed robbery was shot by both the robbery victim and a police officer and was killed. In reversing the defendant's felony-murder conviction, the court reasoned:

"Courts in a majority of the jurisdictions in which the question has been considered have held that under the felony-murder doctrine a participating felon is not guilty of murder when the killing is done by a person other than the participating felon or his co-felons. The rationale underlying this rule is the 'agency' theory of felony murder.

"A classic statement of the agency theory appears in *Commonwealth v. Campbell,* 89 Mass. 541 (1863). There, the accused was participating in a riot growing out of the enforcement of a draft of men for the army. The question presented was whether under the felony-murder doctrine, the rioter could be guilty of murder if another person was killed by a soldier attempting to resist the mob's attack. The Supreme Court of Massachusetts stated:

' * * * *No person can be held guilty of homicide unless the act is either actually or constructively his, and it cannot be his act in either sense unless committed by his own hand or by some one acting in concert with him or in furtherance of a common object or purpose.* Certainly that cannot be said to be an act of a party in any just sense, or on any sound legal principle, which is not only not done by him, or by any one with whom he is associated or connected in a common enterprise, or in attempting to accomplish the same end, *but is committed by a person who is his direct and immediate adversary, and who is, at the moment when the alleged criminal act is done, actually engaged in opposing and resisting him and his confederates and abettors in the accomplishment of the unlawful object for which they are united.* * * *'

"Courts in some jurisdictions that have considered the precise question here have relied on the agency theory and have held that a participating felon is not guilty of murder when a police officer kills a fleeing co-felon while attempting to apprehend him. * * *

"Similarly, courts in some jurisdictions have held that under the felony-murder doctrine a participating felon is not guilty of murder when a victim kills a co-felon during the commission of a felony.[a]

"Courts in still other jurisdictions have considered whether under the felony-murder doctrine a participating felon is guilty of murder when a person other than a co-felon has been killed during the commission of a felony. Such courts have held that under that doctrine a participating felon is not guilty of murder when a police officer attempting to thwart the felony accidentally kills the victim, and when a police officer attempting to thwart the felony accidentally kills another police officer. Additionally, courts in some jurisdictions have held that under the felony-murder doctrine a participating felon is not guilty of murder when a victim, attempting to resist the perpetration of the felony, accidentally kills an innocent bystander.

"Courts in some jurisdictions have held that under the felony-murder doctrine a participating felon is guilty of murder when a killing is committed by a person other than the accused felon or his co-felons. The rationale underlying this rule is the 'proximate cause' theory of felony murder.

"A statement of the proximate cause theory appears in *Miers v. State*, 157 Tex. Cr.R. 572, 251 S.W.2d 404 (1952). There, a victim of an attempted robbery accidentally killed himself while he was attempting to resist the perpetration of the

felony. [T]he Court of Criminal Appeals of Texas stated:

'The whole question here is one of causal connection. If the appellant here set in motion the cause which occasioned the death of deceased, we hold it to be a sound doctrine that he would be as culpable as if he had done the deed with his own hands.' * * *

"Employing the proximate cause theory, courts in these jurisdictions have held that under the felony-murder doctrine a participating felon is guilty of murder not only when a police officer attempting to thwart a felony accidentally kills another police officer, or when a victim, attempting to resist the felony, accidentally kills himself, or when a bystander, attempting to thwart the perpetration of the felony, accidentally kills another bystander, but also when a police officer kills a fleeing co-felon while attempting to apprehend him.

"The present trend has been for courts to employ the agency theory and to limit criminal culpability under the felony-murder doctrine to lethal acts committed by the felons themselves or their accomplices, and not to employ the proximate cause theory to extend criminal culpability for lethal acts of nonfelons. * * *

"One reason for declining to extend the felony-murder doctrine is that such an extension would not achieve the rule's basic purpose. Manifestly, the purpose of deterring felons from killing by holding them strictly responsible for killings they or their co-felons commit is not effectuated by punishing them for killings committed by persons not acting in furtherance of the felony.

a. To be distinguished from the case where a co-felon is killed without such intervention by a third party. See *In re Leon*, 122 R.I. 548, 410 A.2d 121 (1980) (where defendant and others committed crime of arson and co-felon died in the fire, "the fact that the victim was an accomplice to the felony does not prevent the defendant from being convicted of felony murder, so long as an

act of the felon foreseeably produced the fatal injury"). A different result has been reached where the defendant was not even present at the crime scene and the co-felon in effect killed himself in his negligent setting of the fire. *People v. Earnest*, 46 Cal.App.3d 792, 120 Cal.Rptr. 485 (1975).

"Another reason to decline to extend the applicability of the felony-murder doctrine is that the tort liability concept of proximate cause has no proper place in prosecutions for criminal homicide. There is a difference between the underlying rationale of tort and criminal law. Tort law is primarily concerned with who shall bear the burden of loss, while criminal law is concerned with the imposition of punishment. 'Tort concepts of foreseeability and proximate cause have shallow relevance to culpability for murder in the first degree.' Because of the extreme penalty attaching to a conviction of felony murder, a closer and more direct causal connection between the felony and the killing is required than the causal connection ordinarily required under the tort concept of proximate cause. Because the tort liability concept of proximate cause is generally too broad and comprehensive to be appropriate in a criminal proceeding, the proximate cause theory ordinarily should not be employed to extend the applicability of the felony-murder doctrine.

"We are persuaded that the felony-murder doctrine should not be extended beyond its traditional common law limitation. We now hold that ordinarily, under the felony-murder doctrine, criminal culpability shall continue to be imposed for all lethal acts committed by a felon or an accomplice acting in furtherance of a common design. However, criminal culpability ordinarily shall not be imposed for lethal acts of nonfelons that are not committed in furtherance of a common design." [b]

NOTES AND QUESTIONS ON THE MISDEMEANOR–MANSLAUGHTER RULE

1. *Generally.* Under the early common law, an unintended killing occurring in the commission of an unlawful act constituted a criminal homicide. When criminal homicide was later subdivided into the

---

b. Consider, however, that a felon might be convicted of murder on a depraved heart—gross recklessness theory where a policeman or victim shoots a co-felon or bystander. This result has been reached, for example, when those shots were fired after the felon's grossly reckless act of initiating a gun battle.

In *Taylor v. Superior Court,* 3 Cal.3d 578, 91 Cal.Rptr. 275, 477 P.2d 131 (1970), the court held the evidence at the preliminary hearing was sufficient to support a murder charge even though the first shot was fired by the victim. This was on the theory that "a gun battle can be initiated by acts of provocation falling short of firing the first shot," such as, in the instant case, one felon's "repeated threats of 'execution'" and another's "intent and nervous apprehension as he held [one robbery victim] at gunpoint."

In *People v. Antick,* 15 Cal.3d 79, 123 Cal.Rptr. 475, 539 P.2d 43 (1975), the court reversed the defendant's murder conviction. When co-felon Bose fired at a police officer, the officer fired back and killed Bose. The court concluded: "As the immediate cause of death was the act of the officer, it is clear that the felony-murder rule does not operate to convert the killing into a murder for which defendant may be liable by virtue of his participation in the underlying burglary.

"Nor may defendant be held legally accountable for Bose's death based upon his vicarious liability for the crimes of his accomplice. In order to predicate defendant's guilt upon this theory, it is necessary to prove that Bose committed a murder in other words, that he caused the death of another human being that he acted with malice.

"It is well settled that Bose's conduct in initiating a shootout with police officers may establish the requisite malice. As we have noted on a number of occasions, a person who initiates a gun battle in the course of committing a felony intentionally and with a conscious disregard for life commits an act that is likely to cause death. However, Bose's malicious conduct did not result in the unlawful killing of *another* human being, but rather in Bose's own death. The only homicide which occurred was the justifiable killing of Bose by the police officer. Defendant's criminal liability certainly cannot be predicated upon the actions of the officer. As Bose could not be found guilty of murder in connection with his own death, it is impossible to base defendant's liability for this offense upon his vicarious responsibility for the crime of his accomplice."

separate crimes of murder and manslaughter, this type was assigned to the involuntary manslaughter category. Because the requisite unlawful act was almost always a misdemeanor,[a] this type of criminal homicide came to be known as misdemeanor manslaughter. It has been aptly characterized as "a reduced analogue of the felony-murder rule." *State v. Gerak,* 169 Conn. 309, 363 A.2d 114 (1975). It is not surprising, therefore, that some of the previously discussed court-devised limits on the felony-murder rule are also applied here. See, e.g., *State v. Light,* 577 S.W.2d 134 (Mo.App.1979) (given that felon is not held for co-felon's death due to outside agency which thwarts the felony, same true in instant case, where during misdemeanor of theft of telephone wire defendant's partner came into contact with high voltage wire and was electrocuted).

Although the misdemeanor involved is commonly a traffic offense, such as speeding or drunken driving, another common type of misdemeanor causing death is simple battery, as where the defendant hits the victim a light blow but unexpectedly causes death. Illustrative are *State v. Frazier,* 339 Mo. 966, 98 S.W.2d 707 (1936) (where battery on person not known to be a hemophiliac resulted in death, defendant guilty of manslaughter); and *State v. Johnson,* 102 Ind. 247, 1 N.E. 377 (1885) (where defendant knocked victim through screen door, resulting in cuts from which victim contracted lockjaw and died, defendant guilty of manslaughter).

Such cases as *Frazier* and *Johnson* point up the harshness of the misdemeanor-manslaughter rule. As stated in *Model Penal Code* § 201.3, Comments (Tent.Draft No. 9, 1959): "Whether the matter is viewed in relation to the just condemnation of the actor's conduct or in relation to deterrence or correction, and all are relevant perspec-

tives, neither the terminology nor the sanctions appropriate for homicide may fairly be applied when the fatality is thus fortuitous. The actor's conduct is a crime and should be dealt with as such, but as a crime defined in reference to the specific evil it portends, e.g., bodily injury. The inequality involved in treating homicides as manslaughter, when they are accidental in the sense supposed, serves no proper purpose of the penal law and is abusive in itself."

2. *The required causal connection.* Mere coincidence of time and place between the misdemeanor and the causing of death will not suffice. Illustrative is *People v. Mulcahy,* 318 Ill. 332, 149 N.E. 266 (1925), holding it is not enough that the death was caused "while" the defendant was engaged in an unlawful act, and thus it was not manslaughter where a policeman's gun accidentally discharged and killed a hatcheck girl while he was committing the unlawful act of failing to arrest drunks and gamblers who were disturbing the peace and gambling in his presence in a cabaret.

3. *Malum in se or malum prohibitum.* In many but not all jurisdictions with misdemeanor manslaughter, it is significant whether the misdemeanor is of the *malum in se* or *malum prohibitum* type. "An offense malum in se is properly defined as one which is naturally evil as adjudged by the sense of a civilized community, whereas an act malum prohibitum is wrong only because made so by statute." *State v. Horton,* 139 N.C. 588, 51 S.E. 945 (1905). When the defendant's unlawful act was only *malum prohibitum,* courts tended to narrow the scope of the misdemeanor-manslaughter doctrine in various ways:

(a) Sometimes it is said the defendant is not guilty unless the death was the foresee-

---

a. But, except where statutory language provides otherwise, certain other unlawful acts (e.g., a felony which for some reason will not suffice for felony-murder, or a violation of a local ordinance) will also suffice.

able or natural consequence of the defendant's unlawful conduct. For example, in *Commonwealth v. Williams,* 133 Pa.Super. 104, 1 A.2d 812 (1938), where the defendant struck and killed the victim while driving with an expired driver's license, the manslaughter conviction was reversed because for manslaughter liability "the death must be the natural result or probable consequence of the unlawful act."

(b) Sometimes it is said the defendant is not guilty unless the death was in fact caused by his conduct's unlawful excess, that is, that portion of the defendant's whole conduct which makes the conduct unlawful. Illustrative is *State v. Gerak,* supra, reversing a conviction for manslaughter based upon defendant's violation of a statute proscribing the discharge of a firearm within city limits without obtaining a permit from the mayor. "The unlawful act, then, is having no permit to discharge a firearm, not the discharge per se. Had the defendant obtained a permit, and assuming he fired the fatal shot as alleged, the discharge of the firearm would not be an unlawful act and since it cannot reasonably be said that failure to obtain a permit was the proximate cause of death, the doctrine cannot apply."

(c) Sometimes it is said the defendant is not guilty unless his unlawful conduct amounted to criminal negligence. Thus, in *People v. Stuart,* 47 Cal.2d 167, 302 P.2d 5 (1956), the court held that a manslaughter conviction could not be grounded upon a violation of the strict liability offense of misbranding drugs unless it was shown, which would not be necessary for conviction of the misdemeanor, that the defendant "had intentionally or through criminal negligence prepared, compounded or sold an adulterated or misbranded drug."

4. *The current trend.* The Model Penal Code rejected the misdemeanor-manslaughter doctrine in its entirety. The great majority of the recodifications adopted in recent years have followed the lead of the Model Penal Code in this regard.

SECTION 5. CAUSATION

Introductory Notes

1. Whenever a crime is defined in such a way that the occurrence of a certain specific result of conduct is required for its commission (e.g., death of a human being for any criminal homicide), it is necessary that the defendant's conduct be the "legal" or "proximate" cause of the result. For one thing, that conduct must be the cause in fact of the result, which usually means that but for the conduct the result would not have occurred.[a] In addition, even when cause in fact is established, it must be determined whether the variation between the result intended or hazarded and the actual result is so extraordinary that it would be unfair to hold the defendant responsible for the result.

2. In a very significant sense the subject of causation fits within the major

---

a. The "but for" test does not work where two causes, each alone sufficient to bring about the harmful result, operate together to cause it (e.g., A shoots X in the chest and B acting independently shoots X in the head; X dies following these separate fatal wounds). As stated in *State v. Batiste,* 410 So.2d 1055 (La.1982), involving such facts: "The law will not stop, in such a case, to measure which wound is the more serious, and to speculate upon which actually caused the death." Thus, the test for cause in fact is more accurately worded: Was the defendant's conduct a substantial factor in bringing about the forbidden result? *State v. Serebin,* 119 Wis.2d 837, 350 N.W.2d 65 (1984).

Moreover, there is also authority that one of several independent injuries may be a cause of death even if it "alone would not have been sufficient to cause the death." *Commonwealth v. McLeod,* 394 Mass. 727, 477 N.E.2d 972 (1985). It is enough if it "caused, contributed to, or accelerated" the death. *Holsemback v. State,* 443 So.2d 1371 (Ala.Crim.App.1983). But a few states by statute have provided that the defendant is not the cause of death if the other cause was sufficient to cause death but defendant's was not. See *State v. Crocker,* 431 A.2d 1323 (Me.1981).

theme of this Chapter: the classification of crimes in terms of their seriousness. This is because, as noted in *Model Penal Code* § 2.03, Comment (1985): "What will usually turn on determinations under this section is not the criminality of the defendant's conduct, but the gravity of his offense. For example, when the actor's purpose is to cause the death of another, the lack of an adequate relation between his conduct and the death of his intended victim results in conviction for attempted murder rather than murder. Similarly, when the actor recklessly creates a risk of death, escape from responsibility for criminal homicide under the present section does not bar criminal liability for lesser offenses. Thus, the issue in penal law is quite different from that in torts. Ordinarily, it is only in form a question of the actor's liability. In substance, it is a question of the severity of the sentence the court may impose."

3. It is very unusual for a criminal code to define proximate cause or even to articulate principles for courts to utilize in deciding causation issues; the law on this subject is almost exclusively a product of the courts. Consider, as you read the following materials, whether the subject lends itself to legislation. In particular, "test" *Model Penal Code* § 2.03 against the cases which follow.[b]

4. Consider also, in assessing the following cases, the criticism in Hassett, *Absolutism in Causation,* 38 Syrac.L.Rev. 683, 686, 710, 712–13 (1987), that while there are gradations of responsibility with respect to the other elements of criminal offenses (e.g., as to the mental element, intentionally causing a harm is deemed more serious than recklessly causing the same harm; as to results, a completed crime is deemed more serious than an attempt), "the causation element has been

b. For a critique of the Code approach, see Note, 78 Colum.L.Rev. 1249 (1978).

uniformly treated as an absolute that either exists (thus imposing full liability), or does not exist (thus resulting in exoneration). * * * No mechanism exists for adjusting either the grade of the defendant's offense or the authorized penalties to reflect the partial nature of the defendant's contribution to the harm, or the existence of contributing causal forces. * * * [T]he estimation of foreseeability is not an exact science and the transition from foreseeable to unforeseeable may be gradual rather than abrupt. A doctrine of partial causal responsibility would permit the reality of the gradual transition to be incorporated into the adjudication of criminal liability * * *."

STATE v. ROSE

Supreme Court of Rhode Island, 1973.
112 R.I. 402, 311 A.2d 281.

ROBERTS, CHIEF JUSTICE. * * *

[Defendant's conviction of manslaughter] followed the death of David J. McEnery, who was struck by defendant's motor vehicle at the intersection of Broad and Summer Streets in Providence at about 6:30 p.m. on April 1, 1970. According to the testimony of a bus driver, he had been operating his vehicle north on Broad Street and had stopped at a traffic light at the intersection of Summer Street. While the bus was standing there, he observed a pedestrian starting to cross Broad Street, and as the pedestrian reached the middle of the southbound lane he was struck by a "dirty, white station wagon" that was proceeding southerly on Broad Street. The pedestrian's body was thrown up on the hood of the car. The bus driver further testified that the station wagon stopped momentarily, the body of the pedestrian rolled off the hood, and the car immediately drove off along Broad Street in a southerly direction. The bus operator testified that he had alighted from his bus, intending to attempt to assist the victim, but was unable to locate the body.

Subsequently, it appears from the testimony of a police officer, about 6:40 p.m. the police located a white station wagon on Haskins Street, a distance of some 610 feet from the scene of the accident. The police further testified that a body later identified as that of David J. McEnery was wedged beneath the vehicle when it was found and that the vehicle had been registered to defendant.

Testifying on behalf of the state was a Robert Buckley, who stated that he had worked with defendant and that about 5 p.m. on the day of the accident he had gone to a place located in Central Falls that he identified as The Palms where he met defendant about 5:15 p.m. Buckley further testified that about 7 p.m. that evening defendant phoned him, told him that he had been involved in an accident, and asked Buckley to help him look for his car. According to Buckley, he picked up defendant's girl friend, identified as Pat, and went to the vicinity of the accident and drove around for some time but was unable to locate the car.

Buckley testified that later he picked up defendant, who asked him to take him to a cafe in Central Falls known as The Well, where he would attempt to establish an alibi. After arriving at The Well, defendant asked Buckley to take him to the Central Falls police station, where defendant reported that his car had been stolen from in front of The Well sometime between 5:30 p.m. and 9 p.m. on that day. Buckley later drove defendant to Pat's home, and while there defendant answered a telephone call. After the telephone call had been completed, defendant told Buckley that "a guy had been killed." According to Buckley, defendant "was denying it on the 'phone" during the conversation. * * *

The defendant * * * directs our attention to the fact that the court charged the jury that there was no evidence in the case of culpable negligence on the part of defendant up to and including the time at which Mr. McEnery was struck by the station wagon. He further charged the jury that, in order to find defendant guilty of manslaughter, it would be necessary to find that McEnery was alive immediately after the impact and that the conduct of defendant following the impact constituted culpable negligence.

The defendant is contending that if the evidence is susceptible of a finding that McEnery was killed upon impact, he was not alive at the time he was being dragged under defendant's vehicle and defendant could not be found guilty of manslaughter. An examination of the testimony of the only medical witness makes it clear that, in his opinion, death could have resulted immediately upon impact by reason of a massive fracture of the skull. The medical witness also testified that death could have resulted a few minutes after the impact but conceded that he was not sure when it did occur.

We are inclined to agree with defendant's contention in this respect. Obviously, the evidence is such that death could have occurred after defendant had driven away with McEnery's body lodged under his car and, therefore, be consistent with guilt. On the other hand, the medical testimony is equally consistent with a finding that McEnery could have died instantly upon impact and, therefore, be consistent with a reasonable conclusion other than the guilt of defendant. It is clear, then, that, the testimony of the medical examiner lacking any reasonable medical certainty as to the time of the death of McEnery, we are unable to conclude that on such evidence defendant was guilty of manslaughter beyond a reasonable doubt. Therefore, we conclude * * * that it was error to deny defendant's motion for a directed verdict of acquittal. * * *[a]

Notes and Questions

1. Bush shot Geller in the chest several times with a .38 caliber revolver. Shortly thereafter, Dlugash shot Geller in the face five times with his .25 caliber revolver. Though the trial court dismissed that portion of the indictment which alleged that Dlugash and Bush acted in concert, Dlugash was convicted of murder. The conviction was reversed in *People v. Dlugash*, 41 N.Y.2d 725, 395 N.Y.S.2d 419, 363 N.E.2d 1155 (1977): "While the defendant admitted firing five shots at the victim approximately two to five minutes after Bush had fired three times, all three medical expert witnesses testified that they could not, with any degree of medical certainty, state whether the victim had been alive at the time the latter shots were fired by the defendant. Thus, the People failed to prove beyond a reasonable doubt that the victim had been alive at the time he was shot by the defendant. Whatever else it may be, it is not murder to shoot a dead body."[b]

2. Compare with *Rose* the similar case of *State v. Southern*, 304 N.W.2d 329 (Minn.1981): "We disagree with the state's contention that the evidence established beyond a reasonable doubt that defendant was driving in a grossly negligent manner up to the point of impact.

"Defendant's conduct in accelerating and leaving the scene clearly was gross negligence, however, and we are satisfied that the state's evidence sufficiently estab-

lished that gross negligence to be a substantial factor causing the child's death. There was testimony that defendant's gross negligence resulted in the child being dragged approximately 175 feet before his body came to rest, a far greater distance than he would have been dragged if defendant had stopped immediately after impact instead of fleeing. The two main injuries which led to the child's death were a head injury which probably, but not necessarily, occurred at impact and a neck injury which may have occurred at impact or while the child was being dragged. But for defendant's gross negligence, the child may well have survived. Of course, we will never know this because defendant, by her gross negligence in failing to stop and in leaving the scene, made it impossible to determine this. Further, her conduct also had the effect of ensuring the child's death. We are satisfied after a careful review of the record that the evidence established defendant's grossly negligent driving to be a substantial causal factor in the child's death."

Is this so? Does this mean that both *Rose* and *Dlugash* were wrongly decided?

3. Fine became involved in a heated argument with Hodges. Hodges became very angry when Fine said Hodges owed him $5; as Fine later testified, Hodges "had a wild, angry look on his face." Fine grabbed Hodges and shook him and then grabbed him by the throat. Fine released him in a matter of seconds, and Hodges then slumped to the ground. He never regained consciousness, and died several weeks later. At Fine's prosecution for manslaughter, the medical evidence

a. The court went on to conclude that the evidence was sufficient to sustain the findings that defendant had knowledge that he struck a pedestrian and that the pedestrian had sustained injuries, and that such evidence supported defendant's conviction for leaving the scene of an accident.

b. The court went on to conclude "that there is sufficient evidence in the record from which

the jury could conclude that the defendant believed Geller to be alive at the time defendant fired shots into Geller's head," and therefore merely modified the judgment "to reflect a conviction for the lesser included offense of attempted murder."

was that Hodges had suffered a cerebral hemorrhage, that his blood pressure had been "alarmingly high," that "excitement of any kind or nature" could have caused the rupture of the blood vessel in his brain, and that "a person of that age with that blood pressure [would] be liable to have a stroke without anybody even touching them." In *Fine v. State,* 193 Tenn. 422, 246 S.W.2d 70 (1952), the court reversed the conviction. "In the light of the proven facts, including that of the medical experts bearing upon the cause of death, it cannot be said with any degree of certainty that the deceased died as the result of any criminal agency. The conclusion reached by the jury, of necessity, had to be based upon an inference upon an inference and upon a third inference which could not be thought of otherwise than a fantastic speculation."

4. *State v. Minster,* 302 Md. 240, 486 A.2d 1197 (1985): "The issue here is whether we should abrogate the common law rule of 'a year and a day', which bars a prosecution for murder when the victim dies more than a year and a day after being injured. * * *

"We agree with Minster that there are a number of sound justifications for retaining this rule. As Chief Judge Orth stated in *Brown,* '[a]bolition of the rule may well result in imbalance between the adequate protection of society and justice for the individual accused, and there would remain a need for some form of limitation on causation.'

"[W]e find there is a great difference of opinion surrounding the appropriate length of the period after which prosecution is barred and some doubt whether the rule should exist at all. Consequently, we believe it is the legislature which should mandate any change in the rule, if indeed any change is appropriate in Maryland. * * *

"We recognize the cogency of the State's argument concerning medical advances in life-saving techniques, and we are aware that other courts have been persuaded by this argument. Yet recent decisions have affirmed the viability of the year and a day rule, and, by our count, the rule remains extant in twenty six states."

KIBBE v. HENDERSON

United States Court of Appeals, Second Circuit, 1976.
534 F.2d 493.

LUMBARD, CIRCUIT JUDGE: * * *

Kibbe and his codefendant, Roy Krall, met the decedent, George Stafford, at a bar in Rochester, New York on the evening of December 30, 1970. Stafford had been drinking heavily and by about 9:00 p.m. he was so intoxicated that the bartender refused to serve him further. Apparently the defendants saw Stafford offer a one hundred dollar bill for payment, which the bartender refused. At some point during the evening, Stafford began soliciting a ride to Canandaigua from the other patrons in the bar. Kibbe and Krall, who confessed to having already decided to rob Stafford, offered a ride and the three men left the bar together. Before starting out for Canandaigua, the three visited a second bar. When the bartender at this bar also refused to serve Stafford because of his inebriated condition, the three proceeded to a third bar, where each was served additional drinks.

Kibbe, Krall and Stafford left for Canandaigua in Kibbe's car about 9:30 that evening. According to statements of the defendants, as Krall was driving the car, Kibbe demanded Stafford's money and, upon receiving it, forced Stafford to lower his trousers and remove his boots to prove he had no more. At some time between 9:30 and 9:40 p.m., Stafford was abandoned on the side of an unlit, rural two-lane highway. His boots and jacket were also placed on the shoulder of the highway; Stafford's eyeglasses, however, remained in the car. There was testimony that it was "very cold" that night and that strong winds were blowing recently fallen snow across the highway, although the night was clear and the pavement was dry. There was an open and lighted service station in the general vicinity, but testimony varied as to its precise distance from the place where Stafford was abandoned. In any case, the station was no more than one-quarter of a mile away.

About half an hour after Kibbe and Krall had abandoned Stafford, Michael Blake, a college student, was driving his pickup truck northbound on the highway at 50 miles an hour, ten miles per hour in excess of the posted speed limit. A car passed Blake in a southbound direction and the driver flashed his headlights at Blake. Immediately thereafter, Blake saw Stafford sitting in the middle of the northbound lane with his hands in the air. Blake testified that he "went into a kind of shock" as soon as he saw Stafford, and that he did not apply his brakes. Blake further testified that he did not attempt to avoid hitting Stafford because he "didn't have time to react." After the collision, Blake stopped his truck and returned to assist Stafford, whereupon he found the decedent's trousers were around his ankles and his shirt was up to his chest. Stafford was wearing neither his jacket nor his boots.

Stafford suffered massive head and body injuries as a result of the collision and died shortly thereafter. An autopsy revealed a high alcohol concentration of .25% in his blood. The Medical Examiner testified that these injuries were the direct cause of death.

Kibbe and Krall were apprehended on December 31, 1970. They were tried for robbery and for the murder of Stafford under New York Penal Law § 125.25(2) which provides:

A person is guilty of murder in the second degree when:

* * *

(2) Under circumstances evincing a depraved indifference to human life, he recklessly engages in conduct which creates a grave risk of death to another person, and thereby causes the death of another person.

In his charge to the jury, the judge failed to define or explain the issue of causation as that term is used in § 125.25(2). No mention was made of the legal effect of intervening or supervening cause. Nevertheless, defense counsel failed to take any exception whatsoever to this omission. The jury returned guilty verdicts on the charges of second degree murder, second degree robbery, and third degree grand larceny. Kibbe was sentenced to concurrent terms of imprisonment of 15 years to life on the murder conviction, 5 to 15 years on the robbery conviction, and up to 4 years on the grand larceny conviction.

The Appellate Division affirmed the conviction on finding that there was sufficient evidence that Stafford's death was caused by appellant's acts "as well as by the acts of Blake." The court stated that while the trial judge's charge concerning causation was "lacking in detail" appellant had not questioned the sufficiency of the charge on appeal and no exceptions to or requests for a charge on causation had been made at trial. * * * The New York Court of Appeals also found sufficient evidence of causation and unanimously affirmed the convictions. * * *

Kibbe then petitioned for habeas corpus in the District Court for the Northern District. Judge Foley denied the petition and, on the question of the jury charge, noted that the correctness of instructions does not raise a constitutional claim cognizable on habeas corpus. Appeal to this court followed. * * *

In this case, by the language of the statute, the state was bound to prove to the jury beyond a reasonable doubt that appellant evinced a depraved indifference to Stafford's life, recklessly engaged in conduct that created a grave risk of Stafford's death, and thereby caused Stafford's death. The court scrupulously instructed the jury with respect to the meaning of "recklessly", "depraved", "grave", and "indifferent" as used in Penal Law § 125.25(2). The omission of any definition of causation, however, permitted the jury to conclude that the issue was not before them or that causation could be inferred merely from the fact that Stafford's death succeeded his abandonment by Kibbe and Krall.

Even if the jury were aware of the need to determine causation,[5] the court's in-

struction did not provide the tools necessary to that task. The possibility that jurors, as laymen, may misconstrue the evidence before them makes mandatory in every case instruction as to the legal standards they must apply. Error in the omission of an instruction is compounded where the legal standard is complex and requires that fine distinctions be made. That is most assuredly the situation in this case. It has been held that where death is produced by an intervening force, such as Blake's operation of his truck, the liability of one who put an antecedent force into action will depend on the difficult determination of whether the intervening force was a sufficiently independent or supervening cause of death. See W. LaFave & A. Scott, *Criminal Law* 257–63 (1972) (collecting cases).[6] The few cases that

---

5. The trial judge made brief mention of the term "causation" in his charge when he stated:

"You will not consider either (first degree manslaughter or second degree manslaughter) unless you feel that these defendants or either of them, was guilty of causing the death of George Stafford recklessly." This instruction, however, was given in the context of explaining the relation between reckless conduct and manslaughter rather than in the context of a definition of causation. In fact, by emphasizing "recklessly", the judge may have implied that the jury could assume causation and had only to determine whether recklessness was involved. ＊ ＊ ＊

6. The complexity of the definition of legal causation in LaFave and Scott, supra, demonstrates that an explanation of the concept of intervening and supervening cause would have been not merely helpful (as contended by Judge Mansfield), but essential to the jury's determination here. Given the proper standard for causation, the jury could have found that Blake had been so reckless as to absolve defendants of legal responsibility for Stafford's death:

As might be expected, courts have tended to distinguish cases in which the intervening act was a *coincidence* from those in which it was a *response* to the defendant's prior action. An intervening act is a *coincidence* when the defendant's act merely put the victim at a certain place at a certain time, and because the victim was so located it was possible for him to be acted upon by the intervening cause. The case put earlier in which B, after being fired upon by A, changed his route and then was struck by lightning is an illustration of a coincidence.

However, it is important to note that there may be a coincidence even when the subsequent act is that of a human agency, as where A shoots B and leaves him lying in the roadway, resulting in B being struck by C's car; or where A shoots at B and causes him to take refuge in a park, where B is then attacked and killed by a gang of hoodlums.

By contrast, an intervening act may be said to be a *response* to the prior actions of the defendant when it involves a reaction to the conditions created by the defendant.

Thus—though the distinction is not carefully developed in many of the decided cases—it may be said that a coincidence will break the chain of legal cause unless it was foreseeable, while a response will do so only if it is abnormal (and, if abnormal, also unforeseeable).

＊ ＊ ＊

This kind of accident must be distinguished from a somewhat different situation, as where A, with intent to kill B, only wounds B, leaving him lying unconscious in the unlighted road on a dark night, and then C, driving along the road, runs over and kills B. Here C's act is a matter of coincidence rather than a response to what A has done, and thus the question is whether the subsequent events were foreseeable, as they undoubtedly were in the above illustration.[73]

> [73] *People v. Fowler*, 178 Cal. 657, 174 P. 892 (1918). Perhaps if C were driving in a reckless way, A would not be liable. If A in the Fowler case had merely an intent to injure, but not to kill, A would be guilty of manslaughter, but no doubt A, having put B in an unconscious or helpless position on a dark road, has an affirmative duty to act to pull him off the road, and failure to act under the circumstances where A knows death is substantially certain to occur (or even where he realizes

provide similar factual circumstances suggest that the controlling questions are whether the ultimate result was foreseeable to the original actor and whether the victim failed to do something easily within his grasp that would have extricated him from danger.[7]

The New York appellate courts applied these standards and found that there was sufficient evidence to uphold the convictions. We have no reason to doubt that conclusion. * * * The sufficiency of the evidence, however, is not the subject of our inquiry. Our sole concern is whether the jury was adequately instructed in order to make the same finding beyond a reasonable doubt. As this function was within the exclusive province of the jury, the appellate courts may not substitute their own findings for the jury's possible failure to consider the issue. * * * If the jury had been cognizant of the proper legal standards, this evidence, if believed, could have injected an element of reasonable doubt into the jury's deliberations as to whether defendants foresaw or could have foreseen that about one-half hour after they abandoned Stafford he would be struck in the middle of a highway lane by the driver of a speeding truck who failed to react in such a way to avoid a collision.

We are convinced that the trial judge's incomplete instructions took a necessary determination of causation of death from the jury and thereby deprived appellant of his right to due process. * * *

MANSFIELD, CIRCUIT JUDGE (dissenting): * * *

Although it might have been helpful to the jury to have a more definitive instruction on the element of causation, including

there is a very high risk though no certainty of such death) should make him guilty of murder of the intent to kill (or of the depraved heart) variety.

Without a proper definition of causation, the jury, if it considered causation at all, could have found that Blake's conduct, no matter how reckless, could merely supplement and not supervene defendants' culpability.

an explanation of the concepts of proximate, superseding, and intervening causation, I cannot agree with the majority that such a detailed instruction was constitutionally required or that the failure to give it permitted "the jury to conclude that the issue was not before them." We are not here dealing with such fundamental unfairness as failure to advise the jury that the defendant was presumed to be innocent or the substitution by the court in its instruction of a preponderance-of-the-evidence for a reasonable doubt standard, see *In re Winship*, 397 U.S. 358, 90 S.Ct. 1068, 25 L.Ed.2d 368 (1970). Here the jury plainly was made aware by the summations of the necessity of finding that the defendants' conduct was the cause of the victim's death even though it may not have been the only cause. In these circumstances the court's instruction was sufficient to enable the jury intelligently to go about its business. * * *

In *Henderson v. Kibbe,* 431 U.S. 145, 97 S.Ct. 1730, 52 L.Ed.2d 203 (1977), the Court, per Stevens, J., reversed:

"The burden of demonstrating that an erroneous instruction was so prejudicial that it will support a collateral attack on the constitutional validity of a state court's judgment is even greater than the showing required to establish plain error on direct appeal. The question in such a collateral proceeding is 'whether the ailing instruction by itself so infected the entire trial that the resulting conviction violates due process', not merely whether ' * * * the instruction is undesirable, erroneous, or even "universally condemned."' '

7. See *State v. Preslar,* 48 N.C.Rep. 421 (1856) (deliberate choice of victim to forego place of safety exonerates defendant of liability for victim's subsequent death from exposure).

"In this case, the respondent's burden is especially heavy because no erroneous instruction was given; his claim of prejudice is based on the failure to give any explanation—beyond the reading of the statutory language itself—of the causation element. An omission, or an incomplete instruction, is less likely to be prejudicial than a misstatement of the law. Since this omission escaped notice on the record until Judge Cardamone filed his dissenting opinion at the intermediate appellate level, the probability that it substantially affected the jury deliberations seems remote.

"Because respondent did not submit a draft instruction on the causation issue to the trial judge, and because the New York courts apparently had no previous occasion to construe this aspect of the murder statute, we cannot know with certainty precisely what instruction should have been given as a matter of New York law. We do know that the New York Court of Appeals found no reversible error in this case; and its discussion of the sufficiency of the evidence gives us guidance about the kind of causation instruction that would have been acceptable.

"The New York Court of Appeals concluded that the evidence of causation was sufficient because it can be said beyond a reasonable doubt that the 'ultimate harm' was 'something which should have been foreseen as being reasonably related to the acts of the accused.' It is not entirely clear whether the court's reference to 'ultimate harm' merely required that Stafford's death was foreseeable, or, more narrowly, that his death by speeding vehicle was foreseeable. In either event, the court

was satisfied that the 'ultimate harm' was one which 'should have been foreseen.' Thus, an adequate instruction would have told the jury that if the ultimate harm should have been foreseen as being reasonably related to defendants' conduct, that conduct should be regarded as having caused the death of Stafford.

"The significance of the omission of such an instruction may be evaluated by comparison with the instructions that were given. One of the elements of respondent's offense is that he acted 'recklessly.' By returning a guilty verdict, the jury necessarily found, in accordance with its instruction on recklessness, that respondent was 'aware of and consciously disregard[ed] a substantial and unjustifiable risk' [15] that death would occur. A person who is 'aware of and consciously disregards' a substantial risk must also foresee the ultimate harm that the risk entails. Thus, the jury's determination that the respondent acted recklessly necessarily included a determination that the ultimate harm was foreseeable to him.

"In a strict sense, an additional instruction on foreseeability would not have been cumulative because it would have related to an element of the offense not specifically covered in the instructions given. But since it is logical to assume that the jurors would have responded to an instruction on causation consistently with their determination of the issues that were comprehensively explained, it is equally logical to conclude that such an instruction would not have affected their verdict.[16] Accordingly, we reject the suggestion that the omission of more complete instructions on

---

15. In charging the jury on recklessness the trial judge quoted the statutory definition of that term in New York Penal Law § 15.00.

16. In fact, it is not unlikely that a complete instruction on the causation issue would actually have been favorable to the prosecution. For example, an instruction might have been patterned after the following example given in W. LaFave & A. Scott, *Criminal Law* 260 (1972):

" * * * A, with intent to kill B, only wounds B, leaving him lying unconscious in the unlighted road on a dark night, and then C, driving along the road, runs over and kills B. Here C's act is a matter of coincidence rather than a response to what A has done, and thus the question is whether the subsequent events were foreseeable, as they undoubtedly were in the above illustration."

the causation issue 'so infected the entire trial that the resulting conviction violated due process.' Even if we were to make the unlikely assumption that the jury might have reached a different verdict pursuant to an additional instruction, that possibility is too speculative to justify the conclusion that constitutional error was committed.''

REGINA v. BLAUE

Court of Appeal, Criminal Division, England, 1975.
[1975] 1 W.L.R. 1411, [1975] 3 All E.R. 446 (C.A.).

LAWTON L.J. read the following judgment of the court. On October 17, 1974, at Teesside Crown Court after a trial before Mocatta J. the defendant was acquitted of the murder of Jacolyn Woodhead but was convicted of her manslaughter on the ground of diminished responsibility.

* * *

The victim was aged 18. She was a Jehovah's Witness. She professed the tenets of that sect and lived her life by them. During the late afternoon of May 3, 1974, the defendant came into her house and asked her for sexual intercourse. She refused. He then attacked her with a knife inflicting four serious wounds. One pierced her lung. The defendant ran away. She staggered out into the road. She collapsed outside a neighbour's house. An ambulance took her to hospital, where she arrived at about 7:30 p.m. Soon after she was admitted to the intensive care ward. At about 8:30 p.m. she was examined by the surgical registrar who quickly decided that serious injury had been caused which would require surgery. As she had lost a lot of blood, before there could be an operation there would have to be a blood transfusion. As soon as the girl appreciated that the surgeon was thinking of organising a blood transfusion for her, she said that she should not be given one

and that she would not have one. To have one, she said, would be contrary to her religious beliefs as a Jehovah's Witness. She was told that if she did not have a blood transfusion she would die. She said that she did not care if she did die. She was asked to acknowledge in writing that she had refused to have a blood transfusion under any circumstances. She did so. The prosecution admitted at the trial that had she had a blood transfusion when advised to have one she would not have died. She did so at 12:45 a.m. the next day. The evidence called by the prosecution proved that at all relevant times she was conscious and decided as she did deliberately, and knowing what the consequences of her decision would be. In his final speech to the jury, Mr. Herrod for the prosecution accepted that her refusal to have a blood transfusion was *a* cause of her death. The prosecution did not challenge the defence evidence that the defendant was suffering from diminished responsibility.

Towards the end of the trial and before the summing up started counsel on both sides made submissions as to how the case should be put to the jury. Counsel then appearing for the defendant invited the judge to direct the jury to acquit the defendant generally on the count of murder. His argument was that her refusal to have a blood transfusion had broken the chain of causation between the stabbing and her death. As an alternative he submitted that the jury should be left to decide whether the chain of causation had been broken. Mr. Herrod submitted that the judge should direct the jury to convict, because no facts were in issue and when the law was applied to the facts there was only one possible verdict, namely, manslaughter by reason of diminished responsibility.

Such an instruction would probably have been more favorable to the prosecution than the instruction on recklessness which the court actually gave.

When the judge came to direct the jury on this issue he did so by telling them that they should apply their common sense. He then went on to tell them they would get some help from the cases to which counsel had referred in their speeches. He reminded them of what Lord Parker C.J. had said in *Reg. v. Smith* [1959] 2 W.B. 35, 42 and what Maule J. had said 133 years before in *Reg. v. Holland* (1841) 2 Mood. & R. 351, 352. He placed particular reliance on what Maule J. had said. The jury, he said, might find it "most material and most helpful." He continued:

> "This is one of those relatively rare cases, you may think, with very little option open to you but to reach the conclusion that was reached by your predecessors as members of the jury in *Reg. v. Holland,* namely, 'yes' to the question of causation that the stab was still, at the time of this girl's death, the operative cause of death—or a substantial cause of death. However, that is a matter for you to determine after you have withdrawn to consider your verdict."

Mr. Comyn has criticised that direction on three grounds: first, because *Reg. v. Holland* should no longer be considered good law; secondly, because *Reg. v. Smith,* when rightly understood, does envisage the possibility of unreasonable conduct on the part of the victim breaking the chain of causation; and thirdly, because the judge in reality directed the jury to find causation proved although he used words which seemed to leave the issue open for them to decide.

In *Reg. v. Holland,* 2 Mood. & R. 351, the defendant in the course of a violent assault, had injured one of his victim's fingers. A surgeon had advised amputation because of the danger to life through complications developing. The advice was rejected. A fortnight later the victim died of lockjaw. Maule J. said, at p. 352: "the real question is, whether in the end the wound inflicted by the prisoner was the cause of death." That distinguished judge left the jury to decide that question as did the judge in this case. They had to decide it as juries always do, by pooling their experience of life and using their common sense. They would not have been handicapped by a lack of training in dialectic or moral theology.

Maule J.'s direction to the jury reflected the common law's answer to the problem. He who inflicted an injury which resulted in death could not excuse himself by pleading that his victim could have avoided death by taking greater care of himself: see *Hale's Pleas of the Crown* (1800 ed.), pp. 427–428. The common law in Sir Matthew Hale's time probably was in line with contemporary concepts of ethics. A man who did a wrongful act was deemed *morally* responsible for the natural and probable consequences of that act. Mr. Comyn asked us to remember that since Sir Matthew Hale's day the rigour of the law relating to homicide has been eased in favour of the accused. It has been—but this has come about through the development of the concept of intent, not by reason of a different view of causation.

* * *

There have been two cases in recent years which have some bearing upon this topic: *Reg. v. Jordan* (1956) 40 Cr.App.R. 152 and *Reg. v. Smith* [1959] 2 Q.B. 35. In *Reg. v. Jordan* the Court of Criminal Appeal, after conviction, admitted some medical evidence which went to prove that the cause of death was not the blow relied upon by the prosecution but abnormal medical treatment after admission to hospital. This case has been criticised but it was probably rightly decided on its facts. Before the abnormal treatment started the injury had almost healed. We share Lord Parker C.J.'s opinion that *Reg. v. Jordan* should be regarded as a case decided on its own special facts and not as an authority relaxing the common law approach to causation. In *Reg. v. Smith* [1959] 2 Q.B. 35 the man who had been stabbed would probably not have died but for a series of mishaps. These mishaps were said to have broken the chain of causation. Lord Parker C.J., in the course of his judgment, commented as follows:

> "It seems to the court that if at the time of death the original wound is still an operating cause and a substantial cause, then the death can properly be said to be the result of the wound, albeit that some other cause of death is also operating. Only if it can be said that the original wounding is merely the setting in which another cause operates can it be said that the death does not flow from the wound. Putting it another way, only if the second cause is so overwhelming as to make the original wound merely part of the history can it be said that the death does not flow from the wound."

The physical cause of death in this case was the bleeding into the pleural cavity arising from the penetration of the lung. This had not been brought about by any decision made by the deceased but by the stab wound.

Mr. Comyn tried to overcome this line of reasoning by submitting that the jury should have been directed that if they thought the deceased's decision not to have a blood transfusion was an unreasonable one, then the chain of causation would have been broken. At once the question arises—reasonable by whose standards? Those of Jehovah's Witnesses? Humanists? Roman Catholics? Protestants of Anglo–Saxon descent? The man on the Clapham omnibus? But he might well be an admirer of Eleazar who suffered death rather than eat the flesh of swine (2 Maccabees, ch. 6, vv. 18–31) or of Sir Thomas More who, unlike nearly all his contempo-

raries, was unwilling to accept Henry VIII as Head of the Church in England. Those brought up in the Hebraic and Christian traditions would probably be reluctant to accept that these martyrs caused their own deaths.

As was pointed out to Mr. Comyn in the course of argument, two cases, each raising the same issue of reasonableness because of religious beliefs, could produce different verdicts depending on where the cases were tried. A jury drawn from Preston, sometimes said to be the most Catholic town in England, might have different views about martyrdom to one drawn from the inner suburbs of London. Mr. Comyn accepted that this might be so: it was, he said, inherent in trial by jury. It is not inherent in the common law as expounded by Sir Matthew Hale and Maule J. It has long been the policy of the law that those who use violence on other people must take their victims as they find them. This in our judgment means the whole man, not just the physical man. It does not lie in the mouth of the assailant to say that his victim's religious beliefs which inhibited him from accepting certain kinds of treatment were unreasonable. The question for decision is what caused her death. The answer is the stab wound. The fact that the victim refused to stop this end coming about did not break the causal connection between the act and death.

If a victim's personal representatives claim compensation for his death the concept of foreseeability can operate in favour of the wrongdoer in the assessment of such compensation: the wrongdoer is entitled to expect his victim to mitigate his damage by accepting treatment of a normal kind. As Mr. Herrod pointed out, the criminal law is concerned with the maintenance of law and order and the protection of the public generally. A policy of the common law applicable to the settlement of tortious liability between subjects may not be, and in our judgment is not, appropriate for the criminal law.

The issue of the cause of death in a trial for either murder or manslaughter is one of fact for the jury to decide. But if, as in this case, there is no conflict of evidence and all the jury has to do is to apply the law to the admitted facts, the judge is entitled to tell the jury what the result of that application will be. In this case the judge would have been entitled to have told the jury that the defendant's stab wound was an operative cause of death. The appeal fails.

Notes and Questions

1. The distinguished English criminal law scholar Glanville Williams comments on *Blaue* as follows in 35 Camb.L.J. 15–16 (1976): "Although the case follows the precedents, * * * it fails to notice that all of them dated from a time when medical science was in its infancy, and when operations performed without hygiene carried great danger to life. It was therefore open to the court for the benefit of the defendant to consider the question afresh, and there were several reasons for doing so.

"It had been held in *Roberts* (1971) 56 Cr.App.R. 95 that the test of imputable causation (where the victim had sustained injury in an attempt to escape) was one of reasonable foresight. It is a useful test, and one might have hoped that it would

be generalised; yet we are now told that it does not apply to the circumstances in *Blaue.* Why not?

"It had been held in the law of tort that the test of reasonable foresight applies to facts like those in *Blaue,* but the court refused to bring the criminal law into line. The criminal law should avoid the appearance of harshness, and to make it more stringent than the civil law in the matter of causation is surprising.[a] Lawton L.J., speaking for the court, explained the difference between crime and tort by saying that 'the criminal law is concerned with the maintenance of law and order and the protection of the public generally.' This overlooks that Blaue was in any event punishable severely for wounding with intent. What social purpose is served by giving an attacker *extra* punishment because the person attacked unreasonably refused treatment?"

2. In *Blaue* it is said to have "long been the policy of the law that those who use violence on other people must take their victims as they find them." This policy most often comes into play with respect to a pre-existing physical weakness of the victim, as in *State v. Chavers,* 294 So. 2d 489 (La.1974). Chavers and Simpson met Johnston, who was intoxicated, in a bar. They lured Johnston to a deserted area, struck him on the jaw, and then took his wallet and watch, after which they placed him in a parked truck at another

a. Consider, in this regard, this statement from *Commonwealth v. Root,* 403 Pa. 571, 170 A.2d 310 (1961):

"While precedent is to be found for application of the tort law concept of 'proximate cause' in fixing responsibility for criminal homicide, the want of any rational basis for its use in determining criminal liability can no longer be properly disregarded. When proximate cause was first borrowed from the field of tort law and applied to homicide prosecutions in Pennsylvania, the concept connoted a much more direct causal relation in producing the alleged culpable result than it does today. Proximate cause, as an essential element of a tort founded in negligence, has un-

dergone in recent times, and is still undergoing, a marked extension. More specifically, this area of civil law has been progressively liberalized in favor of claims for damages for personal injuries to which careless conduct of others can in some way be associated. To persist in applying the tort liability concept of proximate cause to prosecutions for criminal homicide after the marked expansion of *civil* liability of defendants in tort actions for negligence would be to extend possible *criminal* liability to persons chargeable with unlawful or reckless conduct in circumstances not generally considered to present the likelihood of a resultant death."

location. Johnston was found dead in the truck two days later. The coroner determined that he had died of a heart attack two days earlier and that he had a pre-existing severe heart condition. The coroner found no evidence of any blow to the body, but stated that a blow on the jaw could have aggravated enough emotion to cause a heart attack in view of the decedent's severe pre-existing coronary condition. In affirming Chavers' conviction of manslaughter, the court stated:

"Thus, the trial jury could reasonably find that the blow to the jaw precipitated the heart attack in Johnston, due to his pre-existing unusually severe coronary condition.

"A death so caused may be entirely unforeseeable on the part of the person who hit the victim suffering with a pre-existing weakness. Nevertheless, such person's blow is regarded as being a direct cause of the victim's death, for which the person is criminally responsible, at least for purposes of the misdemeanor-manslaughter rule such as is here involved. Although the holdings to this effect have received scholarly criticism, they do represent the prevailing view in American decisional interpretations of the misdemeanor-manslaughter statutes."

Is the *Chavers* result sound? If so, does it follow that *Blaue* is correct?

NOTES AND QUESTIONS ON INTERVENING ACTS BY THE VICTIM

1. In *Commonwealth v. Atencio,* 345 Mass. 627, 189 N.E.2d 223 (1963), Marshall, Atencio and Britch played Russian roulette. "Marshall examined the gun, saw that it contained one cartridge, and, after spinning it on his arm, pointed it at his head, and pulled the trigger. Nothing happened. He handed the gun to Atencio, who repeated the process again without result. Atencio passed the gun to

[Britch], who spun it, put it to his head and pulled the trigger. The cartridge exploded, and he fell over dead." In affirming the convictions of Atencio and Marshall for manslaughter, the court stated:

"The defendants argue as if it should have been ruled, as matter of law, that there were three 'games' of solitaire and not one 'game' of 'Russian roulette.' That the defendants participated could be found to be a cause and not a mere condition of Stewart Britch's death. It is not correct to say that his act could not be found to have been caused by anything which Marshall and Atencio did, nor that he would have died when the gun went off in his hand no matter whether they had done the same. The testimony does not require a ruling that when the deceased took the gun from Atencio it was an independent or intervening act not standing in any relation to the defendants' acts which would render what he did imputable to them. It is an oversimplification to contend that each participated in something that only one could do at a time. There could be found to be a mutual encouragement in a joint enterprise. In the abstract, there may have been no duty on the defendants to prevent the deceased from playing. But there was a duty on their part not to cooperate or join with him in the 'game.' Nor, if the facts presented such a case, would we have to agree that if the deceased, and not the defendants, had played first that they could not have been found guilty of manslaughter. The defendants were much more than merely present at a crime. It would not be necessary that the defendants force the deceased to play or suggest that he play.

"We are referred in both briefs to cases of manslaughter arising out of automobiles racing upon the public highway. When the victim is a third person, there is no difficulty in holding the drivers, including the one whose car did not strike the victim

(*Brown v. Thayer*, 212 Mass. 392, 99 N.E. 237), or in whose car a victim was not a passenger. *Nelson v. Nason*, 343 Mass. 220, 221, 177 N.E.2d 887.

"In two cases the driver of a noncolliding car has been prosecuted for the death of his competitor, and in both cases an appellate court has ruled that he was not guilty of manslaughter. In *Commonwealth v. Root*, 403 Pa. 571, 170 A.2d 310, the competitor drove on the wrong side of the road head-on into an oncoming truck and was killed. The court held that ' * * * the defendant's reckless conduct was not a sufficiently direct cause of the competing driver's death to make him criminally liable therefor.' In *Thacker v. State*, 103 Ga. App. 36, 117 S.E.2d 913, the defendant was indicted for the involuntary manslaughter of his competitor in a drag race who was killed when he lost control of his car and left the highway. The court said that the indictment 'fails to allege any act or acts on the part of the defendant which caused or contributed to the loss of control of the vehicle driven by the deceased, other than the fact that they were engaged in a race at the time.'

"Whatever may be thought of those two decisions, there is a very real distinction between drag racing and 'Russian roulette.' In the former much is left to the skill, or lack of it, of the competitor. In 'Russian roulette' it is a matter of luck as to the location of the one bullet, and except for a misfire (of which there was evidence in the case at bar) the outcome is a certainty if the chamber under the hammer happens to be the one containing the bullet."

Is *Atencio* really distinguishable from *Root* and *Thacker?* As for the drag-racing cases, should it really make any difference whether it is a third party or one of the competitors who is killed? [a]

2. Hallett bent a stop sign over until it was parallel with the ground. At 9 a.m. the following morning, Ms. Carley passed where the sign would ordinarily be without stopping, struck another vehicle in the intersection and was killed. Within a block of that intersection, she had passed a truck traveling at 25 m.p.h., the speed limit. The word "Stop" was printed in large block letters on the pavement leading to the intersection. Is Hallett guilty of negligent homicide? [b]

3. Hamilton knocked down a man, jumped on his face and kicked him in the head. The injured party was taken to a hospital, his airways were cleansed, and tubes were inserted into his nasal passages and trachea in order to maintain the breathing process. Because he was violent, it was necessary to restrain the patient with leather handcuffs, but they were removed when the bed was changed and were not replaced because the patient was no longer violent. Some hours later the patient had a convulsion, pulled out the tubes, and died thereafter from asphyxiation. [c] May Hamilton be convicted of murder?

4. After Armstrong obtained two $100 bills from his sister, Casper and Wilson knocked him down and went through his clothing looking for the money. When

---

a. Also compare with *Root* and *Thacker* the case of *Jacobs v. State*, 184 So.2d 711 (Fla.App. 1966): "While engaged in such unlawful activity one of the three vehicles actively participating in the race was negligently operated in such manner as to cause the death of the person who drove that vehicle, as well as another innocent party who had no connection with the race. The deaths which proximately resulted from the activities of the three persons engaged in the unlawful activity of drag racing made each of the active participants equally guilty of the criminal act which caused the death of the innocent party."

b. *State v. Hallett*, 619 P.2d 335 (Utah 1980), affirming the conviction, 4–1.

c. *United States v. Hamilton*, 182 F.Supp. 548 (D.D.C.1960), finding defendant guilty.

they could not find it, Wilson threatened to castrate Armstrong if he didn't hand over the money. Armstrong managed to free himself and he then ran into the Missouri River to escape his pursuers. They saw no more of him, but did find the two bills in the area the following morning. Armstrong's body was found floating downstream about 10 days later.[d] May Casper and Wilson be convicted of murder?

5. Goodman picked up Ms. Husch, an 18–year–old girl who was walking down the highway in the direction he was driving. While the car was traveling about 25 m.p.h., Goodman said to the girl that he would pay her one dollar to have sexual intercourse. She immediately opened the door of the car, hesitated a moment on the running board, and jumped. Her skull was fractured in the fall and she died.[e] May Goodman be convicted of manslaughter?

6. Mangin parked his Cadillac on a boat ramp and left the motor running and the gearshift in park. The defendants parked their cars behind the Cadillac, pulled Retzel and Griffin from that vehicle and commenced to beat them. Retzel and Griffin jumped into the Cadillac as it started to roll. The car stopped momentarily, but then plunged into the water. Retzel and Griffin drowned. Are the defendants guilty of misdemeanor-manslaughter?[f]

7. Feinberg operated a cigar store in the skid-row section of Philadelphia. One of the products he sold was Sterno, designed for heating purposes, from which he knew some of his customers extracted

the alcohol for drinking. He had been selling Sterno containing 3.75% methanol and 71% ethanol (of the two, methanol is far more toxic if consumed internally), but on Dec. 21 he inadvertently received a shipment of new industrial Sterno which was 54% methanol. The cartons in which the new Sterno were shipped were no different, but each can lid had these words: "Institutional Sterno. Danger. Poison. For use only as a Fuel. Not for consumer use. For industrial and commercial use. Not for home use." After he had sold 400 cans of the new Sterno, Feinberg returned the unsold portion to the wholesaler. Between Dec. 23 and Dec. 30, 31 persons died in the skid-row area as a result of methanol poisoning. No other industrial Sterno had been sold in the area.[g] May Feinberg be convicted of involuntary manslaughter?

8. Guillette and others were indicted for interstate transportation of stolen firearms. LaPolla, an unindicted co-conspirator, was to be the key government witness. LaPolla and government agents feared that Guillette and his cohorts might try to kill LaPolla, so LaPolla was kept in protective custody most of the time. But just a few weeks before the scheduled start of the trial, LaPolla, ignoring instructions to stay away from his home, opened the front door and touched off a massive explosion which killed him instantly. The opening of the door had caused a switch to close and detonate several sticks of dynamite. Guillette and others were then indicted for conspiracy to deprive a citizen of his civil rights with death resulting; the "if death

---

d. *State v. Casper,* 192 Neb. 120, 219 N.W.2d 226 (1974), affirming the conviction.

e. *People v. Goodman,* 182 Misc. 585, 44 N.Y.S.2d 715 (1943), denying the motion to dismiss the indictment. Compare *State v. Selby,* 183 N.J.Super. 273, 443 A.2d 1076 (1981), a similar case except that defendant's conduct was much more aggressive, where the court approved an instruction that to convict the jury "must find that the defendant's actions and threats were

such as to put a reasonably prudent person in fear of her life, serious bodily harm or an assault with intent to rape."

f. *Commonwealth v. Bianco,* 388 Mass. 358, 446 N.E.2d 1041 (1983), reversing the convictions.

g. *Commonwealth v. Feinberg,* 433 Pa. 558, 253 A.2d 636 (1969), affirming defendant's several convictions of involuntary manslaughter.

results" part of the statute embodies the principle of proximate cause. A witness at the trial testified that Guillette confided in him the day of the explosion that he had "just left a package for your buddy up there." At trial, the defense position was that LaPolla was killed when he accidently detonated a bomb which he himself installed as a booby trap aimed at the defendants and others who were searching for him. Guillette has asked the trial judge to instruct the jury that he may not be convicted if the jury accepts that theory as to what happened.[h] Should the instruction be given?

9. Lewis became involved in an altercation with his brother-in-law Farrell, resulting in his shooting Farrell in the abdomen. The wound severed the mesenteric artery and thus would produce death in about an hour. Farrell was put to bed where, in great pain, he procured a knife and cut his throat, inflicting a wound from which he would necessarily have died in five minutes. May Lewis be convicted of murder? Does it make any difference whether the medical testimony is (a) that Farrell died from the combined effect of both wounds, or (b) that he died from the self-inflicted wound?[i]

NOTES AND QUESTIONS ON INTERVENING ACTS BY THIRD PARTIES AND OUTSIDE FORCES

1. In *People v. Stewart*, 40 N.Y.2d 692, 389 N.Y.S.2d 804, 358 N.E.2d 487 (1976), the defendant stabbed Smith in the stomach. Prior to an operation on Smith he was given Curare, which para-

lyzes the chest and makes it impossible for the patient to breathe on his own, necessitating the anesthesiologist to "breathe" for him by squeezing a bag of oxygen into the lungs. During the operation, the surgeons discovered an incarcerated hernia, so after completing the operation on the stomach they proceeded to correct the hernia. During this phase of the operation the patient went into cardiac arrest, and then suffered a loss of oxygen to the brain and massive brain damage. He died a month later without regaining consciousness. At the time of death, the stomach wound had completely healed. In reducing the defendant's manslaughter conviction to assault, the court observed:

"One of the problems in the case now before us is that there is some question as to whether the operation on the hernia was made necessary by the defendant's act. According to the testimony it was 'medically correct', arguably necessary, clearly incidental—but the hernia itself was absolutely unrelated to the stab wound. Dr. Di Maio conceded that the chances were that if it had not been performed, the patient would have survived. This type of necessity is obviously of a different order than is normally required to fix responsibility for homicide. It is, we believe, a factor we must consider in determining whether the causal relationship is sufficiently direct.

"The other difficulty in the case is that it was never determined what actually caused the cardiac arrest. Dr. Di Maio acknowledged several possibilities which individually or combined could have created the condition. Most of the factors cited would indicate that the defendant's act was re-

---

h. *United States v. Guillette*, 547 F.2d 743 (2d Cir.1976), affirming denial of such an instruction.

i. See *People v. Lewis*, 124 Cal. 551, 57 P. 470 (1899). The court upheld the conviction on the ground that Farrell died from both wounds ("Drop by drop the life current went out from both wounds"), but seemed to indicate this was not the only basis upon which Lewis could be

convicted of murder: "But, if the deceased did die from the effect of the knife wound alone, no doubt the defendant would be responsible, if it was made to appear, and the jury could have found from the evidence, that the knife wound was caused by the wound inflicted by the defendant, in the natural course of events."

sponsible either because it created a physical strain or shock or created the need for an operation which had the same effect. But Dr. Di Maio conceded that there was some evidence that the anesthesiologist failed to provide oxygen to the patient and that this alone could have been the cause of death. In our view if this occurred it was a grave neglect, perhaps gross negligence, but in any event sufficient to break whatever tenuous causal relationship existed at the time of this incidental operation. There is of course no showing that this was in fact the cause of death but on this record it cannot be ruled out as a possibility, certainly not beyond a reasonable doubt."

2. When an 85–year–old woman resisted a purse snatching, she was struck from behind. She was taken to the hospital, where her condition degenerated. "Six days later, on January 19, on the basis of the patient's condition and her age, after consultation with other physicians involved in the case and upon agreement by the victim's son, the neurosurgeon discontinued all 'heroic measures' " and disconnected the respirator which was keeping the woman alive. "All agree that under any legally accepted definition of death, the victim was not dead when the 'heroic measures' were discontinued." The woman died 15 to 20 minutes later. May the purse snatcher be convicted of murder? [a]

3. Bush shot a girl with a pistol. She later died, not from the wound, but from scarlet fever communicated by her attending physician.[b] May Bush be convicted of murder? What if the girl had contracted pneumonia and died from that? [c]

a. *Matter of J.N.,* 406 A.2d 1275 (D.C.App. 1979), affirming the murder conviction though not even an instruction on the causation issue was given; rehearing en banc granted and opinion vacated.

b. *Bush v. Commonwealth,* 78 Ky. 268 (1880), reversing the murder conviction.

4. Catherine Michael, with intent that her 9–month–old son be killed, gave the boy's nurse a bottle of poison, which she told the nurse was medicine to be given the baby every night. The nurse decided that the child did not need any medicine and thus concluded she would not follow those instructions. She placed the bottle on a mantel, and some days later, during the absence of the nurse, the nurse's 5–year–old son gave the poison to the baby, resulting in the infant's death.[d] May Catherine be convicted of murder?

NOTES AND QUESTIONS ON INTERVENING ACTS BY THE DEFENDANT

1. In *Thabo Meli v. Regina,* [1954] 1 W.L.R. 228, [1954] 1 All E.R. 373, the evidence was that the four defendants planned to kill their victim and then fake an accident. After treating him to beer they struck him over the head and then, believing him dead, they rolled the body over a cliff. The medical evidence was that exposure at the bottom of the cliff rather than the blows on the head were the cause of death. In dismissing the appeal from murder convictions obtained in the High Court of Basutoland, the court stated:

"The point of law which was raised in this case can be simply stated. It is said that two acts were necessary and were separable: first, the attack in the hut; and, secondly, the placing of the body outside afterwards. It is said that, while the first act was accompanied by mens rea, it was not the cause of death; but that the second act, while it was the cause of death, was not accompanied by mens rea; and on that

c. Cf. *People v. Love,* 71 Ill.2d 74, 15 Ill.Dec. 628, 373 N.E.2d 1312 (1978) (was causation where defendant's attack necessitated operation and operation predisposed the victim to pneumonia).

d. *Regina v. Michael,* 2 Moody 120, 169 Eng. Rep. 48 (1840), affirming the murder conviction.

ground it is said that the accused are not guilty of any crime except perhaps culpable homicide.

"It appears to their Lordships impossible to divide up what was really one transaction in this way. There is no doubt that the accused set out to do all these acts in order to achieve their plan and as parts of their plan; and it is much too refined a ground of judgment to say that, because they were under a misapprehension at one stage and thought that their guilty purpose had been achieved before in fact it was achieved, therefore they are to escape the penalties of the law. Their Lordships do not think that this is a matter which is susceptible of elaboration. There appears to be no case either in South Africa or England, or for that matter elsewhere, which resembles the present. Their Lordships can find no difference relevant to the present case between the law of South Africa and the law of England, and they are of opinion that by both laws there could be no separation such as that for which the accused contend, as to reduce the crime from murder to a lesser crime, merely because the accused were under some misapprehension for a time during the completion of their criminal plot."

2. 1 *Russell on Crime* 57 (12th ed. by J. Turner, 1964) is critical of the decision: "On analysis of this judgment it would seem (a) that the words 'impossible to divide' must surely mean 'legally impossible' (since from the point of view of fact and of logic it is by no means impossible, but quite easy); and 'legally impossible' must mean simply that there is some recognised legal principle which treats the division as irrelevant (What is that principle? Their Lordships did not indicate it): and (b) that, with all respect, it is difficult to see what is meant by a ground of judgment being 'much too refined.' It must be supposed that an exalted tribunal such as, beyond doubt, is the Judicial Com-

mittee, would be precisely the body which would take cognisance of refined points of law: and (c) that, again with great respect, the use of the words 'escape the penalties of law' in this particular context, is circular, a *petitio principii*, since it was precisely for the court to decide, as a matter of law, whether a particular penalty, the penalty of death, had been justly imposed."

3. In *Lingras Das v. King*, 24 Indian L.R. Patna Ser. 131 (1945), defendant's confession stated that he and another planned to kill a certain prostitute and take her gold earrings. They choked the woman until she collapsed and then, mistakenly thinking she was dead, they placed her body on nearby railroad tracks, where it was shortly thereafter severed at the waist by a passing train. The confession did not suggest that this disposal of the body had been part of the original plan. The court dismissed the appeal, stating that if the defendant and his accomplice "had the common intention of killing the woman, then the series of acts by which they assaulted the woman and then placed her body on the line would be one transaction. That transaction would be judged by the common intention which they originally had. If the common intention was to kill, and they gave effect to their intention by a series of acts, the offence will be clearly one of murder."

4. In *Regina v. Chiswibo*, [1961] 2 S.Afr.L.R. 714, the defendant without intending to kill assaulted another person by striking him on the head with the blunt side of an axe. Believing he had killed the person, the defendant then put the body down an ant-bear hole. The medical evidence did not show that the blow with the axe was fatal or that death did not result from the subsequent interment. The court concluded that only a verdict of attempted murder was proper on these facts. As one member of the court explained:

"There may be a temptation to attempt to equate the present case to that of *Thabo Meli* by saying that a constructive intent to kill, no less than actual intent, is sufficient to establish criminal responsibility, and that there is no adequate reason for distinguishing between the accused who, in advance, plans each step which will be taken to accomplish his dual object of killing and avoiding detection and the accused who regulates his actions, from moment to moment, as circumstances demand. Any such exercise overlooks what I believe to be the basis of the decision in *Thabo Meli's* case. * * * In the present case, neither the assault nor the act of burial was an incident of a preconceived plan; the assault, so the learned Judge found, was committed 'on the spur of the moment'; the act of burial, no doubt, was an afterthought. It is clearly not impossible 'to divide up' the accused's actions. When such a division is made, one is driven, so it seems to me, to the conclusion that the trial Court's verdict of guilty of attempted murder was the only proper one in the circumstances."

SECTION 6. THE DEATH PENALTY

Introductory Notes

1. In large measure, the classification of homicides by courts and legislatures has been prompted by a desire to define more narrowly those criminal homicides which would be subject to the mandatory penalty of death. As detailed in *Mullaney v. Wilbur*, p. 238 of this Book, this explains how the distinction between murder and manslaughter came into being. And as the Court has more recently observed in *Woodson v. North Carolina*, infra, it was public dissatisfaction with the mandatory death penalty statutes which led most of the states to divide the crime of murder into degrees.

2. But even this reform was not sufficient. As noted in *Woodson*:

"Despite the broad acceptance of the division of murder into degrees, the reform proved to be an unsatisfactory means of identifying persons appropriately punishable by death. Although its failure was due in part to the amorphous nature of the controlling concepts of willfulness, deliberateness, and premeditation, a more fundamental weakness of the reform soon became apparent. Juries continued to find the death penalty inappropriate in a significant number of first-degree murder cases and refused to return guilty verdicts for that crime.

"The inadequacy of distinguishing between murders solely on the basis of legislative criteria narrowing the definition of the capital offense led the States to grant juries sentencing discretion in capital cases. Tennessee in 1838, followed by Alabama in 1841, and Louisiana in 1846, were the first States to abandon mandatory death sentences in favor of discretionary death penalty statutes. This flexibility remedied the harshness of mandatory statutes by permitting the jury to respond to mitigating factors by withholding the death penalty. By the turn of the century, 23 States and the Federal Government had made death sentences discretionary for first-degree murder and other capital offenses. * * * By 1963, all of these remaining jurisdictions had replaced their automatic death penalty statutes with discretionary jury sentencing."

3. Thus, there remains one other aspect of homicide classification to be considered, namely, the classification under contemporary law of those homicides for which the penalty shall be death. In particular, it must be asked: (a) to what extent are standards to guide the exercise of discretion necessary or desirable as to those offenses for which the death penalty is discretionary; and (b) to what extent is it permissible or desirable that the penalty of death be mandatory for certain crimes; and (c) to what offenses (or, as to murder,

what bases of liability) may even the discretionary death penalty not be applied.

GREGG v. GEORGIA

Supreme Court of the United States, 1976.
428 U.S. 153, 96 S.Ct. 2909, 49 L.Ed.2d 859.

MR. JUSTICE STEWART, MR. JUSTICE POWELL, and MR. JUSTICE STEVENS announced the judgment of the Court and filed an opinion delivered by MR. JUSTICE STEWART. * * *

[Gregg was found guilty by a jury of two counts of armed robbery and two counts of murder. At the penalty stage of the trial, thereafter occurring before the same jury, the jury returned verdicts of death on each count. The jury had been instructed that it could not impose a death sentence unless it found beyond a reasonable doubt that certain specified aggravating circumstances were present. The Georgia Supreme Court affirmed the convictions and the imposition of the death sentences for murder, but vacated the death sentences for armed robbery on the ground that the death penalty had rarely been imposed for that offense.]

We address initially the basic contention that the punishment of death for the crime of murder is, under all circumstances, "cruel and unusual" in violation of the Eighth and Fourteenth Amendments of the Constitution. * * *

The Court on a number of occasions has both assumed and asserted the constitutionality of capital punishment. In several cases that assumption provided a necessary foundation for the decision, as the Court was asked to decide whether a particular method of carrying out a capital sentence would be allowed to stand under the Eighth Amendment. But until *Furman v. Georgia,* 408 U.S. 238, 92 S.Ct. 2726, 33 L.Ed.2d 346 (1972), the Court never confronted squarely the fundamental claim that the punishment of death always, regardless of the enormity of the offense or

the procedure followed in imposing the sentence, is cruel and unusual punishment in violation of the Constitution. Although this issue was presented and addressed in *Furman,* it was not resolved by the Court. Four Justices would have held that capital punishment is not unconstitutional *per se;* two Justices would have reached the opposite conclusion; and three Justices, while agreeing that the statutes then before the Court were invalid as applied, left open the question whether such punishment may ever be imposed. We now hold that the punishment of death does not invariably violate the Constitution. * * *

It is clear * * * that the Eighth Amendment has not been regarded as a static concept. As Chief Justice Warren said, in an oft-quoted phrase, "[t]he Amendment must draw its meaning from the evolving standards of decency that mark the progress of a maturing society." Thus, an assessment of contemporary values concerning the infliction of a challenged sanction is relevant to the application of the Eighth Amendment. As we develop below more fully, this assessment does not call for a subjective judgment. It requires, rather, that we look to objective indicia that reflect the public attitude toward a given sanction.

But our cases also make clear that public perceptions of standards of decency with respect to criminal sanctions are not conclusive. A penalty also must accord with "the dignity of man," which is the "basic concept underlying the Eighth Amendment." This means, at least, that the punishment not be "excessive." When a form of punishment in the abstract (in this case, whether capital punishment may ever be imposed as a sanction for murder) rather than in the particular (the propriety of death as a penalty to be applied to a specific defendant for a specific crime) is under consideration, the inquiry into "excessiveness" has two aspects. First, the punishment must not involve the unnecessary and wanton infliction of pain. Second, the punishment must not be grossly out of proportion to the severity of the crime.

Of course, the requirements of the Eighth Amendment must be applied with an awareness of the limited role to be played by the courts. This does not mean that judges have no role to play, for the Eighth Amendment is a restraint upon the exercise of legislative power. * * *

But, while we have an obligation to insure that constitutional bounds are not overreached, we may not act as judges as we might as legislators. * * *

Therefore, in assessing a punishment selected by a democratically elected legislature against the constitutional measure, we presume its validity. We may not require the legislature to select the least severe penalty possible so long as the penalty selected is not cruelly inhumane or disproportionate to the crime involved. And a heavy burden rests on those who would attack the judgment of the representatives of the people.

This is true in part because the constitutional test is intertwined with an assessment of contemporary standards and the legislative judgment weighs heavily in ascertaining such standards. "[I]n a democratic society legislatures, not courts, are constituted to respond to the will and consequently the moral values of the people." The deference we owe to the decisions of the state legislatures under our federal system, is enhanced where the specification of punishments is concerned, for "these are peculiarly questions of legislative policy."

Caution is necessary lest this Court become, "under the aegis of the Cruel and Unusual Punishment Clause, the ultimate arbiter of the standards of criminal responsibility * * * throughout the country." A decision that a given punishment is impermissible under the Eighth Amendment cannot be reversed short of a constitutional amendment. The ability of the people to express their preference through the normal democratic processes, as well as through ballot referenda, is shut off. Revisions cannot be made in the light of further experience.

In the discussion to this point we have sought to identify the principles and considerations that guide a court in addressing an Eighth Amendment claim. We now consider specifically whether the sentence of death for the crime of murder is a *per se* violation of the Eighth and Fourteenth Amendments to the Constitution. We note first that history and precedent strongly support a negative answer to this question.

The imposition of the death penalty for the crime of murder has a long history of acceptance both in the United States and in England. The common-law rule imposed a mandatory death sentence on all convicted murderers. And the penalty continued to be used into the 20th century by most American States, although the breadth of the common-law rule was diminished, initially by narrowing the class of murders to be punished by death and subsequently by widespread adoption of laws expressly granting juries the discretion to recommend mercy.

It is apparent from the text of the Constitution itself that the existence of capital punishment was accepted by the Framers. At the time the Eighth Amendment was ratified, capital punishment was a common sanction in every State. Indeed, the First Congress of the United States enacted legislation providing death as the penalty for specified crimes. * * *

For nearly two centuries, this Court, repeatedly and often expressly, has recognized that capital punishment is not invalid *per se*. * * *

Four years ago, the petitioners in *Furman* and its companion cases predicated their argument primarily upon the asserted proposition that standards of decency had evolved to the point where capital punishment no longer could be tolerated. The petitioners in those cases said, in effect, that the evolutionary process had come to an end, and that standards of decency required that the Eighth Amendment be construed finally as prohibiting capital punishment for any crime regardless of its depravity and impact on society. This view was accepted by two Justices. Three other Justices were unwilling to go so far; focusing on the procedures by which convicted defendants were selected for the death penalty rather than on the actual punishment inflicted, they joined in the conclusion that the statutes before the Court were constitutionally invalid.

The petitioners in the capital cases before the Court today renew the "standards of decency" argument, but developments during the four years since *Furman* have undercut substantially the assumptions upon which their argument rested. Despite the continuing debate, dating back to the 19th century, over the morality and utility of capital punishment, it is now evident that a large proportion of American society continues to regard it as an appropriate and necessary criminal sanction.

The most marked indication of society's endorsement of the death penalty for murder is the legislative response to *Furman*. The legislatures of at least 35 States have enacted new statutes that provide for the death penalty for at least some crimes that result in the death of another person. And the Congress of the United States, in 1974, enacted a statute providing the death penalty for aircraft piracy that results in death. These recently adopted statutes have attempted to address the concerns expressed by the Court in *Furman* primarily (i) by specifying the factors to be weighed and the procedures to be followed in deciding when to impose a capital sentence, or (ii) by making the death penalty mandatory for specified crimes. But all of the post-*Furman* statutes make clear that capital punishment itself has not been rejected by the elected representatives of the people. * * *

The jury also is a significant and reliable objective index of contemporary values because it is so directly involved. The Court has said that "one of the most important functions any jury can perform in making * * * a selection [between life imprisonment and death for a defendant convicted in a capital case] is to maintain a link between contemporary community values and the penal system." It may be true that evolving standards have influenced juries in recent decades to be more discriminating in imposing the sentence of death.[26] But the relative infrequency of jury verdicts imposing the death sentence does not indicate rejection of capital punishment *per se.* Rather, the reluctance of juries in many cases to impose the sentence may well reflect the humane feeling that this most irrevocable of sanctions should be reserved for a small number of extreme cases. Indeed, the actions of juries in many States since *Furman* is fully compatible with the legislative judgments, reflected in the new statutes, as to the continued utility and necessity of capital punishment in appropriate cases. At the close of 1974 at least 254 persons had been sentenced to death since *Furman,* and by the end of March 1976, more than 460 persons were subject to death sentences.

---

26. The number of prisoners who received death sentences in the years from 1961 to 1972 varied from a high of 140 in 1961 to a low of 75 in 1972, with wide fluctuations in the intervening years: 103 in 1962; 93 in 1963; 106 in 1964; 86 in 1965; 118 in 1966; 85 in 1967; 102 in 1968; 97 in 1969; 127 in 1970; and 104 in 1971. Department of Justice, Capital Punishment 1971–1972, National prisoner Statistics Bulletin, p. 20 (December 1974). It has been estimated that before *Furman* less than 20% of those convicted of murder were sentenced to death in those States that authorized capital punishment.

As we have seen, however, the Eighth Amendment demands more than that a challenged punishment be acceptable to contemporary society. The Court also must ask whether it comports with the basic concept of human dignity at the core of the Amendment. Although we cannot "invalidate a category of penalties because we deem less severe penalties adequate to serve the ends of penology," the sanction imposed cannot be so totally without penological justification that it results in the gratuitous infliction of suffering.

The death penalty is said to serve two principal social purposes: retribution and deterrence of capital crimes by prospective offenders.

In part, capital punishment is an expression of society's moral outrage at particularly offensive conduct. This function may be unappealing to many, but it is essential in an ordered society that asks its citizens to rely on legal processes rather than self-help to vindicate their wrongs. * * * "Retribution is no longer the dominant objective of the criminal law," but neither is it a forbidden objective nor one inconsistent with our respect for the dignity of men. Indeed, the decision that capital punishment may be the appropriate sanction in extreme cases is an expression of the community's belief that certain crimes are themselves so grievous an affront to humanity that the only adequate response may be the penalty of death.

Statistical attempts to evaluate the worth of the death penalty as a deterrent to crimes by potential offenders have occasioned a great deal of debate. The results simply have been inconclusive. * * *

Although some of the studies suggest that the death penalty may not function as a significantly greater deterrent than lesser penalties, there is no convincing empirical evidence either supporting or refuting this view. We may nevertheless assume safely that there are murderers, such as those who act in passion, for whom the threat of death has little or no deterrent effect. But for many others, the death penalty undoubtedly is a significant deterrent. There are carefully contemplated murders, such as murder for hire, where the possible penalty of death may well enter into the cold calculus that precedes the decision to act. And there are some categories of murder, such as murder by a life prisoner, where other sanctions may not be adequate.

The value of capital punishment as a deterrent of crime is a complex factual issue the resolution of which properly rests with the legislatures, which can evaluate the results of statistical studies in terms of their own local conditions and with a flexibility of approach that is not available to the courts. Indeed, many of the post-*Furman* statutes reflect just such a responsible effort to define those crimes and those criminals for which capital punishment is most probably an effective deterrent. * * *

Finally, we must consider whether the punishment of death is disproportionate in relation to the crime for which it is imposed. There is no question that death as a punishment is unique in its severity and irrevocability. When a defendant's life is at stake, the Court has been particularly sensitive to insure that every safeguard is observed. But we are concerned here only with the imposition of capital punishment for the crime of murder, and when a life has been taken deliberately by the offender,[35] we cannot say that the punishment is invariably disproportionate to the

35. We do not address here the question whether the taking of the criminal's life is a proportionate sanction where no victim has been deprived of life—for example, when capital pun-ishment is imposed for rape, kidnapping, or armed robbery that does not result in the death of any human being.

crime. It is an extreme sanction, suitable to the most extreme of crimes.

We hold that the death penalty is not a form of punishment that may never be imposed, regardless of the circumstances of the offense, regardless of the character of the offender, and regardless of the procedure followed in reaching the decision to impose it. * * *

While *Furman* did not hold that the infliction of the death penalty *per se* violates the Constitution's ban on cruel and unusual punishments, it did recognize that the penalty of death is different in kind from any other punishment imposed under our system of criminal justice. Because of the uniqueness of the death penalty, *Furman* held that it could not be imposed under sentencing procedures that created a substantial risk that it would be inflicted in an arbitrary and capricious manner. * * *

Jury sentencing has been considered desirable in capital cases in order "to maintain a link between contemporary community values and the penal system—a link without which the determination of punishment could hardly reflect 'the evolving standards of decency that mark the progress of a maturing society.' " But it creates special problems. Much of the information that is relevant to the sentencing decision may have no relevance to the question of guilt, or may even be extremely prejudicial to a fair determination of that question. This problem, however, is scarcely insurmountable. Those who have studied the question suggest that a bifurcated procedure—one in which the question of sentence is not considered until the determination of guilt has been made—is the best answer. * * * When a human life is at stake and when the jury must have information prejudicial to the question of

guilt but relevant to the question of penalty in order to impose a rational sentence, a bifurcated system is more likely to ensure elimination of the constitutional deficiencies identified in *Furman.*

But the provision of relevant information under fair procedural rules is not alone sufficient to guarantee that the information will be properly used in the imposition of punishment, especially if sentencing is performed by a jury. Since the members of a jury will have had little, if any, previous experience in sentencing, they are unlikely to be skilled in dealing with the information they are given. To the extent that this problem is inherent in jury sentencing, it may not be totally correctible. It seems clear, however, that the problem will be alleviated if the jury is given guidance regarding the factors about the crime and the defendant that the State, representing organized society, deems particularly relevant to the sentencing decision. * * *

While some have suggested that standards to guide a capital jury's sentencing deliberations are impossible to formulate, the fact is that such standards have been developed. When the drafters of the Model Penal Code faced this problem, they concluded "that it is within the realm of possibility to point to the main circumstances of aggravation and of mitigation that should be weighed *and weighed against each other,* when they are presented in a concrete case." *Model Penal Code* § 201.6, Comment 3, p. 71 (Tent. Draft No. 9, 1959).[a] While such standards are by necessity somewhat general, they do provide guidance to the sentencing authority and thereby reduce the likelihood that it will impose a sentence that fairly can be called capricious or arbitrary. Where the sentencing authority is required to specify the factors it relied upon in reaching its deci-

a. Because of renumbering, the aggravating and mitigating circumstances proposed in the *Model Penal Code* appear in § 210.6(3) and (4).

sion, the further safeguard of meaningful appellate review is available to ensure that death sentences are not imposed capriciously or in a freakish manner.

In summary, the concerns expressed in *Furman* that the penalty of death not be imposed in an arbitrary or capricious manner can be met by a carefully drafted statute that ensures that the sentencing authority is given adequate information and guidance. As a general proposition these concerns are best met by a system that provides for a bifurcated proceeding at which the sentencing authority is apprised of the information relevant to the imposition of sentence and provided with standards to guide its use of the information. * * *

We now turn to consideration of the constitutionality of Georgia's capital-sen-

tencing procedures. In the wake of *Furman,* Georgia amended its capital punishment statute, but chose not to narrow the scope of its murder provisions. Thus, now as before *Furman,* in Georgia "[a] person commits murder when he unlawfully and with malice aforethought, either express or implied, causes the death of another human being." Ga.Code Ann., § 26–1101(a) (1972). All persons convicted of murder "shall be punished by death or by imprisonment for life." § 26–1101(c) (1972).

Georgia did act, however, to narrow the class of murderers subject to capital punishment by specifying 10 statutory aggravating circumstances, one of which must be found by the jury to exist beyond a reasonable doubt before a death sentence can ever be imposed.[b] In addition, the jury is authorized to consider any other

b. The statute provides in part:

"(a) The death penalty may be imposed for the offenses of aircraft hijacking or treason, in any case.

"(b) In all cases of other offenses for which the death penalty may be authorized, the judge shall consider, or he shall include in his instructions to the jury for it to consider, any mitigating circumstances or aggravating circumstances otherwise authorized by law and any of the following statutory aggravating circumstances which may be supported by the evidence:

"(1) The offense of murder, rape, armed robbery, or kidnapping was committed by a person with a prior record of conviction for a capital felony, or the offense of murder was committed by a person who has a substantial history of serious assaultive criminal convictions.

"(2) The offense of murder, rape, armed robbery, or kidnapping was committed while the offender was engaged in the commission of another capital felony, or aggravated battery, or the offense of murder was committed while the offender was engaged in the commission of burglary or arson in the first degree.

"(3) The offender by his act of murder, armed robbery, or kidnapping knowingly created a great risk of death to more than one person in a public place by means of a weapon or device which would normally be hazardous to the lives of more than one person.

"(4) The offender committed the offense of murder for himself or another, for the purpose of

receiving money or any other thing of monetary value.

"(5) The murder of a judicial officer, former judicial officer, district attorney or solicitor or former district attorney or solicitor during or because of the exercise of his official duty.

"(6) The offender caused or directed another to commit murder or committed murder as an agent or employee of another person.

"(7) The offense of murder, rape, armed robbery, or kidnapping was outrageously or wantonly vile, horrible or inhuman in that it involved torture, depravity of mind, or an aggravated battery to the victim.

"(8) The offense of murder was committed against any peace officer, corrections employee or fireman while engaged in the performance of his official duties.

"(9) The offense of murder was committed by a person in, or who has escaped from, the lawful custody of a peace officer or place of lawful confinement.

"(10) The murder was committed for the purpose of avoiding, interfering with, or preventing a lawful arrest or custody in a place of lawful confinement, of himself or another.

"(c) The statutory instructions as determined by the trial judge to be warranted by the evidence shall be given in charge and in writing to the jury for its deliberation. The jury, if its verdict be a recommendation of death, shall designate in writing, signed by the foreman of the jury, the aggravating circumstance or circum-

appropriate aggravating or mitigating circumstances. § 27–2534.1(b) (Supp. 1975). The jury is not required to find any mitigating circumstance in order to make a recommendation of mercy that is binding on the trial court, see § 27–2302 (Supp.1975), but it must find a *statutory* aggravating circumstance before recommending a sentence of death.

These procedures require the jury to consider the circumstances of the crime and the criminal before it recommends sentence. No longer can a Georgia jury do as *Furman's* jury did: reach a finding of the defendant's guilt and then, without guidance or direction, decide whether he should live or die. * * *

As an important additional safeguard against arbitrariness and caprice, the Georgia statutory scheme provides for automatic appeal of all death sentences to the State's supreme court. That court is required by statute to review each sentence of death and determine whether it was imposed under the influence of passion or prejudice, whether the evidence supports the jury's finding of a statutory aggravating circumstance, and whether the sentence is disproportionate compared to those sentences imposed in similar cases. § 27–2537(c) (Supp.1975).

In short, Georgia's new sentencing procedures require as a prerequisite to the imposition of the death penalty, specific jury findings as to the circumstances of the crime or the character of the defendant. Moreover to guard further against a situation comparable to that presented in *Furman,* the Supreme Court of Georgia compares each death sentence with the sentences imposed on similarly situated defendants to ensure that the sentence of death in a particular case is not disproportionate. On their face these procedures

seem to satisfy the concerns of *Furman.* No longer should there be "no meaningful basis for distinguishing the few cases in which [the death penalty] is imposed from the many cases in which it is not."

The petitioner contends, however, that the changes in the Georgia sentencing procedures are only cosmetic, that the arbitrariness and capriciousness condemned by *Furman* continue to exist in Georgia—both in traditional practices that still remain and in the new sentencing procedures adopted in response to *Furman.*

First, the petitioner focuses on the opportunities for discretionary action that are inherent in the processing of any murder case under Georgia law. He notes that the state prosecutor has unfettered authority to select those persons whom he wishes to prosecute for a capital offense and to plea bargain with them. Further, at the trial the jury may choose to convict a defendant of a lesser included offense rather than find him guilty of a crime punishable by death, even if the evidence would support a capital verdict. And finally, a defendant who is convicted and sentenced to die may have his sentence commuted by the Governor of the State and the Georgia Board of Pardons and Paroles.

The existence of these discretionary stages is not determinative of the issues before us. At each of these stages an actor in the criminal justice system makes a decision which may remove a defendant from consideration as a candidate for the death penalty. *Furman,* in contrast, dealt with the decision to impose the death sentence on a specific individual who had been convicted of a capital offense. Nothing in any of our cases suggests that the decision to afford an individual defendant mercy violates the Constitution. *Furman* held only that, in order to minimize the risk that

---

stances which it found beyond a reasonable doubt. In non-jury cases the judge shall make such designation. Except in cases of treason or aircraft hijacking, unless at least one of the statu-

tory aggravating circumstances enumerated in section 27–2534.1(b) is so found, the death penalty shall not be imposed." § 27–2534.1 (Supp.1975).

the death penalty would be imposed on a capriciously selected group of offenders, the decision to impose it had to be guided by standards so that the sentencing authority would focus on the particularized circumstances of the crime and the defendant.

The petitioner further contends that the capital-sentencing procedures adopted by Georgia in response to *Furman* do not eliminate the dangers of arbitrariness and caprice in jury sentencing that were held in *Furman* to be violative of the Eighth and Fourteenth Amendments. He claims that the statute is so broad and vague as to leave juries free to act as arbitrarily and capriciously as they wish in deciding whether to impose the death penalty.

* * *

The petitioner attacks the seventh statutory aggravating circumstance, which authorizes imposition of the death penalty if the murder was "outrageously or wantonly vile, horrible or inhuman in that it involved torture, depravity of mind, or an aggravated battery to the victim," contending that it is so broad that capital punishment could be imposed in any murder case. It is, of course, arguable that any murder involves depravity of mind or an aggravated battery. But this language need not be construed in this way, and there is no reason to assume that the Supreme Court of Georgia will adopt such an open-ended construction. In only one case has it upheld a jury's decision to sentence a defendant to death when the only statutory aggravating circumstance found was that of § 7, see *McCorquodale v. State,* 233 Ga. 369, 211 S.E.2d 577 (1974), and that homicide was a horrifying torture-murder.

The petitioner also argues that two of the statutory aggravating circumstances are vague and therefore susceptible to widely differing interpretations, thus creating a substantial risk that the death penalty will

be arbitrarily inflicted by Georgia juries. In light of the decisions of the Supreme Court of Georgia we must disagree. First, the petitioner attacks that part of § 1 that authorizes a jury to consider whether a defendant has a "substantial history of serious assaultive criminal convictions." The Supreme Court of Georgia, however, has demonstrated a concern that the new sentencing procedures provide guidance to juries. It held this provision to be impermissibly vague in *Arnold v. State,* 236 Ga. 534, 540, 224 S.E.2d 386, 391 (1976), because it did not provide the jury with "sufficiently 'clear and objective standards.'" Second, the petitioner points to § 3 which speaks of creating a "great risk of death to more than one person." While such a phrase might be susceptible to an overly broad interpretation, the Supreme Court of Georgia has not so construed it. The only case in which the court upheld a conviction in reliance on this aggravating circumstance involved a man who stood up in a church and fired a gun indiscriminately into the audience. See *Chenault v. State,* 234 Ga. 216, 215 S.E.2d 223 (1975). On the other hand, the court expressly reversed a finding of great risk when the victim was simply kidnapped in a parking lot. See *Jarrell v. State,* 234 Ga. 410, 424, 216 S.E.2d 258, 269 (1975).

The petitioner next argues that the requirements of *Furman* are not met here because the jury has the power to decline to impose the death penalty even if it finds that one or more statutory aggravating circumstances is present in the case. This contention misinterprets *Furman.* Moreover, it ignores the role of the Supreme Court of Georgia which reviews each death sentence to determine whether it is proportional to other sentences imposed for similar crimes. Since the proportionality requirement on review is intended to prevent caprice in the decision to inflict the penalty, the isolated decision of a jury to afford mercy does not render unconstitutional death sentences imposed on defendants who were sentenced under a system that does not create a substantial risk of arbitrariness or caprice.

The petitioner objects, finally, to the wide scope of evidence and argument allowed at presentence hearings. We think that the Georgia court wisely has chosen not to impose unnecessary restrictions on the evidence that can be offered at such a hearing and to approve open and far-ranging argument. So long as the evidence introduced and the arguments made at the presentence hearing do not prejudice a defendant, it is preferable not to impose restrictions. We think it desirable for the jury to have as much information before it as possible when it makes the sentencing decision.

Finally, the Georgia statute has an additional provision designed to assure that the death penalty will not be imposed on a capriciously selected group of convicted defendants. The new sentencing procedures require that the state supreme court review every death sentence to determine whether it was imposed under the influence of passion, prejudice, or any other arbitrary factor, whether the evidence supports the findings of a statutory aggravating circumstance, and "[w]hether the sentence of death is excessive or disproportionate to the penalty imposed in similar cases, considering both the crime and the defendant. § 27–2537(c)(3) (Supp.1975). In performing its sentence review function, the Georgia court has held that "if the death penalty is only rarely imposed for an act or it is substantially out of line with sentences imposed for other acts it will be set aside as excessive." The court on another occasion stated that "we view it to be our duty under the similarity standard to assure that no death sentence is affirmed unless in similar cases throughout the state the death penal-

ty has been imposed generally * * *."
* * *

The provision for appellate review in the Georgia capital-sentencing system serves as a check against the random or arbitrary imposition of the death penalty. In particular, the proportionality review substantially eliminates the possibility that a person will be sentenced to die by the action of an aberrant jury. If a time comes when juries generally do not impose the death sentence in a certain kind of murder case, the appellate review procedures assures that no defendant convicted under such circumstances will suffer a sentence of death. * * *

For the reasons expressed in this opinion, we hold that the statutory system under which Gregg was sentenced to death does not violate the Constitution. Accordingly, the judgment of the Georgia Supreme Court is affirmed.

It is so ordered.

MR. JUSTICE WHITE, with whom THE CHIEF JUSTICE and MR. JUSTICE REHNQUIST join, concurring in the judgment.
* * *

MR. JUSTICE BLACKMUN, concurring in the judgment. * * *

MR. JUSTICE BRENNAN, dissenting.
* * *

This Court inescapably has the duty, as the ultimate arbiter of the meaning of our Constitution, to say whether, when individuals condemned to death stand before our Bar, "moral concepts" require us to hold that the law has progressed to the point where we should declare that the punishment of death, like punishments on the rack, the screw and the wheel, is no longer morally tolerable in our civilized society. My opinion in *Furman v. Georgia* concluded that our civilization and the law had progressed to this point and that therefore the punishment of death, for whatever crime and under all circum-

stances, is "cruel and unusual" in violation of the Eighth and Fourteenth Amendments of the Constitution. I shall not again canvass the reasons that led to that conclusion. I emphasize only that foremost among the "moral concepts" recognized in our cases and inherent in the Clause is the primary moral principle that the State, even as it punishes, must treat its citizens in a manner consistent with their intrinsic worth as human beings—a punishment must not be so severe as to be degrading to human dignity. A judicial determination whether the punishment of death comports with human dignity is therefore not only permitted but compelled by the Clause.
* * *

The fatal constitutional infirmity in the punishment of death is that it treats "members of the human race as nonhumans, as objects to be toyed with and discarded. [It is] thus inconsistent with the fundamental premise of the Clause that even the vilest criminal remains a human being possessed of common human dignity." As such it is a penalty that "subjects the individual to a fate forbidden by the principle of civilized treatment guaranteed by the [Clause]." I therefore would hold, on that ground alone, that death is today a cruel and unusual punishment prohibited by the Clause. * * *

MR. JUSTICE MARSHALL, dissenting.
* * *

Since the decision in *Furman,* the legislatures of 35 States have enacted new statutes authorizing the imposition of the death sentence for certain crimes, and Congress has enacted a law providing the death penalty for air piracy resulting in death. 49 U.S.C. (Supp. IV) §§ 1472, 1473. I would be less than candid if I did not acknowledge that these developments have a significant bearing on a realistic assessment of the moral acceptability of the death penalty to the American people.

But if the constitutionality of the death penalty turns, as I have urged, on the opinion of an *informed* citizenry, then even the enactment of new death statutes cannot be viewed as conclusive. In *Furman,* I observed that the American people are largely unaware of the information critical to a judgment on the morality of the death penalty, and concluded that if they were better informed they would consider it shocking, unjust, and unacceptable.
* * *

The two purposes that sustain the death penalty as nonexcessive in the Court's view are general deterrence and retribution. In *Furman,* I canvassed the relevant data on the deterrent effect of capital punishment. The state of knowledge at that point, after literally centuries of debate, was summarized as follows by a United Nations Committee:

"It is generally agreed between the retentionists and abolitionists, whatever their opinions about the validity of comparative studies of deterrence, that the data which now exist show no correlation between the existence of capital punishment and lower rates of capital crime."
* * *

The other principal purpose said to be served by the death penalty is retribution. The notion that retribution can serve as a moral justification for the sanction of death finds credence in the opinion of my Brothers STEWART, POWELL, and STEVENS. * * * [Their] statement is wholly inadequate to justify the death penalty. As my Brother BRENNAN stated in *Furman,* "[t]here is no evidence whatever that utilization of imprisonment rather than death encourages private blood feuds and other disorders." It simply defies belief to suggest that the death penalty is necessary to prevent the American people from taking the law into their own hands. * * *

Notes and Questions

1. In *Jurek v. Texas,* 428 U.S. 262, 96 S.Ct. 2950, 49 L.Ed.2d 929 (1976), petitioner, who was convicted of murder and whose death sentence was upheld on appeal, challenged the constitutionality of the Texas procedures enacted after *Furman.* The new Texas Penal Code limits capital homicides to intentional and knowing murders committed in five situations.[a] Texas also adopted a new capital-sentencing procedure, which requires the jury to answer the following three questions in a proceeding that takes place after a verdict finding a person guilty of one of the specified murder categories: (1) whether the conduct of the defendant causing the death was committed deliberately and with the reasonable expectation that the death would result; (2) whether it is probable that the defendant would commit criminal acts of violence constituting a continuing threat to society; and (3) if raised by the evidence, whether the defendant's conduct was an unreasonable response to the provocation, if any, by the deceased. If the jury finds that the State has proved beyond a reasonable doubt that the answer to each of the three questions is affirmative the death sentence is imposed; if it finds that the answer to any question is negative a sentence of life imprisonment results. Stevens, J., joined by Stewart and Powell, JJ., announced the judgment of the Court:

"We conclude that Texas' capital-sentencing procedures, like those of Georgia and Florida, do not violate the Eighth and Fourteenth Amendments. By narrowing its definition of capital murder, Texas has essentially said that there must be at least one statutory aggravating circumstance in a first-degree murder case before a death sentence may even be considered. By authorizing the defense to bring before the jury at the separate sentencing hearing whatever mitigating circumstances relating to the individual defendant can be adduced, Texas has ensured that the sentencing jury will have adequate guidance to enable it to perform its sentencing function. By providing prompt judicial review of the jury's decision in a court with statewide jurisdiction, Texas has provided a means to promote the evenhanded, rational, and consistent imposition of death sentences under law. Because this system serves to assure that sentences of death will not be 'wantonly' or 'freakishly' imposed, it does not violate the Constitution."

White, Rehnquist and Blackmun, JJ., and the Chief Justice concurred in the judgment; Brennan and Marshall, JJ., dissented.

2. In *Proffitt v. Florida,* 428 U.S. 242, 96 S.Ct. 2960, 49 L.Ed.2d 913 (1976), petitioner, who was convicted of first-degree murder, attacked the constitutionality of the Florida capital-sentencing procedure enacted after *Furman.* Under the new statute, the trial judge (who is the sentencing authority) must weigh eight statutory aggravating factors against seven statutory mitigating factors [b] to determine whether the death penalty should be imposed, thus

a. They are where:

"(1) the person murdered a peace officer or fireman who was acting in the lawful discharge of an official duty and who the defendant knew was a peace officer or fireman;

"(2) the person intentionally committed the murder in the course of committing or attempting to commit kidnapping, burglary, robbery, forcible rape, or arson;

"(3) the person committed the murder for remuneration or the promise of remuneration or employed another to commit the murder for remuneration or the promise of remuneration;

"(4) the person committed the murder while escaping or attempting to escape from a penal institution;

"(5) the person, while incarcerated in a penal institution, murdered another who was employed in the operation of the penal institution."

b. The aggravating circumstances are:

"(a) The capital felony was committed by a person under sentence of imprisonment.

requiring him to focus on the circumstances of the crime and the character of the individual defendant. Powell, J., joined by Stewart and Stevens, JJ., announced the judgment of the Court:

"Under Florida's capital-sentencing procedures, in sum, trial judges are given specific and detailed guidance to assist them in deciding whether to impose a death penalty or imprisonment for life. Moreover, their decisions are reviewed to ensure that they are consistent with other sentences imposed in similar circumstances. Thus, in Florida, as in Georgia, it is no longer true that there is ' "no meaningful basis for distinguishing the few cases in which [the death penalty] is imposed from the many cases where it is not." ' On its face the Florida system thus satisfies the constitutional deficiencies identified in *Furman*."

3. In *Lockett v. Ohio,* 438 U.S. 586, 98 S.Ct. 2954, 57 L.Ed.2d 973 (1978), the Court invalidated the Ohio death penalty statute, which provided that once a defendant is found guilty of aggravated murder with at least one of seven specified aggravating circumstances present, the death penalty must be imposed absent one of three specified mitigating circumstances (victim induced or facilitated the crime; unlikely offense would have been committed but for duress, coercion or strong provocation; offense a product of defendant's mental deficiency). Chief Justice Burger, with three other members of the Court concurring and three more Justices concurring in the result, concluded that "the Eighth and Fourteenth Amendments require that the sentencer, in all but the rarest kind of capital case, not be precluded from considering, *as a mitigating factor,* any aspect of a defendant's character or record and any of the circumstances of the offense that the defendant proffers as a basis for a sentence less than death. * * * [A] statute that prevents the sentencer in all capital cases from giving independent mitigating weight to aspects of the defendant's character and record and to circumstances of the offense proffered in mitigation creates the risk that the death penalty will be imposed in spite of factors which may call for a less severe penalty. When the choice is between life and death, that risk is unacceptable and incom-

"(b) The defendant was previously convicted of another capital felony or of a felony involving the use or threat of violence to the person.

"(c) The defendant knowingly created a great risk of death to many persons.

"(d) The capital felony was committed while the defendant was engaged, or was an accomplice, in the commission of, or an attempt to commit, or flight after committing or attempting to commit, any robbery, rape, arson, burglary, kidnapping, or aircraft piracy or the unlawful throwing, placing, or discharging of a destructive device or bomb.

"(e) The capital felony was committed for the purpose of avoiding or preventing a lawful arrest or effecting an escape from custody.

"(f) The capital felony was committed for pecuniary gain.

"(g) The capital felony was committed to disrupt or hinder the lawful exercise of any governmental function or the enforcement of laws.

"(h) The capital felony was especially heinous, atrocious, or cruel."

The mitigating circumstances are:

"(a) The defendant has no significant history of prior criminal activity.

"(b) The capital felony was committed while the defendant was under the influence of extreme mental or emotional disturbance.

"(c) The victim was a participant in the defendant's conduct or consented to the act.

"(d) The defendant was an accomplice in the capital felony committed by another person and his participation was relatively minor.

"(e) The defendant acted under extreme duress or under the substantial domination of another person.

"(f) The capacity of the defendant to appreciate the criminality of his conduct or to conform his conduct to the requirements of law was substantially impaired.

"(g) The age of the defendant at the time of the crime."

patible with the commands of the Eighth and Fourteenth Amendments."

4. At issue in *Spaziano v. Florida,* 468 U.S. 447, 104 S.Ct. 3154, 82 L.Ed.2d 340 (1984), was a sentencing scheme whereby the jury's recommendation was advisory only, so that (as occurred in this case) a jury's recommendation of life imprisonment could be overruled by the trial judge who, based upon his assessment of the aggravating and mitigating circumstances, opted for the death penalty. The Court, per Blackmun, J., concluded "that the purpose of the death penalty is not frustrated by, or inconsistent with, a scheme in which the imposition of the penalty in individual cases is determined by a judge.

"We also acknowledge the presence of the majority view that capital sentencing, unlike other sentencing, should be performed by a jury. As petitioner points out, 30 out of 37 jurisdictions with a capital-sentencing statute give the life-or-death decision to the jury, with only 3 of the remaining 7 allowing a judge to override a jury's recommendation of life. The fact that a majority of jurisdictions has adopted a different practice, however, does not establish that contemporary standards of decency are offended by the jury override. The Eighth Amendment is not violated every time a State reaches a conclusion different from a majority of its sisters over how best to administer its criminal laws."

5. In *Woodson v. North Carolina,* 428 U.S. 280, 96 S.Ct. 2978, 49 L.Ed.2d 944 (1976), the petitioners were convicted of first-degree murder. Following *Furman,* the state law which previously had provided that in cases of first-degree murder the jury in its unbridled discretion could choose whether the convicted defendant should be sentenced to death or life imprisonment was changed to make the death penalty mandatory for that crime.[c] Stewart, J., joined by Powell and Stevens, JJ., announced the judgment of the Court reversing the judgment of the state court. Noting that when such mandatory death sentence provisions were common for first-degree murder "[j]uries continued to find the death penalty inappropriate in a significant number of first-degree murder cases and refused to return guilty verdicts for that crime," and that abandonment of such mandatory death sentence provisions commenced in 1838 until by 1963 all states had replaced them with discretionary jury sentencing, they concluded: "The two crucial indicators of evolving standards of decency respecting the imposition of punishment in our society—jury determinations and legislative enactments—both point conclusively to the repudiation of automatic death sentences." Nor did they believe that the mandatory statutes adopted by a number of states following *Furman* evinced "a sudden reversal of societal values regarding the imposition of capital punishment"; rather, "it seems evident that the post-*Furman* enactments reflect attempts by the States to retain the death penalty in a form consistent with the Constitution." They continued:

"A separate deficiency of North Carolina's mandatory death sentence statute is its failure to provide a constitutionally tolerable response to *Furman's* rejection of unbridled jury discretion in the imposition of capital sentences. Central to the limited

c. The statute now reads as follows:

"*Murder in the first and second degree defined; punishment.*—A murder which shall be perpetrated by means of poison, lying in wait, imprisonment, starving, torture, or by any other kind of willful, deliberate and premeditated killing, or which shall be committed in the perpetration or attempt to perpetrate any arson, rape, robbery, kidnapping, burglary or other felony, shall be deemed to be murder in the first degree and shall be punished with death. All other kinds of murder shall be deemed murder in the second degree, and shall be punished by imprisonment for a term of not less than two years nor more than life imprisonment in the State's prison."

holding in *Furman* was the conviction that the vesting of standardless sentencing power in the jury violated the Eighth and Fourteenth Amendments. It is argued that North Carolina has remedied the inadequacies of the death penalty statutes held unconstitutional in *Furman* by withdrawing all sentencing discretion from juries in capital cases. But when one considers the long and consistent American experience with the death penalty in first-degree murder cases, it becomes evident that mandatory statutes enacted in response to *Furman* have simply papered over the problem of unguided and unchecked jury discretion. * * *

"A third constitutional shortcoming of the North Carolina statute is its failure to allow the particularized consideration of relevant aspects of the character and record of each convicted defendant before the imposition upon him of a sentence of death. In *Furman,* members of the Court acknowledge what cannot fairly be denied—that death is a punishment different from all other sanctions in kind rather than degree. A process that accords no significance to relevant facets of the character and record of the individual offender or the circumstances of the particular offense excludes from consideration in fixing the ultimate punishment of death the possibility of compassionate or mitigating factors stemming from the diverse frailties of humankind. It treats all persons convicted of a designated offense not as uniquely individual human beings, but as members of a

faceless, undifferentiated mass to be subjected to the blind infliction of the penalty of death." Brennan and Marshall, JJ., concurred in the judgment. White, J., joined by Rehnquist, J., and the Chief Justice, dissented. They contended that the change in North Carolina law had solved the problem of unfettered jury discretion which was at the heart of *Furman,* and rejected the argument "that the North Carolina statute, although making the imposition of the death penalty mandatory upon proof of guilt and a verdict of first-degree murder, will nevertheless result in the death penalty being imposed so seldom and arbitrarily that it is void under *Furman.*" Blackmun, J., dissented for the reasons set out in his *Furman* dissent.

6. In *Roberts v. Louisiana,* 428 U.S. 325, 96 S.Ct. 3001, 49 L.Ed.2d 974 (1976), petitioner was found guilty of first-degree murder and sentenced to death under amended Louisiana statutes enacted after *Furman.* This legislation mandates imposition of the death penalty whenever, with respect to five categories of homicide, the jury finds the defendant had a specific intent to kill or to inflict great bodily harm.[d] If a verdict of first-degree murder is returned, death is mandated regardless of any mercy recommendation. Every jury is instructed on the crimes of second-degree murder and manslaughter and permitted to consider those verdicts even if no evidence supports the lesser verdicts; if a lesser verdict is returned it is treated as an acquittal of all

---

d. The five categories are:

"(1) When the offender has a specific intent to kill or to inflict great bodily harm and is engaged in the perpetration or attempted perpetration of aggravated kidnapping, aggravated rape or armed robbery; or

"(2) When the offender has a specific intent to kill, or to inflict great bodily harm upon, a fireman or a peace officer who was engaged in the performance of his lawful duties; or

"(3) Where the offender has a specific intent to kill or to inflict great bodily harm and has previ-

ously been convicted of an unrelated murder or is serving a life sentence; or

"(4) When the offender has a specific intent to kill or to inflict great bodily harm upon more than one person; [or]

"(5) When the offender has specific intent to commit murder and has been offered or has received anything of value for committing the murder."

greater charges. Stevens, J., joined by Stewart and Powell, JJ., announced the judgment of the Court reversing the judgment of the state court. They concluded that neither the narrower definition of first-degree murder nor the responsive verdict device freed the Louisiana statute from the constitutional deficiencies discussed in *Woodson:*

"The constitutional vice of mandatory death sentence statutes—lack of focus on the circumstances of the particular offense and the character and propensities of the offender—is not resolved by Louisiana's limitation of first-degree murder to various categories of killings. The diversity of circumstances presented in cases falling within the single category of killings during the commission of a specified felony, as well as the variety of possible offenders involved in such crimes, underscores the rigidity of Louisiana's enactment and its similarity to the North Carolina statute. Even the other more narrowly drawn categories of first-degree murder in the Louisiana law afford no meaningful opportunity for consideration of mitigating factors presented by the circumstances of the particular crime or by the attributes of the individual offender.[9]

" * * * This responsive verdict procedure not only lacks standards to guide the jury in selecting among first-degree murderers, but it plainly invites the jurors to disregard their oaths and choose a verdict for a lesser offense whenever they feel the death penalty is inappropriate. There is an element of capriciousness in making the jurors' power to avoid the death penalty dependent on their willingness to accept this invitation to disregard the trial judge's instructions. The Louisiana procedure

neither provides standards to channel jury judgments nor permits review to check the arbitrary exercise of the capital jury's *de facto* sentencing discretion."

Brennan and Marshall, JJ., concurred in the judgment. White, J., joined by Blackmun and Rehnquist, JJ., and the Chief Justice, dissented.

7. In a case involving a different petitioner but also styled *Roberts v. Louisiana,* 431 U.S. 633, 97 S.Ct. 1993, 52 L.Ed.2d 637 (1977), the Court held, 5–4, that the death penalty may not be mandatory for the murder of a police officer. "To be sure, the fact that the murder victim was a peace officer performing his regular duties may be regarded as an aggravating circumstance. There is a special interest in affording protection to these public servants who regularly must risk their lives in order to guard the safety of other persons and property. But it is incorrect to suppose that no mitigating circumstances can exist when the victim is a police officer. Circumstances such as the youth of the offender, the absence of any prior conviction, the influence of drugs, alcohol or extreme emotional disturbance, and even the existence of circumstances which the offender reasonably believed provided a moral justification for his conduct are all examples of mitigating facts which might attend the killing of a peace officer and which are considered relevant in other jurisdictions."

8. Similarly, in *Sumner v. Shuman,* ___ U.S. ___, 107 S.Ct. 2716, 97 L.Ed.2d 56 (1987), the Court reached the same result as to a provision mandating the death penalty for murder by a life-term inmate. The Court, per Blackmun, J., reasoned that the statutory mitigating circumstances

---

9. Only the third category of the Louisiana first-degree murder statute, covering intentional killing by a person serving a life sentence or by a person previously convicted of an unrelated murder, defines the capital crime at least in significant part in terms of the character or record of the individual offender. Although even this narrow category does not permit the jury to consider possible mitigating factors, a prisoner serving a life sentence presents a unique problem that may justify such a law.

applicable in other murder cases could "be equally applicable to a murder committed by a life-term inmate" and that the state had not shown "any legitimate state interests" that could not "be satisfied through the use of a guided-discretion statute." The mandatory death penalty, the Court explained, "is not necessary as a deterrent" because sufficient deterrence is supplied by the discretionary systems, and is not "justified because of the State's retribution interests" in that "other sanctions less severe than execution [e.g., changes in the terms of confinement] * * * can be imposed even on a life-term inmate."

White, J., joined by the Chief Justice and Scalia, J., dissenting, concluded that "a State does not violate the Eighth Amendment by maintaining the full deterrent effect of the death penalty in this kind of case and by insisting that those who murder while serving a life sentence without parole not be able to escape punishment for that crime."

9. With respect to use of the death penalty for crimes other than homicide, consider *Coker v. Georgia*, 433 U.S. 584, 97 S.Ct. 2861, 53 L.Ed.2d 982 (1977). Petitioner was convicted of rape and then sentenced to death when the jury found two of the statutory aggravating circumstances to be present, i.e., the rape was (i) by a person with prior capital-felony convictions and (ii) in the course of committing another capital-felony, armed robbery. White, J., announcing the judgment of the Court in an opinion in which Stewart, Blackmun and Stevens, JJ., joined, concluded "that death is indeed a disproportionate penalty for the crime of raping an adult woman.

"We do not discount the seriousness of rape as a crime. It is highly reprehensible, both in a moral sense and in its almost total contempt for the personal integrity and autonomy of the female victim and for the latter's privilege of choosing those with whom intimate relationships are to be established. Short of homicide, it is the 'ultimate violation of self.' It is also a violent crime because it normally involves force, or the threat of force or intimidation, to overcome the will and the capacity of the victim to resist. Rape is very often accompanied by physical injury to the female and can also inflict mental and psychological damage. Because it undermines the community's sense of security, there is public injury as well.

"Rape is without doubt deserving of serious punishment; but in terms of moral depravity and of the injury to the person and to the public, it does not compare with murder, which does involve the unjustified taking of human life. Although it may be accompanied by another crime, rape by definition does not include the death or even the serious injury to another person. The murderer kills; the rapist, if no more than that, does not. Life is over for the victim of the murderers; for the rape victim, life may not be nearly so happy as it was, but it is not over and normally is not beyond repair. We have the abiding conviction that the death penalty, which 'is unique in its severity and revocability,' is an excessive penalty for the rapist who, as such, does not take human life."

Brennan and Marshall, JJ., concurred on the ground that the death penalty constitutes cruel and unusual punishment in all circumstances. Burger, C.J., joined by Rehnquist, J., dissented: "Until now, the issue under the Eighth Amendment has not been the state of any particular victim after the crime, but rather whether the punishment imposed is grossly disproportionate to the evil committed by the perpetrator. As a matter of constitutional principle, that test cannot have the primitive simplicity of 'life for life, eye for eye, tooth for tooth.' Rather States must be permitted to engage in a more sophisticated weighing of values in dealing with criminal activity which consistently poses serious danger of death or grave bodily harm. If innocent life and limb is to be preserved I see no constitutional barrier in punishing by death all who engage in such activity, regardless of whether the risk comes to fruition in any particular instance. * * *

"The Court's conclusion to the contrary is very disturbing indeed. The clear implication of today's holding appears to be that the death penalty may be properly imposed only as to crimes resulting in death of the victim. This casts serious doubt upon the constitutional validity of statutes imposing the death penalty for a variety of conduct which, though dangerous, may not necessarily result in any immediate death, e.g., treason, airplane hijacking, and kidnapping. In that respect, today's holding does even more harm than is initially apparent. We cannot avoid judicial notice that crimes such as airplane hijacking, kidnapping, and mass terrorist activity constitute a serious and increasing danger to the safety of the public. It would be unfortunate indeed if the effect of today's holding were to inhibit States and the Federal Government from experimenting with various remedies—including possibly imposition of the penalty of death—to prevent and deter such crimes."

Powell, J., concurred on the facts of the case because there was "no indication that petitioner's offense was committed with excessive brutality or that the victim sustained serious or lasting injury," but objected to the Court's broader holding: "The deliberate viciousness of the rapist may be greater than that of the murderer. Rape is never an act committed accidentally. Rarely can it be said to be unpremeditated. There also is wide variation in the effect on the victim. The plurality opinion says that '[l]ife is over for the victim of the murderer; for the rape victim, life may not be nearly so happy as it was, but it is not over and normally is not beyond repair.' But there is indeed 'extreme varia-

tion' in the crime of rape. Some victims are so grievously injured physically or psychologically that life *is* beyond repair."

10. After *Coker,* it was only a matter of time before the Court would confront the issue reached in *Enmund v. Florida,* 458 U.S. 782, 102 S.Ct. 3368, 73 L.Ed.2d 1140 (1982): "whether death is a valid penalty under the Eighth and Fourteenth Amendments for one who neither took life, attempted to take life, nor intended to take life." Enmund was convicted of two counts of felony-murder and sentenced to death on proof that he drove the getaway car in a robbery during which two of his co-felons shot and killed the two victims. The Court, per White, J., first took note of "society's rejection of the death penalty for accomplice liability in felony murders," as indicated by the fact that "only a small minority of jurisdictions—eight—allow the death penalty to be imposed solely because the defendant somehow participated in a robbery in the course of which a murder was committed," and that a survey of death penalty cases since 1954 "revealed only 6 cases out of 362 where a nontriggerman felony murderer was executed." The Court continued:

"Enmund himself did not kill or attempt to kill; and, as construed by the Florida Supreme Court, the record before us does not warrant a finding that Enmund had any intention of participating in or facilitating a murder. Yet under Florida law death was an authorized penalty because Enmund aided and abetted a robbery in the course of which murder was committed. It is fundamental that "causing harm intentionally must be punished more severely than causing the same harm unintentionally." H. Hart, *Punishment and Responsibility* 162 (1968). Enmund did not kill or intend to kill and thus his culpability is plainly different from that of the robbers who killed; yet the State treated them alike and attributed to Enmund the culpability of those who killed the Kerseys. This was impermissible under the Eighth Amendment.

"In *Gregg v. Georgia* the opinion announcing the judgment observed that '[t]he death penalty is said to serve two principal social purposes: retribution and deterrence of capital crimes by prospective offenders.' Unless the death penalty when applied to those in Enmund's position measurably contributes to one or both of these goals, it 'is nothing more than the purposeless and needless imposition of pain and suffering,' and hence an unconstitutional punishment. *Coker v. Georgia, supra.* We are quite unconvinced, however, that the threat that the death penalty will be imposed for murder will measurably deter one who does not kill and has no intention or purpose that life will be taken.

*   *   *

"It would be very different if the likelihood of a killing in the course of a robbery were so substantial that one should share the blame for the killing if he somehow participated in the felony. But competent observers have concluded that there is no basis in experience for the notion that death so frequently occurs in the course of a felony for which killing is not an essential ingredient that the death penalty should be considered as a justifiable deterrent to the felony itself. *   *   *

"As for retribution as a justification for executing Enmund, we think this very much depends on the degree of Enmund's culpability—what Enmund's intentions, expectations, and actions were. American criminal law has long considered a defendant's intention—and therefore his moral guilt—to be critical to 'the degree of [his] criminal culpability,' and the Court has found criminal penalties to be unconstitutionally excessive in the absence of intentional wrongdoing."

O'Connor, J., for the four dissenters, concluded that "the petitioner and the Court have failed to show that contempo-

rary standards, as reflected in both jury determinations and legislative enactments, preclude imposition of the death penalty for accomplice felony murder. Moreover, examination of the qualitative factors underlying the concept of proportionality do not show that the death penalty is disproportionate as applied to Earl Enmund. In contrast to the crime in *Coker,* the petitioner's crime involves the very type of harm that this Court has held justifies the death penalty. Finally, because of the unique and complex mixture of facts involving a defendant's actions, knowledge, motives, and participation during the commission of a felony murder, I believe that the factfinder is best able to assess the defendant's blameworthiness."

11. But later, in *Tison v. Arizona,* ___ U.S. ___, 107 S.Ct. 1676, 95 L.Ed.2d 127 (1987), the Court decided *Enmund* was not applicable to every defendant convicted of felony murder on an accomplice liability theory. The petitioners affected the escape of their father from prison and armed him and another convicted murderer with guns and later helped abduct a family and watched as the two convicts murdered that family. The state supreme court affirmed their death sentences, reasoning that under *Enmund* it was sufficient that the defendants had anticipated that lethal force might be used. The Supreme Court, per O'Connor, J., affirmed:

"A narrow focus on the question of whether or not a given defendant 'intended to kill,' however, is a highly unsatisfactory means of definitively distinguishing the most culpable and dangerous of murderers. Many who intend to, and do, kill are not criminally liable at all—those who act in self-defense or with other justification or excuse. Other intentional homicides, though criminal, are often felt undeserving of the death penalty—those that are the result of provocation. On the other hand, some nonintentional murderers may be among the most dangerous and inhumane of all—the person who tortures another not caring whether the victim lives or dies, or the robber who shoots someone in the course of the robbery, utterly indifferent to the fact that the desire to rob may have the unintended consequence of killing the victim as well as taking the victim's property. This reckless indifference to the value of human life may be every bit as shocking to the moral sense as an 'intent to kill.' Indeed it is for this very reason that the common law and modern criminal codes alike have classified behavior such as occurred in this case along with intentional murders. * * * *Enmund* held that when 'intent to kill' results in its logical though not inevitable consequence—the taking of human life—the Eighth Amendment permits the State to exact the death penalty after a careful weighing of the aggravating and mitigating circumstances. Similarly, we hold that the reckless disregard for human life implicit in knowingly engaging in criminal activities known to carry a grave risk of death represents a highly culpable mental state, a mental state that may be taken into account in making a capital sentencing judgment when that conduct causes its natural, though also not inevitable, lethal result.

"The petitioners own personal involvement in the crimes was not minor, but rather, as specifically found by the trial court, 'substantial.' Far from merely sitting in a car away from the actual scene of the murders acting as the getaway driver to a robbery, each petitioner was actively involved in every element of the kidnaping-robbery and was physically present during the entire sequence of criminal activity culminating in the murder of the Lyons family and the subsequent flight. The Tisons' high level of participation in these crimes further implicates them in the resulting deaths. Accordingly, they fall well within the overlapping second intermediate position which focuses on the defendant's degree of participation in the felony.

"Only a small minority of those jurisdictions imposing capital punishment for felony murder have rejected the possibility of a capital sentence absent an intent to kill and we do not find this minority position constitutionally required. We will not attempt to precisely delineate the particular types of conduct and states of mind warranting imposition of the death penalty here. Rather, we simply hold that major participation in the felony committed, combined with reckless indifference to human life, is sufficient to satisfy the *Enmund* culpability requirement. The Arizona courts have clearly found that the former exists; we now vacate the judgments below and remand for determination of the latter in further proceedings not inconsistent with this opinion."

The four dissenters asserted that "the basic flaw in today's decision is the Court's failure to conduct the sort of proportionality analysis that the Constitution and past cases require. Creation of a new category of culpability is not enough to distinguish this case from *Enmund*. The Court must also establish that death is a proportionate punishment for individuals in this category. In other words, the Court must demonstrate that major participation in a felony with a state of mind of reckless indifference to human life deserves the same punishment as intending to commit a murder or actually committing a murder. The Court does not attempt to conduct a proportionality review of the kind performed in past cases raising a proportionality question * * *."

Chapter 6

MENTAL DISEASE OR DEFECT

SECTION 1. COMPETENCY TO STAND TRIAL

Introductory Notes

1. Although the matter of principal concern in this Chapter is the defense of insanity, it is appropriate to begin with a consideration of competency to stand trial. As noted in S. Brakel, J. Parry & B. Weiner, *The Mentally Disabled and the Law* 693–94 (3d ed. 1985): "While the insanity defense has received more attention from the media and has inflamed public debate, the issue of competency, or what has sometimes been called 'present insanity,' affects far greater numbers of mentally disabled defendants,[2] and some consider this issue the most significant mental health inquiry pursued in the criminal justice process. Since the previous edition of this book there has been increased recognition of the detrimental consequences of a finding of incompetency for the defendant,

which has resulted in an increasing number of challenges to the state procedures for hospitalizing incompetent defendants and to provisions permitting indeterminate hospitalization without resolution of the criminal charges. As with the concept of criminal responsibility, the question of present competency engages conflicting philosophies and varying standards for application to individual cases, and it raises both substantive and procedural questions at each stage of the criminal process.

* * *

"Because it is often missed by practitioners in both the legal and the psychiatric professions, it is important to keep in mind the conceptual distinction between competency to participate in the criminal justice process and criminal responsibility. Competency concerns only the defendant's present ability to assist in his defense and understand the process he is involved in or the punishment he receives, whereas crimi-

2. For example, a 1979 study estimated that out of more than two million felony and misdemeanor cases disposed of in the state and federal courts 6,420 were institutionalized because they were incompetent to stand trial, as compared with 1,625 who were there as a result of being found not guilty by reason of insanity. Steadman, Monahan, Hartstone, Davis, & Robbins, Mentally Disordered Offenders: A National Survey of Patients and Facilities, 6 Law & Hum. Behav. 31, 33 (1982).

It has been estimated that as many as 9,000 persons a year are found incompetent, a figure

that reflects that not all of them are institutionalized or that a percentage of those who are institutionalized are discharged after relatively brief periods. H.J. Steadman, Beating A Rap? Defendants Found Incompetent to Stand Trial 4 (1979). In Illinois, for example, approximately 300 people a year are found incompetent, while only about 40 are found not guilty by reason of insanity (statistics kept by the Illinois Dep't of Mental Health & Developmental Disabilities, Statistical Branch, Springfield, Illinois).

nal responsibility concerns only the mental state of the defendant at the time of the commission of the crime, which may have been months or years before the trial. Thus, a defendant may be competent to stand trial but be found not criminally responsible for his acts. Conversely, he could be adjudged incompetent but once restored to competency be held responsible for his criminal actions. Finally, he could be declared incompetent and once restored to competency be found not criminally responsible."

2. In practice, the competency inquiry often obviates any need for a subsequent defense of insanity. Consider Matthews, *Mental Disability and the Criminal Law* 90–92 (1970): "Even when there is real doubt about the accused's fitness for trial, strategical considerations are highly influential in determining whether the issue will be opened up and how it is pursued. Except where competency proceedings are initiated solely for obstruction or delay—and this accounts for a very small portion of motions for competency determination—the movant characteristically seeks expert opinion on some collateral issue. The major reason is to obtain psychiatric opinion in order to determine whether some alternative disposition is feasible, a reason common to the prosecution and the defense. The initiation of competency proceedings is the major access route in the criminal process to psychiatric intervention, a necessary prerequisite if some informal psychiatric disposition is to occur. Since competency proceedings provide that access, both sides have reasons for invoking them. When the prosecution and the defense are agreed on allowing the accused to be treated on an outpatient basis or to be civilly committed, and thus on disposing of the criminal charges, both want to know if such treatment is psychiatrically indicated and feasible. Since the prosecutor has no funds in his budget for this purpose, and the defendant typically is indigent, both sides may agree to raise the competency issue to get a medical consultation. The judge may also want some help in disposing of the offender, initially or subsequently, in a perhaps more humane and effective way than sentencing him to the county jail. Neither judges nor prosecutors have illusions about the limited sentencing alternatives available to them and both are usually eager to take advantage of any opportunity to experiment with a disposition which may 'help' the offender. In many cases this is a conscious use of competency proceedings in which the judge, the prosecutor, and defense counsel concur. Whether by plan or by accident, the psychiatric report, irrespective of its impact on the competency issue, is a highly influential factor in determining the final disposition.

"Another shared reason for initiating competency proceedings is to develop evidence on the issue of criminal responsibility. Many lawyers think the standard for incompetency is broader than that for criminal responsibility * * *. Lawyers sometimes told us they thought an incompetency disposition by a judge was more likely in certain cases than an irresponsibility disposition by a jury. The judge, in the view of his brothers in the legal profession, is less likely than a jury to be prejudiced by the fact, for example, that the offense is particularly violent or atrocious. At times the competency hearing itself (when there is one) approaches a proceeding in which the court reaches a 'summary judgment' of insanity. The prosecutor can avoid a public trial which may carry with it public pressure, usually in the direction of severity; if the accused can be found incompetent, the case can later be disposed of quietly. The result in some cases is a conscious substitution of a finding of incompetency for a trial by jury on the responsibility issue—a result tacitly agreed to by both sides. This practice tends to occur in the more serious cases, especially those involving capital crimes, and helps explain why findings of incompetency outnumber findings of not guilty by reason of insanity.

"Where prosecutor and defense attorney are not equally interested in obtaining expert opinion on the insanity issue, the psychiatric report nevertheless sometimes becomes a basis for working out a disposition short of going to trial. If the psychiatric experts seem to think that the accused did not know what he was doing when the crime was committed or that he did not understand that it was wrong to do so, the prosecutor may be willing to accept a plea to a lesser offense or an outright dismissal. Furthermore, the psychiatrist performing the examination may frequently suggest alternatives, such as civil commitment or probation on condition that the accused seek outpatient psychiatric treatment. After the psychiatric examination, both parties can forecast pretty well the course of a trial, whereas in the absence of psychiatric opinion the bargaining process must be conducted with a major variable unknown."

PATE v. ROBINSON

Supreme Court of the United States, 1966.
383 U.S. 375, 86 S.Ct. 836, 15 L.Ed.2d 815.

MR. JUSTICE CLARK delivered the opinion of the Court.

In 1959 respondent Robinson was convicted of the murder of his common-law wife, Flossie May Ward, and was sentenced to imprisonment for life. Being an indigent he was defended by court-appointed counsel. It was conceded at trial that Robinson shot and killed Flossie May, but his counsel claimed that he was insane at the time of the shooting and raised the issue of his incompetence to stand trial. On writ of error to the Supreme Court of Illinois it was asserted that the trial court's rejection of these contentions deprived Robinson of due process of law under the Fourteenth Amendment. His conviction was affirmed * * *.

The uncontradicted testimony of four witnesses called by the defense revealed that Robinson had a long history of disturbed behavior. His mother testified that when he was between seven and eight years of age a brick dropped from a third floor hit Robinson on the head. "He blacked out and the blood run from his head like a faucet." Thereafter "he acted a little peculiar." The blow knocked him "cockeyed" and his mother took him to a specialist "to correct the crossness of his eyes." He also suffered headaches during his childhood, apparently stemming from the same event. His conduct became noticeably erratic about 1946 or 1947 when he was visiting his mother on a furlough from the Army. While Robinson was sitting and talking with a guest, "he jumped up and run to a bar and kicked a hole in the bar and he run up in the front." His mother asked "what on earth was wrong with him and he just stared at [her], and paced the floor with both hands in his pockets." On other occasions he appeared in a daze, with a "glare in his eyes," and would not speak or respond to questions. In 1951, a few years after his discharge from the service, he "lost his mind and was pacing the floor saying something was after him." This incident occurred at the home of his aunt, Helen Calhoun. Disturbed by Robinson's conduct, Mrs. Calhoun called his mother about six o'clock in the morning, and she "went to see about him." Robinson tried to prevent Mrs. Calhoun from opening the door, saying "that someone was going to shoot him or someone was going to come in after him." His mother testified that after gaining admittance, "I went to him and hugged him to ask him what was wrong and he went to pushing me back, telling me to get back, somebody was going to shoot him, somebody was going to shoot him." Upon being questioned as to

Robinson's facial expression at the time, the mother stated that he "had that starey look and seemed to be just a little foamy at the mouth." A policeman was finally called. He put Robinson, his mother and aunt in a cab which drove them to Hines Hospital. On the way Robinson tried to jump from the cab, and upon arrival at the hospital he was so violent that he had to be strapped in a wheel chair. He then was taken in an ambulance to the County Psychopathic Hospital, from which he was transferred to the Kankakee State Hospital. * * *

After his release from the state hospital Robinson's irrational episodes became more serious. His grandfather testified that while Robinson was working with him as a painter's assistant, "all at once, he would come down [from the ladder] and walk on out and never say where he is going and whatnot and he would be out two or three hours, and at times he would be in a daze and when he comes out, he comes back just as fresh. He just says he didn't do anything. I noticed that he wasn't at all himself." The grandfather also related that one night when Robinson was staying at his house Robinson and his wife had a "ruckus," which caused his wife to flee to the grandfather's bedroom. Robinson first tried to kick down the door. He then grabbed all of his wife's clothes from their room and threw them out in the yard, intending to set them on fire. Robinson got so unruly that the grandfather called the police to lock him up.

In 1953 Robinson, then separated from his wife, brought their 18–month–old son to Mrs. Calhoun's home and asked permission to stay there for a couple of days. She observed that he was highly nervous, prancing about and staring wildly. While she was at work the next day Robinson shot and killed his son and attempted suicide by shooting himself in the head.
* * *

Robinson served almost four years in prison for killing his son, being released in September 1956. A few months thereafter he began to live with Flossie May Ward at her home. In the summer of 1957 or 1958 Robinson "jumped on" his mother's brother-in-law and "beat him up terrible." She went to the police station and swore out a warrant for his arrest. She described his abnormalities and told the officers that Robinson "seemed to have a disturbed mind." * * *

The killing occurred about 10:30 p.m. at a small barbecue house where Flossie May Ward worked. At that time there were 10 customers in the restaurant, six of them sitting at the counter. It appears from the record that Robinson entered the restaurant with a gun in his hand. As he approached the counter, Flossie May said, "Don't start nothing tonight." After staring at her for about a minute, he walked to the rear of the room and, with the use of his hand, leaped over the counter. He then rushed back toward the front of the restaurant, past two other employees working behind the counter, and fired once or twice at Flossie May. She jumped over the counter and ran out the front door with Robinson in pursuit. She was found dead on the sidewalk. Robinson never spoke a word during the three-to-four minute episode. * * *

Four defense witnesses expressed the opinion that Robinson was insane. In rebuttal the State introduced only a stipulation that Dr. William H. Haines, Director of the Behavior Clinic of the Criminal Court of Cook County would, if present, testify that in his opinion Robinson knew the nature of the charges against him and was able to cooperate with counsel when he examined him two or three months before trial. However, since the stipulation did not include a finding of sanity the prosecutor advised the court that "we should have Dr. Haines' testimony as to his opinion whether this man is sane or insane. It is possible that the man might be insane and know the nature of the charge or be able to cooperate with his counsel. I think it should be in evidence, your Honor, that Dr. Haines' opinion is that this defendant was sane when he was examined." However, the court told the prosecutor, "You have enough in the record now. I don't think you need Dr. Haines." In his summation defense counsel emphasized "our defense is clear * * *. It is as to the sanity of the defendant at the time of the crime and also as to the present time." The court, after closing argument by the defense, found Robinson guilty and sentenced him to prison for his natural life.

The State insists that Robinson deliberately waived the defense of his competence to stand trial by failing to demand a sanity hearing as provided by Illinois law. But it is contradictory to argue that a defendant may be incompetent, and yet knowingly or intelligently "waive" his right to have the court determine his capacity to stand trial. In any event, the record shows that counsel throughout the proceedings insisted that Robinson's present sanity was very much in issue. He made a point to elicit Mrs. Robinson's opinion of Robinson's "present sanity." And in his argument to the judge, he asserted that Robinson "should be found not guilty and presently insane on the basis of the testimony that we have heard." Moreover, the prosecutor himself suggested at trial that "we should have Dr. Haines' testimony as to his opinion whether this man is sane or insane." With this record we cannot say that Robinson waived the defense of incompetence to stand trial.

We believe that the evidence introduced on Robinson's behalf entitled him to a hearing on this issue. The court's failure to make such inquiry thus deprived Robinson of his constitutional right to a fair trial. The Supreme Court of Illinois held that the evidence here was not sufficient to require a hearing in light of the mental alertness and understanding displayed in Robinson's "colloquies" with the trial judge. But this reasoning offers no justification for ignoring the uncontradicted testimony of Robinson's history of pronounced irrational behavior. While Robinson's demeanor at trial might be relevant to the ultimate decision as to his sanity, it cannot be relied upon to dispense with a hearing on that very issue. Likewise, the stipulation of Dr. Haines' testimony was some evidence of Robinson's ability to assist in his defense. But, as the state prosecutor seemingly admitted, on the facts presented to the trial court it could not properly have been deemed dispositive on the issue of Robinson's competence.

Having determined that Robinson's constitutional rights were abridged by his failure to receive an adequate hearing on his competence to stand trial, we direct that the writ of habeas corpus must issue and Robinson be discharged, unless the State gives him a new trial within a reasonable time. * * * It has been pressed upon us that it would be sufficient for the state court to hold a limited hearing as to Robinson's mental competence at the time he was tried in 1959. If he were found competent, the judgment against him would stand. But we have previously emphasized the difficulty of retrospectively determining an accused's competence to stand trial. The jury would not be able to observe the subject of their inquiry, and expert witnesses would have to testify solely from information contained in the printed record. That Robinson's hearing would be held six years after the fact aggravates these difficulties. * * *

MR. JUSTICE HARLAN, whom MR. JUSTICE BLACK joins, dissenting. * * *

I do not believe the facts known to the trial judge in this case suggested Robinson's incompetence at time of trial with anything like the force necessary to make out a violation of due process in the failure to pursue the question. * * *

The Court's affirmative answer seemingly rests on two kinds of evidence, principally adduced by Robinson to prove an insanity defense after the State rested its main case. First, there was evidence of a number of episodes of severe irrationality in Robinson's past. Among them were the slaying of his infant son, his attempted suicide, his efforts to burn his wife's clothing, his fits of temper and of abstraction, and his seven-week incarceration in a state hospital eight years before the trial. This evidence may be tempered by the State's counterarguments, for example, that Robinson was found guilty of his son's killing and that alcoholism may explain his hospitalization, but it cannot be written off entirely. The difficulty remains that while this testimony may suggest that Flossie May Ward's killing was just one more irrational act, I cannot say as a matter of common knowledge that it evidences incapacity during the trial. Indeed, the pattern revealed may best indicate that Robinson did function adequately during most of his life interrupted by periods of severe derangement that would have been quite apparent had they occurred at trial. The second class of data pertinent to the Court's theory, remarks by witnesses and counsel that Robinson was "presently insane," deserves little comment. I think it apparent that these statements were addressed to Robinson's responsibility for the killing, that is, his ability to do insane acts, and not to his general competency to stand trial.

Whatever mild doubts this evidence may stir are surely allayed by positive indications of Robinson's competence at the trial. Foremost is his own behavior in the courtroom. The record reveals colloquies between Robinson and the trial judge which undoubtedly permitted a reasonable

inference that Robinson was quite cognizant of the proceedings and able to assist counsel in his defense. Turning from lay impressions to those of an expert, it was stipulated at trial that a Dr. Haines, Director of the Behavior Clinic of the Criminal Court of Cook County, had examined Robinson several months earlier and, if called, would testify that Robinson "knows the nature of the charge and is able to cooperate with his counsel." The conclusive factor is that Robinson's own lawyers, the two men who apparently had the closest contact with the defendant during the proceedings, never suggested he was incompetent to stand trial and never moved to have him examined on incompetency grounds during trial; indeed, counsel's remarks to the jury seem best read as an affirmation of Robinson's present "lucidity" which would be highly peculiar if Robinson had been unable to assist properly in his defense. * * *

Notes and Questions

1. Drope was indicted with two others for rape of his wife. Following severance of his case, he filed a motion for a continuance so that he might be further examined and receive psychiatric treatment, attaching thereto the report of a psychiatrist who had examined him at his counsel's request and had suggested such treatment. The motion was denied and the case proceeded to trial. Drope's wife, in her testimony, confirmed information in the report concerning his "strange behavior" and also stated that he had tried to kill her a few days prior to the trial. On the second day of the trial, Drope shot himself in a suicide attempt, after which the trial continued without his presence. In *Drope v. Missouri,* 420 U.S. 162, 95 S.Ct. 896, 43 L.Ed.2d 103 (1975), a unanimous Court held "that when considered together with the information available prior to trial and the testimony of petitioner's wife at trial, the information concerning petitioner's suicide

attempt created a sufficient doubt of his competence to stand trial to require further inquiry on the question. * * *

"Even when a defendant is competent at the commencement of his trial, a trial court must always be alert to circumstances suggesting a change that would render the accused unable to meet the standards of competence to stand trial. Whatever the relationships between mental illness and incompetence to stand trial, in this case the bearing of the former on the latter was sufficiently likely that, in light of the evidence of petitioner's behavior including his suicide attempt, and there being no opportunity without his presence to evaluate that bearing in fact, the correct course was to suspend the trial until such an evaluation could be made."

2. In neither *Robinson* nor *Drope* did the Court have occasion to rule on exactly what the due process standard regarding competency is, though *Drope* does quote from *Dusky v. United States,* 362 U.S. 402, 80 S.Ct. 788, 4 L.Ed.2d 824 (1960), where it is stated: "We also agree with the suggestion of the Solicitor General that it is not enough for the district judge to find that 'the defendant [is] oriented to time and place and [has] some recollection of events,' but that the 'test must be whether he has sufficient present ability to consult with his lawyer with a reasonable degree of rational understanding—and whether he has a rational as well as factual understanding of the proceedings against him.' "

There is, however, some variation from state to state as to the standard used. Compare *State v. Champagne,* 127 N.H. 266, 497 A.2d 1242 (1985) (no competency unless defendant has "the ability to communicate *meaningfully* with his lawyer so as to be able to make informed choices regarding trial strategy"); with *State v. Ortiz,* 104 Wash.2d 479, 706 P.2d 1069 (1985) (rejecting defense contention "that a person must be able to help with trial

strategy in order to be found competent to stand trial").

Because of such variations, some have concluded that "the broad definition of *Dusky* has not worked." Mickenberg, *Competency to Stand Trial and the Mentally Retarded Defendant,* 17 Cal.W.L.Rev. 365, 402 (1981). What, then, is the solution?

3. The argument "that a finding of 'incompetence to stand trial but for drug maintenance' precludes a finding of competence to stand trial" has been rejected. *United States v. Hayes,* 589 F.2d 811 (5th Cir.1979). Can a waiver of *Robinson* rights occur in that context? Compare *State v. Hayes,* 118 N.H. 458, 389 A.2d 1379 (1978) ("If the defendant by his own voluntary choice, made while competent, becomes incompetent to stand trial because he withdraws from the medication, he may be deemed to have waived his right to be tried while competent"); with *Lane v. State,* 388 So.2d 1022 (Fla. 1980) ("Intentional action by a defendant does not avoid or eliminate the necessity of applying the test of whether a defendant has the sufficient *present* ability to assist counsel with his defense and to understand the proceedings against him").

4. Does defense counsel have a responsibility similar or comparable to that of the judge under *Robinson* and *Drope?* Consider *State v. Johnson,* 133 Wis.2d 207, 395 N.W.2d 176 (1986): "The state argues that defense counsel's strategic decision not to raise a competency question should be honored by this court. Although the fifth circuit has recently held that defense counsel may, for tactical reasons, decide not to request a competency hearing, *Enriquez v. Procunier,* 752 F.2d 111 (5th Cir.1984), we decline to follow the fifth circuit's conclusion. We believe that considerations of strategy are inappropriate in mental competency situations. Thus, we hold that strategic considerations

do not eliminate defense counsel's duty to request a competency hearing."

5. In *People v. Francabandera,* 33 N.Y.2d 429, 354 N.Y.S.2d 609, 310 N.E.2d 292 (1974), defendant (charged with attempted murder, reckless endangerment and possession of a dangerous weapon) moved for a determination of his fitness to stand trial. Though it was established that he was suffering from retrograde amnesia so as to be unable to recall the events surrounding the crimes with which he was charged, the trial court concluded the defendant was not incapacitated within the meaning of the statutory definition ("a defendant who as a result of mental disease or defect lacks capacity to understand the proceedings against him or to assist in his own defense"). The defendant then entered a guilty plea to reckless endangerment. On appeal, the court affirmed: "In no case yet reported has it been held that inability to recall the events charged because of amnesia constitutes mental incapacity to stand trial. * * * In *Wilson* [*v. United States,* 391 F.2d 460 (D.C.Cir.1968),] a case-by-case approach to the amnesic defendant was advocated so that in each situation the Judge would have to prognosticate on the basis of all the circumstances whether defendant was likely to receive a fair trial; and then, at the conclusion of the trial and before imposition of sentence, the Judge would have to decide whether defendant did, in fact, receive a fair trial—this by the application of certain tests advocated by the court.[4]

* * *

"When it is considered that the result of an order finding defendant unfit for trial in these circumstances would be outright release, assuming the amnesia is permanent and there is no other mental defect sufficient to warrant commitment, it can be more easily understood why all the courts which have passed on this question have refused to allow amnesia to be classified as the sort of mental defect causing incapacity to stand trial. This certainly is a consideration in balancing the public safety against the individual's rights; but we do not wish to be understood as making this our prime consideration since it would not fully meet the constitutional arguments. Rather, we are in accord with the reasoning in *Wilson* which addresses itself to the question whether defendant can conceivably receive a fair trial; and, after trial, whether defendant did in fact receive a fair trial. This allows for essential case-by-case evaluation. Applying those concepts to this case we can see that the court could easily have determined (as indeed it did) that defendant's trial would be fair. The alleged crime was played out in front of an audience and the overwhelming evidence, all of which was available to defendant, pointed to his guilt. From this evidence it could be determined that defendant was probably intoxicated. Had they been willing to risk the consequences, defendant and his counsel might have gone to trial

---

4. "In making these findings the court should consider the following factors:

"(1) The extent to which the amnesia affected the defendant's ability to consult with and assist his lawyer.

"(2) The extent to which the amnesia affected the defendant's ability to testify in his own behalf.

"(3) The extent to which the evidence in suit could be extrinsically reconstructed in view of the defendant's amnesia. Such evidence would include evidence relating to the crime itself as well as any reasonably possible alibi.

"(4) The extent to which the Government assisted the defendant and his counsel in that reconstruction.

"(5) The strength of the prosecution's case. Most important here will be whether the Government's case is such as to negate all reasonable hypotheses of innocence. If there is any substantial possibility that the accused could, but for his amnesia, establish an alibi or other defense, it should be presumed that he would have been able to do so.

"(6) Any other facts and circumstances which would indicate whether or not the defendant had a fair trial."

on the question of defendant's inability to form the requisite intent to commit the crimes charged because of intoxication. Coupling the prosecution's evidence on this point with defendant's history of alcoholism, which defendant was perfectly capable of supplying counsel and of course capable, also, of testifying to, would have appeared to be the only course open if the decision to stand trial were made and, indeed, this is argued to us in defendant's brief. It is not explained to us, however, how defendant's lack of memory could actually have crippled his defense in this case in light of the nature of the crime and the evidence possessed by the prosecutor. It cannot be said that the decision to plead guilty to a lesser charge would not have been the most astute decision under these circumstances even had defendant been able to recall the events. There is in this case, then, no indication that defendant was deprived of any of his constitutional rights or that the court was in error in denying defendant's motion."

JACKSON v. INDIANA

Supreme Court of the United States, 1972.
406 U.S. 715, 92 S.Ct. 1845, 32 L.Ed.2d 435.

MR. JUSTICE BLACKMUN delivered the opinion of the Court.

We are here concerned with the constitutionality of certain aspects of Indiana's system for pretrial commitment of one accused of crime.

Petitioner, Theon Jackson, is a mentally defective deaf mute with a mental level of a pre-school child. He cannot read, write, or otherwise communicate except through limited sign language. In May 1968, at age 27, he was charged in the Criminal Court of Marion County, Indiana, with separate robberies of two women. The offenses were alleged to have occurred the preceding July. The first involved property (a purse and its contents) of the value of four dollars. The second concerned five

dollars in money. The record sheds no light on these charges since, upon receipt of not-guilty pleas from Jackson, the trial court set in motion the Indiana procedures for determining his competency to stand trial.

As the statute requires, the court appointed two psychiatrists to examine Jackson. A competency hearing was subsequently held at which petitioner was represented by counsel. The court received the examining doctors' joint written report and oral testimony from them and from a deaf-school interpreter through whom they had attempted to communicate with petitioner. The report concluded that Jackson's almost nonexistent communication skill, together with his lack of hearing and his mental deficiency, left him unable to understand the nature of the charges against him or to participate in his defense. One doctor testified that it was extremely unlikely that petitioner could ever learn to read or write and questioned whether petitioner even had the ability to develop any proficiency in sign language. He believed that the interpreter had not been able to communicate with petitioner to any great extent and testified that petitioner's "prognosis appears rather dim." The other doctor testified that even if Jackson were not a deaf mute, he would be incompetent to stand trial, and doubted whether petitioner had sufficient intelligence ever to develop the necessary communication skills. The interpreter testified that Indiana had no facilities that could help someone as badly off as Jackson to learn minimal communication skills.

On this evidence, the trial court found that Jackson "lack[ed] comprehension sufficient to make his defense," and ordered him committed to the Indiana Department of Mental Health until such time as that Department should certify to the court that "the defendant is sane."

Petitioner's counsel then filed a motion for a new trial, contending that there was no evidence that Jackson was "insane," or that he would ever attain a status which the court might regard as "sane" in the sense of competency to stand trial. * * * On appeal the Supreme Court of Indiana affirmed, with one judge dissenting. * * *

I. INDIANA COMMITMENT PROCEDURES

Section 9–1706a contains both the procedural and substantive requirements for pretrial commitment of incompetent criminal defendants in Indiana. If at any time before submission of the case to the court or jury the trial judge has "reasonable ground" to believe the defendant "to be insane,"[2] he must appoint two examining physicians and schedule a competency hearing. The hearing is to the court alone, without a jury. The examining physicians' testimony and "other evidence" may be adduced on the issue of incompetency. If the court finds the defendant "has not comprehension sufficient to understand the proceedings and make his defense," trial is delayed or continued and the defendant is remanded to the state department of mental health to be confined in an "appropriate psychiatric institution." The section further provides that "[w]henever the defendant shall become sane" the superintendent of the institution shall certify that fact to the court, and the court shall order him brought on to trial. The court may also make such an order *sua sponte.* There is no statutory provision for periodic review of the defendant's condition by either the court or mental health authorities. * * *

Petitioner's central contention is that the State, in seeking in effect to commit him to a mental institution indefinitely, should

have been required to invoke the standards and procedures of Ind.Ann.Stat. § 22–1907, now Ind.Code 16–15–1–3 (1971), governing commitment of "feeble-minded" persons. * * * If the judge determines that the individual is indeed "feeble-minded," he enters an order of commitment and directs the clerk of the court to apply for the person's admission "to the superintendent of the institution for feeble-minded persons located in the district in which said county is situated." A person committed under this section may be released "at any time," provided that "in the judgment of the superintendent, the mental and physical condition of the patient justifies it." The statutes do not define either "feeble-mindedness" or "insanity" as used in § 22–1907. But a statute establishing a special institution for care of such persons, refers to the duty of the State to provide care for its citizens who are "feeble-minded, and are therefore unable properly to care for themselves." These provisions evidently afford the State a vehicle for commitment of persons in need of custodial care who are "not insane" and therefore do not qualify as "mentally ill" under the State's general involuntary civil commitment scheme.

Scant attention was paid this general civil commitment law by the Indiana courts in the present case. An understanding of it, however, is essential to a full airing of the equal protection claims raised by petitioner. Section 22–1201(1) defines a "mentally ill person" as one who

> "is afflicted with a psychiatric disorder which substantially impairs his mental health; and, because of such psychiatric disorder, requires care, treatment, training or detention in the interest of the welfare of such person or the welfare of others of the community in which such person resides."

2. The section refers at several points to the defendant's "sanity." This term is nowhere defined. In context, and in the absence of a contra-

ry statutory construction by the state courts, it appears that the term is intended to be synonymous with competence to stand trial.

Section 22–1201(2) defines a "psychiatric disorder" to be any mental illness or disease, including any mental deficiency, epilepsy, alcoholism, or drug addiction. Other sections specify procedures for involuntary commitment of "mentally ill" persons that are substantially similar to those for commitment of the feeble-minded. * * * An individual adjudged mentally ill under these sections is remanded to the department of mental health for assignment to an appropriate institution. Discharge is in the discretion of the superintendent of the particular institution to which the person is assigned. The individual, however, remains within the court's custody, and release can therefore be revoked upon a hearing.

II.   EQUAL PROTECTION

Because the evidence established little likelihood of improvement in petitioner's condition he argues that commitment under § 9–1706a in his case amounted to a commitment for life. This deprived him of equal protection, he contends, because, absent the criminal charges pending against him, the State would have had to proceed under other statutes generally applicable to all other citizens: either the commitment procedures for feeble-minded persons, or those for mentally ill persons.

* * *

In *Baxstrom v. Herold,* 383 U.S. 107, 86 S.Ct. 760, 15 L.Ed.2d 620 (1966), the Court held that a state prisoner civilly committed at the end of his prison sentence on the finding of a surrogate was denied equal protection when he was deprived of a jury trial that the State made generally available to all other persons civilly committed. Rejecting the State's argument that Baxstrom's conviction and sentence constituted adequate justification for the difference in procedures, the Court said that "there is no conceivable basis for distinguishing the commitment of a person who is nearing the end of a penal term

from all other civil commitments."

* * *

If criminal conviction and imposition of sentence are insufficient to justify less procedural and substantive protection against indefinite commitment than that generally available to all others, the mere filing of criminal charges surely cannot suffice.

* * *

Respondent argues, however, that because the record fails to establish affirmatively that Jackson will never improve, his commitment "until sane" is not really an indeterminate one. It is only temporary, pending possible change in his condition. Thus, presumably, it cannot be judged against commitments under other state statutes that are truly indeterminate.

* * *

Were the State's factual premise that Jackson's commitment is only temporary a valid one, this might well be a different case. But the record does not support that premise. One of the doctors testified that in his view Jackson would be unable to acquire the substantially improved communication skills that would be necessary for him to participate in any defense. The prognosis for petitioner's developing such skills, he testified, appeared "rather dim." In answer to a question whether Jackson would ever be able to comprehend the charges or participate in his defense, even after commitment and treatment, the doctor said, "I doubt it, I don't believe so." The other psychiatrist testified that even if Jackson were able to develop such skills, he would *still* be unable to comprehend the proceedings or aid counsel due to his mental deficiency. * * * There is nothing in the record that even points to any possibility that Jackson's present condition can be remedied at any future time.

* * *

We note also that neither the Indiana statute nor state practice makes the likelihood of the defendant's improvement a relevant factor. The State did not seek to make any such showing, and the record clearly establishes that the chances of Jackson's ever meeting the competency standards of § 9–1706a are at best minimal, if not nonexistent. The record also rebuts any contention that the commitment could contribute to Jackson's improvement. Jackson's § 9–1706a commitment is permanent in practical effect.

We therefore must turn to the question whether, because of the pendency of the criminal charges that triggered the State's invocation of § 9–1706a, Jackson was deprived of substantial rights to which he would have been entitled under either of the other two state commitment statutes. *Baxstrom* held that the State cannot withhold from a few the procedural protections or the substantive requirements for commitment that are available to all others. In this case commitment procedures under all three statutes appear substantially similar: notice, examination by two doctors, and a full judicial hearing at which the individual is represented by counsel and can cross-examine witnesses and introduce evidence. Under each of the three statutes, the commitment determination is made by the court alone, and appellate review is available.

In contrast, however, what the State must show to commit a defendant under § 9–1706a, and the circumstances under which an individual so committed may be released, are substantially different from the standards under the other two statutes.

Under § 9–1706a, the State needed to show only Jackson's inability to stand trial. We are unable to say that, on the record before us, Indiana could have civilly committed him as mentally ill under § 22–1209 or committed him as feeble-minded under § 22–1907. The former requires at least (1) a showing of mental illness and (2) a showing that the individual is in need of "care, treatment, training or de-

tention." Whether Jackson's mental deficiency would meet the first test is unclear; neither examining physician addressed himself to this. Furthermore, it is problematical whether commitment for "treatment" or "training" would be appropriate since the record establishes that none is available for Jackson's condition at any state institution. The record also fails to establish that Jackson is in need of custodial care or "detention." He has been employed at times, and there is no evidence that the care he long received at home has become inadequate. The statute appears to require an independent showing of dangerousness ("requires ＊ ＊ ＊ detention in the interest of the welfare of such person or ＊ ＊ ＊ others ＊ ＊ ＊"). Insofar as it may require such a showing, the pending criminal charges are insufficient to establish it, and no other supporting evidence was introduced. For the same reasons, we cannot say that this record would support a feeble-mindedness commitment under § 22–1907 on the ground that Jackson is "unable properly to care for [himself]."

More important, an individual committed as feeble-minded is eligible for release when his condition "justifies it," and an individual civilly committed as mentally ill when the "superintendent or administrator shall discharge such person *or* [when] cured of such illness." Thus, in either case release is appropriate when the individual no longer requires the custodial care or treatment or detention that occasioned the commitment, or when the department of mental health believes release would be in his best interests. The evidence available concerning Jackson's past employment and home care strongly suggests that under these standards he might be eligible for release at almost any time, even if he did not improve. On the other hand, by the terms of his present § 9–1706a commitment, he will not be entitled to release at all, absent an unlikely substantial change for the better in his condition. * * *

As we noted above, we cannot conclude that pending criminal charges provide a greater justification for different treatment than conviction and sentence. Consequently, we hold that by subjecting Jackson to a more lenient commitment standard and to a more stringent standard of release than those generally applicable to all others not charged with offenses, and by thus condemning him in effect to permanent institutionalization without the showing required for commitment or the opportunity for release afforded by § 22–1209 or § 22–1907, Indiana deprived petitioner of equal protection of the laws under the Fourteenth Amendment.

III. DUE PROCESS

For reasons closely related to those discussed in Part II above, we also hold that Indiana's indefinite commitment of a criminal defendant solely on account of his incompetency to stand trial does not square with the Fourteenth Amendment's guarantee of due process.

A. *The Federal System.* In the federal criminal system, the constitutional issue posed here has not been encountered precisely because the federal statutes have been construed to require that a mentally incompetent defendant must also be found "dangerous" before he can be committed indefinitely. But the decisions have uniformly articulated the constitutional problems compelling this statutory interpretation. * * *

B. *The States.* Some States appear to commit indefinitely a defendant found incompetent to stand trial until he recovers competency. Other States require a finding of dangerousness to support such a commitment or provide forms of parole. New York has recently enacted legislation mandating release of incompetent defendants charged with misdemeanors after 90 days of commitment, and release and dis-missal of charges against those accused of felonies after they have been committed for two-thirds of the maximum potential prison sentence. The practice of automatic commitment with release conditioned solely upon attainment of competence has been decried on both policy and constitutional grounds. Recommendations for changes made by commentators and study committees have included incorporation into pretrial commitment procedures of the equivalent of the federal "rule of reason," a requirement of a finding of dangerousness or of full-scale civil commitment, periodic review by court or mental health administrative personnel of the defendant's condition and progress, and provisions for ultimately dropping charges if the defendant does not improve. One source of this criticism is undoubtedly the empirical data available which tend to show that many defendants committed before trial are never tried, and that those defendants committed pursuant to ordinary civil proceedings are, on the average, released sooner than defendants automatically committed solely on account of their incapacity to stand trial. Related to these statistics are substantial doubts about whether the rationale for pretrial commitment—that care or treatment will aid the accused in attaining competency—is empirically valid given the state of most of our mental institutions. However, very few courts appear to have addressed the problem directly in the state context.

In *United States ex rel. Wolfersdorf v. Johnston,* 317 F.Supp. 66 (S.D.N.Y.1970), an 86–year–old defendant committed for nearly 20 years as incompetent to stand trial on state murder and kidnapping charges applied for federal habeas corpus. He had been found "not dangerous," and suitable for civil commitment. The District Court granted relief. It held that petitioner's incarceration in an institution for the criminally insane constituted cruel and unusual punishment, and that the "shocking circumstances" of his commitment violated the Due Process Clause. The court quoted approvingly the language of *Cook v. Ciccone,* 312 F.Supp., at 824, concerning the "substantial injustice in keeping an unconvicted person in * * * custody to await trial where it is plainly evident his mental condition will not permit trial within a reasonable period of time."

In a 1970 case virtually indistinguishable from the one before us, the Illinois Supreme Court granted relief to an illiterate deaf mute who had been indicted for murder four years previously but found incompetent to stand trial on account of his inability to communicate, and committed. *People ex rel. Myers v. Briggs,* 46 Ill.2d 281, 263 N.E.2d 109 (1970). The institution where petitioner was confined had determined, "[I]t now appears that [petitioner] will never acquire the necessary communication skills needed to participate and cooperate in his trial." Petitioner, however, was found to be functioning at a "nearly normal level of performance in areas other than communication." The State contended petitioner should not be released until his competency was restored. The Illinois Supreme Court disagreed. It held:

"This court is of the opinion that this defendant, handicapped as he is and facing an indefinite commitment because of the pending indictment against him, should be given an opportunity to obtain a trial to determine whether or not he is guilty as charged or should be released."

C. *This Case.* * * *

The States have traditionally exercised broad power to commit persons found to be mentally ill. The substantive limitations on the exercise of this power and the procedures for invoking it vary drastically among the States. The particular fashion in which the power is exercised—for instance, through various forms of civil commitment, defective delinquency laws, sexual psychopath laws, commitment of persons acquitted by reason of insanity—reflects different combinations of distinct bases for commitment sought to be vindicated. The bases that have been articulated include dangerousness to self, dangerousness to others, and the need for care or treatment or training. Considering the number of persons affected, it is perhaps remarkable that the substantive constitutional limitations on this power have not been more frequently litigated.

We need not address these broad questions here. It is clear that Jackson's commitment rests on proceedings that did not purport to bring into play, indeed did not even consider relevant, *any* of the articulated bases for exercise of Indiana's power of indefinite commitment. The state statutes contain at least two alternative methods for invoking this power. But Jackson was not afforded any "formal commitment proceedings addressed to [his] ability to function in society," or to society's interest in his restraint, or to the State's ability to aid him in attaining competency through custodial care of compulsory treatment, the ostensible purpose of the commitment. At the least, due process requires that the nature and duration of commitment bear some reasonable relation to the purpose for which the individual is committed.

We hold, consequently, that a person charged by a State with a criminal offense who is committed solely on account of his incapacity to proceed to trial cannot be held more than the reasonable period of time necessary to determine whether there is a substantial probability that he will attain that capacity in the foreseeable future. If it is determined that this is not the case, then the State must either institute the customary civil commitment proceeding that would be required to commit indefinitely any other citizen, or release the defendant. Furthermore, even if it is determined that the defendant probably soon will be able to stand trial, his continued commitment must be justified by progress toward that goal. In light of differing state facilities and procedures and a lack of evidence in this record, we do not think it appropriate for us to attempt to prescribe arbitrary time limits. We note, however, that petitioner Jackson has now been confined for three and one-half years on a record that sufficiently establishes the lack of a substantial probability that he will ever be able to participate fully in a trial.

* * *

IV. DISPOSITION OF THE CHARGES

Petitioner also urges that fundamental fairness requires that the charges against him now be dismissed. The thrust of his argument is that the record amply establishes his lack of criminal responsibility at the time the crimes are alleged to have been committed. The Indiana court did not discuss this question. Apparently it believed that by reason of Jackson's incompetency commitment the State was entitled to hold the charges pending indefinitely. On this record, Jackson's claim is a substantial one. For a number of reasons, however, we believe the issue is not sufficiently ripe for ultimate decision by us at this time.

A. Petitioner argues that he has already made out a complete insanity defense. Jackson's criminal responsibility at the time of the alleged offenses, however, is a distinct issue from his competency to stand trial. The competency hearing below was not directed to criminal responsibility, and evidence relevant to it was presented only incidentally. Thus, in any event, we would have to remand for further consideration of Jackson's condition in the light of Indiana's law of criminal responsibility.

B. Dismissal of charges against an incompetent accused has usually been thought to be justified on grounds not squarely presented here: particularly, the Sixth–Fourteenth Amendment right to a speedy trial, or the denial of due process inherent in holding pending criminal charges indefinitely over the head of one who will never have a chance to prove his innocence. Jackson did not present the Sixth–Fourteenth Amendment issue to the state courts. Nor did the highest state court rule on the due process issue, if indeed it was presented to that court in precisely the above-described form. We think, in light of our holdings in Parts II and III, that the Indiana courts should have the first opportunity to determine these issues.

C. Both courts and commentators have noted the desirability of permitting some proceedings to go forward despite the defendant's incompetency. For instance, § 4.06(3) of the Model Penal Code would permit an incompetent accused's attorney to contest any issue "susceptible of fair determination prior to trial and without the personal participation of the defendant." An alternative draft of § 4.06(4) of the Model Penal Code would also permit an evidentiary hearing at which certain defenses, not including lack of criminal responsibility, could be raised by defense counsel on the basis of which the court might quash the indictment. Some States have statutory provisions permitting pretrial motions to be made or even allowing the incompetent defendant a trial at which to establish his innocence, without permitting a conviction. We do not read this Court's previous decisions to preclude the States from allowing at a minimum, an incompetent defendant to raise certain defenses such as insufficiency of the indictment, or make certain pretrial motions through counsel. Of course, if the Indiana courts conclude that Jackson was almost certainly not capable of criminal responsibility when the offenses were committed, dismissal of the charges might be warranted. But even if this is not the case, Jackson may have other good defenses that could sustain dismissal or acquittal and that might now be asserted. We do not know if Indiana would approve procedures such as those mentioned here, but these possibilities will be open on remand.

Reversed and remanded

Notes and Questions

1. In *State ex rel. Matalik v. Schubert,* 57 Wis.2d 315, 204 N.W.2d 13 (1973), the court held: (a) that even though the civil commitment statute provides for jury trial, failure to provide for jury trial in a proceeding to determine competency to stand trial does not amount to a denial of equal protection, as this proceeding "contemplates a commitment of a temporary nature" and "is to maximize rather than minimize the rights afforded criminally accused persons"; and (b) that petitioner's hearing (where the psychiatric report was accepted, over defendant's objection, as a basis for finding incompetency) was "insufficient to meet the 'meaningful hearing' requirements of the due process clause. It is insufficient because it provides an alleged incompetent with none of the procedural safeguards assuring an accurate adjudication of incompetency. While it may not often happen that one alleged to be incompetent to stand trial will object to the medical report, the due process clause requires a meaningful hearing where such an objection is made. Certain essentials are required to provide a meaningful hearing. These include the right to an attorney; notice of the hearing which must be promptly held; the right to introduce evidence contradicting the medical report; sworn testimony; and beyond a reasonable doubt as the quantum of proof necessary for the incompetency determination."

2. In *People v. Garlick,* 46 Ill.App.3d 216, 4 Ill.Dec. 746, 360 N.E.2d 1121 (1977), overturning the trial court's finding that defendant was competent to stand trial, the court concluded that "due process will not abide the placing of the burden of proof on a criminal defendant in a hearing to determine his competency to stand trial," and thus held unconstitutional a statute providing that the "burden of proving the defendant is not fit is on the defendant if he raises the question and on the State if the State or the court raises the question." The burden on the prosecution, the court added, is to establish the defendant's competence by a preponderance of the evidence.

3. Are *Matalik* and *Garlick* consistent or inconsistent? Note that in *Matalik* the burden was on the prosecution to prove *in*competency and in *Garlick* the burden was on the prosecution to prove competency. Consider also *Spencer v. Zant,* 715 F.2d 1562 (11th Cir.1983) (state may, consistent with due process, place burden of proving incompetency on defendant, as it "does not implicate his state of mind at the time of the offense and thus is not an element of the crime").

4. *United States v. DeBellis,* 649 F.2d 1 (1st Cir.1981), concludes: "No case that we have found has presented a factual setting in which commitment for competency determination alone has exceeded the maximum possible sentence, and we think our holding that it may not do so merely represents an inevitable application of the [*Jackson*] reasonableness limitation to that setting. Every court to have considered this specific question in dictum has reached the same conclusion."

5. Burt & Morris, *A Proposal for the Abolition of the Incompetency Plea,* 40 U.Chi. L.Rev. 66, 67 (1972): "States will likely be tempted, in the wake of *Jackson,* to resort to civil commitment proceedings rather than dismiss charges against and release permanently incompetent defendants. It is the thesis of this article, however, that the interests of both permanently incompetent defendants and the states would be better served by abandonment of

the traditional rule against trying incompetent defendants. Incompetency should instead be grounds for obtaining a trial continuance during which the state must provide resources to assist the defendant toward greater trial competence. If trial competence is not achieved within six months, the state should be required to dismiss charges or proceed to a trial governed, where necessary, by procedures designed to compensate for the incompetent defendant's trial disabilities."

As for the compensating procedures, they suggest at 94–95: "(a) Prior to trial, the court shall review all the evidence that the prosecution intends to offer at trial and shall order pretrial disclosure of evidence that would materially assist the defendant in overcoming the disabilities under which he labors. Disclosure of evidence that may endanger the lives of witnesses, or in any way promote substantial injustice, shall not be ordered;

"(b) On motion for directed verdict, either before or after jury deliberation, the court shall demand from the prosecution a higher burden of proof than would obtain in an ordinary criminal prosecution, and the court shall insist on extensive corroboration of the prosecution's case with respect to issues on which the defendant is likely to be prevented by his disability from effective rebuttal;

"(c) If the trial is before a jury, the court shall instruct the jury that in weighing the evidence against the defendant, it should take into account, in the defendant's favor, the disabilities under which he went to trial. If trial is before the judge sitting alone, he shall take account of those disabilities."

6. Or, is the solution simply to allow the incompetent defendant to waive his *Robinson–Drope* rights, as proposed in Winick, *Restructuring Competency to Stand Trial,* 32 U.C.L.A.L.Rev. 921, 967–69 (1985): "A presumption should apply in

favor of accepting the defendant's choice to stand trial or to plead guilty, if clearly expressed, notwithstanding his mental impairment, particularly when defense counsel concurs in his choice. Counsel's concurrence presumably eliminates instances in which the defendant's choice is based on irrelevant reasons ('I will plead guilty because I am an insect'), irrational beliefs ('I will stand trial and thereby become a movie star'), or outright delusions ('I am an extraterrestrial and will return to my planet'). Moreover, the concurrence of the defendant's attorney in his decision to stand trial or plead is strong evidence that the risk/benefit ratio of his choice is acceptable compared to an adjudication of incompetency (*i.e.,* that the defendant's decision is not an unreasonable one).

* * *

" * * * *Pate* does not hold that a defendant may not waive the right to be tried while incompetent, or that he may not waive the procedural due process right to a formal determination of competency."

7. Incompetency to stand trial must be distinguished from incompetency to be executed, addressed in *Ford v. Wainwright,* 477 U.S. 399, 106 S.Ct. 2595, 91 L.Ed.2d 335 (1986): "Today, no State in the Union permits the execution of the insane. It is clear that the ancient and humane limitation upon the State's ability to execute its sentences has as firm a hold upon the jurisprudence of today as it had centuries ago in England. The various reasons put forth in support of the common-law restriction have no less logical, moral, and practical force than they did when first voiced. For today, no less than before, we may seriously question the retributive value of executing a person who has no comprehension of why he has been singled out and stripped of his fundamental right to life. See Note, *The Eighth Amendment and the Execution of the Presently Incompetent,* 32 Stan.L.Rev. 765, 777, n. 58 (1980). Similarly, the natural abhorrence civilized

societies feel at killing one who has no capacity to come to grips with his own conscience or deity is still vivid today. And the intuition that such an execution simply offends humanity is evidently shared across this Nation. Faced with such widespread evidence of a restriction upon sovereign power, this Court is compelled to conclude that the Eighth Amendment prohibits a State from carrying out a sentence of death upon a prisoner who is insane. Whether its aim be to protect the condemned from fear and pain without comfort of understanding, or to protect the dignity of society itself from the barbarity of exacting mindless vengeance, the restriction finds enforcement in the Eighth Amendment."

SECTION 2. TESTS FOR THE INSANITY "DEFENSE"

Introductory Notes

1. Although it is customary to speak of the insanity "defense," the actual consequence of a successful insanity defense is quite different than with respect to any other defense. In every other case, a successful defense results in acquittal and outright release of the defendant, but with the insanity defense the probable result is commitment of the defendant to a mental institution until he has recovered his sanity. Acceptance of the defendant's insanity defense is specially noted by a jury verdict (or, in a trial without jury, a judge's finding) of "not guilty by reason of insanity," after which he will (in some jurisdictions) be automatically committed or (in others)

be subjected to proceedings which are most likely to result in commitment.

2. It is thus apparent that the insanity defense serves a unique purpose. Few efforts to articulate that purpose have been made, although the general assumption seems to be that the defense makes it possible to separate out for special treatment certain persons who would otherwise be subjected to the usual penal sanctions which may follow conviction: "The problem is the drawing of a line between the use of public agencies and force (1) to condemn the offender by conviction, with resulting sanctions in which the ingredient of reprobation is present no matter how constructive one may seek to make the sentence and the process of correction, and (2) modes of disposition in which the condemnatory element is absent, even though restraint may be involved. * * * Stating the matter differently, the problem is to etch a decent working line between the areas assigned to the authorities responsible for public health and those responsible for the correction of offenders." [a]

3. In examining the following materials, assess the relative merits of the following alternatives:

(a) adoption of the "right-wrong" or *M'Naghten* test (currently used in about half of the states), set out in *Daniel M'Naghten's Case*, infra;

(b) adoption of *M'Naghten* with the unfortunately labeled "irresistible impulse" test (currently used in just a few of the jurisdictions following *M'Naghten*), discussed in *Parsons v. State*, infra;

a. *Model Penal Code* § 4.01, Comment (1985).

Another view, however, is that the "real function" of the insanity defense "is to authorize the state to hold those 'who must be found not to possess the guilty mind *mens rea*,' even though the criminal law demands that no person be held criminally responsible if doubt is cast on any material element of the offense charged." Goldstein & Katz, *Abolish the "Insanity Defense"— Why Not?*, 72 Yale L.J. 853, 864 (1963). That is,

the defense is seen as a device whereby certain persons are singled out for commitment, not as an alternative to conviction and imprisonment, but rather as an alternative to outright acquittal. This characterization takes on greater force in those jurisdictions where, as discussed in Section 4 of this Chapter, the courts have declined to admit evidence of mental disease on the issue of whether the defendant had the mental state required for commission of the crime charged.

(c) adoption of the "product" or *Durham* test, used in the District of Columbia until abandoned in *United States v. Brawner,* infra;

(d) adoption of the Model Penal Code "substantial capacity" test (currently used in nearly half of the states), discussed in *Brawner,* infra;

(e) adoption of the "justice" approach of Judge Bazelon, dissenting in *Brawner,* infra; or

(f) abolition of the insanity defense, discussed in *Brawner,* infra.

DANIEL M'NAGHTEN'S CASE

House of Lords, 1843.
8 Eng.Rep. 718, 10 Cl. & Fin. 200.

[Daniel M'Naghten shot and killed Edward Drummond, private secretary to Sir Robert Peel. M'Naghten, believing that Peel was heading a conspiracy to kill him, had intended to take Peel's life, but he instead shot Drummond because he mistakenly believed him to be Peel. At the trial of his case, M'Naghten claimed that he was insane and could not be held responsible because it had been his delusions which caused him to act. The jury agreed, and M'Naghten was found not guilty by reason of insanity. Due to the importance of both the victim and the intended victim, the decision was not a popular one. The House of Lords debated the decision and posed five questions concerning the standards for acquitting a defendant due to his insanity to the justices of the Queen's Bench. The answers to these questions were appended to the report of the original case, and have come to be considered as if they were a part of that decision.]

LORD CHIEF JUSTICE TINDAL:

* * *

The first question proposed by your Lordships is this: "What is the law respecting alleged crimes committed by persons afflicted with insane delusion in respect of one or more particular subjects or persons: as, for instance, where at the time of the commission of the alleged crime the accused knew he was acting contrary to law, but did the act complained of with a view, under the influence of insane delusion, of redressing or revenging some supposed grievance or injury, or of producing some supposed public benefit?"

In answer to which question, assuming that your Lordships' inquiries are confined to those persons who labour under such partial delusions only, and are not in other respects insane, we are of opinion that, notwithstanding the party accused did the act complained of with a view, under the influence of insane delusion, of redressing or revenging some supposed grievance or injury, or of producing some public benefit, he is nevertheless punishable according to the nature of the crime committed, if he knew at the time of committing such crime that he was acting contrary to law; by which expression we understand your Lordships to mean the law of the land.

Your Lordships are pleased to inquire of us, secondly, "What are the proper questions to be submitted to the jury, where a person alleged to be afflicted with insane delusion respecting one or more particular subjects or persons, is charged with the commission of a crime (murder, for example), and insanity is set up as a defence?" And, thirdly, "In what terms ought the question to be left to the jury as to the prisoner's state of mind at the time when the act was committed?" And as these two questions appear to us to be more conveniently answered together, we have to submit our opinion to be, that the jurors ought to be told in all cases that every man is to be presumed to be sane, and to possess a sufficient degree of reason to be responsible for his crimes, until the contrary be proved to their satisfaction; and that to establish a defence on the ground of insanity, it must be clearly proved that, at the time of the committing of the act, the party accused was labouring under such a defect of reason, from disease of the mind, as not to know the nature and quality of the act he was doing; or, if he did know it, that he did not know he was doing what was wrong. The mode of putting the latter part of the question to the jury on these occasions has generally been, whether the accused at the time of doing the act knew the difference between right and wrong: which mode, though rarely, if ever, leading to any mistake with the jury, is not, as we conceive, so accurate when put generally and in the abstract, as when put with reference to the party's knowledge of right and wrong in respect to the very act with which he is charged. If the question were to be put as to the knowledge of the accused solely and exclusively with reference to the law of the land, it might tend to confound the jury, by inducing them to believe that an actual knowledge of the law of the land was essential in order to lead to a conviction; whereas the law is administered upon the principle that every one must be taken conclusively to know it, without proof that he does know it. If the accused was conscious that the act was one which he ought not to do, and if that act was at the same time contrary to the law of the land, he is punishable; and the usual course therefore has been to leave the question to the jury, whether the party accused had a sufficient degree of reason to know that he was doing an act that was wrong: and this course we think is correct, accompanied with such observations and explanations as the circumstances of each particular case may require.

The fourth question which your Lordships have proposed to us is this:—"If a person under an insane delusion as to existing facts, commits an offence in consequence thereof, is he thereby excused?" To which question the answer must of course depend on the nature of the delusion: but, making the same assumption as we did before, namely, that he labours under such partial delusion only, and is not in other respects insane, we think he must be considered in the same situation as to responsibility as if the facts with respect to which the delusion exists were real. For example, if under the influence of his delusion he supposes another man to be in the act of attempting to take away his life, and he kills that man, as he supposes, in self-defense, he would be exempt from punishment. If his delusion was that the deceased had inflicted a serious injury to his character and fortune, and he killed him in revenge for such supposed injury, he would be liable to punishment.

The question lastly proposed by your Lordships is:—"Can a medical man conversant with the disease of insanity, who never saw the prisoner previously to the trial, but who was present during the whole trial and the examination of all the witnesses, be asked his opinion as to the state of the prisoner's mind at the time of the commission of the alleged crime, or his opinion whether the prisoner was conscious at the time of doing the act that he was acting contrary to law, or whether he was labouring under any and what delusion at the time?" In answer thereto, we state to your Lordships, that we think the medical man, under the circumstances supposed, cannot in strictness be asked his opinion in the terms above stated, because each of those questions involves the determination of the truth of the facts deposed to, which it is for the jury to decide, and the questions are not mere questions upon a matter of science, in which case such evidence is admissible. But where the facts are admitted or not disputed, and the question becomes substantially one of science only, it may be convenient to allow the question to be put in that general form, though the same cannot be insisted on as a matter of right.

Notes and Questions

1. In *State v. Coombs,* 18 Ohio St.3d 123, 480 N.E.2d 414 (1985), the trial court in a nonjury trial asked defendant's expert witness whether the defendant's disorder could be characterized as either a psychosis or a neurosis. The doctor answered in the negative. At the conclusion of the trial, the judge said a *M'Naghten–* type insanity defense had not been established, adding that the "defendant, whatever his emotional problems are, and were on that night, does not have a psychosis or even a neurosis by the testimony of his own expert witness." The supreme court responded that the "law of this state does not require such a showing," but concluded the trial judge had not actually utilized such a limited standard.

2. In *People v. Skinner,* 39 Cal.3d 765, 217 Cal.Rptr. 685, 704 P.2d 752 (1985), the court held that where the defendant murdered his wife believing that the marriage view "till death do us part" bestowed on a marital partner a God-given right to kill the other partner if he or she was inclined to violate the marital vows, he could not distinguish right from wrong under the *M'Naghten* test: "Courts in a number of jurisdictions which have considered the question have come to the conclusion as we do, that a defendant who is incapable of understanding that his act is morally wrong is not criminally liable merely because he knows the act is unlawful. Justice Cardozo, in an opinion for the New York Court of Appeal, eloquently expressed the underlying philosophy: 'In the light of all these precedents, it is im-

possible, we think, to say that there is any decisive adjudication which limits the word "wrong" in the statutory definition to legal as opposed to moral wrong * * *. The interpretation placed upon the statute by the trial judge may be tested by its consequences. A mother kills her infant child to whom she has been devotedly attached. She knows the nature and quality of the act; she knows that the law condemns it; but she is inspired by an insane delusion that God has appeared to her and ordained the sacrifice. *It seems a mockery to say that, within the meaning of the statute, she knows that the act is wrong.* If the definition propounded by the trial judge is right, it would be the duty of a jury to hold her responsible for the crime. We find nothing either in the history of the rule, or in its reason or purpose, or in judicial exposition of its meaning, to justify a conclusion so abhorrent * * *. [¶] Knowledge that an act is forbidden by law will in most cases permit the inference of knowledge that, according to the accepted standards of mankind, it is also condemned as an offense against good morals. Obedience to the law is itself a moral duty. If, however, there is an insane delusion that God has appeared to the defendant and ordained the commission of a crime, we think it cannot be said of the offender that he knows the act to be wrong.' (*People v. Schmidt* (1915) 216 N.Y. 324, 338–340 [110 N.E. 945, 949–950], emphasis added.) [16]"

3. Compare *State v. Boan,* 235 Kan. 800, 686 P.2d 160 (1984), also a murder case, where defendant's experts testified that Boan had a feeling of being God or a

---

16. Justice Cardozo's opinion continued: "It is not enough, to relieve from criminal liability, that the prisoner is morally depraved [citation]. It is not enough that he has views of right and wrong at variance with those that find expression in the law. The variance must have its origin in some disease of the mind [citation]. The anarchist is not at liberty to break the law because he reasons that all government is wrong. The devotee of a religious cult that enjoins polygamy or

human sacrifice as a duty is not thereby relieved from responsibility before the law [citations]. In such cases the belief, however false according to our own standards, is not the product of disease. Cases will doubtless arise where criminals will take shelter behind a professed belief that their crime was ordained by God, just as this defendant attempted to shelter himself behind that belief. We can safely leave such fabrications to the common sense of juries."

representative of God, who was present at the Last Supper, and that he believed other persons were in his body trying to displace him, requiring him to defend himself in the fashion he did from "salvation level attacks." They said defendant was aware of the laws of the state and that it was wrong to shoot someone, but that because of his "religious delusion" he "modified the definition of what was right, according to his belief that he, as God, made the rights." In affirming Boan's murder conviction, the court upheld this instruction: "Right and wrong are used here in their legal sense, not the social or moral sense. 'Wrong' means that which is prohibited by law."

4. A seminal case adding the so-called "irresistible impulse" test to *M'Naghten* (as some jurisdictions have done) is *Parsons v. State,* 81 Ala. 577, 2 So. 854 (1887):

"We first consider what is *the proper legal rule of responsibility in criminal cases.* No one can deny that there must be two constituent elements of legal responsibility in the commission of every crime, and no rule can be just and reasonable which fails to recognize either of them: (1) Capacity of intellectual discrimination; and (2) freedom of will. Mr. Wharton, after recognizing this fundamental and obvious principle, observes: 'If there be either incapacity to distinguish between right and wrong as to the particular act, or delusion as to the act, or inability to refrain from doing the act, there is no responsibility.' I Whart. *Crim.Law* (9th Ed.) § 33. Says Mr. Bishop, in discussing this subject: 'There cannot be, and there is not, in any locality, or age, a law punishing men for what they cannot avoid.' 1 Bish. *Crim.Law* (7th Ed.) § 383b. If therefore, it be true, as matter of fact, that the disease of insanity can, in its action on the human brain through a shattered nervous organization, or in any other mode, so affect the mind as to subvert the freedom of the will, and thereby destroy the power of the victim *to choose*

between the right and wrong, although he perceive it,—by which we mean the power of volition to adhere in action to the right and abstain from the wrong—is such a one criminally responsible for an act done under the influence of such controlling disease? We clearly think not, and such we believe to be the just, reasonable, and humane rule, towards which all the modern authorities in this country, legislation in England, and the laws of other civilized countries of the world, are gradually but surely tending, as we shall further on attempt more fully to show. * * *

"In the present state of our law, under the rule in *M'Naghten's Case,* we are confronted with this practical difficulty, which itself demonstrates the defects of the rule. The courts, in effect charge the juries, as matter of law, that no such mental disease exists, as that often testified to by medical writers, superintendents of insane hospitals, and other experts; that there can be, as matter of scientific fact, no cerebral defect, congenital or acquired, which destroys the patient's power of self control,— his liberty of will and action,—provided only he retains a mental consciousness of right and wrong. The experts are immediately put under oath, and tell the juries just the contrary, as matter of evidence; asserting that no one of ordinary intelligence can spend an hour in the wards of an insane asylum without discovering such cases, and in fact that 'the whole management of such asylums presupposes a knowledge of right and wrong on the part of their inmates.' * * *

"In the learned treatise of Drs. Bucknill and Tuke on *Psychological Medicine,* 269, (4th Ed., London, 1879), the legal tests of responsibility are discussed, and the adherence of the courts to the right and wrong test is deplored as unfortunate, the true principle being stated to be 'whether, in consequence of congenital defect or acquired disease, *the power of self-control* is absent altogether, or is so far wanting as to render the individual irresponsible.'

* * *

"It is no satisfactory objection to say that the rule above announced by us is of difficult application. The rule in *McNaghten's Case* is equally obnoxious to a like criticism. The difficulty does not lie in the rule, but is inherent in the subject of insanity itself. * * * We think we can safely rely in this matter upon the intelligence of our juries, guided by the testimony of men who have practically made a study of the disease of insanity; and enlightened by a conscientious desire, on the one hand, to enforce the criminal laws of the land, and, on the other, not to deal harshly with any unfortunate victim of a diseased mind, acting without the light of reason or the power of volition. * * *

"In conclusion of this branch of the subject, that we may not be misunderstood, we think it follows very clearly from what we have said that the inquiries to be submitted to the jury, then, in every criminal trial where the defense of insanity is interposed, are these: *First.* Was the defendant at the time of the commission of the alleged crime, as matter of fact, afflicted with a *disease of the mind,* so as to be either idiotic, or otherwise insane? *Second.* If such be the case, did he know right from wrong as applied to the particular act in question? If he did not have such knowledge, he is not legally responsible. *Third.* If he did have such knowledge, he may nevertheless not be legally responsible if the two following conditions concur: (1) If, by reason of the duress of such mental disease, he had so far lost the *power to choose* between the right and wrong, and to avoid doing the act in question, as that his free agency was at the time destroyed; (2) and if, at the same time, the alleged crime was so connected with such mental disease, in the relation of cause and effect, as to have been the product of it *solely.*"

UNITED STATES v. BRAWNER

United States Court of Appeals, District of Columbia Circuit, 1972.
471 F.2d 969.

LEVENTHAL, CIRCUIT JUDGE:

The principal issues raised on this appeal from a conviction for second degree murder and carrying a dangerous weapon relate to appellant's defense of insanity. After the case was argued to a division of the court, the court *sua sponte* ordered rehearing en banc * * * to reconsider the appropriate standard for the insanity defense * * *.

We have stretched our canvas wide; and the focal point of the landscape before us is the formulation of the American Law Institute. The ALI's primary provision is stated thus in its Model Penal Code, see § 4.01(1).

Section 4.01 Mental Disease or Defect Excluding Responsibility.

(1) A person is not responsible for criminal conduct if at the time of such conduct as a result of mental disease or defect he lacks substantial capacity either to appreciate the criminality [wrongfulness] of his conduct or to conform his conduct to the requirements of the law.

We have decided to adopt the ALI rule as the doctrine excluding responsibility for mental disease or defect, for application prospectively to trials begun after this date. * * *

B. PRIOR DEVELOPMENTS OF THE INSANITY DEFENSE IN THIS JURISDICTION * * *

1. The landmark opinion was written by Judge Bazelon in *Durham v. United States,* 94 U.S.App.D.C. 228, 214 F.2d 862 (1954). Prior to *Durham* the law of the District of Columbia * * * stated a traditional test of insanity, in terms of right and wrong and irresistible impulse. *Durham* adopted the "product rule," pioneered in *State v. Pike,* 49 N.H. 399, 402

(1869–70), and exculpated from criminal responsibility those whose forbidden acts were the product of a mental disease or defect.

Few cases have evoked as much comment as *Durham*. It has sparked widespread interest in the legal-judicial community and focused attention on the profound problems involved in defining legal responsibility in case of mental illness. It has been hailed as a guide to the difficult and problem-laden intersection of law and psychiatry, ethics and science. It has been scored as an unwarranted loophole through which the cunning criminal might escape from the penalty of the law. We view it more modestly, as the court's effort, designed in the immemorial manner of the case method that has built the common law, to alleviate two serious problems with the previous rule.

The first of these was a problem of language which raised an important symbolic issue in the law. We felt that the language of the old right-wrong/irresistible impulse rule for insanity was antiquated, no longer reflecting the community's judgment as to who ought to be held criminally liable for socially destructive acts. We considered the rule as restated to have more fruitful, accurate and considered reflection of the sensibilities of the community as revised and expanded in the light of continued study of abnormal human behavior.

The second vexing problem that *Durham* was designed to reach related to the concern of the psychiatrists called as expert witnesses for their special knowledge of the problem of insanity, who often and typically felt that they were obliged to reach outside of their professional expertise when they were asked, under the traditional insanity rule established in 1843 by *M'Naghten's* Case, whether the

defendant knew right from wrong. They further felt that the narrowness of the traditional test, which framed the issue of responsibility solely in terms of cognitive impairment, made it impossible to convey to the judge and jury the full range of information material to an assessment of defendant's responsibility.

2. Discerning scholarship now available asserts that the experts' fears and concerns reflected a misapprehension as to the impact of the traditional standard in terms of excluding relevant evidence.

> Wigmore states the rule to be that when insanity is in issue, "any and all conduct of the person is admissible in evidence." And the cases support Wigmore's view. The almost unvarying policy of the courts has been to admit *any* evidence of abberational behavior so long as it is probative of the defendant's mental condition, without regard to the supposed restrictions of the test used to define insanity for the jury.[5]

Moreover if the term "know" in the traditional test of "know right from wrong" is taken as denoting affective knowledge, rather than merely cognitive knowledge, it yields a rule of greater flexibility than was widely supposed to exist. Livermore and Meehl, *The Virtues of M'Naghten,* 51 Minn. L.Rev. 789, 800–08 (1967).

We need not occupy ourselves here and now with the question whether, and to what extent, the *M'Naghten* rule, ameliorated by the irresistible impulse doctrine, is susceptible of application to include medical insights and information as justice requires. In any event, the experts felt hemmed in by the traditional test; they felt that they could not give the jury and judge the necessary information in response to the questions which the traditional test posed.

---

5. A. Goldstein, *The Insanity Defense* 54 (1967).

The rule as reformulated in *Durham* permitted medical experts to testify on medical matters properly put before the jury for its consideration, and to do so without the confusion that many, perhaps most, experts experienced from testimony structured under the *M'Naghten* rule. That was a positive contribution to jurisprudence—and one that was retained when the American Law Institute undertook to analyze the problem and proposed a different formulation.

3. A difficulty arose under the *Durham* rule in application [because] the court failed to explicate what abnormality of mind was an essential ingredient of these concepts. In the absence of a definition of "mental disease or defect," medical experts attached to them the meanings which would naturally occur to them—medical meanings—and gave testimony accordingly. The problem was dramatically highlighted by the weekend flip flop case, *In re Rosenfield,* 157 F.Supp. 18 (D.D.C.1957). The petitioner was described as a sociopath. A St. Elizabeths psychiatrist testified that a person with a sociopathic personality was not suffering from a mental disease. That was Friday afternoon. On Monday morning, through a policy change at St. Elizabeths Hospital, it was determined as an administrative matter that the state of a psychopathic or sociopathic personality did constitute a mental disease.

The concern that medical terminology not control legal outcomes culminated in *McDonald v. United States,* 114 U.S.App. D.C. 120, 321 F.2d 847, 851 (en banc, 1962), where this court recognized that the term, mental disease or defect, has various meanings, depending upon how and why it is used, and by whom. Mental disease means one thing to a physician bent on treatment, but something different, if somewhat overlapping, to a court of law. We provided a legal definition of mental disease or defect, and held that it included "any abnormal condition of the mind which substantially affects mental or emotional processes and substantially impairs behavior controls." "Thus the jury would consider testimony concerning the development, adaptation and functioning of these processes and controls."

While the *McDonald* standard of mental disease was not without an attribute of circularity, it was useful in the administration of justice because it made plain that clinical and legal definitions of mental disease were distinct, and it helped the jury to sort out its complex task and to focus on the matters given it to decide.

4. The *Durham* rule also required explication along other lines, notably the resolution of the ambiguity inherent in the formulation concerning actions that were the "product" of mental illness. It was supplemented in *Carter v. United States,* 102 U.S.App.D.C. 227 at 234, 235, 252 F.2d 608 at 615–616 (1957):

The simple fact that a person has a mental disease or defect is not enough to relieve him of responsibility for a crime. There must be a relationship between the disease and the criminal act; and the relationship must be such as to justify a reasonable inference that the act would not have been committed if the person had not been suffering from the disease.

Thus *Carter* clarified that the mental illness must not merely have entered into the production of the act, but must have played a necessary role. *Carter* identified the "product" element of the rule with the "but for" variety of causation.

The pivotal "product" term continued to present problems, principally that it put expert testimony on a faulty footing. Assuming that a mental disease, in the legal sense, had been established, the fate of the defendant came to be determined by what came to be referred to by the legal jargon of "productivity." On the other hand, it was obviously sensible if not imperative that the experts having pertinent knowledge should speak to the crucial question whether the mental abnormality involved is one associated with aberrant behavior. But since "productivity" was so decisive a factor in the decisional equation, a ruling permitting experts to testify expressly in language of "product" raised in a different context the concern lest the ultimate issue be in fact turned over to the experts rather than retained for the jurors representing the community. * * *

It was in this context that the court came to the decision in *Washington v. United States,* 129 U.S.App.D.C. 29, 390 F.2d 444 (1967), which forbade experts from testifying as to productivity altogether. Chief Judge Bazelon's opinion illuminates the basis of the ruling, as one intended "to help the psychiatrists understand their role in court, and thus eliminate a fundamental cause of unsatisfactory expert testimony," namely, the tendency of the expert to use "concepts [which] can become slogans, hiding facts and representing nothing more than the witness's own conclusion about the defendant's criminal responsibility." * * *

C. INSANITY RULE IN OTHER CIRCUITS * * *

The core rule of the ALI has been adopted, with variations, by all save one of the Federal circuit courts of appeals, and by all that have come to reconsider the doctrine providing exculpation for mental illness. * * *

D. COMMENTS CONCERNING REASON FOR ADOPTION OF ALI RULE AND SCOPE OF RULE AS ADOPTED BY THIS COURT * * *

1. Need to depart from "product" formulation and undue dominance by experts.

A principal reason for our decision to depart from the *Durham* rule is the undesirable characteristic, surviving even the

McDonald modification, of undue dominance by the experts giving testimony.

* * *

The expert witnesses—psychiatrists and psychologists—are called to adduce relevant information concerning what may for convenience be referred to as the "medical" component of the responsibility issue. But the difficulty—as emphasized in *Washington*—is that the medical expert comes, by testimony given in terms of a non-medical construct ("product"), to express conclusions that in essence embody ethical and legal conclusions. There is, indeed, irony in a situation under which the *Durham* rule, which was adopted in large part to permit experts to testify in their own terms concerning matters within their domain which the jury should know, resulted in testimony by the experts in terms not their own to reflect unexpressed judgments in a domain that is properly not theirs but the jury's. The irony is heightened when the jurymen, instructed under the esoteric "product" standard, are influenced significantly by "product" testimony of expert witnesses really reflecting ethical and legal judgments rather than a conclusion within the witnesses' particular expertise.

It is easier to identify and spotlight the irony than to eradicate the mischief. The objective of *Durham* is still sound—to put before the jury the information that is within the expert's domain, to aid the jury in making a broad and comprehensive judgment. But when the instructions and appellate decisions define the "product" inquiry as the ultimate issue, it is like stopping the tides to try to halt the emergence of this term in the language of those with a central role in the trial—the lawyers who naturally seek to present testimony that will influence the jury who will be charged under the ultimate "product" standard, and the expert witnesses who have an awareness, gained from forensic psychiatry and related disciplines, of the ultimate "product" standard that dominates the proceeding.

The experts have meaningful information to impart, not only on the existence of mental illness or not, but also on its relationship to the incident charged as an offense. In the interest of justice this valued information should be available, and should not be lost or blocked by requirements that unnaturally restrict communication between the experts and the jury. The more we have pondered the problem the more convinced we have become that the sound solution lies not in further shaping of the *Durham* "product" approach in more refined molds, but in adopting the ALI's formulation as the linchpin of our jurisprudence.

The ALI's formulation retains the core requirement of a meaningful relationship between the mental illness and the incident charged. The language in the ALI rule is sufficiently in the common ken that its use in the courtroom, or in preparation for trial, permits a reasonable three-way communication—between (a) the law-trained, judges and lawyers; (b) the experts and (c) the jurymen—without insisting on a vocabulary that is either stilted or stultified, or conducive to a testimonial mystique permitting expert dominance and encroachment on the jury's function. There is no indication in the available literature that any such untoward development has attended the reasonably widespread adoption of the ALI rule in the Federal courts and a substantial number of state courts.

2. Retention of McDonald definition of "mental disease or defect."

Our ruling today includes our decision that in the ALI rule as adopted by this court the term "mental disease or defect" includes the definition of that term provided in our 1962 en banc *McDonald* opinion, as follows:

[A] mental disease or defect includes any abnormal condition of the mind which substantially affects mental or emotional processes and substantially impairs behavior controls. * * *

The *McDonald* rule has helped accomplish the objective of securing expert testimony needed on the subject of mental illness, while guarding against the undue dominance of expert testimony or specialized labels. It has thus permitted the kind of communication without encroachment, as between experts and juries, that has prompted us to adopt the ALI rule, and hence will help us realize our objective. This advantage overrides the surface disadvantage of any clumsiness in the blending of the *McDonald* component, defining mental disease, with the rest of the ALI rule, a matter we discuss further below. * * *

4. Consideration and rejection of other suggestions.

a. Proposal to abolish insanity defense.

A number of proposals in the journals recommend that the insanity defense be abolished altogether. * * *

This proposal has been put forward by responsible judges for consideration, with the objective of reserving psychiatric overview for the phase of the criminal process concerned with disposition of the person determined to have been the actor. However, we are convinced that the proposal cannot properly be imposed by judicial fiat.

The courts have emphasized over the centuries that "free will" is the postulate of responsibility under our jurisprudence. 4 Blackstone's *Commentaries* 27. The concept of "belief in freedom of the human will and a consequent ability and duty of the normal individual to choose between good and evil" is a core concept that is "universal and persistent in mature systems of law." *Morissette v. United States,* 342

U.S. 246, 250, 72 S.Ct. 240, 243, 96 L.Ed. 288 (1952). Criminal responsibility is assessed when through "free will" a man elects to do evil. And while, as noted in *Morissette,* the legislature has dispensed with mental element in some statutory offenses, in furtherance of a paramount need of the community, these instances mark the exception and not the rule, and only in the most limited instances has the mental element been omitted by the legislature as a requisite for an offense that was a crime at common law.

The concept of lack of "free will" is both the root of origin of the insanity defense and the line of its growth. This cherished principle is not undercut by difficulties, or differences of view, as to how best to express the free will concept in the light of the expansion of medical knowledge. We do not concur in the view of the National District Attorneys Association that the insanity defense should be abandoned judicially, either because it is at too great a variance with popular conceptions of guilt or fails "to show proper respect for the personality of the criminal [who] is liable to resent pathology more than punishment."

These concepts may be measured along with other ingredients in a legislative reexamination of settled doctrines of criminal responsibility, root, stock and branch. Such a reassessment, one that seeks to probe and appraise the society's processes and values, is for the legislative branch, assuming no constitutional bar. The judicial role is limited, in Justice Holmes's figure, to action that is molecular, with the restraint inherent in taking relatively small steps, leaving to the other branches of government whatever progress must be made with seven-league leaps. Such judicial restraint is particularly necessary when a proposal requires, as a mandatory ingredient, the kind of devotion of resources, personnel and techniques that can be accomplished only through whole-hearted legislative commitment. * * *

b. Proposal for defense if mental disease impairs capacity to such an extent that the defendant cannot "justly be held responsible."

We have also pondered the suggestion that the jury be instructed that the defendant lacks criminal responsibility if the jury finds that the defendant's mental disease impairs his capacity or controls to such an extent that he cannot "justly be held responsible."

This was the view of a British commission,[23] adapted and proposed in 1955 by Professor Wechsler, the distinguished Reporter for the ALI's Model Penal Code, and sustained by some, albeit a minority, of the members of the ALI's Council.[24] In the ALI, the contrary view prevailed because of a concern over presenting to the jury questions put primarily in the form of "justice."

The proposal is not to be condemned out of hand as a suggestion that the jury be informed of an absolute prerogative that it can only exercise by flatly disregarding the applicable rule of law. It is rather a suggestion that the jury be informed of the matters the law contemplates it will take into account in arriving at the com-

---

23. In 1953 the British Royal Commission on Capital Punishment proposed:

[A person is not responsible for his unlawful act if] at the time of the act the accused was suffering from disease of the mind (or mental deficiency) *to such a degree that he ought not to be held responsible.*

24. The minority, together with the Reporter for the Model Penal Code (Professor Herbert Wechsler), proposed the following test of insanity:

A person is not responsible for criminal conduct if at the time of such conduct as a result of mental disease or defect his capacity either to appreciate the criminality of his conduct or to conform his conduct to the requirements of law is *so substantially impaired that he cannot justly be held responsible.*

This proposal appears as alternative (a) to paragraph (1) of *Model Penal Code* § 4.01 (Tent.Draft No. 4, 1955) (emphasis added).

munity judgment concerning a composite of factors.

However, there is a substantial concern that an instruction overtly cast in terms of "justice" cannot feasibly be restricted to the ambit of what may properly be taken into account but will splash with unconfinable and malign consequences. The Government cautions that "explicit appeals to 'justice' will result in litigation of extraneous issues and will encourage improper arguments to the jury phrased solely in terms of 'sympathy' and 'prejudice.'"

Nor is this solely a prosecutor's concern.

Mr. Flynn, counsel appointed to represent defendant, puts it that even though the jury is applying community concepts of blameworthiness "the jury should not be left at large, or asked to find out for itself what those concepts are."

The amicus submission of the Public Defender Service argues that it would be beneficial to focus the jury's attention on the moral and legal questions intertwined in the insanity defense. It expresses concern, however, over a blameworthiness instruction without more, saying "it may well be that the 'average' American condemns the mentally ill." It would apparently accept an approach not unlike that proposed by the ALI Reporter, under which the justice standard is coupled with a direction to consider the individual's capacity to control his behavior. Mr. Dempsey's recommendation is of like import, with some simplification.[27] But the problem remains, whether, assuming justice calls for the exculpation and treatment of the mentally ill, that is more likely to be gained from a jury, with "average" no-

tions of mental illness, which is explicitly set at large to convict or acquit persons with impaired mental capacity according to its concept of justice.

The brief of the D.C. Bar Association as amicus submits that with a "justly responsible" formulation the test of insanity "would be largely swallowed up by this consideration." And it observes that the function of giving to the jury the law to be applied to the facts is not only the duty of the court, but is also "a bedrock right of every citizen"—and, possibly, his "only protection."

We are impressed by the observation of Professor Abraham S. Goldstein, one of the most careful students of the problem:

> [The] overly general standard may place too great a burden upon the jury. If the law provides no standard, members of the jury are placed in the difficult position of having to find a man responsible for no other reason than their personal feeling about him. Whether the psyches of individual jurors are strong enough to make that decision, or whether the "law" should put that obligation on them, is open to serious question. It is far easier for them to perform the role assigned to them by legislature and courts if they know—or are able to rationalize—that their verdicts are "required" by law.[28]

Professor Goldstein was referring to the broad "justice" standard recommended by the Royal Commission. But the problems remain acute even with the modifications in the proposal of the ALI Reporter, for that still leads to "justly responsible" as the ultimate and critical term. * * *

---

27. He proposes an instruction with this crucial sentence: "It is up to you to decide whether defendant had such an abnormal mental condition, and if he did whether the impairment was substantial enough, and was so related to the

commission of the crime, *that he ought not to be held responsible.*" (Emphasis added.)

28. A. Goldstein, *The Insanity Defense* 81–82 (1967).

6. *Elements of the ALI rule adopted by this court ✱ ✱ ✱.*

a. *Intermesh of components.*

The first component of our rule, derived from *McDonald,* defines mental disease or defect as an abnormal condition of the mind, and a condition which substantially (a) affects mental or emotional processes and (b) impairs behavioral controls. The second component, derived from the Model Penal Code, tells which defendant with a mental disease lacks criminal responsibility for particular conduct: it is the defendant who, as a result of this mental condition, at the time of such conduct, either (i) lacks substantial capacity to appreciate that his conduct is wrongful, or (ii) lacks substantial capacity to conform his conduct to the law.

The first component establishes eligibility for an instruction concerning the defense for a defendant who presents evidence that his abnormal condition of the mind has substantially impaired behavioral controls. The second component completes the instruction and defines the ultimate issue, of exculpation, in terms of whether his behavioral controls were not only substantially impaired but impaired to such an extent that he lacked substantial capacity to conform his conduct to the law.[39]

b. *The "result" of the mental disease.*

The rule contains a requirement of causality, as is clear from the term "result." Exculpation is established not by mental disease alone but only if "as a result" defendant lacks the substantial capacity required for responsibility. Presumably the mental disease of a kleptomaniac does not entail as a "result" a lack of capacity to conform to the law prohibiting rape.

c. *At the time of the conduct.*

Under the ALI rule the issue is not whether defendant is so disoriented or void of controls that he is never able to conform to external demands, but whether he had that capacity at the time of the conduct. The question is not properly put in terms of whether he would have capacity to conform in some untypical restraining situation—as with an attendant or policeman at his elbow. The issue is whether he was able to conform in the unstructured condition of life in an open society, and whether the result of his abnormal mental condition was a lack of substantial internal controls. ✱ ✱ ✱

d. *Capacity to appreciate wrongfulness of his conduct.*

As to the option of terminology noted in the ALI code, we adopt the formulation that exculpates a defendant whose mental condition is such that he lacks substantial capacity to appreciate the wrongfulness of his conduct. We prefer this on pragmatic grounds to "appreciate the criminality of his conduct" since the resulting jury instruction is more like that conventionally given to and applied by the jury. While such an instruction is of course subject to the objection that it lacks complete precision, it serves the objective of calling on the jury to provide a community judgment on a combination of factors. And since the possibility of analytical differences between the two formulations is insubstantial in fact in view of the control capacity test, we are usefully guided by the pragmatic considerations pertinent to jury instructions.[40] ✱ ✱ ✱

---

39. Defendant is also exculpated if he lacks substantial capacity to appreciate the conduct is wrongful.

40. In *M'Naghten's* case, 10 Cl. & F. 200, 211, 8 Eng.Rep. 718, 722 (H.L.1843), the majority opinion of Lord Chief Justice Tindal ruled that the jury should be instructed in terms of the ability of the accused "to know that he was doing an act that was wrong," adding: "If the question were to be put as to the knowledge of the accused solely and exclusively with reference to the law of the land, it might tend to confound the jury, by inducing them to believe that an actual knowl-

e. Caveat paragraph.

Section 4.01 of the Model Penal Code as promulgated by ALI contains in subsection (2) what has come to be known as the "caveat paragraph":

> (2) The terms "mental disease or defect" do not include an abnormality manifested only by repeated criminal or otherwise anti-social conduct.

The purpose of this provision was to exclude a defense for the so-called "psychopathic personality." [41]

There has been a split in the Federal circuits concerning this provision. Some of the courts adopting the ALI rule refer to both subsections but without separate discussion of the caveat paragraph. As to the decisions considering the point, those of the Second and Third Circuits conclude the paragraph should be retained while the decisions, of the Sixth and Ninth Circuits, conclude it should be omitted. The Sixth

Circuit's position is (404 F.2d at 727, fn. 8) that there is "great dispute over the psychiatric soundness" of the caveat paragraph. The *Wade* opinion considers the matter at great length and puts forward three grounds for rejecting the caveat paragraph: (1) As a practical matter, it would be ineffectual in keeping sociopaths out of the definition of insanity; it is always possible to introduce some evidence, other than past criminal behavior, to support a plea of insanity. (2) The criminal sanction ought not be sought for criminal psychopaths—constant recidivists—because such people should be taken off the streets indefinitely, and not merely for a set term of years. (3) Its third ground is stated thus (426 F.2d at 73):

> It is unclear whether [the caveat paragraph] would require that a defendant be considered legally sane if, although the only overt acts manifesting his disease or defect were "criminal or other-

---

edge of the law of the land was essential in order to lead to a conviction."

When the question arose as to whether "wrong" means moral or legal wrong, the American courts split. One group, following *M'Naghten*, held the offender sane if he knew the act was prohibited by law. A second group, following the lead of Judge Cardozo in *People v. Schmidt*, 216 N.Y. 324, 110 N.E. 945, 948–950 (1915) ruled that, e.g., the defense was available to a defendant who knew the killing was legally wrong but thought it morally right because he was so ordered by God. The issue is discussed and authorities collected in A. Goldstein, *The Insanity Defense*, and notes thereto. In *Sauer v. United States*, 241 F.2d 640, 649 (9th Cir.1957), Judge Barnes summed up the practicalities: "[The] practice has been to state merely the word 'wrong' and leave the decision for the jury. While not entirely condonable, such practice is explained in large measure by an awareness that the jury will eventually exercise a moral judgment as to the sanity of the accused."

This issue rarely arose under *M'Naghten*, and its substantiality was reduced if not removed by the control capacity test, since anyone under a delusion as to God's mandate would presumably lack substantial capacity to conform his conduct to the requirements of the law.

We are not informed of any case where a mental illness left a person with capacity to ap-

preciate wrongfulness but not a capacity to appreciate criminality. If such a case ever arises, supported by credible evidence, the court can then consider its correct disposition more meaningfully, in the light of a concrete record.

41. See Comments to Fourth Draft, p. 160:

6. Paragraph (2) of section 4.01 is designed to exclude from the concept of "mental disease or defect" the case of so-called "psychopathic personality." The reason for the exclusion is that, as the Royal Commission put it, psychopathy "is a statistical abnormality; that is to say, the psychopath differs from a normal person only quantitatively or in degree, not qualitatively; and the diagnosis of psychopathic personality does not carry with it any explanation of the causes of the abnormality." While it may not be feasible to formulate a definition of "disease," there is much to be said for excluding a condition that is manifested only by the behavior phenomena that must, by hypothesis, be the result of disease for irresponsibility to be established. Although British psychiatrists had agreed, on the whole, that psychopathy should not be called "disease," there is considerable difference of opinion on the point in the United States. Yet it does not seem useful to contemplate the litigation of what is essentially a matter of terminology; nor is it right to have the legal result rest upon the resolution of a dispute of this kind.

wise anti-social," there arises from his acts a reasonable inference of mental derangement either because of the nature of the acts or because of credible medical or other evidence.

Our own approach is influenced by the fact that our rule already includes a definition of mental disease (from *McDonald*). Under that definition, as we have pointed out, the mere existence of "a long criminal record does not excuse crime." We do not require the caveat paragraph as an insurance against exculpation of the deliberate and persistent offender.[42] Our *McDonald* rule guards against the danger of misunderstanding and injustice that might arise, say, from an expert's classification that reflects only a conception defining all criminality as reflective of mental illness. There must be testimony to show both that the defendant was suffering from an abnormal condition of the mind and that it substantially affected mental or emotional processes and substantially impaired behavioral controls.

In this context, our pragmatic approach is to adopt the caveat paragraph as a rule for application by the judge, to avoid miscarriage of justice, but not for inclusion in instructions to the jury.

The judge will be aware that the criminal and antisocial conduct of a person—on the street, in the home, in the ward—is necessarily material information for assessment by the psychiatrist. On the other hand, rarely if ever would a psychiatrist base a conclusion of mental disease solely on criminal and anti-social acts. Our pragmatic solution provides for reshaping the rule, for application by the court, as follows: The introduction or proffer of past criminal and anti-social actions is not admissible as evidence of mental disease unless accompanied by expert testimony, supported by a showing of the concordance of a responsible segment of professional opinion, that the particular characteristics of these actions constitute convincing evidence of an underlying mental disease that substantially impairs behavioral controls.

This formulation retains the paragraph as a "caveat" rather than an inexorable rule of law. It should serve to obviate distortions of the present state of knowledge that would constitute miscarriages of justice. Yet it leaves the door open—on shouldering the "convincing evidence" burden—to accommodate our general rule to developments that may lie ahead. It is the kind of imperfect, but not unfeasible, accommodation of the abstract and pragmatic that is often found to serve the administration of justice.

We do not think it desirable to use the caveat paragraph as a basis for instructions to the jury. It would be difficult for a juryman—or anyone else—to reconcile the caveat paragraph and the basic (*McDonald*) definition of mental disease if a psychiatrist testified that he discerned from particular past criminal behavior a pattern that established defendant as suffering from an abnormal condition of the mind that substantially impaired behavioral controls. If there is no such testimony, then there would be no evidence that mere misconduct betokens mental illness, it would be impermissible for defense counsel to present such a hypothesis to the jury, and there would be very little likelihood that a jury would arrive at such a proposition on its own. On the other hand, an instruction along the lines of the caveat paragraph runs the risk of appearing to call for the rejection of testimony that is based materially, but only partially, on the history of criminal conduct.

---

42. We note that the Second Circuit adopted the caveat paragraph on the ground that a contrary holding would reduce to absurdity a test designed to encourage full analysis of all psychiatric data and would exculpate those who knowingly and deliberately seek a life of crime. (*Freeman*, 357 F.2d at 625).

f. Broad presentation to the jury.

Our adoption of the ALI rule does not depart from the doctrines this court has built up over the past twenty years to assure a broad presentation to the jury concerning the condition of defendant's mind and its consequences. Thus we adhere to our rulings admitting expert testimony of psychologists, as well as psychiatrists, and to our many decisions contemplating that expert testimony on this subject will be accompanied by presentation of the facts and premises underlying the opinions and conclusions of the experts, and that the Government and defense may present, in Judge Blackmun's words, "all possibly relevant evidence" bearing on cognition, volition and capacity. We agree with the amicus submission of the National District Attorneys Association that the law cannot "distinguish between physiological, emotional, social and cultural sources of the impairment"—assuming, of course, requisite testimony establishing exculpation under the pertinent standard—and all such causes may be both referred to by the expert and considered by the trier of fact.

Breadth of input under the insanity defense is not to be confused with breadth of the doctrines establishing the defense. As the National District Attorneys Association brief points out, the latitude for salient evidence of e.g., social and cultural factors pertinent to an abnormal condition of the mind significantly affecting capacity and controls, does not mean that such factors may be taken as establishing a separate defense for persons whose mental condition is such that blame can be imposed. We have rejected a broad "injustice" approach that would have opened the door to expositions of e.g., cultural deprivation, unrelated to any abnormal condition of the mind.

We have recognized that "Many criminologists point out that even normal human behavior is influenced by such factors as training, environment, poverty and the like, which may limit the understanding and options of the individual." Determinists may contend that every man's fate is ultimately sealed by his genes and environment, over which he has no control. Our jurisprudence, however, while not oblivious to deterministic components, ultimately rests on a premise of freedom of will. This is not to be viewed as an exercise in philosophic discourse, but as a governmental fusion of ethics and necessity, which takes into account that a system of rewards and punishments is itself part of the environment that influences and shapes human conduct. Our recognition of an insanity defense for those who lack the essential, threshold free will possessed by those in the normal range is not to be twisted, directly or indirectly, into a device for exculpation of those without an abnormal condition of the mind. * * *

BAZELON, CHIEF JUDGE, concurring in part and dissenting in part: * * *

Our instruction to the jury should provide that a defendant is not responsible *if at the time of his unlawful conduct his mental or emotional processes or behavior controls were impaired to such an extent that he cannot justly be held responsible for his act.* This test would ask the psychiatrist a single question: what is the nature of the impairment of the defendant's mental and emotional processes and behavior controls? It would leave for the jury the question whether that impairment is sufficient to relieve the defendant of responsibility for the particular act charged.

* * * The Court * * * rejects an instruction "overtly cast in terms of 'justice'" on the grounds that such an instruction "cannot feasibly be restricted to the ambit of what may properly be taken into account but will splash with unconfinable and malign consequences." That argument seems to present two separate justifi-

cations for pretending that the inquiry is confined to fact.

First, the argument apparently reflects a concern that adoption of the "justice" approach would permit the introduction at trial of extraneous information. But under the approach urged by a minority of the ALI Council, a defendant must still demonstrate that proffered evidence is relevant to an impairment of capacity. The test does not provide him with a license to introduce evidence merely for the purpose of engendering sympathy for him in the jury. Adoption of the "justice" approach would still leave standing all of the traditional obstacles to the introduction of irrelevant evidence.

The Court's second ground of objection is apparently that an instruction cast in terms of justice would permit the jury to convict or acquit without regard to legal standard. * * * I take it that in the Court's view the majority version of the ALI test offers the jury "legal rules that crystallize the requirements of justice as determined by the lawmakers of the community," and that the minority version sets the jury adrift without such crystallized rules. What, then, are these crystallized rules? I pointed out above that while the minority version asks the jury to measure the impairment in terms of its own sense of justice, the majority version requires acquittal if the incapacity is *substantial*, and requires conviction if the incapacity is *insubstantial*. Can we seriously maintain that the majority ALI instruction is preferable because its determination that the impairment must be "substantial" reflects a crystallization of the requirements of justice by the lawmakers of the community? Naturally, we would all prefer a rule that could, as a matter of law, draw a bright line between responsible and non-responsible defendants. But the ALI test adopted by this Court is plainly not such a rule. It offers the jury no real help in making the "intertwining moral, legal, and medical judgments" that all of us expect. In fact, because it describes the question as one of fact it may lull the jury into the mistaken assumption that the question of responsibility can best be resolved by experts, leaving the jury at the mercy of the witness who asserts most persuasively that, in his expert judgment, the defendant's capacity was or was not *substantially* impaired. * * *

Notes and Questions

1. Following the public outcry (not unlike that after M'Naghten's acquittal) when John Hinckley was found not guilty by reason of insanity as to his attempted assassination of President Reagan, Congress enacted the Insanity Defense Reform Act of 1984, which provides in 18 U.S.C.A. § 20(a): "It is an affirmative defense to a prosecution under any Federal statute that, at the time of the commission of the acts constituting the offense, the defendant, as a result of a severe mental disease or defect, was unable to appreciate the nature and quality or the wrongfulness of his acts. Mental disease or defect does not otherwise constitute a defense."

2. "The most recent legislative efforts to abolish the insanity defense followed public outcry over the verdict in the *Hinckley* case in 1981. In April 1982, Idaho became the first state in recent times to abolish the insanity defense. Its new law provides that '[m]ental condition shall not be a defense to any charge of criminal conduct' and states that 'nothing herein is intended to prevent the admission of expert evidence on the issues of mens rea or any state of mind which is an element of the offense, subject to the rules of evidence.' The states of Montana and Utah have since followed suit." S. Brakel, J. Parry & B. Weiner, *The Mentally Disabled and the Law* 717 (3d ed. 1985). Is this constitutional? Is it wise?

3. In *State v. Korell,* ___ Mont. ___, 690 P.2d 992 (1984), the court rejected the defendant's contention that the insanity defense was so firmly established in the common law at the time our Constitution was adopted that it was a fundamental right protected by the Fourteenth Amendment due process clause. The court noted that the Supreme Court, in *Powell v. Texas,* p. 419 of this Book, characterized the defense as one of those doctrines which "have historically provided the tools for a constantly shifting adjustment of the tension between the evolving aims of the criminal law and changing religious, moral, philosophical, and medical views of the nature of man," a process always "thought to be the province of the States." Early court decisions holding abolition of the insanity defense unconstitutional were distinguished because the statutes there challenged, unlike their modern counterparts, did not even permit trial testimony on mental condition to cast doubt on whether a defendant had the requisite mental state. As for the contention that abolition of the insanity defense constitutes cruel and unusual punishment under the Eighth Amendment, the *Korell* court concluded this was not so because the Supreme Court's teaching in *Robinson v. California,* p. 420 of this Book, and *Powell* were merely that neither status nor illness could themselves be made criminal.

4. N. Morris & G. Hawkins, *The Honest Politician's Guide to Crime Control* 184–85 (1970): "We find it impossible morally to distinguish the insane from others who may be convicted though suffering deficiencies of intelligence, adversities of social circumstances, indeed all the ills to which the flesh and life of man is prey. It seems to us that our approach better accords with the total role of the criminal law in society than does a system which makes a special exculpatory case out of one rare and unusual criminogenic process,

while it determinedly denies exculpatory effects to other, more potent processes. In the long run we will better handle these problems, as well as the whole and more complex problem of criminality in the community, if we will recognize that within crime itself there lies the greatest disparity of human wickedness and the greatest range of human capacities for self-control.

"Our perennial perseverations about the defense of insanity impede recognition of this diversity, since they push us to a false dichotomy between the responsible and the irresponsible. They should be abandoned. One occupation for the energies thus released might be suggested, a task in which the psychiatrist has an important role to play: the defining of those categories of psychologically disturbed criminals who are serious threats to the community and to whom special treatment measures should therefore be applied."

5. Compare S. Brakel et al., supra, at 718–19: "It is unlikely that the United States Supreme Court will permit the insanity defense to be abolished or allow the concept to be so narrowed that the defendant's rational knowledge and understanding of the prohibited act are not considered essential to establishing the mens rea.

*   *   *

"As one leading psychiatrist has pointed out in defending the insanity defense:

The contradiction between this experience of being without choice and the moral intuition of free will is one of the inescapable contradictions of human existence. That contradiction is expressed and denied by the insanity defense. The insanity defense is the exception that 'proves' the rule of law. . . . the insanity defense does more than test the law; it *demonstrates* that all other criminals had free will—the ability to choose between good and evil—but that they choose evil and therefore deserve to be punished.[311]

"A just society must have the ability to express compassion and exercise moral judgment so as to excuse those rare individuals who could not comprehend the wrongfulness of their actions. This vision of law has led civilized societies for centuries and will likely continue to sustain resistance to demands to abolish the insanity defense in the future."

6. What, then, of partial abolition? Consider Wexler, *An Offense–Victim Approach to Insanity Defense Reform*, 26 Ariz.L. Rev. 18, 21–23 (1984):

"We should, therefore, be able rather easily to dissipate public fear over and objection to the insanity defense if, through legislation, we render the defense *unassertable in the prosecution of specified crimes* (e.g., homicide, attempted homicide, and perhaps aggravated assault) *unless the victim of the offense is somehow 'related to' the defendant.*

" * * * In terms of the public protection interest, the distinction is particularly potent. Surely, the public at large will be less fearful of one who has killed a family member than of one who has killed a stranger. Moreover, although this is an area that can profit from empirical research, a person who has killed a nonrelative seems in actuality to be more likely to pose a threat—particularly to the general public—than does a person who has killed a family member."

NOTES ON THE BORDERLAND OF RESPONSIBILITY

1. *The XYY Syndrome.* In *People v. Yukl*, 83 Misc.2d 364, 372 N.Y.S.2d 313 (1975), in response to an indigent murder defendant's request for appointment of a cytogeneticist to conduct tests on defendant's blood for chromosomal abnormalities, for possible use in an insanity defense, the court reasoned:

"The existence of the XYY genetic phenomenon was firmly established in 1961. Early studies of chromosome imbalance focused almost exclusively on prison populations. The XYY male, in prison samples, appears to be a very tall, slightly retarded individual with a severely disordered personality characterized by violent, aggressive behavior. However, the sampling, thus far, has been inadequate and inconclusive. A built-in bias exists because samples comprised of institutionalized persons will, of course, contain more than a fair number of violent and aggressive types. The statistical significance to be attached to the results of these studies is in doubt until such time as adequate control group data can be compiled. Scientists and legal commentators appear to be in agreement that further study is required to confirm the initial findings and to concretely establish a causal connection between one's genetic complement and a predisposition toward violent criminal conduct.

"The courts have therefore been noticeably reluctant to admit evidence of genetic abnormality as a factor to negate criminal responsibility. In Maryland, Carl Millard sought to introduce evidence of his XYY condition in his trial for armed robbery. The court excluded the evidence and held that research into the relationship between genetics, criminality, and insanity did not yet 'meet reasonable medical certainty standards' necessary for its admission into evidence. The Appellate Court, affirming the order, did not find that a defense based on XYY was beyond the pale of proof, but that on the basis of the record the trial court acted properly in declining to permit the information to go to the jury

311. Stone, *The Insanity Defense on Trial*, 33 Hosp. & Community Psychiatry 636, 640 (1982).

(*Millard v. State,* 8 Md.App. 419, 261 A.2d 227 [1970]).

"In *People v. Tanner,* 13 Cal.App.3d 596, 91 Cal.Rptr. 656 (1970), the California intermediate appellate court upheld a lower court ruling barring admission of XYY testimony to support a defense of insanity, stating:

'The studies of the '47 XYY individuals' undertaken to this time are few, they are rudimentary in scope, and their results are at best inconclusive.'

"Moreover, the court indicated three specific objections that precluded admission of the testimony of genetic abnormality. First, the experts merely suggested that aggressive behavior may be one manifestation of the XYY syndrome. However, they could not confirm that all XYY individuals are involuntarily aggressive; in fact, some identified XYY individuals have not exhibited such tendencies. Second, the experts could not determine whether or not the defendant's aggressive behavior even resulted from chromosome imbalance. Third, the experts were unable to state that possession of the XYY anomaly resulted in mental disease which would constitute legal insanity under California law.

"The California Appellate Court considered the problem and found it an entirely proper use of discretion for the lower court to exclude evidence of an XYY condition because the evidence was 'not clear and convincing.' The court analogized to other scientific data—i.e., voice print analysis, lie detector testing—which had likewise been denied admission because they failed to reach the necessary standards of acceptance and reliability in their field.

"The objections raised in *People v. Tanner,* supra, appear to be equally valid in this jurisdiction. The Penal Law, section 30.05 states:

'1. A person is not criminally responsible for conduct if at the time of such conduct, as a result of mental disease or defect, he lacks substantial capacity to know or appreciate either:

'a. The nature and consequence of such conduct; or

'b. That such conduct was wrong.'

"Thus, in New York an insanity defense based on chromosome abnormality should be possible only if one establishes with a high degree of medical certainty an etiological relationship between the defendant's mental capacity and the genetic syndrome. Further, the genetic imbalance must have so affected the thought processes as to interfere substantially with the defendant's cognitive capacity or with his ability to understand or appreciate the basic moral code of his society.

"While there is strong evidence which indicates a relationship between genetic composition and deviant behavior, the exact biological mechanism has yet to be determined. Moreover, studies have failed to indicate why only some XYY individuals appear to have a propensity for violence and aggression and not others. The answers to these problems are currently being sought by scientists and their solution will assist immeasurably in providing a firmer footing for the incorporation of chromosome abnormality under the defense of insanity.

"However, in New York, Judge Farrell has taken a different approach and permitted, in *People v. Farley,* Supreme Court, Queens County, Indictment Number 1827 (April 30, 1969), evidence of an XYY condition to go to the jury. The defendant's insanity defense consisted of the testimony of two witnesses. A reputable psychiatrist rendered his opinion as to the defendant's mental state at the time of the commission of the crime without regard to the chromosome imbalance of the defendant. The other witness, a medical doctor engaged in genetics research, testified that, based on recent studies in the field, inmates in penal institutions have higher incidence of chromosome imbalance and in the expert's opinion, the defendant's chromosome abnormality affected his antisocial behavior. The jury rejected the insanity defense and found the defendant guilty of murder as charged.

"Judge Farrell, writing for St. John's Law Review, indicated that

'Its [the XYY syndrome] relevancy as part of an insanity defense should not be opened to serious dispute. At present, the law is geared to continuous expansion of the latitude of proof to be allowed to a defendant in such cases.'

In addition, a court in Australia has accepted the XYY syndrome as part of a valid insanity defense. Laurence E. Hannett was charged with murder and was acquitted after a psychiatrist testified that every cell in his body was abnormal. Likewise in France, Daniel Hugon presented the XYY abnormality as a defense and the court permitted its use in mitigation of sentence.

"Notwithstanding the comments of and the practices followed by Judge Farrell in the trial over which he presided and the acceptance by some foreign courts of the XYY syndrome, it appears on the whole that the genetic imbalance theory of crime causation has not been satisfactorily established and accepted in either the scientific or legal communities to warrant its admission in criminal trials.

"Accordingly, the motion for the appointment of a cytogeneticist is denied."

2. *Pathological Gambling Disorder.* In *United States v. Gould,* 741 F.2d 45 (4th Cir.1984), defendant was convicted of entry of a bank with intent to commit robbery and intent to commit larceny. On appeal, he challenged the trial judge's instruction to the jury "that as a matter of law pathological gambling disorder is not a

disease or defect within the meaning of the American Law Institute test which would constitute a basis for the insanity defense." The court responded:

"Two other circuits, the Eighth and the Second, recently have held in closely analogous cases that, under the ALI test, evidence of a compulsive gambling disorder could not be considered as the basis for an insanity defense to charges of theft-type federal offenses. *See United States v. Torniero,* 735 F.2d 725 (2d Cir.1984) (interstate transportation of stolen property); *United States v. Lewellyn,* 723 F.2d 615 (8th Cir.1983) (embezzlement; false statement; mail fraud). In both cases, the courts reserved decision upon the general question whether the compulsive gambling disorder might under any circumstance and in respect of any offenses constitute a 'mental disease or defect' within the ALI substantive test. Each focused more narrowly upon whether the evidence sufficed under the appropriate procedural-evidentiary test to establish the requisite causal connection between the 'disorder' and the specific offenses in issue, a causal connection that is required by the 'as a result of' language in the ALI test. Both courts also concentrated only upon the 'volitional' prong of the ALI test since in both cases, as in the instant case, the defense was proffered only in that respect.

"The gist of the Eighth Circuit's rationale was that, applying the test of *Frye v. United States,* 293 F. 1013, 1014 (D.C.Cir. 1923), the expert testimony offered to establish the requisite causal link between the gambling disorder and the defendant's volition in respect of the 'collateral' criminal offenses there charged did not sufficiently show that the underlying scientific principle had gained 'general acceptance' in the relevant discipline.

"The Second Circuit, analyzing the problem as one of foundational relevance of the proffered evidence, upheld a district court's exclusion of comparable expert testimony on the basis that it did not show that the 'hypothesis' of a causal link between this disorder and commission of the type offenses there charged commanded 'substantial acceptance' in the relevant discipline.

"While there are undoubtedly shadings of conceptual difference between us, we basically agree with the approaches which led both of these courts to reject compulsive gambling as the basis for an insanity defense to criminal offenses collateral to gambling."

3. *Premenstrual Syndrome.* In Holtzman, *Premenstrual Symptoms: No Legal Defense,* 60 St. John's L.Rev. 712, 712–14 (1986), the Kings County, New York, district attorney comments:

"The first reported criminal case in the United States in which a defendant asserted premenstrual syndrome as a defense occurred in the jurisdiction where I serve. In that case a mother was accused of assaulting her four-year-old child with a stick. The defense raised the claim of premenstrual syndrome as one of several grounds for its motion to dismiss in the interests of justice.

"In 1982 my office did extensive research on the issue of premenstrual syndrome in preparing the case for trial. We reviewed some 3,000 medical periodicals published since 1971 in English and foreign languages and interviewed gynecologists, psychiatrists and endocrinologists. From this research we learned that there is no single well-defined medical condition which can be called 'premenstrual syndrome.'

"We also found that there is no scientific evidence for the proposition that the onset of the menstrual cycle provokes aggressive or violent behavior in women. The scientific evidence is confirmed by common sense experience—if women became violent each month our jails would be filled with women. But, as it is, the overwhelming number of jail inmates are men; no menstrual cycle caused their aggression.

"The scientific evidence does show, however, that women experience different symptoms in different degrees in connection with their menstrual cycle. The symptoms cited are myriad. Among them are anxiety, irritability and depression. Insanity is not a symptom of the menstrual cycle. And there *is* no syndrome—'a group of signs and symptoms that occur together and characterize a particular abnormality.'

"Moreover, research has shown that there is no diminution of the cognitive abilities of women in connection with the menstrual cycle. In a study of this question, fifty women between the ages of thirty and forty-five years old were placed in groups matched by age, education and numbers of their children. The two groups were tested for anxiety, depression and cognition, one group tested premenstrually and the other tested intermenstrually. As to depression and anxiety, the distress of the premenstrual women was comparable to that reported for freshmen college women during orientation and testing. But the study found that the 'mood change[s] had no effect on cognitive test performance.' These tests 'measured sensory-perceptive factors, memory, problem solving, induction, concept formation and creativity.' * * *

"In a recent Denver, Colorado bankruptcy case a defendant sought to have a judgment debt she owed to plaintiff discharged under bankruptcy on the ground that the defendant was suffering from 'premenstrual syndrome' when she stabbed the plaintiff, her roommate. In that case, the court decisively rejected the claim of premenstrual syndrome as a way to limit responsibility. The court observed that premenstrual syndrome was not established either medically or legally as an explanation for improper conduct. It further held, after hearing expert testimony on the issue of premenstrual syndrome, that the expert testimony demonstrated a lack of any general acceptance of premenstrual syndrome in the psychiatric community as an explanation for inappropriate behavior."

4. *Post Traumatic Stress Disorder.* As reported in S. Brakel, J. Parry & B. Weiner, *The Mentally Disabled and the Law* 713 (3d ed. 1985): "Post-traumatic stress disorder (PTSD), since officially recognized as a mental illness by the psychiatric profession, strikes survivors of traumatic events, such as natural disasters, plane crashes, and wartime combat, who may reexperience elements of the trauma in dreams, uncontrollable and emotionally intrusive images, dissociative states of consciousness, and unconscious behavioral reenactments of the traumatic situation. PTSD has received the most attention in cases involving Vietnam veterans who raise the condition as the basis for an insanity defense, in which it is argued that the defendant engaged in criminal behavior as a result of a stressful event that caused him to revert to the behavior he exhibited under conditions of war in Vietnam.

"An insanity defense based on PTSD is most plausible and is most likely to be successful in cases in which the defendant exhibited behavior during the crime indicating that he was reliving his war experience. In cases where the defense is less plausible, it will still provide the attorney with an opportunity to present a wide range of evidence contrasting the defendant's behavior before and after the war,

in the hopes of getting a conviction for a lesser offense or a lighter sentence. Because of its relatively recent recognition as an 'illness,' there are yet few reported cases involving PTSD as a defense. This situation may change, particularly given the concept's potential for extension to other kinds of cases, such as those involving women who have committed criminal acts after being raped." [a]

SECTION 3. THE INSANITY DEFENSE—PROCEDURAL ASPECTS

A. RAISING THE DEFENSE— WHY AND BY WHOM?

1. A. Matthews, *Mental Disability and the Criminal Law* 34, 36–37, 47 (1970): "Criminal responsibility cases are rare [b] because defendants, given the alternatives, choose not to plead insanity as a defense. The plea has drawbacks stemming both from the procedural difficulties it involves and from the consequences that follow if it is successful. This seems strange in view of the widespread belief—a belief that has colored procedural approaches to criminal responsibility in this century—that the defense is a great benefit to the defendant, who can readily purchase psychiatric testimony and thus have an easy way out of criminal liability. * * *

"How is it, then, that more defendants do not rely on this tactic if in a serious case in which trial may not occur for a year, or perhaps two, a defendant may have himself psychiatrically examined by experts of his own choosing and not raise the defense until the prosecution has put on its case at trial? In practice, this advantage belongs only to defendants who are well-off. The

---

a. See also Erlinder, *Paying the Price for Vietnam: Post–Traumatic Stress Disorder and Criminal Behavior,* 25 B.C.L.Rev. 305 (1984).

b. He notes at 25–26 that his field research disclosed that the insanity defense was raised with the following frequency in the cities and during the interval indicated:

Place	Period of Observation	Number
Chicago	4 Months	1
San Francisco	4 months	1
New York City	3 months	1
Detroit	3 months	0
Miami	2 months	0

vast majority of persons charged with crime, including those who are mentally disabled, are indigent. Indigence means, as a practical matter, that the accused typically cannot hire his own psychiatric experts freely as he could if he had money, but must depend for psychiatric evidence on 'impartial' experts appointed by the court. Indigence has other consequences which also adversely affect a defendant's chances of preparing and successfully presenting a defense of insanity in court (assuming that, in view of the consequences of success, he wants to do so). It is difficult for the defendant either to obtain, as a preliminary matter, expert advice on his chances for success should he raise the defense of insanity or to obtain psychiatric evidence that might be persuasive in court. * * *

"Furthermore, aside from capital cases, the defense of insanity in New York, Chicago, and Detroit seemed to many lawyers and psychiatrists an empty undertaking since the dispositional consequences of the successful insanity plea did not look any better than those which follow upon conviction. While there is no single explanation of this aspect of the 'last resort' quality of the insanity plea, the following were given to us: (1) the inevitability of indefinite commitment if the defense is successful and the defendant found 'insane'; (2) the belief that psychiatric treatment at the maximum-security hospital 'does not exist' or is likely to prove ineffective; (3) the reluctance of many defendants to label themselves 'maniacs' or even fit candidates for mental treatment; and (4) fear that the

a. The reference is to *North Carolina v. Alford,* 400 U.S. 25, 91 S.Ct. 160, 27 L.Ed.2d 162 (1970), allowing a defendant asserting his innocence to plead guilty when a factual basis for such a plea is shown, and quoting in support from a case stating courts "should not 'force any defense on a defendant in a criminal case.'"

b. The reference is to *Faretta v. California,* 422 U.S. 806, 95 S.Ct. 2525, 45 L.Ed.2d 562 (1975),

prospects of release are dim even if the mental health of the offender improves."

2. In *State v. Jones,* 99 Wash.2d 735, 664 P.2d 1216 (1983), holding the trial court committed prejudicial error by entering a not guilty by reason of insanity plea over defendant's objection, the court explained:

"Courts have taken two basic approaches to the particular question of whether a court may *sua sponte* impose an NGI plea on an unwilling defendant. The first is that taken by the District of Columbia Circuit (hereinafter D.C. Circuit) of the United States Court of Appeals. It recognizes a broad discretion in the trial court to enter an NGI plea sua sponte whenever necessary in the pursuit of justice. In exercising its discretion, the court is to weigh various factors, including the defendant's opposition to asserting an insanity defense, the quality of the defendant's reasoning, the viability of the defense, the court's personal observations of the defendant, and the reasonableness of the defendant's decision. *United States v. Wright,* 627 F.2d 1300 (D.C.Cir.1980). The rationale for the rule is that society has '[an] obligation, through the insanity defense, to withhold punishment of someone not blameworthy.' This, the D.C. Circuit has concluded, distinguishes *Alford* [a] and *Faretta.* [b]

"In *Frendak v. United States,* 408 A.2d 364 (D.C.App.1979), in contrast, the District of Columbia Court of Appeals concluded that *Alford* and *Faretta* required reevaluation of the D.C. Circuit rule.

holding a defendant in a criminal case has a constitutional right to represent himself at his trial, which, as one court has asserted, embodies "the conviction that a defendant has the right to decide, within limits, the type of defense he wishes to mount." *United States v. Laura,* 607 F.2d 52 (3d Cir.1979).

[T]he underlying philosophy of *Alford* and *Faretta* is inconsistent with *Whalem* as currently interpreted. *Whalem* and succeeding cases have laid substantially more emphasis on the strength of the evidence supporting an insanity defense than on the defendant's choice. In contrast, *Alford* and *Faretta* reason that respect for a defendant's freedom as a person mandates that he or she be permitted to make fundamental decisions about the course of the proceedings.

Thus, the D.C. Court of Appeals concluded, any competent defendant has the absolute right to refuse an NGI plea, as long as he is competent to make and does make an intelligent and voluntary waiver.[c]

"The D.C. Circuit rejected the *Frendak* approach and questioned whether it would differ significantly in practice. Nonetheless, we believe that the approaches differ in two important respects. First, the focus in *Frendak* is solely on *present* mental condition while much, if not most, of the D.C. Circuit's focus is on the defendant's mental condition *at the time of the alleged offense.* Second, the two approaches differ in the standard by which they assess the defendant's mental condition. Under *Frendak,* the court focuses on competency to make decisions while, under the D.C. Circuit approach, the court focuses on legal insanity.

"We favor *Frendak* for several reasons. First, we find its reasoning more in accord with *Faretta* and *Alford.* The D.C. Circuit's attempt to distinguish cases involving an insanity defense is unpersuasive. A defendant who is not guilty because of insanity is no more blameless than a defendant who has a valid alibi defense or who acted in legitimate self-defense. Yet

courts do not impose these other defenses on unwilling defendants.

"More generally we concur in the belief that basic respect for a defendant's individual freedom requires us to permit the defendant himself to determine his plea. As noted by the court in *Frendak,* there exist numerous reasons why a defendant might choose to forgo an NGI plea. Absent bifurcation, such a choice may be a wise tactical maneuver where the insanity defense conflicts with some other defense the defendant wishes to interpose. The defendant may find confinement in a mental institution more distasteful than confinement in prison. The stigma of insanity may in some cases be more damaging. Finally, a defendant may have legitimate philosophical reasons for opposing entry of an NGI plea. He may view such a plea as a tacit admission of guilt which he does not wish to make. Alternatively, he may admit the act but maintain its justifiability or intend it to symbolize his strong opposition to some policy of the State. The forced mental commitment of critics in other countries to discredit their dissent is well documented.

"The existence in this state of a right to plead guilty provides an independent rationale for adopting the *Frendak* approach. * * * In entering such a plea, a defendant necessarily waives both his right to plead not guilty and his right to plead not guilty by reason of insanity. To hold that a defendant has a right to waive both rights together but not to waive them separately strikes us as wholly absurd. * * *

"As with waiver of all rights, waiver of an NGI plea must satisfy certain conditions in order to be constitutionally valid. In

c. Should this be so even if defense counsel objects? Consider *State v. Lowenfield,* 495 So.2d 1245 (La.1985): "It appears beyond argument that when a competent defendant wishes to plead not guilty rather than not guilty by reason of insanity, and clearly understands the conse-

quences of his choice, then the counsel must acquiesce to the wishes of his competent client. The court had no choice but to allow the defendant to withdraw his pleas and in this we find no error."

particular, the defendant must be capable of making and must actually make an intelligent and voluntary decision. This requires the trial judge to 'conduct an inquiry designed to assure that the defendant has been fully informed of the alternatives available, comprehends the consequences of failing to assert the [insanity] defense, and freely chooses to raise or waive the defense.' In some instances, the defendant may not be competent to make an intelligent and voluntary decision.

"Among the courts adopting the *Frendak* approach, however, there is disagreement about the relationship between competency to waive the insanity defense and competency to stand trial. The split arises not from a difference of opinion regarding the level of competency necessary to waive the insanity defense but rather from differences regarding the level of competency necessary to stand trial. In *Frendak* itself, the court concluded that a greater degree of competency was necessary to waive the insanity defense because the test for competency to stand trial 'is not intended to measure whether the defendant is also capable of making intelligent decisions on important matters relating to the defense.' In *State v. Kahn,* 175 N.J.Super. 72, 417 A.2d 585 (1980), on the other hand, the court concluded that the test for competency to waive the insanity defense and the test for competency to stand trial were identical because in New Jersey the latter does require the ability to help plan the defense.

"*Frendak's* conclusion, that the competency standards for waiver of the insanity defense and standing trial do differ, rests upon a shaky foundation. It is premised in large part on decisions holding that the level of competency necessary to plead

guilty is greater than that necessary to stand trial, because the former requires an 'ability to make a reasoned choice among the alternatives presented'. *Sieling v. Eyman,* 478 F.2d 211, 215 (9th Cir.1973). *Sieling* and its progeny have been severely criticized, however, and do not represent the majority view. We believe the better view is that both competency standards should require an ability to make necessary decisions at trial.

"In any event, the test for competency to stand trial in Washington does rise to the level of competency to waive the insanity defense. As in New Jersey, a Washington defendant must be capable of 'assist[ing] in his own defense'. *Compare Frendak* (quoting *Dusky v. United States,* 362 U.S. 402, 80 S.Ct. 788, 4 L.Ed.2d 824 (1960) (per curiam) (defendant need only have ability 'to consult with his lawyer with a reasonable degree of rational understanding')). We construe this to include the same ability to understand and choose among alternative defenses which is necessary to intelligently and voluntarily waive the insanity defense.

"Thus, the only permissible inquiries when a defendant seeks to waive his insanity defense are whether he is competent to stand trial and whether his decision is intelligent and voluntary.[3] If the court finds that the defendant is not competent to stand trial, trial must be stayed or dismissed. If the court finds that the defendant is competent to stand trial but that his decision to forgo an NGI plea is not intelligent and voluntary, it should provide him with whatever additional information or assurances are necessary to enable such a decision. In only the rarest of cases, if ever,[4] will it be impossible to make the decision intelligent and voluntary and

---

3. We deal here only with waiver by defendants represented by counsel. Where a defendant represents himself, his decisions to waive various rights should be scrutinized more carefully and a higher competency standard applied.

4. For example, some courts have held that threats of a private party may render a plea involuntary. We need not decide that issue here.

State v. Khan appears to suggest that the defendant's refusal to recognize that he is insane

hence be necessary to enter an NGI plea sua sponte."

3. In *Wright*, discussed in *Jones*, the court noted that in an earlier case involving the same defendant, 511 F.2d 1311 (D.C.Cir.1975), the court held that procedures for automatic commitment after a verdict of not guilty by reason of insanity "*do not* apply where the insanity defense is raised by the court over defendant's objection." Does this make the *Wright* position more palatable?

B. RAISING THE DEFENSE— WHEN AND HOW?

4. Arraignment (the time at which the defendant is called upon to enter his plea) is the earliest point at which the defendant is likely to be able to interpose the defense of insanity. In most jurisdictions, however, he is under no obligation to do so at that time. A minority of jurisdictions, in recognition of the fact that it is extremely important for the prosecution to know in advance of trial whether an insanity defense will be raised, require the defendant to give advance notice. In some states, a special plea of not guilty by reason of insanity is a prerequisite to raising the defense at trial. Some other states require the defendant to file a written notice at a certain time prior to trial of his intention to defend on the ground of insanity.

5. In *Williams v. Florida*, 399 U.S. 78, 90 S.Ct. 1893, 26 L.Ed.2d 446 (1970), the Court held that the Florida requirement that a defendant give advance notice of an alibi defense (including the names and addresses of alibi witnesses) did not violate the privilege against self-incrimination. The Court stressed that the Florida rule only required the defendant to disclose evidence that he intended to produce subsequently at trial, and, if he changed

might prevent him from making an intelligent and voluntary decision. We see no reason, however, why this would prevent a competent defen-

his mind, the rule permitted the defendant to abandon the alibi defense without any harm to his case.

Courts have rather consistently rejected the claim that to require advance notice of an insanity defense violates the privilege against self-incrimination, *State ex rel. Sikora v. District Court*, 154 Mont. 241, 462 P.2d 897 (1969); the recent cases rely upon *Williams* as support, *Gilday v. Commonwealth*, 360 Mass. 170, 274 N.E.2d 589 (1971). But consider the dissent in *Sikora*, concluding that there "is a fundamental difference" between the defense of alibi and insanity or self-defense in this regard: "The defense of alibi denies that the defendant committed the crime with which he is charged, claiming that he was elsewhere at the time the crime was committed. Clearly no self-incrimination is involved here. Not so with the other two defenses. In pleading self-defense, the defendant admits committing the act constituting the crime but claims his act is legally justifiable. * * * Thus, under Montana law the defendant necessarily must admit he committed the act constituting the crime with which he is charged before self-defense applies. The same is true of the defense of insanity—defendant necessarily admits he did the killing but claims it to be legally excusable because of his lack of the requisite mental capacity."

6. *Wardius v. Oregon*, 412 U.S. 470, 93 S.Ct. 2208, 37 L.Ed.2d 82 (1973), established that any state rule providing for prosecution discovery must be reciprocal to meet due process requirements; the Court thus held invalid a notice-of-alibi provision that failed to require the prosecution to provide reciprocal disclosure of its rebuttal witnesses on the alibi issue. In *State v. Curtis*, 544 S.W.2d 580 (Mo. 1976), the court relied on *Wardius* in holding due process was violated where

dant from understanding that, despite his own disbelief, a jury might find him insane.

the defendant was required to give advance notice of his insanity defense and of the expert witnesses he would call in support, but the state was not required to disclose the identity of a psychiatrist called as a rebuttal witness.

7. In both *Williams* and *Wardius,* the Supreme Court emphasized that "[w]hether and to what extent a State can enforce discovery rules against a defendant who fails to comply, by excluding relevant, probative evidence is a question raising Sixth Amendment issues which we have no occasion to explore." Lower courts have utilized the sanction; illustrative is *United States v. Winn,* 577 F.2d 86 (9th Cir. 1978), upholding exclusion of an insanity defense because of defendant's unjustified [b] failure to comply with the notice provisions. But consider Note, 81 Yale L.J. 1342 (1972), arguing that the exclusion sanction violates defendant's Sixth Amendment right to compulsory process in light of the "less drastic means" available for enforcing pretrial discovery, such as: (i) granting the prosecution a continuance when surprised by the defense; (ii) allowing court or prosecution comment on the failure; and (iii) holding defense counsel in contempt for the failure.

C. EXAMINATION AND DIAGNOSIS BEFORE TRIAL

8. Most jurisdictions have enacted statutes providing for examination of the defendant by a court-appointed psychiatrist. Appointment under these provisions may come because the defense, prosecutor, or court has asserted that the defendant is not competent to stand trial (in which case the examination will nonetheless probably re-

sult in the psychiatrist gaining information relating to the accused's condition at the time of the alleged crime), or it may be triggered by the defendant's action of pleading or giving notice of an insanity defense. Under the most common type of procedure, the court designates a specific psychiatrist who will thereafter examine the defendant in his office or in a court clinic or the jail. Elsewhere, the defendant is temporarily committed to a mental hospital for examination by a member of the staff. Under both procedures, the examination is usually by a government psychiatrist, either because he is the only one available or because the law so requires.

9. *Riles v. McCotter,* 799 F.2d 947 (5th Cir.1986): "Riles first argues that the rights guaranteed him under the Fifth and Sixth Amendments were abridged under the standards set forth in *Estelle v. Smith,* 451 U.S. 454, 101 S.Ct. 1866, 68 L.Ed.2d 359 (1981) because: (1) the state's medical experts interviewed him absent counsel; (2) he was not advised of his right to remain silent; and (3) he was not informed that the results of the interviews could be used against him. * * *

"[T]his case is distinguishable from *Smith,* where the prosecution introduced harmful psychiatric evidence during the punishment phase of the trial and the defendant had no clue, because he had never raised a defense of insanity, that such evidence would be introduced. The damaging testimony was based on an unrequested court-ordered psychiatric interview of the defendant conducted without the benefit of *Miranda* warnings. Because advance notice as to the purpose of the examination was not provided to the defendant's counsel, the Court in *Smith*

---

b. Compare *Taylor v. District Court,* 182 Colo. 406, 514 P.2d 309 (1973) (where, prior to arraignment, counsel for defendant had discussed insanity defense with defendant who did not want to plead not guilty by reason of insanity, but on date of severance defendant disclosed new evidence to counsel leading to discovery of other evidence

indicative of a foundation for insanity pleas, and defendant then stated he wanted to plead insanity defense, trial court acted arbitrarily in denying leave to so plead, as defendant showed good cause why the defense was not raised at arraignment).

held that the defendant was also denied assistance of counsel in making a decision of whether to submit to the examination. Here, the record reflects that Riles, represented by counsel, requested most (if not all) of the psychiatric examinations, the results of which he now finds objectionable. Moreover, unlike the defendant in *Smith,* Riles raised the insanity defense; the state, therefore, had every right to rebut that defense. By pursuing this avenue of defense, and by offering psychiatric evidence to support this defense, Riles opened the door to the state's evidence and waived his Fifth Amendment privilege against self-incrimination. Neither was Rile's Sixth Amendment right to assistance of counsel abridged. Finally, a defendant has 'no constitutional right to have his attorney present *during* the psychiatric examination.' "

Is this reasoning convincing? Compare *United States v. Byers,* 740 F.2d 1104 (D.C. Cir.1984), asserting that it is "at best a fiction to say that when the defendant introduces his expert's testimony he 'waives' his Fifth Amendment rights," but that denial of a defendant's Fifth Amendment claim is nonetheless justified "because of the unreasonable and debilitating effect it would have upon society's conduct of a fair inquiry into the defendant's culpability."

10. But what should the consequences be if the defendant refuses to talk with the court-appointed psychiatrist? Consider *State v. Karstetter,* 110 Ariz. 539, 521 P.2d 626 (1974) (not a violation of defendant's privilege against self-incrimination to permit the psychiatrist to so testify at trial); and *State ex rel. Johnson v. Richardson,* 276 Or. 325, 555 P.2d 202 (1976) (trial court ordered "to order the defendant to answer questions asked by the psychiatrist about matters 'other than acts or conduct immediately near the scene of the crime' and if he does not, to strike the defense of lack of responsibility due to mental defect");

Motes v. State, 256 Ga. 831, 353 S.E.2d 348 (1987) (trial judge's response, striking defendant's insanity defense, too severe; defendant is simply barred from relying on expert testimony, as "the state should have an equal opportunity to tell that story through the mouth of an expert" as is exercised by the defendant).

11. In *Ake v. Oklahoma,* 470 U.S. 68, 105 S.Ct. 1087, 84 L.Ed.2d 53 (1985), indigent defendant Ake was convicted of murder despite his attempted defense of insanity. Ake's request for a psychiatric evaluation at state expense was denied, and at trial defense counsel's inquiry of state psychiatrists who had examined Ake concerning his competency to stand trial was not fruitful, for they had not inquired into Ake's mental state at the time of the crime. Emphasizing that consequently "there was no expert testimony for either side on Ake's sanity at the time of the offense," the Supreme Court ruled Ake had been denied due process: "[W]ithout the assistance of a psychiatrist to conduct a professional examination on issues relevant to the defense, to help determine whether the insanity defense is viable, to present testimony, and to assist in preparing the cross-examination of a State's psychiatric witnesses, the risk of an inaccurate resolution of sanity issues is extremely high. With such assistance, the defendant is fairly able to present at least enough information to the jury, in a meaningful manner, as to permit it to make a sensible determination.

"A defendant's mental condition is not necessarily at issue in every criminal proceeding, however, and it is unlikely that psychiatric assistance of the kind we have described would be of probable value in cases where it is not. The risk of error from denial of such assistance, as well as its probable value, are most predictably at their height when the defendant's mental condition is seriously in question. When the defendant is able to make an *ex parte* threshold showing to the trial court that his sanity is likely to be a significant factor in his defense, the need for the assistance of a psychiatrist is readily apparent. It is in such cases that a defense may be devastated by the absence of a psychiatric examination and testimony; with such assistance, the defendant might have a reasonable chance of success. In such a circumstance, where the potential accuracy of the jury's determination is so dramatically enhanced, and where the interests of the individual and the State in an accurate proceeding are substantial, the State's interest in its fisc must yield.

"We therefore hold that when a defendant demonstrates to the trial judge that his sanity at the time of the offense is to be a significant factor at trial, the State must, at a minimum, assure the defendant access to a competent psychiatrist who will conduct an appropriate examination and assist in evaluation, preparation, and presentation of the defense. This is not to say, of course, that the indigent defendant has a constitutional right to choose a psychiatrist of his personal liking or to receive funds to hire his own. Our concern is that the indigent defendant have access to a competent psychiatrist for the purpose we have discussed, and as in the case of the provision of counsel we leave to the State the decision on how to implement this right."

12. In *State v. Gambrell,* 318 N.C. 249, 347 S.E.2d 390 (1986), the court concluded: "We reject defendant's contention that he is entitled to such an independent, privately employed psychiatrist. The appointment of state employed psychiatrists may fulfill the state's constitutional obligation. Their employment by the state, we are satisfied, creates no conflict of interest which would disable them from fulfilling the constitutional requirements." Is this a fair reading of *Ake*? See Notes, 84 Mich. L.Rev. 1326 (1986); 61 N.Y.U.L.Rev. 703 (1986).

Is this a sensible result? Consider A. Matthews, *Mental Disability and the Criminal Law* 43 (1970): "The doctors in private practice, perhaps because they treat a variety of mentally ill persons, tend to have a broader notion of mental disease than their counterparts in state mental hospitals. Their patients may resemble the person charged with crime more closely than do patients in a state hospital, who are more likely to be the victims of obvious and disabling mental illnesses. Since doctors in private practice have no need to fit patients into diagnostic categories for administrative or statistical purposes, they are less concerned with the importance of psychiatric systems of classification than with the individual dynamics of each patient. Their objective being treatment, their diagnostic procedures tend to be more thorough, more deeply probing, and more time-consuming than the diagnostic procedures of a typical state hospital. Psychiatrists in private practice are well aware of the limitations of a forty-five-minute interview with a person in the local county jail. In contrast, many institutional psychiatrists affirm that forty-five-minute interviews qualify them to render an opinion on the accused's mental condition, perhaps because such interviews are their routine hospital mode."

D. BURDEN OF PROOF

13. The initial burden of going forward with evidence of insanity is everywhere placed upon the defendant. This proposition is often stated in terms of a presumption of sanity: most men are sane, and thus the defendant in this case is presumed to be sane until some amount of evidence to the contrary is produced. Were it otherwise, the prosecution would be confronted with the intolerable burden of establishing the defendant's sanity in every criminal case. As to what is required to discharge this burden, the prevailing rule is that the evidence must raise

a reasonable doubt of defendant's mental responsibility, though a few jurisdictions use a lesser standard (sometimes stated as "some evidence" or a "scintilla" of evidence).

14. If the defendant meets his burden of going forward, the question then becomes which party has the burden of persuasion. In about half the states this burden rests with the prosecution; the prosecution must then proceed to prove responsibility beyond a reasonable doubt. Elsewhere, the burden of persuasion is on the defendant to convince the jury of his insanity, usually by the civil standard of a preponderance of the evidence. But in the federal system, by virtue of the Insanity Defense Reform Act of 1984, 18 U.S.C.A. § 20, the burden is on the defendant to establish the insanity defense by "clear and convincing evidence." Which view is preferable?

15. In *Leland v. Oregon,* 343 U.S. 790, 72 S.Ct. 1002, 96 L.Ed.2d 1302 (1952), the Court held a state could constitutionally require a defendant to prove insanity beyond a reasonable doubt. *Mullaney v. Wilbur,* p. 238 of this Book, and the *Winship* case relied upon therein created some doubt regarding the constitutionality of placing the burden of persuasion on the defendant, but the matter has now been resolved. In *Rivera v. Delaware,* 429 U.S. 877, 97 S.Ct. 226, 50 L.Ed.2d 160 (1976), the Court dismissed, as not presenting a substantial federal question, an appeal claiming a state statute burdening the defendant with proving insanity by a preponderance of the evidence was unconstitutional. As noted in *Patterson v. New York,* p. 245 of this Book, in so doing

"the Court confirmed that it remained constitutional to burden the defendant with proving his insanity defense."

E. PRESENTATION OF EVIDENCE AT TRIAL

16. *United States v. Milne,* 487 F.2d 1232 (5th Cir.1973): "It has long been the rule in most jurisdictions that the lay opinion of a witness who is sufficiently acquainted with the person involved and has observed his conduct is admissible as to the sanity of such individual. ＊ ＊ ＊ While familiarity with such person and an opportunity to observe usual or normal human behavior may support a lay opinion as to sanity, additional or more substantial proof may be required to support a lay opinion as to insanity. Insanity is a variance from usual or normal conduct. For that reason a lay witness should be required to testify as to unusual, abnormal or bizarre conduct before being permitted to express an opinion as to insanity. As in other cases involving the qualification of a witness, the trial judge must exercise a sound discretion in concluding whether or not a particular witness is qualified."

17. *Jones v. State,* 289 So.2d 725 (Fla. 1974): "Unless a person is a raving maniac or complete imbecile, a jury can hardly be deemed competent to reach a satisfactory decision on the question of his mental condition without the aid of expert witnesses.[d] It is accordingly well settled that the opinions of psychiatrists are admissible in evidence on an issue of sanity or insanity. Such opinions may be drawn (1) from the evidential facts placed before the expert witness in a hypothetical question or based upon the testimony given in the

d. This is not to suggest that the jury must inevitably accept the expert's conclusions. As stated in *United States v. Shackelford,* 494 F.2d 67 (9th Cir.1974), the jury "may, of course, reject expert opinion if it finds that the opinion was based on an incorrect view of the facts." See also *Commonwealth v. Cullen,* 395 Mass. 225, 479 N.E.2d 179 (1985) (even though burden of proof

on prosecution, trier of fact could reject defendant's insanity defense where defendant had two psychiatrists testify in his behalf and the prosecution produced no lay or expert testimony directly in point, as factfinder may take account of the circumstances of the crime and defendant's conduct before and after the crime).

case to establish the sanity or insanity of the person in question, upon the hypothesis that such testimony is all true, even though he made no personal examinations and knew nothing of the actual facts; or (2) upon symptoms and circumstances observed by the witness and testimony in the case, if he has been in Court and heard it all; or (3) upon examination made of the person whose condition is in question. However, the expert cannot give an opinion as to sanity or insanity based upon the opinion or belief of others or based upon statements of third persons out of court."

18. Although it is generally agreed that the witness may not be asked the ultimate question of whether the defendant was responsible, the prevailing rule is that the witness may be asked to respond to a question phrased in the language of the applicable legal test of insanity. As to the latter, A. Goldstein, *The Insanity Defense* 103–04 (1967), objects: "The essential vice of allowing the test questions is that they tend to supplant the factual detail upon which the decision on responsibility should ideally be based. Too often, psychiatric testimony consists of little else, as the test questions convert the insanity issue into what seems to be a search for something the psychiatric witnesses can 'see'— like speed or weather, some seeing it one way and some another. The issue is treated as little more than a matter of credibility: which of the witnesses is to be believed? Which of them had a better vantage point, sharper eyes, less bias, etc.? The jury is left with the impression that it must choose between the experts, because it is not told enough about the defendant's mental life to enable it to make an intelligent judgment about *him,* rather than about the psychiatric witnesses."

e. Compare *State v. Law,* 270 S.C. 664, 244 S.E.2d 302 (1978) (it sufficient that "both the fact of medication and its effect upon the appellant were fully imparted to the jury by the testimony of the medical witnesses"); with *Commonwealth*

19. The jury rejected defendant's insanity defense and convicted him of first degree murder. It later came to light that during the course of the trial state doctors were administering a drug to the defendant for the purpose of rendering him quiet and tractable. In *In re Pray,* 133 Vt. 253, 336 A.2d 174 (1975), the court reversed the conviction because "the jury never looked upon an unaltered, undrugged Gary Pray at any time during the trial. Yet his deportment, demeanor, and day-to-day behavior during that trial, before their eyes, was a part of the basis of their judgment with respect to the kind of person he really was, and the justifiability of his defense of insanity. At the very least, they should have been informed that he was under heavy, sedative medication, that his behavior in their presence was strongly conditioned by drugs administered to him at the direction of the State, and that his defense of insanity was to be applied to a basic behavior pattern that was not the one they were observing. In fact, it may well have been necessary, in view of the critical nature of the issue, to expose the jury to the undrugged, unsedated Gary Pray, at least, insofar as safety and trial progress might permit." [e]

F. THE BIFURCATED TRIAL

20. In a very few jurisdictions the defense of insanity is tried separately from the other issues in the case. The guilt-stage of the trial is first concluded without any reference to the insanity defense, after which (if defendant was found guilty) a separate proceeding takes place before the same or a different jury for purposes of trying the insanity defense. The reasoning underlying adoption of this bifurcated trial

v. Louraine, 390 Mass. 28, 453 N.E.2d 437 (1983) (holding the "ability to present expert testimony describing the effect of medication on the defendant is not an adequate substitute" for defendant's "own demeanor in an unmedicated state").

procedure was that it would eliminate from the basic trial on the issue of whether the defendant engaged in the conduct a great mass of evidence having no bearing on that question and which may confuse the jury or be made the basis of appeals to the sympathy or prejudice of the jury. However, in those jurisdictions where psychiatric testimony may be received on the question of whether the defendant had the requisite mental state (a matter discussed in the next Section), this objective has not been realized. Louisell & Hazard, *Insanity as a Defense: The Bifurcated Trial,* 49 Cal.L. Rev. 805 (1961). In this regard, consider Dix, *Mental Illness, Criminal Intent, and the Bifurcated Trial,* 1970 Law & Soc. Order 559, 575, suggesting that the solution is not to bar receipt of such evidence on the mental state issue, but rather to bifurcate the trial differently so that issues unrelated to mental illness are tried in the first portion and issues involving proof of such illness are tried in the second portion.

21. In jurisdictions where bifurcation is not required, the defendant may wish to seek such a trial. As noted in *State v. Helms,* 284 N.C. 508, 201 S.E.2d 850 (1974), this is a matter within the sound discretion of the judge, but bifurcation is called for only when "a defendant shows that he has a substantial insanity defense and a substantial defense on the merits to any element of the charge, either of which would be prejudiced by simultaneous presentation with the other."

22. Courts have not been receptive to the claim that a defendant has a constitutional right to a bifurcated trial merely because he will interpose a defense of insanity. See, e.g., *Vardas v. Estelle,* 715 F.2d 206 (5th Cir.1983). But bifurcation will sometimes be the best way to avoid a serious constitutional issue, as is illustrated by *United States v. Bennett,* 460 F.2d 872 (D.C.Cir.1972). An important part of the government's case in establishing sanity was the testimony of a psychiatrist as to the

significance of the defendant's recall of his conduct and of the manner in which the defendant related it to the psychiatrist during his examination. The court noted that as between bifurcation and a jury instruction to consider that evidence only on the insanity issue, the latter was "an unsatisfactory solution" because even "the most conscientious juror will have enormous difficulty forgetting a confession when turning from the insanity issue to the case on the merits."

G. INSTRUCTIONS AND VERDICT

23. In most jurisdictions, if the insanity issue reaches the jury then it will be given three alternative verdict forms: guilty; not guilty; and not guilty by reason of insanity. The jury will be instructed that their first order of business is to determine whether the defendant committed the acts charged and that they should reach the insanity question only if they make that initial determination in the affirmative.

24. At the conclusion of all the evidence, the jury will be told what the legal test for the insanity defense is and who has the burden of proving what. It is improper, however, to instruct the jury on the presumption of sanity. This is because, as explained in *United States v. Lawrance,* 480 F.2d 688 (5th Cir.1973), the presumption vanishes once the defendant has met his burden of going forward and has successfully injected the insanity issue into the case.

25. In *Lyles v. United States,* 254 F.2d 725 (D.C.Cir.1957), the court stated: "Jurors, in common with people in general, are aware of the meanings of verdicts of guilty and not guilty. It is common knowledge that a verdict of not guilty means that the prisoner goes free and that a verdict of guilty means that he is subject to such punishment as the court may impose. But a verdict of not guilty by rea-

son of insanity has no such commonly understood meaning. [In the District of Columbia it] means the accused will be confined in a hospital for the mentally ill until the superintendent of such hospital certifies, and the court is satisfied, that such person has recovered his sanity and will not in the reasonable future be dangerous to himself or others. We think the jury has a right to know the meaning of this possible verdict as accurately as it knows by common knowledge the meaning of the other two possible verdicts." [e]

Some states follow the *Lyles* approach, e.g., *State v. Nuckolls,* 166 W.Va. 259, 273 S.E.2d 87 (1980), but the prevailing view is to the contrary, e.g., *State v. Robinson,* 399 N.W.2d 324 (S.D.1987), apparently on the ground that such an instruction would distract the jury from the insanity issue and would invite a compromise verdict.

26. In recent years, a substantial minority of states have enacted legislation requiring that in trials involving an insanity defense a fourth alternative verdict form be provided: "guilty but mentally ill." The jury is given both an insanity defense instruction and an instruction as to what lesser or different type of mental illness permits a GBMI verdict. If a GBMI verdict is returned, the defendant is then sentenced just as if an unqualified guilty verdict had been returned. The only significance of the GBMI verdict is that the defendant is examined by psychiatrists before beginning his prison term and, if he is found to be in need of treatment, is transferred to a mental health facility. If the defendant's mental illness persists, absent

civil commitment he may be held only until his sentence expires; if the defendant regains his sanity he nonetheless serves the balance of his sentence.

Several commentators have questioned the constitutionality of these provisions. See, e.g., Fentiman, *"Guilty But Mentally Ill": The Real Verdict is Guilty,* 26 B.C.L. Rev. 601 (1985). However, GBMI statutes have been upheld against claims that they deny equal protection, violate due process and impose cruel and unusual punishment, *Cooper v. State,* 253 Ga. 736, 325 S.E.2d 137 (1985), and also against the contention that the statutes are impermissibly vague in setting out two ambiguous and overlapping definitions of insanity, *People v. Ramsey,* 422 Mich. 500, 375 N.W. 2d 297 (1985). If, as conceded in *Ramsey,* the GBMI alternative "complicates a trial and creates greater opportunity for confusion," then what of *Keener v. State,* 254 Ga. 699, 334 S.E.2d 175 (1985), simultaneously upholding the GBMI procedure and ruling that the jury is *not* to be told what disposition follows from such a verdict because it is "irrelevant to the jury's deliberations"?

On policy grounds, what do you think of the GBMI alternative? Is it undesirable because "decisions concerning the proper placement of incarcerated offenders should be made by correctional and mental health authorities, not by juries or trial judges"? [f] Because it weakens the insanity defense in that "it is possible, and indeed likely, for a trier of fact to resolve any doubts it may have about a defendant's sanity at the time of the offense in favor of a finding of

e. In *United States v. Brawner,* 471 F.2d 969 (D.C.Cir.1972), the court suggested a revised instruction in the following form to take account of changes in D.C. law regarding commitment: "If the defendant is found not guilty by reason of insanity, it becomes the duty of the court to commit him to St. Elizabeths Hospital. There will be a hearing within 50 days to determine whether defendant is entitled to release. In that

hearing the defendant has the burden of proof. The defendant will remain in custody, and will be entitled to release from custody only if the court finds by a preponderance of the evidence that he is not likely to injure himself or other persons due to mental illness."

f. Bonnie, *The Moral Basis of the Insanity Defense,* 69 A.B.A.J. 194 (1983).

'mere' mental illness"? [g]   Or, is it desirable because it "provides a workable middle ground for fact-finders who must face the vagaries of conflicting psychiatric opinion"? [h]

Consider in this regard Mickenberg, *A Pleasant Surprise: The Guilty but Mentally Ill Verdict Has Both Succeeded in Its Own Right and Successfully Preserved the Traditional Role of the Insanity Defense,* 55 U.Cin.L.Rev. 943, 991–92 (1987): "Ironically, the fears of those who opposed GBMI and the hopes of those who supported it have both been proven wrong. Because GBMI is a supplement to the insanity defense and not a replacement for it, defendants who would have been acquitted by reason of insanity before GBMI was adopted should still be NGRI after the supplementary plea is in use. GBMI defendants should come exclusively from among those who would otherwise have been found guilty, and the rate of NGRI verdicts should be unchanged. In Michigan, this is exactly what has happened. Since the GBMI verdict was adopted in 1975, the percentage of defendants who successfully assert the insanity defense has remained constant. Aided by clear and thorough jury instructions, Michigan jurors have not become confused over the difference between mental illness and insanity, and have not used the GBMI verdict as an excuse to reach improper compromises. Defendants who should be acquitted by reason of insanity are still being acquitted, and those who are mentally ill but not legally insane are being found GBMI."

H. COMMITMENT AND RELEASE

27. S. Brakel, J. Parry & B. Weiner, *The Mentally Disabled and the Law* 725–26 (3d ed. 1985):

"State statutes dealing with the disposition of persons acquitted by reason of insanity are of four basic types. The first approach, formerly followed by the federal courts, has no special provisions: the insanity acquittee is treated like any other defendant found not guilty, and the court has no hold on him. The second type provides for automatic commitment of the acquittee for a period of evaluation to determine if he is a candidate for civil commitment, followed by a hearing to determine need for continued hospitalization. The third provides for automatic commitment, with no set procedure or date for determining the need for continued hospitalization. The fourth type provides for a hearing immediately after the verdict in which commitment must be predicated on an affirmative finding that the acquittee is mentally ill and/or dangerous.

"The statutes vary in their approach to the duration of commitment. In most states, to be discharged the acquittee must be found by hospital doctors or by the court to be no longer in need of mental treatment or no longer dangerous. In some states the acquittee is to be released when he no longer meets the civil commitment criteria. A number of states specify that the person cannot be held longer than the period for which he could be imprisoned had he been convicted and received the maximum sentence for the crime of which he was accused. If he is to be retained after that, it must be through regular civil commitment. Some states set limits on the amount of time the acquittee can be subject to court-supervised outpatient care.

"In a few states where commitment of a person acquitted by reason of insanity is mandatory, the commitment is indeterminate and is based on information gathered at the criminal trial, with no separate evidence or further hearing required. In other states, the automatic commitment is only for an evaluation period, usually last-

---

g. Fentiman, supra, at 652.

h. Comment, 85 Dick.L.Rev. 289, 290 (1981).

ing from 30 to 90 days, to be followed by a full commitment hearing."

28. At issue in *Jones v. United States,* 463 U.S. 354, 103 S.Ct. 3043, 77 L.Ed.2d 694 (1983), were provisions in the D.C. Code whereunder a defendant acquitted by reason of insanity (upon a showing of insanity by a preponderance of the evidence) is automatically committed to a mental hospital and within 50 days thereafter (and periodically subsequently) receives a judicial hearing regarding eligibility for release, at which he has the burden of proving by a preponderance of the evidence that he is no longer mentally ill or dangerous. Jones, who had he been convicted on the shoplifting charge could have received a jail term not exceeding one year, had been hospitalized for longer following his acquittal on insanity grounds.

"It is clear that 'commitment for any purpose constitutes a significant deprivation of liberty that requires due process protection.' *Addington v. Texas,* 441 U.S. 418, 425, 99 S.Ct. 1804, 1809, 60 L.Ed. 2d 323 (1979).

"Petitioner's argument rests principally on *Addington v. Texas,* in which the Court held that the Due Process Clause requires the Government in a civil-commitment proceeding to demonstrate by clear and convincing evidence that the individual is mentally ill and dangerous. * * *

"We turn first to the question whether the finding of insanity at the criminal trial is sufficiently probative of mental illness and dangerousness to justify commitment. A verdict of not guilty by reason of insanity establishes two facts: (i) the defendant committed an act that constitutes a criminal offense, and (ii) he committed the act because of mental illness. Congress has determined that these findings constitute

an adequate basis for hospitalizing the acquittee as a dangerous and mentally ill person. * * * We cannot say that it was unreasonable and therefore unconstitutional for Congress to make this determination.

"The fact that a person has been found, beyond a reasonable doubt, to have committed a criminal act certainly indicates dangerousness.[12] Indeed, this concrete evidence generally may be at least as persuasive as any predictions about dangerousness that might be made in a civil-commitment proceeding. We do not agree with petitioner's suggestion that the requisite dangerousness is not established by proof that a person committed a non-violent crime against property. This Court never has held that 'violence,' however that term might be defined, is a prerequisite for a constitutional commitment.

"Nor can we say that it was unreasonable for Congress to determine that the insanity acquittal supports an inference of continuing mental illness. It comports with common sense to conclude that someone whose mental illness was sufficient to lead him to commit a criminal act is likely to remain ill and in need of treatment. The precise evidentiary force of the insanity acquittal, of course, may vary from case to case, but the Due Process Clause does not require Congress to make classifications that fit every individual with the same degree of relevance. Because a hearing is provided within 50 days of the commitment, there is assurance that every acquittee has prompt opportunity to obtain release if he has recovered. * * *

"Petitioner next contends that his indefinite commitment is unconstitutional because the proof of his insanity was based only on a preponderance of the evidence,

12. The proof beyond a reasonable doubt that the acquittee committed a criminal act distinguishes this case from *Jackson v. Indiana,* in which the Court held that a person found incompetent to stand trial could not be committed

indefinitely solely on the basis of the finding of incompetency. In *Jackson* there never was any affirmative proof that the accused had committed criminal acts or otherwise was dangerous.

as compared to *Addington's* civil-commitment requirement of proof by clear and convincing evidence. In equating these situations, petitioner ignores important differences between the class of potential civil-commitment candidates and the class of insanity acquittees that justify differing standards of proof. The *Addington* Court expressed particular concern that members of the public could be confined on the basis of 'some abnormal behavior which might be perceived by some as symptomatic of a mental or emotional disorder, but which is in fact within a range of conduct that is generally acceptable.' In view of this concern, the Court deemed it inappropriate to ask the individual 'to share equally with society the risk of error.' But since automatic commitment under § 24–301(d)(1) follows only if the *acquittee himself* advances insanity as a defense and proves that his criminal act was a product of his mental illness, there is good reason for diminished concern as to the risk of error. More important, the proof that he committed a criminal act as a result of mental illness eliminates the risk that he is being committed for mere 'idiosyncratic behavior.' A criminal act by definition is not 'within a range of conduct that is generally acceptable.' * * *

"The remaining question is whether petitioner nonetheless is entitled to his release because he has been hospitalized for a period longer than he could have been incarcerated if convicted. The Due Process Clause 'requires that the nature and duration of commitment bear some reasonable relation to the purpose for which the individual is committed.' *Jackson v. Indiana*. The purpose of commitment following an insanity acquittal, like that of civil commitment, is to treat the individual's mental illness and protect him and society from his potential dangerousness. The committed acquittee is entitled to release when he has recovered his sanity or is no longer dangerous. And because it is im-

possible to predict how long it will take for any given individual to recover—or indeed whether he ever will recover—Congress has chosen, as it has with respect to civil commitment, to leave the length of commitment indeterminate, subject to periodic review of the patient's suitability for release.

"In light of the congressional purposes underlying commitment of insanity acquittees, we think petitioner clearly errs in contending that an acquittee's hypothetical maximum sentence provides the constitutional limit for his commitment. A particular sentence of incarceration is chosen to reflect society's view of the proper response to commission of a particular criminal offense, based on a variety of considerations such as retribution, deterrence, and rehabilitation. The State may punish a person convicted of a crime even if satisfied that he is unlikely to commit further crimes.

"Different considerations underlie commitment of an insanity acquittee. As he was not convicted, he may not be punished. His confinement rests on his continuing illness and dangerousness. Thus, under the District of Columbia statute, no matter how serious the act committed by the acquittee, he may be released within 50 days of his acquittal if he has recovered. In contrast, one who committed a less serious act may be confined for a longer period if he remains ill and dangerous. There simply is no necessary correlation between severity of the offense and length of time necessary for recovery. The length of the acquittee's hypothetical criminal sentence therefore is irrelevant to the purposes of his commitment."

29. What result, then, if the trial court rather than the defendant had intruded the insanity defense into the case? What if the burden of proof had been on the prosecution to establish beyond a reasonable doubt the absence of an insanity defense?

I. THE RIGHT TO TREATMENT

30. In *Rouse v. Cameron,* 373 F.2d 451 (D.C.Cir.1967), the habeas corpus petitioner (committed upon a finding he was not guilty by reason of insanity of carrying a dangerous weapon) objected to the district court's refusal to consider his allegation that he had received no psychiatric treatment. The court of appeals, per Bazelon, J., indicated that absence of treatment might render mandatory commitment unconstitutional under various theories: (i) commitment without an express finding of present insanity might violate due process if treatment were not promptly undertaken; (ii) confinement longer than would have been permissible upon conviction might violate due process if no treatment was provided; (iii) failure to provide treatment might constitute a denial of equal protection; and (iv) indefinite confinement without treatment may be so inhumane as to be cruel and unusual punishment. However, the right to treatment recognized by the court was based upon statutory language providing that a "person hospitalized in a public hospital for a mental illness shall, during his hospitalization, be entitled to medical and psychiatric care and treatment." The court declined "to detail the possible range of circumstances in which release would be the appropriate remedy."

31. A. Goldstein, *The Insanity Defense* 169 (1967): "One approach, which has been taken recently in *Rouse v. Cameron,* is to hold the state to its promise of treatment, upon which the indeterminate detention is ordinarily based, and to release patients if the promise is not fulfilled. That approach is so easily avoided, however, by legislative action to withdraw the promise of treatment and to base the detention instead on probable danger, that it is not likely to serve for long. Moreover, it would assign too great a role to litiga-

tion and to the judiciary to superintend treatment processes."

32. Hoffman & Dunn, *Beyond Rouse and Wyatt: An Administrative–Law Model for Expanding and Implementing the Mental Patient's Right to Treatment,* 61 Va.L.Rev. 297, 302 (1975): "The final and most troublesome difficulty with the *Rouse* approach is the single remedy the court allowed—release upon a finding of inadequate treatment. The medical community views premature release of a patient who is proved to be within statutory commitment criteria as ultimately harmful to both the patient and society if the result is to leave the patient without further access to treatment which is medically necessary." What other remedies should the court have allowed?

SECTION 4. DIMINISHED CAPACITY

STATE v. McVEY

Supreme Court of Iowa, 1985.
376 N.W.2d 585.

McCORMICK, JUSTICE. * * *

Defendant Donald Lee McVey was charged in October 1983 with second-degree theft based on exercising control over a stolen motor vehicle under Code sections 714.1(4) and 714.2(2) and with attempting to elude a pursuing law enforcement vehicle in violation of Code section 321.279. The State's evidence was that defendant and a companion escaped from a prison farm and stole an automobile in Fort Madison. They were subsequently observed in the automobile in Urbandale and were apprehended and charged after a high speed chase.

Before trial defendant gave the State notice of a defense of diminished responsibility in accordance with Iowa Rule of Criminal Procedure 11(b)(1). The State moved to strike the defense on the ground it is unavailable as a defense to the charges involved. The trial court sustained the State's motion, and defendant was precluded at trial from offering the testimony of a psychologist on the issue of diminished responsibility. * * *

In relevant part, section 714.1(4) makes it theft for a person to "[exercise] control over stolen property, knowing such property to have been stolen, or having reasonable cause to believe that such property has been stolen, unless the person's purpose is to promptly restore it to the owner or to deliver it to an appropriate public officer." In *State v. Hutt,* 330 N.W.2d 788, 790 (Iowa 1983), we held that the mens rea of this offense requires proof that the accused actually believe the property is stolen. We have also held that the offense does not require proof of specific intent.

The offense is a general intent crime because it is complete without intent to do a further act or achieve a further consequence. General criminal intent exists when from the circumstances the prohibited result may reasonably be expected to flow from the voluntary act itself "irrespective of any subjective desire to have accomplished such result." Thus the crime of theft based on exercising control over stolen property does not require proof of any intent beyond the voluntary act of exercising the prohibited control over property the accused knows is stolen.

In contending the defense of diminished responsibility is available in this case, defendant recognizes that this court has previously held that the defense is not available to crimes that require only a general criminal intent. He argues nevertheless that the statutory requirement of proof of knowledge the property was stolen introduces a special mental element that should be subject to the defense. This argument necessitates review of the nature and scope of the diminished responsibility defense.

The diminished responsibility defense was first recognized by this court in *State v. Gramenz,* 256 Iowa 134, 126 N.W.2d 285 (1964). It is a common law doctrine that "permits proof of defendant's mental condition on the issue of [the defendant's] capacity to form a specific intent in those instances in which the state must prove defendant's specific intent as an element of the crime charged." The court held that evidence of an accused's mental unsoundness may be received to negate specific intent, premeditation and deliberation on a charge of first degree murder, refusing, however, to allow the evidence on the elements of malice aforethought and general criminal intent. The court noted:

> While malice aforethought is the specific state of mind necessary to convict of murder, it is far different from the specific intent which is a necessary element of murder in the first degree. It may be express or implied from the acts and conduct of defendant.
>
> * * *
>
> It appears * * * that testimony sufficient to establish defendant's lack of mental capacity to have malice aforethought would also be sufficient to satisfy the requirements of the right and wrong test and entitle defendant to an acquittal on a plea of insanity rather than a reduction of the sentence to manslaughter.

Subsequently this court held that the defense is available to any crime in which specific intent is an element. The court has continued to recognize the defense even though it is not listed among the special defenses to crime delineated in Code chapter 701. The court has also continued to contrast the defense with the insanity defense, distinguishing diminished responsibility on the ground it allows evidence of mental unsoundness establishing lack of capacity to form a requisite criminal intent rather than requiring proof of the more aggravated kind of distortion of the thinking process required for the absolute defense of insanity.

As of January 1, 1978, the General Assembly codified the insanity defense. The statute incorporates the M'Naghten standard previously adopted by this court as a common law rule. * * * This is obviously a much more stringent standard than is involved in the diminished responsibility defense. Section 701.4 was recently amended to impose the burden on the defendant to prove an insanity defense by a preponderance of the evidence.

Both defenses nevertheless are absolute defenses to specific intent crimes. This was the situation when the M'Naghten rule was codified. The question is whether diminished responsibility should be extended, despite codification of the insanity defense, so that it is also an absolute defense to a general intent crime that requires proof of guilty knowledge. We conclude the defense should not be extended beyond specific intent crimes.

In formulating the insanity defense the legislature defined limits upon the effect of evidence of mental disease or defect relating to criminal culpability generally. This court earlier drew the same line at common law in the *Gramenz* case. It would undercut the legislative policy inherent in the insanity defense for this court to extend the defense of diminished responsibility.

Insanity and mens rea are legal concepts without psychiatric counterparts. As legal concepts they are used to establish limits to legal culpability. The extent to which evidence of mental impairment will be permitted to affect criminal responsibility is therefore a legal question. The argument that evidence of mental impairment should be received because it bears on the mens rea of an offense presupposes that the mens rea requirement has a legal meaning which makes the evidence from the psychological model relevant.

A prominent psychiatrist observed that, "When the law says that the absence of intent renders one incapable of committing a crime, it really means that the triers are incapable of attaching guilt upon the offender, i.e., of inflicting punishment on one who actually committed a harm which if done by a sane person would be punishable." P. Roche, *The Criminal Mind* 87 (1958). In practical terms a court's refusal to recognize the relevancy of evidence of mental impairment short of legal insanity results from the court's understanding of the legislative intention concerning the blameworthiness of the defendant's conduct. To the extent evidence of mental impairment that does not meet the legal insanity standard permits an accused to avoid responsibility for otherwise culpable conduct, the policy inherent in the insanity defense is undermined.

In view of the fact the Iowa common law recognized mental impairment other than legal insanity as a defense only to specific intent crimes at the time the insanity defense was codified, we believe the General Assembly drew the line at that point. The legislature thus established the applicable legal standard for deciding culpability upon evidence of mental impairment in cases requiring proof only of guilty knowledge or general criminal intent accompanying a prohibited act. The mens rea of those crimes is not affected by evidence of mental impairment that does not meet the insanity standard. Therefore we hold that the diminished responsibility defense is available only to specific intent crimes. A similar limitation appears to exist in most other jurisdictions that recognize the defense.

No reversible error has been established.

CARTER, JUSTICE (dissenting). * * *

There is a popular maxim among debaters that, if you allow your opponent to state the issue, your chances of success are indeed slight. The majority opinion utilizes this principle to support its result by treating the issue in the present case as if it were whether the "defense of diminished responsibility" should be further extended. In reality, the issue presented is whether a court in the trial of a criminal case may exclude relevant and material evidence concerning a basic element of the offense charged. Placing labels on similar concepts in order to foster accurate analysis and facilitate uniformity of treatment among like things is acceptable only as long as the concepts which are identically labeled are in fact similar. What something in fact is and how something in fact operates cannot be established by labels.

Commencing with the seminal decision in *State v. Gramenz,* our characterization of the use of expert testimony negating an essential element of a criminal charge has been inaccurate. Unfortunately, this error in description has produced error in application. The fundamental flaw in the analysis upon which these decisions are based is the acceptance of the premise that "diminished responsibility" is a partial defense which reduces responsibility in some types of crimes. Clearly, it is not and never has been.

An illuminating description of the use of expert testimony to negate an element of a criminal charge is contained in the following commentary:

> Mental illness commonly negates an element without amounting to insanity. As a failure of proof defense, at least in cases where the defendant is still guilty of a lesser included offense, it is often called "partial responsibility" or "diminished capacity." Its name highlights the fact that it is something short of insanity; but it is nonetheless an unfortunate choice of terms because there is nothing

partial about the defense. The mental illness either negates a required element of an offense or it does not, thereby providing a complete defense *to that offense* or providing no defense. It is true that many offenses, especially homicide offenses, have lesser included offenses with less demanding culpability elements. Thus mental illness may negate the culpability element of the greater offense but not the lesser offense. When this occurs, the net effect of the mental illness is to reduce the defendant's liability from the greater to the lesser * * *. However, this ultimate reduction effect results from the different offenses, not from a special rule that, when faced with diminished responsibility due to mental illness, generates diminished liability. If there is no lesser included offense, or if the mental illness also negates an element of any lesser included offense, the mental illness will prevent conviction altogether.

Robinson, *Criminal Law Defenses: A Systematic Analysis,* 82 Colum.L.Rev. 199, 206 (1982) (footnotes omitted) (emphasis in original).

The point which professor Robinson makes is fully applicable to the use of this type of evidence under Iowa law. The concept of partial defense exists only as an inaccurate label, spawned from the rhetoric of our decisions, but thoroughly, contradicted in the actual application of the doctrine. In the so-called specific intent crimes in which it has been allowed to operate, the doctrine of diminished responsibility in actual practice is a defense only in the respect that, in the common usage of language, any evidence presented by a defendant to negate the State's evidence is defensive in nature.

The majority seeks to show meaningful differences between specific intent crimes and general intent crimes through the use of definitions from our cases which have no bearing on the present problem. What difference does it make that a general intent crime has been said to be complete without intent to do a further act or achieve a further consequence? * * *

* * * No reason has been suggested by the majority why there is any less need, in the interest of a fair trial, for the accused to be allowed to defend himself when charged with general intent crimes than is the case with respect to specific intent crimes. * * *

Notes and Questions

1. Many jurisdictions do not recognize the concept of "diminished capacity" at all, meaning that evidence of mental illness is inadmissible with respect to the claimed non-existence of *any* mental state (or, stated differently, is admissible *only* in connection with an insanity defense). Lewin, *Psychiatric Evidence in Criminal Cases for Purposes Other than the Defense of Insanity,* 26 Syrac.L.Rev. 1051, 1055 (1975), notes that "today less than 25 state and federal jurisdictions have approved the [diminished capacity] doctrine." More recently it has been observed that enthusiasm for the doctrine is on the wane. *State v. Wilcox,* 70 Ohio St.2d 182, 436 N.E.2d 523 (1982). This explanation is offered in *Curl v. State,* 40 Wis.2d 474, 162 N.W.2d 77 (1968): "Judge and jury ought not be required to identify, classify and evaluate all categories and classifications of human behavior beyond the establishing of the fact of sanity."

2. At the opposite extreme, there are several states which recognize the "diminished capacity" doctrine across the board; that is, they admit evidence of mental disease or defect to negate any culpable state of mind which is an element of the offense. See, e.g., *Hendershott v. People,* 653 P.2d 385 (Colo.1982). These jurisdictions ordinarily require that the mental state on which the evidence is being re-

ceived be a subjective one, so that the particular defendant's state of mind is really at issue, *State v. Burge,* 195 Conn. 232, 487 A.2d 532 (1985) (recklessness). (But see *Robinson v. Commonwealth,* 569 S.W.2d 183 (Ky.App.1978), receiving evidence on the issue of objective negligence.) This means that careful attention is needed to whether or not the matter at issue is at least partially subjective in nature. See *Commonwealth v. McCusker,* 448 Pa. 382, 292 A.2d 286 (1972) (though heat-of-passion voluntary manslaughter distinguished from murder primarily by objective criteria, it also necessary that particular defendant have been in an actual heat of passion which prompted the slaying, and as to that evidence of mental disease is admissible).

3. The remaining jurisdictions utilize the "diminished capacity" doctrine only part of the time. In those states, the prevailing view is that the doctrine is inapplicable to *any* so-called "general intent" crime (e.g., as in *McVey*) and applicable to *all* so-called "specific intent" crimes (e.g., *State v. Barney,* 244 N.W.2d 316 (Iowa 1976), holding it was reversible error for the trial judge to bar psychiatric testimony on mental state where the defendant was charged with the crime of assault with intent to murder.)

A few other jurisdictions limit the "diminished capacity" doctrine to murder cases and, even there, typically permit its use only on the question of whether there existed the requisite premeditation and deliberation for first degree murder. See, e.g., *Waye v. Commonwealth,* 219 Va. 683, 251 S.E.2d 202 (1979).

Sometimes, notwithstanding reference to the general intent-specific intent dichotomy, it appears that the distinction actually being drawn is between those cases in which the diminished capacity would simply reduce the crime to some lesser offense (as in the aforementioned first degree murder case) and those in which acknowledging defendant's diminished capacity would result in outright acquittal. As stated in *McCarthy v. State,* 372 A.2d 180 (Del.1977), "acceptance of the doctrine requires that there be some lesser-included offense which lacks the requisite specific intent of the greater offense charged. Otherwise, the doctrine of diminished responsibility becomes an impermissible substitute test of criminal responsibility." Compare *People v. Wetmore,* 22 Cal.3d 318, 149 Cal.Rptr. 265, 583 P.2d 1308 (1978): "The presence or absence of a lesser included offense within the charged crime cannot affect the result."

4. Are any of the distinctions in the preceding Note defensible, or must "diminished capacity" be an all or nothing proposition? If the latter, is it all or nothing which is the correct position? Consider:

MUENCH v. ISRAEL

United States Court of Appeals, Seventh Circuit, 1983.
715 F.2d 1124.

ESCHBACH, CIRCUIT JUDGE.

[Muench and Worthy, separately convicted of first degree murder in Wisconsin, sought relief via federal habeas corpus because in their trials the court had excluded expert testimony offered for the purpose of establishing that they lacked capacity to form specific intent. They relied on *Hughes v. Mathews,* 576 F.2d 1250 (7th Cir.1978). The district court denied relief.]

Hughes successfully petitioned for a writ of habeas corpus and this court affirmed the judgment granting the writ. This court based its decision on two alternative grounds, only the second of which is argued in this case. We held that the exclusion of the psychiatric evidence offered to show that Hughes lacked the capacity to form the specific intent to kill was constitu-

LaFave—Mod.Crim.Law, 2nd Ed. ACB—16

tionally infirm, as a violation of a criminal defendant's right to present evidence under *Washington v. Texas,* 388 U.S. 14, 87 S.Ct. 1920, 18 L.Ed.2d 1019 (1967), and *Chambers v. Mississippi,* 410 U.S. 284, 93 S.Ct. 1038, 35 L.Ed.2d 297 (1973). Specifically, we followed Justice Harlan's position that a "defendant's right to present evidence is violated where 'the State has recognized as relevant and competent the testimony of this type of witness, but has arbitrarily barred its use by the defendant.'" We recognized that state law determines the relevance and competence of evidence, and we first considered the relevance of psychiatric testimony regarding the issue of intent under Wisconsin law. Noting that Wis.Stats. § 904.01 defines relevant evidence as that which is material and probative, we thought that psychiatric testimony regarding a defendant's mental state "would pertain to and have some bearing" on distinguishing between the intent requirements of first-degree and second-degree murder. We based this conclusion on (1) [the fact] that proof of insanity is not proof that the defendant lacks the capacity to intend, (2) the fact that Wisconsin viewed psychiatric evidence highly relevant on the issue of competency to stand trial, and (3) *King v. State,* 75 Wis. 2d 26, 248 N.W.2d 458 (1977), in which the defendant was permitted to introduce psychiatric testimony as character evidence. We recognized, however, that *Curl v. State,* 40 Wis.2d 474, 162 N.W.2d 77 (1968), suggested a contrary conclusion on the relevance question, but concluded that *Curl's* objections to psychiatric testimony were based on the competency of such evidence and public policy considerations.

On the issue of competency under state law, we recognized that *Curl* stated that the reason for excluding psychiatric testimony on the intent issue was a disbelief in the ability of psychiatry to define degrees of mental abnormality less than insanity, and we "question[ed] the validity of a system which views psychiatric testimony as trustworthy evidence as to whether a person is mentally capable of appreciating the wrongfulness of his conduct but untrustworthy to express an opinion regarding a person's mental capacity to form specific intent to kill when such testimony is the only relevant evidence available." However, we did not pass on that question; instead we interpreted *Curl* "as stating that the true reason for excluding psychiatric evidence on the issue of intent in Wisconsin courts is the fear that persons who are legally sane will escape punishment," and expressed the view that "[t]his is more of a justification for excluding competent evidence than a reason why the evidence is incompetent." We then concluded that "psychiatric testimony is generally considered competent evidence in Wisconsin" because of its use on the questions of insanity and competence to stand trial, and the fact that psychiatric diagnosis satisfies the general test for admissibility of scientific evidence.

Having thus determined that psychiatric testimony was relevant and competent under state law, we acknowledged that the right of a defendant to present such evidence may " 'bow to accommodate other legitimate interests in the criminal trial process,' " and proceeded to "closely examine[ ]" the "two main justifications" for the Wisconsin practice. The first justification—the fear that the guilty would be absolved of criminal liability—was considered "unpersuasive in the present case where the testimony was offered only to show that a second-degree murder conviction was proper," but we expressly reserved judgment on the sufficiency of this justification in other circumstances. Regarding the second justification—ensuring the integrity of Wisconsin's bifurcated trial system—"confining ourselves to the facts of [Hughes'] case" we noted that no bifurcated trial occurred, and that Hughes had

"admitted the act" and argued only he lacked intent to kill. We thus concluded that the state's second justification (based on the concerns about duplicative evidence, and self-incrimination concerns) was "not applicable here."

In relevant part, we concluded our opinion as follows:

> In conclusion, we emphasize first what we have not done. We have not sought to impose a "diminished responsibility" defense for emotional problems upon Wisconsin. The fashioning of such affirmative defenses involves the type of "subtle balancing of society's interests against those of the accused [which has] been left to the legislative branch." Nor have we attempted to further "constitutionalize" the law of evidence by constructing a constitutional right to introduce psychiatric testimony * * *. We have * * * recognized the due process right of the defendant to present relevant and competent evidence in the absence of valid state justification for excluding such evidence. Upon the particular facts of this case, we find Wisconsin's justifications to be inapplicable.

* * *

The Wisconsin Supreme Court faced yet another challenge to the exclusion of psychiatric testimony during the guilt phase of a bifurcated first-degree murder trial in *Steele v. State*, 97 Wis.2d 72, 294 N.W.2d 2 (1980). * * *

[There the court] examined our conclusion in *Hughes* that such expert testimony was relevant and competent under Wisconsin law, canvassing much of the same authority about the question as we had in *Hughes,* and other authorities as well. The court stated that while it recognized the utility of psychiatric testimony regarding some questions, such as insanity, it had serious doubts about the use of such testimony on the question of criminal intent. The different forms of *mens rea* upon which the criminal law distinguishes certain offenses from one another "requires a fine tuning of an entirely different nature than that required for the admission of evidence on the general question of insanity * * *." The court doubted whether psychiatry could contribute trustworthy, scientifically-substantiated expert knowledge concerning an individual's capacity to form an intent, noted the tendency of juries to place great reliance on such experts, and doubted the efficacy of cross-examination on this question. It concluded that "under the present state of the law, the proffered evidence is neither competent, relevant, nor probative for the purpose asserted in the instant case," emphasizing that this conclusion provided a basis for excluding such testimony independent of its concerns for maintaining its bifurcation scheme. * * *

The question the instant case presents is not the question we decided in *Hughes.* In *Hughes* we determined that when evidence is considered relevant and competent under state law, a criminal defendant may not be precluded from presenting it in his defense if the *policy* considerations advanced in support of exclusion are inapplicable in the context of the situation. We took pains in *Hughes* to point out that we were not seeking to constitutionalize the law of evidence nor to impose a diminished responsibility doctrine on Wisconsin. Yet that is just what petitioners in the instant case seek: they argue that they have a constitutional right to present psychiatric evidence of their abnormal personalities in order to prove that they lacked the capacity to form an intent to kill. * * *

In their attempt to have this court impose the doctrine of diminished capacity on the Wisconsin courts in fact but not in name, petitioners attempt to distinguish the position taken by *Steele* and that taken by the court in *Bethea v. United States,* 365 A.2d 64 (D.C.App.1976). In *Bethea,* the

District of Columbia Court of Appeals expressly rejected the doctrine of diminished responsibility. Petitioners maintain that if *Steele* had done this, the instant case would present a different question. *Steele,* of course, is nothing but a lengthy explication of the reasons for rejecting the doctrine. To avoid the very contention petitioners now make in attempting to cloud the issue, the *Bethea* court stressed the manner in which it was using the terms diminished capacity and diminished responsibility: "to connote the admissibility of expert evidence of the accused's mental abnormalities for the specific purpose of negativing the required *mens rea.*" Since *Steele* and *Bethea* did in fact decide the same question, it is not surprising that *Bethea* is based on the same considerations which motivated *Steele:* that injecting questions about mental abnormalities into a trial on first-degree murder detracts attention from the real issues and has as its basis a theory about culpability which the court is unprepared to accept against the interwoven and delicately crafted fabric of its substantive definition of murder, its view of *scienter,* its conception of legal insanity, its assessment of the limitations of jurors, and its evaluation of the state of the developing discipline of psychology.

Recognition of the doctrine turns not only on whether it is believed that the discipline of psychology has reached the point where it can provide meaningful insights into the kinds of mental states which beget criminal culpability, but on other factors as well. The doctrine emerged in large measure to ameliorate the relatively narrow concept of insanity under the *M'Naghten* test, and found its most fertile ground in capital cases, and cases in which the *mens rea* required premeditation. In short, the doctrine emerged from experience as an attempt to fashion a rational and coherent method for society to treat with compassion those among us who operate in the twilight of rationality.

Of course, there is much logic to the doctrine as well, and it is the logic of the doctrine which petitioners emphasize in their attempt to impose it upon Wisconsin as a matter of constitutional law. They challenge *Steele*'s conclusion that psychiatric evidence is irrelevant and incompetent.

An analysis concerning the relevancy of evidence begins by ascertaining the facts which are in issue as a result of the substantive law and the pleadings. Evidence which establishes a proposition not in issue is said to be immaterial—*i.e.,* the fact wished to be established is not an issue in the case under the substantive law.

Petitioners' argument regarding the materiality of the proffered psychiatric testimony is straightforward. Whether they actually committed their homicidal acts with the mental purpose of ending a human life was a fact in issue. Logically, their "capacity" to "form" that intention is a fact in issue, for if they lacked the capacity to form the intent, then they did not actually form that intent. Hence, their capacity to form an intent to kill is a fact in issue, and evidence standing for that proposition is material.

It is naturally tautological that one who lacks the capacity to do something could not have done that something. Thus conceptualized, the process of cognition is described in essentially, physiological terms. "Forming" an "intention" can be likened to "performing" an "action," and just as evidence of a physical handicap which rendered a person incapable of performing a particular action would be material in a case where the person is accused of performing that action, it would logically seem that evidence of a mental handicap which rendered a person incapable of forming a particular intention would be material where the person is accused of forming that intention.

If specific types of intentions were as discrete as particular types of actions; if

one's mental abilities were as demonstrable as one's physical abilities; if the relationship between one's mental handicaps and a specific intent were as identifiable as the relationship between one's physical handicaps and a specific physical movement; and if one formed an intention the way one performs an action, the analogy would be compelling, but it is not.

The essential flaw in petitioners' argument is that the basic fact which they wish to establish is that they suffered from a personality disorder. It is not disputed that experts in psychology are competent to testify regarding that basic fact. What is the dispute—indeed, the entire debate over the doctrine of diminished capacity has as its focal point—is whether a personality disorder is probative of the defendant's capacity to form an intent to kill. Petitioners' experts contended that personality disorders rendered them unable to form such an intent. That is, their experts contended that the fact of their personality disorders was a material issue in their cases because the fact was probative of whether they were capable of entertaining a mental state in issue. In short, petitioners essentially maintain that the psychiatric testimony they proffered is relevant because their witnesses said so. The proposition does not survive its statement.

CUDAHY, CIRCUIT JUDGE, dissenting.

* * *

For several reasons, however, I do not think the "gross" versus "fine tuning" distinction withstands careful analysis. Therefore, since—as I understand the Supreme Court—the burden is on the state to justify the exclusion for certain uses of evidence it otherwise deems reliable, I am impelled to reach a conclusion which the majority rejects.

First, the state's assertion that it must exclude *expert* testimony on the defendant's *mens rea* lest this testimony interfere with the jury's determination of specific intent to kill seems inconsistent with its willingness to allow the jury to hear all manner of testimony on the very same subject without any expert component.

* * *

Second, the state's broad exclusionary rule apparently will have the effect of excluding certain psychiatric testimony which would appear to be of exceptional value in clarifying the *mens rea* issues for the jury.

* * *

In this connection, the *Steele* court rejected the position that the admission of psychiatric testimony on intent should be left to the discretion of the trial court. This position was advocated by Justice Abrahamson, dissenting in *Steele*. * * *

Third, although the state asserted a distinction between expert testimony on *mens rea* capacity and expert testimony with respect to insanity, the Wisconsin Supreme Court also made the point that the former sort of testimony was "substantially congruent with evidence supportive of the * * * test for insanity to be utilized in the second phase of the bifurcated trial * * *. Both tests focus on exactly the same mental defect—lack of capacity." But this observation seems to suggest that insanity and *mens rea* incapacity are merely labels for the same disorganization of mind and personality; therefore, the evidentiary analysis with respect to one may very well virtually duplicate the analysis of the other.

* * *

Notes and Questions

1. Are the concerns which prompted the Wisconsin Supreme Court to reject the "diminished capacity" doctrine legitimate? Do they necessitate a *total* prohibition upon psychiatric testimony on mental state issues? Consider that in *State v. Flattum,* 122 Wis.2d 282, 361 N.W.2d 705 (1985), the court held that "*Steele* does not render inadmissible *all* expert opinion evidence from a psychiatrist on the issue of a defendant's capacity to form intent. We reemphasize that the *Steele* decision was predicated on this court's disbelief in the ability of psychiatry to causally link psychiatric disorders to a lack of capacity to form specific intent. We hold that a psychiatrist, properly qualified as an expert on the effects of intoxicants, may render an expert opinion as to whether a defendant's voluntary intoxicated condition negatived the defendant's capacity to form the requisite intent, but only if that opinion is based solely on the defendant's voluntary intoxicated condition.

"However, we offer a cautionary note to trial courts when expert opinion testimony from a psychiatrist is offered to causally link a defendant's intoxicated condition with a lack of capacity to form the requisite intent. As we have noted in our review of the basis and scope of *Steele,* there may be a problem with the inconsistency between the law's conception of intent and the psychiatrist's understanding of the term. Nevertheless, it would not be logical to prohibit psychiatrists who are properly qualified as experts on the effects of intoxication from giving expert medical opinion testimony on the effects of intoxication just because of their psychiatric background. However, unlike other witnesses who are expert on the effect of intoxication on capacity to intend, psychiatrists may have a natural tendency, due to their training, to consider a defendant's mental health history in formulating their opinions. Trial courts must carefully scrutinize such testimony to ensure that a defendant's mental health history is not being considered by any expert, psychiatrist or not, in reaching his or her conclusion that the defendant lacked the capacity to form the requisite criminal intent due to his or her voluntary intoxication."

2. 1 P. Robinson, *Criminal Law Defenses* § 64(a) (Supp.1987), observes that "recognition of the fact that this 'defense' works only on an evidentiary level, i.e.,

that only evidence of mental disease or defect that is relevant to a state of mind necessary for the offense charge is admissible under this 'defense,' would not only provide a rational basis for admitting defense evidence, but would also provide a rational basis for exclusion of much psychiatric testimony. At least where a jurisdiction has adopted a modern culpability scheme patterned on Model Penal Code § 2.02, evidence of mental disease or defect often has little bearing on whether the defendant acted with purpose, knowledge, recklessness, or negligence. The definitions of these terms do not call for a 'normative' assessment of blameworthiness; rather they call for specific findings concerning the actor's state of mind with respect to the objective elements of the offense, e.g., was the actor aware that his conduct would cause the death of a human being. Evidence concerning disorders that lead to impaired ability to control conduct, for example, is simply not relevant to the culpability required by such offense definitions. A rule of strict relevance may well do more to limit improper psychiatric testimony than an arbitrary and artificial rule based on such distinctions as specific and general intent."

3. To what extent is the concern not merely about the value of psychiatric evidence, but about the use of such evidence when the possible result is different from that which obtains when there is a successful insanity defense? Consider *People v. Wetmore,* 22 Cal.3d 318, 149 Cal.Rptr. 265, 583 P.2d 1308 (1978):

"The same danger may arise, however, when a diminished capacity defense does not result in the defendant's acquittal, but in his conviction for a lesser included offense. A defendant convicted of a lesser included misdemeanor, for example, will be confined for a relatively short period in a facility which probably lacks a suitable treatment program, and may later, having served his term, be released to become a public danger. The solution to this problem thus does not lie in barring the defense of diminished capacity when the charged crime lacks a lesser included offense, but in providing for the confinement and treatment of defendants with diminished capacity arising from mental disease or defect."

Chapter 7

ALCOHOLISM AND ADDICTION; INTOXICATION; IMMATURITY

SECTION 1. CHRONIC ALCOHOLISM AND DRUG ADDICTION

POWELL v. TEXAS

Supreme Court of the United States, 1968.
392 U.S. 514, 88 S.Ct. 2145, 20 L.Ed.2d 1254.

MR. JUSTICE MARSHALL announced the judgment of the Court and delivered an opinion in which THE CHIEF JUSTICE, MR. JUSTICE BLACK, and MR. JUSTICE HARLAN join.

In late December 1966, appellant was arrested and charged with being found in a state of intoxication in a public place, in violation of Vernon's Ann.Texas Penal Code, Art. 477 (1952), which reads as follows:

"Whoever shall get drunk or be found in a state of intoxication in any public place, or at any private house except his own, shall be fined not exceeding one hundred dollars."
* * *

The trial judge in the county court, sitting without a jury, * * * found appellant guilty, and fined him $50.
* * *

The principal testimony was that of Dr. David Wade, a Fellow of the American Medical Association, duly certificated in psychiatry. * * * Dr. Wade sketched the outlines of the "disease" concept of alcoholism; noted that there is no generally accepted definition of "alcoholism"; alluded to the ongoing debate within the medical profession over whether alcohol is actually physically "addicting" or merely psychologically "habituating"; and concluded that in either case a "chronic alcoholic" is an "involuntary drinker," who is "powerless not to drink," and who "loses his self-control over his drinking." He testified that he had examined appellant, and that appellant is a "chronic alcoholic," who "by the time he has reached [the state of intoxication] * * * is not able to control his behavior, and [who] * * * has reached this point because he has an uncontrollable compulsion to drink." Dr. Wade also responded in the negative to the question whether appellant has "the willpower to resist the constant excessive consumption of alcohol." He added that in his opinion jailing appellant without medical attention would operate neither to rehabilitate him nor to lessen his desire for alcohol.

On cross-examination, Dr. Wade admitted that when appellant was sober he knew the difference between right and wrong, and he responded affirmatively to the question whether appellant's act in taking the first drink in any given instance when he was sober was a "voluntary exercise of his will." Qualifying his answer, Dr. Wade stated that "these individuals have a compulsion, and this compulsion, while not completely overpowering, is a very strong influence, an exceedingly strong influence, and this compulsion coupled with the firm belief in their mind that they are going to be able to handle it from now on causes their judgment to be somewhat clouded."

Appellant testified concerning the history of his drinking problem. He reviewed his many arrests for drunkenness; testified that he was unable to stop drinking; stated that when he was intoxicated he had no control over his actions and could not remember them later, but that he did not become violent; and admitted that he did not remember his arrest on the occasion for which he was being tried. On cross-examination, appellant admitted that he had had one drink on the morning of the trial and had been able to discontinue drinking.

Evidence in the case then closed. [T]he State contented itself with a brief argument that appellant had no defense to the charge because he "is legally sane and knows the difference between right and wrong."

Following this abbreviated exposition of the problem before it, the trial court indicated its intention to disallow appellant's claimed defense of "chronic alcoholism." Thereupon defense counsel submitted, and the trial court entered, the following "findings of fact":

"(1) That chronic alcoholism is a disease which destroys the afflicted person's will power to resist the constant, excessive consumption of alcohol.

"(2) That a chronic alcoholic does not appear in public by his own volition but under a compulsion symptomatic of the disease of chronic alcoholism.

"(3) That Leroy Powell, defendant herein, is a chronic alcoholic who is afflicted with the disease of chronic alcoholism."

Whatever else may be said of them, those are not "findings of fact" in any recognizable, traditional sense in which that term has been used in a court of law; they are the premises of a syllogism transparently designed to bring this case within the scope of this Court's opinion in *Robinson v. California*, 370 U.S. 660, 82 S.Ct. 1417, 8 L.Ed.2d 758 (1962). Nonetheless, the dissent would have us adopt these "findings" without critical examination; it would use them as the basis for a constitutional holding that "a person may not be punished if the condition essential to constitute the defined crime is part of the pattern of his disease and is occasioned by a compulsion symptomatic of the disease."

The difficulty with that position, as we shall show, is that it goes much too far on the basis of too little knowledge. In the first place, the record in this case is utterly inadequate to permit the sort of informed and responsible adjudication which alone can support the announcement of an important and wide-ranging new constitutional principle. We know very little about the circumstances surrounding the drinking bout which resulted in this conviction, or about Leroy Powell's drinking problem, or indeed about alcoholism itself.

* * *

Furthermore, the inescapable fact is that there is no agreement among members of the medical profession about what it means to say that "alcoholism" is a "disease." One of the principal works in this field states that the major difficulty in articulating a "disease concept of alcoholism" is that "alcoholism has too many definitions and disease has practically none." This same author concludes that *a disease is what the medical profession recognizes as such.* In other words, there is widespread agreement today that "alcoholism" is a "disease," for the simple reason that the medical profession has concluded that it should attempt to treat those who have drinking problems. There the agreement stops. Debate rages within the medical profession as to whether "alcoholism" is a separate "disease" in any meaningful biochemical, physiological or psychological sense, or whether it represents one peculiar manifestation in some individuals of underlying psychiatric disorders. * * *

The trial court's "finding" that Powell "is afflicted with the disease of chronic alcoholism," which "destroys the afflicted person's will power to resist the constant, excessive consumption of alcohol" covers a multitude of sins. Dr. Wade's testimony that appellant suffered from a compulsion which was an "exceedingly strong influence," but which was "not completely overpowering" is at least more carefully stated, if no less mystifying. [C]onceptual clarity can only be achieved by distinguishing carefully between "loss of control" once an individual has commenced to drink and "inability to abstain" from drinking in the first place. Presumably a person would have to display both characteristics in order to make out a constitutional defense, should one be recognized. Yet the "findings" of the trial court utterly fail to make this crucial distinction, and there is serious question whether the record can be read to support a finding of either loss of control or inability to abstain.

Dr. Wade did testify that once appellant began drinking he appeared to have no control over the amount of alcohol he finally ingested. Appellant's own testimony concerning his drinking on the day of the trial would certainly appear, however, to cast doubt upon the conclusion that he was without control over his consumption of alcohol when he had sufficiently important reasons to exercise such control. However that may be, there are more serious factual and conceptual difficulties

with reading this record to show that appellant was unable to abstain from drinking. Dr. Wade testified that when appellant was sober, the act of taking the first drink was a "voluntary exercise of his will," but that this exercise of will was undertaken under the "exceedingly strong influence" of a "compulsion" which was "not completely overpowering." Such concepts, when juxtaposed in this fashion, have little meaning. * * *

It is one thing to say that if a man is deprived of alcohol his hands will begin to shake, he will suffer agonizing pains and ultimately he will have hallucinations; it is quite another to say that a man has a "compulsion" to take a drink, but that he also retains a certain amount of "free will" with which to resist. It is simply impossible, in the present state of our knowledge, to ascribe a useful meaning to the latter statement. This definitional confusion reflects, of course, not merely the undeveloped state of the psychiatric art but also the conceptual difficulties inevitably attendant upon the importation of scientific and medical models into a legal system generally predicated upon a different set of assumptions. * * *

There is as yet no known generally effective method for treating the vast number of alcoholics in our society. * * * Thus it is entirely possible that, even were the manpower and facilities available for a full-scale attack upon chronic alcoholism, we would find ourselves unable to help the vast bulk of our "visible"—let alone our "invisible"—alcoholic population.

However, facilities for the attempted treatment of indigent alcoholics are woefully lacking throughout the country. It would be tragic to return large numbers of helpless, sometimes dangerous and frequently unsanitary inebriates to the streets of our cities without even the opportunity to sober up adequately which a brief jail term provides. Presumably no State or city will tolerate such a state of affairs. Yet the medical profession cannot, and does not, tell us with any assurance that, even if the buildings, equipment and trained personnel were made available, it could provide anything more than slightly higher-class jails for our indigent habitual inebriates. Thus we run the grave risk that nothing will be accomplished beyond the hanging of a new sign—reading "hospital"—over one wing of the jailhouse.

One virtue of the criminal process is, at least, that the duration of penal incarceration typically has some outside statutory limit; this is universally true in the case of petty offenses, such as public drunkenness, where jail terms are quite short on the whole. "Therapeutic civil commitment" lacks this feature; one is typically committed until one is "cured." Thus, to do otherwise than affirm might subject indigent alcoholics to the risk that they may be locked up for an indefinite period of time under the same conditions as before, with no more hope than before of receiving effective treatment and no prospect of periodic "freedom."

Faced with this unpleasant reality, we are unable to assert that the use of the criminal process as a means of dealing with the public aspects of problem drinking can never be defended as rational. * * *

Ignorance likewise impedes our assessment of the deterrent effect of criminal sanctions for public drunkenness. The fact that a high percentage of American alcoholics conceal their drinking problems, not merely by avoiding public displays of intoxication but also by shunning all forms of treatment, is indicative that some powerful deterrent operates to inhibit the public revelation of the existence of alcoholism. Quite probably this deterrent effect can be largely attributed to the harsh moral attitude which our society has traditionally taken toward intoxication and the

shame which we have associated with alcoholism. * * *

Obviously, chronic alcoholics have not been deterred from drinking to excess by the existence of criminal sanctions against public drunkenness. But all those who violate penal laws of any kind are by definition undeterred. The longstanding and still raging debate over the validity of the deterrence justification for penal sanctions has not reached any sufficiently clear conclusions to permit it to be said that such sanctions are ineffective in any particular context or for any particular group of people who are able to appreciate the consequences of their acts. Certainly no effort was made at the trial of this case, beyond a monosyllabic answer to a perfunctory one-line question, to determine the effectiveness of penal sanctions in deterring Leroy Powell in particular or chronic alcoholics in general from drinking at all or from getting drunk in particular places or at particular times. * * *

Appellant, however, seeks to come within the application of the Cruel and Unusual Punishment Clause announced in *Robinson v. California,* which involved a state statute making it a crime to "be addicted to the use of narcotics." This Court held there that "a state law which imprisons a person thus afflicted [with narcotic addiction] as a criminal, even though he has never touched any narcotic drug within the State or been guilty of any irregular behavior there, inflicts a cruel and unusual punishment * * *."

On its face the present case does not fall within that holding, since appellant was convicted, not for being a chronic alcoholic, but for being in public while drunk on a particular occasion. The State of Texas thus has not sought to punish a mere status, as California did in *Robinson;* nor has it attempted to regulate appellant's behavior in the privacy of his own home. Rather, it has imposed upon appellant a criminal sanction for public behavior which may create substantial health and safety hazards, both for appellant and for members of the general public, and which offends the moral and esthetic sensibilities of a large segment of the community. This seems a far cry from convicting one for being an addict, being a chronic alcoholic, being "mentally ill, or a leper * * *."

Robinson so viewed brings this Court but a very small way into the substantive criminal law. And unless *Robinson* is so viewed it is difficult to see any limiting principle that would serve to prevent this Court from becoming, under the aegis of the Cruel and Unusual Punishment Clause, the ultimate arbiter of the standards of criminal responsibility, in diverse areas of the criminal law, throughout the country.

It is suggested in dissent that *Robinson* stands for the "simple" but "subtle" principle that "[c]riminal penalties may not be inflicted upon a person for being in a condition he is powerless to change." In that view, appellant's "condition" of public intoxication was "occasioned by a compulsion symptomatic of the disease" of chronic alcoholism, and thus, apparently, his behavior lacked the critical element of *mens rea.* Whatever may be the merits of such a doctrine of criminal responsibility, it surely cannot be said to follow from *Robinson.* The entire thrust of *Robinson's* interpretation of the Cruel and Unusual Punishment Clause is that criminal penalties may be inflicted only if the accused has committed some act, has engaged in some behavior, which society has an interest in preventing, or perhaps in historical common law terms, has committed some *actus reus.* It thus does not deal with the question of whether certain conduct cannot constitutionally be punished because it is, in some sense, "involuntary" or "occasioned by a compulsion."

Likewise, as the dissent acknowledges, there is a substantial definitional distinction between a "status," as in *Robinson,* and a "condition," which is said to be involved in this case. Whatever may be the merits of an attempt to distinguish between behavior and a condition, it is perfectly clear that the crucial element in this case, so far as the dissent is concerned, is whether or not appellant can legally be held responsible for his appearance in public in a state of intoxication. The only relevance of *Robinson* to this issue is that because the Court interpreted the statute there involved as making a "status" criminal, it was able to suggest that the statute would cover even a situation in which addiction had been acquired involuntarily. That this factor was not determinative in the case is shown by the fact that there was no indication of how Robinson himself had become an addict.

Ultimately, then, the most troubling aspects of this case, were *Robinson* to be extended to meet it, would be the scope and content of what could only be a constitutional doctrine of criminal responsibility. In dissent it is urged that the decision could be limited to conduct which is "a characteristic and involuntary part of the pattern of the disease as it afflicts" the particular individual, and that "[i]t is not foreseeable" that it would be applied "in the case of offenses such as driving a car while intoxicated, assault, theft, or robbery." That is limitation by fiat. In the first place, nothing in the logic of the dissent would limit its application to chronic alcoholics. If Leroy Powell cannot be convicted of public intoxication, it is difficult to see how a State can convict an individual for murder, if that individual, while exhibiting normal behavior in all other respects, suffers from a "compulsion" to kill, which is an "exceedingly strong influence," but "not completely overpowering." Even if we limit our consideration to chronic alcoholics, it would seem impossible to confine the principle within the arbitrary bounds which the dissent seems to envision. * * *

Traditional common-law concepts of personal accountability and essential considerations of federalism lead us to disagree with appellant. We are unable to conclude, on the state of this record or on the current state of medical knowledge, that chronic alcoholics in general, and Leroy Powell in particular, suffer from such an irresistible compulsion to drink and to get drunk in public that they are utterly unable to control their performance of either or both of these acts and thus cannot be deterred at all from public intoxication. And in any event this Court has never articulated a general constitutional doctrine of *mens rea.*

We cannot cast aside the centuries-long evolution of the collection of interlocking and overlapping concepts which the common law has utilized to assess the moral accountability of an individual for his antisocial deeds. The doctrines of *actus reus, mens rea,* insanity, mistake, justification, and duress have historically provided the tools for a constantly shifting adjustment of the tension between the evolving aims of the criminal law and changing religious, moral, philosophical, and medical views of the nature of man. This process of adjustment has always been thought to be the province of the States. * * *

Affirmed.

MR. JUSTICE BLACK, whom MR. JUSTICE HARLAN joins, concurring.

* * * The argument is made that appellant comes within the terms of our holding in *Robinson* because being drunk in public is a mere status or "condition." Despite this many-faceted use of the concept of "condition," this argument would require converting *Robinson* into a case protecting actual behavior, a step we explicitly refused to take in that decision.

* * *

The rule of constitutional law urged upon us by appellant would have a revolutionary impact on the criminal law, and any possible limits proposed for the rule would be wholly illusory. If the original boundaries of *Robinson* are to be discarded, any new limits too would soon fall by the wayside and the Court would be forced to hold the States powerless to punish any conduct that could be shown to result from a "compulsion," in the complex, psychological meaning of that term. * * *

The real reach of any such decision, however, would be broader still, for the basic premise underlying the argument is that it is cruel and unusual to punish a person who is not morally blameworthy. I state the proposition in this sympathetic way because I feel there is much to be said for avoiding the use of criminal sanctions in many such situations. But the question here is one of constitutional law. The legislatures have always been allowed wide freedom to determine the extent to which moral culpability should be a prerequisite to conviction of a crime. The criminal law is a social tool that is employed in seeking a wide variety of goals, and I cannot say the Eighth Amendment's limits on the use of criminal sanctions extend as far as this viewpoint would inevitably carry them.

But even if we were to limit any holding in this field to "compulsions" that are "symptomatic" of a "disease," in the words of the findings of the trial court, the sweep of that holding would still be startling. Such a ruling would make it clear beyond any doubt that a narcotics addict could not be punished for "being" in possession of drugs or, for that matter, for "being" guilty of using them. A wide variety of sex offenders would be immune from punishment if they could show that their conduct was not voluntary but part of the pattern of a disease. More generally speaking, a form of the insanity defense would be made a constitutional requirement throughout the Nation, should the

Court now hold it cruel and unusual to punish a person afflicted with any mental disease whenever his conduct was part of the pattern of his disease and occasioned by a compulsion symptomatic of the disease. * * *

MR. JUSTICE WHITE, concurring in the result.

If it cannot be a crime to have an irresistible compulsion to use narcotics, *Robinson v. California,* I do not see how it can constitutionally be a crime to yield to such a compulsion. Punishing an addict for using drugs convicts for addiction under a different name. Distinguishing between the two crimes is like forbidding criminal conviction for being sick with flu or epilepsy but permitting punishment for running a fever or having a convulsion. Unless *Robinson* is to be abandoned, the use of narcotics by an addict must be beyond the reach of the criminal law. Similarly, the chronic alcoholic with an irresistible urge to consume alcohol should not be punishable for drinking or for being drunk.

Powell's conviction was for the different crime of being drunk in a public place. Thus even if Powell was compelled to drink, and so could not constitutionally be convicted for drinking, his conviction in this case can be invalidated only if there is a constitutional basis for saying that he may not be punished for being in public while drunk. * * *

2. Analysis of this difficult case is not advanced by preoccupation with the label "condition." In *Robinson* the Court dealt with "a statute which makes the 'status' of narcotic addiction a criminal offense * * *." By precluding criminal conviction for such a "status" the Court was dealing with a condition brought about by acts remote in time from the application of the criminal sanctions contemplated, a condition which was relatively permanent in duration, and a condition of great magnitude and significance in terms of human behavior and values. Although the same may be said for the "condition" of being a chronic alcoholic, it cannot be said for the mere transitory state of "being drunk in public." "Being" drunk in public is not far removed in time from the acts of "getting" drunk and "going" into

The trial court said that Powell was a chronic alcoholic with a compulsion not only to drink to excess but also to frequent public places when intoxicated. Nothing in the record before the trial court supports the latter conclusion, which is contrary to common sense and to common knowledge. The sober chronic alcoholic has no compulsion to be on the public streets; many chronic alcoholics drink at home and are never seen drunk in public. Before and after taking the first drink, and until he becomes so drunk that he loses the power to know where he is or to direct his movements, the chronic alcoholic with a home or financial resources is as capable as the nonchronic drinker of doing his drinking in private, of removing himself from public places and, since he knows or ought to know that he will become intoxicated, of making plans to avoid his being found drunk in public. For these reasons, I cannot say that the chronic alcoholic who proves his disease and a compulsion to drink is shielded from conviction when he has knowingly failed to take feasible precautions against committing a criminal act, here the act of going to or remaining in a public place. On such facts the alcoholic is like a person with smallpox, who could be convicted for being on the street but not for being ill, or, like the epileptic, who would be punished for driving a car but not for his disease.[2]

public, and it is not necessarily a state of any great duration. And, an isolated instance of "being" drunk in public is of relatively slight importance in the life of an individual as compared with the condition of being a chronic alcoholic. If it were necessary to distinguish between "acts" and "conditions" for purposes of the Eighth Amendment, I would adhere to the concept of "condition" implicit in the opinion in *Robinson*; I would not trivialize that concept by drawing a nonexistent line between the man who appears in public drunk and that same man five minutes later who is then "being" drunk in public. The proper subject of inquiry is whether volitional acts brought about the "condition" and whether those acts are sufficiently proximate to the "con-

For the purposes of this case, it is necessary to say only that Powell showed nothing more than that he was to some degree compelled to drink and that he was drunk at the time of his arrest. He made no showing that he was unable to stay off the streets on the night in question.[5] * * *

MR. JUSTICE FORTAS, with whom MR. JUSTICE DOUGLAS, MR. JUSTICE BRENNAN, and MR. JUSTICE STEWART join, dissenting. * * *

The sole question presented is whether a criminal penalty may be imposed upon a person suffering the disease of "chronic alcoholism" for a condition—being "in a state of intoxication" in public—which is a characteristic part of the pattern of his disease and which, the trial court found, was not the consequence of appellant's volition but of "a compulsion symptomatic of the disease of chronic alcoholism." We deal here with the mere *condition* of being intoxicated in public.[2]

As I shall discuss, consideration of the Eighth Amendment issue in this case requires an understanding of "the disease of chronic alcoholism" with which, as the trial court found, appellant is afflicted, which has destroyed his "will power to resist the constant, excessive consumption of alcohol," and which leads him to "appear in public [not] by his own volition but under a compulsion symptomatic of the disease of chronic alcoholism." * * * Although there is some problem

in defining the concept, its core meaning, as agreed by authorities, is that alcoholism is caused and maintained by something other than the moral fault of the alcoholic, something that, to a greater or lesser extent depending upon the physiological or psychological makeup and history of the individual, cannot be controlled by him. * * *

Authorities have recognized that a number of factors may contribute to alcoholism. Some studies have pointed to physiological influences, such as vitamin deficiency, hormone imbalance, abnormal metabolism, and hereditary proclivity. Other researchers have found more convincing a psychological approach, emphasizing early environment and underlying conflicts and tensions. Numerous studies have indicated the influence of sociocultural factors. It has been shown, for example, that the incidence of alcoholism among certain ethnic groups is far higher than among others.

The manifestations of alcoholism are reasonably well identified. * * * It is well established that alcohol may be habituative and "can be physically addicting." It has been said that "the main point for the nonprofessional is that alcoholism is not within the control of the person involved. He is not willfully drinking." * * *

Robinson stands upon a principle which, despite its sublety, must be simply stated

---

dition" for it to be permissible to impose penal sanctions on the "condition."

5. I do not question the power of the State to remove a helplessly intoxicated person from a public street, although against his will, and to hold him until he has regained his powers. The person's own safety and the public interest require this much. A statute such as the one challenged in this case is constitutional insofar as it authorizes a police officer to arrest any seriously intoxicated person when he is encountered in a public place. Whether such a person may be charged and convicted for violating the statute will depend upon whether he is entitled to the protection of the Eighth Amendment.

2. It is not foreseeable that findings such as those which are decisive here—namely that the appellant's being intoxicated in public was a part of the pattern of his disease and due to a compulsion symptomatic of that disease—could or would be made in the case of offenses such as driving a car while intoxicated, assault, theft, or robbery. Such offenses require independent acts or conduct and do not typically flow from and are not part of the syndrome of the disease of chronic alcoholism. If an alcoholic should be convicted for criminal conduct which is not a characteristic and involuntary part of the pattern of the disease as it afflicts him, nothing herein would prevent his punishment.

and respectfully applied because it is the foundation of individual liberty and the cornerstone of the relations between a civilized state and its citizens: Criminal penalties may not be inflicted upon a person for being in a condition he is powerless to change. In all probability, Robinson at some time before his conviction elected to take narcotics. But the crime as defined did not punish this conduct. The statute imposed a penalty for the offense of "addiction"—a condition which Robinson could not control. Once Robinson had become an addict, he was utterly powerless to avoid criminal guilt. He was powerless to choose not to violate the law.

In the present case, appellant is charged with a crime composed of two elements— being intoxicated and being found in a public place while in that condition. The crime, so defined, differs from that in *Robinson.* The statute covers more than a mere status. But the essential constitutional defect here is the same as in *Robinson,* for in both cases the particular defendant was accused of being in a condition which he had no capacity to change or avoid. The trial judge sitting as trier of fact found upon the medical and other relevant testimony, that Powell is a "chronic alcoholic." He defined appellant's "chronic alcoholism" as "a disease which destroys the afflicted person's will power to resist the constant, excessive consumption of alcohol." He also found that "a chronic alcoholic does not appear in public by his own volition but under a compulsion symptomatic of the disease of chronic alcoholism." I read these findings to mean that appellant was powerless to avoid drinking; that having taken his first drink, he had "an uncontrollable compulsion to drink" to the point of intoxication; and that, once intoxicated, he could not prevent himself from appearing in public places.

The findings in this case, read against the background of the medical and sociological data to which I have referred, com-

pel the conclusion that the infliction upon appellant of a criminal penalty for being intoxicated in a public place would be "cruel and inhuman punishment" within the prohibition of the Eighth Amendment. This conclusion follows because appellant is a "chronic alcoholic" who, according to the trier of fact, cannot resist the "constant excessive consumption of alcohol" and does not appear in public by his own volition but under a "compulsion" which is part of his condition.

I would reverse the judgment below.

Notes and Questions

1. In *Robinson,* the opinion of the Court, by Stewart, J., asserted that a state "might impose criminal sanctions, for example, against the unauthorized manufacture, prescription, sale, purchase, or possession of narcotics within its borders." White, J., dissenting, noted: "It is significant that in purporting to reaffirm the power of the States to deal with the narcotics traffic, the Court does not include among the obvious powers of the State the power to punish for the use of narcotics. I cannot think that the omission was inadvertent."

In *People v. Davis,* 27 Ill.2d 57, 188 N.E.2d 225 (1963), a statute making it an offense to be "under the influence of * * * narcotic drugs" was held unconstitutional; the court stressed that the defendant could have used the drugs outside the state. But in *Salas v. State,* 365 S.W.2d 174 (Tex.Cr.App.1963), notwithstanding an offer of evidence that defendant was under the influence when he crossed the international bridge into Texas, the court upheld a conviction under a similar provision, reasoning that the defendant had not been convicted for his status but rather for "the 'act' of being under the influence."

What bearing does *Powell* have on this issue?

2. *State ex rel. Harper v. Zegeer,* ___ W.Va. ___, 296 S.E.2d 873 (1982): "Since *Powell,* no state court has held that alcoholics could not be punished criminally for public intoxication, except Minnesota. Minn.Stat. § 340.96 provided that 'every person who becomes intoxicated by *voluntarily drinking* intoxicating liquors is guilty of the crime of drunkenness.' (Emphasis added.) In *State v. Fearon,* 283 Minn. 90, 166 N.W.2d 720 (1969), that court determined 'voluntarily drinking' applied only to those who consumed liquor by choice, not to alcoholics:

> However, on the evidence presented in this case, defendant was no more able to make a free choice as to when or how much he would drink than a person would be who is forced to drink under threat of physical violence. To ignore such evidence or distort the meaning of words used by the legislature in order to avoid application of advances in man's knowledge of himself and his environment to existing laws would, we think, be a disservice to the law.

"Although statutes and ordinances involved here do not use the word 'voluntary', we agree with the reasoning of the Minnesota court.

"Other courts, however, have held that alcoholism is not a defense to public drunkenness charges. They have emphasized one or more of these notions: drinking is a voluntary action; if alcoholism is allowed to be a defense to public intoxication charges it might become a defense to other crimes; fear that an alcoholism defense will be expanded to other crimes; jail benefits drunks; and there is a distinction between the status of being an alcoholic and the act of appearing drunk in public. We believe that none of these reasons justifies incarceration of alcoholics.

"* * * Relying on the protections mandated by the West Virginia Constitution, we hold that no chronic alcoholic can be criminally prosecuted for public drunkenness."

3. Note, 94 Harv.L.Rev. 1660, 1665, 1669–70 (1981): "The greatest change in the criminal treatment of alcohol abuse has occurred in the area of public intoxication. Only fifteen years ago public intoxication was handled almost entirely through the criminal justice system. More than two million persons were arrested each year. Since then, however, a fairly well-developed model of noncriminal treatment has emerged. Many states have adopted programs for the decriminalized treatment of public inebriates, and drunkenness arrests have dropped dramatically, both in absolute numbers and as a percentage of total arrests. Yet the criminal model is far from dead. Public intoxication arrests still exceed one million each year, and the movement to decriminalize has stalled; after a period of sharp decline in the late sixties and early seventies, the arrest total seems to have stabilized. This stagnation is unfortunate, for the criminal treatment of public intoxication serves the best interests of neither society nor the inebriates themselves. * * *

"*Powell v. Texas* ended constitutional challenges to a state's power to make public intoxication a criminal act, but it did not halt the decriminalization movement; rather, it moved the focus to the legislatures. Here the most significant victory for the reformers was the approval of the Uniform Alcoholism and Intoxication Treatment Act (Uniform Act) by the National Conference of Commissioners on Uniform State Laws in 1971 and by the American Bar Association in 1972. Under the Uniform Act, the alcoholic was not to be criminally prosecuted; all laws that included drinking or drunkenness as an element of the offense were prohibited except those banning drunken driving or controlling the purchase or sale of alcoholic beverages. States were given an incentive to implement the provisions of the

Uniform Act in 1974 when Congress offered federal grants for alcohol treatment programs to states that decriminalized public intoxication. Many states responded by enacting some form of decriminalization, although far fewer states adopted the Uniform Act.[88]

"Although the treatment of public inebriates under the new statutes varies widely, a model of noncriminal treatment has emerged. This model focuses on providing increased medical and rehabilitative services to needy problem drinkers in a civil setting, while continuing to protect society's interest in orderly streets. Under this model, inebriates are taken to detoxification centers rather than to jails.

"These centers focus on 'drying out' and on emergency medical care. When possible, both entrance and treatment are voluntary, although persons incapacitated by alcohol may be placed in protective custody by the police or civilian patrols. Patients may not be held against their will for periods longer than the two or three days needed to detoxify them. After detoxification, they may simply leave the center or choose to continue treatment. Even when alcoholics decide to undergo further treatment, the focus is on outpatient programs, such as counseling and group meetings, that interfere only minimally in the patients' lives."

UNITED STATES v. MOORE

United States Court of Appeals, District of Columbia Circuit, 1973.
486 F.2d 1139.

WILKEY, CIRCUIT JUDGE, with whom CIRCUIT JUDGES MacKINNON and ROBB join.

This is an appeal from a conviction under two federal statutes for possession of heroin. * * * Arguing that he has lost the power of self-control with regard to his addiction, appellant maintains that by applying "the broad principles of common law criminal responsibility" we must decide that he is entitled to dismissal of the indictment or a jury trial on this issue. The gist of appellant's argument here is that "the common law has long held that the capacity to control behavior is a prerequisite for criminal responsibility."

It is inescapable that the logic of appellant's argument, if valid, would carry over to all other illegal acts of any type whose purpose was to obtain narcotics for his own use, a fact which is admitted by Judge Wright in his opinion.

* * * Drug addiction of varying degrees may or may not result in loss of self-control, depending on the strength of character opposed to the drug craving. Under appellant's theory, adopted by the dissenters, only if there is a resulting loss of self-control can there be an absence of *free will* which, under the extension of the common law theory, would provide a valid defense to the addict. If there is a demonstrable absence of free will (loss of self-control), the illegal acts of possession and acquisition cannot be charged to the user of the drugs.

But if it is absence of free will which excuses the mere possessor-acquirer, the more desperate bank robber for drug money has an even more demonstrable lack of free will and derived from precisely the same factors as appellant argues should excuse the mere possessor.

* * * In fact, it seems clear that the addict who restrains himself from committing any other crimes except acquisition and possession, assuming he obtains his funds by lawful means, has demonstrated a greater degree of self-control than the addict who in desperation robs a bank to buy at retail. If the addict can restrain himself

---

88. Thirteen states have substantially adopted the Uniform Act. Several other states, although not substantially adopting the Uniform Act, have provided for noncriminal treatment of intoxication.

from committing any other illegal act except purchase and possession, then he is demonstrating a degree of self-control greater than that of the one who robs a pharmacy or a bank, and thus his defense of loss of control and accountability is even less valid than that of the addict who robs the pharmacy or the bank. * * *

All of this points up the wisdom of Justice Black's observations in *Powell,* where he reached the conclusion that questions of "voluntariness" or "compulsion" should not be "controlling on the question [of] whether a specific instance of human behavior should be immune from punishment as a constitutional matter" * * *.

Just as Justice Black turned away from the proposed constitutional rule, we spurn the proposed "common law" rule, not only because the recently created statutory scheme of dealing with narcotics addicts stands a reasonable chance of reaching the objectives of "deterrence, isolation, and treatment," but also because the particular nature of the problem of the heroin traffic makes certain policies necessary that should not be weakened by the creation of this defense. There is no compelling policy requiring us to intervene here. * * *

To evaluate the proposed defense in light of the Eighth Amendment we review the case law, in particular, *Robinson v. California* and *Powell v. Texas.* This review demonstrates that the case law simply does not support the position advanced by appellant. * * *

Standing alone, * * * *Robinson* is no authority for the proposition that the Eighth Amendment prevents punishment of an addict for acts he is "compelled" to do by his addiction, since *Robinson* recognizes no compulsion in addiction. *Robinson* simply illustrates repugnance at the prospect of punishing one for his status as an addict. * * *

Where the asserted analogy with *Powell* breaks down * * * is, first, that the acts in *Powell* were held to be punishable, as Justice White's separate opinion for the majority makes clear. Second, here the acquisition and possession of the addictive substance by Moore are *illegal* activities, whereas in *Powell* the "addict" induced his addictive state through *legal* means. Powell's violation was in actions taken later, which to four members of the Court were punishable without question, and which to Justice White were punishable so long as the acts had not been proved to be the product of an established irresistible compulsion. In *Moore,* however, the acquisition and possession of the addictive substance (narcotics) are themselves illegal, whether considered as initial acts *causing* addiction or acts *resulting* from addiction.

* * * Moore could never put the needle in his arm the first and many succeeding times without an exercise of will. His *illegal acquisition and possession* are thus the direct product of a *freely willed illegal act.*

According to the appellant's thesis, an addict only has a choice as to the manner in which he obtains the funds (or the drugs) to support his habit; this neglects the choice that each addict makes *at the start* as to whether or not he is going to take narcotics and run the risk of becoming addicted to them. Although the narcotics user may soon through continued use acquire a compulsion to have the drug, and thus be said to have lost his self-control (insofar as he must take the drug regularly) due to a "disease," it is a disease which he has induced himself through a violation of the law. In contrast to the alcoholic Powell, the drug addict Moore has contracted a disease which virtually always commences with an illegal act. * * *

LEVENTHAL, CIRCUIT JUDGE; with whom McGOWAN, CIRCUIT JUDGE, concurs. * * *

Appellant's key defense concepts are impairment of behavioral control and loss of self-control. These have been considered by this court most fully in discussion of the insanity defense, and the philosophy of those opinions is invoked, although appellant disclaims the insanity defense as such.

* * *

Appellant's presentation rests, in essence, on the premise that the "mental disease or defect" requirement of [the cases defining the insanity defense] is superfluous. He discerns a broad principle that excuses from criminal responsibility when conduct results from a condition that impairs behavior control. * * * The broad assertion is that in general the mens rea element of criminal responsibility requires freedom of will, which is negatived by an impairment of behavioral control and loss of self-control.

If drug dependence really negatived mens rea, it would be a defense not only to the offense of possession or purchase of prohibited drugs but to other actions taken under the compulsion of the need to obtain the drug. If there is an impairment and lack of capacity to alter conduct, there is no way in which the line can be drawn in mens rea terms so as to exclude the very large percentage of addicts who must support their habit by engaging in retail sales, or, indeed, committing other crimes in order to satisfy their compulsion for drugs.

* * *

Appellant's surface logic loses luster with analysis. It does not follow that because one condition (mental disease) yields an exculpatory defense if it results in impairment of and lack of behavioral controls the same result follows when some other condition impairs behavior controls.

* * *

The legal conception of criminal capacity cannot be limited to those of unusual endowment or even average powers. A few may be recognized as so far from normal as to be entirely beyond the reach of criminal justice, but in general the criminal law is a means of social control that must be potentially capable of reaching the vast bulk of the population. Criminal responsibility is a concept that not only extends to the bulk of those below the median line of responsibility, but specifically extends to those who have a realistic problem of substantial impairment and lack of capacity due, say, to weakness of intellect that establishes susceptibility to suggestion; or to a loss of control of the mind as a result of passion, whether the passion is of an amorous nature or the result of hate, prejudice or vengeance; or to a depravity that blocks out conscience as an influence on conduct.

The criminal law cannot "vary legal norms with the individual's capacity to meet the standards they prescribe, absent a disability that is both gross and verifiable, such as the mental disease or defect that may establish irresponsibility. The most that it is feasible to do with lesser disabilities is to accord them proper weight in sentencing." * * *

In our view, the rule for drug addiction should not be modeled on the rule for mental disease because of crucial distinctions between conditions. The subject of mental disease, though subject to some indeterminacy, and difficulty of diagnosis when extended to volitional impairment as well as cognitive incapacity, has long been the subject of systematic study, and in that framework it is considered manageable to ask psychiatrists to address the distinction, all-important and crucial to the law, between incapacity and indisposition, between those who can't and those who won't, between the impulse irresistible and the impulse not resisted. These are matters as to which the court has accepted the analysis of medicine, medical conditions and symptoms, and on the premise that they can be considered on a verifiable basis, and with reasonable dispatch, the courts have recognized a defense even in conditions not as obvious and verifiable as those covered in the older and limited test of capacity to know right from wrong.

As to the subject of drug dependence and psychic incapacity to refrain from narcotics, even the 1970 Study Draft of the Staff of the National Commission on Reform of Federal Criminal Laws, which favors on balance a drug dependence defense to the crime of possession, for incapacity to refrain from use, candidly recognizes the problems involved. One is "the paradox of jail for the least dangerous possessors (non-addict experimenters and the like) while addicts go free." More important, for present purposes, is the Staff's caution first, that even physical symptoms might "be successfully feigned," and, more broadly, that there is considerable difficulty of verification of the claim of a drug user that he is unable to refrain from use. * * *

The difficulty of the verification problem of lack of capacity to refrain from use is sharpened on taking into account that the issue comprehends the addict's failure to participate in treatment programs. This raises problems of the addict's personal knowledge, disposition, motivation, as well as extent of community programs, that may usefully be assessed by someone considering what program to try now or next, but would irretrievably tangle a trial. * * *

The difficulty is sharpened by the appreciable number of narcotic "addicts" who do abandon their habits permanently, and much larger number who reflect their capacity to refrain by ceasing use for varying periods of time. The reasons are not clear but the phenomenon is indisputable. It is noted in the Staff Report, and reported by

specialists voicing different approaches to addiction problems.

There is need for reasonable verifiability as a condition to opening a defense to criminal responsibility. The criminal law cannot gear its standards to the individual's capacity "absent a disability that is both gross and verifiable, such as the mental disease or defect that may establish irresponsibility."

* * * Not dissimilar considerations undergird the maxim, ignorance of the law is no excuse, which contradicts salient principles underlying mens rea, yet rejects the defense claim in the interest of society. "The plea would be universally made, and would lead to interminable questions incapable of solution." The needs of society require overriding the subjective good faith of the individual as a legal defense, remitting his position to mitigation of punishment and executive clemency.

Reliability and validity of a legal defense require that it can be tested by criteria external to the actions which it is invoked to excuse. And so the Model Penal Code's caveat paragraph rejects an insanity defense based on an abnormality manifested only by repeated criminal or otherwise anti-social conduct. * * *

WRIGHT, CIRCUIT JUDGE, with whom BAZELON, CHIEF JUDGE, and TAMM and ROBINSON, CIRCUIT JUDGES, join, dissenting:

* * * I suggest that the development of the common law of *mens rea* has reached the point where it should embrace a new principle: a drug addict who, by reason of his use of drugs, lacks substantial capacity to conform his conduct to the requirements of the law may not be held criminally responsible for mere possession of drugs for his own use. The trial judge refused appellant's request to give the jury an instruction based on this principle. I would, therefore, reverse this conviction

and remand the case for a new trial.
* * *

Although *Powell* left unsettled the precise relationship between criminal responsibility and the Constitution, no member of the Court expressed even the slightest disagreement with the basic proposition that the Eighth Amendment provides only the floor and not the ceiling for development of common law notions of criminal responsibility. Indeed, Mr. Justice Marshall, adopting a restrictive view of the constitutional issue, emphasized that the

"doctrines of *actus reus, mens rea,* insanity, mistake, justification, and duress have historically provided the tools for a constantly shifting adjustment of the tension between the evolving aims of the criminal law and changing religious, moral, philosophical, and medical views of the nature of man. * * *"

Thus, no matter what interpretation of *Powell* eventually is adopted, the decision must "be read not as a bar, but as an exhortation toward further experiment with common-law doctrines of criminal responsibility."

The concept of criminal responsibility is, by its very nature, "an expression of the moral sense of the community." In western society, the concept has been shaped by two dominant value judgments—that punishment must be morally legitimate, and that it must not unduly threaten the liberties and dignity of the individual in his relationship to society. As a result, there has historically been a strong conviction in our jurisprudence that to hold a man criminally responsible his actions must have been the product of a "free will." * * * Thus criminal responsibility is assessed only when through "free will" a man elects to do evil, and if he is not a free agent, or is unable to choose or to act voluntarily, or to avoid the conduct which constitutes the crime, he is outside the postulate of the law of punishment.

Despite this general principle, however, it is clear that our legal system does not exculpate all persons whose capacity for control is impaired, for whatever cause or reason. Rather, in determining responsibility for crime, the law assumes "free will" and then recognizes known deviations "where there is a broad consensus that free will does not exist" with respect to the particular condition at issue. The evolving nature of this process is amply demonstrated in the gradual development of such defenses as infancy, duress, insanity, somnambulism and other forms of automatism, epilepsy and unconsciousness, involuntary intoxication, delirium tremens, and chronic alcoholism.

A similar consensus exists today in the area of narcotics addiction. * * * Thus it can no longer seriously be questioned that for at least some addicts the "overpowering" psychological and physiological need to possess and inject narcotics cannot be overcome by mere exercise of "free will."

Moreover, recognition of a defense of "addiction" for crimes such as possession of narcotics is consistent not only with our historic common law notions of criminal responsibility and moral accountability, but also with the traditional goals of penology—retribution, deterrence, isolation and rehabilitation.

Unlike other goals of penology, the retributive theory of criminal justice looks solely to the past for justification, without regard to considerations of prevention or reformation. Although the primordial desire for vengeance is an understandable emotion, it is a testament to the constantly evolving nature of our social and moral consciousness that the law has, in recent decades, come to regard this "eye-for-an-eye" philosophy as an improper basis for punishment. But even if this barbaric notion of justice retained its validity, it clearly would be inapplicable to those persons who act under a compulsion. Revenge, if it is ever to be legitimate, must be premised on moral blameworthiness, and what segment of our society would feel its need for retribution satisfied when it wreaks vengeance upon those who are diseased because of their disease? * * *

The most widely employed argument in favor of punishing addicts for crimes such as possession of narcotics is that such punishment or threat of punishment has a substantial deterrent effect. Given our present knowledge, however, the merits of this argument appear doubtful. Deterrence presupposes rationality—it proceeds on the assumption that the detriments which would inure to the prospective criminal upon apprehension can be made so severe that he will be dissuaded from undertaking the criminal act. In the case of the narcotic addict, however, the normal sense of reason, which is so essential to effective functioning of deterrence, is overcome by the psychological and physiological compulsions of the disease. As a result, it is widely agreed that the threat of even harsh prison sentences cannot deter the addict from using and possessing the drug.

A similar situation prevails insofar as deterrence of *potential* addicts is concerned. * * * Since the nonaddict may still be punished for his possession of narcotics, the only consolation he might find in exculpation of addict possessors is that if he eventually attains the status of "addict" he must be treated rather than punished. But given what we now know about the pitiable life of an addict, this somewhat dubious consolation is hardly likely to "encourage" persons to use narcotics.

There is another side to the question of deterrence, however, which should not be ignored. The criminal law may serve as a deterrent not only through the fear of apprehension and prosecution, but also through the more general educative or moralizing effect the law may have upon society. Viewed in this manner, punishment as a concrete expression of society's disapproval of particular conduct helps to instill a desired moral code in the citizenry against commission of the proscribed acts.

* * * Since the addict's possession of narcotics is simply a symptom of his disease and not an act of "free will," however, this conduct cannot properly be deemed "culpable," and it would therefore seem inappropriate for society to utilize him as a mere vehicle through which to deter others. * * *

Shifting our focus now to the goal of isolating the offender, we arrive here at not only a justifiable basis for action but one which, in some cases at least, may be vital to the interests of society. * * *

This does not mean, however, that the goal of isolation justifies infliction of criminal punishment upon the addict. On the contrary, this interest may be fully vindicated through a program of civil commitment with treatment as well as by criminal incarceration. And since the addict is not a culpable offender, treatment is clearly a preferable alternative to mere imprisonment. * * *

This, then, brings us to the final and most important goal of modern penology—to rehabilitate the offender. In this age of enlightened correctional philosophy, we now recognize that society has a responsibility to both the individual and the community to treat the offender so that upon his release he may function as a productive, law-abiding citizen. And this is all the more true where, as with the non-trafficking addict possessor, the offender has acted under the compulsion of a disease. The task of rehabilitating the narcotic addict is not, as once was thought, a hopeless task. Great strides have been made in recent years toward development of effective and humane treatment techniques at both community-based and institutional levels, and the cure rate for addiction is now far higher than that of many other illnesses. Thus, with the possible exception of those addicts who remain incurable, society clearly cannot meet its responsibilities simply by confining the addict without treatment. Such an approach does nothing to cure the chronic relapsing aspects of the disease, and where confinement takes the form of imprisonment the addict is thrust inevitably into a "revolving door" of arrest, conviction, imprisonment, release and arrest, with the period of incarceration serving as but a temporary and futile stopping point in an otherwise interminable cycle. * * *

Perhaps the most troublesome question arising out of recognition of the addiction defense I suggest is whether it should be limited only to those acts—such as mere possession for use—which are inherent in the disease itself. It can hardly be doubted that, in at least some instances, an addict may in fact be "compelled" to engage in other types of criminal activity in order to obtain sufficient funds to purchase his necessary supply of narcotics. In such cases, common law principles of criminal responsibility would clearly be applicable. Indeed, it would seem intolerable that such addicts, who are "already crippled by an almost hopeless cycle of poverty, ignorance and drugs, should be further burdened by the moral stigma of guilt, *not* because they are morally blameworthy, but merely because we cannot afford to treat them as if they are not." Nevertheless, I am convinced that Congress has manifested a clear intent to preclude common law extension of the defense beyond those crimes which, like the act of possession,

cause direct harm only to the addict himself. * * *[a]

The basic question of criminal responsibility under the addiction defense is a legal, and not a purely medical, determination. Not all drug users are "addicts" and, as with any compulsion, the degree of dependence may vary among different individuals and, indeed, even in a given individual at different stages of his addiction. Thus what we are concerned with here is not an abstract medical or psychiatric definition of addiction which sets forth a clinical checklist of relevant symptoms but, rather, a behavioral model, based upon traditional legal and moral principles, which tests the ability of the defendant to control his behavior. The essential inquiry, then, is simply whether at the time of the offense, the defendant, as a result of his repeated use of narcotics, lacked substantial capacity to conform his conduct to the requirements of the law. * * *

BAZELON, CHIEF JUDGE (concurring in part and dissenting in part):

* * * I would also permit a jury to consider addiction as a defense to a charge of, for example, armed robbery or trafficking in drugs, to determine whether the defendant was under such duress or compulsion, because of his addiction, that he was unable to conform his conduct to the requirements of the law. * * *

Notes and Questions

1. In *People v. Davis,* 33 N.Y.2d 221, 351 N.Y.S.2d 663, 306 N.E.2d 787 (1973), the court offered yet another reason for the conclusion that an addict may be convicted of drug possession: "More-

a. In an omitted portion of Judge Wright's opinion, he observed (i) that in the 1956 amendments to the Jones–Miller and Harrison Acts, Congress stated unequivocally that addict traffickers should be treated no differently than nonaddict traffickers; and (ii) that in enacting Titles I and II of the Narcotics Addict Rehabilitation Act, "Congress expressly intended that ad-

dicts charged with specified crimes of violence or certain types of trafficking should be held criminally liable despite their addiction. For lesser crimes such as shoplifting or fraud, civil commitment was made available *in lieu of prosecution or sentencing* and only *after* the addict offender had been brought into the criminal process."

over, while it may be that the policy of rehabilitation would be well-served by affording addicts a cruel and unusual punishment and drug dependence defense to possession for their own use, we should not lose sight of the utility of such penalties to law enforcement. For example, these possible penalties may, through the exercise of prosecutorial discretion, enable law enforcement to enlist addict-informers in ferreting out the wholesalers of illicit drugs, thereby facilitating the policy of elimination of the drug traffic. Then, too, punishment may persuade some addicts to undertake rehabilitation through various State or private programs. On the other hand, recognition of the defense might conceivably make the addict the witting or unwitting tool of the drug trafficker."

2. Fingarette, *Addiction and Criminal Responsibility,* 84 Yale L.J. 413, 443–44 (1975): "In spite of a vast literature, professionals in the field of drug addiction acknowledge that no satisfactory scientific understanding of drug addiction has been reached. Thus there is no medical foundation for adopting the general proposition at the crux of the exculpatory legal arguments, the proposition that addictive conduct is involuntary. On the other hand, massive descriptive evidence indicates that individuals often make choices to abandon addictive conduct or abstain from drug use permanently or temporarily. Moreover, authorities observe that narcotic addiction often involves little in the way of chemical or biological influences. Yet it may provide an important individual or group identity for many who lack socially approved skills or are socially alienated. Popular beliefs about the chemically-induced hell of withdrawal agony or the insatiable craving for ecstatic pleasures are profoundly at odds with the facts, though they have deeply colored the thinking of the courts. All this information forces abandonment of the argument that drug

addiction—and acts associated with it—be regarded as legally involuntary. * * *

"Undoubtedly there are those who regard possible legal approaches to addiction in polar terms: Either we inflict harsh, punitive and degrading measures on the addict, or we declare the person sick and therefore not responsible for his conduct. What is needed here is the abandonment of such extreme and fixed positions. In the present antipunitive atmosphere in many enlightened circles, it is appropriate to recall that the lawful and proper threat of sanctions may be not only a pragmatically effective approach, but also a morally humane approach. It regards the addict as an autonomous person, responsible for guiding his own life, and subject to law. The medical approach can also reflect a humane concern, a concern for the weak and ailing and for those who cannot, in some respects, handle their own lives. By now it is no news that both of these approaches, however inspired, can in practice disregard human dignity when ignorance, social prejudice, well-intentioned dogma, lack of funding, or routinization take over. We need to rethink the implications of both approaches against the background of the limited knowledge that we have. Coordinating the attack on the complex problem of drug abuse is preeminently a legislative responsibility. For the courts to assume that addictive drug use or addiction-related conduct is involuntary and to build such an unworthy assumption into constitutional and common law doctrine would be a grave error."

3. In *Robinson,* the Court noted that "a State might establish a program of compulsory treatment for those addicted to narcotics." Is this the best solution? Consider Note, 60 Geo.L.J. 667, 670–72 (1972): "Efforts to provide treatment for drug addicts in a systematic way have concentrated primarily on the development of involuntary commitment procedures. Since 1961, several states and the federal government

have enacted statutes authorizing the involuntary commitment of drug addicts convicted of a crime to an institution for a period of inpatient treatment, followed by compulsory aftercare. While such involuntary commitment procedures do provide an alternative to imprisonment, they have been found wanting for several reasons. First, it has been questioned whether involuntary commitment to an institution is in fact nonpunitive and significantly different from criminal incarceration. Distrust of these programs because of their punitive aspects has resulted in defendants often trying to avoid the 'treatment' alternative at any cost. Second, the rehabilitative successes of the programs have been small. This has led some to question whether the long period of confinement authorized in the statutes can be justified. Third, the requirement that a full adversary hearing be held to order certification, upon the demand of the defendant, has resulted in additional court congestion and consequent underutilization of this treatment route. There are ways to modify the involuntary commitment programs, but because the problems with these programs are so manifold, there is good reason to look in other directions for a response to the needs of the addict, the courts, and society."

4. In *Gorham v. United States,* 339 A.2d 401 (D.C.App.1975), following *Moore,* the court made much of the fact that a "pretrial diversion program for drug abusers" was available. Is this the best solution? How should such a program be structured? Consider, for example, the California program:

"The diversion statute applies only to defendants charged with simple possession of narcotics, possession of narcotics paraphernalia, or 'being present' in a place where narcotics are being used. By implication, diversion may not be considered if the defendant is charged with a drug offense of which cultivation, manufacture,

transportation, sale, or possession for sale is an element.

"After a defendant has been charged with a divertible offense, the statute requires the district attorney to determine whether he should be considered for diversion by applying the following four criteria: (1) the defendant must have 'no prior conviction for any offense involving narcotics or restricted dangerous drugs,' (2) the 'offense charged must not involve a crime of violence or threatened violence,' (3) there must be 'no evidence of a violation relating to narcotics or restricted dangerous drugs other than a [divertible] violation,' and (4) the defendant must have 'no record of probation or parole violations.' If the district attorney concludes that these requirements are satisfied, he so advises the defendant or his attorney. The defendant then decides whether he wishes further consideration for diversion; if he does, he must waive his right to a speedy trial. The district attorney then refers the case to the probation department for investigation.

"The probation department makes two inquiries. First, it investigates the defendant's character and background to determine whether he would benefit from an educational, treatment, or rehabilitation program. Second, the department reviews the available community drug programs to determine which programs would both benefit the defendant and be willing to accept him. Upon completion of the investigation, the probation department reports its findings to the court having jurisdiction over the defendant's case and recommends whether or not the defendant should be diverted and, if so, to which program.

"The court holds a hearing to decide whether the defendant should be diverted. At the hearing it considers the probation department's report and any other information deemed relevant. Before the court may actually order a defendant diverted, however, the statute requires the court to obtain the district attorney's concurrence.

"If the court orders diversion, further criminal proceedings against the defendant are stayed for a period of between 6 months and 2 years at the discretion of the court. During this time, the probation department must file progress reports on the defendant at least every 6 months. Termination of diversion and reactivation of the criminal proceedings are specifically required by the statute only if the defendant is 'arrested and convicted of any criminal offense' during the period of diversion. The court, however, appears to have implicit power within its general grant of jurisdiction to rescind its diversion order at any time for good cause, such as a failure to cooperate or to abide by the conditions of diversion. Upon satisfactory completion of the diversion program, the defendant is entitled to have the charges against him dismissed." [a]

5. What then of methadone maintenance? Consider Vorenberg & Lukoff, *Addiction, Crime, and the Criminal Justice System,* 37 Fed.Prob. 3, 7 (Dec.1973): "The public's first exposure to methadone created high expectations. Some reports suggested the new drug had almost magical qualities—heroin hunger would in some mysterious way be blocked, patients would turn dramatically from crime to a constructive, happy life. What little we have learned to date shows that the early picture was too rosy. For the addicts in Bedford–Stuyvesant—who clearly are eco-

nomically, socially and medically a more depressed group than those groups who were first the subjects of methadone treatment programs and experiments—the results have been far less dramatic. Our data suggest that different subgroups in the sample respond differently to the program with regard to such things as drug use, criminal activity, and even kinds of crimes whose incidence are reduced. Many addicts on methadone maintenance continue to use heroin and other drugs, although at lower levels than before entering treatment. The level of criminal charges for patients in the first year of treatment is actually *higher* than the average rate over the full period of the patients' addiction, but shows a drop as compared with the year immediately preceding entry to the program. What this suggests is that addicts may not come into such programs until they reach a point at which the level of drug use and required criminal activity to support that use has gotten uncomfortably high.

"What we have found to date suggests that it is unrealistic to expect radical changes in behavior from a methadone-based program. The rejection of a long-term life in deviance—aggravated by addiction [b]—is at best a slow process. Any effective results would appear to be a function of a long tenure in treatment in which the administration of methadone is but one rehabilitative tool. Such a trend is indicated by the early figures we have on the criminal behavior of the patients who remained in the program for 2 years."

---

a. Note, 26 Stan.L.Rev. 923–25 (1974). For a description and evaluation of other such programs, see Note, 60 Geo.L.J. 667 (1972).

b. They earlier noted "that for a substantial segment of the patient group criminal behavior *antedates* the onset of heroin use."

SECTION 2. VOLUNTARY AND INVOLUNTARY INTOXICATION

DIRECTOR OF PUBLIC PROSECUTIONS v. MAJEWSKI

House of Lords, 1976.
[1977] A.C. 443, [1976] 2 W.L.R. 623, [1976] 2 All E.R. 142.

[The appellant and another man were involved in a brawl in a public-house. They were ejected and the landlord telephoned the police. They attempted to re-enter the public-house and assaulted and injured the landlord and another customer. When the police arrived they were also assaulted by the appellent. He was charged with three counts of assault occasioning actual bodily harm and with three assaults on police constables in the execution of their duty. His defence was that for some time he had been taking drugs and that the combination of a mixture of drugs and alcohol had affected him adversely. He had had no recollection of what happened on the evening in question and had had no intention of assaulting or hurting anybody. The jury were directed that if a man has induced in himself a state in which he is under the influence of drink or drugs then that state was no defence, and further, that assault did not require the proof by the prosecution of any specific intention and the fact that the appellant might have taken drink and drugs was irrelevant. The jury convicted the appellant, and he appealed to the House of Lords against the dismissal of his appeal by the Court of Appeal.]

LORD ELWYN–JONES L.C.: * * * What * * * is the mental element required in our law to be established in assault? This question has been most helpfully answered in the speech of Lord Simon of Glaisdale, in *D.P.P. v. Morgan* [p. 165 of this Book]: " * * * The *actus reus* of assault is an act which causes another person to apprehend immediate and unlawful violence. The *mens rea* corre-

sponds exactly. The prosecution must prove that the accused foresaw that his act would probably cause another person to have apprehension of immediate and unlawful violence or would possibly have that consequence, such being the purpose of the act, or that he was reckless as to whether or not his act caused such apprehension. This foresight (the term of art is 'intention') or recklessness is the *mens rea* in assault. * * * "

How does the factor of self-induced intoxication fit into that analysis? * * * The authority which for the last half century has been relied upon in this context has been the speech of Lord Birkenhead L.C. in *Director of Public Prosecutions v. Beard,* 14 Cr.App.R. 159; [1920] A.C. 479. * * * Lord Birkenhead concluded that (except in cases where insanity is pleaded) the decisions he cited "establish that where a specific intent is an essential element in the offence, evidence of a state of drunkenness rendering the accused incapable of forming such an intent should be taken into consideration in order to determine whether he had in fact formed the intent necessary to constitute the particular crime. If he was so drunk that he was incapable of forming the intent required he could not be convicted of a crime which was committed only if the intent was proved. * * * "

From this it seemed clear—and this is the interpretation which the judges have placed upon the decision during the ensuing half century—that it is only in the limited class of cases requiring proof of specific intent that drunkenness can exculpate. Otherwise in no case can it exempt completely from criminal liability. * * *

I do not for my part regard that general principle as either unethical or contrary to the principles of natural justice. If a man of his own volition takes a substance which causes him to cast off the restraints of reason and conscience, no wrong is done to him by holding him answerable criminally for any injury he may do while in that condition. His course of conduct in reducing himself by drugs and drink to that condition in my view supplies the evidence of *mens rea,* of guilty mind certainly sufficient for crimes of basic intent. It is a reckless course of conduct and recklessness is enough to constitute the necessary *mens rea* in assault cases. The drunkenness is itself an intrinsic, an integral part of the crime, the other part being the evidence of the unlawful use of force against the victim. Together they add up to criminal recklessness. * * *

This approach is in line with the American Model Penal Code (S. 2.08(2)) * * *.

LORD DIPLOCK: My Lords, I have had the advantage of reading the speech of my noble and learned friend, the Lord Chancellor. I agree with it and with his conclusions. I also agree with my noble and learned friend, Lord Russell of Killowen, in his analysis of the speech of Lord Birkenhead L.C. in *Beard's* case. I would dismiss this appeal.

LORD SIMON OF GLAISDALE: My Lords, I have had the advantage of reading the speech prepared by my noble and learned friend on the Woolsack. I agree with it, and I would therefore dismiss the appeal. What follows is by way of marginal comment. * * *

(3) The Butler Committee on Mentally Abnormal Offenders (Cmnd. 6244 of 1975) recognised that even the traditional view of the effect of intoxication in relation to conduct prohibited by law left a gap in the protection which the criminal law should afford to innocent citizens; this required, in their view, to be closed by legislation. Their recommendation 56 was: " * * * We propose that it should be an offence for a person while voluntarily intoxicated do an act (or make an omis-

sion) that would amount to a dangerous offence if it were done or made with the requisite state of mind for such offence."

The maximum sentence recommended for such offence was imprisonment for one year for a first offence or for three years on a second or subsequent offence (para. 18.58).

But, on the traditional view, much antisocial conduct is still criminal notwithstanding the intoxication * * *.

On the appellant's argument, on the other hand, "the Butler gap" is enormously widened. I have already given the example of *Lipman* [infra]. Another would be an erroneous belief, brought about by self-induced intoxication that a woman is consenting to sexual intercourse (cf. *Morgan,* [supra]). Examples could be readily multiplied. Indeed, the instant appeal is a case where the criminal law would, in my view, seriously depart from the common consent which it should desirably command were it to hold that the appellant's intoxication exculpated him. Certainly, the Butler Committee's recommendations as to sentence might require reconsideration were "the Butler gap" so dramatically widened. * * *

LORD KILBRANDON: My Lords, I have had the advantage of reading the speech of my noble and learned friend the Lord Chancellor. I entirely agree with it and with his conclusions.

I would accordingly dismiss this appeal.

LORD SALMON: * * * A man who by voluntarily taking drink and drugs gets himself into an aggressive state in which he does not know what he is doing and then makes a vicious assault can hardly say with any plausibility that what he did was a pure accident which should render him immune from any criminal liability. Yet this in effect is precisely what Mr. Tucker contends that the learned judge should have told the jury.

A number of distinguished academic writers support this contention on the ground of logic. As I understand it, the argument runs like this: Intention whether special or basic (or whatever fancy name you choose to give it) is still intention. If voluntary intoxication by drink or drugs can, as it admittedly can, negative the special or specific intention necessary for the commission of crimes such as murder and theft; how can you justify in strict logic the view that it cannot negative a basic intention, e.g. the intention to commit offences such as assault and unlawful wounding? The answer is that in strict logic this view cannot be justified. But this is the view that has been adopted by the common law of England, which is founded on common sense and experience rather than strict logic. There is no case in the nineteenth century when the courts were relaxing the harshness of the law in relation to the effect of drunkenness upon criminal liability in which the courts ever went so far as to suggest that drunkenness, short of drunkenness producing insanity, could ever exculpate a man from any offence other than one which required some special or specific intent to be proved.

* * *

As I have already indicated, I accept that there is a degree of illogicality in the rule that intoxication may excuse or expunge one type of intention and not another. This illogicality is, however, acceptable to me because the benevolent part of the rule removes undue harshness without imperilling safety and the stricter part of the rule works without imperilling justice. It would be just as ridiculous to remove the benevolent part of the rule (which no one suggests) as it would be to adopt the alternative of removing the stricter part of rule for the sake of preserving absolute logic. Absolute logic in human affairs is an uncertain guide and a very dangerous master. The law is primarily concerned with human affairs. I believe that the main object of our legal system is to preserve individual liberty. One important aspect of individual liberty is protection against physical violence.

If there were to be no penal sanction for any injury unlawfully inflicted under the complete mastery of drink or drugs, voluntarily taken, the social consequence could be appalling. That is why I do not consider that there is any justification for the criticisms which have been made of the Court of Appeal's decision in *Lipman* (1969) 53 Cr.App.R. 600; [1970] 1 Q.B. 152. Lipman was convicted of manslaughter because he had killed his companion by stuffing bedclothes down her throat under the illusion, induced by the hallucinatory drugs he had taken, that he was fighting for his life against snakes. Had she survived his attack he could have been properly convicted of causing grievous bodily harm or of assault occasioning actual bodily harm under sections 20 and 47 respectively of the Act of 1861. These, like manslaughter, are all offences of basic intent and do not require the proof of any specific intent in order to establish guilt. According to our law as it has stood for about 150 years, in such cases evidence that the injuries were inflicted by a man not knowing what he was doing because he was intoxicated by drinks or drugs which he has voluntarily taken is wholly irrelevant. Certainly this rule seems, in practice, to have worked well without causing any injustice. The judge always carefully takes into account all the circumstances (which vary infinitely from case to case) before deciding which of the many courses open should be adopted in dealing with the convicted man.

If, as I think, this long standing rule was salutory years ago when it related almost exclusively to drunkenness and hallucinatory drugs were comparatively unknown, how much more salutory is it today when such drugs are increasingly becoming a public menace? My Lords, I am satisfied that this rule accords with justice, ethics and common sense, and I would leave it alone even if it does not comply with strict logic. It would, in my view, be disastrous if the law were changed to allow men who did what Lipman did to go free. It would shock the public, it would rightly bring the law into contempt and it would certainly increase one of the really serious menaces facing society today. This is too great a price to pay for bringing solace to those who believe that, come what may, strict logic should always prevail.

LORD EDMUND–DAVIES: * * * The criticism by the academics of the law presently administered in this country is of a two-fold nature: (1) It is illogical and therefore inconsistent with legal principle to treat a person who of his own volition has taken drink or drugs any differently from a man suffering from some bodily or mental disorder of the kind earlier mentioned or whose beverage had, without his connivance, been "laced" with intoxicants. (2) It is unethical to convict a man of a crime requiring a guilty state of mind when, *ex hypothesi*, he lacked it. I seek to say something about each of these two criticisms.

(1) *Illogicality*

Logically, if a man who wounds does not know what he is doing he should be acquitted not only of wounding with intent (Offences against the Person Act 1861, s. 18) but also of unlawful wounding (ibid. section 20), and even of common assault. * * * So we find the Court of Appeal decision in *Lipman* criticised because Lord Widgery C.J. justified the conviction for manslaughter on the basis of death being caused by what was described as the unlawful act of the accused in stuffing bedclothes down his companion's throat under the delusion (induced by the drugs he had taken) that he was dealing with snakes. The criticism is that, although had the verdict been based on a finding that Lip-

man's act was grossly negligent, it would have been unassailable, on the other hand—"Had (the victim) survived her 'trip' and Lipman been faced with any other charge based on her injuries, whether of causing grievous bodily harm with intent (1861 Act, s. 18) or of an assault occasioning actual bodily harm (ibid. section 47) he would, in the absence of evidence that he had realised that harm was likely to befall his fellow-tripper, have been acquitted."

But would Lipman's conviction even on the basis of culpable negligence be *logically* acceptable? This critic clearly thinks it would be, but how can a man who *ex hypothesi* does not know what he is doing be guilty of criminal negligence? If logic is indeed to be the sole guide, I find it easier to understand the view of another writer (G.F. Orchard. *"Drunkenness, Drugs and Manslaughter"* [1970] Crim.L.R. at 214) who states that, "It has been accepted that automatism provides a defence to offences of strict liability, and *a fortiori* it will be a defence where *negligence* is required," and then continues: "Thus the facts in *Lipman* present a problem if it is sought to convict D. of manslaughter by gross negligence, for it would seem that at the relevant time D. was 'acting' in a state of automatism: he had no consciousness of what his limbs were actually doing—his limbs were not controlled by his conscious mind. It appears, therefore, that either D. *cannot* be convicted of manslaughter *or* the extent to which automatism may provide a defence is limited to exclude such a case." [Lord Edmund–Davies' italics]. The undeviating application of logic leads inexorably to the conclusion that a man behaving even as Lipman unquestionably did must be completely discharged from all criminal liability for the dreadful consequences of his conduct. It was, as I recall, submissions of this startling character which led my noble and learned friend, Lord Simon of Glaisdale, to comment trenchantly to appellant's counsel, "It is all right to say 'Let justice be done though the heavens fall.' But you ask us to say 'Let logic be done even though public order be threatened,' which is something very different."

Are the claims of logic, then, so compelling that a man behaving as the Crown witnesses testified Majewski did must be cleared of criminal responsibility?

* * *

If such be the inescapable result of the strict application of logic in this branch of the law, it is indeed not surprising that illogicality has long reigned, and the prospect of its dethronement must be regarded as alarming.

(2) *Lack of Ethics*

It is sometimes said in such cases as the present that it is morally wrong to convict of a crime involving a certain state of mind even where it be established that the charge is based on a man's behaviour when he lacked that guilty mind.

* * * As to the complaint that it is unethical to punish a man for a crime when his physical behaviour was not controlled by a conscious mind, I have long regarded as a convincing theory in support of penal liability for harms committed by voluntary inebriates, the view of Austin, who argued (*Lectures on Jurisprudence,* 1879, pp. 512–513) that a person who voluntarily became intoxicated is to be regarded as acting recklessly, for he made himself dangerous in disregard of public safety.

But, to my way of thinking, the nearest approach to a satisfactory refutation of charges of lack of both logic and ethics in punishing the most drunken man for actions which, were he sober, would call for his criminal conviction is that of Stroud, who wrote (*Mens Rea,* 1914, p. 115): "It has been suggested by various writers, in explanation of the doctrine respecting vol-

untary drunkenness as an excuse for crime, that the effect is 'to make drunkenness itself an offence, which is punishable with a degree of punishment varying as the consequences of the act done.' (Clark, *Analysis of Criminal Liability,* 1880, p. 30). This is not exactly correct, although it is not far from the true explanation of the rule. The true explanation is, that drunkenness is not incompatible with *mens rea,* in the sense of ordinary culpable intentionality, because mere recklessness is sufficient to satisfy the definition of *mens rea,* and drunkenness is itself an act of recklessness. The law therefore establishes a conclusive presumption against the admission of proof of intoxication for the purpose of disproving *mens rea* in ordinary crimes. Where this presumption applies, it does not make 'drunkenness itself' a crime, but the drunkenness is itself an integral part of the crime, as forming, together with the other unlawful conduct charged against the defendant, a complex act of criminal recklessness. This explanation affords at once a justification of the rule of law, and a reason for its inapplicability when drunkenness is pleaded by way of showing absence of full intent, or of some exceptional form of *mens rea* essential to a particular crime, according to its definition." * * *

LORD RUSSELL OF KILLOWEN: My Lords, Your Lordships have dealt so fully with the considerations to which this appeal has given rise that I will be brief. I entirely agree that the answer to the question posed is in the affirmative. That the facts of the case give rise to the question, I doubt. Majewski's participation in the events of the evening begin when he is told by the other man that the latter is to be ejected: whereupon Majewski stationed himself before the door to prevent that, which shows comprehension and intention on his part. When the police arrived Majewski called them adjectival pigs, a word which has of recent years been revived as a reference to law enforcement officers, having been current in the early nineteenth century (see Pierce Egan's *Life in London* 1821): this also negatives lack of understanding. Nevertheless, the question requires to be answered, and I agree with the answer proposed. * * *

Notes and Questions

1. The American cases generally follow the rule of the *Beard* case, relied upon in *Majewski*. Thus, it is commonly held that voluntary intoxication is no defense where the offense is of the general intent type, e.g., *United States v. Meeker,* 527 F.2d 12 (9th Cir.1975) (crime of assault of air crew member); *State v. Sterling,* 235 Kan. 526, 680 P.2d 301 (1984) (crime of criminal damage to property). On the other hand, a "defense" of intoxication may be interposed where the crime is characterized as one requiring a specific intent, e.g., *United States v. Scott,* 529 F.2d 338 (D.C. Cir.1975) (crime of entering bank with intent to rob); *State v. Caldrain,* 115 N.H. 390, 342 A.2d 628 (1975) (crime of breaking and entering with intent to rape).

2. In *People v. Langworthy,* 416 Mich. 630, 331 N.W.2d 171 (1982), the court asserted "the illogic and incongruity of the general intent-specific intent dichotomy," but then said "the remedy is not clear cut." Is either of those propositions correct? Consider *United States v. Nix,* 501 F.2d 516 (7th Cir.1974), involving the convictions of Nix and Peterson under 18 U.S.C.A. § 751 for attempted escape and escape, respectively, from a federal institution. Nix was apprehended inside a locked truck a few hours after it had been driven out of the institution and parked adjacent thereto; Peterson was caught 8 miles away on the day following his disappearance. In both trials, the court instructed that the defendants' claimed intoxication was no defense, and on appeal these instructions were held to be erroneous.

"Under the traditional analysis, specific intent is indeed required for attempted escape. We could end the inquiry here and remand this case because the instruction given erroneously states the law. Simplistic as the traditional analysis is, however, it does not further a logical resolution of the problem. This is true for several reasons.

"Implicit in Nix' argument is an acknowledgement that escape is a general-intent crime. Nix would say that, by choosing to charge him with *attempted* escape, the prosecutor injected the element of specific intent into the case. Therefore intoxication would be relevant in his case but not in Peterson's.

"The trouble with this approach is the impossibility of drawing a line between escape and attempted escape. Was the difference between Nix' act and Peterson's the eight miles Peterson traveled? Or an overnight absence versus the hours Nix was missing? * * * We believe the distinction between the two crimes is too flimsy to support a rule of law that would attach great importance to the prosecutor's choice between a charge of escape and one of attempted escape.

"This deficiency in the traditional analysis might be overcome by labeling both crimes as general-intent crimes, as the district judge did, or as specific-intent crimes, as Peterson urges. These labels are 'often used in the cases but seldom defined.' They were developed, at least with regard to intoxication, primarily to allow drunkenness as a defense to first-degree murder but not to lesser degrees of homicide. The attempt to apply the terms to nonviolent crimes such as escape has produced confused reasoning and disparate results.

Categorizing all crimes as either having 'general' or 'specific' intent seems too mechanical and often forecloses evaluation by the court of the important consideration involved, i.e., what elements are involved in the crime and whether the prosecution has satisfactorily established them. *Intoxication as a Criminal Defense,* 55 Colum.L.Rev. 1210, 1217 (1955).

"Whenever intoxication (or coercion or mistake) is raised as a mitigating factor, use of the 'specific' and 'general' intent labels interferes with the crucial analysis a court should make in escape cases: what constitutes the 'escape' element of the crime?

"Most courts, confronted with evidence that a defendant could not or did not form an intent to leave and not to return, have held such an intent essential to proof of the crime of escape.   *   *   *

"These cases lead us to a definition of escape as a voluntary departure from custody with an intent to avoid confinement. Whatever label is placed on this intent, a defendant under § 751 is entitled to an instruction that includes this mental component as an element of the crime which the government must prove. If the defendant offers evidence that he was intoxicated at the time of the offense, the jury must be instructed to consider whether he was so intoxicated he could not form an intent to escape."

3. In states with modern recodifications, it is more likely the matter of when voluntary intoxication is a defense will be resolved by analysis of specific statutory language. Illustrative are *State v. Coates,* 107 Wash.2d 882, 735 P.2d 64 (1987) (no defense to assault charge, as mental state for that crime is criminal negligence; "Because this mental state is based on a reasonable person standard, evidence of defendant's voluntary intoxication can not work in any way to negate or obviate the mental state"); *State v. Shine,* 193 Conn. 632, 479 A.2d 218 (1984) (no defense to manslaughter by recklessness, as statute says that "when recklessness or criminal negligence is an element of the crime

charged, if the actor, due to self-induced intoxication, is unaware of or disregards or fails to perceive a risk which he would have been aware of had he not been intoxicated, such unawareness, disregard or failure to perceive shall be immaterial"); *White v. State,* 290 Ark. 130, 717 S.W.2d 784 (1986) (no defense to murder or, indeed, any crime, as statute declares purpose "to eliminate the defense of self-induced or voluntary intoxication").

4. Is the *White* position sound? Consider *State v. Vaughn,* 268 S.C. 119, 232 S.E.2d 328 (1977): "Reason requires that a man who voluntarily renders himself intoxicated be no less responsible for his acts while in such condition. To grant immunity for crimes committed while the perpetrator is in such a voluntary state would not only mean that many offenders would go unpunished but would also transgress the principle of personal accountability which is the bedrock of all law. 'The effect of drunkenness on the mind and on men's actions *   *   * is a fact known to everyone, and it is as much the duty of men to abstain from placing themselves in a condition from which such danger to others is to be apprehended as it is to abstain from firing into a crowd or doing any other act likely to be attended with dangerous or fatal consequences.' "

5. Is the *White* position constitutional? *Terry v. State,* 465 N.E.2d 1085 (Ind. 1984), concludes: "Any factor which serves as a denial of the existence of *mens rea* must be considered by a trier of fact before a guilty finding is entered. Historically, facts such as age, mental condition, mistake or intoxication have been offered to negate the capacity to formulate intent. The attempt by the legislature to remove the factor of voluntary intoxication, except in limited situations, goes against this firmly ingrained principle. We thus hold Ind. Code § 35–41–3–5(b) is void and without effect."

Compare *Wyant v. State,* 519 A.2d 649 (Del.1986) ("The argument that voluntary intoxication must remain an available 'fact' defense for defendant to assert because it may negate the element of intent or volition does not stand analysis"); and cf. *Muench v. Israel,* p. 413 of this Book.

6. Is the necessary outcome on the abolition issue the same as the outcome on the issue of whether, if involuntary intoxication *is* a defense, the burden of proof may be placed on the defendant? On the latter question, consider *State v. Schulz,* 102 Wis.2d 423, 307 N.W.2d 151 (1981): "When the defendant introduces evidence to demonstrate that, because of his intoxicated state, he did not intend to kill his victim, the accused seeks to negate a fact which the state must prove in order to convict the defendant of murder. This is the type of negative defense which was contemplated by the decisions in *Mullaney* [p. 238 of this Book] and *Patterson* [p. 245 of this Book]. When such a defense is asserted, the burden of persuasion cannot be placed upon the defendant without violating his right to due process of law." Consider also *State v. Coates,* supra ("intoxication is not a 'defense' to a crime. Evidence of intoxication may bear upon whether the defendant acted with the requisite mental state, but the proper way to deal with the issue is to instruct the jury that it may consider evidence of the defendant's intoxication in deciding whether the defendant acted with the requisite mental state," as to which the state "always has the burden").

Compare *United States ex rel. Goddard v. Vaughn,* 614 F.2d 929 (3d Cir.1980) ("since the Court has held that the defense may be required to establish insanity, it follows that a state may impose the burden of proof upon the accused when the effect upon rational behavior may be less severe. Indeed, in the case of voluntary intoxication, the state has displayed an even greater degree of leniency because the impaired intellectual functioning was caused by the defendant's own voluntary act, unlike deficiencies caused by forces beyond one's control"). See also *Martin v. Ohio,* p. 472 of this Book, holding that consistent with *Patterson* the burden of proof re the defense of self defense may be placed on the defendant, and explaining: "The State did not exceed its authority in defining the crime of murder as purposely causing the death of another with prior calculation or design. It did not seek to shift to Martin the burden of proving any of those elements, and the jury's verdict reflects that none of her self-defense evidence raised a reasonable doubt about the state's proof that she purposefully killed with prior calculation and design."

7. Is *Vaughn* sound, or, on the other hand, should any departure from the majority view head in the other direction? Consider J. Hall, *General Principles of Criminal Law* 554–55 (2d ed. 1960): "Certain very important distinctions must next be drawn between two types of normal offenders, *i.e.* those who had no previous experience with intoxication that rendered them dangerous, and those with such experience. As regards the inexperienced inebriate, it is submitted that on principle he cannot be held criminally liable for a harm committed under gross intoxication. For such persons, there can be no valid reliance on the drinking, to support liability, because, though 'voluntary,' it was quite innocent. Complete exculpation in such cases might offend public opinion. But there are certain practical considerations that render the indicated reform palatable. First, is the likelihood that serious injuries are very rarely, if ever, committed by inexperienced inebriates. The reported cases, where such injuries were committed, exhibit addiction or long histories of repeated dangerous intoxication. In addition, non-punitive treatment of the inexperi-

enced inebriate may be indicated and should be available."

8. Assuming a situation in which the defense of intoxication may be interposed, precisely how severe must the intoxication have been? Recall that in *Beard* it was said that there must be "evidence of a state of drunkenness rendering the accused incapable of forming such an intent." Similar expressions are common in the modern cases, e.g., *People v. Johnson,* 32 Ill.App.3d 36, 335 N.E.2d 144 (1975) ("whether the intoxication is so extreme as to entirely suspend the power of reason"); *State v. McLaughlin,* 286 N.C. 597, 213 S.E.2d 238 (1975) supra ("intoxication to a degree precluding the ability to form a specific intent to kill"); *State v. Cameron,* 104 N.J. 42, 514 A.2d 1302 (1986) ("prostration of faculties such that defendant was rendered incapable of forming an intent"). *Cameron* adds that the factors pertinent to a determination of whether such circumstances were present are: "the quantity of intoxicant consumed, the period of time involved, the actor's conduct as perceived by others (what he said, how he said it, how he appeared, how he acted, how his coordination or lack thereof manifested itself), any odor of alcohol or other intoxicating substance, the results of any tests to determine blood-alcohol content, and the actor's ability to recall significant events."

Compare *People v. Crittle,* 390 Mich. 367, 212 N.W.2d 196 (1973), noting that such formulations "all have one thing in common. They refer to a *capacity* standard. Their test is not Justice Cooley's— 'The crime cannot have been committed when the intent *did not exist.*' Their test is rather 'the crime cannot have been committed when the intent *could not exist.*' It is obviously a different standard and not to be followed.

"As a consequence, trial judges would do well to follow Justice Cooley's language and posit their instructions in terms of whether in the light of defendant's intoxication he in fact had the required specific felonious intent."

Crittle was overruled in *People v. Savoie,* 419 Mich. 118, 349 N.W.2d 139 (1984), as an unjustified departure from "the proper standard * * * articulated more than a century ago."

7. *Parker v. State,* 7 Md.App. 167, 254 A.2d 381 (1969): "Regardless of what test is applicable to determining insanity, the majority [of courts] distinguish between (1) the mental effect of voluntary intoxication which is the immediate result of a particular alcoholic bout; and (2) an alcoholic psychosis resulting from long continued habits of excessive drinking. The first does not excuse responsibility for a criminal act; the second may. In other words, if a person drinks intoxicating liquor and is sane both prior to drinking and after the influences of the intoxicant has worn off, but is insane by the applicable test while under the influence of the intoxicant, he comes under the first category. If he is insane whether or not he is directly under the influence of an intoxicant, even though that insanity was caused by voluntary drinking, he comes under the second category. The cases usually refer to the first category as a 'temporary' insanity and the second category as a 'permanent', 'fixed' or 'settled' insanity. These terms may be an oversimplification. What 'permanent', 'fixed' or 'settled' means within the frame of reference is that the insanity not only existed while a person was under the influence of intoxicating spirits as an immediate result of imbibing, but existed independent of such influence, even though the insanity was caused by past imbibing. So if a person while in the throes of delirium tremens which may meet the test for insanity, commits a crime, he is not responsible for his criminal conduct, although such defect, resulting remotely from excessive drinking is only a temporary toxic state. It would seem that

the distinction, notwithstanding the language of the cases, is not so much between temporary and permanent insanity as it is one between the direct results of drinking, which are voluntarily sought after, and its remote and undesired consequences."

8. Paulsen, *Intoxication as a Defense to Crime,* 1961 U.Ill.L.F. 1, 21: "While alcoholism may not be a mental disease recognized clinically, heavy drinking is often a symptom of deep mental disturbance. If the evidence concerning the defendant's psychic disorientation is such as to satisfy the medical experts that the defendant suffers from some recognized mental disorder, he should not be treated by the law in a way different from others simply because his disorder brings him to an excessive use of alcohol. The appellate cases leave the writer with the impression that advocates have not been skillful in pressing this point. Defense lawyers tend to lay stress on the gross intoxication without attempting to probe carefully into the underlying psychic disorder which may be allied with the drunkenness. Perhaps the failure is explained simply by the lack of defense funds available in most cases of this sort. At any rate it is true, in today's law, that insanity will exculpate completely; drunkenness will not. Therefore, defense strategy should focus attention clearly on the former factor in the intoxication cases."

9. In *State v. Hall,* 214 N.W.2d 205 (Iowa 1974), defendant testified that before he shot and killed his companion he had taken a pill (apparently LSD) which induced hallucinations, and that he had fired at what appeared to him as a rabid dog. On appeal from his murder conviction, the court held the trial judge properly refused defendant's requested insanity instruction. Deeming the rule developed regarding insanity and use of alcohol (see *Parker,* supra) equally applicable in cases where drugs were ingested, the court concluded defendant's evidence did not show "settled or established" insanity. The dis-

senters objected: 'Our intoxication rationale as applied to alcohol simply does not fit the use of modern hallucinatory drugs; and it was never meant to. It was adopted before such drugs, as we now know them, were in common use. That is why I would say they *are* dissimilar and should be so regarded. There is no justifiable reason for equating the effects of so-called 'hard' drugs, particularly those classified as hallucinatory, with the use of alcohol."

CITY OF MINNEAPOLIS v. ALTIMUS

Supreme Court of Minnesota, 1976.
306 Minn. 462, 238 N.W.2d 851.

KELLY, JUSTICE.

Defendant, who was found guilty by a Hennepin County Municipal Court jury of careless driving and hit and run as to an attended vehicle, and not guilty of simple assault, was sentenced by the trial court to terms of 30 and 90 days in the workhouse, sentences to be served concurrently with revocation of parole from Federal prison.

* * *

At 12:15 p.m. on September 28, 1973, defendant, driving south on Hiawatha Avenue, made an illegal left turn from the right-hand lane and crashed into a garbage truck proceeding northward on Hiawatha. Immediately after impact, defendant backed up and drove easterly on Lake Street at a slow speed. This slow speed resulted from the fact that the automobile defendant was driving had been badly damaged in the collision. Policemen who observed the accident followed defendant and stopped him about a block from the point of impact. Defendant, who appeared to one of the officers to be somewhat confused, told the officers that his head and shoulder hurt and asked to be taken to the hospital. In response to questions by the officers, defendant, who gave "William Jones" as his name, stated that he did not have his driver's license with him but showed the officers a paper purporting to be a transfer of title from Robert Altimus to William Jones.

Because of a gap in the evidence, we do not know for certain what happened next, but it appears that an ambulance took defendant to General Hospital and defendant ran away after police discovered his true identity. In any event, we have the testimony of an off-duty uniformed police officer that at about 1:30 p.m. he was on his way to the Minnesota Auto Body Shop at Seventh Street and Park Avenue when another officer told him to be on the lookout for a man fitting defendant's description and that when he got to the body shop he saw the defendant. He testified that defendant refused to identify himself and ran toward the General Hospital construction area, where an altercation occurred when the officer caught him; that defendant then ran to a church at Seventh Street and Chicago Avenue where he broke the officer's nose; and that finally he was apprehended at the St. Barnabas School of Nursing.

At trial, the defense did not dispute the evidence adduced by the state, but introduced evidence designed to show that defendant did not have the requisite state of mind to be guilty of either simple assault or the two remaining traffic charges. Defendant testified that on September 25, 1973, three days before the incident, he had seen a doctor at the Veterans Administration Hospital for treatment of a back problem and the flu and that the doctor had prescribed Valium, which he had taken as prescribed. He testified that on September 28 the Valium began to have a strange effect on him, making it impossible for him to control himself. He testified

that he did not know who owned the automobile which he had driven, and that he remembered nothing about the accident or the events that followed.

The only other defense witness was Dr. Humberto Ortiz, the doctor who treated defendant at the Veterans Administration Hospital. He testified that he prescribed the Valium because it was a skeletal muscle relaxant and was the type of drug which would relieve the acute back pain defendant had been experiencing. He testified that he also prescribed empirin, bed rest, and heat. Dr. Ortiz listed drowsiness, fatigue, ataxia, and confusion as the normal side effects of Valium. He testified, however, that hyperexcitability, although more rare, was also a possible side effect. On cross-examination, he stated that he did not know if the drug might cause one to be confused as to his identity; but in response to a hypothetical question stating the facts of the case, he expressed the opinion that defendant might have been suffering from the effects of the drug.

After resting, the defense requested the trial court to instruct on the defense of involuntary intoxication and submitted proposed instructions to that effect,[2] but the trial court refused to instruct on the defense or to give these instructions. The trial judge did instruct the jury that defendant's alleged intoxication would be a defense to the charge of assault if it rendered him unable to formulate the specific intent to inflict bodily harm on the person of another which is an essential element of the crime of assault. We do not express an opinion as to the propriety of this voluntary intoxication instruction on the assault charge, but we note that we have not

2. The defense submitted the following proposed instructions as to involuntary intoxication: "Intoxication is involuntary when it is produced in a person without his willing and knowing use of intoxicating liquor, drugs or other substance and without his willing assumption of the risk of possible intoxication.

"Proof of the involuntary intoxication of a defendant should be considered by the jury in determining whether the defendant had the capacity or ability to commit any of the four offenses with which he is charged or to form a criminal intent at the time the offenses are alleged to have been committed."

decided whether that defense applies to simple assault cases.

The general rule in Minnesota is that voluntary intoxication is a defense * * * only if a specific intent or purpose is an essential element of the crime charged and the trier of fact concluded that the defendant's intoxication deprived him of the specific intent or purpose requisite to the alleged offense.[4] Because [the] traffic offenses with which defendant was charged do not require a specific intent to do a prohibited act, the defense of voluntary intoxication cannot and does not apply to those offenses.

While general traffic offenses do not require that the wrongdoer specifically intend to commit the crime for which he is charged, we have held that before criminal liability can attach it is essential that the defendant intentionally or negligently do the act which constitutes the crime. *State v. Kremer,* 262 Minn. 190, 114 N.W.2d 88 (1962). In *Kremer* we reversed the conviction of a defendant who unintentionally and non-negligently drove through a stop signal because his brakes failed. We acknowledged there that a defendant may be held criminally responsible for some activities, even though he does not criminally intend the harm caused by his acts, because he "usually is in a position to prevent it with no more care than society might reasonably expect and no more exertion than it might reasonably exact from one who assumed his responsibilities." When that duty of due care is breached, the driver may properly be found criminally responsible for a traffic offense. We reversed the defendant's conviction in *Kremer* because the above rationale did not apply when there was no negligence by the defendant and no intent to do the act which turned out to be criminal. The

unusual issue presented on this appeal is whether the defendant is entitled to assert the defense of involuntary intoxication if due to such intoxication he unintentionally and non-negligently did the acts for which he is charged. In brief, we hold that defendant was entitled to an instruction on involuntary intoxication, that the trial court erred in refusing to grant such an instruction, and that a new trial is required.

We begin our analysis of the defense of involuntary intoxication by considering its origins and its relationship to the partial defense of voluntary intoxication. The common-law rule was that voluntary intoxication was never a defense to a criminal charge. * * * The common law distinguished involuntary from voluntary intoxication, however, and found the former to be a defense to criminal liability if it caused the defendant to become temporarily insane. * * *

Four different kinds of involuntary intoxication have been recognized: Coerced intoxication, pathological intoxication, intoxication by innocent mistake, and unexpected intoxication resulting from the ingestion of a medically prescribed drug. Coerced intoxication is intoxication involuntarily induced by reason of duress or coercion. Some courts have declared in general terms that coerced intoxication may be a complete defense to all criminal liability. See, e.g., *Burrows v. State,* 38 Ariz. 99, 297 P. 1029 (1931). In *Burrows,* the Arizona Supreme Court approved the trial court's instruction which stated that involuntary intoxication would be a complete defense if the defendant was compelled to drink against his will and "his reason was destroyed" so "that he did not understand and appreciate the consequences of his act." Courts have strictly

---

4. Minn.St. 609.075 provides: "An act committed while in a state of voluntary intoxication is not less criminal by reason thereof, but when a particular intent or other state of mind is a necessary element to constitute a particular crime, the fact of intoxication may be taken into consideration in determining such intent or state of mind."

construed the requirement of coercion, however, so that acquittal by reason of coerced intoxication is an exceedingly rare result.

Pathological intoxication has been defined as "intoxication grossly excessive in degree, given the amount of the intoxicant, to which the actor does not know he is susceptible." Pathologically intoxicated offenders have been held not criminally responsible for their acts when they ingested the intoxicant not knowing of their special susceptibility to its effects. The defense of pathological intoxication has been limited in some jurisdictions, however, by the requirement that the intoxicated defendant must be deprived of mental capacity to the degree necessary for an insanity defense.

Involuntary intoxication may also occur when intoxication results from an innocent mistake by the defendant about the character of the substance taken, as when another person has tricked him into taking the liquor or drugs. See, *People v. Penman,* 271 Ill. 82, 110 N.E. 894 (1915). In *Penman,* the defendant killed his victim after apparently taking cocaine tablets which, due to the deception of another, he believed to be breath purifiers. The Illinois Supreme Court held that this would constitute involuntary intoxication and a full defense to criminal liability if it caused the defendant to become temporarily insane.

The last kind of involuntary intoxication recognized in the case law arises when the defendant is unexpectedly intoxicated due to the ingestion of a medically prescribed drug. Several courts have declared that such intoxication constitutes a valid defense to criminal liability if the prescribed drug is taken pursuant to medical advice

and without defendant's knowledge of its potentially intoxicating effects.

Appellant asserts that due to the ingestion of a prescribed drug, Valium, he was unexpectedly intoxicated to the point of unconsciousness, incapable of controlling his actions, and thus not criminally responsible for his actions. To assess fully the merits of this claim, it is necessary to review carefully the circumstances in which a defense of involuntary intoxication due to ingestion of a prescribed drug is properly available.

The first requirement is that the defendant must not know, or have reason to know, that the prescribed drug is likely to have an intoxicating effect. If the defendant knows, or has reason to know, that the prescribed drug will have an intoxicating effect, then he is voluntarily intoxicated [8] and may plead his voluntary intoxication as a partial defense only as provided for in Minn.St. 609.075.

The second requirement is that the prescribed drug, and not some other intoxicant, is in fact the cause of defendant's intoxication at the time of his alleged criminal conduct.

The third requirement is that the defendant, due to involuntary intoxication, is temporarily insane. The numerous cases cited above in which the common-law defense of involuntary intoxication has been recognized are virtually unanimous in holding that this defense is available only when the defendant is legally insane at the time of the alleged criminal offense. We believe that the Minnesota Legislature has already prescribed in Minn.St. 611.026 the test applicable to the defense of involuntary intoxication. Section 611.026 states:

"No person shall be tried, sentenced, or punished for any crime while mentally ill or mentally deficient so as to be

8. The *Model Penal Code,* § 2.08(5)(b) defines self-induced intoxication as "intoxication caused by substances which the actor knowingly in-

troduces into his body, the tendency of which to cause intoxication he knows or ought to know * * *."

incapable of understanding the proceedings or making a defense; but he shall not be excused from criminal liability except upon proof that at the time of committing the alleged criminal act he was laboring under such a defect of reason, from one of these causes, as not to know the nature of his act, or that it was wrong."

We hold that if the defendant is mentally deficient due to involuntary intoxication, then he may be excused from criminal responsibility only if temporarily insane as defined in § 611.026.

Mr. Justice Rogosheske in his special concurrence argues that the insanity test and § 611.026 are not applicable to the defense of involuntary intoxication. He asserts that the better test is that found in the *Model Penal Code,* § 2.08(4). * * * Several states in enacting statutes expressly defining the defense of involuntary intoxication have followed the above test proposed in the Model Penal Code. The Minnesota Legislature, however, has passed no statute expressly addressing the test to be applied when a defendant asserts the defense of involuntary intoxication. In the absence of such an express statute on involuntary intoxication, we adhere to the legislative policy articulated in Minn. St. 611.026. * * *

In the case of voluntary intoxication, the defendant must establish the defense by a fair preponderance of the evidence. Similarly, when insanity is a matter of defense we have held that the defendant must prove by the preponderance of the evidence that he was legally insane; it is not enough that he raise a reasonable doubt as to his sanity. In light of the above, we today hold that the defendant in the instant case bears the burden of establishing by the preponderance of the evidence that he was temporarily insane due to involuntary intoxication.

Involuntary intoxication, we note in summary, is a most unusual condition. The circumstances in which an instruction on the defense of involuntary intoxication will be appropriate will accordingly be very rare. We hold, nevertheless, that in the instant case such an instruction was necessary because defendant introduced evidence sufficient to raise the defense of temporary insanity due to involuntary intoxication. Defendant's evidence indicated that at the time he committed the acts in question he was intoxicated and unaware of what he was doing due to an unusual and unexpected reaction to drugs prescribed by a physician. We further believe that failure to give an instruction on involuntary intoxication was prejudicial error in view of the finding of not guilty on the charge of simple assault, a finding which suggests very strongly that the jury believed defendant's evidence that the Valium was responsible for his behavior.

Reversed and remanded for a new trial.

ROGOSHESKE, JUSTICE (concurring specially). * * *

The premise underlying the defense of involuntary intoxication is that a person should not be held criminally liable in the absence of volitional fault, that is, conscious fault. * * * In recognition of the above principle, the authors of the Model Penal Code declared that involuntary intoxication is an affirmative defense if—

"* * * by reason of such intoxication the actor at the time of his conduct lacks substantial capacity either to appreciate its criminality [wrongfulness] or to conform his conduct to the requirements of law." *Model Penal Code,* § 2.08(4).

I would apply the above principle to the case at bar by instructing the jury that defendant should be excused from criminal liability if defendant establishes by the preponderance of the evidence that due to the ingestion of Valium he was intoxicated to such an extent that he was incapable of exercising reasonable care in operating his automobile, and that he did not know or have reasonable grounds to foresee that in taking the Valium pursuant to his doctor's prescription his mental condition would become such as to render him incapable of exercising reasonable care in driving an automobile.

The majority opinion declares that involuntary intoxication is a defense only when it causes temporary insanity as insanity is defined in Minn.St. 611.026. In my view, § 611.026 has no application to the defense asserted because involuntary intoxication due to the ingestion of a medically prescribed drug is simply not a form of mental "illness" or "deficiency" as those terms are commonly used. To describe the asserted mental state of defendant in this case as one of insanity stretches that word far beyond its ordinary meaning and gives § 611.026 a construction it is doubtful was ever contemplated by the legislature.

In my opinion, the defense of involuntary intoxication does not rest upon so tenuous a statutory basis. Involuntary intoxication is a defense anchored firmly in the theory of mens rea, which has long been a part of Anglo–American common law.

*   *   *

The majority opinion suggests that this court must defer to the legislative judgment expressed in § 611.026 and allow the defense of involuntary intoxication only when it creates temporary insanity. I do not agree because it has traditionally been the duty of the courts and not the legislature to define the defenses which necessarily follow from the doctrine of mens rea. *   *   *

Notes and Questions

1. May it not be argued that the defense is too narrowly stated by both Justice Kelly and Justice Rogosheske? Specifical-

ly, if Altimus was not at fault in becoming intoxicated, then why shouldn't the question be whether he would have driven carelessly and hit and run if he had been sober?

2. In *Altimus* the court holds that the defendant must establish the involuntary intoxication defense by a preponderance of the evidence. Is this a proper allocation of the burden of proof? Compare the cases in Note 6, p. 446 of this Book.

3. The intoxication of a person who is an alcoholic, *Evans v. State*, 645 P.2d 155 (Alaska 1982), or a drug addict, *State v. Bishop*, 632 S.W.2d 255 (Mo.1982), is not, because of that condition, deemed to be *in*voluntary so as to bring the case within the *Altimus* rule. Why should this be so?

4. With respect to what should constitute intoxication by duress, consider Paulsen, *Intoxication as a Defense to Crime*, 1961 U.Ill.L.F. 1, 18–19: "The opinions that can be found take a hard line of defining 'voluntary.' A case summarized by Professor Hall makes the point.

'A college student under eighteen, who had never before tasted intoxicating liquor, was given a ride by the deceased in his automobile. The latter had been drinking heavily and insisted that the boy participate, became abusive and threatened to put him off in the Arizona desert if he refused. The court, noting that the "defendant, being alone, penniless, and fearing that he might be ejected and left on the desert did drink some beer and whiskey," nonetheless held that involuntary intoxication "must be induced by acts amounting in effect to duress." '

The Model Penal Code has taken a similarly tough stand. Section 2.08(4) makes intoxication a defense if it is not self-induced. In section 2.08(5) the definition of 'self-induced intoxication' excludes the case of one brought to drunkenness by 'such duress as would afford a defense to a charge of crime.' The definition of duress is found in section 2.09(1) of the Code.

* * *

"In the case of the college boy crossing the desert it is hardly possible to assert that the driver used or threatened to use such force against the boy's person 'which a person of reasonable firmness in his situation would have been *unable* to resist.' The requirement of inability puts the test of voluntariness for this purpose too high. What may be needed in the Code is a separate definition of duress for purposes of the intoxication section. Reference could be made to a 'person of reasonable firmness' in the 'situation' of the actor but the test should ask whether that person *would have* resisted not whether he was *able* to do so. To do that would take into account the choice of evils facing the actor."

5. With respect to what should constitute intoxication by innocent mistake, consider *State v. Hall,* 214 N.W.2d 205 (Iowa 1974). The defendant testified he killed his companion while hallucinating that the object of his attack was a rabid dog, and that prior to the killing he took a pill "that casual acquaintances in California gave him * * * and told him it was a 'little sunshine' and would make him feel 'groovy.' " The majority concludes this was not a case of involuntary intoxication, as "no one tricked him into taking it or forced him to do so." The dissenters objected:

"The testimony shows defendant took a pill which he knew to be a drug but which he did not know to be LSD and which he testified he thought to be harmless, although he had been told it would make him feel groovy. There is nothing to indicate he knew it could induce hallucinations or lead to the frightening debilitating effects of mind and body to which the doctors testified. The majority nevertheless holds the defendant's resulting drug intoxication was voluntary. I disagree.

* * *

"In other words, does voluntary in this context refer to the *mechanical* act of ingesting the pill or does it refer to a willing and intelligent assumption of the possible harmful consequences of that act?

"I am convinced voluntary as here used should relate to a knowledgeable acceptance of the danger and risk involved. Applied to the instant case, that rule would demand submission of the issue to a jury."

6. In *People v. Walker,* 33 Ill.App.3d 681, 338 N.E.2d 449 (1975), the court noted that the "only basis for the idea of involuntarily produced intoxication was the defendant's testimony that a week or so previous to the shooting he had obtained some pills from his brother to alleviate a stomach ache; that he had taken these pills with beneficial effect, and that on the evening in question he had taken two more of these pills from the jar where they were kept in his brother's house. Afterwards, he had drunk some beer and some wine. The tenuous basis for the involuntariness of his intoxication was that his brother did not tell him—and probably did not know—that the pills in question contained Seconal, a tranquillizing drug which, mixed with alcohol, could have the effect of intensifying the defendant's intoxication and reducing his control over his impulses." The court held that the trial judge properly refused to give an instruction on involuntary intoxication because defendant's drunkenness was not "caused by trick, artifice or force."

Is the result in *Walker* supported by *Hall,* or are the two cases different? How would each be decided under *Model Penal Code* § 2.08(4) and (5)?

SECTION 3. IMMATURITY

STATE v. Q.D.

Supreme Court of Washington, 1984.
102 Wash.2d 19, 685 P.2d 557.

DIMMICK, JUSTICE.

Two juveniles appeal from separate adjudications which found that they had committed offenses which if committed by an adult would be crimes. The Court of Appeals, in these consolidated appeals, certified to this court the questions whether the statutory presumption of infant incapacity, RCW 9A.04.050,[1] applies to juvenile adjudications, and if it does, what standard of proof is required to rebut the presumption. * * *

Appellant Q.D. was found to have capacity per RCW 9A.04.050 in a pretrial hearing. He was 11½ years old at the time of the alleged offense. At trial a different judge determined he had committed trespass in the first degree. The evidence introduced to show capacity consisted of testimony from a case worker and a detective who had worked with him in connection with his plea of guilty to a burglary committed at age 10 years. The case worker testified that Q.D. was familiar with the justice system, was street wise, and that he used his age as a shield. The detective told the court that Q.D. was cooperative in the burglary investigation, and he appeared to know his rights. The evidence in the guilt phase consisted of testimony from the principal and a custodial engineer of the school in which Q.D. was charged with trespass. The engineer testified that he saw Q.D. sitting on the school grounds about 2 p.m. playing with some keys that looked like the set belonging to the night custodian. When the engineer checked his desk which was in an

unlocked office, he found that the keys were missing as was the burglar alarm key. The engineer could not be certain that he had seen the keys since the morning. He called the principal and they brought Q.D. into the office. When Q.D. arose from the chair he had been sitting on in the office, the burglar alarm key was discovered on a radiator behind the chair.

Appellant M.S., in a single proceeding, was found to have capacity and to have committed indecent liberties on a 4½–year–old child for whom she was babysitting. Evidence included the testimony of the victim, the victim's mother, a physician who had examined the victim, and a social worker who had interviewed the victim. M.S. was less than 3 months from 12 years old at the time of the offense. The issue of capacity was first raised by the defendant in a motion to dismiss at the close of the State's evidence. The State argued that defendant's proximity to the age when capacity is assumed, the defendant's threats to the victim not to tell what had happened, and her secrecy in carrying out the act were ample proof of capacity. The trial judge, in his oral ruling finding capacity, stated that the responsibility entrusted to the defendant by the victim's mother and her own parents in permitting her to babysit showed a recognition of the defendant's maturity.

I

Counsel for both the State and the defendants urge us to hold that the infant incapacity defense in RCW 9A.04.050 applies to juvenile proceedings. We so hold.

At common law, children below the age of 7 were conclusively presumed to be incapable of committing crime, and children over the age of 14 were presumed

---

1. RCW 9A.04.050 provides in part:

"Children under the age of eight years are incapable of committing crime. Children of eight and under twelve years of age are presumed to be

incapable of committing crime, but this presumption may be removed by proof that they have sufficient capacity to understand the act or neglect, and to know that it was wrong."

capable and treated as adults. Children between these ages were rebuttably presumed incapable of committing crime. Washington codified these presumptions amending the age of conclusive incapacity to 7, and presumed capacity to 12 years of age. As recently as 1975, the Legislature again included the infancy defense in the criminal code. The purpose of the presumption is to protect from the criminal justice system those individuals of tender years who are less capable than adults of appreciating the wrongfulness of their behavior.

The infancy defense fell into disuse during the early part of the century with the advent of reforms intended to substitute treatment and rehabilitation for punishment of juvenile offenders. This parens patriae system, believed not to be a criminal one, had no need of the infancy defense.

The juvenile justice system in recent years has evolved from parens patriae scheme to one more akin to adult criminal proceedings. The United States Supreme Court has been critical of the parens patriae scheme as failing to provide safeguards due an adult criminal defendant, while subjecting the juvenile defendant to similar stigma, and possible loss of liberty. *See In re Gault,* 387 U.S. 1, 87 S.Ct. 1428, 18 L.Ed.2d 527 (1966); and *In re Winship,* 397 U.S. 358, 90 S.Ct. 1068, 25 L.Ed.2d 368 (1977). This court has acknowledged Washington's departure from a strictly parens patriae scheme to a more criminal one, involving both rehabilitation and punishment. Being a criminal defense, RCW 9A.04.050 should be available to juvenile proceedings that are criminal in nature.

The principles of construction of criminal statutes, made necessary by our recognition of the criminal nature of juvenile court proceedings, also compel us to conclude that RCW 9A.04.050 applies to proceedings in juvenile courts.

A finding that RCW 9A.04.050 does not apply to juvenile courts would render that statute meaningless or superfluous contrary to rules of construction. Juvenile courts have exclusive jurisdiction over all individuals under the chronological age of 18 who have committed acts designated criminal if committed by an adult. Declination of jurisdiction and transfer to adult court is limited to instances where it is in the best interest of the juvenile or the public. Thus, all juveniles who can avail themselves of the infancy defense will come under the jurisdiction of the juvenile court, and most will remain there. Implied statutory repeals are found not to exist where two statutes can be reconciled and given effect. Goals of the Juvenile Justice Act of 1977 include accountability for criminal behavior and punishment commensurate with age and crime. A goal of the criminal code is to safeguard conduct that is not culpable. The infancy defense which excludes from criminal condemnation persons not capable of culpable, criminal acts, is consistent with the overlapping goals of the Juvenile Justice Act of 1977 and the Washington Criminal Code.

II

The State has the burden of rebutting the statutory presumption of incapacity of juveniles age 8 and less than 12 years. Capacity must be found to exist separate from the specific mental element of the crime charged. While capacity is similar to the mental element of a specific crime or offense, it is not an element of the offense, but is rather a general determination that the individual understood the act and its wrongfulness. Both defendants liken the incapacity presumption to a jurisdictional presumption. Were capacity an element of the crime, proof beyond a reasonable doubt would be required. *In re Winship, supra.* But capacity, not being an element of the crime, does not require as stringent a standard of proof.

Few jurisdictions have ruled on the appropriate standard of proof necessary to rebut the presumption of incapacity, and fewer still have discussed their reasoning for preferring one standard over another. It appears that other states have split between requiring proof beyond a reasonable doubt, and clear and convincing proof.

Our recent discussion of the standard of proof to be applied in involuntary commitment proceedings offers guidance. In *Dunner v. McLaughlin,* 100 Wash.2d 832, 676 P.2d 444 (1984), we held that the burden of proof should be by clear, cogent and convincing evidence. In so holding, we recognized that the preponderance of the evidence standard was inadequate, but the proof beyond a reasonable doubt standard imposed a burden which, as a practical matter, was unreasonably difficult, thus undercutting the State's legitimate interests.

The Legislature, by requiring the State to rebut the presumption of incapacity, has assumed a greater burden than the minimal proof imposed by the preponderance of the evidence standard. On the other hand, to require the State to prove capacity beyond a reasonable doubt when the State must also prove the specific mental element of the charged offense by the same standard, is unnecessarily duplicative. Frequently, the same facts required to prove mens rea will be probative of capacity, yet the overlap is not complete. Capacity to be culpable must exist in order to maintain the specific mental element of the charged offense. Once the generalized determination of capacity is found, the State must prove beyond a reasonable doubt that the juvenile defendant possessed the specific mental element. The clear and convincing standard reflects the State's assumption of a greater burden

than does the preponderance of the evidence standard. At the same time, the liberty interest of the juvenile is fully protected by the requirement of proof beyond a reasonable doubt of the specific mental element. We therefore require the State to rebut the presumption of incapacity by clear and convincing evidence.

III

We do not need to reach the question of whether there was substantial evidence to show that Q.D. understood the act of trespass or understood it to be wrong, as we reverse on other grounds. Nevertheless, a discussion of capacity in this case may prove instructive to trial courts. Q.D. argues that the evidence showed only that he was familiar with the juvenile system through his previous plea of guilty to a burglary charge, but did not show he understood the act and wrongfulness of trespass. The language of RCW 9A.04.050 clearly indicates that a capacity determination must be made in reference to the specific act charged: "understand *the act* * * * and to know that *it* was wrong." (Italics ours.) If Q.D. is correct that the evidence showed no more than a general understanding of the justice system, he would be correct in concluding that the State did not show an understanding and knowing wrongfulness of trespass. In addition, an understanding of the wrongfulness of burglary does not alone establish capacity in regard to trespass. While both offenses include entry or unlawfully remaining in a building, burglary also requires an intent to commit a crime against a person or property therein. Defendant may well understand that it is wrong to enter a locked building with the intention of committing a crime, but not know that entering an unlocked school building is wrong.

The issue of capacity was first raised on M.S.'s motion to dismiss at the end of the trial. The judge stated in response to arguments of counsel that he was persuaded by the confidence in defendant's maturity held by the mother of the victim and her own parents in permitting her to assume the responsibility for babysitting. Contrary to defendant's arguments that the trial judge created a prima facie proof of capacity based solely on babysitting, there was other evidence to support his finding of capacity. The defendant waited until she and the victim were alone evidencing a desire for secrecy. The defendant later admonished the victim not to tell what happened, further supporting the finding that the defendant knew the act was wrong. Lastly, the defendant was less than 3 months from the age at which capacity is presumed to exist. There was clear and convincing circumstantial evidence that M.S. understood the act of indecent liberties and knew it to be wrong.

* * *

Notes and Questions

1. Compare *In re Michael,* ___ R.I. ___, 423 A.2d 1180 (1981): "Once one accepts the principle that a finding of delinquency or waywardness in a juvenile proceeding is not the equivalent of a finding that the juvenile has committed a crime, there is no necessity of a finding that the juvenile had such maturity that he or she knew what he or she was doing was wrong. A juvenile is delinquent or wayward, not because the juvenile has committed a crime, but because the juvenile has committed an act that would be a crime if committed by a person not a juvenile and because the juvenile requires 'such care, guidance and control * * * as will serve the child's welfare and the best interests of the state * * *.' General Laws 1956 (1969 Reenactment) § 14–1–2."

2. The commentators are not in agreement as to whether the *Q.D.* or *Michael* approach is best. Consider: (a) Ludwig, *Responsibility for Young Offenders,* 29 Neb.L.

Rev. 521, 534 (1950), asserts that when "the purpose of treatment of immature offenders is solely rehabilitation, it is unnecessary to set limits of absolute irresponsibility. The same is true of conditional responsibility. Age lines and rebuttable presumptions of incapacity become superfluous in the light of this treatment purpose. Indeed if all offenders should be treated by the criminal law like patients by a physician, the concept of criminal responsibility would vanish * * *. The problem of responsibility can exist only in connection with treatment for the sake of deterrence."

(b) Walkover, *The Infancy Defense in the New Juvenile Court,* 31 U.C.L.A.L.Rev. 503, 538 (1984): "Like its adult counterpart, the juvenile justice system operates as a screening device. It shares with and complements the adult system's functions of imposing social controls and attributing blame. Moreover, as a consequence of juvenile justice proceedings, convicted youth may suffer the social stigma and loss of liberty associated with the adult criminal process. It follows that the commitment to punishing only the culpable that animates adult criminal jurisprudence should also be applicable to the juvenile process."

3. Couch, age 16 at the time of his conduct, was convicted in criminal court of murder, armed robbery and motor vehicle theft. On appeal, *Couch v. State,* 253 Ga. 764, 325 S.E.2d 366 (1985), the court stated: "Couch insists that the trial court erred in excluding evidence regarding the circumstances of his childhood, his emotional maturity and his mental capacity, maintaining that it would have shown that he had the *mental* age of a ten-year-old child. This evidence was proffered for the sole purpose of showing that Couch was incapable of forming the requisite intent under OCGA § 16–3–1, which provides that '[a] person shall not be considered or found guilty of a crime unless he has

attained the age of 13 years at the time of the act. * * * '

"The age referred to in the code section is, of course, biological age. Nothing evidences a legislative intent to refer to 'mental age'—if, indeed, such a thing could ever be determined."

Chapter 8

JUSTIFICATION AND EXCUSE

SECTION 1. INTRODUCTION

KENT GREENAWALT— DISTINGUISHING JUSTIFICATIONS FROM EXCUSES

49 Law & Contemp.Probs. 89, 91 (Summer 1986).

When something is fully justified, it is warranted. A justified belief is a belief based on good grounds; a justified action is a morally appropriate action. When something is fully excused, it is not warranted, but the person involved is not blameworthy. An excusable belief is one that a person cannot be blamed for holding; [6] an excusable action is one for which a person is not fully responsible. This is the central distinction between justification and excuse. Insofar as others are responsible and have the power of choice, they would do well to replicate a justified action but to avoid an act like that excused.

Occasionally commentators have suggested other distinguishing characteristics as central to the distinction. For example, it has been argued that justifications are general, applying to everyone in the same situation, and excuses are individual, relating to the characteristics of the particular actor. Although a substantial correlation of this type does exist, some legal excuses

as well as some moral appraisals have objective components: their application depends on how ordinary people would react to difficult conditions. If, as this article claims, justifications depend partly on an actor's state of mind, then they do take account of an important individual characteristic.

Another proposed distinction concerns the rights of others. Generally, justified acts may be aided and not prevented, and excused acts may be prevented but not aided. These correlations, however, are imperfect. In the field of moral evaluation, one can speak of clashing courses of action as justified. A person may be morally justified in shielding a family member from the police, and the police may be morally justified in searching the person's apartment to find the family member. On occasion, the law may also privilege competing courses of action. And if excused action may be stopped, it may not always be stopped with the same tactics as unexcused action. Perhaps Richard is morally and legally justified in shooting an ordinary assailant who runs toward him with a knife in his apartment, even if he could retreat. He may not, however, be justified in shooting if he knows the assailant is crazy.

---

6. Someone might, for example, lack solid rational basis for a belief, but be "excused" because his parents powerfully instilled that belief during childhood.

MODEL PENAL CODE

Article 3, Introduction (1985).

The Model Code does not ＊ ＊ ＊ attempt to draw a fine line between all those situations in which a defense might more precisely be labelled a justification and all those situations in which a defense might more precisely be labelled an excuse. Thus, it treats in justification sections those cases in which an actor mistakenly perceives the circumstances or the necessity for force; in some of the cases, at least, it might be said that the actor is really offering an excuse for his conduct rather than a full-fledged justification. The Code's approach is based on a skepticism that any fine line between excuse and justification can sensibly be drawn, and on the belief that any possible value of attempting such a line would be outweighed by the cost of complicating the content of relevant provisions.

To say that someone's conduct is "justified" ordinarily connotes that the conduct is thought to be right, or at least not undesirable; to say that someone's conduct is "excused" ordinarily connotes that the conduct is thought to be undesirable but that for some reason the actor is not to be blamed for it. Usually one can say whether a defense that is offered is justificatory or excusatory, but there are some troublesome borderline cases. Suppose an actor makes a mistake of fact that is not only reasonable but also consistent with the highest standards of perception and apprehension. For example, relying on the consistently prevailing wind, a person sets a fire that will destroy private property but will also stop the advance of a large forest fire that looks as if it will destroy much more property. A sudden unexpected shift in the wind renders the forest fire harmless, while the set fire does the expected amount of property damage. In retrospect it is regrettable that the second fire was set, and one might consider a defense of setting it an "excuse" for an unfortunate occurrence. But based on all available information, the act of setting the fire was appropriate, and society would hope that similar fires would be set by persons with similar available information; thus the conduct of setting the fire was justified. Whether in this circumstance, one speaks of "justification" or "excuse" is a question of vague linguistic boundary lines rather than of substantive judgment.

In other circumstances there may be genuine doubt as to how behavior should be judged. Self-defense serves as an acceptable reason for the use of deadly force both because it is often desirable that people defend their lives and because it is thought that people will "naturally" defend themselves if they believe their lives are in danger. For many cases of self-defense it would probably be generally agreed that the use of deadly force was actually desirable, but for others, e.g., resistance by one family member to attack by another, there would be disagreement whether the use of deadly force was actually desirable or should merely be accepted as a natural response to a grave threat.

There is little point in trying to "purify" justification provisions of all situations in which it might be said that the defense offered is really an excuse. The main aim of a criminal code is to differentiate conduct that warrants criminal sanctions from conduct that does not. If it is clear that conduct will not be subject to criminal sanctions, the effort to establish precisely in each case whether that conduct is actually justified or only excused does not seem worthwhile, especially since, in regard to the difficult cases, members of society may disagree over the appropriate characterization. Moreover, insofar as determinations of justification and excuse are made by juries and both sorts of defenses are offered in difficult cases, a general verdict of acquittal would conceal the precise defense accepted even if the criminal code drew a fine line between justification and excuse.

SECTION 2. DEFENSE OF SELF AND OTHERS

UNITED STATES v. PETERSON

United States Court of Appeals, District of Columbia Circuit, 1973.
483 F.2d 1222.

SPOTTSWOOD W. ROBINSON, III, CIRCUIT JUDGE: * * *

The events immediately preceding the homicide are not seriously in dispute. The version presented by the Government's evidence follows. Charles Keitt, the deceased, and two friends drove in Keitt's car to the alley in the rear of Peterson's house to remove the windshield wipers from the latter's wrecked car. While Keitt was doing so, Peterson came out of the house into the back yard to protest. After a verbal exchange, Peterson went back into the house, obtained a pistol, and returned to the yard. In the meantime, Keitt had reseated himself in his car, and he and his companions were about to leave.

Upon his reappearance in the yard, Peterson paused briefly to load the pistol. "If you move," he shouted to Keitt, "I will shoot." He walked to a point in the yard slightly inside a gate in the rear fence and, pistol in hand, said, "If you come in here I will kill you." Keitt alighted from his car, took a few steps toward Peterson and exclaimed, "What the hell do you think you are going to do with that?" Keitt then made an about-face, walked back to his car and got a lug wrench. With the wrench in a raised position, Keitt advanced toward Peterson, who stood with the pistol pointed toward him. Peterson warned Keitt not to "take another step" and, when Keitt continued onward shot him in the face from a distance of about ten feet. Death was apparently instantane-

ous. Shortly thereafter, Peterson left home and was apprehended 20-odd blocks away.

This description of the fatal episode was furnished at Peterson's trial by four witnesses for the Government. Peterson did not testify or offer any evidence, but the Government introduced a statement which he had given the police after his arrest, in which he related a somewhat different version. Keitt had removed objects from his car before, and on the day of the shooting he had told Keitt not to do so. After the initial verbal altercation, Keitt went to his car for the lug wrench, so he, Peterson, went into his house for his pistol. When Keitt was about ten feet away, he pointed the pistol "away of his right shoulder;" adding that Keitt was running toward him, Peterson said he "got scared and fired the gun. He ran right into the bullet." "I did not mean to shoot him," Peterson insisted, "I just wanted to scare him."

At trial [for murder], Peterson moved for a judgment of acquittal on the ground that as a matter of law the evidence was insufficient to support a conviction. The trial judge denied the motion. After receiving instructions which in two respects are challenged here, the jury returned a verdict finding Peterson guilty of manslaughter. Judgment was entered conformably with the verdict, and this appeal followed. * * *

More than two centuries ago, Blackstone, best known of the expositors of the English common law, taught that "all homicide is malicious, and of course, amounts to murder, unless * * * *justified* by the command or permission of the law; *excused* on the account of accident or self-preservation; or *alleviated* into manslaughter, by being either the involuntary consequence of some act not strictly lawful, or (if voluntary) occasioned by some sudden and sufficiently violent provocation.

Tucked within this greatly capsulized schema of the common law of homicide is the branch of law we are called upon to administer today. No issue of justifiable homicide, within Blackstone's definition is involved.[35] But Peterson's consistent position is that as a matter of law his conviction of manslaughter—alleviated homicide—was wrong, and that his act was one of self-preservation—excused homicide. The Government, on the other hand, has contended from the beginning that Keitt's slaying fell outside the bounds of lawful self-defense. The questions remaining for our decision inevitably track back to this basic dispute.

Self-defense, as a doctrine legally exonerating the taking of human life, is as viable now as it was in Blackstone's time, and in the case before us the doctrine is invoked in its purest form. But "[t]he law of self-defense is a law of necessity;" the right of self-defense arises only when the necessity begins, and equally ends with the necessity; and never must the necessity be greater than when the force employed defensively is deadly.[40] The "necessity must bear all semblance of reality, and appear to admit of no other alternative, before taking life will be justifiable as excusable." Hinged on the exigencies of self-preservation, the doctrine of homicidal self-defense emerges from the body of the criminal law as a limited though important exception to legal outlawry of the arena of self-help in the settlement of potentially fatal personal conflicts.

So it is that necessity is the pervasive theme of the well defined conditions which the law imposes on the right to kill or maim in self-defense. There must have been a threat, actual or apparent, of the use of deadly force against the defender. The threat must have been unlawful and immediate. The defender must have believed that he was in imminent peril of death or serious bodily harm, and that his response was necessary to save himself therefrom. These beliefs must not only have been honestly entertained, but also objectively reasonable in light of the surrounding circumstances. It is clear that no less than a concurrence of these elements will suffice.

Here the parties' opposing contentions focus on the roles of two further considerations. One is the provoking of the confrontation by the defender. The other is the defendant's failure to utilize a safe route for retreat from the confrontation. The essential inquiry, in final analysis, is whether and to what extent the rule of necessity may translate these considerations into additional factors in the equation. To these questions, in the context of the specific issues raised, we now proceed.

The trial judge's charge authorized the jury, as it might be persuaded, to convict Peterson of second-degree murder or manslaughter, or to acquit by reason of self-defense. On the latter phase of the case, the judge instructed that with evidence of self-defense present, the Government bore the burden of proving beyond a reasonable doubt that Peterson did not act in self-defense; and that if the jury had a reasonable doubt as to whether Peterson acted in self-defense, the verdict must be not

35. By the early common law, justification for homicide extended only to acts done in execution of the law, such as homicides in effecting arrests and preventing forcible felonies, and homicides committed in self-defense were only excusable. The distinction between justifiable and excusable homicide was important because in the latter case the slayer, considered to be not wholly free from blame, suffered a forfeiture of his goods. However, with the passage of 24 Henry VIII, ch. 5 (1532), the basis of justification was enlarged, and the distinction has largely disappeared. More usually the terms are used interchangeably, each denoting a legally non-punishable act, entitling the accused to an acquittal.

40. When we speak of deadly force, we refer to force capable of inflicting death or serious bodily harm.

guilty. The judge further instructed that the circumstances under which Peterson acted, however, must have been such as to produce a reasonable belief that Keitt was then about to kill him or do him serious bodily harm, and that deadly force was necessary to repel him. In determining whether Peterson used excessive force in defending himself, the judge said, the jury could consider all of the circumstances under which he acted.

These features of the charge met Peterson's approval, and we are not summoned to pass on them. There were, however, two other aspects of the charge to which Peterson objected, and which are now the subject of vigorous controversy. The first of Peterson's complaints centers upon an instruction that the right to use deadly force in self-defense is not ordinarily available to one who provokes a conflict or is the aggressor in it. Mere words, the judge explained, do not constitute provocation or aggression; and if Peterson precipitated the altercation but thereafter withdrew from it in good faith and so informed Keitt by words or acts, he was justified in using deadly force to save himself from imminent danger or death or grave bodily harm. And, the judge added, even if Keitt was the aggressor and Peterson was justified in defending himself, he was not entitled to use any greater force than he had reasonable ground to believe and actually believed to be necessary for that purpose. Peterson contends that there was no evidence that he either caused or contributed to the conflict, and that the instructions on that topic could only mislead the jury.

It has long been accepted that one cannot support a claim of self-defense by a self-generated necessity to kill. The right of homicidal self-defense is granted only to those free from fault in the difficulty; it is denied to slayers who incite the fatal attack, encourage the fatal quarrel or otherwise promote the necessitous occasion for taking life. The fact that the deceased struck the first blow, fired the first shot or made the first menacing gesture does not legalize the self-defense claim if in fact the claimant was the actual provoker. In sum, one who is the aggressor in a conflict culminating in death cannot invoke the necessities of self-preservation. Only in the event that he communicates to his adversary his intent to withdraw and in good faith attempts to do so is he restored to his right of self-defense.

This body of doctrine traces its origin to the fundamental principle that a killing in self-defense is excusable only as a matter of genuine necessity. Quite obviously, a defensive killing is unnecessary if the occasion for it could have been averted, and the roots of that consideration run deep with us. A half-century ago, in *Laney v. United States,*[53] this court declared

> that, before a person can avail himself of the plea of self-defense against the charge of homicide, he must do everything in his power, consistent with his safety, to avoid the danger and avoid the necessity of taking life. If one has reason to believe that he will be attacked, in a manner which threatens him with bodily injury, he must avoid the attack if it is possible to do so, and the right of self-defense does not arise until he has done everything in his power to prevent its necessity.

And over the many years since *Laney,* the court has kept faith with its precept.

In the case at bar, the trial judge's charge fully comported with these governing principles. The remaining question, then, is whether there was evidence to make them applicable to the case. A recapitulation of the proofs shows beyond peradventure that there was.

---

53. 54 App.D.C. 56, 294 F. 412 (1923).

It was not until Peterson fetched his pistol and returned to his back yard that his confrontation with Keitt took on a deadly cast. Prior to his trip into the house for the gun, there was, by the Government's evidence, no threat, no display of weapons, no combat. There was an exchange of verbal aspersions and a misdemeanor against Peterson's property was in progress but, at this juncture, nothing more. Even if Peterson's post-arrest version of the initial encounter were accepted—his claim that Keitt went for the lug wrench before he armed himself—the events which followed bore heavily on the question as to who the real aggressor was.[60]

The evidence is uncontradicted that when Peterson reappeared in the yard with his pistol, Keitt was about to depart the scene. Richard Hilliard testified that after the first argument, Keitt reentered his car and said "Let's go." This statement was verified by Ricky Gray, who testified that Keitt "got in the car and * * * they were getting ready to go;" he, too, heard Keitt give the direction to start the car. The uncontroverted fact that Keitt was leaving shows plainly that so far as he was concerned the confrontation was ended. It demonstrates just as plainly that even if he had previously been the aggressor, he no longer was.

Not so with Peterson, however, as the undisputed evidence made clear. Emerging from the house with the pistol, he paused in the yard to load it, and to command Keitt not to move. He then walked through the yard to the rear gate and, displaying his pistol, dared Keitt to come in, and threatened to kill him if he did. While there appears to be no fixed rule on the subject, the cases hold, and we agree, that an affirmative unlawful act reasonably calculated to produce an affray

foreboding injurious or fatal consequences is an aggression which, unless renounced, nullifies the right of homicidal self-defense. We cannot escape the abiding conviction that the jury could readily find Peterson's challenge to be a transgression of that character. * * *

The second aspect of the trial judge's charge as to which Peterson asserts error concerned the undisputed fact that at no time did Peterson endeavor to retreat from Keitt's approach with the lug wrench. The judge instructed the jury that if Peterson had reasonable grounds to believe and did believe that he was in imminent danger of death or serious injury, and that deadly force was necessary to repel the danger, he was required neither to retreat nor to consider whether he could safely retreat. Rather, said the judge, Peterson was entitled to stand his ground and use such force as was reasonably necessary under the circumstances to save his life and his person from pernicious bodily harm. But, the judge continued, if Peterson could have safely retreated but did not do so, that failure was a circumstance which the jury might consider, together with all others, in determining whether he went further in repelling the danger, real or apparent, than he was justified in going.

Peterson contends that this imputation of an obligation to retreat was error, even if he could safely have done so. He points out that at the time of the shooting he was standing in his own yard, and argues he was under no duty to move. We are persuaded to the conclusion that in the circumstances presented here, the trial judge did not err in giving the instruction challenged.

Within the common law of self-defense there developed the rule of "retreat to the

---

60. Notwithstanding that the deceased provoked the original quarrel, the accused cannot, after that quarrel has ended or the deceased has withdrawn, invoke the right of self-defense in a subsequent difficulty which he himself causes or brings on.

wall," which ordinarily forbade the use of deadly force by one to whom an avenue for safe retreat was open. This doctrine was but an application of the requirement of strict necessity to excuse the taking of human life, and was designed to insure the existence of that necessity. Even the innocent victim of a vicious assault had to elect a safe retreat, if available, rather than resort to defensive force which might kill or seriously injure.

In a majority of American jurisdictions, contrarily to the common law rule, one may stand his ground and use deadly force whenever it seems reasonably necessary to save himself. While the law of the District of Columbia on this point is not entirely clear, it seems allied with the strong minority adhering to the common law.

*   *   *

That is not to say that the retreat rule is without exceptions. Even at common law it was recognized that it was not completely suited to all situations. Today it is the more so that its precept must be adjusted to modern conditions non-existent during the early development of the common law of self-defense.[86] One restriction on its operation comes to the fore when the circumstances apparently foreclose a withdrawal with safety. The doctrine of retreat was never intended to enhance the risk to the innocent; its proper application has never required a faultless victim to increase his assailant's safety at the expense of his own. On the contrary, he could stand his ground and use deadly force otherwise appropriate if the alternative were perilous, or if to him it reasonably appeared to be. A slight variant of the same consideration is the principle that

there is no duty to retreat from an assault producing an imminent danger of death or grievous bodily harm. "Detached reflection cannot be demanded in the presence of an uplifted knife," nor is it "a condition of immunity that one in that situation should pause to consider whether a reasonable man might not think it possible to fly with safety or to disable his assailant rather than to kill him."

The trial judge's charge to the jury incorporated each of these limitations on the retreat rule. Peterson, however, invokes another—the so-called "castle" doctrine. It is well settled that one who through no fault of his own is attacked in his home is under no duty to retreat therefrom. The oft-repeated expression that "a man's home is his castle" reflected the belief in olden days that there were few if any safer sanctuaries than the home. The "castle" exception, moreover, has been extended by some courts to encompass the occupant's presence within the curtilage outside his dwelling. Peterson reminds us that when he shot to halt Keitt's advance, he was standing in his yard and so, he argues, he had no duty to endeavor to retreat.

Despite the practically universal acceptance of the "castle" doctrine in American jurisdictions wherein the point has been raised, its status in the District of Columbia has never been squarely decided. But whatever the fate of the doctrine in the District law of the future, it is clear that in absolute form it was inapplicable here. The right of self-defense, we have said, cannot be claimed by the aggressor in an affray so long as he retains that unmitigated role. It logically follows that any rule

86. "We are aware of the wide diversity of opinion as to the duty to retreat, but this difference arises from the circumstances of the particular case under consideration, rather than from any difference of conception as to the rule itself. Time, place, and conditions may create a situation which would clearly justify a modification of the rule. For example, the common-law rule,

which required the assailed to retreat to the wall, had its origin before the general introduction of firearms. If a person is threatened with death or great bodily harm by an assailant, armed with a modern rifle, in open space, away from safety, it would be ridiculous to require him to retreat. Indeed, to retreat would be to invite almost certain death." *Laney v. United States,* supra.

of no-retreat which may protect an innocent victim of the affray would, like other incidents of a forfeited right of self-defense, be unavailable to the party who provokes or stimulates the conflict. Accordingly, the law is well settled that the "castle" doctrine can be invoked only by one who is without fault in bringing the conflict on. That, we think, is the critical consideration here.

We need not repeat our previous discussion of Peterson's contribution to the altercation which culminated in Keitt's death. It suffices to point out that by no interpretation of the evidence could it be said that Peterson was blameless in the affair. And while, of course, it was for the jury to assess the degree of fault, the evidence well nigh dictated the conclusion that it was substantial.

The only reference in the trial judge's charge intimating an affirmative duty to retreat was the instruction that a failure to do so, when it could have been done safely, was a factor in the totality of the circumstances which the jury might consider in determining whether the force which he employed was excessive. We cannot believe that any jury was at all likely to view Peterson's conduct as irreproachable. We conclude that for one who, like Peterson, was hardly entitled to fall back on the "castle" doctrine of no retreat, that instruction cannot be just cause for complaint. * * *

The judgment of conviction appealed from is accordingly

Affirmed.

Notes and Questions

1. *The reasonable belief requirement.* In *Coleman v. State,* 320 A.2d 740 (Del. 1974), the court held it was reversible error to instruct that the defendant must have had a reasonable belief the defensive force was necessary. Such a holding, the court noted, was required in light of the new state criminal code, which adopted the Model Penal Code position (a) that self defense only requires a subjective belief, and (b) that if the defendant is negligent or reckless in having such belief, the defense is unavailable in a prosecution for an offense for which negligence or recklessness, as the case may be, suffices to establish culpability. Most jurisdictions, however, still require a reasonable belief, although a modern trend is to treat death-causing conduct prompted by an unreasonable belief as an "imperfect" defense situation which downgrades the crime from murder to voluntary manslaughter.

As explained in *State v. Faulkner,* 301 Md. 482, 483 A.2d 759 (1984): "The doctrine of imperfect self defense gained a foothold in the United States in the late 1800's. The 'cornerstone' case for this defense is an 1882 decision by the Court of Criminal Appeals of Texas. *Reed v. State,* 11 Tex.Crim.App. 509 (1882). * * * Shortly after *Reed,* courts fashioned three variations of the doctrine.

"First, some courts indicated that the doctrine would apply where the homicide would fall within the perfect self defense doctrine but for the fault of the defendant in provoking or initiating the difficulty at the non-deadly force level. Second, courts noted that the doctrine would apply when the defendant committed a homicide because of a honest but unreasonable belief that he was about to suffer death or serious bodily harm. Third, other courts recognized the doctrine when the defendant used unreasonable force in defending himself and, as a result, killed his opponent.

"Since the acceptance of this doctrine by several jurisdictions during the late 1800's and early 1900's, comparatively few modern jurisdictions have analyzed the doctrine. Of those jurisdictions that have considered the doctrine in recent times, however, several have adopted the honest but unreasonable belief variation of the imperfect self defense doctrine. * * *

"Many states that recognize the doctrine on the basis of statutory law have adopted the subjectively honest but objectively unreasonable standard of the imperfect self defense doctrine. * * *

"We agree that this statement represents an analytically sound view, and reflects the position taken by a majority of those jurisdictions that have addressed and embraced this defense. Logically, a defendant who commits a homicide while honestly, though unreasonably, believing that he is threatened with death or serious bodily harm, does not act with malice. Absent malice he cannot be convicted of murder. Nevertheless, because the killing was committed without justification or excuse, the defendant is not entitled to full exoneration. Therefore, as we see it, when evidence is presented showing the defendant's subjective belief that the use of force was necessary to prevent imminent death or serious bodily harm, the defendant is entitled to a proper instruction on imperfect self defense.[7]"

To what extent might the *Coleman* and *Faulkner* approaches produce different results? Which is to be preferred?

2. *Provokers and aggressors.* In *Peterson,* it is said that the "right of homicidal self-defense is granted only to those free from fault in the difficulty." In the context of this rule, what should suffice to make one a provoker or aggressor? Consider:

(a) *People v. Townes,* 391 Mich. 578, 218 N.W.2d 136 (1974): Townes entered Burnett's store and loudly accused employee McMillion of dating his wife. Burnett ordered Townes to leave, and when Townes refused to do so, Burnett obtained a pistol from his office and again ordered

Townes to leave, which he did. The state's evidence is that once Burnett holstered his gun, Townes reentered and shot him. Townes' version is that he shot in self-defense when Burnett made a "sudden motion" toward his holster. The jury, instructed that Townes could not invoke the doctrine of self-defense if he were "the aggressor in the conflict," convicted Townes of murder. On appeal it was held the instruction was erroneous, in that it was based upon "the incorrect assumption that there had been some evidence introduced at trial from which the jury could reasonably infer that appellant was the 'aggressor' in the fatal confrontation with Burnett. * * * The only reasonable conclusion from the trial testimony is that appellant's actions created a potential threat to Burnett's property and it was to this threat that Burnett responded; but, a threat to property in such a situation, is not a legally sufficient provocation to render appellant an aggressor."

(b) *Townsend v. Commonwealth,* 474 S.W.2d 352 (Ky.App.1971): As Townsend and friends were about to enter their cars after rabbit hunting near the farm of the deceased, they were fired upon with a shotgun from the direction of decedent's home. Some buckshot struck Townsend. He stopped his car in front of decedent's house and asked why decedent had fired upon him, to which the decedent responded that he had not fired the shotgun. Townsend then called him a "God–Damned–Liar." The decedent started toward Townsend, who reached into his car for his shotgun and warned decedent not to come any closer. Because the decedent continued to advance while keeping his hand under his shirt front, Townsend fired. His conviction of voluntary manslaughter was affirmed on appeal. "The

___

7. Because this case presents the sole issue of imperfect self defense, we express no opinion as to the applicability of other suggested forms of "imperfect" mitigation defenses, such as imper-

fect duress, imperfect defense of others, imperfect defense of property, imperfect right to prevent a felony, and imperfect necessity.

fact that appellant stopped in front of decedent's home and got out of his car when he could have driven on by; and the fact that he called the decedent a 'God–Damned–Liar' were circumstances from which the jury could have believed that appellant attempted to provoke the incident. * * * The law does not allow a man to create a bad or dangerous situation and then fight his way out.''

(c) *McMahan v. State,* 617 P.2d 494 (Alaska 1980). Bill and Sheila lived together. When Bill moved out, Steve moved in. Steve told Bill not to return to Sheila's, saying: "I have a new rifle and I wouldn't want to use it—have to use it on you." Bill later went to Sheila's; he had a rifle with him because "I'd be foolish to go back up there if I wasn't able to defend myself." Bill claimed he shot and killed Steve because, when he entered Sheila's apartment Steve came at him with a knife. It was held on appeal of Bill's murder conviction that he was not entitled to a self-defense instruction, for "when a defendant has a prior grievance with the deceased and takes a deadly weapon to an encounter with the deceased, the defendant should be deemed to have provoked the violence which resulted in the death of the deceased."

3. *The retreat doctrine.* Does the retreat doctrine represent sound policy? If so, why is it, as noted in *Peterson,* that a majority of American jurisdictions have rejected it? If it is sound, should it be extended so that even nondeadly force may not be used defensively when retreat is possible, as apparently is now the law in England? See Ashworth, *Self-defence and the Right to Life,* 34 Camb.L.J. 282 (1975).

4. *Safe avenue of retreat.* Assuming the retreat doctrine is sound, precisely when should the victim of an attack be held criminally liable because he used deadly force instead of retreating? Consider *Commonwealth v. Palmer,* 467 Pa. 476, 359 A.2d 375 (1976), in which (a) the trial judge instructed that the defendant was obligated to retreat "unless he is excused from retreating by showing that retreat was not possible and would not have saved him from death or serious bodily harm''; (b) the defendant on appeal objected that the correct rule was that he "need not have retreated if he reasonably believed no avenue of retreat remained open to him''; but (c) the court concluded that the applicable statute instead provided that "the use of deadly force, otherwise allowable, is disallowed only where the defendant *knows* an avenue of retreat is available.''

5. *The "castle" doctrine exception.* In *Peterson* it is noted that "one who through no fault of his own is attacked in his home is under no duty to retreat therefrom." Why should this be so? Compare *Commonwealth v. Shaffer,* 367 Mass. 508, 326 N.E.2d 880 (1975), rejecting the majority view and holding "that one assaulted in his own home does not have the unlimited right to react with deadly force without any attempt at retreat. However, the importance of the location of the assault and the surrounding circumstance should be stressed to the jury.''

6. *Dimensions of the exception.* It is noted in *Peterson* that some courts have extended the "castle" doctrine "to encompass the occupant's presence within the curtilage outside his dwelling." Compare *State v. Bonano,* 59 N.J. 515, 284 A.2d 345 (1971): "It may be seriously doubted whether a concept arising in the mediaeval land law furnishes an intelligent guide in determining whether the taking of a life is to be justified. What, also, of a disputed boundary line? Is the justification for a slaying to rest upon the resolution of a title issue? If a defendant can show good title to the ground upon which he stood when he fired the fatal shot, is he to be exonerated, whereas if the land is later determined to be that of his neighbor, is he to be

found guilty? Might not the better rule be that a duty to retreat should exist except as to the dwelling house itself, defined, as stated above, to include a porch or other similar appurtenance?"

Does the reasoning underlying the "castle" exception warrant its extension to places other than one's home, such as one's place of business? See Annots., 52 A.L.R.2d 1458 (1957); 41 A.L.R.3d 584 (1972).

7. *Attacker's status re the "castle".* In *Cooper v. United States,* 512 A.2d 1002 (D.C.App.1986), defendant was convicted of voluntary manslaughter for shooting his brother during an altercation in their mother's home, where they both resided. The conviction was affirmed on appeal over defendant's objection that a retreat instruction should not have been given:

"Courts following the common law rule have split, however, regarding whether a defendant is entitled to a castle doctrine instruction when the defendant is assaulted by a co-occupant. An early case addressing this question was *People v. Tomlins,* 107 N.E. 496 (N.Y.1914). In *Tomlins,* a father shot and killed his son in their cottage. The New York Court of Appeals held that an instruction which informed the jury that the father had a duty to retreat was erroneous. The court first noted that if a man is assaulted in his home, 'he may stand his ground and resist the attack. He is under no duty to take to the fields and the highways, a fugitive from his own home.' The court then held that the rule is the same whether the attack is initiated by an intruder or a co-occupant; 'why . . . should one retreat from his own house, when assailed by a partner or co-tenant, any more than when assailed by a stranger who is lawfully on the premises? Whither shall he flee, and how far, and when may he be permitted to return?'

"As other courts grappled with this question, they often returned to the ques-

tions posed by the *Tomlins* court, although frequently reaching a different result. A majority of courts favors giving a castle doctrine instruction when a defendant claims self-defense when attacked in his home by a co-occupant, while a substantial minority holds that the castle doctrine does not apply in this special circumstance. Those decisions which favor giving a castle doctrine instruction stress the occupant's interest in remaining in the home, while those that oppose giving the instruction focus on the entitlement of both combatants to occupy the house and the fact that they usually are related, and reason that the parties have some obligation to attempt to defuse the situation.

"Having examined these authorities, we are convinced that the reasoning of those jurisdictions holding that a castle doctrine instruction should *not* be given in instances of co-occupant attacks is the more compelling."

8. *Relationship of self-defense and crime prevention.* In *State v. Harris,* 222 N.W.2d 462 (Iowa 1974), the defendant "adduced proof that Frondle accosted her at the tavern, she left and went to her apartment, he followed and demanded sexual relations, she resisted, and they wrestled. Defendant further contends that she got a shotgun from the corner of the room and told Frondle to leave, which he refused to do. She then got a shell out of a drawer, loaded the gun, pointed it at Frondle, and again told him to leave. When Frondle went to the door and put his hand on the knob, she shot him in the back. Frondle staggered from the building to the street and died shortly thereafter. Defendant contends she shot Frondle because she thought he was going to lock the door and rape her." The trial judge instructed that before a person may take another's life in self-defense, the person must believe he is in imminent danger of "death or great bodily harm," but refused defendant's request to add "or some felony about to be

committed against the defendant." On appeal, this was held not to be reversible error because the requested charge was overbroad:

"Essentially, two situations are involved in this area of homicide. One situation involves the defense of one's own person from attack, self-defense. The law's respect for human life is such that the attacker's life may not be taken unless the victim reasonably and honestly believes he is in imminent danger of loss of life or great bodily injury, quite apart from the question of whether the conduct of the other person is felonious. * * *

"In the other situation, a person may kill if he observes an atrocious, violent felony about to be or being committed—whether upon such person himself or not. From earliest common law, the person may take the life of the offender if necessary to prevent such a crime. * * * The commentators generally treat this type of homicide separately from self-defense. * * * The law's rationale for allowing human life to be taken to prevent commission of atrocious, violent felonies is that such crimes themselves imperil human life or involve danger of great bodily harm. * * *

"From this it is clear that not every felony will permit the taking of human life. The elements of force and atrocity must exist. Blackstone lists those felonies as murder, robbery, burglary, arson, breaking a house with intent to rob, rape, and other forcible and detestable capital crimes. Adultery, as an example, is not within that class of felonies."

Consider also *Model Penal Code* § 3.07(5), which provides that force may be used to prevent another from "committing or consummating the commission of a crime involving or threatening bodily harm," except that "any limitations imposed * * * on the justifiable use of force in self-protection * * * shall apply

notwithstanding the criminality of the conduct against which such force is used."

9. *Injury to or death of third party.* In *People v. Adams,* 9 Ill.App.3d 61, 291 N.E.2d 54 (1972), defendant was charged with the murder of Robinson and Davis. Defendant fired several shots at Robinson and one of them passed through Robinson and killed Davis. Defendant, who defended on the ground that he had been defending himself from a threat of deadly force by Robinson, was convicted only of involuntary manslaughter of Davis. This conviction was reversed on appeal:

"The State argues that self-defense does not necessarily protect an individual from criminal responsibility for all his acts performed in defending his life against a felonious assault, and that even though defendant's conduct here may have been justified as to Robinson nonetheless it constituted a reckless disregard for the consequences towards Mary Davis, and, as such, supported his conviction for involuntary manslaughter.

" * * * The generally accepted view is that if a person without legal excuse or justification, shoots at one individual and inadvertently kills another, he is guilty of the same degree of unlawful homicide as if he had killed the object of his aim, but if he was acting in self-defense and accidentally killed another, he is guilty of no crime. * * *

"We are aware that the above rule is not absolute and that, as pointed out in the ALR Annotation, it may be subject to modification depending on the circumstances involved. But we do not believe such circumstances present themselves in the case before us. There were other persons present in the car with defendant's assailant, but it was dark and defendant was being fired on at close range. He had very little time to think or assess the situation. He had to act immediately to protect himself from a man who had been drinking all day and who was not just threatening him but was shooting at him. Even under such circumstances defendant did not shoot wildly or carelessly. From the record it can be inferred that he hit his assailant with every shot and that the innocent victim was killed only as a result of a bullet passing through the body of the assailant. We conclude that under the circumstances of this case the killing of Mary Davis constituted no crime."

If, as the court suggests, the rule is not absolute, what circumstances would require a modification of it?

10. *Threatening deadly force.* In *United States v. Black,* 692 F.2d 314 (4th Cir. 1982), involving a charge of assault upon a correctional officer, there was testimony that officer Henry swung a putty knife at prisoner Black, that Black then threatened Henry with a homemade knife, and that when Henry backed off Black returned to his cell as ordered by Henry. "At the close of the evidence, Black requested an instruction on self-defense. Under the requested instruction, the jury would have been required to acquit if it found that the corrections officer employed excessive force and Black responded with an amount of force he reasonably deemed necessary to avoid bodily harm to himself. The court, however, rejected the suggested instruction. It gave instead a charge to the effect that Black was entitled to defend himself with 'deadly force' if he reasonably believed that such force was necessary to escape imminent death or serious bodily harm." Black was convicted. What result on appeal?

11. *Self-defense and weapon possession.* Panter was convicted of violating 18 U.S. C.A.App. § 1201(a)(1), which prohibits convicted felons from possessing firearms. The trial court refused to instruct the jury on Panter's self-defense claim, namely, that he possessed the firearm only momentarily to defend himself from an attack by a drunken patron in a bar. The conviction was reversed in *United States v. Panter,* 688 F.2d 268 (5th Cir.1982), holding "that where a convicted felon, reacting out of a reasonable fear for the life or safety of himself, in the actual physical course of a conflict that he did not provoke, takes temporary possession of a firearm for the purpose or in the course of defending himself, he is not guilty of violating § 1202(a)(1)."

12. *Burden of proof.* A very few states place the burden on the defendant to prove the defense of self defense by a preponderance of the evidence. In *Martin v. Ohio,* ___ U.S. ___, 107 S.Ct. 1098, 94 L.Ed.2d 267 (1987), the Supreme Court, in a 5–4 decision, held that under the reasoning of *Patterson v. New York,* p. 245 of this Book, such allocation of the burden is constitutionally permissible:

"We agree with the State and its Supreme Court that this conviction did not violate the Due Process Clause. The State did not exceed its authority in defining the crime of murder as purposely causing the death of another with prior calculation or design. It did not seek to shift to Martin the burden of proving any of those elements, and the jury's verdict reflects that none of her self-defense evidence raised a reasonable doubt about the state's proof that she purposefully killed with prior calculation and design. She nevertheless had the opportunity under state law and the instructions given to justify the killing and show herself to be blameless by proving that she acted in self-defense. The jury thought she had failed to do so, and Ohio is as entitled to punish Martin as one guilty of murder as New York was to punish Patterson.

"It would be quite different if the jury had been instructed that self-defense evidence could not be considered in determining whether there was a reasonable doubt about the state's case, *i.e.,* that self-defense evidence must be put aside for all purposes unless it satisfied the preponderance standard. Such instruction would relieve the state of its burden and plainly run afoul of *Winship's* mandate. The instructions in this case could be clearer in this respect, but when read as a whole, we think they are adequate to convey to the jury that all of the evidence, including the evidence going to self-defense, must be considered in deciding whether there was a reasonable doubt about the sufficiency of the state's proof of the elements of the crime.

"We are thus not moved by assertions that the elements of aggravated murder and self-defense overlap in the sense that evidence to prove the latter will often tend to negate the former. It may be that most encounters in which self-defense is claimed arise suddenly and involve no prior plan or specific purpose to take life. In those cases, evidence offered to support the defense may negate a purposeful killing by prior calculation and design, but Ohio does not shift to the defendant the burden of disproving any element of the state's case. * * *

"Petitioner submits that there can be no conviction under Ohio law unless the defendant's conduct is unlawful and that because self-defense renders lawful what would otherwise be a crime, unlawfulness is an element of the offense that the state must prove by disproving self-defense. This argument founders on state law, for it has been rejected by the Ohio Supreme Court and by the Court of Appeals for the Sixth Circuit. It is true that unlawfulness is essential for conviction, but the Ohio courts hold that the unlawfulness in cases like this is the conduct satisfying the ele-

ments of aggravated murder—an interpretation of state law that we are not in a position to dispute."

The four dissenters, though later expressing a preference for the methodology of the *Patterson* dissent, argued that the instant case was wrongly decided even under the principles set forth in *Patterson,* especially the "clear implication * * * that when an affirmative defense *does* negate an element of the crime, the state may not shift the burden. In such a case, *In re Winship,* 397 U.S. 358, 90 S.Ct. 1068, 25 L.Ed.2d 368 (1970), requires the state to prove the nonexistence of the defense beyond a reasonable doubt.

"The reason for treating a defense that negates an element of the crime differently from other affirmative defenses is plain. If the jury is told that the prosecution has the burden of proving all the elements of a crime, but then also is instructed that the defendant has the burden of *dis*proving one of those same elements, there is a danger that the jurors will resolve the inconsistency in a way that lessens the presumption of innocence. For example, the jury might reasonably believe that by raising the defense, the accused has assumed the ultimate burden of proving that particular element. Or, it might reconcile the instructions simply by balancing the evidence that supports the prosecutor's case against the evidence supporting the affirmative defense, and conclude that the state has satisfied its burden if the prosecution's version is more persuasive. In either case, the jury is given the unmistakable but erroneous impression that the defendant shares the risk of nonpersuasion as to a fact necessary for conviction.[1]
* * *

---

1. Indeed, this type of instruction has an inherently illogical aspect. It makes no sense to say that the prosecution has the burden of proving an element beyond a reasonable doubt *and* that the defense has the burden of proving the contrary by a preponderance of the evidence. If the jury finds that the prosecutor has *not* met his

burden, it of course will have no occasion to consider the affirmative defense. And if the jury finds that each element of the crime *has* been proved beyond a reasonable doubt, it necessarily has decided that the defendant has not disproved an element of the crime. In either situation the instructions on the affirmative defense are sur-

"The Court gives no explanation for this apparent rejection of *Patterson.* * * * The Court seems to conclude that as long as the jury is told that the state has the burden of proving all elements of the crime, the overlap between the offense and defense is immaterial.

"This reasoning is flawed in two respects. First, it simply ignores the problem that arises from inconsistent jury instructions in a criminal case. The Court's holding implicitly assumes that the jury in fact understands that the ultimate burden remains with the prosecutor at all times, despite a conflicting instruction that places the burden on the accused to disprove the same element. But as pointed out above, the *Patterson* distinction between defenses that negate an element of the crime and those that do not is based on the legitimate concern that the jury *will* mistakenly lower the state's burden. In short, the Court's rationale fails to explain why the overlap in this case does not create the risk that *Patterson* suggested was unacceptable.

"Second, the Court significantly, and without explanation, extends the deference granted to state legislatures in this area. Today's decision could be read to say that virtually all state attempts to shift the burden of proof for affirmative defenses will be upheld, regardless of the relationship between the elements of the defense and the elements of the crime. As I understand it, *Patterson* allowed burden-shifting because evidence of an extreme emotional disturbance did not negate the *mens rea* of the underlying offense. After today's decision, however, even if proof of the defense *does* negate an element of the offense, burden-shifting still may be permitted because the jury can consider the defendant's evidence when reaching its verdict."

plusage. Because a reasonable jury will attempt to ascribe some significance to the court's instruc-

STATE v. HODGES

Supreme Court of Kansas, 1986.
239 Kan. 63, 716 P.2d 563.

SCHROEDER, CHIEF JUSTICE:

This is a criminal action in which Joan Hodges (defendant-appellant) appeals from her conviction by a Wyandotte County jury of voluntary manslaughter in the shooting of her husband, Harvey Hodges. * * *

At approximately 3:00 a.m. on July 19, 1983, the defendant shot and killed her husband with a 12-gauge shotgun. The defendant claims she shot him in self-defense. Around 2:00 a.m. that same morning, defendant's stomach was upset and she went to a convenience store to get some Di-Gel for herself and some Skoal for her husband. She returned, went into the bedroom where her husband was lying in bed watching TV, and handed him the Skoal. Before she was out of the bedroom doorway, he jumped off the bed, grabbed her by the back of the hair and slammed her head against the doorjamb of the bedroom door twenty times saying, "God damn you. It's all right if you've got Di-Gel [but] you don't care if my blood sugar is 264. I'm going to kill you." Defendant soiled her clothes and told Harvey she needed to go to the bathroom. Harvey shoved her; she sprawled onto the floor and he repeatedly kicked her toward the bathroom with his bare feet. While the defendant cleaned herself up in the bathroom, Harvey continued to yell and threaten her from the bedroom. After changing into a nightgown, the defendant left the bathroom, went into a smaller bedroom and threw her clothes down on the bed. When she heard Harvey say, "God damn you. Get in here now," she reached for the shotgun in the closet, ran into the open bedroom doorway, and fired twice. Without knowing

tions, the likelihood that it will impermissibly shift the burden is increased. * * *

whether she had hit Harvey, defendant ran out of the house and to her mother's, Mrs. Bushey, who lived next door. The defendant and her mother called the police from a neighbor's house because Mrs. Bushey had no telephone.

Harvey died from massive blood loss due to two wounds located near each armpit. At the time of the shooting, he was lying horizontally on the bed. Harvey was a strong, well-muscled man measuring 5'8" and weighing 245 pounds. * * *

Defendant first contends the trial court erred in refusing to allow expert testimony on the battered woman syndrome. * * *

Dr. Ann Bristow, an assistant professor of psychology at Kansas State University, testified at the hearing on the motion [to allow such testimony] as defendant's expert. * * *

Dr. Bristow explained the battered woman syndrome is a post-traumatic stress disorder with the particular stressor being wife abuse. Symptoms manifested by a woman suffering from the syndrome include an attempt to minimize the violence and to live for the positive aspects of the relationship. She lives in a highly fearful state, becoming very sensitive to when the situation is becoming more violent and to those things that precede arguments. The batterer isolates the woman and will not allow her to go places, and she becomes more and more withdrawn. Few women will discuss their problems even with close family members because of their feeling that there is nothing that can be done about the situation. They have a "learned helplessness"; the more the repeated trauma occurs, the more the woman learns she has no control.

Dr. Bristow testified it is hard for the average lay person to understand why a battered woman doesn't get out of the situation, or call the police. There are misconceptions that these women deserve

such treatment. Dr. Bristow spent a total of seven and one-half hours with the defendant and expressed the opinion defendant's behavior fell within the battered woman syndrome.

The admission of expert testimony is governed in Kansas by K.S.A. 60–456(b), which states:

> "If the witness is testifying as an expert, testimony of the witness in the form of opinions or inferences is limited to such opinions as the judge finds are (1) based on facts or data perceived by or personally known or made known to the witness at the hearing and (2) within the scope of the special knowledge, skill, experience or training possessed by the witness."

The basis for the admission of expert testimony is necessity, arising out of the particular circumstances of the case. Where the normal experience and qualifications of lay persons serving as jurors permit them to draw proper conclusions from given facts and circumstances, expert conclusions or opinions are inadmissible. First, to be admissible, expert testimony must be helpful to the jury. Second, before expert scientific opinion may be received into evidence at trial, the basis of that opinion must be shown to be generally acceptable within the expert's particular scientific field. * * *

The State argues the above testimony is not helpful to the jury because the jury heard ample evidence concerning the alleged abuse, and defendant had explained why she stayed with Harvey. The defendant did testify at trial concerning her marriage to the victim. They were first married in 1950 when defendant was seventeen, and early on Harvey beat her and tried to strangle her. Although defendant left him many times, he would find her and she would return home with him. The defendant related one incident where, after Harvey found her, he took her to a wooded location where he beat her, broke her jaw, and said she was either going to live with him or she wasn't going to live. He left her there unconscious, but eventually returned, took her to the hospital, and told her to tell the hospital staff she fell down. She returned home with him because he had her children. The defendant didn't call the police after any beatings because Harvey had threatened her life if she did. They were divorced in 1957 and remarried in 1970. Harvey had explained he was hot-headed before and wanted to make up for the previous things he had done. The defendant left him again in 1974, but he found her and eventually she stopped trying to run from him. The beatings did not stop. On June 4, 1978, Harvey threw a Coke bottle at her, hitting her in the back near the left shoulder blade. Her mother took her to the emergency room and just as the defendant was ready to make a police report, Harvey walked in and said, "You tell the police that and you will never tell anybody anything again." A medical report dated August 15, 1979, reflected the defendant slipped and fell, but defendant testified Harvey beat her unconscious. Another medical report dated December 21, 1980, reflected the defendant was beaten by her husband. Harvey had beaten her and kicked her down the porch stairs. Finally, a medical report dated February 6, 1983, showed the defendant slipped on ice and lacerated her left knee on concrete. The defendant testified she was coming home from her mother's and Harvey pushed her down onto the icy concrete, causing a cut in her knee which required 63 stitches. The defendant's family members—her mother and daughter—testified that Harvey had threatened them if they ever called the police or helped the defendant to leave him.

We disagree with the State's contention the jury does not need help in addressing the foregoing evidence.

The Supreme Court recently recognized the dilemma of jurors understanding a battered woman's situation in *State v. Hundley,* 236 Kan. 461, 467, 693 P.2d 475 (1985).

"[T]here is no easy answer to why battered women stay with their abusive husbands. Quite likely emotional and financial dependency and fear are the primary reasons for remaining in the household. They feel incapable of reaching out for help and justifiably fear reprisals from their angry husbands if they leave or call the police. The abuse is so severe, for so long a time, and the threat of great bodily harm so constant, it creates a standard mental attitude in its victims. Battered women are terror-stricken people whose mental state is distorted and bears a marked resemblance to that of a hostage or a prisoner of war. The horrible beatings they are subjected to brainwash them into believing there is nothing they can do. They live in constant fear of another eruption of violence. They become disturbed persons from the torture."

Expert testimony on the battered woman syndrome would help dispel the ordinary lay person's perception that a woman in a battering relationship is free to leave at any time. The expert evidence would counter any "common sense" conclusions by the jury that if the beatings were really that bad the woman would have left her husband much earlier. Popular misconceptions about battered women would be put to rest, including the beliefs the women are masochistic and enjoy the beatings and that they intentionally provoke their husbands into fits of rage. See Walker, *The Battered Woman,* 19–31 (1979).

Of the jurisdictions which have considered this question, the majority have ruled a battering relationship is a subject beyond the understanding of the average juror. We agree.

The second requirement to be met here before expert scientific opinion may be admitted into evidence is that the basis of that opinion must be shown to be generally acceptable within the expert's particular scientific field. * * *

Dr. Bristow explained at the hearing on the motion that this field has been researched for ten years with extensive publications and articles, and four or five books written on the subject matter of the battered woman syndrome. When questioned whether there is a common acceptance within the scientific community, Dr. Bristow enumerated two ways to tell. One indication is the extent to which the battered woman syndrome is referred to in professional literature. She testified it is noted in the American Medical Association Journal, in social workers' journals, and in experimental and clinical psychologists' journals, and that papers from conferences on domestic violence cover the topic. Second, by looking at which professionals are involved in either intervention or research of battered women, one can determine the extent of its acceptance. Dr. Bristow testified psychiatrists and psychologists are doing research in this area.[a]

As we stated in State v. Washington, 229 Kan. 47, 622 P.2d 986, it is the basis of the expert's opinion that must be shown to be generally accepted. The record before us reveals the theory underlying the battered woman syndrome has gained a substantial enough scientific acceptance to warrant admissibility. It also appears from the record Dr. Bristow is a qualified expert on the subject of the battered woman syndrome. Furthermore, she spent a total of seven and one-half hours with the defendant and found the defendant suffered from the syndrome. The State had an ample opportunity to question Dr. Bristow about the methodology used. We hold it was error for the trial court to exclude the expert testimony on the battered woman syndrome.

The State argues the testimony is not relevant to defendant's claim of self-defense, which in Kansas is determined by an objective standard of reasonableness, rather than a subjective standard.

Whether a subjective standard or an objective standard is applied, evidence of the battered woman syndrome is relevant to a claim of self-defense. In a state that follows the subjective standard, an evaluation of defendant's actions is made in light of her subjective impressions and the facts and circumstances known to her. In states following the objective standard, the jury must determine whether the defendant's belief in the need to defend one's self was reasonable and the expert's testimony, if accepted by the jury, would aid it in determining whether, under the circumstances, a reasonable person in the defendant's position would have believed her life to be in imminent danger.

In State v. Hundley, 236 Kan. at 467, 693 P.2d 475, we stated:

"The objective test is how a reasonably prudent battered wife would perceive [the aggressor's] demeanor. Expert testimony is admissible to prove the nature and effect of wife-beating just as it is admissible to prove the standard mental state of hostages, prisoners of war, and

a. Compare Note, 72 Va.L.Rev. 619, 647 (1986), concluding: "The prevailing theories of battered woman syndrome have little evidentiary value in self-defense cases. The work of Lenore Walker, the leading researcher on battered woman syndrome, is unsound and largely irrelevant to the central issues in such cases. The Walker cycle theory suffers from significant methodological and interpretive flaws that render it incapable of explaining why an abused woman strikes out at her mate when she does. Similarly, Walker's application of learned helplessness to the situation of battered women does not account for the actual behavior of many women who remain in battering relationships. Thus, in self-defense cases a court should not allow the jury to consider evidence on battered woman syndrome."

others under long-term life-threatening conditions."

Actually, to ask how a reasonably prudent battered woman would have perceived the aggressor's demeanor results in applying a subjective standard of reasonableness, *i.e.,* from the viewpoint of defendant's mental state. The same facts perceived by a person who has been repeatedly abused in a relationship would certainly be perceived differently by an ordinary and prudent non-battered person.

Therefore, we hold where the battered woman syndrome is in issue, the proper standard to determine whether the accused's belief in asserting self-defense was reasonable is a subjective standard. The jury must determine, from the viewpoint of the defendant's mental state, whether the defendant's belief in the need to defend herself was reasonable. * * *

The defendant argues the trial court erred in giving the self-defense instruction using the word "immediate" rather than "imminent."

The jury instructions given on self-defense followed PIK Crim.2d 54.17, as follows:

> "The defendant has claimed her conduct was justified as self-defense.
>
> "A person is justified in the use of force against an aggressor when and to the extent it appears to her and she reasonably believes that such conduct is necessary to defend herself against such aggressor's immediate use of unlawful force. Such justification requires both a belief on the part of defendant and the existence of facts that would persuade a reasonable person to that belief."

* * *

We held in *State v. Osbey,* 238 Kan. 280, the giving of PIK Crim.2d 54.17 using the word "immediate" rather than the statutory word "imminent" was clearly erroneous because it precluded the jury from consid-

ering the effect of the history of violence inflicted on the appellant by the decedent. The word "immediate" places undue emphasis on the decedent's immediate conduct and obliterates the build-up of terror and fear the decedent systematically injected into the relationship over a long period of time. The word "immediate" does not conform to the statutory word "imminent", as the State contends. The use of the word "imminent" does not place undue emphasis on the nature and effect of the history of violence. Rather, it allows the jury to determine, based upon all the evidence before it, including the history of violence *and* the events just prior to the shooting, whether defendant's claim of self-defense was reasonable in light of *all* the circumstances.

The trial court improperly excluded expert testimony on the battered woman syndrome and improperly instructed the jury on self-defense. The judgment of the trial court is reversed and the case is remanded for a new trial.

Notes and Questions

1. Consider Note, 72 Va.L.Rev. 619, 632–33 (1986): "Helen Martin separated from her husband Ronald in September, 1980, after a violent five-year marriage. Ronald moved in with another woman and talked about blowing up Helen's house for the insurance money. Helen feared he would do it while she was in the house. Helen hired Robert Bratcher for $10,000 to kill Ronald. On December 5, 1980, after Ronald came to the house to sign some papers, Bratcher emerged from his basement hiding place and shot Ronald in the neck. Bratcher shot him a second time after Helen complained, 'He's not dying fast enough—hit him again.' Helen later went out to celebrate a friend's birthday. The next day, December 6, Helen reported her husband missing. On December 7 she paid the premiums on her

husband's life insurance policies. Ronald's body was found on the 8th and she confessed to her involvement in his murder on the 9th.

" * * * That the leading theoretician of battered woman syndrome would be willing to characterize *Martin* as a case of legitimate self-defense seems to call into question the credibility of her testimony in other cases. Certainly, few cases are as far removed from the paradigm of self-defense as *Martin,* but it is precisely this willingness of experts to take the stand in extreme cases that reinforces the perception among many lawyers that psychologists and psychiatrists are simply 'hired guns.' "

2. Acker & Toch, *Battered Women, Straw Men, and Expert Testimony,* 21 Crim. L.Bull. 125, 146–48 (1985), object: "In defining the defendant as a battered woman, the expert would necessarily identify the deceased as a battering husband and highlight the years of abuse which the accused suffered at her spouse's hands. Both the character and the conduct of the deceased would be described, interpreted, and defined through the vehicle of scientific testimony. The jury's attention would in this manner be deflected from the *responses* of the *accused* at the *time of the homicide* to the general bad character and repeated acts of misconduct *of the deceased* at times *far removed* from the homicide. Imbued with the 'aura of infallibility' typically ascribed to expert witnesses, and benefiting from the tendency of scientific testimony to be exceptionally persuasive, the effect of the expert's testimony could thus be to enhance the relevance of conclusions that are not germane to a claim of lawful justification. * * *

"When the prior bad acts (the repeated beatings) and the bad character ('battering husband') of the deceased are made principal issues, this through the supportive testimony of an expert witness, the classic defense stratagem of 'blaming the victim' for his own demise has been interjected before the jury. This 'defense' has been dignified by the 'syndrome' concept which draws attention to the prevalence of domestic victimization in society, and which makes the victim and the deceased examples of this problem. The killing of a battering husband could be 'justified' in the jurors' minds not because it was necessary that a battered woman act with responsive deadly force when she was threatened with death or serious bodily injury by her mate but because it was a fitting act of retribution directed at a member of a sadistic fraternity who had finally reaped his just deserts."

3. Comment, 135 U.Pa.L.Rev. 427, 436–37 (1987), observes: "If, as often occurs, a woman has killed her batterer during a lull in the beatings—such as when he was asleep or when he had his back turned—a claim of self-defense is likely to be unsuccessful. In particular, the current formulation of the imminence requirement will, in many situations, impede the success of self-defense claims asserted by women who have killed their batterers.

"Under the current formulation of the self-defense standard, a defendant asserting a claim of self-defense must show that she had a reasonable belief that she was faced with an imminent threat of death or serious bodily harm. Imminence does not mean inevitability or certainty; the fact that a battered woman might be in certain danger of having death or serious bodily injury inflicted upon her by the batterer at some future time is not legally relevant to a claim of self-defense as that defense is currently construed. Rather, the relevant factor is the circumstances at the particular instant in which the killing took place. As one court has observed: '[T]hreats alone, unaccompanied by some act which induces in defendant a reasonable belief that bodily injury is about to be inflicted, do not justify a homicide. The danger which justifies homicide must be imminent and a mere fear that danger will become imminent is not enough.'

"The rationale behind the restrictive definition of imminence is obvious. As long as the threatened acts of violence are only anticipated future events, avenues of prevention or escape might be open to the defendant. Even if avenues of escape are not available when the danger of future harm is first perceived, they may become available before the anticipated violence occurs. Furthermore, the threatened harm might never occur and, even if it does, it might not rise to a level justifying the use of deadly force in response. Accordingly, a defendant asserting a claim of self-defense must show that death or serious bodily injury was imminent at the particular instant at which the killing occurred."

What result, then, upon retrial in *Hodges?* Given the battered woman syndrome, should not the defense of self-defense be more expansively stated?

4. Compare with *Hodges* the case of *Jahnke v. State,* 682 P.2d 991 (Wyo.1984), where the 16–year–old defendant killed his father with a shotgun when his parents returned home from dinner. The defendant had been involved in a violent altercation with his father earlier in the evening, and had been warned by his father not to be there when the father returned. The defendant pleaded self-defense and sought to introduce evidence that his father had beaten him (and his mother and sister) for years. Expert psychiatric testimony about a "battered child syndrome" was excluded, and defendant was convicted of voluntary manslaughter. On appeal, the court declared: "It is clear that self-defense is circumscribed by circumstances involving a confrontation, usually encompassing some overt act or acts by the deceased, which would induce a reasonable person to fear that his life was in danger or

that at least he was threatened with great bodily harm.

" * * * Although many people, and the public media, seem to be prepared to espouse the notion that a victim of abuse is entitled to kill the abuser, that special justification defense is antethetical to the mores of modern civilized society. It is difficult enough to justify capital punishment as an appropriate response of society to criminal acts even after the circumstances have been carefully evaluated by a number of people. To permit capital punishment to be imposed upon the subjective conclusion of the individual that prior acts and conduct of the deceased justified the killing would amount to a leap into the abyss of anarchy."

5. Does *Hodges* mean that under the prevailing objective approach any evidence bearing upon the defendant's personal characteristics and experiences is admissible? Compare:

(a) *People v. Goetz,* 68 N.Y.2d 96, 506 N.Y.S.2d 18, 497 N.E.2d 41 (1986). This is the widely-publicized and much-debated case of the New York City subway rider who was charged with attempted murder and assault. After Goetz boarded the subway and took a seat in a section of a car occupied by four youths, one of the four approached and said "give me five dollars." Goetz pulled a gun and shot at each of the four, wounding all but one. The lower court dismissed the charges on the ground that the prosecutor's instructions to the grand jury on self-defense were erroneously stated in terms of a "reasonable man in [Goetz's] situation." The court of appeals reversed, concluding that the statutory language that a person may use deadly force if he "reasonably believes that such other person is using or about to use deadly physical force" stated an objective test. But the court went on to emphasize that in support of Goetz's assertion that though "he was certain that none of the youths had a gun, he had a fear based on prior experience, of being 'maimed,'" he would be allowed to introduce into evidence "any prior experiences he had which could provide a reasonable basis for [such] belief," e.g., that a few years earlier he had been injured in a mugging. (Goetz was later tried and acquitted.)

(b) *Werner v. State,* 711 S.W.2d 639 (Tex.Crim.App.1986). "Appellant testified that he pursued the deceased's vehicle 'to hold whoever hit my friend's car for the police.' After he found the vehicle he stated he 'yelled at him to get up against the car,' and the deceased replied, 'You're just going to have to shoot me, you son of a bitch.' Appellant testified the deceased made a 'shrugging' motion with his shoulders and took a step towards him. With the flashlight he saw the deceased's face and the deceased 'looked crazy.' He couldn't see the deceased's hands and didn't know whether the deceased was armed. Appellant stated he was in fear of his life, and to protect himself he shot the deceased in the chest." Excluded from appellant's murder trial was testimony by a psychiatrist, who had examined appellant, concerning the "Holocaust syndrome," specifically, that appellant, as the child of a survivor of Nazi concentration camps and one who had often been told stories about the camps, by virtue of that background had a "state of mind to defend himself because he comes from a family that did not." In affirming the murder conviction, the court took note of the objective "reasonable belief" standard in the self-defense statute and concluded: "All that can be inferred from this evidence is that appellant may have been more susceptible to actions in self-defense. * * * The evidence excluded only tended to show that

possibly appellant was not an ordinary and prudent man with respect to self-defense. This did not entitle appellant to an enlargement of the statutory defense on account of his psychological peculiarities."

COMMONWEALTH v. MARTIN

Supreme Court of Massachusetts, 1976.
369 Mass. 640, 341 N.E.2d 885.

KAPLAN, JUSTICE.

The defendant Daniel R. Martin appeals from his multiple convictions, described in the margin,[1] arising from a clash between inmates and guards at Massachusetts Correctional Institution at Concord on October 15, 1972. * * *

According to the prosecution's case, a struggle erupted between two correction officers and two inmates as the inmates were being escorted from a second-floor segregation unit down to a first-floor area for showers and exercise. One of the inmates, Tremblay, fought with an officer near the stairwell and the officer fell or was shoved down the stairs, with Tremblay following him down. The fallen officer yelled to officers on the first floor for help, and one of them, John Quealey, restrained Tremblay, while others went to summon aid. Officer Quealey held Tremblay by the hair while pushing him toward and into an open cell on the first floor. According to the prosecution's proof, Tremblay was held in the cell but not beaten; no clubs or other weapons were used by the officers in the affray although it appeared that clubs were kept in a nearby desk.

Meantime the second inmate involved in the fight on the second floor had taken the cell keys from the other officer and released other inmates of the segregation

1. With regard to the alleged attack on Officer Quealey, the defendant was convicted of assault and battery on a guard of a correctional institution, assault and battery with a dangerous weapon, and armed assault with intent to kill. As to the alleged attack on Officer Taylor, the

defendant was convicted of assault and battery on a guard of a correctional institution, and assault with a dangerous weapon, the judge having directed a verdict on the charge of battery with a dangerous weapon.

unit. Several of the inmates, including the defendant, ran down the stairs and met officers who had arrived to give help. In the melee, Officer Quealey was stabbed a number of times in the chest and once on the arm. Officer Quealey testified that as he was struggling with an inmate, he saw the defendant strike at him three times, and he saw a knife in the defendant's hand as the defendant stepped back. Other officers testified that they saw an attack by the defendant on Officer Quealey, or saw the defendant with a knife immediately after the attack (the testimony was not entirely consistent). There was further testimony that the defendant struck Frederick Taylor, a correction officer, with his fist and threatened him with a knife, saying "Back off, or I will give it to you, too."

The defendant took the stand to give his version of the facts. He was corroborated in part by the codefendant Tremblay. Because the defendant's view was obstructed by a partition between the rows of cells on either side of the second floor, he had not been able to see the fight there and did not know who had started it. When his cell was opened, he walked to the end of the partition but, seeing blood on the floor and hearing sounds of a struggle on the stairs, he started back to his cell. He then heard Tremblay calling for help and surmised that Tremblay was in grave danger. The defendant raced down the stairs and saw Officer Quealey and two other officers striking Tremblay with clubs and a metal mop handle as he lay on the floor of an open cell. Tremblay had his arms over his head and was trying to fend off the blows. He was yelling for help. The defendant struck several officers, including Officers Quealey and Taylor, with his fists in his effort to pull the officers off Tremblay. The defendant denied that he had a knife at this time; he did not stab Officer Quealey or threaten Officer Taylor with a knife. He testified that he first saw the

knife on the floor where another inmate had dropped it after the stabbing of Officer Quealey.

The violence ended when assistant deputy superintendent Nicholas Genakos ordered the officers to withdraw while he and Jon Cooke, a social worker, negotiated with the inmates. During the negotiation Cooke saw the defendant with a knife and, when Genakos asked for it, the defendant said, "We'll see how this goes." The defendant testified that he made the statement and that he did have a knife, but only for a short interval when Cooke saw it. A search by the State police after the inmates had returned peaceably to their cells failed to turn up a knife. * * *

The judge instructed the jury with respect to self-defense and even related these instructions to the question whether the defendant was privileged to use a dangerous weapon to protect himself from attack by Officer Quealey. But he gave the jury no instructions on the subject of the privileged use of force to protect another. This failure seems to have been due to the judge's belief that the claimed justification was not recognized in the law of Massachusetts.

The defendant made due request in writing for jury instructions on the subject. His request was submitted the day before the judge charged the jury. The main requested instruction (No. 9) was a quotation from the relevant statute law of Illinois as reproduced in the case of *People v. Johnson,* 4 Ill.App.3d 249, 251, 280 N.E. 2d 764 (1972): "A person is justified in the use of force against another when and to the extent that he reasonably believes that such conduct is necessary to defend himself or another against such other's imminent use of unlawful force. * * *" Smith-Hurd Ill.Ann.Stat. c. 38, § 7–1 (1972). * * *

We hold that a justification corresponding roughly to that quoted from the Illinois statute is recognized by the law of the Commonwealth. Of course the justification may exist although it is not found in so many words in our statute law: it may be read into the definition of a statutory offense or considered a common-law adjunct to, or qualification of, the offense. This is easily accepted and understood as to the more commonplace justification of self-defense.

There is some but not much light in the decided cases in this jurisdiction about justified force used in aid of another. * * * The paucity of direct authority is perhaps explained by the likelihood that one coming to the defense of another may himself be, or come to be, under attack, and may thus simply claim self-defense, a less esoteric justification.

Whatever the precise precedents, it is hardly conceivable that the law of the Commonwealth, or, indeed, of any jurisdiction, should mark as criminal those who intervene forcibly to protect others; for the law to do so would aggravate the fears which lead to the alienation of people from one another * * *. To the fear of "involvement" and of injury to oneself if one answered a call for help would be added the fear of possible criminal prosecution.

It becomes necessary to sketch the conditions justifying the use of intervening protective force. The essence is this: An actor is justified in using force against another to protect a third person when (a) a reasonable person in the actor's position would believe his intervention to be necessary for the protection of the third person, and (b) in the circumstances as that reasonable person would believe them to be, the

third person would be justified in using such force to protect himself. The reasonableness of the belief may depend in part on the relationships among the persons involved (a matter to which we return below). The actor's justification is lost if he uses excessive force, e.g., aggressive or deadly force unwarranted for the protective purpose.

Of course, the subject cannot be exhausted in a paragraph. Without subscribing in advance to all the relevant provisions of the Model Penal Code of the American Law Institute, we recommend it for study.[13] Accelerated by that Code, the trend, which is exemplified by legislation adopted in many States,[14] has been to interweave closely the justification of defense of a third person with self-defense; to eliminate some earlier authority restricting the justification of third-person defense to situations where the third person is seen retrospectively to have been entitled to use force in his own defense (regardless of the belief, which might be mistaken, of the "reasonable person" at the time); and to remove earlier artificial or factitious restrictions of the justification, e.g., restrictions to protection of spouse, child, parent, master, or servant.

One such possible factitious restriction was rejected, we think correctly, in *United States v. Grimes*, 413 F.2d 1376 (7th Cir. 1969), a case resembling the present. The defendant Grimes, an inmate of the Federal penitentiary in Marion, Illinois, seeing (as he claimed) a fellow inmate, Reid, being beaten by prison guards with metal flashlights, ran to Reid's aid and struck one of the guards. Grimes was indicted and convicted of assault upon an

---

13. The principal sections of the Code (Proposed Official Draft 1962) to be consulted are §§ 3.05(1), 3.09(1)–(2), 3.04(1), (2)(a)(i), (b); and see Tentative Draft No. 8 (1958) for commentary on these sections.

14. It is reported that in the past twenty years some twenty-one States have adopted legis-

lation in the field of "justification"; another fifteen States, and the Federal government as well, are considering such legislation. See Note, *Justification: The Impact of the Model Penal Code on Statutory Reform*, 75 Colum.L.Rev. 914, 914–915 (1975). The legislation on the use of force in defense of a person is analyzed at 932–939.

employee of a United States Correctional institution (18 U.S.C. §§ 111, 1114 [1970]). On appeal, it was held that the trial judge erred in refusing a jury instruction regarding justified use of force to protect a third person. The court spoke as follows to the point that, while the justification might be suitable generally, it should be rejected in the prison context because of its effect on institutional discipline: "We perceive no serious threat to prison discipline from a defense which merely protects inmates from unauthorized physical abuse by overzealous officials. Our decision in no way limits the power of prison officials to restrain or subdue unruly inmates, to carry out all reasonable orders necessary for the maintenance of prison discipline, or to cope with attempted assaults or escapes by prison inmates. See *Model Penal Code* §§ 3.07, 3.08 (Proposed Official Draft 1962). The Government's concern that recognition of this limited defense will emasculate Section 111 is belied by the fact that since 1905, when this statute was originally enacted, this is apparently the first such case."

We agree with the court in the *Grimes* case that the justification of defense of a third person does not necessarily stop short at the prison gates. But the fact that an episode occurs in prison may have considerable significance. So the question of the reasonableness of a belief that an inmate would be justified in using force against a prison guard, thus justifying intervening protective force, is conditioned by the fact that the guard, by the nature of his job, is himself privileged to apply force to inmates when necessary to preserve order in the institution.[17] Therefore the guard's mere taking an inmate into custody or holding him in custody would not be a proper occasion for intervening force.

17. See *Model Penal Code* § 3.08(5) (Proposed Official Draft 1962) (use of force by persons with special responsibility for care, discipline or safety of others—warden or other authorized official of

This may have an important bearing on the present case in the event of retrial.
* * *

SECTION 3. DEFENSE OF PROPERTY

LAW v. STATE
Court of Special Appeals of Maryland, 1974.
21 Md.App. 13, 318 A.2d 859.

LOWE, JUDGE.

When James Cecil Law, Jr. purchased a thirty-nine dollar shotgun for "house protection," he could not possibly have conceived of the ordeal it would cause him to undergo.

Mr. Law, a 32 year old black man, had recently married and moved to a predominantly white middle-class neighborhood. Within two weeks his home was broken into and a substantial amount of clothing and personal property was taken. The investigating officer testified that Mr. Law was highly agitated following the burglary and indicated that he would take the matter in his own hands. The officer quoted Mr. Law as saying: " 'I will take care of the job. I know who it is.' " The officer went on to say that Law told him " * * * he knew somebody he could get a gun from in D.C. and he was going to kill the man and he was going take care of it." Two days later he purchased a 12 gauge shotgun and several "double ought" shells.

The intruder entered the Law's home between 6:30 and 9:00 in the evening by breaking a windowpane in the kitchen door which opened onto a screened back porch. The intruder then apparently reached in and unlocked the door. Law later installed "double locks" which required the use of a key both inside and

a correctional institution). Cf. *State v. Rigler*, 266 A.2d 887 (Super.Ct.Del.1970) (parent disciplines child; defendant not justified in intervening).

outside. He replaced the glass in the door window in a temporary manner by holding it in place with a few pieces of molding, without using the customary glazing compound to seal it in.

One week after the break-in a well meaning neighbor saw a flickering light in the Law's otherwise darkened house and became suspicious. Aware of the previous burglary, he reported to the police that some one was breaking into the Laws' home. Although the hour was 8:00 p.m., Mr. Law and his bride had retired for the evening. When the police arrived, a fuse of circumstances ignited by fear exploded into a tragedy of errors.

The police did not report to or question the calling neighbor. Instead they went about routinely checking the house seeking the possible illegal point of entry. They raised storm windows where they could reach them and shook the inside windows to see if they were locked. They shined flashlights upon the windows out of reach, still seeking evidence of unlawful entry. Finding none, two officers entered the back screened porch to check the back door, whereupon they saw the window-pane which appeared to have been temporarily put in place with a few pieces of molding. These officers apparently had not known of the repair or the cause of damage.

Upstairs Mr. and Mrs. Law heard what sounded like attempts to enter their home. Keenly aware of the recent occurrence, Mr. Law went downstairs, obtained and loaded his newly acquired shotgun and, apparently facing the rear door of the house, listened for more sounds.

In the meantime, the uniformed officers found what they thought to be the point of entry of a burglar, and were examining the recently replaced glass. While Officer Adams held the flashlight on the recently replaced pane of glass, Officer Garrison removed the molding and the glass, laid them down and stated that he was going to reach in and unlock the door from the inside to see if entry could be gained. Officer Adams testified that they "were talking in a tone a little lower than normal at this point." Officer Adams stated that Officer Garrison then tested the inside lock, discovered it was a deadlock and decided no one could have gotten in the door without a key. A law enforcement student, riding with Officer Garrison that evening, testified that he then heard a rattling noise and someone saying "if there was somebody here, he's still in there." As Officer Garrison removed his hand from the window he was hit by a shotgun blast which Law fired through the door. Officer Garrison was dead on arrival at the hospital.

Officer Potts, the officer next to arrive at the scene, saw Officer Adams running to his car to call for reinforcements. He heard another shot and Officer Adams yell "they just shot at me."

The tragedy of errors had only begun. The officers, having obtained reinforcements and apparently believing they had cornered a burglar, subjected the house to a fussillade of gun fire evinced by over forty bullet holes in the bottom of the kitchen door and the police department transcription of a telephone conversation during the ensuing period of incomprehensible terror.

Mr. Law testified that while he stood listening to the sounds and voices at the door, fearful that someone was about to come in " * * * the gun went off, like that, and when it went off like that it scared me and I was so scared because I had never shot a shotgun before and then I heard a voice on the outside say that someone had been shot." Mr. Law was not able to hear who had been shot but he then " * * * hollered up to my wife, call a police officer, I think I shot a burglar." His wife called the police and most of her conversation was recorded. * * *

The appellant, James Cecil Law, Jr. was found guilty of murder in the second degree and of assault with intent to murder. He was convicted by a jury in the Circuit Court for Charles County following removal from Prince George's County. Judge James C. Mitchell sentenced him to concurrent ten year terms. * * *

The appellant's first question assigning error for failure to grant his motion for judgment of acquittal is a request for our review of the trial court's constitutional responsibility to pass upon the sufficiency of the evidence. In doing so we are not permitted to substitute our judgment of whether there was reasonable doubt of the defendant's guilt for that exercised by the jury. The limit of our review is to determine whether there was relevant and legally sufficient evidence, properly before the jury, to sustain a conviction.

The necessity of responding to this question is diminished by the result we reach here;[a] however, appellant's assertion of the defense of habitation requires that we do more than summarily declare the question moot.

There is a dearth of Maryland authority upon the question of what constitutes justifiable homicide in the defense of one's home. We hasten to note, however, that the single case directly meeting the question does so concisely and clearly. In 1962, the Court of Appeals in *Crawford v. State,* 231 Md. 354, 190 A.2d 538, reversed a conviction of manslaughter against a 42 year old man, suffering from a nervous condition and ulcers, whose home was being broken into by a 23 year old man and a partner. The decedent had knocked out a piece of masonite replacing one of four glass panes in the door. Craw-

ford fired a shotgun through the door killing the attacker before he was able to enter.

Certain of the circumstances of that case coincide remarkably with the case at bar. It is as remarkably distinguished, however, by the character and purpose of the decedent, who had previously beaten Crawford and was returning to rob and beat him again after threatening to do so. Without digression on tangential issues, Chief Judge Brune noted with little discussion, as we do here, the appropriateness of the holding of *Gunther v. State,* 228 Md. 404, 409, 179 A.2d 880, that one not seeking a fight may arm himself in anticipation of a violent attack. * * *

The regal aphorism that a man's home is his castle has obscured the limitations on the right to preserve one's home as a sanctuary from fear of force or violence.

Crawford articulates the rule well, distilling it from a review of cases in many jurisdictions:

"Most American jurisdictions in which the question has been decided have taken the view that if an assault on a dwelling and an attempted forcible entry are made under circumstances which would create *a reasonable apprehension* that it is the design of the assailant *to commit a felony* or to inflict on the inhabitants injury which may result in loss of life or great bodily harm, and that the danger that the design will be carried into effect is imminent, a lawful occupant of the dwelling may prevent the entry even by the taking of the intruder's life." (Emphasis partially added.)

The felonies the prevention of which justifies the taking of a life "are such and only such as are committed by forcible means, violence, and surprise such as murder, robbery, burglary, rape or arson."

a. This is a reference to the fact that the court, in a part of the opinion omitted here, reversed the convictions and remanded for a new trial because unconstitutionally obtained admissions by the defendant were received in evidence at trial.

[I]t is "essential that killing is *necessary* to prevent the commission of the felony in question. If other methods would prevent its commission, a homicide is not justified; all other means of preventing the crime must first be exhausted."

The right thus rests upon real or apparent necessity. It is this need for caution in exercising the right that has been relegated to obscurity. The position espoused by appellant typifies the misunderstanding of the extent of the right to defend one's home against intrusion. He says:

"The defendant is not required to act as a reasonable, prudent and cautious individual, nor was he required to limit his force to only that that was required under the circumstances—not when the defendant was in his own home, and believed he was being set upon, or about to be set upon by would be robbers or burglars who were in the act of breaking into his home at the time."

The judgment which must usually be made precipitously under frightening conditions nevertheless demands a certain presence of mind and reasonableness of judgment. Although one is "not obliged to retreat * * * but * * * may even pursue the assailant until he finds himself or his property out of danger * * *, this will not justify a person['s] firing upon everyone who forceably enters his house, even at night." * * *

Appellant points to a portion of the court's instructions which he feels indicates an erroneous shifting of the burden of proof. He contends this is tantamount to removing the presumptive cloak of innocence constitutionally enveloping a defendant. The judge issued a variant of the stock instruction that once an illegal homicide is established the law presumes it to be murder in the second degree. He then went on to say that:

"*the burden rests upon the accused as part of his defense to prove by a fair preponderance of*

the evidence circumstances of a deviation or mitigation, which would lower, reduce the crime to manslaughter or he may show, by way of defense, that the killing was justifiable or excusable and that therefore he should not be held criminally accountable for any crime and the State has the burden of proving not by merely a preponderance of the greater weight of the evidence, but proving beyond a reasonable doubt the element which will raise the crime from second degree murder to first degree." (Emphasis supplied by appellant.)

We are unable to see how the "trial judge illegally shifted the burden of proof to the defendant." Appellant points to cases that draw semantic distinctions between the shifting of the burden of proof and the burden of going forward with the evidence. Undoubtedly the judge chose to avoid confusing the jury with the fine academic distinctions of shifting burdens. His choice of words was not such as appear misleading or prejudicial. This court has itself used that very expression.

Any possibility of a misunderstanding was averted by emphatically placing upon the State the burden of proving guilt beyond a reasonable doubt. The judge elaborated upon that instruction as well as the presumption of innocence favoring the accused. * * *

The same authorities answer appellant's third assignment of error that answered his first. Appellant argues that in defense of his home he "is not subject to the standards of a reasonable, prudent and cautious person, nor is his degree of force limited only to that required under the circumstances to repel the intruder." Quite the contrary, we do not find the right to defend one's habitation to be so absolute as to sanction promiscuous shooting upon a baseless apprehension by an unreasonable person. The permissible degree of force used to repel an intruder must not be excessive. * * * The question of excessive force to resist the intrusion, in most instances, as in *Crawford,* supra, is the most difficult problem the jury has to cope with when death of the intruder was the result. Apropos of the appellant's question is the statement in *State v. Sorrentino,* 31 Wyo. 129, 224 P. 420, 423, that a defendant is not justified in taking a life "[i]f a cautious and prudent man, under the same circumstances, would not believe the danger to have been real * * *." [4]

Notes and Questions

1. What should Mr. Law have done? How significant is it that he failed to call out to the supposed burglar to desist? Consider in this regard the request to desist provision in *Model Penal Code* § 3.06(3)(a).

2. How would Mr. Law fare otherwise under *Model Penal Code* § 3.06?

3. Should Mr. Law's crime be deemed murder or some lesser degree of criminal homicide? Consider *Model Penal Code* § 3.09.

BISHOP v. STATE

257 Ga. 136, 356 S.E.2d 503.
Supreme Court of Georgia, 1987.

GREGORY, JUSTICE.

Robert C. Bishop was convicted of malice murder and sentenced to life imprisonment. We affirm.

Bishop lived in a trailer park in Coweta County. Because he was concerned about past break-ins to his trailer, he erected a spring gun or trap gun. He positioned a Mauser 8mm high-powered rifle on two chairs with the barrel pointed in the direction of the trailer's front door. A string attached to the door knob ran over the back of one of the chairs and was connected to the trigger.

Bishop went to work on the night of February 13, 1986 with the spring gun in place. Later, James Freeman, an acquaintance of Bishop, attempted to enter the front door of the trailer. The rifle discharged and hit the metal molding at the foot of the door. Freeman was hit by either a recocheting bullet fragment or a piece of flying metal. Neighbors heard the shot and found Freeman lying wounded in Bishop's driveway. The neighbors said the house was dark, but that Bishop's car was in the driveway.

Freeman * * * died of a pulmonary embolism or blood clot.

Bishop was tried by a jury and found guilty of malice murder. * * *

Bishop * * * contends erecting the spring gun was not unlawful in his case because the killing of Freeman was justified. He cites OCGA § 16–3–23, which provides: "A person is justified in threatening or using force against another when and to the extent that he reasonably believes that such a threat or force is necessary to prevent or terminate such other's unlawful entry into or attack upon a habitation; however, he is justified in the use of force which is intended or likely to cause death or great bodily harm only if: * * * (2) He reasonably believes that the entry is made or attempted for the purpose of committing a felony therein and such force is necessary to prevent the commission of the felony."

Apparently Bishop's trailer had been broken into on several occasions. Accord-

---

4. Equally apropos are the circumstances in *Sorrentino* which created the reasonable belief of danger:

"The effect upon the human mind of darkness in the stillness of the night is a factor well known * * *. A sudden appearance from out the

darkness is apt to give at least a temporary nervous shock to the stoutest heart. Much more is that apt to be true when, roused from rest or slumber, on a dark night, footsteps and other sounds are heard which are calculated, as in this case, of giving the impression of boding no good."

ing to Bishop, the evidence indicates Freeman was burglarizing the trailer when he was shot, although the State disputes this. Bishop argues had he been at home in the darkened trailer and Freeman attempted to enter unannounced he could have reasonably believed a felony was being committed upon his habitation and been justified in using deadly force pursuant to § 16–3–23.

The weakness in Bishop's argument is that he was working and not at home when the spring gun activated. Bishop contends the traditional rule observed in other jurisdictions is that a person is not justified in taking a life indirectly with a mechanical device unless he would have been justified had he been personally present and taken the life with his own hand.

We decline Bishop's invitation to adopt such a rule in these circumstances. Section 16–3–23 justifies the use of deadly force to protect a habitation only when the inhabitant "reasonably believes" the entry is made for the purpose of committing a felony. We find that under these circumstances, however, it was impossible for Bishop to form a reasonable belief in light of his absence from the trailer. "Allowing persons, at their own risk, to employ deadly mechanical devices imperils the lives of children, firemen and policemen acting within the scope of their employment, and others. Where the actor is present, there is always a possibility he will realize that deadly force is not necessary, but deadly mechanical devices are without mercy or discretion. * * * It seems clear that the use of such devices should not be encouraged. Moreover, whatever may be thought in torts, the foregoing rule setting forth an exception to liability for death or injuries inflicted by such devices 'is inappropriate in penal law for it is obvious it does not prescribe a workable standard of conduct; liability depends upon fortuitous results.' " *People v. Ceballos,* 12 Cal.3d 470, 116 Cal.Rptr. 233, 526 P.2d 241, 244–245 (1974), quoting Model Penal Code (Tent. Draft No. 8), § 3.06, comment 15. * * *

Smith, Justice, dissenting.

"Every man's home is his castle." This statement all of us have heard since childhood. This case involves the extent to which a man may use deadly force to protect that "castle."

In the venerable case *Collins v. Rennison,* 1 Sayer 138 (K.B.1754), an English court described the allowable extent by employing the phrase "moliter manus imposuit." The use of this phrase indicated that a person should gently push a non-felonious intruder out the door. Blackstone, in advocating a tougher response to intrusions into the home, noted that all felonies were punishable by death. He advocated sanction of the use of deadly force to prevent an intruder from entering a home to commit a felony. 4 Blackstone's Commentaries 188.

In 1820, the first "spring gun" case came on the scene. In *Ilott v. Wilkes,* 3 Barn. & Ald. 304, 106 Eng.Rep. 674 (K.B.1820), the defendant set up a spring gun in some woods on his property. The gun worked as planned, injuring a trespasser. The Court of King's Bench entered a non-suit in favor of the defendant when evidence emerged showing that the plaintiff had notice of the spring gun.

In the case of *Bird v. Holbrook,* 4 Bing. 628, 130 Eng.Rep. 911 (C.P.1828), the Court of Common Pleas heard a case similar to *Ilott* in which the plaintiff was injured by a spring gun while searching a neighbor's garden for his fowl. In *Bird,* unlike *Ilott,* however, the plaintiff had no notice of the spring gun. In the opinion of Chief Justice Best, who had taken part in the *Ilott* decision, the lack of notice distinguished the two cases, and the plaintiff was entitled to a verdict. In these early cases, the spring gun owner was arguably not subject to civil damages, much less a murder or assault charge.

Around this time, Parliament became involved in the spring gun debate, passing a statute which criminalized the use of spring guns. 7 & 8 Geo. 4, c. 18 (1827). Parliament did, however, create an exception allowing the use of the guns between dusk and dawn in the home for the prevention of a felony. *Id.;* Bohlen & Burns, *The Privilege to Protect Property by Dangerous Barriers and Mechanical Devices,* 35 Yale L.J., 525, 541 n. 46 (1926).

The first spring gun case in the United States appeared in Kentucky in 1832. *Gray v. Combs,* 30 Ky. 478 (1832). The Kentucky court neither approved nor disapproved of the earlier English cases in holding use of a spring gun to protect property justified under the circumstances. In *Johnson v. Patterson,* 14 Conn. 1 (1940), the Supreme Court of Connecticut in dicta rejected the use of spring guns sanctioned in *Gray.*

Since the early cases, the courts and legislatures in this country have in the absence of complete prohibition, drawn a line between spring guns used in the home and spring guns used elsewhere. Some cases have stated that spring guns could be used to protect dwelling places when the owner could have used deadly force had he been present. See *Prosser on Torts,* p. 136 n. 40 (5th ed. 1984). Others like the majority opinion here, flatly forbid the use of spring guns.

From the broad range of standards dealing with spring guns and criminal law, I would select the rule that views as justified a homicide committed by spring gun at night in the home of the defendant when the defendant can establish under the totality of the circumstances that he possessed a reasonable expectation that someone would be breaking into his home to commit a felony and that the victim was, indeed, breaking into his home to commit a felony. To do this, we simply should look to the intent of the defendant at the time that he sets the spring gun, setting the chain of events leading to the death in motion, rather than to the time at which the victim is shot. Viewed in this manner, OCGA § 16–3–23 would justify a homicide such as the one involved in this case. I would reverse.

Notes and Questions

1. Should the case turn upon whether Freeman, as Bishop claims, "was burglarizing the trailer"? Even if he was, did Bishop utilize means which are inappropriate because of the danger to firefighters or others who might have occasion lawfully to enter the premises? If so, is the solution prosecution of Bishop for reckless endangerment instead of murder?

2. Is it relevant that Bishop was the victim of "past break-ins to his trailer"? Should such circumstances ever be relevant? Consider this account from *N.Y. Times,* Oct. 5, 1986, at L37, col. 1:

"After his small general merchandise store was robbed eight times since it opened a year ago, four times in two recent weeks, Prentice F. Rasheed decided to catch the thief himself.

"Last week he installed an electric booby trap in the ceiling of his shop, situated in an area where the police record many crimes. On Tuesday the trap electrocuted a man who managed to get into the store at night and was leaving with stolen goods.

"Mr. Rasheed was arrested the next day by the Miami police on a manslaughter charge. He was released on $6,500 bond paid by fellow merchants who sided with him, including members of the Edison Model City Merchants Association, of which William J. Calhoun is a director.

"Mr. Calhoun, owner of a tailor shop 50 yards from Mr. Rasheed's, called the death 'regrettable' but added:

"'We are all in sympathy with Prentice. We understand his frustration. We have put iron bars on the windows and doors of our establishments, but that does not stop burglars because there is virtually no protection here.'＊　＊　＊

"The man who died, Odell Hicks, 27 years old, lived a block from Mr. Rasheed's store. Mr. Hicks had a long record of criminal offenses, the police say. In 1976 he was found guilty of burglary and sexual battery and sentenced to eight years in prison on each charge. In 1981, several months after his release, he was arrested again and accused of breaking into a house.

"Mr. Rasheed, who is 43, said he regretted the incident. 'I can't be happy that a young man lost his life,' he said. He said that by rigging the booby trap and connecting it to a 110-volt outlet, he only wanted to scare would-be robbers.

"The police theorized that when Mr. Hicks entered the store he was protected from the current by his rubber-soled sneakers. But when he was leaving, he touched metal with sweaty hands and died."

SECTION 4. LAW ENFORCEMENT AND RESPONSE THERETO

KOHLER v. COMMONWEALTH

Court of Appeals of Kentucky, 1973.
492 S.W.2d 198.

VANCE, COMMISSIONER.

The appellant was convicted of the offense of unlawful sale of heroin, a narcotic drug, and sentenced to confinement for a period of not more than twenty years and was fined $20,000.00.

The defendant admitted he procured two ounces of heroin from Ollie Craycraft and offered it for sale to Harold Brown, for the sum of $8,000.00. He claimed, however, that all of his activities in the procurement of the drug and the at-tempted sale thereof were prompted solely by his desire to aid and assist the police in their efforts to obtain information concerning illicit-drug traffic.

Approximately ten months before his arrest on this charge the appellant was confined in jail in Fayette County, Kentucky, on a charge of assault and battery. While in jail he was contacted by another prisoner who claimed to have six ounces of heroin and also claimed to be raising a half-acre of marijuana. This prisoner solicited appellant's help, upon release from jail, in the sale of the heroin and the harvest and sale of the marijuana.

When appellant was discharged from custody he informed police officers of his conversations with his fellow-prisoner. Officer Thornton advised him to try to keep in touch with the prisoner and to attempt a "buy" of the narcotics. Officer Thornton also advised appellant to keep him informed of appellant's activities in that regard.

Appellant testified that he made a good faith effort during the ten-month period following his release from jail to locate and purchase drugs; that his efforts were of no avail until the transaction which resulted in his arrest; that he periodically advised officer Thornton of his activities and attempted to get in touch with officer Thornton on the day he was arrested to inform him of the pending sale but was unable to do so. Officer Thornton denied that appellant contacted him at any time after their initial meeting.

The attempted sale being admitted, the whole case boils down to a question of appellant's motive and intent. His only real defense was that he acted in good faith with the intent only to be of assistance to law enforcement officers. He requested the court to affirmatively instruct the jury in a manner which fairly presented his theory of defense. The request for an affirmative instruction was denied.

The jury was instructed as follows:

"If the jury shall believe from the evidence in this case to the exclusion of a reasonable doubt that in Fayette County, Kentucky, on or about the 4th day of June, 1971, the defendant, Lance Kohler, unlawfully and feloniously sold a narcotic drug, to-wit, heroin, to Harold Brown, you shall find him guilty as charged in the indictment and fix his punishment at confinement in the penitentiary for not less than five years nor more than twenty years, and by a fine of not more than $20,000.00, in your discretion.

"The word 'feloniously' as used in this instruction means done with an intent to commit a crime or wrong.

" 'Sale' includes barter, exchange or gift, or offer thereof, and each such transaction made by any person, whether as principal, proprietor, agent, servant or employee."

By references to that portion of the instruction wherein the word feloniously was defined as an act done with an intent to commit a crime or wrong, the jurors, if they had believed appellant's testimony, could have determined that his act was not felonious and thus could have acquitted him. But at best, the appellant's theory of defense was presented by these instructions in an oblique rather than an affirmative fashion. * * *

We have consistently recognized, however, that when a defendant confesses the doing of the act of which he stands accused but asserts a legal excuse or justification exonerating him from criminal intent the court should submit his theory of defense in concrete form. *Cooley v. Commonwealth*, Ky., 459 S.W.2d 89 (1970).

The instant case in which appellant seeks to avoid criminal liability upon the ground

that the act with which he is charged was done to assist law enforcement officers is precisely the type of case in which an affirmative instruction is necessary.

In *Evitts v. Commonwealth*, 257 Ky. 586, 78 S.W.2d 798 (1935), we held that one who claimed that he had received stolen goods at the request of the chief of police in an effort to apprehend the thief was entitled to an affirmative instruction on that defense and failure to give it was prejudicial error. This requirement was approved in *Ward v. Commonwealth*, Ky., 399 S.W.2d 463 (1966), in which we said:

"The jury was instructed to find appellants guilty if they 'willfully, unlawfully and feloniously' received the two shotguns knowing they had been stolen. The word 'feloniously', was defined as proceeding from an evil heart or purpose, and this definition provided the only avenue through which the jury could have found appellants not guilty on the basis of their story that Ward had purchased the guns with the intention of communicating with the sheriff before disposing of them. This, in our opinion, was not clear enough to constitute a fair presentation of the appellants' theory of defense. *Evitts v. Commonwealth*, supra. Upon another trial a specific instruction should be given, and the definition of 'feloniously' should be amplified to include the additional words, 'done with deliberate intention of committing a crime.' Cf. *McVey v. Commonwealth*, Ky., 272 S.W.2d 33, 35 (1954)."

Under the requirement of *Evitts* and *Ward* we hold the denial of the requested instruction was prejudicial error.

Notes and Questions

What limits should be placed upon the defense of aiding law enforcement? Consider:

1. *Reigan v. People,* 120 Colo. 472, 210 P.2d 991 (1949): The defendants, game wardens assigned to investigate the illegal taking and transporting of beaver pelts, told two youths they would pay as much as $30 each for beaver hides and explained to the youths how to skin the beavers and care for the hides. The defendants were convicted of conspiring together to commit the crime of unlawfully trapping and killing beaver. On appeal, the court, in affirming the judgment, explained: "Where officers of the law cooperate to induce another to commit a criminal act which would not have been conceived by said person except for the instigation or inducement of the officers, can the officers who cooperated to induce the act be lawfully convicted of conspiracy to cause a violation of the law?

"This question must be answered in the affirmative. The argument advanced by defendants is that since the ultimate purpose of defendants was to arrest and bring to justice those who violated the law, there could be 'no unity of intent between these defendants and the other conspirators.' It is further argued that 'one who participates in a crime as a feigned accomplice, in order to entrap another, or for the purpose of detecting crime, does not thereby become criminally liable.' The foregoing statement is based upon a misconception and misuse of the terms 'entrapment' and 'detection', as applied to the activities of law enforcement officers. Defendants treat these terms as being synonymous, however there is a great difference in their meaning and that distinction is the answer to the question under discussion. While there is some confusion in the authorities in the use of these terms, when considered in the light of the facts in each case the rule of law is clear. A suspected person may be tested by being offered opportunity to transgress the law in such manner as is usual in the activity alleged to be unlawful. However, law enforcement officers may not induce persons, who would not otherwise have committed crime, to violate the law. The former is legitimate 'detection' of crime, and is often necessary to efficient law enforcement. The latter is 'entrapment' to commit crime in which the officer's conduct instigates the offense, the commission of which was nonexistent in the mind of the intended victim of the 'entrapment'. * * *

"Applying these principles to the case at bar, if the cooperation of the defendants amounted to no more than an effort to 'detect' a violation of law on the part of the two boys then the defendants could not be convicted of a conspiracy. If, however, the conduct of the defendants amounted to an attempted 'entrapment' of the boys the judgment must stand. Whether there is here present an attempt at crime 'detection' or 'entrapment' is a question of fact. There was competent evidence to support either finding. Under proper instructions concerning the law the jury found an 'entrapment' and it is not our province to determine to the contrary."

2. *Lilly v. West Virginia,* 29 F.2d 61 (4th Cir.1928): The defendant, a federal prohibition agent, while chasing an auto he had reasonable cause to believe was transporting illegal liquor, struck and killed a pedestrian at a street intersection. He was indicted for involuntary manslaughter; the case was removed to federal court, and he was there convicted of the charge. The court refused to instruct the jury, as requested by the defendant, that if the defendant "was honestly and in good faith executing and attempting to perform a duty imposed upon him by the laws of the United States at the time of the accident, and in so doing, used reasonable care and diligence commensurate with his duty and the apparent danger, if any, then you will find him not guilty." On appeal, the conviction was reversed:

"In refusing to instruct the jury substantially as requested in the requests made by defendant from which we have quoted, and in charging the jury as thus set forth, we think that the learned District Judge committed error prejudicial to the defendant. Prohibition agents are, of course, not above the law. It is their duty, in attempting to apprehend criminals, as it is the duty of other officers of the law, having regard to existing ordinances and the circumstances in which they are placed, to exercise reasonable care and caution for the safety of the public; and, if they fail to do so, and such failure results in the death of any one, they are undoubtedly guilty of manslaughter. But we think that the court went too far in charging the jury that it was the duty of defendant, while chasing a suspected criminal, to have his car under such control in approaching a street intersection that he could avoid any possibility of hurting any one; that deceased had the right of way, if crossing at an intersection not controlled by an officer or traffic device; that the sounding of the whistle and acts relied upon as exercise of care by defendant made no difference, if deceased had the right of way; and, in effect, that the defendant should be convicted, if the death of deceased resulted from defendant's being unable to stop because of excessive speed, and that what was excessive should be determined, not by the circumstances of the case, but by the speed ordinances of the city of Huntington.

"In this charge of the court, sight was apparently lost of the fact that the city's speed ordinances should be interpreted, not alone in the interest of the pedestrian, but for the protection of the public, having due regard to the rights of others, lawfully having to use the streets and highways, and this is especially true as to those engaged in the execution and enforcement of the criminal laws of the land. The failure to recognize speed ordinances under such circumstances must be viewed in the light of the rights of others to be affected, and a contrary view would operate unreasonably and be highly prejudicial to the public. The officer in this case was warranted in attempting to make the arrest under the circumstances, and he is by reason thereof excepted from the limitations of the speed prescribed by the city ordinance in issue, provided the jury believed that he acted in good faith in what he did, and with the prudence, care, and caution that an ordinarily prudent person would have exercised under the circumstances in which he was placed; the degree of care required being commensurate with the dangers existing, and to be increased in proportion to such dangers should there be an increase thereof.

"The traffic ordinances of a city prescribing who shall have the right of way at crossings and fixing speed limits for vehicles are ordinarily binding upon officials of the federal government as upon all other citizens. Such ordinances, however, are not to be construed as applying to public officials engaged in the performance of a public duty where speed and the right of way are a necessity. The ordinance of Huntington makes no exemption in favor of firemen going to a fire or peace officers pursuing criminals, but it certainly could not have been intended that pedestrians at street intersections should have the right of way over such firemen or officers, or that firemen or officers under such circumstances should be limited to a speed of 25 miles, or required to slow down at intersections so as to have their vehicles under control. Such a construction would render the ordinances void for unreasonableness in so far as they applied to firemen or officers engaged in duties, in the performance of which speed is necessary; and we think that they should be construed as not applicable to such officers, either state or federal, under such circumstances."

TENNESSEE v. GARNER

Supreme Court of the United States, 1985.
471 U.S. 1, 105 S.Ct. 1694, 85 L.Ed.2d 1.

JUSTICE WHITE delivered the opinion of the Court.

This case requires us to determine the constitutionality of the use of deadly force to prevent the escape of an apparently unarmed suspected felon. We conclude that such force may not be used unless it is necessary to prevent the escape and the officer has probable cause to believe that the suspect poses a significant threat of death or serious physical injury to the officer or others.

I

At about 10:45 p.m. on October 3, 1974, Memphis Police Officers Elton Hymon and Leslie Wright were dispatched to answer a "prowler inside call." Upon arriving at the scene they saw a woman standing on her porch and gesturing toward the adjacent house. She told them she had heard glass breaking and that "they" or "someone" was breaking in next door. While Wright radioed the dispatcher to say that they were on the scene, Hymon went behind the house. He heard a door slam and saw someone run across the back yard. The fleeing suspect, who was appellee-respondent's decedent, Edward Garner, stopped at a 6–feet–high chain link fence at the edge of the yard. With the aid of a flashlight, Hymon was able to see Garner's face and hands. He saw no sign of a weapon, and, though not certain, was "reasonably sure" and "figured" that Garner was unarmed. He thought Garner was 17 or 18 years old and about 5'5" or 5'7" tall. While Garner was crouched at the base of the fence, Hymon called out "police, halt" and took a few steps toward him. Garner then began to climb over the fence. Convinced that if Garner made it over the fence he would elude capture, Hymon shot him.

The bullet hit Garner in the back of the head. Garner was taken by ambulance to a hospital, where he died on the operating table. Ten dollars and a purse taken from the house were found on his body.

In using deadly force to prevent the escape, Hymon was acting under the authority of a Tennessee statute and pursuant to Police Department policy. The statute provides that "[i]f, after notice of the intention to arrest the defendant, he either flee or forcibly resist, the officer may use all the necessary means to effect the arrest." The Department policy was slightly more restrictive than the statute, but still allowed the use of deadly force in cases of burglary. The incident was reviewed by the Memphis Police Firearm's Review Board and presented to a grand jury. Neither took any action.

Garner's father then brought this action in the Federal District Court for the Western District of Tennessee, seeking damages under 42 U.S.C. § 1983 for asserted violations of Garner's constitutional rights.
* * *

The District Court * * * found that the statute, and Hymon's actions, were constitutional. * * *

The Court of Appeals reversed and remanded. * * *

The State of Tennessee, which had intervened to defend the statute, appealed to this Court.

II

Whenever an officer restrains the freedom of a person to walk away, he has seized that person. While it is not always clear just when minimal police interference becomes a seizure, there can be no question that apprehension by the use of deadly force is a seizure subject to the reasonableness requirement of the Fourth Amendment.

A

A police officer may arrest a person if he has probable cause to believe that person committed a crime. Petitioners and appellant argue that if this requirement is satisfied the Fourth Amendment has nothing to say about *how* that seizure is made. This submission ignores the many cases in which this Court, by balancing the extent of the intrusion against the need for it, has examined the reasonableness of the manner in which a search or seizure is conducted. * * * Because one of the factors is the extent of the intrusion, it is plain that reasonableness depends on not only when a seizure is made, but also how it is carried out. * * *

B

The same balancing process applied in the cases cited above demonstrates that, notwithstanding probable cause to seize a suspect, an officer may not always do so by killing him. The intrusiveness of a seizure by means of deadly force is unmatched. The suspect's fundamental interest in his own life need not be elaborated upon. The use of deadly force also frustrates the interest of the individual, and of society, in judicial determination of guilt and punishment. Against these interests are ranged governmental interests in effective law enforcement.[8] It is argued that overall violence will be reduced by encouraging the peaceful submission of suspects who know

that they may be shot if they flee. Effectiveness in making arrests requires the resort to deadly force, or at least the meaningful threat thereof. "Being able to arrest such individuals is a condition precedent to the state's entire system of law enforcement."

Without in any way disparaging the importance of these goals, we are not convinced that the use of deadly force is a sufficiently productive means of accomplishing them to justify the killing of nonviolent suspects. The use of deadly force is a self-defeating way of apprehending a suspect and so setting the criminal justice mechanism in motion. If successful, it guarantees that that mechanism will not be set in motion. And while the meaningful threat of deadly force might be thought to lead to the arrest of more live suspects by discouraging escape attempts, the presently available evidence does not support this thesis. The fact is that a majority of police departments in this country have forbidden the use of deadly force against nonviolent suspects. If those charged with the enforcement of the criminal law have abjured the use of deadly force in arresting nondangerous felons, there is a substantial basis for doubting that the use of such force is an essential attribute of the arrest power in all felony cases. Petitioners and appellant have not persuaded us that shooting nondangerous fleeing suspects is

---

8. The dissent emphasizes that subsequent investigation cannot replace immediate apprehension. We recognize that this is so; indeed, that is the reason why there is any dispute. If subsequent arrest were assured, no one would argue that use of deadly force was justified. Thus, we proceed on the assumption that subsequent arrest is not likely. Nonetheless, it should be remembered that failure to apprehend at the scene does not necessarily mean that the suspect will never be caught.

In lamenting the inadequacy of later investigation, the dissent relies on the report of the President's Commission on Law Enforcement and Administration of Justice. It is worth noting that, notwithstanding its awareness of this problem,

the Commission itself proposed a policy for use of deadly force arguably even more stringent than the formulation we adopt today. See President's Commission on Law Enforcement and Administration of Justice, Task Force Report: The Police 189 (1967). The Commission proposed that deadly force be used only to apprehend "perpetrators who, in the course of their crime threatened the use of deadly force, or if the officer believes there is a substantial risk that the person whose arrest is sought will cause death or serious bodily harm if his apprehension is delayed." In addition, the officer would have "to know, as a virtual certainty, that the suspect committed an offense for which the use of deadly force is permissible."

so vital as to outweigh the suspect's interest in his own life.

The use of deadly force to prevent the escape of all felony suspects, whatever the circumstances, is constitutionally unreasonable. It is not better that all felony suspects die than that they escape. Where the suspect poses no immediate threat to the officer and no threat to others, the harm resulting from failing to apprehend him does not justify the use of deadly force to do so. It is no doubt unfortunate when a suspect who is in sight escapes, but the fact that the police arrive a little late or are a little slower afoot does not always justify killing the suspect. A police officer may not seize an unarmed, nondangerous suspect by shooting him dead. The Tennessee statute is unconstitutional insofar as it authorizes the use of deadly force against such fleeing suspects.

It is not, however, unconstitutional on its face. Where the officer has probable cause to believe that the suspect poses a threat of serious physical harm, either to the officer or to others, it is not constitutionally unreasonable to prevent escape by using deadly force. Thus, if the suspect threatens the officer with a weapon or there is probable cause to believe that he has committed a crime involving the infliction or threatened infliction of serious physical harm, deadly force may be used if necessary to prevent escape, and if, where feasible, some warning has been given. As applied in such circumstances, the Tennessee statute would pass constitutional muster.

III

A

It is insisted that the Fourth Amendment must be construed in light of the common-law rule, which allowed the use of whatever force was necessary to effect the arrest of a fleeing felon, though not a misdemeanant. * * *

The State and city argue that because this was the prevailing rule at the time of the adoption of the Fourth Amendment and for some time thereafter, and is still in force in some States, use of deadly force against a fleeing felon must be "reasonable." It is true that this Court has often looked to the common law in evaluating the reasonableness, for Fourth Amendment purposes, of police activity. On the other hand, it "has not simply frozen into constitutional law those law enforcement practices that existed at the time of the Fourth Amendment's passage." Because of sweeping change in the legal and technological context, reliance on the common-law rule in this case would be a mistaken literalism that ignores the purposes of a historical inquiry.

B

It has been pointed out many times that the common-law rule is best understood in light of the fact that it arose at a time when virtually all felonies were punishable by death. * * * Courts have also justified the common-law rule by emphasizing the relative dangerousness of felons.

Neither of these justifications makes sense today. Almost all crimes formerly punishable by death no longer are or can be. And while in earlier times "the gulf between the felonies and the minor offences was broad and deep," today the distinction is minor and often arbitrary. Many crimes classified as misdemeanors, or nonexistent, at common law are now felonies. These changes have undermined the concept, which was questionable to begin with, that use of deadly force against a fleeing felon is merely a speedier execution of someone who has already forfeited his life. They have also made the assumption that a "felon" is more dangerous than a misdemeanant untenable. Indeed, numerous misdemeanors involve conduct more dangerous than many felonies.

There is an additional reason why the common-law rule cannot be directly translated to the present day. The common-law rule developed at a time when weapons were rudimentary. Deadly force could be inflicted almost solely in a hand-to-hand struggle during which, necessarily, the safety of the arresting officer was at risk. Handguns were not carried by police officers until the latter half of the last century. Only then did it become possible to use deadly force from a distance as a means of apprehension. As a practical matter, the use of deadly force under the standard articulation of the common-law rule has an altogether different meaning—and harsher consequences—now than in past centuries.

One other aspect of the common-law rule bears emphasis. It forbids the use of deadly force to apprehend a misdemeanant, condemning such action as disproportionately severe.

In short, though the common law pedigree of Tennessee's rule is pure on its face, changes in the legal and technological context mean the rule is distorted almost beyond recognition when literally applied.

B

In evaluating the reasonableness of police procedures under the Fourth Amendment, we have also looked to prevailing rules in individual jurisdictions. The rules in the States are varied. Some 19 States have codified the common-law rule, though in two of these the courts have significantly limited the statute. Four States, though without a relevant statute, apparently retain the common-law rule. Two States have adopted the Model Penal Code's provision [§ 3.07(2)(b)] verbatim. Eighteen others allow, in slightly varying language, the use of deadly force only if the suspect has committed a felony involving the use or threat of physical or deadly force, or is escaping with a deadly weapon, or is likely to endanger life or inflict serious physical injury if not arrested. Louisiana and Vermont, though without statutes or case law on point, do forbid the use of deadly force to prevent any but violent felonies. The remaining States either have no relevant statute or case-law, or have positions that are unclear.

It cannot be said that there is a constant or overwhelming trend away from the common-law rule. In recent years, some States have reviewed their laws and expressly rejected abandonment of the common-law rule. Nonetheless, the long-term movement has been away from the rule that deadly force may be used against any fleeing felon, and that remains the rule in less than half the States.

This trend is more evident and impressive when viewed in light of the policies adopted by the police departments themselves. Overwhelmingly, these are more restrictive than the common-law rule. * * * Overall, only 7.5% of departmental and municipal policies explicitly permit the use of deadly force against any felon; 86.8% explicitly do not. In light of the rules adopted by those who must actually administer them, the older and fading common-law view is a dubious indicium of the constitutionality of the Tennessee statute now before us.

C

Actual departmental policies are important for an additional reason. We would hesitate to declare a police practice of long standing "unreasonable" if doing so would severely hamper effective law enforcement. But the indications are to the contrary. There has been no suggestion that crime has worsened in any way in jurisdictions that have adopted, by legislation or departmental policy, rules similar to that announced today. * * *

Nor do we agree with petitioners and appellant that the rule we have adopted requires the police to make impossible, split-second evaluations of unknowable facts. We do not deny the practical difficulties of attempting to assess the suspect's dangerousness. However, similarly difficult judgments must be made by the police in equally uncertain circumstances. Nor is there any indication that in States that allow the use of deadly force only against dangerous suspects, the standard has been difficult to apply or has led to a rash of litigation involving inappropriate second-guessing of police officers' split-second decisions. Moreover, the highly technical felony/misdemeanor distinction is equally, if not more, difficult to apply in the field. An officer is in no position to know, for example, the precise value of property stolen, or whether the crime was a first or second offense. Finally, as noted above, this claim must be viewed with suspicion in light of the similar self-imposed limitations of so many police departments.

IV

* * * In reversing, the Court of Appeals accepted the District Court's factual conclusions and held that "the facts, as found, did not justify the use of deadly force." We agree. Officer Hymon could not reasonably have believed that Garner—young, slight, and unarmed—posed any threat. Indeed, Hymon never attempted to justify his actions on any basis other than the need to prevent an escape.

* * *

The dissent argues that the shooting was justified by the fact that Officer Hymon had probable cause to believe that Garner had committed a nighttime burglary.

---

23. The dissent points out that three-fifths of all rapes in the home, three-fifths of all home robberies, and about a third of home assaults are committed by burglars. These figures mean only that if one knows that a suspect committed a rape in the home, there is a good chance that the suspect is also a burglar. That has nothing to do with the question here, which is whether the fact that someone has committed a burglary indicates that he has committed, or might commit, a violent crime.

While we agree that burglary is a serious crime, we cannot agree that it is so dangerous as automatically to justify the use of deadly force. The FBI classifies burglary as a "property" rather than a "violent" crime. Although the armed burglar would present a different situation, the fact that an unarmed suspect has broken into a dwelling at night does not automatically mean he is physically dangerous. This case demonstrates as much. In fact, the available statistics demonstrate that burglaries only rarely involve physical violence. During the 10–year period from 1973–1982, only 3.8% of all burglaries involved violent crime.[23]

V

* * *

The judgment of the Court of Appeals is affirmed * * *.

JUSTICE O'CONNOR, with whom THE CHIEF JUSTICE and JUSTICE REHNQUIST join, dissenting. * * *

For purposes of Fourth Amendment analysis, I agree with the Court that Officer Hymon "seized" Garner by shooting him. Whether that seizure was reasonable and therefore permitted by the Fourth Amendment requires a careful balancing of the important public interest in crime prevention and detection and the nature and quality of the intrusion upon legitimate interests of the individual. * * *

The public interest involved in the use of deadly force as a last resort to apprehend a fleeing burglary suspect relates primarily to the serious nature of the crime. Household burglaries represent not only

---

The dissent also points out that this 3.8% adds up to 2.8 million violent crimes over a 10–year period, as if to imply that today's holding will let loose 2.8 million violent burglars. The relevant universe is, of course, far smaller. At issue is only that tiny fraction of cases where violence has taken place and an officer who has no other means of apprehending the suspect is unaware of its occurrence.

the illegal entry into a person's home, but also "pos[e] real risk of serious harm to others." According to recent Department of Justice statistics, "[t]hree-fifths of all rapes in the home, three-fifths of all home robberies, and about a third of home aggravated and simple assaults are committed by burglars." During the period 1973–1982, 2.8 million such violent crimes were committed in the course of burglaries. Victims of a forcible intrusion into their home by a nighttime prowler will find little consolation in the majority's confident assertion that "burglaries only rarely involve physical violence." Moreover, even if a particular burglary, when viewed in retrospect, does not involve physical harm to others, the "harsh potentialities for violence" inherent in the forced entry into a home preclude characterization of the crime as "innocuous, inconsequential, minor, or 'nonviolent.'"

Because burglary is a serious and dangerous felony, the public interest in the prevention and detection of the crime is of compelling importance. Where a police officer has probable cause to arrest a suspected burglar, the use of deadly force as a last resort might well be the only means of apprehending the suspect. With respect to a particular burglary, subsequent investigation simply cannot represent a substitute for immediate apprehension of the criminal suspect at the scene. Indeed, the Captain of the Memphis Police Department testified that in his city, if apprehension is not immediate, it is likely that the suspect will not be caught. Although some law enforcement agencies may choose to assume the risk that a criminal will remain at large, the Tennessee statute reflects a legislative determination that the use of deadly force in prescribed circumstances will serve generally to protect the public. Such statutes assist the police in apprehending suspected perpetrators of serious crimes and provide notice that a lawful police order to stop and submit to

arrest may not be ignored with impunity.

*   *   *

Against the strong public interests justifying the conduct at issue here must be weighed the individual interests implicated in the use of deadly force by police officers. The majority declares that "[t]he suspect's fundamental interest in his own life need not be elaborated upon." This blithe assertion hardly provides an adequate substitute for the majority's failure to acknowledge the distinctive manner in which the suspect's interest in his life is even exposed to risk. For purposes of this case, we must recall that the police officer, in the course of investigating a nighttime burglary, had reasonable cause to arrest the suspect and ordered him to halt. The officer's use of force resulted because the suspected burglar refused to heed this command and the officer reasonably believed that there was no means short of firing his weapon to apprehend the suspect. Without questioning the importance of a person's interest in his life, I do not think this interest encompasses a right to flee unimpeded from the scene of a burglary.   *   *   *

A proper balancing of the interests involved suggests that use of deadly force as a last resort to apprehend a criminal suspect fleeing from the scene of a nighttime burglary is not unreasonable within the meaning of the Fourth Amendment. Admittedly, the events giving rise to this case are in retrospect deeply regrettable. No one can view the death of an unarmed and apparently nonviolent 15-year old without sorrow, much less disapproval. Nonetheless, the reasonableness of Officer Hymon's conduct for purposes of the Fourth Amendment cannot be evaluated by what later appears to have been a preferable course of police action. The officer pursued a suspect in the darkened backyard of a house that from all indications had just been burglarized. The police officer was not certain whether the suspect was alone or unarmed; nor did he know what had transpired inside the house. He ordered the suspect to halt, and when the suspect refused to obey and attempted to flee into the night, the officer fired his weapon to prevent escape. The reasonableness of this action for purposes of the Fourth Amendment is not determined by the unfortunate nature of this particular case; instead, the question is whether it is constitutionally impermissible for police officers, as a last resort, to shoot a burglary suspect fleeing the scene of the crime.

* * *

Even if I agreed that the Fourth Amendment was violated under the circumstances of this case, I would be unable to join the Court's opinion. The Court holds that deadly force may be used only if the suspect "threatens the officer with a weapon or there is probable cause to believe that he has committed a crime involving the infliction or threatened infliction of serious physical harm." The Court ignores the more general implications of its reasoning. Relying on the Fourth Amendment, the majority asserts that it is constitutionally unreasonable to *use* deadly force against fleeing criminal suspects who do not appear to pose a threat of serious physical harm to others. By declining to limit its holding to the use of firearms, the Court unnecessarily implies that the Fourth Amendment constrains the use of any police practice that is potentially lethal, no matter how remote the risk.

Although it is unclear from the language of the opinion, I assume that the majority intends the word "use" to include only those circumstances in which the suspect is actually apprehended. Absent apprehension of the suspect, there is no "seizure" for Fourth Amendment purposes.

* * *

The Court's silence on critical factors in the decision to use deadly force simply invites second-guessing of difficult police decisions that must be made quickly in the most trying of circumstances. Police are given no guidance for determining which objects, among an array of potentially lethal weapons ranging from guns to knives to baseball bats to rope, will justify the use of deadly force. The Court also declines to outline the additional factors necessary to provide "probable cause" for believing that a suspect "poses a significant threat of death or serious physical injury," when the officer has probable cause to arrest and the suspect refuses to obey an order to halt. But even if it were appropriate in this case to limit the use of deadly force to that ambiguous class of suspects, I believe the class should include nighttime residential burglars who resist arrest by attempting to flee the scene of the crime. We can expect an escalating volume of litigation as the lower courts struggle to determine if a police officer's split-second decision to shoot was justified by the danger posed by a particular object and other facts related to the crime. Thus, the majority opinion portends a burgeoning area of Fourth Amendment doctrine concerning the circumstances in which police officers can reasonably employ deadly force. * * *

Notes and Questions

1. Does *Garner* give the police sufficient guidance as to just when they are permitted to use deadly force? Consider Uviller, *Seizure by Gunshot: The Riddle of the Fleeing Felon*, 14 N.Y.U.Rev.L. & Soc. Chg. 705, 711–13 (1986): "Unfortunately, the category of a 'dangerous' or 'violent' suspect upon which deadly force may be used to foil escape is not a clearly described or readily recognized breed. Apart from the easy cases where the fleeing felon brandishes a firearm in attempting to evade capture or is in flight from a crime, just committed, that included an armed assault, the Court's view on this point is obscure. Indeed, it would not put the opinion under great strain to interpret

it as authorizing the use of deadly force in only these easy cases. But, proceeding on the assumption that the Court did not intend to compel the states to allow all other criminals to escape if they were swift enough, we must probe the decision a bit deeper.

"For our test, let us start with this cryptic message from the heart of the opinion: 'Where the suspect poses no immediate threat to the officer and no threat to others, the harm resulting from failing to apprehend him does not justify the use of deadly force to do so.' The nature of the 'threat' the Court has in mind is clear from the opening paragraph: 'a significant threat of death or serious physical injury.' Thus, as to his own person, the officer must have a well-grounded fear of immediate and mortal injury before he may fire. In the instance of the fleeing felon, these conditions, one would suppose, cannot be met except by the actual possession of firearms or explosives, coupled with a manifest, aggressive disposition. A knife or bat, for example, cannot pose a grave threat except at close quarters. And even the armed felon who keeps his gun in his belt and runs without looking back poses no real threat of imminent injury. Nor can the police officer use his gun to capture someone because he reasonably fears that otherwise he may be subjected to attack some appreciable time thereafter. The fourth amendment's tolerance for deadly force on this basis is limited, but it's fairly clear.

"Did Justice White deliberately omit the critical adjective 'immediate' when speaking of the threat to the safety of persons other than the pursuing officer? Unless reason be strained to the fracture point, conscious craft should be assumed. Justice White probably intended to offer a wide window for speculation on the types of harm to 'others' that a police officer may shoot to avoid. I think of the automobile speeding in an erratic path toward a town,

pulling away from the pursuing patrol car. Shooting to kill a reckless, perhaps even intoxicated, driver may seem extreme, but the potential harm to others is clear. Does the constitutional litmus come up: 'reasonable'? Imagine a person wanted for a series of violent crimes, but showing no signs of being armed or violent at the moment; let him get away and he might well strike a future unknown victim in a harmful way. Does the fourth amendment allow the use of deadly force to capture that 'dangerous' person?

"About halfway into his opinion, Justice White, by way of example, indicates in the following language that the nature of the crime from which the felon flees has some bearing on the degree of force appropriate to apprehend him: 'Thus if . . . there is probable cause to believe that he has committed a crime involving the infliction or threatened infliction of serious physical harm, deadly force may be used if necessary to prevent escape, and if, where feasible, some warning has been given.' Passing the odd insertion of a requirement of warning (found nowhere else in the decision), several other curiosities appear. The first may be the unstated assumption that only those crimes of substantial physical injury are socially serious enough to risk killing the perpetrator to halt him. One can think of a number of crimes such as sexual abuse of children, extortion, major drug trafficking, racketeering, or treason that on some scales are the equal in social harm to a knifepoint street robbery. Even some 'crimes against property' such as arson might qualify as serious. Or for that matter the nighttime flatburglary— Garner's crime—might seem to some so frightening, so volatile, so deeply invasive, that it should be regarded as very serious even if the burglar is unarmed (as most legislatures do when they set up punishment quotients), notwithstanding its FBI classification as a property crime or the statistics showing the relative infrequency of actual physical violence during the commission of the crime. (Both factors were cited by the Court in reaching a contrary conclusion.)

"Does the 'prevent escape' phrase suggest a requirement of immediacy? Is the use of deadly force reasonable only if the perpetrator is in actual flight from the crime, moments after its commission, when he might still be armed and dangerous? Or is it enough that the officer have probable cause to believe that the person he shoots committed such a violent crime and is trying to evade capture? May execution of a warrant of arrest for rape, for instance, be aided by a gun if the suspect takes off, regardless of when the rape occurred, or the present inclination of the suspect to resist arrest by dangerous aggression?"

2. Does *Garner* have significance with respect to the use of nondeadly force? Consider Uviller, supra, at 709–10, noting "it is tempting to read *Garner* as creating a constitutional rule of proportionality to govern the use of any force in effecting an arrest. Under such a rule of reason, with its customary consideration of particular circumstances, a court might find excessively rough handling of a petty pickpocket to be unconstitutional, though no deadly weapon was employed. * * *

"Even taking the decision at face value, the notion of 'deadly' force is far from self-defining, particularly in the context of less-than-lethal consequences. * * *

"More chased suspects probably die in high speed vehicle pursuits (not to count the innocent bystanders) than are brought down by police gunfire. Is the trooper, stepping on the gas and opening the siren behind a wayward car, using 'deadly' means to capture the fleeing driver? A hickory club brought down upon the head of a struggling suspect is quite capable of inflicting a mortal blow. Is the swing controlled by the fourth amendment?

Some may even argue that not every gunshot amounts to 'deadly force'; an expert police marksman, drawing a clear and careful bead on his target's lower extremities, it could be said, incurs little risk of fatality.

"To compound the definitional uncertainty, Justice White in several places couples the phrase 'deadly force' with the alternative: 'or the threat of it.' This would seem to prohibit even the pointed pistol or the raised stick. 'Stop or I'll shoot' would offend the fourth amendment to the same extent as a bullet through the head. Can that be the Court's intended meaning?"

3. In *Commonwealth v. Klein,* 372 Mass. 823, 363 N.E.2d 1313 (1977), defendant, a private citizen, saw two men break into a drug store across the street from his home during the early morning hours. He telephoned the police and then went outside with a pistol, where he intercepted the thieves and told them to stop or he would shoot. They did not stop, so he fired several shots at them, wounding both of them. Defendant was thereafter convicted on two counts of assault and battery by means of a deadly weapon. The court noted "that we have never clearly set the limits of the arresting citizen's right to use deadly force.

"Thus, we must consider in this context what rules of law will best serve the public interest in this Commonwealth. Our common law has long recognized a private citizen's right to arrest. Nevertheless, limits must be set, as to the use of deadly force, against the dangers of uncontrolled vigilantism and anarchistic actions and particularly against the danger of death or injury of innocent persons at the hands of untrained volunteers using firearms. In our view, for example, there would be no wisdom in approving the unqualified right of a private citizen to use deadly force to prevent the escape of one who has committed a crime against property only.

"Some jurisdictions have adopted such limiting rules. In *Commonwealth v. Chermansky,* 430 Pa. 170, 242 A.2d 237 (1968), for example, it was held that the prerequisites to justify the use of deadly force by a private person in order to effect the arrest or prevent the escape of a felon are that the person must be in fresh pursuit of the felon and that he must give notice of his purpose to make the arrest for the felony if the attendant circumstances are themselves insufficient to warn the felon of the intention of the pursuing party to arrest him; that such felony must actually have been committed by the person against whom the force is used; *and the felony must be one which normally causes or threatens death or great bodily harm.*

"We have examined comparable law elsewhere, and we think the relevant provisions of the Model Penal Code will best serve this Commonwealth. * * * Accordingly, we establish as the law of Massachusetts the rules (in so far as they are material to the instant case) as found in § 3.07 of the Model Penal Code * * *."

The court then decided it would be unfair to apply these new standards retroactively to the defendant's conduct, but asserted that he "met the standards for justification of his use of the firearm (as we now for the first time establish them) in all respects except that the felons were not themselves engaged in a crime which threatened death or great bodily harm." Is this so?

PEOPLE v. CURTIS

Supreme Court of California, 1969.
70 Cal.2d 347, 74 Cal.Rptr. 713, 450 P.2d 33.

MOSK, JUSTICE.

Defendant Albert Allen Curtis appeals from a conviction of battery upon a peace officer, a felony. He challenges both the construction and the constitutionality of Penal Code, section 834a * * *, as applied to an allegedly unlawful arrest. We conclude that the proper construction of these sections requires a reversal of defendant's conviction.

Defendant was arrested on the night of July 9, 1966, by Lt. Riley of the Stockton Police Department. Riley was investigating a report of a prowler and had received a cursory description of the suspect as a male Negro, about six feet tall, wearing a white shirt and tan trousers. While cruising the neighborhood in his patrol car, the officer observed defendant, who matched the foregoing general description, walking along the street. Riley pulled up next to defendant and called to him to stop; defendant complied. The officer then emerged from his patrol car in full uniform and told defendant he was under arrest and would have to come along with him. Riley reached for the arm of defendant, and the latter attempted to back away. A violent struggle ensued, during which both men were injured, and defendant was finally subdued and taken into custody by several officers.

Defendant was subsequently acquitted of a charge of burglary, but was convicted of battery upon a peace officer. He challenges this conviction on several grounds.

Defendant initially contends that his arrest was unlawful due to a lack of probable cause and that it was accomplished by the use of excessive force, and therefore his resistance was justified. Under the general common law rule prevailing in most states, an unlawful arrest may be resisted reasonably, and excessive force used by an officer in effecting an arrest may be countered lawfully. Until 1957, this rule prevailed in California. However, as we shall first discuss, Penal Code section 834a, enacted in 1957, revised the first aspect of that rule.

Section 834a provides: "If a person has knowledge, or by the exercise of reasonable care, should have knowledge, that he is being arrested by a peace officer, it is the duty of such person to refrain from using force or any weapon to resist such arrest." This section, adapted almost verbatim from the *Uniform Arrest Act* (1942) 28 Virginia Law Review 315, 345, omitted the language in section five thereof which explicitly imposed the duty to refrain from resisting an arrest by force "regardless of whether or not there is a legal basis for the arrest." Moreover, section 834a follows immediately section 834, which defines "arrest" as "taking a person into custody, in a case and in the manner *authorized by law*." (Italics added.)

Nonetheless, it has been consistently held that section 834a prohibits forceful resistance to unlawful as well as lawful arrests. The legislative history of section 834a strongly supports this construction. General acceptance of this apparent intent and its adoption by courts without serious question for more than a decade cannot be ignored at this late date. We find no reason to reject the firmly-established judicial construction of section 834a.

We hold, therefore, that section 834a prohibits forceful resistance to unlawful as well as lawful arrests. Immediately, however, we are met with a challenge to the constitutionality of that construction; it is said to violate the Fourth Amendment's prohibition against unreasonable seizures and the due process clause of the Fourteenth Amendment.

An arrest is a "seizure" and an arrest without a warrant or probable cause is "unreasonable" within the purview of the Fourth Amendment. If section 834a, by eliminating the remedy of self-help, facilitates or sanctions arrests which are by definition unlawful, it could be urged with considerable persuasion that defendant's constitutional rights would be violated by the statute.

While defendant's rights are no doubt violated when he is arrested and detained a matter of days or hours without probable cause, we conclude the state in removing the right to resist does not contribute to or effectuate this deprivation of liberty. In a day when police are armed with lethal and chemical weapons, and possess scientific communication and detection devices readily available for use, it has become highly unlikely that a suspect, using *reasonable* force, can escape from or effectively deter an arrest, whether lawful or unlawful. His accomplishment is generally limited to temporary evasion, merely rendering the officer's task more difficult or prolonged. Thus self-help as a practical remedy is anachronistic, whatever may have been its original justification or efficacy in an era when the common law doctrine permitting resistance evolved. Indeed, self-help not infrequently causes far graver consequences for both the officer and the suspect than does the unlawful arrest itself. Accordingly, the state, in deleting the right to resist, has not actually altered or diminished the remedies available against the illegality of an arrest without probable cause; it has merely required a person to submit peacefully to the inevitable and to pursue his available remedies through the orderly judicial process.

We are not unmindful that under present conditions the available remedies for unlawful arrest—release followed by civil or criminal action against the offending officer—may be deemed inadequate. However, this circumstance does not elevate physical resistance to anything other than the least effective and desirable of all possible remedies; as such its rejection, particularly when balanced against the state's interest in discouraging violence, cannot realistically be considered an affirmative "seizure" or deprivation of liberty.

Thus there is no denial of due process because the deprivation of liberty which an individual suffers upon an unlawful arrest is in no substantial or practical way effectuated, sanctioned or increased by section 834a. There is no constitutional impediment to the state's policy of removing controversies over the legality of an arrest from the streets to the courtroom.

* * *

Defendant contends that his arrest was not only lacking in probable cause and thus unlawful, but also was accomplished with excessive force and hence he was justified in employing counterforce in self-defense. Some courts appear to have incorrectly treated these two problems unitarily, as if a technically unlawful arrest were identical with an overly forceful arrest.

There are, however, two distinct and separate rights at stake. The common law rule allowing resistance to technically unlawful arrests protects a person's freedom from unreasonable seizure and confinement; the rule allowing resistance to excessive force, which applies during a technically lawful *or* unlawful arrest, protects a person's right to bodily integrity and permits resort to self-defense. Liberty can be restored through legal processes, but life and limb cannot be repaired in a courtroom. Therefore any rationale, pragmatic or constitutional, for outlawing resistance to unlawful arrests and resolving the dispute over legality in the courts has no

determinative application to the right to resist excessive force. The commentators are unanimous on this point, and the Model Penal Code states it explicitly.[7] Under Penal Code, sections 835 and 835a, an officer may lawfully use only *reasonable* force to make an arrest or to overcome resistance. Sections 692 and 693 set forth the basic privilege one has to defend against unlawful force. In the absence of unequivocal language, we cannot ascribe to the Legislature an intention to penalize the exercise of a right it has specifically bestowed. * * *

The question of the exercise of reasonable force and the right to self-defense, which we emphasize is distinct from that of the lawfulness of the arrest, is for the trier of fact to determine. Here the jury had before it evidence which could justify a finding either way, depending upon the credibility of witnesses and the weight of the evidence. The court's instructions merely quoted or paraphrased the Penal Code sections regarding the privilege of self-defense, the duty not to resist an arrest, and an officer's privilege to use reasonable force in effecting an arrest. In view of our conclusions on the law, we must hold that the jury was not adequately instructed as to the rights and duties of the respective parties. * * *

Notes and Questions

1. Compare Douglas, J., dissenting from dismissal of the writ of certiorari in

7. *Model Penal Code* (Tent.Draft No. 8, 1958) section 3.04. The comments thereto state, at page 19: "The paragraph, it should be noted, forbids the use of force for the purpose of preventing an arrest; it has *no application when the actor apprehends bodily injury,* as when the arresting officer unlawfully employs or threatens deadly force, unless the actor knows that he is in no peril greater than arrest if he submits to the assertion of authority." (Italics added.)

Compare the cases holding that although only "reasonable" nondeadly force may be used to resist a technically unlawful arrest, there is no limit to the force that may be employed in self-

defense against deadly force by the arresting officer. To the same effect are the numerous cases which hold that even if an arrest is lawful, if the offense is only a misdemeanor and the officer uses deadly force in an attempt to apprehend the suspect, deadly force against the officer by the arrestee is justified. * * *

These and similar cases clearly demonstrate the distinction between the minimal degree of force, if any, permitted where the arrestee need fear loss of liberty only, and the greater, generally unlimited degree of force permitted where the arrestee's life or limb is imperiled without legal justification.

Wainwright v. New Orleans, 392 U.S. 598, 88 S.Ct. 2243, 20 L.Ed.2d 1322 (1968):

"Police officers while cruising late one night saw petitioner standing on a street corner and concluded that he fitted the general description of a murder suspect. They accosted him and asked him to identify himself. He had no identification on his person, only at home. He gave the officers his name and address, and informed them that he was a law student. The officers told him he was being questioned because he fitted the description of a murder suspect who had on his left forearm a tattoo which read, 'born to raise hell.' The officers asked him to remove the coat he was wearing so they could check his forearm, but he refused. He was then 'seized' and taken to the police station, where he was asked to remove his jacket. He refused, folding his arms and crouching in a corner. The officers then attempted to take his jacket off, each pulling on one arm. There was no battle or fracas of any consequence. Petitioner, however, did resist this attempt by moving about and by pushing one officer to one side and then pushing the other officer to the other side. But so far as the record shows no more violence happened than that produced by the combined efforts of petitioner and the officers which caused the officers to be butted around the room. He did not strike at the officers, nor kick them, and none of them had any marks or bruises or torn clothing.

"He was booked on three charges—vagrancy, resisting an officer, and reviling the police.

"At the end of the State's case petitioner moved for dismissal of the charges. That ruling was held under advisement and petitioner was at once arraigned on three new charges, one of resisting an officer and two for disturbing the peace by assaulting an officer. The trial on this second case was had and petitioner fined $25

on each charge or given 30 days in jail on each charge, the sentences being suspended. On appeal the conviction of resisting an officer was reversed, but his conviction on two charges of disturbing the peace was affirmed by the Criminal District Court and later by the Supreme Court of Louisiana, the complaint in the first case apparently being abandoned. While petitioner tried to get the appellate courts to incorporate the record in the first case into the record in the second, that was not done. But that defect has been remedied here, the transcripts of all the hearings now being before the Court.

"The records before us do not even approach establishing probable cause for arrest. The officers had no warrant. They did not see petitioner commit any crime. There was no arrest which could be justified under the heading of vagrancy. That could be made use of only by the factor of loitering, but petitioner was seen standing still for only five to 10 seconds. To be sure he did not have identification papers on him and 'very little funds.' But those factors obviously could not be ingredients of a crime under our present system of government. * * *

"Under our authorities (cf. *John Bad Elk v. United States,* 177 U.S. 529, 534–535, 20 S.Ct. 729, 44 L.Ed. 874; and see *United States v. Di Re,* 332 U.S. 581, 594, 68 S.Ct. 222, 92 L.Ed. 210), * * *, a citizen had the right to offer some resistance to an unconstitutional 'seizure' or 'search.' Must he now stand quietly and supinely while officers 'pat him down,' whirl him around, and throw him in the wagon?

"The present episode may be an insignificant one and the hurt to petitioner nominal. But the principle that a citizen can defy an unconstitutional act is deep in our system. *Thomas v. Collins,* 323 U.S. 516, 532–537, 65 S.Ct. 315, 89 L.Ed. 430.

"When in a recent case (*Wright v. State of Georgia,* 373 U.S. 284, 291–292, 83 S.Ct. 1240, 10 L.Ed.2d 349), it was said that 'failure to obey the command of a police officer constitutes a traditional form of breach of the peace,' we made a qualification: 'Obviously, however, one cannot be punished for failing to obey the command of an officer if that command is itself violative of the Constitution.'

"We should not let those fences of the law be broken down."

2. Consider Chevigny, *The Right to Resist an Unlawful Arrest,* 78 Yale L.J. 1128, 1141 (1969): "The impairment of fourth amendment rights, however, is not enough to justify resistance to an unlawful arrest. The problem is to determine the circumstances under which such a seizure becomes so provocative as to make unfair the imposition of a criminal penalty for resisting it." Is the solution, as proposed in Lerblance, *Impeding Unlawful Arrest: A Question of Authority and Criminal Liability,* 61 Denver L.J. 655, 697 (1984), to recognize a defense when "the resistance was reasonable in view of the totality of the circumstances of the encounter"?

3. The issue of whether self-help should be a defense also arises when the charge is escape. Compare:

(a) *People v. Alexander,* 39 Mich.App. 607, 197 N.W.2d 831 (1972): "On appeal, the defendant claims that his being detained after April 1, 1970, was illegal and, therefore, he was justified in escaping. The basis of defendant's argument is that under *Browning v. Michigan Department of Corrections,* 385 Mich. 179, 188 N.W.2d 552 (1971) which established the proper method of computing 'dead time', defendant's sentence should have ended on April 1, 1970. Defendant therefore argues that he was wrongfully kept in jail for more than ten months and had a right to escape.

In the case of *People v. Hamaker,* 92 Mich. 11, 52 N.W. 82 (1892), the Supreme Court held that one could not be convicted of the crime of escape if his incarceration is unlawful. Although it is not always clear just what circumstances will justify self-help on the part of a prisoner improperly detained, it is clear that personal liberty is given the utmost importance under the laws of this country:

'The right to personal liberty, is accorded a pre-eminent position under our system of law and government, and the history of the last few decades has vividly demonstrated the danger of invasions of the right by governmental agents acting under color of law, so that there is something to be said for the view that the citizen improperly deprived of his liberty should be entitled to recover it by any means available to him, *ruat coelum,* and it seems hard that one improperly imprisoned should be subjected to further punishment for merely asserting the right to liberty guaranteed him by the Constitution.' 70 A.L.R.2d 1432.

"It is our opinion that defendant should not have been prosecuted for the crime of escape if at the time he left prison he was illegally incarcerated."

(b) *Johnson v. State,* 258 Ind. 515, 282 N.E.2d 802 (1972): "Counsel for both the defense and the State have dwelled at length on the proceedings leading up to the order of confinement, attempting to convince us of their illegality or legality, as supports their respective positions. We believe these labors to be lost, however, as such is not determinative of the issue herein. Although grave doubts appear with regard to the legality of the defendant's confinement upon the contempt charge, we do not meet that issue. True, the statute applies only to escapes from 'lawful' confinement, but that does not entitle all who may question the legality of the proceedings leading to their confinement to resort to self-help. Although numerous cases involving justification for escape have arisen in other jurisdictions, the question has not previously been passed upon by this Court. We find a substantial number of decisions from other states where, under circumstances obviously lacking due process, breaking jail was found not to be a criminal offense. We have made no attempt to analyze all these cases or to reconcile them with the majority view to the contrary, which is the view we believe to square with reason. Not necessarily inconsistent with the rule that escape is justifiable where the imprisonment is 'unlawful' are a number of cases holding that where the imprisonment is under color of law, the prisoner is not entitled to resort to self-help but must apply for his release through regular legal channels, even though he might be able to show such defects in the procedure by which he was arrested, tried, sentenced, committed, or imprisoned as to justify or require his release on appeal or habeas corpus.

*   *   *

"As was said by the court in *State v. Palmer* (1950) 6 Terry 308, 45 Del. 308, 72 A.2d 442, this rather severe attitude on the part of the courts was founded upon sound public policy, since jailbreaks are extremely disruptive to prison routine, dangerous to guards, police and the public, and to make it the province of every prisoner in every jail to decide for himself whether conditions justified his escape would only serve to increase the number of attempts to break jail, so that a plea of justification for escape, if permissible at all, would be recognized only in the most extreme situations."

SECTION 5. DOMESTIC AUTHORITY

PEOPLE v. BALL

Appellate Court of Illinois, Fifth District, 1973. 15 Ill.App.3d 143, 303 N.E.2d 516.

JONES, JUSTICE: *   *   *

At the time of the incident in question the defendant was a schoolteacher, aged 54, with 23 years teaching experience, the last 7 as a sixth grade teacher in the Henry Robb School in Belleville, the site of the occurrence in question.

The prosecuting witness was a student of defendant, age 11. On the day in question the defendant's class was practicing unison exercises for an approaching school festival. The boy disrupted the practice by talking, facing in a direction opposite that of the rest of the class and doing "jumping jacks." He was directed by defendant to go to a bench alongside the schoolhouse and remain seated there until he was directed otherwise by defendant. Shortly thereafter the boy left the bench and commenced talking to a friend of his who had approached. The defendant thereupon decided that disciplinary action was necessary. He took the boy into the school and got another teacher as an observer. In the hallway of the school, outside the classroom of the observing teacher, the defendant had the boy bend down with his hands on his knees and he then struck him 10 times on the buttocks with a wooden paddle about 20 inches long, one-fourth inch thick and three inches wide. Following the paddling the defendant took the boy to the classroom and in a conversation explained why the punishment was administered and why it would help the boy. The defendant stated, and the teacher-observer confirmed, that he was not angry, had not lost his temper and remained calm and rational throughout. The boy admitted that he was wrong and deserving of punishment.

The paddling occurred at approximately 2:30 in the afternoon. When school dismissed at 3:15 the boy walked to his home and reported the paddling to his parents. His father took him to the police station and then to the home of their family doctor where they were directed to the emergency room of a local hospital. There the boy was treated by a doctor who applied a surface anesthesia and gauze bandage. The condition as described by the doctor was that the boy had severe burn-type bruises of both buttocks, the right side being worse than the left. The skin temperature was hot to the touch, there was marked discoloration and redness requiring treatment. There may have been minute abrasions in the bruised area but the main effect was one of swelling, redness, heat and a thickening of the area above the surface surrounding the skin. The redness and swelling disappeared in due course with no after effects, except that the mother testified that the boy had some lingering emotional problems stemming from the paddling. We note at this point that defendant has conceded that bodily injury was inflicted.

A written judgment order was entered in which the court merely found defendant guilty [of battery] as charged. However, in his remarks delivered from the bench the court stated that a teacher is a substitute parent and "may administer just and reasonable punishment, switch or paddle accepted." * * *

Defendant next argues that under an applicable statute and the governing case law he was acting within legally prescribed limits and the corporal punishment therefore was administered with legal justification and his conviction cannot stand. The concern of this argument is that in determining whether defendant's actions were "just and reasonable" the trial court applied an erroneous test to the evidence to determine criminal liability. With this we must agree.

Art. 24, sec. 24 of the Illinois School Code of 1961 (Ill.Rev.Stat.1971, ch. 122, art. 24, sec. 24) provides:

"Teachers and other certificated educational employees shall maintain discipline in the schools. In all matters relating to the discipline in and conduct of the schools and the school children, they stand in the relation of parents and guardians to the pupils. This relationship shall extend to all activities connected with the school program and may be exercised at any time for the safety and supervision of the pupils in the absence of their parents or guardians."

It is defendant's position that under the foregoing statute he was acting in the place of the boy's parents in administering the paddling and that under the rule established by the applicable Illinois cases the paddling he administered did not go beyond permissible limits. We are referred to three Illinois cases concerned with the administration of corporal punishment by schoolteachers, *Fox v. People,* 1899, 84 Ill. App. 270; *Drake v. Thomas,* 1941, 310 Ill. App. 57, 33 N.E.2d 889, and *City of Macomb v. Gould,* 1969, 104 Ill.App.2d 361, 244 N.E.2d 634. The rule of the *Fox* and *Drake* cases is concisely stated as the governing law in the *Gould* case as follows:

"He (a teacher) may not wantonly or maliciously inflict corporal punishment and may be guilty of battery if he does so. Whether he has done so may be inferred from the unreasonableness of the method adopted or the force employed under the circumstances. This presents a question of fact requiring reference to the evidence."

It thus becomes apparent that when the trial court, in delivering his findings from the bench, stated that a teacher may administer "just and reasonable" punishment and that the purpose of his ruling was to insure that student discipline will be "just and reasonable," he was applying criteria other than that adopted by the above cases. Those cases prohibit a teacher from wantonly or maliciously inflicting corporal punishment or from acting out of malice.

* * *

Reversed and remanded with directions.

CREBS, J., concurs.

GEORGE J. MORAN, JUSTICE (dissenting):

In my opinion the trial court properly applied the standard of "reasonableness" to determine the defendant's criminal liability for battery. In holding otherwise, the majority grants teachers more power in disciplining school children than possessed by their parents. * * *

More important than the facts of this case is the question of which standard to apply in determining whether a teacher's corporal punishment of a student constitutes battery. Two divergent standards have been applied in this country, which I shall refer to as the "reasonableness" and the "malice" tests.

The reasonableness test is clearly the rule in the majority of American courts. Its philosophical basis is that the right or privilege of a parent or teacher to discipline a child is grounded not in the adult's liberty of action, but in the child's welfare. Therefore, this discipline must not exceed what is reasonable and moderate under the circumstances, considering the age, sex, physical and mental condition of the child, the nature of his offense and his apparent motive, and whether the punishment is disproportionate to the offense, unnecessarily degrading, or likely to cause serious or permanent harm. If the punishment is unreasonable the adult is criminally liable.

The minority "malice" rule is that a parent or teacher in punishing a child acts in a judicial or quasi-judicial capacity and

is not criminally liable for an assault because of an error in judgment or because the punishment was disproportionate to the offense, but is liable only if the punishment either results in permanent injury or was inflicted with malice, either express or implied. This view is grounded more in a desire to protect the adult from liability for otherwise criminal actions than in a desire to protect children from excessive punishment and in my opinion is so concerned with the adult's "right" to punish that it overlooks the reason for the "right", which is the welfare of the child. This outmoded concept was criticized by the Supreme Court of Indiana in *Cooper v. McJunkin,* 4 Ind. 290, as long ago as 1853:

> "The public seem to cling to the despotism in the government of schools which has been discarded everywhere else. * * * The husband can no longer moderately chastise his wife; nor * * * the master his servant or apprentice. Even the degrading cruelties of the naval service have been arrested. Why the person of the schoolboy * * * should be less sacred in the eye of the law than that of the apprentice or the sailor, is not easily explained."

The rationale underlying both tests was discussed extensively in the scholarly opinion of *People v. Curtiss,* 116 Cal.App. (Supp.) 771, 300 P. 801. The court there stated that under the malice test, the teacher is the sole arbiter of the right to punish as well as the degree of punishment to be administered, subject only to the limitation as to punishment maliciously inflicted or punishment which results in disfigurement or permanent injury. The court rejected the malice test, saying:

> "The second group of cases, and the one which, to our mind, expresses the more enlightened view—a view more consonant with modern ideas relating to the relationship between parents or those standing in their place and chil-

dren—refuses to make the teacher the sole arbiter. The courts deciding these cases hold that both the reasonableness of, and the necessity for, the punishment is to be determined by a jury, under the circumstances of each case. This rule * * * seems to be universally recognized by the courts of this country. If the authority to punish be limited by reason and moderation, who, then, on sound principles, should determine whether such authority has been used in excess of its proper limits—the parents administering the punishment, or the triers of fact in a court where complaint has been made? * * *."

Fortunately, most modern decisions (except the present one) have turned away from the "malice" test. * * * Furthermore, even among the older cases applying the "malice" test almost all allow malice to be inferred, usually from excessive punishment. This is also the rule in Illinois. The majority opinion apparently overlooked the second sentence of their quotation from *City of Macomb v. Gould,* wherein it says that a teacher

"* * * may not wantonly or maliciously inflict corporal punishment and may be guilty of battery if he does so. Whether he has done so may be inferred from the unreasonableness of the method adopted or the force employed under the circumstances." * * *

The majority opinion infers that the defendant was legally justified in inflicting punishment which would otherwise be a battery upon a provision of the School Code of 1961 which provides in part:

"Teachers * * * shall maintain discipline in the schools. In all matters relating to the discipline in and conduct of the schools and the school children, they stand in the relation of parents and guardians to the pupils." Ill.Rev.Stat. 1971, ch. 122, par. 24–24.

However, the majority opinion apparently overlooks the fact that under Illinois law not even a parent may punish a child unreasonably. A parent, a step-parent, one standing in loco parentis or a school teacher are all held to the same standard of reasonableness. As the court stated in affirming an aggravated battery conviction of one standing in loco parentis in *People v. Machroli* (1968), 100 Ill.App.2d 227 at 232, 241 N.E.2d 609:

"Even if the defendant stood in loco parentis to Sharie Bianca the force he used in reprimanding the child was far beyond the acceptable standards of parental conduct. The beating applied to Sharie went far beyond reasonable force allowed under Illinois law."

Because the punishment in the present case was unreasonable, I feel that it constituted the criminal offense of battery. Had the punishment been reasonable it might have been legal, but I would still question its wisdom. Although beyond the scope of this opinion, the following sources cast light on the problem. In Aron and Katz, *"Corporal Punishment in the Public Schools,"* 6 Harvard Civil Rights—Civil Liberties Law Review 583 (1971), the authors conclude at 584–585:

"Corporal punishment in the public schools is ineffective and harmful. If mildly and irregularly applied, it is useless in controlling behavior. In order to prevent the recurrence of unwanted behavior, corporal punishment must either be applied continually or its exemplary application must have a 'terrifying and traumatic' effect. Not surprisingly, the National Education Association has concluded that corporal punishment is ineffective in reducing behavioral problems. Furthermore, an English study found that a deterioration of behavior and an increase in delinquency accompany increased use of corporal punishment.

"Corporal punishment has further deleterious effects on children. Insofar as it relies on fear, it disrupts the learning process by repressing the natural tendency of children to explore. This fear may be channeled into aggression against the teacher, against the school, or against society. At the extreme, juvenile delinquency may result. Finally, and perhaps most seriously, the use of corporal punishment may inhibit the development of self-criticism and self-direction in the child. Corporal punishment may drive students to concentrate their energies on conflict with the teacher instead of encouraging them to adjust to their classroom situation.

"While theoretically corporal punishment need not be brutal, there is no assurance that it will be inflicted moderately or responsibly. In the heat of anger, especially if provoked by personal abuse, some teachers are likely to exceed legal bounds. Moreover, if limited corporal punishment were permitted, controls would be unlikely to prevent the 'really unmistakable kind of satisfaction which some teachers feel in applying the rattan.' A total ban of this punishment would provide far more effective control.

"Finally, corporal punishment undermines human dignity. Students are placed at the mercy of teachers who have the power to beat them without explanation or justification. In an institution which purports to inculcate the value of reason in human affairs and the worth of each individual in society, it is antithetical to educate by brutality and unreason."

I would affirm the judgment of the trial court.[a]

a. On further appeal, it was held that "the trial court properly applied a reasonableness standard." 58 Ill.2d 36, 317 N.E.2d 54 (1974).

Notes and Questions

1. Considering the article quoted by Judge Moran, should any use of corporal punishment in the schools be deemed reasonable?

2. If *Ball* had been a jury case, exactly what should the jury have been told about the dimensions of the applicable defense? Consider *State v. Thorpe,* ___ R.I. ___, 429 A.2d 785 (1981), upholding, re a charge of assault upon defendant's 4–month–old daughter, an instruction that "no one has the right to inflict excessive corporal punishment upon a child." The court reasoned that there "is no inflexible rule that defines what, under all circumstances, is unreasonable or excessive force," and that the word "excessive" is "sufficient to convey the meaning that a parent may inflict corporal punishment to discipline and correct the child but may not do so to vent his/her own anger or frustration on the child."

3. Apply the "reasonableness" and "malice" tests to the following facts, taken from *People v. DeCaro,* 17 Ill.App.3d 553, 308 N.E.2d 196 (1974):

"The defendant, Donn DeCaro, was a sixth grade teacher at the Everett Elementary School in the City of Chicago on March 8, 1972. On that date he called Neal and Newton Suwe, eleven year old twin brothers, into his classroom to discuss their conduct with respect to him. Neither boy was a student in his class. The defendant testified they used obscene and defamatory language toward him and he had been informed by another student they had written obscene words about him in the snow near their home. He stated he talked to them at his desk in front of his own students, but Neal used vulgar language so he took them into the adjoining coatroom where they could not be heard by the class. The defendant placed himself in the doorway between the classroom and the coatroom in order that his own class could see him and remain orderly. When Neal lunged for the door, he picked up a 12–inch ruler from a nearby desk to frighten him. Neal collided with him and they both fell to the floor with Neal kicking and struggling. He testified he did not hit Neal with the ruler and never touched Newton.

"The boys testified the defendant hit them eight to twelve times on their buttocks and back of their legs with a stick eight to twelve inches long, which was not a ruler. The boys' mother testified Neal had bruises on his backside which lasted two weeks and Newton had bruises which lasted about six days. Pictures of the bruises were admitted into evidence.

"Three students testified they saw the Suwes struggle with the defendant and saw him wave a ruler, but none saw the defendant strike either of the Suwes. Both of the boys' teachers stated they observed them when they returned to their respective classes and noted no unusual behavior.

"Dr. Sebornik, the district superintendent of schools in the 12th District, was called to the school on the morning of March 9, 1972, and he examined the boys. He testified he saw black and blue marks on Neal and faint bruises on Newton. He also stated the defendant told him he had struck Neal several times with a 12–inch ruler."

4. In *Ingraham v. Wright,* 430 U.S. 651, 97 S.Ct. 1401, 51 L.Ed.2d 711 (1977), the Court held that the Eighth Amendment prohibition on "cruel and unusual punishment" was "designed to protect those convicted of crimes" and thus "does not apply to the paddling of children as a means of maintaining discipline in public schools." The Court added that "[t]he schoolchild has little need for the protection of the Eighth Amendment," in

that "[p]ublic school teachers and administrators are privileged at common law to inflict only such corporal punishment as is reasonably necessary for the proper education and discipline of the child; any punishment going beyond the privilege may result in both civil and criminal liability."

5. What other relationships permit resort to reasonable corporal punishment? Consider *State v. Pittard,* 45 N.C.App. 701, 263 S.E.2d 809 (1980) (day care center employee not in loco parentis re child placed in the temporary care of the center, as such "relationship is established only when the person with whom the child is placed intends to assume the status of a parent—by taking on the obligations incidental to the parental relationship, particularly that of support and maintenance"; and was not a teacher, as her "employment at the center carried with it none of the attributes of teaching nor did the evidence show that she possessed any of the credentials of a teacher").

SECTION 6. DURESS, NECESSITY AND CHOICE OF EVILS

DIRECTOR OF PUBLIC PROSECUTIONS v. LYNCH

House of Lords, 1975.
[1975] A.C. 653, [1975] 2 W.L.R. 641, [1975] 1 All E.R. 913.

Lord Morris of Borthy–Y–Gest.

* * *

The facts as described or asserted by the appellant can be briefly summarised. Many of them had been set out in a signed statement which he had made to the police. He said that while at his house he had received a message that one Sean Meehan required his presence. It was in the forefront of his case that Sean Meehan was and was known to be both a member of the I.R.A. and a ruthless gunman. The appellant had not previously known Meehan personally but had known of him.

He said that what Meehan asked to be done had to be done. "You have no other option. I firmly believe that I would have been shot for defying him." So he went with the messenger to an address in Belfast and there saw Meehan and two other men. Meehan, he said, had a rifle in his hand. After it was learned that the appellant could drive a car he was told to go with another man named Mailey (who had a small automatic gun) and seize a car. They went away. Mailey held up a car and ordered its driver to get out. The appellant was told to drive the car to the address where Meehan had remained. The appellant did so. He parked the car and was told that he would not be doing any more driving. So he returned to his own house. Some half-hour later the messenger returned and told the appellant that Meehan wanted him. He went to the same house as before. Meehan, Bates, Mailey and another man were there. Meehan who had a rifle told the appellant that he was to drive the car which he then did after Mailey (who had a gun in his pocket) had got in beside him and after Bates and Meehan had got into the back. Meehan, Bates and Mailey had combat jackets and balaclava helmets. The appellant was told to go to a particular road. He asked Meehan what he was going to do and was told: "Bates knows a policeman." Following directions given to him he drove past a garage (at which point Bates said: "That's him") and then stopped near to the garage. Meehan told him to stay there. The other three pulled up their woollen helmets and left the car and ran across the road. Then there were a number of shots fired in quick succession. The three men came running back to the car and got into it. The appellant was told to drive on—which he did. They returned to their starting point.

Witnesses gave evidence that the three men who got out of the car driven by the appellant moved swiftly towards the ser-vice bay of the garage where Constable Carroll was doing work on his own car: that shots were fired: that the constable was fatally wounded: that the three men made off towards the waiting car which was then driven away. * * *

[Appellant was charged with the murder of the constable in that he aided and abetted the killing. He was convicted and sentenced to life imprisonment. The Court of Criminal Appeal in Northern Ireland upheld the conviction, and appellant then took an appeal to the House of Lords.]

In a series of decisions and over a period of time courts have recognised that there can be circumstances in which duress is a defence. In examining them and more particularly in approaching the issue raised in this appeal the question naturally presents itself—why and on what basis can duress be raised? If someone acts under duress—does he intend what he does? Does he lack what in our criminal law is called mens rea? If what he does amounts to a criminal offence ought he to be convicted but be allowed in mercy and in mitigation to be absolved or relieved from some or all of the possible consequences?

The answer that I would give to these questions is that it is proper that any rational system of law should take fully into account the standards of honest and reasonable men. By those standards it is fair that actions and reactions may be tested. If then someone is really threatened with death or serious injury unless he does what he is told to do is the law to pay no heed to the miserable agonizing plight of such a person? For the law to understand not only how the timid but also the stalwart may in a moment of crisis behave is not to make the law weak but to make it just. In the calm of the court-room measures of fortitude or of heroic behavior are surely not to be demanded when they could not in moments for decision reasonably have been expected even of the resolute and the well disposed. * * *

The issue in the present case is therefore whether there is any reason why the defence of duress, which in respect of a variety of offences has been recognised as a possible defence, may not also be a possible defence on a charge of being a principal in the second degree to murder. I would confine my decision to that issue. It may be that the law must deny such a defence to an actual killer, and that the law will not be irrational if it does so.

Though it is not possible for the law always to be worked out on coldly logical lines there may be manifest factual differences and contrasts between the situation of an aider and abettor to a killing and that of the actual killer. Let two situations be supposed. In each let it be supposed that there is a real and effective threat of death. In one a person is required under such duress to drive a car to a place or to carry a gun to a place with knowledge that at such place it is planned that X is to be killed by those who are imposing their will. In the other situation let it be supposed that a person under such duress is told that he himself must there and then kill X. In either situation there is a terrible agonising choice of evils. In the former to save his life the person drives the car or carries the gun. He may cling to the hope that perhaps X will not be found at the place or that there will be a change of intention before the purpose is carried out or that in some unforeseen way the dire event of a killing will be averted. The final and fatal moment of decision has not arrived. He saves his own life at a time when the loss of another life is not a certainty. In the second (if indeed it is a situation likely to arise) the person is told that to save his life he himself must personally there and then take an innocent life. It is for him to pull the trigger or otherwise personally to do the act of killing. There, I think, before allowing duress as a

defence it may be that the law will have to call a halt. May there still be force in what long ago was said by Hale?

"Again, if a man be desperately assaulted, and in peril of death, and cannot otherwise escape, unless to satisfy his assailant's fury he will kill an innocent person then present, the fear and actual force will not acquit him of the crime and punishment of murder, if he commit the fact; for he ought rather to die himself, than kill an innocent."

I would allow the appeal accordingly.

LORD WILBERFORCE. * * *

It is clear that a possible case of duress, on the facts, could have been made. I say "a possible case" because there were a number of matters which the jury would have had to consider if this defence had been left to them. Among these would have been whether Meehan, though uttering no express threats of death or serious injury, impliedly did so in such a way as to put the appellant in fear of death or serious injury; whether, if so, the threats continued to operate throughout the enterprise; whether the appellant had voluntarily exposed himself to a situation in which threats might be used against him if he did not participate in a criminal enterprise (the appellant denied that he had done so); whether the appellant had taken every opportunity open to him to escape from the situation of duress.

In order to test the validity of the judge's decision to exclude this defence, we must assume on this appeal that these matters would have been decided in favour of the appellant.

What, then, does exclusion of the defence involve? It means that a person, assumedly not himself a member of a terrorist group, summoned from his home, with explicit or implied threats of death or serious injury at gunpoint, to drive armed men on what he finds to be a criminal enterprise, having no opportunity to escape, but with the certainty of being shot if he resists or tries to get away, is liable to be convicted of murder. * * *

What reason then can there be for excepting murder? One may say that murder is the most heinous of crimes: so it may be, and in some circumstances, a defence of duress in relation to it should be correspondingly hard to establish. Indeed, to justify the deliberate killing by one's own hand of another human being may be something that no pressure or threat even to one's own life which can be imagined can justify—no such case ever seems to have reached the courts. But if one accepts the test of heinousness, this does not, in my opinion, involve that all cases of what is murder in law must be treated in the same way. Heinousness is a word of degree, and that there are lesser degrees of heinousness, even of involvement in homicide, seems beyond doubt. An accessory before the fact, or an aider or abettor, may (not necessarily must) bear a less degree of guilt than the actual killer: and even if the rule of exclusion is absolute, or nearly so in relation to the latter, it need not be so in lesser cases. Nobody would dispute that the greater the degree of heinousness of the crime, the greater and less resistible must be the degree of pressure, if pressure is to excuse. Questions of this kind where it is necessary to weigh the pressures acting upon a man against the gravity of the act he commits are common enough in the criminal law, for example with regard to provocation and self-defence: their difficulty is not a reason for a total rejection of the defence. To say that the defence may be admitted in relation to some degrees of murder, but that its admission in cases of direct killing by a first degree principal is likely to be attended by such great difficulty as almost to justify a ruling that the defence is not available, is not illogical. It simply involves the recognition that by sufficiently

adding to the degrees, one may approach an absolute position.

So I find no convincing reason, on principle, why, if a defence of duress in the criminal law exists at all, it should be absolutely excluded in murder charges whatever the nature of the charge; hard to establish, yes, in case of direct killing so hard that perhaps it will never be proved: but in other cases to be judged, strictly indeed, on the totality of facts. * * *

It is said that such persons as the appellant can always be safeguarded by action of the executive which can order an imprisoned person to be released. I firmly reject any such argument. A law, which requires innocent victims of terrorist threats to be tried for murder and convicted as murderers, is an unjust law even if the executive, resisting political pressures, may decide, after it all, and within the permissible limits of the prerogative to release them. Moreover, if the defence is excluded in law, much of the evidence which would prove the duress would be inadmissible at the trial, not brought out in court, and not tested by cross-examination. The validity of the defence is far better judged by a jury, after proper direction and a fair trial, than by executive officials; and if it is said that to allow the defence will be to encourage fictitious claims of pressure I have enough confidence in our legal system to believe that the process of law is a better safeguard against this than inquiry by a government department. * * *

LORD SIMON OF GLAISDALE. * * * [I]t is convenient to have a working definition of duress—even though it is actually an extremely vague and elusive juristic concept. I take it for present purposes to denote such [well-grounded] fears, produced by threats, of death or grievous bodily harm [or unjustified imprisonment] if a certain act is not done, as overbears the actor's wish not to perform the act, and is effective, at the time of the act, in constraining him to perform it. I am quite uncertain whether the words which I have put in square brackets should be included in any such definition. It is arguable that the test should be purely subjective, and that it is contrary to principle to require the fear to be a reasonable one. Moreover, I have assumed that threat of future injury may suffice, although *Stephen's Digest of the Criminal Law* art. 10 is to the contrary. Then the law leaves it also quite uncertain whether the fear induced by threats must be of death or grievous bodily harm, or whether threatened loss of liberty suffices: cases of duress in the law of contract suggest that duress may extend to fear of unjustified imprisonment; but the criminal law returns no clear answer. It also leaves entirely unanswered whether, to constitute such a general criminal defence, the threat must be of harm to the person required to perform the act, or extends to the immediate family of the actor (and how immediate?), or to any person. Such questions are not academic ones, in these days when hostages are so frequently seized. Is it worse to have a pistol thrust into your back and a grenade into your hand, or to have your child (or a neighbour's child) seized by terrorists and held at peril until you have placed in a public building a parcel which you believe to contain a bomb?

I shall have to consider such situations in another connection in a moment. As of now I refer to them to demonstrate the uncertainty of the proffered rule of law in critical and far from fanciful situations. Surely, certainty in the law is hardly less important in the rules which exonerate from criminal responsibility than in those which impose it. Candid recognition, at the outset of the vague and amorphous nature of the proffered rule should have at least three consequences: first, to cast doubt on whether there is, or should be, any general defence of duress; secondly,

to encourage exploration whether the law has not other means of mitigating its rigours towards those who commit prohibited acts under threats which call for far more than ordinary courage to resist; and, thirdly, to cause hesitation before, in deference to logic, extending the defence beyond where it has been heretofore recognised.

And not only do your Lordships meet with uncertainty at the very outset of your inquiry, you also meet with anomaly. Where so little is clear, this at least seems to be established: that the type of threat which affords a defence must be one of human physical harm (including, possibly, imprisonment), so that threat of injury to property is not enough. But a threat to property may, in certain circumstances, be as potent in overbearing the actor's wish not to perform the prohibited act as a threat of physical harm. For example, the threat may be to burn down his house unless the householder merely keeps watch against interruption while a crime is committed. Or a fugitive from justice may say, "I have it in my power to make your son bankrupt. You can avoid that merely by driving me to the airport." Would not many ordinary people yield to such threats, and act contrary to their wish not to perform an action prohibited by law? Faced with such anomaly, is not the only answer, "Well, the law must draw a line somewhere; and, as a result of experience and human valuation, the law draws it between threats to property and threats to the person." But if any arbitrary line is thus drawn, is not one between murder and traditionally lesser crimes equally justifiable? How can an arbitrary line drawn between murder as a principal in the first degree and murder as a principal in the second degree be justified either morally or juridically? Faced with anomaly and uncertainty, may it not be that a narrow, arbitrary and anomalous general defence of duress, negativing the crime, is far less acceptable in practice and far less justifiable in juristic theory than a broadly based plea which mitigates the penalty?

Any sane and humane system of criminal justice must be able to allow for all such situations as the following, and not merely for some of them. A person, honestly and reasonably believing that a loaded pistol is at his back which will in all probability be used if he disobeys, is ordered to do an act prima facie criminal. Similarly, a person whose child has been kidnapped, and whom as a consequence of threats he honestly and reasonably believes to be in danger of death or mutilation if he does not perform an act prima facie criminal. Or his neighbour's child in such a situation. Or any child. Or any human being. Or his home, a national heritage, threatened to be blown up. Or a stolen masterpiece of art destroyed. Or his son financially ruined. Or his savings for the old age of himself and his wife put in peril. In other words, a sane and humane system of criminal justice needs some general flexibility, and not merely some quirks of deference to certain odd and arbitrarily defined human weaknesses. In fact our own system of criminal justice has such flexibility, provided that it is realised that it does not consist only in the positive prohibitions and injunctions of the criminal law, but extends also to its penal sanctions. May it not be that the infinite variety of circumstances in which the lawful wish of the actor is overborne could be accommodated with far greater flexibility, with much less anomaly, and with avoidance of the social evils which would attend acceptance of the appellant's argument (that duress is a general criminal defence), by taking those circumstances into account in the sentence of the court? Is not the whole rationale of duress as a criminal defence that it recognises that an act prohibited by the criminal law may be morally innocent? Is not an absolute discharge just such an acknowledgment of moral innocence? Nor should one even stop short at

the sentence of the court. Does not our system of criminal justice extend more widely still—to the discretion of prosecutors, to the exercise of the prerogative of mercy, to the operations of the Parole Board?

I spoke of the social evils which might be attendant on the recognition of a general defence of duress. Would it not enable a gang leader of notorious violence to confer on his organisation by terrorism immunity from the criminal law? Every member of his gang might well be able to say with truth, "It was as much as my life was worth to disobey." Was this not in essence the plea of the appellant? We do not, in general, allow a superior officer to confer such immunity on his subordinates by any defence of obedience to orders: why should we allow it to terrorists? Nor would it seem to be sufficient to stipulate that no one can plead duress as a defence who had put himself into a position in which duress could be exercised on himself. Might not his very initial involvement with, and his adherence to, the gang be due to terrorism? Would it be fair to exclude a defence of duress on the ground that its subject should have sought police protection, were the police unable to guarantee immunity, or were co-operation with the police reasonably believed itself to be a warrant for physical retribution? * * * In my respectful submission your Lordships should hesitate long lest you may be inscribing a charter for terrorists, gangleaders and kidnappers. * * *

[The concept of] *necessity* came to be used, most misleadingly, to denote a situation where circumstances faced a person, not with no choice at all, but with the choice between two evils; so that he could hardly be blamed if he chose the lesser. The classic case was the pulling down of another man's house to prevent a fire spreading. * * * But it has been decisively rejected in the criminal law generally. It is certainly not the law that what would otherwise be the theft of a loaf ceases to be criminal if the taker is starving.[a] Morally, there is a world of difference between a man who steals to satisfy his children's hunger and a man who steals to satisfy his own cupidity; but the moral distinction is marked, not by the provision of some eccentric defence in the positive law, but by the discretion of the court in its sentence. And Bacon's "necessity of conservation of life," with his example of the "necessity" of pushing a shipwrecked man off a boat's side in order to secure his place, was called in aid on behalf of the appellants in the famous and terrible case of *Reg. v. Dudley and Stephens,* 14 Q.B.D. 273. The two accused were in a ship's boat without food or water; they killed and ate the ship's boy, who was with them. The accused would otherwise probably have died before they were picked up, and the boy would probably have died before them. At the time of the homicide there was no appreciable chance of saving life except by killing someone for the others to eat. Their conviction for murder was upheld on appeal,[b] though the sentence was respited.

Attempts have been made to explain this case away; but the appellants' argument rested on Bacon's "necessity of conservation of life"; and the rejection of any such doctrine was, in my view, the ratio

decidendi. Unless some distinction can be drawn in principle between "necessity" and duress as defences to a charge of murder, the instant appellant can, I think, only succeed if *Reg. v. Dudley and Stephens* is overruled—unless, indeed, a distinction is to be drawn in these regards between principals in the first and second degrees.

In my opinion no distinction can be based on the degree of participation. I have already rehearsed the arguments in support of the concept of duress as a defence (the absence of moral blameworthiness and the inappropriateness of punishment in such circumstances); there are no different arguments relating to "necessity" as a defence: and none affords any ground for distinguishing between principals in the first or second degrees respectively. It is, with all respect, irrational to say, "The man who actually pulls the trigger is in a class by himself; he is outside the pale of any such defence as I am prepared to countenance." He cannot on any sensible ground be put in a class by himself: the man who pulls the trigger because his child will be killed otherwise is deserving of exactly the same consideration as the man who merely carries the gun because he is frightened. * * *

---

a. In *State v. Moe,* 174 Wash. 303, 24 P.2d 638 (1933), the unemployed defendants were convicted of grand larceny and riot for taking groceries from a store. They were not allowed to prove the conditions of poverty under which they were living. The court affirmed, noting:

"Economic necessity has never been accepted as a defense to a criminal charge. The reason is that, were it ever countenanced, it would leave to the individual the right to take the law into his own hands. In larceny cases economic necessity is frequently invoked in mitigation of punishment, but has never been recognized as a defense. Nor is it available as a defense to the charge of riot. The fact that a riot is spontaneous makes it none the less premeditated. Premeditation may and frequently does, arise on the instant. A lawful assembly may turn into a riotous one in a moment of time over trivial incident or substantial provocation. When it does, those participating are guilty of riot, and neither the cause of the

riot nor their reason for participation in it can be interposed as a defense. The causes, great or small, are available to the participants only in mitigation of punishment. The court did not err in rejecting the offer of proof."

b. In that case, Lord Coleridge, C.J., stated:

"It must not be supposed that in refusing to admit temptation to be an excuse for crime it is forgotten how terrible the temptation was; how awful the suffering; how hard in such trials to keep the judgment straight and the conduct pure. We are often compelled to set up standards we cannot reach ourselves, and to lay down rules which we could not ourselves satisfy. But a man has no right to declare temptation to be an excuse, though he might himself have yielded to it, nor allow compassion for the criminal to change or weaken in any manner the legal definition of the crime."

So the question must be faced whether there is a sustainable distinction in principal between "necessity" and duress as defences to a charge of murder as a principal. In the circumstances where either "necessity" or duress is relevant, there is both actus reus and mens rea. In both sets of circumstances, there is power of choice between two alternatives; but one of those alternatives is so disagreeable that even serious infraction of the criminal law seems preferable. In both the consequence of the act is intended, within any permissible definition of intention. The only difference is that in duress the force constraining the choice is a human threat, whereas in "necessity" it can be any circumstance constituting a threat to life (or, perhaps, limb). Duress is, thus considered, merely a particular application of the doctrine of "necessity". In my view, therefore, if your Lordships were to allow the instant appeal, it would be necessary to hold that *Reg. v. Dudley and Stephens* either was wrongly decided or was not a decision negativing "necessity" as a defence to murder; and, if the latter, it would be further incumbent, I think, to define "necessity" as a criminal defence, and lay down whether it is a defence to all crimes, and if not why not. It would, in particular, be necessary to consider Hale's dissent from Bacon as to the starving man stealing a loaf of bread. It would be a travesty of justice and an invitation to anarchy to declare that an innocent life may be taken with impunity if the threat to one's own life is from a terrorist but not when from a natural disaster like ship- or plane-wreck.

In my respectful submission such questions—why, if duress is available as a defence to a principal in the second degree, it should not also be available to a principal in the first degree; and what is the difference in principle between "necessity" and duress that should make the latter but not the former a defence to murder—cannot simply be shrugged off by an assertion that one's judgment goes no further than the facts instantly under consideration. One of the tests of the validity of a legal rule is to see whether its implications stand up to examination. A refusal to submit a rule to such an examination can only be justified if anomaly is considered as a positive virtue in the law. * * *

A sane system of criminal justice does not permit a subject to set up a countervailing system of sanctions nor by terrorism to confer criminal immunity on his gang. A humane system of criminal justice does not exact retribution from those who infringe the substantive provisions of its code under stresses greater than ordinary human nature can bear, nor attempt, by making an example of them, to deter those who in the nature of things are beyond deterrent. A sane and humane system of criminal justice is sufficiently flexible to reconcile such considerations, and to allow for all their infinite degrees of interaction. I have ventured to suggest that our own system of criminal justice is capable of such sanity and humanity—provided always that it is recognized to extend beyond the mere injunctions and prohibitions and immunities of the substantive criminal code.

There is, however, an apparent exception to such flexibility. This is constituted where a crime has a fixed penalty—specifically, murder with its fixed penalty of life imprisonment. It is true that prosecutors have a discretion whether to indict; but such discretion is hardly real in the circumstances which fall for your Lordships' instant consideration. It is true that the Home Secretary can advise exercise of the royal prerogative of mercy, and that the Parole Board can mitigate the rigour of the penal code; but these are executive not forensic processes, and can only operate after the awful verdict with its dire sentence has been pronounced. Is a sane and humane law incapable of encompassing this situation? I do not believe so.

An infraction of the criminal code under duress does not involve that the conduct is either involuntary or unintentional. The actor is therefore responsible for his act. But his responsibility is diminished by the duress: his is no longer actus volui, but coactus volui. Provocation operates similarly to diminish the responsibility, transmuting the great crime of murder to the lesser crime of manslaughter with no fixed penalty.

The English common law evolved the concept of provocation. Since the Homicide Act of 1957 the provocation may originate in a third party, making the doctrine even closer to that of duress. The Scottish common law evolved another concept of diminished responsibility for homicide (*H. M. Advocate v. Dingwall* (1867) 5 Irv. 466). In my judgment the English common law is well capable of accommodating duress under the concept of diminished responsibility reducing murder to manslaughter. This was the way duress was treated in the South African case of *Reg. v. Hercules,* 1954 (3) S.A. 826; and it seems to me to be the conception of duress in relation to homicide which has greatest juridical cogency. * * *

LORD KILBRANDON. My Lords, the learned trial judge directed the jury to the effect that the defence of duress is not available as exculpation in a charge of murder, whether the accused has been charged as a principal in the first or in the second degree. In my opinion, that direction correctly stated the law as it then stood and now stands. * * * [I]f the present law be altered, coercion will be a good defence to one who, at the behest of a mafia or I.R.A. boss, places a bomb in an aircraft and 250 people are killed. It is more likely, too, that the accused will have assisted by preparing and delivering the bomb knowing its intended use; in that case the question would be, coercion is a good defence to murder as a principal in the second degree or as accessary. This

situation was long ago foreseen. The closing passage of the judgment in *Reg. v. Dudley and Stephens* points out that, if the defence were a good one, the strongest man on board the boat might have eaten his way through all the crew, killing them one by one, and after his rescue have been held guiltless. How many may a man kill in order to save his own life? I pose such a question for the purpose of suggesting that it cannot be answered in this place. It raises issues, some legal, others social, even more ethical, upon which the public will clamour to be heard. In short, the policy questions are so deeply embedded in the legal doctrines we are being asked to review that we may be in danger of reforming the law upon an inadequate appreciation of public needs and public opinion. What would purport to be a judgment declaratory of the common law would in reality be a declaration of public policy. * * *

LORD EDMUND–DAVIES. * * *

If the circumstances are such that "the ordinary power of human resistance" is overborne, why should they not render excusable even the unlawful killing of an innocent person? Several reasons have been advanced for asserting that no duress, however terrible, can save such a participator in unlawful killing as the appellant from being convicted of murder. One of these has already been referred to and is epitomised by the observation of Lord Coleridge C.J., in *Reg. v. Dudley and Stephens,* 14 Q.B.D. 273, 287 that: "To preserve one's life is generally speaking a duty, but it may be the plainest and the highest duty to sacrifice it." Such an approach was elaborately dealt with in *S. v. Goliath,* 1972 (3) S.A. 1 where the Appellate Division held that on a charge of murder compulsion can be a complete defence. In giving the majority judgment, Rumpff J. developed the submission of defence counsel, at p. 6 that, "the criminal law, should not be applied as if it were a blueprint for saintliness but rather in a manner in which it can be obeyed by the reasonable man," by saying at p. 25:

"It is generally accepted * * * that for the ordinary person in general his life is more valuable than that of another. Only those who possess the quality of heroism will intentionally offer their lives for another. Should the criminal law then state that compulsion could never be a defence to a charge of murder, it would demand that a person who killed another under duress, whatever the circumstances, would have to comply with a higher standard than that demanded of the average person. I do not think that such an exception to the general rule which applies in criminal law is justified."

It has also to be remembered that lack of "heroism" may not necessarily be selfishly self-directed, for the duress exerted may well extend to and threaten the lives and safety of others, and, as has been said, " * * * when a third person's life is also at stake even the path of heroism is obscure" * * *.

A second ground advanced in support of the proposition that duress affords no defence in murder is said to have public policy as its basis. Murder, it is rightly said, is a crime so grave that no facilities should be afforded to the murderer to escape conviction and punishment. It is then added that duress is a plea easy to raise and that (the onus to destroy it being upon the prosecution) it may prove impossible to rebut it, however dark the suspicion that it is not well-founded, and that in this way the murderer may well escape retribution. But this is true of many other pleas which extenuate or even extinguish criminal culpability—drunkenness, for example, as destroying criminal intent, or an alibi which may serve to eliminate criminal

involvement of any kind—and no course is open other than to repose confidence in the tribunal of fact to discharge its duty of scrutinising with care the evidence adduced. In this respect, the risk of a miscarriage of justice by a guilty man being acquitted is no greater in murder trials than in those cases in which the plea of duress is, on the authorities, clearly available, despite their gravity—for example, even in attempted murder, where an intent actually to kill is an essential ingredient. Nor should the present grave state of affairs prevailing in Northern Ireland, to which prosecuting counsel very understandably referred, lead this House to arrive at a conclusion different from that which would be proper were Ireland trouble-free. * * *

Notes and Questions

1. Dennis, *Duress, Murder and Criminal Responsibility,* 96 L.Q.Rev. 208, 208–09 (1980), reports: "Two years later, in *Abbott v. R.,*[4] another court of five Law Lords, sitting this time as the Judicial Committee of the Privy Council, held by a majority that at common law duress was not available as a defence to a person charged with murder as a principal in the first degree. The minority in *Abbott* consisted of Lord Wilberforce and Lord Edmund–Davies, who had formed part of the majority in *Lynch.* In their strongly-worded dissenting opinion, they abandoned the usual judicial reticence and accused the majority of 'sidestepping the decision in *Lynch* . . . and even were that constitutionally appropriate, to do it without advancing cogent grounds.' * * *

"Abbott was charged with the murder of a girl named Gale Benson. He had been a member of a commune occupying a house in Trinidad. The commune had been presided over by one Michael Malik,

4. [1977] A.C. 755 (hereafter referred to as *Abbott*).

alias Michael X. The case against Abbott was that, on the directions of Malik, he had taken an active part in the brutal murder of Gale Benson. She had been repeatedly stabbed and then buried alive. On his own testimony, Abbott had held the girl while she was stabbed by another and he had then helped three other men to throw earth on her while she was still alive. He claimed in his defence that he had acted as he had because Malik had made threats to kill him and his mother if Malik's instructions were not obeyed. The trial judge in Trinidad refused to leave the issue of duress to the jury, and subsequently sentenced Abbott to death after the jury had convicted him of murder."

2. American case law generally states the defense of duress in narrow terms, so that it "does not excuse taking the life of an innocent person" and excuses lesser crimes only if the coercion is "present, imminent, and impending and of such a nature as to induce a well grounded apprehension of death or serious bodily injury if the act is not done" and if in addition the actor had no "reasonable opportunity to avoid doing the act without undue exposure to death or serious bodily injury." State v. St. Clair, 262 S.W.2d 25 (Mo. 1953). In State v. Dissicini, 126 N.J.Super. 565, 316 A.2d 12 (1974), the contention that the defense should be available to one who aided and abetted a killing was summarily dismissed "because the argument has little merit." In Tully v. State, 730 P.2d 1206 (Okl.Crim.1986), the court held that "this limitation to the duress defense is restricted to crimes of intentional killing, and not to felony-murder."

Model Penal Code § 2.09 states the defense somewhat more broadly, and comparable provisions are to be found in several of the modern codes. Even where such provisions are lacking, courts have some-times been influenced by the Model Penal Code approach. Illustrative is State v. Toscano, 74 N.J. 421, 378 A.2d 755 (1977), where the defendant, charged with conspiracy to obtain money by false pretenses, testified that he prepared a fraudulent insurance claim after being directed to do so by one Leonardo, who threatened him several times over the telephone. The trial judge refused to charge the jury on the defense of duress because there had been no showing of a "present, imminent and impending" threat of harm. Reversing, the court concluded that "a per se rule based on immediate injury may exclude valid claims of duress by persons for whom resistance to threats or resort to official protection was not realistic," and ruled that henceforth "duress shall be a defense to a crime other than murder if the defendant engaged in conduct because he was coerced to do so by the use of, or threat to use, unlawful force against his person or the person of another, which a person of reasonable firmness in his situation would have been unable to resist."

Consider the fact situations set out in notes 3 through 7 below with a view to determining what the boundaries of the duress and necessity defenses ought to be.

3. Knapp was riding with Stratton and Thompson in Stratton's car. Stratton assaulted the driver of another car, and the victim's car was then taken to a remote area. Stratton sent Knapp in his car to a nearby town to obtain tools to aid in stripping the car. When Knapp returned, the stripping was nearly completed. The items were then loaded into Stratton's car; Stratton later dropped Knapp off at home with the stolen car stereo. Knapp, charged with larceny, testified that he participated in the larceny "because he feared what Stratton would do to him if he refused," a fear which "even extended to the moment when Stratton dropped the

defendant off at home with the stolen car stereo." [a]

4. Unger, who was serving a term of 1 to 3 years in the state penitentiary, was charged with the crime of escape. At trial, he "testified that at some time during the first two months of his imprisonment, while he was working in the clothing room, he was threatened by an inmate who possessed a 6–inch knife and defendant was told he would be required to engage in homosexual activity with the inmate. Defendant requested and received a transfer to the minimum security honor farm where, one week later, on March 2, 1972, he was beaten and forcibly sexually assaulted by a gang of prisoners. In his testimony he named three of the assailants. He stated that he did not tell the authorities about the incident because he was told he would be killed if he did so and was afraid he would be killed. Several days following the attack, on March 7, 1972, he received a phone call in the evening while working at the dairy farm. The caller (whose voice he did not recognize) informed him that he would be killed that evening as the caller had heard that defendant had gone to the authorities about the sexual assault and the beating. After receiving the call, Unger walked off the dairy farm. He was apprehended two days later in a motel room in St. Charles, Illinois. He was still wearing his prison clothes. He stated in his testimony that he left the honor farm in fear of his life and intended to return to the institution." [b]

5. Francese and Tripodi, engaged in illegal gambling activities, have been charged with bribery of members of the city gambling squad. They "testified that they were fearful of legal reprisals from the police should they fail to pay them. Francese testified that one of the [officers] threatened to plant incriminating evidence on him if he stopped paying. When he did cease his payments, the police raided his establishment five times in succession, sometimes without a warrant. He testified that he was also beaten by the police for having stopped the payments. Once, when Tripodi would not pay off on a bet allegedly placed by Detective Court (but denied by Tripodi), the gambling squad parked its van in front of Tripodi's store, obviously to deter any gambling operations thereat, until he relented and paid Detective Court $1,000. This Tripodi believed, was the kind of occurrence which he was paying to prevent. Once, when he was raided, he approached Detectives Bradford and Weber to ascertain the reason therefor—as he had been making his payments. He was informed that the gambling squad had not initiated the raid. All of the gamblers involved herein recognized that if they did not pay they would be harassed and put out of business by the police." [c]

6. "On August 10, 1971 defendant, then 19 years-of-age, while at the Green Isle Bar in the company of his brother, witnessed a murder. Notwithstanding the fact that there were 30 other patrons in the bar at the time of the shooting, defendant emerged as the sole eyewitness. All the other patrons claimed they had not witnessed the incident.

a. *State v. Knapp,* 147 Vt. 56, 509 A.2d 1010 (1986), holding defendant was not entitled to a duress instruction.

b. In *People v. Unger,* 33 Ill.App.3d 770, 338 N.E.2d 442 (1975), aff'd 66 Ill.2d 333, 5 Ill.Dec. 848, 362 N.E.2d 319 (1977), the defendant's conviction was reversed. The court held it was error for the trial judge to instruct that the reasons given for the escape were immaterial and not to be considered as justifying or excusing the escape.

c. Cf. *People v. Court,* 52 A.D.2d 891, 383 N.Y.S.2d 66 (1976), where the defendants were the police, charged with receiving the bribes. The court ruled that the situation "reeks with coercion" and that consequently the gamblers were not accomplices of the police, so that an indictment based upon the gamblers' testimony alone was valid.

"Defendant appeared before the Grand Jury on September 8, 1971 and testified that a man known to him as Ricciardi (alias Tony Long) took out a pistol, shot one Reda, and then left the tavern.

"From the time of his Grand Jury testimony and continuing up to February, 1973, defendant intermittently received threats against his own life and well-being as well as against his family. He relayed the threats to the office of the District Attorney, advised the District Attorney that he was unwilling to identify Ricciardi as the killer and voiced his intention of leaving the jurisdiction.

"Forthwith, the District Attorney had him arrested as a material witness and confined to jail on high bail. Defendant remained in jail for approximately one month, unable to furnish the bail set. During his confinement he changed his mind and indicated his willingness to cooperate with the prosecution and to testify in accordance with his testimony before the Grand Jury. Thereupon his bail was reduced and, by the posting of $2,000 cash, his father effected his release.

"On April 18, 1973 defendant importuned both the District Attorney and the Trial Judge that he not be forced to testify against Ricciardi as he feared for his life. Notwithstanding such request, defendant was sworn. In essence he recanted his Grand Jury testimony. Thereupon the trial court granted an order of dismissal and released Ricciardi. Based on defendant's trial testimony, he was indicted for perjury." [d]

d. In *People v. Colgan,* 50 A.D.2d 932, 377 N.Y.S.2d 602 (1975), the conviction was reversed because defendant had not been allowed to introduce evidence bearing upon the defense of duress. Compare *People v. Carradine,* 52 Ill.2d 231, 287 N.E.2d 670 (1972), affirming a contempt citation against a woman who refused to testify about a homicide she had witnessed because she feared retaliation by members of the Blackstone Rangers, a youth gang. As for the prosecutor's offer of protection, she testified: "Well, look, Judge, I am going to tell you, I live in the middle of the slums,

7. "Mrs. Stevison (appellant) was cashier of the Bank of Sesser, in Sesser, Illinois, for more than 25 years. In the period from May 12 to October 10, 1970, her daughter wrote 48 checks—ranging in amounts from $100 to $20,000—drawn on the Sesser Bank against her account. The account had insufficient funds to cover the checks. Her daughter drew three other checks against an account of the fictitious Indiana and Kentucky Health Care Development, an account maintained at another bank, payable to herself which the appellant cashed at the Sesser Bank when the account of the Health Care Development had insufficient funds to cover the checks. All of the checks drawn on the Sesser Bank account, amounting to $52,800, were paid by appellant from the Sesser Bank's cash items and deducted by her from undivided profits. * * * She asserts that her daughter 'coerced' her into covering the overdrafts by threatening to commit suicide." [e]

8. Under the common law doctrine of "coverture," when a married woman engaged in criminal conduct in her husband's presence, there arose a rebuttable presumption that the wife had been coerced by her husband. Most jurisdictions now reject this doctrine as "outdated and inapplicable to modern society." *Commonwealth v. Santiago,* 462 Pa. 216, 340 A.2d 440 (1975). Compare *Goodwin v. State,* 506 P.2d 571 (Okl.Cr.1973), retaining the coverture doctrine but concluding that "the presumption is slight and may be rebutted by slight circumstances."

down in the slums. Where I live the police don't even come in there even if we call. I called the police one night about a fight. You'd think they were going to kill one another. But the police don't even come up in there where I live. So how are they going to protect me and my family when they don't even come up in the building where we live?"

e. *United States v. Stevison,* 471 F.2d 143 (7th Cir.1972), holding the trial court did not unduly limit development of the coercion defense.

STATE v. WARSHOW

Supreme Court of Vermont, 1979.
138 Vt. 22, 410 A.2d 1000.

BARNEY, CHIEF JUSTICE.

The defendants were part of a group of demonstrators that travelled to Vernon, Vermont, to protest at the main gate of a nuclear power plant known as Vermont Yankee. The plant had been shut down for repairs and refueling, and these protestors had joined a rally designed to prevent workers from gaining access to the plant and placing it on-line.

They were requested to leave the private premises of the power plant by representatives of Vermont Yankee and officers of the law. The defendants were among those who refused, and they were arrested and charged with unlawful trespass.

The issue with which this appeal of their convictions is concerned relates to a doctrine referred to as the defense of necessity. At trial the defendants sought to present evidence relating to the hazards of nuclear power plant operation which, they argued, would establish that defense. After hearing the defendants' offer of proof the trial court excluded the proffered evidence and refused to grant compulsory process for the witnesses required to present the defense. The jury instruction requested on the issue of necessity was also refused, and properly preserved for appellate review.

In ruling below, the trial court determined that the defense was not available. It is on this basis that we must test the issue.

The defense of necessity is one that partakes of the classic defense of "confession and avoidance." It admits the criminal act, but claims justification. * * *

The doctrine is one of specific application insofar as it is a defense to criminal behavior. This is clear because if the qualifications for the defense of necessity are not closely delineated, the definition of criminal activity becomes uncertain and even whimsical. The difficulty arises when words of general and broad qualification are used to describe the special scope of this defense.

In the various definitions and examples recited as incorporating the concept of necessity, certain fundamental requirements stand out:

(1) there must be a situation of emergency arising without fault on the part of the actor concerned;

(2) this emergency must be so imminent and compelling as to raise a reasonable expectation of harm, either directly to the actor or upon those he was protecting;

(3) this emergency must present no reasonable opportunity to avoid the injury without doing the criminal act; and

(4) the injury impending from the emergency must be of sufficient seriousness to outmeasure the criminal wrong.

It is the defendants' position that they made a sufficient offer of proof to establish the elements of the necessity defense to raise a jury question. The trial court rejected this contention on the ground, among others, that the offer did not sufficiently demonstrate the existence of an emergency or imminent danger.

This ruling was sound, considering the offer. The defendants wished to subpoena witnesses to testify to the dangers of nuclear accidents and the effect of low-level radiation. It was conceded that there had been no serious accident at Vermont Yankee, but defendants contended that the consequences could be so serious that the mere possibility should suffice. This is not the law.

There is no doubt that the defendants wished to call attention to the dangers of low-level radiation, nuclear waste, and nuclear accident. But low-level radiation and nuclear waste are not the types of imminent danger classified as an emergency sufficient to justify criminal activity. To be imminent, a danger must be, or must reasonably appear to be, threatening to occur immediately, near at hand, and impending. We do not understand the defendants to have taken the position in their offer of proof that the hazards of low-level radiation and nuclear waste buildup are immediate in nature. On the contrary, they cite long-range risks and dangers that do not presently threaten health and safety. Where the hazards are long term, the danger is not imminent, because the defendants have time to exercise options other than breaking the law.

Nor does the specter of nuclear accident as presented by these defendants fulfill the imminent and compelling harm element of the defense. The offer does not take the position that they acted to prevent an impending accident. Rather, they claimed that they acted to foreclose the "chance" or "possibility" of accident. This defense cannot lightly be allowed to justify acts taken to foreclose speculative and uncertain dangers. Its application must be limited to acts directed to the prevention of harm that is reasonably certain to occur. Therefore the offer fails to satisfy the imminent danger element. The facts offered would not have established the defense.

These acts may be a method of making public statements about nuclear power and its dangers, but they are not a legal basis for invoking the defense of necessity. Nor can the defendants' sincerity of purpose excuse the criminal nature of their acts. * * *

Judgment affirmed.

HILL, JUSTICE, concurring.

While I agree with the result reached by the majority, I am unable to agree with their reasoning. * * *

The defense of necessity proceeds from the appreciation that, as a matter of public policy, there are circumstances where the value protected by the law is eclipsed by a superseding value, and that it would be inappropriate and unjust to apply the usual criminal rule. The balancing of competing values cannot, of course, be committed to the private judgment of the actor, but must, in most cases, be determined at trial with due regard being given for the crime charged and the higher value sought to be achieved.

Determination of the issue of competing values and, therefore, the availability of the defense of necessity is precluded, however, when there has been a deliberate legislative choice as to the values at issue. The common law defense of necessity deals with imminent dangers from obvious and generally recognized harms. It does not deal with non-imminent or debatable harms, nor does it deal with activities that the legislative branch has expressly sanctioned and found not to be harms.

Both the state of Vermont and the federal government have given their imprimatur to the development and normal operation of nuclear energy and have established mechanisms for the regulation of nuclear power. Implicit within these statutory enactments is the policy choice that the benefits of nuclear energy outweigh its dangers.

If we were to allow defendants to present the necessity defense in this case we would, in effect, be allowing a jury to redetermine questions of policy already decided by the legislative branches of the federal and state governments. This is not how our system of government was meant to operate. * * *

In my opinion the majority puts the cart before the horse. It measures the offer made against the requisite elements of the defense of necessity and concludes that the defendants failed to show a likelihood of imminent danger; yet it reserves judgment on the legislative policy exception to the defense. It is illogical to consider whether the necessary elements of a defense have been shown before determining whether the defense is even available in the particular situation.

The dissent, on the other hand, assumes that defendants' offer was sufficient to show not only imminent danger but also a failure of the regulatory scheme. I cannot agree with this assumption because the offer failed to show a danger not contemplated by the legislative scheme. The legislative framework was set up to deal with the very situation defendants offered to prove "might" happen. But because neither the state legislature nor Congress acted to shut down the power plant based on speculative possibilities does not, in my opinion, give rise to the questionable inference that there was an emergency which the regulatory scheme failed to avert.

* * *

BILLINGS, JUSTICE, dissenting.

* * *

The defendants offered evidence on all the requisite elements of the defense of necessity. They stated as follows:

[They had] a feeling that there was a situation of an emergency or imminent danger that would have occurred with the start up of the reactor on October 8th the time of [their] alleged crime * * * the chance * * * of the nuclear power plant having a serious accident which would cause * * * great untold damage to property and lives and health for many generations.

The defendants also stated that "there was reasonable belief that it would have been an emergency had they started that reactor up * * * there was a very good chance of an accident there for which there is no insurance coverage or very little." Specifically, the defendants offered to show by expert testimony that there were defects in the cooling system and other aspects of the power plant which they believed could

and would result in a meltdown within seven seconds of failure on the start up of the plant. In addition, the defendants went to great lengths to base their defense on the imminent danger that would result from the hazardous radiation emitted from the plant and its wastes when the plant resumed operations.

While the offer made by the defendants was laced with statements about the dangers they saw in nuclear power generally, it is clear that they offered to show that the Vermont Yankee facility at which they were arrested was an imminent danger to the community on the day of the arrests; that, if it commenced operation, there was a danger of meltdown and severe radiation damage to persons and property. In support of this contention, the defendants stated that they would call experts familiar with the Vermont Yankee facility and the dangerous manner of its construction, as well as other experts who would testify on the effects of meltdown and radiation leakage, on the results of governmental testing, and on the regulation of the Vermont Yankee facility. These witnesses were highly qualified to testify about the dangers at the Vermont Yankee facility based either on personal knowledge or on conditions the defendants offered to show existed at the time of the trespass.

Furthermore, the defendants offered to show that, in light of the imminent danger of an accident, they had exhausted all alternative means of preventing the start up of the plant and the immediate catastrophe it would bring. Under the circumstances of imminent danger arising from the start up of the plant, coupled with the resistance of Vermont Yankee and government officials, which the defendants offered to prove, nothing short of preventing the workers access to start up the plant would have averted the accident that the defendants expected.

Through this offer, it cannot be said, without prejudgment, that the defendants failed to set forth specific and concrete evidence, which, if proven, would establish the existence of an imminent danger of serious proportions through no fault of the defendants which could not be averted without the trespass. Whether the defendants' expectations and opportunities were reasonable under the circumstances of this case is not for the trial court to decide without hearing the evidence. From a review of the record, I am of the opinion that the offer here measured up to the standard required and that the trial court struck too soon in excluding the offered evidence.

I would also dissent from the concurring opinion in so far as it attempts to hide behind inferences that the legislature precluded the courts from hearing the defense of necessity in the instant case. Even assuming that such inferences can be drawn from the regulatory schemes cited, they have no bearing on this case. We were asked to infer under the facts, which the defendants offered to prove (that they were acting to avert an imminent nuclear disaster), that the legislative branch of government would not permit the courts of this state to entertain the defense of necessity because it had legislatively determined nuclear power to be safe. Were the defense raised without any offer to show an imminent danger of serious accident, it might fail both because defendants did not offer evidence on imminent danger and on the basis of legislative preclusion. But, where, as here, the defendants offer to prove an emergency which the regulatory scheme failed to avert, the inference of preclusion is unwarranted. The defendants are entitled to show that although there is a comprehensive regulatory scheme, it had failed to such an extent as to raise for them the choice between criminal trespass and the nuclear disaster which

the regulatory scheme was created to prevent. * * *

Notes and Questions

1. The defendants in *United States v. Montgomery,* 772 F.2d 733 (11th Cir. 1985), were convicted of depredation of United States Army property because they broke into a defense plant and hammered and poured blood onto nuclear missile launchers and components belonging to the Army. On appeal, the court first rejected the defendants' claim they were entitled to a necessity defense because, inter alia, the defendants "could not hold a reasonable belief that a direct consequence of their actions would be nuclear disarmament." The court of appeals then turned to the defendants' other contention:

"Defendants claim they should have been allowed to submit evidence bearing upon the defense of justification arising under international law. Defendants' argument is that their attempt to halt the manufacture of nuclear missile components, admittedly in violation of domestic law, was an effort to insulate themselves from personal responsibility for United States nuclear military policy which defendants believe is in violation of international law. Other federal courts have considered the availability of an international law defense in cases like this one and have uniformly rejected it. As authority for this defense, defendants cite the cases of several of the defendants at the Nuremberg trials after World War II. In those cases, when war crime defendants argued that they had merely followed German domestic law in committing war crimes in violation of international law, the prosecution argued that even individual private citizens have obligations under international law which may require them to violate domestic law to prevent their government from committing violations of international law. *See The Flick Case,* 6 Trials of War

Criminals Before the Nuremberg Military Tribunals Under Control Council Law No. 10, at 1192 (1952). In *The Flick Case,* German industrialists were charged with using slave labor and war prisoners in armament production. The Tribunal stated:

> International law, as such, binds every citizen just as does ordinary municipal law. Acts adjudged criminal when done by an officer of the government are criminal also when done by a private individual. The guilt differs in magnitude, not in quality. The offender in either case is charged with personal wrong and punishment falls on the offender in *propria persona.* The application of international law to individuals is no novelty.

"Despite this statement, the Tribunal acquitted the defendant plant owners and managers on a theory of necessity, because they 'had no actual control of the administration of [the slave labor program] even where it affected their own plants.' This defense was applicable except when the defendants had actively participated in procuring an increased production quota which required additional slave laborers.

"In another Nuremberg case cited by defendants, the Allies prosecuted German jurists who enforced laws which made it illegal to interfere with German domestic policies of exterminating minority groups and dissidents. *The Justice Case,* 3 Trials of War Criminals Before the Nuremberg Military Tribunals Under Control Council Law No. 10 (1951). The defendant jurists pointed to the pressure exerted on them by Hitler and his Ministry of Justice to punish severely any opposition to his policies to eliminate Jews, Poles and other undesirables. Given this influence and the jurists' propensity to submit to it, the War Crimes Tribunal concluded there was 'no merit in the suggestion that Nazi judges [were] entitled to the benefit of the An-

glo—American doctrine of judicial immunity.' The Tribunal went on to find the jurists were not justified in punishing private individuals pursuant to domestic law who had acted to impede or escape Nazi programs that were in violation of international law.

"Defendants here misperceive the persons for whom such a Nuremberg 'defense' is appropriate. There the German defendants were in positions which required them to participate in sentencing dissidents to death or in utilizing slave labor because domestic law or superior authority ordered them to do so. The question is whether what they were required to do by domestic law could escape international criminal proscription. The War Crimes Tribunal ruled, however, that in certain circumstances those defendants were charged with a duty not to act in accordance with domestic law to avoid liability under international law. Defendants in the case before us stand this doctrine on its head in arguing that a person charged with no duty or responsibility by domestic law may voluntarily violate a criminal law and claim that violation was required to avoid liability under international law. The domestic law simply did not require defendants to do anything that could even arguably be criminal under international law. The attempt to transfer the Nuremberg defense out of context to the case before us was properly rejected by the district court."

2. Consider the fact situations set out in the notes following with a view to determining what the boundaries of the necessity defense ought to be. In that connection, compare the defense as defined in *Warshow* with Model Penal Code § 3.02 (concerning choice of evils) and with the proposal in Comment, 29 U.C. L.A.L.Rev. 409, 435 (1981), that the defense be reformulated to consist of these three elements: (i) "the result of the criminal act must be the socially desirable out-

come" (thus excluding "those fact situations where the alternative outcomes cannot be comparatively measured"); (ii) "the benefit of the criminal act must outweigh the social cost associated with it"; and (iii) "the criminal act need not be the only alternative," just "the least costly alternative."

3. Debra Braun has been charged with trespass because of her participation with others in a demonstration within the reception area of a health clinic which offers a variety of health care services, including first trimester abortions. Braun has explained that she engaged in this conduct because she wished both "to save the life of unborn fetuses" and "to protect the health and well-being of the women who were going into the Clinic that day for abortions." [a]

4. An American ship left Liverpool for Philadelphia with a crew of 17 and 65 passengers. The vessel struck an iceberg and began sinking rapidly. The captain, the second mate, 7 crew members and one passenger got into a lowered jolly-boat. The first mate, 8 seamen and 32 passengers got into a long-boat. The remaining 31 passengers went down with the ship. The next morning, the long-boat began to leak, and that night the situation worsened because of wind and rain. Because it appeared the overloaded boat might sink, the crew threw 14 male passengers overboard in response to the first mate's directions that man and wife should not be parted and that women should be spared. The next morning everyone yet on the longboat was rescued by a passing ship. A member of the crew who participated in these acts was charged with manslaughter.[b]

5. On Monday, Michel challenged Lindsey to a fight and, when Lindsey declined, charged him with a knife. Lindsey fended Michel off and escaped and then filed a complaint with the police. On Tuesday, Lindsey was told by fellow employees that Michel said he would "get" Lindsey. When Lindsey left for work on Wednesday, he carried a firearm although he was not licensed to do so. Michel approached Lindsey on the street and pulled a knife, and when Michel was six feet away and still advancing, Lindsey drew his gun and fired at Michel. Lindsey has now been charged with unlawfully carrying a firearm.[c]

6. Theodore Patrick, charged with kidnapping, "was contacted by a group of parents who believed their daughters were members of a 'dangerous religious cult,' and, at a meeting with the parents on July 16, 1973, defendant agreed to 'deprogram' the women. Later defendant came to Denver and, as a result of arrangements made by the parents previous-

---

a. *Sigma Reproductive Health Center v. State,* 297 Md. 660, 467 A.2d 483 (1983), holding the defense of necessity was not available on such facts. See Note, 48 U.Cin.L.Rev. 501 (1979).

b. See *United States v. Holmes,* 26 F.Cas. 360 (No. 15,383) (C.C.E.D.Pa.1842), where the seaman was convicted and sentenced to six months at hard labor and a fine of $20. A petition to Pres. Tyler for a pardon, joined in by the convicting jury, was denied because not joined in by the presiding judges. The seaman served his sentence of imprisonment, but the fine was remitted. See F. Hicks, *Human Jettison* 275–76 (1927).

c. *Commonwealth v. Lindsey,* 396 Mass. 840, 489 N.E.2d 666 (1986) (affirming defendant's conviction and mandatory one-year sentence; though it "is possible that the defendant is alive today only because he carried the gun that day for protection," necessity instruction properly refused, for were the court "to establish an exception * * * for an unlicensed person to carry a firearm in public if he reasonably believed he was likely to be threatened with serious bodily harm," this "would exonerate every unlicensed person who wants to carry a gun. Such a person wants to carry a gun precisely because he fears that at some time he might be threatened with serious bodily injury"). Compare *State v. Crawford,* 308 Md. 683, 521 A.2d 1193 (1987) (necessity instruction required re charge of unlawful possession of handgun where defendant testified that after being attacked and shot in his apartment he wrestled the gun away and in doing so fell out the window onto the street and then, upon hearing footsteps approaching picked up the gun to defend himself).

ly, on August 23, 1973, drove one of the parents' cars to the parking lot of a medical center in Denver, where Dena Thomas (age 21) worked. While Dena Thomas and Kathy Markis (age 23) were attempting to drive out of the parking lot in their automobile, defendant effectively blocked their exit with the car he was driving. This made it possible for Dena's father, (who had been chasing the women's car on foot) to unlock the door of the women's car, and, together with Kathy's father, to push their way into the car and drive the women away without their consent. The young women were driven to Eldorado Springs, Colorado, where they were detained for two days, while defendant undertook his 'deprogramming' procedure." [d]

7. Sam Diana was charged with possession of marijuana. He is a victim of multiple sclerosis and says he uses marijuana because it "is the only reasonably effective drug for relief of the disabling spasticity associated with multiple sclerosis." He is prepared to prove that his experience in finding relief via use of marijuana is supported by recent medical research, that the drugs which his doctors legally prescribed for him had unpleasant side effects and were not as effective as marijuana in relieving his symptoms, and that he had tried to obtain marijuana from his doctors but they refused because of the illegal status of the drug. The state Controlled Substances Therapeutic Research Act recognizes marijuana as a medicinal drug and makes it available under controlled circumstances to

alleviate the effects of glaucoma and cancer chemotherapy. [e]

8. Ronald Cooley escaped with others from the District of Columbia jail by crawling through a window from which a bar had been removed and then sliding down a knotted bedsheet. He later explained that he escaped because of prison conditions. "Construed in the light most favorable to [him], this evidence demonstrated that the inmates of Northeast One, and on occasion the guards in that unit, set fire to trash, bedding, and other objects thrown from the cells. According to the inmates, the guards simply allowed the fires to burn until they went out. Although the fires apparently were confined to small areas and posed no substantial threat of spreading through the complex, poor ventilation caused smoke to collect and linger in the cellblock." Cooley was apprehended a month after his escape. He "testified that his 'people' had tried to contact the authorities, but 'never got in touch with anybody,'" and suggested his sister had been told the FBI would kill him when he was apprehended. [f]

SECTION 7. CONSENT AND CONDONATION

MODEL PENAL CODE

[Examine § 2.11 in the Appendix.]

Notes and Questions

Consider the utility of the consent concept as a means for resolving the matter of

---

d. *People v. Patrick*, 541 P.2d 320 (Colo.App. 1975), holding the trial court properly refused to instruct on a choice of evils defense. Compare *United States v. Patrick*, 532 F.2d 142 (9th Cir. 1976) (trial judge found defendant not guilty on ground parents had reasonable belief their daughter in danger and that they not able to recapture her alone, so their necessity defense could be claimed by their agent Patrick). See Note, 80 Mich.L.Rev. 271 (1981).

e. *State v. Diana*, 24 Wash.App. 908, 604 P.2d 1312 (1979), remanding for receipt of such evi-

dence of medical necessity. Compare *State v. Tate*, 102 N.J. 64, 505 A.2d 941 (1986), and see Note, 46 Geo.Wash.L.Rev. 273 (1978).

f. *United States v. Bailey*, 444 U.S. 394, 100 S.Ct. 624, 62 L.Ed.2d 575 (1980), holding such evidence insufficient to require an instruction on the necessity defense. See Fletcher, *Should Intolerable Prison Conditions Generate a Justification or an Excuse for Escape?*, 26 U.C.L.A.L.Rev. 1355 (1979).

criminal liability in each of the following fact situations.

1. *Consent by nonresistance?* Evans, a glib bachelor of 37, struck up a conversation with a 20–year old college student, Lucy, upon her arrival at LaGuardia Airport. Posing as a psychologist, Evans said he was doing a magazine article and asked Lucy to answer questions for an interview. He offered to drive her to her destination, Grand Central Station, but on the way he stopped at a singles bar, which he explained was for the purpose of conducting a sociological experiment in which he would observe her reactions and the reactions of males towards her in that setting. After several hours there, Lucy accompanied Evans to an apartment where the psychological interviewing continued. Evans explained that he was searching for the missing link between the "girl-woman" and the "woman-girl." After they had been in the apartment over an hour, Evans pulled Lucy onto an open sofa-bed and attempted to disrobe her, but she resisted. Evans then said that he was disappointed that she had failed this part of his psychological experiment, by which he was trying to reach her inner-most consciousness. He added: "Look where you are. You are in the apartment of a strange man. How do you know that I am really who I say I am? How do you know that I am really a psychologist? I could kill you. I could rape you. I could hurt you physically." Evans then played on Lucy's sympathy by telling her a story about his lost love, how Lucy reminded him of her, and the hurt that he had sustained when she had driven her car off a cliff. Acting instinctively, Lucy stepped forward and

reached out for him; he grabbed her and said, "You're mine, you are mine." Sexual intercourse followed. Lucy left the apartment the following morning and some time thereafter contacted the police. Evans, arrested and later charged with rape, admitted the intercourse to the police and explained that the psychology routine was a "game that he played with girls' heads." [a]

2. *Consent by mistake?* "The complainant, a young girl of eighteen, went to bed at her mother's home after she had spent the evening with her boyfriend. The bed was very near the window of her room which was wide open. It was her habit to sleep without wearing night attire. The defendant, a young man who was walking down the street, looked in through the window and decided to enter it. He took off his clothes before pulling himself on to the window sill. While he crouched there she became aware of him and thought that he was her boy-friend with whom she had been on terms of intimacy. She sat up in bed and held out her arms to him. After they had relations there was something that made her think that he was not her boy-friend. She turned on the bedside light and slapped his face." [b] Assume that the defendant has been charged with rape.

3. *Consent and unperceived risks.* A university student seeking employment was told by the university employment office that there were no jobs available but that he could earn $50 by being the subject of a test at the university hospital. The student then spoke to the doctor who would conduct the test, who explained that he was testing a new drug by a "perfectly safe" procedure which involved putting

a. These facts are from *People v. Evans,* 85 Misc.2d 1088, 379 N.Y.S.2d 912 (1975), finding the defendant not guilty of rape. On the nature and scope of effective consent as a defense to a charge of rape, see Comment, 43 U.Chi.L.Rev. 613, 637–45 (1976).

b. 88 L.Q.Rev. 458 (1972), commenting on *Reg. v. Collins,* [1972] 3 W.L.R. 243, [1972] 2 All E.R.

1105. The charge in *Collins* was burglary rather than rape, and the court held the defendant could not be convicted if his entry was based on the belief he had been invited to enter. See Scutt, *Fraudulent Impersonation and Consent in Rape,* 9 U.Queens.L.J. 59 (1975).

electrodes on the subject's arms, legs and head and inserting a catheter into the vein of his left arm. The student agreed to undergo the test and signed a consent form so indicating. The test involved a new anaesthetic agent which the doctor had not previously used or tested in any way, and the procedures were as had been described to the student, except that the catheter was advanced through the various heart chambers out into the pulmonary artery. When the student began coughing, indicating he was on the verge of waking up, the concentration of anaesthesia was increased, resulting in the student suffering a complete cardiac arrest. The doctor took appropriate medical steps to get the heart functioning again, but the student remained unconscious for four days. He was discharged from the hospital 10 days later, at which time he was paid the $50. It is undisputed that the use of any anaesthetic agent involves a certain amount of risk and that in general medical practice the risk involved is balanced against the threat to life presented by the ailment to be treated.[c]

4. *Consent and sports violence.* "On January 4, 1975, a hockey game was played in Bloomington, Minnesota, between two National Hockey League teams, the Minnesota North Stars and the Boston Bruins. A skirmish occurred during the first period between Henry Boucha of the North Stars and Dave Forbes of the Bruins. As a result of that altercation, both men were assessed penalties and sent to respective penalty boxes. After their penalties had expired, and after numerous threats were made by Forbes against Boucha, both men, at a time when the game was no longer in play, were permitted to leave the penalty box and return to their team benches. Boucha left first, followed shortly by Forbes. Within a few seconds, Forbes, skating from the right rear of Boucha and carrying his hockey stick in his right hand, threw a punch in the direction of the right side of Boucha's head.

"According to the facts presented by the prosecution at the trial, the butt end of Forbes' hockey stick struck Boucha just above the right eye. The force of the blow caused Boucha to drop to the ice, stunned and bleeding profusely. Forbes then dropped his stick and pounced on the helpless Boucha. He punched him in the back of the head with his clenched fist, then grabbed the back of Boucha's head by the hair and proceeded to pound his head into the ice until Forbes was restrained by another North Star player."[d] Forbes has been charged with aggravated assault.

5. *Consent and the masochist.* "Defendant Dr. Samuels, a self-confessed sadist, released his desire to inflict physical pain on others by producing and acting in motion pictures depicting sado-masochistic behavior. One of these films—showing defendant whipping a naked man gagged and suspended from the ceiling—was voluntarily turned over to the police by the developer, Eastman Kodak. The victim was never located or formally identified, but the defendant testified that the victim was a masochist who consented to the physical

---

c. These facts are essentially those in *Halushka v. Univ. of Saskatchewan*, 53 D.L.R.2d 436 (1965), holding the doctor liable in tort. For a discussion of possible criminal liability in cases of this sort, see Skegg, *'Informed Consent' to Medical Procedures*, 15 Med.Sci.Law 125 (1975).

d. Flakne and Caplan, *Sports Violence and the Prosecution*, Trial 33, 34 (Jan.1977). The court declared a mistrial when the jury, after 18 hours of deliberations, could not reach agreement, and the prosecutor elected not to try Forbes again.

See also DiNicola & Mendeloff, *Controlling Violence in Professional Sports*, 21 Duquesne L.Rev. 843 (1983); Hallowell and Meshbesher, *Sports Violence and the Criminal Law*, Trial 27 (1977); Comment, 13 Am.Crim.L.Rev. 235 (1975); Comment, 1975 Wis.L.Rev. 771; Note, 22 Ariz.L.Rev. 919 (1980); Note, 1986 Duke L.J. 1030.

abuse depicted in the film." [e] Dr. Samuels has been charged with aggravated assault.

6. *"Consent" to die.* (a) A patient in a hospital has been advised by his doctor that he is suffering from a terminal illness. The doctor has undertaken, by the use of drugs and other treatment, to prolong the patient's life and to reduce his pain to the extent possible. The patient, preferring to forego prolonged suffering, has asked the doctor to refrain from any further treatment which would have the effect of delaying the time of death. The doctor honored this request, and the patient died shortly thereafter as a result. The doctor has been charged with criminal homicide.[f]

(b) The defendant's "eighty-one year-old sister, who had a painful, deteriorating heart condition, had 'pleaded' for assistance in ending her life. The defendant

e. Recent Case, 81 Harv.L.Rev. 1339 (1968), commenting on *People v. Samuels,* 250 Cal.App. 2d 501, 58 Cal.Rptr. 439 (1967), upholding the defendant's conviction on the ground that the consent was legally ineffective because "[i]t is a matter of common knowledge that a normal person in full possession of his mental faculties does not freely consent to the use, upon himself, of force likely to produce great bodily injury."

Compare Leigh, *Sado–Masochism, Consent, and the Reform of the Criminal Law,* 39 Modern L.Rev. 130 (1976), contending that if the victim consents to sado-masochistic activities there should be no criminal liability unless the conduct results in "mutilation," "disfigurement, either permanently or for an extended period," or "serious impairment of mental or physical powers either permanently or for a protracted period."

f. See Kennedy, *The Legal Effect of Requests by the Terminally Ill and Aged Not to Receive Further Treatment from Doctors,* 1976 Crim.L. Rev. 217.

g. Note, 86 Colum.L.Rev. 348, 360 (1986), observing this occurred in a state which does not specifically make suicide assistance a statutory offense, and that the defendant received a 6–year suspended sentence after her no-contest plea to voluntary manslaughter.

"Suicide is not a crime under the statutes of any state in the United States. Nor does any state, by statute, make attempting suicide a

hooked a vacuum cleaner hose to the end of the exhaust pipe of the family car, gave her sister the other end of the hose, said goodbye, and left, closing the garage door." [g]

(c) A "member of the Hmong tribe from the mountains of Laos living in the United States exercised his right under Hmong culture to execute his adulterous wife." [h] The wife was also a member of that culture and subscribed to its tenets.

7. *Retroactive consent?* Mr. *A* enticed Ms. *B* to his apartment and attempted to entice her to have sexual intercourse with him. *B* refused to consent and asked to leave, but *A* proceeded with his intentions nonetheless, to which *B* manifested her consent only after penetration had occurred. *A* has now been charged with rape.[i]

crime. In twenty-two states and three United States territories, however, assisting a suicide is a crime. If an assistant participates affirmatively in the suicide, for instance by pulling the trigger or administering a fatal dose of drugs, courts agree that the appropriate charge is murder." Id. at 348.

The Note proposes: "An act otherwise constituting criminal assistance to suicide is not punishable if the defendant proves by clear and convincing evidence that: i) the suicidal individual was a competent adult who was suffering from permanent physical incapacitation, or ii) the suicidal individual and the defendant were engaged in a genuine suicide pact at the time of the act." Id. at 372.

h. Note, 99 Harv.L.Rev. 1293 (1986), proposing recognition of a cultural defense in the criminal law. As for the boundaries of such a defense, "if there is a victim, courts should inquire whether the crime is confined to voluntary participants within the defendant's culture. A cultural defense should more readily be admitted when the crime is limited to persons capable of meaningful consent who belong to that culture and subscribe to its tenets." Id. at 1309.

i. Essentially the fact situation assumed in 2 W. Burdick, *The Law of Crime* 236 (1946), concluding: "If penetration alone completes the act, it is illogical and unsound to say that consent may follow the penetration." Why?

STATE v. GAROUTTE

Supreme Court of Arizona, 1964.
95 Ariz. 234, 388 P.2d 809.

BERNSTEIN, JUSTICE.

The defendant, Wayne Garoutte, was charged by direct information in the Superior Court of Maricopa County, Arizona, with the crime of manslaughter in the driving of a motor vehicle, a misdemeanor, said crime happening on or about May 21, 1961. The defendant filed a motion to dismiss on the basis of A.R.S. § 13–1591 [1] which was granted. The order of the trial judge dismissing the charge was as follows:

"The misdemeanor with which defendant herein is charged arises as an alleged law violation based upon defendant's negligence and which negligence is defined under the manslaughter statute (13–456ARS) as a necessary element of the offense charged. In such respect, therefore, and unlike the usual criminal charge where criminal intent is a necessary element of the crime, the elements of negligence under civil and common law principals [sic] appear to enter into a determination of this particular type of offense.

"The statute in question (13–1591ARS) can not be considered as an isolated fragment of our legal system. The manslaughter statute involving operation of motor vehicles (13–456ARS) passed by the legislature in 1957 must necessarily be considered and construed in the light of the whole body of the law on this subject

matter as it existed when that 1957 act was enacted into law, and the legislature is presumed to know of long established laws and procedures when passing new legislation. This is in accordance with well established rules of statutory construction.

"The statute in question (13–1591ARS), which has been in effect since 1901 and applied by the courts for sixty years, specifically recognizes civil satisfaction in a misdemeanor charge based upon compromise of the civil rights and causes of action growing out of the same alleged negligent act of the defendant which forms the basis for the criminal charge. If such satisfaction is accomplished according to the provisions of this statute, then the action appropriately may be dismissed.

"The Court, upon the evidence and stipulation of facts entered into between the County Attorney and counsel for defendant, FINDS:

"That the widow and legal representative of the minor children of the decedent appeared before the court and acknowledged receipt of financial satisfaction and payment of damages for the injuries sustained and in compromise and settlement of all civil causes of action arising from the act in question; that the satisfaction and damages paid, as aforesaid, were fair and substantial in amount; that there was no criminal intent on the part of defendant in committing the act in question; that the death in question resulted solely from negligence on the part of defendant; and that the widow and said decedent requested

---

1. "A. When a defendant is accused of a misdemeanor for which the person injured by the act constituting the offense has a remedy by a civil action, the offense may be compromised as provided in this section, except when the offense is committed by or upon any officer of justice while in the execution of the duties of his office, or when the offense is committed riotously, or with intent to commit a felony.

"B. If the party injured appears before the court in which the action is pending at any time before trial, and acknowledges that he has re-

ceived satisfaction for the injury, the court may, on payment of the costs incurred, order the prosecution dismissed, and the defendant discharged. The reasons for the order shall be set forth and entered of record on the minutes and the order shall be a bar to another prosecution for the same offense.

"C. No public offense shall be compromised or the prosecution or punishment upon a compromise dismissed or stayed except as provided by law.

that defendant not be prosecuted under the pending charge.

"IT IS ORDERED, therefore, that for the foregoing reasons the complaint against defendant herein be and the same is hereby dismissed, pursuant to defendant's motion.

"DONE IN OPEN COURT this 10 day of August, 1961."

The state appealed. * * *

In principle, civil suits and criminal prosecutions should be kept separate. The law should treat rich and poor alike, and the fact that a man might be able to pay for damages due to his negligence should not save him from criminal prosecution. But in practice, this principle is not always applied in misdemeanors, and some states, Arizona among them, have adopted statutes similar to A.R.S. § 13–1591, supra, authorizing the dismissal of misdemeanor cases where the injured party has been compensated. Miller, *"The Compromise of Criminal Cases,"* 1 Southern California L.Rev. 1.

New York was among the first states to adopt this policy. * * *

In 1849, the New York Commissioners on Practice and Pleading, in explaining the policy of the statute, said:

> " 'There are many cases, which are technically public offences, but which are in reality rather of a private than a public nature, and where the public interests are better promoted by checking than by encouraging criminal prosecutions. Of this class are libels, and simple assaults and batteries; or those which are not committed by or upon an officer of justice, while in the execution of the duties of his office, or riotously, or with an intent to commit a felony. With these exceptions, cases of this nature have by the policy of our statutes, always been considered fit subjects of compromise. * * * ' "

The California Act from which the Arizona statute was derived, was first adopted in 1850. The Arizona compromise statute was adopted in 1864. Other states with similar legislation include Alaska, Georgia, Louisiana, Montana, Oregon, Pennsylvania, Virginia and Wisconsin.

Until modern traffic problems arose, manslaughter, as the lowest degree of homicide, was a felony in Arizona. It was never thought that the taking of a human life could be paid for and forgotten.

"Misdemeanor Manslaughter" made its appearance in Arizona law with the adoption of A.R.S. § 28–691 in 1950. * * * On both occasions where the statute was before this court, the crime created was described as a "high misdemeanor".

In the light of this history the problem presented to us here is whether the compromise statute includes "high misdemeanors". The statute, A.R.S. § 13–103, divides crimes only into felonies and misdemeanors, and bases its classification on the term and place of imprisonment. The classification of misdemeanors as "high misdemeanors" or "misdemeanors" is a common law judicial classification. It is based on the seriousness of the crime and has nothing to do with the term or place of confinement or judgment. Arizona statutes make no distinction between high misdemeanors and mere misdemeanors. The legislature is presumed to have known of the compromise statute when it created misdemeanor manslaughter.

After the adoption of the Arizona compromise statute, courts in other states warned against the public evils of extending the compromise statute to all crimes which might be classed by statute as misdemeanors. See e.g. *Commonwealth v. Heckman,* 114 Pa.Super. 70, 172 A. 28 (1934).

The situation calls for clarification by the legislature. A bill which would specifically exclude misdemeanor manslaughter from the compromise statute is now pending before it. The present state of the law has this incongruous result. If a drunk or reckless driver does not hit anyone, he may go to jail. If guilty, he cannot escape punishment. There is no "injured person" or "injured party" or possible "remedy by civil action," and the compromise statute may not be invoked. But if he damages property, hits someone, or even kills them, under the compromise statute he may completely escape criminal punishment by paying civil damages.   *   *   *

Chapter 9

ATTEMPTS

SECTION 1. MENTAL STATE

PEOPLE v. HARRIS

Supreme Court of Illinois, 1978.
72 Ill.2d 16, 17 Ill.Dec. 838, 377 N.E.2d 28.

WARD, CHIEF JUSTICE.

[T]he defendant was convicted on a charge, made by information, of the attempted murder of Joyce Baker on the night of November 18, 1975, in a country area east of Champaign. In a separate count the defendant was charged with aggravated kidnapping.

The alleged murder attempt took place while Miss Baker was sitting inside her car and the defendant was standing behind the car with a pistol in his hand. The defendant and Miss Baker had been keeping company. For much of the evening they had been engaged in an argument in which the defendant accused the victim of infidelity. As the argument became more heated, the defendant, who was driving, reached down and picked up a revolver from the floor of the car and placed it in his lap with the barrel pointed toward Miss Baker. He made several remarks which Miss Baker interpreted as threats to kill her.

Alarmed, she opened the door on her side of the car, got out and began to run away, but ran into a barbed wire fence, injuring her leg. The defendant also got out of the car. He did not pursue her, but remained standing by the car. After her collision with the fence, Miss Baker returned to the car, and made an unsuccessful attempt to capture the gun, which the defendant was holding in his hand and pointing in her general direction. Miss Baker then got into the car on the driver's side, and drove off toward a nearby farmhouse. She testified that as she drove off she looked in the rear vision mirror and saw the defendant standing behind the car. He was holding the gun with both hands, and pointing it at her. Then she heard something strike the rear window, and the broken pane of glass in the rear window fell out of its frame. There were no other witnesses, but following this episode the police were summoned, and they found the defendant walking down the road near the scene of the episode just described. When the car was located, the police officers testified, the rear glass was broken, and a bullet fragment was found on the left side of the rear seat.

The jury returned a verdict of guilty on the charge of attempted murder and a verdict of not guilty on the aggravated kidnapping charge. The defendant was sentenced to serve a term of not less than 4 years and not more than 12 years.
* * *

540

The following instructions to the jury were tendered by the State and were given, over the objection of the defendant:

"A person commits the crime of attempt who, with intent to commit the crime of murder, does any act which constitutes a substantial step toward the commission of the crime of murder. The crime attempted need not have been committed."

"To sustain the charge of attempt, the State must prove the following propositions:

First: That the defendant performed an act which constituted a substantial step toward the commission of the crime of murder; and

Second: That the defendant did so with intent to commit the crime of murder.

*   *   *

"A person commits the crime of murder who kills an individual if, in performing the acts which cause the death, he intends to kill or do great bodily harm to that individual."

The defendant objected to the last of the instructions on the ground that it told the jury it could find him guilty of attempted murder if the jury found that he had acted only with the intent to do great bodily harm and did not have the intent to cause death. *   *   *

The central difficulty *   *   * arises out of the difference between the elements of the offense of attempt and those of the specific offense attempted, murder. The definition of attempt, contained in section 8–4(a) of the Criminal Code of 1961, is:

"A person commits an attempt when, with intent to commit a specific offense, he does any act which constitutes a substantial step toward the commission of that offense."

The statutory definition of murder is found in section 9–1(a) of the Code, and reads:

"A person who kills an individual without lawful justification commits murder if, in performing the acts which caused the death:

(1) He either intends to kill or do great bodily harm to that individual or another, or knows that such acts will cause death to that individual or another; or

(2) He knows that such acts create a strong probability of death or great bodily harm to that individual or another; or

(3) He is attempting or committing a forcible felony other than voluntary manslaughter."

The crime of murder is thus committed not only when a person intends to kill another individual, but also when he intends to do great bodily harm (par. 9–1(a)(1)), or when he knows that his acts create a strong probability of death or great bodily harm (par. 9–1(a)(2)), or when he is attempting or committing a forcible felony (par. 9–1(a)(3)).

This court held in *People v. Koshiol* (1970), 45 Ill.2d 573, 262 N.E.2d 446, that in a trial for attempted murder it is not error to give an instruction defining the elements of murder. As was stated there, "[I]t would seem utterly meaningless to instruct a jury on attempt to commit a 'specific offense' without defining the specific offense *   *   *." Since an attempted murder requires an intent to kill, however, it is obvious that the "specific offense" referred to in section 8–4(a) cannot be construed as incorporating the alternative definitions of murder contained in section 9–1(a) in their entirety.

The point is illustrated by *People v. Viser* (1975), 62 Ill.2d 568, 343 N.E.2d 903, in which the indictment in a prosecution for attempted murder charged that the defendants' acts were committed while they were engaged in a forcible felony. With respect to the indictment in *Viser,* it was observed: "[T]he offense of attempt requires 'an intent to commit a specific offense' * * * while the distinctive characteristic of felony murder is that it does not involve an intention to kill. There is no such criminal offense as an attempt to achieve an unintended result."

This court in *People v. Muir* (1977), 67 Ill.2d 86, 8 Ill.Dec. 94, 365 N.E.2d 332, and *People v. Trinkle* (1977), 68 Ill.2d 198, 12 Ill.Dec. 181, 369 N.E.2d 888, considered, among other questions, whether it was proper in prosecutions for attempted murder to include in instructions to the jury the definition of murder under section 9–1(a)(2), that is, that one commits murder if he knows that his acts "create a strong probability of death or great bodily harm."

In *Muir* the evidence was that the defendant was being approached by a police officer who was investigating a reported burglary at a nearby building. When the officer was about 30 feet away, the defendant pointed a pistol at him and pulled the trigger, but the gun failed to discharge. The defendant then began to run away. While running he pointed his gun at the officer for a second time, and pulled the trigger. Again the pistol failed to go off. It was subsequently ascertained that the barrel of the pistol contained two cartridges which were jammed in the barrel.

The indictment charged that the defendant " * * * did with the intent to commit the offense of Murder in violation of Section 9–1a2 of Chapter 38, Illinois Revised Statutes take a substantial step towards the commission of said offense in that he did without lawful justification point a loaded gun at [name of officer] and pull the trigger knowing such acts

created a strong probability of death or great bodily harm * * *."

The appellate court had reversed the conviction on the ground that the necessary ingredient of specific intent was lacking in the indictment. This court in turn reversed the decision of the appellate court. It approved those parts of the appellate court opinion which held that it was necessary in a charge of attempted murder to allege a specific intent to commit murder, and that such intent could be inferred from the character of the defendant's actions. It was held, however, that since the indictment did charge that the defendant intended to commit murder, the additional charge that the defendant had acted with the knowledge that his acts created a strong probability of death or great bodily harm did not invalidate the indictment.

In *Muir* the court also rejected a contention by the defendant that it was error for the court to have given at the request of the prosecution an instruction that "[a] person commits the crime of murder who kills an individual if, in performing the acts which cause the death, he knows that such acts create a strong probability of death or great bodily harm to that individual."

The circumstances in *Trinkle* were these: The defendant had been refused further service at a tavern after the bartender concluded that he was already intoxicated. The defendant, after threatening to "shoot or blow up the bar," left the premises, purchased a gun, returned to the vicinity of the tavern and fired a shot at the front door of the building. The shot struck a patron who, without the defendant's knowing of it, was standing behind the door.

The indictment in *Trinkle* charged in part:

"David Francis Trinkle committed the offense of ATTEMPT (MURDER) in that said defendant did perform a substantial step toward the commission of that offense in that he did without lawful justification shoot Gayle Lane with a gun knowing that such act created a strong probability of death or great bodily harm to Gayle Lane or another * * *."

The following instructions were given to the jury:

"A person commits the crime of attempt who, with intent to commit the crime of murder, does any act which constitutes a substantial step toward the commission of the crime of murder.

The crime attempted need not have been committed."

"A person commits the crime of murder who kills an individual if, in performing the acts which cause the death he knows that such acts create a strong possibility of death or great bodily harm to that individual or another."

"To sustain the charge of attempted murder, the State must prove the following propositions:

FIRST: That the defendant performed the acts which caused the injury of Gayle E. Lane;

SECOND: That when the defendant did so, he knew that his act created a strong probability of causing death or great bodily harm to Gayle E. Lane, or another; * * *."

This court correctly held that both the indictment and the instructions were defective in that they permitted the jury to find the defendant guilty of attempted murder if it concluded that the defendant knew that his acts created a strong probability of great bodily harm to another person even if the evidence did not show that the defendant had acted with an intent to kill.

Although [the instruction in this case] follows the language of section 9–1(a)(1) rather than that of section 9–1(a)(2), as in *Trinkle*, it is subject to the same objection that it permits the jury to return a verdict of guilty upon evidence that the defendant intended only to cause great bodily harm short of death. An instruction must make it clear that to convict for attempted murder nothing less than a criminal intent to kill must be shown.

The part of the holding in *Muir* that an instruction was not erroneous which charged that proof only that a defendant knowingly and intentionally created a strong probability of death or great bodily harm to another person satisfies the intent element required for attempted murder was error and is hereby overruled. Erroneous also was that part of the holding that an indictment for attempted murder was not defective which alleged that the defendant's acts to his knowledge created a strong probability of death or great bodily harm to another person. That part too of the holding in *Muir* is overruled. Observations of LaFave and Scott (*Criminal Law* sec. 59, at 428–29 (1972)) are representative of authority that it is not sufficient to prove attempted murder to show that the accused intended to cause serious bodily harm:

"Some crimes, such as murder, are defined in terms of acts causing a particular result plus some mental state which need not be an intent to bring about that result. Thus, if A, B, and C have each taken the life of another, A acting with intent to kill, B with an intent to do serious bodily injury, and C with a reckless disregard of human life, all three are guilty of murder because the crime of murder is defined in such a way that any one of these mental states will suffice. However, if the victims do not die from their injuries, then only A is guilty of attempted murder; on a charge of attempted murder it is not sufficient to show that the defendant intended to do serious bodily harm or that he acted in reckless disregard for human life. Again, this is because intent is needed for the crime of attempt, so that attempted murder requires an intent to bring about that result described by the crime of murder (*i.e.,* the death of another)." * * *

Reversed and remanded. * * *

Notes and Questions

1. Compare with *Harris* the case of *People v. Castro,* 657 P.2d 932 (Colo. 1983), holding there *is* such a crime as attempted extreme indifference murder. A statute says one commits an attempt "if, acting with the kind of culpability otherwise required for commission of an offense, he intentionally engages in conduct constituting a substantial step toward the commission of the offense." The crime of extreme indifference murder then consisted of these elements: (1) under circumstances manifesting extreme indifference to the value of human life; (2) "intentionally" engaging in conduct that creates a grave risk of death to another; and (3) thereby causing the death of another. The court reasoned:

"It is quite obvious that the statutory ingredients of attempted extreme indifference murder do not postulate a logical or legal inconsistency by requiring an intent to engage in an unintentional act. The crime of extreme indifference murder requires an intentional state of mind with respect to proscribed conduct. The actor must be aware of his conduct and have a conscious object to engage in it. This form of consciously directed action is the antithesis of the unintentional conduct which the defendant erroneously ascribes to the crime of extreme indifference murder. Because the underlying offense of

extreme indifference murder entails intentional rather than unintentional conduct, the defendant's assertion that the crime of attempted extreme indifference murder requires an intent to commit an unintentional act is without legal foundation."

2. Compare with *Viser,* discussed in *Harris,* the case of *Amlotte v. State,* 456 So. 2d 448 (Fla.1984): "We find that whenever an individual perpetrates or attempts to perpetrate an enumerated felony, and during the commission of the felony the individual commits, aids, or abets a specific overt act which could, but does not, cause the death of another, that individual will have committed the crime of attempted felony murder. Because the attempt occurs during the commission of a felony, the law, as under the felony murder doctrine, presumes the existence of the specific intent required to prove attempt."

3. In *People v. Weeks,* 86 Ill.App.2d 480, 230 N.E.2d 12 (1967), defendant was convicted of attempting to commit voluntary manslaughter,[a] on a charge which alleged that "he, acting under a sudden and intense passion, resulting from serious provocation by Omar Joel, attempted to shoot Omar Joel with intent to kill or do great bodily harm." The court reversed: "We have previously held that the 'intent' required for conviction of the offense of Attempt must be a 'specific intent'. The act that constitutes the attempt must result from some calculation on the part of the accused. Voluntary Manslaughter, on the other hand, precludes any calculation but can only result from 'a sudden and intense passion' that is itself triggered by a 'serious provocation'. The passion engendered by the provoca-

---

a. The Illinois voluntary manslaughter statute provided: "A person who kills an individual without lawful justification commits voluntary manslaughter if at the time of the killing he is acting under a sudden and intense passion resulting from serious provocation by:

"(1) The individual killed, or

"(2) Another whom the offender endeavors to kill, but he negligently or accidentally causes the death of the individual killed.

"Serious provocation is conduct sufficient to excite an intense passion in a reasonable person."

tion must be sufficiently intense to vitiate the normal, self-imposed controls against the criminal act. An act cannot be both the result of a 'sudden and intense passion' and a calculated goal of prior deliberation. It is either one or the other but it cannot be both. Consequently, we agree that there can be no such crime as an Attempt to commit a Voluntary Manslaughter."

Sachs, *Is Attempt to Commit Voluntary Manslaughter a Possible Crime?*, 71 Ill.B.J. 166, 167 (1982), asserts that the "rule of *Weeks*," which "has been rejected in most other states," "is not logically or legally persuasive." Is this so? Why? May the same be said for *Harris*?

4. *Weeks* relied upon *People v. Brown*, 21 A.D.2d 738, 249 N.Y.S.2d 922 (1964), holding that there is no crime of attempted manslaughter with respect to a manslaughter statute which defined that crime as a killing "committed without a design to effect death." (See, with regard to the current New York code, *People v. Zimmerman*, 46 A.D.2d 725, 360 N.Y.S.2d 127 [1974], holding there is no crime of attempted manslaughter when manslaughter is defined as causing death "by a reckless act." Citing *Brown,* the court concluded one "may not intentionally attempt to cause the death of another human being by a reckless act.") Was the reliance upon *Brown* in *Weeks* justified?

5. Yet another variety of manslaughter recognized in several jurisdictions is that in which the defendant's defense of self defense to a charge of murder is "imperfect" because the defendant's belief in the need for the force used was unreasonable. *State v. Grant*, 418 A.2d 154 (Me.1980), holds there can be no such thing as an attempt to commit this kind of manslaughter, as it is "a logical impossibility." Is this so?

6. Do not such cases as *Castro* and *Amlotte* represent the better view, i.e., that the mens rea requirement for an attempt should be not greater than for the com-

pleted crime? Enker, *Mens Rea and Criminal Attempt*, 1977 A.B.F.Res.J. 845, 848, states the argument in favor of such a rule: "The protection of society by incapacitating and correcting the socially dangerous is thought to be best achieved by subjecting them to the correctional process before they do harm. If the lesser forms of mens rea are a sufficient predicate for criminal liability for harm done, arguably they should equally be so for harm risked. For it is the mens rea that is the true indicium of the defendant's dangerousness. The actor's guilt ought not to depend on the fortuitous chance that the harm risked did not ensue."

7. But Enker ultimately decides, at 859, that the *Harris–Viser* approach is best because "attempt differs from substantive crime in that it combines mens rea of intent with an undefined actus reus. While this risks violation of the principle that punishment should be based on previously defined criminal conduct, it is made necessary and is justified by the fact that the actor's harmful intent is not merely the basis for ascribing to him culpability but is itself the source of potential harm. The extreme tendency of attempt to reach purely subjective guilt is controlled to a degree by notions of mere preparation and impossibility.

"Situations in which the actor did not intend to cause harm do not call for the use of this technique. Recklessly dangerous conduct should indeed be penalized, but as a substantive crime in which the actus reus is defined as precisely as the circumstances permit while the actor's mens rea determines his personal guilt. The ordinary requirements of harm and of conduct, in conjunction with the principle of legality, will determine just how broadly the actus reus should be defined."

8. Consider *Model Penal Code* § 5.01. Comment (1985): "The requirement of purpose extends to the conduct of the

actor and to the results that his conduct causes, but his purpose need not encompass all of the circumstances included in the formal definition of the substantive offense. As to them, it is sufficient that he acts with the culpability that is required for commission of the completed crime.

"Several illustrations may serve to clarify the point. Assume, for example, a statute that provides that sexual intercourse with a female under a prescribed age is an offense, and that a mistake as to age will not afford a defense no matter how reasonable its foundation. The policy of the substantive offense as to age, therefore, is one of strict liability, and if the actor has sexual intercourse with a female, he is guilty or not, depending upon her age and irrespective of his views as to her age. Suppose, however, that he is arrested before he engages in the proscribed conduct, and that the charge is an attempt to commit the offense. Should he then be entitled to rely on a mistake as to age as a defense? Or should the policy of the substantive crime on this issue carry over to the attempt as well? Or, assume a statute that makes it a federal offense to murder an FBI agent and treats the agent's status as a member of the FBI as a jurisdictional ingredient, with no culpability required in respect to that element. The question again is whether the policy of the substantive crime should control the same issue when it arises on a charge of attempt, or whether there is a special policy that the law of attempt should embrace to change the result on this point.

"Under the formulation in Subsection (1)(c), the proffered defense would not succeed in either case. In the statutory rape example, the actor must have a purpose to engage in sexual intercourse with a female in order to be charged with the attempt, and must engage in a substantial step in a course of conduct planned to culminate in his commission of that act. With respect to the age of the victim,

however, it is sufficient if he acts 'with the kind of culpability otherwise required for the commission of the crime,' which in the case supposed is none at all. Since, therefore, mistake as to age is irrelevant with respect to the substantive offense, it is likewise irrelevant with respect to the attempt. The same result would obtain in the murder illustration. The actor must, in the case supposed, engage in a substantial step in a course of conduct planned to culminate in the death of his victim. But with respect to his awareness of the status of his victim as an FBI agent, a mistake would not be relevant since the policy of the substantive offense controls on such matters and that policy is one of strict liability.

"The judgment is thus that if the defendant manifests a purpose to engage in the type of conduct or to cause the type of result that is forbidden by the criminal law, he has sufficiently exhibited his dangerousness to justify the imposition of criminal sanctions, so long as he otherwise acts with the kind of culpability that is sufficient for the completed offense. The objective is to select out those elements of the completed crime that, if the defendant desires to bring them about, indicate with clarity that he poses the type of danger to society that the substantive offense is designed to prevent. This objective is well served by the Code's approach, followed in a number of recently enacted and proposed revisions, of allowing the policy of the substantive offense to control with respect to circumstance elements. * * *

"Subsection (1)(b) provides that when causing a particular result is an element of the crime, as in homicide offenses or criminally obtaining property, an actor commits an attempt when he does or omits to do anything with the purpose of causing 'or with the belief that it will cause' such result without further conduct on his part. Thus, a belief that death will ensue from the actor's conduct, or that property will be obtained, will suffice, as well as would a purpose to bring about those results. If, for example, the actor's purpose were to demolish a building and, knowing that persons were in the building and that they would be killed by the explosion, he nevertheless detonated a bomb that turned out to be defective, he could be prosecuted for attempted murder even though it was no part of his purpose that the inhabitants of the building would be killed.

"It is difficult to say what the decision would be under prevailing attempt principles in a case of this kind. It might be held that the actor did not specifically intend to kill the inhabitants of the building; on the other hand, the concept of 'intent' has always been an ambiguous one and might be thought to include results that the actor believed to be the inevitable consequence of his conduct. In any event, the inclusion of such conduct as the basis for liability under Subsection (1)(b) is based on the conclusion that the manifestation of the actor's dangerousness is just as great—or very nearly as great—as in the case of purposive conduct. In both instances a deliberate choice is made to bring about the consequence forbidden by the criminal laws, and the actor has done all within his power to cause this result to occur. The absence of any desire that the result occur is not, under these circumstances, a sufficient basis for differentiating between the two types of conduct involved. Only a minority of recent revisions have explicitly followed the Model Code on this point."

9. In *Gardner v. Akeroyd,* [1952] 2 Q.B. 743, a butcher was acquitted of attempting to violate a regulation prohibiting the sale of meat above a certain price. Inspectors visited his shop and found 33 parcels of meat, prepared by the butcher's assistant, ready for delivery and bearing name tickets and excessive prices. Had the parcels been sold, clearly the butcher would have been guilty of violating the regulation, for it had previously been interpreted as imposing strict and vicarious liability. But the court held the butcher was rightly acquitted, for the charge of attempting a strict liability offense requires proof of mens rea.

Is this result sound? Consider J. Smith and B. Hogan, *Criminal Law* 149 (1965): "If there is a valid policy underlying the imposition of liability for negligence and strict liability in the substantive offence, it is difficult to see why it does not apply equally to the attempt. The only difference between the man who attempts and fails and another who attempts and succeeds may be chance. There is, *ex hypothesi,* no difference in moral blameworthiness between them and the one may be as dangerous as the other."

IN RE SMITH

Supreme Court of California, 1970.
3 Cal.3d 192, 90 Cal.Rptr. 1, 474 P.2d 969.

MOSK, JUSTICE.

Petitioner, John Alexander Smith, is presently incarcerated at San Quentin under sentence imposed in 1967 after he was convicted of two counts of kidnaping, one count of rape, and one count of attempted kidnaping. We issued an order to show cause in response to his petition in propria persona for a writ of habeas corpus to consider the contention that he was deprived of his right to the effective assistance of counsel on appeal. This is a case of first impression on the subject of incompetency of appellate counsel.

The crimes of which petitioner was convicted occurred between November 1, 1966, and February 1, 1967, in Los Angeles. On November 1, Miss Audrey George, while waiting for a bus, was accosted from behind by a man. He pressed a file to her neck and compelled her to walk about a block and a half to a vacant house, where he forcibly committed an act of sexual intercourse upon her. He then walked with her back to the vicinity of the bus stop and permitted her to call a friend to pick her up. At the lineup in February 1967, Miss George identified petitioner as her assailant. At the trial, she again identified petitioner and confirmed her lineup identification.

On January 21, 1967, Mrs. Carla Braswell was approached by a man on the sidewalk after she had parked and locked her car near her home. After asking directions, the man grabbed her arm and brandished a screwdriver. He ordered her to unlock the door on the driver's side of her automobile and told her "that we were going in my car." Mrs. Braswell indicated that she was too frightened to unlock the door and she gave her purse to her assailant, telling him to do it. While he searched for the keys, another car pulled alongside and during the confusion Mrs. Braswell was able to escape to her home. At the February lineup Mrs. Braswell did not unequivocally identify petitioner as her assailant, but she was positive at the trial.

At 11 p.m. on February 1, Miss Delores Burton was grabbed from behind by a man and threatened with a screwdriver held to her neck. She was forced to walk to an alley about two blocks away, where she was told to take off her clothes. She removed her coat, but when an automobile light at the end of the alley prompted the attacker to retrieve the screwdriver he had put down, Miss Burton was able to escape. She ran to a nearby market with the attacker in pursuit, but he did not enter the market. John Wesley saw Miss Burton being chased and described her assailant to the police. Miss Burton identified petitioner at a lineup and in court as the man who attacked her. Wesley could not make a positive identification.

Petitioner was arrested on February 1, about a half hour after the Burton incident. He was walking near the market where Miss Burton had fled and he was wearing a blue shirt, dark pants, and a hat, with a dark coat under his arm. He was perspiring. Miss Burton was brought to the police station to identify him that night.

In April 1967, petitioner was tried by the court and was convicted of the kidnaping and rape of Miss George, the attempted kidnaping of Mrs. Braswell, and the kidnaping of Miss Burton. His defense was alibi on the occasions of all three offenses. The convictions were affirmed on appeal and no petition for hearing was filed.

Petitioner contends that he was denied the effective assistance of counsel in his appeal because his court-appointed appellate counsel was incompetent and failed to raise substantial allegations of error which arguably might have resulted in reversal of his convictions. * * *

Petitioner's conviction of attempted kidnaping in the episode involving Mrs. Braswell was likewise subject to plausible assignments of error. It is well settled that "[t]o constitute an attempt, there must be (a) the specific intent to commit a particular crime, and (b) a direct ineffectual act done towards its commission. * * * To amount to an attempt the act or acts must go further than mere *preparation;* they must be such as would ordinarily result in the crime except for the interruption."

It is at least arguable that petitioner's conduct in regard to Mrs. Braswell exhibited neither the intent nor the action requisite to attempted kidnaping. The only direct evidence of his intention was his statement, paraphrased by Mrs. Braswell, as follows: "Then he told me to unlock my car door, that we were going in my car." Certainly, it could be maintained that this statement is not an unequivocal expression of an intention to abduct Mrs. Braswell, unless moving her from the sidewalk to the inside of the car was sufficient to constitute kidnaping. Also plausible was the inference that petitioner intended to rape his victim inside her car without driving it away, or that he intended to steal from her person or her car. Furthermore, petitioner's actions to effectuate his criminal purpose arguably did not reach that stage of development beyond mere preparation. His search for the keys might as logically have been for the purpose of robbing or sexually assaulting his victim, rather than kidnaping her.

* * *

In the instant action we hold that the inexcusable failure of petitioner's appellate counsel to raise crucial assignments of error, which arguably might have resulted in a reversal, deprived petitioner of the effective assistance of appellate counsel to which he was entitled under the Constitution. * * *

Notes and Questions

1. The court directed the court of appeals to "vacate its decision, reinstate the appeal, and appoint other counsel for appellant." If on the new appeal it is argued that the evidence is not sufficient to show the defendant's intent to kidnap, what should the result be?

2. Did the prosecutor err in the charge he brought against Smith regarding the Braswell incident? Would he have been any better off if he had charged attempted robbery? Or, attempted rape?

SECTION 2. ACTS

Introductory Notes

1. Consider Buxton, *Incitement and Attempt*, 1973 Crim.L.Rev. 656, 660:

"The law of Attempt has over the years proved more confused, and therefore more controversial, than almost any other part of the criminal law; primarily because of a reluctance to recognise that the social reasons for punishing attempts, and therefore the proper analysis of Attempt as a crime, are generically different from the considerations that control the analysis of substantive crimes. In the latter, certain forms of conduct, or the production of certain effects in the physical world, are deemed to be socially undesirable, and are therefore prohibited, the persons who produce those effects being however protected from the morally or socially undesirable exercise of state power against them by the (usual) requirement that they should not be punished unless they acted consciously or intentionally in producing those forbidden results. The crime of Attempt, on the other hand, looks not to the accused's past conduct but to his threatened future conduct, and the analytical roles of *actus reus* and *mens rea* are thus, as it were, reversed. We have a law of Attempt because persons who threaten to commit acts forbidden by the substantive criminal law should be open to social prevention and deterrence, since such persons are, by reason of their intentions, socially dangerous. The *primary* justification for punishing a man for Attempt is thus not his *actus reus* but his *mens rea*. At the same time, however, quite as many threats to liberty seem to be presented by the possibility of punishing a man for *mens rea,* without more, as are presented, in the case of substantive crime, by the possibility of punishing him for *actus reus* alone. The law of Attempt therefore limits its deterrent and preventive role in the interests of freedom by requiring action, of some sort, as well as intention, on the part of the accused; in the same way as in substantive crime the deterrent and preventive role of the law is to some degree limited by the requirement of *mens rea*."

2. What test should be used in determining whether a defendant, charged with attempting some crime, has engaged in sufficient acts? Consider the reasoning

and results in the following six cases, which illustrate these approaches:

(a) the "last act" test, whereunder the defendant must have done everything that he believes necessary to bring about the criminal result (*Regina v. Eagleton*);

(b) the "dangerous proximity" test, which focuses upon what the defendant has done and how close he thereby came to succeeding in his criminal objective (*People v. Rizzo*);

(c) the "indispensible element" test, which focuses instead upon what remains to be done in order to accomplish the criminal objective (*People v. Orndorff*);

(d) the "probable desistance" test, under which a judgment must be made as to whether the defendant had reached a point where it was unlikely he would thereafter abandon his efforts to achieve the criminal objective (*Commonwealth v. Skipper*);

(e) the "equivocality" test, whereunder the question is whether the defendant's actions manifest the intent to achieve the criminal objective (*People v. Bowen*); and

(f) the "substantial step" test (see *Model Penal Code* § 5.01), whereunder the defendant's acts must be strongly corroborative of his criminal purpose (*United States v. Mandujano*).

REGINA v. EAGLETON

Court of Criminal Law, England, 1855.
6 Cox C.C. 559.

[The defendant, a baker, contracted with the guardians of the poor of the parish of Great Yarmouth to supply the poor with loaves of bread, each loaf to weigh three and a half pounds, to be paid for at sevenpence a loaf. Under the contract, each poor person who presented defendant with a "ticket" was to receive such a loaf. The defendant would then turn in the tickets, together with a statement of the number of loaves supplied, to the relieving officer, who would credit the de-

fendant in his books for the amount owed him. The money was to be paid to the defendant at a future time as stipulated in the contract, but before such payment was made it was discovered that the defendant had intentionally furnished loaves deficient in weight and that he had returned the tickets intending to represent that he had delivered loaves of the weight provided for in the contract. Defendant, convicted of attempting to obtain money by false pretenses, appealed.]

PARKE, B., now delivered the judgment of the court. * * * On the part of the defendant, his learned counsel contended—1st. That the attempt to obtain credit in account for a sum of money by delivering up the tickets as vouchers, was not in itself an attempt to obtain money within the meaning of the statute, for that credit in account was not equivalent to money; and no doubt the credit in the relieving officer's book was not equivalent to money, and the defendant could not have been convicted of the offence of actually obtaining money by false presences. * * * But our doubt has been whether the obtaining that credit, though undoubtedly a necessary step towards obtaining the money, can be deemed an attempt to do so. The mere intention to commit a misdemeanor is not criminal, some act is required; and we do not think that all acts towards committing a misdemeanor are indictable. Acts remotely leading towards the commission of the offence are not to be considered as attempts to commit it; but acts immediately connected with it are; and if in this case, after the credit with the relieving officer for the fraudulent overcharge, any further step on the part of the defendant had been necessary to obtain payment, as the making out a further account, or producing the vouchers to the board, we should have thought that the obtaining credit in account with the relieving officer would not have been sufficiently proximate to the obtaining of the money.

But on the statement in this case no other act on the part of the defendant would have been required. It was the last act depending on himself towards the payment of the money, and therefore it ought to be considered as an attempt. The receipt of the money appears to have been prevented by a discovery of the fraud, by the relieving officer, and it is very much the same case as if, supposing rendering an account to the guardians at their office with the vouchers annexed were a preliminary necessary step to receiving the money, the defendant had gone to the office, rendered the account and vouchers, and then been discovered, and the money consequently refused.

Notes and Questions

1. The "last act" test did not long survive. See *Regina v. Roberts*, 7 Cox C.C. 39 (1855).

2. Should the test have been retained? Consider *Rex v. White*, [1910] 2 K.B. 124. Defendant's mother died of heart failure; on a nearby table was a glass of wine with two grains of cyanide in it, and there was evidence showing that defendant had put the cyanide in the wine glass. However, there was no evidence that his mother had consumed any of the liquid, and it was also shown that the quantity of cyanide in the drink would not suffice to cause death. On appeal of his conviction for attempted murder, the defendant objected "that the jury must have acted upon a suggestion of the learned judge in his summing up that this was one, the first or some later, of a series of doses which he intended to administer and so cause her death by slow poisoning; and that if they did act on that suggestion there was no attempted murder." The court affirmed, holding that "the completion or attempted completion of one of a series of acts intended by a man to result in killing is an attempt to murder even although this completed act would not, unless followed by the others acts, result in killing. It might be the beginning of the attempt, but would none the less be an attempt."

PEOPLE v. RIZZO

Court of Appeals of New York, 1927.
246 N.Y. 334, 158 N.E. 888.

CRANE, J. The police of the city of New York did excellent work in this case by preventing the commission of a serious crime. It is a great satisfaction to realize that we have such wide-awake guardians of our peace. Whether or not the steps which the defendant had taken up to the time of his arrest amounted to the commission of a crime, as defined by our law, is, however, another matter. He has been convicted of an attempt to commit the crime of robbery in the first degree, and sentenced to state's prison. There is no doubt that he had the intention to commit robbery, if he got the chance. An examination, however, of the facts is necessary to determine whether his acts were in preparation to commit the crime if the opportunity offered, or constituted a crime in itself, known to our law as an attempt to commit robbery in the first degree. Charles Rizzo, the defendant, appellant, with three others, Anthony J. Dorio, Thomas Milo, and John Thomasello, on January 14th planned to rob one Charles Rao of a pay roll valued at about $1,200 which he was to carry from the bank for the United Lathing Company. These defendants, two of whom had firearms, started out in an automobile, looking for Rao or the man who had the pay roll on that day. Rizzo claimed to be able to identify the man, and was to point him out to the others, who were to do the actual holding up. The four rode about in their car looking for Rao. They went to the bank from which he was supposed to get the money and to various buildings being constructed by the United Lathing Company. At last they came to One Hundred and Eightieth street and Morris Park avenue. By this time they were watched and followed by two police officers. As Rizzo jumped out of the car and ran into the building, all four were arrested. The defendant was taken out from the building in which he was hiding. Neither Rao nor a man named Previti, who was also supposed to carry a pay roll, were at the place at the time of the arrest. The defendants had not found or seen the man they intended to rob. No person with a pay roll was at any of the places where they had stopped, and no one had been pointed out or identified by Rizzo. The four men intended to rob the pay roll man, whoever he was. They were looking for him, but they had not seen or discovered him up to the time they were arrested.

Does this constitute the crime of an attempt to commit robbery in the first degree? The Penal Law, § 2, prescribes:

"An act, done with intent to commit a crime, and tending but failing to effect its commission, is 'an attempt to commit that crime.' "

The word "tending" is very indefinite. It is perfectly evident that there will arise differences of opinion as to whether an act in a given case is one *tending* to commit a crime. "Tending" means to exert activity in a particular direction. Any act in preparation to commit a crime may be said to have a tendency towards its accomplishment. The procuring of the automobile, searching the streets looking for the desired victim, were in reality acts tending toward the commission of the proposed crime. The law, however, has recognized that many acts in the way of preparation are too remote to constitute the crime of attempt. The line has been drawn between those acts which are remote and those which are proximate and near to the consummation. The law must be practical,

and therefore considers those acts only as tending to the commission of the crime which are so near to its accomplishment that in all reasonable probability the crime itself would have been committed, but for timely interference. The cases which have been before the courts express this idea in different language, but the idea remains the same. The act or acts must come or advance very near to the accomplishment of the intended crime. * * *

How shall we apply this rule of immediate nearness to this case? The defendants were looking for the pay roll man to rob him of his money. This is the charge in the indictment. Robbery is defined in section 2120 of the Penal Law as "the unlawful taking of personal property from the person or in the presence of another, against his will, by means of force, or violence, or fear of injury, immediate or future, to his person;" and it is made robbery in the first degree by section 2124 when committed by a person aided by accomplices actually present. To constitute the crime of robbery, the money must have been taken from Rao by means of force or violence, or through fear. The crime of attempt to commit robbery was committed, if these defendants did an act tending to the commission of this robbery. Did the acts above described come dangerously near to the taking of Rao's property? Did the acts come so near the commission of robbery that there was reasonable likelihood of its accomplishment but for the interference? Rao was not found; the defendants were still looking for him; no attempt to rob him could be made, at least until he came in sight; he was not in the building at One Hundred and Eightieth street and Morris Park avenue. There was no man there with the pay roll for the United Lathing Company whom these defendants could rob. Apparently no money had been drawn from the bank for the pay roll by anybody at the time of the arrest. In a word, these defendants had planned to commit a crime, and were looking around the city for an opportunity to commit it, but the opportunity fortunately never came. Men would not be guilty of an attempt at burglary if they had planned to break into a building and were arrested while they were hunting about the streets for the building not knowing where it was. Neither would a man be guilty of an attempt to commit murder if he armed himself and started out to find the person whom he had planned to kill but could not find him. So here these defendants were not guilty of an attempt to commit robbery in the first degree when they had not found or reached the presence of the person they intended to rob.

For these reasons, the judgment of conviction of this defendant appellant must be reversed and a new trial granted.

* * *

PEOPLE v. ORNDORFF

Court of Appeal, Second District, 1968.
261 Cal.App.2d 212, 67 Cal.Rptr. 824.

KINGSLEY, ASSOCIATE JUSTICE.

Defendant was charged with attempted grand theft. The case was submitted on the transcript of the preliminary examination, together with testimony by defendant. He was found guilty as charged, probation was denied and he was sentenced to state prison. He has appealed. We reverse the judgment.

The victim, Juniper Griffis, testified that he was accosted on a street in Long Beach by a Negro sailor, who asked him concerning a hotel. In the conversation that followed, the sailor displayed a roll of bills and told Griffis that he had been given it by his ship's captain as the proceeds of insurance on the life of the sailor's brother. Griffis advised the sailor to put the money (allegedly $19,000) in a bank but the sailor demurred, saying that he understood that if a Negro deposited money in a bank, the bank would not let him with-

draw it. At this stage, defendant appeared, walked by the two men and was accosted by Griffis, who asked defendant to help "straighten out" the sailor. After further conversation, the three men drove, in defendant's car, to Griffis' home to procure his bank book so that Griffis, by making a withdrawal from his account, could satisfy the sailor that the sailor could safely make a deposit. They then drove to the vicinity of Griffis' bank. The sailor remained in the car, Griffis and defendant walked toward the bank but, before reaching it, defendant stopped, telling Griffis to go to the bank alone, as defendant wanted to watch the sailor. Griffis went to the bank where he met his wife; after Griffis and his wife talked to the assistant manager they left the bank to find that defendant, the sailor and the car had disappeared.

Thereafter police officers went to defendant's home, advised him of his constitutional rights, secured permission to search the apartment, discovered a roll of "play money" and arrested defendant. The roll of play money was introduced into evidence. During conversations that took place, then and later, defendant admitted his participation in the affair, but claimed that he recognized that the sailor was attempting a scheme known as the "Jamaica Switch," did not want to get involved because he was on parole, and dropped out of the proceedings as he and Griffis approached the bank.

A police officer, properly qualified as an expert on "bunco" schemes, described the so-called "Jamaica Switch," as follows:

"A The No. 1 Negro I will refer to as the sailor, stops an elderly white man and gives a conversation similar or in scale to what Mr. Griffin [sic] described, in which he will talk about how he is a poor old Negro. He says he is from Jamaica or Martinique or one of the islands down there. He has been left this amount of money, that the captain keeps the money and he is interested in keeping the money in the captain's safe; the night before the girl had tried to take him, getting the victim's sympathy. He then talks about the girl and the hotel, bringing in the sex angle. The third subject will come along, the No. 2 Negro comes by, a man that looks prosperous, has a fine fitting suit, probably wearing a hat and as Mr. Griffis stated, the sailor will constantly refer to himself as a nigger.

" * * *

"A Yes sir. There is a discussion about finding a hotel, they then go around and get the victim's bank book. Usually a roll of 100 and 500 dollars is shown to the victim by the sailor, after showing him that he can get his money in and out of the bank. They will take the victim to the bank, he gets his money out and shows it to the sailor. The sailor will then grab the money and get the victim's money in his hand and tell the victim what a wonderful man he is, and he will have a handkerchief or a bag or a container he can put the money in. So he will take the victim's money, put it in the handkerchief and tell him what a wonderful man he is. He also will take the award money and put the money in the sack and hand it back to the victim. At that time the victim has his own money and then the money the suspect had carried. The victim will start to put it into his pocket, coat pocket, inside pocket or even in his hand. The sailor grabs the package back and says, 'Oh no, man, like my momma used to tell me,' and he will open the victim's shirt and put the package back into there in between the flesh and the shirt, then button it back up. As he grabs the shirt, the No. 2 suspect will turn the victim's attention by saying something to him just after the sailor has taken the money back. At that time the switch is made

and the package is inserted and when the victim gets back to deposit his money he finds he has newspapers or worthless articles and his money has gone south with the sailor."

It is the prosecution's theory that defendant and the sailor (who is not involved in the present case) attempted to practice a Jamaica Switch on Griffis but were prevented from success. On appeal, defendant urges, among other contentions, that the evidence shows, at the most, mere preparation not going far enough to constitute an attempt. Since we agree with that contention, it is not necessary to discuss the objections made in the trial court and here to the introduction of certain evidence.

Both parties cite and rely on *People v. Fulton* (1961) 188 Cal.App.2d 105, 10 Cal.Rptr. 319. We conclude that that case supports the defendant rather than the prosecution. *Fulton* also involved an alleged Jamaica Switch, practiced on two alleged intended victims. The schemes failed, on one instance because a bank officer told the intended victim that it was a bunco scheme, in the other because the intended victim became suspicious and refused to enter his bank and make the proposed withdrawal. In *Fulton,* the court unanimously held that the first instance was a punishable attempt; by a divided court, the second instance was also held to have reached the status of attempt. All three judges lay stress on the element of the procuring cause of failure, saying that it must be "by extraneous circumstances," or "by circumstances independent of any actions on their [defendants'] part." But while, in *Fulton,* the schemes failed because the victim withdrew, here the only evidence is that it failed because defendant abandoned the scheme before it reached the first significant step. It is, of course, possible that Griffis' wife and the bank manager had (as in the first count in *Fulton*) warned Griffis that he was involved in a classic bunco scheme and that he had abandoned the scheme. But there is no evidence to that effect. We do not know what either the wife or the bank officer told Griffis or what he told them. The Attorney General suggests that "inferably" defendant had seen Mrs. Griffis at the bank and had been frightened off by that fact; but there is no evidence that he saw her or knew that she was to intervene in the events.

Looking at the expert's description of the classic scheme, it is to be noticed that not one, but many steps still remained to be performed: the victim must withdraw his money, deliver it to the thief, the thief must perform his slight-of-hand "switch" of the victim's money for the substitute play money or newspaper, and the thief must leave the scene before the victim opens the substituted package. None of these had taken place. Only the first two steps had been accomplished: the victim had procured his bank book and had gone to his bank. Too many potential slips remained before the cup of success would reach the defendant's lip for us to say that there was here anything more than preparation.

The judgment is reversed.

COMMONWEALTH v. SKIPPER

Superior Court of Pennsylvania, 1972.
222 Pa.Super. 242, 294 A.2d 780.

HOFFMAN, JUDGE:

In this *pro se* appeal appellant contends that the evidence was insufficient to sustain his conviction as the principal perpetrator of an attempted prison breach.

At appellant's trial a Commonwealth witness testified that appellant had approached him in prison, asking that he procure some hacksaw blades for the sum of $150.00, which was to be paid by William Schaeffer, a fellow inmate. The witness was a day release prisoner employed at a nearby bakery which made bread for prison use. The plan, allegedly, was that the witness would conceal the blades in loaves of bread to be retrieved inside the prison by appellant, who worked in the kitchen. The witness testified that he placed the blades in the bread at the bakery, and that at a later time the appellant indicated that he had received the blades. Appellant then told the witness to talk to Schaeffer. Schaeffer gave the witness a note to obtain the $150.00. Prison officials intercepted another note, this one written by the witness to Schaeffer, when the witness attempted to illicitly transfer the note to Schaeffer. This note contained a reference to blades.

One June 2, 1970, prison officials caught Schaeffer while he was attempting to go over the prison wall, and they found a hacksaw blade on his person. The officials then conducted a "shake-down" of the prison and discovered two hacksaw blades and a small file in a bread wrapper inside the radiator of appellant's cell.

On the basis of this evidence, the trial judge instructed the jury as to the law of attempts. * * * The jury returned a verdict of guilty.

In *Commonwealth v. Eagan,* 190 Pa. 10, 21–22, 42 A. 374, 377 (1899), our Supreme Court defined an attempt as being " * * * an overt act done in pursuance of an intent to do a specific thing, tending to the end but falling short of complete accomplishment of it. In law, the definition must have this further qualification, that the overt act must be sufficiently proximate to the intended crime to form one of the natural series of acts which the intent requires for its full execution. So long as the acts are confined *to preparation only,* and can be abandoned before any transgression of the law or of others' rights, they are within the sphere of intent and do not amount to attempts."

The trial judge charged the jury in conformity with the definition of attempt accepted in Pennsylvania. Under this definition, however, appellant could not have been found guilty * * *. The discovery of the hacksaw blades in appellant's cell did no more than interrupt appellant's alleged plan in a preparatory stage. If the hacksaw blades were in fact procured by the appellant for use in an intended prison breach, appellant would have had sufficient time to withdraw before the commission of the offense. * * *

Notes and Questions

1. If the question is whether the defendant still "had sufficient time to withdraw before the commission of the offense," then isn't this essentially the same as asking whether the last act has occurred?

2. Consider the somewhat different formulation proposed in Skilton, *The Requisite Act in a Criminal Attempt,* 3 U.Pitt.L. Rev. 308, 309–10 (1937), namely, "that the defendant's conduct must pass that point where most men, holding such an intention as the defendant holds, would think better of their conduct and desist. All of us, or most of us, at some time or other harbor what may be described as a criminal intent to effect unlawful consequences. Many of us take some steps— often slight enough in character—to bring the consequences about; but most of us, when we reach a certain point, desist, and return to our roles as law-abiding citizens. The few who do not and pass beyond that point are, if the object of their conduct is not achieved, guilty of a criminal attempt." Had Skipper reached that point?

PEOPLE v. BOWEN

Court of Appeal of Michigan, 1968.
10 Mich.App. 1, 158 N.W.2d 794.

LEVIN, JUDGE.

Defendants, Sherrel Bowen and William Rouse, appeal their convictions of attempted larceny in a building.

On January 19, 1965, at approximately eight o'clock p.m., the defendants and two female companions were admitted to the home of one Matilda Gatzmeyer, an 80 year old woman. The defendants' car was observed parked in front of Miss Gatzmeyer's residence and a neighbor, believing the defendants to have designs upon her property, called the police. Two police officers arrived and entered the home along with the neighbor. The defendants were found in the rear of the house near or on the basement steps. The two female companions were seated on either side of Miss Gatzmeyer, apparently engaged with her in conversation. The bedroom of the house was in a state of disarray.

The police ordered defendants to come to the front of the house and sit in the living room. Defendant Rouse seated himself within a foot of the TV, and some time thereafter one of the police officers spotted under the TV set two rings belonging to Miss Gatzmeyer. The neighbor testified she found a necklace on the staircase near where defendant Bowen had been standing when he was first sighted by the police. When the neighbor's discovery was called to the attention of one of the police officers, he and Miss Gatzmeyer went to the staircase and found the necklace in that location.

After interrogation, the defendants were arrested and charged with larceny of "rings and a necklace" in a building.

Bowen had been to the Gatzmeyer home on a number of prior occasions, ostensibly as a handy man, the same reason he gave Miss Gatzmeyer for appearing on the night in question. Miss Gatzmeyer testified that on this occasion the defendants sought to hire themselves out to clean and to do some masonry work on the chimney. She complained about the high prices charged by Bowen and his failure to do work as agreed, and that

Bowen's helper (the role allegedly filled by Rouse at the time of the incident) generally helped himself to things that belonged to her.

The neighbor testified that she had met Bowen on three occasions prior to the one in question and that on one occasion Bowen had induced Miss Gatzmeyer to go with him to the bank, but it was not clear whether the visit to the bank was to withdraw money to pay Bowen that which was due him or unlawfully to separate Miss Gatzmeyer from her money.

The neighbor testified that she visited with Miss Gatzmeyer daily and assisted her in various chores and generally in getting around. She stated that when she and the police officers arrived on the night in question the dresser drawers in the bedroom were all pulled out and everything thrown all over the bed. This was not the way Miss Gatzmeyer generally kept the house according to the neighbor: "she has a very neat house, everything is in its place." The neighbor further testified that "after Miss Gatzmeyer cleaned up (presumably after the police left) she found more jewelry back of the pillows" on the couch Bowen sat on during his interrogation by the police.

Miss Gatzmeyer testified that the defendants removed the jewelry from her bedroom without her consent.

At the beginning of his charge to the jury, the trial judge stated that because he doubted whether the case properly could be submitted to the jury on the original charge of larceny in a building he had decided to submit it to the jury solely on the included offense of attempt to commit larceny in a building. * * *

We do find error in the judge's failure properly to charge the jury on the necessity of finding an overt act. It has been said that the overt act "is the essence of the offense" or the "gravamen of the offense." Not only did the trial judge fail

to charge the jury at all concerning the necessity of finding an overt act, but he also incorrectly charged that the jury could convict if it found that the defendants came to or entered Miss Gatzmeyer's house with the intention of committing larceny. * * *

There was ample evidence from which the jury could have found felonious intent. * * *

In the absence of a request, the trial judge's failure to charge the jury on the necessity of finding commission of an overt act, as a separate ingredient or element, might not be error if he were correct in charging the jury that if it found defendants "came" to or "entered" Miss Gatzmeyer's house with intent to commit larceny it could bring in a verdict of guilty. If defendants' coming to, or entering, Miss Gatzmeyer's house with felonious intent was an "overt act", the jury verdict of guilty could be viewed as a finding of the requisite overt act.

Thus, the narrow question before us is whether the defendants when they came to or entered Miss Gatzmeyer's house with the intent to commit larceny committed an overt act that would support their conviction of attempted larceny. In our opinion, their mere coming to or entry of Miss Gatzmeyer's house was not an overt act, under the circumstances that Mr. Bowen and other helpers had rightfully been in the house on prior occasions and were admitted to the house by Miss Gatzmeyer on the night in question.

Whether the defendants came to or entered Miss Gatzmeyer's house with a felonious intent is, of course, a question of fact to be decided by the jury. However, whether the facts found by the jury constitute an overt act, or whether the jury from particular circumstances could find that an overt act had been committed, is a question of law to be decided by the court.

In *People v. Coleman,* 350 Mich. 268, 86 N.W.2d 281 (1957), the Supreme Court stated that a defendant may not be convicted of an attempt unless he has "gone beyond acts of an ambiguous nature" or those that are "equivocal", and that a "thoughtful test for the resolution of the equivocal act has been phrased by Turner in his article, *'Attempts to Commit Crimes'* in 5 Camb.L.J., 230, 237 [238,] in these words:

'If the acts of the accused, taken by themselves, are unambiguous, and cannot, in reason, be regarded as pointing to any other end than the commission of the specific crime in question, then they constitute a sufficient *actus reus.* In other words, his acts must be *unequivocally referable* to the commission of the specific crime. They must, as the late Sir John Salmond said, "speak for themselves." If the example may be permitted, it is as though a cinematograph film, which has so far depicted merely the accused person's acts without stating what was his intention, had been suddenly stopped, and the audience were asked to say to what end those acts were directed. If there is only one reasonable answer to this question then the accused has done what amounts to an "attempt" to attain that end. If there is more than one reasonably possible answer, then the accused has not yet done enough.' "

* * *

It has been suggested that the basic function of the overt act is corroboration of the felonious intent. However, that analysis can become somewhat circular if we permit intent to be gleaned from the overt act itself.

The testimony in this case was that defendant Bowen had, on a number of prior occasions, been in Miss Gatzmeyer's house with helpers. With that in mind and even if it be assumed (on the basis of the jury finding) that the defendants entered her house with a felonious intent, their mere presence there did not indicate, let alone "corroborate", that intention. The defendants did not break into Miss Gatzmeyer's house—they were voluntarily admitted by her. At the time of defendants' admission to Miss Gatzmeyer's house their *acts* were entirely "ambiguous" and "equivocal". It is the acts thereafter allegedly committed (but as to which we have no finding from the jury) that were neither ambiguous nor equivocal.

Our analysis of the authorities convinces us that the function of the overt act is not to "corroborate", but rather to demonstrate that the defendant has converted resolution into action. Man being what he is, evil thoughts and intentions are easily formed. Fortunately, for society, most felonious thoughts are not fulfilled. The law does not punish evil intent or even every act done with the intent to commit a crime. The requirement that the jury find an overt act proceeds on the assumption that the devil may lose the contest, albeit late in the hour.

The overt act is not any act. In this connection "overt" is used in the sense of "manifest" or symbolic. The act must manifest, or be symbolic of, the crime. Considering that Bowen and helpers had been in Miss Gatzmeyer's house on previous occasions (and, whatever her differences with Bowen may have been, she nevertheless again admitted him on the night in question), the fact that the defendants came to and entered Miss Gatzmeyer's house would not manifest or symbolize the crime of which they were convicted of attempting to commit.

* * *

Reversed and remanded for a new trial.

Notes and Questions

1. Does the *Bowen* court mean that Bowen and Rouse could not be convicted of the attempt even if, following their

arrest, they had given a voluntary confession admitting that it had been their intention to steal Miss Gatzmeyer's jewelry?

2. Consider *Campbell and Bradley v. Ward,* [1955] N.Z.L.R. 471. Upon approaching his parked car at about 11 p.m., Eastwick saw McCallion emerging from the front seat. There was no evidence that he had taken anything from the car or that he had done anything beyond entering and leaving the car. McCallion fled, but Eastwick pursued him and pulled him from a moving car just as it was driving off. At 3 a.m., Bradley was arrested at his home and taken to the police station. In a signed statement, he said that he, McCallion and Campbell agreed it would be "a good idea" to get a battery and that McCallion tried to get into several cars for that purpose and for the subsidiary purpose of getting a radio. Bradley also described the events previously related by Eastwick. Campbell was brought to the station at 4:30 a.m., and he gave a statement which generally accorded with Bradley's.

The court deemed it settled, pursuant to *Rex v. Barker,* [1924] N.Z.L.R. 865, "that there can be a conviction for attempt to commit a crime if, and only if, the act done with intent to commit it is in itself sufficient evidence of the intent: it must be a case of *res ipsa loquitor,* in the sense that, with no other evidence before it, a jury could properly infer the intent.

*   *   *

"In these circumstances, though the Court knows full well as against both appellants that it was theft that was contemplated, it is impossible to convict them of attempted theft. Accordingly, the convictions for the attempt cannot stand. If this be regarded as unsatisfactory, the remedying of it seems to rest with the Legislature."

3. The legislature did ultimately remedy the situation. N.Z. Crimes Act of 1961, § 72(3) provides: "An act done or omitted with intent to commit an offense may constitute an attempt if it is immediately or proximately connected with the intended offense, whether or not there was any act unequivocally showing the intent to commit that offense." Was this a change for the better? Consider Stuart, *The Actus Reus in Attempts,* 1970 Crim.L. Rev. 505, 507: "The main criticism of the 'equivocality' test is that, in requiring the act to show unequivocal purpose on its face without reference to evidence *aliunde,* it places the *actus reus* in too watertight a compartment. Any rule that the *actus reus* must be established independently of what is known about the *mens rea* is undesirable and likely to lead to the capricious results reached in New Zealand. If a locksmith is found next to a bank safe with his tools of trade it would be ludicrous to exclude a confession or other evidence that his intention had been to steal. It has also been pointed out that an act in itself will rarely reveal an unequivocal purpose and that it therefore seems unwise to use equivocality as the basis for non-liability in attempts. Even if the purpose is unequivocal from the face of the act the act may still be so remote that policy would be against a conviction."

4. In *Bowen,* the court says that the requisite "overt act is not any act." But why not? Consider G. Williams, *Criminal Law: The General Part* 632 (2d ed. 1961): "Another way of supporting the proximity rule is to say that it results from the notion of crime as a punishable wrong. Society has not thought it desirable to extend the scope of punishment too widely. So long as the law was purely deterrent or retributive in its aim, this circumscription of the offence of attempt was perhaps justified. At the present day, when courts have wide powers of probation, there is much to be said for a broader measure of responsibility. Any act done with the fixed intention of committing a crime, and by way of

preparation for it, however remote it may be from the crime, might well be treated as criminal. The rational course would be to catch intending offenders as soon as possible, and set about curing them of their evil tendencies: not leave them alone on the ground that their acts are mere preparation. It must be said, however, that this opinion is not generally held in the legal profession.

"A particularly unfortunate effect of the present law is that it often puts the police into a most awkward position. If they apprehend the suspect too soon, he may be acquitted; if they delay, they may be criticised for allowing a crime to be committed that they could have prevented."

UNITED STATES v. MANDUJANO

United States Court of Appeals, Fifth Circuit, 1974.
499 F.2d 370.

RIVES, CIRCUIT JUDGE:

Mandujano appeals from the judgment of conviction and fifteen-year sentence imposed by the district court, based upon the jury's verdict finding him guilty of attempted distribution of heroin in violation of 21 U.S.C. § 846. We affirm.

The government's case rested almost entirely upon the testimony of Alfonso H. Cavalier, Jr., a San Antonio police officer assigned to the Office of Drug Abuse Law Enforcement. Agent Cavalier testified that, at the time the case arose, he was working in an undercover capacity and represented himself as a narcotics trafficker. At about 1:30 P.M. on the afternoon of March 29, 1973, pursuant to information Cavalier had received, he and a government informer went to the Tally–Ho Lounge, a bar located on Guadalupe Street in San Antonio. Once inside the bar, the informant introduced Cavalier to Roy Mandujano. After some general conversation, Mandujano asked the informant if he was looking for "stuff." Cavalier said,

"Yes." Mandujano then questioned Cavalier about his involvement in narcotics. Cavalier answered Mandujano's questions, and told Mandujano he was looking for an ounce sample of heroin to determine the quality of the material. Mandujano replied that he had good brown Mexican heroin for $650.00 an ounce, but that if Cavalier wanted any of it he would have to wait until later in the afternoon when the regular man made his deliveries. Cavalier said that he was from out of town and did not want to wait that long. Mandujano offered to locate another source, and made four telephone calls in an apparent effort to do so. The phone calls appeared to be unsuccessful, for Mandujano told Cavalier he wasn't having any luck contacting anybody. Cavalier stated that he could not wait any longer. Then Mandujano said he had a good contact, a man who kept narcotics around his home, but that if he went to see this man, he would need the money "out front." To reassure Cavalier that he would not simply abscond with the money, Mandujano stated, "[Y]ou are in my place of business. My wife is here. You can sit with my wife. I am not going to jeopardize her or my business for $650.00." Cavalier counted out $650.00 to Mandujano, and Mandujano left the premises of the Tally–Ho Lounge at about 3:30 P.M. About an hour later, he returned and explained that he had been unable to locate his contact. He gave back the $650.00 and told Cavalier he could still wait until the regular man came around. Cavalier left, but arranged to call back at 6:00 P.M. When Cavalier called at 6:00 and again at 6:30, he was told that Mandujano was not available. Cavalier testified that he did not later attempt to contact Mandujano, because, "Based on the information that I had received, it would be unsafe for either my informant or myself to return to this area."

The only other government witness was Gerald Courtney, a Special Agent for the

Drug Enforcement Administration. Agent Courtney testified that, as part of a surveillance team in the vicinity of the Tally–Ho Lounge on March 29, 1973, he had observed Mandujano leave the bar around 3:15 or 3:30 P.M. and drive off in his automobile. The surveillance team followed Mandujano but lost him almost immediately in heavy traffic. Courtney testified that Mandujano returned to the bar at about 4:30 P.M. * * *

Mandujano urges that his conduct as described by agent Cavalier did not rise to the level of an attempt to distribute heroin under section 846. He claims that at most he was attempting to acquire a controlled substance, not to distribute it; that it is impossible for a person to attempt to distribute heroin which he does not possess or control; that his acts were only preparation, as distinguished from an attempt; and that the evidence was insufficient to support the jury's verdict. * * *

Although the * * * cases give somewhat varying verbal formulations, careful examination reveals fundamental agreement about what conduct will constitute a criminal attempt. First, the defendant must have been acting with the kind of culpability otherwise required for the commission of the crime which he is charged with attempting. * * *

Second, the defendant must have engaged in conduct which constitutes a substantial step toward commission of the crime. A substantial step must be conduct strongly corroborative of the firmness of the defendant's criminal intent. * * * The use of the word "conduct" indicates that omission or possession, as well as positive acts, may in certain cases provide a basis for liability. The phrase "substantial step," rather than "overt act," is suggested by *Gregg v. United States,* 113 F.2d 687

(8th Cir.1940) ("a step in the direct movement toward the commission of the crime"); *United States v. Coplon,* 185 F.2d 629 (2d Cir.1950) ("before he has taken the last of his intended steps") and *People v. Buffum,* 40 Cal.2d 709, 256 P.2d 317 (1953) ("some *appreciable fragment* of the crime") and indicates that the conduct must be more than remote preparation. The requirement that the conduct be strongly corroborative of the firmness of the defendant's criminal intent also relates to the requirement that the conduct be more than "mere preparation," and is suggested by the Supreme Court's emphasis upon ascertaining the intent of the defendant, *United States v. Quincy,* 31 U.S. 445, 8 L.Ed. 458 (1832), and by the approach taken in *United States v. Coplon,* supra (" * * * some preparation may amount to an attempt. It is a question of degree").[6] * * *

After the jury brought in a verdict of guilty, the trial court propounded a series of four questions to the jury:

"(1) Do you find beyond a reasonable doubt that on the 29th day of March, 1973, Roy Mandujano, the defendant herein, knowingly, wilfully and intentionally placed several telephone calls in order to obtain a source of heroin in accordance with his negotiations with Officer Cavalier which were to result in the distribution of approximately one ounce of heroin from the defendant Roy Mandujano to Officer Cavalier?"

"(2) Do you find beyond a reasonable doubt that the telephone calls inquired about in question no. (1) constituted overt acts in furtherance of the offense alleged in the indictment?"

"(3) Do you find beyond a reasonable doubt that on the 29th day of March, 1973, Roy Mandujano, the de-

6. Our definition is generally consistent with and our language is in fact close to the definitions proposed by the National Commission on Reform

of Federal Criminal Laws and the American Law Institute's Model Penal Code.

fendant herein, knowingly, wilfully and intentionally requested and received prior payment in the amount of $650.00 for approximately one ounce of heroin that was to be distributed by the defendant Roy Mandujano to Officer Cavalier?"

"(4) Do you find beyond a reasonable doubt that the request and receipt of a prior payment inquired about in question no. (3) constituted an overt act in furtherance of the offense alleged in the indictment?"

Neither the government nor the defendant objected to this novel procedure. After deliberating, the jury answered "No" to question (1) and "Yes" to questions (3) and (4). The jury's answers indicate that its thinking was consistent with the charge of the trial court.

The evidence was sufficient to support a verdict of guilty under section 846. Agent Cavalier testified that at Mandujano's request, he gave him $650.00 for one ounce of heroin, which Mandujano said he could get from a "good contact." From this, plus Mandujano's comments and conduct before and after the transfer of the $650.00 the jury could have found that Mandujano was acting knowingly and intentionally and that he engaged in conduct—the request for and the receipt of the $650.00—which in fact constituted a substantial step toward distribution of heroin. From interrogatory (4), it is clear that the jury considered Mandujano's request and receipt of the prior payment a substantial step toward the commission of the offense. Certainly, in the circumstances of this case, the jury could have found the transfer of money strongly corroborative of the firmness of Mandujano's intent to complete the crime. Of course, proof that Mandujano's "good contact" actually existed, and had heroin for sale, would have further strengthened the gov-

ernment's case; however, such proof was not essential. * * *

Notes and Questions

1. Is the "substantial step" test of *Model Penal Code* § 5.01 the best solution? Consider Stuart, *The Actus Reus in Attempts,* 1970 Crim.L.Rev. 505, 522–23: "It is also questionable whether it is really necessary to have a requirement of corroboration. It might well revive some of the absurdities experienced with the 'equivocality' theory. The normal caution in approaching an uncorroborated confession seems to be a sufficient safeguard against induced or false confessions. * * * In fact, the problem of the proximity rule is retained in a different guise together with * * * 'the element of imprecision found in most other approaches to the preparation-attempt problem.' One cannot help a feeling of scepticism as to the value of the suggested switch in emphasis 'from what remains to be done, the chief concern of the proximity tests, to what the actor has already done.' The unfortunate truth is that there is no definable quality that will distinguish a 'substantial step,' 'a step,' 'an act of preparation' and 'an act of perpetration.' "

2. Would Mandujano's conviction have been affirmed under any of the other tests? Does the answer to this question affect your judgment as to the adequacy of the "substantial step" test?

3. In support of the Model Penal Code formulation, it is said that "apprehension of dangerous persons will be facilitated and law enforcement officials and others will be able to stop the criminal effort at an earlier stage, thereby minimizing the risk of substantive harm, but without providing immunity for the offender." Model Penal Code § 5.01, Comment (1985). Compare Misner, *The New Attempt Laws: Unsuspected Threat to the Fourth*

Amendment, 33 Stan.L.Rev. 201, 201–02 (1981):

"Commentators and jurists have expressed legitimate concern about recent *judicial* erosion of the fourth amendment protection against unreasonable search and seizure. Unrecognized, however, is the equally serious threat created by *legislatures* which, following the lead of the Model Penal Code, have adopted broad, expansive definitions of inchoate crimes such as attempt. Because the Supreme Court has upheld the right of police to conduct a full search of an individual incident to *any* arrest, broader attempt laws narrow the procedural protection of the fourth amendment. Conduct that formerly warranted no more than a brief detention for questioning or a patdown search for weapons (a 'frisk') may now justify an attempt arrest and therefore a full search."

In *Terry v. Ohio,* 392 U.S. 1, 88 S.Ct. 1868, 20 L.Ed.2d 889 (1968), where a police officer saw several men repeatedly look into a store as if they were "casing" it for a holdup, the Supreme Court held that such reasonable suspicion short of probable cause to arrest authorized the police to make a brief stop of the suspects and to frisk them for weapons.

"Under most common law tests, Terry's conduct falls short of attempted robbery. Because Terry and his confederates did not brandish their weapons or enter the store they were casing, their actions were neither 'unequivocal' nor 'dangerously proximate' to completion of the crime. And they never committed the 'last proximate act' prior to the robbery. While their conduct came closest to an attempt under the 'probable desistance' test, it is arguable that the defendants left the front of the store, indicating desistance, *before* the police confronted them.

"But in a jurisdiction that follows the Model Penal Code approach, the case for attempt is clear. Because the police could

reasonably conclude that Terry's behavior amounted to 'reconnoitering,' they would have probable cause to arrest him for attempted robbery and conduct a full search incident to the arrest." Misner, supra, at 216.

SECTION 3. IMPOSSIBILITY

UNITED STATES v. THOMAS

United States Court of Military Appeals, 1962.
13 U.S.C.M.A. 278, 32 C.M.R. 278.

KILDAY, JUDGE:

The accused herein, Thomas and McClellan, were tried in common by general court-martial. Separate charges against the pair alleged the offense of conspiracy to commit rape, rape, and lewd and lascivious conduct, in violation of Articles 81, 120, and 134, Uniform Code of Military Justice, respectively. Upon arraignment, both men entered pleas of not guilty. Each was acquitted of rape, but the court-martial found them guilty of attempted rape, contrary to Article 80 of the Uniform Code, and likewise convicted them of the other two charges upon which they were brought to trial. Both received identical sentences to dishonorable discharge, confinement at hard labor for three years, forfeiture of all pay and allowances for a like period, and reduction to the grade of airman recruit.

Thereafter, the findings and sentences adjudged by the trial court were approved by the officer exercising general court-martial jurisdiction. The board of review, however, set aside the findings of guilty of attempted rape and conspiracy as to both accused. It approved a modified finding of lewd and lascivious conduct as to each and reassessed the punishment, reducing the sentences of the pair to bad-conduct discharge, confinement at hard labor for five months, total forfeitures, and reduction. *　*　*

The evidence adduced at the trial presents a sordid and revolting picture which need not be discussed in detail other than as necessary to decide the certified issues. In brief, both these young accused—Thomas being twenty years of age, and McClellan only nineteen, at the time of the instant offenses—started their fateful evening on a "bar hopping" spree. They were accompanied by an eighteen-year-old companion, Abruzzese, who, like both accused, held the grade of airman in the Navy. The latter was a co-actor in these offenses, but was granted immunity from prosecution for his criminality in the incidents, and testified as a witness for the Government.

After several stops the trio entered a tavern known as "Taylor's Place" where McClellan began dancing with a girl. Almost at once she collapsed in McClellan's arms. Thereafter, he, with his two companions, volunteered to take her home. They placed the apparently unconscious female in McClellan's car and left. Abruzzese was seated beside McClellan, who drove; Thomas was in the left rear seat next to the girl. Before they had proceeded very far McClellan, in frank, expressive language, suggested that this was a good chance for sexual intercourse as apparently this woman was just drunk and would never know the difference. Each of the three subsequently did or attempted to consummate this act and then started their return to town. The three became concerned as the woman had not regained consciousness.

In the meantime they dropped Abruzzese off at the USO. The accused, unable to find the female's home and becoming more concerned about her condition, stopped at a service station seeking help. The attendant called the police who, upon arriving at the service station, examined the girl and determined she was dead. An ambulance was called and she was taken to a hospital for further examination. An autopsy, later performed, revealed that she apparently died of "acute interstitial myocarditis." In general terms this is a weakening of the heart muscles with edema and inflammation which occurs more in young people without its presence being suspected. It was the general undisputed opinion that her death probably occurred at the time she collapsed on the dance floor at Taylor's Place or very shortly thereafter. Apparently, in deaths of this type, rigor mortis does not usually begin for some time and as a result the accused were unaware of the fact she was dead.

* * *

Despite the fact that defense counsel at trial vigorously urged to the law officer that the offenses of attempt and conspiracy could not be found validly if the victim's death occurred prior to the commission of the alleged acts, the law officer ruled otherwise. * * *

Before the board of review, appellate defense counsel contended that the law officer erred in his instructions to the court on the attempt and conspiracy offenses. In support of that position, the defense argued that where circumstances beyond the accused's control make it legally impossible to commit a crime, as distinguished from factual impossibility to do so, there can be no attempt nor can there be a conspiracy to commit the substantive offense. * * * The board of review held that an attempt to commit a crime must be directed to an object on which it is possible to commit the crime. Reasoning that a corpse is not a person, the board of review determined that the law officer erred in his instruction that there was no requirement that the victim be alive before the accused could be convicted of attempted rape. * * * Similarly, it was found that the accused could not be found guilty of conspiring to do that which if effected or consummated would not be an offense. Accordingly, the board of review set aside both accused's convictions for attempt to commit rape and for conspiracy to commit rape. * * *

Practically all writers on this subject, whether in law journal articles, texts, or judicial opinions, cite and discuss the same relatively limited number of decisions. These decisions are generally placed in the two following categories:

1. "Legal impossibility" in which attempt convictions have been set aside on the ground that it was legally impossible for the accused to have committed the crime contemplated. These are as follows:

(a) A person accepting goods which he believed to have been stolen, but which were not then "stolen" goods, was not guilty of an attempt to receive stolen goods. *People v. Jaffe,* 185 N.Y. 497, 78 N.E. 169 (1906).

(b) An accused who offered a bribe to a person believed to be a juror, but who was not a juror, could not be said to have attempted to bribe a juror. *State v. Taylor,* 345 Mo. 325, 133 S.W.2d 336 (1939).

(c) An official who contracted a debt which was unauthorized and a nullity, but which he believed to be valid, could not be convicted of an attempt to illegally contract a valid debt. *Marley v. State,* 58 N.J.L. 207, 33 Atl. 208 (1895).

(d) A hunter who shot a stuffed deer believing it to be alive had not attempted to take a deer out of season. *State v. Guffey,* 262 S.W.2d 152 (Mo.1953).

(e) It is not an attempt to commit subornation of perjury where the false testimony solicited, if given, would have been immaterial to the case at hand and hence not perjurious. *People v. Teal,* 196 N.Y. 372, 89 N.E. 1086 (1909).

2. Instances in which a claim of impossibility has been rejected and convictions sustained, are included below. Apparently these can all be classified as "impossibility in fact." These decisions are:

(a) It is now uniformly held that one is guilty if he attempts to steal from an empty pocket. *Commonwealth v. McDonald,* 5 Cushing 365 (Mass. 1850). The same is true as to an empty receptacle, *Clark v. State,* 86 Tenn. 511, 8 S.W. 145 (1888); and an empty house, *State v. Utley,* 82 N.C. 556 (1880). * * *

(b) One can attempt to possess narcotics, even though accused obtained possession of talcum believing it to be narcotics. *People v. Siu,* 126 Cal.App. 2d 41, 271 P.2d 575 (1954). * * *

(c) An accused may be guilty of attempted murder who, suspecting that a policeman on the roof was spying upon him through a hole, but ignorant that the policeman was then upon another part of the roof, fired at the hole with intent to kill. *People v. Lee Kong,* 95 Cal. 666, 30 Pac. 800 (1892). It is attempted murder to shoot into the intended victim's bed believing he is there asleep when in fact he is some place else. *United States v. Cruz-Gerena,* C.M. 228955, 49 B.R. 245 (1943); *State v. Mitchell,* 173 Mo. 633, 71 S.W. 175 (1902). An accused is not absolved from the charge of attempted murder when he points an unloaded gun at his wife's head and pulls the trigger, if he actually thought at the time that it was loaded. *State v. Damms,* 9 Wis.2d 183, 100 N.W.2d 592 (1960).

(d) In attempted abortion cases an accused may be guilty in the absence of proof that the woman was pregnant. *Commonwealth v. Tibbetts,* 157

Mass. 519, 32 N.E. 910 (1893) * * *.

It must be noted, however, that efforts to arrange these various authorities into some sort of classification have met with little real or satisfactory success. * * *

" * * * There are no degrees of impossibility and no sound basis for distinguishing among the conditions necessary for commission of the intended harm." [Hall, *General Principles of Criminal Law,* 2d ed., page 589 (1960).]

"The distinctions * * * are ingenious, but * * * they lead us either to absurd results or else to no results. * * * " [40 Yale Law Journal, supra, at page 71.]

So, too, Professor Sayre indicates that regardless of artificial classifications, one stabbing a corpse thinking it a live person should be liable for attempted murder. Thus he states in a footnote, at 41 Harvard Law Review, supra, page 853:

" * * * [W]here one comes upon his enemy lying apparently asleep and stabs him to the heart, and it is later shown that the victim was dead before the defendant stabbed him, although the defendant could not of course be convicted for murder, he should be held liable for an attempt to kill if his belief that the victim was still living was under all the circumstances a natural and reasonable one."

The lack of logic between some of the holdings, supra; the inherent difficulty in assigning a given set of facts to a proper classification; the criticism of existing positions in this area; and, most importantly, the denial of true and substantial justice by these artificial holdings have led, quite naturally, to proposals for reform in the civilian legal concepts of criminal attempts.

In addition to a progressive and modern view now evident in some judicial decisions and writings, The American Law In-

stitute in its proposal of a "Model Penal Code" defines Criminal Attempts, in Article 5.01 * * *. The import of that suggested statute is made clear in Tentative Draft No. 10 of the Model Penal Code of The American Law Institute, supra, at page 25, where it is stated:

" * * * It should suffice, therefore, to indicate at this stage what we deem to be the major results of the draft. They are:

(a) to extend the criminality of attempts by sweeping aside the defense of impossibility (including the distinction between so-called factual and legal impossibility) and by drawing the line between attempt and non-criminal preparation further away from the final act; the crime becomes essentially one of criminal purpose implemented by an overt act strongly corroborative of such purpose; * * *."

After having given this entire question a great deal more than casual attention and study, we are forced to the conclusion that the law of attempts in military jurisprudence has tended toward the advanced and modern position, which position will be achieved for civilian jurisprudence if The American Law Institute is completely successful in its advocacy of this portion of the Model Penal Code. * * *

We hold, therefore, in accordance with the foregoing authorities, that in this instance the fact that the female, upon whom these detestable acts were performed, was already dead at the time of their commission, is no bar to conviction for attempted rape.

However, for purposes of clarity, we should make mention of that portion of paragraph 159, Manual for Courts–Martial, supra, which reads:

"It is not an attempt when every act intended by the accused could be completed without committing an offense, even though the accused may at the time believe he is committing an offense."

That provision has no reference to questions we have here discussed. Such language says no more than that if what an accused believed to be a substantive crime was actually no crime at all, he cannot be guilty of an attempt to commit such crime. That is, when the intended action, even if completed, is not an offense despite the fact accused believed otherwise, he cannot be held for a criminal attempt. Under those circumstances a substantive offense is nonexistent, and an accused's acts, whether carried to fruition or not, constitute wholly lawful conduct. It is interesting to observe that the same situation will exist under the Model Penal Code. See Tentative Draft No. 10, supra, page 31, which states, in the commentary:

> "Of course, it is still necessary that the result desired or intended by the actor constitute a crime. If, according to his beliefs as to facts and legal relationships, the result desired or intended is not a crime, the actor will not be guilty of an attempt even though he firmly believes that his goal is criminal." * * *

FERGUSON, JUDGE (concurring in part and dissenting in part):

Professor Jerome Hall traces the difficulty in analyzing the defense of impossibility in criminal attempts to Baron Bramwell's original use of illustrative fact situations "from Never–Never Land" in *Regina v. Collins,* 9 Cox.C.C. 497, 169 Eng.Rep. 1477 (1864). Hall, *General Principles of Criminal Law,* 2d ed., page 593. I am inclined to attribute it to a growing tendency on the part of legal theoreticians to attach more importance to the evilness of a man's intent than to his acts—a belief, if you will, that the law should punish sinful thoughts if accompanied by any sort of antisocial conduct which evidences the design to execute forbidden acts. When certain courts adopt such broad penal theories

and others reject them, the result is the legal morass to which my brothers refer.

* * *

Impossibility cases have generally involved homicide, larceny and related crimes, rape, and what might be classified as a hodgepodge of statutory offenses, ranging from abortion to corruption of jurors.

The homicide cases have usually involved the absence of the victim. In *State v. Mitchell,* 170 Mo. 633, 71 S.W. 175 (1902), it was established that the defendant fired two shots into his intended victim's bedroom for the purpose of slaying him. The victim, however, was elsewhere in the house, and the attack went for nought. Rejecting the contention that accused should not have been convicted of attempted murder, the court stated, at page 177:

> " * * * So in this case the intent evidenced by the firing into the bedroom with a deadly weapon, accompanied by a present capacity in defendant to murder Warren if he were in the room, and the failure to do so only because Warren happily retired upstairs instead of in the bed into which defendant fired, made out a perfect case of an attempt within the meaning of the statute. * * * " * * *

In *State v. Damms,* 9 Wis.2d 183, 100 N.W.2d 592 (1960), a different situation was presented. Accused, with intent to kill, held a pistol to his wife's head, and pulled the trigger twice. The weapon did not fire, as it did not contain any cartridges. The evidence indicated that accused in fact thought it was fully loaded.

Relying on a great number of decisions involving similar facts, the Wisconsin Supreme Court held that the defendant was properly convicted of attempted murder. It said, at page 596:

> "Sound public policy would seem to support the majority view that impossi-

bility not apparent to the actor should not absolve him from the offense of attempt to commit the crime he intended. An unequivocal act accompanied by intent should be sufficient to constitute a criminal attempt. Insofar as the actor knows, he has done everything necessary to insure the commission of the crime intended, and he should not escape punishment because of the fortuitous circumstance that by reason of some fact unknown to him it was impossible to effectuate the intended result."

* * *

In *People v. Jaffe,* 185 N.Y. 497, 78 N.E. 169 (1906), it was concluded that the defendant could not be guilty of an attempt to receive stolen property when the cloth which he received was in fact not stolen. In the *Jaffe* case, the court noted, at page 169:

" * * * In passing upon the question here presented for our determination, it is important to bear in mind precisely what it was that the defendant attempted to do. He simply made an effort to purchase certain specific pieces of cloth. He believed the cloth to be stolen property, but it was not such in fact. The purchase, therefore, if it had been completely effected, could not constitute the crime of receiving stolen property, knowing it to be stolen, since there could be no such thing as knowledge on the part of the defendant of a nonexistent fact, although there might be a belief on his part that the fact existed. As Mr. Bishop well says, it is a mere truism that there can be no receiving of stolen goods which have not been stolen. 2 Bishop's New Crim.Law, § 1140. It is equally difficult to perceive how there can be an attempt to receive stolen goods, knowing them to have been stolen, when they have not been stolen in fact.

"The crucial distinction between the case before us and the pickpocket cases, and others involving the same principle, lies not in the possibility or impossibility [factual?] *of the commission of the crime, but in the fact that, in the present case, the act, which it was doubtless the intent of the defendant to commit would not have been a crime if it had been consummated."* [Emphasis supplied.]

Some jurisdictions have concluded that attempts to commit larceny by false pretenses occur where the victim knows the defendant's representations are false but parts with his money or property without reliance thereon. Thus, in *State v. Peterson,* 109 Wash. 25, 186 Pac. 264 (1919), the appellant called a department store and sought to obtain delivery of merchandise by falsely representing herself as another credit customer. The store was not deceived by her pretense and notified police officers. Appellant was apprehended when she called for the merchandise. In concluding that attempted larceny had been made out, the Washington Supreme Court stated, at page 265:

" * * * Had the ruse succeeded in its entirety, there would have been a consummated offense, and it does not follow from the fact that the employes of the merchandise house were not deceived there is taken away from the transaction the element of attempt to deceive." * * *

In *Marley v. State,* 58 N.J.L. 207, 33 Atl. 208 (1895), the defendants were indicted for incurring a debt on behalf of their county in excess of the limit permitted by law. It was shown in defense that the debt which the defendants contracted was void in law. In upsetting a conviction of attempt to incur a debt beyond the permissible limit, the court pointed out that, as the debt was a nullity from the standpoint of the body politic, it was legally impossible for it to have been incurred. Hence, the conviction of attempt would not lie.

In like manner, it has been held that one does not commit the crime of attempted embracery when the individual whom he sought to corrupt was in fact not a juror, having been previously excused from attendance upon the trial. *State v. Taylor,* 345 Mo. 325, 133 S.W.2d 336 (1939); *State v. Porter,* 125 Mont. 503, 242 P.2d 984 (1942). And where defendants intended to sell pears in violation of a pricing order and did in fact sell them, it was concluded that there could be no conviction of an attempt to violate the order upon a showing that the actual sale was within the order's terms. *Rex v. Dalton,* 33 Crim.App.R. 102 (1949). Nor could there be a conviction of an attempt to pursue and take a deer out of season upon proof that the defendant shot a stuffed deer. *State v. Guffey,* 262 S.W.2d 152 (1953) (Missouri). In the last cited case, the court remarked, at page 156:

" * * * The State's evidence shows that one of the defendants did shoot the dummy but did they pursue, chase or follow a *deer* by shooting this stuffed defunct doe hide? It was not a deer. If the dummy had been actually taken, (it could not be pursued) defendants would not have committed any offense. It is no offense to attempt to do that which is not illegal. Neither is it a crime to attempt to do that which it is legally impossible to do. For instance, it is no crime to attempt to murder a corpse because it cannot be murdered." * * *

Charges of attempted rape seem uniformly to have allowed legal impossibility as a defense when a juridical impediment was found to prevent the consummation of the crime. Thus, in *Frazier v. State,* 48 Tex.Crim. 142, 86 S.W. 754 (1905), it was concluded to be legally impossible for a husband to be convicted of the attempted criminal violation of his wife's person. And in *Foster v. Commonwealth,* 96 Va. 306, 31 S.E. 503 (1898), a jurisdiction applying the common-law's conclusive presumption of legal incapacity of a boy under the age of fourteen to commit rape determined that, because of such presumption, he could not be convicted of attempted rape. The court said, at page 505:

"The accused being under 14 years of age, and conclusively presumed to be incapable of committing the crime of rape, it logically follows, as a plain legal deduction, that he was also incapable in law of an attempt to commit it. He could not be held to be guilty of an attempt to commit an offense which he was physically impotent to perpetrate."

Where, however, a jurisdiction holds to the view that a boy's age as less than fourteen years creates only a *rebuttable factual* presumption of noncapacity, it also is concluded that there may be a conviction of attempted rape by such an individual. *Davidson v. Commonwealth,* 20 Ky.Law.Rep. 540, 47 S.W. 213 (1898). So, also, is the defense of legal impossibility unavailable in the case of individuals above the common-law age of legal capacity who, for physical reasons, are impotent and thus unable to consummate the crime of rape. *Preddy v. Commonwealth,* 184 Va. 765, 36 S.E.2d 549 (1946).

It seems to me that, from the foregoing authorities—representative as they are of the welter of decisions in this field—definite principles may be derived which, when applied to the facts depicted in the record before us, lead inevitably to the conclusion that accused's conviction of attempted rape must be vitiated on the basis of legal impossibility. In the homicide cases, we find in every instance a victim in being upon whom the crime could have been committed * * *.

In the false pretense cases, again we find victims in being and defendants who have done everything necessary to the commission of the consummated crime except to convince their quarry of the validity of the confidence game. Their crimes were unsuccessful not because of legal considerations but only because of the fact that, in each instance, the actors underestimated the acumen of their human targets.

* * *

In contrast to these cases upholding convictions of attempts wherein, but for the fact of absence, disbelief, poor aim, and physical inability to accomplish the result sought, are those in which there is, so to speak, no "victim in being." Thus, we find that one cannot attempt to influence a juror who is not a juror. *State v. Taylor,* supra; *State v. Porter,* supra. One cannot attempt to pursue a deer which is nothing more than a stuffed hide. *State v. Guffey,* supra. One cannot attempt to kill by firing into a corpse or commit rape upon a mannequin. Nor can one attempt to receive stolen goods which are not in fact stolen, *People v. Jaffe,* supra, or attempt rape where he legally has no capacity so to act, *Foster v. Commonwealth,* supra.

In each of these instances, there is simply no "victim" or thing which the particular law intended to be broken is designed to protect. Thus, embracery statutes are designed to protect jurors rather than those whom an accused believes to be jurors. Only *stolen* goods are within the proscription against attempts to receive. Only a deer can be the subject of an attempt to hunt deer. In short, the subject matter of accused's acts must be one within the prohibition of the particular statute which he is alleged to have violated, no matter what his personal belief may be, so that he could have been convicted of the consummated crime had he been entirely successful.

No series of cases more clearly portray this distinction than those which deal with the legal incapacity of a boy under fourteen years of age to attempt rape as compared to those which hold simple physical impotency to be no such bar to conviction.

In the one instance, the actor, because of a pure rule of law, is incapable of violating a woman, regardless of his actual precocity. In the other, there is no legal bar, the inability being a fact resulting from some disease, disability, or infirmity of which the law refuses to take notice.

In like manner, the barrier to consummation of the crime charged here is not factual but legal. Indeed, accused did everything they set out to do, but they admittedly could not commit the actual crime of rape because their victim was dead and thus outside the protection of the law appertaining to that offense. Because the objective of their loathsome attentions was no longer subject to being raped, it seems to me that there cannot be any liability for an attempt, for, just as in the case of the lad under the age of fourteen, the stuffed "deer," and the nonjuror, a legal rather than a factual impediment existed to the offense's consummation. In brief, this is not the case of an empty pocket but one in which there was no pocket to pick. And, as is succinctly stated in the Manual, supra, at page 305:

> "It is not an attempt when every act intended by the accused [sexual intercourse with a woman in fact dead] could be completed without committing an offense [rape], even though the accused may at the time believe he is committing an offense [rape]."

Finally, I believe that the position which my brothers take unnecessarily emphasizes the accused's mental frame of reference at the expense of what they actually did. The common-law concept that danger to society lay chiefly in action rather than in thought has much to commend it, based as it is upon centuries of experiential development. Particularly, however, is this true in the armed services, furnished as they are with general articles of the Code within whose scope conduct potentially invasive of any important social interest easily falls. Indeed, such is the course which was wisely followed here, for accused's reprehensible behavior was charged as— and so sustained by the board of review— lewd and lascivious conduct in violation of Code, supra, Article 134. With the propriety of that conclusion, I am certain that none of us argue. When, however, it is found that such acts, albeit legally incapable of consummation, are also punishable as attempted rape, I believe we so widen the thrust of Code, supra, Article 80, that we permit punishment to be predicated upon one's plans quite without regard to whether they may legally be completed. The door, therefore, is left open for the protection of logs against homicidal attack and of the supposed honor of dressmaker's dummies. And to those who, as does Professor Hall, believe that these are hypotheses from Never–Never Land, I recommend the reading of the transcript before us. * * *

Notes and Questions

1. Compare *United States v. Berrigan,* 482 F.2d 171 (3d Cir.1973), the appeal by Fr. Philip Berrigan and Sister Elizabeth McAlister from their convictions for attempting to send seven letters into and out of Lewisburg Federal Penitentiary "without the knowledge and consent of the warden." The court reversed:

"Applying the principles of the law of attempt to the instant case, the writing of the letters, and their copying and transmittal by the courier, Boyd Douglas, constituted the *Act.* This much the government proved. What the government did not prove—and could not prove because it was a legal impossibility—was the 'external, objective situation which the substantive law may require to be present,' to-wit, absence of knowledge and consent of the warden. Thus, the government failed to prove the *'Circumstances or attendant circumstances'* vital to the offense. Without such

proof, the *Consequence* or *Result* did not constitute an offense that violated the federal statute. The warden and the government were aware of the existence of the letters. The courier acted with the consent of the warden. Although there was no entrapment, the public authorities were privy to the *Act* which gave rise to these charges. There are many supporters of the view that irrespective of the absence of a necessary element of the offense prohibited by statute—the 'external, objective situation which the substantive law may require be present'—criminal responsibility should attach 'if the attendant circumstances were as [the actor] believes them to be.' The bills presently before the Congress contain such a provision. But the efforts of the distinguished scholars who drafted these proposals must be kept in perspective; they are recommending changes to fill an apparent void in existing law. They suggest a statutory change which would remove one of the elements of the offense which still must be proved under the present federal statutory law of crimes."

2. The *Jaffe* case, discussed in *Thomas,* is one of the most famous and most commented upon impossibility cases. Does it present an easier or more difficult problem than *Thomas?* Consider the views on *Jaffe* in notes 3 through 8 following.

3. *Model Penal Code* § 5.01, Comment (1985), concludes that the *Jaffe* approach "is unsound in that it seeks to evaluate a mental attitude—'intent' or 'purpose'—not by looking to the actor's mental frame of reference, but to a situation wholly at variance with the actor's beliefs. In so doing, the courts exonerate defendants in situations where attempt liability most certainly should be imposed. In all of these cases the actor's criminal purpose has been clearly demonstrated; he went as far as he could in implementing that purpose; and as a result, his 'dangerousness' is plainly manifested."

4. Keedy, *Criminal Attempts at Common Law,* 102 U.Pa.L.Rev. 464, 477 (1954), says that *Jaffe* is "easily explainable, without reference to any conception of 'legal impossibility.' In the *Jaffe* case the necessary intent * * * was lacking."

5. Enker, *Impossibility in Criminal Attempts—Legality and the Legal Process,* 53 Minn.L.Rev. 665, 679–80, 682 (1969):

"Those who would eliminate the defense of legal impossibility from the legal lexicon and would convict Jaffe of attempted possession of stolen goods because he thought they were stolen presumably would convict any other defendant of the same crime with respect to goods that had never been stolen if it could be proved that the defendant thought they were stolen. Having dispensed with the need for establishing the circumstance that the goods are stolen, they must permit this result if there is evidence of guilty belief. Assume two cases in which the sole direct evidence of the defendant's alleged belief that the goods are stolen is a confession or the testimony of an informer or an accomplice. In one case the goods possessed are in fact stolen; in the other they are not. It is reasonably clear that most of us would rest easier with a conviction in the first case than in the second although we might have a difficult time articulating reasons for this distinction. [This may be because] possession of stolen goods furnishes some evidence of belief that they are stolen while, clearly, possession of goods not in fact stolen furnishes no reason to believe that the defendant thought they were stolen.

"This requires some elaboration. Concededly, the probative relationship between the fact that the goods are stolen and the possessor's knowledge that they are stolen differs from the probative relationship between, say, the fact that certain goods are machine guns or narcotics and the possessor's knowledge of their nature.

Ordinarily, knowledge that goods are within one's possession carries with it knowledge of their physical nature. Where the defendant is proved to have had in his possession certain objects, say, narcotics, it seems reasonable to conclude that he knew the physical nature of those objects and to cast on him the risk of conviction if he does not adduce some evidence to dispel this normal inference. It is clear, then, that to convict someone of attempted possession of narcotics for possessing nonnarcotic goods which he allegedly believed were narcotics would be to redefine the crime of possession of narcotics to eliminate an objective element that had major evidentiary significance and to increase the risk of mistaken conclusions that the defendant believed the goods were narcotics.

" * * * The point is, however, that by eliminating these objective elements we create newly defined crimes in which we replace the statutorily defined fixed reference points for judging the defendant's mens rea with an open-ended sufficiency-of-the-evidence test which may include the less reliable forms of evidence such as questionable admissions, the testimony of informers and accomplices, and proof of prior convictions."

6. Similar analysis is found in *United States v. Oviedo,* 525 F.2d 881 (5th Cir. 1976). Oviedo was contacted by an undercover agent who desired to purchase narcotics, and thereafter sold to the agent what he said was one pound of heroin. Though a field test of the substance was positive, later chemical analysis revealed it was in fact procaine hydrochloride, an uncontrolled substance. Oviedo was charged with attempt to distribute heroin. At trial, he testified he knew the substance was not heroin and that he had been trying to "rip off" the agent. In reversing his conviction, the court reasoned:

"When the defendant sells a substance which is actually heroin, it is reasonable to infer that he knew the physical nature of the substance, and to place on him the burden of dispelling that inference. However, if we convict the defendant of attempting to sell heroin for the sale of a non-narcotic substance, we eliminate an objective element that has major evidentiary significance and we increase the risk of mistaken conclusions that the defendant believed the goods were narcotics.

"Thus, we demand that in order for a defendant to be guilty of a criminal attempt, the objective acts performed, without any reliance on the accompanying *mens rea,* mark the defendant's conduct as criminal in nature. The acts should be unique rather than so commonplace that they are engaged in by persons not in violation of the law."

7. Weigand, *Why Lady Eldon Should be Acquitted: The Social Harm in Attempting the Impossible,* 27 DePaul L.Rev. 231, 268–69 (1977), proposes this test: "An attempt which cannot succeed is punishable if the offender's conduct, seen in the light of his statements accompanying the acts he deemed necessary for achieving his purpose, would cause alarm or apprehension to an average observer." He continues at 271: "Under the standards here suggested, Oviedo's attorney would face a most difficult task. Too much evidence speaks against his client. Not only had Oviedo promised heroin to the government agent, but he had also stored a large amount of the procaine hydrochloride in his television set—certainly an odd place to keep substances which one regards as innocent. Both elements, taken together, would strongly suggest to our hypothetical observer that Oviedo intended to sell a controlled substance, particularly since the hiding of the powder is not consistent with the possible alternative purpose of 'ripping off' the supposed customer. Inasmuch as the observer feels threatened by persons dealing in drugs, he would be alarmed by Oviedo's conduct. The original conviction, which was overturned by the Fifth Circuit, therefore was probably the correct decision of the case."

8. Enker, supra, at 685–87: "[I]n drafting the substantive statute involved in *Jaffe,* nothing prevented the legislature from defining the crime as the possession of goods in the belief that they are stolen without also requiring that they be in fact stolen. As earlier suggested, a crucial factor justifying legislative delegation of the power to define the act element of attempts in the preparation-attempt cases was the inability of the legislature to provide for the infinitely varying acts in advance. In the case of the circumstantial elements of the crimes here considered—whether the goods are in fact dutiable, are stolen, or are narcotics—the legislature is perfectly capable of deciding in advance whether or not to require the particular element. There is no need to delegate that power to the courts under the attempt rubric.

* * *

"We may, therefore, characterize the issue presented by legal impossibility thus: the legislature has defined the substantive crime to require the presence of a particular circumstance; there is no reason why—for cases in which that circumstance is absent but the defendant allegedly thinks it is present—the legislature should delegate to the courts the power or the duty to decide whether that circumstance may be dispensed with; if the legislature were to delegate the issue to the courts—or the courts were to assume it—the courts would have no analytic tools for deciding the issue; delegation to the court of the power to define the elements of a crime after the act raises serious issues of legality, particularly when such analytic tools are lacking; and there are in any event good policy reasons favoring retention of the circumstance as an element of the crime."

9. In *Damms*, the unloaded gun case discussed in *Thomas*, the applicable statute defined an attempt in terms of an act demonstrating that the defendant "would commit the crime except for the intervention of another person or some extraneous factor." Was the dissent in that case correct in saying that the cause of failure was not extraneous because it was defendant's own conduct in omitting to load the gun? Compare Note, 70 Yale L.J. 160, 165 (1960): "Neither opinion adequately utilizes the 'extraneous factor' criterion to examine the potential dangerousness of the offender. The dissent, by ignoring defendant's state of mind, failed to consider the possibility that the act of omission, although directly traceable to the actor, may have been caused by a factor other than the exercise of internal control. Likewise, the majority's definition, by focusing solely upon defendant's awareness at the conscious level of the omission, did not consider the possibility that failure to load the gun might have resulted from internal control at the unconscious level."

10. Consider the case put by Maxey, J., dissenting in *Commonwealth v. Johnson*, 312 Pa. 140, 167 A. 344 (1933): "Even though a 'voodoo doctor' just arrived here from Haiti actually believed that his malediction would surely bring death to the person on whom he was invoking it, I cannot conceive of an American court upholding a conviction of such a maledicting 'doctor' for attempted murder or even attempted assault and battery. Murderous maledictions might have to be punished by the law as disorderly conduct, but they could not be classed as attempted crimes unless the courts so far departed from the law of criminal attempts as to engage in legislation. A malediction arising out of a murderous intent is not such a substantial overt act that it would support a charge of attempted murder."

11. Consider *Wilson v. State*, 85 Miss. 687, 38 So. 46 (1905): "Wilson was convicted of an attempt to commit forgery, the court below properly charging the jury that it could not convict of the crime itself. The instrument of which attempt to commit forgery is predicated is a draft for 'two and $^{50}/_{100}$ dollars,' as written out in the body of it, having in the upper right-hand corner the figures '$2.$^{50}/_{100}$,' as is customary in checks, drafts, and notes, and having plainly printed and stamped on the face of the instrument the words 'Ten Dollars or Less.' Wilson, with a pen, put the figure '1' before the figure '2' in the upper right-hand corner, making these immaterial figures appear '$12.50' instead of '$2.50,' and undertook to negotiate it as $12.50. This was not forgery, because it was an immaterial part of the paper, and because it could not possibly have injured anybody. In order to constitute the crime, there must not only be the intent to commit it, but also an act of alteration done to a material part, so that injury might result. [I]t is enough to say * * * that an instrument void on its face is not the subject of forgery, and in order to be so subject, it must have been capable of working injury if it had been genuine, and that the marginal numbers and figures are not part of the instrument, and their alteration is not forgery.

"This being true, can the conviction of an attempt to commit forgery be sustained in the case before us? We think not. No purpose appears to change anything on the paper except the figures in the margin, and this could not have done any hurt. Our statute confines the crime of forgery to instances where "any person may be affected, bound, or in any way injured in his person or property." This is not such a case, and section 974 forbids convicting of an attempt 'when it shall appear that the crime intended or the offense attempted was perpetrated.' In this record the innocuous prefix of the figure '1' on the margin was fully accomplished, and no other effort appears, and, if genuine, could have done no harm; and so the appellant is guiltless, in law, of the crime of which he was convicted."

12. Some have asserted that the *Jaffe* rule is wrong but that nonetheless *Wilson* is correct because, were *Wilson* decided otherwise, "the law of attempt would be used to manufacture a new crime, when the legislature has left the situation outside of the ambit of the law." G. Williams, *Criminal Law: The General Part* 634 (2d ed. 1961). Is this consistent? Such persons, complains Kelman, *Interpretive Construction in the Substantive Criminal Law,* 33 Stan.L.Rev. 591, 622 (1981), "simply interpret, without rationale, Wilson's intent narrowly and Jaffe's intent broadly. They view Wilson as intending the most precise deed imaginable—altering the numbers on the check—rather than as intending a broader category of acts—intending to receive money from a bank by aptly altering an instrument. They view Jaffe as intending a broader category of acts—receiving stolen property—rather than intending a precise act—receiving the particular goods that were actually delivered to him. Viewed narrowly, Jaffe 'thought he was committing a crime' but was not because the criminal law does not prohibit receiving unstolen goods. Similarly, viewed broadly, Wilson intended to violate the law of forgery; had he *correctly* altered the instrument (so as to make a bank pay him money), he would have been guilty of the completed crime."

SECTION 4. ABANDONMENT

PEOPLE v. STAPLES

Court of Appeal, Second District, 1970.
6 Cal.App.3d 61, 85 Cal.Rptr. 589.

REPPY, ASSOCIATE JUSTICE.

Defendant was charged in an information with attempted burglary. Trial by jury was waived, and the matter submitted on the testimony contained in the transcript of the preliminary hearing together with exhibits. Defendant was found guilty. Proceedings were suspended before pronouncement of sentence, and an order was made granting defendant probation. The appeal is from the order which is deemed a final judgment.

In October 1967, while his wife was away on a trip, defendant, a mathematician, under an assumed name, rented an office on the second floor of a building in Hollywood which was over the mezzanine of a bank. Directly below the mezzanine was the vault of the bank. Defendant was aware of the layout of the building, specifically of the relation of the office he rented to the bank vault. Defendant paid rent for the period from October 23 to November 23. The landlord had 10 days before commencement of the rental period within which to finish some interior repairs and painting. During this prerental period defendant brought into the office certain equipment. This included drilling tools, two acetylene gas tanks, a blow torch, a blanket, and a linoleum rug. The landlord observed these items when he came in from time to time to see how the repair work was progressing. Defendant learned from a custodian that no one was in the building on Saturdays. On Saturday, October 14, defendant drilled two groups of holes into the floor of the office above the mezzanine room. He stopped drilling before the holes went through the floor. He came back to the office several times thinking he might slowly drill down, covering the holes with the linoleum rug. At some point in time he installed a hasp lock on a closet, and planned to, or did, place his tools in it. However, he left the closet keys on the premises. Around the end of November, apparently after November 23, the landlord notified the police and turned the tools and equipment over to them. Defendant did not pay any more rent. It is not clear when he last entered the office, but it could have been after November 23, and even after the landlord had removed the equipment. On February 22, 1968, the police arrested defendant. After receiving advice as to his constitutional rights, defendant voluntarily made an oral statement which he reduced to writing.

Among other things which defendant wrote down were these:

"Saturday, the 14th * * * I drilled some small holes in the floor of the room. Because of tiredness, fear, and the implications of what I was doing, I stopped and went to sleep.

"At this point I think my motives began to change. The actutal [sic] commencement of my plan made me begin to realize that even if I were to succeed a fugitive life of living off of stolen money would not give the enjoyment of the life of a mathematician however humble a job I might have.

"I still had not given up my plan however. I felt I had made a certain investment of time, money, effort and a certain pschological [sic] commitment to the concept.

"I came back several times thinking I might store the tools in the closet and slowly drill down (covering the hole with a rug of linoleum square. As time went on (after two weeks or so). My wife came back and my life as bank robber seemed more and more absurd."

Defendant's position in this appeal is that, as a matter of law, there was insufficient evidence upon which to convict him of a criminal attempt under Penal Code section 664. Defendant claims that his actions were all preparatory in nature and never reached a stage of advancement in relation to the substantive crime which he concededly intended to commit (burglary of the bank vault) so that criminal responsibility might attach.

In order for the prosecution to prove that defendant committed an attempt to burglarize as proscribed by Penal Code section 664, it was required to establish that he had the specific intent to commit a burglary of the bank and that his acts toward that goal went beyond mere preparation.

The required specific intent was clearly established in the instant case. Defendant admitted in his written confession that he rented the office fully intending to burglarize the bank, that he brought in tools and equipment to accomplish this purpose, and that he began drilling into the floor with the intent of making an entry into the bank.

The question of whether defendant's conduct went beyond "mere preparation" raises some provocative problems. The briefs and the oral argument of counsel in this case point up a degree of ambiguity and uncertainty that permeates the law of attempts in this state. Each side has cited us to a different so-called "test" to determine whether this defendant's conduct went beyond the preparatory stage. Predictably each respective test in the eyes of its proponents yielded an opposite result.

Defendant relies heavily on the following language: "Preparation alone is not enough [to convict for an attempt], there must be some appreciable fragment of the crime committed, *it must be in such progress that it will be consummated unless interrupted by circumstances independent of the will of the attempter,* and the act must not be equivocal in nature." Defendant argues that while the facts show that he did do a series of acts directed at the commission of a burglary—renting the office, bringing in elaborate equipment and actually starting drilling—the facts do not show that he was interrupted by any outside circumstances. Without such interruption and a voluntary desistence on his part, defendant concludes that under the above stated test, he has not legally committed an attempt. The attorney general has replied that even if the above test is appropriate, the trial judge, obviously drawing reasonable inferences, found that defendant was interrupted by outside circumstances—the landlord's acts of discovering the burglary equipment, resuming control over the premises, and calling the police.

However, the attorney general suggests that another test is more appropriate: " * * * Whenever the design of a person to commit crime is clearly shown, slight acts in furtherance of the design will constitute an attempt." (Note absence of reference to interruption.) The People argue that defendant's felonious intent was clearly set out in his written confession; that the proven overt acts in furtherance of the design, although only needing to be slight, were, in fact, substantial; that this combination warrants the affirmance of the attempt conviction.

We suggest that the confusion in this area is a result of the broad statutory language of section 664, which reads in part: "Every person who attempts to commit any crime, but fails, or is prevented or intercepted in the perpetration thereof, is punishable * * *."

An examination of the decisional law reveals *at least two* general categories of attempts, both of which have been held to fall within the ambit of the statute.

In the first category are those situations where the actor does all acts necessary (including the last proximate act) to commit the substantive crime, but nonetheless he somehow is unsuccessful. This lack of success is either a "failure" or a "prevention" brought about because of some extraneous circumstance, e.g., a malfunction of equipment, a miscalculation of operations by the actor or a situation wherein circumstances were at variance with what the actor believed them to be. Certain convictions for attempted murder illustrate

the first category. Some turn on situations wherein the actor fires a weapon at a person but misses; takes aim at an intended victim and pulls the trigger, but the firing mechanism malfunctions; plants on an aircraft a homemade bomb which sputters but does not explode. * * *

In the above situations application of the rule * * * which defendant herein seeks to have applied, would appear to be quite appropriate. After a defendant has done all acts necessary under normal conditions to commit a crime, he is culpable for an attempt if he is unsuccessful *because* of an extraneous or fortuitous circumstance.

However, it is quite clear that under California law an overt act, which, when added to the requisite intent, is sufficient to bring about a criminal attempt, need not be the last proximate or ultimate step towards commission of the substantive crime. "It is not necessary that the overt act proved should have been the ultimate step toward the consummation of the design. It is sufficient if it was 'the first or some subsequent step in a direct movement towards the commission of the offense after the preparations are made.'" * * *

This rule makes for a second category of "attempts." * * *

* * * There was definitely substantial evidence entitling the trial judge to find that defendant's acts had gone beyond the preparation stage. Without specifically deciding where defendant's preparations left off and where his activities became a completed criminal attempt, we can say that his "drilling" activity clearly was an unequivocal and direct step toward the completion of the burglary. It was a fragment of the substantive crime contemplated i.e., the beginning of the "breaking" element. Further, defendant himself characterized his activity as the *actual commencement of his plan.* The drilling by defendant was obvi-

ously one of a series of acts which logic and ordinary experience indicate would result in the proscribed act of burglary.

The instant case provides an out-of-the-ordinary factual situation within the second category. Usually the actors in cases falling within that category of attempts are intercepted or caught in the act. Here, there was no direct proof of any actual interception. But it was clearly inferable by the trial judge that defendant became aware that the landlord had resumed control over the office and had turned defendant's equipment and tools over to the police. This was the equivalent of interception.

The inference of this nonvoluntary character of defendant's abandonment was a proper one for the trial judge to draw. However, it would seem that the character of the abandonment in situations of this type, whether it be voluntary (prompted by pangs of conscience or a change of heart) or nonvoluntary (established by inference in the instant case), is not controlling. The relevant factor is the determination of whether the acts of the perpetrator have reached such a stage of advancement that they can be classified as an attempt. Once that attempt is found there can be no exculpatory abandonment. "One of the purposes of the criminal law is to protect society from those who intend to injure it. When it is established that the defendant intended to commit a specific crime and that in carrying out this intention he committed an act that caused harm or sufficient danger of harm, it is immaterial that for some collateral reason he could not complete the intended crime."

The order is affirmed.

Notes and Questions

1. Should abandonment be a defense? If so, under what circumstances? Compare *Model Penal Code* § 5.01(4) with *People v. Von Hecht,* 133 Cal.App.2d 25, 283 P.2d 764 (1955): "Abandonment is a defense if the attempt to commit a crime is freely and voluntarily abandoned before the act is put in process of final execution and where there is no outside cause prompting such abandonment." In deciding upon the answers to these questions, consider the fact situations set out in notes 2 through 5 following.

2. "At the time of the alleged offense, appellant was serving a one- to three-year sentence for larceny in the Luzerne County Prison. At about 12:15 a.m., on December 26, 1972, James Larson, a Guard Supervisor at the prison, heard an alarm go off that indicated that someone was attempting an escape in the recreation area of the prison. The alarm was designed so that it could be heard in the prison office, but not in the courtyard. Larson immediately contacted Guards Szmulo and Banik. Initially, the guards checked the prison population, but found no one missing. The three men then conducted a search of the area where the alarm had been 'tripped'. Near the recreation yard between two wings of the prison, they found one piece of barbed wire that had been cut. In addition, Guard Szmulo found a laundry bag filled with civilian clothing. The bags are issued by the prison and are marked with a different number for each prisoner. A check revealed that the bag belonged to appellant.

"At approximately 5:15 a.m., on December 26, the appellant voluntarily approached Larson. Appellant had spent that night on the nine p.m. to five a.m. shift at work in the boiler room, situated near the point where the alarm had been triggered. Appellant explained to Larson 'I was gonna make a break last night, but I changed my mind because I thought of my family, and I got scared of the consequences.' Appellant testified at trial that he had become depressed prior to his decision to escape because he had been denied a Christmas furlough on December 24,

1972. His testimony at trial was consistent with Larson's version of the episode: '* * * in the yard, I realized that I had shamed my family enough, and I did not want to shame them any more * * *. So I went back to the boiler room and continued working.' [a]

3. "In the fall of 1980 McDowell purchased two kilograms of cocaine from Fernando Dalmau. Dalmau was arrested later for an unrelated offense and agreed to act as an undercover agent for the Drug Enforcement Administration (DEA).

"In the summer of 1981 Dalmau and McDowell began negotiating another cocaine deal. They discussed the deal in a series of telephone conversations that DEA recorded. McDowell, a resident of Knoxville, Tennessee, agreed to travel to Atlanta, Georgia to make the purchase.

"McDowell, Dalmau and Crane, an undercover DEA agent, met in McDowell's motel room in Atlanta and negotiated the sale of one kilo of cocaine for $58,500. Crane told McDowell that he wanted to see the money before bringing the cocaine into the room. McDowell insisted on examining the cocaine first. Crane and Dalmau left the motel. A few minutes later they returned with two packages of sham cocaine and advised McDowell that he could examine the packages but not test the cocaine until Crane had seen the money. McDowell examined the packages closely and stated: 'This does not look like anything I ever done before. I don't want to buy it.'

"Crane later arrested McDowell in his motel room."

McDowell was charged with attempt to possess cocaine with intent to distribute same.[b]

4. "Around midnight Thorne saw appellant and Pust drive back and forth past the service station several times. Later, about 2:30 or 3 a.m., appellant and Pust drove into the pump area of the service station. At that time Thorne was busy waiting on a customer. He finished with the customer and returned the money to the till inside the station. When he came out the door appellant and Pust drove up in front of him, got out of the car and offered Thorne a pair of pliers in exchange for some money to buy gasoline. Thorne refused the offer. However, he noticed a gun partially covered by a shirt on the back seat of the car and asked if it was a .22. Appellant opened the car door, sat on the edge of the back seat, picked up the gun and pointed it at Thorne's chest. Appellant mumbled something which sounded to Thorne like 'this is a stickup' or 'this is a holdup.' Then when Thorne asked if it was a holdup appellant replied, 'That's what it means. That's what it looks like.'

"Thorne tried to talk the boys out of the holdup. He told them, 'Boys, let's just talk this all over and think twice before you do it. I am talking to you father's advice'. However, Pust told Thorne that they had 'some girls' and needed the money to get out of town. Pust also suggested that Thorne claim colored people had held him up. Thorne answered, 'The girls ain't worth going through this. As far as that, I'll put the gas, I'll give you some gas.'

---

a. *Commonwealth v. McCloskey,* 234 Pa.Super. 577, 341 A.2d 500 (1975). Defendant's conviction for attempted prison breach was reversed on the ground he had never engaged in sufficient acts for such an attempt. Cercone, J., concurring, "would have found little difficulty, for instance, in affirming appellant's conviction had he been apprehended by the guards immediately after he had snipped the barbed wire and crossed the inner fence," but concluded that "appellant's

abandonment of his plan is a sufficient defense to the crime of attempted prison breach and should be recognized as such."

b. *United States v. McDowell,* 705 F.2d 426 (11th Cir.1983), affirming defendant's conviction because "McDowell spurned the deal not to renounce his criminal intent but because he doubted either the genuineness or quality of the cocaine."

Then Thorne took $2 from his pocket and said he would put $2 worth of gasoline in the car and make up the shortage with the $2. A woman drove into the station just as Thorne was finishing putting the gasoline in the car. Pust gave Thorne the pliers and he and appellant drove away. Thorne, however, testified he would not have given the boys the gas but for the threat with the gun." [c]

5. "On March 3, 1965 at 6:55 p.m., the complaining witness, Jodean Randen, a housewife, was walking home across a fairly well-traveled railroad bridge in Eau Claire. She is a slight woman whose normal weight is 95 to 100 pounds. As she approached the opposite side of the bridge she passed a man who was walking in the opposite direction. The man turned and followed her, grabbed her arm and demanded her purse. She surrendered her purse and at the command of the man began walking away as fast as she could. Upon discovering that the purse was empty, he caught up with her again, grabbed her arm and told her that if she did not scream he would not hurt her. He then led her—willingly, she testified, so as to avoid being hurt by him—to the end of the bridge. While walking he shoved her head down and warned her not to look up or do anything and he would not hurt her.

"On the other side of the bridge along the railroad tracks there is a coal shack. As they approached the coal shack he grabbed her, put one hand over her mouth, and an arm around her shoulder and told her not to scream or he would kill her. At this time Mrs. Randen thought he had a knife in his hand. He then forced her into the shack and up against the wall. As she struggled for her breath he said, 'You know what else I want,' unzipped his pants and started pulling up her skirt. She finally succeeded in removing his hand from her mouth, and after reassuring him that she would not scream, told him she was pregnant and pleaded with him to desist or he would hurt her baby. He then felt of her stomach and took her over to the door of the shack, where in the better light he was able to ascertain that, under her coat, she was wearing maternity clothes. He thereafter let her alone and left after warning her not to scream or call the police, or he would kill her." [d]

6. Consider Kelman, *Interpretive Construction in the Substantive Criminal Law,* 33 Stan.L.Rev. 591, 628–30 (1981): "Suppose a defendant sets out to shoplift from a department store. He has taken steps sufficient to constitute an attempt, were he to be interrupted by external forces. However, he stops of his own accord because: (a) he decides that stealing is bad; (b) he decides that stealing is too risky; (c) he spots a warning that 'Shoplifters will be apprehended and prosecuted'; or (d) he spots the store detective watching him. Many jurisdictions would exculpate the defendant in any of the first three situations. But none would allow a voluntary abandonment defense in the last case. They

c. *People v. Crary,* 265 Cal.App.2d 534, 71 Cal. Rptr. 457 (1968). Appellant's conviction of robbery was reversed because of the failure of the trial court to instruct on attempted robbery, on the ground that "if appellant and Pust had changed their minds about robbing the service station when Thorne put the gasoline in appellant's automobile, and if they left with the impression that they had paid for it with a pair of pliers, they did not have the felonious intent required to commit robbery." The court noted in passing that even voluntary abandonment would not be a defense to the attempt crime.

d. *Le Barron v. State,* 32 Wis.2d 294, 145 N.W.2d 79 (1966), affirming defendant's conviction of attempted rape. The defendant on appeal did not claim that he should have a defense of abandonment. Rather, he unsuccessfully claimed (i) that the evidence did not show beyond a reasonable doubt an intent to rape, and (ii) that the woman's pregnancy was not an "extraneous factor" under the Wisconsin attempt statute, which defines an attempt as conduct demonstrating the defendant "would commit the crime except for the intervention of another person or some other extraneous factor."

would find the defendant guilty of attempt if he decided that unpredicted legal consequences would befall him and so decided 'to postpone the criminal conduct until a more advantageous time or to transfer the criminal effort to another but similar objective or victim.' In other words, using interpretive construction language, if the defendant abandons because of fear of legal consequences on the particular occasion, he has still demonstrated an intent to commit the categorical crime of theft, but has simply shifted the instance of the category. * * *

"This particular interpretive construction seems defensible, at least at first blush. The person who reads the sign has not discovered anything unique to the particular situation. There appears to be no reason *not* to equate the abandonment of this larceny with the abandonment of larcenies in general, because other larcenies appear to pose the same threats. But imagine that one defendant decides not to crack a safe because he discovers there is an alarm system he cannot crack, while another desists when he discovers there are alarm systems in general, none of which he *ever* can hope to crack. The first safecracker is looking for an easier safe system to break, the second for an object of his larcenous desires that is unprotected. Both could be seen as simply looking for safer targets. Yet it is implausible that a defendant who abandoned his attempted crime because he read a sign, 'This Safe Protected by Alarms' could be convicted while one who read a sign, 'Safe-crackers will be Apprehended and Prosecuted' would be acquitted. Both are simply being informed of the riskiness of their activity. It is simply unwarranted assertive construction to treat these defendants as renouncing larceny because they renounce *this* larceny. It is not clear how we would ever know that someone is moving on to a more advantageous time and place for his mischief, rather than abandoning a life of crime because he has

at least understood the social signals about the costs of crime. It is quite plain we cannot *know* that, because the social signals concerning the propriety of cost-benefit calculation are ambivalent and uninterpretable. We suppress the recognition of this ambivalence by asserting clear cases of total acceptable renunciation and by blocking the knowledge that in a world where selfish calculation is acceptable, all renunciations are in significant senses partial."

SECTION 5. PROSECUTION AND PUNISHMENT

1. *Charge of completed crime, conviction of attempt.* Assume that *A* has been charged with and is on trial for the offense of burglary, but during the course of the trial the evidence develops in such a way that it appears *A* may have only attempted the offense of burglary. May *A* be convicted of attempted burglary? At one time the answer was no, for while it was generally recognized that when a charge of an offense included within it a lesser offense the defendant could be convicted of that lesser crime, this rule was subject to one important qualification: upon an indictment for a felony, the defendant could not be convicted of a misdemeanor. Thus a conviction for the common law misdemeanor of attempt could not be had upon an indictment charging the felony of burglary.

Insofar as can be determined, that exception was based upon the fact that under early English criminal procedure a defendant in a felony trial had fewer rights than a defendant on trial for a misdemeanor. That quite clearly is not the case in the United States, and thus there has been no reason to honor this exception in this country. The courts are in general agreement that an attempt conviction may be had on a charge of the completed crime, and statutes to this effect are not uncommon.

This is not to say, however, that upon any charge of a completed crime the trier of fact will inevitably be confronted with the possibility of returning a verdict or finding of only an attempt. The judge may give an instruction on the attempt alternative only if the evidence would support such a verdict. For example, if on *A's* trial for burglary *A* merely interposes an alibi defense or admits to being within the dwelling but claims to have been acting with an innocent intent, then the only logical alternatives are guilty of burglary or not guilty. On the other hand, if *A* asserts that he had not yet entered at the time of his apprehension, then the third alternative of guilt of attempted burglary exists. In such a case the attempt alternative may go to the jury even over the defendant's objection.

2. *Charge of attempt, proof of completed crime.* Quite obviously, a defendant charged only with an attempt may not be convicted of the completed crime. That is, if *A* had been on trial only for attempted burglary but it was shown at trial that he had actually entered the dwelling, clearly *A* may not be convicted of the greater uncharged offense of burglary. But, under those facts may he even be convicted of attempted burglary? As we have seen, the crime of attempt is often defined as if failure were an essential element, and on this basis it has sometimes been held that proof of the completed crime requires reversal of an attempt to commit it. The assumption that failure is required may be derived from the old common law rule of merger, whereby if an act resulted in both a felony and a misdemeanor the misdemeanor was said to be absorbed into the felony. (Taking that as the basis of the rule, then the problem would not arise if the completed crime would also be only a misdemeanor or, in the alternative, if the completed crime would be a felony but an attempt to commit it had by statute also been made a felony.)

The English merger rule was laid to rest by statute in 1851, and there seems no reason to follow it in this country. As one court observed, a defendant can hardly complain "where the determination of his case was more favorable to him than the evidence warranted." *People v. Vanderbilt,* 199 Cal. 461, 249 P. 867 (1926). Thus, many recent cases have held that a defendant may be convicted of the attempt even if the completed crime is proved, and many jurisdictions expressly so provide by statute.

3. *Punishment.* Considerable variation is to be found across the country concerning the authorized penalties for attempt. As to statutory provisions concerning the sentences which may be imposed for all or a broad class of attempts, the most common permits a penalty up to one-half the maximum penalty for the completed crime, except that a specific maximum is set for attempts to commit crimes punishable by death or life imprisonment. Another common provision establishes categories according to the severity of the penalty for the completed crime and specifies a range of penalties for attempts to commit crimes within each category, while some states have a combination of these two patterns. A few jurisdictions have set a maximum penalty for all attempts encompassed by the general attempt statute, and a few others merely provide that the penalty for attempt may be as great as for the completed crime. As to statutes dealing with attempts to commit particular crimes, the authorized punishment is usually lower than for the completed crime, but in some instances the same or even a higher punishment is possible.

Taking into account the rationale of the crime of attempt, what kind of penalty provisions would be most sensible? [a]

SECTION 6. ATTEMPT–LIKE CRIMES

Introductory Notes

1. In light of the difficulties which courts and legislatures have encountered in trying to formulate a rational law of attempts, should the general crime of attempt be abolished in favor of more comprehensive substantive crimes? Consider Glazebrook, *Should We Have a Law of Attempted Crime?*, 85 L.Q.Rev. 28, 35–36, 42–43 (1969):

"Not least among the aims of a Criminal Code is the rescuing of the law from its present confusion and uncertainty, and the primary objection to any general provision imposing liability for attempting to commit any and every offence is, I suggest (*pace* Stephen, who thought it a positive merit [36]), its inescapable vagueness and uncertainty. The vast literature which has grown up on both sides of the Atlantic concerning the *actus reus* of attempts is a reflection, not simply of the confused state of the case law, but of the very intractability of the problem which the courts have set themselves. No one has ever supposed that some single formula might, given a clever enough lawyer, be devised which would embrace the *actus reus* of, for instance, the offences of murder, obtaining property by deception, and the commission of acts of gross indecency between males. Why, then, should it be supposed that a single formula might, when combined with the definitions of those very different crimes, serve to identify the *actus reus* of such disparate offences as attempting to murder, attempting to obtain property by deception, and attempting to commit an act of gross indecency?

" * * * I suggest [this as a] preferable solution: that there should be no general provision imposing liability for attempting to commit the substantive offences. Rather, the question of how far the law should go in penalising acts done with the intention of effecting the evils with which the Special Part of the Code will be concerned (or which recklessly or negligently create the risk of bringing about those evils) should be considered as part and parcel of the overall question: what should be the definition of each substantive offence, or group of offences? If, as is devoutly to be wished, the draftsmen of the Special Part are not to be confined to tidying up the definitions of the traditional offences, but are to undertake a critical reappraisal of the types of conduct which are to be the subject of the substantive offences, the elimination of the distinction between attempted and completed crimes can only simplify their task. Similarly, the draftsman of regulatory legislation would no longer be able to shrug off the definition of the *actus reus* with the thought that the villain who does not come within his definition will nevertheless fall into the safety net of the law of attempt. And would this not be a good thing, both for him, and for the courts as well? For it can hardly conduce to the efficiency of the

---

a. See Burkhardt, *Is There a Rational Justification for Punishing an Accomplished Crime More Severely Than an Attempted Crime?*, 1986 Brigham Young U.L.Rev. 553; Schulhofer, *Harm and Punishment: A Critique of Emphasis on the Results of Conduct in the Criminal Law*, 122 U.Pa.L.Rev. 1497 (1974).

36. "The exact point at which [such preliminary steps] become criminal cannot, in the nature of things, be precisely ascertained, nor is it desirable that such a matter should be made the

subject of great precision. There is more harm than good in telling people precisely how far they may go without risking punishment in the pursuit of an unlawful object"—Stephen, J.F., *A General View of the Criminal Law of England*, 2nd ed. (London 1890), p. 83. Smith, J.C. and Hogan, B., *Criminal Law* (London 1965), content themselves with the oracular observation that "The law is necessarily vague; but perhaps it is better that it should be vague than capricious"—p. 152.

criminal trial that a large amount of attention should be directed to a question—whether the accused has been proved to have committed the *actus reus* of the completed offence—if the answer to that question is going to make precious little or no difference to what is done with him.

'' * * * Sexual offences against women provide an example. Anyone who has sat through a trial for rape, where one of the main questions was whether the accused succeeded in having connection with the prosecutrix, is likely to have asked himself what good was served by investigating that issue. The crucial question in such cases should surely be whether the woman has been assaulted with a sexual intent. And while, no doubt, a case can be mounted for distinguishing between indecent assaults of a technical kind, and assaults where the accused intended to have some form of sexual intercourse with the prosecutrix, even against her will, there is nothing to be said for distinguishing between those cases where he did, and those where he did not, succeed in having the physical connection with her which English law specifies.''

2. All jurisdictions have a great many attempt-like substantive crimes *in addition to* the general crime of attempt. Some of these offenses (e.g., assault, burglary) apparently came into being originally because the law of attempts had not yet developed adequately to reach such conduct. Others (e.g., vagrancy) often serve to make criminal certain conduct which would not be covered by even the modern law of attempts because the requisite mental state or the requisite acts (or both) could not be proved.

A. VAGRANCY

PAPACHRISTOU v. CITY OF JACKSONVILLE

Supreme Court of the United States, 1972.
405 U.S. 156, 92 S.Ct. 839, 31 L.Ed.2d 110.

MR. JUSTICE DOUGLAS delivered the opinion of the Court.

This case involves eight defendants who were convicted in a Florida municipal court of violating a Jacksonville, Florida vagrancy ordinance.[1] Their convictions, entailing fines and jail sentences (some of which were suspended), were affirmed by the Florida Circuit Court in a consolidated appeal, and their petition for certiorari was denied by the District Court of Appeals on the authority of *Johnson v. State,* Fla., 202 So.2d 852.[2] The case is here on a petition

---

1. Jacksonville Ordinance Code § 26–57 provided at the time of these arrests and convictions as follows:

"Rogues and vagabonds, or dissolute persons who go about begging, common gamblers, persons who use juggling or unlawful games or plays, common drunkards, common night walkers, thieves, pilferers or pickpockets, traders in stolen property, lewd, wanton and lascivious persons, common railers and brawlers, persons wandering or strolling around from place to place without any lawful purpose or object, habitual loafers, disorderly persons, persons neglecting all lawful business and habitually spending their time by frequenting houses of ill fame, gaming houses, or places where alcoholic beverages are sold or served, persons able to work but habitually living upon the earnings of their wives or minor children shall be deemed vagrants and, upon conviction in the Municipal Court shall be punished as provided for Class D offenses."

Class D offenses at the time of these arrests and convictions were punishable by 90 days imprisonment, $500 fine, or both. Jacksonville Ordinance Code § 1–8 (1965). * * *

2. Florida also has a vagrancy statute, Fla. Stat. § 856.02, F.S.A. which reads closely on the Jacksonville ordinance. Jacksonville Ordinance Code § 27–43, makes the commission of any Florida misdemeanor a Class D offense against the City of Jacksonville.

Section 856.02 was declared unconstitutionally overbroad in *Lazarus v. Faircloth,* D.C., 301 F.Supp. 266. The Court said: "All loitering, loafing, or idling on the streets and highways of a city, even though habitual, is not necessarily detrimental to the public welfare nor is it under all circumstances an interference with travel upon them. It may be and often is entirely innocuous. The statute draws no distinction between conduct that is calculated to harm and that which is essentially innocent."

for certiorari, which we granted. For reasons which will appear, we reverse.

At issue are five consolidated cases. Margaret Papachristou, Betty Calloway, Eugene Eddie Melton, and Leonard Johnson were all arrested early on a Sunday morning, and charged with vagrancy— "prowling by auto."

Jimmy Lee Smith and Milton Henry were charged with vagrancy— "vagabonds."

Henry Edward Heath and a co-defendant were arrested for vagrancy—"loitering" and "common thief."

Thomas Owen Campbell was charged with vagrancy—"common thief."

Hugh Brown was charged with vagrancy—"disorderly loitering on street" and "disorderly conduct—resisting arrest with violence."

The facts are stipulated. Papachristou and Calloway are white females. Melton and Johnson are black males. Papachristou was enrolled in a job-training program sponsored by the State Employment Service at Florida Junior College in Jacksonville. Calloway was a typing and shorthand teacher at a state mental institution located near Jacksonville. She was the owner of the automobile in which the four defendants were arrested. Melton was a Vietnam war veteran who had been released from the Navy after nine months in a veterans' hospital. On the date of his arrest he was a part-time computer helper while attending college as a full-time student in Jacksonville. Johnson was a tow-motor operator in a grocery chain warehouse and was a lifelong resident of Jacksonville.

At the time of their arrest, the four of them were riding in Calloway's car on the main thoroughfare in Jacksonville. They had left a restaurant owned by Johnson's uncle where they had eaten and were on their way to a night club. The arresting officers denied that the racial mixture in the car played any part in the decision to make the arrest. The arrest, they said, was made because the defendants had stopped near a used-car lot which had been broken into several times. There was, however, no evidence of any breaking and entering on the night in question.

Of these four charged with "prowling by auto" none had been previously arrested except Papachristou who had once been convicted of a municipal offense.

Jimmy Lee Smith and Milton Henry (who is not a petitioner) were arrested between 9 and 10 a.m. on a weekday in downtown Jacksonville, while waiting for a friend who was to lend them a car so they could apply for a job at a produce company. Smith was a part-time produce worker and part-time organizer for a Negro political group. He had a common-law wife and three children supported by him and his wife. He had been arrested several times but convicted only once. Smith's companion, Henry, was an 18–year–old high school student with no previous record of arrest.

This morning it was cold, and Smith had no jacket, so they went briefly into a dry cleaning shop to wait, but left when requested to do so. They thereafter walked back and forth two or three times over a two-block stretch looking for their friend. The store owners, who apparently were wary of Smith and his companion, summoned two police officers who searched the men and found neither had a weapon. But they were arrested because the officers

The Florida disorderly conduct ordinance, covering "loitering about any hotel, block, barroom, dramshop, gambling house or disorderly house, or wandering about the streets either by night or by day without any known lawful means of support or without being able to give a satisfactory account of themselves" has also been held void for "excessive broadness and vagueness" by the Florida Supreme Court, *Headley v. Selkowitz,* 171 So. 2d 368, 370.

said they had no identification and because the officers did not believe their story.

Heath and a codefendant were arrested for "loitering" and for "common thief." Both were residents of Jacksonville, Heath having lived there all his life and being employed at an automobile and body shop. Heath had previously been arrested but his codefendant had no arrest record. Heath and his companion were arrested when they drove up to a residence shared by Heath's girlfriend and some other girls. Some police officers were already there in the process of arresting another man. When Heath and his companion started backing out of the driveway, the officers signaled to them to stop and asked them to get out of the car, which they did. Thereupon they and the automobile were searched. Although no contraband or incriminating evidence was found, they were both arrested, Heath being charged with being a "common thief" because he was reputed to be a thief. The codefendant was charged with "loitering" because he was standing in the driveway, an act which the officers admitted was done only at their command.

Campbell was arrested as he reached his home very early one morning and was charged with "common thief." He was stopped by officers because he was traveling at a high rate of speed, yet no speeding charge was placed against him.

Brown was arrested when he was observed leaving a downtown, Jacksonville, hotel by a police officer seated in a cruiser. The police testified he was reputed to be a thief, narcotics pusher, and generally opprobrious character. The officer called Brown over to the car, intending at that time to arrest him unless he had a good explanation for being on the street. Brown walked over to the police cruiser, as commanded, and the officer began to search him, apparently preparatory to placing him in the car. In the process of the search he came on two small packets which were later found to contain heroin. When the officer touched the pocket where the packets were, Brown began to resist. He was charged with "disorderly loitering on the street" and "disorderly conduct—resisting arrest with violence." * * *

This ordinance is void-for-vagueness, both in the sense that it "fails to give a person of ordinary intelligence fair notice that his contemplated conduct is forbidden by the statute," and because it encourages arbitrary and erratic arrests and convictions.

Living under a rule of law entails various suppositions, one of which is that "All [persons] are entitled to be informed as to what the State commands or forbids." *Lanzetta v. New Jersey,* 306 U.S. 451, 453, 59 S.Ct. 618, 619, 83 L.Ed. 888.

Lanzetta is one of a well-recognized group of cases insisting that the law give fair notice of the offending conduct. In the field of regulatory statutes governing business activities, where the acts limited are in a narrow category, greater leeway is allowed.

The poor among us, the minorities, the average householder are not in business and not alerted to the regulatory schemes of vagrancy laws; and we assume they would have no understanding of their meaning and impact if they read them. Nor are they protected from being caught in the vagrancy net by the necessity of having a specific intent to commit an unlawful act. * * *

This aspect of the vagrancy ordinance before us is suggested by what this Court said in 1875 about a broad criminal statute enacted by Congress: "It would certainly be dangerous if the legislature could set a net large enough to catch all possible offenders, and leave it to the courts to step inside and say who could be rightfully detained, and who should be set at large."

United States v. Reese, 92 U.S. 214, 221, 23 L.Ed. 563.

While that was a federal case, the due process implications are equally applicable to the States and to this vagrancy ordinance. Here the net cast is large, not to give the courts the power to pick and choose but to increase the arsenal of the police. * * *

Another aspect of the ordinance's vagueness appears when we focus, not on the lack of notice given a potential offender, but on the effect of the unfettered discretion it places in the hands of the Jacksonville police. Caleb Foote, an early student of this subject, has called the vagrancy-type law as offering "punishment by analogy." Such crimes, though long common in Russia, are not compatible with our constitutional system. We allow our police to make arrests only on "probable cause," a Fourth and Fourteenth Amendment standard applicable to the States as well as to the Federal Government. Arresting a person on suspicion, like arresting a person for investigation, is foreign to our system, even when the arrest is for past criminality. Future criminality, however, is the common justification for the presence of vagrancy statutes. Florida has indeed construed her vagrancy statute "as necessary regulations," *inter alia,* "to deter vagabondage and prevent crimes."

A direction by a legislature to the police to arrest all "suspicious" persons [15] would not pass constitutional muster. A vagran-

cy prosecution may be merely the cloak for a conviction which could not be obtained on the real but undisclosed grounds for the arrest. * * *

A presumption that people who might walk or loaf or loiter or stroll or frequent houses where liquor is sold, or who are supported by their wives or who look suspicious to the police are to become future criminals is too precarious for a rule of law. The implicit presumption in these generalized vagrancy standards—that crime is being nipped in the bud—is too extravagant to deserve extended treatment. Of course, vagrancy statutes are useful to the police. Of course they are nets making easy the round-up of so-called undesirables. But the rule of law implies equality and justice in its application. Vagrancy laws of the Jacksonville type teach that the scales of justice are so tipped that even-handed administration of the law is not possible. The rule of law, evenly applied to minorities as well as majorities, to the poor as well as the rich, is the great mucilage that holds society together.

The Jacksonville ordinance cannot be squared with our constitutional standards and is plainly unconstitutional.

Reversed.

Notes and Questions

1. Because *Papachristou* appeared to seal the fate of the state vagrancy statute as well (see footnote 2 in the opinion), the

---

15. On arrests for investigation, see Secret Detention by the Chicago Police, A Report by the American Civil Liberties Union (1959). The table below contains nationwide data on arrests for "vagrancy" and for "suspicion" in the three-year period 1968–1970.

Year [*]	Vagrancy		Suspicion		Combined Offenses	
	Total rptd. arrests	Rate per 100,000	Total rptd. arrests	Rate per 100,000	Total rptd. arrests	Rate per 100,000
1968	99,147	68.2	89,986	61.9	189,133	130.1
1969	106,269	73.9	88,265	61.4	194,534	135.3
1970	101,093	66.1	70,173	46.3	171,266	113.0
3 year averages	102,170	69.6	82,808	56.5	184,978	126.1

[*] Reporting agencies represent population of:

1968—145,306,000; 1969—143,815,000; 1970—151,604,000.

Source: FBI Annual Crime Reports, 1968–1970.

Florida legislature enacted a new provision patterned after *Model Penal Code* § 250.6. The new statute reads as follows:

"(1) It is unlawful for any person to loiter or prowl in a place, at a time or in a manner not usual for law-abiding individuals, under circumstances that warrant a justifiable and reasonable alarm or immediate concern for the safety of persons or property in the vicinity.

"(2) Among the circumstances which may be considered in determining whether such alarm or immediate concern is warranted is the fact that the person takes flight upon appearance of a law enforcement officer, refuses to identify himself, or manifestly endeavors to conceal himself or any object. Unless flight by the person or other circumstance makes it impracticable, a law enforcement officer shall, prior to any arrest for an offense under this section, afford the person an opportunity to dispel any alarm or immediate concern which would otherwise be warranted by requesting him to identify himself and explain his presence and conduct. No person shall be convicted of an offense under this section if the law enforcement officer did not comply with this procedure or if it appears at trial that the explanation given by the person is true and, if believed by the officer at the time, would have dispelled the alarm or immediate concern."

2. Is the new statute constitutional? Consider *Kolender v. Lawson,* 461 U.S. 352, 103 S.Ct. 1855, 75 L.Ed.2d 903 (1983), involving a conviction under a California statute requiring persons who loiter or wander on the streets to provide a "credible and reliable" identification and to account for their presence. As construed by the state courts, identification is required *only* of persons lawfully stopped by the police on reasonable suspicion, and is "credible and reliable" if it carries "reasonable assurance that the identification is authentic and provid[es] means for later

getting in touch with the person who has identified himself." The Supreme Court held this statute to be void for vagueness:

"At oral argument, the appellants confirmed that a suspect violates § 647(e) unless "the officer [is] satisfied that the identification is reliable." In giving examples of how suspects would satisfy the requirement, appellants explained that a jogger, who was not carrying identification, could, depending on the particular officer, be required to answer a series of questions concerning the route that he followed to arrive at the place where the officers detained him, or could satisfy the identification requirement simply by reciting his name and address.

"It is clear that the full discretion accorded to the police to determine whether the suspect has provided a 'credible and reliable' identification necessarily 'entrust[s] lawmaking "to the moment-to-moment judgment of the policeman on his beat." ' Section 647(e) 'furnishes a convenient tool for "harsh and discriminatory enforcement by local prosecuting officials, against particular groups deemed to merit their displeasure," ' and 'confers on police a virtually unrestrained power to arrest and charge persons with a violation.' * * * [T]he State fails to establish standards by which the officers may determine whether the suspect has complied with the subsequent identification requirement."

The two dissenters in *Kolender* objected that the "narrowing construction given this statute by the state court cannot be likened to the 'standardless' statutes involved in" such cases as *Papachristou.*

3. The *Kolender* majority also emphasized that § 647(e) "is not simply a 'stop-and-identify' statute," referring to the kind of *procedural* provision permitted by *Terry v. Ohio,* 392 U.S. 1, 88 S.Ct. 1868, 20 L.Ed.2d 889 (1968), concluding it is not an unreasonable seizure under the Fourth Amendment for police to stop and inquire

"where a police officer observes unusual conduct which leads him reasonably to conclude in light of his experience that criminal activity may be afoot." Does this suggest that underlying *Kolender* is the notion that conduct which is, at best, only preparation for other criminal activity should be treated by the law as a procedural matter rather than one properly addressed by the substantive criminal law? Is that a sound notion? See LaFave, *Penal Code Revision: Considering the Problems and Practices of the Police,* 45 Texas L.Rev. 434, 451–54 (1967).

4. Assuming any vagueness problems are overcome, is such legislation objectionable because it, at best, makes punishable what would constitute noncriminal "mere preparation" under the law of attempts? In *State v. Young,* 57 N.J. 240, 271 A.2d 569 (1970), the defendant, charged with violating a statute prohibiting entry of a school building with the intent of disrupting classes, claimed the state was powerless to punish such "innocent" conduct. The court noted that there are "a host of statutes, federal and State, which condemn acts, themselves innocent, if done with a forbidden intent" (e.g., possession of burglary tools with intent to commit a burglary), and concluded:

"To meet the added dangers of a complex and congested society, legislatures have gone beyond the common law in punishing conduct which by common law standards might fall short of an attempt. Professor Perkins observes that 'it is becoming increasingly common for legislative enactment to provide a penalty (often a severe one) for what the common law regarded as an unpunishable act of preparation.' [M]any statutes * * * have the common feature of punishing an act only because of the evil purpose it pursues, without regard to whether the act would constitute an attempt to commit the offense the statutes seek to head off, and

even though the act, absent such purpose, may be one protected by the Constitution.

"We see no serious challenge to the power of a legislature to make it an offense to take a step, otherwise lawful, in furtherance of a hostile end. * * *

"We appreciate, of course, that all of the statutes we have cited which condemn an act, otherwise innocent, because of a forbidden intent, could be misused. But courts exist to see that they are not, and the Constitution must be read with the confidence that the judicial process will be equal to its fact-finding responsibility."

5. Does *Young* means that the state may reach such activity *only* if the "evil purpose" is a part of the definition of the crime? Compare *People v. Johnson,* 6 N.Y. 2d 549, 190 N.Y.S.2d 694, 161 N.E.2d 9 (1959), where the challenged statute merely prohibited loitering within a school building without permission. In upholding the defendant's conviction, the court reasoned:

"Nor is there any merit to defendant's contention that the statute was not intended to make criminal an otherwise innocent activity. Loitering in school buildings, or on school grounds, is not an innocent activity. It is common knowledge that law enforcement agencies and school authorities are continuously and increasingly harassed by the presence of unauthorized persons invading the precincts of our schools such, for instance, as dope peddlers, sex offenders, idlers and trouble makers in general, and other persons harboring some illegitimate purpose involving the innocence of immature school children and youth. Then, too, there is the ever present threat of fire and disaster from indiscriminate and careless use of cigarettes in and about the school corridors and buildings. The authorities, we know, are not only charged with the duty of providing children with a proper education, but while so doing must be watchful of their moral and physical safety and well-being. It was for these and other reasons that the enactment of section 722–b was sponsored by the law enforcement authorities and parent organizations, leading boards of education and other civic-minded groups. The nature of the activity carried on in a school building incident to the teaching and protection of children compels restriction against persons loitering in and about the building and grounds wherein these activities are carried on."

B. ASSAULT

IN RE M.

Supreme Court of California, 1973.
9 Cal.3d 517, 108 Cal.Rptr. 89, 510 P.2d 33.

MOSK, JUSTICE.

We are called upon to determine whether "attempted assault" is a crime in the State of California. We conclude that it is not.

About 10:30 a.m. on the morning of December 7, 1971, Los Angeles Police Officer Sietz and his partner were conducting a field interview with two juveniles loitering in the area of a school. Across the street, some 35 feet away, a crowd of 75 to 100 other juveniles gathered behind a 12-foot high chain link fence enclosing the school yard. The youths taunted the officers, shouted obscenities, and threw miscellaneous items over the fence in the general direction of the officers. According to the testimony of Officer Sietz, "Most of it was small things like paper, of no consequence."

Officer Sietz then saw James M., a dimunitive 13-year-old boy, climb partway up the fence, and, while hanging on, throw an opaque object about three inches in diameter. The missile struck the left front fender of the patrol car, some eight feet from the officer, causing a small dent. The officer crossed the street and climbed over the fence, at which moment, predict-ably, most of the youngsters scattered and ran. The officer observed James coming around a nearby building and placed him under arrest. Although the object was never found, Sietz "formed the opinion" it was a rock. When interrogated at the scene, James denied throwing a rock and said it was a piece of glass.

On the basis of these facts a petition was filed to declare James M. a ward of the court on the ground he had violated two laws defining crime. (Welf. & Inst.Code, § 602.) The particular offenses charged were assault with a deadly weapon upon the person of a police officer (Pen.Code, § 245, subd. (b)) and disturbing the peace (Pen.Code, § 415).

At the adjudication hearing, James denied throwing any substance and produced two juvenile witnesses to corroborate his story. The officer testified that he searched the area after arresting James but could not find the object which dented the fender of the patrol car. He also stated the missile hit the fender three feet off the ground and probably would have struck him in the foot or lower leg but for deflection by the patrol car.

The juvenile court dismissed the count alleging disturbing the peace because of insufficient evidence. As to the aggravated assault charge, the court resolved the conflict in the evidence and found that James had indeed thrown something at the police officer, but concluded that a violation of section 245, subdivision (b), of the Penal Code had not been established assertedly because the object missed its target. But rather than dismissing the petition or convicting James of the lesser included offense of simple assault on a peace officer (Pen.Code, §§ 240, 241), the court found James guilty of an *attempt* to commit an assault with a deadly weapon on a peace officer, and amended the petition by interlineation to so provide.

At the disposition hearing defense counsel contended that the prior finding "does not establish an offense under the Penal Code * * *. [E]ither the crime [i.e., a violation of section 245] was committed or it wasn't, and there can be no such thing as an attempted assault." The court, with no recognition of this issue, adjudged James to be a ward and placed him in the probation department day center program.

On appeal, defense counsel renews his contention there is no crime identified as "attempted assault" in California, whether simple or aggravated, and asks for a reversal with directions to dismiss the petition.

* * *

We must therefore decide whether "attempted assault" is recognized and punishable as a crime in the State of California. Whether it is possible to attempt an assault has long been a source of academic discussion and a somewhat recondite topic for an exercise in legal analysis. Case law on the subject is by no means uniform.

At common law an assault was defined as an attempted battery. It was said that one cannot attempt to commit an attempt, and, therefore, attempted assault was a deductive impossibility. A century ago one court described the matter thus: "As an assault is itself an attempt to commit a crime, an attempt to make an assault can only be an attempt to attempt to do it * * *. This is simply absurd." (*Wilson v. State* (1974) 53 Ga. 205, 206.) Yet esoteric theories have been advanced to demonstrate that the concept of an attempted assault is not wholly illogical.

One such theory is based on the concept of "proximity," i.e., that a greater degree of proximity is required to commit an assault than to commit a general criminal attempt. Hence, it is reasoned, conduct which goes further than preparation, but falls short of assault, may be punished as a general criminal attempt. A second theory, apparently relied on by the trial court

herein, suggests that inasmuch as an assault is defined in California as an attempt to commit battery coupled with the present ability to do so, an attempted assault means, in substance, an attempt to commit a battery *without* such present ability.

Whether or not the foregoing theories are entirely tenable, it is apparent that the abstract concept of an attempted assault is not necessarily a logical absurdity. Yet to concede, in an academic sense, the possibility that there can be an attempted assault is not the equivalent of declaring it to be a punishable offense under the laws of this state.

Section 6 of the Penal Code declares that "No act or omission * * * is criminal or punishable, except as prescribed or authorized by this Code" or by other statutes or ordinances. Since its first session, our Legislature has defined criminal assault as an attempt to commit a battery by one *having present ability* to do so and no offense known as attempt to assault was recognized in California at the time that statutory definition of assault was adopted. Under the doctrine of manifested legislative intent, an omission from a penal provision evinces a legislative purpose not to punish the omitted act. Hence, there is a clear manifestation of legislative intent under this doctrine for an attempt to commit a battery without present ability to go unpunished.

It is also an established rule of statutory construction that particular provisions will prevail over general provisions. Therefore, the legislative intent not to punish batteries attempted without present ability prevails over the general criminal attempt provisions of section 664. It follows that to judicially find a crime in California in an attempt to commit a battery where the actor lacks the present ability to consummate the battery would be to invade the province of the Legislature by redefining the elements of the underlying crime.

In addition, we foresee serious pragmatic difficulties if attempted assault were judicially established as a punishable crime. Trial courts must instruct on lesser included offenses if the evidence raises questions as to whether all the elements of the charged crime are present. If it were a crime trial courts would be required to instruct on attempted assault in every prosecution for a crime involving any type of assault, whether simple or aggravated, when the proof of one of the elements of the underlying crime is unclear or contested. The injection of an additional issue into such trials, with attendant likelihood of confusion of the jury and unwarranted reversals, does not seem justified, particularly since the lack of seriousness of a mere attempted assault has been evidenced by consistent legislative omission since 1850 to provide for any such crime. Juries should not be required to engage in fruitless metaphysical speculation as to differing degrees of proximity between an assault and a general attempt, nor as to the logical possibility of attempting to commit any crime of assault, either simple or aggravated, the basic nature of which is an attempt in itself.

The judgment is reversed with directions to the trial court to dismiss the petition.

Notes and Questions

1. Compare *State v. Wilson,* 218 Or. 575, 346 P.2d 115 (1959), affirming defendant's conviction for attempted assault with a dangerous weapon. (The defendant, with the intention of shooting his wife, came to her place of employment with a shotgun, but did not find her because she was hiding; it was thus assumed that the "present ability to inflict corporal injury" needed to convict of assault was lacking.) The court reasoned:

"If we should regard assault as an attempted battery, is it reasonable to recognize the crime of attempted assault? It has been categorically asserted that there can be no attempt to commit a crime which is itself merely an attempt. Upon the basis of this premise it is said that there can be no such offense as an attempted assault. * * * In none of these sources is it explained why this conclusion is inevitable. It appears to be assumed that logic permits no other conclusion. But is that so? Thurman Arnold, in an article in 40 Yale L.J. 53, 65 (1930) answers as follows:

'* * * [It is said that] there can be no attempt at a direct attempt. But the query immediately arises, Why not? We do not punish attempts at ordinary assaults which carry light penalties. But suppose the accused is guilty of conduct tending toward an aggravated assault but which does not seem to require the heavier penalty. The court is confronted with the alternative of either discharging the accused or modifying the penalty to make it more nearly fit his conduct. An easy way to accomplish this is by making attempts at aggravated assaults punishable, and this is frequently done. It is academic to call such cases "wrong" because assault is in the nature of an attempt and hence cannot be attempted, particularly when a common sense result is reached. In short the generalization that there can be no attempt at a crime in the nature of an attempt tells us nothing and tends merely to divert the court's mind from the real issue.'

"We agree with the foregoing analysis. The mere fact that assault is viewed as preceding a battery should not preclude us from drawing a line on one side of which we require the present ability to inflict corporal injury, denominating this an assault, and on the other side conduct which falls short of a present ability, yet so advanced toward the assault that it is more than mere preparation and which we denominate an attempt."

2. In *Robinson v. United States,* 506 A.2d 572 (D.C.App.1986), the defendant was convicted of assault on evidence that he pointed a loaded pistol at a police officer. On appeal, the defendant claimed the evidence was insufficient. The court first concluded it would be insufficient under the attempted-battery kind of assault discussed in *In re M.* "To establish an attempted-battery type of assault on the facts of this case, the government would have had to prove that appellant either fired the gun or attempted to fire it." The court then continued:

"In *Anthony v. United States,* 361 A.2d 202 (D.C.1976), this court recognized for the first time that the crime of assault included not only attempted battery but also 'such conduct as could induce in the victim a well-founded apprehension of peril.' We reiterated that holding a few years later in *Williamson v. United States,* 445 A.2d 975 (D.C.1982). Taking note of 'this expanded concept of common law criminal assault,' we enlarged the standard three-part definition to include the intent-to-frighten type of assault as well as the attempted-battery type:

First, there must be an act on the part of the defendant; mere words do not constitute an assault. * * * The act does not have to result in injury[.] * * * [I]t can be either an actual attempt, with force or violence, to injure another, or a menacing threat, which may or may not be accompanied by a specific intent to injure, on the part of the defendant. * * * [Second], at the time the defendant commits the act, the defendant must have the apparent present ability to injure the victim. * * * [Third], at the time the act is committed, the defendant must have the intent to perform the acts which constitute the assault.

"In the case at bar, there was sufficient evidence before the jury to prove each of these three elements beyond a reasonable doubt. First, appellant's act of pointing a gun at Sergeant Monroe constituted 'a menacing threat.' It is irrelevant whether appellant had a specific intent to injure Monroe. An intent to frighten is sufficient, and that intent can be inferred from the pointing of a gun. Second, from the fact that appellant had a gun in his hand, it is reasonable to infer (it would be unreasonable not to infer) that appellant had the 'apparent present ability to injure the victim.' *Anthony* makes clear that the victim, in this case Sergeant Monroe, need not 'be shown factually to have experienced apprehension or fear in order to establish the offense.' Instead, 'the crucial inquiry [is] whether the assailant acted in such a manner as would under the circumstances portend an immediate threat of danger to a person of reasonable sensibility.' Finally, the jury was free to infer that appellant had the intent to perform the act, in this case the pointing of the gun, that constituted the assault; appellant presented no evidence suggesting that his actions were inadvertent, accidental, or involuntary.

"Thus we hold that the evidence was sufficient to permit the case to go to the jury * * *."

C. BURGLARY

MODEL PENAL CODE
§ 221.1, Comment (1980).

The common-law concept of burglary encompassed breaking and entering the dwelling house of another at night with the intent to commit a felony therein. The scope of the offense had been enlarged by judicial interpretation and legislation, however, with the result that, at least under the most comprehensive of the statutes in force at the time the Model Penal Code was drafted, the offense could be committed by entry alone, in the daytime as well as at night, in any building, structure, or vehicle, with the intent to commit any criminal offense. Enlargement of the offense in this manner was accompanied by the adoption of various grading distinctions. Generally, the most serious penalties were reserved for situations involving actual or potential danger to persons, and misdemeanor or lesser felony sanctions were provided for less aggravated conduct.

The initial development of the offense of burglary, as well as much of the later expansion of the offense, probably resulted from an effort to compensate for defects of the traditional law of attempt. The common law of attempt ordinarily did not reach a person who embarked on a course of criminal behavior unless he came very close to his goal. Sometimes it was stated that to be guilty of attempt one had to engage in the final act which would have accomplished his object but for the intervention of circumstances beyond his control. Under that view of the law of attempt, a person apprehended while breaking into a dwelling with intent to commit a felony therein would not have committed an attempt, for he would not have arrived at the scene of his projected theft, rape, or murder. Moreover, even when the actor's conduct reached the stage where an attempt was committed, penalties for attempt were disproportionately low as compared to the penalties for the completed offense.

The development and expansion of the offense of burglary provided a partial solution to these problems. Making entry with criminal intent an independent substantive offense carrying serious sanctions moved back the moment when the law could intervene in a criminal design and authorized penalties more nearly in accord with the seriousness of the actor's conduct. The surface logic of this solution, however, tended to obscure the anomalies introduced by later expansion of the burglary concept to include non-dangerous situations and new target offenses, especially

when concomitant adjustments in the penalty structure were not made.

Since every burglary is by hypothesis an attempt to commit some other crime, it is appropriate to consider the sanction for the completed offense that is the objective of the burglary in evaluating the propriety of the sentence that is authorized for the burglary itself. In some cases, it is of course quite proper for the burglary to be graded severely. Thus, entry into a home at night in order to commit a theft is surely a more aggravated offense than an attempted theft standing alone, because of the additional element of personal danger that attends such conduct. On the other hand, a greatly expanded burglary statute authorizes the prosecutor and the courts to treat as burglary behavior that is distinguishable from theft or attempted theft only on purely artificial grounds.

This point can be illustrated by examination of some of the consequences of burglary laws in effect at the time the Model Penal Code was drafted. In California, a boy who broke into an automobile to steal the contents of the glove compartment would have subjected himself to imprisonment for up to 15 years, although a successful theft of the automobile itself together with its contents would have been punishable by a maximum of only 10 years. Entering a henhouse to steal a chicken became a serious offense, while stealing a chicken at the henhouse door was merely petty larceny. A person who went into an open department store and stole something from the counter would be a burglar or a minor misdemeanant depending upon the largely immaterial question of whether he intended to steal when he entered the store. A person who entered a structure by invitation might have been classified as a burglar rather than a thief if he moved from one room to another in order to steal. The language of some statutes appeared to be broad enough to make a burglar out of one who entered his own house or office with the purpose of committing a crime, whether it be to prepare a fraudulent income tax return or to commit an assault upon his wife. The ultimate absurdity was the provision in some statutes making it burglary to commit an offense "in" a building, regardless of the lawfulness of the actor's entry or the intent with which he entered.

An entirely separate difficulty was caused by the fact that burglary generally was regarded as an offense distinct and independent from the other crime which the actor contemplated or carried out. As a result, cumulative penalties could be imposed, for example, for entering with intent to steal and for either attempted stealing or stealing. Thus, even if there was a rationale for using the burglary offense as an aggravating device because of defects in the law of attempt, the aggravation was excessive. Not only was burglary often more serious than its target offense, but there was the opportunity for consecutive sentences as well. This is to be contrasted with the normal rule that forbids conviction for both the attempt and the completed offense.

It is also worth noting that a haphazardly defined burglary offense impedes scientific study of crime and its treatment by making statistical studies based on this categorization virtually meaningless. The possibilities of arbitrary classification of offenses were so numerous under typical burglary legislation in effect when the Model Code was drafted that it was impossible to understand or evaluate even the limited crime statistics that were available.

Notes and Questions

1. What is the solution? Consider Prof. Nowak's suggestion, 1970 U.Ill.L.F. 391, 400–01: "The best way to deal with the offense of burglary would be to abolish it. The offense lacks any theoretical or historical justification, and modern laws of attempt would better serve in punishing such conduct. This would establish a punishment rationally connected to the seriousness of the offense which was being attempted. An attempted petty theft would no longer be punished as severely as attempted murder, and the moving of the situs of the offense a few feet would no longer determine the degree of punishment."

Compare *Model Penal Code* § 221.1(3).

2. In *DeGidio v. State,* 289 N.W.2d 135 (Minn.1980), the defendant claimed on appeal that the offense of which he had been convicted, attempted burglary, was not a valid crime. The court disagreed, reasoning that "while burglary is in a sense an inchoate crime, the legislature clearly has determined that the conduct covered by the burglary statute merits separate treatment as a substantive offense. Because the legislature in enacting the attempt statute gave no indication that some substantive crimes could not serve as a foundation for attempt convictions and because burglary is a separate substantive offense, it seems clear to us that the legislature intended to permit prosecutions and convictions for attempted burglary."

Chapter 10

CONSPIRACY AND SOLICITATION

SECTION 1. CONSPIRACY: INTRODUCTION

The definition of conspiracy which persists in those jurisdictions retaining common law crimes is: a combination between two or more persons formed for the purpose of doing either an unlawful act or a lawful act by unlawful means. (Where conspiracy is defined by statute, the common law definition is sometimes followed, elsewhere other language is used which makes it apparent that some noncriminal objectives are also covered, while some states have now limited conspiracy to criminal objectives.) Although a more precise definition of conspiracy may be difficult, it is useful to keep in mind that conspiracy, like most other offenses, requires both an act and an accompanying mental state. The agreement constitutes the act, while the intention to achieve the objective is the mental state.

Some years ago, Judge Learned Hand called conspiracy "the darling of the modern prosecutor's nursery," [a] and this characterization certainly is not without justification. It is clear that a conspiracy charge gives the prosecution certain unique advantages and that one who must defend against such a charge bears a particularly heavy burden.

1. *Vagueness.* The criticism which commentators have voiced most often and most strongly is that there is an inherent vagueness in the crime of conspiracy. "In the long category of crimes there is none," wrote Dean Harno, "not excepting criminal attempt, more difficult to confine within the boundaries of definitive statement than conspiracy." [b] Professor Sayre, in his classic article on the subject, noted: "A doctrine so vague in its outlines and uncertain in its fundamental nature as criminal conspiracy lends no strength or glory to the law; it is a veritable quicksand of shifting opinion and ill-considered thought." [c] And Justice Jackson, in his oft-quoted concurring opinion in *Krulewitch v. United States,* [d] referred to conspiracy as an "elastic, sprawling and pervasive offense, * * * so vague that it almost defies definition [and also] chameleon-like [because it] takes on a special coloration from each of the many independent offenses on which it may be overlaid."

2. *Venue.* The Sixth Amendment provides that in "all criminal prosecutions, the accused shall enjoy the right to a speedy

a. *Harrison v. United States,* 7 F.2d 259, 263 (2d Cir.1925).

b. Harno, *Intent in Criminal Conspiracy,* 89 U.Pa.L.Rev. 624 (1941).

c. Sayre, *Criminal Conspiracy,* 35 Harv.L.Rev. 393 (1922).

d. 336 U.S. 440, 69 S.Ct. 716, 93 L.Ed. 790 (1949).

and public trial, by an impartial jury of the State and district wherein the crime shall have been committed." Similarly, most state constitutions also provide that a defendant in a criminal case is entitled to be tried in the county, parish, or district where the crime occurred. These venue provisions constitute an important constitutional guarantee, for they "safeguard against the unfairness and hardship involved when an accused is prosecuted in a remote place." [e]

Given the common reference to the agreement in conspiracy as the "gist" of the offense, it might be thought that the place of trial for conspiracy prosecutions must be the place where the agreement was made. But, while it has long been settled that a conspiracy prosecution may be brought at the place of agreement, it is clear that the prosecution may also elect to have the trial in any locale where any overt act by any of the conspirators took place. Although it is argued in support of this rule that if it were otherwise conspiracy prosecutions would often be impossible because of the frequent difficulty of proving the place of agreement, the rule makes it possible for the prosecution to select a district inconvenient to the defendant or one in which a jury may be more disposed to convict.

3. *Hearsay exception.* The general rule that hearsay is not admissible in a criminal prosecution is marked by many exceptions. One of these is the co-conspirator exception: any act or declaration by one co-conspirator committed during and in furtherance of the conspiracy is admissible against each co-conspirator. The rationale most often given for this exception is that each of the conspirators is the agent of all the others.

However, the co-conspirator hearsay exception as applied often extends beyond

that rationale. The requirement that the act or statement be in furtherance of the conspiracy is often applied broadly, with the result that any evidence somehow relating to the conspiracy comes in. Sometimes statements are admitted into evidence notwithstanding the fact that they were made prior to the formation of the conspiracy or after its termination. And on the ground that the addition of a new member does not create a new conspiracy, statements by one conspirator are held admissible against others who joined the group after they were made.

Another requirement of the co-conspirator hearsay exception is that a statement by one conspirator is not admissible against the others unless the existence of the conspiracy has been independently established. However, courts have been sympathetic to the problems of the prosecution in presenting evidence in a vast conspiracy case, and thus have admitted evidence falling under the exception, subject to an instruction to the jury that such evidence is not to be considered against the other defendants if independent proof of the conspiracy is not thereafter presented. As Justice Jackson saw it, "In other words, a conspiracy often is proved by evidence that is admissible only upon assumption that conspiracy existed. The naive assumption that prejudicial effects can be overcome by instructions to the jury * * * all practicing lawyers know to be unmitigated fiction."

4. *Circumstantial evidence.* Most conspiracy convictions are based upon circumstantial evidence, and this evidence is often admitted under rather loose standards of relevance. As one court put it, "Wide latitude is allowed [the prosecution] in presenting evidence, and it is within the discretion of the trial court to admit evi-

---

e. *United States v. Cores,* 356 U.S. 405, 407, 78 S.Ct. 875, 877, 2 L.Ed.2d 873, 876 (1958).

dence which even remotely tends to establish the conspiracy charged." [f]

5. *Joint trial.* When several defendants have been charged as participants in a single conspiracy, they may be required to defend against the charges in a single trial, which may present added disadvantages for the several defendants. For one thing, what would otherwise be rights individual to each defendant may become, in effect, group rights which must be exercised jointly by all of the defendants. The greatest danger, however, is that the probability of an individual defendant being convicted may be greatly enhanced by his association through joinder with the others. This is particularly true when there is a long, complicated trial involving many defendants, where the jury may have great difficulty in keeping the evidence and jury instructions straight as they apply to particular defendants.

6. *Rationale.* However, even those who have voiced such criticisms have acknowledged that "the basic conspiracy principle has some place in modern criminal law." [g] The crime of conspiracy is said to serve two important but different functions: (1) as with solicitation and attempt, it is a means for preventive intervention against persons who manifest a disposition to criminality; and (2) it is also a means of striking against the special danger incident to group activity.

SECTION 2. THE AGREEMENT

UNITED STATES v. JAMES

United States Court of Appeals, Fifth Circuit, 1976.
528 F.2d 999.

BREWSTER, DISTRICT JUDGE:

[The seven appellants were convicted of conspiracy to commit the offenses of (i)

assault on federal officers engaged in the performance of their duties, (ii) using firearms to commit the assault, and (iii) possessing unregistered firearms. The conspiracy was claimed to have begun about July 15 and to have continued to August 18, when it culminated in a shoot-out between FBI agents and local police, on the one hand, and the appellants, on the other, at the "capitol" of the Republic of New Africa (RNA) in Jackson, Miss. The RNA claims to be an independent foreign nation composed of "citizens" descended from Africans who were at one time slaves in this country. The officers lived and worked in the "capitol," a residential building; some "citizens" and potential "citizens" stayed there for periods of time. The substantial part of a three-day meeting at the "capitol" in mid-July was devoted to discussion of security measures for RNA officials and the "capitol." Drills with weapons were held periodically during the two months following, and "citizens" participating were taught that, upon the command "jump," they should go to certain vantage points where they could fire upon persons trying to intrude. The FBI was kept posted on these developments by an informer posing as a "citizen." A reliable informant told the FBI that one Steiner, for whom they had an arrest warrant for unlawful flight to avoid prosecution, was present in the "capitol," so 15 FBI agents and 12 local police planned a raid on those premises. They took positions around the building and then, using a bullhorn, advised the occupants of their authority and purpose and that the occupants should leave the building. When no response was forthcoming, tear gas cannisters were fired into the building, and simultaneously a heavy barrage of gunfire came from the "capitol." One police officer was killed; one officer and one FBI agent were

f. *Nye & Nissen v. United States,* 168 F.2d 846, 857 (9th Cir.1948).

g. *Krulewitch v. United States,* 336 U.S. 440, 448, 69 S.Ct. 716, 721, 93 L.Ed. 790, 797 (1949) (Jackson, J., concurring).

wounded. About 20 minutes later, several persons exited the building. After *Miranda* warnings were given to them, Norman, Shillingford, James and Jackson (not one of the appellants) admitted firing from the building. Stalling said he did not fire because he was engaged in getting the two females (Austin and Lockhart) into a fortified bunker. The two women denied firing any weapons. After it was determined that Steiner was not in the building, the authorities turned their attention to another building to which the RNA was in the process of moving. A similar announcement by bullhorn was made, and four persons (including Henry) exited. Henry had a fully loaded ammunition clip in his pocket. Various weapons were found in plain view in both premises.]

All of the appellants contend that the evidence is insufficient to support any conviction under the conspiracy count. The principal grounds urged in support of this contention are: (1) the evidence did not show (a) any *agreement* to assault, intimidate or interfere with anyone, or (b) any "knowledge that federal officers would come in conflict with the essentially defensive precautions"; or (2) any connection of any individual defendant with the conspiracy. * * *

The discussion of appellants in support of their contention would be more fitting for a jury argument. They take a view of the evidence most favorable to themselves; and, when evidence supporting the government's theory stands in their way, they insist that it is not credible. Other shortcomings in their contentions are that they assume that a conspiracy must be based on an express agreement; that it must be full and complete from the beginning; that it is not subject to change; and that each participant must have full knowledge of all its details. * * *

The facts above stated, along with others included in the statement of the case at the beginning of the opinion, are adequate to establish a common plan among the appellants alleged as the basis of the conspiracy. The actions of the defendants themselves are always important circumstances from which to draw inferences of a conspiracy. The manner in which the appellants acted during the shoot-out on the morning of August 18 was strong evidence of a common plan and certainly showed concerted action. They did not go about things haphazardly in trying to carry out what some of the RNA "citizens" had called their "combat-win procedures". The evidence of a common plan or unlawful combination is much stronger in this case than it was in many of the cases cited under this heading, where the evidence was held to be sufficient. There is no doubt that there was a common plan to defy, intimidate and shoot it out with any law enforcement officers when the opportunity presented itself.

The following legal principles support the Court's holding that the evidence is sufficient to show the existence of the agreement or common design which formed the basis for the conspiracy alleged in the indictment. To establish the common plan element of a conspiracy, it is not necessary for the government to prove an express agreement between the alleged conspirators to go forth and violate the law. The "common purpose and plan may be inferred from a 'development and collocation of circumstances'." *Glasser v. United States,* 1942, 315 U.S. 60, 80, 62 S.Ct. 457, 469, 86 L.Ed. 680, 704. "A conspiracy is seldom born of 'open covenants openly arrived at.'" "The proof, by the very nature of the crime, must be circumstantial and therefore inferential to an extent varying with the conditions under which the crime may be committed." *Direct Sales Co. v. United States,* 1943, 319 U.S. 703, 714, 63 S.Ct. 1265, 1270, 87 L.Ed. 1674, 1683. Knowledge by a defendant of all details or phases of a conspiracy is not required. It is enough that he knows the essential nature of it. *Blumenthal v. United States,* 1947, 332 U.S. 539, 68 S.Ct. 248, 92 L.Ed. 154. "And, it is black letter law that all participants in a conspiracy need not know each other; all that is necessary is that each know that it has a 'scope' and that for its success it requires an organization wider than may be disclosed by his personal participation."

* * *

The claims of each of the appellants that the evidence is insufficient to connect him or her with the conspiracy, if it was established, must be judged in the light of the legal principles that follow in this paragraph. Once the existence of a common scheme of a conspiracy is shown, slight evidence is all that is required to connect a particular defendant with the conspiracy. The connection may be shown by circumstantial evidence. "A person may be held as a conspirator although he joins the criminal concert at a point in time far beyond the initial act of the conspirators. If he joins later, knowing of the criminal design, and acts in concert with the original conspirators, he may be held responsible, not only for everything which may be done thereafter, but also for everything which has been done prior to his adherence to the criminal design * * *". The fact that a conspirator is not present at, or does not participate in, the commission of any of the overt acts does not, by itself, exonerate him.

A few conclusory comments based on the facts already set out will suffice in the discussion of the question of the sufficiency of the evidence to show the connection, or lack of it, of each defendant with the conspiracy. It would unduly lengthen this opinion to do otherwise.

Henry. He was the President of RNA. All of the "security" measures and "combat-win procedures" were planned and practiced under his direct supervision. He

had made public threats of violence against law enforcement officers who might come to the "capitol". Within less than a month of the shoot-out, he held a meeting wherein instructions were given RNA "citizens" to shoot people, especially police officers and FBI Agents, who might try to intrude the "capitol". The shoot-out went according to the plan and procedure he had helped set up. While he was at the Lynch Street house to which the "capitol" was being moved, instead of the Lewis Street "capitol", at the time of the shoot-out, his presence and participation in the shoot-out were not necessary to support his conviction under the conspiracy count. * * * The overwhelming evidence shows that this tragedy would not have taken place except for the work of Henry.

Norman. He was Vice-President of RNA, and had been actively involved in RNA in Jackson for some time. He and President Henry designated the chain of command for the security forces. He assisted Henry in the RNA meeting in July when instructions were given to shoot intruders attempting to enter the "capitol", especially police and FBI Agents. He admitted just after the shoot-out that he was a participant in it. He said he was firing a British 303 gun from inside the house.

James. He held the title of Interior Minister of the RNA. He lived at the Lewis Street "capitol" for most of six weeks before August 18. He was a participant in the "combat-win procedure" drills. He was in charge of the arsenal of some 30 weapons and ammunition to be used in carrying out the common plan. It was his job to assign the weapons to members of the crack security guard. He discussed the bomb and the Molotov cocktails with such members and told them how to use them. He told the officers shortly after the shoot-out that he had shot at any white man he saw. His fingerprints were on the automatic rifle found under the house beside a pile of spent rounds after the shoot-out. He was one of the main actors in the conspiracy.

Toni Rene Austin. As Minister of Finance of the RNA, she was in charge of the treasury. She lived with her husband, appellant James, in the room in the back part of the "capitol" where the arsenal and ammunition for the security guard were kept. She did guard duty at the "capitol", and participated in the "jump" drills. On July 27, she wrote out a list of ammunition to be bought for use by the security guard. The ammunition was not purchased until the night before the shoot-out.[17] She was in the "capitol" when the officers made their announcements on the morning of August 18, but did not come out until forced by tear gas to do so after the shoot-out.

Shillingford. He was a "citizen" of the RNA. He had come to Jackson a few days before the shoot-out to participate in the RNA activities at the "capitol". He stayed at the "capitol" and was an active "citizen" there. He was the one who went on the night of August 17 and got the ammunition which was on the list prepared by appellant Toni Austin on July 27. He was a member of the crack security guard, and fired an M–1 rifle from his station inside the west part of the "capitol" during the shoot-out.

Stalling. He was an active "citizen" of the RNA. He lived in the Lewis Street "capitol". He helped dig the escape tunnel which was to figure importantly in the security procedures when it was finished. He did active guard duty at the "capitol" and participated in the "jump" drills. He

took the female defendants to the escape tunnel during the shooting.

Under the circumstances, a reasonably-minded jury could well conclude beyond a reasonable doubt that the conspiracy alleged actually existed, and that the appellants, Henry, Norman, James, Austin, Shillingford and Stalling, were each members of it. That leaves the question of the sufficiency of the evidence to connect Ann Lockhart with it.

Lockhart. Her residence was in Wisconsin. She was not a "citizen" of RNA, but she obviously sympathized with its objectives. Her husband was appellant Norman, the Vice-President of RNA. She had spent over a month of the summer in Africa, and was not in Jackson for the People's Center Council in July. She arrived at the Lewis Street "capitol" on August 16, and stayed with her husband until after the shoot-out. On August 16 and 17, she purchased groceries and prepared meals for the occupants of the "capitol". Her stopover there was intended to be very short, as her plans were to leave for North Carolina on the morning of August 18. The evidence is insufficient to show that she had any knowledge of the conspiracy or participation in it. There is nothing in the record to justify making her responsible for her husband's unlawful conduct. Mere presence at the scene of a crime or mere association with the members of a conspiracy is not enough to prove participation in it.

Notes and Questions

1. "Officer Grimball was the Government's principal witness. He testified that

---

17. On the night of August 17, some 30 officers made plans to go to the "capitol" the next morning to serve arrest warrants. The following events also occurred on that night: (1) The fugitive, Steiner, left town unexpectedly around 11:00 o'clock. (2) A purchase order for ammunition for the security guard which had lain around for almost three weeks was executed. (3) President

Henry did not stay at the Lewis Street "capitol" on that night. Whether the "citizens" of RNA had got wind of the plans for the officers' visit to the Lewis Street "capitol" on the early morning of August 18 does not appear; but the possibility that the three occurrences above described were just coincidences seems somewhat remote.

early in the evening of October 9, 1984, he approached Gregory Valentine on the corner of 115th Street and Eighth Avenue and asked him for a joint of 'D'. Valentine asked Grimball whom he knew around the street. Grimball asked if Valentine knew Scott. He did not. Brown 'came up' and Valentine said, 'He wants a joint, but I don't know him.' Brown looked at Grimball and said, 'He looks okay to me.' Valentine then said, 'Okay. But I am going to leave it somewhere and you [meaning Officer Grimball] can pick it up.' Brown interjected, 'You don't have to do that. Just go and get it for him. He looks all right to me.' After looking again at Grimball, Brown said, 'He looks all right to me' and 'I will wait right here.'

"Valentine then said, 'Okay. Come on with me around to the hotel.' Grimball followed him to 300 West 116th Street, where Valentine instructed him, 'Sit on the black car and give me a few minutes to go up and get it.' Valentine requested and received $40, which had been prerecorded, and then said, 'You are going to take care of me for doing this for you, throw some dollars my way?,' to which Grimball responded, 'Yeah.'

"Valentine then entered the hotel and shortly returned. The two went back to 115th Street and Eighth Avenue, where Valentine placed a cigarette box on the hood of a blue car. Grimball picked up the cigarette box and found a glassine envelope containing white powder, stipulated to be heroin. Grimball placed $5 of prerecorded buy money in the cigarette box, which he replaced on the hood. Valentine picked up the box and removed the $5. Grimball returned to his car and made a radio transmission to the backup field team that 'the buy had went down' and informed them of the locations of the persons involved. Brown and Valentine

a. *United States v. Brown,* 776 F.2d 397 (2d Cir.1985), a 3–1 affirmance of the conviction.

were arrested. Valentine was found to possess two glassine envelopes of heroin and the $5 of prerecorded money. Brown was in possession of $31 of his own money; no drugs or contraband were found on him. The $40 of marked buy money was not recovered, and no arrests were made at the hotel." [a] What result on Brown's appeal of his conviction for conspiracy to distribute heroin?

2. "On the evening of April 4, 1966, a man and woman entered a pharmacy on West Colfax Avenue in Denver, Colorado. The man remained in the front portion of the store and the woman proceeded to the rear and presented a prescription for Dilaudid to the druggist in charge, requesting that it be filled. The druggist described Dilaudid as 'an unusual drug in not too much use today.' Because of the nature of the drug and the handwriting which he suspected not to be genuine, the druggist called the doctor whose name appeared on the prescription blank. As he commenced this telephone inquiry, the woman and man proceeded rapidly from the store. The doctor advised that the prescription was false and the druggist immediately notified the police. Investigating officers presented photographs to the druggist and to a clerk, who each identified the man and the woman, respectively, as Ronald Arthur Ziatz and Lorraine Irene Valdez. Both Valdez and Ziatz were thereafter apprehended and placed under arrest. Miss Valdez was charged jointly with Ziatz in this case, but was tried separately and is not a party to this writ of error.

"The People's evidence showed that the handwriting on the prescription was that of Ziatz. He did not testify and presented only one witness, whose testimony related to his employment prior to the time of the transaction under consideration." [b] What

b. *Ziatz v. People,* 171 Colo. 58, 465 P.2d 406 (1970), reversing the conviction.

result on his appeal from his conviction for conspiracy to forge a prescription?

3. If a defendant is sufficiently involved in a crime to be an accomplice in its commission, does it necessarily follow that he is a member of a conspiracy to commit that crime? Consider *Commonwealth v. Cook,* 10 Mass.App.Ct. 668, 411 N.E.2d 1326 (1980), where a 17-year-old girl stopped on the street to chat with the Cook brothers, Maurice and Dennis. Because she had not met them before and had trouble remembering their names, each of the brothers displayed identification to her and indicated where they were employed. After about 45 minutes, Maurice suggested they walk to a nearby store so he could purchase cigarettes, and he directed the group along a path through a wooded area toward the store. The girl tripped and fell and sat on the ground laughing; Maurice then jumped on her, scratched her with a stick and said, "No blood, no blood." Dennis laughed and said, "The bitch doesn't want to bleed, we'll make her bleed." Maurice then raped the girl; she lost consciousness, awoke later and went home. When Dennis appealed his conviction of conspiracy to rape, claiming insufficient evidence, the prosecution countered that it sufficed the evidence showed Dennis to be an accomplice in the rape under the rule (as stated by the appellate court) that "accomplice liability is based on the defendant's desire to make the crime succeed and is usually established by proof that the defendant was present at the scene, that he assented to the crime occurring, and that he put himself in a position where he could render aid to the perpetrator if it should become necessary." Is this so? Is the evidence sufficient without relying upon that theory?

4. The assertion in *James* that only "slight evidence" is needed to connect a particular defendant with a proven conspiracy is commonly found in conspiracy decisions. Given the due process requirement that a particular defendant's guilt be proved beyond a reasonable doubt, how can this be so? Consider *United States v. Alvarez,* 548 F.2d 542 (5th Cir.1977), where defendant appealed his conviction of conspiracy to possess marijuana. Customs agents intervened when a boat which had crossed the Rio Grande was being unloaded. Villareal was arrested, but the others (including a short, stocky man) escaped in the darkness. At Alvarez' trial, Villareal denied having said that Alvarez had been involved, but this testimony was impeached by testimony of the arresting agents that Villareal had told them Alvarez was the stocky man who fled. Said the appellate court: "We note first that the existence of a conspiracy has certainly been established—that the presence of seven men working under cover of darkness on the banks of the Rio Grande to unload 1,600 pounds of marijuana which was floated across the river 'is sufficient to show a concert of action, all parties working together understandingly, with a single design.' Thus, at first blush, it might appear that in reviewing Alvarez' conviction on the conspiracy count we should concern ourselves only with searching for the 'slight evidence' required on appellate review to connect a person with an existing conspiracy, including, at the least, some showing of Alvarez' knowledge of the conspiracy's purpose and some action in his participation therein. Mature reflection has convinced us, however, that the 'slight evidence' rule is of doubtful application to the state of facts presented here, where the issue for review is whether Alvarez was connected with the demonstrated conspiracy *at all.* It being of the nature of a conspiracy to conceal itself, the 'slight evidence' rule finds its proper application where persons are clearly connected to the conspiring group or are found acting in such a manner as unmistakably to forward its purposes. In such instances, given the

clandestine character of such projects, slight additional evidence suffices to base an inference that one who had been shown beyond reasonable doubt to be a participant was as well a *knowing* participant. But where, as here, the question is whether a defendant was connected with the conspiracy at all, to apply such a rule is to risk convicting him of the crime itself upon 'slight evidence.' We conclude that Alvarez' presence at the river must be established by evidence which a jury could conclude rules out any reasonable hypothesis of innocence. Once presence is so established as to his knowing participation, the 'slight evidence' rule may have its day." [c]

Is the distinction convincing?

STATE v. ST. CHRISTOPHER

Supreme Court of Minnesota, 1975.
305 Minn. 226, 232 N.W.2d 798.

ROGOSHESKE, JUSTICE.

Defendant was found guilty by the court, sitting without a jury, of conspiracy to commit murder, and attempted first-degree murder, and sentenced under the conspiracy conviction to a maximum indeterminate term of 20 years' imprisonment. He contends upon this appeal from the judgment (1) that he was improperly convicted of conspiracy because the evidence shows that the only party with whom he conspired never intended to aid defendant but merely feigned agreement while cooperating with police; (2) that the trial court erred in finding him guilty of attempted murder because the information did not charge him with that crime and attempted murder is not, a lesser included offense of the charge of conspiracy to commit murder * * *. We affirm the conviction of

conspiracy and reverse the conviction of attempted first-degree murder.

The facts in this case are relatively simple. On March 16, 1974, defendant (who formerly was named Marlin Peter Olson but legally changed his name to Daniel St. Christopher) stated to his cousin, Roger Zobel, that he wanted to kill his mother, Mrs. Marlin Olson, and that he wanted Zobel's help. He would pay him $125,000 over the years, money defendant would get from his father after his mother was dead. Zobel, the key witness against defendant at his trial on the charge of conspiracy, testified that at no time did he ever intend to participate in the murder but that he discussed the matter with defendant on that and subsequent occasions and acted as if he intended to participate in the plan. On March 18, Zobel contacted the police and told them of defendant's plan and they later told him to continue to cooperate with defendant. The plan, which became definite in some detail as early as March 20, was for Zobel to go to the Olson farmhouse on Saturday, March 23, when defendant's father was at the weekly livestock auction. Since defendant's mother was Zobel's aunt, Zobel could gain entrance readily. The idea was for Zobel to break her neck, hide her body in his automobile trunk, and then attach bricks to it and throw it in a nearby river after dark. Later it developed that defendant's father might not go to the sale on Saturday, so a plan was developed whereby defendant would feign car trouble, call his father for help, then signal Zobel when the father was on his way. Police followed defendant on Saturday when he left his apartment and observed him make a number of telephone calls. In one of these he called his father and told

c. The conviction was affirmed. The court relied upon this collection of circumstantial evidence regarding Alvarez' presence: (1) a van found at the scene belonged to him and his 7 brothers; (2) he used the truck more than his brothers; (3) the stocky man fled toward the

house of Alvarez' father; (4) Alvarez was the only one of the brothers who was short and stocky; (5) he lied about his identity when arrested; (6) his alibi testimony was somewhat dubious; and (7) Villareal worked at a truck stop owned by one of Alvarez' relatives.

him he was having car trouble and asked him to come and help him pay the bill. In a call to Zobel, which was taped, defendant told Zobel that his father was coming and that Zobel should proceed with the plan. Shortly thereafter, police arrested defendant. * * *

We have not found any Minnesota cases in point on the issue of the validity of the conspiracy conviction. However, in two criminal conspiracy cases this court has stated, or at least implied, that a person cannot be guilty of conspiracy where the only person with whom he has conspired or agreed has feigned agreement. The first of these cases is *State v. Burns,* 215 Minn. 182, 186, 9 N.W.2d 518, 520 (1943), where this court stated that "[t]o constitute a conspiracy to cheat and defraud, there must be not only a combination, but a common object to cheat and defraud, which each member of the combination intends shall be accomplished by the concerted action of all." [2]

The more recent Minnesota case is *State v. Willman,* 296 Minn. 322, 208 N.W.2d 300 (1973). In that case, there was a true meeting of the minds by both defendant and one Toles followed by an overt act in furtherance of the conspiracy to commit murder in the first degree. Subsequently, Toles changed his mind and contacted the police. In holding that there was sufficient evidence that defendant was guilty of conspiracy, this court arguably implied (but did not hold or even say) that this might not be the case if there had not been a true meeting of the minds or if an overt act had not occurred until after Toles contacted the police.

There is extensive authority from other jurisdictions which supports defendant's contention. The reasoning employed in these cases was summarized in Fridman, *Mens Rea in Conspiracy,* 19 Modern L.Rev. 276, as follows:

> " * * * Conspiracy is the agreement of two or more to effect an unlawful purpose. Two people cannot agree unless they both intend to carry out the purpose which is stated to be the object of their combination. Therefore there is no agreement, and consequently no conspiracy, where one of the two never intends to carry out the unlawful purpose." [a]

If there had been some evidence to suggest that, contrary to his testimony, Zobel in fact had intended to participate in the conspiracy and had not feigned agreement from the start, then the court as factfinder could have found defendant guilty of conspiracy without rejecting the rule followed in the cited cases. However, the only evidence that the state produced was that Zobel did not intend at any time to participate in the conspiracy and that his agreement was feigned, and the trial court believed this evidence. Therefore, if we accept the rule followed in these cases, we would have to reverse defendant's conviction.

We are persuaded not to accept this rule and base our decision on (a) our belief that the rule is unsound, and (b) our belief that the present conspiracy statute authorizes a conviction in this situation.

(a) One criticism by a number of commentators of the rule followed in the cited cases is that the courts have reached their

---

2. Actually, this dictum does not accurately state the rule which courts have followed. The fact that A's agreement is feigned does not prevent a conspiracy conviction of B where C is also involved and has not feigned agreement. Note, 72 Harv.L.Rev. 920, 925 note 35.

a. But if there are more than two persons involved, then the fact that one is an undercover

agent only feigning agreement is irrelevant, and this is so even if that person served as a link" between genuine conspirators who had no direct dealings with one another. See, e.g., *United States v. Fincher,* 723 F.2d 862 (11th Cir.1984).

conclusion by using as a starting point the definition of conspiracy as an agreement between two or more persons, a definition which was framed in cases not involving the issue. As one commentator put it, "if a conspiracy is arbitrarily defined as 'an agreement of intentions and not merely of language (the intentions being unlawful)' the answer to the problem is undoubtedly that where there is no such agreement of intentions then there is no conspiracy." Fridman, *Mens Rea in Conspiracy,* 19 Modern L.Rev. 276, 278. In other words, the basis for the rule is a strict doctrinal approach toward the conception of conspiracy as an agreement in which two or more parties not only objectively indicate their agreement but actually have a meeting of the minds.

Addressing the rule to be applied as a policy issue, a number of commentators have come to the conclusion that there should be no requirement of a meeting of the minds. Thus, Fridman points to cases holding that factual impossibility is no defense to a charge of attempt to commit a crime and argues that, because of close connections between the origins and purposes of the law of conspiracy and of attempt, a similar rule should obtain in conspiracy. Specifically, he argues that "[t]he fact that, unknown to a man who wishes to enter a conspiracy to commit some criminal purpose, the other person has no intention of fulfilling that purpose ought to be irrelevant as long as the first man does intend to fulfill it if he can" because "a man who believes he is conspiring to commit a crime and wishes to conspire to commit a crime has a guilty mind and has done all in his power to plot the commission of an unlawful purpose."

Professor Glanville Williams makes a somewhat similar argument, basing his opinion on the fact that conspiracy, like attempt, is an inchoate crime and that it is the act of conspiring by a defendant which is the decisive element of criminality, for it makes no difference in logic or public policy that the person with whom the defendant conspires is not himself subject to prosecution. Williams, *Criminal Law—The General Part,* § 157(a).

The draftsmen of the Model Penal Code take a slightly different approach. They recognize that conspiracy is not just an inchoate crime complementing the law of attempt and solicitation but that it is also a means of striking at the special dangers incident to group activity. *Model Penal Code* (Tent.Draft No. 10, 1960) § 5.03, Comment. In view of that recognition, it is probably not quite as easy to reject the approach taken by the cases cited, yet this is what the draftsmen have done. The provision which accomplishes this, § 5.03(1), reads as follows:

"A person is guilty of conspiracy with another person or persons to commit a crime if with the purpose of promoting or facilitating its commission he:

"(a) agrees with such other person or persons that they or one or more of them will engage in conduct which constitutes such crime or an attempt or solicitation to commit such crime; or

"(b) Agrees to aid such other person or persons in the planning or commission of such crime or of an attempt or solicitation to commit such crime."

In comments explaining this provision, the reporters state as follows:

"2. *The Conspiratorial Relationship.*

"*Unilateral Approach of the Draft.* The definition of the Draft departs from the traditional view of conspiracy as an entirely bilateral or multilateral relationship, the view inherent in the standard formulation cast in terms of 'two or more persons' agreeing or combining to commit a crime. Attention is directed instead to each individual's culpability by framing the definition in terms of the conduct which suffices to establish the liability of any given actor, rather than the conduct of a group of which he is charged to be a part—an approach which in this comment we have designated 'unilateral.' * * *

"*Second:* Where the person with whom the defendant conspired secretly intends not to go through with the plan. In these cases it is generally held that neither party can be convicted because there was no 'agreement' between two persons. Under the unilateral approach of the Draft, the culpable party's guilt would not be affected by the fact that the other party's agreement was feigned. He has conspired, within the meaning of the definition, in the belief that the other party was with him; apart from the issue of entrapment often presented in such cases, his culpability is not decreased by the other's secret intention. True enough, the project's chances of success have not been increased by the agreement; indeed, its doom may have been sealed by this turn of events. But the major basis of conspiratorial liability—the unequivocal evidence of a firm purpose to commit a crime—remains the same. The result would be the same under the Draft if the only co-conspirator established a defense of renunciation under Section 5.03(6). While both the Advisory Committee and the Council support the Draft upon this point, it should be noted that the Council vote was 14–11, the dissenting members deeming mutual agreement on the part

of two or more essential to the concept of conspiracy."[6]

(b) We find the scholarly literature persuasive on this subject.[7] The question is whether this court can take the recommended approach. We think the answer lies in the wording of our statute. The Minnesota statute formerly dealing with the crime of conspiracy read as follows (Minn.St.1961, § 613.70):

"When two or more persons shall conspire:

(1) To commit a crime;

* * *

"Every such person shall be guilty of a misdemeanor."

This is the most common type of conspiracy statute, and it is understandable that this type of statute lends itself easily to the result reached by the cases because the statute starts with the phrase, "When two or more persons shall conspire."

However, the Minnesota statute as it presently reads omits this phrase and is now phrased in unilateral terms similar to those used in the Model Penal Code. The provision, Minn.St. 609.175, subd. 2, reads in part:

"Whoever conspires with another to commit a crime and in furtherance of the conspiracy one or more of the parties does some overt act in furtherance of such conspiracy may be sentenced as follows:"

---

6. The proposed Federal Criminal Code takes a similar approach. The full text of the conspiracy section, § 1–2A5, is reproduced and discussed in Note, 47 Tulane L.Rev. 1017. See, also, Final Report of the National Commission on Reform of Federal Criminal Laws (1971) § 1004.

7. An alternative approach would be to say that in cases of this sort the factfinder may find the defendant guilty of attempted conspiracy. This is the approach recommended in Note, 72 Harv.L.Rev. 920, 926, note 35. The approach is undesirable because it would result in disparate

sentences for defendants whose conduct was the same, the length of sentence turning on a fortuity. Thus, if A agreed with B (a policeman who merely feigns agreement) to commit murder, A would be guilty of attempted conspiracy and could receive a maximum of 10 years' imprisonment, whereas if A agreed with C (who does not feign agreement), A could be guilty of conspiracy and could receive a maximum of 20 years' imprisonment. See, Minn.St. 609.17, subd. 4(2), and 609.175, subd. 2(2).

Because of this wording, we hold that the trial court was free to convict defendant of conspiracy under the facts of this case.

The second issue raised by defendant is whether he was properly convicted of attempted murder. We hold that he was not and reverse this part of the judgment.

Because defendant was charged only with conspiracy to commit murder, the trial court could not find him guilty of attempted murder unless attempted murder is an included offense of conspiracy to commit murder. We believe that attempted murder is not, as the state contends, necessarily proved by proof of conspiracy to commit murder. * * *

Notes and Questions

1. Note, 75 Colum.L.Rev. 1122, 1135–37 (1975): "Nearly all jurisdictions [with recent recodifications] have elected to follow the [Model Penal Code] recommendation that conspiracy be redefined as a unilateral, rather than a bilateral (or multilateral), crime. Statutory descriptions of the conspiracy offense have been carefully reworded to focus on the behavior of a single malefactor rather than the collaboration of several wrongdoers. Under a unilateral formulation, the crime of conspiracy is committed *when a person agrees* to proceed in a prohibited manner; under a bilateral formulation, the crime of conspiracy is committed *when two or more persons* agree to proceed in such manner.

"While the basic elements of the offense are identical under either formulation, the unilateral approach is preferred because it solves a number of problems which arise in cases where, for one reason or another, co-conspirators are differently situated with respect to the legal system. By concentrating on individual, rather than group, liability, the guilt of a particular actor is made independent of that of his co-conspirator(s). Such treatment is important when, for example, defendant's

only co-conspirator * * * has feigned agreement, usually as part of some law enforcement scheme * * *."

2. Compare Burgman, *Unilateral Conspiracy: Three Critical Perspectives*, 29 DePaul L.Rev. 75, 77–78 (1979): "This [unilateral] approach ignores the historical rationale of the common law crime of conspiracy: the threat to society of two or more persons pursuing crime. When one of two conspirators has no intention of pursuing the criminal objective, the rationale for increased punishment is absent. Therefore, although this latest extension of the law appears logical when viewed alongside its judicial precursors, it actually defies its own reason. While the move may be heralded as a step toward more effective law enforcement, it is not justified because society's interest in punishing such conduct is already met by the charges of solicitation and attempt.

"Moreover, because the crime of unilateral conspiracy inevitably punishes predisposition to commit crime, without the safeguards incorporated in bilateral conspiracy, it opens the door to entrapment. Unfortunately, recent judicial treatment of the entrapment defense has curtailed its effectiveness. Courts that have considered the entrapment issue in the context of unilateral conspiracy cases have dismissed it summarily or, after discussion, have deemed it inapplicable."

3. Is the *St. Christopher* rejection in fn. 7 of the attempted conspiracy alternative sound? Consider Burgman, supra, at 95–96: "With this tour de force, the court constructed what is tantamount to an equal protection rationale for the unilateral doctrine. What it patently ignored was the fact that the two situations differ considerably: in the first, *none* of the justifications for penalizing conspiracy applies; in the second, *all* the rationales apply. The argument simply makes too much of the idea of 'fortuity.' If X shoots at Y and misses,

while Z shoots Y and kills Y, the criminal jurisprudence does not seek to punish both X and Z equally, even though it is clear that both X and Z have exhibited a dangerous predisposition. The punishment is commensurate with the harm sustained; this principle is true for both the crime of attempt and the crime of conspiracy."

4. Is the attempted conspiracy alternative a rational theory when the applicable conspiracy statute does not follow the unilateral approach? See *Hutchinson v. State,* 315 So.2d 546 (Fla.App.1975), concluding that "there is no case law in Florida or other jurisdictions which proscribes or defines attempted conspiracy. * * * To concede in the academic sense the possibility that there can be an attempted conspiracy is not the equivalent of declaring it to be reasonable and a punishable statutory offense. Moreover, the judicial creation of attempted conspiracy to punish solicitation is not needed here to fill a gap in the definition of a crime or to extend the reach of the conspiracy statute. Appellant's conduct could have been reached * * * as common law solicitation, which as of July 1, 1975, will also be a statutory crime."

Query, would or should a court reach a different result if there is no applicable solicitation crime or if that crime is not applicable to the defendant because he attempted to agree with an undercover agent who first solicited him? See *State v. Sexton,* 232 Kan. 539, 657 P.2d 43 (1983) (though defendant's murder solicitation of undercover agent who feigned agreement is "behavior of a type ordinarily prohibited by the criminal statutes," such conduct occurring prior to recent enactment of solicitation statute cannot be prosecuted as attempted conspiracy, for "it is not our function to create a crime where the legislature has not done so").

5. May a defendant who was not a party to the conspiratorial agreement

nonetheless be convicted of conspiracy on the theory that he aided and abetted the conspiracy and thus was an accomplice in the conspiracy? An instruction to that effect was upheld in *United States v. Kasvin,* 757 F.2d 887 (7th Cir.1985), where the defendant claimed to have been nothing more than a customer of an ongoing marijuana distribution conspiracy. The court stated: "The decision in the case of Kasvin's co-defendant, *United States v. Galiffa,* 734 F.2d 306 (7th Cir.1984), established the following principles of law which apply with equal force in this case:

"1. A defendant can be convicted of aiding and abetting a conspiracy for deeds other than acting as a liaison for the parties to the conspiratorial agreement provided the defendant has knowledge of the conspiracy's existence at the time of his act.

"2. One can aid and abet a conspiracy without necessarily participating in the original agreement.

"3. The charge of aiding and abetting under 18 U.S.C. § 2(a) 'need not be specifically pleaded and a defendant indicted for a substantive offense can be convicted as an aider and abettor' upon a proper demonstration of proof so long as no unfair surprise results.

"4. No fatal amendment to an indictment occurs where a defendant may have been convicted as a principal in a conspiracy by aiding and abetting it even though he was not charged with aiding and abetting in the original indictment.

"* * * [I]f the jury simply regarded Kasvin as a major customer of the ring, it was fully justified in finding that he associated himself with the criminal venture, participated in it as something he wished to bring about and sought by his actions to make it succeed. It is difficult to imagine what greater contribution Kasvin could have made to the financial success of the venture than by becoming its largest regular customer. In short, if he was not a member of the conspiracy, he was clearly an aider and abettor of it."

Swygert, J., dissenting, objected: "There is some authority that the only manner in which a defendant may aid and abet a conspiracy is by bringing two other persons together to conspire. There is some merit to this argument because the crime of conspiracy always requires the act of agreement. But it must be that certain other 'extraneous acts' might also aid and abet a conspiracy if they facilitate agreement by keeping the group of conspirators together and the conspiracy going. Thus, liability for aiding and abetting a conspiracy might be imposed on a defendant who brings two parties together with the intention and knowledge that they will conspire, or warns drug conspirators of undercover police activity, or permits one's home to be used as a rendezvous for drug trafficking, or provides police protection to drug dealers, or acts as a paid bodyguard to the principal of an illegal scheme to distribute stolen securities. In these cases, the clear theoretical and practical difference between aiding and abetting a conspiracy and aiding and abetting the substantive offense that is the object of the conspiracy simply was not and could not be merged. * * *

"In this case, the Government insisted at trial that a customer who frequently purchases large amounts of illegal goods from a conspiracy may under certain circumstances be found guilty as a coconspirator. But, as I note in Part III of this dissent, the trial judge found there was insufficient evidence to create an issue as to whether the defendant was a member of the conspiracy, and, even if it was questionable whether the judge was warranted in granting the directed verdict in favor of the defendant, this court may not engage in *de novo* decisionmaking at this juncture by second-guessing the trial judge.

"Under this state of affairs the only charge that remained was that of aiding and abetting, and the only evidence to support this theory of liability was that the defendant was a frequent customer of the organization who bought large amounts of marijuana on credit and who was apparently a friend of the conspirators. But these distributions to the defendant were overt acts and objectives of the conspiracy. They were not extraneous to it; they are analogous to plunging the knife into the murder victim, not to providing the murderer with the knife. * * * Thus, in applying the analysis of what aiding and abetting a conspiracy means, the defendant's conduct did not come within that meaning."

SECTION 3. MENTAL STATE

UNITED STATES v. CHAGRA
United States Court of Appeals, Fifth Circuit, 1986.
807 F.2d 398.

PATRICK E. HIGGINBOTHAM, CIRCUIT JUDGE:

Elizabeth Chagra appeals from her conviction of conspiracy to murder Federal Judge John H. Wood, Jr., of the Western District of Texas. * * *

Elizabeth Chagra was first indicted for her role in the murder of Judge Wood on April 15, 1982. She was charged in count one of that indictment, with her husband Jimmy Chagra, her brother-in-law Joe Chagra, and Charles Harrelson, with conspiring to commit first-degree murder of a federal judge in violation of 18 U.S.C. §§ 1111, 1114, and 1117. Also charged in a separate count with conspiracy to obstruct justice, she was convicted of both counts, but on appeal we reversed her conviction for conspiracy to murder and remanded the case for a new trial on that count. On the first appeal we found that the instructions to the jury did not require the government to prove premeditation and malice aforethought at the time Elizabeth Chagra joined the conspiracy to murder, essential elements of the substantive crime of murder in the first degree. We observed that *Ingram v. United States,* 360 U.S. 672, 79 S.Ct. 1314, 3 L.Ed.2d 1503 (1959), held that "conspiracy to commit a particular substantive offense cannot exist without at least the degree of criminal intent necessary for the substantive offense itself . . ." We then explained that:

> "[f]irst degree murder under Section 1111 clearly requires the criminal intent of premeditation and malice aforethought. Thus, proof of premeditation and malice aforethought is required to sustain a conviction of conspiracy to commit first degree murder under that section."

Before the trial on remand, a new grand jury returned a superseding indictment with one count charging Elizabeth Chagra with conspiring "to kill with malice aforethought . . . in violation of Title 18, United States Code, Sections 1111 and 1114, and in violation of Title 18, United States Code, Section 1117." The new indictment did not allege premeditation and, at a pretrial conference, the government conceded that the prosecution did "not maintain that Mrs. Chagra premeditated prior to joining the conspiracy." Her motion to dismiss the new indictment because it did not charge an offense was denied.

Elizabeth Chagra argues here, as she did below, that because second degree murder "is distinguished from first degree murder by the absence of premeditation," and a conspiracy is an agreement to commit a crime, there can be no conspiracy to commit second degree murder. This is so because "you cannot plan the unplannable, intend the unintended." She points out that:

[p]remeditation is the formation of the intent or plan to kill, the formation of a positive design to kill. It must have been considered by the defendants.

The present argument has its genesis in the effort of the prosecution to meet the requirement expressed in *Ingram v. United States.* * * * The government recognized that the substantive offense of second degree murder requires proof of an intentional killing with malice aforethought. The superseding indictment on which Elizabeth Chagra was tried in the second trial alleged an intent to kill and the government undertook to make that proof. * * *

But, Elizabeth Chagra argues, the agreement necessary to a conspiracy, and premeditation, are sufficiently the same that one cannot exist without the other; that in the context of this case, she cannot have agreed with her husband to the killing of Judge Wood without premeditation. Conversely, that second-degree murder is an unplanned offense and therefore could not be the subject of a conspiracy.

The surface appeal of this argument rests on an incorrect assumption and is without merit. In *Harrelson* we read *Ingram* and *Feola* to require that the government prove that at the time of the agreement the intent required for the illegal objective of the conspiracy also existed. We did not hold that the intent required for the substantive offense is required for the agreement itself—that the agreement was premeditated. What is required is that the defendant agree with another to accomplish an illegal objective and that at the time of agreement the defendant also have the state of mind required to commit the substantive crime. The two states of mind are almost always one, or tend to collapse into one, but it is nonetheless important that the inquiries be made separately.

Having said this, the quick answer to defendant's argument is that without proving premeditation the government can prove intent to kill with malice aforethought. Under the government's theory it was entitled to prove that at the moment of conspiratorial agreement, her intent to kill Judge Wood was impulsive and with malice aforethought. An impulsive killing is nonetheless the intentional taking of life and with malice aforethought is murder in the second degree. Certainly then the element of agreement and the requisite intent to commit the substantive offense were in harmony. More to the point, they were certainly not mutually exclusive requirements of proof.

Nor does the rhetorical flourish that "one cannot plan an unplanned event" present a different argument, in any event, one of substance. It suggests that second degree murder can be sustained here only on the theory of impulsive killing and one cannot possess the intent to kill impulsively at some future time. Conspiracy, however is a crime independent of the substantive offense that was its object. The focus of a conspiracy offense is upon agreement. The inquiry is into defendant's intent at the time of the illegal agreement or conspiracy, and that state of mind can certainly be to impulsively kill such as, "yes! let's kill the judge."

Elizabeth Chagra argues that if there were a substantive crime charged, the court erred in two material ways in instructing the jury regarding malice aforethought. The court instructed the jury as follows:

"Malice," as that term has been used here, is but another name for a certain state or condition of a person's mind or heart. Since no one can look into the heart or mind of another, the only means of determining whether or not malice existed *at the time of the killing* is by inference drawn from the surrounding facts and circumstances as shown by the evidence in the case.

"Malice aforethought" means an intent *at the time of a killing* willfully to take the life of another human being or an intent willfully to act in callous and wanton disregard of the consequences of human life. Malice aforethought does not necessarily imply any ill will, spite or hatred towards the individual killed or that *the intent to kill was thought out before the killing.*

Now, in determining whether the Defendant, Elizabeth Nichols Chagra, joined the conspiracy with malice aforethought, the jury should consider all the facts and circumstances preceding, surrounding, and following any agreement, if any, as shown by the evidence in the case which tends to shed light upon the condition of the mind and heart of Elizabeth Nichols Chagra before and at the time of the agreement. No fact, no matter how small, no circumstance, no matter how trivial, which bears upon the question of malice aforethought, should escape careful consideration by the jury. (emphasis supplied)

The first error is said to be the instruction that malice aforethought included "an intent willfully to act in callous and wanton disregard of the consequences of human life"; that the court's instruction did not demand proof of an intent to kill but only of reckless acts causing the death of another. This, however, is the correct definition of malice. There is no reason that a defendant cannot have this intent at the time he joins a conspiracy to kill. As the district court put it:

[The] evidence could very well show that . . . Chagra was aware of her husband's dangerous violent tendencies, and that her encouragement of his stated intent to murder Judge Wood demonstrated conduct which was so reckless, so wanton and such a gross deviation from a reasonable standard of care that a jury could find her guilty of conspiracy to commit intent-to-do-serious-bodily-injury murder. . . .

The second urged error is that the instruction is ambivalent as to when Elizabeth Chagra must have had this state of mind, at one place in the charge asking the jury to determine the presence of malice at the time she joined the conspiracy and at another place in the charge asking the jury to determine the presence of malice at the time of the killing.

We review claimed deficiencies in a jury charge by looking to the entire charge as well as the arguments made to the jury. Our inquiry is whether in the context of the true trial scene the jury was given incorrect instructions. This is a common sense approach that recognizes that the jury charge does not stand alone for separate examination; that the charge is part of a larger picture of what the jury was told. Examined apart from context, charges frequently have seemingly ambiguous expressions and understandably so, given the need of trial courts to assemble the divergent requests of counsel into a meaningful whole. Potential ambiguity frequently lurks at the juncture points, but is often resolved in closing argument by counsel's explanation of the case to the jury. For this reason, the use made of jury instruction in summation can be significant in an appellate court's effort to determine whether the ambiguity of a cold transcript actually existed at trial.

The court first gave the pattern instruction defining the phrases "knowingly" and "willfully," defining willfully as including the specific intent to do something which the law prohibits, explaining that "specific intent" is more than the "general intent" to engage in illegal conduct. It instructed that knowingly means that the act was done voluntarily and intentionally, and not because of a mistake or accident or other innocent reason. As we have earlier discussed, the court told the jury that the

government had to prove that Elizabeth Chagra had two intents: the intent requisite to agreement and the intent to commit the substantive offense which was the object of the conspiracy. The jury was told that the government must prove that Elizabeth Chagra willfully, knowingly, and with malice aforethought became a member of the conspiracy. As she points out, the court then defined malice aforethought in an unexceptional way except it referenced intent at the time of the killing. Thereafter, the court told the jury that it had to find beyond a reasonable doubt whether Elizabeth Chagra joined the conspiracy with malice explaining "if the defendant, with an understanding of the unlawful character of the plan to kill Judge Wood on account of the performance of his official duties, knowingly, willfully and with malice aforethought, joined in the unlawful scheme," the jury could convict her.

Whatever uncertainty there may have been from the charge alone, defense counsel's eloquent summation left no uncertainty as he outlined the government's burden. Without objection from the prosecution or correction from the court, he argued:

Now, you are instructed that the government must prove beyond a reasonable doubt that at least two of the defendants charged with conspiracy had at least the criminal intent necessary to commit the offense, that is, the intent to murder the judge with malice aforethought. In order to convict Elizabeth Nichols Chagra, you must find and believe beyond a reasonable doubt that at the instant she joined the conspiracy, if indeed she did, that she intended to accomplish the purpose of the conspiracy, that is, to kill Judge John H. Wood, Jr., with malice aforethought. Therefore, the government must prove beyond a reasonable doubt that Elizabeth Chagra conspired to kill Judge John H. Wood with the requisite intent of malice aforethought, and if the government fails to prove such intent beyond a reasonable doubt, you must acquit the defendant.

Viewing the charge as a whole and in the context of trial, we are persuaded that the charge stated the government's burden to prove beyond a reasonable doubt that at the time Elizabeth Chagra joined the conspiracy she intended to kill with malice aforethought. We are aided in that judgment by the able closing arguments that reduced any risk that the jury would be confused by the reference to the time of killing for the inquiry into malice aforethought. * * *

Notes and Questions

1. In *People v. Horn,* 12 Cal.3d 290, 115 Cal.Rptr. 516, 524 P.2d 1300 (1974), Horn and Feltner appealed from their conviction of conspiracy to commit first degree murder by firebombing. Evidence at their trial showed that at the time of the conspiracy they were so intoxicated as to lack the capacity to entertain malice aforethought, but the trial judge refused to instruct the jury that diminished capacity arising from intoxication can reduce a homicide to voluntary manslaughter (as clearly is the case under prior California decisions regarding what constitutes malice aforethought). The court, per Tobriner, J., reversed, concluding:

"Penal Code section 182, after listing certain felonies, not including murder or manslaughter, provides that when two or more persons 'conspire to commit any other felony, they shall be punishable in the same manner and to the same extent as is provided for the punishment of the said felony. If the felony is one for which different punishments are prescribed for different degrees, the jury or court which finds the defendant guilty thereof shall determine the degree of the felony defendant conspired to commit. If the degree is not so determined, the punishment for

conspiracy to commit such felony shall be that prescribed for the lesser degree, except in the case of conspiracy to commit murder, in which case the punishment shall be that prescribed for murder in the first degree.' To comply with this section, the trier of fact must determine the identity of the conspired felony, and if that felony is divided into degrees, the degree of the felony. * * *

"The Attorney General, however, argues that conspiracy is a crime without degrees or lesser included offenses, and hence that the defense of diminished capacity goes not to the conspired homicide but only to the conspirators' capacity to agree among themselves. This argument mistakes the element of intent in the crime of conspiracy, and overlooks the duty of the jury under Penal Code section 182 to determine the crime, and the degree of the crime, which defendants conspired to commit.

"Conspiracy is a 'specific intent' crime. The specific intent required divides logically into two elements: (a) the intent to agree, or conspire, and (b) the intent to commit the offense which is the object of the conspiracy. To sustain a conviction for conspiracy to commit a particular offense, the prosecution must show not only that the conspirators intended to agree but also that they intended to commit the elements of that offense. * * *

"It is contended that since defendants are charged with conspiracy, not with murder, that only two issues arise: did defendants conspire, and did they have the capacity to conspire? But resolution of only those two issues does not dispose of the case. *Under Penal Code section 182 the jury must also determine which felony defendants conspired to commit,* and if that felony is divided into degrees, which degree of the felony they conspired to commit. The jury cannot perform that task unless it is instructed on the elements of both the offense defendants are charged with conspiring to commit, and any lesser offense defendants assert to be the true object of the conspiracy.

"Moreover, section 182 clearly makes the punishment for conspiracy turn on the nature and degree of the conspired offense. Thus even if a defendant could be convicted of conspiracy in the abstract, he could not be punished until the trier of fact ascertained the criminal object of the conspiracy. To determine whether the object of defendants' conspiracy in the present case was the commission of a first degree murder, the trier of fact obviously would need to know the elements of that offense."

Mosk, J., dissenting, objected: "Of course, diminished capacity is an issue in this case. But where the majority fall into error is in relating diminished capacity to murder, instead of to the charge of conspiracy. The *Wells-Gorshen* instruction, properly given by the trial court, alerted the jury to the necessity of determining the capacity of defendants to conspire. Since there are no degrees of conspiracy created by law, if defendants' capacity to conspire was diminished the jury would have been compelled to bring in a verdict of acquittal. The guilty verdict indicates the jury found no diminished capacity preventing defendants from conspiring.

"[W]e must look to the capacity of the defendants to conspire, i.e., to agree between themselves. It seems obvious that the criminal act they agreed to commit is unrelated to their mental ability to agree. The issue is: *was their capacity to conspire diminished?* The jury was properly instructed on that query, and by its verdict of guilt found the defendants to have adequate capacity to negotiate a criminal agreement.

"But, say the majority, two persons may have the ability to conspire but lack the ability to complete the offense they conspire to commit; therefore they can be convicted of conspiring to commit some lesser offense. In this instance the majority hold that lacking the capacity to conspire to commit first degree murder, the defendants nevertheless may have the capacity to conspire to commit manslaughter. I confess the rationale of this esoteric concept escapes me. If the defendants are unable to conspire to commit one crime because of mental incapacity, it would seem to follow that they would be equally unable to conspire to commit another crime. By the simple device of changing the crime alleged to have been conspiratorially contemplated the law cannot elevate, *mirabile dictu,* the mental capacity of the defendants."

2. Assume instead that Horn and Feltner were not intoxicated, but that the proof was that their sole objective was to destroy the building by firebombing, though they knew that persons in the building would in all likelihood be killed by the firebombing. Should this be treated as a conspiracy to murder? *Model Penal Code* § 5.03, Comment (1985), puts this case and says that under the Code "they are nevertheless guilty only of a conspiracy to destroy the building and not of a conspiracy to kill the inhabitants. While this result may seem unduly restrictive from the viewpoint of the completed crime, it is necessitated by the extremely preparatory behavior that may be involved in conspiracy."

3. Compare *United States v. United States Gypsum Co.,* 438 U.S. 422, 98 S.Ct. 2864, 57 L.Ed.2d 854 (1978), involving a conviction for violating § 1 of the Sherman Act by conspiracy to fix the prices of gypsum board. The Court, per Burger, C.J., first concluded that "the Sherman Act should be construed as including intent as an element," but then concluded "that action undertaken with knowledge of its probable consequences and having the requisite anticompetitive effects can be a suffi-

cient predicate for a finding of criminal liability under the antitrust laws.   *   *   *

"Nothing in our analysis of the Sherman Act persuades us that this general understanding of intent should not be applied to criminal antitrust violations such as charged here. The business behavior which is likely to give rise to criminal antitrust charges is conscious behavior normally undertaken only after a full consideration of the desired results and a weighing of the costs, benefits, and risks. A requirement of proof not only of this knowledge of likely effects, but also of a conscious desire to bring them to fruition or to violate the law would seem, particularly in such a context, both unnecessarily cumulative and unduly burdensome. Where carefully planned and calculated conduct is being scrutinized in the context of a criminal prosecution, the perpetrator's knowledge of the anticipated consequences is a sufficient predicate for a finding of criminal intent."

4. Assume instead that Horn and Feltner merely agreed to handle explosive materials in such a way as would be reckless vis-a-vis persons known to be in the premises. Are they guilty of a conspiracy to commit involuntary manslaughter of the recklessness type? Of a conspiracy to commit the crime of reckless conduct? Does *Chagra* suggest an affirmative answer? Consider *State v. Beccia,* 199 Conn. 1, 505 A.2d 683 (1986), where defendant was acquitted of conspiracy to commit arson in the first degree (that is, starting a fire with intent to damage a building) but convicted of conspiracy to commit arson in the third degree (that is, intentionally starting a fire which recklessly causes damage to a building). The court reversed, declaring that "there is no such thing as a conspiracy to commit a crime which is defined in terms of recklessly or negligently causing a result."

PEOPLE v. LAURIA

Court of Appeal, Second District, 1967.
251 Cal.App.2d 471, 59 Cal.Rptr. 628.

FLEMING, ASSOCIATE JUSTICE.

In an investigation of call-girl activity the police focused their attention on three prostitutes actively plying their trade on call, each of whom was using Lauria's telephone answering service, presumably for business purposes.   *   *   *

Lauria and the three prostitutes were indicted for conspiracy to commit prostitution, and nine overt acts were specified. Subsequently the trial court set aside the indictment as having been brought without reasonable or probable cause. The People have appealed, claiming that a sufficient showing of an unlawful agreement to further prostitution was made.

To establish agreement, the People need show no more than a tacit, mutual understanding between coconspirators to accomplish an unlawful act. Here the People attempted to establish a conspiracy by showing that Lauria, well aware that his codefendants were prostitutes who received business calls from customers through his telephone answering service, continued to furnish them with such service. This approach attempts to equate knowledge of another's criminal activity with conspiracy to further such criminal activity, and poses the question of the criminal responsibility of a furnisher of goods or services who knows his product is being used to assist the operation of an illegal business. Under what circumstances does a supplier become a part of a conspiracy to further an illegal enterprise by furnishing goods or services which he knows are to be used by the buyer for criminal purposes?

The two leading cases on this point face in opposite directions. In *United States v. Falcone,* 311 U.S. 205, 61 S.Ct. 204, 85 L.Ed. 128, the sellers of large quantities of sugar, yeast, and cans were absolved from participation in a moonshining conspiracy among distillers who bought from them, while in *Direct Sales Co. v. United States,* 319 U.S. 703, 63 S.Ct. 1265, 87 L.Ed. 1674, a wholesaler of drugs was convicted of conspiracy to violate the federal narcotic laws by selling drugs in quantity to a codefendant physician who was supplying them to addicts. The distinction between these two cases appears primarily based on the proposition that distributors of such dangerous products as drugs are required to exercise greater discrimination in the conduct of their business than are distributors of innocuous substances like sugar and yeast.

In the earlier case, *Falcone,* the sellers' knowledge of the illegal use of the goods was insufficient by itself to make the sellers participants in a conspiracy with the distillers who bought from them. Such knowledge fell short of proof of a conspiracy, and evidence on the volume of sales was too vague to support a jury finding that respondents knew of the conspiracy from the size of the sales alone.

In the later case of *Direct Sales,* the conviction of a drug wholesaler for conspiracy to violate federal narcotic laws was affirmed on a showing that it had actively promoted the sale of morphine sulphate in quantity and had sold codefendant physician, who practiced in a small town in South Carolina, more than 300 times his normal requirements of the drug, even though it had been repeatedly warned of the dangers of unrestricted sales of the drug. The court contrasted the restricted goods involved in *Direct Sales* with the articles of free commerce involved in *Falcone:* "All articles of commerce may be put to illegal ends," said the court. "But all do not have inherently the same susceptibility to harmful and illegal use. * * * This difference is important for two purposes. One is for making certain that the seller knows the buyer's intended illegal use. The other is to show that by the sale

he intends to further, promote and cooperate in it. This intent, when given effect by overt act, is the gist of conspiracy. While it is not identical with mere knowledge that another purposes unlawful action, it is not unrelated to such knowledge. * * * The step from knowledge to intent and agreement may be taken. There is more than suspicion, more than knowledge, acquiescence, carelessness, indifference, lack of concern. There is informed and interested cooperation, stimulation, instigation. And there is also a 'stake in the venture' which, even if it may not be essential, is not irrelevant to the question of conspiracy."

While *Falcone* and *Direct Sales* may not be entirely consistent with each other in their full implications, they do provide us with a framework for the criminal liability of a supplier of lawful goods or services put to unlawful use. Both the element of *knowledge* of the illegal use of the goods or services and the element of *intent* to further that use must be present in order to make the supplier a participant in a criminal conspiracy.

Proof of *knowledge* is ordinarily a question of fact and requires no extended discussion in the present case. The knowledge of the supplier was sufficiently established when Lauria admitted he knew some of his customers were prostitutes and admitted he knew that Terry, an active subscriber to his service, was a prostitute. In the face of these admissions he could scarcely claim to have relied on the normal assumption an operator of a business or service is entitled to make, that his customers are behaving themselves in the eyes of the law. Because Lauria knew in fact that some of his customers were prostitutes, it is a legitimate inference he knew they were subscribing to his answering service for illegal business purposes and were using his service to make assignations for prostitution. On this record we think the prosecution is entitled to claim positive knowledge by Lauria of the use of his service to facilitate the business of prostitution.

The more perplexing issue in the case is the sufficiency of proof of *intent* to further the criminal enterprise. The element of intent may be proved either by direct evidence, or by evidence of circumstances from which an intent to further a criminal enterprise by supplying lawful goods or services may be inferred. Direct evidence of participation, such as advice from the supplier of legal goods or services to the user of those goods or services on their use for illegal purposes, such evidence as appeared in a companion case we decide today, *People v. Roy,* 59 Cal.Rptr. 636, provides the simplest case.[a] When the intent to further and promote the criminal enterprise comes from the lips of the supplier himself, ambiguities of inference from circumstance need not trouble us. But in cases where direct proof of complicity is lacking, intent to further the conspiracy must be derived from the sale itself and its surrounding circumstances in order to establish the supplier's express or tacit agreement to join the conspiracy.

In the case at bench the prosecution argues that since Lauria knew his customers were using his service for illegal purposes but nevertheless continued to furnish it to them, he must have intended to assist them in carrying out their illegal activities. Thus through a union of knowledge and intent he became a participant in a criminal conspiracy. Essentially, the People argue that knowledge alone of the continuing use of his telephone facilities for criminal purposes provided a sufficient basis from which his intent to participate in those criminal activities could be inferred.

In examining precedents in this field we find that sometimes, but not always, the criminal intent of the supplier may be inferred from his knowledge of the unlawful use made of the product he supplies. Some consideration of characteristic patterns may be helpful.

1. Intent may be inferred from knowledge, when the purveyor of legal goods for illegal use has acquired a stake in the venture. (*United States v. Falcone,* 2 Cir., 109 F.2d 579, 581.) For example, in *Regina v. Thomas* (1957), 2 All.E.R. 181, 342, a prosecution for living off the earnings of prostitution, the evidence showed that the accused, knowing the woman to be a convicted prostitute, agreed to let her have the use of his room between the hours of 9 p.m. and 2 a.m. for a charge of £3 a night. The Court of Criminal Appeal refused an appeal from the conviction, holding that when the accused rented a room at a grossly inflated rent to a prostitute for the purpose of carrying on her trade, a jury could find he was living on the earnings of prostitution.

In the present case, no proof was offered of inflated charges for the telephone answering services furnished the codefendants.

a. In *Roy,* the defendant (also the operator of a telephone answering service) advised a supposed prostitute of precautions she should take in conducting business as a prostitute and also undertook to arrange the sharing of customers between prostitutes using her answering service. Said the court: "By no stretch of the imagination does the making of arrangements for the referral of overflow business from one prostitute to another have anything to do with the legitimate operation of a telephone answering service. The mischief for which Mrs. Roy was indicted had thus been divorced from the operation of the telephone answering service and become a separate venture

of its own, even though some of its acts were derived from and dependent upon the use of facilities of the legitimate business. * * *

"Introducing one prostitute to another to facilitate the sharing of customers can have no legitimate function or purpose. The case thus falls within the rule of *People v. McLaughlin,* 111 Cal. App.2d 781, 245 P.2d 1076, where the furnishing of wire service information having no other use than to service the illegal operations of bookmakers, made the defendants knowing and intentional participants in a criminal conspiracy to further bookmaking."

2. Intent may be inferred from knowledge, when no legitimate use for the goods or services exists. The leading California case is *People v. McLaughlin,* 111 Cal. App.2d 781, 245 P.2d 1076, in which the court upheld a conviction of the suppliers of horse-racing information by wire for conspiracy to promote bookmaking, when it had been established that wire-service information had no other use than to supply information needed by bookmakers to conduct illegal gambling operations.

* * *

Other services of a comparable nature come to mind: the manufacturer of crooked dice and marked cards who sells his product to gambling casinos; the tipster who furnishes information on the movement of law enforcement officers to known lawbreakers. (Cf. *Jackson v. State of Texas,* 164 Tex.Cr.R. 276, 298 S.W.2d 837 (1957), where the furnisher of signaling equipment used to warn gamblers of the police was convicted of aiding the equipping of a gambling place.) In such cases the supplier must necessarily have an intent to further the illegal enterprise since there is no known honest use for his goods.

However, there is nothing in the furnishing of telephone answering service which would necessarily imply assistance in the performance of illegal activities. Nor is any inference to be derived from the use of an answering service by women, either in any particular volume of calls, or outside normal working hours. Nightclub entertainers, registered nurses, faith healers, public stenographers, photographic models, and free lance substitute employees, provide examples of women in legitimate occupations whose employment might cause them to receive a volume of telephone calls at irregular hours.

3. Intent may be inferred from knowledge, when the volume of business with the buyer is grossly disproportionate to

any legitimate demand, or when sales for illegal use amount to a high proportion of the seller's total business. In such cases an intent to participate in the illegal enterprise may be inferred from the quantity of the business done. For example, in *Direct Sales,* supra, the sale of narcotics to a rural physician in quantities 300 times greater than he would have normal use for provided potent evidence of an intent to further the illegal activity. In the same case the court also found significant the fact that the wholesaler had attracted as customers a disproportionately large group of physicians who had been convicted of violating the Harrison Act. * * *

No evidence of any unusual volume of business with prostitutes was presented by the prosecution against Lauria.

Inflated charges, the sale of goods with no legitimate use, sales in inflated amounts, each may provide a fact of sufficient moment from which the intent of the seller to participate in the criminal enterprise may be inferred. In such instances participation by the supplier of legal goods to the illegal enterprise may be inferred because in one way or another the supplier has acquired a special interest in the operation of the illegal enterprise. His intent to participate in the crime of which he has knowledge may be inferred from the existence of his special interest.

Yet there are cases in which it cannot reasonably be said that the supplier has a stake in the venture or has acquired a special interest in the enterprise, but in which he has been held liable as a participant on the basis of knowledge alone. Some suggestion of this appears in *Direct Sales,* supra, where both the knowledge of the illegal use of the drugs and the intent of the supplier to aid that use were inferred. In *Regina v. Bainbridge* (1959), 3 W.L.R. 656 (CCA 6), a supplier of oxygen-cutting equipment to one known to intend to use it to break into a bank was convicted as an accessory to the crime. In *Sykes v. Director of Public Prosecutions* [1962] A.C. 528, one having knowledge of the theft of 100 pistols, 4 submachine guns, and 1960 rounds of ammunition was convicted of misprision of felony for failure to disclose the theft to the public authorities. It seems apparent from these cases that a supplier who furnishes equipment which he *knows* will be used to commit a serious crime may be deemed from that knowledge alone to have intended to produce the result. Such proof may justify an inference that the furnisher intended to aid the execution of the crime and that he thereby became a participant. For instance, we think the operator of a telephone answering service with positive knowledge that his service was being used to facilitate the extortion of ransom, the distribution of heroin, or the passing of counterfeit money who continued to furnish the service with knowledge of its use, might be chargeable on knowledge alone with participation in a scheme to extort money, to distribute narcotics, or to pass counterfeit money. The same result would follow the seller of gasoline who knew the buyer was using his product to make Molotov cocktails for terroristic use.

Logically, the same reasoning could be extended to crimes of every description. Yet we do not believe an inference of intent drawn from knowledge of criminal use properly applies to the less serious crimes classified as misdemeanors. The duty to take positive action to dissociate oneself from activities helpful to violations of the criminal law is far stronger and more compelling for felonies than it is for misdemeanors or petty offenses. In this respect, as in others, the distinction between felonies and misdemeanors, between more serious and less serious crime, retains continuing vitality. In historically the most serious felony, treason, an individual with knowledge of the treason can be prosecuted for concealing and failing to

disclose it. In other felonies, both at common law and under the criminal laws of the United States, an individual knowing of the commission of a felony is criminally liable for concealing it and failing to make it known to proper authority. But this crime, known as misprision of felony, has always been limited to knowledge and concealment of felony and has never extended to misdemeanor. A similar limitation is found in the criminal liability of an accessory, which is restricted to aid in the escape of a principal who has committed or been charged with a *felony*. We believe the distinction between the obligations arising from knowledge of a felony and those arising from knowledge of a misdemeanor continues to reflect basic human feelings about the duties owed by individuals to society. Heinous crime must be stamped out, and its suppression is the responsibility of all. Venial crime and crime not evil in itself present less of a danger to society, and perhaps the benefits of their suppression through the modern equivalent of the posse, the hue and cry, the informant, and the citizen's arrest, are outweighed by the disruption to everyday life brought about by amateur law enforcement and private officiousness in relatively inconsequential delicts which do not threaten our basic security. * * *

With respect to misdemeanors, we conclude that positive knowledge of the supplier that his products or services are being used for criminal purposes does not, without more, establish an intent of the supplier to participate in the misdemeanors. With respect to felonies, we do not decide the converse, viz. that in all cases of felony knowledge of criminal use alone may justify an inference of the supplier's intent to participate in the crime. The implications of *Falcone* make the matter uncertain with respect to those felonies which are merely prohibited wrongs. But decision on this point is not compelled, and we leave the matter open.

From this analysis of precedent we deduce the following rule: the intent of a supplier who knows of the criminal use to which his supplies are put to participate in the criminal activity connected with the use of his supplies may be established by (1) direct evidence that he intends to participate, or (2) through an inference that he intends to participate based on, (a) his special interest in the activity, or (b) the aggravated nature of the crime itself.

When we review Lauria's activities in the light of this analysis, we find no proof that Lauria took any direct action to further, encourage, or direct the call-girl activities of his codefendants and we find an absence of circumstances from which his special interest in their activities could be inferred. Neither excessive charges for standardized services, nor the furnishing of services without a legitimate use, nor an unusual quantity of business with call girls, are present. The offense which he is charged with furthering is a misdemeanor, a category of crime which has never been made a required subject of positive disclosure to public authority. Under these circumstances, although proof of Lauria's knowledge of the criminal activities of his patrons was sufficient to charge him with that fact, there was insufficient evidence that he intended to further their criminal activities, and hence insufficient proof of his participation in a criminal conspiracy with his codefendants to further prostitution. Since the conspiracy centered around the activities of Lauria's telephone answering service, the charges against his codefendants likewise fail for want of proof.

In absolving Lauria of complicity in a criminal conspiracy we do not wish to imply that the public authorities are without remedies to combat modern manifestations of the world's oldest profession. Licensing of telephone answering services under the police power, together with the revocation of licenses for the toleration of prostitution, is a possible civil remedy. The furnishing of telephone answering service in aid of prostitution could be made a crime. (Cf. Pen.Code, § 316, which makes it a misdemeanor to let an apartment with knowledge of its use for prostitution.) Other solutions will doubtless occur to vigilant public authorities if the problem of call-girl activity needs further suppression.

The order is affirmed.

Notes and Questions

1. Consider Marcus, *Criminal Conspiracy: The State of Mind Crime—Intent, Proving Intent, and Anti-Federal Intent*, 1976 U.Ill. L.F. 627, 643–44: "The conclusion of the *Lauria* court is remarkable. Why can a factfinder infer intent if the object crime is a felony, but cannot if the crime is a misdemeanor? The distinction is difficult to understand. The nature of the defendant's conduct and state of mind rather than the category of the ultimate or object crime should determine if a court may infer intent. Whether the object crime is a felony or a misdemeanor is irrelevant in deciding if a defendant is a criminal conspirator."

2. Rush was charged with conspiracy to import marijuana into the United States with intent to distribute it. He loaned $25,000 to others, knowing they would use the money to finance purchases of marijuana from sources in the Bahamas, and was later repaid the principal and $15,000 interest. On appeal from his conviction, Rush emphasized he did not receive a percentage share of the proceeds of the marijuana sales and that his loan had been fully secured. He argued (relying on *Falcone*) that consequently he was not guilty of conspiracy because his only intent was "to profit from a loan transaction." In affirming the conviction, the court of appeals stressed that Rush "was a podiatrist" and "not a money lender" and that

he made "an exorbitant and usurious profit." *United States v. Rush,* 666 F.2d 10 (2d Cir.1982). What if Rush *had* been a money lender? Or, what if he had charged the usual rate for a secured loan?

3. Gallishaw, who supplied a machine gun which others used in robbing a bank, was charged with bank robbery and conspiracy to rob a bank. The jury failed to agree except on the conspiracy count, for which Gallishaw was convicted. During its deliberations, the jury sent this note to the judge: "Does the supplying or renting of a gun, which is subsequently used in a bank robbery, constitute grounds for a conspiracy if the person who rents the gun doesn't know how or where the gun will be used?" The judge answered: "Well, I charge you that it isn't necessary for the Government to prove that the one who rented the gun knew precisely what was intended or all the objectives of the conspiracy or the specific objectives of the conspiracy, or how the gun was to be used. But if you find that the defendant rented the gun and understood and knew that there was a conspiracy to do something wrong and to use the gun to violate the law, you may find that he willfully entered the conspiracy.

"Now, of course, that element must be proved beyond a reasonable doubt. If that is all the evidence that the Government has established, you must be satisfied that by that evidence the Government has proved beyond a reasonable doubt that he entered the conspiracy willfully and knowingly. And willfully and knowingly, as I charged you, means that he entered it intentionally and with the specific knowingly [*sic*] and with the specific intent to do something which the law forbids. That means to violate some law."

In *United States v. Gallishaw,* 428 F.2d 760 (2d Cir.1970), the court reversed:

"On appeal, we are thus faced with the following situation. The Government's

witness, Carballo, testified that when Gallishaw handed over the machine gun, Thomas said he would either 'pull the bank job' or 'pull something else' with it. This imprecision about both Thomas's intentions and Gallishaw's knowledge of them apparently bothered the jury and led it to inquire about the possibility of participation in a conspiracy 'if the person who rents the gun doesn't know how or where the gun will be used.' It may be that the jury was asking only whether a conspirator had to know about specific places and times. However, it is at least as likely that this jury, which failed to convict Gallishaw on the substantive offense counts, was asking whether a weapon supplier who knew in a general way that a machine gun was to be used to 'pull something' could be said to have joined a conspiracy to rob a bank. The judge answered, in the press of the moment, that the jury could convict if Gallishaw rented the gun with the knowledge 'that there was a conspiracy to do something wrong and to use the gun to violate the law.' The jury was thus told, in a singularly pointed way, that it could convict on the conspiracy count without deciding whether to believe Carballo's testimony that Thomas has specifically mentioned a possible bank robbery to Gallishaw along with his generalized statement about pulling something.

"Under this instruction, the jury may simply have drawn the perfectly reasonable inference that one who rents a machine gun knows it is likely to be used 'to do something wrong' or 'to violate the law,' and therefore convicted Gallishaw, totally without regard to anything Thomas said, of the conspiracy charged in the indictment. A verdict on such a basis would have been improper. In *Ingram v. United States,* 360 U.S. 672, 678, 79 S.Ct. 1314, 1319, 3 L.Ed.2d 1503 (1959), the Supreme Court stated:

'[C]onspiracy to commit a particular substantive offense cannot exist without at least the degree of criminal intent necessary for the substantive offense itself.' [Footnote omitted.]

"On this record, to convict Gallishaw for the substantive crime of aiding and abetting a violation of 18 U.S.C. § 2113(a), the Government would have had to show at a minimum that he knew that a bank was to be robbed. To convict him of conspiracy, at the very least no less was required."

UNITED STATES v. FEOLA

Supreme Court of the United States, 1975.
420 U.S. 671, 95 S.Ct. 1255, 43 L.Ed.2d 541.

MR. JUSTICE BLACKMUN delivered the opinion of the Court.

This case presents the issue whether knowledge that the intended victim is a federal officer is a requisite for the crime of conspiracy, under 18 U.S.C. § 371, to commit an offense violative of 18 U.S.C. § 111,[1] that is, an assault upon a federal officer while engaged in the performance of his official duties.

Respondent Feola and three others (Alsondo, Rosa, and Farr) were indicted for violations of §§ 371 and 111. A jury found all four defendants guilty of both charges. * * *

The facts reveal a classic narcotics "ripoff." The details are not particularly important for our present purposes. We need note only that the evidence shows that Feola and his confederates arranged for a sale of heroin to buyers who turned out to be undercover agents for the Bureau of Narcotics and Dangerous Drugs. The group planned to palm off on the

purchasers, for a substantial sum, a form of sugar in place of heroin and, should that ruse fail, simply to surprise their unwitting buyers and relieve them of the cash they had brought along for payment. The plan failed when one agent, his suspicions being aroused, drew his revolver in time to counter an assault upon another agent from the rear. Instead of enjoying the rich benefits of a successful swindle, Feola and his associates found themselves charged, to their undoubted surprise, with conspiring to assault, and with assaulting, federal officers.

At the trial, the District Court, without objection from the defense, charged the jurors that, in order to find any of the defendants guilty on either the conspiracy count or the substantive one, they were not required to conclude that the defendants were aware that their quarry were federal officers.

The Court of Appeals reversed the conspiracy convictions on a ground not advanced by any of the defendants. Although it approved the trial court's instructions to the jury on the substantive charge of assaulting a federal officer, it nonetheless concluded that the failure to charge that knowledge of the victim's official identity must be proved in order to convict on the conspiracy charge amounted to plain error. * * *

The Government's plea is for symmetry. It urges that since criminal liability for the offense described in 18 U.S.C. § 111 does not depend on whether the assailant harbored the specific intent to assault a federal officer, no greater scienter requirement can be engrafted upon the conspiracy of-

---

1. "**§ 111. Assaulting, Resisting, or Impeding Certain Officers or Employees.**

"Whoever forcibly assaults, resists, opposes, impedes, intimidates, or interferes with any person designated in section 1114 of this title while engaged in or on account of the performance of his official duties, shall be fined not more than $5,000 or imprisoned not more than three years, or both.

"Whoever, in the commission of any such acts uses a deadly or dangerous weapon, shall be fined not more than $10,000 or imprisoned not more than ten years, or both."

Among the persons "designated in section 1114" of 18 U.S.C. is "any officer or employee * * * of the Bureau of Narcotics and Dangerous Drugs."

fense, which is merely an agreement to commit the act proscribed by § 111. Consideration of the Government's contention requires us preliminarily to pass upon its premise, the proposition that responsibility for assault upon a federal officer does not depend upon whether the assailant was aware of the official identity of his victim at the time he acted.

* * *

Section 111 has its origin in § 2 of the Act of May 18, 1934, c. 299, 48 Stat. 781. Section 1 of that Act, in which the present 18 U.S.C. § 1114 has its roots, made it a federal crime to kill certain federal law enforcement personnel while engaged in, or on account of, the performance of official duties, and § 2 forbade forcible resistance or interference with, or assault upon, any officer designated in § 1 while so engaged. The history of the 1934 Act, though scanty, offers insight into its multiple purposes. The pertinent committee reports consist, almost in their entirety, of a letter dated January 3, 1934, from Attorney General Cummings urging the passage of the legislation. * * *

Attorney General Cummings, in his letter, emphasized the importance of providing a federal forum in which attacks upon named federal officers could be prosecuted. This, standing alone, would not indicate a congressional conclusion to dispense with a requirement of specific intent to assault a federal officer, for the locus of the forum does not of itself define the reach of the substantive offense. But the view that § 111 requires knowledge of the victim's office rests on the proposition that the reference to the federal forum was merely a shorthand expression of the need for a statute to fill a gap in the substantive law of the States. In that view § 111 is seen merely as a federal aggravated assault statute, necessary solely because some state laws mandate increased punishment only for assaults on state peace officers; assaults on federal personnel would be punishable,

under state law, only for simple assault. As a federal aggravated assault statute, § 111 would be read as requiring the same degree of knowledge as its state-law counterparts. The argument fails, however, because it is fairly certain that Congress was not enacting § 111 as a federal counterpart to state proscriptions of aggravated assault.

The Attorney General's call for a federal forum in which to prosecute an attacker of a federal officer was directed at both sections of the proposed bill that became the 1934 Act. The letter concerned not only the section prohibiting assaults but also the section prohibiting killings. The latter, § 1, was not needed to fill a gap in existing substantive state law. The States proscribed murder, and, until recently, with the enactment of certain statutes in response to the successful attack on capital punishment, murder of a peace officer has not been deemed an aggravated form of murder, for all States usually have punished murderers with the most severe sanction the law allows. Clearly, then, Congress understood that it was not only filling one gap in state substantive law but in large part was duplicating state proscriptions in order to insure a federal forum for the trial of offenses involving federal officers. Fulfillment of the congressional goal to protect federal officers required then, as it does now, the highest possible degree of certainty that those who killed or assaulted federal officers were brought to justice. In the congressional mind, with the reliance upon the Attorney General's letter, certainty required that these cases be tried in the federal courts, for no matter how "respectable and well disposed," it would not be unreasonable to suppose that state officials would not always or necessarily share congressional feelings of urgency as to the necessity of prompt and vigorous prosecutions of those who violate the safety of the federal officer. From the days of prohibition to the days of the modern civil rights movement, the statutes federal agents have sworn to uphold and enforce have not always been popular in every corner of the Nation. Congress may well have concluded that § 111 was necessary in order to insure uniformly vigorous protection of federal personnel, including those engaged in locally unpopular activity.

We conclude, from all this, that in order to effectuate the congressional purpose of according maximum protection to federal officers by making prosecution for assaults upon them cognizable in the federal courts, § 111 cannot be construed as embodying an unexpressed requirement that an assailant be aware that his victim is a federal officer. All the statute requires is an intent to assault, not an intent to assault a federal officer. A contrary conclusion would give insufficient protection to the agent enforcing an unpopular law, and none to the agent acting under cover.

* * *

We hold, therefore, that in order to incur criminal liability under § 111 an actor must entertain merely the criminal intent to do the acts therein specified. We now consider whether the rule should be different where persons conspire to commit those acts.

Our decisions establish that in order to sustain a judgment of conviction on a charge of conspiracy to violate a federal statute, the Government must prove at least the degree of criminal intent necessary for the substantive offense itself. Respondent Feola urges upon us the proposition that the Government must show a degree of criminal intent in the conspiracy count greater than is necessary to convict for the substantive offense; he urges that even though it is not necessary to show that he was aware of the official identity of his assaulted victims in order to find him guilty of assaulting federal officers, in violation of 18 U.S.C. § 111, the Govern-

ment nonetheless must show that he was aware that his intended victims were undercover agents, if it is successfully to prosecute him for conspiring to assault federal agents. And the Court of Appeals held that the trial court's failure to charge the jury to this effect constituted plain error.

The general conspiracy statute, 18 U.S.C. § 371, offers no textual support for the proposition that to be guilty of conspiracy a defendant in effect must have known that his conduct violated federal law. The statute makes it unlawful simply to "conspire * * * to commit any offense against the United States." A natural reading of these words would be that since one can violate a criminal statute simply by engaging in the forbidden conduct, a conspiracy to commit that offense is nothing more than an agreement to engage in the prohibited conduct. Then where, as here, the substantive statute does not require that an assailant know the official status of his victim, there is nothing on the face of the conspiracy statute that would seem to require that those agreeing to the assault have a greater degree of knowledge.

We have been unable to find any decision of this Court that lends support to the respondent. On the contrary, at least two of our cases implicitly repudiate his position. The appellants in *In re Coy,* 127 U.S. 731, 8 S.Ct. 1263, 32 L.Ed. 274 (1888), were convicted of conspiring to induce state election officials to neglect their duty to safeguard ballots and election results. The offense occurred with respect to an election at which Indiana voters, in accordance with state law, voted for both local officials and members of Congress. Much like Feola here, those appellants asserted that they could not be punished for conspiring to violate federal law because they had intended only to affect the outcome of state races. In short, it was urged that the conspiracy statute embodied a requirement of specific intent to violate federal law. The Court rejected this contention and held that the statute required only that the conspirators agree to participate in the prohibited conduct.

Similarly, in *United States v. Freed,* 401 U.S. 601, 91 S.Ct. 1112, 28 L.Ed.2d 356 (1971), we reversed the dismissal of an indictment charging defendants with possession of, and with conspiracy to possess, hand grenades that had not been registered, as required by 26 U.S.C. § 5861(d). The trial court dismissed the indictment for failure to allege that the defendants knew that the hand grenades in fact were unregistered. We held that actual knowledge that the grenades were unregistered was not an element of the substantive offense created by Congress and therefore upheld the indictment both as to the substantive offense and as to the charge of conspiracy. Again, we declined to require a greater degree of intent for conspiratorial responsibility than for responsibility for the underlying substantive offense.

With no support on the face of the general conspiracy statute or in this Court's decisions, respondent relies solely on the line of cases commencing with *United States v. Crimmins,* 123 F.2d 271 (CA2 1941), for the principle that the Government must prove "antifederal" intent in order to establish liability under § 371. In *Crimmins,* the defendant had been found guilty of conspiring to receive stolen bonds that had been transported in interstate commerce. Upon review, the Court of Appeals pointed out that the evidence failed to establish that Crimmins actually knew the stolen bonds had moved into the State. Accepting for the sake of argument the assumption that such knowledge was not necessary to sustain a conviction on the substantive offense, Judge Learned Hand

nevertheless concluded that to permit conspiratorial liability where the conspirators were ignorant of the federal implications of their acts would be to enlarge their agreement beyond its terms as they understood them. He capsulized the distinction in what has become well known as his "traffic light" analogy:

> "While one may, for instance, be guilty of running past a traffic light of whose existence one is ignorant, one cannot be guilty of conspiring to run past such a light, for one cannot agree to run past a light unless one supposes that there is a light to run past."

Judge Hand's attractive, but perhaps seductive, analogy has received a mixed reception in the Courts of Appeals. The Second Circuit, of course, has followed it; others have rejected it. It appears that most have avoided it by the simple expedient of inferring the requisite knowledge from the scope of the conspiratorial venture. We conclude that the analogy, though effective prose, is, as applied to the facts before us, bad law.[24]

The question posed by the traffic light analogy is not before us, just as it was not before the Second Circuit in *Crimmins.* Criminal liability, of course, may be imposed on one who runs a traffic light regardless of whether he harbored the "evil intent" of disobeying the light's command; whether he drove so recklessly as to be unable to perceive the light; whether, thinking he was observing all traffic rules, he simply failed to notice the light; or whether, having been reared elsewhere, he thought that the light was only an ornament. Traffic violations generally fall into that category of offenses that dispense with a *mens rea* requirement. These laws embody the social judgment that it is fair

---

24. The Government rather effectively exposes the fallacy of the *Crimmins* traffic light analogy by recasting it in terms of a jurisdictional element. The suggested example is a traffic light on an Indian reservation. Surely, one may conspire with others to disobey the light but be ignorant of the fact that it is on the reservation. As applied to a jurisdictional element of this kind the formulation makes little sense.

to punish one who intentionally engages in conduct that creates a risk to others, even though no risk is intended or the actor, through no fault of his own, is completely unaware of the existence of any risk. The traffic light analogy poses the question whether it is fair to punish parties to an agreement to engage intentionally in apparently innocent conduct where the unintended result of engaging in that conduct is the violation of a criminal statute.

But this case does not call upon us to answer this question, and we decline to do so, just as we have once before. *United States v. Freed,* 401 U.S., at 609 n. 14, 91 S.Ct. at 1118. We note in passing, however, that the analogy comes close to stating what has been known as the *"Powell* doctrine," originating in *People v. Powell,* 63 N.Y. 88 (1875), to the effect that a conspiracy, to be criminal, must be animated by a corrupt motive or a motive to do wrong. Under this principle, such a motive could be easily demonstrated if the underlying offense involved an act clearly wrongful in itself; but it had to be independently demonstrated if the acts agreed to were wrongful solely because of statutory proscription. Interestingly, Judge Hand himself was one of the more severe critics of the *Powell* doctrine.[25]

That Judge Hand should reject the *Powell* doctrine and then create the *Crimmins* doctrine seems curious enough. Fatal to the latter, however, is the fact that it was announced in a case to which it could not have been meant to apply. In *Crimmins,* the substantive offense, namely, the receipt of stolen securities that had been in interstate commerce, proscribed clearly wrongful conduct. Such conduct could not be engaged in without an intent to accomplish the forbidden result. So, too, it is with

assault, the conduct forbidden by the substantive statute, § 111, presently before us. One may run a traffic light "of whose existence one is ignorant," but assaulting another "of whose existence one is ignorant," probably would require unearthly intervention. Thus, the traffic light analogy, even if it were a correct statement of the law, is inapt, for the conduct proscribed by the substantive offense, here assault, is not of the type outlawed without regard to the intent of the actor to accomplish the result that is made criminal. If the analogy has any vitality at all, it is to conduct of the latter variety; that, however, is a question we save for another day. We hold here only that where a substantive offense embodies only a requirement of *mens rea* as to each of its elements, the general federal conspiracy statute requires no more.

The *Crimmins* rule rests upon another foundation: that it is improper to find conspiratorial liability where the parties to the illicit agreement were not aware of the fact giving rise to federal jurisdiction, because the essence of conspiracy is agreement and persons cannot be punished for acts beyond the scope of their agreement. This "reason" states little more than a conclusion, for it is clear that one may be guilty as a conspirator for acts the precise details of which one does not know at the time of the agreement. See *Blumenthal v. United States,* 332 U.S. 539, 557, 68 S.Ct. 248, 256, 92 L.Ed. 154 (1947). The question is not merely whether the official status of an assaulted victim was known to the parties at the time of their agreement, but whether the acts contemplated by the conspirators are to be deemed legally different from those actually performed solely because of the official identity of the

---

25. "Starting with *People v. Powell* * * * the anomalous doctrine has indeed gained some footing in the circuit courts of appeals that for conspiracy there must be a 'corrupt motive * * *.' Yet it is hard to see any reason for

this, or why more proof should be necessary than that the parties had in contemplation all the elements of the crime they are charged with conspiracy to commit." *United States v. Mack,* 112 F.2d 290, 292 (2nd Cir.1940).

victim. Put another way, does the identity of the proposed victim alter the legal character of the acts agreed to, or is it no more germane to the nature of those acts than the color of the victim's hair?

Our analysis of the substantive offense is sufficient to convince us that for the purpose of individual guilt or innocence, awareness of the official identity of the assault victim is irrelevant. We would expect the same to obtain with respect to the conspiracy offense unless one of the policies behind the imposition of conspiratorial liability is not served where the parties to the agreement are unaware that the intended target is a federal law enforcement official.

It is well settled that the law of conspiracy serves ends different from, and complementary to, those served by criminal prohibitions of the substantive offense. Because of this, consecutive sentences may be imposed for the conspiracy and for the underlying crime. Our decisions have identified two independent values served by the law of conspiracy. The first is protection of society from the dangers of concerted criminal activity. That individuals know that their planned joint venture violates federal as well as state law seems totally irrelevant to that purpose of conspiracy law which seeks to protect society from the dangers of concerted criminal activity. Given the level of criminal intent necessary to sustain conviction for the substantive offense, the act of agreement to commit the crime is no less opprobrious and no less dangerous because of the absence of knowledge of a fact unnecessary to the formation of criminal intent. Indeed, unless imposition of an "anti-federal" knowledge requirement serves social purposes external to the law of conspiracy of which we are unaware, its imposition here would serve only to make it more difficult to obtain convictions on charges of conspiracy, a policy with no apparent purpose.

The second aspect is that conspiracy is an inchoate crime. This is to say, that, although the law generally makes criminal only antisocial conduct, at some point in the continuum between preparation and consummation, the likelihood of a commission of an act is sufficiently great and the criminal intent sufficiently well formed to justify the intervention of the criminal law. The law of conspiracy identifies the agreement to engage in a criminal venture as an event of sufficient threat to social order to permit the imposition of criminal sanctions for the agreement alone, plus an overt act in pursuit of it, regardless of whether the crime agreed upon actually is committed. Criminal intent has crystallized, and the likelihood of actual, fulfilled commission warrants preventive action.

Again, we do not see how imposition of a strict "anti-federal" scienter requirement would relate to this purpose of conspiracy law. Given the level of intent needed to carry out the substantive offense, we fail to see how the agreement is any less blameworthy or constitutes less of a danger to society solely because the participants are unaware which body of law they intend to violate. Therefore, we again conclude that imposition of a requirement of knowledge of those facts that serve only to establish federal jurisdiction would render it more difficult to serve the policy behind the law of conspiracy without serving any other apparent social policy. * * *

The judgment of the Court of Appeals with respect to the respondent's conspiracy conviction is reversed. * * *

MR. JUSTICE STEWART, with whom MR. JUSTICE DOUGLAS joins, dissenting. * * *

The history of § 111 permits no doubt that this is an aggravated assault statute, requiring proof of scienter. The provision derives from a 1934 statute, 18 U.S.C. § 254 (1940 ed.). * * *

Rummaging through the sparse legislative history of the 1934 law, the Court manages to persuade itself that Congress intended to reach unknowing assaults on federal officers. But if that was the congressional intention, which I seriously doubt, it found no expression in the legislative product. *The fact is that the 1934 statute expressly required scienter for an assault conviction.* An assault on a federal officer was proscribed only if perpetrated "*on account of* the performance of his official duties." That is, it was necessary not only that the assailant have notice that his victim possessed official status or duties but also that the assailant's *motive* be retaliation against the exercise of those duties.

It was not until the *1948 recodification* that the proscription was expanded to cover assaults on federal officers "while engaged in," as well as "on account of," the performance of official duties. This was, as the Reviser observed, a technical alteration; it produced no instructive legislative history. As presently written, the statute does clearly reach knowing assaults regardless of motive. But to suggest that it also reaches wholly unknowing assaults is to convert the 1948 alteration into one of major substantive importance, which it concededly was not.

The Court has also managed to convince itself that § 254 was not an aggravated assault statute. The surest evidence that § 254 *was* an aggravated assault statute may be found in its penalty provision. A single unarmed assault was made, and remains, punishable by a sentence of three years' imprisonment and a $5,000 fine. One need not make an exhaustive survey of state law to appreciate that this is a harsher penalty than is typically imposed for an unarmed assault on a private citizen.

* * *

* * * So far as the scienter requirement is concerned, it makes no difference whether the statute aims to protect individuals, or functions, or both. The Court appears to think that extending § 111 to unknowing assaults will deter such assaults—will "give * * * protection * * * to the agent acting under cover." This, of course, is nonsense. The federal statute "protects" an officer from assault only when the assailant knows that the victim is an officer. Absent such knowledge, the only "protection" is that provided by the *general* law of assault, for that is the only law which the potential assailant reasonably, if erroneously, believes applicable in the circumstances.

The Court also suggests that implication of a scienter requirement "would give insufficient protection to the agent enforcing an unpopular law." This is to repeat the same error. Whatever the "popularity" of the laws he is executing, and whatever the construction placed on § 111, a federal officer is "protected" from assault by that statute only where the assailant has some indication from the circumstances that his victim is other than a private citizen. * * *

Turning from the history of the statute to its structure, the propriety of implying a scienter requirement becomes manifest. The statute proscribes not only assault but also a whole series of related acts. It applies to any person who "forcibly assaults, *resists, opposes, impedes, intimidates,* or *interferes* with [a federal officer] * * * while engaged in or on account of the performance of his official duties." (Emphasis added.) It can hardly be denied that the emphasized words imply a scienter requirement. Generally speaking, these acts are legal and moral wrongs only if the actor knows that his "victim" enjoys a moral or legal privilege to detain him or order him about. * * *

For the reasons stated, I believe that before there can be a violation of 18 U.S.C. § 111, an assailant must know or have reason to know that the person he assaults is an officer. It follows *a fortiori* that there can be no criminal conspiracy to violate the statute in the absence of at least equivalent knowledge. Accordingly, I respectfully dissent from the opinion and judgment of the Court.

Notes and Questions

1. Compare *United States v. Prince,* 529 F.2d 1108 (6th Cir.1976), reversing Prince's conviction of violating and conspiring to violate 18 U.S.C.A. § 1952,[a] the Interstate Travel Act. Prince was a madam in a West Virginia house of prostitution; there was no evidence that she used interstate facilities in carrying on that activity or that she was aware any of the women working for her had been transported from another state. "Prince relies primarily on this court's decision in *United States v. Barnes,* 383 F.2d 287 (1967), for the proposition that one who is shown to have violated a local law may not be convicted of violating the Travel Act, or conspiring to do so, without proof of direct agreement to illegal interstate transportation or proof of an indirect agreement evidenced by substantial participation in an unlawful scheme with actual knowledge of illegal interstate transportation.

"The Government argues that the decision of the Supreme Court in *United States v. Feola,* requires that we reexamine and overrule *Barnes.* * * *

a. § 1952. Interstate and Foreign Travel or Transportation in Aid of Racketeering Enterprises.

(a) Whoever travels in interstate or foreign commerce or uses any facility in interstate or foreign commerce, including the mail, with intent to—

(1) distribute the proceeds of any unlawful activity; or

(2) commit any crime of violence to further any unlawful activity; or

(3) otherwise promote, manage, establish, carry on, or facilitate the promotion, management, establishment, or carrying on, of any unlawful activity.

"We are not persuaded, however, that *Feola* requires us to overrule *Barnes.* The Travel Act does not make it a federal offense to engage in prostitution, an activity which is illegal under State law. It provides an additional string to the law enforcement bow, however, by providing that '[w]hoever travels in interstate or foreign commerce or uses any facility in interstate or foreign commerce * * * *with intent* * * *' to engage in enumerated types of unlawful activity including prostitution may be punished thereunder. * * * In *Feola* the Supreme Court was construing a statute which made the performance of an act a federal offense without any requirement of intent separate from that which led to the act itself (the assault of another person). Its federal character depended upon the identity of the victim, whether known or unknown to the assailant. On the other hand, the Travel Act only reaches those who engage in interstate activities *with intent* to perform other illegal acts. Thus there is a requirement of a separate intent related to the use of interstate facilities which is different from the intent required to commit the underlying State offense. So far as this record shows the defendant Prince was nothing more than the madam of a house of prostitution in West Virginia. The Travel Act is not written so broadly as to subject such a person to federal prosecution.

and thereafter performs or attempts to perform any of the acts specified in subparagraphs (1), (2), and (3), shall be fined not more than $10,000 or imprisoned for not more than five years, or both.

(b) As used in this section "unlawful activity" means (1) any business enterprise involving gambling, liquor on which the Federal excise tax has not been paid, narcotics, or controlled substances (as defined in section 102(6) of the Controlled Substances Act), or prostitution offenses in violation of the laws of the State in which they are committed or of the United States, or (2) extortion, bribery, or arson in violation of the laws of the State in which committed or of the United States.

"Since Pandelli was shown to have actually caused a woman to travel from Ohio to West Virginia for the purpose of engaging in prostitution, it was immaterial whether or not he had actual knowledge of the jurisdictional element. The act coupled with the intent was sufficient. However, since Prince was not shown either to have traveled interstate or used interstate facilities, her strictly intrastate activities could not be held to constitute a violation of the Travel Act in the absence of a showing that she knew or reasonably should have known of Pandelli's interstate activities.

"In *Feola* the defendant urged that the Government was required to 'show a degree of criminal intent in the conspiracy count greater than is necessary to convict for the substantive offense; * * *.' This argument was rejected, but the rule was reaffirmed that 'in order to sustain a judgment of conviction on a charge of conspiracy to violate a federal statute, the Government must prove at least the degree of criminal intent necessary for the substantive offense itself.' Since that degree of criminal intent necessary for the substantive offense was not proven, the convictions of Prince both for violating the Travel Act and conspiring to do so must be reversed."

2. *Model Penal Code* § 5.03, Comment (1985): "A doctrine that has had a somewhat confusing effect on the mens rea requirements of conspiracy was first formulated in the New York case of *People v. Powell*.[111] The defendants in the *Powell* case were prosecuted for conspiracy to violate a statute requiring municipal officials to advertise for bids before buying supplies for the city. The defendants urged as a defense that they had acted in good faith since they did not know of the existence of the statute. The court accepted this argument, holding that a confederation to do an act 'innocent in itself' is not criminal unless it is 'corrupt.' The agreement must have been entered into with an evil purpose, as distinguished from a purpose simply 'to do the act prohibited in ignorance of the prohibition. This is implied in the meaning of the word conspiracy.'

"The decision is subject to and has been given a number of interpretations. Some courts have read it literally as requiring knowledge by the conspirators that their object is prohibited by law, while others have rejected this interpretation but required a 'corrupt motive' of uncertain and varying content. The fact that the offense in the *Powell* case was 'innocent in itself' is often emphasized and a number of decisions have imported into the doctrine the distinction between offenses malum prohibitum and malum in se. Despite the considerable amount of attention and deference that the *Powell* doctrine has received, its actual effect upon the decisions and its vitality prior to the Model Code were probably smaller than was generally believed. Although no cases in New York questioned its authority, its status in most of the other jurisdictions that considered it was uncertain. * * *

"The *Powell* rule, and many of the decisions that rely upon it, may be viewed as a judicial endeavor to import fair mens rea requirements into statutes creating regulatory offenses that do not rest on traditional concepts of personal fault and culpability. This should, however, be the function of the statutes defining such offenses. * * * There is no good reason why the fortuity of concert should be used as the device for limiting criminality in this area, just as there is no good reason for using it as the device to expand liability through imprecise formulations of objectives that include activity not otherwise criminal."

111. 63 N.Y. 88 (1875).

3. Churchill was a bookkeeper employed by a company which, with an associated company, sold a quantity of diesel oil for use in vehicles. The oil bears a tax of 2s. 9d. a gallon, but a rebate of 2s. 7d. is allowed if the oil is used for home heating. Churchill was tried with others on a two-count indictment charging: (i) conspiracy to cheat and defraud the government of the rebate allowed on oil which was actually used in vehicles; and (ii) conspiracy to violate a statute which says that diesel oil on which the home use rebate has been allowed shall not be used in vehicles unless an amount equal to that rebate has been paid to the proper government official. This latter statute is a strict liability offense and thus one may be convicted under it for so using the oil even absent knowledge that the necessary repayment has not been made. Apparently because of that fact, the judge instructed the jury that they could convict Churchill on the second count if he was a party to an arrangement to use the fuel in vehicles, notwithstanding his lack of knowledge that a rebate had been allowed and not repaid with respect to the fuel so used. Churchill was acquitted on the first count, but was convicted on the second. The Court of Criminal Appeal dismissed the appeal but certified to the House of Lords this point of law: "Whether mens rea is an essential ingredient in conspiracy to commit the absolute offence charged in count 2 of the indictment and, if so, what knowledge of the facts and/or law on the part of the defendant must be established to prove the charge." In *Churchill v. Walton,* [1967] 2 A.C. 224, [1967] 2 W.L.R. 682, [1967] 1 All E.R. 467, the House allowed the appeal, reasoning:

"In answer to the question posed by the Court of Criminal Appeal in this case, I would say that mens rea is only an essential ingredient in conspiracy in so far as there must be an intention to be a party to an agreement to do an unlawful act; that

knowledge of the law on the part of the accused is immaterial and that knowledge of the facts is only material in so far as such knowledge throws a light on what was agreed.

"In cases of this kind, it is desirable to avoid the use of the phrase 'mens rea,' which is capable of different meanings, and to concentrate on the terms or effect of the agreement made by the alleged conspirators. The question is, 'What did they agree to do?' If what they agreed to do was, on the facts known to them, an unlawful act, they are guilty of conspiracy and cannot excuse themselves by saying that, owing to their ignorance of the law, they did not realise that such an act was a crime. If, on the facts known to them, what they agreed to do was lawful, they are not rendered artificially guilty by the existence of other facts, not known to them, giving a different and criminal quality to the act agreed upon.

"For the reasons I have given, I think that the direction given by the judge in relation to the second count was erroneous in point of law. The guilt of the accused did not depend on whether prohibited fuel was used in road vehicles but on whether he was a party to an agreement to use such fuel in road vehicles."

Is this a sound result? Is it simply another application of the *Powell* rule, or what?

SECTION 4. THE OBJECTIVE

SHAW v. DIRECTOR OF PUBLIC PROSECUTIONS

House of Lords, 1961.
[1962] A.C. 220, [1961] 2 W.L.R. 897, [1961] 2 All E.R. 446.

VISCOUNT SIMONDS: My Lords, the appellant, Frederick Charles Shaw, was, on Sept. 21, 1960, convicted at the Central Criminal Court on an indictment containing three counts which alleged the following offences:—(i) conspiracy to corrupt public morals; (ii) living on the earnings of prostitution contrary to s. 30 of the Sexual Offences Act, 1956; and (iii) publishing an obscene publication contrary to s. 2 of the Obscene Publications Act, 1959. He appealed against conviction to the Court of Criminal Appeal on all three counts. His appeal was dismissed * * *.

* * * When the Street Offences Act, 1959, came into operation, it was no longer possible for prostitutes to ply their trade by soliciting in the streets and it became necessary for them to find some other means of advertising the services that they were prepared to render. It occurred to the appellant that he could with advantage to himself assist them to this end. The device that he adopted was to publish on divers days between the dates mentioned in the particulars of offences a magazine or booklet which was called "Ladies Directory". It contained the names, addresses and telephone numbers of prostitutes with photographs of nude female figures, and in some cases details which conveyed to initiates willingness to indulge not only in ordinary sexual intercourse but also in various perverse practices. * * *

My Lords, as I have already said, the first count in the indictment is "Conspiracy to corrupt public morals", and the particulars of offence will have sufficiently appeared. I am concerned only to assert what was vigorously denied by counsel for the appellant, that such an offence is known to the common law and that it was open to the jury to find on the facts of this case that the appellant was guilty of such an offence. I must say categorically that, if it were not so, Her Majesty's courts would strangely have failed in their duty as servants and guardians of the common law. Need I say, my Lords, that I am no advocate of the right of the judges to create new criminal offences? * * * But I am at a loss to understand how it can be said

either that the law does not recognise a conspiracy to corrupt public morals or that, though there may not be an exact precedent for such a conspiracy as this case reveals, it does not fall fairly within the general words by which it is described. * * * The fallacy in the argument that was addressed to us lay in the attempt to exclude from the scope of general words acts well calculated to corrupt public morals just because they had not been committed or had not been brought to the notice of the court before. It is not thus that the common law has developed. * * * In the sphere of criminal law, I entertain no doubt that there remains in the courts of law a residual power to enforce the supreme and fundamental purpose of the law, to conserve not only the safety and order but also the moral welfare of the state, and that it is their duty to guard it against attacks which may be the more insidious because they are novel and unprepared for. That is the broad head (call it public policy if you wish) within which the present indictment falls. It matters little what label is given to the offending act. To one of your Lordships it may appear an affront to public decency, to another, considering that it may succeed in its obvious intention of provoking libidinous desires, it will seem a corruption of public morals. Yet others may deem it aptly described as the creation of a public mischief or the undermining of moral conduct. The same act will not in all ages be regarded in the same way. The law must be related to the changing standards of life, not yielding to every shifting impulse of the popular will but having regard to fundamental assessments of human values and the purposes of society. [There is] a residual power, where no statute has yet intervened to supersede the common law, to superintend those offences which are prejudicial to the public welfare. Such occasions will be rare, for Parliament has not been slow to legislate when attention has been sufficiently aroused. But gaps remain and will always remain since no one can foresee every way in which the wickedness of man may disrupt the order of society. Let me take a single instance to which my noble and learned friend, Lord Tucker, refers. Let it be supposed that, at some future, perhaps, early, date homosexual practices between adult consenting males are no longer a crime. Would it not be an offence if, even without obscenity, such practices were publicly advocated and encouraged by pamphlet and advertisement? Or must we wait until Parliament finds time to deal with such conduct? I say, my Lords, that, if the common law is powerless in such an event, then we should no longer do her reverence. * * *

The appeal on both counts should, in my opinion, be dismissed.

LORD REID: * * * In my opinion, there is no such general offence known to the law as conspiracy to corrupt public morals. Undoubtedly there is an offence of criminal conspiracy and undoubtedly it is of fairly wide scope. * * * I think that Lord Goddard, C.J., was repeating the generally accepted view when he said: "A conspiracy consists of agreeing or acting in concert to achieve an unlawful act or to do a lawful act by unlawful means." But what is an "unlawful act"? * * *

There are two competing views. One is that conspiring to corrupt public morals is only one facet of a still more general offence, conspiracy to effect public mischief; and that, like the categories of negligence, the categories of public mischief are never closed. The other is that, whatever may have been done two or three centuries ago, we ought not now to extend the doctrine further than it has already been carried by the common law courts. Of course I do not mean that it should only be applied in circumstances precisely similar to those in some decided case.

Decisions are always authority for other cases which are reasonably analogous and are not properly distinguishable. But we ought not to extend the doctrine to new fields. * * * Every argument against creating new offences by an individual appears to me to be equally valid against creating new offences by a combination of individuals. But there is this historical difference. The judges appear to have continued to extend the law of conspiracy after they had ceased to extend offences by individuals. * * * Even if there is still a vestigial power of this kind, it ought not, in my view, to be used unless there appears to be general agreement that the offence to which it is applied ought to be criminal if committed by an individual. Notoriously there are wide differences of opinion today how far the law ought to punish immoral acts which are not done in the face of the public. Some think that the law already goes too far, some that it does not go far enough. Parliament is the proper place, and I am firmly of opinion the only proper place, to settle that. When there is sufficient support from public opinion, Parliament does not hesitate to intervene. Where Parliament fears to tread it is not for the courts to rush in.

* * * It may, perhaps, be said that there is no question here of creating a new offence because there is only one offence of conspiracy—agreeing or acting in concert to do an unlawful act. In a technical sense, that is true. But, in order to extend this offence to a new field, the court would have to create a new unlawful act; it would have to hold that conduct of a kind which has not hitherto been unlawful in this sense must now be held to be unlawful. It appears to me that the objections to that are just as powerful as the objections to creating a new offence. The difference is a matter of words; the essence of the matter is that a type of conduct for the punishment of which there is no previous authority now for the first

time becomes punishable solely by a decision of a court. * * *

LORD MORRIS OF BORTH–Y–GEST: * * *

It is said that there is a measure of vagueness in a charge of conspiracy to corrupt public morals, and also that there might be peril of the launching of prosecutions in order to suppress unpopular or unorthodox views. My Lords, I entertain no anxiety on those lines. Even if accepted public standards may to some extent vary from generation to generation, current standards are in the keeping of juries who can be trusted to maintain the corporate good sense of the community and to discern attacks on values that must be preserved. If there were prosecutions which were not genuinely and fairly warranted, juries would be quick to perceive this. There could be no conviction unless twelve jurors were unanimous in thinking that the accused person or persons had combined to do acts which were calculated to corrupt public morals. My Lords, as time proceeds, our criminal law is more and more being codified. Though it may be that the occasions for presenting a

a. But see *Regina v. Withers,* [1974] 3 W.L.R. 751, where the defendants, in the course of their business as private investigators, obtained for clients confidential information about the financial standing of third parties. They did this by misrepresenting to banks and government departments that they were persons authorized to receive such information. They appealed to the House of Lords their convictions of conspiracy to effect public mischief, and their convictions were quashed. Viscount Dilhorne, after discussing *Shaw* and other cases, stated:

"What conclusions are to be drawn from the cases to which I have referred? I think they are these:

"1. There is no separate and distinct class of criminal conspiracy called conspiracy to effect a public mischief.

"2. That description has in the past been applied to a number of cases which might have been regarded as coming within well-known heads of conspiracy, e.g. conspiracy to defraud, to pervert the course of justice, etc.

charge such as that in count 1 will be infrequent, I concur in the view that such a charge is contained within the armour of the law and that the jury were in the present case fully entitled to decide the case as they did.

I would dismiss the appeal.[a]

Notes and Questions

1. In *Commonwealth v. Bessette,* 351 Mass. 148, 217 N.E.2d 893 (1966), defendant, head of the Division of Waterways of the state Department of Public Works, appealed his conviction of conspiring with officers of two dredging companies to violate a Division regulation which prohibited assignment of contracts without the written consent of the Department. The court reversed:

"In *Commonwealth v. Dyer,* 243 Mass. 472, 485, 138 N.E. 296, 303, it was said, 'It is the consensus of opinion that conspiracy as a criminal offence is established when the object of the combination is either a crime, or if not a crime, is unlawful, or when the means contemplated are either criminal, or if not criminal, are ille-

"3. It is far too late to hold that a conspiracy of the kind that occurred in those cases was not criminal * * *.

"4. The judges have no power to create new offences.

"5. Where a charge of conspiracy to effect a public mischief has been preferred, the question to be considered is whether the objects or means of the conspiracy are in substance of such a quality or kind as has already been recognised by the law as criminal.

"6. If there are, then one has to go on to consider, on an appeal, whether the course the trial took in consequence of the reference to public mischief was such as to vitiate the conviction."

The Law Commission, *Working Paper No. 50* (June 1973), setting out the tentative views of the Commission regarding codification of the criminal law with respect to inchoate offenses, states at p. 10: "A law of conspiracy extending beyond the ambit of conspiracy to commit crimes has, in our view, no place in a comprehensively planned criminal code."

gal, provided that, where no crime is contemplated either as the end or the means, the illegal but noncriminal element involves prejudice to the general welfare or oppression of the individual of sufficient gravity to be injurious to the public interest.' Bessette argues that these general principles have not been broadly applied in Massachusetts in recent years. He in effect would have us interpret the term 'unlawful' as meaning 'criminal.' * * *

"The recent decisions undoubtedly have tended to apply the principles of criminal conspiracy primarily to group arrangements which have a criminal purpose or contemplate the use of criminal methods. Nevertheless, in view of the *Dyer* case, we are not prepared to say that criminal conspiracy has been completely restricted to this extent. The later discussion in the *Dyer* case (conspiracy for a monopoly) shows that the term 'unlawful,' in relation to a conspiracy, was thought to include situations where the purpose of a group plan or the proposed means of accomplishing that plan, even if not criminal, involve 'an evil intent to oppress and injure the public' (or, perhaps, third persons) by activity, which is 'illegal, void and against public policy.'

"In view of the conclusion which we reach, it is not now necessary to determine precisely when, in situations comparable to that presented in the *Dyer* case, joint action may create additional dangers and risks sufficient to make criminal as a conspiracy an agreement upon a plan for unlawful acts which would not be criminal when done by individuals separately. We think it plain, however, that the term 'unlawful,' as used in the criminal conspiracy cases (where neither a criminal object nor criminal means are in contemplation), is limited in any event to a narrow range of situations, (a) where there is strong probability (as in the monopolistic plans involved in the *Dyer* case) that the execution of the

plan by group action will cause such significant harm to an individual or to the general public, as to be seriously contrary to the public interest, and (b) where the unlawfulness of objective or contemplated means is substantial and clear. There is sound reason for such limitation. As Perkins, *Criminal Law,* 544, points out, a more inclusive definition of 'unlawful' might 'be held void for vagueness under the Due Process Clause [of the Federal and Massachusetts Constitutions] unless what is * * * proscribed is spelled out with sufficient clearness to guide those who would be law-abiding and to advise defendants of the offense with which they are charged.' Even as limited by this opinion, the rule of the *Dyer* case is necessarily indefinite and its application in a particular instance may present serious problems. This circumstance suggests strongly that certainty of statement of the criminal law would be greatly promoted by legislative definition of the types of unlawful, but not criminal, objectives and proposed means which may constitute elements of criminal conspiracy. * * *

"From the very general allegations it could be inferred that Bessette knowingly violated, by agreement with others, whatever department policy lay behind the use of art. 65 in the contracts. No allegations, however, tend to show the significance of that policy or that its violation by combined action (a) would cause loss to the Commonwealth, or any material interference with, or obstruction of, departmental operations, or (b) would be 'particularly dangerous to the public interests'."

2. In *State v. Bowling,* 5 Ariz.App. 436, 427 P.2d 928 (1967), the court held unconstitutional a statute providing that it "is unlawful for two or more persons to conspire to: * * * Commit any act injurious to the public health or public morals," reasoning:

"In considering a Utah statute with similar wording, the Supreme Court of the United States said:

'Standing by itself, it would seem to be warrant for conviction for agreement to do almost any act which a judge and jury might find at the moment contrary to his or its notions of what was good for health, morals, trade, commerce, justice or order.'

"*Musser v. State of Utah,* 333 U.S. 95, 68 S.Ct. 397, 398, 92 L.Ed. 562 (1948).

"The Supreme Court of the United States remanded the *Musser* case to the Utah Supreme Court to consider whether the language of this statute was unconstitutionally vague. The United States Supreme Court suggested that there was a possibility that under Utah statutory or case law the broad language of the statute might have been limited so as to give the required degree of specificity thereto.

"The Supreme Court of Utah, however, was unable to point to any limitations upon the subject language and came to the conclusion that this statute, making it a crime to conspire to commit an act '* * * injurious * * * to public morals * * *' was unconstitutional:

'No language in this or any other statute of this state or other law thereof or any historical fact or surrounding circumstance connected with the enactment of this statute has been pointed to as indicating that the legislature intended any limitation thereon other than that expressed on the face of the words used. We are therefore unable to place a construction on these words which limits their meaning beyond their general meaning. The conviction of the defendants thereunder cannot be upheld. This part of the statute is therefore void for vagueness and uncertainty under the Fourteenth Amendment to the Federal Constitution.'

LaFave—Mod.Crim.Law, 2nd Ed. ACB—23

"*State v. Musser,* 118 Utah 537, 223 P.2d 193, 194 (1950).

"Likewise, we know of no statutory or case law in this state which limits the broad sweep of that which is encompassed within the words '* * * injurious to * * * public morals * * *'. Common-law crimes have not survived in this state, and unless certain conduct is singled out by criminal statute, conduct is not a crime no matter how reprehensible."

3. The general conspiracy statute in the federal code, 18 U.S.C.A. § 371, makes it an offense to conspire "to commit any offense against the United States," and also to conspire "to defraud the United States, or any agency thereof in any manner or for any purpose." The meaning of this latter language has often been a matter of dispute. Illustrative is *United States v. Burgin,* 621 F.2d 1352 (5th Cir.1980), where Burgin and Lambert were charged with conspiracy to defraud the United States of its right to have "the official business of the United States Department of Health, Education and Welfare, conducted honestly, impartially, and with integrity." (The indictment further alleged that Lambert received money from Learning Development Corporation to help it get business in Mississippi, that some of this money was paid by Lambert to Mississippi state senator Burgin, and that Burgin in turn used his influence to get state contracts for LDC to provide service to various Head Start centers in Mississippi which were funded by both state and federal monies.) In response to the defendants' challenge of the sufficiency of the indictment, the court of appeals stated:

"In *Hammerschmidt v. U.S.,* 265 U.S. 182, 44 S.Ct. 511, 68 L.Ed. 968 (1924), the Supreme Court interpreted § 371:

To conspire to defraud the United States means primarily to cheat the government out of property or money, *but it also means to interfere with or obstruct one of its lawful governmental functions by deceit, craft or trickery, or at least by means that are dishonest. It is not necessary that the government shall be subjected to property or pecuniary loss by the fraud, but only that its legitimate official action and purpose shall be defeated by misrepresentation, chicane, or the overreaching of those charged with carrying out the governmental intention.* (emphasis added)

More recently, in *Dennis v. U.S.,* 384 U.S. 855, 86 S.Ct. 1840, 16 L.Ed.2d 973 (1966), the Court stated that § 371 reaches 'any conspiracy for the purpose of impairing, obstructing, or defeating the lawful function of any department of government.' It is now clear that the term 'defraud' as used in § 371 not only reaches financial or property loss through employment of a deceptive scheme, but also is designed and intended to protect the integrity of the United States and its agencies, programs and policies.

"In support of the indictment, the government argues that the meaning of 'defraud' includes any scheme of 'influence peddling' whereby a public official receives remuneration for the exertion of influence upon other officials in order for another to gain the upper hand in some financial transaction with the government. Although no pecuniary loss to the government has occurred, the government contends that the mere exertion of influence by a public official *having a covert financial interest* is a violation of § 371.

"The defendants argue that to apply § 371 in circumstances where the government has suffered no pecuniary loss would amount to no more than a code of governmental ethics to be applied to any state official having some connection with federally funded projects. In support of their argument, the defendants rely heavily on *U.S. v. Porter,* 591 F.2d 1048 (5th Cir. 1979), wherein this court held that if the government has suffered no pecuniary loss

from the activities set forth in the indictment, the indictment can stand only if it alleges that some lawful function of the government has been impaired, obstructed or defeated. In the *Porter* case, the government contended that the United States had been defrauded of its right to have the Medicare program conducted honestly and fairly because of the business practices employed by the defendant doctors. This court held that where purely private parties were under no legal duty to act differently than they had been acting the government had failed to demonstrate interference with any of its lawful functions.

"However, in *Porter,* this Court through Chief Judge Coleman, expressly recognized that 'no public officials were bribed or *participated in the scheme.'* The indictment in this case charged overreaching of an agent of the United States by a public official having a financial quid pro quo interest in a federally financed contract. If that allegation does not amount to obstruction of a lawful governmental function, it is hard to imagine an indictment which would. Therefore, we hold that the alleged involvement of Burgin and Lambert in a silent scheme whereby Burgin, in exchange for remuneration, was to use his political influence as an elected official to insure that state funds would be appropriated or to exert influence in his official capacity on various state officials in order to enable another to enter into or maintain contracts financed by federal funds, charges a violation of 18 U.S.C. § 371."

4. Consider Goldstein, *Conspiracy to Defraud the United States,* 68 Yale L.J. 405, 461–62 (1959): " 'Conspiracy to defraud the United States' has evolved in several stages. First, it was a crime reaching only agreements to use falsehood to induce action by the Government which would cause it a loss of money or property. It expanded to include an agreed-upon falsehood which might disadvantage the Gov-

ernment in any way whatever, and ultimately covered virtually any impairment of the Government's operating efficiency. The end to be gained having thus been obscured, it remained only for the means to be made equally shadowy. This was accomplished in the cases which viewed any dishonest act, including concealment, as the measure of an interference with the Government. Suspiciously unethical conduct, the failure to disclose even that which Congress had never required to be disclosed, became the raw material from which criminal liability was fashioned.

"As a result of these interpretations, the federal conspiracy statute has become another governmental weapon in the eternal conflict between authority and the individual. By making unclear the line between what is permitted and what is prohibited, by conceiving the statute's reach to be as broad as that of an expanding government, present doctrine places within the power of police and prosecutor an instrument for intruding upon Everyman. The instrument is all the more dangerous because it wears the garb of conspiracy, with all the tactical and evidentiary benefits that that doctrine implies. Imprecise definition and procedural advantages combine to make it virtually certain that a charge of conspiracy to defraud the United States will get to the jury—where a showing of suspicious behavior by the sort of people who ought to know better and who least appeal to that body's occasional empathy for those who commit crimes of passion and violence, is very likely to produce conviction."

5. Considering *Burgin* and the Goldstein criticism, what should the result be on these facts, taken from *United States v. Conover,* 772 F.2d 765 (11th Cir.1985)?

Seminole Electric Cooperative is a Florida corporation owned by several rural electric cooperatives. Seminole borrowed over $1.1 billion from the Federal Financing Bank, an agency of the U.S. Treasury, to construct a power plant. The loan was guaranteed by the Rural Electrification Administration, an agency of the U.S. Department of Agriculture. Conover, Seminole's manager of procurement, was a friend of Tanner, who owned a limerock mine. Conover prepared contract specifications for a Seminole contract for fill material for an access road which required limerock content instead of any sand-clay mixture, and consequently Tanner submitted the low bid. Conover received money from Tanner in the form of a "loan" and compensation for landscaping work. Conover and Tanner were charged with conspiracy to defraud the United States. Conover's actions constituted a violation of Seminole's conflict of interest policy. There was no showing of any financial loss to an agency of the U.S. government, nor was there any showing of a violation of a federal agency's rules, regulations, or procedures. (Not admitted into evidence was a letter from an REA official to Seminole stating that REA approval was not required of either the contracts awarded to Tanner or the bidding procedures used.)

6. Most jurisdictions which have adopted new codes in recent years have followed *Model Penal Code* § 5.03, which requires that the object of a conspiracy be the commission of a crime.[a]

Does the Model Penal Code go far enough? Consider Note, 75 Colum.L. Rev. 1122, 1130–31 (1975):

"A number of states have gone even further. For an agreement to be criminal

---

a. This is not to suggest that the sole objective or the primary objective must be criminal. In *Anderson v. United States,* 417 U.S. 211, 94 S.Ct. 2253, 41 L.Ed.2d 20 (1974), the Court held:

"In our view, petitioners err in seeking to attach significance to the fact that the primary

motive behind their conspiracy was to affect the result in the local rather than the federal election. A single conspiracy may have several purposes, but if one of them—whether primary or secondary—be the violation of a federal law, the conspiracy is unlawful under federal law."

in Oregon, either a felony or a class A misdemeanor must be included among its objectives. The laws of New Mexico, Texas, and Virginia do not prohibit conspiracies to commit any sort of misdemeanor; they subject agreements to criminal sanctions only where the goal sought constitutes a felony. Ohio has chosen the most drastic approach of all, making criminal only conspiracies designed to achieve one or more of certain enumerated criminal ends, including murder, kidnapping, compelling or promoting prostitution, arson, robbery, burglary, and felonious unauthorized use of a vehicle. Such limitation of the range of possible conspiratorial objectives to a set of offenses narrower than the set of all crimes probably reflects a degree of legislative uneasiness with the basic notion of conspiracy as an independent crime. To the extent that certain crimes are rejected as potential bases for making agreements to commit them criminal, a judgment has been made that the societal benefits, measured in terms of prevention of substantive offenses and protection against group criminal endeavor, to be derived from early law enforcement action (and the other procedural advantages offered by conspiracy) are insufficient to counterbalance the likelihood of invasion of individual liberties inherent in

a more far-reaching conspiracy statute.[b] Of course, such considerations go to the very heart of the justification for denominating conspiracy criminal. Widespread acceptance of the recently enacted Ohio statutory pattern would spell the end of conspiracy as a general inchoate crime."

SECTION 5. IMPOSSIBILITY

VENTIMIGLIA v. UNITED STATES
United States Court of Appeals, Fourth Circuit, 1957.
242 F.2d 620.

SOBELOFF, CIRCUIT JUDGE.

The Taft–Hartley Act forbids the payment of money by an employer subject to its provisions to "any representative of any of his employees." 29 U.S.C.A. § 186(a). The defendants were indicted for three substantive violations of this law and for conspiracy to violate it. At a trial before the District Judge, sitting without a jury, the defendants were acquitted of the substantive offenses, but convicted of the conspiracy. The sufficiency of the evidence to sustain the conviction is the question raised by this appeal.

Weather–Mastic, Inc., is a non-unionized contractor engaged in the insulating and weather-proofing business. Parran is its general manager and Ventimiglia its labor

b. See Comment, 47 Tulane L.Rev. 1017, 1036 (1973), contending, with respect to conspiracy in the proposed federal code, that "the inchoate crime rationale and the group danger rationale should be adequately satisfied by prohibiting conspiratorial agreements to commit crimes involving potential violence to persons or property, or involving serious danger to the nation. No attempt will be made here to specify which offenses should be classified as involving potential violence to persons or property, or serious danger to the nation, but it is easily seen that conspiracy to commit murder should be included while conspiracy to disseminate obscene material should not. Those involved in the latter conspiracy could be liable for the offense itself, for attempt or for their complicity."

See also Filvaroff, *Conspiracy and the First Amendment,* 121 U.Pa.L.Rev. 189, 234–35 (1972):

"The justification for intervening through the criminal process in the case of unexecuted conspiracy to murder, for example, is that should the conspirators carry out their plans immediate and irreparable harm is likely to result to the victim. The case of conspiracy to commit a speech crime is hardly comparable. Prosecution for conspiracy to incite to violence must be justified on remoter grounds. Just as conspiracy itself is an inchoate crime, so too is incitement, like most other speech crimes. Thus, to charge a speech conspiracy is to load one inchoate offense upon another. Even if the conspirators act, the immediate result is not violence but the impact on others of the assertedly inciting words. These may or may not prove effective in achieving the conspirators' ends. Another stage must be reached before the harm— here violence—befalls; the listeners must themselves move to do that which the conspirators seek to induce."

relations adviser. In the prevailing industry practice, workers are required to have in their possession some evidence of union membership, if in fact affiliated with a union, or "working cards," which the union customarily issues to a limited number of non-union men seeking work on union jobs. Having been accepted as a sub-contractor for a job in Alexandria on which Stone and Webster, a unionized company, was general contractor, Weather–Mastic faced the need of obtaining working cards for its men. Joseph Martin, business agent of Local No. 80 of United Slate, Tile and Composition Roofers, Damp and Water Proof Workers, complained to Weather–Mastic that its workmen were carrying "working cards" issued, not by him, but by Ventimiglia, who was then in the service of Weather–Mastic, Inc., but had earlier been the business agent of the union. After discussion, Martin was persuaded by the defendants to issue working cards to Weather–Mastic's employees, for which the defendants agreed to pay Martin One Hundred Dollars each month.

Martin's duties as business agent for Local No. 80 are said to be of the usual type: negotiating wage contracts and working conditions, representing the union members and acting as peacemaker between employers and union members in respect to disputes or grievances. Martin never represented any of Weather–Mastic's employees in any of these respects. He did issue working cards signed by him, which he delivered to Ventimiglia. For this he received several monthly payments from the defendants.

An additional duty of union business agents is to check on the union credentials of men engaged on a union job who are not members of his union. The evidence is that if another business agent was skeptical of an employee's working card, the usual procedure would be to make inquiry of the agent who had issued the card, and

if he verified its validity, that ordinarily would be enough to satisfy the inquirer. While Weather–Mastic's men were never asked to show their cards, except by the Federal Bureau of Investigation (to whom Martin had reported his agreement with the defendants), the significance sought to be attached to this fact is that Martin, it is said, was prepared to stand behind and vouch for Weather–Mastic's employees if questions as to their status should ever arise.

It is, of course, beyond dispute that a punishable conspiracy may exist independent of the actual commission of the substantive offense which was the object of the conspiracy. This need not be labored. However, there can be no conviction for conspiracy to commit an offense against the United States if the act that the alleged conspirators agree to do has not been made unlawful, and is not planned to be accomplished in an unlawful manner.

According to the Court's findings, the testimony affirmatively established that the corporate defendant's employees were not at any time members of Martin's union, and that there is no evidence that they authorized or subsequently ratified Martin's representing them; and the Court added—correctly, we think—that there is here no representation by operation of law. If Martin was no representative of the employees, Section 186(a) did not apply to him. The Court concluded, as we think was required in these circumstances, that the section was not violated, and he entered the not guilty verdict as to the three substantive counts.

In considering the conspiracy count, however, the Court predicated a verdict of guilty upon the theory that while the defendants did not desire Martin to represent the employees in *all* respects, they did intend to deal with him as their employees' representative in issuing cards evidencing the union's willingness to permit them to work on union jobs. The opinion says: [145 F.Supp. 43] "He [Martin] was to furnish the necessary indicia of union membership, and if questions arose, handle the matter so that there would be no interruption to work. * * * He was not to organize them, or to negotiate on their behalf with the employer as to wages. But there can be no doubt that the defendants intended Martin to do acts which a representative of employees would be expected to do—insure the availability and continuity of work. Likewise, Martin could have become the formal representative of the employees had they initiated the issuance of cards, or accepted or used them knowing the reasons for which, and the circumstances under which the cards were issued."

Thereupon, the Court concluded that, for a period at least, defendants intended to deal with and dealt with Martin as a representative of their employees. He added that "the defendants cannot avoid the natural consequences of their conduct by a simple denial that Martin was such a representative when the evidence is that they intended him to be and dealt with him in that capacity; nor does the fact that they did not want him to be (and indeed forbade him to be) the employees' representative in certain respects, prevent him from being such representative in the limited field in which he was to, and did, act."

In analyzing the evidence in connection with the conspiracy count, the District Judge, we think fell into error. The testimony, it seems to us, does not lend itself to the treatment given it. Plainly enough, the defendants did not deal with Martin as their employees' representative, and never intended to deal with him as such. They did not want him to approach their employees or organize them, or represent them, and he did not do so. As the Court declared in a subsidiary finding of fact, the defendants induced Martin *not* to organize

or represent the employees. The cards he issued were not "indicia of union membership;" on the contrary, they were working cards such as are customarily issued to non-members, to workers *not* represented by the union. Employees represented by the union or by its business agent require no such cards. The purpose of the cards is to sanction work by *non*-union men, who are unrepresented. So, far from treating them as union members and thus under representation by Martin, he treated them as the only class of workers who could carry such cards, namely, persons not in the union or represented by it or by its officers. * * *

The Government contends that a conspiracy may be punished even if the objective of the conspirators cannot be achieved, but the conspirators mistakenly think it can be. Even assuming that the defendants intended to treat Martin as their employees' representative, though in fact he was not, such a theory cannot avail to sustain the prosecution. The Government has referred us to cases in which conviction for conspiracy has been upheld despite the fact that, unknown to the conspirators, the object of the conspiracy was impossible of accomplishment, as where pickpockets conspired to rob an intended victim, but were frustrated by the fact that his pocket was empty. Such unexpected physical impossibility would not prevent successful prosecution for conspiracy.

But the present case is not comparable to the attempt to pick an empty pocket. The analogy to the present case would be closer if we assumed an attempt or conspiracy to pick the pocket of what is merely a wooden dummy. Criminal liability in such a case would seem highly implausible, and it would not save the prosecution to prove that the defendants thought that the object of their design and effort was human. A like distinction is that between an unsuccessful murder attempt due to a faulty gun or a blank cartridge, and a failure due to the fact that the intended victim was merely a block of wood, or a shadow. In the former, there would be a criminal attempt, while in the latter there would not. The distinction in these pairs of cases is readily discernible. It lies in the difference between, on the one hand, a physical impediment to completion of the crime due merely to miscalculation or to the choice of ineffective means which would normally be effective, and, on the other hand, a failure due to an inherent impossibility of completing the crime.

A legal impossibility might also, in many cases, be termed an inherent impossibility, in that the act, though consummated, would not be criminal, and consequently an attempt or agreement to commit it would also not be. * * *

* * * See also *O'Kelley v. U.S.*, 8 Cir., 116 F.2d 966, where it was held that there could be no conspiracy to commit larceny of an interstate shipment, because there could be no substantive violation inasmuch as the goods had lost their interstate character. Similarly, if one thinks that a uniformed doorman is a police officer and bribes him not to tag his car, it is no crime, and neither the attempt nor the conspiracy can be, for there is an inherent or legal impossibility of consummating the offense, although the act itself was completed. Likewise, where one mistakenly believes a certain individual is the union representative of his employees, the misconception cannot sufficiently negative the impossibility of committing the substantive offense so as to provide the basis for a conspiracy conviction. But where the object of a bribe is a draft board official of the United States who, but for the defendant's mistake of registering with the wrong board, would have had no jurisdiction over the defendant, the impossibility was not inherent but was due simply to a prior mistaken course of action. See *United States v. Schanerman*, 3 Cir., 150 F.2d 941.

* * *

Even were we to doubt the foregoing propositions and their application here, the present case is on the facts of an even more extreme variety, for it is said merely that the defendants *intended* to deal with Martin as their employees' representative. The previous example of the doorman will suffice to show the fallacy of basing a conviction on such a fact. Had the defendant in that hypothetical case, knowing that the doorman was not a police officer, nevertheless intended to deal with him as such, it could certainly not be said that he attempted to bribe a police officer.

* * *

We conclude, therefore, that there could be no conviction under this indictment even if the defendants mistakenly thought that Martin was a representative of Weather–Mastic's employees. Even less can a conviction be sustained when it is clear beyond dispute, not only that he was not the employees' representative, but that no one concerned thought or pretended that he was.

Reversed.

Notes and Questions

1. Compare *United States v. Thomas,* p. 563 of this Book, where the majority went on to conclude that its holding that impossibility was no defense on the attempt charge was likewise applicable to the conspiracy charge. Significantly, Ferguson, J., who vigorously dissented from the affirmance of the attempt conviction, stated:

"Despite my position with respect to the charge of attempted rape, I would affirm the conviction of conspiracy to commit rape. Unlike criminal attempts, legal impossibility is not recognized as a defense to a charge of conspiracy. Although both crimes are, in a sense, inchoate offenses, their development has been somewhat different. At common law, conspiracy consisted only of the agreement to do an unlawful act or a lawful act in an unlawful manner. Although Code, supra, Article 81, 10 USC § 881, requires proof of an overt act in addition to the agreement to commit an offense under the Code, we have held that the heart of the crime remains the corrupt meeting of the minds. Here, the accused agreed to have intercourse with an unconscious girl against her will and while she was unable to resist. The averred overt act was also made out. As what these two men thus subjectively agreed to be their objective constitutes in law the offense of rape, in violation of Code, supra, Article 120, 10 USC § 920, and as thereafter one of them performed an overt act, guilt of conspiracy is made out. My objection is simply to the action of my brothers in transferring the subjective approach in conspiracy to the objective questions involved in attempts."

2. Is the Ferguson position inconsistent? Consider *State v. Moretti,* 52 N.J. 182, 244 A.2d 499 (1968), affirming convictions of conspiracy to commit an illegal abortion upon a woman who in fact was a nonpregnant police agent: "The case has been argued as though, for purposes of the defense of impossibility, a conspiracy charge is the same as a charge of attempting to commit a crime. It seems that such an equation could not be sustained, however, because, as discussed above, a conspiracy charge focuses primarily on the *intent* of the defendants, while in an attempt case the primary inquiry centers on the defendants' *conduct* tending toward the commission of the substantive crime. The crime of conspiracy is complete once the conspirators, having formed the intent to commit a crime, take any step in preparation; mere preparation, however, is an inadequate basis for an attempt conviction regardless of the intent. Thus, the impossibility that the defendants' conduct will result in the consummation of the contemplated crime is not as pertinent in a conspiracy case as it might be in an attempt prosecution."

3. Might it be argued that there is *more,* rather than less, reason to recognize impossibility as a defense when the charge is conspiracy? Consider *People v. Tinskey,* 394 Mich. 108, 228 N.W.2d 782 (1975), involving facts similar to those in *Moretti:* "It is possible, although we need not decide, that defendants could not have been convicted of attempted abortion; at common law the general rule is that while factual impossibility is not a defense, legal impossibility is a defense.

"The somewhat indeterminate common-law definition of conspiracy, as a combination to accomplish some criminal or unlawful purpose or end or to accomplish a lawful purpose or end by criminal or unlawful means, was replaced by 1966 P.A. 296, which defines the object of the conspiracy as the 'commit[ting of] an offense prohibited by law' or of 'a legal act in an illegal manner.'

"While the crime of conspiracy is distinct from the substantive offense, the Legislature has indicated that in Michigan the penalty for an attempt to commit an offense shall be significantly less than the penalty for the substantive offense. We note, without resting decision on this ground, that to charge a person with conspiracy—which may subject the offender to the same jail or prison sentence as the substantive offense—as a substitute for charging attempt to commit the offense tends to circumvent that legislative policy.

"There are two statutory patterns prevalent in this country: one requiring that the woman be pregnant (Michigan and other states), the other requiring only that the person to be aborted be a woman. The Legislature, having elected the pattern requiring that the person to be aborted be pregnant, has rejected prosecutions where the person is not pregnant. It has indicated that an attempted abortion which does not or cannot succeed because the person is not pregnant is not a crime. The Legislature has not, as to most other offenses, so similarly indicated that impossibility is not a defense.

"In this statutory pattern, the crime of conspiracy to commit abortion cannot be committed with respect to a person who is not pregnant."

SECTION 6. THE OVERT ACT RE-QUIREMENT

DEVELOPMENTS IN THE LAW—CRIMINAL CONSPIRACY

72 Harv.L.Rev. 920, 945–48 (1959).

At common law the crime of conspiracy was indictable upon the formation of the agreement. In enacting conspiracy statutes, several jurisdictions, including the federal government, have required that an overt act in furtherance of the conspiracy be proved. Such a provision has seldom materially increased the difficulty of securing convictions for conspiracy. A non-criminal and relatively minor act is held to satisfy the requirement if it is in furtherance of the conspiracy. An act committed by any one of the conspirators is sufficient both as to all present members of the conspiracy and as to persons subsequently joining the agreement. The act, however, cannot be part of the formation of the agreement, nor can it take place after termination of the conspiracy. But it may be the step which accomplishes the conspiracy's objective. There need not be an affirmative act, since nonfeasance may in some circumstances satisfy the requirement.

The inclusion of the overt-act requirement in the federal general conspiracy statute was unaccompanied by any indication of the function it was to serve. It may have represented merely a legislative interpretation of what was necessary to prove a conspiracy at common law. The secrecy normally surrounding formulation of criminal plans makes proof of the agreement by direct evidence improbable and usually forces the prosecution to rely upon conduct of the conspirators from which an inference of an agreement can be drawn. Thus, since most conspiracy prosecutions involved proof of an overt act, there emerged a practice of alleging such acts in the indictment. The courts, however, have pragmatically used other rationales of the requirement to justify results which seemed desirable.

In *United States v. Donau* [178] the defendant sought to quash an indictment on the ground that the overt acts alleged were not reasonably calculated to effect the specific object of the conspiracy. In overruling the motion, the court held that the statutory offense consisted of the agreement alone, the overt act merely affording a *"locus poenitentiae"* so that before the commission of the act a conspirator might withdraw from the scheme without incurring guilt. * * *

In *Hyde v. United States,* [180] the Court viewed the overt act as an element of the offense in order to hold that venue could be laid in any district in which such an act had been committed. Mr. Justice Holmes, dissenting, reasoned that the act itself was no more a part of the offense than was the fact that the statute of limitations had not run. That the rationale employed in *Hyde* was not the exclusive means of reaching the result of the case is indicated by the similar venue decisions in jurisdictions not requiring an overt act. * * *

The overt-act requirement may also be interpreted as a legislative determination that a mere agreement does not usually represent a sufficient threat of the specific offense or sufficient evidence of a general danger to warrant criminal prosecution. This rationale seems particularly apparent

---

178. 25 Fed.Cas. 890 (No. 14983) (S.D.N.Y. 1873).

180. 225 U.S. 347 (1912).

in the few instances in which legislatures have, for conspiracies to commit certain serious crimes, made specific exceptions to a general rule which requires allegation and proof of an overt act.

Notes and Questions

1. Does the overt act requirement serve a useful purpose? Does it make sense to require an overt act for some types of conspiracies but not for others? Should more than a "mere" overt act be required?

2. In assessing these questions, consider the variety of approaches taken in recent codifications, as reported in Note, 75 Colum.L.Rev. 1122, 1153–54 (1975):

"Some dispute exists among the states over whether an overt act in pursuance of an agreement to commit a crime should be a prerequisite for a conspiracy conviction. Though such an act was not necessary at common law, two-thirds of the jurisdictions which have revised or are considering revision of their conspiracy statutes have elected to impose such an additional requirement before an agreement to commit any offense will be proscribed. Another five states, choosing to follow the [Model Penal Code] pattern, insist on an overt act in all cases other than those involving agreements to commit a first or second degree felony (or one of a similar list of serious crimes). Maine, Ohio, Washington, and Vermont, all members of the former group, set even stricter standards than the rest of the majority. Statutes in these states permit conspiracy convictions only where a 'substantial step' has been taken in furtherance of the conspiracy. Under the laws recently adopted in Ohio and proposed in Vermont, an act, to qualify as 'substantial,' must be 'of such character as to manifest a purpose on the part of the actor that the object of the conspiracy should be completed.' Maine's

new conspiracy provision further narrows the definition of 'substantial step,' demanding 'conduct which, under the circumstances in which it occurs, is *strongly corroborative* of the firmness of the actor's intent to complete commission of the crime,' and adding that 'speech alone may not constitute a substantial step.' This language greatly resembles that found in Maine's attempt section, and indicates that Maine may be tending toward the elimination of all conspiracy liability where a substantive offense has not been at least attempted. Such a development may also be favored by Washington, which uses the phrase 'substantial step' without definition in both its conspiracy and its attempt provisions. At the opposite extreme, eight states have decided, for one reason or another, to preserve the common law scheme on this issue, and so require no overt act whatever. Under such statutes, the crime of conspiracy is complete when the agreement is formed."

SECTION 7. SCOPE: THE OBJECT DIMENSION

BRAVERMAN v. UNITED STATES
Supreme Court of the United States, 1942.
317 U.S. 49, 63 S.Ct. 99, 87 L.Ed. 23.

MR. CHIEF JUSTICE STONE delivered the opinion of the Court.

[The question is:] Whether a conviction upon the several counts of an indictment, each charging conspiracy to violate a different provision of the Internal Revenue laws, where the jury's verdict is supported by evidence of but a single conspiracy, will sustain a sentence of more than two years' imprisonment, the maximum penalty for a single violation of the conspiracy statute * * *.

Petitioners were indicted, with others, on seven counts, each charging a conspiracy to violate a separate and distinct internal revenue law of the United States.[1] On the trial there was evidence from which the jury could have found that for a considerable period of time petitioners, with others, collaborated in the illicit manufacture, transportation, and distribution of distilled spirits involving the violations of statute mentioned in the several counts of the indictment. At the close of the trial petitioners renewed a motion which they had made at its beginning to require the Government to elect one of the seven counts of the indictment upon which to proceed, contending that the proof could not and did not establish more than one agreement. In response the Government's attorney took the position that the seven counts of the indictment charged as distinct offenses the several illegal objects of one continuing conspiracy, that if the jury found such a conspiracy it might find the defendants guilty of as many offenses as it had illegal objects, and that for each such offense the two-year statutory penalty could be imposed.

The trial judge submitted the case to the jury on that theory. The jury returned a general verdict finding petitioners "guilty as charged", and the court sentenced each to eight years' imprisonment. On appeal the Court of Appeals for the Sixth Circuit affirmed * * *.

Both courts below recognized that a single agreement to commit an offense does not become several conspiracies because it continues over a period of time, and that

there may be such a single continuing agreement to commit several offenses. But they thought that in the latter case each contemplated offense renders the agreement punishable as a separate conspiracy.

The question whether a single agreement to commit acts in violation of several penal statutes is to be punished as one or several conspiracies is raised on the present record, not by the construction of the indictment, but by the Government's concession at the trial and here, reflected in the charge to the jury, that only a single agreement to commit the offenses alleged was proven. Where each of the counts of an indictment alleges a conspiracy to violate a different penal statute it may be proper to conclude, in the absence of a bill of exceptions bringing up the evidence, that several conspiracies are charged rather than one, and that the conviction is for each. But it is a different matter to hold, as the court below appears to have done in this case, that even though a single agreement is entered into, the conspirators are guilty of as many offenses as the agreement has criminal objects. * * *

[W]hen a single agreement to commit one or more substantive crimes is evidenced by an overt act, as the statute requires, the precise nature and extent of the conspiracy must be determined by reference to the agreement which embraces and defines its objects. Whether the object of a single agreement is to commit one

1. The seven counts respectively charged them with conspiracy, in violation of § 37 of the Criminal Code, unlawfully (1) to carry on the business of wholesale and retail liquor dealers without having the special occupational tax stamps required by statute, 26 U.S.C. § 3253, 26 U.S.C.A. Int.Rev.Code § 3253; (2) to possess distilled spirits, the immediate containers of which did not have stamps affixed denoting the quantity of the distilled spirits which they contained and evidencing payment of all Internal Revenue taxes imposed on such spirits, 26 U.S.C. § 2803, 26 U.S.C.A. Int.Rev.Code § 2803; (3) to transport quantities of distilled spirits, the immediate containers of which did not have affixed the required

stamps, 26 U.S.C. § 2803, 26 U.S.C.A. Int.Rev. Code § 2803; (4) to carry on the business of distillers without having given bond as required by law, 26 U.S.C. § 2833, 26 U.S.C.A. Int.Rev. Code, § 2833; (5) to remove, deposit and conceal distilled spirits in respect whereof a tax is imposed by law, with intent to defraud the United States of such tax, 26 U.S.C. § 3321, 26 U.S.C.A. Int.Rev.Code § 3321; (6) to possess unregistered stills and distilling apparatus, 26 U.S.C. § 2810, 26 U.S.C.A. Int.Rev.Code § 2810; and (7) to make and ferment mash, fit for distillation, on unauthorized premises, 26 U.S.C. § 2834, 26 U.S.C.A. Int.Rev.Code § 2834.

or many crimes, it is in either case that agreement which constitutes the conspiracy which the statute punishes. The one agreement cannot be taken to be several agreements and hence several conspiracies because it envisages the violation of several statutes rather than one.

The allegation in a single count of a conspiracy to commit several crimes is not duplicitous, for "The conspiracy is the crime, and that is one, however diverse its objects". A conspiracy is not the commission of the crime which it contemplates, and neither violates nor "arises under" the statute whose violation is its object. Since the single continuing agreement, which is the conspiracy here, thus embraces its criminal objects, it differs from successive acts which violate a single penal statute and from a single act which violates two statutes. The single agreement is the prohibited conspiracy, and however diverse its objects it violates but a single statute, § 37 of the Criminal Code. For such a violation only the single penalty prescribed by the statute can be imposed. * * *

Reversed.

Notes and Questions

1. Compare *Lievers v. State,* 3 Md.App. 597, 241 A.2d 147 (1968), where the defendants were convicted of several conspiracies. The evidence was that their scheme involved the obtaining of a counterfeit chauffeur's license which was used in trying to utter (i.e., pass) a check they had forged, by which they would have obtained $104.87:

"As indicated, appellants were convicted of (a) conspiracy to forge a designated check in the amount of $104.87, (b) conspiracy to utter said forged check, (c) conspiracy to obtain $104.87 from a designated corporation by a 'certain' false pretense, and (d) conspiracy to hold and use a designated forged and counterfeited Maryland chauffeur's license. In *Tender v. State,* 2

Md.App. 692, 237 A.2d 65, we held that a person should not be twice punished for the same acts whether the offenses charged by reason of such acts be deemed to be inconsistent, duplicitous, or to have merged. The true test of merger of offenses is whether one crime necessarily involves the other. Thus in *Sutton v. State,* 2 Md.App. 639, 236 A.2d 301, we held, on the facts of that case, that the substantive offense of uttering merged into the offense of false pretenses where the false representation consisted only of the uttering. It appears to us from the evidence in this case that the conspiracy to utter merged into the conspiracy to obtain money by false pretenses since no false representation independent of the uttering of the forged check itself is shown by the evidence.

"Holding and using a forged Maryland chauffeur's license with fraudulent intent is a felony. We think it clear that appellant's conviction for conspiring to hold and use such a document clearly charges an act separate and distinct from any of the [other] conspiracies charged * * * and is indeed broader in scope than the other conspiracies since it is not limited to an agreement to hold and use such forged license solely in connection with an illegal effort to negotiate a forged check made payable to Steven Thompson in the amount of $104.87, dated March 18, 1965."

2. Compare the approach taken in *Braverman, Lievers,* and *Model Penal Code* § 5.03(3) in assessing whether there is more than one conspiracy in each of the following situations:

(a) *A, B* and *C* meet together and conceive a plan which they agree to use in robbing the First National Bank on June 1st and the Second National Bank on August 1st; equipment used for each robbery is thereafter acquired.

(b) *A, B* and *C* meet together and conceive a plan which they agree to use in robbing the First National Bank on June 1st. On May 30th, while working out the last minute details, it occurs to them that the plan is so good that they should also use it in robbing the Second National Bank on August 1st, which they agree to do. They continue meeting after the First National robbery for this latter purpose.

(c) *A, B* and *C* meet together and conceive a plan which they agree to use in robbing the First National Bank on June 1st. They carry out the robbery, distribute the proceeds, and disperse without any plan to meet again. On July 1st, *A* contacts *B* and *C* and proposes that they use the same plan to rob the Second National Bank on August 1st. *B* and *C* agree with *A,* and they thereafter meet to work out the details.

3. What then of the following facts, deemed in *People v. Burleson,* 50 Ill.App.3d 629, 8 Ill.Dec. 776, 365 N.E.2d 1162 (1977), to amount to two conspiracies? "On September 11, 1975, the defendant and Brown, having the necessary intent, agreed to rob the bank on September 13, 1975. In furtherance of this agreement, they committed the overt acts of "casing" the bank, procuring a weapon and disguises, and going to the bank on September 13, 1975, to commit the crime. This first conspiracy was abandoned when the conspirators observed a large number of persons in and around the bank. Thereafter, the same conspirators, with the necessary intent, agreed to rob the bank on September 16, 1975, after which they committed the overt acts of preserving the disguises, participating in a practice escape from the bank and in approaching the bank on September 16, 1975."

4. Consider Note, 75 Colum.L.Rev. 1122, 1163–64 (1975): "The basic rule concerning the object dimension of conspiracy is that multiple criminal objectives do not imply multiple conspiracies, 'so long as such multiple crimes are the object of the same agreement or continuous conspiratorial relationship.' Nearly two-thirds of the jurisdictions surveyed, including the federal, have devoted no statutory attention whatever to this issue, presumably in the belief that the controlling decisions dictate the same result. Fifteen states have included provisions similar or identical to the [Model Penal Code] subsection quoted above, and three more have drafted proposed sections in all likelihood intended to emulate the MPC. The efficacy of these latter sections in completely achieving their probable goal is cast in some doubt by their unexplained omission of the final phrase of MPC § 5.03(3): 'or continuous conspiratorial relationship.' That language was framed to dispose of logical problems encountered in the attempt to reconcile the agreement concept with the idea that a single conspiracy could be directed toward criminal objectives conceived at different times. The fundamental query under the MPC is a highly realistic one, namely, 'whether there was a single and continuous association for criminal purposes.' The statutory sections which fail to incorporate the notion of an ongoing conspiratorial relationship may nevertheless have been formulated with the MPC treatment in mind. The comments to the proposed Missouri provision evidence this fact. They state unequivocally that, 'If various offenses are the product of a continuous relationship they should be considered part of one conspiracy.' "

5. In *Albernaz v. United States,* 450 U.S. 333, 101 S.Ct. 1137, 67 L.Ed.2d 275 (1981), the Court held that notwithstanding a single agreement the defendants could be convicted and consecutively sentenced for violating 21 U.S.C.A. § 963, which proscribes conspiracy to commit any offense defined in Subchapter II of the Comprehensive Drug Abuse Prevention

and Control Act of 1970, including importation of marijuana; and 21 U.S.C.A. § 846, which proscribes conspiracy to commit any offense defined in Subchapter I of the Act, including distribution of marijuana. The Court concluded this result conformed to the *Blockburger* rule of statutory construction—that where each provision requires proof of a fact the other does not, this indicates Congress intended to allow such cumulative conviction and punishment. *Braverman* was distinguished because the conspiracy there "violated but a single statute," while here two separate conspiracy statutes were involved.

In *Mason v. State,* 302 Md. 434, 488 A.2d 955 (1985), where again it was conceded there was but a single agreement, the defendants were charged with two conspiracies: to distribute heroin; and to distribute cocaine. The state, noting that these were common law conspiracy charges because there is no conspiracy statute and noting further that cocaine distribution and heroin distribution are proscribed in separate sections of the Controlled Dangerous Substances Act, relied on *Albernaz.* The defendant relied on *Braverman.* What result?

SECTION 8. SCOPE: THE PARTY DIMENSION

Introductory Notes

1. *Model Penal Code* § 5.03, Comment (1985): "Much of the most perplexing litigation in conspiracy has been concerned less with the essential elements of the offense than with the scope to be accorded to a combination i.e., the singleness or multiplicity of the conspiratorial relationships typical in a large, complex and sprawling network of crime. * * *

"The inquiry may be crucial for a number of purposes. These include not only defining each defendant's liability but also the propriety of joint prosecution, admissibility against a defendant of the hearsay acts and declarations of others, questions of multiple prosecution or conviction and double jeopardy, satisfaction of the overt act requirement or statutes of limitation or rules of jurisdiction and venue, and possibly liability for substantive crimes executed pursuant to the conspiracy. The scope problem is thus central to the present concern of courts and commentators about the use of conspiracy, a concern based on the conflict between the need for effective means of prosecuting large criminal organizations, and the dangers of prejudice to individual defendants."

2. Johnson, *The Unnecessary Crime of Conspiracy,* 61 Calif.L.Rev. 1137, 1168–71 (1973): "Most cases in which joinder by conspiracy is disputed reflect a variation or combination of two familiar models, the 'wheel' and the 'chain.' In a wheel conspiracy, various defendants accused of individual criminal transactions are linked together by the fact that one defendant or one group of defendants participated in every transaction. For graphic purposes, the defendant or defendants implicated in every charge are described as the hub of the wheel and those charged with individual crimes as the spokes. The United States Supreme Court discovered such a wheel in unusually pure form in *Kotteakos v. United States.* * * *

" * * * As the name indicates, a chain conspiracy involves the chain of distribution of some commodity, such as narcotics, from the initial manufacture or smuggling to the ultimate consumer. A chain conspiracy is similar to a wheel conspiracy in that the participants at opposite ends of the chain may not know or have any dealings with each other, but the two are different in that the participants in a chain conspiracy all deal with the same goods. A chain may, and frequently does, incorporate one or more subsidiary wheels. Thus in *United States v. Bruno,* the most famous chain case, the conspiracy consisted of smugglers who brought narcotics into New York, middlemen who purchased from the smugglers and resold to retailers, and two groups of retailers, one operating in New York and the other in Texas and Louisiana."

KOTTEAKOS v. UNITED STATES

Supreme Court of the United States, 1946.
328 U.S. 750, 66 S.Ct. 1239, 90 L.Ed. 1557.

MR. JUSTICE RUTLEDGE delivered the opinion of the Court.

The only question is whether petitioners have suffered substantial prejudice from being convicted of a single general conspiracy by evidence which the Government admits proved not one conspiracy but some eight or more different ones of the same sort executed through a common key figure, Simon Brown. Petitioners were convicted of conspiring to violate the provisions of the National Housing Act.

* * *

The indictment named thirty-two defendants, including the petitioners. The gist of the conspiracy, as alleged, was that the defendants had sought to induce various financial institutions to grant credit, with the intent that the loans or advances would then be offered to the Federal Housing Administration for insurance upon applications containing false and fraudulent information.

Of the thirty-two persons named in the indictment nineteen were brought to trial and the names of thirteen were submitted to the jury. Two were acquitted; the jury disagreed as to four; and the remaining seven, including petitioners, were found guilty.

The Government's evidence may be summarized briefly, for the petitioners have not contended that it was insufficient, if considered apart from the alleged errors relating to the proof and the instructions at the trial.

Simon Brown, who pleaded guilty, was the common and key figure in all of the transactions proven. He was president of the Brownie Lumber Company. Having had experience in obtaining loans under the National Housing Act, he undertook to act as broker in placing for others loans for modernization and renovation, charging a five per cent commission for his services. Brown knew, when he obtained the loans, that the proceeds were not to be used for the purposes stated in the applications.

In May, 1939, petitioner Lekacos told Brown that he wished to secure a loan in order to finance opening a law office, to say the least a hardly auspicious professional launching. Brown made out the application, as directed by Lekacos, to state that the purpose of the loan was to modernize a house belonging to the estate of Lekacos' father. Lekacos obtained the money. Later in the same year Lekacos secured another loan through Brown, the application being in the names of his brother and sister-in-law. Lekacos also received part of the proceeds of a loan for which one Gerakeris, a defendant who pleaded guilty, had applied.

In June, 1939, Lekacos sent Brown an application for a loan signed by petitioner Kotteakos. It contained false statements. Brown placed the loan, and Kotteakos thereafter sent Brown applications on behalf of other persons. Two were made out in the names of fictitious persons. The proceeds were received by Kotteakos and petitioner Regenbogen, his partner in the cigarette and pinball machine business. Regenbogen, together with Kotteakos, had indorsed one of the applications. Kotteakos also sent to Brown an application for a loan in Regenbogen's name. This was for modernization of property not owned by Regenbogen. The latter, however, repaid the money in about three months after he received it.

The evidence against the other defendants whose cases were submitted to the jury was similar in character. They too had transacted business with Brown relating to National Housing Act loans. But no connection was shown between them and petitioners, other than that Brown had been the instrument in each instance for obtaining the loans. In many cases the other defendants did not have any relationship with one another, other than Brown's connection with each transaction.

* * *

The proof therefore admittedly made out a case, not of a single conspiracy, but of several, notwithstanding only one was charged in the indictment. The Court of Appeals aptly drew analogy in the comment, "Thieves who dispose of their loot to a single receiver—a single 'fence'—do not by that fact alone become confederates: they may, but it takes more than knowledge that he is a 'fence' to make them such." It stated that the trial judge "was plainly wrong in supposing that upon the evidence there could be a single conspiracy; and in the view he took of the law, he should have dismissed the indictment." Nevertheless the appellate court held the error not prejudicial, saying among other things that "especially since guilt was so manifest, it was 'proper' to join the conspiracies," and "to reverse the conviction would be a miscarriage of justice." * * *

The Government's theory seems to be, in ultimate logical reach, that the error presented by the variance is insubstantial and harmless, if the evidence offered specifically and properly to convict each defendant would be sufficient to sustain his conviction, if submitted in a separate trial. [I]n apparent support of its view the Government argues that there was no prejudice here because the results show that the jury exercised discrimination as among the defendants whose cases were submitted to it. As it points out, the jury

acquitted some, disagreed as to others, and found still others guilty. From this it concludes that the jury was not confused and, apparently, reached the same result as would have been reached or would be likely, if the convicted defendants had been or now should be tried separately.

One difficulty with this is that the trial court itself was confused in the charge which it gave to guide the jury in deliberation. The court instructed: "The indictment charges but one conspiracy, and to convict each of the defendants of a conspiracy, the Government would have to prove, and you would have to find, that each of the defendants was a member of that conspiracy. You cannot divide it up. It is one conspiracy, and the question is whether or not each of the defendants or which of the defendants, are members of that conspiracy." * * *

This view, specifically embodied throughout the instructions, obviously confuses the common purpose of a single enterprise with the several, though similar, purposes of numerous separate adventures of like character. It may be that, notwithstanding the misdirection, the jury actually understood correctly the purport of the evidence, as the Government now concedes it to have been; and came to the conclusion that the petitioners were guilty only of the separate conspiracies in which the proof shows they respectively participated. But, in the face of the misdirection and in the circumstances of this case, we cannot assume that the lay triers of fact were so well informed upon the law or that they disregarded the permission expressly given to ignore that vital difference. * * *

On those instructions it was competent not only for the jury to find that all of the defendants were parties to a single common plan, design and scheme, where none was shown by the proof, but also for them to impute to each defendant the acts and statements of the others without reference to whether they related to one of the schemes proven or another, and to find an overt act affecting all in conduct which admittedly could only have affected some. True, the Court of Appeals painstakingly examined the evidence directly relating to each petitioner and concluded he had not been prejudiced in this manner. That judgment was founded largely in the fact that each was clearly shown to have shared in the fraudulent phase of the conspiracy in which he participated. Even so, we do not understand how it can be concluded, in the face of the instruction, that the jury considered and was influenced by nothing else. * * *

Reversed.

Notes and Questions

1. A year later, *Kotteakos* was distinguished by its author in *Blumenthal v. United States,* 332 U.S. 539, 68 S.Ct. 248, 92 L.Ed. 154 (1947). Francisco Distributing Co., operated by Weiss and Goldsmith, obtained two carloads of whiskey from an unidentified source. Feigenbaum (operator of a drugstore), Blumenthal (operator of a pawn shop) and Abel (operator of a jewelry store) acted as "salesmen" in selling this liquor to tavern owners at inflated prices. Weiss and Goldsmith later admitted to a federal agent that they were merely acting for their supplier, who they declined to name. The salesmen had no dealings with one another, and it was not shown that they knew of the unknown owner's existence or part in the scheme. The aforementioned persons were convicted of conspiring with one another and the unidentified owner to sell the whiskey at a price above the maximum permitted under wartime price control regulations. The Supreme Court affirmed:

"We think that in the special circumstances of this case the two agreements were merely steps in the formation of the larger and ultimate more general conspiracy. In that view it would be a perversion of justice to regard the salesmen's ignorance of the unknown owner's participation as furnishing adequate ground for reversal of their convictions. Nor does anything in the *Kotteakos* decision require this. The scheme was in fact the same scheme; the salesmen knew or must have known that others unknown to them were sharing in so large a project; and it hardly can be sufficient to relieve them that they did not know, when they joined the scheme, who those people were or exactly the parts they were playing in carrying out the common design and object of all. By their separate agreements, if such they were, they became parties to the larger common plan, joined together by their knowledge of its essential features and broad scope, though not of its exact limits, and by their common single goal.

"The case therefore is very different from the facts admitted to exist in the *Kotteakos* case. Apart from the much larger number of agreements there involved, no two of those agreements were tied together as stages in the formation of a larger all-inclusive combination, all directed to achieving a single unlawful end or result. On the contrary each separate agreement had its own distinct, illegal end. Each loan was an end in itself, separate from all others, although all were alike in having similar illegal objects. Except for Brown, the common figure, no conspirator was interested in whether any loan except his own went through. And none aided in any way, by agreement or otherwise, in procuring another's loan. The conspiracies therefore were distinct and disconnected, not parts of a larger general scheme, both in the phase of agreement with Brown and also in the absence of any aid given to others as well as in specific object and result. There was no drawing of all together in a single, overall, comprehensive plan.

"Here the contrary is true. All knew of and joined in the overriding scheme. All intended to aid the owner, whether Francisco or another, to sell the whiskey unlawfully, though the two groups of defendants differed on the proof in knowledge and belief concerning the owner's ability. All by reason of their knowledge of the plan's general scope, if not its exact limits, sought a common end, to aid in disposing of the whiskey. True, each salesman aided in selling only his part. But he knew the lot to be sold was larger and thus that he was aiding in a larger plan. He thus became a party to it and not merely to the integrating agreement with Weiss and Goldsmith.

"We think therefore that in every practical sense the unique facts of this case reveal a single conspiracy of which the several agreements were essential and integral steps, and accordingly that the judgments should be affirmed."

2. Stern was engaged in the business of performing illegal abortions. Many persons referred women desiring abortions to Stern, for which they were paid a fee. One of these individuals was Anderson, who referred several women to Stern. Anderson was later charged with conspiracy to commit abortions with Stern and the others who had made referrals. Anderson did not know the identity of the others, but did know that Stern was engaged in the performance of abortions on a regular basis and that thus he would be receiving referrals from others.[a] Is this one conspiracy or several?

3. "Appellants [Cole, Hawkins, Hensley, and Holley], along with Kenneth Hart and Jerry Owens, were active members of the Tampa (Florida) Chapter of the Outlaw Motorcycle Club. To join the Outlaws one must be male, own a Harley–

Davidson motorcycle, and embrace the Outlaw lifestyle.

"The Tampa Outlaws are an insular group with members living at or near their clubhouse, occupying themselves primarily with their motorcycles, touring, and 'partying'. Gainful employment among the Outlaws is rare.

"Women closely associated with the Outlaws are termed 'patched old ladies' and sport insignia, sometimes tattoos, proclaiming them 'Property of Outlaws.' These women are treated as 'property' by the Outlaws. At a given time an individual woman is typically associated with a particular Outlaw. But she may be sold, traded, or given to another. Unlike the males, the women are expected to work— sometimes as waitresses, dancers, barmaids—often as prostitutes. An 'old lady's' duties to the man with whom she is associated include giving him her money and following orders without question. Mostly the women are compliant in all this; if not, compliance may be enforced with physical violence.

"In the spring of 1979, Mary Carley was living at the Outlaw clubhouse in Tampa with Kenneth Hart as his 'old lady' and supplying Hart's income by working locally as a prostitute. But local work became difficult. She was out on bond from a firearms charge, and the local police were cracking down on prostitution. Through Lori, another 'old lady,' she and Hart learned of the Club Caprice, a brothel in Meridian, Mississippi. Lori, Carley and Hart telephoned the club owner and arranged jobs there for Carley and Lori.

"The two women went to Meridian and began work at the club. Lori was fired soon after for misconduct. Carley continued to work there but didn't like working alone. She called Hart and asked him to

---

a. *Anderson v. Superior Court,* 78 Cal.App.2d 22, 177 P.2d 315 (1947), denying a writ of prohibition on such facts.

send some other 'old ladies' to join her. Soon afterwards two more Outlaw women arrived from Tampa. Carley worked intermittently at the Club Caprice for more than a year, joined at different times by various Outlaw women including those associated with Hawkins, Cole, Hensley, and Owens. During that year she was traded by Hart and became Holley's 'old lady.' At times some of the men came to Meridian to see the women, and phone calls were exchanged between the women in Meridian and the men in Florida.

"At times Carley and the other women would return to Tampa. When this occurred Carley would personally deliver her prostitution proceeds to her 'old man.' Other times Hart, and later Holley, would telephone Carley asking for money, and she would wire the money via Western Union. She also instructed other Outlaw women on how to send money back to the men and on occasions accompanied them to the Meridian Western Union office." [b] Is this a single conspiracy to violate the Travel Act, proscribing use of the mails to "distribute the proceeds of any unlawful activity"?

4. Meyrick and Ribuffi are both operators of night clubs located with other clubs in the entertainment area of the community. Each of them individually approached the policeman responsible for enforcement in that area, Sgt. Goddard, and gave him a bribe in exchange for his promise to overlook violations of the laws regarding the sale of intoxicating liquors in their respective premises.[c] Does this alone establish the existence of a single conspiracy to corrupt the police involving those three individuals? What if Meyrick and Ribuffi each knew that Goddard was tolerating liquor law violations throughout the entertainment area? That Goddard was re-

ceiving bribes from one or more other club owners? That their bribery of Goddard was known by the other, who was also bribing Goddard?

UNITED STATES v. BRUNO

United States Court of Appeals, Second Circuit, 1939.
105 F.2d 921, rev'd on other grounds, 308 U.S. 287, 60 S.Ct. 198, 84 L.Ed. 257 (1939).

PER CURIAM.

Bruno and Iacono were indicted along with 86 others for a conspiracy to import, sell and possess narcotics; some were acquitted; others, besides these two, were convicted, but they alone appealed. They complain, (1), that if the evidence proved anything, it proved a series of separate conspiracies, and not a single one, as alleged in the indictment; * * *

The first point was made at the conclusion of the prosecution's case: the defendants then moved to dismiss the indictment on the ground that several conspiracies had been proved, and not the one alleged. The evidence allowed the jury to find that there had existed over a substantial period of time a conspiracy embracing a great number of persons, whose object was to smuggle narcotics into the Port of New York and distribute them to addicts both in this city and in Texas and Louisiana. This required the cooperation of four groups of persons; the smugglers who imported the drugs; the middlemen who paid the smugglers and distributed to retailers; and two groups of retailers—one in New York and one in Texas and Louisiana—who supplied the addicts. The defendants assert that there were, therefore, at least three separate conspiracies; one between the smugglers and the middlemen, and one between the middlemen and each group of retailers. The evidence did

---

b. *United States v. Cole,* 704 F.2d 554 (11th Cir.1983), concluding "there was sufficient evidence of one overall conspiracy that each appellant joined."

c. *Rex v. Meyrick and Ribuffi,* 21 Crim.App. 94 (1929), rejecting the contention of separate conspiracies. But see *Regina v. Griffiths,* 49 Crim.App. 279 (1965).

not disclose any coöperation or communication between the smugglers and either group of retailers, or between the two groups of retailers themselves; however, the smugglers knew that the middlemen must sell to retailers, and the retailers knew that the middlemen must buy of importers of one sort or another. Thus the conspirators at one end of the chain knew that the unlawful business would not, and could not, stop with their buyers; and those at the other end knew that it had not begun with their sellers. That being true, a jury might have found that all the accused were embarked upon a venture, in all parts of which each was a participant, and an abettor in the sense that the success of that part with which he was immediately concerned, was dependent upon the success of the whole. That distinguishes the situation from that in *United States v. Peoni,* 2 Cir., 100 F.2d 401, where Peoni, the accused, did not know that Regno, his buyer, was to sell the counterfeit bills to Dorsey, and had no interest in whether he did, since Regno might equally well have passed them to innocent persons himself. It might still be argued that there were two conspiracies; one including the smugglers, the middlemen and the New York group, and the other, the smugglers, the middlemen and the Texas & Louisiana group, for there was apparently no privity between the two groups of retailers. That too would be fallacious. Clearly, quoad the smugglers, there was but one conspiracy, for it was of no moment to them whether the middlemen sold to one or more groups of retailers, provided they had a market somewhere. So too of any retailer; he knew that he was a necessary link in a scheme of distribution, and the others, whom he knew to be convenient to its execution, were as much parts of a single undertaking or enterprise as two salesmen in the same shop. We think therefore that there was only one conspiracy * * *.

UNITED STATES v. MICHELENA–OROVIO

United States Court of Appeals, Fifth Circuit, 1983.
719 F.2d 738.

Before CLARK, CHIEF JUDGE, BROWN, WISDOM, GEE, RUBIN, REAVLEY, POLITZ, RANDALL, TATE, JOHNSON, WILLIAMS, GARWOOD, JOLLY and HIGGINBOTHAM, CIRCUIT JUDGES.

RANDALL, CIRCUIT JUDGE:

[Undercover agents met with persons representing themselves as engaged in smuggling marijuana from Columbia. The agents were hired to provide ships to meet at sea other ships carrying marijuana and to transfer the cargo and then store it. When the smugglers said the mother ship had left Columbia, the agents alerted the Coast Guard. The described vessel, the Alex Luz, was boarded, and 363 bales of marijuana were found in the hold. The defendant, found aboard the Alex Luz, was charged with others with conspiracy to import marijuana into the United States and conspiracy to possess marijuana with intent to distribute it, and was convicted on both counts. A panel of the court of appeals held the evidence sufficient on the first count but not on the second count, 702 F.2d 496 (5th Cir.1983), and the court then agreed to rehear the case en banc.]

A. CONSPIRACY TO IMPORT.

Relying on the factors set forth in *United States v. Alfrey,* 620 F.2d 551, 556 (5th Cir.1980) (the length of the voyage, the quantity of contraband on board, and the relationship between captain and crew), the panel upheld Michelena–Orovio's conviction of conspiracy to import marijuana. We agree with the panel's conclusion that the government established more than the defendant's mere presence on board the ALEX LUZ, and that there was ample evidence to support the defendant's conviction on the importation count.

In particular, we note that Michelena–Orovio was arrested on board a small vessel that had just completed a relatively lengthy voyage from Colombia. The boat was laden with twelve tons of marijuana and reeked of its illicit cargo. Although the boat was a shrimping vessel, there was no fishing equipment aboard and no cargo other than the contraband. The marijuana was found in the ship's cargo hold. The cargo hatch was neither locked nor fastened, and there was open access to the cargo hold from the engine room of the vessel.

The ship's crew, including Michelena–Orovio, engaged in a concerted endeavor to elude capture and protect each other. When the Coast Guard first spotted the vessel, it had its lights reversed so that it appeared to be going in the direction opposite to its actual course, apparently in the hope that it would escape detection. The boat changed direction as soon as its crew became aware of the Coast Guard's presence. When the agents came on board, all eight crew members were waiting on deck with their bags packed, and all eight insisted that there was no captain aboard the vessel.

We are satisfied that a reasonable jury could have found Michelena–Orovio guilty beyond a reasonable doubt of conspiracy to import marijuana on the basis of this evidence. We turn then to our consideration of whether the evidence was also sufficient to support his conviction of conspiracy to possess the marijuana with intent to distribute it.

B. THE CONSPIRACY TO POSSESS WITH INTENT TO DISTRIBUTE.

1. Conflict In the Circuit.

In setting aside Michelena–Orovio's conviction of conspiracy to possess marijuana with intent to distribute it, the panel majority chose to follow *United States v. Cadena,* 585 F.2d 1252 (5th Cir.1978).

In *Cadena,* we reversed the conviction of the captain of a mother ship that had transferred a large quantity of marijuana to a smaller craft 200 miles south of the Florida coast. We noted:

> Unlike the situation presented by an ongoing enterprise, Cadena had no interest in or awareness of what plans, if any, had been reached to dispose of the marijuana once he reached these shores. Although a conspiracy to import facilitates a conspiracy to distribute, one cannot joint [sic] a conspiracy, whether by conduct or verbal accord, unless one knows that it has in fact been concocted * * *. [F]rom Cadena's perspective, it was not apparent that any accord had yet been reached, either tacitly or otherwise. * * *

Relying on a long line of Fifth Circuit cases that had held that the jury may infer intent to distribute the contraband from the size of the cache, the panel dissent argued that Michelena–Orovio's conviction on the second count should be affirmed. * * *

2. Narcotics Conspiracies: Has the Chain Been Broken?

Conspiracies to distribute narcotics have generally been considered to be prime examples of chain, or interconnected, conspiracies, in which a participant in a segment of the conspiracy may be convicted of participation in the whole.

* * * The question in this case is whether Michelena–Orovio's knowledge of and participation in this distribution scheme may be inferred from his participation in the scheme to supply twelve tons of marijuana from Colombia. * * *

The panel majority * * * reasoned that where there is prolonged cooperation, the seller may have a "stake" in the successful outcome of the entire scheme, but where there is nothing more than a "single or casual transaction," the supplier may be indifferent to the buyer's illicit purpose. The panel majority failed to recognize that Michelena–Orovio was not just a supplier of goods to the conspirators; he was himself a member of a segment of an extensive conspiracy to obtain marijuana and to distribute it in the United States.

* * * The absence of any legal market provides an additional link that supports the inference of the illegal importer's involvement in the conspiracy to possess his cargo with intent to distribute it. Michelena–Orovio would have had no job if there had been no plan made for the distribution of his cargo, and the twelve tons of marijuana would have been virtually worthless if there had been no conspiracy to distribute. * * * [C]ommon sense leads to the conclusion that an importer of that much marijuana knows perfectly well, and indeed relies on the fact, that there is a plan for the distribution of his cargo. * * *

Where a single act itself is one from which knowledge and participation may be inferred, the courts have not hesitated in upholding a defendant's conviction. * * * Michelena–Orovio's attempted importation of a huge quantity of marijuana is such an act. The importation of twelve tons of marijuana with an approximate street value of between four to six million dollars is not readily characterized as a "casual" transaction, even if the transaction is planned for one time only.

Contrasting Captain Cadena's situation with the "situation presented by an ongoing enterprise," the *Cadena* court surmised that the captain "had no interest in or awareness of what plans, if any, had been reached to dispose of the marijuana once he reached these shores." The facts of the case before us demonstrate the fallacy in this reasoning. According to Agent Donald's testimony, the conspiracy to distribute the marijuana came into existence long before Michelena–Orovio's boat left

Colombia; indeed, the ALEX LUZ apparently set sail under orders from the United States detailing the size of the cargo and the point of rendevous with the boats that were to take the cargo into the United States. The ALEX LUZ would never have left Colombia, and therefore Michelena–Orovio would have had no opportunity to earn his wages as a crew member, had there been no distributors in the United States placing orders for the contraband.

In summary, the fact that the defendant is involved in importing a huge quantity of marijuana into the United States may establish both the defendant's knowledge of and his joinder in the conspiracy to possess with intent to distribute. Since twelve tons of marijuana is more than mere mortals could personally consume in a lifetime, someone must have an intent to distribute the contraband. The defendant's awareness of the existence of the conspiracy flows from his participation in the conspiracy to import such a large quantity, for in the absence of any legal market in which to dispose of his wares, there is no reason to import the goods if there has been no plan made for their distribution. Similarly, the defendant's joinder or interest in the conspiracy to distribute may be inferred from his involvement in the importation scheme, for he would have no importing job if there was no conspiracy to distribute. Finally, the act of importation itself is an act in furtherance of the conspiracy to possess with intent to distribute, for there would be no distribution scheme if there were no marijuana to distribute.

3. The Mere Colombian Seaman.

Michelena–Orovio argues further that the absence of actual contact with the United States and his status as a "lowly non-English speaking seaman" further weakens the case against him. Michelena–Orovio's first argument concerns the fact that he, a Colombian national, was discovered on a foreign vessel on the high seas. He maintains that the evidence proved only that he was on a vessel loaded with marijuana headed for the United States, but that plans never actually called for his entry into this country. While the evidence might be sufficient to demonstrate that he knew that the vessel contained contraband and that he had joined in the conspiracy to bring it close enough to the United States for someone else to import it, he maintains that there is no evidence that he knew of or cared about the contraband's fate once it reached American shores.

The location and nationality of the vessel and its crew has no bearing on the issues in this case: knowledge of and participation in the conspiracy to possess marijuana with intent to distribute it. * * * Michelena–Orovio has never disputed the fact that the cargo's ultimate destination was the United States, a fact evidenced by Agent Donald's testimony about the Louisiana-based portion of the conspiracy.

Michelena–Orovio's nationality does not weaken the inference of his knowledge that a conspiracy to distribute the contraband must exist or of his knowing facilitation of that conspiracy. While a foreign national may not have the same detailed knowledge of our laws as a United States citizen might have, it would hardly be irrational for a jury to infer that Michelena–Orovio knew that the possession and distribution of marijuana in the United States is illegal. After all, both are also illegal in Colombia, and indeed, in most parts of the world. Therefore, to the extent that participation in the conspiracy to distribute may normally be inferred from participation in the conspiracy to import a large quantity of contraband, in light of the absence of a legal market for the imported goods, Michelena–Orovio's knowledge of and dependence on the existence of the distribution scheme are the same as those of his American counterpart.

We note further that a defendant's distribution of the contraband need not be made to the ultimate consumer in order to convict him of conspiracy to possess with intent to distribute; it may, in appropriate circumstances, be made to a coconspirator. * * *

Michelena–Orovio's final argument is that the inference of participation in the distribution scheme should not be applied to him because * * * he was simply a lowly member of the crew. * * *

Michelena–Orovio's lowly employee argument is in essence no more than a variation on the "mere presence" argument rejected in our discussion of the importation count. As was discussed in our disposition of the defendant's argument with regard to the importation count, more than mere presence was established in this case. The jury determined that the evidence demonstrated beyond a reasonable doubt that Michelena–Orovio was aware of and participated in the conspiracy to import a large quantity of marijuana. He was not a mere employee, but an employee aware of the nature of his business. It is well settled in this circuit that a conviction will not be reversed for lack of evidence merely because the defendant played only a minor role in the overall scheme. While the trial court might wish to take Michelena–Orovio's status as an employee into account in sentencing the defendant, his status as an employee does not weaken the inference of his knowledge of or complicity in the distribution scheme. * * *

The defendant's conviction on both counts is AFFIRMED.

WISDOM, CIRCUIT JUDGE, with whom RUBIN, POLITZ and TATE, CIRCUIT JUDGES, join, dissenting: * * *

The en banc opinion rests not on the evidence, but on a figure of speech: a conspiracy is a single chain and each conspirator is a link. This premise is a deceptively appealing shortcut to evidence overcoming the presumption of innocence. The notion that the conspiracy in this case is a chain begs the question. If one accepts the premise, of course each person performing a function relating to handling the contraband—from the grower in Colombia, to the first purchaser, to the middleman, to the crewmen on a ship transporting the contraband, down to the retailer—is guilty of conspiring to import and to "possess with intent to distribute" the contraband. No doubt there are some conspiracies that may aptly be described as a chain in which an individual conspirator is an essential link, although he may not have any idea of details of the scheme and may be unknown to some other conspirators. That is not this case. Here the United States did not charge a single massive venture to import, sell, and distribute, as it did in *United States v. Bruno*. The indictment has two separate counts, one for importation and another for distribution, because the facts point to two separate conspiracies, at least with respect to some of the participants, the most conspicuous of whom was seaman Michelena–Orovio.

In dealing with the difficult problem of narcotics control, Congress chose to distinguish between the crime of conspiring to import controlled drugs in violation of 21 U.S.C. § 963 (1976) and the crime of conspiring to possess such drugs with intent to distribute them in violation of 21 U.S.C. § 846 (1976). This is not to say that the same defendant can never be guilty of both offenses. But the effect of the majority decision is that a violation of section 963 now automatically entails a violation of section 846—whenever the principal basis for conviction under section 963 rests on the inference that the large amount of contraband seized necessarily shows intent to import on the part of

seamen on the vessel carrying the contraband. Such an inference is a non sequitur as to distribution, however, because it fails to take into account the element of *intent* necessary for proof of the crime.

In this case, one may reasonably infer from the size of the cargo knowledge and intent on the part of the defendant to participate in the conspiracy to import the contraband. But that inference cannot do double duty and show as well intent to distribute when the defendant had no role to play in distribution. With deference, I suggest that in the circumstances of this case, considering especially that Michelena–Orovio's role was to terminate on delivery of the marijuana to another vessel on the high seas, 150 to 200 miles from our shores, the only rational inference that can be drawn is that the defendant did *not* intend to play any part in any ongoing conspiracy to distribute the marijuana. The distribution in the United States, assuming that it was to take place in the United States, was to be handled by others.   *   *   *

The position I advocate is not contrary to congressional objectives in enacting drug control legislation. The real culprits in this case, as in many similar cases, are the American ringleaders who made arrangements with the grower or broker in Colombia and unquestionably arranged for the purchase, transportation, and distribution in this country. They are guilty of conspiracy to import and conspiracy to distribute and perhaps other conspiracies as well. But Michelena–Orovio, the lowly Colombian seaman on the edge of the conspiracy to import, should not be punished twice by expediently adding a tenuous inference to an attenuated inference. The majority has succumbed to an alluring figure of speech as a substitute for facts and reason.

SECTION 9. DURATION OF THE CONSPIRACY

GRUNEWALD v. UNITED STATES

Supreme Court of the United States, 1957.
353 U.S. 391, 77 S.Ct. 963, 1 L.Ed.2d 931.

MR. JUSTICE HARLAN delivered the opinion of the Court.

The three petitioners were convicted on Count 1 of an indictment brought under 18 U.S.C. § 371, 18 U.S.C.A. § 371 for conspiracy to defraud the United States with reference to certain tax matters.

* * *

In 1947 and 1948 two New York business firms, Patullo Modes and Gotham Beef Co., were under investigation by the Bureau of Internal Revenue for suspected fraudulent tax evasion. Through intermediaries, both firms established contact with Halperin, a New York attorney, and his associates in law practice. Halperin in turn conducted negotiations on behalf of these firms with Grunewald, an "influential" friend in Washington, and reported that Grunewald, for a large cash fee, would undertake to prevent criminal prosecution of the taxpayers. Grunewald then used his influence with Bolich, an official in the Bureau, to obtain "no prosecution" rulings [5] in the two tax cases. These rulings were handed down in 1948 and 1949. Grunewald, through Halperin, was subsequently paid $60,000 by Gotham and $100,000 by Patullo.

Subsequent activities of the conspirators were directed at concealing the irregularities in the disposition of the Patullo and Gotham cases. Bolich attempted to have the Bureau of Internal Revenue report on the Patullo case "doctored," and careful steps were taken to cover up the traces of the cash fees paid to Grunewald. In 1951 a congressional investigation was started by the King Committee of the House of Representatives; the conspirators felt themselves threatened and took steps to hide their traces. Thus Bolich caused the disappearance of certain records linking him to Grunewald, and the taxpayers were repeatedly warned to keep quiet. In 1952 the taxpayers and the conspirators were called before a Brooklyn grand jury. Halperin attempted to induce the taxpayers not to reveal the conspiracy, and Grunewald asked his secretary not to talk to the grand jury. These attempts at concealment were, however, in vain. The taxpayers and some of Halperin's associates revealed the entire scheme, and petitioners' indictment and conviction followed.

The first question before us is whether the prosecution of these petitioners on Count 1 of the indictment was barred by the applicable three-year statute of limitations.

The indictment in these cases was returned on October 25, 1954. It was therefore incumbent on the Government to prove that the conspiracy, as contemplated in the agreement as finally formulated, was still in existence on October 25, 1951, and that at least one overt act in furtherance of the conspiracy was performed after that date. For where substantiation of a conspiracy charge requires proof of an overt act, it must be shown both that the conspiracy still subsisted within the three years prior to the return of the indictment, and that at least one overt act in furtherance of the conspiratorial agreement was performed within that period. Hence, in both of these aspects, the crucial question in determining whether the statute of limitations has run is the scope of the conspiratorial agreement, for it is that which determines both the duration of the conspiracy, and whether the act relied on as an overt act may properly be

---

5. A "no prosecution" ruling is an internal decision by the investigative branch of the Bureau of Internal Revenue not to press criminal charges against a taxpayer.

regarded as in furtherance of the conspiracy.

Petitioners, in contending that this prosecution was barred by limitations, state that the object of the conspiratorial agreement was a narrow one: to obtain "no prosecution" rulings in the two tax cases. When these rulings were obtained, in October 1948 in the case of Gotham Beef, and in January 1949 in the case of Patullo Modes, the criminal object of the conspiracy, petitioners say, was attained and the conspirators' function ended. They argue, therefore, that the statute of limitations started running no later than January 1949, and that the prosecution was therefore barred by 1954, when the indictment was returned.

The Government counters with two principal contentions: First, it urges that even if the main object of the conspiracy was to obtain decisions from the Bureau of Internal Revenue not to institute criminal tax prosecutions—decisions obtained in 1948 and 1949—the indictment alleged, and the proofs showed, that the conspiracy also included as a subsidiary element an agreement to conceal the conspiracy to "fix" these tax cases, to the end that the conspirators would escape detection and punishment for their crime. Says the Government, "from the very nature of the conspiracy * * * there had to be, and was, from the outset a conscious, deliberate, agreement to conceal * * * each and every aspect of the conspiracy * * *." It is then argued that since the alleged conspiracy to conceal clearly continued long after the main criminal purpose of the conspiracy was accomplished, and since overt acts in furtherance of the agreement to conceal were performed well within the indictment period, the prosecution was timely.

Second, and alternatively, the Government contends that the central aim of the conspiracy was to obtain for these taxpayers, not merely a "no prosecution" ruling, but absolute immunity from tax prosecution; in other words, that the objectives of the conspiracy were not attained until 1952, when the statute of limitations ran on the tax cases which these petitioners undertook to "fix." The argument then is that since the conspiracy did not end until 1952, and since the 1949–1952 acts of concealment may be regarded as, at least in part, in furtherance of the objective of the conspirators to immunize the taxpayers from tax prosecution, the indictment was timely.

For reasons hereafter given, we hold that the Government's first contention must be rejected, and that as to its second, which the Court of Appeals accepted, a new trial must be ordered.

We think that the Government's first theory—that an agreement to conceal a conspiracy can, on facts such as these, be deemed part of the conspiracy and can extend its duration for the purposes of the statute of limitations—has already been rejected by this Court in *Krulewitch v. United States,* 336 U.S. 440, 69 S.Ct. 716, 718, 93 L.Ed. 790, and in *Lutwak v. United States,* 344 U.S. 604, 73 S.Ct. 481, 97 L.Ed. 593.

* * *

The crucial teaching of *Krulewitch* and *Lutwak* is that after the central criminal purposes of a conspiracy have been attained, a subsidiary conspiracy to conceal may not be implied from circumstantial evidence showing merely that the conspiracy was kept a secret and that the conspirators took care to cover up their crime in order to escape detection and punishment. As was there stated, allowing such a conspiracy to conceal to be inferred or implied from mere overt acts of concealment would result in a great widening of the scope of conspiracy prosecutions, since it would extend the life of a conspiracy indefinitely. Acts of covering up, even though done in the context of a mutually understood need for secrecy, cannot themselves constitute proof that concealment of the crime after its commission was part of the initial agreement among the conspirators. For every conspiracy is by its very nature secret; a case can hardly be supposed where men concert together for crime and advertise their purpose to the world. And again, every conspiracy will inevitably be followed by actions taken to cover the conspirators' traces. Sanctioning the Government's theory would for all practical purposes wipe out the statute of limitations in conspiracy cases, as well as extend indefinitely the time within which hearsay declarations will bind co-conspirators.

A reading of the record before us reveals that on the facts of this case the distinction between "actual" and "implied" conspiracies to conceal, as urged upon us by the Government, is no more than a verbal tour de force. True, in both *Krulewitch* and *Lutwak* there is language in the opinions stressing the fact that only an *implied* agreement to conceal was relied on. Yet when we look to the facts of the present cases, we see that the evidence from which the Government here asks us to deduce an "actual" agreement to conceal reveals nothing beyond that adduced in prior cases. What is this evidence? First, we have the fact that from the beginning the conspirators insisted on secrecy. Thus the identities of Grunewald and Bolich were sedulously kept from the taxpayers; careful steps were taken to hide the conspiracy from an independent law firm which was also working on Patullo's tax problems; and the taxpayers were told to make sure that their books did not reflect the large cash payments made to Grunewald. Secondly, after the "no prosecution" rulings were obtained, we have facts showing that this secrecy was still maintained. Thus, a deliberate attempt was made to make the above-mentioned independent law firm believe that it was *its*

(quite legitimate) efforts which produced the successful ruling. Finally, we have the fact that great efforts were made to conceal the conspiracy when the danger of exposure appeared. For example, Bolich got rid of certain records showing that he had used Grunewald's hotel suite in Washington; Patullo's accountant was persuaded to lie to the grand jury concerning a check made out to an associate of the conspirators; Grunewald attempted to persuade his secretary not to talk to the grand jury; and the taxpayers were repeatedly told by Halperin and his associates to keep quiet.

We find in all this nothing more than what was involved in *Krulewitch,* that is, (1) a criminal conspiracy which is carried out in secrecy; (2) a continuation of the secrecy after the accomplishment of the crime; and (3) desperate attempts to cover up after the crime begins to come to light; and so we cannot agree that this case does not fall within the ban of those prior opinions. * * *

By no means does this mean that acts of concealment can never have significance in furthering a criminal conspiracy. But a vital distinction must be made between acts of concealment done in furtherance of the *main* criminal objectives of the conspiracy, and acts of concealment done after these central objectives have been attained, for the purpose only of covering up after the crime. Thus the Government argues in its brief that "in the crime of kidnapping, the acts of conspirators in hiding while waiting for ransom would clearly be planned acts of concealment which would be in aid of the conspiracy to kidnap. So here, there can be no doubt that * * * all acts of concealment, whether to hide the identity of the conspirators or the action theretofore taken, were unquestionably in furtherance of the initial conspiracy * * *." We do not think the analogy is valid. Kidnapers in hiding, waiting for ransom, commit acts of concealment in furtherance of the objectives of the conspiracy itself, just as repainting a stolen car would be in furtherance of a conspiracy to steal; in both cases the successful accomplishment of the crime necessitates concealment. More closely analogous to our case would be conspiring kidnapers who cover their traces after the main conspiracy is finally ended—i.e., after they have abandoned the kidnaped person and then take care to escape detection. In the latter case, as here, the acts of covering up can by themselves indicate nothing more than that the conspirators do not wish to be apprehended—a concomitant, certainly, of every crime since Cain attempted to conceal the murder of Abel from the Lord. * * *

In view of how the case was submitted to the jury, we are also unable to accept the Government's second theory for avoiding the statute of limitations. * * *

The Court of Appeals accepted this theory of the case in affirming these convictions. * * *

We find the legal theory of the Court of Appeals unexceptionable. * * *

If, therefore, the jury could have found that the aim of the conspiratorial agreement was to protect the taxpayers from tax prosecution, and that the overt acts occurring in the indictment period were in furtherance of that aim, we would affirm. We do not think, however, that we may safely assume that the jury so found, for we cannot agree with the Court of Appeals' holding that this theory of the case was adequately submitted to the jury. * * *

Notes and Questions

1. Comment, 17 Ga.L.Rev. 539, 556 (1983), observes: "The Court gave no rationale for requiring direct evidence under the 'express original agreement' theory other than the repetition of its reasoning in *Krulewitch* and *Lutwak*. Without the

benefit of clear reasoning, federal courts have subsequently misapplied and even ignored the direct evidence requirement in situations that by analogy to *Grunewald* would appear to require direct evidence."

2. In *United States v. Girard,* 744 F.2d 1170 (5th Cir.1984), Girard was charged with conspiracy to defraud the United States. The indictment stated that Girard, who contracted with the Housing Authority of New Orleans to replace space heaters in a housing complex, funds for which were provided by the U.S. Department of Housing and Urban Development, conspired with Housing Authority employees to rig the bidding process. The contract was signed on March 16, 1977; the work was accepted as complete on Nov. 22, 1977; a check to Girard as final payment was received March 13, 1978, but a June 7, 1978 check for $620 later arrived with an invoice identifying it as an adjustment to the March 13 payment. Girard's last payment to a co-conspirator was May 21, 1978. On the issue of whether the 5–year statute of limitations had run by June 3, 1983, the court concluded:

"Girard's contention that the purpose of the conspiracy ended with the award of the contract represents an overly narrow construction of the alleged agreement. His interest lay not in securing the contract itself, but in obtaining the money thereunder. The payments to his initial coconspirators were not made until after Girard Plumbing had received its first payment under the contract. Thus the conspiracy continued at least until Girard had received the full monetary benefits under the contract, including the $620 payment on June 7, 1978.

"Our earlier decision, *United States v. Davis,* 533 F.2d 921 (1976), does not affect the validity of this conclusion. In *Davis,* we held that a conspiracy to make false statements to a government agency ended with the last false statement, not when the government acted on the false statements to award the desired contract. According to the *Davis* indictment, the sole object of the conspiracy was to make false statements in violation of 18 U.S.C. § 1001. Given the narrow scope of the particular indictment, we could not say that the obtaining of the contract was an objective of the conspiracy as charged. We specifically noted, however, that the indictment could not be read as charging the defendants with a conspiracy to defraud the United States under 18 U.S.C. § 371. In the present case, the broader scope of the indictment allows us to accept the government's allegations that the purposes of the conspiracy included the receipt of the funds.

"Our determination that the conspiracy continued until Girard had realized fully his anticipated economic benefits is consistent with the law of other circuits. The Second Circuit, in *United States v. Mennuti,* 679 F.2d 1032 (2d Cir.1982), a prosecution under 18 U.S.C. § 371 for conspiracy to commit mail fraud, ruled that a conspiracy to fraudulently obtain insurance funds by burning a house did not end when the insurance check was issued. Instead it continued until each participant had received his agreed-upon payoff. Mennuti's compensation was the right to purchase the property after the fire at a reduced price. Accordingly, the conspiracy continued after the receipt of the insurance check and the execution of the contract giving Mennuti the right to purchase the land until the sale actually closed six months later. This closing was the only event within the statutory time period.

* * *

"In deciding *Mennuti,* the Second Circuit relied heavily on *United States v. Walker,* 653 F.2d at 1343. Walker was convicted under 18 U.S.C. § 371 for bid-rigging in connection with a federal timber sale. On appeal, he argued that the charge was time-barred because the only purpose of

the conspiracy was to secure the contract, which had been awarded more than five years before his indictment. The Ninth Circuit rejected this contention, holding that the conspiracy continued after the completion of the central objective, the securing of the contract, because it encompassed an additional objective, the continued acquisition and division of profits obtained by defrauding the United States.

"The defendant in *United States v. Helmich,* 704 F.2d 547 (11th Cir.1983), the defendant was indicted for conspiracy to commit espionage. He contended that his 1981 indictment was untimely because it did not charge him with transmitting information after 1964. The indictment, however, also alleged that the conspiracy included an agreement for the Soviet Union to pay Helmich and that he had travelled to Canada in 1980 to collect outstanding compensation. Therefore, the conspiracy continued until Helmich received his anticipated economic benefits in 1980. The payoff, which was the last overt act under the conspiracy, triggered the limitations period.

"Under the terms of the agreement alleged here, each of Girard's coconspirators was to receive a set payoff on specified dates between March 30, 1977 and March 21, 1978. The economic benefit for Girard was to be the funds obtained under the illegally secured contract. He did not receive this benefit on March 16, 1977, when the contract was awarded, but as the Housing Authority issued partial payments between March 30, 1977 and June 7, 1978. Girard's contention that the June 7 check was not a payment but an account adjustment is irrelevant. The accounting terminology used by the Housing Authority on its invoices is not controlling. Girard received these funds after signing an undated form certifying that the $620 was the balance due under the contract. Therefore, the money was part of the economic benefit which Girard sought and received under the alleged terms of the conspiracy.

"It is true, as the district court noted, that there was no plan to divide the $620 between the coconspirators after its receipt. The fact that Girard was to retain the entire sum himself, however, does not mean that obtaining the funds was not an objective of the conspiracy. As discussed above, according to the indictment, each coconspirator received a payment after payments on the contract had begun and Girard received the rest of the funds. The mere fact that the alleged agreement defined the payoff terms in this manner, instead of providing each coconspirator with a percentage of each Housing Authority payment, does not defeat our determination that one of the purposes of the conspiracy alleged here was to obtain all funds possible under the contract. The conspiracy continued until June 7, 1978 when the last $620 was paid."

3. 18 U.S.C.A. § 2312 makes it an offense to transport in interstate commerce a vehicle known to be stolen; 18 U.S.C.A. § 2313 makes it an offense to receive, conceal, store, barter, sell or dispose of a motor vehicle which has moved in interstate commerce and which is known to be stolen. Yow and Strand have been charged with conspiracy to violate those statutes. The government wishes to offer as part of its case the testimony of two witnesses: (i) Strand's brother, who will testify that Strand told him, a few days after receiving the vehicle at his Nebraska shop and before the car was dismantled, that Yow had delivered it from California; (ii) Scott, who will testify that several months after Strand received the car and at a time when only a few parts of the auto remained to be disposed of, Strand told him Yow had delivered the car from California.[a] What result upon Yow's objec-

tion that such hearsay testimony is not admissible against him because these declarations of his alleged co-conspirator Strand were not made "during and in furtherance of the conspiracy"?

4. Garcia, Pain and Yslas burglarized an elderly woman's home at about 2 a.m. They put a sewing machine, clock, radio, TV and other items into Garcia's car and later dropped them off at Garcia's house, but at about 7 a.m. Garcia and Pain dropped Yslas off at his house and gave him the TV to sell for himself so that it could be determined whether that would provide him with his fair "share" of the spoils. Later that day, Garcia's sister confronted him with a newspaper account of the burglary and death by skull fracture of the victim, to which Garcia responded he was involved only in the burglary. Garcia and Pain then went to Yslas' house; Garcia said he wanted to get rid of the stolen property, and Yslas said he would take it. Garcia and Pain returned to Garcia's house to get the property, and while they were there Garcia's sister confronted Pain, who said Yslas had hit the woman with a tool. Yslas was not home when Garcia and Pain brought the stolen property to his residence, so they discarded it in the desert. Yslas tried to sell the TV to some friends without success. At Yslas' trial for murder, the prosecution offers against him Pain's statement to Garcia's sister on the theory that it is admissible under the evidence rule which says statements by a coconspirator "during the course of and in furtherance of the conspiracy" may be received in evidence. What should the judge rule?[b]

5. After Clyde purchased an auto repair shop, he encountered serious financial problems. In January of 1968, Lauria and Smith loaned him $2,000, to be paid back over a 40–week period and with a "vig"

a. A variation on *United States v. Yow*, 465 F.2d 1328 (8th Cir.1972).

b. *State v. Yslas*, 139 Ariz. 60, 676 P.2d 1118 (1984), holding the statement inadmissible.

(vigorish or excessive interest) of $4,000. Carvelli was to serve as collector. On April 10, 1968, Lauria, Smith and Carvelli visited Clyde's shop and threatened to burn it down if he didn't pay. On May 8, Lauria and Smith came to Clyde's home and told his wife something might happen to their children if the payments were not made. None of this violated federal law, for it was not until May 29, 1968, that the Consumer Credit Protection Act became effective. Clyde made payments to Carvelli in May, June and July, but in late July the Clydes fled their home in the middle of the night to escape further payments. Lauria and Smith were convicted of conspiracy to violate the CCPA, which prohibits knowing participation in the use of any extortionate means to collect any extension of credit. On appeal, they point out that there is no evidence of any threats to the person or property of the Clydes occurring after the effective date of the statute.[c] What result?

6. Note, 75 Colum.L.Rev. 1122, 1164–67 (1975): "The duration of a criminal agreement is important primarily for statute of limitations purposes. The [Model Penal Code] essentially codifies existing case law on the subject. According to MPC § 5.03(7)(a), 'conspiracy is a continuing course of conduct which terminates when the crime or crimes which are its object are committed or the agreement that they be committed is abandoned by the defendant and by those with whom he conspired.' Perhaps because prior decisions have left the key issues reasonably well settled, most state statutes say nothing about conspiracy's time dimension. Eleven states include provisions which track the MPC language, while Maine, North

Dakota, Massachusetts, Vermont, and H.R. 333 add 'frustration' to 'success' and 'abandonment' in the catalog of means by which a conspiracy may reach its conclusion. This latter modification seems reasonable, unless frustration is too broadly defined. Where circumstances simply make the criminal object slightly more difficult to achieve, a conspiracy should not be regarded as terminated. On the other hand, when an intended victim permanently relocates in a distant land or when new security procedures are instituted which make effective implementation of a criminal plan virtually impossible, a permissible inference might be drawn that a conspiracy no longer continues. Of course, evidence would be required to the effect that the conspirators were aware of the relevant developments and that they had not transferred their criminal purpose to another object. In point of fact, the leading case cited in support of the 'frustration' alternative involved parties to a criminal agreement already in custody, and thus left little doubt that the participants would proceed no further.[242] * * *

"The MPC contains a further pronouncement on the duration of conspiracy. Section 5.03(7)(b) states the 'generally accepted' rule that 'abandonment is presumed if neither the defendant nor anyone with whom he conspired does any overt act in pursuance of the conspiracy during the applicable period of limitation.' Though like provisions characterize conspiracy statutes in but few jurisdictions, no implication should be drawn that the rule does not enjoy more widespread acceptance. The comment to Missouri's proposed statute clearly demonstrates that the draftsmen expected the 'presumed aban-

---

c. Based on *United States v. Smith,* 464 F.2d 1129 (2d Cir.1972), affirming the conviction.

242. *Fiswick v. United States,* 329 U.S. 211, 215–17 (1946). For illustrations of the fact that claims of frustration will not be readily sustained, see *United States v. Franzese,* 392 F.2d 954, 963–64 (2d Cir.1968) (conspiracy to rob bank

continued despite arrest of some participants), vacated on other grounds as to defendant Franzese only sub nom. *Giordano v. United States,* 394 U.S. 310 (1969); and *United States v. Goldstein,* 135 F.2d 359, 361 (2d Cir.1943) (conspiracy to defraud government of liquor taxes continued despite seizure of still).

donment' rule to prevail, despite their omission of the MPC language. While closely akin to their MPC counterpart, corresponding sections in H.R. 333, North Dakota law, and pending Vermont legislation may impose a greater rigidity than the ALI reporters thought desirable. Rather than establishing a presumption of abandonment in the absence of an overt act during a given time period, these statutes provide that, '[a] conspiracy *shall be deemed* to have been abandoned if no overt act to effect its objectives has been committed by any conspirator during the applicable period of limitations.' If such legislation is construed to create an irrebuttable presumption, then lack of a sufficiently recent overt act would be fatal to a conspiracy prosecution, despite the possible availability of other evidence of the criminal agreement's continuing vitality. Such an outcome would not be endorsed by the MPC framers."

SECTION 10. WITHDRAWAL

NOTE, CONSPIRACY: STATUTORY REFORM SINCE THE MODEL PENAL CODE

75 Colum.L.Rev. 1122, 1168–72 (1975).

The rationale normally advanced for statutory inclusion of a renunciation defense involves two complementary ideas. First, repudiation of criminal purpose is said to indicate lack of firm antisocial intent, and hence the absence of any real public danger. Secondly, the theory runs, "the law should provide a means for encouraging persons to abandon courses of criminal· activity which they have already undertaken." As a criminal plan nears fruition, the former notion diminishes in persuasive power, while the latter gains.

* * *

Whatever the proper underlying justification, [*Model Penal Code*] § 5.03(6) provides a defense to a conspiracy indictment if "the actor, after conspiring to commit a crime, thwarted the success of the conspiracy, under circumstances manifesting a complete and voluntary renunciation of his criminal purpose." Twenty state statutes and both versions of the proposed Federal Criminal Code contain similar provisions. Under the language just quoted, the individual claiming the defense must have prevented commission of the object offense. Failure of the criminal scheme due to fortuitous natural causes or efficient, independent police work will not protect a defendant who contends he renounced. Pending New Jersey legislation would make the requirements of renunciation even more stringent. To sustain the defense under prospective New Jersey law, an actor would need to block not only his co-conspirators' consummation of the *object* offense(s), but also their commission of *any* substantive offense in furtherance of the conspiracy. Furthermore, the proposed New Jersey statute would insist on notification of a law enforcement officer, irrespective of any demonstration of a particular individual's effectiveness in defusing a criminal agreement through independent action. These additional burdens seem unduly onerous. If a person otherwise guilty of conspiracy should recant and foil the agreement of which he was once a part, the method by which he accomplishes this task should be immaterial to his criminal liability. Moreover, availability of the renunciation defense should not be premised on prevention of all instrumental substantive offenses, no matter how minor in comparison with the conspiracy's object crime(s). To so limit the potential applicability of the defense is to greatly reduce renunciation's utility, especially with respect to large, complex criminal enterprises, which often entail a series of relatively insignificant, but nevertheless criminal, steps before attainment of the ultimate illegal objective. New Jersey's proposed provision would remove the primary incentive for renunciation, immediately upon commission of any substantive offense by a co-conspirator, regardless of how distant the larger goals of the criminal scheme might remain.

An attractive alternative to the MPC outline of renunciation has been endorsed by eight states. With slight variations of phrasing, the relevant statutory sections would allow a defense to conspiracy where an actor "gave a timely warning to law enforcement authorities or made a substantial effort to prevent the performance of the criminal conduct contemplated" by the agreement. Admittedly, difficult issues of fact might be raised by such a formula. Hawaii has tried to anticipate some of these problems by enacting more detailed specifications for determining whether the renunciation prerequisites have been met.[274] A more serious theoretical objection to this minority modification of the MPC is also possible. If the renunciation defense is regarded as essentially a form of statutory grace conferred on deserving transgressors, then the more limited applicability of the MPC definition may be justified. To put it another way, since renunciation by its very nature comprehends absolution for an already-completed conspiracy offense, the defense may legitimately be restricted to those occasions when an actor succeeds in protecting society from the consequences of his prior criminal agreement. Where prevention efforts are unavailing, even a reformed conspirator will not be heard, under this line of reasoning, to gainsay his part in the illegal scheme. In defense of the minority position, on the other hand, one might maintain that the law should not demand more than can reasonably be expected. In par-

ticular, criminal liability should not be imposed because of police ineptitude or other happenstance factors which deprive an actor's attempts to defuse a conspiracy of their ordinary effectiveness. The Hawaii comments expand on this argument.

> It would not be reasonable to hold the defendant strictly liable for his inchoate activities by imposing liability where unforeseeable circumstances thwart prevention of the substantive offense. If the defendant's renunciation is effective but for circumstances not reasonably foreseeable, that is all that may be asked. Moreover, to impose strict liability in such situations would be to ignore the rationales for allowing the defense of renunciation. If the defendant's renunciation is effective under all foreseeable circumstances, he has evidenced a sufficient lack of firmness in his criminal purpose, and the law has succeeded as far as is rationally possible in encouraging him to abandon such purpose.

Finally, fifteen states have adhered to the common law wisdom that the conspiracy offense is completed on agreement (with the performance of an overt act, if necessary), and that no subsequent events should serve to erase a previously committed crime. In embracing this view, these jurisdictions may have demonstrated their conception of conspiracy as a weapon against group criminal activity rather than as inchoate crime. Conceding the desirability of aiding public prosecutors in their struggle with large-scale corruption and organized crime, this end should not be achieved by the elimination of a renunciation defense for the extremely preparatory behavior governed by conspiracy statutes.

---

274. Under Hawaii § 530(5), warning is not "timely" unless "the authorities, reasonably acting upon the warning, would have the opportunity to prevent the conduct or result." Similarly, an effort is not "reasonable" (Hawaii substitutes

this term for "substantial") unless "the defendant, under reasonably foreseeable circumstances, would have prevented the conduct or result." * * *

Notes and Questions

1. Comparing the Model Penal Code, New Jersey, Hawaii and common law positions, which is preferable? Consider in this regard these comments to the Maryland Code reported in the Note at 1168: "The arguments utilized by the [Model Penal] Code framers seem somewhat divorced from reality. Availability or unavailability of the defense would seem to have little impact on conduct. The judgment should turn on whether the desirability of maintaining intellectual consistency by exonerating a relatively small number of persons where renunciation may be taken as evidence of reduced dangerousness of acts or persons is outweighed by the desirability of simplifying the Code provisions and the issues at trial." What then of the Georgia approach, discussed in *Sak v. State*, 129 Ga.App. 301, 199 S.E.2d 628 (1973), of permitting the defense only if the withdrawal occurs before any conspirator performs an overt act?

2. Even if withdrawal is not recognized as a defense to the conspiracy charge, it may be important for other purposes, namely: (i) preventing the admission into evidence against the withdrawn conspirator of acts and statements of his co-conspirators occurring after his withdrawal; (ii) starting the running of the statute of limitations as to the participation in the conspiracy by the withdrawn conspirator; and (iii) in those jurisdictions following the rule of *Pinkerton v. United States*, p. 732 of this Book, that conspirators are accountable for *all* crimes committed by their co-conspirators in furtherance of the conspiracy, preventing post-withdrawal crimes from being so attributed.

3. Should the test for effective withdrawal be different for these purposes? In *United States v. United States Gypsum Co.*, 438 U.S. 422, 98 S.Ct. 2864, 57 L.Ed.2d 854 (1978), where the issue was whether abandonment presented a statute of limita-

tions bar, the trial judge instructed: "To withdraw, a defendant must have affirmatively notified each other member of the conspiracy he will no longer participate in the undertaking so they understand they can no longer expect his participation or acquiescence, or he must make disclosures of the illegal scheme to law enforcement officials." The Supreme Court concluded the instruction was "unnecessarily confining": "Nothing that we have been able to find in the case law suggests, much less commands, that such confining blinders be placed on the jury's freedom to consider evidence regarding the continuing participation of alleged conspirators in the charged conspiracy. Affirmative acts inconsistent with the object of the conspiracy and communicated in a manner reasonably calculated to reach co-conspirators have generally been regarded as sufficient to establish withdrawal or abandonment."

SECTION 11. THE PLURALITY REQUIREMENT

IANNELLI v. UNITED STATES

Supreme Court of the United States, 1975.
420 U.S. 770, 95 S.Ct. 1284, 43 L.Ed.2d 616.

MR. JUSTICE POWELL delivered the opinion of the Court. * * *

Petitioners were tried under a six-count indictment alleging a variety of federal gambling offenses. Each of the eight petitioners, along with seven unindicted co-conspirators and six codefendants, was charged, *inter alia*, with conspiring to violate and violating 18 U.S.C. § 1955, a federal gambling statute making it a crime for five or more persons to conduct, finance, manage, supervise, direct, or own a gambling business prohibited by state law. Each petitioner was convicted of both offenses and each was sentenced under both the substantive and conspiracy counts. The Court of Appeals for the Third Circuit affirmed, finding that a recognized exception to Wharton's Rule permitted prosecution and punishment for both offenses.

*   *   *

Wharton's Rule owes its name to Francis Wharton, whose treatise on criminal law identified the doctrine and its fundamental rationale:

> "When to the idea of an offense plurality of agents is logically necessary, conspiracy, which assumes the voluntary accession of a person to a crime of such a character that it is aggravated by a plurality of agents, cannot be maintained. * * * In other words, when the law says, 'a combination between two persons to effect a particular end shall be called, if the end be effected, by a certain name,' it is not lawful for the prosecution to call it by some other name; and when the law says, such an offense—e.g., adultery—shall have a certain punishment, it is not lawful for the prosecution to evade this limitation by indicting the offense as conspiracy." 2 F. Wharton, *Criminal Law* § 1604, p. 1862 (12th ed. 1932).

The Rule has been applied by numerous courts, state and federal alike. *   *   *

The classic formulation of Wharton's Rule requires that the conspiracy indictment be dismissed before trial. *   *   * Federal courts earlier adhered to this literal interpretation and thus sustained demurrers to conspiracy indictments. More recently, however, some federal courts have * * * held that the Rule's purposes can be served equally effectively by permitting the prosecution to charge both offenses and instructing the jury that a conviction for the substantive offense necessarily precludes conviction for the conspiracy.

Federal courts likewise have disagreed as to the proper application of the recognized "third-party exception," which renders Wharton's Rule inapplicable when the conspiracy involves the cooperation of a greater number of persons than is required

for commission of the substantive offense. In the present case, the Third Circuit concluded that the third-party exception permitted prosecution because the conspiracy involved more than the five persons required to commit the substantive offense. The Seventh Circuit reached the opposite result, however, reasoning that since § 1955 also covers gambling activities involving more than five persons, the third-party exception is inapplicable.

The Courts of Appeals are at odds even over the fundamental question whether Wharton's Rule ever applies to a charge for conspiracy to violate § 1955.

*   *   *

Traditionally the law has considered conspiracy and the completed substantive offense to be separate crimes. *   *   * Thus, it is well recognized that in most cases separate sentences can be imposed for the conspiracy to do an act and for the subsequent accomplishment of that end. Indeed, the Court has even held that the conspiracy can be punished more harshly than the accomplishment of its purpose.

The consistent rationale of this long line of decisions rests on the very nature of the crime of conspiracy. This Court repeatedly has recognized that a conspiracy poses distinct dangers quite apart from those of the substantive offense.

> "This settled principle derives from the reason of things in dealing with socially reprehensible conduct: collective criminal agreement—partnership in crime—presents a greater potential threat to the public than individual delicts. Concerted action both increases the likelihood that the criminal object will be successfully attained and decreases the probability that the individuals involved will depart from their path of criminality. Group association for criminal purposes often, if not normally, makes possible the attainment of ends more complex than those which one

criminal could accomplish. Nor is the danger of a conspiratorial group limited to the particular end toward which it has embarked. Combination in crime makes more likely the commission of crimes unrelated to the original purpose for which the group was formed. In sum, the danger which a conspiracy generates is not confined to the substantive offense which is the immediate aim of the enterprise." * * *

The historical difference between the conspiracy and its end has led this Court consistently to attribute to Congress "a tacit purpose—in the absence of any inconsistent expression—to maintain a long-established distinction between offenses essentially different,—a distinction whose practical importance in the criminal law is not easily overestimated." Wharton's Rule announces an exception to this general principle. * * *

This Court's previous discussions of Wharton's Rule have not elaborated upon its precise role in federal law. In most instances, the Court simply has identified the Rule and described it in terms similar to those used in Wharton's treatise. But in *United States v. Holte,* 236 U.S. 140, 35 S.Ct. 271, 59 L.Ed. 504 (1915), the sole case in which the Court felt compelled specifically to consider the applicability of Wharton's Rule, it declined to adopt an expansive definition of its scope. In that case, Wharton's Rule was advanced as a bar to prosecution of a female for conspiracy to violate the Mann Act. Rejecting that contention, the Court adopted a narrow construction of the Rule that focuses on the statutory requirements of the substantive offense rather than the evidence offered to prove those elements at trial:

> "The substantive offence might be committed without the woman's consent; for instance, if she were drugged or taken by force. Therefore the decisions that it is impossible to turn the concurrence necessary to effect certain crimes such as bigamy or duelling into a conspiracy to commit them do not apply."

* * *

This Court's prior decisions indicate that the broadly formulated Wharton's Rule does not rest on principles of double jeopardy. Instead, it has current vitality only as a judicial presumption, to be applied in the absence of legislative intent to the contrary. The classic Wharton's Rule offenses—adultery, incest, bigamy, duelling—are crimes that are characterized by the general congruence of the agreement and the completed substantive offense. The parties to the agreement are the only persons who participate in commission of the substantive offense,[15] and the immediate consequences of the crime rest on the

---

15. An exception to the Rule generally is thought to apply in the case in which the conspiracy involves more persons than are required for commission of the substantive offense. For example, while the two persons who commit adultery cannot normally be prosecuted both for that offense and for conspiracy to commit it, the third-party exception would permit the conspiracy charge where a "matchmaker"—the third party—had conspired with the principals to encourage commission of the substantive offense. The rationale supporting this exception appears to be that the addition of a third party enhances the dangers presented by the crime. Thus, it is thought that the legislature would not have intended to preclude punishment for a combination of greater dimension than that required to commit the substantive offense.

Our determination that Congress authorized prosecution and conviction for both offenses in all cases makes it unnecessary to decide whether the exception to Wharton's Rule could properly be applied to conspiracies to violate § 1955 involving more than five persons. We note, however, that the statute and its legislative history seem to suggest that it could not. By its terms, § 1955 reaches gambling activities involving "five or more persons." Moreover, the legislative history of the statute indicates that Congress assumed that it would generally be applied in cases in which more than the statutory minimum number were involved. It thus would seem anomalous to conclude that Congress intended the substantive offense to subsume the conspiracy in one case but not in the other.

parties themselves rather than on society at large. Finally, the agreement that attends the substantive offense does not appear likely to pose the distinct kinds of threats to society that the law of conspiracy seeks to avert. It cannot, for example, readily be assumed that an agreement to commit an offense of this nature will produce agreements to engage in a more general pattern of criminal conduct.

The conduct proscribed by § 1955 is significantly different from the offenses to which the Rule traditionally has been applied. Unlike the consequences of the classic Wharton's Rule offenses, the harm attendant upon the commission of the substantive offense is not restricted to the parties to the agreement. Large-scale gambling activities seek to elicit the participation of additional persons—the bettors—who are parties neither to the conspiracy nor to the substantive offense that results from it. Moreover, the parties prosecuted for the conspiracy need not be the same persons who are prosecuted for commission of the substantive offense. An endeavor as complex as a large-scale gambling enterprise might involve persons who have played appreciably different roles, and whose level of culpability varies significantly. It might, therefore, be appropriate to prosecute the owners and organizers of large-scale gambling operations both for the conspiracy and for the substantive offense but to prosecute the lesser participants only for the substantive offense. Nor can it fairly be maintained that agreements to enter into large-scale gambling activities are not likely to generate additional agreements to engage in other criminal endeavors. The legislative history of § 1955 provides documented testimony to the contrary.

Wharton's Rule applies only to offenses that *require* concerted criminal activity, a plurality of criminal agents. In such cases, a closer relationship exists between the conspiracy and the substantive offense because *both* require collective criminal activity. The substantive offense therefore presents some of the same threats that the law of conspiracy normally is thought to guard against, and it cannot automatically be assumed that the Legislature intended the conspiracy and the substantive offense to remain as discrete crimes upon consummation of the latter. Thus, absent legislative intent to the contrary, the Rule supports a presumption that the two merge when the substantive offense is proved.[18]

But a legal principle commands less respect when extended beyond the logic that supports it. In this case, the significant differences in characteristics and consequences of the kinds of offenses that gave rise to Wharton's Rule and the activities proscribed by § 1955 counsel against attributing significant weight to the presumption the Rule erects. More important, as the Rule is essentially an aid to the determination of legislative intent, it must defer to a discernible legislative judgment. We turn now to that inquiry.   *   *   *

In drafting the Organized Crime Control Act of 1970, Congress manifested its clear awareness of the distinct nature of a conspiracy and the substantive offenses that might constitute its immediate end. The identification of "special offenders" in Title X speaks both to persons who commit specific felonies during the course of a pattern of criminal activity and to those who enter into conspiracies to engage in patterns of criminal conduct. And Congress specifically utilized the law of conspiracy to discourage organized crime's corruption of state and local officials for

---

18. We do not consider initial dismissal of the conspiracy charge to be required in such a case. When both charges are considered at a single trial, the real problem is the avoidance of dual

punishment. This problem is analogous to that presented by the threat of conviction for a greater and a lesser included offense, and should be treated in a similar manner.

the purpose of facilitating gambling enterprises.

But the § 1955 definition of "gambling activities" pointedly avoids reference to conspiracy or to agreement, the essential element of conspiracy. Moreover, the limited § 1955 definition is repeated in identifying the reach of § 1511, a provision that specifically prohibits conspiracies. Viewed in this context, and in light of the numerous references to conspiracies throughout the extensive consideration of the Organized Crime Control Act, we think that the limited congressional definition of "gambling activities" in § 1955 is significant. The Act is a carefully crafted piece of legislation. Had Congress intended to foreclose the possibility of prosecuting conspiracy offenses under § 371 by merging them into prosecutions under § 1955, we think it would have so indicated explicitly. It chose instead to define the substantive offense punished by § 1955 in a manner that fails specifically to invoke the concerns which underlie the law of conspiracy.

Nor do we find merit to the argument that the congressional requirement of participation of "five or more persons" as an element of the substantive offense under § 1955 represents a legislative attempt to merge the conspiracy and the substantive offense into a single crime. The history of the Act instead reveals that this requirement was designed to restrict federal intervention to cases in which federal interests are substantially implicated. * * * Recognizing that gambling activities normally are matters of state concern, Congress indicated a desire to extend federal criminal jurisdiction to reach only "those who are engaged in an illicit gambling business of major proportions." * * *

In expressing these conclusions we do not imply that the distinct nature of the crimes of conspiracy to violate and violation of § 1955 should prompt prosecutors to seek separate convictions in every case, or judges necessarily to sentence in a manner that imposes an additional sanction for conspiracy to violate § 1955 and the consummation of that end. Those decisions fall within the sound discretion of each, and should be rendered in accordance with the facts and circumstances of a particular case. We conclude only that Congress intended to retain these traditional options. Neither Wharton's Rule nor the history and structure of the Organized Crime Control Act of 1970 persuade us to the contrary.

Affirmed.

MR. JUSTICE DOUGLAS, dissenting. * * *

In my view the Double Jeopardy Clause forbids simultaneous prosecution under §§ 1955 and 371. * * *

* * * The very same evidence was relied upon to establish the conspiracy—a conspiracy, apparently, enduring as long as the substantive offense continued, and provable by the same acts that established the violation of § 1955. Thus the very same transactions among the defendants gave rise to criminal liability under both statutes.

Under these circumstances, I would require the prosecutor to choose between § 371 and § 1955 as the instrument for criminal punishment. * * *

Apart from my views of the Double Jeopardy Clause, I would reverse on the additional ground that Congress did not intend to permit simultaneous convictions under §§ 371 and 1955 for the same acts. * * *

Conviction under § 1955 satisfies, in my view, the social concerns that punishment for conspiracy is supposed to address. The provision was aimed not at the single unlawful wager but at "syndicated gambling." Congress viewed this activity as harmful because on such a scale it was thought to facilitate other forms of illicit activity, one of the reasons traditionally advanced for the separate prosecution of conspiracies. Where § 1955 has been violated, the elements of conspiracy will almost invariably be found. The enterprises to which Congress was referring in § 1955 cannot, as a practical matter, be created and perpetuated without the agreement and coordination that characterize conspiracy. Section 1955 is thus most sensibly viewed as a statute directed at conspiracy in a particular context.

All this the majority seems to concede when it acknowledges a "presumption that the two [crimes] merge when the substantive offense is proved." But the majority concludes that simultaneous conviction is authorized because it is not "explicitly excluded." The majority thus implicitly concedes that the statute is silent on the matter of simultaneous conviction. To infer from silence an intention to permit multiple punishment is, I think, a departure from the "presupposition of our law to resolve doubts in the enforcement of a penal code against the imposition of a harsher punishment," *Bell v. United States,* 349 U.S. 81, 83, 75 S.Ct. 620, 622, 99 L.Ed. 905 (1955) * * *.

MR. JUSTICE STEWART and MR. JUSTICE MARSHALL join this opinion [except as to the double jeopardy contention].

MR. JUSTICE BRENNAN, dissenting.

* * * I would invoke *Bell's* rule of lenity. I therefore dissent.

Notes and Questions

1. *Iannelli* was distinguished in *Jeffers v. United States,* 432 U.S. 137, 97 S.Ct. 2207, 53 L.Ed.2d 168 (1977), where defendant was convicted in separate trials of violating 21 U.S.C.A. § 846, proscribing conspiracy to distribute heroin and cocaine, and 21 U.S.C.A. § 848, proscribing engaging in a

continuing criminal enterprise "in concert with five or more other persons" to violate the drug laws. Noting that in *Iannelli* "the Court felt constrained to construe the statute to permit the possibility that the five persons 'involved' in the gambling operation might not be acting together," the Court in *Jeffers* concluded the "same flexibility does not exist with respect to the continuing-criminal-enterprise statute" because as to it "a conviction would be impossible unless concerted activity were present. * * * In the absence of any indication from the legislative history or elsewhere to the contrary, the far more likely explanation is that Congress intended the word 'concert' to have its common meaning of agreement in a design or plan." The Court thus concluded that § 846 was a lesser included offense of § 848; that this meant defendant was entitled to a joint trial at which a lesser included offense instruction was given; that defendant nonetheless could not complain because he opposed the government's joinder-for-trial motion; but that defendant was entitled to a sentence reduction because Congress had not authorized cumulative sentences for these two crimes. "[T]he reason for separate penalties for conspiracies lies in the additional dangers posed by concerted activity. Section 848, however, already expressly prohibits this kind of conduct. Thus, there is little legislative need to further this admittedly important interest by authorizing consecutive penalties from the conspiracy statute."

2. In which of the following situations should the defendant prevail by reliance on Wharton's rule? (a) Lupino gave Crippen a .38 caliber revolver which had been manufactured in Germany and transported to New York and then Minnesota. Lupino has been charged with conspiring with Crippen to violate 18 U.S.C.App. § 1202(a) (proscribing, in the part here

applicable, receiving a firearm which had travelled in interstate commerce).[a]

(b) Helmich transmitted secret defense information to a known Soviet agent. Helmich has been charged with conspiring with that agent to violate 18 U.S.C.A. § 794 (covering one who, "with intent or reason to believe that it is to be used to the injury of the United States or to the advantage of a foreign nation, communicates, delivers, or transmits" to an agent of a foreign government "information relating to the national defense").[b]

(c) A power company employee gave Kimble money when Kimble gave her a note indicating that otherwise her sons would be harmed. When Kimble was arrested, he said Carter wrote the note and shared in the proceeds. Carter was charged (i) under the conspiracy statute with conspiring with Kimble to commit extortion, and (ii) under the aiding and abetting statute (intended "to ensure that any person who participates in a substantive offense is held liable as if he had directly committed the offense") with aiding and abetting extortion.[c]

3. Consider Note, 52 Wash.L.Rev. 142, 162–64 (1976): "Where one offense consists only of preparation to commit another offense, the former is not punishable if there is conviction for the latter. This principle is generally recognized for the crime of attempt but has not been embraced by the United States Supreme Court in regard to conspiracy. It has been adopted, however, by several state stat-

utes[86] and the Model Penal Code[87] in order to limit conspiracy convictions.

"Application of the preparatory offense test to actions under section 1955 would serve to prevent unjustified conspiracy convictions. As previously discussed, a conspiracy charge should only be maintained when it serves one of the recognized functions of conspiracy law. Once the substantive offense has been consummated, additional punishment for conspiracy can only be justified by the existence of a clearly identifiable social threat greater than that posed by the consummated crime. Therefore, where the substantive offense encompasses and protects the same concerns that are threatened by the conspiracy, a conviction for the latter has no purpose other than increasing punishment beyond that prescribed by the legislature. This reasoning illustrates that the addition of a conspiracy charge to a section 1955 conviction is an example of unjustified multiple punishment.

"In order to accommodate the argument that a conspiracy with an objective broader than the commission of a specific offense presents an additional danger, the Model Penal Code does not provide for an absolute prohibition of a conspiracy conviction in the event the crime is consummated:[91]

[T]he limitation of the draft is confined to the situation where the completed offense was the sole criminal objective of the conspiracy. Therefore, there may be conviction of both a conspiracy and a completed offense committed pursuant to that conspiracy if the prosecution

a. A variation on *United States v. Lupino*, 480 F.2d 720 (8th Cir.1973).

b. A variation on *United States v. Helmich*, 704 F.2d 547 (11th Cir.1983).

c. See *People v. Carter*, 415 Mich. 558, 330 N.W.2d 314 (1982).

86. * * * These statutes prohibit all multiple convictions for conspiracy and the substantive offense, *irrespective of the conspiracy's scope.* * * *

87. The *Model Penal Code* § 1.07(1)(b) (Proposed Official Draft, 1962), states that a defendant may not "be convicted of more than one offense if: One offense consists only of a conspiracy or other form of preparation to commit the other." * * *

91. *Model Penal Code* § 1.08. Comment at 32 (Tent.Draft No. 5, 1956).

shows that the objective of the conspiracy was the commission of additional offenses.

The Court in *Iannelli,* drawing from conclusions of the Senate Report on the Act, found that '[l]arge-scale gambling enterprises were seen to be both a substantive evil and a source of funds for other criminal conduct.' This finding may be true as a general proposition, but it is insufficient to prove that the objectives of any particular conspiracy include the commission of additional offenses. Thus, in the absence of other evidence to show such an objective, a conspiracy charge should be dismissed upon conviction for violation of section 1955.''

4. Under the Model Penal Code approach, what should the result be on these facts? Morgan, in Cornman's presence, accepted Carney's offer of $5,000 to kill Sims. Cornman and Morgan then stole a rifle, and Cornman made inquiries revealing that Sims would not be at work that day. Morgan shot Haas, a neighbor of Sims, in the mistaken belief he was Sims. Haas survived. Cornman was convicted of first degree assault and conspiracy to murder, and was sentenced to consecutive terms of 30 and 10 years. Cornman appeals.[d]

5. In *Iannelli,* it is noted that the Court "has even held that the conspiracy can be punished more harshly than the accomplishment of its purpose." Is this a sensible sentencing scheme? Consider Note, 75 Colum.L.Rev. 1122, 1183–86 (1975):

"The job of grading the conspiracy offense demands an evaluation of the proper relationship between an inchoate and a substantive crime. The [Model Penal Code] has enjoyed considerable success in pressing the view that the degree of a

criminal agreement should depend on the gravity of the substantive offense which is its object. Several pre-reform statutes classify all conspiracies as misdemeanors, regardless of their purpose. * * * Since the promulgation of the MPC, nearly all jurisdictions concerned with criminal law revision have endorsed conspiracy penalties more closely resembling those assigned to the particular substantive crime intended.

"For sentencing purposes, the MPC would treat conspiracy and its object offense identically, unless the latter were a first-degree felony. In that case, conspiracy would be labeled a felony of the second degree.[360] The justification for such a grading procedure rests on a conception of conspiracy as inchoate crime, and an accompanying conviction regarding the punishment appropriate for that sort of offense. Apart from retribution, the legitimate ends of punishment as commonly enumerated, are deterrence, reformation, and protection of society through incapacitation of the offender. By definition, a conspirator is one who agrees to commit a crime with the purpose of promoting or facilitating the commission of that crime. Theoretically, then, his criminal intent is established. He is as much in need of correction or reformation as a person successful in committing the crime. On the other hand, sanctions attached to the object offense have not dissuaded the conspirator from aligning himself with others in a plan to violate the law. From this perspective, the potential deterrent efficacy of any conspiracy penalty seems slight. The MPC framers believed that, given this lack of significant deterrent function, the harshest of the law's sanctions could safely be removed from inchoate crimes. Hence, the treatment of conspira-

d. *State v. Cornman,* 695 S.W.2d 443 (Mo. 1985), affirming where the statute said a person may not be convicted "on the basis of the same course of conduct of both the actual commission

of an offense and a conspiracy to commit that offense.''

360. MPC § 5.05(1) * * *.

cy to commit a first-degree felony.
* * *

"A * * * prevalent alternative to the MPC pattern is the automatic downgrading of the inchoate offense, without regard to indications of the stage which the criminal project reached. Sixteen states have chosen to reduce conspiracy one degree from its object crime, and five other jurisdictions have favored even further reductions."

6. Wharton's rule should not be confused with the doctrine utilized in *Gebardi v. United States,* 287 U.S. 112, 53 S.Ct. 35, 77 L.Ed. 206 (1932). The petitioners, a man and a woman, were convicted of conspiracy to violate the Mann Act, which makes it an offense to "knowingly transport or cause to be transported, or aid or assist in obtaining transportation for, or in transporting in interstate or foreign commerce * * * any woman or girl for the purpose of prostitution or debauchery or for any other immoral purpose." The evidence was that the man purchased rail tickets for both of them to travel interstate, as the woman had previously consented to do, for immoral purposes, and that they had done so. The Court, per Stone, J., after concluding that the "penalties of the statute are too clearly directed against the acts of the transporter as distinguished from the consent of the subject of the transportation" to warrant the conclusion that on these facts the woman could herself be convicted of violating the Act, then came "to the main question in the case," namely, "whether her concurrence, which was not criminal before the Mann Act, nor punished by it, may without more, support a conviction under the conspiracy section, enacted many years before.

"As was said in the *Holte* Case, an agreement to commit an offense may be criminal, though its purpose is to do what some of the conspirators may be free to do alone. Incapacity of one to commit the substantive offense does not necessarily imply that he may with impunity conspire with others who are able to commit it.[5] For it is the collective planning of criminal conduct at which the statute aims. The plan is itself a wrong which, if any act be done to effect its object, the state has elected to treat as criminal. And one may plan that others shall do what he cannot do himself.

"But in this case we are concerned with something more than an agreement between two persons for one of them to commit an offense which the other cannot commit. There is the added element that the offense planned, the criminal object of the conspiracy, involves the agreement of the woman to her transportation by the man, which is the very conspiracy charged.

"Congress set out in the Mann Act to deal with cases which frequently, if not normally, involve consent and agreement on the part of the woman to the forbidden transportation. In every case in which she is not intimidated or forced into the transportation, the statute necessarily contemplates her acquiescence. Yet this acquiescence, though an incident of a type of transportation specifically dealt with by the statute, was not made a crime under the Mann Act itself. * * * We do not rest our decision upon the theory of those cases [applying Wharton's rule]. We place it rather upon the ground that we perceive in the failure of the Mann Act to condemn the woman's participation in those transportations which are effected

---

5. So it has been held repeatedly that one not a bankrupt may be held guilty under section 37 of conspiring that a bankrupt shall conceal property from his trustee * * *.

In like manner *Chadwick v. United States,* 141 F. 225 (2d Cir.1906) sustained the conviction of

one not an officer of a national bank for conspiring with an officer to commit a crime which only he could commit.

with her mere consent, evidence of an affirmative legislative policy to leave her acquiescence unpunished. We think it a necessary implication of that policy that when the Mann Act and the conspiracy statute came to be construed together, as they necessarily would be, the same participation which the former contemplates as an inseparable incident of all cases in which the woman is a voluntary agent at all, but does not punish, was not automatically to be made punishable under the latter. It would contravene that policy to hold that the very passage of the Mann Act effected a withdrawal by the conspiracy statute of that immunity which the Mann Act itself confers.

"It is not to be supposed that the consent of an unmarried person to adultery with a married person, where the latter alone is guilty of the substantive offense, would render the former an abettor or a conspirator, compare *In re Cooper,* 162 Cal. 81, 85, 121 P. 318, or that the acquiescence of a woman under the age of consent would make her a co-conspirator with the man to commit statutory rape upon herself. Compare *Queen v. Tyrrell,* [1894] 1 Q.B. 710. The principle, determinative of this case, is the same.

"On the evidence before us the woman petitioner has not violated the Mann Act and, we hold, is not guilty of a conspiracy to do so. As there is no proof that the man conspired with anyone else to bring about the transportation, the convictions of both petitioners must be

"Reversed."

But, why should the *man's* conviction also be reversed? Compare *Model Penal Code* § 5.04(1).

7. Deutsch and Holden were charged with conspiracy to commit theft. Deutsch pleaded guilty but Holden was tried and acquitted. Deutsch obtained relief via habeas corpus in *Eyman v. Deutsch,* 92 Ariz. 82, 373 P.2d 716 (1962), where the court stated: "The weight of authority seems to be that if one of the two alleged co-conspirators is acquitted the conviction of the other co-conspirator may not stand." Is this rule sound? Was it properly applied to the above facts? What of the dissenter's objection that the rule should not apply because Deutsch entered his plea *after* Holden's acquittal? Compare *People v. Holzer,* 25 Cal.App.3d 456, 102 Cal.Rptr. 11 (1972): "This rule is a logical imperative when all conspirators are tried together. Where separate trials are had this reasoning loses its force." Compare also *United States v. Espinoza–Cerpa,* 630 F.2d 328 (5th Cir.1980): "The notion that the acquittal of one's alleged coconspirators concludes the fact of their noncomplicity misapprehends the true nature of an acquittal in the scheme of trial by jury in the American criminal justice system." Are these arguments rebutted by the assertion that the rule, "rather than based solely on logic, reflects the community sense of a just outcome," as stated in *Developments in the Law—Criminal Conspiracy,* 72 Harv.L.Rev. 920, 974 (1959)? Even if that is not the case, is it illogical to accept such arguments and reject the *Eyman* rule when either (i) at the alleged co-conspirator's trial the *judge* dismissed the conspiracy charge because of insufficient evidence; or (ii) that jurisdiction does not accept the "unilateral" approach to conspiracy of the *St. Christopher* case, p. 604 of this Book? See *People v. Anderson,* 418 Mich. 31, 340 N.W.2d 634 (1983), rejecting the *Eyman* rule notwithstanding the presence of *both* these circumstances.

Assuming the *Eyman* rule is sound, should it be extended to other situations? What if the other conspirators had their cases nolle prossed after a hung jury, as in *United States v. Fox,* supra? Were granted immunity by the prosecutor in exchange for their testimony, as in *Hurwitz v. State,* 200 Md. 578, 92 A.2d 575 (1952)? Were foreign diplomats who were thus immune from prosecution, as in *Farnsworth v. Zerbst*, 98 F.2d 541 (5th Cir.1938)? Were found not guilty by reason of insanity, as in *Regle v. State*, 9 Md.App. 346, 264 A.2d 119 (1970)?

Note, 75 Colum.L.Rev. 1122, 1135–37 (1975): "Nearly all jurisdictions [with modern codes] have elected to follow the [Model Penal Code] recommendation that conspiracy be redefined as a unilateral, rather than a bilateral (or multilateral), crime. * * * By concentrating on individual, rather than group, liability, the guilt of a particular actor is made independent of that of his co-conspirator(s). Such treatment is important when, for example, defendant's only co-conspirator (a) is legally irresponsible or immune or incapable of committing a particular offense, (b) has feigned agreement, usually as part of some law enforcement scheme, or (c) is unknown, unapprehended, unindicted, unconvicted, or acquitted. A unilateral definition of conspiracy means that none of these circumstances will preclude defendant's conviction where the evidence is otherwise sufficient. Each of the possibilities mentioned in (c) above, especially the possibility of an acquitted co-conspirator, raises questions of consistency of disposition if the defendant is convicted. The framers of the MPC were cognizant of possible objections of this character, but they regarded disparate outcomes as preferable to the discharge of an offender whose own culpability was clearly established. '[T]he Code * * * recognizes that inequalities in the administration of the law are, to some extent, inevitable, that they may reflect unavoidable differences in proof, and that, in any event, they are a lesser evil than granting immunity to one criminal because justice may have miscarried in dealing with another.' "

e. *United States v. MacAndrews & Forbes Co.*, 149 Fed. 823 (S.D.N.Y.1906).

f. *People v. Dunbar Contracting Co.*, 165 App. Div. 59, 151 N.Y.S. 164 (1914).

8. Although it is clear that a corporation may be indicted as a conspirator, problems may arise in determining the existence of the plurality necessary for a conspiracy. No problem exists when two corporations and an officer of each are indicted,[e] or when a corporation is indicted with one of its officers and a third party,[f] for in such situations it is clear (without regard to whether the corporation and its agent are one) that there are at least two distinct participants in the conspiracy. However, plurality has been found to be lacking when the corporate entity and a single agent are the only parties,[g] and also when two corporations and one person acting as the agent of both were the only alleged conspirators.[h]

Consider the soundness of those results and also that reached in *United States v. Hartley*, 678 F.2d 961 (11th Cir.1982), namely, that the necessary plurality for a conspiracy is present when the alleged co-conspirators are the corporation and two or more of that corporation's agents. The *Hartley* court explained that "the fiction of corporate personification * * * originated to broaden the scope of corporate responsibility; we will not use it to shield individuals or corporations from criminal responsibility."

Is *Hartley* consistent with the theory underlying criminal conspiracy? Consider Welling, *Intracorporate Plurality in Criminal Conspiracy Law*, 33 Hastings L.J. 1155, 1198–99 (1982), noting: "The main theme of criminal conspiracy laws is the presumption that an increased number of participants result in increased power and therefore in increased danger to society. * * *

"At a minimum, whether the power of the conspiracy and therefore the danger to

g. *Union Pac. Coal Co. v. United States*, 173 Fed. 737 (8th Cir.1909).

h. *United States v. Santa Rita Store Co.*, 16 N.M. 3, 113 P. 620 (1911).

society actually are increased by more people or remain constant in the intracorporate context depends on the specific employees and company involved, the industry structure, the criminal objective contemplated, and other such factors unique to each case. Thus, the presumption of increased danger may not be accurate when applied to conspiracies that are exclusively intracorporate. Ideally, each case should be examined individually to determine whether the facts warrant the conclusion that society faces more danger because of the participation of more than one agent. If the factual examination reveals that the power to harm society is increased by the participation of multiple agents, the agents should be deemed a plurality and held liable for conspiracy. In contrast, if the facts reveal no increase in the power to harm society resulting from the participation of more than one agent, the agents should not be defined as a plurality and no conspiracy charge should be upheld."

Given that reasoning, does the two-corporation, one-agent situation deserve a closer look? Consider the hypothetical in Brickey, *Conspiracy, Group Danger and the Corporate Defendant*, 52 U.Cin.L.Rev. 431, 443–44 (1983): "Suppose, for example, that Deegan planned the following: Using false invoices from the Santa Rita Store Company, he intends to bill the Mining Company through the mail for goods that were never delivered. The Store Company will divert the payments from the Mining Company into a slush fund to be maintained in a secret foreign financial account for the purpose of bribing domestic and foreign governmental officials. Deegan will be able to conceal these transactions by keeping two false sets of corporate books. The Mining Company books will reflect that the goods that have been paid for actually have been ordered and received, and the Store Company books will reflect neither the issuance of phony invoices nor the receipt of the payments from the Mining Company."

9. Because of the old notion that husband and wife became one person by marriage, the early common law view was that an agreement between husband and wife only could not be a conspiracy. Typical of the modern response to this position is *United States v. Dege,* 364 U.S. 51, 80 S.Ct. 1589, 4 L.Ed.2d 1563 (1960), where the majority, per Frankfurter, J., stated:

"None of the considerations of policy touching the law's encouragement or discouragement of domestic felicities on the basis of which this Court determined appropriate rules for testimonial compulsion as between spouses * * * are relevant to yielding to the claim that an unqualified interdiction by Congress against a conspiracy between two persons precludes a husband and wife from being two persons. Such an immunity to husband and wife as a pair of conspirators would have to attribute to Congress one of two assumptions: either that responsibility of husband and wife for joint participation in a criminal enterprise would make for marital disharmony, or that a wife must be presumed to act under the coercive influence of her husband and, therefore, cannot be a willing participant. The former assumption is unnourished by sense; the latter implies a view of American womanhood offensive to the ethos of our society."

But the three dissenters in *Dege* thought otherwise: "It is not necessary to be wedded to fictions to approve the husband-wife conspiracy doctrine, for one of the dangers which that doctrine averts is the prosecution and conviction of persons for 'conspiracies' which Congress never meant to be included within the statute. A wife, simply by virtue of the intimate life she shares with her husband, might easily perform acts that would technically be sufficient to involve her in a criminal conspiracy with him, but which might be far removed from the arm's-length agreement typical of that crime. It is not a medieval mental quirk or an attitude 'unnourished by sense' to believe that husbands and wives should not be subjected to such a risk, or that such a possibility should not be permitted to endanger the confidentiality of the marriage relationship. While it is easy enough to ridicule Hawkins' pronouncement in Pleas of the Crown from a metaphysical point of view, the concept of the 'oneness' of a married couple may reflect an abiding belief that the communion between husband and wife is such that their actions are not always to be regarded by the criminal law as if there were no marriage."

SECTION 12. CONSPIRACY: A FINAL LOOK

PHILLIP E. JOHNSON—THE UNNECESSARY CRIME OF CONSPIRACY

61 Calif.L.Rev. 1137, 1162–64 (1973).

Against the background of a law of attempt dominated by the proximity approach, an independent inchoate crime of conspiracy made sense. Although the defendants in the New York and California cases described previously [a] could not be convicted under traditional attempt law, they could each have been convicted of conspiracy because they worked with confederates and performed an "overt act" in furtherance of the criminal design. Each of these defendants, however, could also be convicted of attempt under the Model Penal Code * * *.

Under the conspiracy sections of the Model Penal Code and proposed Federal Criminal Code, however, the act of agreement *is* the forbidden conduct whether or not it strongly corroborates the existence of a criminal purpose. In justifying this per se rule, the Model Penal Code commentary relied heavily on the argument, quoted previously, that the act of agreeing is so decisive and concrete a step towards the commission of a crime that it ought always to be regarded as a "substantial step." Whether this point is sense or nonsense depends upon how restrictively one defines the term "agreement." Hiring a professional killer to commit murder is an agreement, and surely few would doubt that it is a substantial step toward accomplishing the killing. But the language of the conspiracy sections of both the Model Penal Code and proposed Federal Criminal Code is broad enough to reach conduct far less dangerous or deserving of punishment than letting a contract for murder. As the Model Penal Code commentary concedes, one may be liable for agreeing with another that *he* should commit a particular crime, although this agreement might be insufficient to establish complicity in the completed offense. Furthermore, neither code would change the well-established rule that the agreement may be tacit or implied as well as express, and that it may be proved by circumstantial evidence. In short, the term "agreement" may connote anything from firm commitment to engage in criminal activity oneself to reluctant approval of a criminal plot to be carried out entirely by others. To be sure, the Model Penal Code also requires that one enter into the agreement with the purpose of promoting or facilitating the crime, but the existence of that purpose need not be substantiated by any conduct beyond the express or implied agreement and performance in some cases of a single overt act by any party to it. This point is of particular importance in conspiracy cases involving political activity or agitation. Members of radical societies may be

---

a. The cases referred to are *People v. Rizzo,* p. 551 of this Book, and *People v. Orndorff,* p. 553 of this Book.

likely to discuss or even to begin to plan criminal activities that they have no serious intention of carrying through.

In summary, insofar as conspiracy adds anything to the attempt provisions of the reform codes under discussion, it adds only overly broad criminal liability. Like its use in every other area of the substantive criminal law, the use of an independent crime of conspiracy to punish inchoate crimes turns out to be unnecessary.

SECTION 13. BEYOND CONSPIRACY: RICO

UNITED STATES v. TURKETTE

Supreme Court of the United States, 1981.
452 U.S. 576, 101 S.Ct. 2524, 69 L.Ed.2d 246.

JUSTICE WHITE delivered the opinion of the Court.

2. Title 18 U.S.C. § 1961(4) provides:

"'enterprise' includes any individual, partnership, corporation, association, or other legal entity, and any union or group of individuals associated in fact although not a legal entity."

a. Title 18 U.S.C. § 1961(1) provides:

"'racketeering activity' means (A) any act or threat involving murder, kidnaping, gambling, arson, robbery, bribery, extortion, dealing in obscene matter, or dealing in narcotic or other dangerous drugs, which is chargeable under State law and punishable by imprisonment for more than one year; (B) any act which is indictable under any of the following provisions of title 18, United States Code: Section 201 (relating to bribery), section 224 (relating to sports bribery), sections 471, 472, and 473 (relating to counterfeiting), section 659 (relating to theft from interstate shipment) if the act indictable under section 659 is felonious, section 664 (relating to embezzlement from pension and welfare funds), sections 891–894 (relating to extortionate credit transactions), section 1084 (relating to the transmission of gambling information), section 1341 (relating to mail fraud), section 1343 (relating to wire fraud), sections 1461–1465 (relating to obscene matter), section 1503 (relating to obstruction of justice), section 1510 (relating to the obstruction of criminal investigations), section 1511 (relating to the obstruction of State or local law enforcement), section 1951 (relating to interference with commerce, robbery, or extortion), section 1952 (relating to racketeering), section 1953 (relating to interstate transportation of wagering paraphernalia), section 1954 (relating to unlawful wel-

Chapter 96 of Title 18 of the United States Code, 18 U.S.C. §§ 1961–1968 (1976 ed. and Supp. III), entitled Racketeer Influenced and Corrupt Organizations (RICO), was added to Title 18 by Title IX of the Organized Crime Control Act of 1970. The question in this case is whether the term "enterprise" as used in RICO encompasses both legitimate and illegitimate enterprises or is limited in application to the former. * * *

I

Count Nine of a nine-count indictment charged respondent and 12 others with conspiracy to conduct and participate in the affairs of an enterprise[2] engaged in interstate commerce through a pattern of racketeering activities,[a] in violation of 18 U.S.C. § 1962(d).[3] The indictment described the enterprise as "a group of indi-

fare fund payments), section 1955 (relating to the prohibition of illegal gambling businesses), sections 2312 and 2313 (relating to interstate transportation of stolen motor vehicles), sections 2314 and 2315 (relating to interstate transportation of stolen property), section 2320 (relating to trafficking in certain motor vehicles or motor vehicle parts), sections 2341–2346 (relating to trafficking in contraband cigarettes), sections 2421–24 (relating to white slave traffic), (C) any act which is indictable under title 29, United States Code, section 186 (dealing with restrictions on payments and loans to labor organizations) or section 501(c) (relating to embezzlement from union funds), (D) any offense involving fraud connected with a case under title 11, fraud in the sale of securities, or the felonious manufacture, importation, receiving, concealment, buying, selling, or otherwise dealing in narcotic or other dangerous drugs, punishable under any law of the United States, or (E) any act which is indictable under the Currency and Foreign Transactions Reporting Act."

Title 18 U.S.C. § 1961(5) provides:

"'pattern of racketeering activity' requires at least two acts of racketeering activity, one of which occurred after the effective date of this chapter and the last of which occurred within ten years (excluding any period of imprisonment) after the commission of a prior act of racketeering activity."

3. Title 18 U.S.C. § 1962(d) provides that "[i]t shall be unlawful for any person to conspire to violate any of the provisions of subsections (a), (b),

viduals associated in fact for the purpose of illegally trafficking in narcotics and other dangerous drugs, committing arsons, utilizing the United States mails to defraud insurance companies, bribing and attempting to bribe local police officers, and corruptly influencing and attempting to corruptly influence the outcome of state court proceedings * * *." The other eight counts of the indictment charged the commission of various substantive criminal acts by those engaged in and associated with the criminal enterprise, including possession with intent to distribute and distribution of controlled substances, and several counts of insurance fraud by arson and other means. The common thread to all counts was respondent's alleged leadership of this criminal organization through which he orchestrated and participated in the commission of the various crimes delineated in the RICO count or charged in the eight preceding counts.

After a 6–week jury trial, in which the evidence focused upon both the professional nature of this organization and the execution of a number of distinct criminal acts, respondent was convicted on all nine counts. He was sentenced to a term of 20 years on the substantive counts, as well as a 2–year special parole term on the drug count. On the RICO conspiracy count he was sentenced to a 20–year concurrent term and fined $20,000.

On appeal, respondent argued that RICO was intended solely to protect legitimate business enterprises from infiltration by racketeers and that RICO does not make criminal the participation in an association which performs only illegal acts and which has not infiltrated or attempted to infiltrate a legitimate enterprise. The Court of Appeals agreed. We reverse.

II

In determining the scope of a statute, we look first to its language. If the statutory language is unambiguous, in the absence of "a clearly expressed legislative intent to the contrary, that language must ordinarily be regarded as conclusive." Of course, there is no errorless test for identifying or recognizing "plain" or "unambiguous" language. Also, authoritative administrative constructions should be given the deference to which they are entitled, absurd results are to be avoided and internal inconsistencies in the statute must be dealt with. We nevertheless begin with the language of the statute.

Section 1962(c) makes it unlawful "for any person employed by or associated with any enterprise engaged in, or the activities of which affect, interstate or foreign commerce, to conduct or participate, directly or indirectly, in the conduct of such enterprise's affairs through a pattern of racketeering activity or collection of unlawful debt." The term "enterprise" is defined as including "any individual, partnership, corporation, association, or other legal entity, and any union or group of individuals associated in fact although not a legal entity." § 1961(4). There is no restriction upon the associations embraced by the definition: an enterprise includes any union or group of individuals associated in fact. On its face, the definition appears to include both legitimate and illegitimate enterprises within its scope; it no more excludes criminal enterprises than it does legitimate ones. Had Congress not intended to reach criminal associations, it could easily have narrowed the sweep of the definition by inserting a single word, "legitimate." But it did nothing to indicate that an enterprise consisting of a

or (c) of this section." Pertinent to these charges, subsection (c) provides:

"It shall be unlawful for any person employed by or associated with any enterprise engaged in, or the activities of which affect, interstate or

foreign commerce, to conduct or participate, directly or indirectly, in the conduct of such enterprise's affairs through a pattern of racketeering activity or collection of unlawful debt."

group of individuals was not covered by RICO if the purpose of the enterprise was exclusively criminal.

The Court of Appeals, however, clearly departed from and limited the statutory language. It gave several reasons for doing so, none of which is adequate. First, it relied in part on the rule of *ejusdem generis* an aid to statutory construction problems suggesting that where general words follow a specific enumeration of persons or things, the general words should be limited to persons or things similar to those specifically enumerated. The Court of Appeals ruled that because each of the specific enterprises enumerated in § 1961(4) is a "legitimate" one, the final catchall phrase—"any union or group of individuals associated in fact"—should also be limited to legitimate enterprises. There are at least two flaws in this reasoning. The rule of *ejusdem generis* is no more than an aid to construction and comes into play only when there is some uncertainty as to the meaning of a particular clause in a statute. Considering the language and structure of § 1961(4), however, we not only perceive no uncertainty in the meaning to be attributed to the phrase, "any union or group of individuals associated in fact" but we are convinced for another reason that *ejusdem generis* is wholly inapplicable in this context.

Section 1961(4) describes two categories of associations that come within the purview of the "enterprise" definition. The first encompasses organizations such as corporations and partnerships, and other "legal entities." The second covers "any union or group of individuals associated in fact although not a legal entity." The Court of Appeals assumed that the second

category was merely a more general description of the first. Having made that assumption, the court concluded that the more generalized description in the second category should be limited by the specific examples enumerated in the first. But that assumption is untenable. Each category describes a separate type of enterprise to be covered by the statute—those that are recognized as legal entities and those that are not. The latter is not a more general description of the former. The second category itself not containing any specific enumeration that is followed by a general description, *ejusdem generis* has no bearing on the meaning to be attributed to that part of § 1961(4).[4]

A second reason offered by the Court of Appeals in support of its judgment was that giving the definition of "enterprise" its ordinary meaning would create several internal inconsistencies in the Act. With respect to § 1962(c), it was said:

> "If 'a pattern of racketeering' can itself be an 'enterprise' for purposes of section 1962(c), then the two phrases 'employed by or associated with any enterprise' and 'the conduct of such enterprise's affairs through [a pattern of racketeering activity]' add nothing to the meaning of the section. The words of the statute are coherent and logical only if they are read as applying to legitimate enterprises."

This conclusion is based on a faulty premise. That a wholly criminal enterprise comes within the ambit of the statute does not mean that a "pattern of racketeering activity" is an "enterprise." In order to secure a conviction under RICO, the Government must prove both the existence of

---

4. The Court of Appeals' application of *ejusdem generis* is further flawed by the assumption that "any individual, partnership, corporation, association or other legal entity" could not act totally beyond the pale of the law. The mere fact that a given enterprise is favored with a legal existence does not prevent that enterprise from proceeding along a wholly illegal course of conduct. Therefore, since legitimacy of purpose is not a universal characteristic of the specifically listed enterprises, it would be improper to engraft this characteristic upon the second category of enterprises.

an "enterprise" and the connected "pattern of racketeering activity." The enterprise is an entity, for present purposes a group of persons associated together for a common purpose of engaging in a course of conduct. The pattern of racketeering activity is, on the other hand, a series of criminal acts as defined by the statute. 18 U.S.C. § 1961(1) (1976 ed., Supp. III). The former is proved by evidence of an ongoing organization, formal or informal, and by evidence that the various associates function as a continuing unit. The latter is proved by evidence of the requisite number of acts of racketeering committed by the participants in the enterprise. While the proof used to establish these separate elements may in particular cases coalesce, proof of one does not necessarily establish the other. The "enterprise" is not the "pattern of racketeering activity"; it is an entity separate and apart from the pattern of activity in which it engages. The existence of an enterprise at all times remains a separate element which must be proved by the Government.

Apart from § 1962(c)'s proscription against participating in an enterprise through a pattern of racketeering activities, RICO also proscribes the investment of income derived from racketeering activity in an enterprise engaged in or which affects interstate commerce as well as the acquisition of an interest in or control of any such enterprise through a pattern of racketeering activity. 18 U.S.C. §§ 1962(a) and (b).[6] The Court of Appeals concluded that these provisions of RICO should be interpreted so as to apply only to legitimate enterprises. If these two sections are so limited, the Court of Appeals held that the proscription in § 1962(c), at issue here, must be similarly limited. Again, we do not accept the premise from which the Court of Appeals derived its conclusion. It is obvious that § 1962(a) and (b) address the infiltration by organized crime of legitimate businesses, but we cannot agree that these sections were not also aimed at preventing racketeers from investing or reinvesting in wholly illegal enterprises and from acquiring through a pattern of racketeering activity wholly illegitimate enterprises such as an illegal gambling business or a loan-sharking operation. There is no inconsistency or anomaly in recognizing that § 1962 applies to both legitimate and illegitimate enterprises. Certainly the language of the statute does not warrant the Court of Appeals' conclusion to the contrary.

Similarly, the Court of Appeals noted that various civil remedies were provided by § 1964,[7] including divestiture, dissolution, reorganization, restrictions on future

6. Title 18 U.S.C. §§ 1962(a) and (b) provide:

"(a) It shall be unlawful for any person who has received any income derived, directly or indirectly, from a pattern of racketeering activity or through collection of an unlawful debt in which such person has participated as a principal within the meaning of section 2, title 18, United States Code, to use or invest, directly or indirectly, any part of such income, or the proceeds of such income, in acquisition of any interest in, or the establishment or operation of, any enterprise which is engaged in, or the activities of which affect, interstate or foreign commerce. A purchase of securities on the open market for purposes of investment, and without the intention of controlling or participating in the control of the issuer, or of assisting another to do so, shall not be unlawful under this subsection if the securities of the issuer held by the purchaser, the members

of his immediate family, and his or their accomplices in any pattern or racketeering activity or the collection of an unlawful debt after such purchase do not amount in the aggregate to one percent of the outstanding securities of any one class, and do not confer, either in law or in fact, the power to elect one or more directors of the issuer.

"(b) It shall be unlawful for any person through a pattern of racketeering activity or through collection of an unlawful debt to acquire or maintain, directly or indirectly, any interest in or control of any enterprise which is engaged in, or the activities of which affect, interstate or foreign commerce."

7. Title 18 U.S.C. §§ 1964(a) and (c) provide:

"(a) The district courts of the United States shall have jurisdiction to prevent and restrain

activities by violators of RICO, and treble damages. These remedies it thought would have utility only with respect to legitimate enterprises. As a general proposition, however, the civil remedies could be useful in eradicating organized crime from the social fabric, whether the enterprise be ostensibly legitimate or admittedly criminal. The aim is to divest the association of the fruits of its ill-gotten gains. Even if one or more of the civil remedies might be inapplicable to a particular illegitimate enterprise, this fact would not serve to limit the enterprise concept. Congress has provided civil remedies for use when the circumstances so warrant. It is untenable to argue that their existence limits the scope of the criminal provisions.

Finally, it is urged that the interpretation of RICO to include both legitimate and illegitimate enterprises will substantially alter the balance between federal and state enforcement of criminal law. This is particularly true, so the argument goes, since included within the definition of racketeering activity are a significant number of acts made criminal under state law. 18 U.S.C. § 1961(1) (1976 ed., Supp. III). But even assuming that the more inclusive definition of enterprise will have the effect suggested, the language of the statute and its legislative history indicate that Congress was well aware that it was entering a new domain of federal involvement through the enactment of this measure. Indeed, the very purpose of the Organized Crime Control Act of 1970 was to enable the Federal Government to address a large and seemingly neglected problem. The

view was that existing law, state and federal, was not adequate to address the problem, which was of national dimensions. That Congress included within the definition of racketeering activities a number of state crimes strongly indicates that RICO criminalized conduct that was also criminal under state law, at least when the requisite elements of a RICO offense are present. As the hearings and legislative debates reveal, Congress was well aware of the fear that RICO would mov[e] large substantive areas formerly totally within the police power of the State into the Federal realm." In the face of these objections, Congress nonetheless proceeded to enact the measure, knowing that it would alter somewhat the role of the Federal Government in the war against organized crime and that the alteration would entail prosecutions involving acts of racketeering that are also crimes under state law. There is no argument that Congress acted beyond its power in so doing. That being the case, the courts are without authority to restrict the application of the statute.

Contrary to the judgment below, neither the language nor structure of RICO limits its application to legitimate "enterprises." Applying it also to criminal organizations does not render any portion of the statute superfluous nor does it create any structural incongruities within the framework of the Act. The result is neither absurd nor surprising. On the contrary, insulating the wholly criminal enterprise from prosecution under RICO is the more incongruous position.

violations of section 1962 of this chapter by issuing appropriate orders, including, but not limited to: ordering any person to divest himself of any interest, direct or indirect, in any enterprise; imposing reasonable restrictions on the future activities or investments of any person, including, but not limited to, prohibiting any person from engaging in the same type of endeavor as the enterprise engaged in, the activities of which affect interstate or foreign commerce; or ordering dissolution or reorganization of any enter-

prise, making due provision for the rights of innocent persons.

*   *   *

"(c) Any person injured in his business or property by reason of a violation of section 1962 of this chapter may sue therefore in any appropriate United States district court and shall recover threefold the damages he sustains and the cost of the suit, including a reasonable attorney's fee."

Section 904(a) of RICO, 84 Stat. 947, directs that "[t]he provisions of this Title shall be liberally construed to effectuate its remedial purposes." With or without this admonition, we could not agree with the Court of Appeals that illegitimate enterprises should be excluded from coverage. We are also quite sure that nothing in the legislative history of RICO requires a contrary conclusion.

III

The statement of findings that prefaces the Organized Crime Control Act of 1970 reveals the pervasiveness of the problem that Congress was addressing by this enactment:

"The Congress finds that (1) organized crime in the United States is a highly sophisticated, diversified, and widespread activity that annually drains billions of dollars from America's economy by unlawful conduct and the illegal use of force, fraud, and corruption; (2) organized crime derives a major portion of its power through money obtained from such illegal endeavors as syndicated gambling, loan sharking, the theft and fencing of property, the importation and distribution of narcotics and other dangerous drugs, and other forms of social exploitation; (3) this money and power are increasingly used to infiltrate and corrupt legitimate business and labor unions and to subvert and corrupt our democratic processes; (4) organized crime activities in the United States weaken the stability of the Nation's economic system, harm innocent investors and competing organizations, interfere with free competition, seriously burden interstate and foreign commerce, threaten the domestic security, and undermine the general welfare of the Nation and its citizens; and (5) organized crime continues to grow because of defects in the evidence-gathering process of the law inhibiting the development of the legally admissible evidence necessary to bring criminal and other sanc-

tions or remedies to bear on the unlawful activities of those engaged in organized crime and because the sanctions and remedies available to the Government are unnecessarily limited in scope and impact."

In light of the above findings, it was the declared purpose of Congress "to seek the eradication of organized crime in the United States by strengthening the legal tools in the evidence-gathering process, by establishing new penal prohibitions, and by providing enhanced sanctions and new remedies to deal with the unlawful activities of those engaged in organized crime." The various Titles of the Act provide the tools through which this goal is to be accomplished. Only three of those Titles create substantive offenses, Title VIII, which is directed at illegal gambling operations, Title IX, at issue here, and Title XI, which addresses the importation, distribution, and storage of explosive materials. The other Titles provide various procedural and remedial devices to aid in the prosecution and incarceration of persons involved in organized crime.

Considering this statement of the Act's broad purposes, the construction of RICO suggested by respondent and the court below is unacceptable. Whole areas of organized criminal activity would be placed beyond the substantive reach of the enactment. For example, associations of persons engaged solely in "loan sharking, the theft and fencing of property, the importation and distribution of narcotics and other dangerous drugs," would be immune from prosecution under RICO so long as the association did not deviate from the criminal path. Yet these are among the very crimes that Congress specifically found to be typical of the crimes committed by persons involved in organized crime, see 18 U.S.C. § 1961(1) (1976 ed., Supp. III), and as a major source of revenue and power for such organizations. * * *

This is not to gainsay that the legislative history forcefully supports the view that the major purpose of Title IX is to address the infiltration of legitimate business by organized crime. The point is made time and again during the debates and in the hearings before the House and Senate. But none of these statements requires the negative inference that Title IX did not reach the activities of enterprises organized and existing for criminal purposes.

On the contrary, these statements are in full accord with the proposition that RICO is equally applicable to a criminal enterprise that has no legitimate dimension or has yet to acquire one. Accepting that the primary purpose of RICO is to cope with the infiltration of legitimate businesses, applying the statute in accordance with its terms, so as to reach criminal enterprises, would seek to deal with the problem at its very source. Supporters of the bill recognized that organized crime uses its primary sources of revenue and power—illegal gambling, loan sharking and illicit drug distribution—as a springboard into the sphere of legitimate enterprise. * * *

As a measure to deal with the infiltration of legitimate businesses by organized crime, RICO was both preventive and remedial. Respondent's view would ignore the preventive function of the statute. If Congress had intended the more circumscribed approach espoused by the Court of Appeals, there would have been some positive sign that the law was not to reach organized criminal activities that give rise to the concerns about infiltration. The language of the statute, however—the most reliable evidence of its intent—reveals that Congress opted for a far broader definition of the word "enterprise," and we are unconvinced by anything in the legislative history that this definition should be given less than its full effect.

The judgment of the Court of Appeals is accordingly

Reversed.

JUSTICE STEWART agrees with the reasoning and conclusion of the Court of Appeals as to the meaning of the term "enterprise" in this statute. Accordingly, he respectfully dissents.

Notes and Questions

1. *Scope of the "enterprise"; conspiracy compared.* (a) Consider *United States v. Elliott,* 571 F.2d 880 (5th Cir.1978): "Here, the government proved beyond a reasonable doubt the existence of an enterprise comprised of at least five of the defendants. This enterprise can best be analogized to a large business conglomerate. Metaphorically speaking, J.C. Hawkins was the chairman of the board, functioning as the chief executive officer and overseeing the operations of many separate branches of the corporation. An executive committee in charge of the 'Counterfeit Title, Stolen Car, and Amphetamine Sales Department' was comprised of J.C., Delph, and Taylor, who supervised the operations of lower level employees such as Farr, the printer, and Green, Boyd, and Jackson, the car thieves. Another executive committee, comprised of J.C., Recea and Foster, controlled the 'Thefts From Interstate Commerce Department', arranging the purchase, concealment, and distribution of such commodities as meat, dairy products, 'Career Club' shirts, and heavy construction equipment. An offshoot of this department handled subsidiary activities, such as murder and obstruction of justice, intended to facilitate the smooth operation of its primary activities. Each member of the conglomerate, with the exception of Foster, was responsible for procuring and wholesaling whatever narcotics could be obtained. The thread tying all of these departments, activities, and individuals together was the desire to make money. * * *

"The evidence in this case demonstrated the existence of an enterprise—a myriopod criminal network, loosely connected but connected nonetheless. By committing arson, actively assisting a car theft ring, fencing thousands of dollars worth of goods stolen from interstate commerce, murdering a key witness, and dealing in narcotics, J.C. and Recea Hawkins directly and indirectly participated in the enterprise's affairs through a pattern, indeed a plethora, of racketeering activity. * * *

"Applying pre-RICO conspiracy concepts to the facts of this case, we doubt that a single conspiracy could be demonstrated. Foster had no contact with Delph and Taylor during the life of the alleged conspiracy. Delph and Taylor, so far as the evidence revealed, had no contact with Recea Hawkins. The activities allegedly embraced by the illegal agreement in this case are simply too diverse to be tied together on the theory that participation in one activity necessarily implied awareness of others. Even viewing the 'common objective' of the conspiracy as the raising of revenue through criminal activity, we could not say, for example, that Foster, when he helped to conceal stolen meat, had to know that J.C. was selling drugs to persons unknown to Foster, or that Delph and Taylor, when they furnished counterfeit titles to a car theft ring, had to know that the man supplying the titles was also stealing goods out of interstate commerce. The enterprise involved in this case probably could not have been successfully prosecuted as a single conspiracy under the general federal conspiracy statute, 18 U.S.C. § 371.

"[W]e are convinced that, through RICO, Congress intended to authorize the single prosecution of a multi-faceted, diversified conspiracy by replacing the inadequate 'wheel' and 'chain' rationales with a new statutory concept: the enterprise.

"To achieve this result, Congress acted against the backdrop of hornbook conspiracy law. Under the general federal conspiracy statute,

the precise nature and extent of the conspiracy must be determined by reference to the agreement which embraces and defines its objects. Whether the object of a single agreement is to commit one or many crimes, it is in either case that agreement which constitutes the conspiracy which the statute punishes. *Braverman v. United States,* 317 U.S. 49, 53, 63 S.Ct. 99, 102, 87 L.Ed. 23 (1942).

In the context of organized crime, this principle inhibited mass prosecutions because a single agreement or 'common objective' cannot be inferred from the commission of highly diverse crimes by apparently unrelated individuals. RICO helps to eliminate this problem by creating a substantive offense which ties together these diverse parties and crimes. Thus, the object of a RICO conspiracy is to violate a substantive RICO provision— here, to conduct or participate in the affairs of an enterprise through a pattern of racketeering activity—and not merely to commit each of the predicate crimes necessary to demonstrate a pattern of racketeering activity. The gravamen of the conspiracy charge in this case is not that each defendant agreed to commit arson, to steal goods from interstate commerce, to obstruct justice, and to sell narcotics; rather, it is that each agreed to participate, directly and indirectly, in the affairs of the enterprise by committing two or more predicate crimes. Under the statute, it is irrelevant that each defendant participated in the enterprise's affairs through different, even unrelated crimes, so long as we may reasonably infer that each crime was intended to further the enterprise's affairs. To find a single conspiracy, we still must look for agreement on an overall objective. What Congress did was to define that objective through the substantive provisions of the Act."

(b) Holderman, *Reconciling RICO's Conspiracy and "Group" Enterprise Concepts with Traditional Conspiracy Doctrine,* 52 U.Cin.L. Rev. 385, 385–86 (1983), asserts: "Although the opinions have been conflicting in their attempts to reconcile RICO's 'group enterprise' and 'conspiracy' concepts with prior conspiracy doctrine, a trend has emerged. That trend rejects the ideas espoused in *Elliott* and returns to traditional conspiracy principles in determining complicity in multi-defendant RICO prosecutions. The trend is evidenced in the increased use by courts of traditional conspiracy concepts such as 'common purpose' and 'consciousness of scope' in applying RICO's 'group enterprise' and 'conspiracy' notions. Moreover, the United States Department of Justice in its policy statements has embraced, as proper interpretations of RICO's scope, judicial opinions that have applied traditional conspiracy principles. This trend, though not uniform, has progressed to the point that it is doubtful whether *any* federal appellate circuit would now advance *Elliott*'s proposition that the statutory concept of enterprise embodied in RICO *replaced* prior conspiracy rationale. If the trend continues, *Elliott* will be viewed as an aberration in RICO law and of only historical interest; traditional conspiracy concepts will be the point of analytical departure when determining the proper reach of a prosecution under RICO's 'group enterprise' and 'conspiracy' concepts."

2. *"Associated in fact" enterprise.* (a) In *United States v. Bledsoe,* 674 F.2d 647 (8th Cir.1982), the government argued "that any association of individuals can be an enterprise." The court responded: "Although several courts have accepted this loose construction of RICO, we believe that the legislative history of the statute and an analysis of the statute itself as well as the surrounding criminal law indicates that such a broad construction is not warranted.

" * * * Each element of the crime, that is, the predicate acts, the pattern of such acts, and the enterprise requirement, was designed to limit the applicability of the statute and separate individuals engaged in organized crime from ordinary criminals. The enterprise requirement must be interpreted in this light. * * *

"The word 'enterprise' ordinarily means an undertaking or project or a unit of organization established to perform any such undertaking or project. However, under RICO, an enterprise cannot simply be the undertaking of the acts of racketeering, neither can it be the minimal association which surrounds these acts. Any two criminal acts will necessarily be surrounded by some degree of organization and no two individuals will ever jointly perpetrate a crime without some degree of association apart from the commission of the crime itself. Thus unless the inclusion of the enterprise element requires proof of some structure separate from the racketeering activity and distinct from the organization which is a necessary incident to the racketeering, the Act simply punishes the commission of two of the specified crimes within a 10–year period. Congress clearly did not intend such an application of the Act.

"A comparison of the severe penalties authorized by RICO with those for conspiracy indicates that the Act must have been directed at participation in enterprises consisting of more than simple conspiracies to perpetrate the predicate acts of racketeering. Violation of RICO may be punished by a fine of up to $25,000 or imprisonment for up to 20 years or both, while conspiracy to commit an offense against the United States carries a maximum penalty of a $10,000 fine and five years imprisonment. * * *

" * * * Although commonality of purpose may be the sine qua non of a criminal enterprise, in many cases this singular test fails to distinguish enterprises from individuals merely associated together for the commission of sporadic crime. Any two wrongdoers who through concerted action commit two or more crimes share a purpose. This suggests that an enterprise must exhibit each of three basic characteristics.

"In addition to having a common or shared purpose which animates those associated with it, it is fundamental that the enterprise 'function as a continuing unit.' In *Turkette,* the Supreme Court stated that an enterprise 'is proved by evidence of an *ongoing* organization, formal or informal, and by evidence that the various associates function as a *continuing* unit.' This does not mean the scope of the enterprise cannot change as it engages in diverse forms of activity nor does it mean that the participants in the enterprise cannot vary with different individuals managing *its* affairs at different times and in different places. What is essential, however, is that there is some continuity of both structure and personality. For example, the operatives in a prostitution ring may change through time, but the various roles which the old and new individuals perform remain the same. But if an entirely new set of people begin to operate the ring, it is not the same enterprise as it was before.

"Finally, an enterprise must have an 'ascertainable structure' distinct from that inherent in the conduct of a pattern of racketeering activity. This distinct structure might be demonstrated by proof that a group engaged in a diverse pattern of crimes or that it has an organizational pattern or system of authority beyond what was necessary to perpetrate the predicate crimes. The command system of a Mafia family is an example of this type of structure as is the hierarchy, planning, and division of profits within a prostitution ring."

(b) Is the *Bledsoe* approach sound? Consider how it should apply to the facts of *United States v. Lemm,* 680 F.2d 1193 (8th Cir.1982), concerning an insurance fraud scheme involving 17 arson fires in five states over a 3–year period, where the court split, 2–1. "The arson and insurance fraud activities underlying the convictions vary from fire to fire, but a general scenario can be summarized. Eugene P. Gamst, the government's chief witness, was a public insurance adjuster licensed in Minnesota. The government's case showed that at some point in the early 1970's Gamst began mixing his legitimate adjustment activities with arson, eventually becoming the center of an arson ring alleged to have existed from April 1, 1975 to September 1, 1978. The basic mode of operation was that Gamst, or occasionally another coconspirator, would recruit an individual to start an arson fire for insurance proceeds. Gamst would instruct the individual how to start the fire, how to act, and what to tell the authorities. After the fire, Gamst would pose as a legitimate public adjuster of an accidental fire. Occasionally, Gamst would also act as a private contractor and repair the fire damage in order to obtain a larger portion of the insurance proceeds. The roles of the other conspirators included providing seed money for the purchases of property, locating property for burning, providing property to be burned, preparing and torching the property, and recruiting others to the scheme."

3. *"Legal entity" enterprise.* At issue in *United States v. Thompson,* 685 F.2d 993 (6th Cir.1982), was the validity of an indictment which referred to "The Office of Governor of the State of Tennessee" as the RICO enterprise. The court concluded:

"We have emphasized the many references Congress made to crimes which primarily or substantially impact upon or make use of units of state or local governments. We believe Congress' inclusion of such crimes as bribery or extortion (through influence on state or local offices), obstruction of justice, obstruction of state or local law enforcement, obstruction of criminal investigation tends to rebut appellants' argument that Congress never intended to assert jurisdiction over a state activity such as that involved in the present indictment. * * *

"The case law which has already developed nationwide on the question of identifying a governmental unit as the RICO 'enterprise' is unanimous in rejecting appellants' single appellate contention in this case. * * *

"[W]e conclude that the language and plain meaning of the statute does not exclude identification of a governmental office as a RICO enterprise, that the weight of authority thus far developed is unanimously of the view that an indictment cast in this form is within congressional intent and valid, and that a review of legislative history of this statute indicates no contrary legislative intent. Under these circumstances defendants' voluntary pleas of guilty must be affirmed.

"We also hold, however, that description of 'The Office of Governor' of one of the states of the union as the 'enterprise' referred to in RICO is disruptive of comity in federal-state relations. In some cases, such language may also needlessly cast unfair reflection upon innocent individuals."

A dissent concluded to the contrary, and gave "three reasons for reaching this conclusion. In the first place, there is no language in the text of the statute which indicates that governmental units were intended to be treated as enterprises for purposes of RICO prosecutions. * * *

"In the second place, I find the legislative history as inconclusive as the language of the Act itself in determining whether a governmental unit was intended to be treated as an enterprise for purposes of a RICO prosecution. * * *

"Finally, and perhaps most importantly, the Act should be interpreted in such a way as to avoid straining delicate state-federal relations. There is no provision in the Constitution or statutes of Tennessee establishing 'The Office of the Governor.' However, Article III, Section 1 provides, 'The Supreme Executive power of the state shall be vested in a Governor.' The office of the governor is no ordinary enterprise; it is the embodiment of state sovereignty. As the majority opinion makes clear, these three defendants could have been prosecuted under RICO as an 'enterprise' consisting of a group of individuals associated in fact. RICO is intended to be broadly construed. However, since neither the language of the statute nor its legislative history requires an interpretation which treats governmental units as RICO enterprises, and since corruption in government can be effectively reached through other provisions of the Organized Crime Control Act of 1970 and other federal criminal laws such as those dealing with extortion and mail fraud, consideration of comity should lead the courts to give RICO a less intrusive interpretation than that adopted by the majority."

4. *Enterprise with political goals.* (a) In *United States v. Ivic,* 700 F.2d 51 (2d Cir. 1983), the court held that because the "core purpose" of RICO is "preventing and reversing the infiltration of legitimate businesses by organized crime elements," "political terrorism, at least when unaccompanied by any financial motive * * *, is beyond its contemplated reach."

(b) In *United States v. Bagaric,* 706 F.2d 42 (2d Cir.1983), where "the charges and proof all relate to a terrorist organization, 'motivated' by political as well as economic crimes 'to obtain money to further [its] activities,' " the court concluded: "Relying on isolated language in *Ivic,* appellants argue the Government is required to prove an ultimate and overriding financial motive to secure a RICO conviction. The *Ivic* court nowhere stated, however, that economic gain must be the sole motive of every RICO enterprise. Such a rule, we believe, would run counter to fundamental principles of criminal law and risk the politicization of criminal trials. We reject appellants' contention. * * *

"RICO demands no such inquiry. * * * Moreover, such an exercise would embroil courts and jurors in a controversy essentially irrelevant to the purpose of the statute under consideration. Whether appellants extorted money for the long-term political purpose of effecting the separation of Croatia from Yugoslavia, whether this formed part, but not all, of their 'motivation,' or whether the freedom of their former province is an issue they care about not at all, the effect of their activities on the national economy is identical. The *Ivic* court described RICO as a device to prevent (and reverse) 'the drain[ing of] billions of dollars from America's economy by unlawful conduct.' This effect is accomplished whatever considerations compel the creation and execution of an extortion scheme. * * *

"Further, investigation into motive would serve only to politicize, and otherwise inflame, RICO prosecutions. [D]efense counsel sought to inject peripheral political and religious considerations into the trial of this case, implying that appellants' anti-Communism or Catholicism, or their persecution by American and Yugoslavian officials acting in concert, justifiably drove them to commit the acts of extortion and violence charged in the indictment. These suggestions—which ultimately formed no part of the defense

case of appellants who testified or presented witnesses—were, viewed charitably, misguided. They can only have served to patronize the jury and to add a distracting element of emotionalism to the proceedings. An interpretation of RICO requiring proof of long-term pecuniary objectives which in some sense can be said to supersede accompanying political or religious ones would invite a repetition of this conduct. It would authorize the admission of evidence of political beliefs, racial animosities, and family and blood feuds as justifications for criminal acts. Because we believe Congress, and the traditions of our criminal law, contemplate trials free of consideration of such issues, we reject appellants' argument that economic motive must surmount all others.

"Appellants appear to argue also that the enterprise itself, rather than the predicate acts of racketeering, must be shown to yield financial gain. This contention is supported neither by a careful reading of the *Ivic* opinion nor by reference to the underlying purposes of RICO."

5. *"Pattern of racketeering activity."* In *Sedima, S.P.R.L. v. Imrex Co., Inc.,* 473 U.S. 479, 105 S.Ct. 3275, 87 L.Ed.2d 346 (1985), this footnote dictum appears:

"As many commentators have pointed out, the definition of a 'pattern of racketeering activity' differs from the other provisions in § 1961 in that it states that a pattern *requires* at least two acts of racketeering activity' § 1961(5) (emphasis added), not that it 'means' two such acts. The implication is that while two acts are necessary, they may not be sufficient. Indeed, in common parlance two of anything do not generally form a 'pattern.' The legislative history supports the view that two isolated acts of racketeering activity do not constitute a pattern. As the Senate Report explained: 'The target of [RICO] is thus not sporadic activity. The infiltration of legitimate business normally requires more than one "racketeering activity" and the threat of continuing activity to be effective. It is this factor of *continuity plus relationship* which combines to produce a pattern.' (emphasis added). Similarly, the sponsor of the Senate bill, after quoting this portion of the Report, pointed out to his colleagues that '[t]he term "pattern" itself requires the showing of a relationship * * *. So, therefore, proof of two acts of racketeering activity, without more, does not establish a pattern * * *.' Significantly, in defining 'pattern' in a later provision of the same bill, Congress was more enlightening: 'criminal conduct forms a pattern if it embraces criminal acts that have the same or similar purposes, results, participants, victims, or methods of commission, or otherwise are interrelated by distinguishing characteristics and are not isolated events.' 18 U.S.C. § 3575(e). This language may be useful in interpreting other sections of the Act."

6. *Effect on "interstate or foreign commerce."* In *United States v. Barton*, 647 F.2d 224 (2d Cir.1981), the defendants challenged the jurisdictional predicate of the charge that they conspired in violation of 18 U.S.C.A. § 1962(d) to violate § 1962(c). The evidence was that the defendants were connected with several bombings and attempted bombings in the state of New York, and the defendants argued on appeal that there was no proof they "were part of a nationwide crime syndicate" or that "their activities reached into other states." In affirming, the court of appeals pointed out that "there was evidence, for example, that Gignello's car, blown up by appellants, was insured by an interstate insurance carrier. [T]he broader focus of § 1962(c) persuades us that the latter section encompasses this bombing activity. *See United States v. DiFrancesco*, 604 F.2d 769, 775 (2d Cir. 1979) (payment by insurance companies in New York and other states of $480,000 in claims resulting from arson and mail fraud

had requisite effect on interstate commerce under § 1962(c)). Further, the attempted bombings of the Blue Gardenia restaurant had an admitted impact on interstate commerce. Witnesses who had supplied the restaurant with liquor and fish that had come from other countries and other states testified that after the bombing attempts, the restaurant's purchases declined significantly. Appellants concede that 'the loss of business was due to unfavorable reporting about the attempted assassination of Salvatore Gignello.' In addition, appellants made several interstate telephone calls to and from New York in their quest for explosive devices needed for their activities, and Vaccaro, Celestino, and Frassetto traveled from New York to Ohio, Virginia, and West Virginia, in order to obtain explosives."

7. *Assessment of RICO.* (a) Tarlow, *RICO: The New Darling of the Prosecutor's Nursery*, 49 Fordham L.Rev. 165, 305–06 (1980), concludes: "The present overbroad application of Title IX with its accompanying severe penalties has resulted from an abrogation of responsibility at all stages of the criminal justice system. Congress has promulgated a vague statute that gives no clear warning of the proscribed activities. The courts have broadly interpreted it in derogation of their obligation to narrowly construe criminal statutes. The actions of the prosecuting authorities have belied their public pronouncements that they would not 'power rape nickel and dime cases.' This situation can only be remedied by legislative action to clarify and revise the statute and by increased sensitivity of the courts directed toward protecting defendants from unfair and unconstitutional applications of Title IX."

(b) Compare Dombrink & Meeker, *Racketeering Prosecution: The Use and Abuse of RICO*, 16 Rutgers L.J. 633, 650–51 (1985): "Despite claims to the contrary, it appears that Criminal RICO has been used in a conservative manner without systematic abuse or creative extension. If anything, such constrained use reinforces traditional concepts of organized crime.

"As part of a social movement against white-collar and organized crime, RICO has been both a powerful and a controversial weapon. It produces an intense response both from those who criticize its underutilization and those who seek to restrict its use. Yet, the appellate litigation we studied indicates a pattern of conservative use, providing little support for the advocates on either side of the issue."

SECTION 14. SOLICITATION

PEOPLE v. LUBOW

Court of Appeals of New York, 1971.
29 N.Y.2d 58, 323 N.Y.S.2d 829, 272 N.E.2d 331.

BERGAN, JUDGE.

The revised Penal Law creates a new kind of offense, simpler in structure than an attempt or a conspiracy, and resting solely on communication without need for any resulting action (art. 100, Criminal Solicitation * * *).

The basic statutory definition of criminal solicitation is that with intent that another person shall "engage in conduct constituting a crime" the accused "solicits, requests, commands, importunes or otherwise attempts to cause such other person to engage in such conduct". This basic definitory language is continued through three grades of solicitation, the gravity depending on what crime the conduct sought to be induced would effectuate.

* * *

As it has been noted, nothing need be done under the statute in furtherance of the communication ("solicits, commands, importunes") to constitute the offense. The communication itself with intent the other person engage in the unlawful conduct is enough. It needs no corroboration.

And an attempt at communication which fails to reach the other person may also constitute the offense for the concluding clause "or otherwise attempts to cause such other person to engage in such conduct" would seem literally to embrace as an attempt an undelivered letter or message initiated with the necessary intent.

Appellants have been convicted after a trial by a three-Judge panel in the Criminal Court of the City of New York of violation of section 100.05 which describes solicitation to commit a felony. The information on which the prosecution is based is made by complainant Max Silverman. It describes the charge as criminal solicitation and states that "defendants attempted to cause deponent to commit the crime of grand larceny" in that they "attempted to induce the deponent to obtain precious stones on partial credit with a view towards appropriating the property to their own use and not paying the creditors, said conduct constituting the crime of larceny by false promise". * * *

The evidence showed that complainant Silverman and both defendants were engaged in the jewelry business. It could be found that defendant Lubow owed Silverman $30,000 for diamonds on notes which were unpaid; that Lubow had told Silverman he was associated with a big operator interested in buying diamonds and introduced him to defendant Gissinger.

It could also be found that in October, 1967, Silverman met the two defendants together at their office, demanded his money, and said that because of the amount owed him he was being forced into bankruptcy.

Silverman testified in response to this Lubow said "Well, let's make it a big one, a big bankruptcy", and Gissinger said this was a good idea. When Silverman asked "how it is done" he testified that Lubow, with Gissinger participating, outlined a method by which diamonds would be purchased partly on credit, sold for less than cost, with the proceeds pyramided to boost Silverman's credit rating until very substantial amounts came in, when there was to be a bankruptcy with Silverman explaining that he had lost the cash gambling in Puerto Rico and Las Vegas. The cash would be divided among the three men. The gambling explanation for the disappearance of cash would be made to seem believable by producing credit cards for Puerto Rico and Las Vegas. Silverman testified that Lubow said "we would eventually wind up with a quarter of a million dollars each" and that Gissinger said "maybe millions".

Silverman reported this proposal to the District Attorney in October, 1967 and the following month a police detective equipped Silverman with a tape recorder concealed on his person which was in operation during conversations with defendants on November 16 and which tends to substantiate the charge. The reel was received in evidence on concession that it was taken from the machine Silverman wore November 16.

A police detective testified as an expert that a "bust out operation" is a "pyramiding of credit by rapid purchasing of merchandise, and the rapid selling of the same merchandise sometimes 10 and 20 per cent the cost of the merchandise itself, and they keep selling and buying until they establish such a credit rating that they are able to purchase a large order at the end of their operation, and at this time they go into bankruptcy or they just leave".

There thus seems sufficient evidence in the record to find that defendants intended Silverman to engage in conduct constituting a felony by defrauding creditors of amounts making out grand larceny and that they importuned Silverman to engage in such conduct. Thus the proof meets the actual terms of the statute.

The statute itself is a valid exercise of legislative power. Commentators closely associated with the drafting of the Model Penal Code of the American Law Institute, from which the New York solicitation statute stems, have observed: "Purposeful solicitation presents dangers calling for preventive intervention and is sufficiently indicative of a disposition towards criminal activity to call for liability. Moreover, the fortuity that the person solicited does not agree to commit or attempt to commit the incited crime plainly should not relieve the solicitor of liability, when otherwise he would be a conspirator or an accomplice."

Solicitation to commit a felony was a misdemeanor at common law. Summarizing this historical fact Judge Cardozo observed: "So at common law, incitement to a felony, when it did not reach the stage of an attempt, was itself a separate crime, and like conspiracy, which it resembled, was a misdemeanor, not a felony." * * *

Although this Penal Law provision is the first statutory enactment in New York, there have been statutes aimed at criminal solicitation in some other States, notably California.

In commenting on the criminal solicitation enactment of article 100, two lawyers who were active in the work of the State Commission on Revision of the Penal Law and Criminal Code which prepared the present statute observed that article 100 "closes that gap" for those who believe, as apparently the commission and the American Law Institute did, that "solicitation to commit a crime involves sufficient culpability to warrant criminal sanctions".

There are, however, potential difficulties inherent in this penal provision which should be looked at, even though all of them are not decisive in this present case. One, of course, is the absence of any need for corroboration. The tape recording here tends to give some independent support to the testimony of Silverman, but there are types of criminal conduct which might be solicited where there would be a heavy thrust placed on the credibility of a single witness testifying to a conversation. Extraordinary care might be required in deciding when to prosecute; in determining the truth; and in appellate review of the factual decision.

One example would be the suggestion of one person to another that he commit a sexual offense; another is the suggestion that he commit perjury. The Model Penal Code did not require corroboration; but aside from the need for corroboration which is traditional in some sexual offenses, there are dangers in the misinterpretation of innuendos or remarks which could be taken as invitations to commit sexual offenses. * * *

In two opinions for the California Supreme Court, Justice Traynor has analyzed that State's criminal solicitations statute (Penal Code, § 653f; *Benson v. Superior Ct. of Los Angeles County,* 57 Cal.2d 240, 18 Cal.Rptr. 516, 368 P.2d 116 [1962], and *People v. Burt,* 45 Cal.2d 311, 288 P.2d 503 [1955]).

The first case was for solicitation to commit perjury and the second for solicitation to commit extortion.

The California statute is based on a specific list of serious crimes to which criminal solicitation expressly applies; but as to all of them the statute requires that the offense "must be proved by the testimony of two witnesses, or of one witness and corroborating circumstances".

The basic public justification for legislative enactment is, however, very similar to New York's and was developed in the *Burt* opinion: "Legislative concern with the proscribed soliciting is demonstrated not only by the gravity of the crimes specified but by the fact that the crime, unlike conspiracy, does not require the commission of any overt act. It is complete when the solicitation is made, and it is immateri-

al that the object of the solicitation is never consummated, or that no steps are taken toward its consummation." The California Legislature was concerned "not only with the prevention of the harm that would result should the inducements prove successful, but with protecting inhabitants of this state from being exposed to inducements to commit or join in the commission of the crimes specified."

Another potential problem with the statute is that it includes an attempt to commit unlawful solicitation, i.e., solicits, etc., "or otherwise attempts to cause" the conduct. This has the same effect as the Model Penal Code, but the language there is different. The code spells the purpose out more specifically that: "It is immaterial * * * that the actor fails to communicate with the person he solicits to commit a crime if his conduct was designed to effect such communication" (*Model Penal Code,* § 5.02, subd. [2], Tent. Draft No. 10 * * *). This could be an attempt in the classic sense and might be committed by a telephone message initiated but never delivered. The present Penal Law, stated in different language, has the same effect. * * *

Notes and Questions

1. *Need.* Are you convinced, given the availability of the crimes of attempt and conspiracy to deal with inchoate criminality, that there is also a need for the crime of solicitation? What of the contention that a mere solicitation need not be made criminal because the "force set in motion is neither continuous nor mechanical, and its operation may be broken before the stage of attempt has been attained by the withdrawal or repentence" of the person solicited? *People v. Werblow,* 241 N.Y. 55, 148 N.E. 786 (1925).

2. *Risks.* Is whatever need exists outweighed by the risk of false charges arising

out of misunderstanding or harassment? Consider:

(a) *Smith v. Commonwealth,* 54 Pa. 209 (1867), where, in holding there was no common law crime of soliciting fornication, the court commented: "It is observable that no assault or overt act is charged—no writing, or picture, or indecent exposure of person is alleged, nothing indeed is suggested but mere solicitation. And the manner of this is not even hinted. It may have been by direct request, by innuendo, by argument, founded, as has sometimes happened, upon scriptural texts and analogies, or it may have been by gay and frivolous anecdote or appeal. Possibly nothing was *said,* but only impure thoughts insinuated by looks or gestures. What evidence shall be sufficient to sustain such a charge?"

(b) *Kelly v. United States,* 194 F.2d 150 (D.C.Cir.1952), where, with respect to the charge against the defendant that he solicited sodomy from an undercover policeman (who had made six arrests upon such a charge the same evening), the court said: "The public has a peculiar interest in the problem before us. The alleged offense, consisting of a few spoken words, may be alleged to have occurred in any public place, where any citizen is likely to be. They may be alleged to have been whispered, or to have occurred in the course of a most casual conversation. Any citizen who answers a stranger's inquiry as to direction, or time, or a request for a dime or a match is liable to be threatened with an accusation of this sort. There is virtually no protection, except one's reputation and appearance of credibility, against an uncorroborated charge of this sort. At the same time, the results of the accusation itself are devastating to the accused. The gratuitous solicitation of a total stranger for a perverted act is a phenomenon on the outer fringes of behavior. While technically this offense is a minor misdemeanor and in the catalog of crimes is graded as

less serious than reckless driving, in the practical world of everyday living it is a major accusation.

"It follows that threatened accusation of this offense is the easiest of blackmail methods. The horror of the ordinary citizen at the thought of such an accusation may impel him to comply with a demand for money under such a threat. The public has a great interest in the prevention of any such criminal operation."

3. *Minimizing the risks.* What can be done about these risks? Consider (a) the California corroboration rule discussed in *Lubow;* (b) the requirement in Wis.Stat. Ann. § 939.30 that the solicitation take place "under circumstances which indicate unequivocally" the defendant's intent that a crime be committed; and (c) the proposal in National Comm'n on Reform of Federal Criminal laws, *Final Report* § 1003 (1971), that an overt act by the person solicited be required.

4. *Acts.* (a) Does the New York statute specify sufficiently what acts will suffice for the crime? Would a broader statement be desirable? Compare the statute discussed in *Turner v. LaBelle,* 251 F.Supp. 443 (D.Conn.1966), which uses the words "advocates, encourages, justifies, praises, incites or solicits."

(b) Must the solicitation be directed toward a particular person? See *State v. Schleifer,* 99 Conn. 432, 121 A. 805 (Dist. Ct.1923) holding sufficient an information charging the defendant with soliciting from a public platform a number of persons to commit the crimes of murder and robbery. Is it correct to say that "solicitations of this type are more dangerous than solicitations of a special kind, for here solicitation is to a greater number"? Blackburn, *Solicitation to Crimes,* 40 W.Va. L.Rev. 135, 146 (1934).

What result, then, on these facts: The defendants have been charged under the New York solicitation statute with soliciting the illegal possession of DMT, a psychedelic agent. The evidence is that they circulated a pamphlet highly critical of contemporary American life which included the assertion: "What's needed is a generation of people who are freaky, crazy, irrational, sexy, angry, irreligious, childish and mad: people who burn draft cards, burn high school and college degrees: people who say: 'To hell with your goals'; people who lure youth with music, pot and acid." This was followed by a paragraph entitled "How to make a fire bomb," and a recipe for producing DMT, which concluded: "This cannot be drunk or injected, but may be smoked by sprinkling on mint or cannabis leaves and letting the solution evaporate." [a]

(c) Assume that *A* gives *B* a letter for delivery to *C* which solicits *C* to commit a crime, but that *B* does not make delivery. Would *A* be guilty under the New York statute? Should this be deemed solicitation? Attempted solicitation?

5. *Objectives.* May a statute prohibit the solicitation of conduct which is itself not criminal? In *City of Columbus v. Scott,* 47 Ohio App.2d 287, 353 N.E.2d 858 (1975), the court affirmed the dismissal of a complaint charging violation of an ordinance providing: "No person shall solicit a person to engage in sexual activity with the offender, when the offender knows such solicitation is offensive to the other person, or is reckless in that regard." In holding that "the ordinance makes a criminal offense of the social interrelationships and protected free speech rights of otherwise consenting adults," the court emphasized, as the trial court concluded, that "sexual activity is illegal only under specific circumstances" and that "the ordinance is not limited to *illegal* sexual activity." Consider also *Cherry v. State,* 18 Md.App. 252, 306 A.2d 634 (1973), upholding

defendant's conviction of solicitation for purposes of prostitution on the theory that "if consummated crimes themselves are constitutional in terms of their criminality * * *, then constitutionality follows as to their incipient or inchoate phases."

But does this mean that on either policy or constitutional grounds particular solicitation-type statutes should be confined to objectives which are and constitutionally may be made criminal? Consider *United States v. Carson,* 319 A.2d 329 (D.C.App. 1974), reversing the dismissal of several charges of soliciting for lewd and immoral purposes:

"In holding that this soliciting statute amounts to a violation of a right of privacy, the trial court used as its major premise 'the fundamental principle that the Constitution protects the right of an individual to control *the use and function* of his or her body without unreasonable interference from the state.' (Emphasis supplied.) The trial court's ruling thus appears to have been based on the assumption that an act of sodomy between consenting adults in privacy (i.e., 'use and function') may not constitutionally be proscribed. Irrespective of the validity of a criminal sanction against a private and consensual sodomitic act, the overbreadth doctrine may not properly be applied to the soliciting statute. The acts charged were public solicitations of strangers for sodomy. That any of the accused ultimately may have contemplated a private and consensual act is of no legal significance. Any such hope or expectation by an accused may not in contemplation of law project him into a posture in which he can assert a right of privacy which arguably might arise from such a projected position."

6. *Impossibility.* In *Benson,* cited in *Lubow,* an undercover investigator visited

a. *People v. Quentin,* 58 Misc.2d 601, 296 N.Y.S.2d 443 (1968), concluding the statute was not "designed to cover a situation where the

defendant makes a general solicitation (however reprehensible) to a large undefinable group to commit a crime."

defendant, an attorney, and told him she was pregnant, that she wanted to have the child adopted, and that the child's father was unknown because she had been living with her husband and another man. Defendant told her there were ways of getting around the statutory requirement of obtaining her husband's consent to the adoption. At defendant's suggestion, the woman arranged for a friend (actually, another investigator) to meet with the defendant, and he instructed her as to the perjured testimony she should give at the custody proceedings. Defendant, charged with solicitation of perjured testimony, objected that he had not committed that crime because the investigator was not actually pregnant and thus the anticipated custody proceedings would never occur. Held: "If the solicitor believes that the act can be committed 'it is immaterial that the crime urged is not possible of fulfilment at the time when the words are spoken' or becomes impossible at a later time."

7. *Abandonment.* In *State v. Boehm,* 127 Wis.2d 351, 379 N.W.2d 874 (App. 1985), Lynn Boehm solicited Larry Poor to murder Ron Hitchler. She later told Poor she was "done with" the Hitchler killing and that the whole thing was off; the murder was not committed. On appeal of Boehm's conviction for solicitation of first-degree murder, the court took note of the renunciation defense in Model Penal Code § 5.02(3), but then held: "Renunciation or withdrawal cannot undo that which has been done and therefore has no effect on the elements of solicitation, once completed."

8. *Nonliability for offense solicited.* In *Leffel v. Municipal Court,* 54 Cal.App.3d 569, 126 Cal.Rptr. 773 (1976), it was held that a statute providing that "[e]very person * * * [w]ho solicits * * * an act of prostitution" is guilty of disorderly conduct, is applicable to a potential customer of a prostitute who solicits her. Is this a fair construction of the statute? A

desirable result? Is it a proper result if the defendant would not have been an accomplice to the act of prostitution had it occurred? See *Model Penal Code* § 5.04(2).

9. *Punishment.* As noted in *Lubow,* New York has three grades of solicitation. Each grade authorizes punishment which is not as great as that provided for the crimes specified as the object of that grade of solicitation. Compare *Model Penal Code* § 5.05. Which penalty scheme is most rational?

10. *Solicitation as an attempt.* "While a few of the courts have treated solicitation to commit a crime as an attempt, the great weight of authority warrants the assertion that mere solicitation, unaccompanied by an act moving directly toward the commission of the intended crime, is not an overt act constituting an element of the crime of attempt." *State v. Davis,* 319 Mo. 1222, 6 S.W.2d 609 (1928). What additional acts should suffice? Compare *State v. Otto,* 102 Idaho 250, 629 P.2d 646 (1981) (defendant not guilty of attempted murder where he told person referred to him as a "hitman" who he wanted killed, negotiated fee of $1,000, paid $250 as an advance, and discussed type of weapon to be utilized and manner in which hit to be made); with *State v. Kilgus,* 128 N.H. 577, 519 A.2d 231 (1986) (defendant's conviction of attempted murder affirmed where he solicited killing of specified person, paid fee of $1,000 and stressed that body must be found out of state).

11. *The innocent solicitee.* In *State v. Bush,* 195 Mont. 475, 636 P.2d 849 (1981), defendant appealed his conviction of soliciting the possession of dangerous drugs. The evidence at trial was that defendant had hired a Ms. Kohse as a photographer of animals and sent her to Lima, Peru to take pictures at the zoo, during which time an accomplice placed cocaine into the lining of her camera case, which she transported into the United States.

"Appellant's final contention is that the crime of solicitation is not complete unless the person solicited is aware of the solicitor's criminal purpose and scheme. Since Kohse was unaware that she was to do anything but work for a movie company and since she was unaware of the drugs, appellant maintains she was not solicited.

"At common law the use of an innocent agent to accomplish a crime was considered an attempt but not a solicitation. The common law has been affirmatively changed in some jurisdictions by statutes which provide that it is no defense to a charge of solicitation that the solicitee is unaware of the criminal nature of the conduct solicited or of the defendant's purpose. The theory behind the change is that one is no less guilty of a crime because he employs an innocent agent.

"The Montana statute is not explicit in this regard. The language 'facilitates the commission of that offense' does not imply that the person solicited must be aware of the criminal purpose. As above noted, the Montana legislature has changed the common law, as is its prerogative, and has not required that the solicitee be aware of the criminal purpose of the solicitor or of the criminal nature of the conduct solicited. To do so would defeat the purpose of the statute which is to protect the citizens of this state from victimization and from exposure to inducements to commit or join in the commission of crime. The gravamen of the offense of solicitation is the intent of the solicitor and not the knowledge of the victim."

Consider also *State v. Rossi,* __ R.I. __, 520 A.2d 582 (1987) (rejecting defendant's claim his conviction of soliciting an 8–year–old girl to commit perjury cannot stand because the girl, as a minor, could not be convicted of perjury, and noting that a "similar view" is taken in Model Penal Code § 5.04(1)(b)).

12. *The cautious solicitor.* Persons seeking "customers" for some criminal activity, fearful of being discovered by undercover police, often phrase their solicitations in the most ambiguous terms possible. It is not uncommon, therefore, for courts to be confronted with the question of whether the events proved will support a solicitation conviction. Consider, for example, whether a conviction of soliciting for lewd and immoral purposes could be had on these facts:

"On November 7, 1972, Officer Keeton of the Vice Squad, Metropolitan Police Department, was driving his private car south in the 1000 block of 14th Street, N.W., when he was waived to the curb by two persons standing with others at a corner. Both persons, attired as women, approached the passenger side of the car and one of them (appellant) asked the officer who was in civilian clothes, 'You want to go out for a while?' The other person, identified as one Walter Modin, asked, 'How much money you spending?' When Officer Keeton replied that he had 'about $75', appellant's companion asked where he was staying to which Officer Keeton replied '[T]he Hilton.' Mr. Modin said, 'We can't get in there, so we'll have to find another place.' He left the car to speak to other persons attired also as women who were gathered on the corner. Appellant, while standing at the side of the car, was asked by Officer Keeton what he was going to get for his money, to which appellant replied, 'I'll do anything at all.' According to Officer Keeton's testimony the following then transpired:

At that time I asked if he would [submit to rectal sodomy], and he [appellant] said, 'I'll do anything at all.' So, I asked him what he was best at, and * * * in the meantime, while this conversation was going on, Mr. Modin approached the auto again, and Mr. Shannon then said he would [participate in natural and perverted sexual acts] * * *. 'I'm good at everything, baby.'

"Both appellant and Mr. Modin then got into the car and Officer Keeton drove for a short distance to the 1000 block of Vermont Avenue, N.W., where he placed both men under arrest with the assistance of his partner, Officer Martin, who had followed Keeton's vehicle after observing the two approach it, engaged in apparent conversation, and then enter the vehicle." [b]

b. *Shannon v. United States*, 311 A.2d 501 (D.C.App.1973), modified, 319 A.2d 135 (1974), reversing the conviction.

Chapter 11

PARTIES; LIABILITY FOR CONDUCT OF ANOTHER

SECTION 1. THE COMMON LAW CLASSIFICATION

In the commission of each criminal offense there may be several persons or groups which play distinct roles before, during, and after the offense. Collectively these persons or groups are termed the parties to the crime.

The common law classification of parties to a felony consisted of four categories: (1) principal in the first degree; (2) principal in the second degree; (3) accessory before the fact; and (4) accessory after the fact. This classification scheme gave rise to many procedural difficulties, but if they were overcome a person in any one of the four categories could be convicted and subjected to the penalties authorized for commission of the felony. It was later recognized that the accessory after the fact, by virtue of his involvement only after the felony was completed, was not truly an accomplice in the felony. This category has thus remained distinct from the others, and today the accessory after the fact is not deemed a participant in the felony but rather one who has obstructed justice, subjecting him to different and lesser penalties.[a] The distinctions between the other three categories, however, have now been

largely abrogated, although statutes frequently resort to the common law terminology in defining the scope of complicity. It thus remains important to understand what is collectively encompassed within these three categories.

The common law classification scheme described above existed only as to felonies. When treason was committed, those who would be included within any of the four felony categories were all classified as principals. As to misdemeanors, all parties were again held to be principals, although conduct which would constitute one an accessory after the fact to a felony was not criminal when the post-crime aid was to a misdemeanant.

1. *Principal in the First Degree.* A principal in the first degree may simply be defined as the criminal actor. He is the one who, with the requisite mental state, engages in the act or omission concurring with the mental state which causes the criminal result.

There can be more than one principal in the first degree. This occurs when more than one actor participates in the actual commission of the offense. Thus, when one man beats a victim and another shoots him, both may be principals in first degree

---

a. See Section 11 of this Chapter.

to murder. And when two persons forge separate parts of the same instrument, they are both principals in the first degree to the forgery.

Although it has been said that a principal in the first degree must be present at the commission of the offense, this is not literally so. He may be "constructively" present when some instrument which he left or guided caused the criminal result. Thus, when an actor leaves poison for another who later drinks it, he is a first degree principal, as is the person whose unwitting agent acts for him in his absence.

While there may be more than one principal in the first degree, there must always be at least one for a crime to have taken place.

2. *Principal in the Second Degree.* To be a principal in the second degree, one must be present at the commission of a criminal offense and aid, counsel, command, or encourage the principal in the first degree in the commission of that offense. This requirement of presence may be fulfilled by constructive presence. A person is constructively present when he is physically absent from the situs of the crime but aids and abets the principal in the first degree at the time of the offense from some distance. This may happen when one stands watch for the primary actor, signals to the principal from a distance that the victim is coming, or stands ready (though out of sight) to render aid to the principal if needed. However, one must be close enough to render aid if needed.

3. *Accessory Before the Fact.* An accessory before the fact is one who orders, counsels, encourages, or otherwise aids and abets another to commit a felony and who is not present at the commission of the offense. The primary distinction between the accessory before the fact and the principal in the second degree is presence. If

a person was actually or constructively present at the offense, due to his participation he is a principal in the second degree; if he was not present, he is an accessory before the fact. Through prior counseling followed by appearance at the scene of the crime to aid the primary actor, one may become both an accessory before the fact and also a principal in the second degree.

Although the accessory before the fact is often the originator of the offense, this need not be the case. Indeed, if one is enlisted by another to lend aid toward the commission of the offense and the aid is given, the person giving the assistance may thereby become an accessory before the fact.

4. *Legislative Reform.* Virtually all states have now expressly abrogated the distinction between principals and accessories before the fact. The most common form of legislation declares that accessories before the fact are now principals, although substantially the same result has been reached by providing that those who would have been accessories before the fact may be prosecuted, tried and punished as if they were principals.

A much more modern approach to the entire subject of parties to crime is to abandon completely the old common law terminology and simply provide that a person is legally accountable for the conduct of another when he is an accomplice of the other person in the commission of the crime. Such is the view taken in the Model Penal Code,[b] which provides that a person is an accomplice of another person in the commission of an offense if, with the purpose of promoting or facilitating the commission of the offense, he solicits the other person to commit it, or aids or agrees or attempts to aid the other person in planning or committing it, or (having a legal duty to prevent the crime) fails to make proper effort to prevent it. A simi-

b.   § 2.06(2)(c).

lar approach has been taken in many of the recent recodifications.

SECTION 2. ACTS OR OMISSIONS

HICKS v. UNITED STATES

Supreme Court of the United States, 1893.
150 U.S. 442, 14 S.Ct. 144, 37 L.Ed. 1137.

MR. JUSTICE SHIRAS delivered the opinion of the court.

In the circuit court of the United States for the western district of Arkansas, John Hicks, an Indian, was jointly indicted with Stand Rowe, also an Indian, for the murder of Andrew J. Colvard, a white man, by shooting him with a gun on the 13th of February, 1892. Rowe was killed by the officers in the attempt to arrest him, and Hicks was tried separately, and found guilty, in March, 1893. * * *

At the trial the government's evidence clearly disclosed that John Hicks, the accused, did not, as charged in the indictment, shoot the deceased, nor take any part in the physical struggle. To secure a conviction it hence became necessary to claim that the evidence showed such participation in the felonious shooting of the deceased as to make the accused an accessory, or that he so acted in aiding and abetting Rowe as to make him guilty as a principal. The prosecution relied on evidence tending to show that Rowe and Hicks co-operated in inducing Colvard to leave the house, where they and a number of others had passed the night in a drunken dance, and to accompany them up the road to the spot where the shooting took place. Evidence was likewise given by two or three men, who, from a house about 100 yards distant, were eyewitnesses of the occurrence, that the three men were seated on their horses a few feet apart; that Rowe twice raised his gun and aimed at Colvard; that Hicks was heard to laugh on both occasions; that Rowe thereupon

withdrew his gun; that Hicks pulled off his hat, and, striking his horse with it, said to Colvard, "Pull off your hat, and die like a man;" that thereupon Rowe raised his gun a third time, and fired at Colvard, whose horse then ran some distance before Colvard fell. As the horse ran, Rowe fired a second time. When Colvard's body was subsequently examined, it was found that the first bullet had passed through his chest, inflicting a fatal wound, and that the second had not taken effect.

The language attributed to Hicks, and which he denied having used, cannot be said to have been entirely free from ambiguity. It was addressed, not to Rowe, but to Colvard. Hicks testified that Rowe was in a dangerous mood, and that he did not know whether he would shoot Colvard or Hicks. The remark made,—if made,—accompanied with the gesture of taking off his own hat, may have been an utterance of desperation, occasioned by his belief that Rowe would shoot one or both of them. That Hicks and Rowe rode off together after seeing Colvard fall was used as a fact against Hicks, pointing to a conspiracy between them. Hicks testified that he did it in fear of his life; that Rowe had demanded that he should show him the road which he wished to travel. Hicks further testified—and in this he was not contradicted—that he separated from Rowe a few minutes afterwards, on the first opportunity, and that he never afterwards had any intercourse with him, nor had he been in the company of Rowe for several weeks before the night of the fatal occurrence. * * *

Another error is contained in that portion of the charge now under review, and that is the statement "that, if Hicks was actually present at that place at the time of the firing by Stand Rowe, and he was there for the purpose of either aiding, abetting, advising, or encouraging the shooting of Andrew J. Colvard by Stand Rowe, and that, as a matter of fact, he did not do it, but was present for the purpose of aiding or abetting or advising or encouraging his shooting, but he did not do it because it was not necessary, it was done without his assistance, the law says there is a third condition where guilt is fastened to his act in that regard."

We understand this language to mean that where an accomplice is present for the purpose of aiding and abetting in a murder but refrains from so aiding and abetting because it turned out not to be necessary for the accomplishment of the common purpose, he is equally guilty as if he had actively participated by words or acts of encouragement. Thus understood, the statement might, in some instances, be a correct instruction. Thus, if there had been evidence sufficient to show that there had been a previous conspiracy between Rowe and Hicks to waylay and kill Colvard, Hicks, if present at the time of the killing, would be guilty, even if it was found unnecessary for him to act. But the error of such an instruction, in the present case, is in the fact that there was no evidence on which to base it. The evidence, so far as we are permitted to notice it, as contained in the bills of exception and set forth in the charge, shows no facts from which the jury could have properly found that the rencounter was the result of any previous conspiracy or arrangement. The jury might well, therefore, have thought that they were following the court's instructions in finding the accused guilty because he was present at the time and place of the murder, although he contributed neither by word nor action to the crime, and although there was no substantial evidence of any conspiracy or prior arrangement between him and Rowe. * * *

The judgment of the court below is reversed, and the cause remanded, with directions to set aside the verdict and award a new trial. * * *

Notes and Questions

1. Should Hicks be deemed an accomplice because he failed to intervene or even manifest his disapproval? Consider *Pace v. State,* 248 Ind. 146, 224 N.E.2d 312 (1967), an appeal from a conviction for being an accessory to a robbery:

"Viewing the evidence most favorable to the State, the record shows the following: appellant, his wife and two infant children were in a car driving from South Bend to LaPorte. Eugene Rootes was riding with them. The appellant was driving with his wife and one child in the front seat. Rootes and appellant's other child were in the back seat. While in South Bend, appellant after asking his wife for permission stopped to pick up a hitchhiker, Mr. Reppert, who sat next to Rootes in the back seat with one of appellant's infant children. Later Rootes pulled a knife and took Reppert's wallet. After driving further, Reppert got out of the car, Rootes then took his watch. The appellant said nothing during the entire period and they continued driving to LaPorte. This is all of the evidence presented by the record which would have any bearing on the crime charged, i.e., accessory before the fact of robbery by placing in fear.

"The main question presented in the facts at bar is what evidence beyond the mere presence of a person at the scene of a crime is sufficient to sustain a connection as an accessory before the fact? This court has previously stated that negative acquiescence is not enough to constitute a person guilty of aiding and abetting the commission of a crime. * * * However, it has been further stated by this court in *Mobley v. State* (1949), 227 Ind. 335, 344, 85 N.E.2d 489, 492:

'* * * in the absence of anything in his conduct showing a design to encourage, incite, aid, abet or assist in the crime, the trier of the facts may consider failure of such person to oppose the commission of the crime in connection with other circumstances and conclude therefrom that he assented to the commission of the crime, lent his countenance and approval thereto and thereby aided and abetted it * * *'

It should be noted that the court in *Mobley,* supra, in stating that a failure to oppose the commission of a crime may be considered as aiding and abetting, impliedly qualified this statement wherein the Court stated:

'This, it seems to us, is particularly true when the person who fails to interfere owes a duty to protect as a parent owes to a child.'

In other cases relying on *Mobley,* supra, there has normally been some course of conduct of an affirmative nature to connect the defendant with the crime.

"In the facts at bar we have found no evidence or reasonable inferences therefrom which might demonstrate that the appellant aided and abetted in the alleged crime. While he was driving the car, nothing was said nor did he act in any manner to indicate his approval or countenance of the robbery. While there is evidence from which a jury might reasonably infer that he knew the crime was being committed, his situation was not one which would demonstrate a duty to oppose it. We do not intend to draw any hard and fast rules in this area of the law. Each case must be reviewed on its own facts; in so doing we hold that the verdict is not sustained by substantial evidence of probative value and is therefore contrary to law."

2. Compare *State v. Walden,* 306 N.C. 466, 293 S.E.2d 780 (1982), where defendant was convicted of aiding and abetting an assault by one Hoskins upon defendant's one-year-old son. The evidence was that the assault occurred in defendant's presence without her objection or intervention. On appeal, she challenged a jury instruction that one's mere presence is insufficient but that it is sufficient if one "is present with the reasonable opportunity and duty to prevent the crime and fails to take reasonable steps to do so." In affirming the conviction, the court reasoned:

"Parents in this State have an affirmative legal duty to protect and provide for their minor children. * * *

"We find no case from any jurisdiction directly in point on the precise question before us, i.e., whether a mother may be found guilty of assault on a theory of aiding and abetting solely on the ground that she was present when her child was attacked and had a reasonable opportunity to prevent or attempt to prevent the attack but failed to do so. * * *

"[W]e believe that to require a parent as a matter of law to take affirmative action to prevent harm to his or her child or be held criminally liable imposes a reasonable duty upon the parent. Further, we believe this duty is and has always been inherent in the duty of parents to provide for the safety and welfare of their children, which duty has long been recognized by the common law and by statute. This is not to say that parents have the legal duty to place themselves in danger of death or great bodily harm in coming to the aid of their children. To require such, would require every parent to exhibit courage and heroism which, although commendable in the extreme, cannot realistically be expected or required of all people. But parents do have the duty to take every step reasonably possible under the circumstances of a given situation to prevent harm to their children.

"In some cases, depending upon the size and vitality of the parties involved, it might be reasonable to expect a parent to physically intervene and restrain the person attempting to injure the child. In other circumstances, it will be reasonable for a parent to go for help or to merely verbally protest an attack upon the child. What is reasonable in any given case will be a question for the jury after proper instructions from the trial court.

"We think that the rule we announce today is compelled by our statutes and prior cases establishing the duty of parents to provide for the safety and welfare of their children. Further, we find our holding today to be consistent with our prior cases regarding the law of aiding and abetting. It remains the law that one may not be found to be an aider and abettor, and thus guilty as a principal, solely because he is present when a crime is committed. It will still be necessary, in order to have that effect, that it be shown that the defendant said or did something showing his consent to the criminal purpose and contribution to its execution. But we hold that the failure of a parent who is present to take all steps reasonably possible to protect the parent's child from an attack by another person constitutes an act of omission by the parent showing the parent's consent and contribution to the crime being committed. *Cf. State v. Haywood,* 295 N.C. 709, 249 S.E.2d 429 (1978) (When a bystander is a friend of the perpetrator and knows his presence will be regarded as encouragement, presence alone may be regarded as aiding and abetting.)."

3. In *State v. Tazwell,* 30 La.Ann. 884 (1878), defendant was convicted as an accessory before the fact to the burglary of a barn, in that he had provided the burglar with an instrument to be used in committing the crime. On appeal, the defendant objected that the judge had refused to give the following requested charge: "That if there be no evidence to show that an instrument furnished by one accused as accessory before the fact was used for the purpose for which it was made, but another and different one is used to commit the offense, that it has not been sufficiently proved to justify a verdict of guilty as accessory before the fact. That the instru-

ment said in the indictment to have been furnished for the purpose of committing an offense must be proved to have been used for that purpose."

The court affirmed, concluding that the requested charge "is manifestly wrong. It would be strange, indeed, if one who had so far counseled, aided, and abetted a burglary as to provide and furnish implements to effect it, could escape because when the burglar reached the place of his crime he found more convenient tools, and did not actually use those furnished him for the purpose by his confederate."

4. *Hicks* indicates that "words or acts of encouragement" can suffice as a basis for accomplice liability. What result then on the facts in *State v. Ulvinen,* 313 N.W.2d 425 (Minn.1981)? Helen told her son David that she was moving out of David's home because David's wife Carol "had been so nasty to me." David then said that he was going to kill Carol, and Helen responded "it will be for the best." Later that day David told Helen that "Tonight's got to be the night," and Helen answered that "it would be the best for the kids." That night, while Helen was sleeping, David strangled Carol. David later dismembered the body; while this was occurring, Helen remained upstairs to intercept the children should they awaken. Helen then helped David clean up the bathroom, where the dismemberment took place.

5. *State ex rel. Martin v. Tally,* 102 Ala. 25, 15 So. 722 (1894), involved an appeal by Judge Tally from his impeachment for his complicity in a murder. At the impeachment proceedings it was shown that Ross had seduced the judge's sister-in-law and that consequently her brothers (the Skeltons) followed him to the nearby town of Stevenson for the purpose of killing Ross. While at the telegraph office in Scottsboro, the judge learned that a relative of Ross had just sent Ross a telegram

reading: "Four men on horseback with guns following. Look out." The judge then sent a telegram to the telegraph operator in Stevenson, an acquaintance by the name of Huddleston, reading: "Do not let the party warned get away." Huddleston received both messages, but failed to deliver the one addressed to Ross. The Skeltons caught up with Ross and killed him. The court concluded that these facts sufficed to make Judge Tally an accomplice:

"We are therefore clear to the conclusion that, before Judge Tally can be found guilty of aiding and abetting the Skeltons to kill Ross, it must appear that his vigil at Scottsboro to prevent Ross from being warned of his danger was by preconcert with them, or at least known to them, whereby they would naturally be incited, encouraged, and emboldened—'given confidence'—to the deed, or that he aided them to kill Ross, contributed to Ross' death, in point of physical fact, by means of the telegram he sent to Huddleston. The assistance given, however, need not contribute to the criminal result in the sense that but for it the result would not have ensued. It is quite sufficient if it facilitated a result that would have transpired without it. It is quite enough if the aid merely rendered it easier for the principal actor to accomplish the end intended by him and the aider and abettor, though in all human probability the end would have been attained without it. If the aid in homicide can be shown to have put the deceased at a disadvantage, to have deprived him of a single chance of life which but for it he would have had, he who furnishes such aid is guilty, though it can-

not be known or shown that the dead man, in the absence thereof, would have availed himself of that chance; as, where one counsels murder, he is guilty as an accessory before the fact, though it appears to be probable that murder would have been done without his counsel; and as, where one being present by concert to aid if necessary is guilty as a principal in the second degree, though, had he been absent murder would have been committed, so, where he who facilitates murder even by so much as destroying a single chance of life the assailed might otherwise have had, he thereby supplements the efforts of the perpetrator, and he is guilty as principal in the second degree at common law, and is principal in the first degree under our statute, notwithstanding it may be found that in all human probability the chance would not have been availed of, and death would have resulted anyway."

6. What if Huddleston had not acted on the judge's instructions but had instead delivered the warning telegram to Ross? If the Skeltons had nonetheless caught up with Ross and killed him, would the judge be an accomplice to murder? Consider *Model Penal Code* § 2.06(3)(a)(ii), which includes "attempts to aid" as a basis for accomplice liability.[a] The draftsmen explain: "The inclusion of attempts to aid may go in part beyond present law, but attempted complicity ought to be criminal, and to distinguish it from effective complicity appears unnecessary where the crime has been committed. Where complicity is based upon agreement or solicitation, one does not ask for evidence that they were actually operative psychologically on the person who committed the of-

---

a. Several modern codes have adopted this innovation. Illustrative of its impact is *State v. Gelb*, 212 N.J.Super. 582, 515 A.2d 1246 (1986) (defendant convicted of being homicide accomplice to Wade, who pulled switch causing train to leave main track and hit brick wall, killing engineer; testimony was that one Held yelled "Throw the switch," and that Wade then began pulling

the switch, after which he heard Gelb yell "to wait until the train passed Morlot Avenue so the engineer doesn't know the switch is pulled"; because of "attempt to aid" language in statute, defendant not entitled to jury instruction that he must be acquitted if his actions were "subsequent to the actual and irreversible lifting of the switch").

fense; there ought to be no difference in the case of aid." *Model Penal Code* § 2.06, Comment (1985).

What, then, should be the result if Ross escapes because Huddleston warns him notwithstanding the judge's instructions? Under *Model Penal Code* § 5.01(3) the judge is guilty of attempted murder. The draftsmen note: "If the judge had been unsuccessful in his effort to prevent Ross from being warned and Ross had escaped, or if, notwithstanding the effective suppression of the warning, Ross had not been killed, the judge would have engaged in conduct designed to aid the others to murder Ross and liability would be established under subsection (3)." *Model Penal Code* § 5.01, Comment (1985).

7. In *People v. Bohmer*, 46 Cal.App.3d 185, 120 Cal.Rptr. 136 (1975), defendant appealed his conviction under a statute making it an offense to maliciously place an obstruction upon the tracks of any railroad. Bohmer chaired a meeting at which the means to be used in stopping a train carrying war supplies was discussed, and he addressed a group of 350 to 500 people gathered near the Santa Fe tracks and depot. When a railroad signal indicated a train was approaching, several people placed railroad ties on the tracks and set them on fire.

"Bohmer was not one of those who engaged physically in placing obstructions on the railroad tracks. Although he had been at the general location of that activity earlier, he had left the scene just before the work of obstruction began. His guilt, if any, could only have resulted from incitement or abetting of the placing of the obstructions based upon his antecedent speech and conduct.

"Hence arises his claim that his conviction violates his First Amendment rights of speech and assembly. In *Brandenburg v. Ohio*, 395 U.S. 444, 447, 89 S.Ct. 1827, 1829, 23 L.Ed.2d 430, it was held that the mere advocacy of violence or a law violation as a means, may not be proscribed 'except where such advocacy is directed to inciting or producing imminent lawless action and is likely to incite or produce such action.' It is contended that Bohmer's criminal liability is based on his verbal conduct and thus falls within, and must be measured against, the test set out in *Brandenburg*.

"Accepting that theory, the trial court instructed the jury in part as follows:

'Advocating a violation of law does not constitute encouraging or instigating unless it is directed to inciting or producing imminent lawless action and is likely to incite or produce such action.'[1]

"In any event Bohmer's speech, under the circumstances in which his oral declarations were made, was reasonably calculated to incite or produce imminent lawless action, and was not protected by the First Amendment. * * *

"*Brandenburg* did not deal with a conviction for a crime involving a physical, nonverbal act, but with the constitutionality of a statute proscribing the *advocacy* of violent action as a means of obtaining certain desired ends.

"There is an obvious distinction between a statute such as that under scrutiny in *Brandenburg* that makes criminal the speaking, writing, printing, publishing, editing, issuing or displaying of spoken or written communications advocating or teaching unlawful methods of effecting political change, and a statute that proscribes the doing, for whatever purpose, of unlaw-

---

1. We doubt that the "imminent lawless action" test of *Brandenburg* is required in determining the guilt of one who advises the commission of a specific overt physical act which is by definition a crime. Such aiding and abetting is sometimes separated by a substantial distance in time from the actual substantive crime.

ful acts defined in terms that do not include verbal or other means of communication.

"Verbal incitement to such acts is rarely defended on the ground of First Amendment protection. Even when the proscribed act is not done, the verbal inducement to do it has often been punished as an attempt, or made separately punishable, as in the cases of the offer or solicitation of a bribe.

"The man who advocates death for all rapists may do so. However, when he stands before a crowd that holds a like view and also holds a confessed rapist prisoner and he shouts, "Let's lynch him," he will not be shielded by the First Amendment if the prisoner is then and there lynched.   *   *   *

"The action to which Bohmer incited was not as extreme as that in the suppositious case, but the incitement was as real."

8. To convict the perpetrator of a crime defined in terms of results (e.g., homicide), we saw in Chapter 5, Section 5, that the prosecution must establish that the defendant was the cause of death. By contrast, as the material in the present Section illustrates, one can become an accomplice to a murder even if one's acts did not, in a but-for sense, cause the perpetrator to do the killing. Is this (to use Professor Dressler's words [b]) "simplistic uniform treatment of all accomplices alike regardless of participation in the crime" inappropriate? Is the solution, as he suggests, a lesser offense of Noncausal Assistance where the accomplice's "assistance or influence did not cause the harm specified by the other offense to be committed"?

b. Dressler, *Reassessing the Theoretical Underpinnings of Accomplice Liability: New Solu-*

BAILEY v. UNITED STATES

United States Court of Appeals, District of Columbia Circuit, 1969.
416 F.2d 1110.

Spottswood W. Robinson, III, Circuit Judge:

Appellant was tried in the District Court on a single-count indictment charging robbery of an employee of the Center Market Provision Company. The prosecutive theory was that he aided and abetted the principal assailant, who remains unknown, in the commission of the crime. At the close of the Government's case in chief, appellant moved unsuccessfully for a judgment of acquittal on the ground that the proof did not establish a prima facie case against him. This motion he renewed, and the court again denied, after all the evidence was in. The jury returned a verdict finding appellant guilty as charged, and from the conviction this appeal was taken.   *   *   *

Appellant spent some of the afternoon of September 26, 1966, the date of the robbery, in the vicinity of the Center Market Provision Company, a wholesale meat distributor. He was first seen across the street from the company's place of business "shooting craps" with a short, stocky man—the "other man" in the case, who was to become the actual robber. At one point appellant left the other man but returned minutes later. Appellant subsequently left him again to join several men in a game of "five-and-ten-cent crap" on a parking lot in front of the Center Market building. When the game terminated, appellant rejoined the other man, who in the meanwhile had remained across the street, and somewhat later they walked over to the parking lot and stood by a truck owned by Center Market. The offense for which appellant was prosecuted took place shortly thereafter.

tions to an Old Problem, 37 Hastings L.J. 91, 121 (1985).

Wilson C. Lawson, Jr., a part-time book-keeper for Center Market, was the victim of the robbery. Each day he checked in the cash receipts of Center Market's drivers and prepared the company's bank deposit. His regular routine was to take the deposit with him when he left and to deliver it to a bank, at which he was employed full-time, on the following day.

As Lawson left Center Market on September 26, he carried a paper bag containing a deposit of approximately $4,200. He noticed appellant and the other man by the truck, but attached no significance to that circumstance. While Lawson stood on a loading platform locking the door, a driver whom he recognized came out of another building and conversed with him briefly. A second truck driver was sitting in a car parked facing the platform.

Lawson walked down the platform steps toward his car, which was parked next to the truck where appellant and the other man were. When Lawson reached his car, the other man took the bag with the deposit at gunpoint. Appellant, just prior to the holdup, had walked away from the gunman toward the curb of the street, and was then about ten feet away. The man who had conversed with Lawson yelled "Look, they're robbing him," and both appellant and the other man ran away in the same direction. The two truck drivers attempted to follow but lost them. Appellant was subsequently apprehended, but the other man was never identified or caught.

Appellant's conviction must stand, if at all, on the premise that he aided and abetted the unknown robber, for the record is barren of proof that appellant was an active perpetrator of the offense. * * *

Appellant's conduct, as portrayed in the view most favorable to the Government, amounted to presence at the scene of the crime, slight prior association with the actual perpetrator, and subsequent flight. A *sine qua non* of aiding and abetting, however, is guilty participation by the accused. "In order to aid and abet another to commit a crime it is necessary that a defendant 'in some sort associate himself with the venture, that he participate in it as in something that he wishes to bring about, that he seek by his action to make it succeed.'" The crucial inquiries in this case relate to the legal capabilities of the evidence to sustain a jury determination that appellant collaborated to that degree in the robbery.

An inference of criminal participation cannot be drawn merely from presence; a culpable purpose is essential. * * * Presence is thus equated to aiding and abetting when it is shown that it designedly encourages the perpetrator, facilitates the unlawful deed—as when the accused acts as a lookout—or where it stimulates others to render assistance to the criminal act. But presence without these or similar attributes is insufficient to identify the accused as a party to the criminality. And this case is devoid of evidence, beyond what the previous associative acts and the subsequent flight might themselves reflect, that appellant's presence on the scene was designed to in any way sanction or promote the robbery.

The Government urges the efficacy of appellant's presence when it is coupled with his association with the perpetrator on the date of and shortly prior to the robbery. But an accused's prior association with one who is to become a criminal offender, even when coupled with the accused's later presence at the scene of the offense, does not warrant an inference of guilty collaboration. Moreover, here the uncontradicted evidence shows that each of appellant's several brief meetings with the eventual robber occurred on the street or the parking lot in the open view of others, including the men with whom appellant fraternized for some time in a dice game—evidence becoming even more eloquent when scrutinized in the light of what was not shown at trial. The Government's proof did not expose appellant as a planner of the robbery, or as an aide or lookout in its consummation,[28] or as one who shared in its proceeds, or even as one who knew the unidentified robber. In these circumstances, we cannot say that reasonable jurors could find a taint of criminality in appellant's limited association with him.

The Government contends finally that the strength of its case against appellant was enhanced by the fact that appellant fled the scene after the crime was committed. The evidentiary value of flight, however, has depreciated substantially in the face of Supreme Court decisions delineating the dangers inherent in unperceptive reliance upon flight as an indicium of guilt. We no longer hold tenable the notion that "the wicked flee when no man pursueth, but the righteous are as bold as a lion." The proposition that "one who flees shortly after a criminal act is committed or when he is accused of committing it does so because he feels some guilt concerning that act" is not absolute as a legal doctrine "since it is a matter of common knowledge that men who are entirely innocent do sometimes fly from the scene of a crime through fear of being apprehended as the guilty parties, or from an unwillingness to appear as witnesses."

With cautious application in appreciation of its innate shortcomings, flight may under particular conditions be the basis for an inference of consciousness of guilt. But guilt, as a factual deduction, must be

predicated upon a firmer foundation than a combination of unelucidated presence and unelucidated flight. Here there was no evidentiary manifestation that the appellant was prompted by subjective considerations related in any wise to the crime.[34] Moreover, as the evidence disclosed, appellant had several convictions prior to the affair in suit, and these might well have dictated what seemed to him to be best. Absent anything more, there was no more basis for attributing his flight to complicity in the robbery than to a purpose consistent with innocence.

If we consider presence, association and flight separately, the Government's case quite obviously did not qualify for submission to the jury. And while "the jury must take the Government's case as a whole and determine whether as a whole it proves guilt beyond a reasonable doubt," any effort to repair the Government's fragmented case still leaves a prosecution constructed from evidence which is pregnant with the probability that appellant was an innocent bystander. After all, it shows only that he openly gambled with the eventual robber, talked to him, and stood with him beside the truck at intermittent periods during the afternoon. Suddenly when the robbery victim appeared on the scene with the bag of money, it was the unidentified man who pointed a gun at him and grabbed the bag. Appellant, prompted by reasons which only random speculation could summon, ran away in the midst of shouts that "they" had committed a robbery.[37] The admoni-

---

28. The Government's aiding and abetting theory, as argued to the jury, was that appellant either planned the robbery or functioned as a lookout. But the record is devoid of evidence disclosing circumstances that could give that sort of color to appellant's conduct. There is no trustworthy indication that appellant was a party to the scheme to rob, and the Government did not ask any of its eyewitnesses to try to elucidate appellant's behavior as he walked away from the unidentified robber immediately before the crime took place.

34. There was no evidence of such things as manifest cooperation, division of the spoils, or the like, activities which have been factors in decisions reaching the contrary conclusion under their particular circumstances.

37. Our dissenting colleague emphasizes the word "they" in the shout but we are unable to attach particular significance to it. The witness who made that outcry testified that appellant had walked away from the gunman prior to the holdup and explained appellant's role thusly:

tion that "innocent people caught in a web of circumstances frequently become terror-stricken" carries its usual force here.

In the annals of the case law we find well reasoned decisions exonerating from conviction persons accused in circumstances not significantly divergent from those appearing here. We hold concordantly that the Government's ambiguous evidence against appellant left too much room for the jury to engage in speculation, with the result that the motion for judgment of acquittal was erroneously denied. The totality of that evidence could only conjecturally support a finding that appellant "associate[d] himself with the [criminal] venture, that he participate[d] in it as in something that he wish[ed] to bring about, [and] that he [sought] by his action to make it succeed." The circumstances may arouse suspicions but, as we have counseled, even "grave suspicion is not enough."

We reverse the judgment of appellant's conviction and remand the case to the District Court with direction that a judgment of acquittal be entered.

Reversed and remanded.

BASTIAN, SENIOR CIRCUIT JUDGE (dissenting): * * *

In this case, prior to the commission of the crime, appellant was closely associated with the actual perpetrator and was with him immediately before the robbery. Furthermore, appellant was present at the scene of the crime. Finally, he ran away together with the other man after the robbery. Yet, my colleagues decide that only

> Q. Did Mr. Bailey at any time ever go over to Mr. Lawson?
>
> A. Not as I knows of. Only thing I seen was both running down the street.
>
> Q. You ever see Mr. Bailey do anything to Mr. Lawson?
>
> A. No, sir.
>
> Q. You ever see Mr. Bailey anytime snatch anything out of Mr. Lawson's hands?

by impermissible conjecture could the evidence support a finding that appellant "in some sort associate himself with the venture, that he participate in it as in something that he wishes to bring about, that he seek by his action to make it succeed."

I, on the other hand, state forcefully that the totality of this evidence, when considered in the light most favorable to the prosecution, is surely adequate, yea, more than adequate, to meet the governing standard, " * * * [that] a reasonable mind might fairly conclude guilt beyond a reasonable doubt * * * [and if the trial judge] concludes that either of the two results, a reasonable doubt or no reasonable doubt, is fairly possible, he must let the jury decide the matter." * * *

Notes and Questions

Consider in which of the following cases the evidence should be deemed sufficient to support defendant's conviction as an accomplice.

1. At 4:15 p.m. Settles and Whitley approached Ms. Smith from behind as she was walking with her 3–year-old son. Settles put his hand over Smith's mouth and shoved her and her son into the basement of a nearby apartment building. As she was being pushed, she turned and saw Whitley, and told Settles she knew Whitley. Settles hit her and said, "Shut up; Whitley is not with me." Smith saw Whitley standing "right outside of the door" to the basement. Inside the basement, Settles struck Ms. Smith several times, and her son then began to cry. Settles raped Ms. Smith and then left the

> A. No, sir.
>
> Q. The only thing you saw Mr. Bailey do was run up the street?
>
> A. That is all.
>
> This coincides with all else said at trial.
> * * *

basement. She looked out and saw "Settles and Whitely running away together, side by side." Whitely appeals his conviction as an accessory to rape, arguing "that the evidence against him in the case was no stronger than the evidence in *Bailey*— 'presence at the scene of the crime, slight prior association with the actual perpetrator, and subsequent flight.' " [a]

2. "The defendant was convicted of armed robberies of three stores which occurred on December 25 and 26, 1974. There was evidence that she rode to the scene of each robbery in a car with her brother and one Cote; that in each instance the car was parked in a street on which the store to be robbed either fronted or sided; that during each robbery she remained in the car while her brother and Cote entered the store and stole money, groceries and cigarettes at gunpoint; that she knew beforehand of their purpose in entering each store; and that she was present at the division of the proceeds, but received no share other than some cigarettes in unspecified amounts. There was no evidence that she drove (or did not drive) the car or that she knew (or did not know) how to drive. Except for what may be inferred from the foregoing, the evidence is silent as to her ability from her vantage point in the parked car to act as lookout or otherwise assist in any of the robberies." [b]

3. "Shortly before 5 a.m. on January 4, 1970, the burglar alarm sounded at Smith's Country Store in Cave City. Cave City Police Officer Shaw was notified and came to the scene quickly. He stated that a hole had been made in a side wall of the store building and that he observed James Orville Moore emerging from the building through that hole. Moore ran from the scene, up a hill back of the building. Of-

ficer Shaw fired at Moore but missed him. Moore left the scene and was not apprehended until five hours later. Shaw 'stayed at the hole until the sheriff got there' because he thought 'there was still maybe some more inside.' However, no one else was found inside, and Moore was the only person seen at or near the premises. There was a pick-up truck (which had been stolen in Hart County) parked near the hole. A tape recorder and perhaps one or two country hams which had been taken from the store were found in the truck. About thirty hams, averaging between twelve and fifteen pounds each, were found lying near the hole in the store. Apparently these hams had been carried from a rack on the opposite side of the storeroom. There was no testimony linking Moore or Hodges with the stolen truck.

"A substantial posse of peace officers was quickly assembled. An airplane was obtained which circled the area in the effort to thwart an escape from the area by the culprit or culprits.

"About 10 a.m. (some five hours after Officer Shaw observed Moore leaving the store building) he came upon Moore and Hodges [the defendant here] who were hiding under a log in a field at a point variously estimated as two or three-and-a-half miles from Smith's Country Store. The actual apprehension was thus described by Officer Shaw:

'Q 32. What did they do when they saw you?

'A. Well, I hollered at them and throwed my gun on them, and they started to run, and I shot over them, and they stopped.' " [c]

4. At about 8:30 p.m. Mrs. Jackson was confronted by two men, one of whom

---

a. *Settles v. United States,* 522 A.2d 348 (D.C. App.1987), affirming the conviction.

b. *Commonwealth v. Drew,* 4 Mass.App.Ct. 30, 340 N.E.2d 524 (1976), affirming the convictions.

c. *Hodges v. Commonwealth,* 473 S.W.2d 811 (Ky.App.1971), reversing the conviction.

was armed with a pistol. They wrenched a purse from her arms while striking a blow to her head. She saw a vehicle drive away, but could not describe the car or its occupants. A speeding vehicle was stopped five blocks away and the driver, McCall, was issued a traffic ticket at 8:40; the officer noted that there were 4 or 5 men in the car and that 1 or 2 of them left the vehicle immediately thereafter. The car was out of sight only seconds when the officer received a call regarding the robbery; he and other police then stopped the car. In addition to McCall, the occupants were Cephas (in the front seat) and Bonham (in the back seat). Mrs. Jackson's purse was seen on the right rear floor, and a loaded sawed-off shotgun was protruding from under the right front seat. McCall had a 4-inch blade knife on his person, but no pistol was found. Mrs. Jackson was unable to identify either Cephas or McCall, but they have been charged with armed robbery.[d]

SECTION 3. MENTAL STATE

STATE v. GREBE

Supreme Court of Missouri, 1970.
461 S.W.2d 265.

DONNELLY, PRESIDING JUDGE.

Appellant, Ruth I. Grebe, was convicted of manslaughter by the Circuit Court of Boone County, Missouri, and her punishment was assessed at imprisonment in the custody of the State Department of Corrections for a term of three years. Following rendition of judgment and imposition of sentence, an appeal was perfected to this Court.

Appellant, with her husband and children, lived on a farm adjoining and west of the Salem Cumberland Presbyterian Church in Johnson County, Missouri. A dispute arose between the Grebes and the

trustees of the church as to ownership of a strip of land between the two properties.

On the morning of July 7, 1967, Larry Martin and his father, Robert Hugh Martin, members of the church, went to the church to mow the grass. An altercation occurred between the Martins and appellant, Kenneth Grebe, her thirteen-year-old son, and the Grebe dog. Robert Hugh Martin was killed. The parties do not question on this appeal that Robert Hugh Martin died as a result of a stab wound inflicted by Kenneth Grebe. * * *

The parties agree that Larry Martin testified essentially as follows: Immediately prior to the altercation, the Martins, father and son, walked toward appellant, Ruth Grebe, her son, and their dog. They stopped within four or five feet of the Grebes and there was no conversation between them except one of the Grebes stated that the Martins should get off the property. Kenneth Grebe removed a six-inch knife from his trousers and began swinging it back and forth. The Grebe dog advanced rapidly toward Larry Martin, who removed a rubber hose from his pocket, and struck the dog. Kenneth Grebe stabbed Larry Martin in the groin with the knife. The dog grabbed Larry Martin's right arm and he concentrated on it. At that time Larry Martin didn't know where Ruth Grebe was, and he did not hear her say anything or see her do anything at that point. Larry Martin raised up and looked toward the west where he saw defendant Ruth Grebe pushing Robert Hugh Martin backward down the fence line with her hands shoving on his collar bone. Larry Martin hit Ruth Grebe with his hose. Ruth Grebe moved away from Robert Hugh Martin and "stood there and looked" at Larry Martin. Ruth Grebe then pulled Larry Martin backward by his shoulders. He then saw Ruth Grebe be-

---

d. *United States v. McCall*, 460 F.2d 952 (D.C. Cir.1972), affirming both convictions.

hind Robert Hugh Martin pulling him backward by his shoulders. At that time, there was blood on Robert Hugh Martin's clothing. The dog jumped on Robert Hugh Martin, Larry Martin hit the dog with his hose, and the dog got off. Larry Martin then assisted his father to rise and they left the scene and walked east toward the front of the churchyard. Robert Hugh Martin died as a result of a knife wound in the abdomen. * * *

Appellant next contends the trial court erred in giving and reading to the jury Instruction 11A, which reads, in part, as follows:

"The Court instructs the jury that if you find the defendant not guilty of murder in the second degree, then you will consider whether or not under the testimony in this case, the defendant is guilty of manslaughter.

"You are instructed that if you find and believe from the evidence beyond a reasonable doubt, Kenneth Grebe at the County of Johnson and State of Missouri did wilfully and feloniously, but without premeditation and malice aforethought, stab with a knife and kill one Robert Hugh Martin, and if you further find that the defendant, Ruth I. Grebe, was present at the said time and place, and knowing the unlawful intent of Kenneth Grebe, did aid, abet, help and assist Kenneth Grebe in the commission of such act, then you will find the defendant, Ruth I. Grebe, guilty of manslaughter and assess her punishment at imprisonment in the penitentiary * * *."

Appellant urges that the trial court should have instructed the jury that " * * * if you further find that the defendant, Ruth I. Grebe, was present at the said time and place, and knowing the unlawful intent of Kenneth Grebe, did *intentionally* aid, abet, help and assist Kenneth Grebe in the commission of such act * * *." (Emphasis ours.)

In *State v. Chernick,* Mo.Sup., 303 S.W.2d 595, 599, this Court approved Instruction No. 1, which read, in part, as follows:

" ' * * * In this connection you are instructed that if upon consideration of all the evidence in the case, in the light of the instructions of the Court, you believe and find from the evidence, beyond a reasonable doubt, that at the City of St. Louis and State of Missouri, on the 24th day of April, 1953, the defendant, Glenn Chernick, if you find he was present at or near the scene of the Southwest Bank in the City of St. Louis, Missouri, did aid, abet, assist, advise or encourage Fred Bowerman, Frank Vito and William Fred Scholl, or any of them, *with the intent that his presence should aid, abet, assist or encourage* said Fred Bowerman, Frank Vito and William Fred Scholl, or any of them, to feloniously assault one Alice Ruzicka by means of a dangerous and deadly weapon * * *.' " (Emphasis ours.) * * *

We also note approval of the use of the words "with the intent that the words or acts should encourage and abet the crime committed," in *State v. Russell,* Mo.Sup., 324 S.W.2d 727, 732 (Instruction No. 2), and *State v. Cooley,* Mo.Sup., 387 S.W.2d 544, 549 (Instruction No. 2).

Our research has disclosed no Missouri case specifically ruling the question presented in this case. The question has been ruled in the Supreme Court of the United States and in the Supreme Court of Ohio.

In *Hicks v. United States,* 150 U.S. 442, 14 S.Ct. 144, 37 L.Ed. 1137, the Supreme Court of the United States reviewed a case arising out of the Circuit Court of the United States for the Western District of Arkansas. On February 13, 1892, in the Cherokee Nation, Stand Rowe, an Indian, shot and killed Andrew J. Colvard, a white man. John Hicks, an Indian, was tried as an aider and abettor and was convicted. The Court held that the instruction given to the jury by the trial court was erroneous because it "omitted to instruct the jury that the acts or words of encouragement and abetting must have been used by the accused with the *intention* of encouraging and abetting Rowe." (Emphasis ours.)

* * *

The State tried appellant as an aider and abettor in this case. Instruction 11A did not require the jury to find that appellant *intentionally* aided and abetted Kenneth Grebe in the commission of the act of stabbing Robert Hugh Martin. We consider appellant's intent in this regard an essential element of the State's case. We hold the instruction prejudicially erroneous.

The judgment is reversed and the cause remanded.

Morgan, Judge (dissenting).

* * *

The sole question is—did Instruction 11A require the jury to find defendant (the mother) acted "intentionally"? I am convinced that it did. After it was found that Kenneth (the son) acted "wilfully and feloniously," the jury also was required to find that the defendant (mother) did aid, abet, help and assist while "knowing the unlawful intent of Kenneth * * *" It seems not only logical but fair to conclude that the mother (*knowing* of the unlawful intent of the son) did adopt such intent as her own when she continued to actively assist in the commission of the crime. Her doing so provided the basis for the jury to conclude she acted "intentionally." I do not believe that any jury of reasonable men and women could have been misled by the absence of the one word "intentionally" from the instruction as given. The use of that specific word is not dictated nor required by the precedents cited.

Notes and Questions

1. Can one have "intentionally aided and abetted" a certain offense, as required

by *Grebe,* without knowing of all the facts and circumstances which must be present for that offense to occur? Consider:

(a) *State v. Davis,* 101 Wash.2d 654, 682 P.2d 883 (1984), upholding defendant's conviction for being an accomplice to armed robbery by standing lookout, notwithstanding a jury instruction that it sufficed to elevate defendant's complicity to the armed robbery level that the principal "in fact had a gun." The court took note of *State v. McKim,* 98 Wash.2d 111, 653 P.2d 1040 (1982), where "we held that the deadly weapon statute requires that the State prove the defendant was either actually or constructively armed with a deadly weapon. Constructive possession exists if the defendant knew his coparticipant was armed.

"Our conclusion in *McKim* rested in part upon our recognition of the differences between accomplice liability for a substantive crime and accomplice liability for enhancement statutes. We reasoned that the new complicity statute, unlike the old one, made an accomplice equally liable only for the substantive crime. We reaffirm this distinction. As to the substantive crime, the law has long recognized that an accomplice, having agreed to participate in a criminal act, runs the risk of having the primary actor exceed the scope of the preplanned illegality. * * *

"Furthermore, this distinction recognizes that the Legislature has a valid interest in discouraging the use of deadly weapons by imposing strict liability on all those involved in robbery which, by its very nature, generally requires use of weapons to facilitate the act of illegally obtaining money from another by force."

A dissent objected: "We have held, in *McKim,* that it is improper to enhance a defendant's sentence under the deadly weapon statute absent a showing that the defendant either had a weapon or knew that a coparticipant had a weapon. I see no reason why a different rule should apply to substantive offenses. The majority's rule allows the State to do indirectly what *McKim* says it may not do directly, namely, impose upon a defendant an enhanced sentence (by convicting the defendant of first degree robbery instead of second degree robbery) because of a deadly weapon which the defendant knew nothing about."

(b) *United States v. Gregg,* 612 F.2d 43 (2d Cir.1979), where Bates and other officers of REA Express in New York formulated a scheme to steal REA funds. Bates contacted a Florida acquaintance, Gregg, who agreed to and did "wash" some REA checks for 10% of the proceeds. Gregg was charged as an accomplice to violation of 18 U.S.C.A. § 660, which covers misappropriation by "a president, director, officer, or manager of any firm, association, or corporation engaged in commerce as a common carrier" of that organization's funds or assets. In upholding a jury instruction that Gregg could be convicted even if he did not know Bates was the manager of REA, the court concluded "that the requirement that the principal violator under the statute hold the position of president, director, officer, or manager of the interstate carrier is jurisdictional only. Upon the authority of *Feola,* [p. 623 of this Book] therefore, it was not essential that the court charge the jury that they must find that appellant knew of the status of the principal. As the Court stated in *Feola:*

'This interpretation poses no risk of unfairness to defendants. It is no snare for the unsuspecting. * * * The situation is not one where legitimate conduct becomes unlawful solely because of the identity of the individual or agency affected. * * * The concept of criminal intent does not extend so far as to require that the actor understand not only the nature of his act but also its consequence for the choice of a judicial forum.'

Similarly, we note that appellant here was not engaged in legitimate conduct that was rendered unlawful 'solely because of the identity of the individual' with whom he conspired. Hence, there is no element of unfairness in holding appellant liable for conduct which he knew to be illegal."

2. During an evening of drinking, Wilson accused Pierce of having stolen his watch, but Pierce denied it. They then discussed feats of crime, and decided to burglarize a certain drug store. Wilson boosted Pierce through a transom and then, while Pierce was inside, telephoned the police. After Pierce had handed several bottles of whiskey out to Wilson, the police arrived. Wilson told them Pierce was inside, and after Pierce escaped Wilson led the police to him and identified him. Wilson told the police that his purpose was to get even with Pierce for taking his watch. Wilson was convicted of aiding and abetting Pierce in the commission of burglary (breaking and entering the premises with intent to commit larceny) and larceny (trespassory taking and carrying away of the personal property of another with intent to deprive the owner of it permanently). On appeal, he objected to a jury instruction that one "who attempts to detect the commission of crime in others must himself stop short of lending assistance, or participation in the commission of the crime." In *Wilson v. People,* 103 Colo. 441, 87 P.2d 5 (1939), the court agreed and reversed.

Didn't Wilson, in the language of *Grebe,* "intentionally aid, abet, help and assist" Pierce? Why, then, should his conviction be reversed?

3. If the mental states of the principal and the accomplice are not the same, another possible result is that they will be found guilty of different offenses. For example, it has been held that one is not an accomplice to the crime of assault with intent to kill (as compared to mere assault)

if the accomplice did not share that intent.[a] But disparity in mental states has been a matter of greatest significance in the homicide area, where the precise state of mind of the defendant has great significance in determining the degree of the offense. To determine the kind of homicide of which the accomplice is guilty, it is necessary to look to his state of mind; it may have been different from the state of mind of the principal and they thus may be guilty of different offenses.[b] Thus, because first degree murder requires a deliberate and premeditated killing, an accomplice is not guilty of this degree of murder unless he acted with premeditation and deliberation.[c] And, because a killing in a heat of passion is manslaughter and not murder, an accomplice who aids while in such a state is guilty only of manslaughter even though the killer is himself guilty of murder.[d] Likewise, it is equally possible that the killer is guilty only of manslaughter because of his heat of passion but that the accomplice, aiding in a state of cool blood, is guilty of murder.[e]

STATE v. GLADSTONE

Supreme Court of Washington, 1970.
78 Wash.2d 306, 474 P.2d 274.

HALE, JUSTICE.

A jury found defendant Bruce Gladstone guilty of aiding and abetting one Robert Kent in the unlawful sale of marijuana. Deferring imposition of sentence, the court placed defendant on probation. He appeals the order deferring sentencing contending that the evidence as a matter of law was insufficient to sustain a verdict of guilty. His point, we think, is well taken.

* * *

Gladstone's guilt as an aider and abettor in this case rests solely on evidence of a conversation between him and one Douglas MacArthur Thompson concerning the possible purchase of marijuana from one Robert Kent. There is no other evidence to connect the accused with Kent who ultimately sold some marijuana to Thompson. * * *

The conversation between defendant and Thompson occurred at defendant's residence. Douglas MacArthur Thompson, a 25-year-old student at the University of Puget Sound in Tacoma and an employee of the Internal Revenue Service of the United States, had done some investigative work for the government. From time to time, the Tacoma Police Department engaged him to investigate the use, possession and sale of narcotics, principally marijuana, among college students. When working for the Tacoma Police Department, he operated under the control and direction of the department's narcotics detail.

Thompson testified that Lieutenant Seymour and Detective Gallwas of the narcotics detail asked him to attempt a purchase of marijuana from Gladstone. During the evening of April 10, 1967—between 10 and 11 o'clock—the two officers and Thompson drove in a police car to the vicinity of defendant's apartment. Thompson went to Gladstone's door alone, beyond the hearing and out of the sight of the two officers. He knocked at the door and Gladstone responded. Thompson asked Gladstone if he would sell him some marijuana. Describing this incident, Thompson testified as follows:

---

a. *State v. Taylor,* 70 Vt. 1, 39 A. 447 (1898).

b. Some difficulty in this regard was experienced under the old common law view of parties, for an accessory before the fact could not be convicted of a higher crime than his principal. 4 Blackstone, *Commentaries on the Laws of England* 36 (1765).

c. *Leavine v. State,* 109 Fla. 447, 147 So. 897 (1933).

d. *Dorsey v. Commonwealth,* 13 Ky.L.R. 359, 17 S.W. 183 (1891); *Moore v. Lowe,* 116 W.Va. 165, 180 S.E. 1 (1935).

e. *State v. McAllister,* 366 So.2d 1340 (La. 1978).

Well, I asked—at the time Gladstone told me that he was—he did not have enough marijuana on hand to sell me any, but he did know an individual who had quite a sufficient quantity and that was very willing to sell and he named the individual as Robert Kent, or Bob Kent as he put it, and he gave me directions to the residence and he—due to the directions I asked him if, you know, if he could draw me a map and he did.

When Thompson said he asked Gladstone to draw the map for him, he added, "I'm not sure whether he did give me the exact address or not, he told me where the residence was." He said that Gladstone then with pencil and paper sketched the location of Kent's place of residence. Thompson had no prior knowledge of where Kent lived, and did not know if he might have marijuana or that he had ever possessed it.

The two officers then took Thompson to Kent's residence where marijuana was purchased. The actual purchase was made by Thompson directly from Kent while Officer Gallwas and Lieutenant Seymour stayed in the police car. Kent was subsequently arrested and convicted of selling Thompson approximately 8 ounces of marijuana—the very sale which defendant here was convicted of aiding and abetting.

That ended the prosecution's case. Even if it were accorded all favorable inferences, there appears at this point a gap in the evidence which we feel as a matter of law is fatal to the prosecution's cause. Neither on direct examination nor under cross-examination did Thompson testify that he knew of any prior conduct, arrangements or communications between Gladstone and Kent from which it could be even remotely inferred that the defendant had any understanding, agreement, purpose, intention or design to participate or engage in or aid or abet any sale of marijuana by Kent. Other than to obtain a simple map from Gladstone and to say that Gladstone told him Kent might have some marijuana available, Thompson did not even establish that Kent and the defendant were acquainted with each other. Testimony of the brief conversation and Gladstone's very crude drawing consisting of 8 penciled lines indicating where Kent lived constitute the whole proof of the aiding and abetting presented. * * *

[E]ven without prior agreement, arrangement or understanding, a bystander to a robbery could be guilty of aiding and abetting its commission if he came to the aid of a robber and knowingly assisted him in perpetrating the crime. But regardless of the modus operandi and with or without a conspiracy or agreement to commit the crime and whether present or away from the scene of it, there is no aiding and abetting unless one " 'in some sort associate himself with the venture, that he participate in it as in something that he wishes to bring about, that he seek by his action to make it succeed.' " *Nye & Nissen v. United States,* 336 U.S. 613, 619, 69 S.Ct. 766, 769, 93 L.Ed. 919 (1949). * * *

Gladstone's culpability, if at all, must be brought within RCW 9.01.030, which makes a principal of one who aids and abets another in the commission of the crime. Although an aider and abettor need not be physically present at the commission of the crime to be held guilty as a principal, his conviction depends on proof that he did something in association or connection with the principal to accomplish the crime. Learned Hand, J., we think, hit the nail squarely when, in *United States v. Peoni,* 100 F.2d 401, 402 (2d Cir. 1938), he wrote that, in order to aid and abet another to commit a crime, it is necessary that a defendant

in some sort associate himself with the venture, that he participate in it as in something that he wishes to bring about, that he seek by his action to make it succeed. All the words used—even the most colorless, "abet"—carry an implication of purposive attitude towards it.

* * *

This court has recognized the necessity of proof of a nexus between aider and abettor and other principals to sustain a conviction. In *State v. Hinkley,* 52 Wash. 2d 415, at 418, 325 P.2d 889 (1958), amplifying the term *abet,* we said:

> Although the word "aid" does not imply guilty knowledge or felonious intent, the word "abet" includes *knowledge* of the wrongful purpose of the perpetrator, as well as counsel and encouragement in the crime.

and approved the instruction that:

> To abet another in the commission of a crime implies a consciousness of guilt in instigating, encouraging, promoting or aiding in the commission of such criminal offense.

It would be a dangerous precedent indeed to hold that mere communications to the effect that another might or probably would commit a criminal offense amount to an aiding and abetting of the offense should it ultimately be committed.

There being no evidence whatever that the defendant ever communicated to Kent the idea that he would in any way aid him in the sale of any marijuana, or said anything to Kent to encourage or induce him or direct him to do so, or counseled Kent in the sale of marijuana, or did anything more than describe Kent to another person as an individual who might sell some marijuana, or would derive any benefit, consideration or reward from such a sale, there was no proof of an aiding and abetting, and the conviction should, therefore, be reversed as a matter of law. Remanded with directions to dismiss. * * *

HAMILTON, JUSTICE (dissenting).

* * * The statutory language and the overt action it contemplates does, however, give rise to the requirement that the aider or abettor entertain a conscious intent, i.e., knowledge and intent that his action will instigate, induce, procure or encourage perpetration of the primary crime.

The question to be resolved, then, in the instant case is whether the evidence sustains the jury's conclusion that the appellant entertained the requisite intent to render him culpable as an aider or abettor. In the resolution of this question, it is to be borne in mind that appellant's challenge to the sufficiency of the evidence requires that the evidence, and all reasonable inferences to be drawn therefrom, be interpreted in a light most favorable to the state. Furthermore, this court has held that an aider's or abettor's culpability may be established by circumstantial evidence.

Although the evidence in the case is conflicting, the jury was entitled to believe that on April 10, 1967, one Robert Kent sold marijuana to Douglas Thompson, who at the time was acting as an undercover agent for and in concert with officers of the Tacoma Police Department; that appellant Gladstone, Kent, and Thompson were students at the same school in Tacoma; that prior to the evening of April 10, 1967, when Thompson talked to appellant, *Thompson and the Tacoma Police Department were unaware of Kent or his association with marijuana;* that appellant knew Kent, whom he met and associated with on the campus of the school they respectively attended; that both appellant and Kent lived off campus; that appellant knew where Kent lived and on at least one occasion had driven him home; that at the time in question the Tacoma Police Department had information that appellant was supposed to be holding a supply of marijuana for sale; that Thompson, who was but slightly acquainted with appellant, approached appellant at his residence about 10:50 p.m. on April 10, 1967, and asked appellant to sell him some marijuana; that appellant then stated that he did not have enough marijuana on hand to sell but that he knew an individual who did have an ample supply and who was willing to sell some and named the individual as Robert Kent; that upon request appellant orally gave Thompson directions to Kent's apartment and drew a map to aid Thompson in finding the address, utilizing as a reference point a building known to appellant to be a student rendezvous where drugs had been sold; that by using the map and oral directions Thompson and the police went to Kent's residence; *that Thompson approached Kent and told him "Gladstone had sent me" whereupon Kent invited him to a room and sold him some marijuana for $30;* and that Thompson and one of the police officers later returned to the Kent residence, after again visiting appellant, and made a second purchase of marijuana at which time Kent was arrested.

Based upon the foregoing circumstances and the inferences reasonably derivable therefrom, I am satisfied that the jury was fully warranted in concluding that appellant, when he affirmatively recommended Kent as a source and purveyor of marijuana, entertained the requisite conscious design and intent that his action would instigate, induce, procure or encourage perpetration of Kent's subsequent crime of selling marijuana to Thompson. Furthermore, insofar as an element of preconcert be concerned, certainly the readiness with which the passwords, "Gladstone had sent me," gained a stranger's late evening entree to Kent's domain and produced two illegal sales strongly suggests, if not conclusively establishes, the missing communal nexus which the majority belabors.

*   *   *

Notes and Questions

1. *Peoni,* relied upon in *Gladstone,* is a well-known case on this subject. Peoni sold counterfeit bills to Regno in the Bronx; Regno sold the same bills to Dorsey in the Bronx; and Dorsey was arrested while trying to pass them in Brooklyn. Peoni was convicted as an accessory to the crime of possessing counterfeit money in Brooklyn. The court of appeals concluded that "Peoni was not an accessory to Dorsey's possession; his connection with the business ended when he got his money from Regno, who might dispose of the bills as he chose; it was of no moment to him whether Regno passed them himself, and so ended the possibility of further guilty possession, or whether he sold them to a second possible passer. His utterance of the bills was indeed a step in the causal chain which ended in Dorsey's possession, but that was all. Perhaps he was Regno's accessory. * * * Be that as it may nobody, so far as we can find, has ever held that a contract is criminal, because the seller has reason to know, not that the buyer will use the goods unlawfully, but that some one further down the line may do so. Nor is it at all desirable that the seller should be held indefinitely. The real gravamen of the charge against him is his utterance of the bills; and he ought not to be tried for that wherever the prosecution may pick up any guilty possessor— perhaps thousands of miles away."

2. Compare *Backun v. United States,* 112 F.2d 635 (4th Cir.1940). Backun sold Zucker stolen silverware in New York, knowing that the goods were not saleable in New York and that Zucker intended to take the silverware with him to the South and dispose of it there. Backun's conviction of being an accessory to the interstate transportation of property known to have been stolen was affirmed:

"Whether one who sells property to another knowing that the buyer intends to use it for the commission of a felony renders himself criminally liable as aiding and abetting in its commission, is a question as to which there is some conflict of authority. It must be remembered, however, that guilt as accessory before the fact has application only in cases of felony; and since it is elementary that every citizen is under moral obligation to prevent the commission of felony, if possible, and has the legal right to use force to prevent its commission and to arrest the perpetrator without warrant, it is difficult to see why, in selling goods which he knows will make its perpetration possible with knowledge that they are to be used for that purpose, he is not aiding and abetting in its commission within any fair meaning of those terms. Undoubtedly he would be guilty, were he to give to the felon the goods which make the perpetration of the felony possible with knowledge that they would be used for that purpose; and we cannot see that his guilt is purged or his breach of social duty excused because he receives a price for them. In either case, he knowingly aids and assists in the perpetration of the felony.

"Guilt as an accessory depends, not on 'having a stake' in the outcome of crime, but on aiding and assisting the perpetrators; and those who make a profit by furnishing to criminals, whether by sale or otherwise, the means to carry on their nefarious undertakings aid them just as truly as if they were actual partners with them, having a stake in the fruits of their enterprise. To say that the sale of goods is a normally lawful transaction is beside the point. The seller may not ignore the purpose for which the purchase is made if he is advised of that purpose, or wash his hands of the aid that he has given the perpetrator of a felony by the plea that he has merely made a sale of merchandise. One who sells a gun to another knowing that he is buying it to commit a murder, would hardly escape conviction as an accessory to the murder by showing that he received full price for the gun; and no difference in principle can be drawn between such a case and any other case of a seller who knows that the purchaser intends to use the goods which he is purchasing in the commission of felony. In any such case, not only does the act of the seller assist in the commission of the felony, but his will assents to its commission, since he could refuse to give the assistance by refusing to make the sale. This is the view taken of the matter in a number of well considered cases in the federal courts. * * *

"But even if the view be taken that aiding and abetting is not to be predicated on an ordinary sale made with knowledge that the purchaser intends to use the goods purchased in the commission of felony, we think that the circumstances relied on by the government here are sufficient to establish the guilt of Backun. The sale here was not of a mere instrumentality to be used in the commission of felony, but of the very goods which were to be feloniously transported. Backun knew not only that the commission of felony was contemplated by Zucker with respect to such goods, but also that the felony could not be committed by Zucker unless the sale were made to him. The sale thus made possible the commission of the felony by Zucker; and, if Zucker is to be believed, the commission of the felony was one of the purposes which Backun had in mind in making the sale. After testifying that he had told Backun that he wished to go on the road with the silverware (i.e. transport it in interstate commerce), he says 'He (Backun) knew that. That is the reason he wanted to sell it to me.' There can be no question, therefore, but that the evidence sustains the view that the felony committed by Zucker flowed from the will of Backun as well as from his own will, and that Backun aided its commission by making the sale. There was thus evidence of direct participation of Backun in the criminal purpose of Zucker; and whatever view be taken as to the case of a mere sale, certainly such evidence is sufficient to establish guilt."

3. The draftsmen of the Model Penal Code proposed a provision which would make a person an accomplice not only when he aided with the purpose of facilitating the crime, but also if "acting with knowledge that such other person was committing or had the purpose of committing the crime, he knowingly, substantially facilitated its commission." They explained that the "substantially facilitated" qualification "provides a basis for discrimination that should satisfy the common sense of justice. A vendor who supplies materials readily available upon the market arguably does not make substantial contribution to commission of the crime since the materials could have as easily been gotten elsewhere. The minor employee may win exemption on this ground, though he minded his own business to preserve his job. What is required is to give the courts and juries a criterion for drawing lines that must be drawn. The formula proposed accomplishes this purpose by a standard that is relevant, it is submitted, to all the legal ends involved. There will, of course, be arguable cases; they should, we think, be argued in these terms." *Model Penal Code* § 2.04, Comments (Tent. Draft No. 1, 1953). But that language was omitted from the Code pursuant to a vote of the American Law Institute; the revised provision was renumbered as § 2.06(3).

4. Does the knowing aid approach of *Backun* have more appeal when the crime is a most serious one? Reconsider *People v. Lauria,* p. 616 of this Book, where the court argued "that a supplier who furnishes equipment which he *knows* will be used to commit a serious crime may be deemed from that knowledge alone to have intended to produce the result. Such proof may justify an inference that the furnisher intended to aid the execution of the crime and that he thereby became a participant. For instance, we think the operator of a telephone answering service with positive knowledge that his service was being used to facilitate the extortion of ransom, the distribution of heroin, or the passing of counterfeit money who continued to furnish the service with knowledge of its use, might be chargeable on knowledge alone with participation in a scheme to extort money, to distribute narcotics, or to pass counterfeit money. The same result would follow the seller of gasoline who knew the buyer was using his product to make Molotov cocktails for terroristic use."

5. Should mere knowing aid be dealt with as a lesser offense than the crime aided? This is the solution in the New York Penal Law:

"§ 115.00   Criminal facilitation in the second degree.

"A person is guilty of criminal facilitation in the second degree when, believing it probable that he is rendering aid to a person who intends to commit a crime, he engages in conduct which provides such person with means or opportunity for the commission thereof and which in fact aids such person to commit a felony.

"Criminal facilitation in the second degree is a class A misdemeanor [punishable by up to one-year imprisonment].

"§ 115.05   Criminal facilitation in the first degree.

"A person is guilty of criminal facilitation in the first degree when, believing it probable that he is rendering aid to a person who intends to commit murder or kidnapping in the first degree, he engages in conduct which provides such person with means or opportunity for the commission thereof and which in fact aids such person to commit murder or kidnapping in the first degree.

"Criminal facilitation in the first degree is a class C felony [punishable by up to 15 years imprisonment].

"§ 115.10　Criminal facilitation; no defense.

"It is no defense to a prosecution for criminal facilitation that: * * *

"3.　The defendant is not guilty of the felony which he facilitated because he did not act with the intent or other culpable mental state required for the commission thereof."

6.　What if the defendant in *Gladstone*, upon being approached by Thompson, acted for Thompson in getting the marijuana from Kent to Thompson and the purchase money from Thompson to Kent, and as a consequence was charged with having made (rather than aided in) the sale? Consider *Commonwealth v. Simione*, 447 Pa. 473, 291 A.2d 764 (1972):

"In *Commonwealth v. Harvard*, 356 Mass. 452, 253 N.E.2d 346 (1969), the Supreme Court of Massachusetts was recently faced with a case whose facts were virtually identical with those of the case before us. In *Harvard* an undercover agent named Martin had persuaded the defendant to obtain some marihuana for him. The defendant introduced the agent to a third individual named Zacharo. The transfer of marihuana took place with the defendant standing between the agent's car and Zacharo's car. '[D]efendant persuaded Zacharo to sell marihuana to Martin. Zacharo thereupon handed a plastic bag of marihuana to the defendant who passed it to Martin in Martin's car. Martin then gave $15 to the defendant who passed it to Zacharo. There was no evidence that the defendant received any of the proceeds of the sale.'

"On these facts the Massachusetts Supreme Court concluded that the evidence was insufficient to warrant a conviction on an indictment charging a 'sale' of marihuana. That court reasoned: 'The record

shows that the defendant facilitated an illegal sale by introducing a willing buyer and seller and by aiding in the physical transfer of drug and money. There is nothing to show that the defendant had any financial interest in the transaction, or was employed by the seller to promote sales.'

"Under similar facts many other jurisdictions have held the prosecution's evidence insufficient to establish a 'sale.' * * *

"We agree with those jurisdictions which have held that one who acts solely as the agent of the buyer cannot be convicted of a 'sale' of an unlawful drug. Though Pennsylvania's Drug, Device and Cosmetic Act sets forth no definition of the term 'sale,' it should be noted that our Legislature has singled out the 'sale' of narcotic drugs as deserving of especially severe punishment. The minimum penalty for the 'sale' of drugs is five years imprisonment as compared to a minimum penalty of two years imprisonment for the 'possession' of narcotic drugs. Webster's New International Dictionary of the English Language (2d ed. 1954) defines 'sale' as 'a contract whereby the * * * ownership of property is transferred from one person to another for a price, or sum of money, or loosely, for any consideration * * *.' This Court is obligated to construe words employed in the laws of this Commonwealth 'according to their common and approved usage.' Where as here there is no evidence that the defendant received any of the proceeds of the sale or was employed by the seller to promote sales, we do not believe it can be fairly said that defendant is guilty of a 'sale,' and we hold that as a matter of law defendant cannot be included in the category of 'sellers' of narcotic drugs that the Legislature singled out for especially severe punishment."

7.　Compare *State v. Hecht*, 116 Wis.2d 605, 342 N.W.2d 721 (1984), where the defendant was charged with being an accomplice to possession of a controlled substance with intent to deliver, based upon his efforts on behalf of the intended purchaser. The court concluded "that all circuits which have addressed the issue have concluded that the 'procuring agent' theory is no longer a valid defense under the federal law.

"* * * Wisconsin's statutes dealing with controlled substances are based upon the Uniform Controlled Substances Act. * * * When we review the decisions of those states which have adopted the act, we find that a majority of the jurisdictions have held that the procuring agent theory is no longer a valid defense.

"Based upon the similarity of the Wisconsin and federal statutes and the fact that this state has adopted in part the Uniform Controlled Substances Act, we hold that the procuring agent theory is not a valid defense in this state. Our statutes, like the federal statutes, no longer distinguish between buying and selling as separate offenses. Rather, the statute instead addresses the act of possession with the intent to deliver, with no mention of the terms buying and selling. The transfer itself has become the prohibited act, and participation in this transfer may amount to an offense. This is evidenced by the language of section 161.01(6), defining 'delivery' in terms of the 'actual, constructive or attempted transfer' of a controlled substance. There is no mention of the requirement of buying or selling. Accordingly, we hold that the procuring agent defense will not be recognized by this court."

8. As between *Simione* and *Hecht,* which represents better policy? What considerations bear upon making this judgment? What, for example, of this observation in Note, 22 Kan.L.Rev. 272, 280

(1974): "Conviction of a drug seller may depend entirely on a procuring agent's testimony. An agent's incentive to testify against a seller in exchange for a plea bargain may be diminished because he can now be charged with only possession. If the procuring agent does not wish to bargain for dismissal of the possession charge, the seller may have to be approached directly by undercover agents. This direct approach may be the only method to obtain sufficient evidence upon which to convict sellers who are insulated from buyers."

PEOPLE v. MARSHALL

Supreme Court of Michigan, 1961.
362 Mich. 170, 106 N.W.2d 842.

SMITH, JUSTICE.

At approximately 3:00 a.m. on the morning of February 4, 1958, a car driven by Neal McClary, traveling in the wrong direction on the Edsel Ford Expressway, crashed head-on into another vehicle driven by James Coldiron. The drivers of both cars were killed. Defendant William Marshall has been found guilty of involuntary manslaughter of Coldiron. At the time that the fatal accident took place, he, the defendant William Marshall, was in bed at his place of residence. His connection with it was that he owned the car driven by McClary, and as the evidence tended to prove, he voluntarily gave his keys to the car to McClary, with knowledge that McClary was drunk.

The principal issue in the case is whether, upon these facts, the defendant may be found guilty of involuntary manslaughter. It is axiomatic that "criminal guilt under our law is personal fault." As Sayre [2] puts the doctrine "it is of the very essence of our deep-rooted notions of criminal liability that guilt be personal and individual." This was not always true in our law, nor is

2. Sayre, *Criminal Responsibility for the Acts of Another,* 43 Harv.L.Rev. 689, 717.

it universally true in all countries even today, but for us it is settled doctrine.

The State relies on a case, *Story v. United States,* [3] in which the owner, driving with a drunk, permitted him to take the wheel, and was held liable for aiding and abetting him "in his criminal negligence." The owner, said the court, sat by his side and permitted him "without protest so recklessly and negligently to operate the car as to cause the death of another." If defendant Marshall had been by McClary's side an entirely different case would be presented, but on the facts before us Marshall, as we noted, was at home in bed. The State also points out that although it is only a misdemeanor to drive while drunk, yet convictions for manslaughter arising out of drunk driving have often been sustained. It argues from these cases that although it was only a misdemeanor for an owner to turn his keys over to a drunk driver, nevertheless a conviction for manslaughter may be sustained if such driver kills another. This does not follow from such cases as *Story,* supra. In the case before us death resulted from the misconduct of driver. The accountability of the owner must rest as a matter of general principle, upon his complicity in such misconduct. In turning his keys over, he was guilty of a specific offense, for which he incurred a specific penalty. Upon these facts he cannot be held a principal with respect to the fatal accident: the killing of Coldiron was not counselled by him, accomplished by another acting jointly with him, nor did it occur in the attempted achievement of some common enterprise.

This is not to say that defendant is guilty of nothing. He was properly found guilty of violation of paragraph (b) of section 625 of the Michigan vehicle code which makes it punishable for the owner of an automobile knowingly to permit it to be driven by a person "who is under the influence of intoxicating liquor." The State urges that this is not enough, that its manslaughter theory, above outlined, "was born of necessity," and that the urgency of the drunk-driver problem "has made it incumbent upon responsible and concerned law enforcement officials to seek new approaches to a new problem within the limits of our law." What the State actually seeks from us is an interpretation that the manslaughter statute imposes an open-end criminal liability. That is to say, whether the owner may ultimately go to prison for manslaughter or some lesser offense will depend upon whatever unlawful act the driver commits while in the car. Such a theory may be defensible as a matter of civil liability but Gellhorn's [10] language in another criminal context is equally applicable here: "It is a basic proposition in a constitutional society that crimes should be defined in advance, and not after action has been taken." We are not unaware of the magnitude of the problem presented, but the new approaches demanded for its solution rest with the legislature, not the courts.   *   *   *

Notes and Questions

1. Compare with *Marshall* the case of *State v. Foster,* 202 Conn. 520, 522 A.2d 277 (1987). Defendant beat up Bill, a man he thought had raped his girl friend, and then gave his friend Otha a knife and told him to prevent Bill from leaving while defendant summoned his girl friend to make identification. After defendant left, Otha became apprehensive and stabbed Bill, who died. Defendant was convicted of being an accessory to criminally negligent homicide. Noting that the accomplice statute "merely requires that a defendant have the mental state required for the commission of a crime while inten-

3. 57 App.D.C. 3, 16 F.2d 342, 344, 53 A.L.R. 246.

10. Gellhorn, *American Rights,* 85, 86.

tionally aiding another," the court affirmed, reasoning that accordingly "an accessory may be liable in aiding another if he acts intentionally, knowingly, recklessly or with criminal negligence toward the result, depending on the mental state required by the substantive crime. When a crime requires that a person act with criminal negligence, an accessory is liable if he acts 'with respect to a result or to a circumstance described by a statute defining an offense when he fails to perceive a substantial and unjustifiable risk that such result will occur or that such circumstance exists.'

*   *   *

"[B]ecause accessorial liability is not a distinct crime, but only an alternative means by which a substantive crime may be committed, it would be illogical to impose liability on the perpetrator of the crime, while precluding liability for an accessory, even though both possess the mental state required for the commission of the crime. Connecticut 'long ago adopted the rule that there is no practical significance in being labeled an "accessory" or a "principal" for the purpose of determining criminal responsibility. The modern approach "is to abandon completely the old common law terminology and simply provide that a person is legally accountable for the conduct of another when he is an accomplice of the other person in the commission of the crime.

*   *   *" '

"From the evidence presented, the jury could reasonably have found that the defendant intentionally had aided Cannon by giving him the knife. Additionally, the jury could reasonably have inferred that the defendant had failed to perceive a substantial and unjustifiable risk that death would occur by handing Cannon the knife to prevent Middleton from escaping."

2. In *State v. Etzweiler,* 125 N.H. 57, 480 A.2d 870 (1984), on facts very similar to those in *Marshall,* the driver was indicted in the alternative with (i) having committed negligent homicide, and (ii) having acted as an accomplice to the intoxicated driver's negligent homicide. Was the appellate court correct in upholding the dismissal of both indictments?

3. In *People v. Turner,* 125 Mich.App. 8, 336 N.W.2d 217 (1983), defendant was convicted of being an accomplice to involuntary manslaughter. He furnished loaded firearms to two women with whom he lived and directed that a "trial by battle" be held. The trial court found that one of the women, Tomkins, intentionally pointed her gun at the other, Smith, at which point it accidentally discharged, killing Smith. The applicable statute says that death from a firearm "pointed or aimed, intentionally but without malice," is involuntary manslaughter. Was the court correct in concluding that notwithstanding *Marshall* the "extent of defendant's complicity in the instant case is clearly sufficient to render her liable as an accomplice to involuntary manslaughter" ?

4. A builder offered a house for sale, and obtained from the purchaser an agreement to pay more for the house than was allowed by law. After the amount in excess was paid to the builder in advance, he instructed a firm of solicitors to act for him in the sale. He concealed from them the fact that he had received the additional amount. Two of the partners in the firm never learned otherwise at any material time, but the third partner received a letter from the purchaser's solicitors stating they had not proceeded because the builder was in breach. This partner sought an explanation from the builder, who said that the amount paid in advance was for work to be done on the house in the future. The solicitor accepted that explanation, formed the opinion that such payment was lawful, and called on the purchaser to complete. The builder was charged with offering to sell the house for a greater price than permitted by law, and

the three solicitors were charged with aiding and abetting him. The builder was convicted, but the charges against the three solicitors were dismissed on the ground that mens rea was required. The prosecutor appealed, arguing: "Mens rea is not an essential ingredient of the offence of aiding and abetting the commission of a substantive offence of which mens rea is not a necessary ingredient." In *Johnson v. Youden,* [1950] 1 K.B. 544, the court ruled:

"Before a person can be convicted of aiding and abetting the commission of an offence he must at least know the essential matters which constitute that offence. He need not actually know that an offence has been committed, because he may not know that the facts constitute an offence and ignorance of the law is not a defence. If a person knows all the facts and is assisting another person to do certain things, and it turns out that the doing of those things constitutes an offence, the person who is assisting is guilty of aiding and abetting that offence, because to allow him to say, 'I knew of all those facts but I did not know that an offence was committed,' would be allowing him to set up ignorance of the law as a defence.

"The reason why, in our opinion, the justices were right in dismissing the informations against the first two defendants is that they found, and found on good grounds, that they did not know of the matters which in fact constituted the offence; and, as they did not know of those matters, it follows that they cannot be guilty of aiding and abetting the commission of the offence.

"With regard to their partner, the third defendant, a different state of affairs arises. His client, the builder, told him a story which, even if it were true, was on the face of it obviously a colourable evasion of the Act. The builder told him that he had received another 250*l.*, that he had placed

the sum in a separate deposit account, 'and that it was to be spent on payment for work as and when he, the builder, would be lawfully able to execute it in the future on the house on behalf of the said purchaser.' It seems impossible to imagine that anyone could believe such a story. Who has ever heard of a purchaser putting money into the hands of the builder when he bought a house from him because he might want some work done thereafter? Surely, if the builder did not think that the purchaser could pay for the work, he would say: 'Will you pay something on account?' A story of that kind, on the face of it, is a mere colourable evasion of the Act.

"It is more than likely, I think, that, in reading the Act, the third defendant did not read as carefully as he might have done sub-s. 5, of s. 7. If he had read that subsection carefully, I cannot believe that he—or indeed any solicitor, or even a layman,—would not have understood that the arrangement which the builder said that he had made was just the kind of thing which that sub-section prohibited.

"How could anybody say that the story which the builder told the third defendant was not a story with regard to a transaction with which the sale was associated? If that sub-section had been read by the third defendant and appreciated by him, he would have seen at once that the extra 250*l.* which the builder was obtaining was an unlawful payment; but unfortunately he did not realize it, but either misread the Act or did not read it carefully; and the next day he called on the purchaser to complete. Therefore he was clearly aiding and abetting the builder in the offence which the latter was committing.

"The result is that, as far as the first two defendants are concerned, the appeal fails and must be dismissed; but as far as the third defendant is concerned, the case must go back to the justices with an intimation that an offence has been committed, and that he must be convicted."

SECTION 4. THE CONSPIRACY–COMPLICITY RELATIONSHIP

PINKERTON v. UNITED STATES

Supreme Court of the United States, 1946.
328 U.S. 640, 66 S.Ct. 1180, 90 L.Ed. 1489.

MR. JUSTICE DOUGLAS delivered the opinion of the Court.

Walter and Daniel Pinkerton are brothers who live a short distance from each other on Daniel's farm. They were indicted for violations of the Internal Revenue Code. The indictment contained ten substantive counts and one conspiracy count. The jury found Walter guilty on nine of the substantive counts and on the conspiracy count. It found Daniel guilty on six of the substantive counts and on the conspiracy count. Walter was fined $500 and sentenced generally on the substantive counts to imprisonment for thirty months. On the conspiracy count he was given a two year sentence to run concurrently with the other sentence. Daniel was fined $1,000 and sentenced generally on the substantive counts to imprisonment for thirty months. On the conspiracy count he was fined $500 and given a two year sentence to run concurrently with the other sentence. The judgments of conviction were affirmed by the Circuit Court of Appeals. * * *

It is contended that there was insufficient evidence to implicate Daniel in the conspiracy. But we think there was enough evidence for submission of the issue to the jury.

There is, however, no evidence to show that Daniel participated directly in the commission of the substantive offenses on which his conviction has been sustained, although there was evidence to show that these substantive offenses were in fact committed by Walter in furtherance of the

unlawful agreement or conspiracy existing between the brothers. The question was submitted to the jury on the theory that each petitioner could be found guilty of the substantive offenses, if it was found at the time those offenses were committed petitioners were parties to an unlawful conspiracy and the substantive offenses charged were in fact committed in furtherance of it.

Daniel relies on *United States v. Sall,* 116 F.2d 745 (3d Cir.1940). That case held that participation in the conspiracy was not itself enough to sustain a conviction for the substantive offense even though it was committed in furtherance of the conspiracy. The court held that, in addition to evidence that the offense was in fact committed in furtherance of the conspiracy, evidence of direct participation in the commission of the substantive offense or other evidence from which participation might fairly be inferred was necessary.

We take a different view. We have here a continuous conspiracy. There is here no evidence of the affirmative action on the part of Daniel which is necessary to establish his withdrawal from it. *Hyde v. United States,* 225 U.S. 347, 369, 32 S.Ct. 793, 803, 56 L.Ed. 1114, Ann.Cas.1914A, 614. As stated in that case, "Having joined in an unlawful scheme, having constituted agents for its performance, scheme and agency to be continuous until full fruition be secured, until he does some act to disavow or defeat the purpose he is in no situation to claim the delay of the law. As the offense has not been terminated or accomplished, he is still offending. And we think, consciously offending,—offending as certainly, as we have said, as at the first moment of his confederation, and consciously through every moment of its existence." And so long as the partnership in crime continues, the partners act for each other in carrying it forward. * * * The criminal intent to do the act is established by the formation of the conspiracy. Each conspirator instigated the commission of the crime. The unlawful agreement contemplated precisely what was done. It was formed for the purpose. The act done was in execution of the enterprise. The rule which holds responsible one who counsels, procures, or commands another to commit a crime is founded on the same principle. That principle is recognized in the law of conspiracy when the overt act of one partner in crime is attributable to all. An overt act is an essential ingredient of the crime of conspiracy under § 37 of the Criminal Code, 18 U.S.C. § 88. If that can be supplied by the act of one conspirator, we fail to see why the same or other acts in furtherance of the conspiracy are likewise not attributable to the others for the purpose of holding them responsible for the substantive offense.

A different case would arise if the substantive offense committed by one of the conspirators was not in fact done in furtherance of the conspiracy, did not fall within the scope of the unlawful project, or was merely a part of the ramifications of the plan which could not be reasonably foreseen as a necessary or natural consequence of the unlawful agreement. But as we read this record, that is not this case.

Affirmed.

MR. JUSTICE RUTLEDGE, dissenting in part.

The judgment concerning Daniel Pinkerton should be reversed. In my opinion it is without precedent here and is a dangerous precedent to establish.

Daniel and Walter, who were brothers living near each other, were charged in several counts with substantive offenses, and then a conspiracy count was added naming those offenses as overt acts. The proof showed that Walter alone committed the substantive crimes. There was none to establish that Daniel participated in them, aided and abetted Walter in committing

them, or knew that he had done so. Daniel in fact was in the penitentiary, under sentence for other crimes, when some of Walter's crimes were done.

There was evidence, however, to show that over several years Daniel and Walter had confederated to commit similar crimes concerned with unlawful possession, transportation, and dealing in whiskey, in fraud of the federal revenues. On this evidence both were convicted of conspiracy. Walter also was convicted on the substantive counts on the proof of his committing the crimes charged. Then, on that evidence without more than the proof of Daniel's criminal agreement with Walter and the latter's overt acts, which were also the substantive offenses charged, the court told the jury they could find Daniel guilty of those substantive offenses. They did so.

I think this ruling violates both the letter and the spirit of what Congress did when it separately defined the three classes of crime, namely, (1) completed substantive offenses; (2) aiding, abetting or counseling another to commit them; and (3) conspiracy to commit them. Not only does this ignore the distinctions Congress has prescribed shall be observed. It either convicts one man for another's crime or punishes the man convicted twice for the same offense.

The three types of offense are not identical. Nor are their differences merely verbal. The gist of conspiracy is the agreement; that of aiding, abetting or counseling is in consciously advising or assisting another to commit particular offenses, and thus becoming a party to them; that of substantive crime, going a step beyond mere aiding, abetting, counseling to completion of the offense.

These general differences are well understood. But when conspiracy has ripened into completed crime, or has advanced to the stage of aiding and abetting, it becomes easy to disregard their differences and loosely to treat one as identical with the other, that is, for every purpose except the most vital one of imposing sentence. * * *

The court's theory seems to be that Daniel and Walter became general partners in crime by virtue of their agreement and because of that agreement without more on his part Daniel became criminally responsible as a principal for everything Walter did thereafter in the nature of a criminal offense of the general sort the agreement contemplated, so long as there was not clear evidence that Daniel had withdrawn from or revoked the agreement. Whether or not his commitment to the penitentiary had that effect, the result is a vicarious criminal responsibility as broad as, or broader than, the vicarious civil liability of a partner for acts done by a co-partner in the course of the firm's business. * * *

Notes and Questions

1. Consider *Model Penal Code* § 2.06, Comment (1985): "The most important point at which the Model Penal Code formulation diverges from the language of many courts is that it does not make 'conspiracy' as such a basis of complicity in substantive offenses committed in furtherance of its aims. It asks, instead, more specific questions about the behavior charged to constitute complicity, such as whether the defendant solicited commission of the particular offense or whether he aided, or agreed or attempted to aid, in its commission.

"The reason for this treatment is that there appears to be no better way to confine within reasonable limits the scope of liability to which conspiracy may theoretically give rise. In *People v. Luciano,* [25] for example, Luciano and others were convicted of sixty-two counts of compulsory pros-

25. 277 N.Y. 348, 14 N.E.2d 433 (1938).

titution, each count involving a specific instance of placing a girl in a house of prostitution, receiving money for so doing or receiving money from the earnings of a prostitute—acts proved to have been committed pursuant to a combination to control commercialized vice in New York City.

"Liability was properly imposed with respect to these defendants, who directed and controlled the combination. They solicited and aided the commission of numberless specific crimes, including the ones for which they were held. But would so extensive a liability be just for each of the prostitutes or runners involved in the plan? They have, of course, committed their own crimes; they may actually have assisted in others but they exerted no substantial influence on the behavior of a hundred other prostitutes or runners, each pursuing his own ends within the shelter of the combination. A court would and should hold that they are parties to a conspiracy; this is itself a crime, under this Code as well as most others. And they should also be held for those crimes they actually committed, or within the principle of this section for those to which they were accomplices. However, law would lose all sense of just proportion if simply because of the conspiracy itself each were held accountable for thousands of additional offenses of which he was completely unaware and which he did not influence at all.

"Again, in *United States v. Bruno,* [p. 655 of this Book,] eighty-eight defendants were indicted for conspiracy to import, sell and possess narcotics. The evidence showed a large combination composed of four groups of persons: the smugglers who imported the drugs; the middlemen who paid the smugglers and distributed to retailers; and two groups of retailers, one in Texas and Louisiana and the other in

New York. The Court held that this evidence sustained a verdict that there was one large conspiracy in which the members of each group were criminal participants. That judgment commands support in a prosecution for conspiracy, and is one that would follow from the application of the standards of Section 5.03 of this Code. But should it follow that each retailer in Texas commits the offenses of each retailer in New York, though he has not promoted or facilitated their commission and has no interest in them? Yet if the conspiracy involved one combination, the commission of those crimes was certainly included in its objects, and a traditionally worded inquiry might lead to liability for them all.

"No decision has been found in which the liability of co-conspirators for acts of one another has been pressed to limits such as these, though the limits have been approached.[30] The cases that declare the doctrine normally involve defendants who have had a hand in planning, directing, or executing the crimes charged. When that is so, the other principles of accessorial liability establish guilt, and under this section the defendant has 'solicited,' 'aided,' 'agreed to aid,' or 'attempted to aid' in planning or committing the crime. Indeed, when that is not so, courts may be expected to seek ways to avoid the conclusion of complicity, though traditional doctrine hardly points the way. The right way, it is submitted, is to measure liability by the criteria of this section. Conspiracy may prove solicitation, aid or agreement to aid, etc.; it is evidentially important and may be sufficient for that purpose. But whether it suffices ought to be decided by the jurors; they should not be told that it establishes complicity as a matter of law.

However proper it may be to draw the necessary inference from proof of the conspiracy, the jury ought to face in concrete cases whether or not, on the evidence, the inference is one that should be drawn.

"Virtually all recently enacted and proposed revisions adopt the principle of the Code that the liability of co-conspirators for substantive offenses should be controlled by the same limits that are otherwise the measure of liability for complicity."

2. Note, 75 Colum.L.Rev. 1122, 1150–51 (1975): "[The Model Penal Code approach] stands in stark contrast to current federal practice. Despite the fact that the relevant statute makes no mention of conspiracy as a potential source of complicitous liability, the leading case of *Pinkerton v. United States* proclaimed, nearly thirty years ago, that a conspirator, by virtue of his participation in a criminal agreement, is responsible for *all* substantive offenses committed by his co-conspirators *in furtherance* of that agreement. Whether reasonable foreseeability of such substantive offenses is indispensable to conviction as a principal on the basis of conspiracy alone (i.e., with no showing of actual aiding or abetting) is a subject of some dispute in the federal courts. However, even when this limitation is added to the 'in furtherance of the agreement' prerequisite, the embrace of vicarious liability under federal law remains unjustifiably broad."

3. In *United States v. Alvarez*, 755 F.2d 830 (11th Cir.1985), members of a drug conspiracy were convicted of murder on a *Pinkerton* theory after an undercover agent was killed during a shootout that unexpect-

---

30. *See, e.g., Anderson v. Superior Court,* 78 Cal.App.2d 22, 177 P.2d 315 (1947). The defendant referred several women to an abortionist, receiving part of his fee. This evidence was held sufficient to support an indictment charging the defendant, the abortionist and sixteen others with a conspiracy to perform abortions and twen-

ty-six substantive counts based on individual abortions. It was deemed immaterial that this defendant had no contact with any other codefendant and had no part in any substantive offenses other than those involving the women whom she herself had referred.

edly erupted between the dealers and undercover agents during a cocaine deal. The court of appeals stated:

"We acknowledge that the instant case is not a typical *Pinkerton* case. Here, the murder of Agent Rios was not within the originally intended scope of the conspiracy, but instead occurred as a result of an unintended turn of events. We have not found, nor has the government cited, any authority for the proposition that all conspirators, regardless of individual culpability, may be held responsible under *Pinkerton* for reasonably foreseeable but originally unintended substantive crimes.[25] Furthermore, we are mindful of the potential due process limitations on the *Pinkerton* doctrine in cases involving attenuated relationships between the conspirator and the substantive crime.

"Nevertheless, these considerations do not require us to reverse the murder convictions of Portal, Concepcion, and Hernandez, for we cannot accept the three appellants' assessment of their individual culpability. All three were more than 'minor' participants in the drug conspiracy. Portal served as a look-out in front of the Hurricane Motel during part of the negotiations that led to the shoot-out, and the evidence indicated that he was armed. Concepcion introduced the agents to Alvarez, the apparent leader of the conspiracy, and was present when the shoot-out started. Finally, Hernandez, the manager of the motel, allowed the drug transactions to

take place on the premises and acted as a translator during part of the negotiations that led to the shoot-out.

"In addition, all three appellants had actual knowledge of at least some of the circumstances and events leading up to the murder. The evidence that Portal was carrying a weapon demonstrated that he anticipated the possible use of deadly force to protect the conspirators' interests. Moreover, both Concepcion and Hernandez were present when Alvarez stated that he would rather be dead than go back to prison, indicating that they, too, were aware that deadly force might be used to prevent apprehension by Federal agents.

"We find the individual culpability of Portal, Concepcion, and Hernandez sufficient to support their murder convictions under *Pinkerton,* despite the fact that the murder was not within the originally intended scope of the conspiracy. In addition, based on the same evidence, we conclude that the relationship between the three appellants and the murder was not so attenuated as to run afoul of the potential due process limitations on the *Pinkerton* doctrine. We therefore hold that *Pinkerton* liability for the murder of Agent Rios properly was imposed on the three appellants, and we decline to reverse their murder convictions on this ground."

4. Anderberg was convicted of assault on LaRoche with intent to inflict great bodily harm, in that he aided the person who broke a pool cue over LaRoche's

---

25. The imposition of *Pinkerton* liability for such crimes is not wholly unprecedented. *See, e.g., Government of Virgin Islands v. Dowling,* 633 F.2d 660, 666 (3d Cir.1980) (conspiracy to commit bank robbery; substantive crime of assault with deadly weapons against police officers, committed during escape attempt); *Park v. Huff,* 506 F.2d 849, 859 (5th Cir.1975) (liquor conspiracy; substantive crime of first degree murder of local district attorney, committed in attempt to stop investigation of illegal liquor sales). In each of the aforementioned cases, however, vicarious liability was imposed only on "major" participants in the conspiracy.

At trial in the instant case, the government's attorney argued that *Pinkerton* liability for Agent Rios' murder properly could be imposed on all of the conspirators, and expressed the view that prosecutorial discretion would protect truly "minor" participants, such as appellants Rios and Raymond, from liability for the far more serious crimes committed by their coconspirators. We do not find this argument persuasive. In our view, the liability of such "minor" participants must rest on a more substantial foundation than the mere whim of the prosecutor.

head. In affirming the conviction, the court in *State v. Anderberg*, 89 S.D. 75, 228 N.W.2d 631 (1975), said: "On behalf of the defendant it is asserted that he can not be held as an aider and abettor in the assault on LaRoche without a showing that he and the others involved acted in furtherance of a conspiracy. The short answer to this is that one may aid and abet without having previously entered into a conspiracy to commit a crime. Being involved as an aider and abettor in the commission of a crime and being involved as a conspirator to commit the same crime are separate and distinct offenses."

SECTION 5. FORESEEABLE OR RELATED CRIMES

UNITED STATES v. CARTER

United States Court of Appeals, District of Columbia Circuit, 1971.
445 F.2d 669.

WILKEY, CIRCUIT JUDGE:

This is the sorry story of a brutal, senseless and unprofitable crime so characteristic of life and death in our urban centers such as Washington, D.C. Since the principal question in this appeal is the sufficiency of the evidence against appellant, and since he received a sentence of imprisonment from 20 years to life, we have examined the evidence with some care. Finding it sufficient, and appellant's other points of error not persuasive, we affirm.

The appellant and one Whiteside were charged with three offenses: robbery, premeditated murder, and felony murder. On premeditated murder the District Court directed an acquittal; the jury convicted of robbery and felony murder.

On 29 December 1967 John Pointer, a part-time cab driver, made the mistake of picking up appellant and Whiteside at Fourteenth Street and Park Road, N.W., Washington, D.C. On the trip to the Southeast section of the city Whiteside rode in the back while appellant sat in front beside the cab driver. According to appellant's own story, in the Southeast section Whiteside called on the cab driver to stop, and when he did not do so immediately, Whiteside took out a .22 caliber pistol and shot Pointer twice. One bullet entered the right side of the victim's neck just under the right ear, the other to the rear of the right ear.

At approximately 10:00 p.m. Whiteside and appellant were seen by a witness leaving the cab; Whiteside had blood all over one side of his trench coat. Around midnight other witnesses noticed the cab with the driver slumped over and called the police. The homicide squad examination found a pack of Pall Malls, later determined as belonging to appellant, on the right side of the dashboard. A large amount of blood was on both the front and back seats; the inside of the right front door and the outside of the left rear door were smeared with blood. The victim's right-hand jacket pocket was turned inside out. The driver's record of fares for the day totaled $24.60, but only a one-dollar bill was discovered—that being in his wallet. His change carrier was missing.

Shortly after ten o'clock appellant Carter and Whiteside entered a house about two blocks away from the scene of the crime. Six people were present at a small party, three of whom later testified. One of these was James Makel, the credibility of whose testimony assumed some importance in the trial. At the time they entered the house appellant's coat had a little blood on the sleeve, and Whiteside still wore the trench coat with the blood-spattered front. Whiteside washed his coat in the bathtub. Both gentlemen felt the need to wash their hands. Appellant also washed blood from four one-dollar bills.

After an interval appellant Carter asked James Makel to drive them uptown. As the three left, appellant carried the two outer coats and put them in the back seat of Makel's car. On the way toward town Makel stopped for gas. Whiteside paid for the gas with six quarters which he took from a silver change carrier. Appellant Carter had four one-dollar bills lying in his lap, but explained they could not be used because they were still wet from his having washed off the blood.

According to Makel's testimony, as they drove toward town appellant kept reiterating that Whiteside did not have to kill the cab driver; he said that he had the cab driver "up tight" and that Whiteside didn't have to shoot him. Appellant demonstrated what he meant by "up tight" by putting his arm around Makel's neck and shoulders to show that he (appellant) had grabbed the cab driver by the shoulder and neck and yoked him. He further explained, "That's how I got blood on my arm." Makel demonstrated this yoking at the trial in the same manner he testified appellant Carter had demonstrated to him. As they drove along, appellant kept repeating that Whiteside did not have to kill the man, saying "He killed him for some junk change."

When they arrived in the Northwest section near the house of Makel's brother-in-law, the appellant and Whiteside asked Makel if he would dispose of the two coats. When Makel declined, Whiteside put the coats into a trash can behind Makel's brother-in-law's house. Makel later put the coats on the back porch of the house, where they were found by the police on 2 January 1968, the day Whiteside was apprehended. In a search of Whiteside's apartment pursuant to his arrest, a .22 caliber derringer pistol, identified as the one Whiteside carried on the evening of 29 December 1967, was found in his closet, and the cab driver's silver change carrier in a trash can in his kitchen.

After appellant Carter was arrested two days later, he made a voluntary statement in which he admitted being in the cab with Whiteside when Whiteside killed the driver. He described going with Whiteside to the house where they encountered Makel and the drive uptown with Makel. He claimed that after the shooting Whiteside had given him four one-dollar bills with blood on them and recalled that Whiteside had a silver change carrier with him when they were in Makel's car. The appellant denied that he had participated in any plan to rob or kill the driver, and denied he had actually seen Whiteside commit robbery, although he confirmed Whiteside's act of murder. * * *

Appellant argues strenuously that from the verbal descriptions of the various witnesses it was impossible for Whiteside to have shot the cab driver as described by both Makel and appellant, and for appellant to have yoked the cab driver at the same time as described and demonstrated by Makel. But it was for the jury and the trial judge, who had the opportunity of seeing Makel's demonstration in the courtroom, to determine if there was any inconsistency, and apparently there was not.

Appellant also inveighs heavily against the interpretation put by Makel on the words "up tight" used by appellant. But whatever appellant meant by saying he had the cab driver "up tight," those words could only mean that appellant was participating in some fashion in the robbery. If appellant had him "up tight," and he was participating in the attack on or in the robbery of the cab driver, appellant was participating in a felony. It may be true that the ultimate tragedy of the cab driver's senseless murder was far from appellant's mind, but under our statutory law, his participation in the robbery resulting in a killing made him guilty of murder in the first degree, of which he was duly convicted.[8]

This testimony of Makel was completely sufficient to implicate appellant Carter in the robbery of the cab driver. We cannot ascribe to the witness Makel an intimate knowledge of the intricacies of the felony murder doctrine, i.e., we cannot impugn Makel's testimony by attributing to him a scheme to put appellant's neck in the noose for murder by implicating appellant in the robbery, and having sufficient legal knowledge to rest confident that the felony murder doctrine would do the rest.

* * *

Appellant's convictions for robbery and felony murder are therefore

Affirmed.

FAHY, SENIOR CIRCUIT JUDGE (concurring in part, dissenting in part):

I concur in the affirmance of appellant's conviction of robbery. As to his conviction of felony-murder based on the killing by appellant's co-felon of the victim of the robbery, during the course of its commission, I would reverse. The instruction to the jury on that phase of the case, insofar as the instruction applied to appellant who did not himself kill the victim, did not require the jury to find, as I believe to be essential to his conviction of first degree felony-murder, that the killing was committed in furtherance of a design or purpose which appellant held in common with the one who actually killed the victim.

22 D.C.Code § 2401 provides that "[w]hoever * * * in perpetrating or attempting to perpetrate any offense punishable by imprisonment in the penitentiary * * * kills another * * * is guilty of murder in the first degree." Under this provision only the person who actually kills another is guilty of first degree murder. To hold a co-felon such as appellant guilty of first degree murder more must be shown, namely, an aiding and abetting in the commission of the crime of murder defined by Section 2401. That section does not provide that one who aids and abets the commission of a robbery during which another commits a homicide is sufficient for conviction of the former of first degree murder.

The instruction to the jury, nevertheless, was as follows:

If two or more persons acting together and jointly are perpetrating a robbery or are attempting to perpetrate a robbery, and one or more of them, in the course of the robbery or attempted robbery, kills another person, then all the persons involved in the robbery or attempted robbery are guilty of murder in the first degree.

If one person is perpetrating or attempting to perpetrate a robbery and one or more other persons aids and abets him in so doing, and the first of these persons in the course of the robbery or attempted robbery kills a human being, then the person or persons who aided and abetted him in the robbery or attempted robbery and the person who committed the killing are both equally guilty of murder in the first degree.

Under the circumstances of this case, the elements of the offense of murder in the first degree which the Government must prove * * * are as follows:

* * *

(4) That the killing was within the scope of the robbery or attempted robbery which Whiteside and [appellant] undertook to commit, if you find they so undertook to do so.

8. This is so even though appellant was the accomplice of Whiteside, who did the actual shooting. 22 D.C.Code § 105. In pertinent part, 22 D.C.Code § 2401, defining first degree murder, reads:

Whoever, being of sound memory and discretion, * * * without purpose so to do, kills another in perpetrating or attempting to perpetrate any * * * robbery * * * is guilty of murder in the first degree.

Appellant did not himself kill the deceased cab driver, and indeed he seemed to repudiate the shooting. Possibly the homicide was the independent act of appellant's co-felon, committed to the dismay of appellant. This is not to say that appellant could not be found guilty of murder. The problem is that his guilt of that offense was not submitted to the jury in terms which would allow, but not require, the jury to find that he aided and abetted commission of the homicide. The proper test in such a case in my opinion should be, not whether the homicide was within the scope of the robbery, but whether it was in furtherance of a common design or purpose.[3]

For the foregoing reason I would reverse appellant's conviction of first degree murder and grant him a new trial of that charge with an instruction conformably with the views above expressed.

I concur in affirmance of the conviction of robbery.

Notes and Questions

1. One jurisdiction has attempted to mitigate the harshness of this aspect of the felony-murder rule. N.Y. Penal Law § 125.25(3) provides:

"A person is guilty of murder in the second degree when: * * *

"3. Acting either alone or with one or more other persons, he commits or attempts to commit robbery, burglary, kidnapping, arson, rape in the first degree, sodomy in the first degree, sexual abuse in the first degree, escape in the first degree, or escape in the second degree, and, in the course of and in furtherance of such crime or of immediate flight therefrom, he, or another participant, if there be any, causes

the death of a person other than one of the participants; except that in any prosecution under this subdivision, in which the defendant was not the only participant in the underlying crime, it is an affirmative defense that the defendant:

"(a) Did not commit the homicidal act or in any way solicit, request, command, importune, cause or aid the commission thereof; and

"(b) Was not armed with a deadly weapon, or any instrument, article or substance readily capable of causing death or serious physical injury and of a sort not ordinarily carried in public places by law-abiding persons; and

"(c) Had no reasonable ground to believe that any other participant was armed with such a weapon, instrument, article or substance; and

"(d) Had no reasonable ground to believe that any other participant intended to engage in conduct likely to result in death or serious physical injury."

PEOPLE v. KESSLER

Supreme Court of Illinois, 1974.
57 Ill.2d 493, 315 N.E.2d 29.

DAVIS, JUSTICE.

In a jury trial in the circuit court of Winnebago County, defendant, Rudolph Louis Kessler, was convicted on one count of burglary and two counts of attempted murder. The appellate court affirmed the burglary conviction and reversed the attempted-murder convictions, and we allowed the People's petition for leave to appeal. The facts are stated in the opinion of the appellate court and will be restated here only to the extent necessary to more fully delineate the issues. Defendant waited in an automobile outside a tavern while

---

3. This is not to say that the jury must find that appellant and Whiteside planned specifically to use the force of shooting the victim, but only that as a minimum they planned to use such force if necessary to consummate the robbery.

This concert between co-felons, of course, could be shown by circumstantial evidence. The point, however, is that the determination should be left to the jury under instructions properly framing the issue.

his two unarmed companions entered the building to commit the burglary. While inside the tavern, they were surprised by the owner, and one of the burglars shot and wounded him with a gun taken during the burglary. Later, while defendant's companions were fleeing on foot, one of them fired a shot at a pursuing police officer. At that time defendant was sitting in the automobile. * * *

In reversing the attempted-murder convictions, the appellate court held that "The application of the 'common design' principle is not justified by the language of section 5—2 to hold a defendant accountable for crimes committed by an accomplice which the defendant was not shown to have intended." * * *

The People argue "that a person is responsible for all criminal violations actually committed by another if he assists another in the commission of a single criminal violation," and that "if the legislature had intended to limit accomplice liability only to further criminal acts which were specifically intended the word 'conduct' would not have been included in the language of section 5—2."

Sections 5—1 and 5—2 of the Criminal Code provide in pertinent part:

"Sec. 5—1. Accountability for *Conduct* of Another.

"A person is responsible for *conduct* which is an element of an offense if the conduct is either that of the person himself, or that of another and he is legally accountable for such *conduct* as provided in Section 5—2 or both." (Emphasis added.)

"Sec. 5—2. When Accountability Exists.

"A person is legally accountable for the conduct of another when:

* * *

(b) The statute defining the offense makes him so accountable; or

(c) Either before or during the commission of *an offense* and with the intent to promote or facilitate such commission, he solicits, aids, abets, agrees or attempts to aid, such other person in the planning or commission of the offense. * * *" (Emphasis added.)

"Conduct" is defined as:

" * * * an act or a series of acts, and the accompanying mental state." Ill.Rev.Stat.1971, ch. 38, par. 2–4.

* * *

We believe the statute, as it reads, means that where one aids another in the planning or commission of an offense, he is legally accountable for the conduct of the person he aids; and that the word "conduct" encompasses any criminal act done in furtherance of the planned and intended act.

An early application of this rule is found in *Hamilton v. People* (1885), 113 Ill. 34. The defendant and two companions invaded a watermelon patch intending to steal some melons. The owner discovered them and a scuffle or fight ensued during which the owner pinned one of the three to the ground, and when in this position another of the three fired a gun at the owner, but the shot missed the owner and struck the potential watermelon thief, who the owner had thrown to the ground. During this occurrence, the third potential watermelon thief stood by. All three of the putative watermelon thieves were charged and convicted of assault with intent to commit murder. This court stated:

"The fact is undisputed that the three defendants, one of whom was armed with a pistol, invaded the premises of the prosecuting witness with a criminal purpose. The business upon which the parties had deliberately entered was a hazardous one. They had a right to expect that in the event they were detected in stealing the melons, it would result in violence endangering life or limb,—as it actually turned out afterwards. That they were all co-conspirators in a dangerous criminal enterprise, is an undisputed fact. Such being the case, whatever was done by one, in contemplation of law was done by all, and all are therefore equally responsible."

In the case at bar, the record shows a common design to commit a robbery or burglary. Kessler, Mass and Abney sat in on the plan, and Kessler led Mass and Abney to the Anchor Tap where he stated the days' receipts were kept.

In *People v. Cole* (1964), 30 Ill.2d 375, 196 N.E.2d 691, the court stated:

"While it is true that mere presence or negative acquiescence is not enough to constitute a person a principal, one may aid and abet without actively participating in the overt act and if the proof shows that a person was present at the commission of the crime without disapproving or opposing it, it is competent for the trier of fact to consider this conduct in connection with other circumstances and thereby reach a conclusion that such person assented to the commission of the crime, lent to it his countenance and approval and was thereby aiding and abetting the crime. Stated differently, circumstances may show there is a common design to do an unlawful act to which all assent, and whatever is done in furtherance of the design is the act of all, making each person guilty of the crime."

A similar conclusion was reached in *People v. Hubbard* (1975), 55 Ill.2d 142, 302 N.E.2d 609, where in considering the problem at issue, we referred to *People v. Armstrong* (1968), 41 Ill.2d 390, 243 N.E.2d 825, wherein the court stated as follows:

"The next contention of defendants involves a request to depart from the long established common-design rule, i.e., that where defendants have a common design to do an unlawful act, then whatever act any one of them does in furtherance of the common design is the act of all and all are equally guilty of whatever crime is committed. * * * We have fully reiterated our support of this rule in recent cases, and we continue to do so in this case. Nor do we accept defendants' argument that the statutorily defined rules on accountability in any way modify or abrogate the common-design rule. This section provides that a person is legally accountable for the conduct of another when '(c) Either before or during the commission * * * he solicits, aids, abets, or agrees or attempts to aid, such other person in the planning or commission of the offense.' Applying this section to this case the attempted robbery was the offense which the defendants were jointly committing and each was legally accountable for the conduct of the other. The result was murder, the killing of an individual without lawful justification while attempting or committing a forcible felony other than voluntary manslaughter."

In applying the rationale of *Armstrong* to the case at bar, the burglary was the offense which the defendant, Mass, and Abney had jointly planned and were jointly committing, and each was legally accountable for the conduct of the other in connection therewith. The result was the offense of attempted murder of Louis Cotti, the tap owner, and of State Trooper Max L. Clevenger, who answered a report of the incident and who tried to apprehend the fleeing parties.

For the foregoing reasons, we affirm the part of the appellate court decision which affirmed the burglary conviction of the defendant, and we reverse the part of its decision which reversed the conviction of the defendant for attempted murder, and we affirm the judgment of the circuit court.

Appellate court affirmed in part and reversed in part; circuit court affirmed.

GOLDENHERSH, JUSTICE (dissenting): * * *

It is clear that defendant's accountability cannot stem from section 5—2(b) for the simple reason that the statute defining the offense of attempt murder does not make him so accountable. In support of its position the majority cites *People v. Armstrong,* and quotes at length from *People v. Hubbard.* These cases are clearly not in point. They involved defendants charged with murder and fall under section 5—2(b) for the reason that section 9—1(3) of the Criminal Code creates the "felony murder" classification and obviates the need of proof of intent. It should be further noted that [the cases] cited in and relied upon in *Armstrong* were also murder cases and are not relevant here.

The majority also quotes from *Hamilton v. People,* and *People v. Cole.* In *Hamilton* there was a common design to burglarize a watermelon patch, one of the co-defendants was armed, all were present and took part in the fight which followed their being accosted by the farmer whose melons they were stealing and the court applied a common design theory. The rationale of *Cole* is the basis on which the appellate court affirmed, correctly, defendant's conviction on the burglary charge but neither *Cole* nor *Hamilton* can be read so as to stretch the statute to cover the facts of this case.

The Committee Comments to section 5—2(c) *inter alia* state:

"Subsection 5—2(c) is a comprehensive statement of liability based on counseling, aiding and abetting and the like, which includes those situations that, at common law, involve the liability of principals in the second degree and accessories before the fact. It will be observed that liability under this subsection requires proof of an 'intent to promote or facilitate * * * commission' of the substantive offense. Moreover, 'conspiracy' between the actor and defendant is not of itself made the basis of accountability for the actor's conduct, although the acts of conspiring may in many cases satisfy the particular requirements of this subsection."

It should be noted that emphasis is placed on the requirement of proof of an "intent to promote or facilitate * * * commission of the substantive offense" and the Criminal Code provides:

"A person intends, or acts intentionally or with intent, to accomplish a result or engage in conduct described by the statute defining the offense, when his conscious objective or purpose is to accomplish that result or engage in that conduct." Ill.Rev.Stat.1971, ch. 38, par. 4—4.

The substantive offense involved is attempt murder and section 8—4(a) of the Code provides that the requisite elements of the offense of attempt are the intent to commit a specific criminal offense and the doing of an act which constitutes a substantial step toward the commission of that offense. * * * As pointed out by the appellate court, had either of the intended victims died, the provisions of section 9—1(3) of the Criminal Code would have served to make the defendant accountable, but the attempt statute contains no such provision. * * *

I submit that on this record the defendant was not proved guilty of attempt murder. The evidence is uncontradicted that when his companions embarked on the burglary they were unarmed and that he was not inside the tavern when the shot was fired. Again, when the shot was fired at the pursuing officer, defendant was in the automobile, and under the circumstances neither occurrence is shown to be a consequence of any action of the defendant from which the requisite specific intent could be inferred. * * *

Notes and Questions

1. Compare *United States v. Greer,* 467 F.2d 1064 (7th Cir.1972), where Greer and two others were charged with violating 18 U.S.C.A. § 2314, in that they "did transport and caused to be transported in interstate commerce" 40,400 pounds of copper which they knew to have been stolen. The government's theory with respect to Greer was that he was an aider and abettor, in that he told the others that they could find a broken down tractor-trailer filled with copper at an Indiana freight depot. The others stole the copper from the disabled trailer and later hauled it to Chicago, where they arranged to store it. On appeal, Greer claimed that the proof was only that he had aided the theft, but the government responded that he thereby could be held accountable for the "foreseeable consequences" of the theft, which prompted the court of appeals to "consider how far accomplice liability can be extended to include crimes other than the one (or ones) the accomplice immediately aided.

"Accomplice liability is necessarily limited by the general principles of criminal liability. To allow a jury to infer an intent to aid in the commission of one offense from the demonstrated intent to aid in another earlier offense because the later crime is a foreseeable consequence of the earlier one, is to base criminal liability only on a showing of negligence rather than criminal intent. The court will relax the intent component of aiding and abetting in a limited number of situations. We agree, for instance, that a defendant can be held responsible as an aider and abettor of

a crime even where there is no direct proof that he intended to aid in the crime, if he is substantially involved in the chain of events leading immediately to it. Thus, the driver of a 'getaway' car during a robbery who intends only to aid in the theft, can be charged with the crime of transporting the stolen goods although his participation in the subsequent transportation was inadvertent. The requisite intent may be inferred when the defendant's physical participation in the course of events is substantial.[4] But where the relationship between the defendant's acts and the ultimate crime for which he is charged is as attenuated as it is in the instant case, we would require some showing of specific intent to aid in, or specific knowledge of, the crime charged.

"Greer's participation was limited to triggering the theft by providing the thieves with information about the copper. Young testified that Greer alerted him to the existence of the copper, described its location, and later, after the theft, phoned him in order to claim the proceeds. Since the Government does not claim Greer was physically present at the crime, Greer's participation amounts to that of an 'accessory before the fact.' As such, in order to prove Greer's complicity with the later stages of the crime—namely, the transportation of the goods—the Government must show that he intended to aid in post-theft plans, or that he knew details of the thieves' travel plans, such as the specific destination of the goods. Since the Government made no such showing, we find the proof insufficient to sustain a conviction on this count."

2. *Model Penal Code* § 2.06, Comment (1985): "Stephen thought the common law to be that if 'a person instigates another to commit a crime, and the person so

---

4. There are two additional situations in which the intent requirement for accomplice liability is relaxed, the felony-murder and misdemeanor-manslaughter situations. Aiding in the commission of a felony which results in an unintended death subjects the accomplice to liability for murder.

instigated commits a crime different from the one he was instigated to commit, but likely to be caused by such instigation, the instigator is an accessory before the fact.' The cases put in illustration involve homicide, however, where doctrines of transferred intent, felony murder and liability for recklessness present a special situation that does not readily lend itself to broad generalization. So too, the American decisions that declare the principle that co-conspirators are liable for crimes that it is merely probable will be committed in the execution of the plan have mainly involved homicide; and the point of the declaration has often been to limit the constructive liability for murder, rather than to extend a liability that otherwise would not obtain.

"There is, on the other hand, impressive indication that, apart from the case of homicide, a liability based upon probability alone is not sustained. Judge Learned Hand, for example, has said of criminal conspiracy: 'At times it seemed to be supposed that, once some kind of criminal concert is established, all parties are liable for everything anyone of the original participants does, and even for what those do who join later. Nothing could be more untrue. Nobody is liable in conspiracy except for the fair import of the concerted purpose or agreement as he understands it; if later comers change that, he is not liable for the change * * *.' If that is true of conspiracy, it is true *a fortiori* of substantive offenses allegedly committed in the course of the conspiracy. Many decisions so hold.

"Whatever may have been the law on the point, in any event, it is submitted that the liability of an accomplice ought not to

be extended beyond the purposes that he shares. Probabilities have an important evidential bearing on these issues; to make them independently sufficient is to predicate the liability on negligence when, for good reason, more is normally required before liability is found. More extensive liability for consequences may be defensible in special situations; if so, the liability should be created by the section dealing with the special situation, not comprehended in a principle designed for application throughout the Code. Most modern revisions share this approach." [a]

SECTION 6. MUST THE PRINCIPAL BE GUILTY?

PEOPLE v. TAYLOR

Supreme Court of California, 1974.
12 Cal.3d 686, 117 Cal.Rptr. 70, 527 P.2d 622.

WRIGHT, CHIEF JUSTICE.

Defendant Alvin Taylor appeals from a judgment upon jury convictions of the murder of John H. Smith, one of the individuals who, with defendant, perpetrated a robbery of Jack West and of the robbery of said Jack West. * * *

While *Taylor I*[a] was pending in this court Daniels was separately tried and convicted of the robbery but was acquitted of the murder charge. Since defendant was sitting in the getaway car outside the store at the time of the shooting, his subsequent conviction for murder could result only upon a finding that one of his confederates, Daniels or Smith, harbored malice which the trier of fact then attributed to defendant because of his role as an aider

a. Some clearly do not, but their provisions have withstood constitutional challenge. See, e.g., *State v. Linscott*, 520 A.2d 1067 (Me.1987), upholding an accomplice liability statutory provision stating: "A person is an accomplice under this subsection to any crime the commission of which was a reasonably foreseeable consequence of his conduct."

a. The reference is to *Taylor v. Superior Court*, p. 313 of this Book, holding that the felony-murder rule was inapplicable but that defendant might be found guilty on a theory of accomplice liability if his confederates entertained malice aforethought.

and abettor. At Daniels' trial the People already have sought and have failed to establish that either Daniels or Smith entertained the requisite malice aforethought. Defendant thus argues that the doctrine of collateral estoppel should have precluded the People from relitigating this identical issue at his later trial.[5] We agree.

Collateral estoppel has been held to bar relitigation of an issue decided at a previous trial if (1) the issue necessarily decided at the previous trial is identical to the one which is sought to be relitigated; if (2) the previous trial resulted in a final judgment on the merits; and if (3) the party against whom collateral estoppel is assessed was a party or in privity with a party at the prior trial. The first two of these requirements are fully satisfied in the instant case. The question of whether the conduct of Daniels or Smith was sufficiently provocative to support a finding of implied malice was resolved adversely to the People in Daniels' trial, and the People have sought to relitigate the identical issue in these proceedings. Daniels' acquittal was a final judgment on the merits. * * *

In criminal cases the bar of collateral estoppel is constitutionally compelled when the same defendant was involved in both trials. (*Ashe v. Swenson* (1970) 397 U.S. 436, 443–447, 90 S.Ct. 1189, 25 L.Ed.2d 469.) However, courts have sometimes declined to apply the doctrine

in behalf of a criminal defendant who was not involved in the prior trial. * * *

We have failed to discover any controlling precedents on this issue. Although some cases contain dicta unfavorable to defendant's position, they are readily distinguishable. These cases (1) involved situations in which the basic requirements of collateral estoppel were not satisfied because identity of the issue was lacking [6] or because there was no prior final judgment on the merits as to the alleged perpetrators,[7] or (2) involved joint trials which failed to raise the issue of collateral estoppel; [8] or (3) did not involve the question of an accused's vicarious liability for the acts of a previously acquitted perpetrator.

The reported cases in other jurisdictions are divided on the question of whether an accused may be convicted by holding him vicariously responsible for the acts of a previously acquitted accomplice.

Some jurisdictions apply the defense of collateral estoppel in these circumstances, primarily to avoid the inconsistency and apparent unfairness of holding the accused liable for a crime which a previous adjudication has determined was not committed. Such distaste for inconsistent verdicts has caused the conviction of an aider and abettor to be vacated when the perpetrator is subsequently acquitted in a separate trial or is later convicted of a lesser offense than the aider and abettor.[10]

---

5. Although defendant did not raise the plea of collateral estoppel at trial, he should not be faulted for failing to do so since it does not appear that there were then any controlling precedents in California on the issue raised by such a plea.

6. In these cases, the accused's conviction was not based solely on the acts of his acquitted confederate because (1) the accused himself was on the scene of the crime and actively engaged in its commission or (2) the accomplice was acquitted because of the lack of a culpable mental state for reasons personal only to the accomplice (— lack of criminal intent by reason of deception practiced by the accused;—duress induced by the accused;—lack of criminal intent because of intoxication).

7. In these cases there was no final judgment of acquittal on the merits as to the alleged perpetrators because (1) at least one of the alleged perpetrators was convicted of the same crime for which the accused was later prosecuted or (2) the perpetrator pleaded guilty to a lesser related offense than that with which the accused was charged.

8. One of these cases held that an accused could not be convicted as an aider and abettor when the perpetrator was acquitted in the same trial, although there is dicta that such a result would not be sanctioned if the two had been tried separately. * * *

10. Other jurisdictions have rejected the defense of collateral estoppel in a situation similar

Although as stated there are no controlling cases on point there are nevertheless persuasive related cases which favor the application of collateral estoppel to foreclose the conviction of an accused based on his vicarious responsibility for the acts of a previously acquitted confederate.

It is settled that a defense judgment in a tort action will bar the plaintiff from relitigating the issue of the defendant's negligence in a subsequent suit against the defendant's employer based solely on a *respondeat superior* theory. * * *

An application of the doctrine of collateral estoppel similar to that in civil tort cases involving vicarious liability also has been made in criminal conspiracy cases which, like the instant case, involve criminal responsibility for other than purely unilateral conduct. Since a criminal conspiracy requires the participation of two or more conspirators, a conviction necessarily involves a finding that another person conspired with the accused. The courts also have applied the doctrine to preclude the conviction of an alleged conspirator when all other alleged coconspirators have been acquitted or the charges against all the other coconspirators have been dismissed because of insufficient evidence. The courts have thus refused to uphold the conviction of a sole remaining conspirator as he could be convicted only through a finding that at least one of the previously acquitted coconspirators had, in fact, engaged in a conspiracy.

There are strong policy considerations which, in addition to the holdings in related cases, favor application of the doctrine in the instant circumstances. We deem the purposes of an application of the doctrine to be: (1) to promote judicial economy by minimizing repetitive litigation; (2) to prevent inconsistent judgments which

undermine the integrity of the judicial system; and (3) to provide repose by preventing a person from being harassed by vexatious litigation. In deciding whether the doctrine is applicable in a particular situation a court must balance the need to limit litigation against the right of a fair adversary proceeding in which a party may fully present his case.

The need for judicial economy by minimizing repetitive litigation is even more important in criminal than in civil trials. Crowded court dockets inevitably will impose a heavy burden on criminal defendants as substantial periods of incarceration may result while they await trial, and long delays between arrest and sentencing will decrease the effectiveness of the punishment which is ultimately meted out. Although the saving of the resources of the court system may be somewhat reduced when, in addition to the crime against which a plea of collateral estoppel is urged, other crimes must also be litigated, the other goals of an application of the doctrine can nevertheless be achieved.

Perhaps the most compelling reason for an application of collateral estoppel where vicarious liability is at issue is to prevent the compromising of the integrity of the judicial system caused by the rendering of inconsistent verdicts. Criminal trials generally receive more publicity than civil ones, and the public's view of the judicial system in general is often shaped by the impression of the fairness of the criminal justice system in particular. Few things undermine the layman's faith in the integrity of our legal institutions more than the spector of a system which results in a person being punished for the acts of another, when the actor himself under identical charges had been previously exonerated from responsibility for those very acts. This is particularly so under the facts of

to the instant case thereby permitting conviction of an aider and abettor based solely on the acts of a previously acquitted accomplice * * *.

the instant case when the People seek to punish defendant, who was not even present on the immediate scene, for the death of an accomplice caused by the acts of another confederate who himself has been exonerated.

Although the third purpose of collateral estoppel, preventing harassment through vexatious litigation, does not appear to be fulfilled if the doctrine is applied when different defendants are tried but once in separate trials, the other general purposes of an application of the doctrine are as readily achievable in criminal as in civil trials and, as will be seen, the reasons for its greater limitation in criminal proceedings fail to justify the refusal to apply it in the instant circumstances.

In the past some courts have refused to dispense with identity of parties as a requirement for application of the doctrine of collateral estoppel, because of (1) difficulty of identifying the issues resolved against the People in the prior trial; (2) unfairness of binding the state when the defendant is not also bound by the first trial; or (3) undesirability of multiplying the results of a possibly erroneous verdict of acquittal.[12] None of these considerations, however, is applicable in the instant situation.

Where, as here, the accused's guilt is predicated only on vicarious liability, identity of issues is clear. Since defendant was outside the store in the getaway car at the

time of the shooting, defendant's murder conviction can be based only on his being held responsible for Daniels' or Smith's conduct which must be vicariously attributed to defendant. There is no indication that Daniels' acquittal is based on anything other than a final determination that his and Smith's acts were not sufficiently provocative to support a finding of implied malice.[13]

As to the second of the reasons for reluctance to retreat from the requirement of identity of parties, it does not appear that the defense of collateral estoppel in defendant's case would result in any unfairness to the prosecution. At Daniels' murder trial the People had both the incentive and opportunity to litigate fully the issue of the provocativeness of the conduct of Daniels and Smith as Daniels appeared to be the leader in the robbery which resulted in the shootout. Furthermore, defendant appears to have played a minor role in the events leading to the death of Smith and there is no evidence that defendant directed or instigated the holdup of the liquor store.[14]

There is little support for the People's contention that relaxing the identity-of-parties requirement is unfair as it gives defendant two chances for exoneration, either through the prior acquittal of the perpetrator or through his own acquittal if the perpetrator should be convicted. We have rejected similar arguments in civil

---

12. The high burden of proof required for a criminal conviction has influenced some courts to hesitate to relax the identity-of-parties requirement for collateral estoppel in criminal cases. Such courts assert that the prior judgment of acquittal merely means that the crime was not proved beyond a reasonable doubt, not that the alleged perpetrator and therefore the accused are innocent. Such reasoning is not convincing. As is the case in civil litigation where identity of parties is not a prerequisite to the invocation of collateral estoppel, the burden of proof in a subsequent criminal trial is the same as the burden of proof in the previous criminal trial upon which the plea of collateral estoppel is based. Moreover, the previous acquittal of the perpetrator

should create a reasonable doubt about his guilt thereby raising a reasonable doubt about the guilt of an alleged aider and abettor when his guilt is based solely on acts of the alleged perpetrator.

13. We note that Daniels did not offer a defense such as insanity, intoxication, or duress based on his personal lack of culpability irrespective of the criminality of his acts.

14. We do not reach the question of whether the doctrine of collateral estoppel should be applied to bar the prosecution of a person who directed, instigated or participated in a crime for which the perpetrators were acquitted.

cases where we held that there is little real inequity in permitting strangers to take advantage of prior judgments where the party adversely affected had every motive and opportunity to litigate the matter fully in the prior trial. We note further that Daniels' acquittal affects only the case against defendant and therefore this is not a situation in which collateral estoppel may affect many potential defendants.[15]

It is unlikely that the application of the doctrine of collateral estoppel to the case at bar will result in spreading the effects of a possibly erroneous acquittal, the third of the reasons urged for not relaxing the identity-of-parties requirement. Contrary to the contention of the People the inconsistency in the results of Daniels' trial and defendant's trial cannot be explained by differences in evidence[16] or jury instructions.[17] The description of Daniels' conduct given by the prosecution witnesses was substantially the same in both trials. Although Daniels disputed the People's version of the events in the store while defendant did not,[18] Daniels' conviction of robbery reveals that the jury did not believe his account of the occurrences in the liquor store. Although defendant was exposed in a fabrication in his testimony and was forced to admit that he lied during some of his pretrial statements, Daniels likewise was caught in a falsehood during his trial and was also compelled to reveal that he had lied to investigators. Similarly, there is no significant difference in the instructions on malice given in the two

trials. Both set out the standard that a finding of implied malice must be supported by a determination that the conduct in question involved a high risk of death and must be done with a conscious disregard for life.

We conclude that the lack of identity of parties defendant does not preclude the application of the doctrine of collateral estoppel; we limit today's holding to the particular circumstances of the instant case where an accused's guilt must be predicated on his vicarious liability for the acts of a previously acquitted confederate.

The judgment is reversed as to the conviction of murder and affirmed as to the conviction of robbery.

Compare *Standefer v. United States*, 447 U.S. 10, 100 S.Ct. 1999, 64 L.Ed.2d 689 (1980), where the Court declined to apply this doctrine of nonmutual collateral estoppel, used in federal *civil* cases, to criminal cases:

"This, however, is a criminal case, presenting considerations different from those in [civil cases]. First, in a criminal case, the Government is often without the kind of 'full and fair opportunity to litigate' that is a prerequisite of estoppel. Several aspects of our criminal law make this so: the prosecution's discovery rights in criminal cases are limited, both by rules of court and constitutional privileges; it is prohibited from being granted a directed verdict or from obtaining a judgment not-

----

15. We thus do not reach the question of whether the doctrine should be applied where the issue decided in the previous trial may affect many persons whose criminal liability is not based solely on the acts of the previously acquitted defendant.

16. This case therefore does not present the issue of whether and under what circumstances the prosecution's discovery of new evidence after the first trial will preclude a plea of collateral estoppel which otherwise may have been valid.

17. As the prosecution does not contend there were legal errors concerning matters other than

jury instructions committed at Daniels' trial, we do not reach the question of whether the bar of collateral estoppel is applicable when the People allege that the prior verdict of acquittal was based on erroneous rulings which they were unable to correct through appellate review.

18. Daniels claimed he was an innocent bystander, did not participate in the robbery, and did not make the remarks attributed to him by the prosecution witnesses. Defendant, relying on alibi, denied any knowledge of the transactions in the store, and therefore did not dispute the Wests' description of Daniels' conduct.

withstanding the verdict no matter how clear the evidence in support of guilt; it cannot secure a new trial on the ground that an acquittal was plainly contrary to the weight of the evidence; and it cannot secure appellate review where a defendant has been acquitted.

"The absence of these remedial procedures in criminal cases permits juries to acquit out of compassion or compromise or because of ' "their assumption of a power which they had no right to exercise, but to which they were disposed through lenity." ' It is of course true that verdicts induced by passion and prejudice are not unknown in civil suits. But in civil cases, post-trial motions and appellate review provide an aggrieved litigant a remedy; in a criminal case the Government has no similar avenue to correct errors. Under contemporary principles of collateral estoppel, this factor strongly militates against giving an acquittal preclusive effect.

"The application of nonmutual estoppel in criminal cases is also complicated by the existence of rules of evidence and exclusion unique to our criminal law. It is frequently true in criminal cases that evidence inadmissible against one defendant is admissible against another. The exclusionary rule, for example, may bar the Government from introducing evidence against one defendant because that evidence was obtained in violation of his constitutional rights. And the suppression of that evidence may result in an acquittal. The same evidence, however, may be admissible against other parties to the crime 'whose rights were [not] violated.' In such circumstances, where evidentiary rules prevent the Government from presenting all its proof in the first case, application of nonmutual estoppel would be plainly unwarranted."

UNITED STATES v. BRYAN

United States Court of Appeals, Third Circuit, 1973.
483 F.2d 88 (3d Cir.1973).

Present SEITZ, CHIEF JUDGE, and VAN DUSEN, ALDISERT, ADAMS, GIBBONS, ROSENN and HUNTER, CIRCUIT JUDGES.

OPINION OF THE COURT

ROSENN, CIRCUIT JUDGE.

[Bryan and Echols were jointly indicted and tried; Echols was charged with having stolen 950 cases of scotch from a pier, and Bryan was charged with having aided and abetted him. In a nonjury trial, the judge found Echols not guilty because the evidence created at least a reasonable doubt whether he was anything more than an innocent dupe; Echols was the truck driver who picked up the whiskey upon presentation of what he apparently did not know were false documents. But the judge concluded that the scotch had been stolen and that Bryan had aided and abetted that crime by supplying certain documents, and thus Bryan was convicted.]

Two permissible interpretations of the indictment and of the proof offered by the Government at trial would sustain the conviction: (1) that Bryan aided and abetted Echols in the commission of the offense; or (2) that Bryan was in fact the principal, but the discrepancy between indictment as an aider and abettor, and proof as a principal, was a non-prejudicial variance. On either interpretation, we find the conviction should be affirmed.

Appellant's argument suggests that Bryan could not have aided and abetted Echols because Echols was found innocent by the trial court and there is no aiding and abetting offense unless the Government first proves the principal committed the crime. *United States v. Jones*, 425 F.2d 1048, 1056–1057 (9th Cir.1970); *United States v. Rodgers*, 419 F.2d 1315 (10th Cir. 1969). To the extent that there is dictum in *Jones* indicating that the Government cannot convict an aider and abettor without proving that the principal had committed the crime, the later opinion of the Ninth Circuit in *United States v. Azadian*, 436 F.2d 81 (9th Cir.1971), suggests re-examination of that dictum. The court permitted conviction of an aider and abettor even though the principal had been acquitted because of entrapment. The dissenter suggested that the court had wholly disregarded the *Jones* case.

In *Rodgers*, a number of prison inmates were each charged and convicted of aiding and abetting each other in instigating a riot, in violation of 18 U.S.C. § 1792. Because the statute makes instigation of a riot illegal, but does not prohibit mere participation therein, and because no principal was shown to have instigated the riot, the court reversed the convictions for aiding and abetting. This holding is consistent with the general criminal law principles that one cannot be convicted of aiding and abetting unless the proof establishes that the substantive crime was committed by someone.

The facts in the present case, however, are significantly different from those in *Rodgers*. The commission of the substantive offense was established. The whiskey was stolen. Echols played a significant role in perpetrating the offense. Although he was found not guilty, because the trial judge had a reasonable doubt as to Echols' criminal intent, there is no doubt that he removed the goods with false documents. Although Echols may have been an innocent dupe, it was he who at least physically removed the whiskey.

Appellant would seem to argue that the aider and abettor is guilty only if the principal is also *convicted*. The criminal law has no such requirement.   *   *   *

We turn now to the remaining issue as to whether Bryan's conviction on Count II was so inconsistent with the terms of the indictment as to contravene the fifth amendment requirement of indictment by grand jury. We believe the proof adequately demonstrated that Bryan aided and abetted Echols in the commission of the crime, exactly as is charged in the indictment. Black's Law Dictionary (Revised 4th Ed. 1968), defines "abet," as "to encourage, incite or set another on to commit a crime." To term Bryan's actions as abetting Echols, therefore, is to describe them precisely. We therefore have difficulty with appellant's assertion that the proof at trial demonstrated that Bryan was the principal, and not the aider and abettor, in the crime charged. Nonetheless, even if the evidence at trial is so viewed and a discrepancy between indictment and proof therefore recognized, we still believe the conviction must stand.

We note first that the distinction between aiders and abettors and principals in cases such as this is to a great extent semantic. Is the driver of the truck the principal because of his physical contact with the stolen goods? Or, should he be viewed as the aider and abettor because the plan for taking the goods was conceived by another person? Conversely, is the man who engineered the theft the principal, or rather the aider and abettor? Such semantic difficulties were largely eliminated from the federal criminal code by passage of 18 U.S.C. § 2,[8] which makes aiders and abettors punishable as principals. At least for purposes of sentencing, therefore, the federal criminal code makes

---

8. 18 U.S.C. § 2 provides:

(a) Whoever commits an offense against the United States or aids, abets, counsels, commands, induces or procures its commission, is punishable as a principal.

(b) Whoever wilfully causes an act to be done which if directly performed by him or another would be an offense against the United States, is punishable as a principal.

no distinctions between aiders and abettors and principals.

We further note that courts have had no difficulty sustaining convictions when defendants have been charged as principals and proven to have been aiders and abettors, * * *. Nor have courts had difficulty sustaining convictions when the indictment did not specify whether the defendant was the aider and abettor or the principal.

18 U.S.C. § 2 has eliminated the archaic common law distinctions between principals and accessories before and after the fact, and makes them all principals, whether the offense is a felony or a misdemeanor, and subject to the same liability. Thus, in *United States v. Bell*, 457 F.2d 1231, 1235 (5th Cir.1972), the court sustained the proposition that one charged as an aider and abettor could be found guilty as a principal. It rejected the contention that the defendant could not be convicted as a principal under a count charging him solely as an aider and abettor, holding: "While the better practice would have been to frame the charge in the alternative, the contention is without merit. Under 18 U.S.C.A. § 2 (1969) an aider and abettor is a principal and can be punished as such." * * *

The general rule that the Government may not amend an indictment, either explicitly by motion, or implicitly by presenting proof of a crime different from that charged, has its roots in the fifth amendment requirement of indictment by grand jury and Supreme Court interpretation as early as *Ex parte Bain*, 121 U.S. 1, 7 S.Ct. 781, 30 L.Ed. 849 (1887). The doctrine that a discrepancy between proof and indictment may be deemed an amendment, reversible *per se*, however, has been recognized and adjudicated extensively only in recent years. The Supreme Court's discussion of indictment and proof discrepancies in *Stirone v. United States*, 361 U.S. 212, 80

S.Ct. 270, 4 L.Ed.2d 252 (1960), has since been interpreted to distinguish between amendments, reversible *per se*, and variances, reversible only if prejudicial to the defendant. Prior to *Stirone*, most courts adjudged discrepancies between indictment and proof only by the prejudice standards of *Berger v. United States*, 295 U.S. 78, 82, 55 S.Ct. 629, 630, 79 L.Ed. 1314 (1935):

> The general rule that allegations and proof must correspond is based upon the obvious requirements (1) that the accused shall be definitely informed as to the charges against him, so that he may be enabled to present his defense and not be taken by surprise by the evidence offered at the trial; and (2) that he may be protected against another prosecution for the same offense.

Were we to find the discrepancy between indictment of Bryan as an aider and abettor, and proof as the principal in the theft of the scotch whiskey from the U.S. Lines dock, to be a variance judged by *Berger* standards, it would seem clear there was no prejudicial error. Acquittal in the trial would have protected Bryan from trial again for the theft of the scotch whiskey. The indictment fully informed him of the crime for which he was to be tried. By explicitly stating that he would be tried for aiding and abetting a man named Echols in the taking of 950 cases of scotch whiskey from Pier 80 in Philadelphia on May 1, 1970, the indictment could not have been more specific in giving notice to Bryan. The proof conformed to the charge; Echols did take the 950 cases of whiskey from Pier 80 in Philadelphia on the date alleged by means of false documents supplied by Bryan. The trial revealed that Bryan not only aided Echols but was in fact the mastermind.

The question, therefore, is only whether the proof here varied from the indictment in such a manner that the indictment was constructively amended and, thus, the conviction was reversible *per se*, regardless of whether Bryan was actually prejudiced. * * * The focus of our inquiry is whether an element of the offense for which Bryan was convicted was different from an element of the offense for which it appears from the face of the indictment he was charged.

We find no difference between the elements of the crime charged and the crime proven. We are unable to see how the crime Bryan committed was any different whether he be labeled the aider and abettor of Echols or the principal who used Echols as his dupe. In either case, Bryan's actions, as presented first to the grand jury, and then to the judge at trial, would have been exactly the same; only the legal nomenclature would be changed. Under the federal statute, moreover, the common law nomenclature no longer has any significance.

We therefore hold (1) that a felonious taking was proven; (2) that this taking was a criminal act despite failure to prove Echols' criminal intent beyond a reasonable doubt; and (3) that Bryan was guilty as charged.

The judgment of the district court will be affirmed.

GIBBONS, CIRCUIT JUDGE, dissenting.

* * * If the grand jury had indicted Bryan as a principal, proof that he aided and abetted would suffice to convict. If, without naming a specific principal, an indictment charged him as an aider and abettor, proof that he aided and abetted anyone who may have committed the substantive offense would suffice to convict. But where the grand jury has charged that a specific person committed the substantive offense and that the defendant aided and abetted that specific person, a different problem is presented.

* * * The complicating factor is that clause of the Fifth Amendment requiring indictment by a grand jury for infamous crimes. The crime with which Bryan is charged falls within that clause, and if the grand jury charges one offense, the trial court may not try another. The grand jury did not indict Bryan as a principal. It did not indict him as an aider and abettor of persons unknown. It indicted him as an aider and abettor of a specific named principal. The Government in response to a motion for a bill of particulars reiterated that Echols was the thief who stole the whiskey with an intent to convert it to his own use and that Bryan aided and abetted Echols by supplying the means by which Echols converted the whiskey to Echols' own use. Bryan has been convicted, however, on evidence which does not establish beyond a reasonable doubt that the specific principal named in the indictment and in the bill of particulars committed the offense. The district court may not convict him of being an aider and abettor on the basis of evidence relevant only to a charge of being a principal; a charge for which he was not indicted.

Keeping in mind the language of both the indictment and the bill of particulars, and putting myself in the position of Bryan's trial attorney, the tactical decision not to offer Bryan's testimony seems eminently sound. Bryan did not have the burden of persuading the court that he hadn't committed a theft. The Government had the burden of proving beyond a reasonable doubt the one offense with which he was charged in the indictment. The Government attempted to prove not that persons unknown committed a theft, or that Bryan committed a theft, but that Echols committed a theft to which Bryan was an aider and abettor. The Government's proof on Echols' theft was insufficient to withstand a motion. Now, after the case is closed, and after Bryan has lost the opportunity to testify in his own behalf, the majority sustains the conviction on a theory that the grand jury did not consider, that the Government's case did not present, and of which neither before nor during the trial was Bryan given notice.   *   *   *

CHIEF JUDGE SEITZ and JUDGE ALDISERT concur in this dissent.

Notes and Questions

1. Although the prevailing view is to require acquittal of the alleged accomplice if the principal was acquitted in the same trial, *People v. Allsip*, 268 Cal.App.2d 830, 74 Cal.Rptr. 550 (1969), it is now generally accepted that an accomplice may be convicted notwithstanding the fact that the principal in the first degree has not yet been tried or has been acquitted in a separate trial. See, e.g., *Rozell v. State*, 502 S.W.2d 16 (Tex.Cr.App.1973); *State v. Young*, 211 N.W.2d 352 (Iowa 1973). Often this is as the result of a statutory provision along the lines of *Model Penal Code* § 2.06(7).

2. In *Azadian,* cited in *Bryan*, appellant was convicted of aiding and abetting the bribery of a public official. On appeal, he urged that his conviction could not stand because the principal in the case was found not guilty by reason of entrapment. The court of appeals affirmed, relying upon *Carbajal–Portillo v. United States*, 396 F.2d 944 (9th Cir.1968), where it was emphasized that the entrapment defense "is made available not because inducement negatives criminal intent and thus establishes the fact of innocence; but because Government agents should not be permitted to act in such a fashion. The defense does not so much establish innocence as grant immunity from prosecution for criminal acts concededly committed." Ely, J., dissenting, noted that in *Carbajal* the entrapped principal had solicited the aider's help on his own, while in *Azadian* government agents solicited both the principal and the aider from the beginning. He concluded: "I deplore the prospect that my Brother's opinion could encourage an

eager Government agent to engage in reprehensible conduct in order to lure others, as aiders and abettors, into a web of criminality, even while knowing that his principal entrapee would escape conviction."

See also *People v. Jones*, 184 Colo. 96, 518 P.2d 819 (1974); and *Babcock v. State*, 485 S.W.2d 85 (Mo.1972), both holding that an accomplice may be convicted notwithstanding the fact the principal has been found not guilty by reason of insanity.

3. Hayes proposed to Hill that he join in the burglary of a store. Hill, actually a relative of one of the owners, feigned agreement. On the night in question, they arrived at the store together; Hayes raised the window and boosted Hill in, after which Hill handed a side of bacon out to Hayes. Hayes was convicted of burglary and larceny upon an instruction that he was guilty of burglary if he, with felonious intent, assisted Hill to enter, even if Hill had no intent to steal. In *State v. Hayes*, 105 Mo. 76, 16 S.W. 514 (1891), the court reversed:

"We may assume, then, for the sake of the argument, that Hill committed no crime in entering the wareroom. The act of Hill, however, was by the instruction of the court imputed to defendant. This act, according to the theory of the instructions, so far as Hill was concerned, was not a criminal act, but when it was imputed to defendant it became criminal because of the latter's felonious intent. This would probably be true if Hill had acted under the control and compulsion of defendant, and as his passive and submissive agent. But he was not a passive agent in this transaction. He was an active one. He acted of his own volition. He did not raise the window and enter the building with intent to commit crime, but simply to entrap defendant in the commission of crime, and have him captured.   *   *   * [W]e find that defendant did not commit every overt act that went to make up the crime. He did not enter the warehouse, either actually or constructively, and hence he did not commit the crime of burglary, no matter what his intent was, it clearly appearing that Hill was guilty of no crime. To make defendant responsible for the acts of Hill, they must have had a common motive and common design. The design and the motives of the two men were not only distinct, but dissimilar, even antagonistic. * * * The court should instruct the jury that if Hill broke into and entered the wareroom with a felonious intent, and defendant was present, aiding him with the same intent, then he is guilty; but if Hill entered the room with no design to steal, but simply to entrap defendant, and capture him in the commission of crime, and defendant did not enter the room himself, then he is not guilty of burglary and larceny as charged. He may be found guilty, however, of petit larceny, in taking and removing the bacon after it was handed to him. This overt act he did in fact commit."

Is this a desirable result? Compare *Model Penal Code* § 5.01(3).

4. Of what, if anything, may the defendant be convicted on the facts of *Bailey v. Commonwealth*, 229 Va. 258, 329 S.E.2d 37 (1985): "Bailey and Murdock lived about two miles apart in the Roanoke area. On the evening in question, each was intoxicated. Bailey had consumed a 'twelve-pack' of beer and a 'fifth of liquor' since mid-afternoon; a test of Murdock's blood made during an autopsy showed alcoholic content of '.271% * * * by weight.' Murdock was also 'legally blind,' with vision of only 3/200 in the right eye and 2/200 in the left. Bailey knew that Murdock had 'a problem with vision' and that he was intoxicated on the night in question.

"Bailey also knew that Murdock owned a handgun and had boasted 'about how he would use it and shoot it and scare people off with it.' Bailey knew further that Murdock was easily agitated and that he became especially angry if anyone disparaged his war hero, General George S. Patton. During the conversation in question, Bailey implied that General Patton and Murdock himself were homosexuals.

"Also during the conversation, Bailey persistently demanded that Murdock arm himself with his handgun and wait on his front porch for Bailey to come and injure or kill him. Murdock responded by saying he would be waiting on his front porch, and he told Bailey to 'kiss [his] mother or [his] wife and children goodbye because [he would] never go back home.'

"Bailey then made two anonymous telephone calls to the Roanoke City Police Department. In the first, Bailey reported 'a man . . . out on the porch [at Murdock's address] waving a gun around.' A police car was dispatched to the address, but the officers reported they did not 'see anything.'

"Bailey called Murdock back on the radio and chided him for not 'going out on the porch.' More epithets and threats were exchanged. Bailey told Murdock he was 'going to come up there in a blue and white car'[1] and demanded that Murdock 'step out there on the . . . porch' with his gun 'in [his] hands' because he, Bailey, would 'be there in just a minute.'

"Bailey telephoned the police again. This time, Bailey identified Murdock by name and told the dispatcher that Murdock had 'a gun on the porch,' had 'threatened to shoot up the neighborhood,' and was 'talking about shooting anything that moves.' Bailey insisted that the police 'come out here and straighten this man

---

1. Bailey owned a blue and white vehicle; the police vehicles were also blue and white.

out.' Bailey refused to identify himself, explaining that he was 'right next to [Murdock] out here' and feared revealing his identity.

"Three uniformed police officers, Chambers, Beavers, and Turner, were dispatched to Murdock's home. None of the officers knew that Murdock was intoxicated or that he was in an agitated state of mind. Only Officer Beavers knew that Murdock's eyesight was bad, and he did not know 'exactly how bad it was.' Beavers also knew that Murdock would get 'a little 10–96 (mental subject) occasionally' and would 'curse and carry on' when he was drinking.

"When the officers arrived on the scene, they found that Murdock's 'porch light was on' but observed no one on the porch. After several minutes had elapsed, the officers observed Murdock come out of his house with 'something shiny in his hand.' Murdock sat down on the top step of the porch and placed the shiny object beside him.

"Officer Chambers approached Murdock from the side of the porch and told him to '[l]eave the gun alone and walk down the stairs away from it.' Murdock 'just sat there.' When Chambers repeated his command, Murdock cursed him. Murdock then reached for the gun, stood up, advanced in Chambers' direction, and opened fire. Chambers retreated and was not struck.

"All three officers returned fire, and Murdock was struck. Lying wounded on the porch, he said several times, 'I didn't know you was the police.' He died from 'a gunshot wound of the left side of the

chest.' In the investigation which followed, Bailey stated that he was 'the hoss that caused the loss.' "

5. Reconsider the facts of *Director of Public Prosecutions v. Morgan*, p. 165 of this Book. Assuming that Parker, McDonald and McLarty had been found not guilty of rape because of their belief in Mrs. Morgan's consent, then of what—if anything— would Morgan be guilty? [a]

Consider also whether the defendant may be convicted of rape on these facts from *Dusenbery v. Commonwealth*, 220 Va. 770, 263 S.E.2d 392 (1980): "At approximately 10:30 p.m. on September 16, 1978, T* * *M* * * and J* * * G* * *, both 16 years of age, parked their car in a secluded area and partially undressed in preparation for sexual intercourse. Defendant, a part-time security guard wearing a uniform, badge, handcuffs, and a holstered pistol, appeared at the window with a flashlight, ordered the couple to get out, and demanded identification. Defendant told them that he would take them to the authorities or report their conduct to their parents unless they finished what they had started and allowed him to watch. The couple entered the back seat of the car, discussed the options, and agreed to attempt to perform the act in defendant's presence. Defendant watched as the couple undressed and the boy assumed the superior position. Complaining that the boy had not penetrated the girl, defendant thrust his head and shoulders through the open window, seized the boy's penis, and forced it 'partially in' the girl's vagina."

---

a. Consider Comment, 1975 Crim.L.Rev. 584, 585, contending that in such a case Morgan is guilty of rape "but that the correct theoretical basis of [his] liability was that of an aider and abettor rather than that of a principal in the first degree."

SECTION 7. WITHDRAWAL

STATE v. THOMAS

Superior Court of New Jersey, Appellate Division, 1976.
140 N.J.Super. 429, 356 A.2d 433.

MORGAN, J.A.D.

Convicted by jury verdict of murder in the first degree, defendant appeals * * *.

During the early evening hours of September 12, 1973 one Frank Jennette shot and killed Officer Casper Buonocore from the rooftop of 49 Armstrong Avenue in Jersey City. It was at all times undisputed that Buonocore was in uniform and in the performance of his duties when he was killed. The events which terminated in this tragic occurrence commenced innocently with the ticketing of a double-parked car in the area of the crime. The driver of the vehicle, one Sam Williams, was arrested when a radio check revealed an outstanding motor vehicle warrant for him. Williams' daughter, 13 years of age, intervened in an apparent attempt to prevent her father's arrest and struck one of the arresting officers. When the patrol car arrived to transport Williams to the police station, the daughter was also placed under arrest for assault. When she renewed her attack she was struck by another officer and rendered unconscious. Officer Buonocore, who had neither arrested the father nor struck the daughter, summoned an ambulance and rendered first aid to the girl. Eventually, the father was transported to the police station and the daughter removed in the ambulance. Buonocore and his partner were then instructed to resume their normal patrol duties and were departing the scene on their motorcycles when Buonocore was felled by the fatal shot.

Defendant and two other young men, Frank Jennette and David Cheatham, were arrested in the neighboring building and taken to the Fifth Precinct. The State conceded that Jennette had fired the fatal shot; later he pleaded guilty to the charge. Cheatham and defendant were charged as aiders and abettors. Defendant's conviction rested largely on some inculpatory matter in his own statement. In it he admitted both seeing Jennette with the gun earlier in the evening while with him in a neighborhood bar and, after the incident in which the young girl was rendered unconscious, responding to Jennette's invitation to go up on the roof "to shoot the police." When asked why he went up on the roof with Jennette defendant responded that he did not know. Notwithstanding, defendant asserted in the statement that he was not on the roof with Jennette and Cheatham at the time the shot was fired. At trial defendant denied the truth of the inculpatory portions of his statement, contending that he did not see Jennette's gun until they were on the roof, was unaware of Jennette's intention to shoot a police officer, and that as soon as he became aware of that intention he fled the roof.

The State adduced no direct evidence that defendant was on the roof at the time the fatal shot was fired. It argues that his presence there as an aider and abettor of the murder was reasonably inferable from the fact of his friendship with Jennette, knowledge of Jennette's intentions to "shoot the police" and the latter's possession of a gun with which to achieve this purpose, together with his admission that with such knowledge he accompanied Jennette to the roof. Accordingly, the State properly contends, the jury was entitled to disbelieve that portion of defendant's statement and testimony that he left the roof

before the actual shooting occurred.
* * *

We turn now to defendant's contention that the trial judge erred in rejecting a request to charge which concerned the implications from defendant's testimony that he was not present on the roof at the time the fatal shot was fired, having left immediately before that event. Both in his pretrial statement and in his testimony defendant averred that he had left the roof before the murder occurred. Evidence apart from defendant's own statements does provide some independent support of that fact. Defendant submitted the two following requests to charge, both of which were rejected by the judge:

> 1. That if you find that the Defendant went up to the roof of 49 Armstrong Avenue with the intention of killing or harming anyone, but that on the roof he quit that intention or idea and abandoned that purpose before an attempt was made to fire the weapon, then you must acquit the Defendant.

> 2. * * *

Implicit in the first request to charge is the proposition that if a defendant, who participates as an aider and abettor, absents himself from the immediate vicinity of the crime before it occurs, he cannot be found guilty. The requested charge does not accurately state the law, particularly in the present context, and the trial judge properly refused to so charge. Generally, presence at the scene of a crime is not an essential element to the crime of aiding and abetting. Clearly, one who would previously have been characterized as an accessory before the fact, one who planned the criminal event, or supplied necessary equipment or otherwise procured its commission, need not be present in order to be held as an aider and abettor. Similarly one who positions himself at a distance from the scene in order to stand watch against intervention or to avoid apprehen-

sion does not escape being stigmatized as an aider and abettor.

Even one who cannot be viewed as an accessory before the fact but rather as one who assented to the crime, "lent to it his countenance and approval," thereby aiding and abetting the crime may not escape liability by simply fleeing the scene shortly before the crime occurs. In *People v. Rybka,* 16 Ill.2d 394, 158 N.E.2d 17 (Sup. Ct.1959), defendant was convicted of murder by the court sitting without a jury despite the fact that he was not present when the fatal blow was struck. In *Rybka* two carloads of persons, bent on attacking the victim, started out together on that quest. The car in which defendant was seated became separated from the car in which the actual perpetrator was seated. Defendant was nowhere near the scene of the murder which subsequently took place. Defendant was nonetheless found guilty of the murder. The court stated:

> It is alternatively contended on behalf of Budz and Gorski that, even though it be concluded that they encouraged Schwartz (the actual perpetrator) in the perpetration of a crime, the evidence indicates that they withdrew from any concert or common venture with those in the Oldsmobile when the Chrysler turned off at California Avenue and that the fact of their withdrawal was communicated to Schwartz. Our attention is called to the general rule that "one who withdraws from a criminal enterprise is not responsible for the act of another subsequently committed in furtherance of the enterprise, provided the fact of withdrawal is communicated to the other conspirators." * * * However, it is the communication of intent to withdraw and not the naked fact of withdrawal that determines whether one who advised, encouraged or incited another to commit a crime is to be released from liability as an accessory before the fact.

In *People v. Lacey,* 49 Ill.App.2d 301, 200 N.E.2d 11 (App.Ct.1964), defendant was convicted of rape. The evidence disclosed that defendant had cooperated with others in the robbery of the ultimate rape victim. Following the robbery there appeared to have been a spontaneous decision to commit rape and the victim was taken to a basement. Defendant, however, after receiving his share of the fruits of the robbery left the scene of the rape without himself sexually assaulting the victim. He never touched the victim. He was, nevertheless, convicted of the rape, the court saying:

> Defendant contends his actions in leaving the basement constituted an effective withdrawal from the common design. A person who encourages the commission of an unlawful act cannot escape responsibility by quietly withdrawing from the scene. Here Lacey told Jones he was leaving and just walked out. He then proceeded to a restaurant, where in the course of conversation he told two other boys what was happening back in the basement. Far from withdrawing from the rape his conduct indirectly sent two more rapists to the scene.
>
> To be timely a withdrawal must be such as to give his co-conspirators a reasonable opportunity, if they desire, to follow his example and refrain from further action before the act is committed, and it must be possible for the trier of fact to say that the accused had wholly and effectively detached himself from the criminal enterprise before the act with which he is charged is in the process of consummation or has become so inevitable that it cannot reasonably be stayed. In order to constitute an effective withdrawal some kind of disapproval or opposition must be shown to the activities which the defendant knew had either preceded or were about to proceed. No such disapproval appears here at all.

Defendant's own testimony at trial, taken at face value, indicates that he simply left the roof when he saw Jennette take out his gun. Nothing in his testimony suggests that he communicated to Jennette that he was leaving or that he disapproved of the contemplated act, or that he otherwise sought to actively withdraw the support to the proposed event which his presence on the roof supplied. According to defendant, he merely left the scene within minutes before the shooting occurred. As a matter of law, such a spontaneous, unannounced withdrawal, without more, only briefly before the commission of the offense which had been previously encouraged by defendant's presence or other support, is insufficient to insulate the defendant from criminal liability as an aider and abettor. In order to warrant an instruction to a jury concerning the effect of withdrawal from a criminal enterprise, evidence must disclose some effort on the part of the defendant to communicate the fact of his withdrawal and some attempt to neutralize the effects of his previous support. With such evidence the effect of a withdrawal is for the jury; without such evidence no issue for jury consideration is presented and any such instruction would be inappropriate. * * *

Notes and Questions

1. In *Commonwealth v. Huber,* 15 D. & C.2d 726 (1958), the defendant was convicted of being an accessory before the fact to a robbery. On appeal, he claimed he was not proved guilty beyond a reasonable doubt. The evidence was that defendant loaned his rifle to Goodwin, who explained, "I am going to rob somebody," and that when Goodwin asked defendant to go along the defendant answered, "No, I ain't going to get involved in anything like that." In affirming, the court reasoned:

"The fact that this defendant was asked to participate in the robbery as a principal, and that he refused, does not constitute such a withdrawal as would relieve him of criminal liability as an accessory before the fact. Had this defendant demanded and received back his rifle, or had he reported the principals to the police in time to thwart the robbery, then he could be said to have withdrawn successfully. Having placed the rifle in the hands of John Goodwin who, according to defendant's own testimony, told defendant 'he was going to rob somebody', defendant committed himself to a sequence of events from which he could only extricate himself by getting his rifle out of the hands of John Goodwin before the robbery, or by thwarting the robbery in some other way."

2. In contrast to *Model Penal Code* § 2.06(6)(c), some recent recodifications impose an additional requirement, namely, that the withdrawal occur "under circumstances manifesting a voluntary and complete renunciation of his criminal purpose," e.g., N.Y.Penal Law § 35.45. Is this desirable?

SECTION 8. EXCEPTIONS TO ACCOMPLICE LIABILITY

QUEEN v. TYRRELL

Queen's Bench Division, High Court of Justice, England, 1893.
[1894] 1 Q.B. 710.

The defendant, Jane Tyrrell, was on September 15, 1893, tried and convicted at the Central Criminal Court on an indictment charging her, in the first count, with having unlawfully aided and abetted, counselled, and procured the commission by one Thomas Ford of the misdemeanor of having unlawful carnal knowledge of her whilst she was between the ages of thirteen and sixteen, against the form of the statute, &c.; and, in the second count, with having falsely, wickedly, and unlaw-

fully solicited and incited Thomas Ford to commit the same offence.

It was proved at the trial that the defendant did aid, abet, solicit, and incite Thomas Ford to commit the misdemeanor made punishable by s. 5 of the Criminal Law Amendment Act, 1885 (48 & 49 Vict. c. 69).

The question for the opinion of the Court was, "Whether it is an offence for a girl between the ages of thirteen and sixteen to aid and abet a male person in the commission of the misdemeanor of having unlawful carnal connection with her, or to solicit and incite a male person to commit that misdemeanor." * * *

LORD COLERIDGE, C.J. The Criminal Law Amendment Act, 1885, was passed for the purpose of protecting women and girls against themselves. At the time it was passed there was a discussion as to what point should be fixed as the age of consent. That discussion ended in a compromise, and the age of consent was fixed at sixteen. With the object of protecting women and girls against themselves the Act of Parliament has made illicit connection with a girl under that age unlawful; if a man wishes to have such illicit connection he must wait until the girl is sixteen, otherwise he breaks the law; but it is impossible to say that the Act, which is absolutely silent about aiding or abetting, or soliciting or inciting, can have intended that the girls for whose protection it was passed should be punishable under it for the offences committed upon themselves. I am of opinion that this conviction ought to be quashed.

MATHEW, J. I am of the same opinion. I do not see how it would be possible to obtain convictions under the statute if the contention for the Crown were adopted, because nearly every section which deals with offences in respect of women and girls would create an offence in the woman or girl. Such a result cannot have been intended by the legislature. There is no trace in the statute of any intention to treat the woman or girl as criminal.

Notes and Questions

1. Consider also *State v. Bearcub,* 1 Or. App. 579, 465 P.2d 252 (1970):

"The defendants, before their marriage, were jointly indicted under ORS 418.140, for unlawfully sharing public assistance.

"They demurred separately to the indictment on grounds that no crime was stated and that every statute can embrace only one subject and this statute is 'buried in a chapter relating to child welfare services.' Each demurrer was sustained.

"ORS 418.140 provides:

'(1) No male person over the age of 18 years * * * shall habitually accept subsistence or lodging in the dwelling place of any female householder, who is the recipient of aid * * *.'

Sandra contends that only a male can be prosecuted under this statute; hence, no crime can be stated under it as to her. The state contends that a female can be guilty of the crime by aiding and abetting the male who violates the statute. ORS 161.220 makes principals of all persons concerned in the commission of a crime.

"In *State v. Fraser,* 105 Or. 589, 209 P. 467 (1922), a corporation and its president were alleged to have violated the Blue Sky Law. The court said that a person who cannot alone commit a particular crime, can, by aiding and abetting another against whose class the statute is directed, become criminally liable under the statute. This case * * * might be authority for the state's contention but for the fact that ORS 418.140 indicates the statute is directed only at the male. Subsection (2) makes it a defense if 'the per-

son accused has fully paid to the female householder' the costs of subsistence, etc. By this language of the statute, the legislature obviously intended that only the male would be accused. It would be absurd if the female householder, in this case, Sandra, who was receiving welfare aid, could be accused under the statute, but have a good defense by paying her welfare money from one of her pockets into another. The first demurrer was correctly sustained." [a]

2. Many cases are to be found following the rule of the *Fraser* case discussed in *Bearcub.* See e.g., *Rozell v. State,* 502 S.W.2d 16 (Tex.Cr.App.1973) (holding "that a husband cannot be guilty of rape of his wife where he by himself forcibly has an act of intercourse with her, but if he acts as a co-principal with another man who ravishes his wife, he may be convicted of the rape as a principal"); *State v. Tronca,* 84 Wis.2d 68, 267 N.W.2d 216 (1978) (rejecting defendant's argument "that he could not be convicted as a party to a crime on the charge of misconduct in office, because he is not a public officer").

3. Why, then, the result in *Bearcub?* Consider *Model Penal Code* § 2.06, Comment (1985):

"Exclusion of the victim does not wholly meet the problems that arise. Should a woman be deemed an accomplice when a criminal abortion is performed upon her? Should the man who has intercourse with a prostitute be viewed as an accomplice in the act of prostitution, the purchaser an accomplice in the unlawful sale, the unmarried party to a bigamous marriage an accomplice of the bigamist, the bribe-giver an accomplice of the taker?

"These are typical situations where conflicting policies and strategies, or both, are involved in determining whether the nor

---

a. See also *Gebardi v. United States,* p. ___ of this Book, holding that on the facts there presented the woman would not be an accomplice to the Mann Act violation, and thus could not be deemed a member of a conspiracy to commit such a violation.

mal principles of accessorial accountability ought to apply. One factor that has weighed with some state courts is that affirming liability makes applicable the requirement that testimony be corroborated; the consequence may be to diminish rather than enhance the law's effectiveness by making any convictions unduly difficult. More than this, however, is involved. In situations like prostitution, prohibition, even late abortion, there is an ambivalence in public attitudes that makes enforcement very difficult at best; if liability is pressed to its logical extent, public support may be wholly lost. Yet to trust only to the discretion of prosecutors makes for anarchical diversity and enlists sympathy for those against whom prosecution may be launched.

"To seek a systematic legislative resolution of these issues seems a hopeless effort; the problem must be faced and weighed as it arises in each situation. What is common to these cases, however, is that the question is before the legislature when it defines the individual offense involved. No one can draft a prohibition of adultery without awareness that two parties to the conduct necessarily will be involved. The provision, therefore, is that the general section on complicity is inapplicable, leaving to the definition of the crime itself the selective judgment that must be made. If legislators know that buyers will not be viewed as accomplices in sales unless the statute indicates that this behavior is included in the prohibition, they will focus on the problem as they frame the definition of the crime. And since the exception is confined to behavior 'inevitably incident to' the commission of the crime, the problem inescapably presents itself in defining the crime.

"This method of treatment might be unacceptable in legislating on accomplices for an established system, where the legislature may or may not have dealt with the issue in particular definitions and will not

have been consistent in its practice. But in a model code or general revision, former legislative practice appears immaterial; the problem may be faced as each branch of the work proceeds."

SECTION 9. VICARIOUS LIABILITY

STATE v. BEAUDRY

Supreme Court of Wisconsin, 1985.
123 Wis.2d 40, 365 N.W.2d 593.

ABRAHAMSON, JUSTICE.   *   *   *

The facts are undisputed. The defendant, Janet Beaudry, and her husband, Wallace Beaudry, are the sole shareholders of Sohn Manufacturing Company, a corporation which has a license to sell alcoholic beverages at the Village Green Tavern in the village of Elkhart Lake, Sheboygan county. Janet Beaudry is the designated agent for the corporate licensee pursuant to sec. 125.04(6)(a), Stats. 1981–82.

Janet Beaudry's conviction grew out of events occurring during the early morning hours of February 9, 1983. At approximately 3:45 a.m., a deputy sheriff for the Sheboygan County Sheriff's Department drove past the Village Green Tavern. He stopped to investigate after noticing more lights than usual inside the building and also seeing two individuals seated inside. As he approached the tavern, he heard music, saw an individual standing behind the bar, and saw glasses on the bar. Upon finding the tavern door locked, the deputy sheriff knocked and was admitted by Mark Witkowski, the tavern manager. The tavern manager and two men were the only persons inside the bar. All three were drinking. The deputy sheriff reported the incident to the Sheboygan county district attorney's office for a formal complaint.

At about noon on February 9, the tavern manager reported to Wallace Beaudry about the deputy's stop earlier that morning. After further investigation Wallace

Beaudry discharged the tavern manager on February 11.

On March 2, 1983, the Sheboygan County Sheriff's Department served the defendant with a summons and a complaint charging her with the crime of keeping the tavern open after hours contrary to sec. 125.68(4)(c), Stats., and sec. 125.11(1), Stats. The tavern manager was not arrested or charged with an offense arising out of this incident.

The case was tried before a jury on May 20, 1983. At trial Janet Beaudry testified that she was not present at the tavern the morning of February 9. Wallace Beaudry testified that Janet Beaudry had delegated to him, as president of Sohn Manufacturing, the responsibilities of business administration associated with the Village Green Tavern; that he had hired Mark Witkowski as manager; that he had informed Witkowski that it was his duty to abide by the liquor laws; and that he never authorized Witkowski to remain open after 1:00 a.m., to throw a private party for his friends, or to give away liquor to friends.

Witkowski testified that he had served drinks after hours to two men. During cross-examination Witkowski confirmed that Wallace Beaudry had never authorized him to stay open after hours; that he had been instructed to close the tavern promptly at the legal closing time; that he knew it was illegal to serve liquor after 1:00 a.m. to anyone, including friends; that his two friends drank at the bar before 1:00 a.m. and had paid for those drinks; that he was having a good time with his friends before closing hours and wanted to continue partying and conversing with them after 1 a.m.; that after closing hours he was simply using the tavern to have a private party for two friends; that he did not charge his friends for any of the liquor they drank after 1:00 a.m.; and that by staying open he was trying to benefit not Wallace Beaudry but himself.

At the close of evidence, the jury was instructed that the law required the premises to be closed for all purposes between 1:00 a.m. and 8:00 a.m. and that if the jury found that there were patrons or customers on the premises after 1:00 a.m., it must find the premises open contrary to statute.

The jury was also instructed regarding Janet Beaudry's liability for the conduct of the tavern manager: As designated agent of the corporation, the defendant had full authority over the business and would be liable for the tavern manager's violation of the closing hour statute if he was acting within the scope of his employment. The instructions, which are pattern instructions Wis.J.I.Cr. 440 (1966), describe what activities are within the scope of employment and what are outside the scope of employment. Specifically, the jury was instructed as follows regarding the defendant's liability for the conduct of the tavern manager:

"It is also the law of the State of Wisconsin that violations of statutes regulating the sale of liquor do not require a showing of a willful or intentional act.

"It is a law that when a corporation is a licensee, the corporation vests in its agent, in this case Janet Beaudry, full control and authority over the premises and of the conduct of all business on the premises relative to alcohol beverages that the licensee could have exercised if it were a natural person.

"Under Wisconsin law if a person employs another to act for him [*sic*] in the conduct of his [*sic*] business, and such servant or agent violates the law, as in this case relating to open after hours, then the employer is guilty of that violation as if he [*sic*] had been present or had done the act himself [*sic*], if such act was within the scope of the employment of the servant or agent. It is no defense to prosecution under the statute that the employer was not upon the premises, did not know of the acts of his [*sic*] servant or agent, had not consented thereto, or even had expressly forbidden such act.

"A servant or agent is within the scope of his employment when he is performing work or rendering services he was hired to perform and render within the time and space limits of his authority and is actuated by a purpose in serving his employer in doing what he is doing. He is within the scope of his employment when he is performing work or rendering services in obedience to the express orders or directions of his master of doing that which is warranted within the terms of his express or implied authority, considering the nature of the services required, the instructions which he has received, and the circumstances under which his work is being done or the services are being rendered.

"A servant or agent is outside the scope of his employment when he deviates or steps aside from the prosecution of his master's business for the purpose of doing an act or rendering a service intended to accomplish an independent purpose of his own, or for some other reason or purpose not related to the business of his employer.

"Such deviation or stepping aside from his employer's business may be momentary and slight, measured in terms of time and space, but if it involves a change of mental attitude in serving his personal interests, or the interests of another instead of his employer's, then his conduct falls outside the scope of his employment.

"If you are satisfied beyond a reasonable doubt from the evidence in this case that Mark Witkowski, the employee of the registered agent, committed the acts charged in the complaint, that Mark Witkowski was the servant or agent of the defendant, and that the acts charged

in the complaint were committed by him in the scope of his employment, then you should find the defendant guilty.

"If, however, you are not so satisfied, then you must find the defendant not guilty."

Having been so instructed, the jury returned a verdict of guilty.

In light of the facts and these instructions, we consider first the question of whether the statutes impose vicarious criminal liability on a designated agent for the illegal conduct of the tavern manager in this case, *i.e.,* remaining open after 1:00 a.m.

The state's prosecution of the defendant under the criminal laws rests on a theory of vicarious liability, that is respondeat superior. Under this theory of liability, the master (here the designated agent) is liable for the illegal conduct of the servant (here the tavern manager). The defendant asserts, contrary to the position of the state, that the statutes do not impose vicarious criminal liability on her as designated agent of the corporation for the tavern manager's illegal conduct.

While the focus in this case is on the defendant's vicarious criminal liability, it is helpful to an understanding of vicarious liability to compare it with the doctrine of strict liability. Strict liability allows for criminal liability absent the element of *mens rea* found in the definition of most crimes. Thus under strict liability the accused has engaged in the act or omission; the requirement of mental fault, *mens rea,* is eliminated.

This court has construed violations of several statutes regulating the sale of alcoholic beverages which command that an act be done or omitted and which do not include words signifying scienter as imposing strict liability on the actor. As early as 1869, this court explained that the legislature imposed strict liability for the sale of spiritous liquors to a minor because protection of the public interest warrants the imposition of liability unhindered by examination of the subjective intent of each accused.[6] * * *

Vicarious liability, in contrast to strict liability, dispenses with the requirement of the *actus reus* and imputes the criminal act of one person to another.

Whether the defendant in this case is vicariously liable for the tavern manager's violation of sec. 125.68(4)(c), Stats.1981–82, depends on whether the specific statutes in question impose vicarious liability. We look first at the language of the statutes themselves.

The principal statutory provisions are secs. 125.68(4)(c)1., 125.11(1)(a), and 125.02(14). Sec. 125.68(4)(c), Stats. 1981–82, provides that "no premises for which a 'Class B' license or permit has been issued may remain open between the hours of 1 a.m. and 8 a.m. * * *" Sec. 125.11(1)(a), provides that "[a]ny person who violates any provision of this chapter for which a specific penalty is not provided, shall be fined not more than $500 or imprisoned for not more than 90 days or both." Sec. 125.02(14), states that " '[p]erson' means a natural person, sole proprietorship, partnership, corporation or association."

It is apparent that no statute expressly imposes criminal liability upon the designated agent for the illegal conduct of the tavern manager. None of the statutes states, for example, that "whoever by herself or by an employee of the corporation for which she is the designated agent keeps the premises open shall be punished by * * *" or "whoever keeps the premises open is punishable by * * *

and any act by a corporate employee shall be deemed the act of the designated agent as well as the act of the employee."

The state contends that the defendant's liability as designated agent for the illegal conduct of the tavern manager is predicated on sec. 125.04(6)(a), which requires a corporate licensee selling alcoholic beverages to designate an agent to whom the corporation delegates full authority and control of the premises and of the conduct of the business. Sec. 125.04(6)(a) equates the power and authority of the corporation's designated agent with that of a natural person who is a licensee or permittee. * * *

The state has not cited a statute expressly making the natural person licensee vicariously criminally liable for the conduct of an employee who illegally sells alcoholic beverages, and we have found none. Nevertheless, as the state correctly points out, over a long period the court has interpreted several statutes regulating the sale of alcoholic beverages as imposing on the natural person licensee vicarious criminal liability for the illegal conduct of an employee. * * *

[S]ince [those] decisions the legislature has had the opportunity to adopt or to preclude vicarious liability for violations of laws regarding sale of alcoholic beverages. The legislature took neither course of action. Instead the legislature left the statutes in question substantially the same. We read this legislative history to mean that in enacting the current laws the legislature intended to retain the * * * decisional law interpreting the statutes as imposing vicarious liability on the natural person licensee for the conduct of the

---

6. Whether or not remaining open after hours is a strict liability offense is not squarely before the court. The jury was instructed that "violations of statutes regulating the sale of liquor do not require a showing of a willful or intentional act." The parties do not dispute the illegality of the bar manager's conduct in this case. We

discuss the strict liability nature of the several alcoholic beverage sale statutes in order to distinguish strict liability from vicarious liability and to delineate the nature of the offense for which the defendant is determined to be vicariously liable.

employee who illegally sells alcoholic beverages.

In addition to the legislative history, another consideration persuades us that the legislature intended the statutes in question to impose vicarious criminal liability on the natural person licensee for an employee's violation of the closing hour law. The purpose of the statute is promoted if the doctrine of vicarious liability is applied.

Several factors influence this court to conclude that the purpose of the statute is promoted by the imposition of vicarious liability. First, the state has imposed numerous restrictions on the sale of alcoholic beverages to protect the public health and safety. The state has been particularly concerned with when and to whom alcoholic beverages may be sold. Statutes regulating the sale of alcoholic beverages have been recognized as creating strict liability "public welfare offenses." Second, violation of the closing hours law is a misdemeanor; the penalty is a monetary fine and a relatively short period of imprisonment. Third, in many cases it may be difficult for the state to prove that the natural person licensee or corporate agent was negligent in hiring or supervising the employee, or knew about or authorized the employee's violation of the statute. Lastly, the number of prosecutions may be large so that the legislature would want to relieve the prosecution of the task of proving that the employer knew of or authorized the violation or was negligent.

* * *

After reviewing the language of the current statutes, the legislative history of the current statutes, the cases interpreting the statutes, and the purpose of the statutes regulating the sale of alcoholic beverages, we conclude that the line of cases interpreting alcoholic beverage statutes as imposing vicarious criminal liability on the natural person licensee for an employee's

violation of an alcoholic beverage sale law have continuing validity under the statutes in question in this case.

Inasmuch as the natural person licensee is subject to vicarious criminal liability for the conduct of her or his employee who illegally sells alcoholic beverages, it logically follows that a corporation licensee should be similarly liable for the illegal conduct of its employee. But in this case the defendant is not the corporation licensee; the defendant is the designated agent of the corporation. The question for the present case, therefore, is whether a designated corporate agent is subject to vicarious criminal liability for the illegal conduct, *i.e.,* remaining open after closing hours, of the tavern manager who is an employee of the corporation.

We agree with the court of appeals that the legislature intended to impose such liability on the designated agent. The court of appeals correctly noted that unless vicarious criminal liability was imposed on the designated agent, a natural person licensee could avoid criminal liability by simply incorporating the business. The legislative intent in vesting the designated agent with full authority and responsibility for conduct of the business was to treat the designated agent as a natural person licensee for all purposes, including criminal liability. The legislature could not have intended to allow a natural person licensee to avoid criminal liability by incorporating the business.

While legislative purpose and public policy support our holding that a designated agent is vicariously liable for the conduct of the corporate employee who violates the closing hours law, the defendant's final argument is that due process requires blameworthy conduct on the part of the defendant as a prerequisite to criminal liability. Although the imposition of criminal liability for faultless conduct does not comport with the generally accepted premise of Anglo-American criminal justice that criminal liability is based on personal fault, this court and the United States Supreme Court have upheld statutes imposing criminal liability for some types of offenses without proof that the conduct was knowing or wilful or negligent.

The defendant's chief challenge to the constitutionality of the statute in issue in this case appears to be that the defendant could have received a jail sentence of up to 90 days for the violation. As the state points out, the defendant was fined $200, and the due process issue the defendant raises, whatever its validity, is not presented by the facts in this case. A decision by this court on the constitutionality of a jail term where the statute imposes vicarious liability would not affect the judgment of conviction in this case or the sentence imposed on this defendant. We therefore do not consider this issue.

We turn now to the question of whether the evidence supports the verdict that the tavern manager was acting within the scope of his employment. * * *

The "scope of employment" standard as applied to alcoholic beverage regulation in this state can be traced to *Doscher v. State,* 194 Wis. 67, 214 N.W. 359 (1927). In *Doscher,* the defendant was licensed to conduct a business selling non-intoxicating beverages. Contrary to instructions, an employee brought intoxicating liquor on the premises. The defendant, a natural person licensee, was convicted of unlawfully having intoxicating liquor on his premises. The state urged the court to uphold the conviction on the ground that the conscious possession of contraband liquor by the defendant's employee who was in charge of the licensed premises must be held to be the conscious possession of the defendant. The court reversed the conviction. * * *

"In the [other] cases . . . the agent was employed to have possession of and dispose of liquor for the defendant. The very employment, therefore, contemplated and covered the field of possession, disposal, and sale of the articles, so that the respective violations by the agents of the specific regulations as to the manner of carrying on such employment could properly be charged against the defendant employers who knowingly furnished the agents with the means and opportunity of violating the law. Here the defendant as employer did not confer upon the one left in charge of the premises any power, authority, or means for any such violation. The act of the employee in going outside of the premises and obtaining the forbidden alcohol was a stepping outside of any express or implied authority given him by defendant. For such an act, entirely independent of and beyond the purpose of the employment, the defendant ought not to stand charged merely because of an existing relationship of master and servant for an entirely different and lawful purpose."

The application of the standard of scope of employment limits liability to illegal conduct which occurred while the offending employee was engaged in some job-related activity and thus limits the accused's vicarious liability to conduct with which the accused has a factual connection and with which the accused has some responsible relation to the public danger envisaged by the legislature. * * *

We agree with the conclusion reached by the court of appeals. The credibility of the bar manager's testimony was a matter for the jury. The bar manager's testimony which supports the defendant's position that the manager was acting outside the scope of employment was based on a statement the bar manager gave defendant's counsel the night before trial. The jury may not have believed this testimony which was favorable to the defendant. Considering that the conduct occurred on the employer's premises and began immediately after "closing time"; that the employee had access to the tavern after hours only by virtue of his role as an employee of the corporate licensee, which role vested him with the means to keep the tavern open; and that the defendant may anticipate that employees may be tempted to engage in such conduct; the jury could conclude that the tavern manager's conduct was sufficiently similar to the conduct authorized as to be within the scope of employment. The jury could view the tavern manager's conduct as more similar to that of an employee to whom the operation of the business had been entrusted and for whose conduct the defendant should be held criminally liable than to that of an interloper for whose conduct the defendant should not be held liable.

* * *

CECI, JUSTICE (dissenting).

I respectfully dissent from the majority's conclusion that there is sufficient evidence to support the verdict in this case finding that Mark Witkowski, the tavern manager, was acting within the scope of his employment. In reviewing the evidence in the light most favorable to sustaining Janet Beaudry's conviction, I believe that the record is devoid of evidence to sustain the verdict. I would reverse the decision of the court of appeals which affirmed the defendant's conviction because I am convinced that, as a matter of law, no trier of fact, acting reasonably, could conclude beyond a reasonable doubt that Mark Witkowski was acting within the scope of his employment when he kept the Village Green tavern open after 1:00 a.m. in violation of section 125.68(4)(c), Stats.

We have previously held that a servant is *not* within the scope of his employment if (a) his acts were different in kind than those authorized by the master, (b) his acts were far beyond the authorized time or space limits, or (c) his acts were too little actuated by a purpose to serve the master.

It is important to note that this test is set out in the disjunctive and not the conjunctive, and, thus, not all three elements must be satisfied before there can be a finding that the servant was outside the scope of his authority.

* * * Unfortunately, the majority fails to evaluate the uncontroverted facts in this case with respect to these three criteria. In doing so, I conclude that Mark Witkowski was not within the scope of employment when he kept the tavern open after 1:00 a.m. * * *

Notes and Questions

1. Compare *Vachon v. New Hampshire,* 414 U.S. 478, 94 S.Ct. 664, 38 L.Ed.2d 666 (1974), where the operator of a store was sentenced to 30 days in jail and fined $100 after conviction under a statute applicable to "anyone * * * who shall knowingly or wilfully encourage, aid, cause or abet or connive at, or who has knowingly or wilfully done any act to produce, promote or contribute to the delinquency of [a] child." The conviction was based on the fact that a 14-year-old girl had purchased a button inscribed "Copulation Not Masturbation" at defendant's store. The Supreme Court reversed the conviction on the due process ground that it was "based on a record lacking any relevant evidence as to a crucial element," in that "there is no evidence whatever that the defendant sold the button, that he knew it had been sold to a minor, that he authorized such sales to minors, or that he was even in the store at the time of the sale." The three dissenters objected that the "entire thrust" of the state supreme court decision affirming the conviction "is that appellant need not *personally* have sold the button to the minor nor *personally* have authorized its sale to a minor in order to be guilty of the statutory offense. The only fair reading of the * * * language from the Supreme Court of New Hampshire is that the word

'wilfully' in the statute does *not* mean *'personally,'* and the facts that the appellant controlled and operated the shop, that the same type of pin had been previously purchased at the shop, and that the pins were prominently offered for sale were sufficient evidence on the issue of wilfullness."

2. In *Beaudry,* the court carefully distinguished between strict and vicarious liability. But, are not the two related, in that the latter naturally follows from the former? Compare *People v. Travers,* 52 Cal. App.3d 111, 124 Cal.Rptr. 728 (1975) (employer vicariously liable for employee's sale of misbranded oil, as while it "is a settled rule of law that a principal is not criminally liable for the criminal act of his agent unless he authorized, consented to, advised, aided or encouraged the specific act," an "exception to this rule is the doctrine of criminal liability without fault which has been applied to criminal statutes enacted for the public morals, health, peace and safety. In general, such statutes deal with offenses of a regulatory nature and are enforceable irrespective of criminal intent or criminal negligence"); with *People v. Wilcox,* 83 Mich.App. 654, 269 N.W.2d 256 (1978) (employer not vicariously liable for employee's sale of second hand merchandise without keeping proper record of same, and this so even though "the statute does not require scienter or intent, but rather imposes strict liability for violations").

3. On the constitutional issue, does it make a difference whether the defendant is actually imprisoned? In *Commonwealth v. Koczwara,* 397 Pa. 575, 155 A.2d 825 (1959), the court concluded the defendant, the operator of a tavern, could be held for sales to minors at his establishment during his absence, for the applicable statute declared it unlawful for "any person, by himself or by an employe or agent, to expose or keep for sale, or directly or indirectly sell or offer to sell any liquor within this Commonwealth, except in accordance with the provisions of this act." But as to defendant's sentence of a $500 fine and 3 months imprisonment, the court ruled: "The Courts of the Commonwealth have already strained to permit the legislature to carry over the civil doctrine of *respondeat superior* and to apply it as a means of enforcing the regulatory scheme that covers the liquor trade. We have done so on the theory that the Code established petty misdemeanors involving only light monetary fines. It would be unthinkable to impose vicarious criminal responsibility in cases involving true crimes. Although to hold a principal criminally liable might possibly be an effective means of enforcing law and order, it would do violence to our more sophisticated modern-day concepts of justice. Liability for all true crimes, wherein an offense carries with it a jail sentence, must be based exclusively upon personal causation. It can be readily imagined that even a licensee who is meticulously careful in the choice of his employees cannot supervise every single act of the subordinates. A man's liberty cannot rest on so frail a reed as whether his employee will commit a mistake in judgment."

Musmanno, J., dissenting, objected: "If it is wrong to send a person to jail for acts committed by another, is it not wrong to convict him at all? There are those who value their good names to the extent that they see as much harm in a degrading criminal conviction as in a jail sentence. The laceration of a man's reputation, the blemishing of his good name, the wrecking of his prestige by a criminal court conviction may blast a person's chances for honorable success in life to such an extent that a jail sentence can hardly add much to the ruin already wrought to him by the conviction alone."

4. Authority supporting the latter position is emerging. See *Davis v. Peachtree City,* 251 Ga. 219, 304 S.E.2d 701 (1983) (employer was convicted for employee's

sale of liquor to minor and was sentenced to $200 fine and 60 days imprisonment, latter suspended upon payment of fine and so long as employer did not again violate the law; because defendant "faces a possible restraint of his liberty, particularly if another employee fails to exercise good judgment; damage will be done to his good name by having a criminal record; and his future will be imperiled because of possible disabilities or legal disadvantages arising from the conviction," this violates due process, especially "when, as here, there are other, less onerous alternatives which sufficiently promote these interests. * * * The Model Penal Code recommends that civil violations providing civil penalties such as fines or revocation of licenses be used for offenses for which the individual was not morally blameworthy and does not deserve the social condemnation 'implicit in the concept "crime" ' "); *State v. Guminga,* 395 N.W.2d 344 (Minn. 1986) (employer charged for employee's act of selling liquor to minor; charge dismissed on due process grounds: "Not only could Guminga be given a prison sentence or a suspended sentence, but, in the more likely event that he receives only a fine, his liberty could be affected by a longer presumptive sentence in a possible future felony conviction. Such an intrusion on personal liberty is not justified by the public interest protected, especially when there are alternative means by which to achieve the same end, such as civil fines or license suspension, which do not entail the legal and social ramifications of a criminal conviction").

5. Even if *Beaudry,* the prevailing view, is to be preferred over *Davis* and *Guminga,* is the situation different outside a business context? At issue in *State v. Akers,* 119 N.H. 161, 400 A.2d 38 (1979), was a provision pertaining to use of highway recreational vehicles that the "parents or guardians will be responsible for any damage incurred or for any violations of this

chapter by any person under the age of 18." The defendants were convicted for their minor sons' improper operation of such vehicles. The court reversed:

"Without passing upon the validity of statutes that might seek to impose vicarious criminal liability on the part of an employer for acts of his employees, we have no hesitancy in holding that any attempt to impose such liability on parents simply because they occupy the status of parents, without more, offends the due process clause of our State constitution.

"Parenthood lies at the very foundation of our civilization. The continuance of the human race is entirely dependent upon it. It was firmly entrenched in the Judaeo-Christian ethic when 'in the beginning' man was commanded to 'be fruitful and multiply.' Genesis I. Considering the nature of parenthood, we are convinced that the status of parenthood cannot be made a crime. This, however, is the effect of RSA 269–C:24 IV. Even if the parent has been as careful as anyone could be, even if the parent has forbidden the conduct, and even if the parent is justifiably unaware of the activities of the child, criminal liability is still imposed under the wording of the present statute. There is no other basis for criminal responsibility other than the fact that a person is the parent of one who violates the law."

CITY OF MISSOULA v. SHEA
Supreme Court of Montana, 1983.
202 Mont. 286, 661 P.2d 410.

B.W. THOMAS, DISTRICT JUDGE.

Defendant was charged in Missoula Municipal Court with sixty parking ordinance violations dating from June 1, 1976, to April 22, 1978. * * * After her conviction in Municipal Court, defendant appealed to district court. The district court upheld her conviction. * * *

Although there were two charges brought under Missoula Municipal Code sections 20–115 and 20–118, the majority of charges were brought under sections 20–132(c) and 20–184, M.M.C. This opinion applies to all the ordinances. They read as follows:

"Sec. 20–115. Marking no parking zones. Whenever curbs or curbing are painted yellow in color by the city engineer pursuant to an ordinance or resolution of the city council, no person shall at any time stop, stand or park; or whenever signs are erected by the city engineer pursuant to an ordinance or resolution of the city council which prohibits parking, establish limited time parking zones or in any way limit or restrict parking, no person shall stop, stand or park in violation of the provisions indicated on such signs."

"Sec. 20–118. Registered owner to be responsible for illegally parked vehicle. Every person in whose name a vehicle is registered or licensed shall be responsible for any parking of the vehicle in violation of this division. It shall be no defense to such charge that the vehicle is illegally parked by another unless it is shown that at such time the vehicle was being used without the consent of the registered owner thereof."

"Sec. 20–132. Extension of time beyond the legal limit; parking after expiration of time.

"(a) No person shall deposit or cause to be deposited in a parking meter a coin for the purpose of increasing or extending the parking time for any vehicle beyond the legal maximum parking time which has been established for the parking space adjacent to which the parking meter is placed.

"(b) No person shall permit a vehicle to remain or be placed in any parking space adjacent to any parking meter while the parking meter is indicating a signal indicating violation.

"(c) No person shall cause, allow, permit or suffer any vehicle registered in his name or operated or controlled by him to be upon any street within the parking meter zone in any space adjacent to which a parking meter is installed, at any time during which the meter is showing a signal indicating that such space is illegally in use, other than such time as is necessary to operate the meter to show legal parking, between the hours of 9:00 a.m. and 6:00 p.m. of any day, Sundays and legal holidays excepted."

"Sec. 20–184. Presumption in reference to illegal parking. (a) In any prosecution charging a violation of any law or regulation governing the standing or parking of a vehicle, proof that the particular vehicle described in the complaint was parked in violation of any such law or regulation, together with proof that the defendant named in the complaint was at the time of such parking the registered owner of the vehicle, shall constitute in evidence a prima facie presumption that the registered owner of such vehicle was the person who parked or placed such vehicle where, and for the time during which, such violation occurred.

(b) The foregoing stated presumption shall apply only when the procedure indicated in sections 20–182 and 20–183 has been followed."

The second sentence of section 20–118, M.M.C. was eliminated by the city council on July 10, 1978, because of this Court's decision in the case of *State v. Jetty* (1978), 176 Mont. 519, 579 P.2d 1228.

The District Court found that the presumption provided for by section 20–184(a), M.M.C. was unconstitutional in that it resulted in an impermissible shifting of the burden of persuasion under the holding in *Sandstrom v. State of Montana* [p. 117 of this Book]. The District Court further found that the remaining provisions of the ordinances established a prima facie responsibility upon the registered owner, which that owner had a right to rebut by way of an affirmative defense, following the decision in *Jetty*. The defendant did not offer any evidence in rebuttal in district court to show that she was not the person who parked the car.

Defendant contends that a prima facie case that the registered owner parked the vehicle is no different than a presumption that the registered owner parked the car. She makes three arguments in support of her contention: (1) the presumption shifts the burden of persuasion to the defendant, thus violating the due process requirement that the state prove each element of a criminal offense beyond a reasonable doubt; (2) the presumption is not based on a sufficient constitutional nexus between the fact presumed and the fact proved; and (3) the presumption presumes guilt itself, when it should only presume one of the several elements of the crime.

To accept defendant's arguments would require that we reverse or modify the position taken by this court in *State v. Jetty.*

In *Jetty,* this Court had under consideration a City of Livingston parking ordinance. The opinion stated:

"Defendant's second issue on appeal becomes academic due to this Court's holding on the first issue. However, because of the wide use of this traffic ordinance throughout the state, we feel it necessary to comment on its constitutionality.

"The Livingston city code, Section 28–264, provides:

'(a) Every person in whose name a vehicle is registered (licensed) shall be responsible for any parking of such vehicle in violation of this division.

'(b) It shall be no defense to such charge that such vehicle was illegally parked by another, unless it is shown that at such time the vehicle was being used without the consent of the registered (licensed) owner thereof.'

"The Livingston ordinance is identical to a Seattle, Washington, ordinance which was declared unconstitutional in part by the Washington Supreme Court in *City of Seattle v. Stone* (1966), 67 Wash.2d 886, 410 P.2d 583.

"We cite *City of Seattle v. Stone,* supra, with approval and adopt the following rationale:

'The second sentence of the Seattle ordinance [section 28–264(b), Livingston ordinance] preceding the proviso is patently incompatible with the concept of due process. It purports to make a defendant responsible even though he in fact might not have been responsible for the parking violation.

'For the reasons indicated, we are forced to strike down as unconstitutional that portion of the second sentence of § 21.66.180 [Livingston ordinance subsection (b)] preceding the proviso, for it deprives an automobile owner of due process of law.

'We then interpret the remainder of § 21.66.180 [Livingston ordinance 28–264, subsection (a)], as do the authorities heretofore cited, to establish only a prima facie responsibility upon the registered owner, which he has the right to rebut, if he can. *This in nowise interrupts the city's exercise of its police power or its right and power to enforce its parking ordinances.'* (Emphasis added.) [Bracketed material added.]

"As pointed out, the owner is still prima facie liable under the ordinance and subject to arrest and prosecution. However, he *cannot* be deprived of his defense that some one else he permitted to use his car was the actual violator."

As the above quotation shows, in *Jetty* this Court adopted the reasoning of the Washington court in the case of *City of Seattle v. Stone,* supra, including its holding that a city parking ordinance can make the registered owner prima facie liable so long as he is not deprived of the defense that he was not the actual violator.

We agree with the defendant that to make the owner of a vehicle prima facie liable upon proof that his vehicle has been parked illegally is equivalent to a presumption that the owner parked the vehicle. This requires us to consider whether that presumption, in the light of its effect, meets the constitutional requirements for the use of presumptions in criminal cases.

Since its decision in *Seattle v. Stone,* supra, the Washington Supreme Court has developed a strict three-part test of the constitutionality of criminal presumptions: (1) although a presumption may shift the initial burden of producing evidence to the defendant, it may not operate to relieve the prosecution of its burden of persuasion on that element by proof beyond a reasonable doubt; (2) the facts presumed must follow from the facts proven beyond a reasonable doubt, and (3) the trier of fact must know that the presumption allows, but does not require, it to infer the presumed fact from proof of the operative fact. Based on those requirements, the Washington Court of Appeals in *City of Spokane v. Potter,* found that a presumption similar to the one we are dealing with here, appearing in a Spokane parking ordinance, was unconstitutional. Although these Washington decisions are not binding on us, they indicate an erosion of the foundation for the *Jetty* holding.

Decisions of the United States Supreme Court on due process questions are binding on us. * * * However, the United States Supreme Court has not gone so far as to require that the nexus between the fact proved and the fact presumed must be established beyond a reasonable doubt. Instead, that Court has said that there must at least be "substantial assurance that the presumed fact is more likely than not to flow from the proved fact on which it is made to depend." *Leary v. United States* (1969), 395 U.S. 6, 89 S.Ct. 1532, 23 L.Ed.2d 57.

Under the rule in *Jetty,* the City need only prove the act of parking and the registered ownership of the vehicle to make a prima facie case of guilt. The burden then shifts to the owner to establish that she was not the driver. The act of illegal parking becomes an essential element of the offense, which the City is permitted to prove by means of the presumption. Rule 301(b)(2), Mont.R.Evid., states that a disputable presumption "may be overcome by a preponderance of evidence contrary to the presumption. Unless the presumption is overcome, the trier of fact must find the assumed fact in accordance with the presumption." Thus, the trier of fact is not free to accept or reject the presumption. The effect of the presumption is to violate constitutional due process requirements by shifting the burden of persuasion to defendant and contradicting the presumption of innocence.

We therefore come to the conclusion that the prima facie presumption is unconstitutional and invalid. The ruling in *Jetty* relative to the validity of the portion of the above-quoted Livingston ordinance and the prima facie responsibility of the registered owner was given for the express purpose of providing future guidance to cities. The ruling was not necessary to the decision in that case. It cannot stand.

We have also reached the conclusion that we should reconsider the holding in *Jetty* which struck from the Livingston ordinance, on due process grounds, the following provision:

"It shall be no defense to such charge that such vehicle was illegally parked by another, unless it is shown that at such time the vehicle was being used without the consent of the registered (licensed) owner thereof." Livingston City Code, section 28–264(b).

That provision made the registered owner vicariously liable for the illegal parking of a vehicle by one who was driving with the permission of the owner. Under such a provision, no presumption is involved in determining the liability of the owner. The offense constitutes only two elements, the registered ownership and the illegal parking. There is absolute liability on the part of the registered owner upon proof of those two elements.

"While as a general rule, one person is not liable for the criminal acts of another in which he did not participate either directly or indirectly, there is a class of cases which form an exception to such general rule; [those] cases relat[e] to criminal responsibility for the maintenance of a public nuisance and for the violation of revenue and police regulations by one's agent or servant." This principle has been applied to traffic regulations.

Montana statutes contemplate the imposition of vicarious liability in certain criminal offenses. Section 45–2–301, MCA, provides: "Accountability for conduct of another. A person is responsible for conduct which is an element of an offense if the conduct is either that of the person himself or that of another and he is legally accountable for such conduct as provided in 45–2–302, or both."

Section 45–2–302, MCA, provides: "When accountability exists. A person is legally accountable for the conduct of another when: * * * (2) The statute defining the offense makes him so accountable;"

The Commission Comment for this subsection states:

"Subsection (2) makes clear a person may be held legally accountable in circumstances not otherwise included in section 94–2–107 [R.C.M.1947, now 45–2–302, MCA], where the particular statute so provides * * * An example of such a statute might be one imposing vicarious criminal liability on a tavern owner for the act of an employee resulting in sale of liquor to a minor."

We hold that vicarious criminal responsibility can be imposed, without breaching due process restrictions, in the regulation of traffic and the parking of motor vehicles. *Jetty* is overruled insofar as it holds to the contrary.

In addition to the statutes quoted above, section 45–2–104, MCA, is pertinent here. That section reads as follows:

"Absolute liability. A person may be guilty of an offense without having, as to each element thereof, one of the mental states described in subsections (33), (37), and (58) of 45–2–101 only if the offense is punishable by a fine not exceeding $500 and the statute defining the offense clearly indicates a legislative purpose to impose absolute liability for the conduct described."

Joseph B. Gary, District Judge, dissenting. * * *

The effect of the majority's decision is to strike from the ordinances as unconstitutional, that portion of the ordinance which established a prima facie presumption that the registered owner of the vehicle was the person who parked the vehicle. The effect of this is to place the municipalities in the State of Montana in a complete state of disarray and is inconsistent with what the majority of the courts are doing in the United States. * * *

Looking at other jurisdictions, the courts there have discussed the problems that exist if the majority opinion is followed to its logical conclusion in that the municipalities are really offered no alternative when a parking violation occurs. Therefore, the practical aspect would require the cities to place a large number of policemen at all cars so that the offender can be apprehended when he returns to the vehicle or in the alternative to remove the vehicles and charge large storage and removal fees etc. which will undoubtedly cause the citizens to rise up in arms. * * *

In other words, practically all of the courts are unanimous and hold that if it is merely a prima facie establishment of liability that can be rebutted there is no unconstitutional shifting of burden in a case such as this. * * *

JOHN M. MCCARVEL, DISTRICT JUDGE, concurring in JUDGE JOSEPH B. GARY'S dissent:

The Defendant relies on two United States Supreme Court decisions, *Sandstrom v. Montana* (1979), 442 U.S. 510, 99 S.Ct. 2450, 61 L.Ed.2d 39, and *In Re Winship* (1970), 397 U.S. 358, 364, 90 S.Ct. 1068, 1072, 25 L.Ed.2d 368. These cases have no relevance to the misdemeanor defense of illegal parking. In *Sandstrom* the Supreme Court clearly defined what element was involved in that case.

"The question presented is whether, *in a case in which intent is an element of the crime charged,* the jury instruction 'the law presumes that a person intends the ordinary consequences of his voluntary acts,' violates the Fourteenth Amendment's requirements that the State prove every element of a criminal offense beyond a reasonable doubt."

Those cases refer to the specific intent offenses. Intent is not an element of the offense charged in this case.

a. See § 2.07.

SECTION 10. LIABILITY OF ORGANIZATIONS, THEIR OFFICERS AND AGENTS

COMMONWEALTH v. BENEFICIAL FINANCE CO.

Supreme Court of Massachusetts, 1971.
360 Mass. 188, 275 N.E.2d 33.

SPIEGEL, JUSTICE. [Various individual and corporate defendants were convicted of conspiracy to engage in bribery, in that three finance companies (Household Finance, Beneficial Finance, and Liberty Loan) sought favorable treatment from state agencies. Household was held criminally responsible for the criminal conduct of Barber and Pratt, employees but neither directors nor officers; Liberty was held liable for the criminal acts of Woodstock, a director and executive vice-president; and Beneficial was held criminally responsible for the conduct of Farrell and Glynn, who were neither directors, officers nor employees of that corporation, but who were vice-president and an employee, respectively, of Beneficial Management, a wholly-owned subsidiary.]

The defendants and the Commonwealth have proposed differing standards upon which the criminal responsibility of a corporation should be predicated. The defendants argue that a corporation should not be held criminally liable for the conduct of its servants or agents unless such conduct was performed, authorized, ratified, adopted or tolerated by the corporations' directors, officers or other "high managerial agents" who are sufficiently high in the corporate hierarchy to warrant the assumption that their acts in some substantial sense reflect corporate policy. This standard is that adopted by the American Law Institute Model Penal Code, approved in May, 1962.[a] * * *

The Commonwealth, on the other hand, argues that the standard applied by the judge in his instructions to the jury was correct. These instructions, which prescribe a somewhat more flexible standard than that delineated in the Model Penal Code, state in part, as follows: "[T]he Commonwealth must prove beyond a reasonable doubt that there existed between the guilty individual or individuals and the corporation which is being charged with the conduct of the individuals, such *a relationship that the acts and the intent of the individuals were the acts and intent of the corporation.* * * *

"How is that to be shown? How is the jury to determine whether the Commonwealth has proved that? First let me say that the Commonwealth does not have to prove that the individual who acted criminally was expressly requested or authorized in advance by the corporation to do so, nor must the Commonwealth prove that the corporation expressly ratified or adopted that criminal conduct on the part of that individual or those individuals. *It does not mean that the Commonwealth must prove that the individual who acted criminally was a member of the corporation's board of directors, or that he was a high officer in the corporation, or that he held any office at all.* If the Commonwealth did prove that an individual for whose act it seeks to hold a corporation criminally liable was an officer of the corporation, the jury should consider that. *But more important than that, it should consider what the authority of that person was as such officer in relation to the corporation.* The mere fact that he has a title is not enough to make the corporation liable for his criminal conduct. The Commonwealth must prove that the individual for whose conduct it seeks to charge *the corporation criminally was placed in a position by the corporation where he had enough power, duty, responsibility and authority to act for and in behalf of the corporation to handle the particular business or operation or project of the corpo-*

ration in which he was engaged at the time that he committed the criminal act, with power of decision as to what he would or would not do while acting for the corporation, and that he was acting for and in behalf of the corporation in the accomplishment of that particular business or operation or project, and that he committed a criminal act while so acting. * * *"

The difference between the judge's instructions to the jury and the Model Penal Code lies largely in the latter's reference to a "high managerial agent" and in the Code requirement that to impose corporate criminal liability, it at least must appear that its directors or high managerial agent "authorized * * * or recklessly tolerated" the allegedly criminal acts. The judge's instructions focus on the authority of the corporate agent in relation to the *particular* corporate business in which the agent was engaged. The Code seems to require that there be authorization or reckless inaction by a corporate representative having some relation to framing corporate policy, or one "having duties of such responsibility that his conduct may fairly be assumed to represent the policy of the corporation." Close examination of the judge's instructions reveals that they preserve the underlying "corporate policy" rationale of the Code by allowing the jury to infer "corporate policy" from the *position* in which the corporation placed the agent in commissioning him to handle the particular corporate affairs in which he was engaged at the time of the criminal act. * * *

It may also be observed that the judge's standard is somewhat similar to the traditional common law rule of respondeat superior. However, in applying this rule to a criminal case, the judge added certain requirements not generally associated with that common law doctrine. He further qualified the rule of respondeat superior by requiring that the conduct for which the corporation is being held accountable be performed *on behalf of the corporation.*

This factor is noted as important in the commentary to § 2.07(1) of the Model Penal Code. It may well be that there is often little distinction between an act done *on behalf of a principal* and an act done *within the scope of employment,* which is the traditional requirement of the doctrine of respondeat superior. Nevertheless, in the circumstances of this case it might reasonably be concluded that the explicit instruction of the judge that the jury look to the authority vested in the agent by the corporation to act within the particular sphere of corporate affairs relating to the criminal act, together with the explicit instruction that such act be performed on behalf of the corporation, required, in effect, the type of evidence which would support an inference that the criminal act was done as a matter of corporate policy. We deem this to be a valid conclusion, especially in view of the quantum of proof required in a criminal case in order to prove guilt beyond a reasonable doubt. * * *

The thrust of [earlier Mass. cases] involving a human principal is that it is fundamental to our criminal jurisprudence that for more serious offences guilt is personal and not vicarious. "One is punished for his own blameworthy conduct, not that of others." Professor Sayre's article [b] is heavily relied on by Beneficial for the proposition that the considerations proposed by Sayre apply with equal weight to corporations. However, we do not think that the Sayre article, or the rule in the master-servant cases, is helpful to these corporations. The essence of Sayre's discussion is that, as to certain crimes, a theory of vicarious liability is an inadequate basis for imposing criminal liability on a natural person who can suffer imprisonment or ignominy for the acts of his agents. * * *

b. Sayre, *Criminal Responsibility for the Acts of Another,* 43 Harv.L.Rev. 689 (1930).

As alluded to by Professor Sayre, and pointed out by the Commonwealth in its brief, the very nature of a corporation as a "person" before the law renders it impossible to equate the imposition of vicarious liability on a human principal with the imposition of vicarious liability on a corporate principal. "A corporation can act only through its agents. * * * [C]orporate criminal liability is necessarily vicarious." Since a corporation is a legal fiction, comprised only of individuals, it has no existence separate and distinct from those whom it has clothed with authority and commissioned to act for it whether such individuals are directors, officers, shareholders or employees. Thus, the issue is not whether vicarious liability should be imposed on a corporation under the "direct participation and assent rule" of the master-servant cases cited above, but rather, whether the acts and intent of natural persons, be they officers, directors or employees, can be treated as the acts and intent of the corporation itself. For the foregoing reasons, despite the strenuous urging of the defendants, we are unconvinced that the standard for imposing criminal responsibility on a human principal adequately deals with the evidentiary problems which are inherent in ascribing the acts of individuals to a corporate entity.

Since we have exhausted our review of Massachusetts cases in point, we turn to cases in other jurisdictions discussing the problem of corporate criminal responsibility. We note, however, that in view of the fact that the crimes alleged here, namely, conspiracy and the substantive offences of bribery, are mala in se, we necessarily exclude discussion of those cases which *clearly* involve "public welfare" offences by a corporation, unless such cases cast some insight into the question before us. Generally, these cases concern public nuisances resulting from the nonperformance of a nondelegable duty, rather than the rule of respondeat superior.

We first treat with the case of *New York Cent. & H.R.R. Co. v. United States,* 212 U.S. 481, 29 S.Ct. 304, 53 L.Ed. 613, a case relied upon by both the judge and the Commonwealth.   There, the Supreme Court of the United States upheld the constitutionality of a statute which specifically made corporations liable for the acts of their officers, agents or employees acting within the scope of their employment. The statute in question prohibited shippers from receiving rebates from common carriers and specifically provided as follows: "In construing and enforcing the provisions of this section the act, omission, or failure of any officer, agent, or other person acting for or employed by any common carrier acting within the scope of his employment shall in every case be also deemed to be the act, omission, or failure of such carrier as well as that of the person."   [T]he court made a number of pertinent observations and rulings from which we quote at some length: "A corporation is held responsible for acts not within the agent's corporate powers strictly construed, but which the agent has assumed to perform for the corporation when employing the corporate powers actually authorized, and in such cases there need be no written authority under seal or vote of the corporation in order to constitute the agency or to authorize the act. * * * We see no valid objection in law, and every reason in public policy, why the corporation, which profits by the transaction, and can only act through its agents and officers, shall be held punishable by fine because of the knowledge and intent of its agents to whom it has intrusted authority to act in the subject-matter of making and fixing rates of transportation, and whose knowledge and purposes may well be attributed to the corporation for which the agents act.   While the law should have regard to the rights of all, and

to those of corporations no less than to those of individuals, it cannot shut its eyes to the fact that the great majority of business transactions in modern times are conducted through these bodies, and particularly that interstate commerce is almost entirely in their hands, and to give them immunity from all punishment because of the old and exploded doctrine that a corporation cannot commit a crime would virtually take away the only means of effectually controlling the subject-matter and correcting the abuses aimed at." * * *

Household argues that the *New York Central* case is one in which Congress clearly dispensed with the necessity of proving corporate intent and is therefore distinguishable from the case before us. While we agree that the thrust of the opinion in that case is addressed to the constitutionality of the statutory imputation of the agent's acts to the corporation, we think that the case falls outside the class of offences generally denominated as "public welfare" offences and serves as precedent for the proposition that a corporation may be held criminally responsible for the acts of one who is neither a director, officer nor "high managerial agent" of the corporation.   In this regard, the case illustrates the public policy rationale for imposing vicarious liability upon a corporation and thus warranting the treatment of corporations in a manner different from that of individuals for the acts of their agents.   This rationale was subsequently developed and applied in lower Federal court cases which dealt with crimes requiring specific intent. * * *

Household, Beneficial and Liberty all vigorously attack these cases in an attempt to distinguish them from the cases before us.   The thrust of their argument is that all of these cases fall into 1 of 2 categories; either they involve public welfare and regulatory statute crimes in which intent was not an element, or if the crimes did include intent as a necessary element, then they assert that the corporations were only held liable if one high in the corporate hierarchy directed, approved or acquiesced in the agent's criminal act. * * *

We think that the answer to these contentions is twofold. First, the defendants' attempted categorization of the above cases into two neat little groups greatly oversimplifies the complex and multifaceted issues which confronted the various courts in the cases we have cited. The principal cases all entail prosecutions for the crimes of conspiracy, a crime requiring specific intent. In addition, the object of the conspiracies in those cases involved a wide scope of serious criminal activity, usually in matters tending to be of benefit to the corporation, extending from violations of the Espionage Act through the making of illegal political contributions, various types of fraudulent acquisitive crimes, and conspiracy to violate the Sherman Act through price fixing. * * * Secondly, the argument that only high corporate officers were involved has no basis in fact. In [one] case, a minor branch manager was involved, and in [another] case, a salesman. * * *

It may be that the theoretical principles underlying this standard are, in general, the same as embodied in the rule of respondeat superior. Nevertheless, as we observed at the outset, the judge's instructions, as a whole and in context, required a greater quantum of proof in the practical application of this standard than is required in a civil case. In focusing on the "kinship" between the authority of an individual and the act he committed, the judge emphasized that the jury must be satisfied "beyond a reasonable doubt" that the act of the individual *"constituted"* the act of the corporation. Juxtaposition of the traditional criminal law requirement of ascertaining guilt beyond a reasonable doubt (as opposed to the civil law standard of the preponderance of the evidence), with the rule of respondeat superior, fully

justifies application of the standard enunciated by the judge to a criminal prosecution against a corporation for a crime requiring specific intent.

The foregoing is especially true in view of the particular circumstances of this case. In order to commit the crimes charged in these indictments, the defendant corporations either had to offer to pay money to a public official or conspire to do so. The disbursal of funds is an act peculiarly within the ambit of corporate activity. These corporations by the very nature of their business are constantly dealing with the expenditure and collection of moneys. It could hardly be expected that any of the individual defendants would conspire to pay, or would pay, the substantial amount of money here involved, namely $25,000, out of his own pocket. The jury would be warranted in finding that the disbursal of such an amount of money would come from the corporate treasury. A reasonable inference could therefore be drawn that the payment of such money by the corporations was done as a matter of corporate policy and as a reflection of corporate intent, thus comporting with the underlying rationale of the Model Penal Code, and probably with its specific requirements.

Moreover, we do not think that the Model Penal Code standard really purports to deal with the evidentiary problems which are inherent in establishing the quantum of proof necessary to show that the directors or officers of a corporation authorize, ratify, tolerate, or participate in the criminal acts of an agent when such acts are apparently performed on behalf of the corporation. Evidence of such authorization or ratification is too easily susceptible of concealment. As is so trenchantly stated by the judge: "Criminal acts are not usually made the subject of votes of authorization or ratification by corporate Boards of Directors; and the lack of such votes does not prevent the act from being the act of the corporation."

It is obvious that criminal conspiratorial acts are not performed within the glare of publicity, nor would we expect a board of directors to meet officially and record on the corporate records a delegation of authority to initiate, conduct or conclude proceedings for the purpose of bribing a public official. Of necessity, the proof [of] authority to so act must rest on all the circumstances and conduct in a given situation and the reasonable inferences to be drawn therefrom.

Additional factors of importance are the size and complexity of many large modern corporations which necessitate the delegation of more authority to lesser corporate agents and employees. As the judge pointed out: "There are not enough seats on the Board of Directors, nor enough offices in a corporation, to permit the corporation engaged in widespread operations to give such a title or office to every person in whom it places the power, authority, and responsibility for decision and action." This latter consideration lends credence to the view that the title or position of an individual in a corporation should not be conclusively determinative in ascribing criminal responsibility. In a large corporation, with many numerous and distinct departments, a high ranking corporate officer or agent may have no authority or involvement in a particular sphere of corporate activity, whereas a lower ranking corporate executive might have much broader power in dealing with a matter peculiarly within the scope of his authority. Employees who are in the lower echelon of the corporate hierarchy often exercise more responsibility in the *everyday operations* of the corporation than the directors or officers. Assuredly, the title or

58. The term "endocratic" was coined by Dean Rostow and means a "large, publicly-held corporation, whose stock is scattered in small fractions among thousands of stockholders."

office that the person holds may be considered, but it should not be the decisive criterion upon which to predicate corporate responsibility. * * *

To permit corporations to conceal the nefarious acts of their underlings by using the shield of corporate armor to deflect corporate responsibility, and to separate the subordinate from the executive, would be to permit "endocratic" corporations to inflict widespread public harm without hope of redress. It would merely serve to ignore the scramble and realities of the market place.[58] This we decline to do. We believe that stringent standards must be adopted to discourage any attempt by "endocratic" corporations' executives to place the sole responsibility for criminal acts on the shoulders of their subordinates. * * *

Considering everything we have said above, we are of opinion that the quantum of proof necessary to sustain the conviction of a corporation for the acts of its agents is sufficiently met if it is shown that the corporation has placed the agent in a position where he has enough authority and responsibility to act for and in behalf of the corporation in handling the *particular* corporate business, operation or project in which he was engaged at the time he committed the criminal act. The judge properly instructed the jury to this effect and correctly stated that this standard does not depend upon the responsibility or authority which the agent has with respect to the entire corporate business, but only to his position with relation to the particular business in which he was serving the corporation. Some of the factors that the jury were entitled to consider in applying the above test, although perhaps not in themselves decisive, are the following: (1) the extent of control and authority exercised

Note, *Increasing Community Control Over Corporate Crime—A Problem in the Law of Sanctions,* 71 Yale L.J. 280, 281, n. 3.

by the individual over and within the corporation; (2) the extent and manner to which corporate funds were used in the crime; (3) a repeated pattern of criminal conduct tending to indicate corporate toleration or ratification of the agent's acts.[c]

Notes and Questions

1. Does corporate criminal liability, under either the Model Penal Code or *Beneficial Finance* approach, represent sound policy? Evaluate the following objections: (1) that the imposition of a criminal fine on the corporation is often ineffective as a profit-diminishing sanction, in that the economic cost of the fine may be "passed on" to the consumer by means of higher prices or rates;[a] (2) that in the "endocratic" corporation (the large publicly-held corporation whose stock is scattered in small fractions among thousands of stockholders) the stockholders simply cannot control the management, and thus should not be penalized for their failure to do so;[b] (3) that the availability of the corporation as a defendant provides a convenient "scapegoat" whereby corporate

agents engaged in the wrongdoing escape the personal criminal liability which would be a greater deterrent;[c] (4) that depriving wrongdoers of their ill-gotten gains is not a function of the criminal law,[d] and that in any event fines are usually unrelated to the gains and may penalize stockholders other than those who profited from the illegal activity;[e] and (5) that the criminal prosecutions of corporations are not adequately reported to the public to result in damage to the "corporate image."[f]

2. Under the traditional respondeat superior approach, "the prosecution must show that the illegal act was committed within the agent's scope of employment. The traditional agency definition limits scope of employment to conduct that is authorized, explicitly or implicitly, by the principal or that is similar or incidental to authorized conduct. However, courts generally find conduct to fall within the scope of employment even if it was specifically forbidden by a superior and occurred despite good faith efforts on the part of the corporation to prevent the crime. Thus, scope of employment in practice

c. The court then went on to conclude:

(1) that there was sufficient evidence that Barber, divisional director of public relations, and Pratt, a subordinate of the vice-president in charge of public relations, acted "within the authority conferred on them" by Household in conspiring to bribe public officials, as the public relations men were responsible for dealings between the corporation and persons in "public life";

(2) that there was sufficient evidence that Woodstock, in light of his position, had authority to act for Liberty; and

(3) that Farnell and Glynn possessed sufficient authority to act for Beneficial Management, the wholly-owned subsidiary of Beneficial Finance, and that the former was the agent of the latter under the test of *My Bread Baking Co. v. Cumberland Farms, Inc.*, 353 Mass. 614, 233 N.E.2d 748 (1968):

"Although common ownership of the stock of two or more corporations together with common management, standing alone, will not give rise to liability on the part of one corporation for the acts of another corporation or its employees, addi-

tional facts may be such as to permit the conclusion that an agency or similar relationship exists between the entities. Particularly is this true (a) when there is active and direct participation by the representatives of one corporation, apparently exercising some form of pervasive control, in the activities of another and there is some fraudulent or injurious consequence of the intercorporate relationship, or (b) when there is a confused intermingling of activity of two or more corporations engaged in a common enterprise with substantial disregard of the separate nature of the corporate entities, or serious ambiguity about the manner and capacity in which the various corporations and their respective representatives are acting."

a. G. Williams, *Criminal Law: The General Part* § 283 (2d ed. 1961).

b. Note, 71 Yale L.J. 280, 281 (1961).

c. Id. at 292 n. 50.

d. G. Williams, supra note a, at § 186.

e. Id. at § 283.

f. Note, supra note b, at 287 n. 35.

means little more than that the act occurred while the offending employee was carrying out a job-related activity." *Developments in the Law—Corporate Crime,* 92 Harv.L.Rev. 1227, 1249–50 (1979). Is this unduly harsh?

3. Is the solution to give the corporation an affirmative defense along the lines of *Model Penal Code* § 2.07(5)? Consider:

(a) Miller, *Corporate Criminal Liability: A Principle Extended to Its Limits,* 38 Fed. B.J. 49, 66 (1979): "One of the principal justifications for the imposition of corporate criminal liability is that the corporate fine will encourage diligent supervision of corporate employees by managerial personnel. This goal is obviously furthered by encouraging corporate management to engage in self-policing functions. If corporate managers know that the company faces criminal sanctions despite their best efforts to insure compliance with the law, their motivation to undertake such efforts would be chilled. As Professor Mueller has pointed out: 'The imposition of punishment despite the exercise of due care, when the efforts were unsuccessful, creates frustration. If punishment followed as a matter of course upon every *discovered* technical breach of the law, no matter whether due care has been exercised or not, the managerial agents may well conclude that it is far more simple to let things take their own course, than it is to exercise care.'"

(b) Coffee, *Corporate Criminal Responsibility,* 1 Encyclopedia of Crime & Justice 253, 262 (1983): "Without such a defense, the corporation would still have an incentive to monitor and police its employees since, as a practical matter, it will probably be held strictly liable for any offense committed by employees in the course of their work. But by recognizing the defense, one raises the possibility of feigned compliance and thus encourages cosmetic attempts at monitoring. Worse yet, there is the danger that honest efforts at monitoring and compliance will be mistaken by middle-level management as only a cynical attempt to prepare a due-diligence defense in advance.

"On a more theoretical level, once such a defense is recognized, the corporation might invest less funds in monitoring and detecting illegal and potentially illegal behavior since, once the minimal standard of diligence is met, the corporation becomes legally immune and has no remaining incentive to prevent criminal acts by its agents, even though further investment might prevent such crime. In theory, the ideal position for the corporation would be to invest just enough to establish the defense but not to prevent those crimes profitable to the corporation. Yet without the defense, the rational corporation would invest in crime prevention by any means (including research or experimentation with new techniques) up to the level at which such expenditures equaled the expected penalty—that is, the likely fine discounted by the likelihood of apprehension and conviction. In short, the absence of the defense creates an incentive to seek new methods of prevention not yet established or required by a due-diligence standard. Ironically, the more diligence is made a defense, the less it is encouraged."

4. In *Granite Construction Co. v. Superior Court,* 149 Cal.App.3d 465, 197 Cal.Rptr. 3 (1983), denying a writ of prohibition re a grand jury indictment of the corporation for manslaughter after seven workers were killed in an accident at a power plant construction site, the petitioner asserted "that a corporation may be charged with crimes against 'property,' but 'not against the person.' This attempt to distinguish crimes against property from crimes against the person relies on the corporation's nature as an economically motivated entity. While a corporation may directly benefit from a crime against property, crimes against persons are not as directly linked to the profit motive. This argu-

ment is unsuccessful. It overlooks the substantial *indirect* economic benefits that may accrue to the corporation through crimes against the person. To get these economic benefits, corporate management may shortcut expensive safety precautions, respond forcibly to strikes, or engage in criminal anticompetitive behavior. If any such risk-taking is a corporate action, the corporation becomes a proper criminal defendant."

5. Recall that in *Beneficial Finance* the court found the cases "involving a human principal" not controlling. Does this mean that if the organizations had been partnerships rather than corporations and if the defendants had been the partners, the court would have taken a different approach?

Consider, in this regard, *Gordon v. United States,* 203 F.2d 248 (10th Cir.1953), where the defendants, partners in an appliance business, were convicted of "willfully" violating regulations concerning the selling of sewing machines on credit. The case was submitted to the jury on the theory that the knowledge of one partner was imputable to the other and that the knowledge and acts of the salesmen employed by the partnership were imputable to the partners. The court affirmed on the ground it was proper "to charge the employer with knowledge of records he is required to keep and acts he is required or forbidden to do, and which he necessarily keeps, does or omits to do by and through his agents and employees." The Supreme Court granted certiorari and reversed per curiam, 347 U.S. 909, 74 S.Ct. 473, 98 L.Ed. 1067 (1954): "The jury was instructed that the knowledge of petitioners' employees was chargeable to petitioners in determining petitioners' wilfulness. Because of the instruction, the Government has confessed error. We agree, and accordingly reverse the judgment and remand the case to the District Court for retrial."

6. What, then, of a prosecution of the partnership rather than the partners? In *United States v. A. & P. Trucking Co.,* 358 U.S. 121, 79 S.Ct. 203, 3 L.Ed.2d 165 (1958), the government appealed the dismissal of criminal charges against two partnerships. As for charges brought under 49 U.S.C.A. § 322(a), a part of the Motor Carrier Act, which provided a penalty for "any person knowingly and willfully violating" certain provisions, the government pointed out that the Act defined person to mean "any individual, firm, copartnership, corporation, company, association or joint-stock association." As for charges brought under 18 U.S.C.A. § 835, dealing with "whoever knowingly violates" ICC regulations on the transport of dangerous articles, the government relied on 1 U.S.C.A. § 1, which provides that "in determining the meaning of any Act of Congress, unless the context indicates otherwise * * * the words 'person' and 'whoever' include corporations, companies, firms, partnerships, societies, and joint stock companies, as well as individuals." The Court reversed:

"We think that partnerships as entities may be proceeded against under both § 322(a) and § 835. The purpose of both statutes is clear: to ensure compliance by motor carriers, among others, with safety and other requirements laid down by the Interstate Commerce Commission in the exercise of its statutory duty to regulate the operations of interstate carriers for hire. In the effectuation of this policy it certainly makes no difference whether the carrier which commits the infraction is organized as a corporation, a joint stock company, a partnership, or an individual proprietorship. The mischief is the same, and we think that Congress intended to make the consequences of infraction the same.

"True, the common law made a distinction between a corporation and a partnership, deeming the latter not a separate entity for purposes of suit. But the power of Congress to change the common-law rule is not to be doubted. We think it beyond dispute that it has done so in § 322(a) for, as we have seen, 'person' in that section is expressly defined in the Motor Carrier Act to include partnerships. We think it likewise has done so in § 835, since we find nothing in that section which would justify us not applying to the word 'whoever' the definition given it in 1 U.S. C.A. § 1, which includes partnerships. Section 835 makes regulations promulgated by the ICC for the transportation of dangerous articles binding on '*all* common carriers.' In view of the fact that many motor carriers are organized as partnerships rather than as corporations, the conclusion is not lightly to be reached that Congress intended that some carriers should not be subject to the full gamut of sanctions provided for infractions of ICC regulations merely because of the form under which they were organized to do business. More particularly, we perceive no reason why Congress should have intended to make partnership motor carriers criminally liable for infractions of § 322(a), but not for violations of § 835."

Four members of the Court dissented in part: "If the rule of strict construction of a criminal statute is to obtain, 18 U.S.C. § 835 must be read narrowly to reflect the prevailing view of partnership law. If the entity theory is to be applied for the purpose of imposing criminal penalties on partnership assets, where the partners are

wholly innocent of any wrongful act, it should be done only on the unequivocal command of Congress, as is the case under the Motor Carrier Act."

UNITED STATES v. PARK

Supreme Court of the United States, 1975.
421 U.S. 658, 95 S.Ct. 1903, 44 L.Ed.2d 489.

MR. CHIEF JUSTICE BURGER delivered the opinion of the Court. * * *

Acme Markets, Inc., is a national retail food chain with approximately 36,000 employees, 874 retail outlets, 12 general warehouses, and four special warehouses. Its headquarters, including the office of the president, respondent Park, who is chief executive officer of the corporation, are located in Philadelphia, Pennsylvania. In a five-count information filed in the United States District Court for the District of Maryland, the Government charged Acme and respondent with violations of the Federal Food, Drug and Cosmetic Act. Each count of the information alleged that the defendants had received food that had been shipped in interstate commerce and that, while the food was being held for sale in Acme's Baltimore warehouse following shipment in interstate commerce, they caused it to be held in a building accessible to rodents and to be exposed to contamination by rodents. These acts were alleged to have resulted in the food being adulterated within the meaning of 21 U.S.C. §§ 342(a)(3) and (4),[1] in violation of 21 U.S.C. § 331(k).[2]

---

1. Section 402 of the Act, 21 U.S.C. § 342, provides in pertinent part:

"A food shall be deemed to be adulterated—(a) * * * (3) if it consists in whole or in part of any filthy, putrid, or decomposed substance, or if it is otherwise unfit for food; or (4) if it has been prepared, packed, or held under insanitary conditions whereby it may have become contaminated with filth, or whereby it may have been rendered injurious to health * * *."

2. Section 301(k) of the Act, 21 U.S.C. § 331(k), provides:

"The following acts and the causing thereof are prohibited:

* * *

"(k) The alteration, mutilation, destruction, obliteration, or removal of the whole or any part of the labeling of, or the doing of any other act with respect to, a food, drug, device, or cosmetic, if such act is done while such article is held for sale (whether or not the first sale) after shipment in interstate commerce and results in such article being adulterated or misbranded."

Acme pleaded guilty to each count of the information. Respondent pleaded not guilty. The evidence at trial demonstrated that in April 1970 the Food and Drug Administration (FDA) advised respondent by letter of insanitary conditions in Acme's Philadelphia warehouse. In 1971 FDA found that similar conditions existed in the firm's Baltimore warehouse. An FDA consumer safety officer testified concerning evidence of rodent infestation and other insanitary conditions discovered during a 12-day inspection of the Baltimore warehouse in November and December 1971. He also related that a second inspection of the warehouse had been conducted in March 1972.[5] On that occasion the inspectors found that there had been improvement in the sanitary conditions, but that "there was still evidence of rodent activity in the building and in the warehouse and we found some rodent-contaminated lots of food items."

The Government also presented testimony by the Chief of Compliance of FDA's Baltimore office, who informed respondent by letter of the conditions at the Baltimore warehouse after the first inspection. There was testimony by Acme's Baltimore division vice president, who had responded to the letter on behalf of Acme and respondent and who described the steps taken to remedy the insanitary conditions discovered by both inspections. The Government's final witness, Acme's vice president for legal affairs and assistant secretary, identified respondent as the president and chief executive officer of the company and read a bylaw prescribing the

duties of the chief executive officer.[7] He testified that respondent functioned by delegating "normal operating duties," including sanitation, but that he retained "certain things, which are the big, broad principles of the operation of the company," and had "the responsibility of seeing that they all work together." * * *

Respondent was the only defense witness. He testified that, although all of Acme's employees were in a sense under his general direction, the company had an "organizational structure for responsibilities for certain functions" according to which different phases of its operation were "assigned to individuals who, in turn, have staff and departments under them." He identified those individuals responsible for sanitation and related that upon receipt of the January 1972 FDA letter, he had conferred with the vice president for legal affairs, who informed him that the Baltimore division vice president "was investigating the situation immediately and would be preparing a summary of the corrective action to reply to the letter." Respondent stated that he did not "believe there was anything [he] could have done more constructively than what [he] found was being done."

On cross-examination, respondent conceded that providing sanitary conditions for food offered for sale to the public was something that he was "responsible for in the entire operation of the company," and he stated that it was one of many phases of the company that he assigned to "dependable subordinates." Respondent was asked about and, over the objections of his coun-

---

5. The first four counts of the information alleged violations corresponding to the observations of the inspectors during the November and December 1971 inspection. The fifth count alleged violations corresponding to observations during the March 1972 inspection.

7. The bylaw provided in pertinent part:

"The Chairman of the board of directors or the president shall be the chief executive officer of the company as the board of directors may from

time to time determine. He shall, subject to the board of directors, have general and active supervision of the affairs, business, offices and employees of the company * * *.

"He shall, from time to time, in his discretion or at the order of the board, report the operations and affairs of the company. He shall also perform such other duties and have such other powers as may be assigned to him from time to time by the board of directors."

sel, admitted receiving, the April 1970 letter addressed to him from FDA regarding insanitary conditions at Acme's Philadelphia warehouse. He acknowledged that, with the exception of the division vice president, the same individuals had responsibility for sanitation in both Baltimore and Philadelphia. Finally, in response to questions concerning the Philadelphia and Baltimore incidents, respondent admitted that the Baltimore problem indicated the system for handling sanitation "wasn't working perfectly" and that as Acme's chief executive officer he was responsible for "any result which occurs in our company."

At the close of the evidence, respondent's renewed motion for a judgment of acquittal was denied. The relevant portion of the trial judge's instructions to the jury challenged by respondent is set out in the margin.[9] Respondent's counsel objected to the instructions on the ground that they failed fairly to reflect our decision in *United States v. Dotterweich,* 320 U.S. 277, 64 S.Ct. 134, 88 L.Ed. 48, and to define " 'Responsible relationship.' " The trial judge overruled the objection. The jury found respondent guilty on all counts of the information, and he was subsequently sentenced to pay a fine of $50 on each count.

9. "In order to find the Defendant guilty on any count of the Information, you must find beyond a reasonable doubt on each count ∗ ∗ ∗.

∗ ∗ ∗

"Thirdly, that John R. Park held a position of authority in the operation of the business of Acme Markets, Incorporated.

"However, you need not concern yourselves with the first two elements of the case. The main issue for your determination is only with the third element, whether the Defendant held a position of authority and responsibility in the business of Acme Markets.

∗ ∗ ∗

"The statute makes individuals, as well as corporations, liable for violations. An individual is liable if it is clear, beyond a reasonable doubt, that the elements of the adulteration of the food

The Court of Appeals reversed the conviction and remanded for a new trial. That court viewed the Government as arguing "that the conviction may be predicated solely upon a showing that ∗ ∗ ∗ [respondent] was the President of the offending corporation," and it stated that as "a general proposition, some act of commission or omission is an essential element of every crime." ∗ ∗ ∗

The question presented by the Government's petition for certiorari in *United States v. Dotterweich,* supra, and the focus of this Court's opinion, was whether "the manager of a corporation, as well as the corporation itself, may be prosecuted under the Federal Food, Drug, and Cosmetic Act of 1938 for the introduction of misbranded and adulterated articles into interstate commerce." In *Dotterweich,* a jury had disagreed as to the corporation, a jobber purchasing drugs from manufacturers and shipping them in interstate commerce under its own label, but had convicted Dotterweich, the corporation's president and general manager. The Court of Appeals reversed the conviction on the ground that only the drug dealer, whether corporation or individual, was subject to the criminal provisions of the Act, and that where the dealer was a corporation, an individual connected therewith might be held personally only if he

as to travel in interstate commerce are present. As I have instructed you in this case, they are, and that the individual had a responsible relation to the situation, even though he may not have participated personally.

"The individual is or could be liable under the statute, even if he did not consciously do wrong. However, the fact that the Defendant is pres[id]ent and is a chief executive officer of the Acme Markets does not require a finding of guilt. Though, he need not have personally participated in the situation, he must have had a responsible relationship to the issue. The issue is, in this case, whether the Defendant, John R. Park, by virtue of his position in the company, had a position of authority and responsibility in the situation out of which these charges arose."

was operating the corporation "as his 'alter ego.' "

In reversing the judgment of the Court of Appeals and reinstating Dotterweich's conviction, this Court looked to the purposes of the Act and noted that they "touch phases of the lives and health of the people which, in the circumstances of modern industrialism, are largely beyond self-protection." It observed that the Act is of "a now familiar type" which "dispenses with the conventional requirement for criminal conduct—awareness of some wrongdoing. In the interest of the larger good it puts the burden of acting at hazard upon a person otherwise innocent but standing in responsible relation to a public danger."

Central to the Court's conclusion that individuals other than proprietors are subject to the criminal provisions of the Act was the reality that "the only way in which a corporation can act is through the individuals who act on its behalf." The Court also noted that corporate officers had been subject to criminal liability under the Federal Food and Drugs Act of 1906, and it observed that a contrary result under the 1938 legislation would be incompatible with the expressed intent of Congress to "enlarge and stiffen the penal net" and to discourage a view of the Act's criminal penalties as a " 'license fee for the conduct of an illegitimate business.' "

At the same time, however, the Court was aware of the concern which was the motivating factor in the Court of Appeals' decision, that literal enforcement "might operate too harshly by sweeping within its condemnation any person however remotely entangled in the proscribed shipment." A limiting principle, in the form of "settled doctrines of criminal law" defining those who "are responsible for the commission of a misdemeanor", was available. In this context, the Court concluded, those doctrines dictated that the offense was committed "by all who have * * * a responsible share in the furtherance of the transaction which the statute outlaws".

The Court recognized that, because the Act dispenses with the need to prove "consciousness of wrongdoing", it may result in hardship even as applied to those who share "[a] responsibility in the business process resulting in" a violation. It regarded as "too treacherous" an attempt "to define or even to indicate by way of illustration the class of employees which stands in such a responsible relation." The question of responsibility, the Court said, depends "on the evidence produced at the trial and its submission—assuming the evidence warrants it—to the jury under appropriate guidance." The Court added: "In such matters the good sense of prosecutors, the wise guidance of trial judges, and the ultimate judgment of juries must be trusted."

The rule that corporate employees who have "a responsible share in the furtherance of the transaction which the statute outlaws" are subject to the criminal provisions of the Act was not formulated in a vacuum. Cases under the Federal Food and Drugs Act of 1906 reflected the view both that knowledge or intent were not required to be proved in prosecutions under its criminal provisions, and that responsible corporate agents could be subjected to the liability thereby imposed. Moreover, the principle had been recognized that a corporate agent, through whose act, default, or omission the corporation committed a crime, was himself guilty individually of that crime. The principle had been applied whether or not the crime required "consciousness of wrongdoing", and it had been applied not only to those corporate agents who themselves committed the criminal act, but also to those who by virtue of their managerial positions or other similar relation to the actor could be deemed responsible for its commission.

In the latter class of cases, the liability of managerial officers did not depend on their knowledge of, or personal participation in, the act made criminal by the statute. Rather, where the statute under which they were prosecuted dispensed with "consciousness of wrongdoing", and omission or failure to act was deemed a sufficient basis for a responsible corporate agent's liability. It was enough in such cases that, by virtue of the relationship he bore to the corporation, the agent had the power to have prevented the act complained of. * * *

Thus *Dotterweich* and the cases which have followed reveal that in providing sanctions which reach and touch the individuals who execute the corporate mission—and this is by no means necessarily confined to a single corporate agent or employee—the Act imposes not only a positive duty to seek out and remedy violations when they occur but also, and primarily, a duty to implement measures that will insure that violations will not occur. The requirements of foresight and vigilance imposed on responsible corporate agents are beyond question demanding, and perhaps onerous, but they are no more stringent than the public has a right to expect of those who voluntarily assume positions of authority in business enterprises whose services and products affect the health and well-being of the public that supports them.

The Act does not, as we observed in *Dotterweich,* make criminal liability turn on "awareness of some wrongdoing" or "conscious fraud". The duty imposed by Congress on responsible corporate agents is, we emphasize, one that requires the highest standard of foresight and vigilance, but the Act, in its criminal aspect, does not require that which is objectively impossible. The theory upon which responsible

corporate agents are held criminally accountable for "causing" violations of the Act permits a claim that a defendant was "powerless" to prevent or correct the violation to "be raised defensively at a trial on the merits." If such a claim is made, the defendant has the burden of coming forward with evidence, but this does not alter the Government's ultimate burden of proving beyond a reasonable doubt the defendant's guilt, including his power, in light of the duty imposed by the Act, to prevent or correct the prohibited condition. Congress has seen fit to enforce the accountability of responsible corporate agents dealing with products which may affect the health of consumers by penal sanctions cast in rigorous terms, and the obligation of the courts is to give them effect so long as they do not violate the Constitution.

We cannot agree with the Court of Appeals that it was incumbent upon the District Court to instruct the jury that the Government had the burden of establishing "wrongful action" in the sense in which the Court of Appeals used that phrase. The concept of a "responsible relationship" to, or a "responsible share" in, a violation of the Act indeed imports some measure of blameworthiness; but it is equally clear that the Government establishes a prima facie case when it introduces evidence sufficient to warrant a finding by the trier of the facts that the defendant had, by reason of his position in the corporation, responsibility and authority either to prevent in the first instance, or promptly to correct, the violation complained of, and that he failed to do so. The failure thus to fulfill the duty imposed by the interaction of the corporate agent's authority and the statute furnishes a sufficient causal link. The considerations which prompted the imposition of this duty, and the scope of the duty, provide the measure of culpability. * * *

Reading the entire charge satisfies us that the jury's attention was adequately focused on the issue of respondent's authority with respect to the conditions that formed the basis of the alleged violations. Viewed as a whole, the charge did not permit the jury to find guilt solely on the basis of respondent's position in the corporation; rather, it fairly advised the jury that to find guilt it must find respondent "had a responsible relation to the situation," and "by virtue of his position * * * had authority and responsibility" to deal with the situation. The situation referred to could only be "food * * * held in unsanitary conditions in a warehouse with the result that it consisted, in part, of filth or * * * may have been contaminated with filth." * * *

We conclude that, viewed as a whole and in the context of the trial, the charge was not misleading and contained an adequate statement of the law to guide the jury's determination. Although it would have been better to give an instruction more precisely relating the legal issue to the facts of the case, we cannot say that the failure to provide the amplification requested by respondent was an abuse of discretion. Finally, we note that there was no request for an instruction that the Government was required to prove beyond a reasonable doubt that respondent was not without the power or capacity to affect the conditions which founded the charges in the information.[17] In light of the evidence adduced at trial, we find no basis to conclude that the failure of the trial court to give such an instruction *sua sponte* was

plain error or a defect affecting substantial rights. * * *

Respondent testified in his defense that he had employed a system in which he relied upon his subordinates, and that he was ultimately responsible for this system. He testified further that he had found these subordinates to be "dependable" and had "great confidence" in them. By this and other testimony respondent evidently sought to persuade the jury that, as the president of a large corporation, he had no choice but to delegate duties to those in whom he reposed confidence, that he had no reason to suspect his subordinates were failing to insure compliance with the Act, and that, once violations were unearthed, acting through those subordinates he did everything possible to correct them.

Although we need not decide whether this testimony would have entitled respondent to an instruction as to his lack of power had he requested it,[19] the testimony clearly created the "need" for rebuttal evidence. [Thus, it was not error, as the Court of Appeals had believed, to admit into evidence the fact that the respondent had been advised in 1970 of insanitary conditions in the *Philadelphia* warehouse.]

Reversed.

MR. JUSTICE STEWART, with whom MR. JUSTICE MARSHALL and MR. JUSTICE POWELL join, dissenting.

The trial judge instructed the jury to find Park guilty if it found beyond a reasonable doubt that Park "had a responsible relation to the situation * * *. The issue is, in this case, whether the Defen-

---

17. Counsel for respondent submitted only two requests for charge: (1) "Statutes such as the ones the Government seeks to apply here are criminal statutes and should be strictly construed," and (2) "The fact that John Park is President and Chief Executive Officer of Acme Markets, Inc. does not of itself justify a finding of guilty under Counts I through V of the Information."

19. Assuming, *arguendo,* that it would be objectively impossible for a senior corporate agent to control fully day-to-day conditions in 874 retail outlets, it does not follow that such a corporate agent could not prevent or remedy promptly violations of elementary sanitary conditions in 16 regional warehouses.

dant, John R. Park, by virtue of his position in the company, had a position of authority and responsibility in the situation out of which these charges arose." Requiring, as it did, a verdict of guilty upon a finding of "responsibility," this instruction standing alone could have been construed as a direction to convict if the jury found Park "responsible" for the condition in the sense that his position as chief executive officer gave him formal responsibility within the structure of the corporation. But the trial judge went on specifically to caution the jury not to attach such a meaning to his instruction, saying that "the fact that the Defendant is present [*sic*] and is a chief executive officer of the Acme Markets does not require a finding of guilt." "Responsibility" as used by the trial judge therefore had whatever meaning the jury in its unguided discretion chose to give it.

The instructions, therefore, expressed nothing more than a tautology. They told the jury: "You must find the defendant guilty if you find that he is to be held accountable for this adulterated food." In other words: "You must find the defendant guilty if you conclude that he is guilty." * * *

We deal here with a criminal conviction, not a civil forfeiture. It is true that the crime was but a misdemeanor and the penalty in this case light. But under the statute even a first conviction can result in imprisonment for a year, and a subsequent offense is a felony carrying a punishment of up to three years in prison. So the standardless conviction approved today can serve in another case tomorrow to support a felony conviction and a substantial prison sentence. However highly the Court may regard the social objectives of the Food, Drug, and Cosmetic Act, that regard cannot serve to justify a criminal conviction so wholly alien to fundamental principles of our law.

The *Dotterweich* case stands for two propositions, and I accept them both. First, "any person" within the meaning of 21 U.S.C. § 333 may include any corporate officer or employee "standing in responsible relation" to a condition or transaction forbidden by the Act. Second, a person may be convicted of a criminal offense under the Act even in the absence of "the conventional requirement for criminal conduct—awareness of some wrongdoing."

But before a person can be convicted of a criminal violation of this Act, a jury must find—and must be clearly instructed that it must find—evidence beyond a reasonable doubt that he engaged in wrongful conduct amounting at least to common-law negligence. There were no such instructions, and clearly, therefore, no such finding in this case.

For these reasons, I cannot join the Court in affirming Park's criminal conviction.

Notes and Questions

1. Would the Court have reached the same result if Park had received the more serious penalties allowed under the Act? Consider in this regard a survey of the reported decisions in the 32-year period between *Dotterweich* and *Park*, O'Keefe & Shapiro, *Personal Criminal Liability Under the Federal Food, Drug, and Cosmetic Act,* 30 Food Drug Cosm.L.J. 5, 18–19 (1975), noting: "Jail sentences, terms of probation, and criminal fines have been imposed, all without the necessity of proof of *scienter,* and in situations where persons other than the convicted defendant performed the violative acts. In one case, a jail sentence was imposed although the offense charged related to economic misbranding, without risk to public health or safety. In another case, the court ruled that intent was not a necessary element, even for conviction of a felony under the Act."

2. Is the availability of criminal sanctions for corporate officers an essential part of the enforcement machinery under the Act, or would criminal liability on the corporation suffice? Compare:

(a) Cohen, *Enforcement Under the Food, Drug and Cosmetic Act—The Park Case in Perspective,* 30 Food Drug Cosm.L.J. 676, 681 (1975): "Del Monte cannot go to jail. General Mills cannot go to jail. Pillsbury cannot go to jail. Acme Markets cannot go to jail. All four could absorb sizable fines: their financial losses, if any, are in any case borne by the stockholders rather than by the corporate officials who bear ultimate responsibility for the firm's compliance with laws written to protect the consumer. But the fear of being branded a criminal—even though I doubt John Park is a social outcast because of his misdemeanor conviction—and the mere possibility, albeit remote, of a prison term, strikes terror in executive hearts, creating a potent deterrent for which civil sanctions and criminal sanctions against the corporation alone cannot substitute. The mere existence of this sanction helps to create the desired behavior of full compliance with the Act."

(b) McVisk, *Toward a Rational Theory of Criminal Liability for the Corporate Executive,* 69 J.Crim.L. & C. 75, 88 (1978): "By imposing vague and seemingly arbitrary standards of conduct, enforced by criminal sanctions, the Court's doctrine may well discourage responsible people from taking jobs in highly regulated industries. The long run result may be less careful operation of these businesses. Because the Court's system of liability does not specifically provide a defense for individual officers who have taken reasonable steps to prevent violations from occurring, it fails to provide adequate incentive to take these steps. Further, because the standards imposed seem arbitrary and impossible to fulfill, judges are likely to refuse to use the sanction of imprisonment and will proba-

bly impose very light fines, thus reducing the effectiveness of the regulation still further. Most importantly, the Court has failed to provide any clear direction which would guide corporate officials in their attempts to comply with the law."

3. Does *Park* include a requirement of culpability, or does it impose strict liability? Compare the views of the following two commentators (who also disagree about many other aspects of *Park*):

(a) Abrams, *Criminal Liability of Corporate Officers for Strict Liability Offenses—A Comment on Dotterweich and Park,* 28 U.C. L.A.L.Rev. 463, 469–70 (1981): "Most courts are likely to agree with Justice Stewart—who in dissent characterized the Chief Justice's opinion as embodying a negligence standard—and conclude that *Park* supports the imposition of criminal liability only where there is a departure from a standard of care. Certainly the Burger opinion is also replete with language which smacks of negligence—'the defendant's . . . power, in light of the duty imposed by the Act, to prevent or correct . . . some measure of blameworthiness . . . the scope of the duty, provide[s] the measure of culpability.' * * *

"Given language that speaks of 'the highest standard of foresight' and that which is not 'objectively impossible', the most plausible interpretation is that the culpability standard thereby established is one of extraordinary care. Under this view, all that must be proved by the government is a deviation from that standard—something certainly less than common law negligence; it can be characterized as 'very slight' or 'slight' negligence to be distinguished from 'ordinary' negligence."

(b) Brickey, *Criminal Liability of Corporate Officers for Strict Liability Offenses—Another View,* 35 Vand.L.Rev. 1337, 1363–64 (1982): "The Chief Justice explained that proof that the officer had the responsibility and the power to prevent the violation and that he failed to fulfill the duty to do so establishes the required causal link between the officer and the violation. Thus, while a corporate officer cannot be blamed for a violation unless he is factually connected with it, the prosecution may establish the required factual connection without also proving a culpable state of mind.

"That the Court did not intend its reference to blameworthiness in this passage to connote any requirement of a culpable mental state is reinforced by its explicit rejection, in the same passage, of the Fourth Circuit's position regarding the Government's burden of proof. The court of appeals had stated that Park could not be found guilty unless the Government established 'some wrongful action' on his part."

4. FDA agents inspected a food storage warehouse on the island of Maui, Hawaii, in May and June of 1972. They discovered that birds were flying in and out of the warehouse, perching on overhead sprinkler pipes and on bags of rice, and eating from rice bags. The corporation and its president were charged with violating the Federal Food, Drug and Cosmetic Act. The evidence showed that the president had been aware of the bird infestation problem as early as August 1971, and that numerous devices to prevent birds from gaining entry to the warehouse had been tried, but none of them was completely successful. In the spring of 1972, it was decided to enclose the food storage area of the warehouse in a huge wire cage. The materials necessary to do this were ordered from the mainland, but they had not been received by the time of the inspections. Both the corporation and the president have asked for an "objective impossibility" instruction, but the govern-

ment contends "that the defense is available only to the corporate officer and not to the corporation itself, and applies only when the officer was in fact powerless to prevent or correct the violation, even by suspending the corporation's food warehousing activity if necessary." [a] Should the judge give the instruction?

5. Sometimes an officer or employee will escape liability because the statute in question is construed as being applicable only to the organization he serves. Illustrative is *State v. Riley,* 158 W.Va. 823, 215 S.E.2d 460 (1975), overturning the conviction of truck drivers, employees of a motor carrier, found not to have the required identification card displayed in their vehicles. Noting that the statute said it "shall be unlawful for any motor carrier to operate any power unit within this State unless such identification card is displayed" (in contrast to another part of the same statute making it "unlawful for the motor carrier, his agent, servant, or employee, or any other person to use or display said identification card" after it had expired), the court concluded: "The appellants as mere employees do not come within the definition of 'motor carrier' and thus could not be prosecuted individually for failure to display the required identification card."

Similarly, in *Day v. State,* 168 Ind.App. 68, 341 N.E.2d 209 (1976), the court held that the president of a professional association which employed a lobbyist could not be convicted of failing to file an expense statement within a specified time, as the statute imposed that duty on the "person, firm, corporation or association employing legislative counsel or legislative agents." The court concluded that the "statute clearly imposes the duty on the association as a separate entity—not on the officers or members of the association."

---

a. See *United States v. Y. Hata & Co., Ltd.,* 535 F.2d 508 (9th Cir.1976), affirming the convictions.

Can these cases be squared with *Park?* In light of the fact, as we saw earlier, that a person may be an accomplice to a crime he cannot commit directly, are these decisions correct? Is it significant that there was no showing that the truck drivers knew they were driving without the permits, or that the association president knew the expense statement had not been filed? What if such knowledge had been established?

6. If a person has engaged in conduct which would otherwise suffice for personal criminal liability, it is no defense that he was acting on behalf of a corporation. Illustrative is *People v. Cheff,* 37 Mich.App. 1, 194 N.W.2d 401 (1971), where the defendant, president of a mortgage corporation, obtained money under false pretenses with intent to defraud. The court held: "Even though the money was received and misappropriated by the corporation, the scheme for acquisition of the funds was a fraudulent act perpetrated by Mr. Cheff, the president and principal officer of the corporation. Thus, in the light of the generally recognized principle that a corporate officer is criminally responsible for the fraudulent larceny of the property of another through a corporate act where the act was done by the individual officer, at his discretion, or by his permission, it was no defense here that the money was paid to the corporation and not to the defendant, Cheff, personally."

SECTION 11. POST–CRIME AID

STEPHENS v. STATE

Supreme Court of Wyoming, 1987.
734 P.2d 555.

BROWN, CHIEF JUSTICE.

This is an appeal from a conviction of accessory after the fact to the commission of a burglary. The issues raised by appellant are whether or not there was sufficient evidence of the element of "rendering assistance" and of the element of "intent" to sustain the conviction. We hold that there was not sufficient evidence of either element, and reverse the conviction.

On December 1, 1985, appellant was at his ex-wife's residence with Harry Van Buren. Appellant agreed to let Van Buren stay with him that evening and in return Van Buren agreed to help appellant look for a part for appellant's truck the following morning. Appellant left the house about three o'clock that afternoon, while Van Buren remained. The next time appellant saw Van Buren was about 8:00 that evening. At that time, Van Buren informed appellant and appellant's girl friend that he had burglarized Yellowstone Electric hours earlier. Appellant told Van Buren he "didn't want to hear about it." The next morning appellant and his girlfriend awoke to find Van Buren gone. He returned around 7:30 a.m., and went with appellant to look for the truck part, as previously arranged.

When appellant was unable to find the truck part he needed he asked Van Buren to give him some money to purchase a car. Van Buren complied, giving appellant $100. Thereafter, an automobile was purchased and the two traveled back to the home, appellant driving the recently purchased car while Van Buren drove the truck. Upon arriving home, appellant noticed that Van Buren, having arrived home already, was being questioned by police officers in a police car. Subsequently, appellant was approached by the police officers.

When the officers questioned appellant about the burglary and Van Buren's possible role in it, appellant replied that he did not know anything about it. Upon further questioning, appellant informed the officers that a few years earlier he had received money from Van Buren from a similar burglary. Appellant told the officers that he had learned his lesson after the earlier burglary and would not get involved in that situation again.

About fifteen minutes later the police confronted appellant with some information they had received from his girlfriend, and appellant then admitted that he knew of the burglary and of Van Buren's role in it. Appellant also told the officers that he had told Van Buren he did not want to know about it.

The statute under which appellant was convicted reads, in part:

"(a) A person is an accessory after the fact if, with intent to hinder, delay or prevent the discovery, detection, apprehension, prosecution, detention, conviction or punishment of another for the commission of a crime, he renders assistance to the person * * *."

The two elements that appellant contends are missing are the elements of intent and rendering assistance.

"Render assistance" is defined in § 6–5–201 as follows:

"(a) As used in this article:

" * * *

"(iv) 'Render assistance' means to:

"(A) Harbor or conceal the person;

"(B) Warn the person of impending discovery or apprehension, excluding an official warning given in an effort to bring the person into compliance with the law;

" * * *

"(D) By force, intimidation or deception, obstruct anyone in the performance of any act which might aid in the discovery, detection, apprehension, prosecution, conviction or punishment of the person."

The state contends that appellant rendered assistance by harboring or concealing Van Buren and by helping Van Buren to avoid discovery and apprehension. The facts that the state relies on are that appel-lant provided Van Buren a place to stay the night after the burglary and that he denied knowledge of Van Buren's involvement in the burglary. Case law from other jurisdictions does not support this argument.

In the case of *State v. Clifford,* 263 Or. 436, 502 P.2d 1371 (1972), the defendant saw Douglas Wright a day after Wright murdered two people and kidnapped a five-year-old boy. After learning of the murder, defendant was arrested on other charges and asked by the police if he had seen Wright. Defendant told the police either that he had not seen Wright, or that he had not seen him in a long time. The Oregon Supreme Court, after reciting the common-law history of the offense of being an accessory after the fact, concluded that there was no sharp line between conduct which constituted aiding or concealing and that which does not. However, some type of line may be drawn from examples given.

" * * * The examples describing criminal conduct uniformly consist of an affirmative act from which the intention to aid an offender, to escape arrest, conviction or punishment is obvious. None of the examples indicate that a mere denial of knowledge of the whereabouts of an offender at some time in the past would amount to accessorial conduct."

Furthermore, other cases uniformly support the conclusion reached by the Oregon Supreme Court, that is, merely denying knowledge of the principal's involvement in a crime will not give rise to a charge of accessory after the fact. A mere denial of knowledge is to be differentiated from an "[a]ffirmative statement of facts tending to raise any defense for (the principal), or a statement within itself indicating an effort to shield or protect (the principal)." Such an affirmative statement would be such as supplying a false alibi. This amounts to more than passive nondisclosure.

In the case here, appellant did nothing more than passively deny knowledge of Van Buren's involvement in the burglary. When finally confronted by the statement made by his girlfriend, appellant relented and told the police what he really knew. This does not rise to the level of helping Van Buren avoid discovery and detection, especially in light of appellant's probable intent, which will be discussed later.

Further, we question whether appellant actually harbored Van Buren. Again, case law supports appellant. Here, the distinction is between active concealment and merely allowing a person to stay in one's home. This distinction is examined in the case of *United States v. Bissonette*, 586 F.2d 73 (8th Cir.1978). There, the defendant kept several juveniles, including her grandson, in her basement following a shooting and jail break, of which she was aware. "She [the defendant] told [the juveniles] and the others to stay in the basement when she was out of the house, to keep the doors locked, and the blinds drawn. In the following days, she purchased food and cooked for [the juveniles] and cashed a check for [her grandson.]"

The federal court found that the defendant's conduct went beyond merely offering the juveniles the comforts of her home. " * * * [s]he instructed the fugitives to stay in the basement when she was out of the house, to keep the blinds drawn, and the doors locked; she berated them when they tried to contact friends outside the house, lest their discovery result." This all resulted in an affirmative, continuing pattern of conduct establishing the intent of the defendant to prevent apprehension of her grandson by the authorities.

The *Bissonette* case is far different than the case before us. Here, appellant had agreed to let Van Buren spend the night at his home. This agreement was made before appellant had any knowledge of a burglary. Further, appellant did not keep Van Buren concealed, but rather, was accompanied by him in public to look for a truck part, and then to purchase a car. There was no active concealment.

Appellant also contends there was insufficient evidence of intent to uphold his conviction. The requisite intent, from a plain reading of the statute, is to hinder, prevent or delay the discovery or apprehension, etc., of the principal. Once more, case law is in appellant's favor.

"If, however, the act is a mere false denial of knowledge which may have been motivated by self-interest, there must also be evidence from which the jury could infer that the actor told the lie with the intent to aid the offender and that the lie was, under the existing circumstances, likely to aid the offender to escape arrest or punishment. * * *"

The intent evident from the testimony presented at trial was clearly self-motivated. First, Van Buren had already been apprehended by the police when they questioned appellant. Second, appellant knew that he was guilty himself of receiving stolen property (the $100 that Van Buren gave him to buy a car). Further, appellant knew that four years ago when an almost identical situation arose, he ended up with a felony on his record and a two to four year sentence, suspended, with four years probation. Appellant certainly had plenty of self-interest in denying any knowledge of Van Buren's activities in the present instance. Further, no other evidence presented at trial indicated any intent of appellant to benefit Van Buren.

The standard of review with respect to the sufficiency of the evidence is that we examine the evidence in a light most favorable to the state to determine if there is sufficient evidence to uphold the verdict. Even when we apply this standard, we are unable to find evidence sufficient to uphold appellant's conviction, either on the element of intent or of rendering assistance.

The conviction is reversed and the charge of accessory after the fact is dismissed.

Notes and Questions

1. In *Commonwealth v. Devlin*, 366 Mass. 132, 314 N.E.2d 897 (1974), defendant was convicted of being an accessory after the fact [a] to assault with intent to murder. Bartoloni stabbed another inmate in block B–2 of the state prison. Defendant, also an inmate, then entered the block, asked what had happened, was summoned to cell No. 3 as the block representative, and was told a knife had been kicked into the cell. Defendant picked up the knife with a T-shirt, apparently rubbed it with the shirt, and then handed it over to a guard. The court reversed:

"1. We assume, although we need not so decide, that the evidence was sufficient to show that the actions of the defendant constituted aid to the principal felon, presumably by removing his fingerprints from the knife. However, we do not believe there was sufficient evidence that the defendant either knew that a felony had been committed, or that he knew the identity of the principal felon, to warrant submission of the case to the jury. The record does not indicate that the blood later shown by chemical tests to have been present on the knife was visible to the defendant. Even assuming that it was, the Commonwealth presented no testimony that would indicate the defendant knew how the knife had been used. While mere possession of the knife was no doubt a violation of prison regulations, and even assuming it was a crime, it was certainly not a felony to which the defendant could have been an accessory after the fact. The defendant's own testimony was that he was not present when the disturbance began and was inquiring of other inmates as to what had occurred when he was called to the scene of his alleged crime. It would be mere speculation to conclude that he had learned of the felony or such details as who had committed it.

"We hold that knowledge of the particular felony which has occurred is an element of the crime of being an accessory after the fact which must be proved beyond a reasonable doubt. That is to say, one charged as such an accessory must be shown to have been aware, by his observations or by information transmitted to him, of the substantial facts of the felonious crime.[4] Since there was a failure to prove that knowledge in this case, a directed verdict for the defendant is required.

"2. The accessory after the fact must also be shown to have had knowledge of the identity of the principal felon. There was not the slightest showing here that the defendant was aware that the principal, Bartoloni, was concerned in the matter.

a. The applicable statute reads: "Whoever, after the commission of a felony, harbors, conceals, maintains or assists the principal felon or accessory before the fact, or gives such offender any other aid, knowing that he has committed a felony or has been accessory thereto before the fact, with intent that he shall avoid or escape detention, arrest, trial or punishment, shall be an accessory after the fact, and, except as otherwise provided, be punished by imprisonment in the state prison for not more than seven years or in jail for not more than two and one half years or by a fine of not more than one thousand dollars. The fact that the defendant is the husband or wife, or by consanguinity, affinity or adoption, the parent or grandparent, child or grandchild, brother or sister of the offender, shall be a defence to a prosecution under this section. If such a defendant testifies solely as to the existence of such relationship, he shall not be subject to cross examination on any other subject matter, nor shall his criminal record, if any, except for perjury or subornation of perjury, be admissible to impeach his credibility."

4. There is no suggestion here that the knowledge of the accessory must be such that he is able to put a name or label on the felony—only that he is aware of the substantial facts which make up the elements of the felony.

For that reason too, the defendant must have a directed verdict.

"Since there is total absence of knowledge here, we need not reach discussion of the minimum evidence which might be required to establish sufficient knowledge of identity. Nor need we discuss the nature of such proof.[5]

"The common law emphasized, as a basis for liability, the personal relationship between principal and accessory. In fact, the accessory was often considered 'an accomplice in the original crime.' The accessory was defined by his direct, personal assistance as one who receives and comforts, or conceals the principal felon. This assistance could be provided in a variety of ways: '[G]enerally, any assistance whatever given to a felon, to hinder his being apprehended, tried, or suffering punishment, makes the assistor an accessory. As furnishing him with a horse to escape his pursuers, money or victuals to support him, a house or other shelter to conceal him, or open force and violence to rescue or protect him.' 4 Blackstone, *Commentaries,* 37–38 (1769).

"The requirement that relief or assistance be given to the felon personally is also illustrated by the common law doctrine that one could never be convicted as an accessory after the fact for receiving stolen goods 'because he only received the stolen goods and did nothing to receive the felon.' This crime is, of course, now separately provided for by statute.

"A proper interpretation of G.L. c. 274, § 4, also demands incorporation of this knowledge requirement. The language of the statute is in the common law form. The words themselves require aid to the principal felon 'knowing that he has committed a felony.' The plain meaning of these words requires knowledge of the identity of the principal. * * *

"3. In summary, it is clear that there was insufficient proof of the requisite elements of the statutory crime charged in the indictment. It may be considered that the defendant's acts constituted what is in some jurisdictions called 'obstruction of justice.' He was not so charged and therefore we need not consider whether such a common law crime exists in Massachusetts."

2. *United States v. Hobson,* 519 F.2d 765 (9th Cir.1975): "Both Hobson and Newman were convicted of being accessories after the fact, in violation of 18 U.S.C. § 3 which provides in part:

'Whoever, knowing that an offense against the United States has been committed, receives, relieves, comforts or assists the offender in order to hinder or prevent his apprehension, trial or punishment is an accessory after the fact. * * *'

They contend that in order for them to have violated the statute they must be shown to have known that Beaty's escape (and shooting of the guard) constituted an offense *against the United States.* The district court rejected Hobson's proposed instruction to this effect and refused to grant a judgment of acquittal. The district court was correct in both rulings.

"Beaty was clearly guilty of escape. He has been convicted and sentenced to life imprisonment for that escape. There is no requirement that he had to have known that he was committing a federal offense in escaping. *See United States v. Fernandez,* 497 F.2d 730, 736–739 (9 Cir.1974). It borders on the ridiculous to suggest that Hobson and Newman could be acquitted, despite knowledge that they were aiding Beaty in hiding from the authorities, be-

---

5. For example, suppose a defendant witnessed the flight of a robber, who was a stranger to him, whereupon the defendant wilfully impeded pursuit of the robber by a police officer. Is this sufficient knowledge by the defendant as to the identity of the felon?

LaFave—Mod.Crim.Law, 2nd Ed. ACB—28

cause they thought he had *only* committed murder and escape from a *State* prison. In fact, the Supreme Court has recently rejected just such a contention with respect to a conspiracy prosecution. *See United States v. Feola,* [p. 623 of this Book]."

Is this so?

3. In *United States v. Prescott,* 581 F.2d 1343 (9th Cir.1978), federal agents sought to arrest Duvernay, but found his apartment padlocked from the outside. They then asked defendant, a neighbor, if Duvernay was in her apartment. She said no, and the agents then asked permission to search her apartment. She asked if they had a warrant, they said no, and she then refused to admit them. The agents kicked down the door and found Duvernay inside. On reversal of defendant's accessory after the fact conviction, the court held that upon retrial defendant's refusal to admit the police should not be admitted into evidence because under the Fourth Amendment one has a constitutional right to refuse to consent to a search:

"One cannot be penalized for passively asserting this right, regardless of one's motivation. Just as a criminal suspect may validly invoke his Fifth Amendment privilege in an effort to shield himself from criminal liability, so one may withhold consent to a warrantless search, even though one's purpose be to conceal evidence of wrongdoing.

"Had Prescott forcibly resisted the entry into her apartment, we might have a different case. We express no opinion on that question. We only hold that her passive refusal to consent to a warrantless search is privileged conduct which cannot be considered as evidence of criminal wrongdoing. If the government could use such a refusal against the citizen, an unfair and impermissible burden would be placed upon the assertion of a constitutional right and future consents would not be 'freely and voluntarily given.' "

A dissent reasoned that the refusal did have evidentiary significance and that defendant was merely entitled to a jury instruction that "assertion of Fourth Amendment rights, even if without foundation, cannot constitute the crime with which the defendant is charged."

4. Carullo and Johnston stole gold coins in Mission, Kansas, and transported them to Kansas City, Missouri, and then to Kansas City, Kansas, to Sol's Loan Office, where Balano and Rosen provided them with clothing to replace that used in the crime and a suitcase within which to hide the coins. Balano and Rosen were charged as accessories after the fact to interstate transportation of stolen goods. On appeal of Balano's conviction, *United States v. Balano,* 618 F.2d 624 (10th Cir. 1979), the court stated:

"Balano's argument that Carullo and Johnston were still in the escape phase of their crime when they reached the loan office is similarly without merit. There is no doubt that one who assists in an escape should be charged under 18 U.S.C. § 2 [as a principal] rather than 18 U.S.C. § 3 [as an accessory after the fact]. It is not necessary, however, for the principals to have come to a final resting place for the escape to have ended. The escape phase doctrine was developed to deal with those who are entangled in the consummation of the crime itself, such as getaway car drivers. In contrast, accessories after the fact '[obstruct] justice by rendering assistance to hinder or prevent the arrest of the offender after he has committed the crime.'

"Carullo and Johnston crossed the state line again after leaving Sol's Loan Office, and the sale of the coins took place shortly thereafter. However, sufficient evidence was admitted at Balano's trial to permit the jury to infer that Carullo and Johnston had made prior arrangements to 'fence' the coins at Sol's. Although they did not ultimately fence the coins there, a finding that the events at Sol's were beyond the escape phase is entirely consistent with the testimony of Carullo and Johnston. The getaway car had been abandoned, and no more furtive action was taken. We cannot consider an escape to continue until an ultimate buyer is found. The court's dismissal of the third count, based on 18 U.S.C. § 2, at the end of the first trial was therefore proper, and we cannot say the submission of the second count to the jury was improper."

5. Exemptions along the lines of those stated in the statute applied in *Devlin* are found in most jurisdictions. Compare *Model Penal Code* § 242.3, Comment (1980): "Section 242.3 does not contain a statutory exemption, in part on the ground that this is a factor that can be taken into account at sentencing. It is hard to justify any particular limitation on an exemption provision. Furthermore, exemption rules create trial difficulties if the government bears the burden of proving that none of the specified relations exist."

Assume now a statute with exemptions like those in *Devlin.* Compare *State v. Williams,* 142 Vt. 81, 451 A.2d 1142 (1982) (where defendant's brother, a juvenile not subject to criminal prosecution, and one Bristol together committed a homicide, the defendant could not be convicted as an accessory after the fact because his acts "consisted entirely of deeds helping both his brother and Bristol"); with *State v. Mobbley,* 98 N.M. 557, 650 P.2d 841 (App.1982) (where police told defendant warrants had been issued for Mobbley and Needham and asked if "both were there" and defendant "denied that the men were there, although she knew that both men were there," defendant—the wife of Mobbley—was properly convicted).

6. In *State v. Cole,* 502 S.W.2d 443 (Mo.App.1973), an appeal of defendant's

conviction for armed robbery, defendant noted that the evidence was susceptible to the interpretation that he had not been aware in advance that the passenger in his car would commit the robbery and that thus the trial judge should have given the jury an instruction that they might instead convict him of being an accessory after the fact for his conduct in driving the robber away while being pursued by the police. "Under the evidence he was either guilty as charged or he was not guilty. The crime of accessory after the fact is a distinct and separate offense and not a lesser included offense of Robbery in the First Degree by means of dangerous and deadly weapon. It would therefore have been error for the trial court to instruct on the crime of accessory after the fact."

May the prosecutor *charge* a defendant with both being a principal and an accessory after the fact? See *Thomas v. State,* 275 Ind. 499, 417 N.E.2d 1124 (1981), rejecting the notion a defendant should not have to defend against "two inconsistent theories of prosecution."

7. Most jurisdictions have rejected the old common law view that an accessory after the fact could not be tried until after the principal was found guilty. See, e.g., *State ex rel. Brown v. Thompson,* 149 W.Va. 649, 142 S.E.2d 711 (1965).

But, "the jury in the trial of the accessory must find as a fact that the principal did actually commit the crime involved." *State v. Massey,* 267 S.C. 432, 229 S.E.2d 332 (1976). What then of *State v. Price,* 278 S.C. 266, 294 S.E.2d 426 (1982), where defendant helped conceal the body after her 12–year–old son Randy strangled a playmate, and the court upheld exclusion of testimony that at the time of the killing the son was unconscious due to an epileptic seizure, reasoning that "the defense of Randy's incapacity is not available to appellant" because it "does not constitute a defense to his crime, it only relates to the degree of culpability"?

8. Most jurisdictions prescribe penalties for the accessory after the fact without reference to the penalty attached to the principal offense; five years is the most common maximum, with a range from six months to ten years. See *Osborne v. State,* 304 Md. 323, 499 A.2d 170 (1985).

9. Today, the accessory after the fact situation is dealt with by statute in most jurisdictions. These statutes often retain the accessory terminology, although the more modern approach is to abandon the traditional terminology and to cover the subject by one or more statutes creating such offenses as "hindering prosecution," "obstructing justice," "concealing or aiding a fugitive," "harboring or aiding a felon," "tampering with evidence," and "aiding escape." While some of these statutes do not extend liability beyond that which was possible under the common law accessory after the fact offense, many of them do. In contrast to the common law requirement that the accessory have known that the person aided was a felon, some statutes also cover the case in which the aider only believed that a felony had been committed or had reasonable grounds to believe that a felony had been committed, or where the person aided was in fact a felon. Some of the statutes cover aid to both felons and misdemeanants. In a few states, the mental element has been broadened to include the situation in which the intent is "to assist a person in profiting or benefiting from the commission" of a felony or any crime.

UNITED STATES v. MAGNESS

United States Court of Appeals, Ninth Circuit, 1972.
456 F.2d 976.

PER CURIAM:

Leslie V. Magness appeals from his conviction, after trial without a jury, of con-

cealing Wayland Jean Ballard in order to prevent his apprehension, knowing that a warrant had been issued for Ballard's arrest, in violation of 18 U.S.C. § 1071. The ultimate question presented on appeal is whether the evidence is sufficient to support the finding of guilt. We reverse.

The testimony favorable to the Government is as follows: On December 19, 1970, Magness went to the Cress Motel in the small town of Cabazon, California, and rented Room 7, telling the operator that the room was for some people from out of the state. Magness paid fifteen dollars for a week's rent. On December 22, 1970, a federal warrant for the arrest of Ballard, on a charge of unlawful flight to avoid prosecution for murder, was issued.

About December 26, 1970, Ballard, using the name Wilkins, registered at the Cress Motel as one of the persons for whom Magness had rented Room 7. Magness visited Room 7 several times while Ballard was there. Magness and Ballard were also seen together around town, although Ballard was always introduced as Wilkins. There is, however, no evidence to establish that no one in Cabazon, other than Magness, knew of Ballard's presence; and, in fact, Ballard's girl friend was also in the town during this period.

On January 4, 1971, Federal Bureau of Investigation Special Agent J. Clayton Taylor arrived in Cabazon to investigate whether Ballard was there in hiding. Taylor was accompanied throughout this investigation by several other special agents and law enforcement officers. On January 4, 1971, Taylor spoke to only one person other than defendant about Ballard. That person was a service station attendant who reported that he did not know a Mr. Ballard.

Later on the same day, Taylor spoke to Magness at the latter's home and at that time told Magness about the outstanding federal warrant. Taylor also warned Magness about the federal harboring and concealment statute. When Taylor asked Magness if the latter had been in contact with Ballard, Magness replied that he had known Ballard about twenty years ago in Texas, but had not seen Ballard for many years.

Following this conversation, Taylor and the others with him left Magness' home and proceeded with the investigation elsewhere. Approximately one hour later, Taylor returned to Magness' home and had a second conversation with him. Taylor told Magness that he had new information linking Magness with Ballard. Magness then admitted that he had been in contact with Ballard, and stated that Ballard was at the Oasis Motel, living under the name of Wilkins.

Taylor and the other officers then proceeded to the Oasis Motel but ascertained that Ballard had been living in Room 7 of the adjacent Cress Motel. Upon their arrival at Room 7, they found it unoccupied. The light was on in the bathroom, the coffee pot was still warm, and food was on the table. Agent Taylor put out an all points radio broadcast regarding Ballard and his automobile. Later the same evening Ballard and his girl friend were apprehended about forty or fifty miles south of Indio, California.

The conduct proscribed by 18 U.S.C. § 1071 is harboring or concealing a person for whose arrest a warrant or process has been issued "after notice or knowledge of the fact that a warrant or process has been issued. ∗ ∗ ∗." It follows that none of Magness' conduct prior to January 4, 1971, when he first learned of the outstanding warrant for the arrest of Ballard, could constitute an offense under the statute, although it might throw light

on Magness' conduct after he gained such knowledge.

The Government asserts that, on January 4, 1971, Magness engaged in two acts, each of which constituted a violation of section 1071. The first of these was Magness' false statement to Agent Taylor during their first conversation on that day, that he had known Ballard about twenty years ago in Texas, but had not seen Ballard for many years. Such a false statement, standing alone, however, could not constitute the active conduct of hiding, or secreting contemplated by the statute. *United States v. Foy,* 416 F.2d 940 (7th Cir. 1969).

The other act relied upon by the Government is Magness' asserted conduct in actively warning Ballard about the possibility of impending arrest by F.B.I. agents.

There was no direct evidence that Magness gave such a warning, and the circumstantial evidence of this is, in our opinion, entirely too thin to support the finding of guilt. There is, in this record, no evidence that Ballard had a telephone in his Room 7 at the Cress Motel. While it might be assumed that the operator of the Cress Motel had a telephone, the Government did not call the operator as a witness to ascertain whether Magness telephoned a message to Ballard on January 4, 1971. There is no evidence as to the distance between Magness' residence and the Cress Motel, and therefore proof is lacking that Magness could have personally travelled to the Cress Motel in time to warn Ballard. Under the evidence, the possibility that Ballard had been forewarned by learning, through personal observation or from persons other than Magness,[2] that F.B.I. agents were in town, remains very real.

Under this state of the record we think the showing that Magness warned Ballard on January 4, 1971, is purely speculative

---

2. Such as, for example, Ballard's girl friend who, as noted, was also in town.

and does not support such a finding beyond a reasonable doubt. Indeed, there is nothing in the record to indicate that the trial court made such a finding.

Reversed.

HOLLAND v. STATE

District Court of Appeal of Florida, Second District, 1974.
302 So.2d 806.

McNULTY, CHIEF JUDGE.

Petitioner seeks review by common law certiorari of an order of the Circuit Court of Pinellas County, sitting in its appellate capacity, which reversed the county court's dismissal of an indictment charging petitioner with the crime of "misprision of felony." We grant certiorari and reinstate the order quashing the indictment.

As far as we know or are able to determine, this is the first case in Florida involving the crime of misprision of felony. Such offense is not proscribed by the statutes of Florida, but was a crime at common law. The circuit court order now under review, as did the county court order before it, recognized it as such common law offense and held it to be a "crime under the laws of the State of Florida" pursuant to the provisions of § 775.01, F.S.1971, which declares common law crimes to be of full force in this state in the absence of a specific statute on the subject. We disagree on this fundamental finding and therefore deem it unnecessary to discuss the factual issues which the circuit court considered viable and upon which he predicated his reversal of the court's dismissal of the indictment.

Before continuing further, and to assist in lighting the path we take, we briefly define the offense as it existed at common

law. We will more fully discuss it, *infra;* but for now, let it be said that it was the bare failure of a person with knowledge of the commission of a felony to bring the crime to the attention of the proper authorities.[2]

Now the facts. Petitioner was, at the times material herein, City Manager of the City of Pinellas Park, Florida. On or about the critical date herein, to wit: August 2, 1973, he was attempting to contact his assistant city manager, one Rutherford, and had been unable to do so by telephone. He drove to Rutherford's residence but though Rutherford's car was parked in front he was unable to raise him. He went around to the rear of the house looking for him and, at that time, noticed several plants growing in the rear yard which he suspected to be marijuana. He picked two leaves from two different plants and returned to his office. He contacted one T.W. Kelley, Captain of the Pinellas Park Police Department, to whom he related his findings. The two men then caused the plant samples to be chemically analyzed and their suspicions were confirmed.

Subsequently, Captain Kelley accompanied appellant back to Rutherford's house where they confronted Mr. Rutherford and accused him of the offense of which they suspected he was guilty. After some equivocation Rutherford finally indicated to them his guilt. In Mr. Rutherford's presence, then, appellant and Kelley uprooted a sufficient number of the aforesaid plants to constitute an aggregate of more than five grams of marijuana thus establishing the offense as *felony* possession of marijuana.

Thereafter, appellant requested Rutherford's resignation as assistant city manager,

2. * * * We note here that misprision of felony does exist by statute under Federal law. 18 U.S.C. § 4 (1970). However, this statutory crime of misprision includes the added element of a positive act of concealment. In Florida, this type of behavior is proscribed by §§ 776.03 and 843.14, F.S.1971, which respectively condemn such conduct as "accessory after the fact" or "compounding a felony."

which Rutherford submitted, and then both appellant and Captain Kelley contacted Pinellas Park Police Chief Ernest Van Horn to whom they related all of the foregoing. The decision was then made by appellant, and concurred in by Chief Van Horn and Captain Kelley, that the matter would be handled administratively as an internal affair, that they would avoid unfavorable publicity and dishonor to the City of Pinellas Park and that, to preclude further dishonor and disgrace to Rutherford and his family, no criminal prosecution would ensue.

Within several days thereafter appellant related the entire incident, together with a full disclosure of the decision aforesaid, to three city councilmen, the city clerk, six high level city officials, four lower level city officials, one newspaper editor, one newspaper reporter and one prominent clergyman of the city. Each of these seventeen persons filed an identical affidavit herein in which he acknowledges his full and complete knowledge of the matter and each of whom made the following sworn statement:

> "Douglas J. Holland * * * advised me what action was taken in this matter, at which time I told him in effect that I felt he had taken the appropriate steps and agreed that this was good so as to avoid unfavorable publicity and dishonor to the City of Pinellas Park and to further avoid any dishonor to Rutherford's career and disgrace and serious harm to his family. I certainly felt that we should not proceed to cause the arrest of Mr. Rutherford."

As hereinabove noted, we chose to decide this case on the fundamental issue of whether misprision of felony is a crime in Florida. We parenthetically insert here, however, that had we not so chosen it is difficult to conclude from the foregoing facts, which are not in dispute, that appellant Holland failed to bring knowledge of the commission of a felony to the "proper authorities" or was guilty of concealing such knowledge in any respect.

In any case, we now get on to the merits of the question we decide today. We begin by pointing out that almost every state in the United States has adopted the Common Law of England to some extent. Many of these states have done so by constitutional or statutory provisions similar to ours. But the nearly universal interpretation of such provisions is that they adopt the common law of England only to the extent that such laws are consistent with the existing physical and social conditions in the country or in the given state.

* * *

With the foregoing as a predicate, we now consider the history of the crime of misprision of felony and whether the reasons therefor have ceased to exist, if indeed they ever did exist, in this country. The origin of the crime is well described in 8 U. of Chi.L.Rev. 338, as follows:

> "[M]isprision of felony as defined by Blackstone is merely one phase of the system of communal responsibility for the apprehension of criminals which received its original impetus from William I, under pressure of the need to protect the invading Normans in hostile country, and which endured up to the Seventeenth Century in England. In order to secure vigilant prosecution of criminal conduct, the vill or hundred in which such conduct occurred was subject to fine, as was the tithing to which the criminal belonged, and every person who knew of the felony and failed to make report thereof was subject to punishment for misprision of felony. Compulsory membership in the tithing group, the obligation to pursue criminals when the hue and cry was raised, broad powers of private arrest, and the periodic visitations of the General Eyre for the purpose of penalizing

laxity in regard to crime, are all suggestive of the administrative background against which misprision of felony developed. With the appearance of specialized and paid law enforcement officers, such as constables and justices of the peace in the Seventeenth Century, there was a movement away from strict communal responsibility, and a growing tendency to rely on professional police * * *."

In short the initial reason for the existence of misprision of felony as a crime at common law was to aid an alien, dictorial sovereign in his forcible subjugation of England's inhabitants. Enforcement of the crime was summary, harsh and oppressive; and commentators note that most prosecutors in this country long ago recognized the inapplicability or obsolescence of the law and its harshness in their contemporary society by simply not charging people with that crime. This very case, in fact, serves well to illustrate the potential mischief of the charge and the possible discriminatory, oppressive or absurd results thereof. For example, should not Captain Kelley have been indicted too? Or Chief Van Horn? And if not, why only Holland? Or, perhaps, should not the three city councilmen have been indicted? Or the city clerk? Or the other city officials, the newspaper people or the clergyman in their turn? Should there be fully nineteen indictments herein, or any given lesser number, when for aught we know the principal felon hasn't even been charged?

Many courts faced with this issue have also found, though with varying degrees of clarity, that the reasons for the proscription of this crime do not exist. Moreover, as early as 1822 in this country Chief Justice John Marshall stated in *Marbury v. Brooks:* [8]

8. 20 U.S. (7 Wheat.) 556, 575–576, 5 L.Ed. 522.

"It may be the duty of a citizen to accuse every offender, and to proclaim every offense which comes to his knowledge; but the law which would punish him in every case, for not performing this duty, is too harsh for man."
* * *

We agree with Chief Justice Marshall and with the above cases and commentaries that the crime of misprision of felony is wholly unsuited to American criminal law. While it may be desirable, even essential, that we encourage citizens to "get involved" to help reduce crime, they ought not be adjudicated criminals themselves if they don't. The fear of such a consequence is a fear from which our traditional concepts of peace and quietude guarantee freedom. We cherish the right to mind our own business when our own best interests dictate. Accordingly, we hold that misprision of felony has not been adopted into, and is not a part of, Florida substantive law. * * *

Notes and Questions

1. Compare Goldberg, *Misprision of Felony: An Old Concept in a New Context,* 52 A.B.A.J. 148, 149–50 (1966): "The Supreme Court of Vermont in 1907 defined the offense in its traditional sense:

Misprision of felony is * * * a criminal neglect either to prevent a felony from being committed or to bring the offender to justice after its commission, but without such previous concert with or subsequent assistance of him as will make the concealer an accessory before or after the fact.

"Thus defined, misprision of felony would be a very salutary influence in our distressed society. If limited by its terms to serious crimes, perhaps only serious crimes against the person, few injustices are likely to result. Then Chief Justice

Marshall's concern * * * need not deter legislators from passing a much-needed law. In the case which elicited Marshall's compassion, the defendant had advanced money to his son-in-law in an attempt to save him from the consequences of forgery. The law which would punish such behavior and even require a man to report his family's peculations to the police *is* too harsh. Restricting the operation of the law to serious crimes (and perhaps exempting certain degrees of consanguinity) ought to remove this objection.

"Exceptions must also be made for conflicting legal duties. A lawyer is legally obliged not to divulge information confidentially revealed to him by his client regarding a committed felony. Nor may a doctor broadcast his patient's confidential communications, nor a clergyman his parishioner's. Misprision of felony statutes must allow for these obligations to be respected without fear of lawbreaking.

"It may finally be objected that a legal duty to report criminal acts to the authorities would be so novel in most American jurisdictions that even responsible citizens would unavoidably break the law. But all Americans are familiar with their legal duty to report serious traffic accidents to the police. It is about time we consider violent assault on persons as important as automobile crashes."

2. In *United States v. Kuh*, 541 F.2d 672 (7th Cir.1976), a complaint was initially filed against Kuh and Rea for violation of 18 U.S.C.A. § 2113(c),[a] but the grand jury instead indicted them for violation of the misprision of felony statute, 18 U.S.C.A. § 4.[b] Upon their motion to dismiss, the United States attorney indicated

the evidence would be that they had buried money taken in a bank robbery. In affirming the dismissal, the court of appeals, after noting "that the defendants could reasonably apprehend that they had violated § 2113(c)," concluded that prosecution was barred by the Fifth Amendment privilege against self-incrimination:

"The privilege guaranteed by the Fifth Amendment not only extends to statements that would in themselves support a conviction but likewise embraces those which would furnish a 'link in the chain of evidence' that could lead to prosecution, provided that the individual has reasonable cause to fear he might thereby be convicted of the crime. An effort to use the misprision statute against persons who have knowingly possessed, received, and concealed the proceeds of a bank robbery clearly raises a serious Fifth Amendment question.

"The Government insists that *United States v. Daddano*, 432 F.2d 1119, 1125 (7th Cir.1970), precludes the defendants' argument that the misprision statute is unconstitutional as applied to them. We do not agree and decline to give such a broad reading to that decision.

"The defendants in *Daddano* relied upon a legal theory akin to that advanced by Kuh and Rea. This court rejected the argument and the holding of *United States v. King*, 402 F.2d 694 (9th Cir.1968), observing that the offense of misprision as defined in 18 U.S.C. § 4 consists of an act of concealment in addition to failure to disclose, so that the statute did not purport to punish one solely for failure to report facts which he has reasonable fear might lead to his conviction of crime.

a. "Whoever receives, possesses, conceals, stores, barters, sells, or disposes of, any property or money or other thing of value knowing the same to have been taken from a bank, credit union, or a savings and loan association, in violation of subsection (b) of this section shall be subject to the punishment provided in said subsection (b) for the taker."

b. "Whoever, having knowledge of the actual commission of a felony cognizable by a court of the United States, conceals and does not as soon as possible make known the same to some judge or other person in civil or military authority under the United States, shall be fined not more than $500 or imprisoned not more than three years, or both."

"The *Daddano* ruling, however, must be read within the context of the facts of that case. Indeed, the opinion noted at the outset that the evidence presented an unusual story. The defendants charged in the misprision count had caused lie detector tests to be administered in order to determine whether certain persons were furnishing information concerning the bank robbery and the perpetrators thereof to governmental authorities investigating the same. It appeared from the evidence that whichever bank robber failed the test would be silenced, *viz.,* the others could shoot him if they wished. The arrangement whereby a member of the Special Investigations Unit of Cook County administered the polygraph tests presented a situation wherein an entirely separate offense from that involved in the original bank robbery was the means employed to mislead the federal authorities. In *Daddano* the polygraph procedures engaged in by the defendants constituted a distinct and separate concealment of the commission of a felony. This as the court observed in *Daddano* is the 'act of concealment in addition to failure to disclose.' The concealment in the present case, while it might incidentally have served to cloak the felony commission, was directly the concealment of the stolen money, a clear violation of 18 U.S.C. § 2113(c).

"Moreover, although the *Daddano* court recognized that defendant Montagna had knowingly received part of the stolen money and, as a professional bondsman, had arranged for the bonds of the four defendants originally charged with the robbery, its characterization of his conduct took place in a context wherein he had not been charged in the indictment with that particular misprision but only with concealing information through the use of the polygraph test. Thus, the rejection of his Fifth Amendment claim focused on Montagna's fear of being convicted as an accessory after the fact. True, the *Daddano* court

did make a brief reference to 'some other related offense'; but the absence of any count in the indictment alleging that Montagna had possessed or used funds which he knew to be the fruits of a bank robbery in violation of 18 U.S.C. § 2113(c) points to a conclusion that the quoted phrase was not intended to refer to a subsection (c) violation.

"We are satisfied that *Daddano* is factually and legally distinguishable from the instant case. Here the facts as represented by the prosecutors are that at the time the duty to disclose arose, the defendants Kuh and Rea were simultaneously involved in criminal conduct through the knowing receipt and possession of the stolen money followed by its concealment. The object of the Fifth Amendment is to insure that a person should not be compelled to give information which might tend to show he himself has committed a crime. Under the circumstances of this case, we cannot accept the argument that, although a person who fails to disclose a felony in which he might be implicated is protected from punishment by the Fifth Amendment, his failure to make known the felony, when coupled with an act of concealment, makes him susceptible to prosecution, conviction, and punishment under 18 U.S.C. § 4. If the duty to notify federal authorities is precluded by constitutional privilege, it is difficult to understand how a conviction could be substantiated. The factual allegations were and are sufficient to engender in the defendants reasonable cause to believe that disclosing information as to their knowledge of the Purolator robbery would place them in the position of furnishing the Government with evidence that could lead to their prosecution or conviction."

3. In *United States v. Ciambrone,* 750 F.2d 1416 (9th Cir.1984), defendant contacted a Secret Service agent, showed him a xerox copy of a counterfeit $100 bill and also two actual counterfeit bills and said

for $15,000 he would provide further information about a very substantial counterfeiting operation (the counterfeiters were seeking to trade the fruits of their labors for half a million dollars). Upon his refusal to give any further information without such a payoff, he was convicted of misprision of a felony. The court of appeals reversed:

"The starting point of our analysis is the proposition that '[m]ere silence, without some affirmative act, is insufficient evidence' of the crime of misprision of felony. Thus, a person who witnesses a crime does not violate 18 U.S.C. § 4 if he simply remains silent. Here, Ciambrone did not remain silent; rather, he made a truthful, but partial disclosure of what he knew about the counterfeiting operation. The district court viewed Ciambrone's actions as 'tantamount to an affirmative act,' because 'the case goes beyond the defendant sitting at home knowing about it, not doing anything about it.' We disagree. In our view, Ciambrone's partial disclosure did not result in any greater concealment of the crime than would have occurred had he stayed at home and said nothing. Indeed, in stepping forward to make at least a partial disclosure, Ciambrone provided some information and possibly valuable leads that the Secret Service would not have otherwise obtained from him. Thus, Ciambrone not only informed Agent Devaney that he knew a person with large quantities of counterfeit notes, but also gave him a xerox copy of one and showed him two actual counterfeit notes before they were put into circulation. From the Secret Service's standpoint, this partial disclosure had to be better than no disclosure at all. Rather than helping the counterfeiters conceal their criminal activity, Ciambrone's partial disclosure put them at some greater risk of detection than if he had remained silent.

"Since it is undisputed that Ciambrone was truthful, the Secret Service could not have been misled by his statements. This case is thus distinguishable from *Hodges,* where we determined that 'the giving of an untruthful statement [denying knowledge of the crime] to [F.B.I.] authorities is a sufficient act of concealment to sustain a conviction for misprision of felony.' The important distinction is that lying to the authorities can help those who committed a crime by throwing the authorities off the track. Here, although Ciambrone chose to be selectively silent, he did at least convey some information that might have been useful to the Secret Service, which is better than no information at all."

*

Appendix

AMERICAN LAW INSTITUTE
MODEL PENAL CODE
(OFFICIAL DRAFT, 1962)

TABLE OF CONTENTS

MODEL PENAL CODE

PART I. GENERAL PROVISIONS

ARTICLE 1. PRELIMINARY

Section		Page
1.01.	Title and Effective Date	816
1.02.	Purposes; Principles of Construction	816
1.03.	Territorial Applicability	817
1.04.	Classes of Crimes; Violations	818
1.05.	All Offenses Defined by Statute; Application of General Provisions of the Code	818
1.06.	Time Limitations	818
1.07.	Method of Prosecution When Conduct Constitutes More Than One Offense	819
1.08.	When Prosecution Barred by Former Prosecution for the Same Offense	820
1.09.	When Prosecution Barred by Former Prosecution for Different Offense	821
1.10.	Former Prosecution in Another Jurisdiction: When a Bar	821
1.11.	Former Prosecution Before Court Lacking Jurisdiction or When Fraudulently Procured by the Defendant	822

Section   **Page**

1.12. Proof Beyond a Reasonable Doubt; Affirmative Defenses; Burden
       of Proving Fact When Not an Element of an Offense; Presump-
       tions_____ 822
1.13. General Definitions_____ 823

ARTICLE 2.   GENERAL PRINCIPLES OF LIABILITY

2.01. Requirement of Voluntary Act; Omission as Basis of Liability;
       Possession as an Act_____ 823
2.02. General Requirements of Culpability_____ 824
2.03. Causal Relationship Between Conduct and Result; Divergence
       Between Result Designed or Contemplated and Actual Result or
       Between Probable and Actual Result_____ 825
2.04. Ignorance or Mistake_____ 826
2.05. When Culpability Requirements Are Inapplicable to Violations
       and to Offenses Defined by Other Statutes; Effect of Absolute
       Liability in Reducing Grade of Offense to Violation_____ 826
2.06. Liability for Conduct of Another; Complicity_____ 827
2.07. Liability of Corporations, Unincorporated Associations and Per-
       sons Acting, or Under a Duty to Act, in Their Behalf_____ 828
2.08. Intoxication_____ 829
2.09. Duress_____ 829
2.10. Military Orders_____ 830
2.11. Consent_____ 830
2.12. De Minimis Infractions_____ 830
2.13. Entrapment_____ 831

ARTICLE 3.   GENERAL PRINCIPLES OF JUSTIFICATION

3.01. Justification an Affirmative Defense; Civil Remedies Unaffected 831
3.02. Justification Generally: Choice of Evils_____ 831
3.03. Execution of Public Duty_____ 832
3.04. Use of Force in Self-Protection_____ 832
3.05. Use of Force for the Protection of Other Persons_____ 833
3.06. Use of Force for the Protection of Property_____ 834
3.07. Use of Force in Law Enforcement_____ 835
3.08. Use of Force by Persons With Special Responsibility for Care,
       Discipline or Safety of Others_____ 837
3.09. Mistake of Law as to Unlawfulness of Force or Legality of Arrest;
       Reckless or Negligent Use of Otherwise Justifiable Force;
       Reckless or Negligent Injury or Risk of Injury to Innocent
       Persons_____ 838
3.10. Justification in Property Crimes_____ 839
3.11. Definitions_____ 839

ARTICLE 4.   RESPONSIBILITY

4.01. Mental Disease or Defect Excluding Responsibility_____ 839
4.02. Evidence of Mental Disease or Defect Admissible When Relevant
       to Element of the Offense; [Mental Disease or Defect Impairing
       Capacity as Ground for Mitigation of Punishment in Capital
       Cases]_____ 839
4.03. Mental Disease or Defect Excluding Responsibility is Affirmative
       Defense; Requirement of Notice; Form of Verdict and Judg-
       ment When Finding of Irresponsibility is Made_____ 840
4.04. Mental Disease or Defect Excluding Fitness to Proceed_____ 840

Section   **Page**

4.05. Psychiatric Examination of Defendant With Respect to Mental Disease or Defect _____ 840

4.06. Determination of Fitness to Proceed; Effect of Finding of Unfitness; Proceedings if Fitness is Regained [; Post–Commitment Hearing] _____ 841

4.07. Determination of Irresponsibility on Basis of Report; Access to Defendant by Psychiatrist of His Own Choice; Form of Expert Testimony When Issue of Responsibility is Tried _____ 842

4.08. Legal Effect of Acquittal on the Ground of Mental Disease or Defect Excluding Responsibility; Commitment; Release or Discharge _____ 843

4.09. Statements for Purposes of Examination or Treatment Inadmissible Except on Issue of Mental Condition _____ 844

4.10. Immaturity Excluding Criminal Conviction; Transfer of Proceedings to Juvenile Court _____ 844

ARTICLE 5. INCHOATE CRIMES

5.01. Criminal Attempt _____ 844
5.02. Criminal Solicitation _____ 845
5.03. Criminal Conspiracy _____ 846
5.04. Incapacity, Irresponsibility or Immunity of Party to Solicitation or Conspiracy _____ 847
5.05. Grading of Criminal Attempt, Solicitation and Conspiracy; Mitigation in Cases of Lesser Danger; Multiple Convictions Barred 847
5.06. Possessing Instruments of Crime; Weapons _____ 847
5.07. Prohibited Offensive Weapons _____ 848

ARTICLE 6. AUTHORIZED DISPOSITION OF OFFENDERS

6.01. Degrees of Felonies _____ 848
6.02. Sentence in Accordance With Code; Authorized Dispositions ____ 849
6.03. Fines _____ 849
6.04. Penalties Against Corporations and Unincorporated Associations; Forfeiture of Corporate Charter or Revocation of Certificate Authorizing Foreign Corporation to Do Business in the State 849
6.05. Young Adult Offenders _____ 850
6.06. Sentence of Imprisonment for Felony; Ordinary Terms _____ 851
6.06. (Alternate) Sentence of Imprisonment for Felony; Ordinary Terms _____ 851
6.07. Sentence of Imprisonment for Felony; Extended Terms _____ 851
6.08. Sentence of Imprisonment for Misdemeanors and Petty Misdemeanors; Ordinary Terms _____ 852
6.09. Sentence of Imprisonment for Misdemeanors and Petty Misdemeanors; Extended Terms _____ 852
6.10. First Release of All Offenders on Parole; Sentence of Imprisonment Includes Separate Parole Term; Length of Parole Term; Length of Recommitment and Reparole After Revocation of Parole; Final Unconditional Release _____ 852
6.11. Place of Imprisonment _____ 853
6.12. Reduction of Conviction by Court to Lesser Degree of Felony or to Misdemeanor _____ 853
6.13. Civil Commitment in Lieu of Prosecution or of Sentence _____ 853

ARTICLE 7.   AUTHORITY OF COURT IN SENTENCING

Section   Page
7.01.   Criteria for Withholding Sentence of Imprisonment and for Plac-
        ing Defendant on Probation _____ 853
7.02.   Criteria for Imposing Fines_____ 854
7.03.   Criteria for Sentence of Extended Term of Imprisonment; Felo-
        nies _____ 854
7.04.   Criteria for Sentence of Extended Term of Imprisonment; Misde-
        meanors and Petty Misdemeanors _____ 855
7.05.   Former Conviction in Another Jurisdiction; Definition and Proof
        of Conviction; Sentence Taking into Account Admitted Crimes
        Bars Subsequent Conviction for Such Crimes _____ 856
7.06.   Multiple Sentences; Concurrent and Consecutive Terms _____ 856
7.07.   Procedure on Sentence; Pre-sentence Investigation and Report;
        Remand for Psychiatric Examination; Transmission of Records
        to Department of Correction_____ 858
7.08.   Commitment for Observation; Sentence of Imprisonment for Felo-
        ny Deemed Tentative for Period of One Year; Re-sentence on
        Petition of Commissioner of Correction_____ 859
7.09.   Credit for Time of Detention Prior to Sentence; Credit for Impris-
        onment Under Earlier Sentence for the Same Crime_____ 860

PART II.   DEFINITION OF SPECIFIC CRIMES

OFFENSES AGAINST EXISTENCE OR STABILITY OF THE STATE

OFFENSES INVOLVING DANGER TO THE PERSON

ARTICLE 210.   CRIMINAL HOMICIDE

210.0.   Definitions _____ 860
210.1.   Criminal Homicide_____ 861
210.2.   Murder_____ 861
210.3.   Manslaughter_____ 861
210.4.   Negligent Homicide _____ 861
210.5.   Causing or Aiding Suicide _____ 861
210.6.   Sentence of Death for Murder; Further Proceedings to Determine
         Sentence _____ 862

ARTICLE 211.   ASSAULT; RECKLESS ENDANGERING; THREATS

211.0.   Definitions _____ 864
211.1.   Assault_____ 864
211.2.   Recklessly Endangering Another Person_____ 864
211.3.   Terroristic Threats _____ 864

ARTICLE 212.   KIDNAPPING AND RELATED OFFENSES; COERCION

212.0.   Definitions _____ 864
212.1.   Kidnapping _____ 865
212.2.   Felonious Restraint _____ 865
212.3.   False Imprisonment_____ 865
212.4.   Interference With Custody _____ 865
212.5.   Criminal Coercion_____ 865

ARTICLE 213.   SEXUAL OFFENSES

213.0.   Definitions _____ 866
213.1.   Rape and Related Offenses _____ 866

Section		Page
213.2.	Deviate Sexual Intercourse by Force or Imposition	867
213.3.	Corruption of Minors and Seduction	867
213.4.	Sexual Assault	867
213.5.	Indecent Exposure	868
213.6.	Provisions Generally Applicable to Article 213	868

OFFENSES AGAINST PROPERTY

ARTICLE 220. ARSON, CRIMINAL MISCHIEF, AND OTHER PROPERTY DESTRUCTION

220.1.	Arson and Related Offenses	869
220.2.	Causing or Risking Catastrophe	869
220.3.	Criminal Mischief	870

ARTICLE 221. BURGLARY AND OTHER CRIMINAL INTRUSION

221.0.	Definitions	870
221.1.	Burglary	870
221.2.	Criminal Trespass	870

ARTICLE 222. ROBBERY

222.1.	Robbery	871

ARTICLE 223. THEFT AND RELATED OFFENSES

223.0.	Definitions	871
223.1.	Consolidation of Theft Offenses; Grading; Provisions Applicable to Theft Generally	872
223.2.	Theft by Unlawful Taking or Disposition	873
223.3.	Theft by Deception	873
223.4.	Theft by Extortion	873
223.5.	Theft of Property Lost, Mislaid or Delivered by Mistake	874
223.6.	Receiving Stolen Property	874
223.7.	Theft of Services	874
223.8.	Theft by Failure to Make Required Disposition of Funds Received	874
223.9.	Unauthorized Use of Automobiles and Other Vehicles	875

ARTICLE 224. FORGERY AND FRAUDULENT PRACTICES

224.0.	Definitions	875
224.1.	Forgery	875
224.2.	Simulating Objects of Antiquity, Rarity, Etc.	875
224.3.	Fraudulent Destruction, Removal or Concealment of Recordable Instruments	875
224.4.	Tampering With Records	875
224.5.	Bad Checks	876
224.6.	Credit Cards	876
224.7.	Deceptive Business Practices	876
224.8.	Commercial Bribery and Breach of Duty to Act Disinterestedly	877
224.9.	Rigging Publicly Exhibited Contest	877
224.10.	Defrauding Secured Creditors	877
224.11.	Fraud in Insolvency	877
224.12.	Receiving Deposits in a Failing Financial Institution	878
224.13.	Misapplication of Entrusted Property and Property of Government or Financial Institution	878
224.14.	Securing Execution of Documents by Deception	878

OFFENSES AGAINST THE FAMILY

ARTICLE 230.   OFFENSES AGAINST THE FAMILY

Section   **Page**
230.1.   Bigamy and Polygamy _____ 878
230.2.   Incest _____ 879
230.3.   Abortion _____ 879
230.4.   Endangering Welfare of Children _____ 880
230.5.   Persistent Non-support _____ 880

OFFENSES AGAINST PUBLIC ADMINISTRATION

ARTICLE 240.   BRIBERY AND CORRUPT INFLUENCE

240.0.   Definitions _____ 880
240.1.   Bribery in Official and Political Matters_____ 881
240.2.   Threats and Other Improper Influence in Official and Political
            Matters _____ 881
240.3.   Compensation for Past Official Behavior_____ 881
240.4.   Retaliation for Past Official Action _____ 882
240.5.   Gifts to Public Servants by Persons Subject to Their Jurisdiction 882
240.6.   Compensating Public Servant for Assisting Private Interests in
            Relation to Matters Before Him _____ 883
240.7.   Selling Political Endorsement; Special Influence_____ 883

ARTICLE 241.   PERJURY AND OTHER FALSIFICATION IN OFFICIAL MATTERS

241.0.   Definitions _____ 883
241.1.   Perjury_____ 883
241.2.   False Swearing _____ 884
241.3.   Unsworn Falsification to Authorities_____ 884
241.4.   False Alarms to Agencies of Public Safety _____ 885
241.5.   False Reports to Law Enforcement Authorities _____ 885
241.6.   Tampering With Witnesses and Informants; Retaliation Against
            Them_____ 885
241.7.   Tampering With or Fabricating Physical Evidence_____ 885
241.8.   Tampering With Public Records or Information _____ 885
241.9.   Impersonating a Public Servant _____ 886

ARTICLE 242.   OBSTRUCTING GOVERNMENTAL OPERATIONS; ESCAPES

242.0.   Definitions _____ 886
242.1.   Obstructing Administration of Law or Other Governmental Func-
            tion _____ 886
242.2.   Resisting Arrest or Other Law Enforcement_____ 886
242.3.   Hindering Apprehension or Prosecution _____ 886
242.4.   Aiding Consummation of Crime_____ 887
242.5.   Compounding_____ 887
242.6.   Escape_____ 887
242.7.   Implements for Escape; Other Contraband _____ 887
242.8.   Bail Jumping; Default in Required Appearance _____ 888

ARTICLE 243.   ABUSE OF OFFICE

243.0.   Definitions _____ 888
243.1.   Official Oppression_____ 888
243.2.   Speculating or Wagering on Official Action or Information_____ 888

OFFENSES AGAINST PUBLIC ORDER AND DECENCY

ARTICLE 250. RIOT, DISORDERLY CONDUCT, AND RELATED OFFENSES

Section		Page
250.1.	Riot; Failure to Disperse	888
250.2.	Disorderly Conduct	889
250.3.	False Public Alarms	889
250.4.	Harassment	889
250.5.	Public Drunkenness; Drug Incapacitation	889
250.6.	Loitering or Prowling	889
250.7.	Obstructing Highways and Other Public Passages	890
250.8.	Disrupting Meetings and Processions	890
250.9.	Desecration of Venerated Objects	890
250.10.	Abuse of Corpse	890
250.11.	Cruelty to Animals	890
250.12.	Violation of Privacy	891

ARTICLE 251. PUBLIC INDECENCY

251.1.	Open Lewdness	891
251.2.	Prostitution and Related Offenses	891
251.3.	Loitering to Solicit Deviate Sexual Relations	892
251.4.	Obscenity	892

ADDITIONAL ARTICLES

PART III. TREATMENT AND CORRECTION [OMITTED]

PART IV. ORGANIZATION OF CORRECTION [OMITTED]

PART I. GENERAL PROVISIONS

ARTICLE 1. PRELIMINARY

Section 1.01. Title and Effective Date.

(1) This Act is called the Penal and Correctional Code and may be cited as P.C.C. It shall become effective on ___.

(2) Except as provided in Subsections (3) and (4) of this Section, the Code does not apply to offenses committed prior to its effective date and prosecutions for such offenses shall be governed by the prior law, which is continued in effect for that purpose, as if this Code were not in force. For the purposes of this Section, an offense was committed prior to the effective date of the Code if any of the elements of the offense occurred prior thereto.

(3) In any case pending on or after the effective date of the Code, involving an offense committed prior to such date:

(a) procedural provisions of the Code shall govern, insofar as they are justly applicable and their application does not introduce confusion or delay;

(b) provisions of the Code according a defense or mitigation shall apply, with the consent of the defendant;

(c) the Court, with the consent of the defendant, may impose sentence under the provisions of the Code applicable to the offense and the offender.

(4) Provisions of the Code governing the treatment and the release or discharge of prisoners, probationers and parolees shall apply to persons under sentence for offenses committed prior to the effective date of the Code, except that the minimum or maximum period of their detention or supervision shall in no case be increased.

Section 1.02. Purposes; Principles of Construction.

(1) The general purposes of the provisions governing the definition of offenses are:

(a) to forbid and prevent conduct that unjustifiably and inexcusably inflicts or threatens substantial harm to individual or public interests;

(b) to subject to public control persons whose conduct indicates that they are disposed to commit crimes;

(c) to safeguard conduct that is without fault from condemnation as criminal;

(d) to give fair warning of the nature of the conduct declared to constitute an offense;

(e) to differentiate on reasonable grounds between serious and minor offenses.

(2) The general purposes of the provisions governing the sentencing and treatment of offenders are:

(a) to prevent the commission of offenses;

(b) to promote the correction and rehabilitation of offenders;

(c) to safeguard offenders against excessive, disproportionate or arbitrary punishment;

(d) to give fair warning of the nature of the sentences that may be imposed on conviction of an offense;

(e) to differentiate among offenders with a view to a just individualization in their treatment;

(f) to define, coordinate and harmonize the powers, duties and functions of the courts and of administrative officers and agencies responsible for dealing with offenders;

(g) to advance the use of generally accepted scientific methods and knowledge in the sentencing and treatment of offenders;

(h) to integrate responsibility for the administration of the correctional system in a State Department of Correction [or other single department or agency].

(3) The provisions of the Code shall be construed according to the fair import of their terms but when the language is susceptible of differing constructions it shall be interpreted to further the general purposes stated in this Section and the special purposes of the particular provision involved. The discretionary powers conferred by the Code shall be exercised in accordance with the criteria stated in the Code and, insofar as such criteria are not decisive, to further the general purposes stated in this Section.

Section 1.03. Territorial Applicability.

(1) Except as otherwise provided in this Section, a person may be convicted under the law of this State of an offense committed by his own conduct or the conduct of another for which he is legally accountable if:

(a) either the conduct which is an element of the offense or the result which is such an element occurs within this State; or

(b) conduct occurring outside the State is sufficient under the law of this State to constitute an attempt to commit an offense within the State; or

(c) conduct occurring outside the State is sufficient under the law of this State to constitute a conspiracy to commit an offense within the State and an overt act in furtherance of such conspiracy occurs within the State; or

(d) conduct occurring within the State establishes complicity in the commission of, or an attempt, solicitation or conspiracy to commit, an offense in another jurisdiction which also is an offense under the law of this State; or

(e) the offense consists of the omission to perform a legal duty imposed by the law of this State with respect to domicile, residence or a relationship to a person, thing or transaction in the State; or

(f) the offense is based on a statute of this State which expressly prohibits conduct outside the State, when the conduct bears a reasonable relation to a legitimate interest of this State and the actor knows or should know that his conduct is likely to affect that interest.

(2) Subsection (1)(a) does not apply when either causing a specified result or a purpose to cause or danger of causing such a result is an element of an offense and the result occurs or is designed or likely to occur only in another jurisdiction where the conduct charged would not constitute an offense, unless a legislative purpose plainly appears to declare the conduct criminal regardless of the place of the result.

(3) Subsection (1)(a) does not apply when causing a particular result is an element of an offense and the result is caused by conduct occurring outside the State which would not constitute an offense if the result had occurred there, unless the actor purposely or knowingly caused the result within the State.

(4) When the offense is homicide, either the death of the victim or the bodily impact causing death constitutes a "result," within the meaning of Subsection (1)(a) and if the body of a homicide victim is found within the State, it is presumed that such result occurred within the State.

(5) This State includes the land and water and the air space above such land and water with respect to which the State has legislative jurisdiction.

Section 1.04. Classes of Crimes; Violations.

(1) An offense defined by this Code or by any other statute of this State, for which a sentence of [death or of] imprisonment is authorized, constitutes a crime. Crimes are classified as felonies, misdemeanors or petty misdemeanors.

(2) A crime is a felony if it is so designated in this Code or if persons convicted thereof may be sentenced [to death or] to imprisonment for a term which, apart from an extended term, is in excess of one year.

(3) A crime is a misdemeanor if it is so designated in this Code or in a statute other than this Code enacted subsequent thereto.

(4) A crime is a petty misdemeanor if it is so designated in this Code or in a statute other than this Code enacted subsequent thereto or if it is defined by a statute other than this Code which now provides that persons convicted thereof may be sentenced to imprisonment for a term of which the maximum is less than one year.

(5) An offense defined by this Code or by any other statute of this State constitutes a violation if it is so designated in this Code or in the law defining the offense or if no other sentence than a fine, or fine and forfeiture or other civil penalty is authorized upon conviction or if it is defined by a statute other than this Code which now provides that the offense shall not constitute a crime. A violation does not constitute a crime and conviction of a violation shall not give rise to any disability or legal disadvantage based on conviction of a criminal offense.

(6) Any offense declared by law to constitute a crime, without specification of the grade thereof or of the sentence authorized upon conviction, is a misdemeanor.

(7) An offense defined by any statute of this State other than this Code shall be classified as provided in this Section and the sentence that may be imposed upon conviction thereof shall hereafter be governed by this Code.

Section 1.05. All Offenses Defined by Statute; Application of General Provisions of the Code.

(1) No conduct constitutes an offense unless it is a crime or violation under this Code or another statute of this State.

(2) The provisions of Part I of the Code are applicable to offenses defined by other statutes, unless the Code otherwise provides.

(3) This Section does not affect the power of a court to punish for contempt or to employ any sanction authorized by law for the enforcement of an order or a civil judgment or decree.

Section 1.06. Time Limitations.

(1) A prosecution for murder may be commenced at anytime.

(2) Except as otherwise provided in this Section, prosecutions for other offenses are subject to the following periods of limitation:

(a) a prosecution for a felony of the first degree must be commenced within six years after it is committed;

(b) a prosecution for any other felony must be commenced within three years after it is committed;

(c) a prosecution for a misdemeanor must be commenced within two years after it is committed;

(d) a prosecution for a petty misdemeanor or a violation must be commenced within six months after it is committed.

(3) If the period prescribed in Subsection (2) has expired, a prosecution may nevertheless be commenced for:

(a) any offense a material element of which is either fraud or a breach of fiduciary obligation within one year after discovery of the offense by an aggrieved party or by a person who has legal duty to represent an aggrieved party and who is himself not a party to the offense, but in no case shall this provision extend the period of limitation otherwise applicable by more than three years; and

(b) any offense based upon misconduct in office by a public officer or employee at any time when the defendant is in public office or employment or within two years thereafter, but in no case shall this provision extend the period of limitation otherwise applicable by more than three years.

(4) An offense is committed either when every element occurs, or, if a legislative purpose to prohibit a continuing course of conduct plainly appears, at the time when the course of conduct or the defendant's complicity therein is terminated. Time starts to run on the day after the offense is committed.

(5) A prosecution is commenced either when an indictment is found [or an information filed] or when a warrant or other process is issued, provided that such warrant or process is executed without unreasonable delay.

(6) The period of limitation does not run:

(a) during any time when the accused is continuously absent from the State or has no reasonably ascertainable place of abode or work within the State, but in no case shall this provision extend the period of limitation otherwise applicable by more than three years; or

(b) during any time when a prosecution against the accused for the same conduct is pending in this State.

Section 1.07. Method of Prosecution When Conduct Constitutes More Than One Offense.

(1) **Prosecution for Multiple Offenses; Limitation on Convictions.** When the same conduct of a defendant may establish the commission of more than one offense, the defendant may be prosecuted for each such offense. He may not, however, be convicted of more than one offense if:

(a) one offense is included in the other, as defined in Subsection (4) of this Section; or

(b) one offense consists only of a conspiracy or other form of preparation to commit the other; or

(c) inconsistent findings of fact are required to establish the commission of the offenses; or

(d) the offenses differ only in that one is defined to prohibit a designated kind of conduct generally and the other to prohibit a specific instance of such conduct; or

(e) the offense is defined as a continuing course of conduct and the defendant's course of conduct was uninterrupted, unless the law provides that specific periods of such conduct constitute separate offenses.

(2) **Limitation on Separate Trials for Multiple Offenses.** Except as provided in Subsection (3) of this Section, a defendant shall not be subject to separate trials for multiple offenses based on the same conduct or arising from the same criminal episode, if such offenses are known to the appropriate prosecuting officer at the time of the commencement of the first trial and are within the jurisdiction of a single court.

(3) **Authority of Court to Order Separate Trials.** When a defendant is charged with two or more offenses based on the same conduct or arising from the

same criminal episode, the Court, on application of the prosecuting attorney or of the defendant, may order any such charge to be tried separately, if it is satisfied that justice so requires.

(4) **Conviction of Included Offense Permitted.** A defendant may be convicted of an offense included in an offense charged in the indictment [or the information]. An offense is so included when:

(a) it is established by proof of the same or less than all the facts required to establish the commission of the offense charged; or

(b) it consists of an attempt or solicitation to commit the offense charged or to commit an offense otherwise included therein; or

(c) it differs from the offense charged only in the respect that a less serious injury or risk of injury to the same person, property or public interest or a lesser kind of culpability suffices to establish its commission.

(5) **Submission of Included Offense to Jury.** The Court shall not be obligated to charge the jury with respect to an included offense unless there is a rational basis for a verdict acquitting the defendant of the offense charged and convicting him of the included offense.

Section 1.08. When Prosecution Barred by Former Prosecution for the Same Offense.

When a prosecution is for a violation of the same provision of the statutes and is based upon the same facts as a former prosecution, it is barred by such former prosecution under the following circumstances:

(1) The former prosecution resulted in an acquittal. There is an acquittal if the prosecution resulted in a finding of not guilty by the trier of fact or in a determination that there was insufficient evidence to warrant a conviction. A finding of guilty of a lesser included offense is an acquittal of the greater inclusive offense, although the conviction is subsequently set aside.

(2) The former prosecution was terminated, after the information had been filed or the indictment found, by a final order or judgment for the defendant, which has not been set aside, reversed, or vacated and which necessarily required a determination inconsistent with a fact or a legal proposition that must be established for conviction of the offense.

(3) The former prosecution resulted in a conviction. There is a conviction if the prosecution resulted in a judgment of conviction which has not been reversed or vacated, a verdict of guilty which has not been set aside and which is capable of supporting a judgment, or a plea of guilty accepted by the Court. In the latter two cases failure to enter judgment must be for a reason other than a motion of the defendant.

(4) The former prosecution was improperly terminated. Except as provided in this Subsection, there is an improper termination of a prosecution if the termination is for reasons not amounting to an acquittal, and it takes place after the first witness is sworn but before verdict. Termination under any of the following circumstances is not improper:

(a) The defendant consents to the termination or waives, by motion to dismiss or otherwise, his right to object to the termination.

(b) The trial court finds that the termination is necessary because:

(i) it is physically impossible to proceed with the trial in conformity with law; or

(ii) there is a legal defect in the proceedings which would make any judgment entered upon a verdict reversible as a matter of law; or

(iii) prejudicial conduct, in or outside the courtroom, makes it impossible to proceed with the trial without injustice to either the defendant or the State; or

(iv) the jury is unable to agree upon a verdict; or

(v) false statements of a juror on voir dire prevent a fair trial.

Section 1.09. When Prosecution Barred by Former Prosecution for Different Offense.

Although a prosecution is for a violation of a different provision of the statutes than a former prosecution or is based on different facts, it is barred by such former prosecution under the following circumstances:

(1) The former prosecution resulted in an acquittal or in a conviction as defined in Section 1.08 and the subsequent prosecution is for:

(a) any offense of which the defendant could have been convicted on the first prosecution; or

(b) any offense for which the defendant should have been tried on the first prosecution under Section 1.07, unless the Court ordered a separate trial of the charge of such offense; or

(c) the same conduct, unless (i) the offense of which the defendant was formerly convicted or acquitted and the offense for which he is subsequently prosecuted each requires proof of a fact not required by the other and the law defining each of such offenses is intended to prevent a substantially different harm or evil, or (ii) the second offense was not consummated when the former trial began.

(2) The former prosecution was terminated, after the information was filed or the indictment found, by an acquittal or by

a final order or judgment for the defendant which has not been set aside, reversed or vacated and which acquittal, final order or judgment necessarily required a determination inconsistent with a fact which must be established for conviction of the second offense.

(3) The former prosecution was improperly terminated, as improper termination is defined in Section 1.08, and the subsequent prosecution is for an offense of which the defendant could have been convicted had the former prosecution not been improperly terminated.

Section 1.10. Former Prosecution in Another Jurisdiction: When a Bar.

When conduct constitutes an offense within the concurrent jurisdiction of this State and of the United States or another State, a prosecution in any such other jurisdiction is a bar to a subsequent prosecution in this State under the following circumstances:

(1) The first prosecution resulted in an acquittal or in a conviction as defined in Section 1.08 and the subsequent prosecution is based on the same conduct, unless (a) the offense of which the defendant was formerly convicted or acquitted and the offense for which he is subsequently prosecuted each requires proof of a fact not required by the other and the law defining each of such offenses is intended to prevent a substantially different harm or evil or (b) the second offense was not consummated when the former trial began; or

(2) The former prosecution was terminated, after the information was filed or the indictment found, by an acquittal or by a final order or judgment for the defendant which has not been set aside, reversed or vacated and which acquittal, final order or judgment necessarily required a determination inconsistent with a fact which must be established for

conviction of the offense of which the defendant is subsequently prosecuted.

Section 1.11. Former Prosecution Before Court Lacking Jurisdiction or When Fraudulently Procured by the Defendant.

A prosecution is not a bar within the meaning of Sections 1.08, 1.09 and 1.10 under any of the following circumstances:

(1) The former prosecution was before a court which lacked jurisdiction over the defendant or the offense; or

(2) The former prosecution was procured by the defendant without the knowledge of the appropriate prosecuting officer and with the purpose of avoiding the sentence which might otherwise be imposed; or

(3) The former prosecution resulted in a judgment of conviction which was held invalid in a subsequent proceeding on a writ of habeas corpus, coram nobis or similar process.

Section 1.12. Proof Beyond a Reasonable Doubt; Affirmative Defenses; Burden of Proving Fact When Not an Element of an Offense; Presumptions.

(1) No person may be convicted of an offense unless each element of such offense is proved beyond a reasonable doubt. In the absence of such proof, the innocence of the defendant is assumed.

(2) Subsection (1) of this Section does not:

(a) require the disproof of an affirmative defense unless and until there is evidence supporting such defense; or

(b) apply to any defense which the Code or another statute plainly requires the defendant to prove by a preponderance of evidence.

(3) A ground of defense is affirmative, within the meaning of Subsection (2)(a) of this Section, when:

(a) it arises under a section of the Code which so provides; or

(b) it relates to an offense defined by a statute other than the Code and such statute so provides; or

(c) it involves a matter of excuse or justification peculiarly within the knowledge of the defendant on which he can fairly be required to adduce supporting evidence.

(4) When the application of the Code depends upon the finding of a fact which is not an element of an offense, unless the Code otherwise provides:

(a) the burden of proving the fact is on the prosecution or defendant, depending on whose interest or contention will be furthered if the finding should be made; and

(b) the fact must be proved to the satisfaction of the Court or jury, as the case may be.

(5) When the Code establishes a presumption with respect to any fact which is an element of an offense, it has the following consequences:

(a) when there is evidence of the facts which give rise to the presumption, the issue of the existence of the presumed fact must be submitted to the jury, unless the Court is satisfied that the evidence as a whole clearly negatives the presumed fact; and

(b) when the issue of the existence of the presumed fact is submitted to the jury, the Court shall charge that while the presumed fact must, on all the evidence, be proved beyond a reasonable doubt, the law declares that the jury may regard the facts giving rise to the presumption as sufficient evidence of the presumed fact.

(6) A presumption not established by the Code or inconsistent with it has the consequences otherwise accorded it by law.

Section 1.13. General Definitions.

In this Code, unless a different meaning plainly is required:

(1) "statute" includes the Constitution and a local law or ordinance of a political subdivision of the State;

(2) "act" or "action" means a bodily movement whether voluntary or involuntary;

(3) "voluntary" has the meaning specified in Section 2.01;

(4) "omission" means a failure to act;

(5) "conduct" means an action or omission and its accompanying state of mind, or, where relevant, a series of acts and omissions;

(6) "actor" includes, where relevant, a person guilty of an omission;

(7) "acted" includes, where relevant, "omitted to act";

(8) "person," "he" and "actor" include any natural person and, where relevant, a corporation or an unincorporated association;

(9) "element of an offense" means (i) such conduct or (ii) such attendant circumstances or (iii) such a result of conduct as

(a) is included in the description of the forbidden conduct in the definition of the offense; or

(b) establishes the required kind of culpability; or

(c) negatives an excuse or justification for such conduct; or

(d) negatives a defense under the statute of limitations; or

(e) establishes jurisdiction or venue;

(10) "material element of an offense" means an element that does not relate exclusively to the statute of limitations, jurisdiction, venue or to any other matter similarly unconnected with (i) the harm or evil, incident to conduct, sought to be prevented by the law defining the offense, or (ii) the existence of a justification or excuse for such conduct;

(11) "purposely" has the meaning specified in Section 2.02 and equivalent terms such as "with purpose," "designed" or "with design" have the same meaning;

(12) "intentionally" or "with intent" means purposely;

(13) "knowingly" has the meaning specified in Section 2.02 and equivalent terms such as "knowing" or "with knowledge" have the same meaning;

(14) "recklessly" has the meaning specified in Section 2.02 and equivalent terms such as "recklessness" or "with recklessness" have the same meaning;

(15) "negligently" has the meaning specified in Section 2.02 and equivalent terms such as "negligence" or "with negligence" have the same meaning;

(16) "reasonably believes" or "reasonable belief" designates a belief which the actor is not reckless or negligent in holding.

ARTICLE 2. GENERAL PRINCIPLES OF LIABILITY

Section 2.01. Requirement of Voluntary Act; Omission as Basis of Liability; Possession as an Act.

(1) A person is not guilty of an offense unless his liability is based on conduct which includes a voluntary act or the omission to perform an act of which he is physically capable.

(2) The following are not voluntary acts within the meaning of this Section:

(a) a reflex or convulsion;

(b) a bodily movement during unconsciousness or sleep;

(c) conduct during hypnosis or resulting from hypnotic suggestion;

(d) a bodily movement that otherwise is not a product of the effort or determination of the actor, either conscious or habitual.

(3) Liability for the commission of an offense may not be based on an omission unaccompanied by action unless:

(a) the omission is expressly made sufficient by the law defining the offense; or

(b) a duty to perform the omitted act is otherwise imposed by law.

(4) Possession is an act, within the meaning of this Section, if the possessor knowingly procured or received the thing possessed or was aware of his control thereof for a sufficient period to have been able to terminate his possession.

Section 2.02. General Requirements of Culpability.

(1) **Minimum Requirements of Culpability.** Except as provided in Section 2.05, a person is not guilty of an offense unless he acted purposely, knowingly, recklessly or negligently, as the law may require, with respect to each material element of the offense.

(2) **Kinds of Culpability Defined.**

(a) *Purposely.*

A person acts purposely with respect to a material element of an offense when:

(i) if the element involves the nature of his conduct or a result thereof, it is his conscious object to engage in conduct of that nature or to cause such a result; and

(ii) if the element involves the attendant circumstances, he is aware of the existence of such circumstances or he believes or hopes that they exist.

(b) *Knowingly.*

A person acts knowingly with respect to a material element of an offense when:

(i) if the element involves the nature of his conduct or the attendant circumstances, he is aware that his conduct is of that nature or that such circumstances exist; and

(ii) if the element involves a result of his conduct, he is aware that it is practically certain that his conduct will cause such a result.

(c) *Recklessly.*

A person acts recklessly with respect to a material element of an offense when he consciously disregards a substantial and unjustifiable risk that the material element exists or will result from his conduct. The risk must be of such a nature and degree that, considering the nature and purpose of the actor's conduct and the circumstances known to him, its disregard involves a gross deviation from the standard of conduct that a law-abiding person would observe in the actor's situation.

(d) *Negligently.*

A person acts negligently with respect to a material element of an offense when he should be aware of a substantial and unjustifiable risk that the material element exists or will result from his conduct. The risk must be of such a nature and degree that the actor's failure to perceive it, considering the nature and purpose of his conduct and the circumstances known to him, involves a gross deviation from the standard of care that a reasonable person would observe in the actor's situation.

(3) **Culpability Required Unless Otherwise Provided.** When the culpability sufficient to establish a material element of an offense is not prescribed by law, such element is established if a person acts purposely, knowingly or recklessly with respect thereto.

(4) **Prescribed Culpability Requirement Applies to All Material Elements.** When the law defining an offense prescribes the kind of culpability that is sufficient for the commission of an offense, without distinguishing among the material elements thereof, such provision shall apply to all the material elements of the offense, unless a contrary purpose plainly appears.

(5) **Substitutes for Negligence, Recklessness and Knowledge.** When the law provides that negligence suffices to establish an element of an offense, such element also is established if a person acts purposely, knowingly or recklessly. When recklessness suffices to establish an element, such element also is established if a person acts purposely or knowingly. When acting knowingly suffices to establish an element, such element also is established if a person acts purposely.

(6) **Requirement of Purpose Satisfied if Purpose Is Conditional.** When a particular purpose is an element of an offense, the element is established although such purpose is conditional, unless the condition negatives the harm or evil sought to be prevented by the law defining the offense.

(7) **Requirement of Knowledge Satisfied by Knowledge of High Probability.** When knowledge of the existence of a particular fact is an element of an offense, such knowledge is established if a person is aware of a high probability of its existence, unless he actually believes that it does not exist.

(8) **Requirement of Wilfulness Satisfied by Acting Knowingly.** A requirement that an offense be committed wilfully is satisfied if a person acts knowingly with respect to the material elements of the offense, unless a purpose to impose further requirements appears.

(9) **Culpability as to Illegality of Conduct.** Neither knowledge nor recklessness or negligence as to whether conduct constitutes an offense or as to the existence, meaning or application of the law determining the elements of an offense is an element of such offense, unless the definition of the offense or the Code so provides.

(10) **Culpability as Determinant of Grade of Offense.** When the grade or degree of an offense depends on whether the offense is committed purposely, knowingly, recklessly or negligently, its grade or degree shall be the lowest for which the determinative kind of culpability is established with respect to any material element of the offense.

Section 2.03. Causal Relationship Between Conduct and Result; Divergence Between Result Designed or Contemplated and Actual Result or Between Probable and Actual Result.

(1) Conduct is the cause of a result when:

(a) it is an antecedent but for which the result in question would not have occurred; and

(b) the relationship between the conduct and result satisfies any additional causal requirements imposed by the Code or by the law defining the offense.

(2) When purposely or knowingly causing a particular result is an element of an offense, the element is not established if the actual result is not within the purpose or the contemplation of the actor unless:

(a) the actual result differs from that designed or contemplated, as the case may be, only in the respect that a different person or different property is injured or affected or that the injury or harm designed or contemplated would have been more serious or more extensive than that caused; or

(b) the actual result involves the same kind of injury or harm as that designed or contemplated and is not too remote or accidental in its occurrence to have a [just] bearing on the actor's liability or on the gravity of his offense.

(3) When recklessly or negligently causing a particular result is an element of an offense, the element is not established if the actual result is not within the risk of which the actor is aware or, in the case of negligence, of which he should be aware unless:

(a) the actual result differs from the probable result only in the respect that a different person or different property is injured or affected or that the probable injury or harm would have been more serious or more extensive than that caused; or

(b) the actual result involves the same kind of injury or harm as the probable result and is not too remote or accidental in its occurrence to have a [just] bearing on the actor's liability or on the gravity of his offense.

(4) When causing a particular result is a material element of an offense for which absolute liability is imposed by law, the element is not established unless the actual result is a probable consequence of the actor's conduct.

Section 2.04. Ignorance or Mistake.

(1) Ignorance or mistake as to a matter of fact or law is a defense if:

(a) the ignorance or mistake negatives the purpose, knowledge, belief, recklessness or negligence required to establish a material element of the offense; or

(b) the law provides that the state of mind established by such ignorance or mistake constitutes a defense.

(2) Although ignorance or mistake would otherwise afford a defense to the offense charged, the defense is not available if the defendant would be guilty of another offense had the situation been as he supposed. In such case, however, the ignorance or mistake of the defendant shall reduce the grade and degree of the offense of which he may be convicted to those of the offense of which he would be guilty had the situation been as he supposed.

(3) A belief that conduct does not legally constitute an offense is a defense to a prosecution for that offense based upon such conduct when:

(a) the statute or other enactment defining the offense is not known to the actor and has not been published or otherwise reasonably made available prior to the conduct alleged; or

(b) he acts in reasonable reliance upon an official statement of the law, afterward determined to be invalid or erroneous, contained in (i) a statute or other enactment; (ii) a judicial decision, opinion or judgment; (iii) an administrative order or grant of permission; or (iv) an official interpretation of the public officer or body charged by law with responsibility for the interpretation, administration or enforcement of the law defining the offense.

(4) The defendant must prove a defense arising under Subsection (3) of this Section by a preponderance of evidence.

Section 2.05. When Culpability Requirements Are Inapplicable to Violations and to Offenses Defined by Other Statutes; Effect of Absolute Liability in Reducing Grade of Offense to Violation.

(1) The requirements of culpability prescribed by Sections 2.01 and 2.02 do not apply to:

(a) offenses which constitute violations, unless the requirement involved is included in the definition of the offense or the Court determines that its application is consistent with effective enforcement of the law defining the offense; or

(b) offenses defined by statutes other than the Code, insofar as a legislative purpose to impose absolute liability for such offenses or with respect to any material element thereof plainly appears.

(2) Notwithstanding any other provision of existing law and unless a subsequent statute otherwise provides:

(a) when absolute liability is imposed with respect to any material element of an offense defined by a statute other than the Code and a conviction is based upon such liability, the offense constitutes a violation; and

(b) although absolute liability is imposed by law with respect to one or more of the material elements of an offense defined by a statute other than the Code, the culpable commission of the offense may be charged and proved, in which event negligence with respect to such elements constitutes sufficient culpability and the classification of the offense and the sentence that may be imposed therefor upon conviction are determined by Section 1.04 and Article 6 of the Code.

Section 2.06. Liability for Conduct of Another; Complicity.

(1) A person is guilty of an offense if it is committed by his own conduct or by the conduct of another person for which he is legally accountable, or both.

(2) A person is legally accountable for the conduct of another person when:

(a) acting with the kind of culpability that is sufficient for the commission of the offense, he causes an innocent or irresponsible person to engage in such conduct; or

(b) he is made accountable for the conduct of such other person by the Code or by the law defining the offense; or

(c) he is an accomplice of such other person in the commission of the offense.

(3) A person is an accomplice of another person in the commission of an offense if:

(a) with the purpose of promoting or facilitating the commission of the offense, he

(i) solicits such other person to commit it; or

(ii) aids or agrees or attempts to aid such other person in planning or committing it; or

(iii) having a legal duty to prevent the commission of the offense, fails to make proper effort so to do; or

(b) his conduct is expressly declared by law to establish his complicity.

(4) When causing a particular result is an element of an offense, an accomplice in the conduct causing such result is an accomplice in the commission of that offense, if he acts with the kind of culpability, if any, with respect to that result that is sufficient for the commission of the offense.

(5) A person who is legally incapable of committing a particular offense himself may be guilty thereof if it is committed by the conduct of another person for which he is legally accountable, unless such liability is inconsistent with the purpose of the provision establishing his incapacity.

(6) Unless otherwise provided by the Code or by the law defining the offense, a person is not an accomplice in an offense committed by another person if:

(a) he is a victim of that offense; or

(b) the offense is so defined that his conduct is inevitably incident to its commission; or

(c) he terminates his complicity prior to the commission of the offense and

(i) wholly deprives it of effectiveness in the commission of the offense; or

(ii) gives timely warning to the law enforcement authorities or otherwise makes proper effort to prevent the commission of the offense.

(7) An accomplice may be convicted on proof of the commission of the offense and of his complicity therein, though the person claimed to have committed the offense has not been prosecuted or convicted or has been convicted of a different offense or degree of offense or has an immunity to prosecution or conviction or has been acquitted.

Section 2.07. Liability of Corporations, Unincorporated Associations and Persons Acting, or Under a Duty to Act, in Their Behalf.

(1) A corporation may be convicted of the commission of an offense if:

(a) the offense is a violation or the offense is defined by a statute other than the Code in which a legislative purpose to impose liability on corporations plainly appears and the conduct is performed by an agent of the corporation acting in behalf of the corporation within the scope of his office or employment, except that if the law defining the offense designates the agents for whose conduct the corporation is accountable or the circumstances under which it is accountable, such provisions shall apply; or

(b) the offense consists of an omission to discharge a specific duty of affirmative performance imposed on corporations by law; or

(c) the commission of the offense was authorized, requested, commanded, performed or recklessly tolerated by the board of directors or by a high managerial agent acting in behalf of the corporation within the scope of his office or employment.

(2) When absolute liability is imposed for the commission of an offense, a legislative purpose to impose liability on a corporation shall be assumed, unless the contrary plainly appears.

(3) An unincorporated association may be convicted of the commission of an offense if:

(a) the offense is defined by a statute other than the Code which expressly provides for the liability of such an association and the conduct is performed by an agent of the association acting in behalf of the association within the scope of his office or employment, except that if the law defining the offense designates the agents for whose conduct the association is accountable or the circumstances under which it is accountable, such provisions shall apply; or

(b) the offense consists of an omission to discharge a specific duty of affirmative performance imposed on associations by law.

(4) As used in this Section:

(a) "corporation" does not include an entity organized as or by a governmental agency for the execution of a governmental program;

(b) "agent" means any director, officer, servant, employee or other person authorized to act in behalf of the corporation or association and, in the case of an unincorporated association, a member of such association;

(c) "high managerial agent" means an officer of a corporation or an unincorporated association, or, in the case of a partnership, a partner, or any other agent of a corporation or association having duties of such responsibility that his conduct may fairly be assumed to represent the policy of the corporation or association.

(5) In any prosecution of a corporation or an unincorporated association for the

commission of an offense included within the terms of Subsection (1)(a) or Subsection (3)(a) of this Section, other than an offense for which absolute liability has been imposed, it shall be a defense if the defendant proves by a preponderance of evidence that the high managerial agent having supervisory responsibility over the subject matter of the offense employed due diligence to prevent its commission. This paragraph shall not apply if it is plainly inconsistent with the legislative purpose in defining the particular offense.

(6)(a) A person is legally accountable for any conduct he performs or causes to be performed in the name of the corporation or an unincorporated association or in its behalf to the same extent as if it were performed in his own name or behalf.

(b) Whenever a duty to act is imposed by law upon a corporation or an unincorporated association, any agent of the corporation or association having primary responsibility for the discharge of the duty is legally accountable for a reckless omission to perform the required act to the same extent as if the duty were imposed by law directly upon himself.

(c) When a person is convicted of an offense by reason of his legal accountability for the conduct of a corporation or an unincorporated association, he is subject to the sentence authorized by law when a natural person is convicted of an offense of the grade and the degree involved.

Section 2.08. Intoxication.

(1) Except as provided in Subsection (4) of this Section, intoxication of the actor is not a defense unless it negatives an element of the offense.

(2) When recklessness establishes an element of the offense, if the actor, due to self-induced intoxication, is unaware of a risk of which he would have been aware had he been sober, such unawareness is immaterial.

(3) Intoxication does not, in itself, constitute mental disease within the meaning of Section 4.01.

(4) Intoxication which (a) is not self-induced or (b) is pathological is an affirmative defense if by reason of such intoxication the actor at the time of his conduct lacks substantial capacity either to appreciate its criminality [wrongfulness] or to conform his conduct to the requirements of law.

(5) **Definitions.** In this Section unless a different meaning plainly is required:

(a) "intoxication" means a disturbance of mental or physical capacities resulting from the introduction of substances into the body;

(b) "self-induced intoxication" means intoxication caused by substances which the actor knowingly introduces into his body, the tendency of which to cause intoxication he knows or ought to know, unless he introduces them pursuant to medical advice or under such circumstances as would afford a defense to a charge of crime;

(c) "pathological intoxication" means intoxication grossly excessive in degree, given the amount of the intoxicant, to which the actor does not know he is susceptible.

Section 2.09. Duress.

(1) It is an affirmative defense that the actor engaged in the conduct charged to constitute an offense because he was coerced to do so by the use of, or a threat to use, unlawful force against his person or the person of another, which a person of reasonable firmness in his situation would have been unable to resist.

(2) The defense provided by this Section is unavailable if the actor recklessly

placed himself in a situation in which it was probable that he would be subjected to duress. The defense is also unavailable if he was negligent in placing himself in such a situation, whenever negligence suffices to establish culpability for the offense charged.

(3) It is not a defense that a woman acted on the command of her husband, unless she acted under such coercion as would establish a defense under this Section. [The presumption that a woman, acting in the presence of her husband, is coerced is abolished.]

(4) When the conduct of the actor would otherwise be justifiable under Section 3.02, this Section does not preclude such defense.

Section 2.10. Military Orders.

It is an affirmative defense that the actor, in engaging in the conduct charged to constitute an offense, does no more than execute an order of his superior in the armed services which he does not know to be unlawful.

Section 2.11. Consent.

(1) **In General.** The consent of the victim to conduct charged to constitute an offense or to the result thereof is a defense if such consent negatives an element of the offense or precludes the infliction of the harm or evil sought to be prevented by the law defining the offense.

(2) **Consent to Bodily Injury.** When conduct is charged to constitute an offense because it causes or threatens bodily injury, consent to such conduct or to the infliction of such injury is a defense if:

(a) the bodily injury consented to or threatened by the conduct consented to is not serious; or

(b) the conduct and the injury are reasonably foreseeable hazards of joint participation in a lawful athletic contest or competitive sport or other concerted activity not forbidden by law; or

(c) the consent establishes a justification for the conduct under Article 3 of the Code.

(3) **Ineffective Consent.** Unless otherwise provided by the Code or by the law defining the offense, assent does not constitute consent if:

(a) it is given by a person who is legally incompetent to authorize the conduct charged to constitute the offense; or

(b) it is given by a person who by reason of youth, mental disease or defect or intoxication is manifestly unable or known by the actor to be unable to make a reasonable judgment as to the nature or harmfulness of the conduct charged to constitute the offense; or

(c) it is given by a person whose improvident consent is sought to be prevented by the law defining the offense; or

(d) it is induced by force, duress or deception of a kind sought to be prevented by the law defining the offense.

Section 2.12. De Minimis Infractions.

The Court shall dismiss a prosecution if, having regard to the nature of the conduct charged to constitute an offense and the nature of the attendant circumstances, it finds that the defendant's conduct:

(1) was within a customary license or tolerance, neither expressly negatived by the person whose interest was infringed nor inconsistent with the purpose of the law defining the offense; or

(2) did not actually cause or threaten the harm or evil sought to be prevented by the law defining the offense or did so

only to an extent too trivial to warrant the condemnation of conviction; or

(3) presents such other extenuations that it cannot reasonably be regarded as envisaged by the legislature in forbidding the offense.

The Court shall not dismiss a prosecution under Subsection (3) of this Section without filing a written statement of its reasons.

Section 2.13. Entrapment.

(1) A public law enforcement official or a person acting in cooperation with such an official perpetrates an entrapment if for the purpose of obtaining evidence of the commission of an offense, he induces or encourages another person to engage in conduct constituting such offense by either:

(a) making knowingly false representations designed to induce the belief that such conduct is not prohibited; or

(b) employing methods of persuasion or inducement which create a substantial risk that such an offense will be committed by persons other than those who are ready to commit it.

(2) Except as provided in Subsection (3) of this Section, a person prosecuted for an offense shall be acquitted if he proves by a preponderance of evidence that his conduct occurred in response to an entrapment. The issue of entrapment shall be tried by the Court in the absence of the jury.

(3) The defense afforded by this Section is unavailable when causing or threatening bodily injury is an element of the offense charged and the prosecution is based on conduct causing or threatening such injury to a person other than the person perpetrating the entrapment.

ARTICLE 3. GENERAL PRINCIPLES OF JUSTIFICATION

Section 3.01. Justification an Affirmative Defense; Civil Remedies Unaffected.

(1) In any prosecution based on conduct which is justifiable under this Article, justification is an affirmative defense.

(2) The fact that conduct is justifiable under this Article does not abolish or impair any remedy for such conduct which is available in any civil action.

Section 3.02. Justification Generally: Choice of Evils.

(1) Conduct which the actor believes to be necessary to avoid a harm or evil to himself or to another is justifiable, provided that:

(a) the harm or evil sought to be avoided by such conduct is greater than that sought to be prevented by the law defining the offense charged; and

(b) neither the Code nor other law defining the offense provides exceptions or defenses dealing with the specific situation involved; and

(c) a legislative purpose to exclude the justification claimed does not otherwise plainly appear.

(2) When the actor was reckless or negligent in bringing about the situation requiring a choice of harms or evils or in appraising the necessity for his conduct, the justification afforded by this Section is unavailable in a prosecution for any offense for which recklessness or negligence, as the case may be, suffices to establish culpability.

Section 3.03. Execution of Public Duty.

(1) Except as provided in Subsection (2) of this Section, conduct is justifiable when it is required or authorized by:

(a) the law defining the duties or functions of a public officer or the assistance to be rendered to such officer in the performance of his duties; or

(b) the law governing the execution of legal process; or

(c) the judgment or order of a competent court or tribunal; or

(d) the law governing the armed services or the lawful conduct of war; or

(e) any other provision of law imposing a public duty.

(2) The other sections of this Article apply to:

(a) the use of force upon or toward the person of another for any of the purposes dealt with in such sections; and

(b) the use of deadly force for any purpose, unless the use of such force is otherwise expressly authorized by law or occurs in the lawful conduct of war.

(3) The justification afforded by Subsection (1) of this Section applies:

(a) when the actor believes his conduct to be required or authorized by the judgment or direction of a competent court or tribunal or in the lawful execution of legal process, notwithstanding lack of jurisdiction of the court or defect in the legal process; and

(b) when the actor believes his conduct to be required or authorized to assist a public officer in the performance of his duties, notwithstanding that the officer exceeded his legal authority.

Section 3.04. Use of Force in Self–Protection.

(1) **Use of Force Justifiable for Protection of the Person.** Subject to the provisions of this Section and of Section 3.09, the use of force upon or toward another person is justifiable when the actor believes that such force is immediately necessary for the purpose of protecting himself against the use of unlawful force by such other person on the present occasion.

(2) **Limitations on Justifying Necessity for Use of Force.**

(a) The use of force is not justifiable under this Section:

(i) to resist an arrest which the actor knows is being made by a peace officer, although the arrest is unlawful; or

(ii) to resist force used by the occupier or possessor of property or by another person on his behalf, where the actor knows that the person using the force is doing so under a claim of right to protect the property, except that this limitation shall not apply if:

(1) the actor is a public officer acting in the performance of his duties or a person lawfully assisting him therein or a person making or assisting in a lawful arrest; or

(2) the actor has been unlawfully dispossessed of the property and is making a re-entry or recaption justified by Section 3.06; or

(3) the actor believes that such force is necessary to protect himself against death or serious bodily harm.

(b) The use of deadly force is not justifiable under this Section unless the actor believes that such force is necessary to protect himself against death, serious bodily harm, kidnapping or sexual intercourse compelled by force or threat; nor is it justifiable if:

(i) the actor, with the purpose of causing death or serious bodily harm, provoked the use of force against himself in the same encounter; or

(ii) the actor knows that he can avoid the necessity of using such force with complete safety by retreating or by surrendering possession of a thing to a person asserting a claim of right thereto or by complying with a demand that he abstain from any action which he has no duty to take, except that:

(1) the actor is not obliged to retreat from his dwelling or place of work, unless he was the initial aggressor or is assailed in his place of work by another person whose place of work the actor knows it to be; and

(2) a public officer justified in using force in the performance of his duties or a person justified in using force in his assistance or a person justified in using force in making an arrest or preventing an escape is not obliged to desist from efforts to perform such duty, effect such arrest or prevent such escape because of resistance or threatened resistance by or on behalf of the person against whom such action is directed.

(c) Except as required by paragraphs (a) and (b) of this Subsection, a person employing protective force may estimate the necessity thereof under the circumstances as he believes them to be when the force is used, without retreating, surrendering possession, doing any other act which he has no legal duty to do or abstaining from any lawful action.

(3) **Use of Confinement as Protective Force.** The justification afforded by this Section extends to the use of confinement as protective force only if the actor takes all reasonable measures to terminate the confinement as soon as he knows that he safely can, unless the person confined has been arrested on a charge of crime.

Section 3.05. Use of Force for the Protection of Other Persons.

(1) Subject to the provisions of this Section and of Section 3.09, the use of force upon or toward the person of another is justifiable to protect a third person when:

(a) the actor would be justified under Section 3.04 in using such force to protect himself against the injury he believes to be threatened to the person whom he seeks to protect; and

(b) under the circumstances as the actor believes them to be, the person whom he seeks to protect would be justified in using such protective force; and

(c) the actor believes that his intervention is necessary for the protection of such other person.

(2) Notwithstanding Subsection (1) of this Section:

(a) when the actor would be obliged under Section 3.04 to retreat, to surrender the possession of a thing or to comply with a demand before using force in self-protection, he is not obliged to do so before using force for the protection of another person, unless he knows that he can thereby secure the complete safety of such other person; and

(b) when the person whom the actor seeks to protect would be obliged under Section 3.04 to retreat, to surrender the possession of a thing or to comply with a demand if he knew that he could obtain complete safety by so doing, the actor is obliged to try to cause him to do so before using force in his protection if the actor knows that he can obtain complete safety in that way; and

(c) neither the actor nor the person whom he seeks to protect is obliged to retreat when in the other's dwelling or place of work to any greater extent than in his own.

Section 3.06. Use of Force for the Protection of Property.

(1) **Use of Force Justifiable for Protection of Property.** Subject to the provisions of this Section and of Section 3.09, the use of force upon or toward the person of another is justifiable when the actor believes that such force is immediately necessary:

(a) to prevent or terminate an unlawful entry or other trespass upon land or a trespass against or the unlawful carrying away of tangible, movable property, provided that such land or movable property is, or is believed by the actor to be, in his possession or in the possession of another person for whose protection he acts; or

(b) to effect an entry or re-entry upon land or to retake tangible movable property, provided that the actor believes that he or the person by whose authority he acts or a person from whom he or such other person derives title was unlawfully dispossessed of such land or movable property and is entitled to possession, and provided, further, that:

(i) the force is used immediately or on fresh pursuit after such dispossession; or

(ii) the actor believes that the person against whom he uses force has no claim of right to the possession of the property and, in the case of land, the circumstances, as the actor believes them to be, are of such urgency that it would be an exceptional hardship to postpone the entry or re-entry until a court order is obtained.

(2) **Meaning of Possession.** For the purposes of Subsection (1) of this Section:

(a) a person who has parted with the custody of property to another who refuses to restore it to him is no longer in possession, unless the property is movable and was and still is located on land in his possession;

(b) a person who has been dispossessed of land does not regain possession thereof merely by setting foot thereon;

(c) a person who has a license to use or occupy real property is deemed to be in possession thereof except against the licensor acting under claim of right.

(3) **Limitations on Justifiable Use of Force.**

(a) *Request to Desist.* The use of force is justifiable under this Section only if the actor first requests the person against whom such force is used to desist from his interference with the property, unless the actor believes that:

(i) such request would be useless; or

(ii) it would be dangerous to himself or another person to make the request; or

(iii) substantial harm will be done to the physical condition of the property which is sought to be protected before the request can effectively be made.

(b) *Exclusion of Trespasser.* The use of force to prevent or terminate a trespass is not justifiable under this Section if the actor knows that the exclusion of the trespasser will expose him to substantial danger of serious bodily harm.

(c) *Resistance of Lawful Re-entry or Recaption.* The use of force to prevent an entry or re-entry upon land or the recaption of movable property is not justifiable under this Section, although the actor believes that such re-entry or recaption is unlawful, if:

(i) the re-entry or recaption is made by or on behalf of a person who was actually dispossessed of the property; and

(ii) it is otherwise justifiable under paragraph (1)(b) of this Section.

(d) *Use of Deadly Force.* The use of deadly force is not justifiable under this Section unless the actor believes that:

(i) the person against whom the force is used is attempting to dispossess him of his dwelling otherwise than under a claim of right to its possession; or

(ii) the person against whom the force is used is attempting to commit or consummate arson, burglary, robbery or other felonious theft or property destruction and either:

(1) has employed or threatened deadly force against or in the presence of the actor; or

(2) the use of force other than deadly force to prevent the commission or the consummation of the crime would expose the actor or another in his presence to substantial danger of serious bodily harm.

(4) **Use of Confinement as Protective Force.** The justification afforded by this Section extends to the use of confinement as protective force only if the actor takes all reasonable measures to terminate the confinement as soon as he knows that he can do so with safety to the property, unless the person confined has been arrested on a charge of crime.

(5) **Use of Device to Protect Property.** The justification afforded by this Section extends to the use of a device for the purpose of protecting property only if:

(a) the device is not designed to cause or known to create a substantial risk of causing death or serious bodily harm; and

(b) the use of the particular device to protect the property from entry or trespass is reasonable under the circumstances, as the actor believes them to be; and

(c) the device is one customarily used for such a purpose or reasonable care is taken to make known to probable intruders the fact that it is used.

(6) **Use of Force to Pass Wrongful Obstructor.** The use of force to pass a person whom the actor believes to be purposely or knowingly and unjustifiably obstructing the actor from going to a place to which he may lawfully go is justifiable, provided that:

(a) the actor believes that the person against whom he uses force has no claim of right to obstruct the actor; and

(b) the actor is not being obstructed from entry or movement on land which he knows to be in the possession or custody of the person obstructing him, or in the possession or custody of another person by whose authority the obstructor acts, unless the circumstances, as the actor believes them to be, are of such urgency that it would not be reasonable to postpone the entry or movement on such land until a court order is obtained; and

(c) the force used is not greater than would be justifiable if the person obstructing the actor were using force against him to prevent his passage.

Section 3.07. Use of Force in Law Enforcement.

(1) **Use of Force Justifiable to Effect an Arrest.** Subject to the provisions of this Section and of Section 3.09, the use of force upon or toward the person of another is justifiable when the actor is making or assisting in making an arrest and the actor believes that such force is immediately necessary to effect a lawful arrest.

(2) **Limitations on the Use of Force.**

(a) The use of force is not justifiable under this Section unless:

(i) the actor makes known the purpose of the arrest or believes that it is otherwise known by or cannot reasonably be made known to the person to be arrested; and

(ii) when the arrest is made under a warrant, the warrant is valid or believed by the actor to be valid.

(b) The use of deadly force is not justifiable under this Section unless:

(i) the arrest is for a felony; and

(ii) the person effecting the arrest is authorized to act as a peace officer or is assisting a person whom he believes to be authorized to act as a peace officer; and

(iii) the actor believes that the force employed creates no substantial risk of injury to innocent persons; and

(iv) the actor believes that:

(1) the crime for which the arrest is made involved conduct including the use or threatened use of deadly force; or

(2) there is a substantial risk that the person to be arrested will cause death or serious bodily harm if his apprehension is delayed.

(3) **Use of Force to Prevent Escape from Custody.** The use of force to prevent the escape of an arrested person from custody is justifiable when the force could justifiably have been employed to effect the arrest under which the person is in custody, except that a guard or other person authorized to act as a peace officer is justified in using any force, including deadly force, which he believes to be immediately necessary to prevent the escape of a person from a jail, prison, or other institution for the detention of persons charged with or convicted of a crime.

(4) **Use of Force by Private Person Assisting an Unlawful Arrest.**

(a) A private person who is summoned by a peace officer to assist in effecting an unlawful arrest, is justified in using any force which he would be justified in using if the arrest were lawful provided that he does not believe the arrest is unlawful.

(b) A private person who assists another private person in effecting an unlawful arrest, or who, not being summoned, assists a peace officer in effecting an unlawful arrest, is justified in using any force which he would be justified in using if the arrest were lawful, provided that (i) he believes the arrest is lawful, and (ii) the arrest would be lawful if the facts were as he believes them to be.

(5) **Use of Force to Prevent Suicide or the Commission of a Crime.**

(a) The use of force upon or toward the person of another is justifiable when the actor believes that such force is immediately necessary to prevent such other person from committing suicide, inflicting serious bodily harm upon himself, committing or consummating the commission of a crime involving or threatening bodily harm, damage to or loss of property or a breach of the peace, except that:

(i) any limitations imposed by the other provisions of this Article on the justifiable use of force in self-protection, for the protection of others, the protection of property, the effectuation of an arrest or the prevention of an escape from custody shall apply notwithstanding the criminality of the conduct against which such force is used; and

(ii) the use of deadly force is not in any event justifiable under this Subsection unless:

(1) the actor believes that there is a substantial risk that the person whom he seeks to prevent from

committing a crime will cause death or serious bodily harm to another unless the commission or the consummation of the crime is prevented and that the use of such force presents no substantial risk of injury to innocent persons; or

(2) the actor believes that the use of such force is necessary to suppress a riot or mutiny after the rioters or mutineers have been ordered to disperse and warned, in any particular manner that the law may require, that such force will be used if they do not obey.

(b) The justification afforded by this Subsection extends to the use of confinement as preventive force only if the actor takes all reasonable measures to terminate the confinement as soon as he knows that he safely can, unless the person confined has been arrested on a charge of crime.

Section 3.08. Use of Force by Persons With Special Responsibility for Care, Discipline or Safety of Others.

The use of force upon or toward the person of another is justifiable if:

(1) the actor is the parent or guardian or other person similarly responsible for the general care and supervision of a minor or a person acting at the request of such parent, guardian or other responsible person and:

(a) the force is used for the purpose of safeguarding or promoting the welfare of the minor, including the prevention or punishment of his misconduct; and

(b) the force used is not designed to cause or known to create a substantial risk of causing death, serious bodily harm, disfigurement, extreme pain or mental distress or gross degradation; or

(2) the actor is a teacher or a person otherwise entrusted with the care or supervision for a special purpose of a minor and:

(a) the actor believes that the force used is necessary to further such special purpose, including the maintenance of reasonable discipline in a school, class or other group, and that the use of such force is consistent with the welfare of the minor; and

(b) the degree of force, if it had been used by the parent or guardian of the minor, would not be unjustifiable under Subsection (1)(b) of this Section; or

(3) the actor is the guardian or other person similarly responsible for the general care and supervision of an incompetent person; and:

(a) the force is used for the purpose of safeguarding or promoting the welfare of the incompetent person, including the prevention of his misconduct, or, when such incompetent person is in a hospital or other institution for his care and custody, for the maintenance of reasonable discipline in such institution; and

(b) the force used is not designed to cause or known to create a substantial risk of causing death, serious bodily harm, disfigurement, extreme or unnecessary pain, mental distress, or humiliation; or

(4) the actor is a doctor or other therapist or a person assisting him at his direction, and:

(a) the force is used for the purpose of administering a recognized form of treatment which the actor believes to be adapted to promoting the physical or mental health of the patient; and

(b) the treatment is administered with the consent of the patient or, if the patient is a minor or an incompetent person, with the consent of his parent or guardian or other person legally competent to consent in his behalf, or the treatment is administered in an emergency when the actor believes that no one competent to consent can be consulted and that a reasonable person, wishing to safeguard the welfare of the patient, would consent; or

(5) the actor is a warden or other authorized official of a correctional institution, and:

(a) he believes that the force used is necessary for the purpose of enforcing the lawful rules or procedures of the institution, unless his belief in the lawfulness of the rule or procedure sought to be enforced is erroneous and his error is due to ignorance or mistake as to the provisions of the Code, any other provision of the criminal law or the law governing the administration of the institution; and

(b) the nature or degree of force used is not forbidden by Article 303 or 304 of the Code; and

(c) if deadly force is used, its use is otherwise justifiable under this Article; or

(6) the actor is a person responsible for the safety of a vessel or an aircraft or a person acting at his direction, and

(a) he believes that the force used is necessary to prevent interference with the operation of the vessel or aircraft or obstruction of the execution of a lawful order, unless his belief in the lawfulness of the order is erroneous and his error is due to ignorance or mistake as to the law defining his authority; and

(b) if deadly force is used, its use is otherwise justifiable under this Article; or

(7) the actor is a person who is authorized or required by law to maintain order or decorum in a vehicle, train or other carrier or in a place where others are assembled, and:

(a) he believes that the force used is necessary for such purpose; and

(b) the force used is not designed to cause or known to create a substantial risk of causing death, bodily harm, or extreme mental distress.

Section 3.09. Mistake of Law as to Unlawfulness of Force or Legality of Arrest; Reckless or Negligent Use of Otherwise Justifiable Force; Reckless or Negligent Injury or Risk of Injury to Innocent Persons.

(1) The justification afforded by Sections 3.04 to 3.07, inclusive, is unavailable when:

(a) the actor's belief in the unlawfulness of the force or conduct against which he employs protective force or his belief in the lawfulness of an arrest which he endeavors to effect by force is erroneous; and

(b) his error is due to ignorance or mistake as to the provisions of the Code, any other provision of the criminal law or the law governing the legality of an arrest or search.

(2) When the actor believes that the use of force upon or toward the person of another is necessary for any of the purposes for which such belief would establish a justification under Sections 3.03 to 3.08 but the actor is reckless or negligent in having such belief or in acquiring or failing to acquire any knowledge or belief which is material to the justifiability of his use of force, the justification afforded by those Sections is unavailable in a prosecution for an offense for which recklessness or negligence, as the case may be, suffices to establish culpability.

(3) When the actor is justified under Sections 3.03 to 3.08 in using force upon or toward the person of another but he

recklessly or negligently injures or creates a risk of injury to innocent persons, the justification afforded by those Sections is unavailable in a prosecution for such recklessness or negligence towards innocent persons.

Section 3.10. Justification in Property Crimes.

Conduct involving the appropriation, seizure or destruction of, damage to, intrusion on or interference with property is justifiable under circumstances which would establish a defense of privilege in a civil action based thereon, unless:

(1) the Code or the law defining the offense deals with the specific situation involved; or

(2) a legislative purpose to exclude the justification claimed otherwise plainly appears.

Section 3.11. Definitions.

In this Article, unless a different meaning plainly is required:

(1) "unlawful force" means force, including confinement, which is employed without the consent of the person against whom it is directed and the employment of which constitutes an offense or actionable tort or would constitute such offense or tort except for a defense (such as the absence of intent, negligence, or mental capacity; duress; youth; or diplomatic status) not amounting to a privilege to use the force. Assent constitutes consent, within the meaning of this Section, whether or not it otherwise is legally effective, except assent to the infliction of death or serious bodily harm.

(2) "deadly force" means force which the actor uses with the purpose of causing or which he knows to create a substantial risk of causing death or serious bodily harm. Purposely firing a firearm in the direction of another person or at a vehicle in which another person is believed to be constitutes deadly force. A threat to cause death or serious bodily harm, by the production of a weapon or otherwise, so long as the actor's purpose is limited to creating an apprehension that he will use deadly force if necessary, does not constitute deadly force;

(3) "dwelling" means any building or structure, though movable or temporary, or a portion thereof, which is for the time being the actor's home or place of lodging.

ARTICLE 4. RESPONSIBILITY

Section 4.01. Mental Disease or Defect Excluding Responsibility.

(1) A person is not responsible for criminal conduct if at the time of such conduct as a result of mental disease or defect he lacks substantial capacity either to appreciate the criminality [wrongfulness] of his conduct or to conform his conduct to the requirements of law.

(2) As used in this Article, the terms "mental disease or defect" do not include an abnormality manifested only by repeated criminal or otherwise anti-social conduct.

Section 4.02. Evidence of Mental Disease or Defect Admissible When Relevant to Element of the Offense; [Mental Disease or Defect Impairing Capacity as Ground for Mitigation of Punishment in Capital Cases].

(1) Evidence that the defendant suffered from a mental disease or defect is admissible whenever it is relevant to prove that the defendant did or did not have a state of mind which is an element of the offense.

[(2) Whenever the jury or the Court is authorized to determine or to recommend whether or not the defendant shall be sentenced to death or imprisonment upon conviction, evidence that the capacity of the defendant to appreciate the criminality [wrongfulness] of his conduct or to conform his conduct to the requirements of law was impaired as a result of mental disease or defect is admissible in favor of sentence of imprisonment.]

Section 4.03.   Mental Disease or Defect Excluding Responsibility is Affirmative Defense; Requirement of Notice; Form of Verdict and Judgment When Finding of Irresponsibility is Made.

(1) Mental disease or defect excluding responsibility is an affirmative defense.

(2) Evidence of mental disease or defect excluding responsibility is not admissible unless the defendant, at the time of entering his plea of not guilty or within ten days thereafter or at such later time as the Court may for good cause permit, files a written notice of his purpose to rely on such defense.

(3) When the defendant is acquitted on the ground of mental disease or defect excluding responsibility, the verdict and the judgment shall so state.

Section 4.04.   Mental Disease or Defect Excluding Fitness to Proceed.

No person who as a result of mental disease or defect lacks capacity to understand the proceedings against him or to assist in his own defense shall be tried, convicted or sentenced for the commission of an offense so long as such incapacity endures.

Section 4.05.   Psychiatric Examination of Defendant With Respect to Mental Disease or Defect.

(1) Whenever the defendant has filed a notice of intention to rely on the defense of mental disease or defect excluding responsibility, or there is reason to doubt his fitness to proceed, or reason to believe that mental disease or defect of the defendant will otherwise become an issue in the

cause, the Court shall appoint at least one qualified psychiatrist or shall request the Superintendent of the Hospital to designate at least one qualified psychiatrist, which designation may be or include himself, to examine and report upon the mental condition of the defendant. The Court may order the defendant to be committed to a hospital or other suitable facility for the purpose of the examination for a period of not exceeding sixty days or such longer period as the Court determines to be necessary for the purpose and may direct that a qualified psychiatrist retained by the defendant be permitted to witness and participate in the examination.

(2) In such examination any method may be employed which is accepted by the medical profession for the examination of those alleged to be suffering from mental disease or defect.

(3) The report of the examination shall include the following: (a) a description of the nature of the examination; (b) a diagnosis of the mental condition of the defendant; (c) if the defendant suffers from a mental disease or defect, an opinion as to his capacity to understand the proceedings against him and to assist in his own defense; (d) when a notice of intention to rely on the defense of irresponsibility has been filed, an opinion as to the extent, if any, to which the capacity of the defendant to appreciate the criminality [wrongfulness] of his conduct or to conform his conduct to the requirements of law was impaired at the time of the criminal conduct charged; and (e) when directed by the Court, an opinion as to the capacity of the defendant to have a particular state of mind which is an element of the offense charged.

If the examination can not be conducted by reason of the unwillingness of the defendant to participate therein, the report shall so state and shall include, if possible, an opinion as to whether such unwillingness of the defendant was the result of mental disease or defect.

The report of the examination shall be filed [in triplicate] with the clerk of the Court, who shall cause copies to be delivered to the district attorney and to counsel for the defendant.

Section 4.06. Determination of Fitness to Proceed; Effect of Finding of Unfitness; Proceedings if Fitness is Regained [; Post–Commitment Hearing].

(1) When the defendant's fitness to proceed is drawn in question, the issue shall be determined by the Court. If neither the prosecuting attorney nor counsel for the defendant contests the finding of the report filed pursuant to Section 4.05, the Court may make the determination on the basis of such report. If the finding is contested, the Court shall hold a hearing on the issue. If the report is received in evidence upon such hearing, the party who contests the finding thereof shall have the right to summon and to cross-examine the psychiatrists who joined in the report and to offer evidence upon the issue.

(2) If the Court determines that the defendant lacks fitness to proceed, the proceeding against him shall be suspended, except as provided in Subsection (3) [Subsections (3) and (4)] of this Section, and the Court shall commit him to the custody of the Commissioner of Mental Hygiene [Public Health or Correction] to be placed in an appropriate institution of the Department of Mental Hygiene [Public Health or Correction] for so long as such unfitness shall endure. When the Court, on its own motion or upon the application of the Commissioner of Mental Hygiene [Public Health or Correction] or the prosecuting attorney, determines, after a hearing if a hearing is requested, that the defendant has regained fitness to proceed, the proceeding shall be resumed. If, however, the Court is of the view that so much time has elapsed since the commitment of the defendant that it would be unjust to resume the criminal proceeding, the Court may dismiss the charge and may order the defendant to be discharged or, subject to the law governing the civil commitment of persons suffering from mental disease or defect, order the defendant to be committed to an appropriate institution of the Department of Mental Hygiene [Public Health].

(3) The fact that the defendant is unfit to proceed does not preclude any legal objection to the prosecution which is susceptible of fair determination prior to trial and without the personal participation of the defendant.

[Alternative: (3) At any time within ninety days after commitment as provided in Subsection (2) of this Section, or at any later time with permission of the Court granted for good cause, the defendant or his counsel or the Commissioner of Mental Hygiene [Public Health or Correction] may apply for a special post-commitment hearing. If the application is made by or on behalf of a defendant not represented by counsel, he shall be afforded a reasonable opportunity to obtain counsel, and if he lacks funds to do so, counsel shall be assigned by the Court. The application shall be granted only if the counsel for the defendant satisfies the Court by affidavit or otherwise that as an attorney he has reasonable grounds for a good faith belief that his client has, on the facts and the law, a defense to the charge other than mental disease or defect excluding responsibility.

[(4) If the motion for a special post-commitment hearing is granted, the hearing shall be by the Court without a jury. No evidence shall be offered at the hearing by either party on the issue of mental disease or defect as a defense to, or in mitigation of, the crime charged. After hearing, the Court may in an appropriate case quash the indictment or other charge, or find it to be defective or insufficient, or determine that it is not proved beyond a reasonable doubt by the evidence, or otherwise terminate the proceedings on the evidence or the law. In any such case, unless all defects in the proceedings are promptly cured, the Court shall terminate the commitment ordered under Subsection (2) of this Section and order the defendant to be discharged or, subject to the law governing the civil commitment of persons suffering from mental disease or defect, order the defendant to be committed to an appropriate institution of the Department of Mental Hygiene [Public Health].]

Section 4.07. Determination of Irresponsibility on Basis of Report; Access to Defendant by Psychiatrist of His Own Choice; Form of Expert Testimony When Issue of Responsibility is Tried.

(1) If the report filed pursuant to Section 4.05 finds that the defendant at the time of the criminal conduct charged suffered from a mental disease or defect which substantially impaired his capacity to appreciate the criminality [wrongfulness] of his conduct or to conform his conduct to the requirements of law, and the Court, after a hearing if a hearing is requested by the prosecuting attorney or the defendant, is satisfied that such impairment was sufficient to exclude responsibility, the Court on motion of the defendant shall enter judgment of acquittal on the ground of mental disease or defect excluding responsibility.

(2) When, notwithstanding the report filed pursuant to Section 4.05, the defendant wishes to be examined by a qualified psychiatrist or other expert of his own choice, such examiner shall be permitted to have reasonable access to the defendant for the purposes of such examination.

(3) Upon the trial, the psychiatrists who reported pursuant to Section 4.05 may be called as witnesses by the prosecution, the defendant or the Court. If the issue is being tried before a jury, the jury may be informed that the psychiatrists were designated by the Court or by the Superintendent of the Hospital at the request of the Court as the case may be. If called by the Court, the witness shall be subject to cross-examination by the prosecution and by the defendant. Both the prosecution and the defendant may summon any other qualified psychiatrist or other expert to testify, but no one who has not examined the defendant shall be competent to testify to an expert opinion with respect to the mental condition or responsibility of the defendant, as distinguished from the validity of the procedure followed by, or the general scientific propositions stated by, another witness.

(4) When a psychiatrist or other expert who has examined the defendant testifies concerning his mental condition, he shall be permitted to make a statement as to the nature of his examination, his diagnosis of the mental condition of the defendant at the time of the commission of the offense charged and his opinion as to the extent, if any, to which the capacity of the defendant to appreciate the criminality [wrongfulness] of his conduct or to conform his conduct to the requirements of law or to have a particular state of mind which is an element of the offense charged was impaired as a result of mental disease or defect at that time. He shall be permitted to make any explanation reasonably serving to clarify his diagnosis and opinion and may be cross-examined as to any matter bearing on his competency or credibility or the validity of his diagnosis or opinion.

Section 4.08. Legal Effect of Acquittal on the Ground of Mental Disease or Defect Excluding Responsibility; Commitment; Release or Discharge.

(1) When a defendant is acquitted on the ground of mental disease or defect excluding responsibility, the Court shall order him to be committed to the custody of the Commissioner of Mental Hygiene [Public Health] to be placed in an appropriate institution for custody, care and treatment.

(2) If the Commissioner of Mental Hygiene [Public Health] is of the view that a person committed to his custody, pursuant to paragraph (1) of this Section, may be discharged or released on condition without danger to himself or to others, he shall make application for the discharge or release of such person in a report to the Court by which such person was committed and shall transmit a copy of such application and report to the prosecuting attorney of the county [parish] from which the defendant was committed. The Court shall thereupon appoint at least two qualified psychiatrists to examine such person and to report within sixty days, or such longer period as the Court determines to be necessary for the purpose, their opinion as to his mental condition. To facilitate such examination and the proceedings thereon, the Court may cause such person to be confined in any institution located near the place where the Court sits, which may hereafter be designated by the Commissioner of Mental Hygiene [Public Health] as suitable for the temporary detention of irresponsible persons.

(3) If the Court is satisfied by the report filed pursuant to paragraph (2) of this Section and such testimony of the reporting psychiatrists as the Court deems necessary that the committed person may be discharged or released on condition without danger to himself or others, the Court

shall order his discharge or his release on such conditions as the Court determines to be necessary. If the Court is not so satisfied, it shall promptly order a hearing to determine whether such person may safely be discharged or released. Any such hearing shall be deemed a civil proceeding and the burden shall be upon the committed person to prove that he may safely be discharged or released. According to the determination of the Court upon the hearing, the committed person shall thereupon be discharged or released on such conditions as the Court determines to be necessary, or shall be recommitted to the custody of the Commissioner of Mental Hygiene [Public Health], subject to discharge or release only in accordance with the procedure prescribed above for a first hearing.

(4) If, within [five] years after the conditional release of a committed person, the Court shall determine, after hearing evidence, that the conditions of release have not been fulfilled and that for the safety of such person or for the safety of others his conditional release should be revoked, the Court shall forthwith order him to be recommitted to the Commissioner of Mental Hygiene [Public Health], subject to discharge or release only in accordance with the procedure prescribed above for a first hearing.

(5) A committed person may make application for his discharge or release to the Court by which he was committed, and the procedure to be followed upon such application shall be the same as that prescribed above in the case of an application by the Commissioner of Mental Hygiene [Public Health]. However, no such application by a committed person need be considered until he has been confined for a period of not less than [six months] from the date of the order of commitment, and if the determination of the Court be adverse to the

application, such person shall not be permitted to file a further application until [one year] has elapsed from the date of any preceding hearing on an application for his release or discharge.

Section 4.09. Statements for Purposes of Examination or Treatment Inadmissible Except on Issue of Mental Condition.

A statement made by a person subjected to psychiatric examination or treatment pursuant to Sections 4.05, 4.06 or 4.08 for the purposes of such examination or treatment shall not be admissible in evidence against him in any criminal proceeding on any issue other than that of his mental condition but it shall be admissible upon that issue, whether or not it would otherwise be deemed a privileged communication [, unless such statement constitutes an admission of guilt of the crime charged].

Section 4.10. Immaturity Excluding Criminal Conviction; Transfer of Proceedings to Juvenile Court.

(1) A person shall not be tried for or convicted of an offense if:

(a) at the time of the conduct charged to constitute the offense he was less than sixteen years of age [, in which case the Juvenile Court shall have exclusive jurisdiction *]; or

(b) at the time of the conduct charged to constitute the offense he was sixteen or seventeen years of age unless:

(i) the Juvenile Court has no jurisdiction over him, or,

(ii) the Juvenile Court has entered an order waiving jurisdiction and consenting to the institution of criminal proceedings against him.

(2) No court shall have jurisdiction to try or convict a person of an offense if

---

* The bracketed words are unnecessary if the Juvenile Court Act so provides or is amended accordingly.

---

criminal proceedings against him are barred by Subsection (1) of this Section. When it appears that a person charged with the commission of an offense may be of such an age that criminal proceedings may be barred under Subsection (1) of this Section, the Court shall hold a hearing thereon, and the burden shall be on the prosecution to establish to the satisfaction of the Court that the criminal proceeding is not barred upon such grounds. If the Court determines that the proceeding is barred, custody of the person charged shall be surrendered to the Juvenile Court, and the case, including all papers and processes relating thereto, shall be transferred.

ARTICLE 5. INCHOATE CRIMES

Section 5.01. Criminal Attempt.

(1) **Definition of Attempt.** A person is guilty of an attempt to commit a crime if, acting with the kind of culpability otherwise required for commission of the crime, he:

(a) purposely engages in conduct which would constitute the crime if the attendant circumstances were as he believes them to be; or

(b) when causing a particular result is an element of the crime, does or omits to do anything with the purpose of causing or with the belief that it will cause such result without further conduct on his part; or

(c) purposely does or omits to do anything which, under the circumstances as he believes them to be, is an act or omission constituting a substantial step in a course of conduct planned to culminate in his commission of the crime.

(2) **Conduct Which May Be Held Substantial Step Under Subsection (1) (c).** Conduct shall not be held to consti-

tute a substantial step under Subsection (1) (c) of this Section unless it is strongly corroborative of the actor's criminal purpose. Without negativing the sufficiency of other conduct, the following, if strongly corroborative of the actor's criminal purpose, shall not be held insufficient as a matter of law:

(a) lying in wait, searching for or following the contemplated victim of the crime;

(b) enticing or seeking to entice the contemplated victim of the crime to go to the place contemplated for its commission;

(c) reconnoitering the place contemplated for the commission of the crime;

(d) unlawful entry of a structure, vehicle or enclosure in which it is contemplated that the crime will be committed;

(e) possession of materials to be employed in the commission of the crime, which are specially designed for such unlawful use or which can serve no lawful purpose of the actor under the circumstances;

(f) possession, collection or fabrication of materials to be employed in the commission of the crime, at or near the place contemplated for its commission, where such possession, collection or fabrication serves no lawful purpose of the actor under the circumstances;

(g) soliciting an innocent agent to engage in conduct constituting an element of the crime.

(3) **Conduct Designed to Aid Another in Commission of a Crime.** A person who engages in conduct designed to aid another to commit a crime which would establish his complicity under Section 2.06 if the crime were committed by such other person, is guilty of an attempt to commit the crime, although the crime is not committed or attempted by such other person.

(4) **Renunciation of Criminal Purpose.** When the actor's conduct would otherwise constitute an attempt under Subsection (1)(b) or (1)(c) of this Section, it is an affirmative defense that he abandoned his effort to commit the crime or otherwise prevented its commission, under circumstances manifesting a complete and voluntary renunciation of his criminal purpose. The establishment of such defense does not, however, affect the liability of an accomplice who did not join in such abandonment or prevention.

Within the meaning of this Article, renunciation of criminal purpose is not voluntary if it is motivated, in whole or in part, by circumstances, not present or apparent at the inception of the actor's course of conduct, which increase the probability of detection or apprehension or which make more difficult the accomplishment of the criminal purpose. Renunciation is not complete if it is motivated by a decision to postpone the criminal conduct until a more advantageous time or to transfer the criminal effort to another but similar objective or victim.

Section 5.02. Criminal Solicitation.

(1) **Definition of Solicitation.** A person is guilty of solicitation to commit a crime if with the purpose of promoting or facilitating its commission he commands, encourages or requests another person to engage in specific conduct which would constitute such crime or an attempt to commit such crime or which would establish his complicity in its commission or attempted commission.

(2) **Uncommunicated Solicitation.** It is immaterial under Subsection (1) of this Section that the actor fails to communicate with the person he solicits to commit a crime if his conduct was designed to effect such communication.

(3) **Renunciation of Criminal Purpose.** It is an affirmative defense that the

actor, after soliciting another person to commit a crime, persuaded him not to do so or otherwise prevented the commission of the crime, under circumstances manifesting a complete and voluntary renunciation of his criminal purpose.

Section 5.03. Criminal Conspiracy.

(1) **Definition of Conspiracy.** A person is guilty of conspiracy with another person or persons to commit a crime if with the purpose of promoting or facilitating its commission he:

(a) agrees with such other person or persons that they or one or more of them will engage in conduct which constitutes such crime or an attempt or solicitation to commit such crime; or

(b) agrees to aid such other person or persons in the planning or commission of such crime or of an attempt or solicitation to commit such crime.

(2) **Scope of Conspiratorial Relationship.** If a person guilty of conspiracy, as defined by Subsection (1) of this Section, knows that a person with whom he conspires to commit a crime has conspired with another person or persons to commit the same crime, he is guilty of conspiring with such other person or persons, whether or not he knows their identity, to commit such crime.

(3) **Conspiracy With Multiple Criminal Objectives.** If a person conspires to commit a number of crimes, he is guilty of only one conspiracy so long as such multiple crimes are the object of the same agreement or continuous conspiratorial relationship.

(4) **Joinder and Venue in Conspiracy Prosecutions.**

(a) Subject to the provisions of paragraph (b) of this Subsection, two or more persons charged with criminal conspiracy may be prosecuted jointly if:

(i) they are charged with conspiring with one another; or

(ii) the conspiracies alleged, whether they have the same or different parties, are so related that they constitute different aspects of a scheme of organized criminal conduct.

(b) In any joint prosecution under paragraph (a) of this Subsection:

(i) no defendant shall be charged with a conspiracy in any county [parish or district] other than one in which he entered into such conspiracy or in which an overt act pursuant to such conspiracy was done by him or by a person with whom he conspired; and

(ii) neither the liability of any defendant nor the admissibility against him of evidence of acts or declarations of another shall be enlarged by such joinder; and

(iii) the Court shall order a severance or take a special verdict as to any defendant who so requests, if it deems it necessary or appropriate to promote the fair determination of his guilt or innocence, and shall take any other proper measures to protect the fairness of the trial.

(5) **Overt Act.** No person may be convicted of conspiracy to commit a crime, other than a felony of the first or second degree, unless an overt act in pursuance of such conspiracy is alleged and proved to have been done by him or by a person with whom he conspired.

(6) **Renunciation of Criminal Purpose.** It is an affirmative defense that the actor, after conspiring to commit a crime, thwarted the success of the conspiracy, under circumstances manifesting a complete and voluntary renunciation of his criminal purpose.

(7) **Duration of Conspiracy.** For purposes of Section 1.06(4):

(a) conspiracy is a continuing course of conduct which terminates when the crime or crimes which are its object are committed or the agreement that they be committed is abandoned by the defendant and by those with whom he conspired; and

(b) such abandonment is presumed if neither the defendant nor anyone with whom he conspired does any overt act in pursuance of the conspiracy during the applicable period of limitation; and

(c) if an individual abandons the agreement, the conspiracy is terminated as to him only if and when he advises those with whom he conspired of his abandonment or he informs the law enforcement authorities of the existence of the conspiracy and of his participation therein.

Section 5.04. Incapacity, Irresponsibility or Immunity of Party to Solicitation or Conspiracy.

(1) Except as provided in Subsection (2) of this Section, it is immaterial to the liability of a person who solicits or conspires with another to commit a crime that:

(a) he or the person whom he solicits or with whom he conspires does not occupy a particular position or have a particular characteristic which is an element of such crime, if he believes that one of them does; or

(b) the person whom he solicits or with whom he conspires is irresponsible or has an immunity to prosecution or conviction for the commission of the crime.

(2) It is a defense to a charge of solicitation or conspiracy to commit a crime that if the criminal object were achieved, the actor would not be guilty of a crime under the law defining the offense or as an accomplice under Section 2.06(5) or 2.06(6) (a) or (b).

Section 5.05. Grading of Criminal Attempt, Solicitation and Conspiracy; Mitigation in Cases of Lesser Danger; Multiple Convictions Barred.

(1) **Grading.** Except as otherwise provided in this Section, attempt, solicitation and conspiracy are crimes of the same grade and degree as the most serious offense which is attempted or solicited or is an object of the conspiracy. An attempt, solicitation or conspiracy to commit a [capital crime or a] felony of the first degree is a felony of the second degree.

(2) **Mitigation.** If the particular conduct charged to constitute a criminal attempt, solicitation or conspiracy is so inherently unlikely to result or culminate in the commission of a crime that neither such conduct nor the actor presents a public danger warranting the grading of such offense under this Section, the Court shall exercise its power under Section 6.12 to enter judgment and impose sentence for a crime of lower grade or degree or, in extreme cases, may dismiss the prosecution.

(3) **Multiple Convictions.** A person may not be convicted of more than one offense defined by this Article for conduct designed to commit or to culminate in the commission of the same crime.

Section 5.06. Possessing Instruments of Crime; Weapons.

(1) **Criminal Instruments Generally.** A person commits a misdemeanor if he possesses any instrument of crime with purpose to employ it criminally. "Instrument of crime" means:

(a) anything specially made or specially adapted for criminal use; or

(b) anything commonly used for criminal purposes and possessed by the actor under circumstances which do not negative unlawful purpose.

(2) Presumption of Criminal Purpose from Possession of Weapon. If a person possesses a firearm or other weapon on or about his person, in a vehicle occupied by him, or otherwise readily available for use, it is presumed that he had the purpose to employ it criminally, unless:

(a) the weapon is possessed in the actor's home or place of business;

(b) the actor is licensed or otherwise authorized by law to possess such weapon; or

(c) the weapon is of a type commonly used in lawful sport.

"Weapon" means anything readily capable of lethal use and possessed under circumstances not manifestly appropriate for lawful uses which it may have; the term includes a firearm which is not loaded or lacks a clip or other component to render it immediately operable, and components which can readily be assembled into a weapon.

(3) Presumptions as to Possession of Criminal Instruments in Automobiles. Where a weapon or other instrument of crime is found in an automobile, it shall be presumed to be in the possession of the occupant if there is but one. If there is more than one occupant, it shall be presumed to be in the possession of all, except under the following circumstances:

(a) where it is found upon the person of one of the occupants;

(b) where the automobile is not a stolen one and the weapon or instrument is found out of view in a glove compartment, car trunk, or other enclosed customary depository, in which case it shall be presumed to be in the possession of the occupant or occupants who own or have authority to operate the automobile;

(c) in the case of a taxicab, a weapon or instrument found in the passengers' portion of the vehicle shall be presumed to be in the possession of all the passengers, if there are any, and, if not, in the possession of the driver.

Section 5.07. Prohibited Offensive Weapons.

A person commits a misdemeanor if, except as authorized by law, he makes, repairs, sells, or otherwise deals in, uses, or possesses any offensive weapon. "Offensive weapon" means any bomb, machine gun, sawed-off shotgun, firearm specially made or specially adapted for concealment or silent discharge, any blackjack, sandbag, metal knuckles, dagger, or other implement for the infliction of serious bodily injury which serves no common lawful purpose. It is a defense under this Section for the defendant to prove by a preponderance of evidence that he possessed or dealt with the weapon solely as a curio or in a dramatic performance, or that he possessed it briefly in consequence of having found it or taken it from an aggressor, or under circumstances similarly negativing any purpose or likelihood that the weapon would be used unlawfully. The presumptions provided in Section 5.06(3) are applicable to prosecutions under this Section.

ARTICLE 6. AUTHORIZED DISPOSITION OF OFFENDERS

Section 6.01. Degrees of Felonies.

(1) Felonies defined by this Code are classified, for the purpose of sentence, into three degrees, as follows:

(a) felonies of the first degree;

(b) felonies of the second degree;

(c) felonies of the third degree.

A felony is of the first or second degree when it is so designated by the Code. A crime declared to be a felony, without specification of degree, is of the third degree.

(2) Notwithstanding any other provision of law, a felony defined by any statute

of this State other than this Code shall constitute for the purpose of sentence a felony of the third degree.

Section 6.02. Sentence in Accordance With Code; Authorized Dispositions.

(1) No person convicted of an offense shall be sentenced otherwise than in accordance with this Article.

[(2) The Court shall sentence a person who has been convicted of murder to death or imprisonment, in accordance with Section 210.6.]

(3) Except as provided in Subsection (2) of this Section and subject to the applicable provisions of the Code, the Court may suspend the imposition of sentence on a person who has been convicted of a crime, may order him to be committed in lieu of sentence, in accordance with Section 6.13, or may sentence him as follows:

(a) to pay a fine authorized by Section 6.03; or

(b) to be placed on probation [, and, in the case of a person convicted of a felony or misdemeanor to imprisonment for a term fixed by the Court not exceeding thirty days to be served as a condition of probation]; or

(c) to imprisonment for a term authorized by Sections 6.05, 6.06, 6.07, 6.08, 6.09, or 7.06; or

(d) to fine and probation or fine and imprisonment, but not to probation and imprisonment [, except as authorized in paragraph (b) of this Subsection].

(4) The Court may suspend the imposition of sentence on a person who has been convicted of a violation or may sentence him to pay a fine authorized by Section 6.03.

(5) This Article does not deprive the Court of any authority conferred by law to decree a forfeiture of property, suspend or cancel a license, remove a person from office, or impose any other civil penalty.

Such a judgment or order may be included in the sentence.

Section 6.03. Fines.

A person who has been convicted of an offense may be sentenced to pay a fine not exceeding:

(1) $10,000, when the conviction is of a felony of the first or second degree;

(2) $5,000, when the conviction is of a felony of the third degree;

(3) $1,000, when the conviction is of a misdemeanor;

(4) $500, when the conviction is of a petty misdemeanor or a violation;

(5) any higher amount equal to double the pecuniary gain derived from the offense by the offender;

(6) any higher amount specifically authorized by statute.

Section 6.04. Penalties Against Corporations and Unincorporated Associations; Forfeiture of Corporate Charter or Revocation of Certificate Authorizing Foreign Corporation to Do Business in the State.

(1) The Court may suspend the sentence of a corporation or an unincorporated association which has been convicted of an offense or may sentence it to pay a fine authorized by Section 6.03.

(2)(a) The [prosecuting attorney] is authorized to institute civil proceedings in the appropriate court of general jurisdiction to forfeit the charter of a corporation organized under the laws of this State or to revoke the certificate authorizing a foreign corporation to conduct business in this State. The Court may order the charter forfeited or the certificate revoked upon finding (i) that the board of directors or a high managerial agent acting in behalf of the corporation has, in conducting the corporation's affairs, purposely engaged in a persistent course of criminal conduct and (ii) that for the prevention of future criminal conduct of the same character, the public interest requires the charter of the corporation to be forfeited and the corporation to be dissolved or the certificate to be revoked.

(b) When a corporation is convicted of a crime or a high managerial agent of a corporation, as defined in Section 2.07, is convicted of a crime committed in the conduct of the affairs of the corporation, the Court, in sentencing the corporation or the agent, may direct the [prosecuting attorney] to institute proceedings authorized by paragraph (a) of this Subsection.

(c) The proceedings authorized by paragraph (a) of this Subsection shall be conducted in accordance with the procedures authorized by law for the involuntary dissolution of a corporation or the revocation of the certificate authorizing a foreign corporation to conduct business in this State. Such proceedings shall be deemed additional to any other proceedings authorized by law for the purpose of forfeiting the charter of a corporation or revoking the certificate of a foreign corporation.

Section 6.05. Young Adult Offenders.

(1) **Specialized Correctional Treatment.** A young adult offender is a person convicted of a crime who, at the time of sentencing, is sixteen but less than twenty-two years of age. A young adult offender who is sentenced to a term of imprisonment which may exceed thirty days [alternatives: (1) ninety days; (2) one year] shall be committed to the custody of the Division of Young Adult Correction of the Department of Correction, and shall receive, as far as practicable, such special and individualized correctional and rehabilitative treatment as may be appropriate to his needs.

(2) **Special Term.** A young adult offender convicted of a felony may, in lieu of any other sentence of imprisonment authorized by this Article, be sentenced to a special term of imprisonment without a minimum and with a maximum of four years, regardless of the degree of the felony involved, if the Court is of the opinion that such special term is adequate for his correction and rehabilitation and will not jeopardize the protection of the public.

[(3) **Removal of Disabilities; Vacation of Conviction.**

(a) In sentencing a young adult offender to the special term provided by this Section or to any sentence other than one of imprisonment, the Court may order that so long as he is not convicted of another felony, the judgment shall not constitute a conviction for the purposes of any disqualification or disability imposed by law upon conviction of a crime.

(b) When any young adult offender is unconditionally discharged from probation or parole before the expiration of the maximum term thereof, the Court may enter an order vacating the judgment of conviction.]

[(4) **Commitment for Observation.** If, after pre-sentence investigation, the Court desires additional information concerning a young adult offender before imposing sentence, it may order that he be committed, for a period not exceeding ninety days, to the custody of the Division of Young Adult Correction of the Department of Correction for observation and study at an appropriate reception or classification center. Such Division of the Department of Correction and the [Young Adult Division of the] Board of Parole shall advise the Court of their findings and recommendations on or before the expiration of such ninety-day period.]

Subsection (3) should be eliminated if Section 306.6, dealing with removal of disabilities generally, is adopted.

Subsection (4) should be eliminated if Subsection (1) of Section 7.08, dealing with commitments for observation generally, is adopted.

Section 6.06. Sentence of Imprisonment for Felony; Ordinary Terms.

A person who has been convicted of a felony may be sentenced to imprisonment, as follows:

(1) in the case of a felony of the first degree, for a term the minimum of which shall be fixed by the Court at not less than one year nor more than ten years, and the maximum of which shall be life imprisonment;

(2) in the case of a felony of the second degree, for a term the minimum of which shall be fixed by the Court at not less than one year nor more than three years, and the maximum of which shall be ten years;

(3) in the case of a felony of the third degree, for a term the minimum of which shall be fixed by the Court at not less than one year nor more than two years, and the maximum of which shall be five years.

Alternate Section 6.06. Sentence of Imprisonment for Felony; Ordinary Terms.

A person who has been convicted of a felony may be sentenced to imprisonment, as follows:

(1) in the case of a felony of the first degree, for a term the minimum of which shall be fixed by the Court at not less than one year nor more than ten years, and the maximum at not more than twenty years or at life imprisonment;

(2) in the case of a felony of the second degree, for a term the minimum of which shall be fixed by the Court at not less than one year nor more than three years, and the maximum at not more than ten years;

(3) in the case of a felony of the third degree, for a term the minimum of which shall be fixed by the Court at not less than one year nor more than two years, and the maximum at not more than five years.

No sentence shall be imposed under this Section of which the minimum is longer than one-half the maximum, or, when the maximum is life imprisonment, longer than ten years.

Section 6.07. Sentence of Imprisonment for Felony; Extended Terms.

In the cases designated in Section 7.03, a person who has been convicted of a felony may be sentenced to an extended term of imprisonment, as follows:

(1) in the case of a felony of the first degree, for a term the minimum of which shall be fixed by the Court at not less than five years nor more than ten years, and the maximum of which shall be life imprisonment;

(2) in the case of a felony of the second degree, for a term the minimum of which shall be fixed by the Court at not less than one year nor more than five years, and the maximum of which shall be fixed by the Court at not less than ten nor more than twenty years;

(3) in the case of a felony of the third degree, for a term the minimum of which shall be fixed by the Court at not less than one year nor more than three years, and the maximum of which shall be fixed by the Court at not less than five nor more than ten years.

Section 6.08. Sentence of Imprisonment for Misdemeanors and Petty Misdemeanors; Ordinary Terms.

A person who has been convicted of a misdemeanor or a petty misdemeanor may be sentenced to imprisonment for a definite term which shall be fixed by the Court and shall not exceed one year in the case of a misdemeanor or thirty days in the case of a petty misdemeanor.

Section 6.09. Sentence of Imprisonment for Misdemeanors and Petty Misdemeanors; Extended Terms.

(1) In the cases designated in Section 7.04, a person who has been convicted of a misdemeanor or a petty misdemeanor may be sentenced to an extended term of imprisonment, as follows:

(a) in the case of a misdemeanor, for a term the minimum of which shall be fixed by the Court at not more than one year and the maximum of which shall be three years;

(b) in the case of a petty misdemeanor, for a term the minimum of which shall be fixed by the Court at not more than six months and the maximum of which shall be two years.

(2) No such sentence for an extended term shall be imposed unless:

(a) the Director of Correction has certified that there is an institution in the Department of Correction, or in a county, city [or other appropriate political subdivision of the State] which is appropriate for the detention and correctional treatment of such misdemeanants or petty misdemeanants, and that such institution is available to receive such commitments; and

(b) the [Board of Parole] [Parole Administrator] has certified that the Board of Parole is able to visit such institution and to assume responsibility for the release of such prisoners on parole and for their parole supervision.

Section 6.10. First Release of All Offenders on Parole; Sentence of Imprisonment Includes Separate Parole Term; Length of Parole Term; Length of Recommitment and Reparole After Revocation of Parole; Final Unconditional Release.

(1) **First Release of All Offenders on Parole.** An offender sentenced to an indefinite term of imprisonment in excess of one year under Section 6.05, 6.06, 6.07, 6.09 or 7.06 shall be released conditionally on parole at or before the expiration of the maximum of such term, in accordance with Article 305.

(2) **Sentence of Imprisonment Includes Separate Parole Term; Length of Parole Term.** A sentence to an indefinite term of imprisonment in excess of one year under Section 6.05, 6.06, 6.07, 6.09 or 7.06 includes as a separate portion of the sentence a term of parole or of recommitment for violation of the conditions of parole which governs the duration of parole or recommitment after the offender's first conditional release on parole. The minimum of such term is one year and the maximum is five years, unless the sentence was imposed under Section 6.05(2) or Section 6.09, in which case the maximum is two years.

(3) **Length of Recommitment and Reparole After Revocation of Parole.** If an offender is recommitted upon revocation of his parole, the term of further imprisonment upon such recommitment and of any subsequent reparole or recommitment under the same sentence shall be fixed by the Board of Parole but shall not exceed in aggregate length the unserved balance of the maximum parole term provided by Subsection (2) of this Section.

(4) **Final Unconditional Release.** When the maximum of his parole term has

expired or he has been sooner discharged from parole under Section 305.12, an offender shall be deemed to have served his sentence and shall be released unconditionally.

Section 6.11. Place of Imprisonment.

(1) When a person is sentenced to imprisonment for an indefinite term with a maximum in excess of one year, the Court shall commit him to the custody of the Department of Correction [or other single department or agency] for the term of his sentence and until released in accordance with law.

(2) When a person is sentenced to imprisonment for a definite term, the Court shall designate the institution or agency to which he is committed for the term of his sentence and until released in accordance with law.

Section 6.12. Reduction of Conviction by Court to Lesser Degree of Felony or to Misdemeanor.

If, when a person has been convicted of a felony, the Court, having regard to the nature and circumstances of the crime and to the history and character of the defendant, is of the view that it would be unduly harsh to sentence the offender in accordance with the Code, the Court may enter judgment of conviction for a lesser degree of felony or for a misdemeanor and impose sentence accordingly.

Section 6.13. Civil Commitment in Lieu of Prosecution or of Sentence.

(1) When a person prosecuted for a [felony of the third degree,] misdemeanor or petty misdemeanor is a chronic alcoholic, narcotic addict [or prostitute] or person suffering from mental abnormality and the Court is authorized by law to order the civil commitment of such person to a hospital or other institution for medical, psychiatric or other rehabilitative treatment, the Court may order such commitment and

dismiss the prosecution. The order of commitment may be made after conviction, in which event the Court may set aside the verdict or judgment of conviction and dismiss the prosecution.

(2) The Court shall not make an order under Subsection (1) of this Section unless it is of the view that it will substantially further the rehabilitation of the defendant and will not jeopardize the protection of the public.

ARTICLE 7. AUTHORITY OF COURT IN SENTENCING

Section 7.01. Criteria for Withholding Sentence of Imprisonment and for Placing Defendant on Probation.

(1) The Court shall deal with a person who has been convicted of a crime without imposing sentence of imprisonment unless, having regard to the nature and circumstances of the crime and the history, character and condition of the defendant, it is of the opinion that his imprisonment is necessary for protection of the public because:

(a) there is undue risk that during the period of a suspended sentence or probation the defendant will commit another crime; or

(b) the defendant is in need of correctional treatment that can be provided most effectively by his commitment to an institution; or

(c) a lesser sentence will depreciate the seriousness of the defendant's crime.

(2) The following grounds, while not controlling the discretion of the Court, shall be accorded weight in favor of withholding sentence of imprisonment:

(a) the defendant's criminal conduct neither caused nor threatened serious harm;

(b) the defendant did not contemplate that his criminal conduct would cause or threaten serious harm;

(c) the defendant acted under a strong provocation;

(d) there were substantial grounds tending to excuse or justify the defendant's criminal conduct, though failing to establish a defense;

(e) the victim of the defendant's criminal conduct induced or facilitated its commission;

(f) the defendant has compensated or will compensate the victim of his criminal conduct for the damage or injury that he sustained;

(g) the defendant has no history of prior delinquency or criminal activity or has led a law-abiding life for a substantial period of time before the commission of the present crime;

(h) the defendant's criminal conduct was the result of circumstances unlikely to recur;

(i) the character and attitudes of the defendant indicate that he is unlikely to commit another crime;

(j) the defendant is particularly likely to respond affirmatively to probationary treatment;

(k) the imprisonment of the defendant would entail excessive hardship to himself or his dependents.

(3) When a person who has been convicted of a crime is not sentenced to imprisonment, the Court shall place him on probation if he is in need of the supervision, guidance, assistance or direction that the probation service can provide.

Section 7.02. Criteria for Imposing Fines.

(1) The Court shall not sentence a defendant only to pay a fine, when any other disposition is authorized by law, unless having regard to the nature and circumstances of the crime and to the history and character of the defendant, it is of the opinion that the fine alone suffices for protection of the public.

(2) The Court shall not sentence a defendant to pay a fine in addition to a sentence of imprisonment or probation unless:

(a) the defendant has derived a pecuniary gain from the crime; or

(b) the Court is of opinion that a fine is specially adapted to deterrence of the crime involved or to the correction of the offender.

(3) The Court shall not sentence a defendant to pay a fine unless:

(a) the defendant is or will be able to pay the fine; and

(b) the fine will not prevent the defendant from making restitution or reparation to the victim of the crime.

(4) In determining the amount and method of payment of a fine, the Court shall take into account the financial resources of the defendant and the nature of the burden that its payment will impose.

Section 7.03. Criteria for Sentence of Extended Term of Imprisonment; Felonies.

The Court may sentence a person who has been convicted of a felony to an extended term of imprisonment if it finds one or more of the grounds specified in this Section. The finding of the Court shall be incorporated in the record.

(1) The defendant is a persistent offender whose commitment for an extended term is necessary for protection of the public.

The Court shall not make such a finding unless the defendant is over twenty-one years of age and has previously been convicted of two felonies or of one felony and two misdemeanors, committed at different times when he was over [insert Juvenile Court age] years of age.

(2) The defendant is a professional criminal whose commitment for an extended term is necessary for protection of the public.

The Court shall not make such a finding unless the defendant is over twenty-one years of age and:

(a) the circumstances of the crime show that the defendant has knowingly devoted himself to criminal activity as a major source of livelihood; or

(b) the defendant has substantial income or resources not explained to be derived from a source other than criminal activity.

(3) The defendant is a dangerous, mentally abnormal person whose commitment for an extended term is necessary for protection of the public.

The Court shall not make such a finding unless the defendant has been subjected to a psychiatric examination resulting in the conclusions that his mental condition is gravely abnormal; that his criminal conduct has been characterized by a pattern of repetitive or compulsive behavior or by persistent aggressive behavior with heedless indifference to consequences; and that such condition makes him a serious danger to others.

(4) The defendant is a multiple offender whose criminality was so extensive that a sentence of imprisonment for an extended term is warranted.

The Court shall not make such a finding unless:

(a) the defendant is being sentenced for two or more felonies, or is already under sentence of imprisonment for felony, and the sentences of imprisonment involved will run concurrently under Section 7.06; or

(b) the defendant admits in open court the commission of one or more other felonies and asks that they be taken into account when he is sentenced; and

(c) the longest sentences of imprisonment authorized for each of the defendant's crimes, including admitted crimes taken into account, if made to run consecutively would exceed in length the minimum and maximum of the extended term imposed.

Section 7.04. Criteria for Sentence of Extended Term of Imprisonment; Misdemeanors and Petty Misdemeanors.

The Court may sentence a person who has been convicted of a misdemeanor or petty misdemeanor to an extended term of imprisonment if it finds one or more of the grounds specified in this Section. The finding of the Court shall be incorporated in the record.

(1) The defendant is a persistent offender whose commitment for an extended term is necessary for protection of the public.

The Court shall not make such a finding unless the defendant has previously been convicted of two crimes, committed at different times when he was over [insert Juvenile Court age] years of age.

(2) The defendant is a professional criminal whose commitment for an extended term is necessary for protection of the public.

The Court shall not make such a finding unless:

(a) the circumstances of the crime show that the defendant has knowingly devoted himself to criminal activity as a major source of livelihood; or

(b) the defendant has substantial income or resources not explained to be derived from a source other than criminal activity.

(3) The defendant is a chronic alcoholic, narcotic addict, prostitute or per-

son of abnormal mental condition who requires rehabilitative treatment for a substantial period of time.

The Court shall not make such a finding unless, with respect to the particular category to which the defendant belongs, the Director of Correction has certified that there is a specialized institution or facility which is satisfactory for the rehabilitative treatment of such persons and which otherwise meets the requirements of Section 6.09, Subsection (2).

(4) The defendant is a multiple offender whose criminality was so extensive that a sentence of imprisonment for an extended term is warranted.

The Court shall not make such a finding unless:

(a) the defendant is being sentenced for a number of misdemeanors or petty misdemeanors or is already under sentence of imprisonment for crime of such grades, or admits in open court the commission of one or more such crimes and asks that they be taken into account when he is sentenced; and

(b) maximum fixed sentences of imprisonment for each of the defendant's crimes, including admitted crimes taken into account, if made to run consecutively, would exceed in length the maximum period of the extended term imposed.

Section 7.05. Former Conviction in Another Jurisdiction; Definition and Proof of Conviction; Sentence Taking into Account Admitted Crimes Bars Subsequent Conviction for Such Crimes.

(1) For purposes of paragraph (1) of Section 7.03 or 7.04, a conviction of the commission of a crime in another jurisdiction shall constitute a previous conviction. Such conviction shall be deemed to have

been of a felony if sentence of death or of imprisonment in excess of one year was authorized under the law of such other jurisdiction, of a misdemeanor if sentence of imprisonment in excess of thirty days but not in excess of a year was authorized and of a petty misdemeanor if sentence of imprisonment for not more than thirty days was authorized.

(2) An adjudication by a court of competent jurisdiction that the defendant committed a crime constitutes a conviction for purposes of Sections 7.03 to 7.05 inclusive, although sentence or the execution thereof was suspended, provided that the time to appeal has expired and that the defendant was not pardoned on the ground of innocence.

(3) Prior conviction may be proved by any evidence, including fingerprint records made in connection with arrest, conviction or imprisonment, that reasonably satisfies the Court that the defendant was convicted.

(4) When the defendant has asked that other crimes admitted in open court be taken into account when he is sentenced and the Court has not rejected such request, the sentence shall bar the prosecution or conviction of the defendant in this State for any such admitted crime.

Section 7.06. Multiple Sentences; Concurrent and Consecutive Terms.

(1) **Sentences of Imprisonment for More Than One Crime.** When multiple sentences of imprisonment are imposed on a defendant for more than one crime, including a crime for which a previous suspended sentence or sentence of probation has been revoked, such multiple sentences shall run concurrently or consecutively as the Court determines at the time of sentence, except that:

(a) a definite and an indefinite term shall run concurrently and both sentences shall be satisfied by service of the indefinite term; and

(b) the aggregate of consecutive definite terms shall not exceed one year; and

(c) the aggregate of consecutive indefinite terms shall not exceed in minimum or maximum length the longest extended term authorized for the highest grade and degree of crime for which any of the sentences was imposed; and

(d) not more than one sentence for an extended term shall be imposed.

(2) **Sentences of Imprisonment Imposed at Different Times.** When a defendant who has previously been sentenced to imprisonment is subsequently sentenced to another term for a crime committed prior to the former sentence, other than a crime committed while in custody:

(a) the multiple sentences imposed shall so far as possible conform to Subsection (1) of this Section; and

(b) whether the Court determines that the terms shall run concurrently or consecutively, the defendant shall be credited with time served in imprisonment on the prior sentence in determining the permissible aggregate length of the term or terms remaining to be served; and

(c) when a new sentence is imposed on a prisoner who is on parole, the balance of the parole term on the former sentence shall be deemed to run during the period of the new imprisonment.

(3) **Sentence of Imprisonment for Crime Committed While on Parole.** When a defendant is sentenced to imprisonment for a crime committed while on parole in this State, such term of imprisonment and any period of reimprisonment that the Board of Parole may require the defendant to serve upon the revocation of

his parole shall run concurrently, unless the Court orders them to run consecutively.

(4) **Multiple Sentences of Imprisonment in Other Cases.** Except as otherwise provided in this Section, multiple terms of imprisonment shall run concurrently or consecutively as the Court determines when the second or subsequent sentence is imposed.

(5) **Calculation of Concurrent and Consecutive Terms of Imprisonment.**

(a) When indefinite terms run concurrently, the shorter minimum terms merge in and are satisfied by serving the longest minimum term and the shorter maximum terms merge in and are satisfied by discharge of the longest maximum term.

(b) When indefinite terms run consecutively, the minimum terms are added to arrive at an aggregate minimum to be served equal to the sum of all minimum terms and the maximum terms are added to arrive at an aggregate maximum equal to the sum of all maximum terms.

(c) When a definite and an indefinite term run consecutively, the period of the definite term is added to both the minimum and maximum of the indefinite term and both sentences are satisfied by serving the indefinite term.

(6) **Suspension of Sentence or Probation and Imprisonment; Multiple Terms of Suspension and Probation.** When a defendant is sentenced for more than one offense or a defendant already under sentence is sentenced for another offense committed prior to the former sentence:

(a) the Court shall not sentence to probation a defendant who is under sentence of imprisonment [with more than thirty days to run] or impose a sentence of probation and a sentence of imprisonment [, except as authorized by Section 6.02(3)(b)]; and

(b) multiple periods of suspension or probation shall run concurrently from the date of the first such disposition; and

(c) when a sentence of imprisonment is imposed for an indefinite term, the service of such sentence shall satisfy a suspended sentence on another count or a prior suspended sentence or sentence to probation; and

(d) when a sentence of imprisonment is imposed for a definite term, the period of a suspended sentence on another count or a prior suspended sentence or sentence to probation shall run during the period of such imprisonment.

(7) **Offense Committed While Under Suspension of Sentence or Probation.** When a defendant is convicted of an offense committed while under suspension of sentence or on probation and such suspension or probation is not revoked:

(a) if the defendant is sentenced to imprisonment for an indefinite term, the service of such sentence shall satisfy the prior suspended sentence or sentence to probation; and

(b) if the defendant is sentenced to imprisonment for a definite term, the period of the suspension or probation shall not run during the period of such imprisonment; and

(c) if sentence is suspended or the defendant is sentenced to probation, the period of such suspension or probation shall run concurrently with or consecutively to the remainder of the prior periods, as the Court determines at the time of sentence.

Section 7.07. Procedure on Sentence; Presentence Investigation and Report; Remand for Psychiatric Examination; Transmission of Records to Department of Correction.

(1) The Court shall not impose sentence without first ordering a pre-sentence investigation of the defendant and according due consideration to a written report of such investigation where:

(a) the defendant has been convicted of a felony; or

(b) the defendant is less than twenty-two years of age and has been convicted of a crime; or

(c) the defendant will be [placed on probation or] sentenced to imprisonment for an extended term.

(2) The Court may order a pre-sentence investigation in any other case.

(3) The pre-sentence investigation shall include an analysis of the circumstances attending the commission of the crime, the defendant's history of delinquency or criminality, physical and mental condition, family situation and background, economic status, education, occupation and personal habits and any other matters that the probation officer deems relevant or the Court directs to be included.

(4) Before imposing sentence, the Court may order the defendant to submit to psychiatric observation and examination for a period of not exceeding sixty days or such longer period as the Court determines to be necessary for the purpose. The defendant may be remanded for this purpose to any available clinic or mental hospital or the Court may appoint a qualified psychiatrist to make the examination. The report of the examination shall be submitted to the Court.

(5) Before imposing sentence, the Court shall advise the defendant or his counsel of the factual contents and the conclusions of any pre-sentence investiga-

tion or psychiatric examination and afford fair opportunity, if the defendant so requests, to controvert them. The sources of confidential information need not, however, be disclosed.

(6) The Court shall not impose a sentence of imprisonment for an extended term unless the ground therefor has been established at a hearing after the conviction of the defendant and on written notice to him of the ground proposed. Subject to the limitation of Subsection (5) of this Section, the defendant shall have the right to hear and controvert the evidence against him and to offer evidence upon the issue.

(7) If the defendant is sentenced to imprisonment, a copy of the report of any pre-sentence investigation or psychiatric examination shall be transmitted forthwith to the Department of Correction [or other state department or agency] or, when the defendant is committed to the custody of a specific institution, to such institution.

Section 7.08. Commitment for Observation; Sentence of Imprisonment for Felony Deemed Tentative for Period of One Year; Re-sentence on Petition of Commissioner of Correction.

(1) If, after pre-sentence investigation, the Court desires additional information concerning an offender convicted of a felony or misdemeanor before imposing sentence, it may order that he be committed, for a period not exceeding ninety days, to the custody of the Department of Correction, or, in the case of a young adult offender, to the custody of the Division of Young Adult Correction, for observation and study at an appropriate reception or classification center. The Department and the Board of Parole, or the Young Adult Divisions thereof, shall advise the Court of their findings and recommendations on or before the expiration of such ninety-day

period. If the offender is thereafter sentenced to imprisonment, the period of such commitment for observation shall be deducted from the maximum term and from the minimum, if any, of such sentence.

(2) When a person has been sentenced to imprisonment upon conviction of a felony, whether for an ordinary or extended term, the sentence shall be deemed tentative, to the extent provided in this Section, for the period of one year following the date when the offender is received in custody by the Department of Correction [or other state department or agency].

(3) If, as a result of the examination and classification by the Department of Correction [or other state department or agency] of a person under sentence of imprisonment upon conviction of a felony, the Commissioner of Correction [or other department head] is satisfied that the sentence of the Court may have been based upon a misapprehension as to the history, character or physical or mental condition of the offender, the Commissioner, during the period when the offender's sentence is deemed tentative under Subsection (2) of this Section shall file in the sentencing Court a petition to resentence the offender. The petition shall set forth the information as to the offender that is deemed to warrant his re-sentence and may include a recommendation as to the sentence to be imposed.

(4) The Court may dismiss a petition filed under Subsection (3) of this Section without a hearing if it deems the information set forth insufficient to warrant reconsideration of the sentence. If the Court is of the view that the petition warrants such reconsideration, a copy of the petition shall be served on the offender, who shall have the right to be heard on the issue and to be represented by counsel.

(5) When the Court grants a petition filed under Subsection (3) of this Section,

it shall resentence the offender and may impose any sentence that might have been imposed originally for the felony of which the defendant was convicted. The period of his imprisonment prior to re-sentence and any reduction for good behavior to which he is entitled shall be applied in satisfaction of the final sentence.

(6) For all purposes other than this Section, a sentence of imprisonment has the same finality when it is imposed that it would have if this Section were not in force.

(7) Nothing in this Section shall alter the remedies provided by law for vacating or correcting an illegal sentence.

Section 7.09. Credit for Time of Detention Prior to Sentence; Credit for Imprisonment Under Earlier Sentence for the Same Crime.

(1) When a defendant who is sentenced to imprisonment has previously been detained in any state or local correctional or other institution following his [conviction of] [arrest for] the crime for which such sentence is imposed, such period of detention following his [conviction] [arrest] shall be deducted from the maximum term, and from the minimum, if any, of such sentence. The officer having custody of the defendant shall furnish a certificate to the Court at the time of sentence, showing the length of such detention of the defendant prior to sentence in any state or local correctional or other institution, and the certificate shall be annexed to the official records of the defendant's commitment.

(2) When a judgment of conviction is vacated and a new sentence is thereafter imposed upon the defendant for the same crime, the period of detention and imprisonment theretofore served shall be deducted from the maximum term, and from the minimum, if any, of the new sentence. The officer having custody of the defen-

dant shall furnish a certificate to the Court at the time of sentence, showing the period of imprisonment served under the original sentence, and the certificate shall be annexed to the official records of the defendant's new commitment.

PART II. DEFINITION OF SPECIFIC CRIMES

OFFENSES AGAINST EXISTENCE OR STABILITY OF THE STATE

[This category of offenses, including treason, sedition, espionage and like crimes, was excluded from the scope of the Model Penal Code. These offenses are peculiarly the concern of the federal government. The Constitution itself defines treason: "Treason against the United States shall consist only in levying War against them, or in adhering to their Enemies, giving them Aid and Comfort. * * *" Article III, Section 3; cf. Pennsylvania v. Nelson, 350 U.S. 497 (supersession of state sedition legislation by federal law). Also, the definition of offenses against the stability of the state is inevitably affected by special political considerations. These factors militated against the use of the Institute's limited resources to attempt to draft "model" provisions in this area. However we provide at this point in the Plan of the Model Penal Code for an Article 200, where definitions of offenses against the existence or stability of the state may be incorporated.]

OFFENSES INVOLVING DANGER TO THE PERSON

ARTICLE 210. CRIMINAL HOMICIDE

Section 210.0. Definitions.

In Articles 210–213, unless a different meaning plainly is required:

(1) "human being" means a person who has been born and is alive;

(2) "bodily injury" means physical pain, illness or any impairment of physical condition;

(3) "serious bodily injury" means bodily injury which creates a substantial risk of death or which causes serious, permanent disfigurement, or protracted loss or impairment of the function of any bodily member or organ;

(4) "deadly weapon" means any firearm, or other weapon, device, instrument, material or substance, whether animate or inanimate, which in the manner it is used or is intended to be used is known to be capable of producing death or serious bodily injury.

Section 210.1. Criminal Homicide.

(1) A person is guilty of criminal homicide if he purposely, knowingly, recklessly or negligently causes the death of another human being.

(2) Criminal homicide is murder, manslaughter or negligent homicide.

Section 210.2. Murder.

(1) Except as provided in Section 210.3(1)(b), criminal homicide constitutes murder when:

(a) it is committed purposely or knowingly; or

(b) it is committed recklessly under circumstances manifesting extreme indifference to the value of human life. Such recklessness and indifference are presumed if the actor is engaged or is an accomplice in the commission of, or an attempt to commit, or flight after committing or attempting to commit robbery, rape or deviate sexual intercourse by force or threat of force, arson, burglary, kidnapping or felonious escape.

LaFave Mod.Crim.Law, 2nd Ed. ACB—30

(2) Murder is a felony of the first degree [but a person convicted of murder may be sentenced to death, as provided in Section 210.6].

Section 210.3. Manslaughter.

(1) Criminal homicide constitutes manslaughter when:

(a) it is committed recklessly; or

(b) a homicide which would otherwise be murder is committed under the influence of extreme mental or emotional disturbance for which there is reasonable explanation or excuse. The reasonableness of such explanation or excuse shall be determined from the viewpoint of a person in the actor's situation under the circumstances as he believes them to be.

(2) Manslaughter is a felony of the second degree.

Section 210.4. Negligent Homicide.

(1) Criminal homicide constitutes negligent homicide when it is committed negligently.

(2) Negligent homicide is a felony of the third degree.

Section 210.5. Causing or Aiding Suicide.

(1) **Causing Suicide as Criminal Homicide.** A person may be convicted of criminal homicide for causing another to commit suicide only if he purposely causes such suicide by force, duress or deception.

(2) **Aiding or Soliciting Suicide as an Independent Offense.** A person who purposely aids or solicits another to commit suicide is guilty of a felony of the second degree if his conduct causes such suicide or an attempted suicide, and otherwise of a misdemeanor.

[Section 210.6.   Sentence of Death for Murder; Further Proceedings to Determine Sentence.

(1) **Death Sentence Excluded.** When a defendant is found guilty of murder, the Court shall impose sentence for a felony of the first degree if it is satisfied that:

(a) none of the aggravating circumstances enumerated in Subsection (3) of this Section was established by the evidence at the trial or will be established if further proceedings are initiated under Subsection (2) of this Section; or

(b) substantial mitigating circumstances, established by the evidence at the trial, call for leniency; or

(c) the defendant, with the consent of the prosecuting attorney and the approval of the Court, pleaded guilty to murder as a felony of the first degree; or

(d) the defendant was under 18 years of age at the time of the commission of the crime; or

(e) the defendant's physical or mental condition calls for leniency; or

(f) although the evidence suffices to sustain the verdict, it does not foreclose all doubt respecting the defendant's guilt.

(2) **Determination by Court or by Court and Jury.** Unless the Court imposes sentence under Subsection (1) of this Section, it shall conduct a separate proceeding to determine whether the defendant should be sentenced for a felony of the first degree or sentenced to death. The proceeding shall be conducted before the Court alone if the defendant was convicted by a Court sitting without a jury or upon his plea of guilty or if the prosecuting attorney and the defendant waive a jury with respect to sentence. In other cases it shall be conducted before the Court sitting with the jury which determined the defendant's guilt or, if the Court for good cause shown discharges

that jury, with a new jury empanelled for the purpose.

In the proceeding, evidence may be presented as to any matter that the Court deems relevant to sentence, including but not limited to the nature and circumstances of the crime, the defendant's character, background, history, mental and physical condition and any of the aggravating or mitigating circumstances enumerated in Subsections (3) and (4) of this Section. Any such evidence, not legally privileged, which the Court deems to have probative force may be received, regardless of its admissibility under the exclusionary rules of evidence, provided that the defendant's counsel is accorded a fair opportunity to rebut such evidence. The prosecuting attorney and the defendant or his counsel shall be permitted to present argument for or against sentence of death.

The determination whether sentence of death shall be imposed shall be in the discretion of the Court, except that when the proceeding is conducted before the Court sitting with a jury, the Court shall not impose sentence of death unless it submits to the jury the issue whether the defendant should be sentenced to death or to imprisonment and the jury returns a verdict that the sentence should be death. If the jury is unable to reach a unanimous verdict, the Court shall dismiss the jury and impose sentence for a felony of the first degree.

The Court, in exercising its discretion as to sentence, and the jury, in determining upon its verdict, shall take into account the aggravating and mitigating circumstances enumerated in Subsections (3) and (4) and any other facts that it deems relevant, but it shall not impose or recommend sentence of death unless it finds one of the aggravating circumstances enumerated in Subsection (3) and further finds that there are no mitigating circumstances sufficiently substantial to call for leniency. When the issue is submitted to the jury, the Court shall so instruct and also shall inform the jury of the nature of the sentence of imprisonment that may be imposed, including its implication with respect to possible release upon parole, if the jury verdict is against sentence of death.

Alternative formulation of Subsection (2):

(2) **Determination by Court.** Unless the Court imposes sentence under Subsection (1) of this Section, it shall conduct a separate proceeding to determine whether the defendant should be sentenced for a felony of the first degree or sentenced to death. In the proceeding, the Court, in accordance with Section 7.07, shall consider the report of the pre-sentence investigation and, if a psychiatric examination has been ordered, the report of such examination. In addition, evidence may be presented as to any matter that the Court deems relevant to sentence, including but not limited to the nature and circumstances of the crime, the defendant's character, background, history, mental and physical condition and any of the aggravating or mitigating circumstances enumerated in Subsections (3) and (4) of this Section. Any such evidence, not legally privileged, which the Court deems to have probative force may be received, regardless of its admissibility under the exclusionary rules of evidence, provided that the defendant's counsel is accorded a fair opportunity to rebut such evidence. The prosecuting attorney and the defendant or his counsel shall be permitted to present argument for or against sentence of death.

The determination whether sentence of death shall be imposed shall be in the discretion of the Court. In exercising such discretion, the Court shall take into account the aggravating and mitigating circumstances enumerated in Subsections (3) and (4) and any other facts that it deems relevant but shall not impose sentence of death unless it finds one of the aggravating circumstances enumerated in Subsection (3) and further finds that there are no mitigating circumstances sufficiently substantial to call for leniency.

(3) **Aggravating Circumstances.**

(a) The murder was committed by a convict under sentence of imprisonment.

(b) The defendant was previously convicted of another murder or of a felony involving the use or threat of violence to the person.

(c) At the time the murder was committed the defendant also committed another murder.

(d) The defendant knowingly created a great risk of death to many persons.

(e) The murder was committed while the defendant was engaged or was an accomplice in the commission of, or an attempt to commit, or flight after committing or attempting to commit robbery, rape or deviate sexual intercourse by force or threat of force, arson, burglary or kidnapping.

(f) The murder was committed for the purpose of avoiding or preventing a lawful arrest or effecting an escape from lawful custody.

(g) The murder was committed for pecuniary gain.

(h) The murder was especially heinous, atrocious or cruel, manifesting exceptional depravity.

(4) **Mitigating Circumstances.**

(a) The defendant has no significant history of prior criminal activity.

(b) The murder was committed while the defendant was under the influence of extreme mental or emotional disturbance.

(c) The victim was a participant in the defendant's homicidal conduct or consented to the homicidal act.

(d) The murder was committed under circumstances which the defendant believed to provide a moral justification or extenuation for his conduct.

(e) The defendant was an accomplice in a murder committed by another person and his participation in the homicidal act was relatively minor.

(f) The defendant acted under duress or under the domination of another person.

(g) At the time of the murder, the capacity of the defendant to appreciate the criminality [wrongfulness] of his conduct or to conform his conduct to the requirements of law was impaired as a result of mental disease or defect or intoxication.

(h) The youth of the defendant at the time of the crime.]

ARTICLE 211. ASSAULT; RECKLESS ENDANGERING; THREATS

Section 211.0. Definitions.

In this Article, the definitions given in Section 210.0 apply unless a different meaning plainly is required.

Section 211.1. Assault.

(1) **Simple Assault.** A person is guilty of assault if he:

(a) attempts to cause or purposely, knowingly or recklessly causes bodily injury to another; or

(b) negligently causes bodily injury to another with a deadly weapon; or

(c) attempts by physical menace to put another in fear of imminent serious bodily injury.

Simple assault is a misdemeanor unless committed in a fight or scuffle entered into by mutual consent, in which case it is a petty misdemeanor.

(2) **Aggravated Assault.** A person is guilty of aggravated assault if he:

(a) attempts to cause serious bodily injury to another, or causes such injury purposely, knowingly or recklessly under circumstances manifesting extreme indifference to the value of human life; or

(b) attempts to cause or purposely or knowingly causes bodily injury to another with a deadly weapon.

Aggravated assault under paragraph (a) is a felony of the second degree; aggravated assault under paragraph (b) is a felony of the third degree.

Section 211.2. Recklessly Endangering Another Person.

A person commits a misdemeanor if he recklessly engages in conduct which places or may place another person in danger of death or serious bodily injury. Recklessness and danger shall be presumed where a person knowingly points a firearm at or in the direction of another, whether or not the actor believed the firearm to be loaded.

Section 211.3. Terroristic Threats.

A person is guilty of a felony of the third degree if he threatens to commit any crime of violence with purpose to terrorize another or to cause evacuation of a building, place of assembly, or facility of public transportation, or otherwise to cause serious public inconvenience, or in reckless disregard of the risk of causing such terror or inconvenience.

ARTICLE 212. KIDNAPPING AND RELATED OFFENSES; COERCION

Section 212.0. Definitions.

In this Article, the definitions given in Section 210.0 apply unless a different meaning plainly is required.

Section 212.1. Kidnapping.

A person is guilty of kidnapping if he unlawfully removes another from his place of residence or business, or a substantial distance from the vicinity where he is found, or if he unlawfully confines another for a substantial period in a place of isolation, with any of the following purposes:

(a) to hold for ransom or reward, or as a shield or hostage; or

(b) to facilitate commission of any felony or flight thereafter; or

(c) to inflict bodily injury on or to terrorize the victim or another; or

(d) to interfere with the performance of any governmental or political function.

Kidnapping is a felony of the first degree unless the actor voluntarily releases the victim alive and in a safe place prior to trial, in which case it is a felony of the second degree. A removal or confinement is unlawful within the meaning of this Section if it is accomplished by force, threat or deception, or, in the case of a person who is under the age of 14 or incompetent, if it is accomplished without the consent of a parent, guardian or other person responsible for general supervision of his welfare.

Section 212.2. Felonious Restraint.

A person commits a felony of the third degree if he knowingly:

(a) restrains another unlawfully in circumstances exposing him to risk of serious bodily injury; or

(b) holds another in a condition of involuntary servitude.

Section 212.3. False Imprisonment.

A person commits a misdemeanor if he knowingly restrains another unlawfully so as to interfere substantially with his liberty.

Section 212.4. Interference With Custody.

(1) **Custody of Children.** A person commits an offense if he knowingly or recklessly takes or entices any child under the age of 18 from the custody of its parent, guardian or other lawful custodian, when he has no privilege to do so. It is an affirmative defense that:

(a) the actor believed that his action was necessary to preserve the child from danger to its welfare; or

(b) the child, being at the time not less than 14 years old, was taken away at its own instigation without enticement and without purpose to commit a criminal offense with or against the child.

Proof that the child was below the critical age gives rise to a presumption that the actor knew the child's age or acted in reckless disregard thereof. The offense is a misdemeanor unless the actor, not being a parent or person in equivalent relation to the child, acted with knowledge that his conduct would cause serious alarm for the child's safety, or in reckless disregard of a likelihood of causing such alarm, in which case the offense is a felony of the third degree.

(2) **Custody of Committed Persons.** A person is guilty of a misdemeanor if he knowingly or recklessly takes or entices any committed person away from lawful custody when he is not privileged to do so. "Committed person" means, in addition to anyone committed under judicial warrant, any orphan, neglected or delinquent child, mentally defective or insane person, or other dependent or incompetent person entrusted to another's custody by or through a recognized social agency or otherwise by authority of law.

Section 212.5. Criminal Coercion.

(1) **Offense Defined.** A person is guilty of criminal coercion if, with purpose

unlawfully to restrict another's freedom of action to his detriment, he threatens to:

    (a) commit any criminal offense; or

    (b) accuse anyone of a criminal offense; or

    (c) expose any secret tending to subject any person to hatred, contempt or ridicule, or to impair his credit or business repute; or

    (d) take or withhold action as an official, or cause an official to take or withhold action.

It is an affirmative defense to prosecution based on paragraphs (b), (c) or (d) that the actor believed the accusation or secret to be true or the proposed official action justified and that his purpose was limited to compelling the other to behave in a way reasonably related to the circumstances which were the subject of the accusation, exposure or proposed official action, as by desisting from further misbehavior, making good a wrong done, refraining from taking any action or responsibility for which the actor believes the other disqualified.

(2) **Grading.** Criminal coercion is a misdemeanor unless the threat is to commit a felony or the actor's purpose is felonious, in which cases the offense is a felony of the third degree.

ARTICLE 213. SEXUAL OFFENSES

Section 213.0. Definitions.

In this Article, the definitions given in Section 210.0 apply unless a different meaning plainly is required. Sexual intercourse includes intercourse per os or per anum, with some penetration however slight; emission is not required.

Deviate sexual intercourse means sexual intercourse per os or per anum between human beings who are not husband and wife, and any form of sexual intercourse with an animal.

Section 213.1. Rape and Related Offenses.

(1) **Rape.** A male who has sexual intercourse with a female not his wife is guilty of rape if:

    (a) he compels her to submit by force or by threat of imminent death, serious bodily injury, extreme pain or kidnapping, to be inflicted on anyone; or

    (b) he has substantially impaired her power to appraise or control her conduct by administering or employing without her knowledge drugs, intoxicants or other means for the purpose of preventing resistance; or

    (c) the female is unconscious; or

    (d) the female is less than 10 years old.

Rape is a felony of the second degree unless (i) in the course thereof the actor inflicts serious bodily injury upon anyone, or (ii) the victim was not a voluntary social companion of the actor upon the occasion of the crime and had not previously permitted him sexual liberties, in which cases the offense is a felony of the first degree.

(2) **Gross Sexual Imposition.** A male who has sexual intercourse with a female not his wife commits a felony of the third degree if:

    (a) he compels her to submit by any threat that would prevent resistance by a woman of ordinary resolution; or

    (b) he knows that she suffers from a mental disease or defect which renders her incapable of appraising the nature of her conduct; or

    (c) he knows that she is unaware that a sexual act is being committed upon her or that she submits because she mistakenly supposes that he is her husband.

Section 213.2. Deviate Sexual Intercourse by Force or Imposition.

(1) **By Force or Its Equivalent.** A person who engages in deviate sexual intercourse with another person, or who causes another to engage in deviate sexual intercourse, commits a felony of the second degree if:

(a) he compels the other person to participate by force or by threat of imminent death, serious bodily injury, extreme pain or kidnapping, to be inflicted on anyone; or

(b) he has substantially impaired the other person's power to appraise or control his conduct, by administering or employing without the knowledge of the other person drugs, intoxicants or other means for the purpose of preventing resistance; or

(c) the other person is unconscious; or

(d) the other person is less than 10 years old.

(2) **By Other Imposition.** A person who engages in deviate sexual intercourse with another person, or who causes another to engage in deviate sexual intercourse, commits a felony of the third degree if:

(a) he compels the other person to participate by any threat that would prevent resistance by a person of ordinary resolution; or

(b) he knows that the other person suffers from a mental disease or defect which renders him incapable of appraising the nature of his conduct; or

(c) he knows that the other person submits because he is unaware that a sexual act is being committed upon him.

Section 213.3. Corruption of Minors and Seduction.

(1) **Offense Defined.** A male who has sexual intercourse with a female not his wife, or any person who engages in devi-

ate sexual intercourse or causes another to engage in deviate sexual intercourse, is guilty of an offense if:

(a) the other person is less than [16] years old and the actor is at least [4] years older than the other person; or

(b) the other person is less than 21 years old and the actor is his guardian or otherwise responsible for general supervision of his welfare; or

(c) the other person is in custody of law or detained in a hospital or other institution and the actor has supervisory or disciplinary authority over him; or

(d) the other person is a female who is induced to participate by a promise of marriage which the actor does not mean to perform.

(2) **Grading.** An offense under paragraph (a) of Subsection (1) is a felony of the third degree. Otherwise an offense under this section is a misdemeanor.

Section 213.4. Sexual Assault.

A person who has sexual contact with another not his spouse, or causes such other to have sexual intercourse with him, is guilty of sexual assault, a misdemeanor, if:

(1) he knows that the contact is offensive to the other person; or

(2) he knows that the other person suffers from a mental disease or defect which renders him or her incapable of appraising the nature of his or her conduct; or

(3) he knows that the other person is unaware that a sexual act is being committed; or

(4) the other person is less than 10 years old; or

(5) he has substantially impaired the other person's power to appraise or control his or her conduct, by administering or employing without the other's knowl-

edge drugs, intoxicants or other means for the purpose of preventing resistance; or

(6) the other person is less than [16] years old and the actor is at least [4] years older than the other person; or

(7) the other person is less than 21 years old and the actor is his guardian or otherwise responsible for general supervision of his welfare; or

(8) the other person is in custody of law or detained in a hospital or other institution and the actor has supervisory or disciplinary authority over him.

Sexual contact is any touching of the sexual or other intimate parts of the person for the purpose of arousing or gratifying sexual desire.

Section 213.5. Indecent Exposure.

A person commits a misdemeanor if, for the purpose of arousing or gratifying sexual desire of himself or of any person other than his spouse, he exposes his genitals under circumstances in which he knows his conduct is likely to cause affront or alarm.

Section 213.6. Provisions Generally Applicable to Article 213.

(1) **Mistake as to Age.** Whenever in this Article the criminality of conduct depends on a child's being below the age of 10, it is no defense that the actor did not know the child's age, or reasonably believed the child to be older than 10. When criminality depends on the child's being below a critical age other than 10, it is a defense for the actor to prove by a preponderance of the evidence that he reasonably believed the child to be above the critical age.

(2) **Spouse Relationships.** Whenever in this Article the definition of an offense excludes conduct with a spouse, the exclu-

sion shall be deemed to extend to persons living as man and wife, regardless of the legal status of their relationship. The exclusion shall be inoperative as respects spouses living apart under a decree of judicial separation. Where the definition of an offense excludes conduct with a spouse or conduct by a woman, this shall not preclude conviction of a spouse or woman as accomplice in a sexual act which he or she causes another person, not within the exclusion, to perform.

(3) **Sexually Promiscuous Complainants.** It is a defense to prosecution under Section 213.3 and paragraphs (6), (7) and (8) of Section 213.4 for the actor to prove by a preponderance of the evidence that the alleged victim had, prior to the time of the offense charged, engaged promiscuously in sexual relations with others.

(4) **Prompt Complaint.** No prosecution may be instituted or maintained under this Article unless the alleged offense was brought to the notice of public authority within [3] months of its occurrence or, where the alleged victim was less than [16] years old or otherwise incompetent to make complaint, within [3] months after a parent, guardian or other competent person specially interested in the victim learns of the offense.

(5) **Testimony of Complainants.** No person shall be convicted of any felony under this Article upon the uncorroborated testimony of the alleged victim. Corroboration may be circumstantial. In any prosecution before a jury for an offense under this Article, the jury shall be instructed to evaluate the testimony of a victim or complaining witness with special care in view of the emotional involvement of the witness and the difficulty of determining the truth with respect to alleged sexual activities carried out in private.

OFFENSES AGAINST PROPERTY

ARTICLE 220. ARSON, CRIMINAL MISCHIEF, AND OTHER PROPERTY DESTRUCTION

Section 220.1. Arson and Related Offenses.

(1) **Arson.** A person is guilty of arson, a felony of the second degree, if he starts a fire or causes an explosion with the purpose of:

(a) destroying a building or occupied structure of another; or

(b) destroying or damaging any property, whether his own or another's, to collect insurance for such loss. It shall be an affirmative defense to prosecution under this paragraph that the actor's conduct did not recklessly endanger any building or occupied structure of another or place any other person in danger of death or bodily injury.

(2) **Reckless Burning or Exploding.** A person commits a felony of the third degree if he purposely starts a fire or causes an explosion, whether on his own property or another's, and thereby recklessly:

(a) places another person in danger of death or bodily injury; or

(b) places a building or occupied structure of another in danger of damage or destruction.

(3) **Failure to Control or Report Dangerous Fire.** A person who knows that a fire is endangering life or a substantial amount of property of another and fails to take reasonable measures to put out or control the fire, when he can do so without substantial risk to himself, or to give a prompt fire alarm, commits a misdemeanor if:

(a) he knows that he is under an official, contractual, or other legal duty to prevent or combat the fire; or

(b) the fire was started, albeit lawfully, by him or with his assent, or on property in his custody or control.

(4) **Definitions.** "Occupied structure" includes a ship, trailer, sleeping car, airplane, or other vehicle, structure or place adapted for overnight accommodation of persons or for carrying on business therein, whether or not a person is actually present. Property is that of another, for the purposes of this section, if anyone other than the actor has a possessory or proprietory interest therein. If a building or structure is divided into separately occupied units, any unit not occupied by the actor is an occupied structure of another.

Section 220.2. Causing or Risking Catastrophe.

(1) **Causing Catastrophe.** A person who causes a catastrophe by explosion, fire, flood, avalanche, collapse of building, release of poison gas, radioactive material or other harmful or destructive force or substance, or by any other means of causing potentially widespread injury or damage, commits a felony of the second degree if he does so purposely or knowingly, or a felony of the third degree if he does so recklessly.

(2) **Risking Catastrophe.** A person is guilty of a misdemeanor if he recklessly creates a risk of catastrophe in the employment of fire, explosives or other dangerous means listed in Subsection (1).

(3) **Failure to Prevent Catastrophe.** A person who knowingly or recklessly fails to take reasonable measures to prevent or mitigate a catastrophe commits a misdemeanor if:

(a) he knows that he is under an official, contractual or other legal duty to take such measures; or

(b) he did or assented to the act causing or threatening the catastrophe.

Section 220.3. Criminal Mischief.

(1) **Offense Defined.** A person is guilty of criminal mischief if he:

(a) damages tangible property of another purposely, recklessly, or by negligence in the employment of fire, explosives, or other dangerous means listed in Section 220.2(1); or

(b) purposely or recklessly tampers with tangible property of another so as to endanger person or property; or

(c) purposely or recklessly causes another to suffer pecuniary loss by deception or threat.

(2) **Grading.** Criminal mischief is a felony of the third degree if the actor purposely causes pecuniary loss in excess of $5,000, or a substantial interruption or impairment of public communication, transportation, supply of water, gas or power, or other public service. It is a misdemeanor if the actor purposely causes pecuniary loss in excess of $100, or a petty misdemeanor if he purposely or recklessly causes pecuniary loss in excess of $25. Otherwise criminal mischief is a violation.

ARTICLE 221. BURGLARY AND OTHER CRIMINAL INTRUSION

Section 221.0. Definitions.

In this Article, unless a different meaning plainly is required:

(1) "occupied structure" means any structure, vehicle or place adapted for overnight accommodation of persons, or for carrying on business therein, whether or not a person is actually present.

(2) "night" means the period between thirty minutes past sunset and thirty minutes before sunrise.

Section 221.1. Burglary.

(1) **Burglary Defined.** A person is guilty of burglary if he enters a building or occupied structure, or separately secured or occupied portion thereof, with purpose to commit a crime therein, unless the premises are at the time open to the public or the actor is licensed or privileged to enter. It is an affirmative defense to prosecution for burglary that the building or structure was abandoned.

(2) **Grading.** Burglary is a felony of the second degree if it is perpetrated in the dwelling of another at night, or if, in the course of committing the offense, the actor:

(a) purposely, knowingly or recklessly inflicts or attempts to inflict bodily injury on anyone; or

(b) is armed with explosives or a deadly weapon.

Otherwise, burglary is a felony of the third degree. An act shall be deemed "in the course of committing" an offense if it occurs in an attempt to commit the offense or in flight after the attempt or commission.

(3) **Multiple Convictions.** A person may not be convicted both for burglary and for the offense which it was his purpose to commit after the burglarious entry or for an attempt to commit that offense, unless the additional offense constitutes a felony of the first or second degree.

Section 221.2. Criminal Trespass.

(1) **Buildings and Occupied Structures.** A person commits an offense if, knowing that he is not licensed or privileged to do so, he enters or surreptitiously remains in any building or occupied structure, or separately secured or occupied portion thereof. An offense under this Subsection is a misdemeanor if it is committed in a dwelling at night. Otherwise it is a petty misdemeanor.

(2) **Defiant Trespasser.** A person commits an offense if, knowing that he is not licensed or privileged to do so, he enters or remains in any place as to which notice against trespass is given by:

(a) actual communication to the actor; or

(b) posting in a manner prescribed by law or reasonably likely to come to the attention of intruders; or

(c) fencing or other enclosure manifestly designed to exclude intruders.

An offense under this Subsection constitutes a petty misdemeanor if the offender defies an order to leave personally communicated to him by the owner of the premises or other authorized person. Otherwise it is a violation.

(3) **Defenses.** It is an affirmative defense to prosecution under this Section that:

(a) a building or occupied structure involved in an offense under Subsection (1) was abandoned; or

(b) the premises were at the time open to members of the public and the actor complied with all lawful conditions imposed on access to or remaining in the premises; or

(c) the actor reasonably believed that the owner of the premises, or other person empowered to license access thereto, would have licensed him to enter or remain.

ARTICLE 222. ROBBERY

Section 222.1. Robbery.

(1) **Robbery Defined.** A person is guilty of robbery if, in the course of committing a theft, he:

(a) inflicts serious bodily injury upon another; or

(b) threatens another with or purposely puts him in fear of immediate serious bodily injury; or

(c) commits or threatens immediately to commit any felony of the first or second degree.

An act shall be deemed "in the course of committing a theft" if it occurs in an attempt to commit theft or in flight after the attempt or commission.

(2) **Grading.** Robbery is a felony of the second degree, except that it is a felony of the first degree if in the course of committing the theft the actor attempts to kill anyone, or purposely inflicts or attempts to inflict serious bodily injury.

ARTICLE 223. THEFT AND RELATED OFFENSES

Section 223.0. Definitions.

In this Article, unless a different meaning plainly is required:

(1) "deprive" means: (a) to withhold property of another permanently or for so extended a period as to appropriate a major portion of its economic value, or with intent to restore only upon payment of reward or other compensation; or (b) to dispose of the property so as to make it unlikely that the owner will recover it.

(2) "financial institution" means a bank, insurance company, credit union, building and loan association, investment trust or other organization held out to the public as a place of deposit of funds or medium of savings or collective investment.

(3) "government" means the United States, any State, county, municipality, or other political unit, or any department, agency or subdivision of any of the foregoing, or any corporation or other association carrying out the functions of government.

(4) "movable property" means property the location of which can be changed, including things growing on, affixed to, or found in land, and documents although the

rights represented thereby have no physical location. "Immovable property" is all other property.

(5) "obtain" means: (a) in relation to property, to bring about a transfer or purported transfer of a legal interest in the property, whether to the obtainer or another; or (b) in relation to labor or service, to secure performance thereof.

(6) "property" means anything of value, including real estate, tangible and intangible personal property, contract rights, choses-in-action and other interests in or claims to wealth, admission or transportation tickets, captured or domestic animals, food and drink, electric or other power.

(7) "property of another" includes property in which any person other than the actor has an interest which the actor is not privileged to infringe, regardless of the fact that the actor also has an interest in the property and regardless of the fact that the other person might be precluded from civil recovery because the property was used in an unlawful transaction or was subject to forfeiture as contraband. Property in possession of the actor shall not be deemed property of another who has only a security interest therein, even if legal title is in the creditor pursuant to a conditional sales contract or other security agreement.

Section 223.1. Consolidation of Theft Offenses; Grading; Provisions Applicable to Theft Generally.

(1) **Consolidation of Theft Offenses.** Conduct denominated theft in this Article constitutes a single offense. An accusation of theft may be supported by evidence that it was committed in any manner that would be theft under this Article, notwithstanding the specification of a different manner in the indictment or information, subject only to the power of the Court to ensure fair trial by granting a continuance or other appropriate relief where the conduct of the defense would be prejudiced by lack of fair notice or by surprise.

(2) **Grading of Theft Offenses.**

(a) Theft constitutes a felony of the third degree if the amount involved exceeds $500, or if the property stolen is a fire-arm, automobile, airplane, motorcycle, motorboat or other motor-propelled vehicle, or in the case of theft by receiving stolen property, if the receiver is in the business of buying or selling stolen property.

(b) Theft not within the preceding paragraph constitutes a misdemeanor, except that if the property was not taken from the person or by threat, or in breach of a fiduciary obligation, and the actor proves by a preponderance of the evidence that the amount involved was less than $50, the offense constitutes a petty misdemeanor.

(c) The amount involved in a theft shall be deemed to be the highest value, by any reasonable standard, of the property or services which the actor stole or attempted to steal. Amounts involved in thefts committed pursuant to one scheme or course of conduct, whether from the same person or several persons, may be aggregated in determining the grade of the offense.

(3) **Claim of Right.** It is an affirmative defense to prosecution for theft that the actor:

(a) was unaware that the property or service was that of another; or

(b) acted under an honest claim of right to the property or service involved or that he had a right to acquire or dispose of it as he did; or

(c) took property exposed for sale, intending to purchase and pay for it promptly, or reasonably believing that the owner, if present, would have consented.

(4) **Theft from Spouse.** It is no defense that theft was from the actor's spouse, except that misappropriation of household and personal effects, or other property normally accessible to both spouses, is theft only if it occurs after the parties have ceased living together.

Section 223.2. Theft by Unlawful Taking or Disposition.

(1) **Movable Property.** A person is guilty of theft if he unlawfully takes, or exercises unlawful control over, movable property of another with purpose to deprive him thereof.

(2) **Immovable Property.** A person is guilty of theft if he unlawfully transfers immovable property of another or any interest therein with purpose to benefit himself or another not entitled thereto.

Section 223.3. Theft by Deception.

A person is guilty of theft if he purposely obtains property of another by deception. A person deceives if he purposely:

(1) creates or reinforces a false impression, including false impressions as to law, value, intention or other state of mind; but deception as to a person's intention to perform a promise shall not be inferred from the fact alone that he did not subsequently perform the promise; or

(2) prevents another from acquiring information which would affect his judgment of a transaction; or

(3) fails to correct a false impression which the deceiver previously created or reinforced, or which the deceiver knows to be influencing another to whom he stands in a fiduciary or confidential relationship; or

(4) fails to disclose a known lien, adverse claim or other legal impediment to the enjoyment of property which he transfers or encumbers in consideration for the property obtained, whether such impediment is or is not valid, or is or is not a matter of official record.

The term "deceive" does not, however, include falsity as to matters having no pecuniary significance, or puffing by statements unlikely to deceive ordinary persons in the group addressed.

Section 223.4. Theft by Extortion.

A person is guilty of theft if he purposely obtains property of another by threatening to:

(1) inflict bodily injury on anyone or commit any other criminal offense; or

(2) accuse anyone of a criminal offense; or

(3) expose any secret tending to subject any person to hatred, contempt or ridicule, or to impair his credit or business repute; or

(4) take or withhold action as an official, or cause an official to take or withhold action; or

(5) bring about or continue a strike, boycott or other collective unofficial action, if the property is not demanded or received for the benefit of the group in whose interest the actor purports to act; or

(6) testify or provide information or withhold testimony or information with respect to another's legal claim or defense; or

(7) inflict any other harm which would not benefit the actor.

It is an affirmative defense to prosecution based on paragraphs (2), (3) or (4) that the property obtained by threat of accusation, exposure, lawsuit or other invocation of official action was honestly claimed as restitution or indemnification for harm done in the circumstances to which such accusation, exposure, lawsuit or other official action relates, or as compensation for property or lawful services.

Section 223.5. Theft of Property Lost, Mislaid, or Delivered by Mistake.

A person who comes into control of property of another that he knows to have been lost, mislaid, or delivered under a mistake as to the nature or amount of the property or the identity of the recipient is guilty of theft if, with purpose to deprive the owner thereof, he fails to take reasonable measures to restore the property to a person entitled to have it.

Section 223.6. Receiving Stolen Property.

(1) **Receiving.** A person is guilty of theft if he purposely receives, retains, or disposes of movable property of another knowing that it has been stolen, or believing that it has probably been stolen, unless the property is received, retained, or disposed with purpose to restore it to the owner. "Receiving" means acquiring possession, control or title, or lending on the security of the property.

(2) **Presumption of Knowledge.** The requisite knowledge or belief is presumed in the case of a dealer who:

(a) is found in possession or control of property stolen from two or more persons on separate occasions; or

(b) has received stolen property in another transaction within the year preceding the transaction charged; or

(c) being a dealer in property of the sort received, acquires it for a consideration which he knows is far below its reasonable value.

"Dealer" means a person in the business of buying or selling goods, including a pawnbroker.

Section 223.7. Theft of Services.

(1) A person is guilty of theft if he purposely obtains services which he knows are available only for compensation, by deception or threat, or by false token or other means to avoid payment for the service. "Services" includes labor, professional service, transportation, telephone or other public service, accommodation in hotels, restaurants or elsewhere, admission to exhibitions, use of vehicles or other movable property. Where compensation for service is ordinarily paid immediately upon the rendering of such service, as in the case of hotels and restaurants, refusal to pay or absconding without payment or offer to pay gives rise to a presumption that the service was obtained by deception as to intention to pay.

(2) A person commits theft if, having control over the disposition of services of others, to which he is not entitled, he knowingly diverts such services to his own benefit or to the benefit of another not entitled thereto.

Section 223.8. Theft by Failure to Make Required Disposition of Funds Received.

A person who purposely obtains property upon agreement, or subject to a known legal obligation, to make specified payment or other disposition, whether from such property or its proceeds or from his own property to be reserved in equivalent amount, is guilty of theft if he deals with the property obtained as his own and fails to make the required payment or disposition. The foregoing applies notwithstanding that it may be impossible to identify particular property as belonging to the victim at the time of the actor's failure to make the required payment or disposition. An officer or employee of the government or of a financial institution is presumed: (i) to know any legal obligation relevant to his criminal liability under this Section, and (ii) to have dealt with the property as his own if he fails to pay or account upon lawful demand, or if an audit reveals a shortage or falsification of accounts.

Section 223.9. Unauthorized Use of Automobiles and Other Vehicles.

A person commits a misdemeanor if he operates another's automobile, airplane, motorcycle, motorboat, or other motor-propelled vehicle without consent of the owner. It is an affirmative defense to prosecution under this Section that the actor reasonably believed that the owner would have consented to the operation had he known of it.

ARTICLE 224. FORGERY AND FRAUDULENT PRACTICES

Section 224.0. Definitions.

In this Article, the definitions given in Section 223.0 apply unless a different meaning plainly is required.

Section 224.1. Forgery.

(1) **Definition.** A person is guilty of forgery if, with purpose to defraud or injure anyone, or with knowledge that he is facilitating a fraud or injury to be perpetrated by anyone, the actor:

(a) alters any writing of another without his authority; or

(b) makes, completes, executes, authenticates, issues or transfers any writing so that it purports to be the act of another who did not authorize that act, or to have been executed at a time or place or in a numbered sequence other than was in fact the case, or to be a copy of an original when no such original existed; or

(c) utters any writing which he knows to be forged in a manner specified in paragraphs (a) or (b).

"Writing" includes printing or any other method of recording information, money, coins, tokens, stamps, seals, credit cards, badges, trademarks, and other symbols of value, right, privilege, or identification.

(2) **Grading.** Forgery is a felony of the second degree if the writing is or purports to be part of an issue of money, securities, postage or revenue stamps, or other instruments issued by the government, or part of an issue of stock, bonds or other instruments representing interests in or claims against any property or enterprise. Forgery is a felony of the third degree if the writing is or purports to be a will, deed, contract, release, commercial instrument, or other document evidencing, creating, transferring, altering, terminating, or otherwise affecting legal relations. Otherwise forgery is a misdemeanor.

Section 224.2. Simulating Objects of Antiquity, Rarity, Etc.

A person commits a misdemeanor if, with purpose to defraud anyone or with knowledge that he is facilitating a fraud to be perpetrated by anyone, he makes, alters or utters any object so that it appears to have value because of antiquity, rarity, source, or authorship which it does not possess.

Section 224.3. Fraudulent Destruction, Removal or Concealment of Recordable Instruments.

A person commits a felony of the third degree if, with purpose to deceive or injure anyone, he destroys, removes or conceals any will, deed, mortgage, security instrument or other writing for which the law provides public recording.

Section 224.4. Tampering With Records.

A person commits a misdemeanor if, knowing that he has no privilege to do so, he falsifies, destroys, removes or conceals any writing or record, with purpose to deceive or injure anyone or to conceal any wrongdoing.

Section 224.5. Bad Checks.

A person who issues or passes a check or similar sight order for the payment of money, knowing that it will not be honored by the drawee, commits a misdemeanor. For the purposes of this Section as well as in any prosecution for theft committed by means of a bad check, an issuer is presumed to know that the check or order (other than a post-dated check or order) would not be paid, if:

(1) the issuer had no account with the drawee at the time the check or order was issued; or

(2) payment was refused by the drawee for lack of funds, upon presentation within 30 days after issue, and the issuer failed to make good within 10 days after receiving notice of that refusal.

Section 224.6. Credit Cards.

A person commits an offense if he uses a credit card for the purpose of obtaining property or services with knowledge that:

(1) the card is stolen or forged; or

(2) the card has been revoked or cancelled; or

(3) for any other reason his use of the card is unauthorized.

It is an affirmative defense to prosecution under paragraph (3) if the actor proves by a preponderance of the evidence that he had the purpose and ability to meet all obligations to the issuer arising out of his use of the card. "Credit card" means a writing or other evidence of an undertaking to pay for property or services delivered or rendered to or upon the order of a designated person or bearer. An offense under this Section is a felony of the third degree if the value of the property or services secured or sought to be secured by means of the credit card exceeds $500; otherwise it is a misdemeanor.

Section 224.7. Deceptive Business Practices.

A person commits a misdemeanor if in the course of business he:

(1) uses or possesses for use a false weight or measure, or any other device for falsely determining or recording any quality or quantity; or

(2) sells, offers or exposes for sale, or delivers less than the represented quantity of any commodity or service; or

(3) takes or attempts to take more than the represented quantity of any commodity or service when as buyer he furnishes the weight or measure; or

(4) sells, offers or exposes for sale adulterated or mislabeled commodities. "Adulterated" means varying from the standard of composition or quality prescribed by or pursuant to any statute providing criminal penalties for such variance, or set by established commercial usage. "Mislabeled" means varying from the standard of truth or disclosure in labeling prescribed by or pursuant to any statute providing criminal penalties for such variance, or set by established commercial usage; or

(5) makes a false or misleading statement in any advertisement addressed to the public or to a substantial segment thereof for the purpose of promoting the purchase or sale of property or services; or

(6) makes a false or misleading written statement for the purpose of obtaining property or credit; or

(7) makes a false or misleading written statement for the purpose of promoting the sale of securities, or omits information required by law to be disclosed in written documents relating to securities.

It is an affirmative defense to prosecution under this Section if the defendant proves by a preponderance of the evidence that his conduct was not knowingly or recklessly deceptive.

Section 224.8. Commercial Bribery and Breach of Duty to Act Disinterestedly.

(1) A person commits a misdemeanor if he solicits, accepts or agrees to accept any benefit as consideration for knowingly violating or agreeing to violate a duty of fidelity to which he is subject as:

(a) agent or employee of another;

(b) trustee, guardian, or other fiduciary;

(c) Lawyer, physician, accountant, appraiser, or other professional adviser or informant;

(d) officer, director, manager or other participant in the direction of the affairs of an incorporated or unincorporated association; or

(e) arbitrator or other purportedly disinterested adjudicator or referee.

(2) A person who holds himself out to the public as being engaged in the business of making disinterested selection, appraisal, or criticism of commodities or services commits a misdemeanor if he solicits, accepts or agrees to accept any benefit to influence his selection, appraisal or criticism.

(3) A person commits a misdemeanor if he confers, or offers or agrees to confer, any benefit the acceptance of which would be criminal under this Section.

Section 224.9. Rigging Publicly Exhibited Contest.

(1) A person commits a misdemeanor if, with purpose to prevent a publicly exhibited contest from being conducted in accordance with the rules and usages purporting to govern it, he:

(a) confers or offers or agrees to confer any benefit upon, or threatens any injury to a participant, official or other

person associated with the contest or exhibition; or

(b) tampers with any person, animal or thing.

(2) **Soliciting or Accepting Benefit for Rigging.** A person commits a misdemeanor if he knowingly solicits, accepts or agrees to accept any benefit the giving of which would be criminal under Subsection (1).

(3) **Participation in Rigged Contest.** A person commits a misdemeanor if he knowingly engages in, sponsors, produces, judges, or otherwise participates in a publicly exhibited contest knowing that the contest is not being conducted in compliance with the rules and usages purporting to govern it, by reason of conduct which would be criminal under this Section.

Section 224.10. Defrauding Secured Creditors.

A person commits a misdemeanor if he destroys, removes, conceals, encumbers, transfers or otherwise deals with property subject to a security interest with purpose to hinder enforcement of that interest.

Section 224.11. Fraud in Insolvency.

A person commits a misdemeanor if, knowing that proceedings have been or are about to be instituted for the appointment of a receiver or other person entitled to administer property for the benefit of creditors, or that any other composition or liquidation for the benefit of creditors has been or is about to be made, he:

(a) destroys, removes, conceals, encumbers, transfers, or otherwise deals with any property with purpose to defeat or obstruct the claim of any creditor, or otherwise to obstruct the operation of any law relating to administration of property for the benefit of creditors; or

(b) knowingly falsifies any writing or record relating to the property; or

(c) knowingly misrepresents or refuses to disclose to a receiver or other person entitled to administer property for the benefit of creditors, the existence, amount or location of the property, or any other information which the actor could be legally required to furnish in relation to such administration.

Section 224.12. Receiving Deposits in a Failing Financial Institution.

An officer, manager or other person directing or participating in the direction of a financial institution commits a misdemeanor if he receives or permits the receipt of a deposit, premium payment or other investment in the institution knowing that:

(1) due to financial difficulties the institution is about to suspend operations or go into receivership or reorganization; and

(2) the person making the deposit or other payment is unaware of the precarious situation of the institution.

Section 224.13. Misapplication of Entrusted Property and Property of Government or Financial Institution.

A person commits an offense if he applies or disposes of property that has been entrusted to him as a fiduciary, or property of the government or of a financial institution, in a manner which he knows is unlawful and involves substantial risk of loss or detriment to the owner of the property or to a person for whose benefit the property was entrusted. The offense is a misdemeanor if the amount involved exceeds $50; otherwise it is a petty misdemeanor. "Fiduciary" includes trustee, guardian, executor, administrator, receiver and any person carrying on fiduciary functions on behalf of a corporation or other organization which is a fiduciary.

Section 224.14. Securing Execution of Documents by Deception.

A person commits a misdemeanor if by deception he causes another to execute any instrument affecting or purporting to affect or likely to affect the pecuniary interest of any person.

OFFENSES AGAINST THE FAMILY

ARTICLE 230. OFFENSES AGAINST THE FAMILY

Section 230.1. Bigamy and Polygamy.

(1) **Bigamy.** A married person is guilty of bigamy, a misdemeanor, if he contracts or purports to contract another marriage, unless at the time of the subsequent marriage:

(a) the actor believes that the prior spouse is dead; or

(b) the actor and the prior spouse have been living apart for five consecutive years throughout which the prior spouse was not known by the actor to be alive; or

(c) a Court has entered a judgment purporting to terminate or annul any prior disqualifying marriage, and the actor does not know that judgment to be invalid; or

(d) the actor reasonably believes that he is legally eligible to remarry.

(2) **Polygamy.** A person is guilty of polygamy, a felony of the third degree, if he marries or cohabits with more than one spouse at a time in purported exercise of the right of plural marriage. The offense is a continuing one until all cohabitation and claim of marriage with more than one spouse terminates. This Section does not apply to parties to a polygamous marriage, lawful in the country of which they are residents or nationals, while they are in transit through or temporarily visiting this State.

(3) **Other Party to Bigamous or Polygamous Marriage.** A person is guilty of bigamy or polygamy, as the case may be, if he contracts or purports to contract marriage with another knowing that the other is thereby committing bigamy or polygamy.

Section 230.2. Incest.

A person is guilty of incest, a felony of the third degree, if he knowingly marries or cohabits or has sexual intercourse with an ancestor or descendant, a brother or sister of the whole or half blood [or an uncle, aunt, nephew or niece of the whole blood]. "Cohabit" means to live together under the representation or appearance of being married. The relationships referred to herein include blood relationships without regard to legitimacy, and relationship of parent and child by adoption.

Section 230.3. Abortion.

(1) **Unjustified Abortion.** A person who purposely and unjustifiably terminates the pregnancy of another otherwise than by a live birth commits a felony of the third degree or, where the pregnancy has continued beyond the twenty-sixth week, a felony of the second degree.

(2) **Justifiable Abortion.** A licensed physician is justified in terminating a pregnancy if he believes there is substantial risk that continuance of the pregnancy would gravely impair the physical or mental health of the mother or that the child would be born with grave physical or mental defect, or that the pregnancy resulted from rape, incest, or other felonious intercourse. All illicit intercourse with a girl below the age of 16 shall be deemed felonious for purposes of this subsection. Justifiable abortions shall be performed only in a licensed hospital except in case of emergency when hospital facilities are unavailable. [Additional exceptions from the requirement of hospitalization may be incorporated here to take account of situations in sparsely settled areas where hospitals are not generally accessible.]

(3) **Physicians' Certificates; Presumption from Non-Compliance.** No abortion shall be performed unless two physicians, one of whom may be the person performing the abortion, shall have certified in writing the circumstances which they believe to justify the abortion. Such certificate shall be submitted before the abortion to the hospital where it is to be performed and, in the case of abortion following felonious intercourse, to the prosecuting attorney or the police. Failure to comply with any of the requirements of this Subsection gives rise to a presumption that the abortion was unjustified.

(4) **Self-Abortion.** A woman whose pregnancy has continued beyond the twenty-sixth week commits a felony of the third degree if she purposely terminates her own pregnancy otherwise than by a live birth, or if she uses instruments, drugs or violence upon herself for that purpose. Except as justified under Subsection (2), a person who induces or knowingly aids a woman to use instruments, drugs or violence upon herself for the purpose of terminating her pregnancy otherwise than by a live birth commits a felony of the third degree whether or not the pregnancy has continued beyond the twenty-sixth week.

(5) **Pretended Abortion.** A person commits a felony of the third degree if, representing that it is his purpose to perform an abortion, he does an act adapted to cause abortion in a pregnant woman although the woman is in fact not pregnant, or the actor does not believe she is. A person charged with unjustified abortion under Subsection (1) or an attempt to commit that offense may be convicted thereof upon proof of conduct prohibited by this Subsection.

(6) **Distribution of Abortifacients.** A person who sells, offers to sell, possesses

with intent to sell, advertises, or displays for sale anything specially designed to terminate a pregnancy, or held out by the actor as useful for that purpose, commits a misdemeanor, unless:

(a) the sale, offer or display is to a physician or druggist or to an intermediary in a chain of distribution to physicians or druggists; or

(b) the sale is made upon prescription or order of a physician; or

(c) the possession is with intent to sell as authorized in paragraphs (a) and (b); or

(d) the advertising is addressed to persons named in paragraph (a) and confined to trade or professional channels not likely to reach the general public.

(7) **Section Inapplicable to Prevention of Pregnancy.** Nothing in this Section shall be deemed applicable to the prescription, administration or distribution of drugs or other substances for avoiding pregnancy, whether by preventing implantation of a fertilized ovum or by any other method that operates before, at or immediately after fertilization.

Section 230.4. Endangering Welfare of Children.

A parent, guardian, or other person supervising the welfare of a child under 18 commits a misdemeanor if he knowingly endangers the child's welfare by violating a duty of care, protection or support.

Section 230.5. Persistent Non-support.

A person commits a misdemeanor if he persistently fails to provide support which he can provide and which he knows he is legally obliged to provide to a spouse, child or other defendant.

OFFENSES AGAINST PUBLIC ADMINISTRATION

ARTICLE 240. BRIBERY AND CORRUPT INFLUENCE

Section 240.0. Definitions.

In Articles 240–243, unless a different meaning plainly is required:

(1) "benefit" means gain or advantage, or anything regarded by the beneficiary as gain or advantage, including benefit to any other person or entity in whose welfare he is interested, but not an advantage promised generally to a group or class of voters as a consequence of public measures which a candidate engages to support or oppose;

(2) "government" includes any branch, subdivision or agency of the government of the State or any locality within it;

(3) "harm" means loss, disadvantage or injury, or anything so regarded by the person affected, including loss, disadvantage or injury to any other person or entity in whose welfare he is interested;

(4) "official proceeding" means a proceeding heard or which may be heard before any legislative, judicial, administrative or other governmental agency or official authorized to take evidence under oath, including any referee, hearing examiner, commissioner, notary or other person taking testimony or deposition in connection with any such proceeding;

(5) "party official" means a person who holds an elective or appointive post in a political party in the United States by virtue of which he directs or conducts, or participates in directing or conducting party affairs at any level of responsibility;

(6) "pecuniary benefit" is benefit in the form of money, property, commer-

cial interests or anything else the primary significance of which is economic gain;

(7) "public servant" means any officer or employee of government, including legislators and judges, and any person participating as juror, advisor, consultant or otherwise, in performing a governmental function; but the term does not include witnesses;

(8) "administrative proceeding" means any proceeding other than a judicial proceeding the outcome of which is required to be based on a record or documentation prescribed by law, or in which law or regulation is particularized in application to individuals.

Section 240.1. Bribery in Official and Political Matters.

A person is guilty of bribery, a felony of the third degree, if he offers, confers or agrees to confer upon another, or solicits, accepts or agrees to accept from another:

(1) any pecuniary benefit as consideration for the recipient's decision, opinion, recommendation, vote or other exercise of discretion as a public servant, party official or voter; or

(2) any benefit as consideration for the recipient's decision, vote, recommendation or other exercise of official discretion in a judicial or administrative proceeding; or

(3) any benefit as consideration for a violation of a known legal duty as public servant or party official.

It is no defense to prosecution under this section that a person whom the actor sought to influence was not qualified to act in the desired way whether because he had not yet assumed office, or lacked jurisdiction, or for any other reason.

Section 240.2. Threats and Other Improper Influence in Official and Political Matters.

(1) **Offenses Defined.** A person commits an offense if he:

(a) threatens unlawful harm to any person with purpose to influence his decision, opinion, recommendation, vote or other exercise of discretion as a public servant, party official or voter; or

(b) threatens harm to any public servant with purpose to influence his decision, opinion, recommendation, vote or other exercise of discretion in a judicial or administrative proceeding; or

(c) threatens harm to any public servant or party official with purpose to influence him to violate his known legal duty; or

(d) privately addresses to any public servant who has or will have an official discretion in a judicial or administrative proceeding any representation, entreaty, argument or other communication with purpose to influence the outcome on the basis of considerations other than those authorized by law.

It is no defense to prosecution under this Section that a person whom the actor sought to influence was not qualified to act in the desired way, whether because he had not yet assumed office, or lacked jurisdiction, or for any other reason.

(2) **Grading.** An offense under this Section is a misdemeanor unless the actor threatened to commit a crime or made a threat with purpose to influence a judicial or administrative proceeding, in which cases the offense is a felony of the third degree.

Section 240.3. Compensation for Past Official Behavior.

A person commits a misdemeanor if he solicits, accepts or agrees to accept any pecuniary benefit as compensation for having, as public servant, given a decision, opinion, recommendation or vote favorable to another, or for having otherwise exercised a discretion in his favor, or for having violated his duty. A person commits a misdemeanor if he offers, confers or agrees to confer compensation acceptance of which is prohibited by this Section.

Section 240.4. Retaliation for Past Official Action.

A person commits a misdemeanor if he harms another by any unlawful act in retaliation for anything lawfully done by the latter in the capacity of public servant.

Section 240.5. Gifts to Public Servants by Persons Subject to Their Jurisdiction.

(1) **Regulatory and Law Enforcement Officials.** No public servant in any department or agency exercising regulatory functions, or conducting inspections or investigations, or carrying on civil or criminal litigation on behalf of the government, or having custody of prisoners, shall solicit, accept or agree to accept any pecuniary benefit from a person known to be subject to such regulation, inspection, investigation or custody, or against whom such litigation is known to be pending or contemplated.

(2) **Officials Concerned with Government Contracts and Pecuniary Transactions.** No public servant having any discretionary function to perform in connection with contracts, purchases, payments, claims or other pecuniary transactions of the government shall solicit, accept or agree to accept any pecuniary benefit from any person known to be interested in or likely to become interested in any such contract, purchase, payment, claim or transaction.

(3) **Judicial and Administrative Officials.** No public servant having judicial or administrative authority and no public servant employed by or in a court or other tribunal having such authority, or participating in the enforcement of its decisions, shall solicit, accept or agree to accept any pecuniary benefit from a person known to be interested in or likely to become interested in any matter before such public servant or a tribunal with which he is associated.

(4) **Legislative Officials.** No legislator or public servant employed by the legislature or by any committee or agency thereof shall solicit, accept or agree to accept any pecuniary benefit from any person known to be interested in a bill, transaction or proceeding, pending or contemplated, before the legislature or any committee or agency thereof.

(5) **Exceptions.** This Section shall not apply to:

(a) fees prescribed by law to be received by a public servant, or any other benefit for which the recipient gives legitimate consideration or to which he is otherwise legally entitled; or

(b) gifts or other benefits conferred on account of kinship or other personal, professional or business relationship independent of the official status of the receiver; or

(c) trivial benefits incidental to personal, professional or business contacts and involving no substantial risk of undermining official impartiality.

(6) **Offering Benefits Prohibited.** No person shall knowingly confer, or offer or agree to confer, any benefit prohibited by the foregoing Subsections.

(7) **Grade of Offense.** An offense under this Section is a misdemeanor.

Section 240.6. Compensating Public Servant for Assisting Private Interests in Relation to Matters Before Him.

(1) **Receiving Compensation.** A public servant commits a misdemeanor if he solicits, accepts or agrees to accept compensation for advice or other assistance in preparing or promoting a bill, contract, claim, or other transaction or proposal as to which he knows that he has or is likely to have an official discretion to exercise.

(2) **Paying Compensation.** A person commits a misdemeanor if he pays or offers or agrees to pay compensation to a public servant with knowledge that acceptance by the public servant is unlawful.

Section 240.7. Selling Political Endorsement; Special Influence.

(1) **Selling Political Endorsement.** A person commits a misdemeanor if he solicits, receives, agrees to receive, or agrees that any political party or other person shall receive, any pecuniary benefit as consideration for approval or disapproval of an appointment or advancement in public service, or for approval or disapproval of any person or transaction for any benefit conferred by an official or agency of government. "Approval" includes recommendation, failure to disapprove, or any other manifestation of favor or acquiescence. "Disapproval" includes failure to approve, or any other manifestation of disfavor or nonacquiescence.

(2) **Other Trading in Special Influence.** A person commits a misdemeanor if he solicits, receives or agrees to receive any pecuniary benefit as consideration for exerting special influence upon a public servant or procuring another to do so. "Special influence" means power to influence through kinship, friendship or other relationship, apart from the merits of the transaction.

(3) **Paying for Endorsement or Special Influence.** A person commits a mis-

demeanor if he offers, confers or agrees to confer any pecuniary benefit receipt of which is prohibited by this Section.

ARTICLE 241. PERJURY AND OTHER FALSIFICATION IN OFFICIAL MATTERS

Section 241.0. Definitions.

In this Article, unless a different meaning plainly is required:

(1) the definitions given in Section 240.0 apply; and

(2) "statement" means any representation, but includes a representation of opinion, belief or other state of mind only if the representation clearly relates to state of mind apart from or in addition to any facts which are the subject of the representation.

Section 241.1. Perjury.

(1) **Offense Defined.** A person is guilty of perjury, a felony of the third degree, if in any official proceeding he makes a false statement under oath or equivalent affirmation, or swears or affirms the truth of a statement previously made, when the statement is material and he does not believe it to be true.

(2) **Materiality.** Falsification is material, regardless of the admissibility of the statement under rules of evidence, if it could have affected the course or outcome of the proceeding. It is no defense that the declarant mistakenly believed the falsification to be immaterial. Whether a falsification is material in a given factual situation is a question of law.

(3) **Irregularities No Defense.** It is not a defense to prosecution under this Section that the oath or affirmation was administered or taken in an irregular manner or that the declarant was not competent to make the statement. A document purporting to be made upon oath or affirmation at any time when the actor presents

it as being so verified shall be deemed to have been duly sworn or affirmed.

(4) **Retraction.**   No person shall be guilty of an offense under this Section if he retracted the falsification in the course of the proceeding in which it was made before it became manifest that the falsification was or would be exposed and before the falsification substantially affected the proceeding.

(5) **Inconsistent Statements.**   Where the defendant made inconsistent statements under oath or equivalent affirmation, both having been made within the period of the statute of limitations, the prosecution may proceed by setting forth the inconsistent statements in a single count alleging in the alternative that one or the other was false and not believed by the defendant.   In such case it shall not be necessary for the prosecution to prove which statement was false but only that one or the other was false and not believed by the defendant to be true.

(6) **Corroboration.**   No person shall be convicted of an offense under this Section where proof of falsity rests solely upon contradiction by testimony of a single person other than the defendant.

Section 241.2.   False Swearing.

(1) **False Swearing in Official Matters.**   A person who makes a false statement under oath or equivalent affirmation, or swears or affirms the truth of such a statement previously made, when he does not believe the statement to be true, is guilty of a misdemeanor if:

(a) the falsification occurs in an official proceeding; or

(b) the falsification is intended to mislead a public servant in performing his official function.

(2) **Other False Swearing.**   A person who makes a false statement under oath or equivalent affirmation, or swears or affirms the truth of such a statement previously made, when he does not believe the statement to be true, is guilty of a petty misdemeanor, if the statement is one which is required by law to be sworn or affirmed before a notary or other person authorized to administer oaths.

(3) **Perjury Provisions Applicable.** Subsections (3) to (6) of Section 241.1 apply to the present Section.

Section 241.3.   Unsworn Falsification to Authorities.

(1) **In General.**   A person commits a misdemeanor if, with purpose to mislead a public servant in performing his official function, he:

(a) makes any written false statement which he does not believe to be true; or

(b) purposely creates a false impression in a written application for any pecuniary or other benefit, by omitting information necessary to prevent statements therein from being misleading; or

(c) submits or invites reliance on any writing which he knows to be forged, altered or otherwise lacking in authenticity; or

(d) submits or invites reliance on any sample, specimen, map, boundary-mark, or other object which he knows to be false.

(2) **Statements "Under Penalty."**   A person commits a petty misdemeanor if he makes a written false statement which he does not believe to be true, on or pursuant to a form bearing notice, authorized by law, to the effect that false statements made therein are punishable.

(3) **Perjury Provisions Applicable.** Subsections (3) to (6) of Section 241.1 apply to the present Section.

Section 241.4. False Alarms to Agencies of Public Safety.

A person who knowingly causes a false alarm of fire or other emergency to be transmitted to or within any organization, official or volunteer, for dealing with emergencies involving danger to life or property commits a misdemeanor.

Section 241.5. False Reports to Law Enforcement Authorities.

(1) **Falsely Incriminating Another.** A person who knowingly gives false information to any law enforcement officer with purpose to implicate another commits a misdemeanor.

(2) **Fictitious Reports.** A person commits a petty misdemeanor if he:

(a) reports to law enforcement authorities an offense or other incident within their concern knowing that it did not occur; or

(b) pretends to furnish such authorities with information relating to an offense or incident when he knows he has no information relating to such offense or incident.

Section 241.6. Tampering With Witnesses and Informants; Retaliation Against Them.

(1) **Tampering.** A person commits an offense if, believing that an official proceeding or investigation is pending or about to be instituted, he attempts to induce or otherwise cause a witness or informant to:

(a) testify or inform falsely; or

(b) withhold any testimony, information, document or thing; or

(c) elude legal process summoning him to testify or supply evidence; or

(d) absent himself from any proceeding or investigation to which he has been legally summoned.

The offense is a felony of the third degree if the actor employs force, deception, threat or offer of pecuniary benefit. Otherwise it is a misdemeanor.

(2) **Retaliation Against Witness or Informant.** A person commits a misdemeanor if he harms another by any unlawful act in retaliation for anything lawfully done in the capacity of witness or informant.

(3) **Witness or Informant Taking Bribe.** A person commits a felony of the third degree if he solicits, accepts or agrees to accept any benefit in consideration of his doing any of the things specified in clauses (a) to (d) of Subsection (1).

Section 241.7. Tampering With or Fabricating Physical Evidence.

A person commits a misdemeanor if, believing that an official proceeding or investigation is pending or about to be instituted, he:

(1) alters, destroys, conceals or removes any record, document or thing with purpose to impair its verity or availability in such proceeding or investigation; or

(2) makes, presents or uses any record, document or thing knowing it to be false and with purpose to mislead a public servant who is or may be engaged in such proceeding or investigation.

Section 241.8. Tampering With Public Records or Information.

(1) **Offense Defined.** A person commits an offense if he:

(a) knowingly makes a false entry in, or false alteration of, any record, document or thing belonging to, or received or kept by, the government for information or record, or required by law to be kept by others for information of the government; or

(b) makes, presents or uses any record, document or thing knowing it to be false, and with purpose that it be taken as a genuine part of information or records referred to in paragraph (a); or

(c) purposely and unlawfully destroys, conceals, removes or otherwise impairs the verity or availability of any such record, document or thing.

(2) **Grading.** An offense under this Section is a misdemeanor unless the actor's purpose is to defraud or injure anyone, in which case the offense is a felony of the third degree.

Section 241.9. Impersonating a Public Servant.

A person commits a misdemeanor if he falsely pretends to hold a position in the public service with purpose to induce another to submit to such pretended official authority or otherwise to act in reliance upon that pretense to his prejudice.

ARTICLE 242. OBSTRUCTING GOVERNMENTAL OPERATIONS; ESCAPES

Section 242.0. Definitions.

In this Article, unless another meaning plainly is required, the definitions given in Section 240.0 apply.

Section 242.1. Obstructing Administration of Law or Other Governmental Function.

A person commits a misdemeanor if he purposely obstructs, impairs or perverts the administration of law or other governmental function by force, violence, physical interference or obstacle, breach of official duty, or any other unlawful act, except that this Section does not apply to flight by a person charged with crime, refusal to submit to arrest, failure to perform a legal duty other than an official duty, or any other means of avoiding compliance with law without affirmative interference with governmental functions.

Section 242.2. Resisting Arrest or Other Law Enforcement.

A person commits a misdemeanor if, for the purpose of preventing a public servant from effecting a lawful arrest or discharging any other duty, the person creates a substantial risk of bodily injury to the public servant or anyone else, or employs means justifying or requiring substantial force to overcome the resistance.

Section 242.3. Hindering Apprehension or Prosecution.

A person commits an offense if, with purpose to hinder the apprehension, prosecution, conviction or punishment of another for crime, he:

(1) harbors or conceals the other; or

(2) provides or aids in providing a weapon, transportation, disguise or other means of avoiding apprehension or effecting escape; or

(3) conceals or destroys evidence of the crime, or tampers with a witness, informant, document or other source of information, regardless of its admissibility in evidence; or

(4) warns the other of impending discovery or apprehension, except that this paragraph does not apply to a warning given in connection with an effort to bring another into compliance with law; or

(5) volunteers false information to a law enforcement officer.

The offense is a felony of the third degree if the conduct which the actor knows has been charged or is liable to be charged against the person aided would constitute a felony of the first or second degree. Otherwise it is a misdemeanor.

Section 242.4. Aiding Consummation of Crime.

A person commits an offense if he purposely aids another to accomplish an unlawful object of a crime, as by safeguarding the proceeds thereof or converting the proceeds into negotiable funds. The offense is a felony of the third degree if the principal offense was a felony of the first or second degree. Otherwise it is a misdemeanor.

Section 242.5. Compounding.

A person commits a misdemeanor if he accepts or agrees to accept any pecuniary benefit in consideration of refraining from reporting to law enforcement authorities the commission or suspected commission of any offense or information relating to an offense. It is an affirmative defense to prosecution under this Section that the pecuniary benefit did not exceed an amount which the actor believed to be due as restitution or indemnification for harm caused by the offense.

Section 242.6. Escape.

(1) **Escape.** A person commits an offense if he unlawfully removes himself from official detention or fails to return to official detention following temporary leave granted for a specific purpose or limited period. "Official detention" means arrest, detention in any facility for custody of persons under charge or conviction of crime or alleged or found to be delinquent, detention for extradition or deportation, or any other detention for law enforcement purposes; but "official detention" does not include supervision of probation or parole, or constraint incidental to release on bail.

(2) **Permitting or Facilitating Escape.** A public servant concerned in detention commits an offense if he knowingly or recklessly permits an escape. Any person who knowingly causes or facilitates an escape commits an offense.

(3) **Effect of Legal Irregularity in Detention.** Irregularity in bringing about or maintaining detention, or lack of jurisdiction of the committing or detaining authority, shall not be a defense to prosecution under this Section if the escape is from a prison or other custodial facility or from detention pursuant to commitment by official proceedings. In the case of other detentions, irregularity or lack of jurisdiction shall be a defense only if:

(a) the escape involved no substantial risk of harm to the person or property of anyone other than the detainee; or

(b) the detaining authority did not act in good faith under color of law.

(4) **Grading of Offenses.** An offense under this Section is a felony of the third degree where:

(a) the actor was under arrest for or detained on a charge of felony or following conviction of crime; or

(b) the actor employs force, threat, deadly weapon or other dangerous instrumentality to effect the escape; or

(c) a public servant concerned in detention of persons convicted of crime purposely facilitates or permits an escape from a detention facility.

Otherwise an offense under this section is a misdemeanor.

Section 242.7. Implements for Escape; Other Contraband.

(1) **Escape Implements.** A person commits a misdemeanor if he unlawfully introduces within a detention facility, or unlawfully provides an inmate with, any weapon, tool or other thing which may be useful for escape. An inmate commits a misdemeanor if he unlawfully procures, makes, or otherwise provides himself with, or has in his possession, any such implement of escape. "Unlawfully" means sur-

reptitiously or contrary to law, regulation or order of the detaining authority.

(2) **Other Contraband.** A person commits a petty misdemeanor if he provides an inmate with anything which the actor knows it is unlawful for the inmate to possess.

Section 242.8. Bail Jumping; Default in Required Appearance.

A person set at liberty by court order, with or without bail, upon condition that he will subsequently appear at a specified time and place, commits a misdemeanor if, without lawful excuse, he fails to appear at that time and place. The offense constitutes a felony of the third degree where the required appearance was to answer to a charge of felony, or for disposition of any such charge, and the actor took flight or went into hiding to avoid apprehension, trial or punishment. This Section does not apply to obligations to appear incident to release under suspended sentence or on probation or parole.

ARTICLE 243. ABUSE OF OFFICE

Section 243.0. Definitions.

In this Article, unless a different meaning plainly is required, the definitions given in Section 240.0 apply.

Section 243.1. Official Oppression.

A person acting or purporting to act in an official capacity or taking advantage of such actual or purported capacity commits a misdemeanor if, knowing that his conduct is illegal, he:

(a) subjects another to arrest, detention, search, seizure, mistreatment, dispossession, assessment, lien or other infringement of personal or property rights; or

(b) denies or impedes another in the exercise or enjoyment of any right, privilege, power or immunity.

Section 243.2. Speculating or Wagering on Official Action or Information.

A public servant commits a misdemeanor if, in contemplation of official action by himself or by a governmental unit with which he is associated, or in reliance on information to which he has access in his official capacity and which has not been made public, he:

(1) acquires a pecuniary interest in any property, transaction or enterprise which may be affected by such information or official action; or

(2) speculates or wagers on the basis of such information or official action; or

(3) aids another to do any of the foregoing.

OFFENSES AGAINST PUBLIC ORDER AND DECENCY

ARTICLE 250. RIOT, DISORDERLY CONDUCT, AND RELATED OFFENSES

Section 250.1. Riot; Failure to Disperse.

(1) **Riot.** A person is guilty of riot, a felony of the third degree, if he participates with [two] or more others in a course of disorderly conduct:

(a) with purpose to commit or facilitate the commission of a felony or misdemeanor;

(b) with purpose to prevent or coerce official action; or

(c) when the actor or any other participant to the knowledge of the actor uses or plans to use a firearm or other deadly weapon.

(2) **Failure of Disorderly Persons to Disperse Upon Official Order.** Where [three] or more persons are participating in a course of disorderly conduct likely to cause substantial harm or serious inconvenience, annoyance or alarm, a peace of-

ficer or other public servant engaged in executing or enforcing the law may order the participants and others in the immediate vicinity to disperse. A person who refuses or knowingly fails to obey such an order commits a misdemeanor.

Section 250.2. Disorderly Conduct.

(1) **Offense Defined.** A person is guilty of disorderly conduct if, with purpose to cause public inconvenience, annoyance or alarm, or recklessly creating a risk thereof, he:

(a) engages in fighting or threatening, or in violent or tumultuous behavior; or

(b) makes unreasonable noise or offensively coarse utterance, gesture or display, or addresses abusive language to any person present; or

(c) creates a hazardous or physically offensive condition by any act which serves no legitimate purpose of the actor.

"Public" means affecting or likely to affect persons in a place to which the public or a substantial group has access; among the places included are highways, transport facilities, schools, prisons, apartment houses, places of business or amusement, or any neighborhood.

(2) **Grading.** An offense under this section is a petty misdemeanor if the actor's purpose is to cause substantial harm or serious inconvenience, or if he persists in disorderly conduct after reasonable warning or request to desist. Otherwise disorderly conduct is a violation.

Section 250.3. False Public Alarms.

A person is guilty of a misdemeanor if he initiates or circulates a report or warning of an impending bombing or other crime or catastrophe, knowing that the report or warning is false or baseless and that it is likely to cause evacuation of a building, place of assembly, or facility of public transport, or to cause public inconvenience or alarm.

Section 250.4. Harassment.

A person commits a petty misdemeanor if, with purpose to harass another, he:

(1) makes a telephone call without purpose of legitimate communication; or

(2) insults, taunts or challenges another in a manner likely to provoke violent or disorderly response; or

(3) makes repeated communications anonymously or at extremely inconvenient hours, or in offensively coarse language; or

(4) subjects another to an offensive touching; or

(5) engages in any other course of alarming conduct serving no legitimate purpose of the actor.

Section 250.5. Public Drunkenness; Drug Incapacitation.

A person is guilty of an offense if he appears in any public place manifestly under the influence of alcohol, narcotics or other drug, not therapeutically administered, to the degree that he may endanger himself or other persons or property, or annoy persons in his vicinity. An offense under this Section constitutes a petty misdemeanor if the actor has been convicted hereunder twice before within a period of one year. Otherwise the offense constitutes a violation.

Section 250.6. Loitering or Prowling.

A person commits a violation if he loiters or prowls in a place, at a time, or in a manner not usual for law-abiding individuals under circumstances that warrant alarm for the safety of persons or property in the vicinity. Among the circumstances which may be considered in determining whether such alarm is warranted is the fact that the actor takes flight upon appearance of a peace officer, refuses to identify himself, or manifestly endeavors to conceal himself or any object. Unless flight by the actor or other circumstance makes it impracticable, a peace officer shall prior to any arrest for an offense under this section afford the actor an opportunity to dispel any alarm which would otherwise be warranted, by requesting him to identify himself and explain his presence and conduct. No person shall be convicted of an offense under this Section if the peace officer did not comply with the preceding sentence, or if it appears at trial that the explanation given by the actor was true and, if believed by the peace officer at the time, would have dispelled the alarm.

Section 250.7. Obstructing Highways and Other Public Passages.

(1) A person, who, having no legal privilege to do so, purposely or recklessly obstructs any highway or other public passage, whether alone or with others, commits a violation, or, in case he persists after warning by a law officer, a petty misdemeanor. "Obstructs" means renders impassable without unreasonable inconvenience or hazard. No person shall be deemed guilty of recklessly obstructing in violation of this Subsection solely because of a gathering of persons to hear him speak or otherwise communicate, or solely because of being a member of such a gathering.

(2) A person in a gathering commits a violation if he refuses to obey a reasonable official request or order to move:

(a) to prevent obstruction of a highway or other public passage; or

(b) to maintain public safety by dispersing those gathered in dangerous proximity to a fire or other hazard.

An order to move, addressed to a person whose speech or other lawful behavior attracts an obstructing audience, shall not be deemed reasonable if the obstruction can be readily remedied by police control of the size or location of the gathering.

Section 250.8. Disrupting Meetings and Processions.

A person commits a misdemeanor if, with purpose to prevent or disrupt a lawful meeting, procession or gathering, he does any act tending to obstruct or interfere with it physically, or makes any utterance, gesture or display designed to outrage the sensibilities of the group.

Section 250.9. Desecration of Venerated Objects.

A person commits a misdemeanor if he purposely desecrates any public monument or structure, or place of worship or burial, or if he purposely desecrates the national flag or any other object of veneration by the public or a substantial segment thereof in any public place. "Desecrate" means defacing, damaging, polluting or otherwise physically mistreating in a way that the actor knows will outrage the sensibilities of persons likely to observe or discover his action.

Section 250.10. Abuse of Corpse.

Except as authorized by law, a person who treats a corpse in a way that he knows would outrage ordinary family sensibilities commits a misdemeanor.

Section 250.11. Cruelty to Animals.

A person commits a misdemeanor if he purposely or recklessly:

(1) subjects any animal to cruel mistreatment; or

(2) subjects any animal in his custody to cruel neglect; or

(3) kills or injures any animal belonging to another without legal privilege or consent of the owner.

Subsections (1) and (2) shall not be deemed applicable to accepted veterinary practices and activities carried on for scientific research.

Section 250.12. Violation of Privacy.

(1) **Unlawful Eavesdropping or Surveillance.** A person commits a misdemeanor if, except as authorized by law, he:

(a) trespasses on property with purpose to subject anyone to eavesdropping or other surveillance in a private place; or

(b) installs in any private place, without the consent of the person or persons entitled to privacy there, any device for observing, photographing, recording, amplifying or broadcasting sounds or events in such place, or uses any such unauthorized installation; or

(c) installs or uses outside a private place any device for hearing, recording, amplifying or broadcasting sounds originating in such place which would not ordinarily be audible or comprehensible outside, without the consent of the person or persons entitled to privacy there.

"Private place" means a place where one may reasonably expect to be safe from casual or hostile intrusion or surveillance, but does not include a place to which the public or a substantial group thereof has access.

(2) **Other Breach of Privacy of Messages.** A person commits a misdemeanor if, except as authorized by law, he:

(a) intercepts without the consent of the sender or receiver a message by telephone, telegraph, letter or other means of communicating privately; but this paragraph does not extend to (i) overhearing of messages through a regularly installed instrument on a telephone party line or on an extension, or (ii) interception by the telephone company or subscriber incident to enforcement of regulations limiting use of the facilities

or incident to other normal operation and use; or

(b) divulges without the consent of the sender or receiver the existence or contents of any such message if the actor knows that the message was illegally intercepted, or if he learned of the message in the course of employment with an agency engaged in transmitting it.

ARTICLE 251. PUBLIC INDECENCY

Section 251.1. Open Lewdness

A person commits a petty misdemeanor if he does any lewd act which he knows is likely to be observed by others who would be affronted or alarmed.

Section 251.2. Prostitution and Related Offenses.

(1) **Prostitution.** A person is guilty of prostitution, a petty misdemeanor, if he or she:

(a) is an inmate of a house of prostitution or otherwise engages in sexual activity as a business; or

(b) loiters in or within view of any public place for the purpose of being hired to engage in sexual activity.

"Sexual activity" includes homosexual and other deviate sexual relations. A "house of prostitution" is any place where prostitution or promotion of prostitution is regularly carried on by one person under the control, management or supervision of another. An "inmate" is a person who engages in prostitution in or through the agency of a house of prostitution. "Public place" means any place to which the public or any substantial group thereof has access.

(2) **Promoting Prostitution.** A person who knowingly promotes prostitution of another commits a misdemeanor or felony as provided in Subsection (3). The following acts shall, without limitation of the foregoing, constitute promoting prostitution:

(a) owning, controlling, managing, supervising or otherwise keeping, alone or in association with others, a house of prostitution or a prostitution business; or

(b) procuring an inmate for a house of prostitution or a place in a house of prostitution for one who would be an inmate; or

(c) encouraging, inducing, or otherwise purposely causing another to become or remain a prostitute; or

(d) soliciting a person to patronize a prostitute; or

(e) procuring a prostitute for a patron; or

(f) transporting a person into or within this state with purpose to promote that person's engaging in prostitution, or procuring or paying for transportation with that purpose; or

(g) leasing or otherwise permitting a place controlled by the actor, alone or in association with others, to be regularly used for prostitution or the promotion of prostitution, or failure to make reasonable effort to abate such use by ejecting the tenant, notifying law enforcement authorities, or other legally available means; or

(h) soliciting, receiving, or agreeing to receive any benefit for doing or agreeing to do anything forbidden by this Subsection.

(3) **Grading of Offenses Under Subsection (2).** An offense under Subsection (2) constitutes a felony of the third degree if:

(a) the offense falls within paragraph (a), (b) or (c) of Subsection (2); or

(b) the actor compels another to engage in or promote prostitution; or

(c) the actor promotes prostitution of a child under 16, whether or not he is aware of the child's age; or

(d) the actor promotes prostitution of his wife, child, ward or any person for whose care, protection or support he is responsible.

Otherwise the offense is a misdemeanor.

(4) **Presumption from Living off Prostitutes.** A person, other than the prostitute or the prostitute's minor child or other legal dependent incapable of self-support, who is supported in whole or substantial part by the proceeds of prostitution is presumed to be knowingly promoting prostitution in violation of Subsection (2).

(5) **Patronizing Prostitutes.** A person commits a violation if he hires a prostitute to engage in sexual activity with him, or if he enters or remains in a house of prostitution for the purpose of engaging in sexual activity.

(6) **Evidence.** On the issue whether a place is a house of prostitution the following shall be admissible evidence: its general repute; the repute of the persons who reside in or frequent the place; the frequency, timing and duration of visits by non-residents. Testimony of a person against his spouse shall be admissible to prove offenses under this Section.

Section 251.3. Loitering to Solicit Deviate Sexual Relations.

A person is guilty of a petty misdemeanor if he loiters in or near any public place for the purpose of soliciting or being solicited to engage in deviate sexual relations.

Section 251.4. Obscenity.

(1) **Obscene Defined.** Material is obscene if, considered as a whole, its predominant appeal is to prurient interest, that is, a shameful or morbid interest, in nudity, sex or excretion, and if in addition it goes substantially beyond customary limits of candor in describing or representing such matters. Predominant appeal shall be judged with reference to ordinary adults unless it appears from the character of the material or the circumstances of its dissemination to be designed for children or other specially susceptible audience. Undevel-

oped photographs, molds, printing plates, and the like, shall be deemed obscene notwithstanding that processing or other acts may be required to make the obscenity patent or to disseminate it.

(2) **Offenses.** Subject to the affirmative defense provided in Subsection (3), a person commits a misdemeanor if he knowingly or recklessly:

(a) sells, delivers or provides, or offers or agrees to sell, deliver or provide, any obscene writing, picture, record or other representation or embodiment of the obscene; or

(b) presents or directs an obscene play, dance or performance, or participates in that portion thereof which makes it obscene; or

(c) publishes, exhibits or otherwise makes available any obscene material; or

(d) possesses any obscene material for purposes of sale or other commercial dissemination; or

(e) sells, advertises or otherwise commercially disseminates material, whether or not obscene, by representing or suggesting that it is obscene.

A person who disseminates or possesses obscene material in the course of his business is presumed to do so knowingly or recklessly.

(3) **Justifiable and Non–Commercial Private Dissemination.** It is an affirmative defense to prosecution under this Section that dissemination was restricted to:

(a) institutions or persons having scientific, educational, governmental or other similar justification for possessing obscene material; or

(b) non-commercial dissemination to personal associates of the actor.

(4) **Evidence; Adjudication of Obscenity.** In any prosecution under this Section evidence shall be admissible to show:

(a) the character of the audience for which the material was designed or to which it was directed;

(b) what the predominant appeal of the material would be for ordinary adults or any special audience to which it was directed, and what effect, if any, it would probably have on conduct of such people;

(c) artistic, literary, scientific, educational or other merits of the material;

(d) the degree of public acceptance of the material in the United States;

(e) appeal to prurient interest, or absence thereof, in advertising or other promotion of the material; and

(f) the good repute of the author, creator, publisher or other person from whom the material originated.

Expert testimony and testimony of the author, creator, publisher or other person from whom the material originated, relating to factors entering into the determination of the issue of obscenity, shall be admissible. The Court shall dismiss a prosecution for obscenity if it is satisfied that the material is not obscene.

ADDITIONAL ARTICLES

[At this point, a State enacting a new Penal Code may insert additional Articles dealing with special topics such as narcotics, alcoholic beverages, gambling and offenses against tax and trade laws. The Model Penal Code project did not extend to these, partly because a higher priority on limited time and resources was accorded to branches of the penal law which have not received close legislative scrutiny. Also, in legislation dealing with narcotics, liquor, tax evasion, and the like, penal provisions have been so intermingled with regulatory and procedural provisions that the task of segregating one group from the other presents special difficulty for model legislation.]

*

Index

ABETTING
See Parties to Crime

ABSOLUTE LIABILITY
See Strict Liability

ACCESSORY AFTER THE FACT
See Post–Crime Aid

ACCESSORY BEFORE THE FACT
See Parties to Crime

ACCOMPLICES
See Parties to Crime

ACCOUNTABILITY
See Parties to Crime

ACT
Amnesia, 188
Attempts, 549
Automatism, 188
Brainwashing, 199
Burden of proof, 187, 196
Hypoglycemia, 198
Intoxication and, 198
Mental state distinguished, 201
Model Penal Code, 823
Multiple-personality, 200
Omission as, 217
One, multiple punishment, 225
Parties to crime, 706
Possession, 203
Post-traumatic stress disorder, 200
Premenstrual syndrome, 201
Psychomotor epilepsy, 196
Reflex action, 196
Unconsciousness defense, 187
Voluntary nature, 187

ACTUS REUS
See Act

ADULTERY
Ignorance or mistake and, 185

AGENT
See Parties to Crime

AGREEMENT
See Conspiracy

AIDING AND ABETTING
See Parties to Crime

ALCOHOLISM
See Intoxication

AMERICAN LAW INSTITUTE
See Model Penal Code

AMNESIA
See Act

ANTICIPATORY OFFENSES
See Attempts; Conspiracy; Solicitation

ARREST
See Law Enforcement

ASSAULT
Apprehension by victim, 593
Attempted, 590
Conspiracy to, 623
Intoxication and, 439
Model Penal Code, 804
With intent to kill, 113

ATTEMPTS
Abandonment, 575
Abolition, 583
Act,
    Dangerous proximity test, 551
    Equivocality test, 556
    Indispensible element test, 553
    Last act test, 550
    Model Penal Code test, 560
    Probable desistance test, 555
    Substantial step test, 560
Assault, 590
Burglary, 593
Charge to jury, 581
Conspiracy, 609
Impossibility, 563
Manslaughter, 544
Mental state, 540
Merger, 582
Model Penal Code, 844
Murder, 540
Proof of intent, 547
Prosecution, 581
Punishment, 582
Solicitation as, 701
Strict liability, 547

AUTOMATISM
See Act

BATTERED SPOUSE SYNDROME
Self-defense, 474

BIGAMY
Ignorance or mistake and, 185, 186

BRAINWASHING
See Act

BURDEN OF PROOF
Act, 187
Defense of property, 487
Diminished capacity, 245
Heat of passion, 238
Insanity, 400
Intent, 113, 117
Intoxication, 446, 453
Knowledge, 132
Model Penal Code, 822
Possession, 210
Self defense, 472

BURGLARY
Abolition, 595
Attempted, 595
Attempts and, 594
Common law, 593
Ignorance or mistake, 186
Mental state, 109
Model Penal Code, 870
Statutory, 594

CAUSATION
But for test, 315
Cause in fact, 315
Coincidence or response, 319
Defendant's intervening acts, 332
Foreseeability, 323
Instructions on, 319
Intervening, 319
Legal cause, 315
Model Penal Code, 825
Outside force intervening, 331
Pre-existing weakness, 318
Proximate cause, 315
Supervening, 319
Third party's intervening acts, 331
Time of death, 316
Victim's intervening acts, 324, 328
Year-and-a-day rule, 319

CHILD ABUSE
Omissions and, 217

CHOICE OF EVILS
See Duress; Necessity

COERCION
See Duress

COMMON LAW
Crime of common scold, 42
Crime of homicide, 48
Crime of nonfeasance, 45
Crime of solicitation, 45
Crimes abolished, 47
Federal, 47
Manslaughter, 240
Model Penal Code, 818
Parties to crime, 704

COMPETENCY TO STAND TRIAL
Amnesia, 361
Burden of proof, 369
Commitment for incompetency, 362
Constitutionality of commitment, 362
Due process requires, 356
Model Penal Code, 840
Proceeding notwithstanding incompetency, 369
Relationship to insanity defense, 354

COMPROMISE
See Condonation

CONCEALING A FUGITIVE
See Post–Crime Aid

CONDONATION
Defense, 533

CONSENT
Death, 536
Masochist, 535
Mistake, 534
Mistake of fact and, 165
Model Penal Code, 830
Nonresistance, 534
Rape, 534
Retroactive, 536
Sports violence, 535
Unperceived risks, 534

CONSPIRACY
Acquittal of co-conspirator, 679
Agreement, 598
Antifederal intent, 623
Assault, 623
Attempted, 609
Chain conspiracy, 650, 657
Circumstantial evidence, 597
Conviction of completed crime and, 676
Corporations, 680
Corrupt motive, 627, 631
Defrauding the U.S., 637
Duration, 661
Federal, 637
Feigned agreement, 604
Hearsay exception, 597
Husband and wife, 681
Impossibility, 640
Joint trial, 598
Mental state, 610

CONSPIRACY—Cont'd
Model Penal Code, 606, 608, 631, 639, 646, 648, 649, 650, 667, 668, 669, 670, 676, 677, 678, 679, 680, 682, 846
Objective, 632
Overt act, 645
Party to crime, 732
Plurality requirement, 670
Powell doctrine, 627, 631
Proof of intent, 616
Punishment, 676
Rationale, 598
RICO compared, 689
Scope,
    Object dimension, 646
    Party dimension, 650
Strict liability, 626, 632
Unilateral approach, 606, 680
Unnecessary, 682
Vagueness, 596, 636
Venue, 596
Wharton's rule, 670
Wheel conspiracy, 650
Withdrawal, 668

COOLING TIME
See Manslaughter

CORPORATIONS
Conspiracy, 680
Liability for agent's acts, 775
Liability of agent, 793
Liability of officer, 784
Model Penal Code, 828

CRIMES
Administrative, 68
Federal power to create, 66
Federal pre-emption, 67
Municipal power to create, 66
State-local conflicts, 67
State power to create, 66
State pre-emption, 67

"CRIMES AGAINST NATURE"
Cruel and unusual punishment, 94
Equal protection, 94
Meaning, 71
Model Penal Code, 867
Police power, 93
Right to privacy, 83, 92
Substantive due process, 82
Void for vagueness, 71, 74, 75

CRIMINAL JUSTICE AGENCIES
Defense counsel, 19
Judiciary, 20
Police, 14
Prosecutors, 15

CRIMINAL PROCESS STEPS
Appeals, 12
Arraignment, 10
Arrest, 3

CRIMINAL PROCESS STEPS—Cont'd
Booking, 3
Criminal justice funnel, 13
Decision to charge, 4
Filing complaint, 6
First appearance, 6
Grand jury review, 9
Indictment, 9
Information, 9
Post-arrest investigation, 4
Post-conviction remedies, 12
Pre-arrest investigation, 2
Preliminary hearing, 8
Pretrial motions, 10
Report of crime, 1
Sentencing, 12
Trial, 10

CRUEL AND UNUSUAL PUNISHMENT
"Crimes against nature," 94
Death penalty, 335
Discipline in schools, 513
Drug addiction, 422, 429
Narcotics addiction, 422, 429

CUNNILINGUS
See "Crimes Against Nature"

DEATH PENALTY
Appeal, 341
Constitutionality, 334, 345
Cruel and unusual punishment, 334
Felony-murder, 351
Mandatory, 347
Model Penal Code, 862
Murder, 334, 345
Rape, 350
Standards for jury, 339, 345

DEFENSE OF ANOTHER
Model Penal Code, 833
Prison cases, 481
Reasonable belief, 481

DEFENSE OF PROPERTY
Felony prevention, 486
Model Penal Code, 834
Reasonable apprehension, 486
Trap gun, 488
Warning to desist, 487

DENUNCIATION
See Punishment

DETERRENCE
See Punishment

DEVIATE SEXUAL CONDUCT
See "Crimes Against Nature"

DIMINISHED CAPACITY
See Insanity

DISCRETION
Enforcement, 68
Sentencing, 23

DOMESTIC AUTHORITY
Discipline in school, 509
Model Penal Code, 837

DRUG ADDICTION
See Intoxication

DRUNKENNESS
See Intoxication

DUE PROCESS
See, also, Burden of Proof; Void-for-Vagueness Doctrine
Commitment for incompetency to stand trial, 366
Ex post facto laws, 52, 60
Fair warning, 52, 57, 60
Police power, 93
Right to privacy, 92
Substantive, 93

DURESS
Aiding and abetting and, 514
Intoxication by, 450, 453
Model Penal Code, 829
Murder by, 514
Test for, 524

EQUAL PROTECTION
Commitment for incompetency to stand trial, 364
"Crimes against nature," 94

EXCUSE
Distinguished from justification, 460

EX POST FACTO LAWS
See Due Process

FAIR WARNING
See Void-for-Vagueness Doctrine

FELLATIO
See "Crimes Against Nature"

HEAT OF PASSION
See Manslaughter

HOMICIDE
See Manslaughter; Murder

HOMOSEXUALITY
See "Crimes Against Nature"

IGNORANCE OF FACT
See Ignorance or Mistake

IGNORANCE OF LAW
See Ignorance or Mistake.

IGNORANCE OR MISTAKE
Adultery, 185
Bigamy, 174, 185, 186
Burglary, 186
Constitutionality of not a defense, 181
Ignorance conduct proscribed, 175
Ignorance of law no excuse, 182
Immoral conduct and, 175
Model Penal Code, 826
Omissions and, 181
Possessing obscene material, 186
Rape and, 165, 171
Reasonable reliance, 184
Reasonableness of, 165
Statutory construction, 175
Statutory rape, 174

IMMATURITY
Crimes and, 455
Juvenile delinquency and, 455
Model Penal Code, 844

IMPOSSIBILITY
Attempts, 563
Conspiracy, 640
Solicitation, 700

INCAPACITATION
See Punishment

INDECENT EXPOSURE
Mental state, 102

INFANCY
See Immaturity

INSANITY
Abolition of defense, 387
Bifurcated trial, 402
Burden of proof, 400
Commitment, 405
Compared to other defenses, 371
Diminished capacity, 408, 615
Durham test, 376
Examination of defendant before trial, 398
How defense raised, 397
Instructions, 403
Intoxication and, 448
Irresistible impulse test, 375
Justice test, 386
M'Naghten test, 372
Model Penal Code test, 376, 839
Pathological gambling disorder, 391
Post-traumatic stress disorder, 393
Premenstrual syndrome, 392
Presentation of evidence to jury, 401
Psychopathic personality, 384
Relationship to incompetency to stand trial, 354
Release after commitment, 405
Right to treatment, 408
Unconsciousness distinguished, 188
Verdict, 403
When defense raised, 397

INSANITY—Cont'd
Who raises defense, 393
Why defense raised, 393
XYY chromosome defense, 389

INTENT
Assault, 113
Attempts, 540
Burden of proof and, 113
Burglary, 109
Conditional, 106
Conspiracy, 610
Constructive, 105
Criminal, 105
Foreseeability and, 104
General, 106
Homicide cases, 238
Inferred, 117
Malice and, 98
Meaning, 102, 105
Model Penal Code, 824
Motive and, 105
Multiple, 106
Parties to crime, 717
Presumed, 113, 117
Specific, 106
Transferred, 108

INTERNATIONAL LAW
Justification, 530

INTOXICATION
Act requirement and, 198
Burden of proof, 446, 453
By mistake, 451
Chronic alcoholism, 419
Coerced, 450
Drug addiction, 422, 429
Insanity and, 448
Involuntary, 450
Model Penal Code, 829
Narcotics addiction, 422, 429
Pathological, 451
Public drunkenness, 419, 428
Treatment of addiction, 436
Unexpected, 451
Voluntary, 439

JUSTIFICATION
Distinguished from excuse, 460

JUVENILE DELINQUENCY
See Immaturity

"KNOWINGLY"
See Knowledge

KNOWLEDGE
Attempts, 540
Burden of proof and, 132
Conspiracy, 616
Inferred, 132
Model Penal Code, 824
Objective test, 122

KNOWLEDGE—Cont'd
Parties to crime, 724
Presumed, 118
Recklessness and, 127
Willful blindness rule, 129

LAW ENFORCEMENT
Aid to as defense, 491
Arrest by policeman, 495
Arrest by private citizen, 503
Force to arrest, 495
Model Penal Code, 835
Resisting illegal arrest, 504

MALICE
Aforethought, defined, 279
Constructive, 280
Meaning, 99, 241

MANSLAUGHTER
See, also, Causation
Attempted, 544
Awareness of risk, 291
Common law origin, 240
Degree of risk, 293
Gross negligence, 291
Heat of passion,
  Burden of proof, 238
  Cooling time, 261
  Reasonable man test, 250
  Type of provocation, 256
Misdemeanor manslaughter,
  Abolition, 315
  Causation, 314
  Harshness of rule, 314
  Type of misdemeanor, 314
Model Penal Code, 861
Objective test, 293
Omission, by, 221

MAYHEM
Mental state, 101

MENTAL STATE
See, also, Ignorance or Mistake; Intent;
  Knowledge; Malice; Negligence; Reck-
  lessness; Strict Liability
Common law crimes, 96
Mayhem, 101
Meaning, 96
Model Penal Code approach, 97, 824
Objective fault, 97
Relating to results, 97
Statutory crimes, 97
Subjective fault, 97

MISPRISION OF FELONY
See Post–Crime Aid

MISTAKE OF FACT
See Ignorance or Mistake

MISTAKE OF LAW
See Ignorance or Mistake

MODEL PENAL CODE
Abuse of office, 888
Act, 823
Affirmative defenses, 246, 822
Arrest by force, 498, 835
Arson and related offenses, 869
Assault, 864
Attempts,
   Abandonment, 578, 844
   Impossibility, 571, 844
   Mental state, 545, 844
   Punishment, 847
   Substantial step, 562, 563, 844
Bribery, 880
Burden of proof, 246, 822
Burglary and related offenses, 593, 870
Capital punishment, 339, 862
Causation, 316, 825
Choice of evils, 531, 831
Common law crimes, 47, 818
Competency to stand trial, 840
Consent, 533, 830
Conspiracy,
   Agreement, 606, 846
   Corrupt motive, 631
   Duration, 667, 846
   Objective, 639, 846
   Object dimension, 646
   Overt act, 646
   Party dimension, 650
   Plurality requirement, 679, 680
   Punishment, 847
   Unilateral approach, 606, 846
   Withdrawal, 668, 846
Corporate liability, 776, 828
Crime prevention, 471, 835
"Crimes against nature," 867
Cumulative penalties, 230
De minimus infractions, 830
Death penalty, 339, 862
Defense of another, 490, 833
Defense of property, 488, 834
Definitions, 823
Deliberation, 269
Diminished capacity, 839
Disorderly conduct, 889
Domestic authority, 837
Double jeopardy, 820
Duress, 524, 829
Entrapment, 831
Escape, 887
Family offenses, 878
Felony defined, 818
Felony murder, 303, 306
Force to arrest, 498, 504
Forgery, 875
Fraudulent practices, 875
General intent, 106
Ignorance or mistake, 184, 826
Immaturity, 844
Impact, 46
Imperfect defense, 488
Indecent exposure, 102, 889

MODEL PENAL CODE—Cont'd
Insanity, 372, 376, 839
Intoxication, 451, 452, 453, 454, 829
Kidnapping and related offenses, 864
Knowledge, 129, 130, 824
Law enforcement, 835
Lesser included offenses, 236
Lost property, 164
Manslaughter, 255, 260, 488, 861
Mental states, 97, 824
Military orders, 830
Misdemeanor defined, 818
Misdemeanor manslaughter, 314, 315
Mistake of fact, 173
Multiple convictions, 236, 819
Murder, 288, 290, 861
Necessity, 831
Negligence, 140, 824
Negligent homicide, 861
Not guilty by reason of insanity, 843
Obscenity, 892
Obstructing governmental operations, 886
Parties to crime, 705, 710, 711, 726, 734, 735,
   744, 755, 760, 761, 827
Perjury and related offenses, 883
Petty misdemeanor defined, 818
Possession, 823
Prostitution, 891
Public duty, 832
Public indecency, 891
Punishment, 848–60
Purpose, 46, 816, 824
Rape, 866
Recklessness, 140, 824
Resisting illegal arrest, 506
Riot, 808
Robbery, 871
Same transaction test, 237
Self defense, 467, 832
Sex offenses, 71, 866
Solicitation, 697, 845
Specific intent, 106
Statutory interpretation, 816
Strict liability, 155, 161, 826
Suicide, 861
Territorial applicability, 817
Theft, 60, 164, 871
Time limitations, 818
Vagrancy, 588, 889
Vicarious liability, 770, 827

MOTIVE
Intent and, 105

MULTIPLE OFFENDER
Collateral estoppel, 237
Model Penal Code, 819
Number of convictions, 236
Offenses charged, 235
Offenses to jury, 235
Punishment, 225
Successive prosecutions, 237

MURDER
See, also, Causation; Death Penalty
Attempted, 540
Degrees of, 264
Deliberation,
Proof of, 273
Test criticized, 269
Time for, 264
Depraved heart, 285
Diminished capacity, 271, 412
Duress defense, 514
Felony murder,
Abolition, 303, 306
Accomplice to, 737
Constitutionality, 305
Double jeopardy, 308
Duration of felony, 308
Liability of co-felony, 311
Merger rule, 307
Rationale, 302
Status of deceased, 311
Status of person causing death, 311
Type of felony, 306
Fetus, 47, 58
Gross recklessness, 285
Human being, 53, 59
Intent to do serious bodily injury, 278, 289
Known probability act will cause death, 278
Model Penal Code, 861
Premeditation,
Proof of, 273
Test criticized, 269
Time for, 264
Presumption of malice, 238
Time of death, 59

NARCOTICS ADDICTION
See Intoxication

NECESSITY
Economic, 520
Model Penal Code, 831
Natural forces, 527
Test for, 527

NEGLIGENCE
Civil vs. criminal, 137
Culpable, 137
Gross, 137
Model Penal Code, 824
Objective standard, 144
Statutory definitions, 140

OMISSIONS
See, also, Act
Ignorance or mistake and, 181

PARTIES TO CRIME
Accessory after the fact, 704
Accessory before the fact, 705
Accommodation agent defense, 727
Acquittal of principal, 745, 750
Acts, 706

PARTIES TO CRIME—Cont'd
Attempt to aid, 709
Coercion of accomplice, 514
Common law classification, 704
Conspiracy aider, 609
Conspirator as party, 732
Criminal facilitation distinguished, 726
Exceptions to accomplice liability, 760
Felony murder, 737
Foreseeable offenses, 737, 740
Intent, 717
Knowledge, 724
Mental state, 717
Model Penal Code, 705, 710, 711, 726, 734, 735, 744, 755, 760, 761, 827
Omissions, 706
Presence at crime, 712
Principal in first degree, 704
Principal in second degree, 705
Procuring agent defense, 727
Recklessness, 728
Related crimes, 737, 740
Stake in the outcome, 721
Strict liability, 731
Withdrawal, 757

PARTNERSHIPS
Liability of partners, 783
Liability of partnership, 783

PATHOLOGICAL GAMBLING DISORDER
See Insanity

POLICE POWER
Constitutional limits, 93
Federal, 66
Municipal, 66
State, 66

POSSESSING DRUGS
Addiction and, 429

POSSESSING MARIJUANA
Mental state, 136

POSSESSING OBSCENE MATERIAL
Ignorance or mistake and, 186
Mental state, 135

POSSESSING STOLEN PROPERTY
Mental state, 132

POSSESSION
Act, 203
Constructive, 207
Model Penal Code, 823
Presumption of, 210
Proof of, 206

POST–CRIME AID
Accessory after the fact, 793
Concealing a fugitive, 800
Misprision of felony, 802

POST–TRAUMATIC STRESS DISORDER
See Act; Insanity

PREMENSTRUAL SYNDROME
See Act; Insanity

PRESUMPTIONS
See Burden of Proof

PRINCIPAL IN FIRST DEGREE
See Parties to Crime

PRINCIPAL IN SECOND DEGREE
See Parties to Crime

PROVOCATION
See Manslaughter

PUNISHMENT
Attempts, 582
Bias, 23
Consecutive for one act, 225
Consecutive for related acts, 229
Conspiracy, 676
Equality in, 36
Guidelines for, 39
Individualization of, 32
Medicaid fraud, 28
Model Penal Code, 848–60
Plea bargaining and, 34
Purposes, 23
Solicitation, 701
Theories of,
    Denunciation, 24
    Deterrence, 24, 29
    Incapacitation, 24, 29
    Reformation, 24, 29
    Rehabilitation, 24, 29
    Retribution, 24
Vicarious liability, 769

RAPE
Consent, 534
Death penalty, 350
Mistake of fact and, 165, 171
Model Penal Code, 866

RECKLESSNESS
Conspiracy, 616
Malice and, 99
Model Penal Code, 824
Parties to crime, 728
Presumed, 147
Statutory definitions, 140

REFORMATION
See Punishment

REHABILITATION
See Punishment

RESISTING ARREST
See Law Enforcement

RETRIBUTION
See Punishment

RICO
Assessment, 695
"Associated in fact" enterprise, 691
"Enterprise" meaning, 683
Conspiracy compared, 689
Interstate and foreign commerce effect, 695
"Legal entity" enterprise, 692
"Pattern of racketeering activity," 694
Political-goals enterprise, 693

SELF DEFENSE
Aggressor's right, 465, 468
Battered spouse syndrome, 474
Burden of proof, 472
"Castle" doctrine, 466, 469
Crime prevention and, 470
Model Penal Code, 832
Reasonable belief, 467
Retreat, 465, 469
Third party killed or harmed, 471

SENTENCING
See Punishment

SODOMY
See "Crimes Against Nature"

SOLICITATION
Abandonment, 701
Acts, 699
Attempt, 701
Common law, 45
Definition, 696
Impossibility, 700
Model Penal Code, 698
Need, 698
Objectives, 700
Punishment, 701
Risks, 698

STATUTORY INTERPRETATION
Administrative, 68
Amendment, 60
Construing cases compared, 63
"Crimes against nature" statute, 71
Ejusdem generis, 65
Expressio unius est exclusio alterius, 65
Ignorance or mistake, 175
In pari materia, 66
Judicial enlargement, 52, 60, 77
Legislative history, 50
Legislative intent, 64
Model Penal Code, 816
Plain meaning, 51, 64
Saving clause, 60
Strict construction, 50, 63

STATUTORY RAPE
Ignorance or mistake and, 174

STRICT LIABILITY
Alternatives to, 159
Attempts, 547
Conspiracy, 626, 632
Constitutionality of, 150, 160, 161
Enforcement and, 159
Interpretation of statute as imposing, 150
Mistake of fact or law and, 165
Model Penal Code, 826
Parties to crime, 731
Penalty and, 154, 158, 159
Pros and cons of, 157
Vicarious liability and, 762

SUICIDE
Assistance of, 262, 536

THEFT
Model Penal Code, 871

TRESPASS
Justification defense, 527

UNCONSCIOUSNESS
See Act

VAGRANCY
Constitutionality of statute, 584
Model Penal Code, 889

VICARIOUS LIABILITY
Constitutionality of, 768
Model Penal Code, 827
Punishment of, 769
Strict liability and, 762

VOID–FOR–VAGUENESS DOCTRINE
Common scold, 44
Conspiracy, 636
"Crimes against nature" statute, 74, 75
Reasons for, 44
Vagrancy, 81, 584
Views on, 80

XYY CHROMOSOME DEFENSE
See Insanity

†

0–314–82177–5

90000

9 780314 821775